BLUNKETT, D.   B BLUNKETT, D

The Blunkett tapes: my life in the bear
pit

70002978015   Hbk

Please return/renew this item by the last date shown

worcestershire
c o u n t y c o u n c i l
Cultural Services

THE
BLUNKETT
TAPES

THE
BLUNKETT
TAPES

MY LIFE IN THE BEAR PIT

DAVID BLUNKETT

BLOOMSBURY

No part of this book may be used or reproduced in any manner whatsoever without written permission from the Publisher except in the case of brief quotations embodied in critical articles or reviews

Every reasonable effort has been made to trace copyright holders of material reproduced in this book, but if any have been inadvertently overlooked the publishers would be glad to hear from them. For legal purposes the picture credits on page vi constitute an extension of the copyright page

Bloomsbury Publishing Plc, 36 Soho Square, London W1D 3QY

www.bloomsbury.com

Bloomsbury Publishing, London, New York and Berlin

A CIP catalogue record for this book is available from the British Library

HB ISBN 0 7475 8821 X
HB ISBN-13 9780747588214
Large Print Edition ISBN 0 7475 8840 6
Large Print Edition ISBN-13 9780747588405
TPB ISBN 0 7475 8931 3
TPB ISBN-13 9780747589310

10 9 8 7 6 5 4 3 2 1

Typeset by Hewer Text UK Ltd
Printed in Great Britain by Clays Ltd, St Ives plc

The paper this book is printed on is certified by the © 1996 Forest Stewardship Council A.C. (FSC). It is ancient-forest friendly. The printer holds FSC chain of custody SGS-COC-2061

FSC
Mixed Sources
Product group from well-managed
forests and other controlled sources
Cert no. SGS-COC-2061
www.fsc.org
© 1996 Forest Stewardship Council

CONTENTS

LIST OF ILLUSTRATIONS

This diary is dedicated to my close family and friends, together with my neighbours and the wonderful people of Sheffield and north Derbyshire, who have sustained me through good and bad times alike and to whom I owe a deep debt of gratitude.

PREFACE

Over the winter of 2005/6 I was approached by a large number of publishers who were interested in either my autobiography or diaries. I specifically chose to work with Bloomsbury because they understood and were prepared to publish the kind of book I wanted, and which I hoped would stand the test of time.

What follows are edited diaries compiled from the tapes that I had dictated, usually on a weekly basis on weekends but occasionally with longer intervals, from 1997 to the end of 2005. In the light of the obvious practical difficulties of compiling a book of this nature, and the intense political and sometimes personal pressure under which the tapes were dictated, I hope the reader will forgive any lapse from the lofty language of politics, and likewise excuse the occasional erratic move from strict chronological order: incidents and issues were often recorded not systematically but as they came into my mind.

Naturally periods when Parliament was in recess were less fruitful as far as diary items are concerned – which explains why there is no mention in August 1997 of the death of Princess Diana, and why entries are uncharacteristically sparse in July and August 2001. This does not mean that emotional but non-political traumas did not impinge on my feelings; rather that they seemed outside the scope of my personal tapes.

The diary entries are interspersed with italic passages of my reflections on some of the events and policy decisions with which I was associated and on which, with the benefit of hindsight, I can now see more clearly. Presenting my contemporaneous view of the New Labour government in this way and avoiding the opportunity to rewrite history which a conventional political autobiography would have afforded comes at a price. I can see that I might have handled some policy decisions differently, and I would undoubtedly have had a different view of how to relate to colleagues.

Similarly, I have often revised my somewhat hasty thoughts about their actions or reactions.

My tapes, therefore, tell the story as I saw it at the time. As with any diary, when things were going smoothly (for instance, when real progress was being made on implementing the detailed policy that we had worked on for years on primary education and the raising of standards, prior to entering government) much less attention is paid to what is happening, because the direction was clear and the aggravation was manageable. Perversely, therefore, some issues take on a much greater significance than public debate at the time would have reflected.

On the other hand, in letting off steam – as I often do – I think I truly reflect the 'bear pit' which constitutes frontline politics. We are at the cutting edge of major decisions and this inevitably leads to tension, not least because at this level we all have pretty big egos.

The diary, therefore, is about coping with the pressures of modern government and the reality of New Labour, and dealing with the transformation in the way information is communicated both publicly and privately – entirely different from any experience of previous politicians in the country and within an increasingly global economy and ever more pluralistic democratic framework.

I use the word 'coping' because the diary also gives some insight into how I, as an individual not able to use print, dealt with the avalanche of material, the day-to-day challenges and, particularly at the Home Office, a sixteen-hour seven-day-a-week job.

If in the course of narrating my experience I do less than justice to individuals with whom I have worked, to the civil service which supported me, and to the media with which I had an ambivalent – not to say love-hate – relationship, the fault is mine.

I have chosen in this diary, as I have throughout my life, to do what I can to protect my privacy, and in this I am grateful to Bloomsbury for their understanding. I ask that those reflecting publicly on my diary entries and my commentary on them exercise voluntary restraint when dispensing extraneous comment which draws on previous commentary with regard to my private life, much of which was either untrue or deeply offensive (though rarely quite so offensive as the newspaper editor some years ago who went to great efforts to back up her conviction that I am not blind at all!), although I expect no such quarter to be given in relation to my political activities.

There are many people to thank at this point, both for their part in my political life and for their work on this book in particular.

My gratitude is due to the Brightside Constituency Labour Party, to the people of Sheffield and to those members of the general public (many of whom I have never met) who have shown me such amazing kindness and offered support through good times and bad. They will never know how important such support has been, and how crucial in sustaining me at times of great trauma and stress or where impossible decisions have to be taken.

In addition, I owe deep gratitude to those who have worked so closely with me: my personal assistants Valda Waterfield, Tricia Jones and Georgina Banton; my special advisers Conor Ryan, Sophie Linden, Nick Pearce, Huw Evans, Kath Raymond, Matthew Doyle, Anna Turley, Matt Cavanagh, Tom Bentley and Sue Regan (and of course Hilary Benn); to Sir Michael Barber for his work as Head of the Standards Unit and subsequently at 10 Downing Street; to my previous parliamentary private secretaries Jean Corston, Paul Goggins, Andy Burnham and Laura Moffatt; to my dedicated private secretaries; to my long-standing driver Barry Brazier; and to all my constituency and parliamentary staff, past and present, who carried an enormous workload: currently working with me are Tracy Barker, Janet Pickering, Melanie Ward and Ben Hamilton. Without all of these I could not have done the job, in that they gave support without ever making me feel that I was dependent on their compensating for my lack of sight. I was very lucky to have them, and to have the ministerial teams with which I worked.

I have other debts of gratitude specific to the publication of this book. In the introduction to the first volume of his diaries, Richard Crossman stated that since his original text was 'dictated very much ad lib and often for two or three hours on end, I found that when transcribed it was hardly readable.' A very similar process of composition applied to my own diaries, and any readability which the published text possesses can be primarily ascribed to two people: the aforementioned Valda Waterfield, who painstakingly and untiringly transcribed the dictated tapes and edited them into initial printed form; and Sean Magee, who undertook the subsequent editing and worked closely with me on preparation of the final version. For Valda and Sean the construction of the text constituted the most enormous challenge, and without their commitment and dedication the book would not have appeared. (And I must express my gratitude to Valda's long-suffering husband Trevor!) My appreciation is also due to my agent Ed Victor and his staff, and to Nigel Newton, Michael Fishwick, Trâm-Anh Doan and Emily Sweet at Bloomsbury.

To them and to all others who have made this book possible, my thanks.

DB
September 2006

INTRODUCTION

The immediate post-war baby boom was an inauspicious time for any youngster, not least in a wartime Sheffield which had taken more than its fair share of German bombing. But I was lucky. The Jessop Hospital in Sheffield was then one of the better neo-natal units in the country, despite the fact that at the time my Mum was considered to be very late in life in having me, and suffered medically for it.

I arrived apparently whole and certainly very vocal. My Mum's daughter from her previous marriage, Doreen, remained very close – she was nineteen when I was born – but although I did try to keep in touch with my Dad's four sons from his first marriage who were still alive (he was a widower, and the other children had died), it wasn't easy. I didn't therefore see much of Ron, Roy, Derek and Herbert, although Derek was a groundsman at my beloved Sheffield Wednesday.

It was some months before it was recognised that there might be something wrong with my eyes. Even small babies soon learn to follow what is going on around them and, of course, to smile. It is still a mystery to me how blind children learn to smile. Contrary to the presumption that youngsters simply copy, smiling is obviously something inherent in the human race – although my life experience has taught me that some people obviously missed the gene which allows them to do so. Once it was clear that I could see only a tiny bit (normally referred to as 'light and dark'), efforts to trace the cause were under way. This was a time when other than youngsters who had been placed inappropriately in oxygen tents – there were a number of children at school who had lost their sight because of inadequate medical knowledge – tumours were considered to be the most likely cause. It was only my mother's tenacity that prevented them from what now would probably be described as a medical fetish – namely to remove the eyes of the child in order to avoid further damage. There was no tumour, and it was a one-in-several-million chance which led to the failure of my optic nerve to develop. How I describe it to youngsters who ask me about this is that it is the equivalent of a perished or damaged electric wire leading to a light bulb: the longer the electric wire does not light up the bulb, the more the bulb itself deteriorates. Modern science will soon be able to deal with these matters, but that was certainly not the case back in the late 1940s. My mother's hair temporarily turned white at the news that I was blind, for disability in the post-war era was no longer leading (with some exceptions, as I found at school) to rejection but to fear. There was still great uncertainty about how a blind child would survive, what would happen to them, what possibilities there would be for work, for independence and for a full life.

Thankfully both my mother and father were made of stern stuff. My mother's hair recovered its colour and my Dad took everything in his stride. Both of them were in their middle years. (It is hard to think now that back in the late 1940s and early 1950s, fifty-four (my father) and forty-three (my mother) were considered to be late middle age.) Bizarre as it seems, I remember them both having false teeth and putting them into glasses of Steradent at the side of the bed.

My mother was diagnosed with breast cancer when I was nine years old, and went through the most horrendous surgery and radiotherapy. I shall never forget holding her hand as she was sick time and time again after returning home from the treatment. But she survived another twenty-seven years before dying from stomach cancer at the ripe old age of eighty-three.

My Dad, who was self-taught and had been on trawlers in the North Sea before spending forty-seven years working for what was then known as the Gas Board, gave me no quarter. He walked me for miles, sat me on his knee and taught me what general studies and geography he knew. He also instilled the work ethic. Between my mother's puritanism and deep Christian faith and my Dad's six-day week, three-shift work pattern, I learned that hard work was the norm.

When I was two years old a request came in from the 'School Bobbies' – the forerunner of the Education Social Work Service – that I should be sent to a special boarding school for children who could not see. My mother and father resisted it on the grounds that they could look after me themselves. Thank goodness they did resist, because it later transpired that the school I was to be sent to, caring as its staff were, instilled all sorts of peculiar habits into its blind pupils, who rocked to and fro while standing up, poked their fingers and fists into their eyes, and developed mannerisms which would make it difficult to integrate.

But by the time I was four their resistance could no longer withstand the pressure for residential schooling. In those days, a child simply had to attend the school chosen by the professionals. It was not until I started to fight for it much later as a local councillor that Sheffield pioneered integration of disabled youngsters.

I was fortunate, though, in that Sheffield did at the time have a school for blind children between the ages of four and twelve, the upper limit being twelve because an extra year was added on to each stage of education, presumably to take account of the difficulty of learning how to handle Braille and tactile means of coping with mathematics, geography and the like. So it was that my Mum and Dad, each holding one of my hands, took me one Sunday evening past the cathedral in the city centre as the sun of an early September dropped in the sky. After two bus rides we arrived at what to me seemed like a mansion: the Manchester Road School for the Blind. Ironically, when the school was later closed and converted into flats my eldest son Alastair was to rent an apartment in the building: just one of those strange coincidences of life.

But on that day in 1951 I was left by my parents, at the instruction of the teachers, to find my own way to the dormitory which I would share with another eight youngsters – to learn to clean my teeth, make my bed, clean my own shoes, wear the school uniform provided and start the process of becoming a rebel.

It was a robust life. Learning to ride a two-wheeler bike, crashing at speed into walls on snowy days when we could find a sledge, and of course playing games: football with ball bearings in the ball, cricket with a bell in the smaller ball. These days we'd probably be banned from doing so on health and safety grounds. Cricket was something more than the gentle crack of willow on leather. It was more often the crack of the willow on the nearest boy's head as we swung out to hit the ball and caught the poor devil fielding in the slips or even the wicket keeper if he got too close. Taken alongside the adventure of going down to the depths of the cellars in order to share the big bath and dry my hair in front of the fire, this experience certainly helped to toughen me up. But what was lacking was my mother's love and affection, and my father's stern hand – except of course in the holidays. Instead the sixteen- and seventeen-year-old 'house mothers' who looked after us and put us to bed provided the nearest thing to a goodnight kiss and cuddle – and someone who could share the tears – that I got between the ages of four and twelve.

Approaching the age of twelve we took an exam, one entirely different from the Eleven Plus. The exam itself was less important than the assessment of whether a youngster leaving the Manchester Road School would fit into one of three tiers of secondary education: a very (and I mean very) nineteenth-century-style secondary school, a 'technical' school (as it was called), or the residential grammar school at Worcester. There was a separate school for girls at Chorley Wood in Hertfordshire. It was adjudged that I would be a disruptive element at the grammar school and would not fit in, and therefore that I would not go for the final exam and assessment there at all. I would instead go to the Royal National College. (It was called Normal after French teacher training college, but changed its name to National later when nobody understood that the 'Normal' meant that being blind is pretty normal if you just discount the fact that you cannot see!)

This was to be a horrendous time in my life, a time I shall never forget and which has rested with me in a number of ways ever since. My father had agreed to stay on at the Gas Board past retirement age to train others in the job he did, as a foreman working what was known as a water gas plant. On 9 December 1959, just before I was due to start my new residential school outside Shrewsbury, Shropshire, the following month, my father stepped back to avoid an approaching truck and dropped into a vat of boiling water through a hole where a cover had been inadvertently left off. He lived for a month – a month of me visiting him, holding his bandaged hand, and of crying at home with my mother. It was many years before I was able to afford a stone for the head of his grave, and finally I felt that I had said farewell.

Later, as Work and Pensions Secretary, I inherited responsibility for the Health and Safety Commission and Health and Safety Executive. In my earlier days of lecturing I had been responsible for teaching health and safety representatives (following the 1974 Act), and as a minister I took on with relish a function which had been passed from pillar to post over the previous couple of decades. I was only sorry that I was not able to carry forward the nationwide occupational health programme that I set in train in 2005.

Personal experience and tragedy affect all of us, just as my experience of schooling drove me later in life, both as Leader of Sheffield City Council and as Education Secretary, to a passion (some would say obsession) for raising standards and promoting education as a key driver for equality.

With the death of my grandfather, another seed was sown. He had lived with us for many years and, despite her continuing illness, my mother had done everything possible to look after him. But when he was in his early nineties she was so ill herself that at last he had to go into a geriatric ward in the local hospital, now in my constituency. The 'Fir Vale Wing' was an ex-workhouse and was frankly a disgrace to the twentieth century. Every time I visited him, and following the accident when he fell downstairs, which led to his painful death, I was determined that if ever I got the chance to do so, I would put this wrong to rights. As Chairman of Social Services (known in Sheffield as Family and Community Services) for four years, I was able to work with the health service in eliminating the obscenity of the geriatric ward and in its place creating modern elderly persons' homes, including wards for dementia, as well as the dramatic expansion in domestic care (home helps and wardens) to keep people in their own homes as long as possible. There was also supported independent living, with a core residential facility servicing dozens of flats.

The injustice that I saw around me and experienced as a child, the fact that it took years to get compensation for my father's death (because he was over retirement age), and the struggle my mother had to afford to put food on the table, were and remain key factors in my politics. I didn't need – and don't need today – to hear the patronising tones of those liberal and left-of-centre commentators talking about poverty, when the nearest they have ever come to experiencing it is to buy a copy of the *Big Issue*.

Despite all else, I still have the complete and continuing conviction of the things I believed as a young man and the driving force for equality of opportunity based not on a hand-out but on self-reliance and self-determination, underpinned by the mutual strength of all of us working together, sharing together and understanding that we swim or sink together.

So it was that at the age of sixteen, without a qualification to my name, I set out on the road to self-fulfilment and public service. The head of the school I had attended, who himself had a PhD, did not believe that blind children needed (or, I fear, ought to bother with) qualifications. We therefore did not take O levels, which were the precursor to GCSEs. Instead I took a secretarial course which ensured that I could use a typewriter, learn Braille shorthand and acquire commercial skills. Twice a week I went down to the local technical college in Shrewsbury, and after my first year's success in gaining a couple of O levels (much to my amazement) I then embarked on more ambitious fare. We persuaded the college to lay on English during the day and, oddly, religious knowledge. I continued going to the local tech and, having accumulated six O levels, moved on to take three A levels, which I picked up when I left the college to take up my first paid employment as a clerk with – yes – the East Midlands Gas Board. This was the idea of the Royal National Institute for the Blind's placement officer, who felt that they owed me something – slightly bizarre, but who was I to argue? What they did do was give me one day a week to go to college, coupled with evening school, and I was able to put in sufficient time and effort to get three A levels and the National Certificate in Business Studies.

To cut a long story short, I could have done sociology at Durham or York but chose to stay in Sheffield, one of the reasons being that I had spent so little time with my mother. I therefore endeavoured successfully to get into the course on Political Theory and Institutions at Sheffield University, which turned out to be a tremendously wise move – not only because Sheffield was building a first-class reputation, but because it gave me the opportunity to read philosophy, to study institutions and to understand the relationship of the values I held to political and economic history. I would never again, until the winter of 2005/6 when I took up reading political autobiographies, have the chance to read so thoroughly and to ground myself in the experience of others and the wisdom of thought.

By this time, at twenty-two years old, I was the youngest councillor on Sheffield City Council – indeed, the youngest councillor in Britain, thus undertaking my political studies at the same time as learning about political reality. Six years later I was Chairman of Social Services, having served on both Sheffield and the short-lived South Yorkshire Metropolitan County Council, where I played my part with a handful of others in what at the time was the infamous and highly successful policy of subsidising public transport and providing a free bus service in Sheffield city centre.

In 1970 I married my wife Ruth, and we had three sons, Alastair, Hugh and Andrew, of whom I am deeply proud. Although our marriage failed in 1987 and we were divorced in 1990, I owe Ruth a debt of gratitude, both for the enormous support she gave me in those very early days and for the way in which we were able to co-operate in bringing up our sons in two happy and loving homes. Later Ruth was to refuse a very large sum of money from the *Sunday Express* to 'tell all' about our marriage and its break-up, and again I am deeply grateful to her for her integrity.

In 1980 I became Leader of Sheffield City Council. The early 1980s were turbulent years. Margaret Thatcher was cutting back on local government in a way which is hard to describe to those with only a passing knowledge of local government finance and the politics of the time, and almost impossible to those with knowledge of neither. Suffice to say that Sheffield lost 40 per cent of its funding from central government at a time when, because of the Thatcher government's obsession with non-intervention and the free market and changes brought about in production through the introduction of new technology, over 50,000 jobs in specialist steel and engineering were lost in that city alone. Ironically, we were arguing for what would now be described as 'the third way' – new Labour before New Labour – although our rhetoric was seen to be that of a left-wing radical authority. We were creatures of the time, and there is no point in pretending that you would do something different when you were dealing with the politics of the moment. Hindsight is the most visionary sight of all, and there are many things which, given the chance, I would do differently with the experience I now have and the knowledge that the years have brought me. But in the pamphlet produced by Professor Geoff Green and myself for the Fabian Society in 1982, we spelt out a commitment to building community politics from the bottom up, and even participated in the BBC's A level economics course on an alternative to old Labour and free-market Thatcherism which twenty-five years later appeared to be commonplace.

At this time I had given up my job as a tutor at Barnsley College of Technology. (I was on full-time secondment.) I had worked there since 1973 following the postgraduate course in further education teaching, after graduating from Sheffield University in 1972.

As local councillors we were pretty hair-shirted in those days. We decided to forgo the new special responsibility allowances for Council leaders and chairs of committees, and I personally lost several years of pension rights. But it all seemed worthwhile, not only in terms of keeping up hope – Sheffield was genuinely seen as a beacon within the Labour Party during those dreadful years of prolonged opposition – but also in transforming public services, innovating and finding new ways of delivering decentralised, neighbourhood-based provision. This was pretty much against the odds given the financial pressures and the need to steer a middle course between old-style local government and the very different but equally notorious twin pillars of Militant Tendency in Liverpool and what became known as the Rainbow Coalition in the Greater London Council and some London boroughs.

This is not the place to go into the politics of the 1980s in any depth. Because of the substantial increases in raising local government funding in Sheffield we were seen as 'left wing', but in many respects we were forging new ground, taking on the Militant Tendency and trying to persuade those in London that a coalition of the dispossessed, the disadvantaged and the discriminated against was morally very satisfying but electorally disastrous in the long term. It was inevitable that as you overcame deprivation, disadvantage and discrimination, you eliminated any kind of majority for the programme you were putting forward – hence the need to reach out across economic, social and cultural groupings. So it was that we recognised in Sheffield that to help the dispossessed we had to persuade a large swathe of the electorate that what we were doing was in their best interests as well.

My main regret – and I tried to learn from this later in my political life – was that I did not instil the changes that I believed most strongly were necessary into the process of decision-making, into the delivery of services, and into the very heart of officialdom and public provision.

As ever, I was in a hurry to bring about change and, as will be seen later, the necessity of bringing about change rapidly does not always allow you to inculcate and embed the values or the practical changes that are necessary to carry through reforms for the future.

Leaving aside one or two of the antics of gesturist politics (such as nuclear-free zones), I am proud of what was achieved in Sheffield in the 1980s. The Audit Commission, the body that oversees the probity and efficiency of local services, described Sheffield as 'a shining example of local government at its best'. When people ask whether I have changed since those years, the answer is self-evidently 'yes'. Partly the demise of the Labour Party in the 1980s was due to the fact that people did not want to change as the world changed around them. But if I had the choice, I would like the best of the radical, often opinionated and dedicated David Blunkett of the 1980s to be mixed with the more mature, thoughtful, realistic and certainly older and wiser version of the early twenty-first century.

However, back in the 1980s as a thrusting young man, I was determined to make a mark. The National Executive Committee of the Labour Party was the ruling body (and in opposition played an absolutely seminal role in the reform of the party) and, under Neil Kinnock and then John Smith, provided us with the platform on which Tony Blair was able to stand from 1994 onwards in taking the party into government and the years with which this book is primarily concerned.

In 1983, with a great deal of help from my close friends, I was elected to the National Executive Committee. For someone who was not an MP to be elected to that section of the executive reserved for the party rank and file was unheard of – in fact it was equalled only by Professor Harold Laski at the end of the Second World War.

But at times when my ego is inflated, along with friends it has often been my dogs who bring me down to earth. I recall that I was walking down the promenade at Brighton during party conference, full of my new-found 'power' – which incidentally is an indication of how internalised everything had become, as we all thought we had won great victories if we won something inside the party rather than actually winning elections outside it. There I was, strolling along, thinking that I owned the world, when towards me came a couple of people who I heard saying, 'It can't be . . . It is . . . No, it can't be.' I thought: 'My goodness, they've recognised me.' And then came the punchline: 'It is, you know, it *is* a curly coat retriever!'

At the time of writing, I have had five dogs – Ruby, Teddy, Offa, Lucy and Sadie – and their company, their sometimes amusing antics and their ability often to break the ice in conversation have made a very big difference to me, as well of course as their primary duty of giving me dignity and independence in moving about.

But before moving on to my time in Parliament, it is worth reflecting that my experiences in my early years in local government, and my time teaching industrial relations, politics and public administration in the heart of the South Yorkshire coalfield, taught me a great deal. When in 1978 I missed by one vote being selected as the Labour candidate for a by-election in the South Yorkshire seat of Penistone, I thought the world had fallen apart. In fact that one vote saved me. Not only did it save me from eighteen years in opposition, sitting on the green benches of the House of Commons and no doubt becoming more and more demoralised, it also saved the country from an extremely callow and bumptious young man who thought he knew it all without having had the experience so often lacking in politics at senior level these days. It does make an enormous difference knowing how to handle officialdom, whether it be local government officers or civil servants, and having experience of making decisions, developing policy, campaigning and communicating ideas. Above all, it makes a difference in the real struggle to deliver services on the ground in the teeth of institutionalised resistance to the change and modernisation you are endeavouring to put in place.

I was deeply fortunate to be selected as Labour candidate for the 1987 general election in my home community of Sheffield Brightside, on the retirement of the sitting member Joan Maynard, the firebrand left-wing MP affectionately known as 'Stalin's Granny'. Schooling apart, I had been brought up in the constituency from my earliest childhood, and I cared deeply about doing something to put right the despair and disadvantage which mass unemployment and deteriorating services brought.

I was duly elected, but with my marriage breaking down and my need to establish a home in London as well as a new home in Sheffield, this was a time of turbulence for me. I had two major illnesses in the first year of my time in Parliament which, in one perverse way, took me out of the public eye so that, unlike Ken Livingstone, former Leader of the GLC who became Mayor of London over twenty years later, I avoided getting up the noses of those MPs who had already suffered for eight years on the Opposition benches.

My main interest was still local government, and I began to fight the proposals for the infamous poll tax, which in the end was a major reason for Margaret Thatcher's downfall. Neil Kinnock, at the behest of Jack Cunningham – with whom I had always had a fairly stormy relationship – agreed to make me a Junior Spokesman in the Shadow Team dealing with local government and the environment. That, together with my place on the National Executive Committee, gave me an important role in taking on the Conservative government on one of its flagship policies – and something that was critically important to our wider campaigning. This was one of those opportunities in life which I grasped with both hands.

In 1992, after the bitterness of our defeat, I felt it was important that we had a contest for the leadership. I therefore backed my then boss Bryan Gould, who had taken over from Jack Cunningham and who despite being vehemently anti-European was New Labour on economic and social policy in a way which would have made him a real asset had he and John Smith not fallen out so bitterly. John Smith's great strength, for which I shall always be grateful to him, was to understand why I had campaigned against his 'shoo-in' as leader and to offer me the portfolio of Shadow Health Secretary, which I held between 1992 and 1994. At this point, while we had a phenomenally good anti-government campaign on health which Robin Cook had put together over the previous five years, we had virtually no policies of our own. The task therefore was to develop a coherent policy, which we did in a document *Health 2000*. I am still proud of that piece of work which, although not implemented immediately when we took office in 1997, formed the basis of the reforms of the first two parliaments of the New Labour government.

By now I was recognising what I had let myself in for: the enormity of trying to break new ground and develop radical policy and at the same time get elected each year to the Shadow Cabinet. This process, which had more to do with cronyism and organisation than it had to do with merit, was the beginning of my baptism into the world of serious internecine politics. In order to understand the years of government, it is worth reflecting here that I have never been good at the back-slapping, the ego-smoothing or the tea-room gossip. Had I taken a little more time and trouble in those early days, perhaps it would have stood me in better stead in rougher times when, having ruffled many feathers, I could hear the birds of prey wheeling overhead.

But thoughts of internal difficulties for the future were secondary to the promotion and election of a Labour government, and a new era in Labour Party politics began in the summer of 1994.

That summer was when I first became close to Tony Blair. We had known each other before then, of course, and I recall a memorable moment on a train going down to a Joint Local Government and Young Labour conference, when we spent time talking about the ideas I had put to John Smith's Commission on Social Justice (1993) about a non-military national service for young people. He was interested, but indicated that I had chosen a very strange audience to which to deliver such a speech – the Young Labour delegates. Twelve years later in the Pre-Budget Report of 2005 we were still struggling to square the circle of wanting young people to have a very positive engagement with community and citizenship, while at the same time not wanting to engage in compulsion.

I also remember this particular train journey for an insight into how much his aide Anji Hunter mattered with regard to the support she gave to Tony. It may seem trivial, but the fact that she ensured he had sandwiches for the journey I thought extremely important. So many of us traversed the country throughout the years of opposition, sometimes travelling for hours to a half-empty hall or television studio to find that even a request for a cup of tea was met with bewilderment. Margaret Beckett tells the story of having travelled for three hours to arrive at a hall for a meeting which had been cancelled. When she enquired where she might obtain something to eat, she was told there was a good fish and chip shop round the corner.

It was the fortuitous and completely unimportant position of Party Chairman that led me to know Tony much better. I remember to this day the telephone call from Larry Whitty, then General Secretary of the Party (and now a member of the House of Lords), on the morning of 12 May 1994. At that time I lived in a small one-bedroom terraced house near Wimbledon, and the phone call reached me as I was about to leave for St Albans to visit a hospital as Shadow Health Secretary. Larry told me that John Smith had had a massive heart attack in the early hours, and warned me that I might well be wasting my time going to St Albans as I would be recalled to London; but, nevertheless, until the death of John was confirmed I should go ahead as planned. No sooner had I got on the train than another call came to tell me that John was dead.

This was a resounding shock both to the party and to the nation, but it came as a very signal jolt to me personally. The night before I had been with John at one of the gala dinners which formed part of the essential fundraising for the general election and in this case also for the European campaign, as the European Assembly elections were under way. As Party Chair, I had sat with John and his wife Elizabeth at the top table and heard his brilliant speech, so often quoted: 'We will do our best to reward your faith in us, but please give us the opportunity to serve our country. That is all we ask.'

I knew that John had drunk rather a lot that evening, although it certainly didn't affect his speech – probably the opposite – but what I couldn't have known was that he had also drunk a bottle of champagne when they returned to their flat, elated as is so often the case when a speech has gone well, when the tide has turned and political adrenalin turns to the real thing.

In my tiny office off the Committee corridor at the House of Commons, I started to phone round to find out who was likely to stand for the leadership, and therefore whether or not I had a role in the weeks ahead. As it happened, every senior member of the Shadow Cabinet other than myself was, in one way or another, embroiled in the election campaign, and therefore purely by accident it fell to me to work with Larry Whitty on organising the leadership election. Tony was in Aberdeen, and when I spoke to him he indicated that he would be back that evening and would like to talk to me. This we did, in my tiny office, and it became clear that he had every determination to run.

Near me resided the larger-than-life character of Denis Healey, who had retired as an MP at the 1992 general election. Denis was to throw his full weight behind Tony – and frankly the momentum which Tony already possessed was going to carry him to the leadership whatever the ins and outs of the famous supper with Gordon at Granita.

Much was to be made later of comparisons between David Cameron's emergence as Tory leader and Tony's rise to prominence. In my view this was mistaken for two essential reasons: firstly, that Tony had been in Parliament for eleven years before standing for the leadership, and had held a number of absolutely key reforming portfolios (not least Employment, which at that time included industrial relations) and was Shadow Home Secretary in 1994; and secondly, because the momentum that he already had was essentially with the support of the British media. I remember asking myself, as a fellow Shadow Cabinet member, what was needed from the rest of us to achieve the adoration that already existed for anything that Tony did, including in Standing Committees (which take the day-to-day grinding detail of legislation through its inexorable process) at a time when getting the press to report a Standing Committee at all was becoming an impossible task for the rest of us.

What Tony Blair showed, as has David Cameron more recently, was the belief within his party that his accession to the leadership would be a passport to electoral success. Back in 1994 it was a revelation for the Labour Party to decide that it wanted to be the party of government rather than one of protest.

Tony was duly elected leader in July 1994, and the age of New Labour had well and truly begun.

1

SECRETARY OF STATE

FOR EDUCATION AND EMPLOYMENT

1997–2001

*M*y position as Secretary of State for Education in the 1997 Labour government effectively began with an invitation to supper with Tony Blair at his Islington house in September 1994, a few weeks after he had become party leader. Tony needed to know whether I agreed with his modernising and reform agenda – what had become known, in relation to Tony and Gordon, as 'the Project'.

I gave Tony my full support, and over a simple, unpretentious meal – with Cherie joining us after what had clearly been for her an incredibly hectic day – he asked me what brief I would wish to hold in his reshuffled Shadow Cabinet. After pointing out light-heartedly that one or two jobs were already well spoken for, I said that if I really had a choice I would like to have a crack at Education or Employment (which at that point were two separate portfolios). I was offered the first and inherited the second when, a year later, the Conservative government amalgamated the Department for Education with the Department for Employment into the Department for Education and Employment (DfEE). While in Opposition, the employment brief included both industrial relations and the national minimum wage, so there was a substantial portfolio in the economic as well as the education-and-skills programme.

It is important to understand this, because no Shadow Team did more work preparing for entry into government than the one that I had the privilege of leading. It is history now that Gordon Brown and those working with him developed the concept of the windfall levy, without which we would not have been able to implement the New Deal proposals, covering a range of employment initiatives but centring initially on the 18–25 age group. The New Deal drew its title from Roosevelt's public employment programme, but this New Deal was to focus on training, job placement and environmental task forces. Compulsion (and the withdrawal of automatic pay-out of benefits for those not complying) was central to the new approach. The concept of using such resources in a targeted way to tackle long-standing unemployment was Gordon's, but the shaping of that programme alongside the development of the national minimum wage and industrial relations was, as we will see, a joint venture.

The Shadow Education Team included Ian McCartney, Stephen Byers and my fellow Shadow Cabinet member Michael Meacher, and keeping the peace between these three was no mean feat, as they did not exactly all get on together. Also in the team was my old friend – though later a scathing critic –

Peter Kilfoyle, from whom my eldest son Alastair had enjoyed outstanding hospitality while on a placement in the laboratories at Liverpool University, which was later to assist him in gaining a place as an undergraduate there. I spent the evening of Alastair's eighteenth birthday with the Kilfoyle family, minus Peter himself, who had been called back to London to vote on a knife-edge amendment intended to embarrass the Tories on the issue of VAT on energy charges, a vote we needed to lose in order to keep up the pressure – which is why one or two of us were allowed to be absent (but not those without permission, as Jim Cousins and Ann Clwyd found to their cost when they declined to return from their trip to the Kurdish areas of Turkey and Iraq). It was with particular regret, therefore, that ten years later I found Peter such an implacable opponent.

To understand the early months of the new Labour government on the education-and-skills front requires some grasp of the context of the previous two and a half years.

We had two major hurdles. The first was to persuade the party and the education profession that standards and discipline (a word that had not been used in Labour parlance for many years) were absolutely central to what we stood for. The second was to ensure that structures were designed to assist that goal and to put behind us the enormous divisions and almost obsessive concentration on the status, structure and selective nature of some schools which had diverted the Labour Party and the teaching profession for so long.

It is now hard to remember just how exercised people were by the issue of grant-maintained schools and remaining selection: not until the White Paper produced in the autumn of 2005 did we see a reversion to the old arguments.

But from 1994 to 1996 the battle was raging inside the party, and the document we produced for the party conference in autumn 1995 which spelt out the changes we wished to make was only narrowly carried – indeed, at one stage it genuinely looked as if we were going to lose the vote. Although in the long run this would not have changed our direction, it would have been a tremendous humiliation and, more importantly, would have sent entirely the wrong signal to the electorate, allowing our critics in the press to paint us as obsessed with the very thing that we had been accusing our opponents of having an obsession about – structures and status, rather than standards.

My own conference speech in 1995 had to be one of the best I have ever made, not least because my adversaries had made extraordinarily good speeches of their own – notably Roy Hattersley, who was to become steadfastly opposed not only to virtually everything I did in government but to me personally. This was sad, given that both of us love our home city of Sheffield (and love Sheffield Wednesday FC), and that I had a great affection for Roy's mother Enid, who had been Lord Mayor of Sheffield when I was Leader of the Council in the 1980s. But unfortunately Roy seemed to believe that his mother's attitude to me diminished his standing in her eyes. I do not for a moment believe this to be true, but I think that – perfectly understandably – it could have affected his view of me.

Suffice it to say that the atmosphere of tension as I rose to go to the conference rostrum – tension augmented by the whispered 'Good luck' from Tony Blair – contributed to one error in the speech which came back to haunt me on many future occasions.

It is salutary how one word can make such a difference, and in my case that word was 'more'. My declaration – following the admonition 'Read my lips', as parody of George Bush senior's notorious promise of no new taxes – that under a Labour government schools would be allowed 'no selection, either by examination or by interview', should have read 'no more selection'. The omission really shouldn't have mattered, not least because in the seventeen broadcast interviews I did after my speech I made our position abundantly clear. But it did matter, because it became a stick with which to beat me when it was obvious that we were not going to be in a position simply to eliminate the existing selective schools without going through the procedure we had constructed.

There were two major advantages to the $2\frac{1}{2}$-year run-up to the general election on 1 May 1997.

The first was that we had detailed policies to place before the civil service, with a clear idea of the kind of unit we needed in order to drive them forward as well as the engagement of those from outside the traditional Department for Education and Employment to do the job.

The second was that we had won over enough members of the party to push the policies through the House of Commons legitimately, with all the temptations that later revealed themselves for a very large majority to engage in dissent and revolt.

That second point should not be underestimated. You can bring forward a charismatic leader, you can have someone or even a small group of people who know what it takes to win, but if you have not actually secured the necessary momentum, the early procedural steps of legitimacy in taking the party with you, then the electorate will rightly be suspicious of what, even in those days, was an attempt to sever the head from the body.

This is a lesson for many political parties, reinforced for me in 2005 by a conversation I had with the retiring Minister of Labour in the outgoing SPD government in Germany. His contention was that Gerhardt Schröder had never carried with him the consent of the SPD as a whole, and therefore had never built up the momentum to ensure that not just the parliamentary grouping but also those crucially engaged across the country were fighting for and understood the importance of reform and change.

However, it was the first of these two points – the clear programme with a clear delivery plan – that made such a difference. For instance, the literacy strategy implemented within months of taking office resulted in a 25 per cent uplift in the number of youngsters being able to read adequately by the age of eleven.

Our programme, worked out through that long pre-general-election period, was bitterly fought by those who, extraordinarily, believed that young children were incapable of achieving well in basic subjects such as literacy or numeracy, while the critics themselves were preaching equality of opportunity and at the same time expecting a great deal from their own children. This was a point I was to make over and over again during interviews on radio and television and in the press, but which was history within a couple of years of the end of my tenure as Secretary of State for Education and Employment in 2001.

May 1997

My see-saw government career began in the early hours of 2 May 1997 when I was returned as Member of Parliament for Sheffield Brightside with a majority of nearly 20,000 votes, one of 417 Labour wins which gave us a massive House of Commons majority of 179 seats. While the now-legendary celebration party was taking place on the South Bank in London as dawn broke that Friday morning, I was still in Sheffield, snatching a few hours' sleep before returning to London. I confess that a small part of me regretted not being at the South Bank, but at that momentous time I was happier being where my roots are.

The presumption that I would be offered the education and employment brief has been considerable. Before the election, the Leadership Group (particularly Tony Blair's chief of staff, Jonathan Powell) couldn't make up their minds as to whether they wanted just Gordon Brown, John Prescott and Robin Cook to be called on the Friday, or whether they wanted to include Jack Straw, Margaret Beckett and myself. In the end they did include us and I took the train down to London, arriving in time to give my guide dog Lucy a walk in the park next to the House of Lords and enjoy the wonderful sunshine which carried through from election day itself to the Saturday teatime. Among the crowds there was an almost tangible sense of enjoyment, the sheer exhilaration of people revelling in the feeling that the Tories had disappeared – as if the whole nation was letting out a huge sigh of relief.

Personally I was subdued that day, aware of the enormity of what we are taking on. I have already done a great deal of preparation, seeing people in the Department, talking to the Permanent Secretary and to the Principal Private Secretary, and I have seen the Policy Board three times with the previous team.

I am still considerably perturbed by the low turn-out – 57.5 per cent – in my own constituency of Sheffield Brightside. It transpires that other constituencies with a similar make-up have witnessed similar disillusionment from the electorate, and seen similarly abysmal turn-outs – Liverpool Riverside, for instance, had only 52 per cent – but none the less it is a real blow.

Remarkably the Liverpool Riverside turn-out fell to 34 per cent in the 2001 general election (and my own constituency to 46.7 per cent), so there was a clear trend here.

Fortunately the other candidates in Sheffield Brightside all stood up and said that everywhere they had been – on the doorstep, in the shopping centres and in the community – the message came across that people believed I was doing a very good job and my constituency office were doing a good job, and so the low turn-out was not a personal slight. But if I hadn't been told that, I think I would have been even more downhearted.

When I arrived at No. 10, Tony confirmed my appointment as Secretary of State for Education and Employment, and we ran through briefly, for about half an hour, issues about education and the importance of the New Deal. I raised with him the state of play on the Social Affairs Council in Europe and the importance of a new employability agenda dealing with skills and preparation for new technology in the new century.

After Tony had appointed me I went straight across to the Department. My meeting with Tony had followed his appointing Margaret Beckett as Secretary of State at the Department of Trade and Industry, although in the pecking order of the published Cabinet positions, for what it's worth, Education came after Home Office and before the DTI. The idea of Education Secretary being an Office of State didn't seem to mean a lot.

The DfEE has not done what I had asked them to do before the election. When on the Friday it was clear that we had won and it was likely that I was to be appointed Education Secretary, I asked them to secure me a decent room in the Palace of Westminster. Unfortunately they have not done anything at all except just ring across to the House authorities, who have allocated me a room like a dungeon in the Speaker's Court archway.

I spent all day Saturday in the Department and came back north on Saturday night on a train full of drunks who had been to the Rugby League Cup Final. I got off at Doncaster to be driven across to Sheffield, and they went on to Leeds and Bradford.

When I returned to London on the Monday I needed to work very quickly, and a decision was taken to appoint Michael Barber as head of the Standards and Effectiveness Unit, which subsumed the Improvement Unit in the Department. There was even a tussle about that. Sir Robin Butler, Head of the Civil Service, tried to veto the idea and clearly was exercising enormous power when laying down what could and could not be done.

The Tories and Margaret Thatcher had the same sort of problems with the civil service, and I know I have to be very tough about it. This is one of the few times I have ever blessed Margaret Thatcher, for having at least had some strength in dealing with the civil service. I fear that the influence of the past on these matters is quite considerable.

The DfEE has been very welcoming. Michael Bichard [Permanent Secretary], who has come from outside the civil service himself, is very keen to help us open up the Department and the machinery. I immediately wrote to all the Department's staff and to all schools and colleges, and this seemed to go down very well.

We then organised a series of meetings, starting with one on the Queen's Speech day, 14 May, at 9.30 a.m. in Westminster Central Hall, with over 2,000 of the Department's staff present. We were trying to get the message across that we believed in public service, that we wanted an enabling department, that we wanted everybody involved, and that they could all feel they had a part to play and were all valued. We also wanted to indicate that there should be two-way communication: where changes were clearly needed they should speak out, while for our part we would recognise what they were doing, rather than simply dwelling on how things had been done in the past.

Despite considerable efforts to get round schools and local authorities, to reach out to job centres, and to hold meetings across the country in an unprecedented way (more than any other department), I still believe that this was not enough. I had learned lessons from my time as Leader of Sheffield City Council about the importance of instilling ideas, practices and focus in those at the sharp end, but given the enormous pressure to develop, communicate and then deliver policy there were just not enough hours in the day or week to be able to do the kind of work that my ministers and senior civil servants wanted to do. The consequence of not embedding change, of not getting across fully what we were trying to do and why, and above all reaching out in order to isolate the 'Jonahs' who sit in the corner of every staff room, meant that once the foot came off the accelerator and there was any kind of diversion, the momentum lessened.

This is true of government as a whole and, of course, the longer you are in government, the less likely it is that you are able to keep up the same direct contact. For that matter, the departmental staff themselves begin to wonder whether you are all about 'spin' and communication rather than getting on with the job. There were occasions when secretaries of state and ministers who hovered above problems, detached from the day-to-day pressure and reality, got credit from the media – and, it has to be said, from the civil service – for not actually being up to their elbows and embroiled in detail. There is a real Catch-22 here which takes some resolving. I think there is no choice but to simply get stuck in, and any minister who doesn't care enough to be on top of the detail and to feel deeply about what they are doing isn't worth his/her salt.

The team is turning out to be very good. Steve Byers is Minister of State, and I managed to keep Estelle Morris as number two to Steve with the education brief, dealing with standards and schools, and Tessa Blackstone has been appointed Minister of State at the Lords, dealing with Lifelong Learning. They have been joined by Kim Howells. I was a little bit sceptical about Kim at first but he has certainly knuckled down and is doing the job as part of a team.

Andrew Smith is no surprise at Employment, with Alan Howarth, previously a Tory minister, backing him up. (Ironically, the civil service allocated Alan Howarth the same office that he had been in when he had been a Tory minister.) Andrew is not in the Cabinet, but has been made a member of the Privy Council.

We have had a struggle about how many special advisers we are allowed. Robin Butler has been trying to persuade Tony that there should be a very, very strict regime, but there seem to be exceptions all round for No. 10, including on the question of who could be made a civil servant without going through the normal procedures – in this case Anji Hunter – and the setting-up of a major extension of the Policy Unit as well as extending the Political Unit with Sally Morgan, John Cruddas and Faz Hakim.

For myself, rather than just the two advisers proposed by Robin Butler I want four, whom I will draw together into a Policy Unit in the same way as Tony.

In the end, we compromised on three and a half special advisers for me, which reflected the fact that my team had a tremendous task in going through printed material with me in a way that was clearly not necessary for anyone else.

Thursday 15 May: the second Cabinet meeting. The first, a week after polling day, was something of an anti-climax. I was subdued anyway, as my feet had never left the ground, but the first cabinet meeting really didn't address any major issues. There was a brief mention of Zaire: George Robertson [Secretary of State for Defence] indicated, as he has done at the second meeting, that the Ministry of Defence has already got a grip on the situation and is suggesting things like a major airlift at considerable expense and a large number of troops being sent to Kinshasa. It hasn't been until the second Cabinet meeting that the wisdom of this has really been questioned. There is a danger that the MoD is going to make a complete mess of it by sending a large number of troops to a place where they appear to think there is no threat from the rebels. This indicates that both the ambassador in Kinshasa and the Ministry of Defence really have a very strange view of what is likely to happen, not recognising that stability would come from a rebel victory. The rebels are disciplined and organised, whereas the Mbuto camp is evil, corrupt and genocidal. This issue has been raised in some detail at the second Cabinet meeting, where Robin Cook and in particular Clare Short expressed themselves very strongly. The point was well taken by Tony and it was made clear that the thing needed to be sorted out.

The Cabinet minute for that particular meeting – circulated before the next meeting – doesn't illustrate quite as strongly as it might the feeling of disbelief we had when we realised that George Robertson thought that he couldn't overturn what had already been committed by the previous government, indicating perhaps why Tony moved him from Scotland and the key devolution debate – although to be fair, he had given a very strong impression of competence and humanity in the handling of the tragedy at Dunblane.

These reactions to the first two Cabinet meetings demonstrate what happens time and time again – namely that foreign affairs and defence dominate discussion, forming a standing item, together with the parliamentary business for the immediate period ahead. (We extended this discussion of imminent parliamentary business from a week ahead to a more sensible period of two to three weeks.) No such detailed agenda item exists for major home affairs and domestic matters. This, of course, harks back to the nineteenth century, to imperial Britain. It reflects the Prime Minister's role (particularly in the cases of Margaret Thatcher and Tony Blair, both of whom had a part on the world stage and the stature to go with it), but none the less it is a major distortion of what Cabinet should be about in twenty-first-century Britain, with its population of 60 million. It also accounts in small measure for the irritation that bubbles up in me from time to time that government as a whole is diverted into foreign policy and international matters rather than concentrating on reform and delivery at home.

At the first Cabinet meeting, I think we were all just finding our feet. I sat opposite Sir Robin Butler, next to Derry Irvine, with Gordon Brown on Derry Irvine's other side (Derry being Lord Chancellor), and Frank Dobson sitting sullenly on my left. I think Frank was contemplating that it was going to be difficult in a New Labour government.

While examining the Cabinet Room, I found a ceremonial sword on the table behind me.

In retrospect I should have provided myself with chain-mail armour which I could have slipped on like a sleeveless vest. As it was, the sword lay there menacing, waiting for a hand to grip it. Luckily I had a dog under the table.

The two things I remember most from that meeting are Gordon Brown persuading Tony to cut our salaries and the decision to call each other by our first names – including Tony – rather than having to go through the palaver of saying 'Prime Minister', 'Foreign Secretary', 'Lord Chancellor' and so on, which I frankly welcomed as I thought it would otherwise make meetings rather theatrical.

It is quite clear that not a great deal is going to be discussed at Cabinet. Instead, business is going to be done informally, one to one with Tony, or through Cabinet Committees. What is interesting is the way in which even Cabinet Committees are not discussed at Cabinet, which I think is quite a significant failure to use the Cabinet effectively.

At the first Cabinet meeting, Tony indicated that he would like everyone to notify No. 10 before going on any radio or television programme or undertaking any major interview. I suggested that he, as a past master at the art of managing the media, would recognise better than any of us the way in which speed is of the essence. If we were dealing with an issue at 11.30 a.m., say, and weren't on the television by twelve o'clock, we would have missed the lunchtime news broadcasts and would be left flat-footed. He replied that he understood this and that common sense would have to prevail, but the subsequent minute didn't reflect this latter point. (Since that meeting a circular has been sent round asking us to notify No. 10 of any lunch or dinner dates with journalists. I've told the office simply to ignore it.)

While the first Cabinet stretched to an hour and a half, the second lasted only an hour, and even then Tony was quite keen to get away.

On policy issues we have been moving very rapidly in the two weeks since the election, getting the Standards and Effectiveness Unit up and running, dealing with failing schools, finding out what should be done with the local education authorities, getting the letters out, taking key decisions in relation to nursery vouchers and having the first Queen's Speech slot after the Prime Minister. This was scheduled for Thursday the 15th, which created difficulties for the Awayday [for the Department's ministers and senior civil servants] which we had planned from teatime that day through to Friday teatime, in a Derbyshire hotel as there was no time to book Chevening or Dorneywood. We decided we would have to go away because, had we stayed in the Department, people would have been coming and going all the time, the telephone would have been ringing incessantly, and nothing would have got done.

I didn't get to Derbyshire until 8.45 in the evening – after some considerable awkwardness with Frank Dobson, who was deeply unpleasant about the fact that it wasn't possible for our team to stay in the House until the very end of the day. It was supposed to be an Education, Employment, Social Security and Health day but none of the social-security ministers helped us to cover the bench. (There always has to be a minister on the government front bench, no matter how tedious the debate.) Alan Howarth remained until 6.30 p.m. before he was able to get away – fortuitously, Alan Milburn [Minister of State at the Department of Health] happened to be in the Chamber. He had not been due to take over, but Alan Howarth was able to hand over to him to make sure the Health team covered the last part of the evening.

In the Commons, the general picture is very rosy, but with our majority of 179 there is not enough room in the Chamber for all our members, and many of them have been pressing to be allowed to sit on the other side so that they have a seat. That would be very awkward for me because I wouldn't be able to tell whether the question or intervention was coming from my side of the House or the Opposition side. It's going to take a long time to get to know the voices, even of those who regularly intervene. There are so many new members that it is going to be quite a strain. I am not very good at networking and keeping in touch with backbenchers at the best of times, and have to rely very heavily on my team – and in particular on Jean Corston, my Parliamentary Private Secretary – to help me make sure I don't make terrible errors.

This was to be a recurring problem for me. It is not that I am anti-social – quite the opposite. It is a simple practical problem, and not one which it is possible to make a fuss about if you want to be taken seriously. The problem is this. You walk down a corridor, go into the Members' Tea Room (exclusive to MPs) or into one of the dining rooms, and you simply cannot see who is there. They can see you but you can't see them. When you pass people in a corridor, you can say hello but you can't know whether it is a friend or a foe. Simply keeping on top of the job, reading the mass of material and getting through the tapes night after night inevitably means that you cut yourself off.

In the early days, I think now that this was a plus, not because I should not have been getting to know my own colleagues better or doing the networking, but because it kept me away from the sort of personal difficulties that later came my way. I lived the life that I had had since 1988 when my marriage broke up, when literally every weekend except when I was at party conference my young sons came to stay, all the way through to 1998 when Andrew was sixteen, Hugh eighteen and Alastair twenty-one. It was only at that time, when the boys became free spirits, that this solid, common-sense life started to change – and not for the better. My 100 per cent dedication to work and the austere image that many branches of the media liked so much began to alter. So in these early days of government, my ten years in Parliament, of commitment to family, to close friends and to work, was the rock on which I rested. How I wish that that had remained the case.

On Monday [19 May] I had an interesting conversation with my Principal Private Secretary, Alun Evans. He indicated there was now a very different style of approach from the previous regime, not least because I dictated some of my own letters and even some memos and notes. Later in the day Michael Bichard raised with me the question of a note I had sent to Gordon Brown which Gordon had understandably passed on to the Treasury: this had been typed up in the office and Alun Evans was aware of it. I had handed the note to Gordon personally – a friendly comment regarding the development of the Budget strategy for June and the critical importance of potential capital investment relating to education, which can have a beneficial effect on jobs and might form part of the windfall tax.

Michael Bichard indicated that this was not the correct style at all, and that the Treasury had realised this memo had not been written by the Department but by me. He suggested that in future the Private Office should see such memos before they went. I said I was very happy with the process of ensuring that all concerned, including the Director of Finance, had notes, but that I obviously reserved the right to write my own and didn't have to rely on the Department drafting everything. We parted on good terms, but I was left with the distinct impression that secretaries of state are usually confined to what is written for them and are expected to do as they are told.

What was significant about this exchange is that Michael Bichard was, and remained, the most radical, free-thinking and open-minded of all permanent secretaries. Having worked outside the civil service (including having been chief executive of two local authorities and of the Benefits Agency), he had real experience of doing things in a different way. The truth is – and I can admit it now – that I did eventually pretty well concede. I wrote my own memos internally, and dictated a large number of letters to people outside rather than relying on the cumbersome, lengthy and often frustrating system of having the letters written for me; but when it came to inter-departmental correspondence, I confined myself to slotting in my own paragraphs and altering phrases here and there.

No doubt the senior civil service spotted the inserts – and perhaps even the deletions – because (and here is a little-known fact) the civil service share 'draft memos and letters' across departments before senior politicians see them. They are therefore painfully aware when secretaries of state have overridden their senior officials and they know what the 'departmental line' really is.

This is a world within a world, and it was some considerable time before I fully appreciated just how much was passed between departments prior to policy documents reaching the politicians – with the sole exception of genuine battles with the Treasury, where the civil service recognised that their own

standing and status depended on the success of their Cabinet minister. Of
course, the more senior you are the less likely it is that you will be the loser, and
therefore there will be supplicant departments seeking clearance from their
more powerful colleagues (if they know what is good for them).

I am in the House of Commons office formerly occupied by Gillian
Shephard [Secretary of State for Education and Employment in the Conservative government, 1994–97]. It is boiling hot, doesn't have a telephone,
and other people have clearly taken the best of the furniture and dumped old
furniture from their room in it. This is apparently par for the course and
leaves me with the feeling that somehow, while I am running the Department, leading on policy and trying to get it clearly across to both the staff and
the public, I am far from in charge of the minutiae of life.

I can only look on with admiration at the new Chancellor of the
Exchequer, who wanted to invite all new Labour MPs for drinks at No. 10
and managed to get the invitations out in less than a week. I have a feeling
that if I had asked my Department to do this, it would have taken them the
best part of six weeks even to find out the names of those who had been
elected.

Sunday 25 May: today's papers suggest that Gordon's approach is
rubbing the Treasury up the wrong way, irritating Treasury insiders to
the point where they are briefing the City that things aren't well and that
Gordon has no grip of the normal administration and day-to-day working
of the Department. Given Gordon's style in opposition, this is no surprise,
although clearly the Treasury have their own agenda and want to try to
reassert themselves.

On the other hand, there is no doubt that the axis between Sir Robin
Butler as Cabinet Secretary and Tony's chief of staff Jonathan Powell is a
very powerful one indeed. Jonathan, with his experience in the Diplomatic
Service, has a great empathy with the civil service, with its structures and its
conservatism, and this shows in their close relationship and presumably
agreed demarcation of responsibilities, from which both of them benefit.
But Sir Robin retains the kind of influence and power he could never have
hoped to have had, say, a year earlier. He must have thought that the Blair
government would be quick to sweep aside a traditional mandarin like
him.

Roy Hattersley can't resist launching another attack on me in an article
about education in the *Observer*. This time it is about naming failing
schools and how we're demoralising everyone by doing it. Funny how

defending the profession has taken on a much greater salience with people like Roy than actually defending the children. How you could sneak improvement teams into schools without an awareness that there was a problem there, God only knows.

This has been Adult Learners' Week. The departmental press office has had hordes of people working on it, from the launch on a bus in Trafalgar Square to all the fuss about my learning a few words of French in order to be able to order a bottle of St Emilion. But it didn't seem to get more publicity than a couple of lines in the *Daily Mirror*.

None the less I established the Advisory Group to take forward the establishment of a skills and Lifelong Learning agenda, with Bob Fryer, Principal of the Northern College, appointed as chair, and that seemed to go down very well. It appeared in the *Guardian* because I did my own briefing with John Carvel. I am afraid if Conor Ryan, my special adviser, and I had left it to the press office there would have been very little that got through, other than formal announcements.

I had two meetings with Tony this week, on education and on Welfare to Work. At one of these he asked, quite out of the blue, where I was living. I replied: 'Southfields, near Wimbledon.' Tony said that that was too far out and that they should find me a house. He asked the Private Secretary whether somewhere could be found and was told that there was nothing available, at which point I chipped in and explained that I'm more concerned at the moment with trying to get a decent room in the House. But it all fell on deaf ears.

I'm not sure what the Whips have done about room allocations. George Mudie, the Deputy Chief Whip, keeps on saying that he has been trying to sort it out, but nobody runs the House of Commons; there is no chief executive and the politicians don't have direct control over what goes on. The Whips are allocated a set of rooms that they in turn reallocate to different political parties and then within the political parties. But nobody, including No. 10, appears to have any control over Westminster as an entity.

As far as the New Deal is concerned, it appears we are going to have to phase it in, because Gordon has ruled that £3 billion is the absolute limit and from the papers it is clear that there is a lot of pressure on him now from No. 10 and from the City not to raise as much from the windfall tax as he would like to. I agree with him. I think he should raise as much as he can, reduce the borrowing requirement, and fill some of the gaps that the Tories have left us. Jonathan Powell is clearly against raising more money, because he said so to me in passing during the general-election campaign.

The fact that there is only one person who seems to be a proficient typist in the Secretary of State's Office strikes me as absurd. I've had a brief conversation with Michael Bichard, Alun Evans, and the Personnel Officer, explaining that I wanted the office to be restructured so that it became the pinnacle of what is possible, rather than way down the hill. In this way we can get people regraded and ensure that they have the right skills and thereby retain some stability in the office, and if necessary get some secretarial help in.

I continued to have a struggle getting a personal assistant who had real secretarial skills. Such a person was necessary not only because I work by doing an enormous amount of personal dictation, and annotation of documents and pre-prepared memoranda by dictating changes, but because there should always be someone who has responsibility for the personal, for the particular and, of course, for the simple human aspects such as 'Does the Secretary of State get a lunch?'

It is remarkable that from the days of the 1950s and 1960s when it was assumed that anyone who is the Principal Private Secretary to a Cabinet minister would have a direct route to becoming a Permanent Secretary at the top of the civil service, we now had a situation in the late 1990s when the turnover of staff equated to an eighteen-month stay, and it was necessary to regrade within my own office in order to attract people who had had any kind of meaningful experience at all before joining the Private Office.

In the end they turned out, despite my constant grumbling about things going wrong, to be a really tremendous bunch, as was true at the Home Office and during my brief tenure at the Department for Work and Pensions. In fact I did everything I could to build a team within my own staff and officials, as well as my political ministerial team, as it seemed to me that I needed a committed and united group working for a common purpose. Extraordinarily, this was not only unusual but frowned upon. The idea that the Secretary of State would actually 'manage' and take an interest both in leadership and in the machinery of government was, to some, anathema.

Both when coming into government and later when switching departments, my holding such a view was clearly a shock for many of the incumbents, at first greeted with horror but then embraced as a new way of really valuing the job they were doing, getting satisfaction and seeing the results of lifting their performance, their motivation and their speed of working, in bringing about delivery on the ground. The best civil servants warmed to this; the worst slunk off to tick away their time in moving from job to job until eventually they would be promoted in order to get them out of something they were incapable of doing.

We had a European Committee on Thursday morning. There are far too many of these Cabinet Committees, taking up an enormous amount of the day. I think meetings are becoming a substitute for work for some people.

On the plus side, I am discovering that I am as well briefed as anybody else, and aware of what is going on in a way which one or two members of the Committee don't appear to be. I'm pleased to note that the system of cutting things down to sensible and absorbable proportions is working.

This was very important, because for those who had never before operated the software which linked a computer to a Braille embosser the task must have been pretty daunting. Equally, summarising material on to tape was a skill that staff had to learn, and every time there was a movement of personnel within the office it had to be learned again – as it did four years later when I moved on to the Home Office. The fact that I felt comfortable and on top of things so quickly at the DfEE was not just down to me, but to the fact that people around me had actually engaged with this with real enthusiasm.

At the European leaders' meeting in Holland on Friday, I had to intervene to support Robin Cook when Peter Mandelson suggested that we had to take a hard line in Europe. Peter's suggestion strikes me as crass, because if we go in and take our bat home again we will get nowhere. It is all about manoeuvring and compromise. Robin was becoming angry and I intervened to say that I thought Peter's point about presentation was right, but if we weren't careful we would end up back where the Tories had been – and this took some of the steam out of it.

It is curious how hardline Peter Mandelson was at this stage, given his future role as European Commissioner. It was not that he was being funny. We all knew that he was deeply pro-European, so there must have been some other game being played. I have to admit now that I am not entirely sure what it was, so I must have missed a trick.

Spring bank-holiday week has been very strange. I've been able to have Monday and Tuesday off, working a bit but enjoying a really good couple of days before going down to London on Wednesday.

Bill Clinton has been in London, and came to Cabinet on Thursday, sitting opposite me so that the cameras were over my shoulder. Tony had a cold, but performed very well, as ever. He and the President seemed keen to get away rather than take the opportunity to talk to us, though Clinton himself did pause briefly and start a kind of conversation with Tony that none of us actually joined in. A strange occasion – very low key, which was partly appropriate and partly disappointing.

The office is still not being methodical. They keep dibbing in with urgent letters and other pressing items, rather than putting them carefully on to tape in their proper order and making sure that I am on top of them in that way. I've realised that they are fitting the Secretary of State into their pattern, rather than fitting themselves round the Secretary of State. And on the occasions when they do fit round the Secretary of State, it is the position and not the person which they are servicing – the post rather than the personality.

This was blatantly evident on the Friday when I spoke at the National Association of Head Teachers' conference in Darlington. The Office Manager wanted to come with me, supposedly so that she could read material to me on the journey. Unfortunately she never said that she suffered from car sickness, so she couldn't actually read in the car. It was perfectly understandable and I didn't mind at all, except that if she had said so from the beginning then the material could have been put on tape and I could have dealt with it. As it happened, she had brought some material on tape that had been done on the Thursday, but there was no cassette machine in the car, so I had to do it on my own little machine, taking the cassette out and putting it back in again to record.

On this trip it became clear that the vagueness of the diary as opposed to the hour-by-hour diary that I had been used to resulted in the fact that there was no space made available for a sandwich at lunchtime, and no account taken of potential media interest after my speech, given the controversy about our appointing Chris Woodhead, the Chief Inspector of Schools, to provide special advice, and Tim Brighouse, Chief Education Officer of Birmingham, to work alongside him.

To explain: just before I stood up to speak, the conference passed a resolution unanimously condemning Chris Woodhead – not merely for his vehement condemnation of the failings of the teaching profession, but also in protest at his scathing analysis of their training and their failure to respond to his call for a return to didactic teaching. My own views are that there is no way I could not appoint Tim Brighouse without most of the liberal/left-wing newspapers interpreting this as an insult to the teachers, and there is no way I could avoid appointing Chris Woodhead if I want to demonstrate rigour and toughness in achieving high standards. It is a case of appointing neither of them or both, and, if both, then pulling them together and making them concentrate on what they agreed on. It has at least been worth a try.

After the conference I had dinner with Helen Jackson [Labour MP for Sheffield Hillsborough, my neighbouring constituency], who told me that her friend Ann Coffey [Labour MP for Stockport] had been made Tony Blair's PPS and was given the job, alongside Bruce Grocott [Labour MP for Telford], of keeping an eye on the new MPs and making a report back on how they were performing and what they were doing – a bit like the Soviet Union.

A right palaver after my speech at the conference of the GMB [General, Municipal and Boilermakers] Union. I made a very moderate key speech, not a rabble-rousing speech of any kind. But I got a standing ovation after just happening to say that we would be consulting over the winter on employment rights. When questioned I said that there would be a White Paper, which I thought Margaret Beckett and Ian McCartney had announced, but apparently not.

No. 10 went ballistic, and Tony asked me to come and see him just before the next Cabinet meeting. He was as friendly as anything, but obviously relieved that I had sent a note to Margaret saying that I was sorry and that I had genuinely thought she had made the announcement. He did make it clear that what Peter Mandelson presumably had been intending (in a speech he'd made in relation to the trade unions earlier) was that the presentation of a White Paper and a promise of legislation in the session 1998/9 would be on the basis of the unions agreeing to take certain measures internally to change their structures.

Firstly, I thought that was actually not on, given the minimum rights that we were promising in the document *Building Prosperity*, for which I had been responsible before the general election, and secondly I thought it was the wrong way round. We needed to build up good will and then get people to do things because they wanted to, not try and beat them with a stick.

I may well have done people at work and in the trade-union movement a very great favour, but I didn't do myself any favours.

June 1997

Friday 6 June: my fiftieth birthday – a wonderful occasion, relaxed and easy apart from having to deal with the New Deal paper and one or two other work-related things.

I read some of Roy Hattersley's book *Who Goes Home?* – well written, amusing and highly relevant to the way that things carry on – and had a lovely meal out in the evening with family and friends. My problem is that I just flake out after eleven o'clock. I am getting to the stage where I need much more sleep early and then I am waking up earlier and earlier.

Chaired a meeting with the European Commissioner, Padraig Flynn from Ireland. He stayed an hour and ten minutes and frightened Margaret Beckett to death when he started to list all the things that were coming through from the Commission in relation to employment and employment rights. Obviously I knew something about all these because before the election we had been told about them by Larry Whitty [then General Secretary of the Labour Party]. I am trying to get on to skills, employability and Lifelong Learning rather than be negative, but Margaret was obviously horrified.

The reason for this was very simple. The European Union was still on a very regulatory and paternalistic agenda, trying to carry things through which might have seemed relevant in the 1980s or even in the early 1990s but which were becoming increasingly irrelevant and counterproductive as far as enterprise and innovation were concerned. The EU was concerned with structural protection rather than addressing the global economy.

When taking up the presidency again in 2005, we tried to get the employability agenda going and once again I found myself, this time with the Trade and Industry Secretary, Alan Johnson, producing papers on how we would link the social dimension to helping people cope with risk, insecurity and instability in the rapidly changing economy that we face in the twenty-first century. It was funny how all those years later we were still having the same debate, still prey to the same fears and still looking for the same sort of solutions. The European Union had moved on but the same pressures existed with the European Parliament, and certainly the non-governmental organisations peddled the same old material.

A struggle to finalise the announcement of Sir Peter Davies as Chairman of the New Deal Task Force. We ended up with a farce, with Geoffrey

Robinson from the Treasury intervening and trying first to claim that Davies's appointment wanted only Gordon's signature on it, and then claiming that it could be jointly credited to the DfEE and Treasury but had to go on Treasury-headed paper. In the end they had to concoct a heading with both the DfEE and the Treasury logo and with Gordon's signature on one side of the paper and mine on the other. This is the kind of nonsense you get.

I was not quite sure whether this was something Tony was aware of.

I had a very enjoyable sandwich lunch with Gordon on the day before my birthday. He gave me a cake and a bottle of champagne, which may be the only things I get out of him for a long time – but it was very pleasant.

Another little detail. I hadn't realised when I became Secretary of State that staff in my Private Office would check out what I was wearing on a daily basis. I found this out because shortly after taking up office I was astonished to be told by one of my private secretaries that I ought to change my tie, because I had had the same one on for three days running. Actually I was aware of that and had intended to change it – but as a consequence of being told, I didn't!

An early hiccup came when, during the week after the general election, a Braille transcriber was installed in the office. I had asked for a German model, Theil, to be provided but we ended up with a Swedish model (which shows how much the civil servants listen to what the ministers want). Stephen Byers and I went for a meeting with Tony Blair to spell out the programme that we were going to initiate, and to my horror discovered as I started my presentation that my Braille notes were gibberish. So I had to go it alone and carry on without reference to my notes, but fortunately I was on top of the detail, and eventually was able to hand over to Steve to follow through the print version handed to Tony. He, as ever, did a competent job, so we survived. We discovered afterwards that the reason my notes were gibberish was that the machine was switched to Swedish Braille, rather than English!

Problems continue with getting clarity in the diary. Venues are never put in, so I get what I am supposed to be doing but not an actual venue. More seriously, it seems that the Private Office is incapable of operating a proactive diary, as opposed to simply taking down what comes in, and therefore there are outstanding requests for meetings that just disappear into a black hole, and I end up having to remind people to organise them.

Minuting of the Cabinet by Sir Robin Butler only records those who are specifically asked to make a presentation or who are introducing one of the standard weekly items on foreign affairs, European or home affairs, or in the case of Gordon Brown introducing his contribution on the National Audit Office report or a reassessment of the public finances. None of the discussion, and in particular my contribution concerning what happened back in 1967 on the balance of trade, and again what happened in 1976 with the IMF [International Monetary Fund] and the over-exaggeration of the problems by the Treasury – none of that is recorded in the minutes at all.

Of course, as can be seen from the informal handwritten Cabinet minutes released in 2005 relating to the Second World War, Cabinet secretaries do take their own reflective notes of what was said and done. The problem with this is that it is entirely dependent on the whims of the Cabinet Secretary. It is a moot point as to what future generations will glean from modern Cabinet notes.

For example, the Cabinet agenda on 26 June 1997 included an item on the Millennium Dome.

After the previous week's two-hour discussion of the National Heritage Department presentation about the Greenwich Millennium Exhibition, I had circulated a separate paper, and had spoken. But nothing of what I said was recorded, and Margaret Beckett said that in any case I was being very parochial in dealing with just my Department's role. I was interested in that because my Permanent Secretary had contacted hers in the hope of producing a joint paper on how learning and education information in industry, commerce and technology could all work together – and the DTI declined.

The Millennium Exhibition issue is worth recording, because in the middle of the first Cabinet discussion on it Tony had to go to the parliamentary church service, and we were left in the air. He had made it clear that he wanted the Millennium Exhibition to go ahead, but I would say that 80 per cent of the Cabinet were against it; 10 per cent were against but trying to be positive about what might go into the exhibition if it had to go ahead (which was my position); and the remaining 10 per cent – that is, principally Harriet Harman [Secretary of State for Social Security] and Margaret Beckett – were in favour. After Tony had left the room John Prescott took the chair, and it was very awkward for him because Tony had really made it clear that it was going to go ahead whatever we said. So we spent another hour after he had gone, agonising.

We laid down five key precepts, including the requirement that no public money would go into the Millennium Dome over and above what had already been allocated – and nobody believed for a minute that this would be the case. If the scheme were to run into financial difficulties – and it clearly would – then there was no way in which the government could not bail it out as we approached the year 2000.

This was a very difficult decision. The Conservatives had already effectively made the decision, and to pull out would have incurred cost which in itself would have then been the subject of media attack, irrespective of the alternative programmes that would have been put in place. We are all wise in retrospect. It is easy for pundits and – dare I say it? – columnists to pontificate about what should and should not have been done. One lesson of government is that sometimes it is necessary to take difficult decisions, and there are occasions – and this was one of them – where it is necessary to concur, albeit reluctantly, with a decision that you feel in your bones is unwise. The other lesson is that sometimes when you know that something is not going to work, then perhaps you should stand up for what you believe. The difficulty with that, of course, is that you build up enormous antagonism if you keep on doing it time after time.

I am afraid the issue of the Dome will not go down as one of our finest hours, but neither we as a government, nor the Prime Minister, was to blame. Circumstances overtook us, and if we had to go back to the summer of 1997, I dare say that many of us would reflect again on how much more robust we might have been in arguing that substantial sums of lottery money should instead have been spent across the country on making the life of people in local neighbourhoods a lot better, and giving them the kind of facilities that they have longed for.

From the ridiculous to the even more ridiculous: an extraordinary set of events took place at the Social Affairs Council in Luxembourg, postponed from 12 to 27 June, when the Italians, with the connivance of the Dutch chairman, tried to present a declaration alongside the Burden of Proof Directive (an obscure piece of European legislation concerning industrial relations). This was simply passed round at lunchtime, and Andrew Smith and I went through it and objected to it over lunch. A few other countries – among them Portugal, Germany and Luxembourg – got involved, and we had to have a meeting immediately afterwards with officials. These are the permanent officials based in Brussels, but those with us in Luxembourg had clearly not warned us that this might happen, had not found out through discussion that it was going to happen, and didn't have a clue as to what the implications would be. I was deeply disenchanted with the lot of them.

The implications of the declaration were that the Social Affairs Council would ask the Commission to report to the Parliament and hence back to the Social Affairs Council on widening the scope and interpretation of the Burden of Proof Directive in the light of European Court judgements, so that it would take in issues relating to social security. If I had come back with that, I would have simply lost my job. The idea of widening the scope and, therefore, the competence of the European Union into social security was blatantly against what had been agreed over the years, and of course would have started the process of ensuring that the Social Affairs Council had to consider it. When I challenged them on it, they said: 'Well, we don't have to take the decision. It is not made here' – as though they had no responsibility. They seemed to think that if it got the problem off their backs and satisfied the Italians, then there would be no problem. The Social Affairs Council is particularly critical, not merely because we will be chairing it from January, but because the whole of the Social Chapter and Social Agreement areas fall under it. To say that I wasn't pleased would be the understatement of the year.

All of this may sound very convoluted, but it is not. It was and remains a fundamental issue as to just how much the European Union encroaches on domestic, welfare, social-security and tax policy. At this stage back in June 1997, had the boundaries of what is known as 'competence' been extended, then as with so many other things in politics one step would have led inexorably to another. The snowball would have started to roll down the hill and the avalanche would have swept us away.

With regard to Europe, I have always seen myself as a positive sceptic. I understand entirely why, in the global economy of the twenty-first century, we need not only a trading bloc but a voice that can match that of the only superpower now left in the world, the USA, as well as the increasing co-operation of other countries – and of course the power of China is rapidly increasing. Many things automatically cross boundaries: damage to our environment cannot be confined to one country, and unfair competition cannot simply be dealt with by going back to the old protectionist arguments about stopping goods and services coming into the country. But it is absolutely crucial that people are clearer about what it is that the European Union offers and precisely what it is that it can, in the end, deliver. As someone who believes

passionately in the importance of neighbourhood and community (increas-
ingly difficult in parts of our urban environment), it is vital that decisions are
not taken away from people but are handed back to them.

I have always approached the debates within the European Union in this
spirit, but also with a painful awareness of the grinding bureaucracy that
seems to be almost endemic and that in some countries (particularly France)
appears to be taken as normal. What some citizens and therefore their
politicians are prepared to put up with across Europe we are not, which is
why the alternative network that Tony Blair assiduously cultivated in recent
years is so vital, using our contacts with both the Netherlands and Scandinavia
to form a foundation for further support from the countries which entered the
European Union in 2004.

July 1997

Budget week. On Monday morning I had a long conversation with Gordon
Brown about the £1 billion extra for revenue (day-to-day costs for paying
wages, heating, lighting and the like) and the £1.3 billion over four years
for capital (investment in buildings, repair and renewal, and equipment),
and managed to persuade him that unless the money went to the education
authorities rather than all councils it would be a waste of time. I had to
follow this up in the next forty-eight hours with the Department contacting the Treasury, and eventually they got confirmation. In fact David
Miliband [head of the Downing Street Policy Unit] was really helpful at
No. 10, because Tony was deeply concerned when he realised that Gordon
had done a deal with John Prescott in that, while there would be capping,
the money would go into the basic Revenue Support Grant (the grant that
goes direct to local authorities to support a range of services locally) rather
than directly through us to schools.

So we had to find another way round it. This was to change the ratio of
how much we put in from the centre for those aspects of education where
there was a ratio from central and local government. By reducing our ratio
and increasing what local authorities had to find, we could free up money
to invest in our new projects, including Education Action Zones (the new
initiative to establish public-private partnerships in deprived areas).

But it was too late by then, so the way we thought we would do it was to
change the ratio on grants for education support and training and change
the name so that we could get some money for Education Action Zones out

of the Budget. We would then target the capital investment for Education Action Zones for the schools that needed them, and for getting the public-private partnership off the ground.

It has all gone very well in the Budget, and people are very pleased. There is money for Health as well, and all the weeks and weeks of negotiating and agreeing to keep quiet and not bang the drum publicly have paid off. At least it is a start.

This first Budget was a holding operation. It is absolutely clear that the Conservatives would have to have made a readjustment, given the totally unrealistic financial deal that had been put together before the general election and which would have meant that departments like Education and Employment or Health would have simply imploded. It was therefore absolutely crucial that Gordon brought forward the necessary resources to keep the ship afloat, while also being able to allocate some of the windfall levy for long-term investment in repair and renewal. It was incredibly tight nevertheless. I've never experienced anything like those first two years, where we were having to develop the most bold and imaginative initiatives and institute reform and modernisation with hardly a penny with which to do it. We were literally scraping together £10 million here and £20 million there. How we managed to do some of the things we did at that time with so few resources still amazes me.

On Thursday we had a right palaver about whether I should make a Statement on the New Deal or just do the Budget Debate speech opposite Peter Lilley. (The Conservatives can choose after the Budget which days they wish to lead on – with the government replying. This is a reversal of what normally happens in relation to government business.) In the end, after a ding-dong with Nick Brown as Chief Whip, Ann Taylor [Leader of the House of Commons] and Gordon – who wanted a Statement, while the others didn't – I agreed not to make a Statement because the sleaze stuff on Hamilton and co. was coming out at the same time, so it would have been wiped out anyway. [Neil Hamilton, MP for Tatton until losing his seat to the independent candidate Martin Bell at the 1997 general election, had been accused of accepting cash in return for asking parliamentary questions.]

We did a press conference in the afternoon and then I made the speech, which went OK. Kenneth Clarke followed me and was much better than Peter Lilley.

I came home after ten o'clock, having stayed on for the wind-up speeches – a matter of courtesy when frontbenchers from another team are concluding the debate – and have spent the whole weekend preparing for the White Paper launch on Standards on Monday. It is just one thing after another.

I don't understand why Gordon hasn't put up VAT on luxury goods to 20 per cent, which would have slowed down the economy and would have been seen to put pressure on consumer spending. But at least we've got the money for education, for the New Deal, so now we can get on with it. I do find Gordon very hard to negotiate with. Every time something is raised he becomes defensive, but you simply have to override it and say, 'Look, I am trying to sort this out in the best interests of all of us.'

This was going to be the pattern increasingly until we all settled down and understood each other better. It was some time before Gordon and I had a real rapprochement and, thanks to the intervention of his then girlfriend – and now wife – Sarah, began to be able to clash with each other without falling out for long periods. But it is worth just noting here that Gordon and I have known each other for a very long time: in fact I had spoken for him as the warm-up act in his election campaign when he successfully stood for Parliament back in the infamous election of 1983.

I think Tony was instrumental in getting me the resources. He has realised that we cannot implement the Education Standards Agenda without the money or it would be a public-relations disaster, but the strange thing is the money allocated for childcare and disability. While we have included childcare as part of the New Deal and I have raised the issue with Tony personally, what he has come out with is both more extensive and less well thought through than I had hoped.

Gordon had spotted very clearly that childcare was going to be a major issue for the coming decade, and it took me a little time to realise that I was not going to be sorting this particular policy out alone.

When I came out of the Budget Statement and was just getting in the car, Tony asked if he could have a word. He said he had been talking to Derry Irvine, the Lord Chancellor, who was prepared to consider letting me have his flat in the House of Lords. This is astonishing, and I will follow it up.

Talking of Derry Irvine, he behaved abominably to Steve Byers when he was chairing the Legislation Committee of the Cabinet. It had taken me an hour and three-quarters to get in to central London – which is another reason why I think they are interested in trying to find me somewhere else to live – partly because of the tennis at Wimbledon and partly because of the state of the traffic and the lack of any co-ordination and any central London authority to do anything about it. I arrived half an hour late and Derry was behaving like some sort of medieval Chancellor – lofty and condescending.

This is all about clearing the detail of the Standards and Framework Bill, our flagship piece of legislation implementing the policies on which we have worked so assiduously over the last two and a half years. It was all about raising standards and then putting in place the levers that would make a difference at local level, establishing formally what we were now implementing informally.

In her book Shephard's Watch, *Gillian Shephard concedes that without the levers to pull, the department that she headed before the 1997 election had been able to do very little in substantially raising standards. Our agenda was therefore absolutely vital, and if in subsequent pages I do not consider in detail the blow-by-blow measures we took, this is because when things were going smoothly my diary did not reflect that – it reflected the ups and downs, the irritations, and the cross-departmental and external frustrations. Justice may not therefore be done in reflecting in my diary the true enormity of what we were engaged in, and despite the obvious failure to achieve all we hoped, in the timescale we set ourselves, we managed to achieve a great deal.*

On Sunday morning I did one of my better interviews on *Breakfast with Frost*, then spent the rest of the day in Sheffield, getting ready for the launch of the Education White Paper. (The White Paper was to be the forerunner of the legislation and a key plank in stimulating debate, outlining our direction, and ensuring that those in every part of the school system knew what it was that we were expecting – and what we were prepared to do to help them achieve it.) I found myself getting more and more nervous about reading the Statement rather than dealing with the press or answering Commons questions afterwards, and the tension was not helped by my having to go down to London on the Sunday night because Tony could only do 9.30 for a Monday-morning visit to a school in Hammersmith and Fulham.

To Broadcasting House on Monday for the *Today* programme. John Humphrys seems to be getting more and more laid back and flying by the seat of his pants rather than doing any work. He showed only mild interest in anything, which I think undermines the quality of his interviews.

Then off on the school visit with Tony: he has a driver and apparently a detective who go everywhere with him. The main thing on his mind is Northern Ireland, understandably as things have gone very badly wrong over the weekend, with the beginning of the marching season raising the tension. It wasn't easy to talk to Tony about anything else, but we did discuss his having to go abroad so often and how little he likes living at No. 10 – strictly at No. 11, as the Blair family is occupying the living quarters there, which are much roomier than the No. 10 accommodation. He said that Chequers is a great benefit for them: the children liked the place, and he enjoyed being able to walk or play with them. He said that the difficulty with Chequers was that it was run by a combination of permanent staff and armed-service cadets, and they wouldn't let you make a cup of tea – so the kitchen was a sort of big service kitchen rather than a family kitchen. I think they should have done something about that.

Tony suggested that taking the accommodation that Derry Irvine has proposed would be a solution to the problem of my living so far out, but I've just discovered that what is being offered is just one room with a toilet off, which they would adapt to include a shower. It sounds like a bedsit without a kitchen, so I don't think it's a starter. According to the papers, Derry is going to spend over £600,000 on his House of Lords accommodation and the offices, so goodness knows what is going on there.

The launch of the White Paper has gone well, undermined as far as publicity is concerned by the situation in Northern Ireland and the tragedy of three youngsters being killed in a coach crash in France. The Statement to the House went all right, although I read it too fast and was more nervous than I have ever been. The question-and-answer session afterwards was fine. So there we have it – the first White Paper of the new government, the largest consultation paper in many years on education, and the first major one for any Labour government (the 1945 government inherited the 1944 Act) – and we did it in nine weeks, which, even though I say it myself, is remarkable because we've got off the ground the New Deal, the White Paper, the end of vouchers, the targets for summer schools, the Standards Unit and the Task Force, and I've started the process of preparing for the Dearing Committee with a series of meetings with the Prime Minister.

Sir Ron Dearing had, with my agreement, been given the job by Gillian Shephard before the general election of reviewing options for financing the university sector, which had been up in arms about the eight-year freeze on student numbers and the 40 per cent drop in funding in unit costs per student place. His options, though thoughtful, did not go anywhere near as far as we needed to raise substantial funding and deal with the immediate financial crisis – and it was a crisis – in university budgets.

It has become clear that our preferred option in our document 'Lifelong Learning' was not on its own acceptable because the only people who suffered were the ones who were receiving grants. We are going to be the ones in the firing line, so we've started to look at the options that Ron Dearing has put forward and considered combining his preferred option – for a student to be able to raise £1,000 a year from fees using contingent loans – with our own. (Contingent loans means contingent on income but not replicating income tax with a much more convoluted formula for repayment. This didn't raise very much money and left the present system in place, so we thought we would combine the two loans for both maintenance and the new £1,000 fees and base them on a test of income so that the poorest and middle-rank-income families would pay nothing at all or very little for the fee, but everybody would pay towards the maintenance.) It is going to be a massive battleground and I am going to have to face the unpopularity of it.

We have had some real problems following what I think was a briefing from Charlie Whelan (Gordon's special adviser) to the *Observer*, saying that we are going to attach investment in schools to past examination results, diverting attention from what we have decided to Gordon's own proposal, which we aren't accepting and which wasn't in the White Paper. So I spent the following twenty-four hours having to deal with that.

On Wednesday night I went to supper with Alastair Campbell and Fiona Millar [Alastair Campbell's partner and aide to Tony Blair's wife Cherie], who told me about Downing Street being chronically inefficient, particularly the staff dealing with correspondence. She said that a letter from a headteacher of a special school had been replied to in terse terms and the head had written back, saying, 'Couldn't you at least be pleasant? These are children who are blind and deaf and we have spent ages getting them to understand who they were writing to.' No. 10 then sent a letter back saying it didn't matter where the correspondence came from, it would get the same answer. So the headteacher then sent that reply to Cherie Blair, who has taken it up with Fiona to sort out. It's worse in No. 10 than in my own department.

I later heard an even more astonishing story about correspondence at Downing Street in those very early days. Tony Blair's father Leo had written a really nice letter to his son (at his new address at No. 10), in his own handwriting, saying how proud he was, and had signed it, 'Your Loving Pa'. This letter arrived in the Political Office, who mistook the signing off and addressed the reply – the standard 'Thank you for your letter, which has been noted' – to 'Mr L. Pa'. I was told that Tony related this story at the leaving party of the individual concerned some years later, and was doubled up with laughter as he described his father's bemused reaction.

What Fiona told me has prompted me to address over a hundred of the DfEE staff who deal with the correspondence and with the briefings for the correspondence section. I talked to them about the importance of sending letters that they themselves would like to receive, and I tried to get a few of the messages across on how to deal with things. But it does seem as if there is a very real problem across the board, with regard to both efficiency and sensitivity.

On Thursday we had the first meeting of the Education Standards Task Force. This went very well, but quite a snide piece has appeared in the *Observer* that may well have come from Chris Woodhead, Chief Inspector of Schools, via Melanie Phillips, which amounted to a sneer about one individual looking out of the window and being bored.

Chris Woodhead had many qualities which he did his best to hide, but collegiality and modesty were not among them.

We've had to rewrite the whole agenda for the Standards Task Force ourselves, the civil service not having managed to do it – a debacle. The Director-General of Schools had apparently made Gillian Shephard tear her hair out, not only because he knew very little about schools but because he didn't seem to grasp that failure and underperformance were part of his remit. If Gillian had been frustrated and patient, I am to be frustrated no longer, though ensuring a rapid change is difficult because he is highly popular with the old guard. I keep coming across people who think he is a wonderful chap. He is so wonderful that he announced at the beginning of his presentation that he had been so busy he hadn't managed to look at the slides, so he wasn't sure they were in the right order. I nearly got up out of my seat and walked round and hit him.

The first unpleasant incident since the general election has been a demonstration outside my advice surgery in Sheffield on Saturday morning, when BBC North, Yorkshire Television, local radio and the local paper came along. The demo was supposed to be by the parents of Earl Marshal School, protesting at our sending in the improvement team. This is a school with under 6 per cent of its children getting five A–C grades at GCSE – where diversity and not standards and quality are the central feature, and where the actions we're taking are going to bite deepest. The numbers have dropped and the school is going to close unless we can transform it, and the community will be the loser. But the demo turned out to be about twenty-five people from the Socialist Workers' Party and just three parents. This was all about a school that was falling apart, and denying its pupils a decent education.

I was absolutely determined about what I wanted to do and took action later to transform the school. It was very rewarding, eight years later in November 2005, to go there and see how successfully this transformation had been achieved. I wonder now where those Socialist Workers' Party members are and what they think they were doing.

The main event of the week [Monday 14 to Sunday 20 July] has been sorting out the Dearing Report. I had a meeting with the Prime Minister on the Tuesday and did manage to get agreement that money raised from university fees should go back into Lifelong Learning and not into schools. The Treasury were trying to say that they could divert the money into schools, but Tony was very strong indeed, saying that this simply wasn't acceptable.

Alistair Darling [Chief Secretary to the Treasury] is still arguing about whether the Inland Revenue should be made to collect the money. It is the most obvious solution but the Treasury, who are increasingly demonstrating their conservatism, seem to have captured him, and it is obviously going to be a battle. They have given as one of their reasons against the Inland Revenue collecting the loans the fact that the income tax-return forms would have to be changed.

On the Wednesday I went to speak at the conference of the Council for Local Education Authorities, under the auspices of the new Local Government Association, and a more unresponsive and deadbeat lot it is hard to imagine. I was flabbergasted to learn from feedback afterwards that they seemed to think that the speech was very good, that they had all liked it and it had gone down very well. You could have fooled me from the reaction of the audience.

I then went to Highgrove [country home of the Prince of Wales] for a reception for 200 headteachers of schools that were doing things well. Charles was late and, as a consequence, I ended up hosting it and going round shaking hands with everyone. When Charles arrived, he had to do that as well, and we were therefore delayed. He stood on a box and made a speech and then I had to stand on the box and make a speech after him. I said it reminded me of medieval England and the King gathering his loyal band of troops together to go out into the highways and byways. Charles then decided he would like to show me round his garden, which he duly did, and while he was taking me round I commented on being able to inhale the most wonderful smell of lavender everywhere we went. He replied: 'Secretary of State, I think you will find it is my aftershave.'

Tony specifically asked me not to speak on Dearing at the Cabinet on Thursday, which I had every intention of doing. One or two ministers from the other relevant departments, Scotland and Northern Ireland in particular, raised the fact that they hadn't been informed about the report, and Mo Mowlam [Secretary of State for Northern Ireland] raised it in passing. After the Cabinet meeting I got out a list from the Department, indicating when they had each been informed, and sent it round to them, because while I was happy to be tough with the Department when they were incompetent, it was a bit rich when other people hadn't been told by their officials and they then blamed us.

Tuesday was spent in preparation for the Dearing Report publication on the Wednesday, together with meetings with the Japanese Education and Science Minister and with the Leader of the Australian Labour Party, Kim Beasley, who is quite a character: a tall, blunt, archetypal Australian who would as soon knock you down as have an intellectual debate.

I had dinner with Chris Woodhead, who was being as nice as pie, which was interesting given the performance he put on later in the week, when he excluded a DfEE press officer from a press briefing that Ofsted [Office for Standards in Education – the education 'watchdog'] were giving. I've issued an instruction that this must never happen again, which might account for the bizarre way in which Chris behaved at the dinner at Highgrove with Prince Charles on the Friday night – my second visit there in the week.

Wednesday, the day of Dearing's publication, was somewhat weird. I had to go and meet the Emir of Qatar at the Dorchester (where incidentally he had taken a whole floor): he was looking into the possibility of medical students from Qatar being allowed into Britain with access to courses with lower qualification levels than would be acceptable for British students. The Qatar contingent apparently thought that the meeting went extremely well, but for me it was one of those occasions when you wonder what on earth you are doing there – when you have to force the conversation.

That afternoon saw the Dearing Statement, and getting the text of that agreed was also bizarre. Every time we thought we had got an agreement, a message came back from Tony that he wanted changes, even at the last minute. After two o'clock Alastair Campbell rang to ask if I could change it so that there would be a better soundbite. I don't think anybody had cottoned on that this had to be Brailled before I could read it and you can't highlight Braille, so you have got to read it as it is and you have got to be familiar with it if you are going to read it out loud. So by 2.20 p.m. – a little over an hour before the Statement was due to be made – the damn thing was still being finalised.

I went across from the Department to the House, stood on the Green and ran my guide dog Lucy, then just before Prime Minister's Questions began I went in and received yet another version because they thought they had made a mistake. As it happened the version they passed across to me at the last minute had the wrong opening, so I had to take the front page off the one I had already carried across and substitute it for the one that was handed in at the last moment.

The final paragraphs which I had asked to be changed round had not been changed round, but I didn't know that until I stood up to read. Anyway I got through the Statement and then got through the questions and answers. There was quite a lot of aggro from left-wing backbenchers like Denis Canavan and John Cryer, but not generally, and people on the back benches were very good.

Not everyone seems to understand that we are proposing a hypothecated tax on a progressive income-related basis, and there is clearly going to have to be a lot of work done to persuade people that we are not reneging on basic values. We are trying to raise major income to invest in further and higher education – income that would otherwise not be available because we need all the money we can get out of the Treasury for schools.

Despite the constant changes to the Statement, Tony was very helpful, and it was only with his assistance that we managed to ensure clarification about holding on to the money.

So Dearing went through this stage (though we had of course to legislate). The press reaction wasn't too bad, although television did present it as though this was the end of free higher education, when there hadn't been free higher education for some people for a very long time. They failed to see that we were opening up new access and that there was a financial crisis, so I wasn't too pleased about the television coverage, which unfortunately is what most people see.

Thursday, apart from Cabinet and a lunchtime meeting at No. 10 with Tony about the forthcoming European presidency, we had Education and Employment Questions and after the Scottish Devolution White Paper was published it was the return of the Assisted Places Scheme to the Commons from the Lords. I just had to keep calm and not go over the top. We had a debate and a vote and it went back to the Lords. The Tories in the Lords said that, having given the Commons a chance to rethink and the Bill having been returned with the Lords' amendment deleted, they would, in the words of the Tory spokesman, 'go to dinner', so after the fuss in the Commons and the Tories' cant about how they cared so deeply and how we were breaking promises, when it got back to the Lords they were only concerned with getting to dinner in time.

Friday the 25th saw my first ever trip in a helicopter – from Sheffield to Highgrove, for dinner with the Prince of Wales. The helicopter was very noisy, and made tolerable only by earphones, but it was a lovely evening, we had the wind behind us and it took only an hour to get to Gloucestershire. Michael Bichard had travelled with me from Sheffield and we arrived slightly earlier than the other guests, which gave me the opportunity for a walk in the kitchen garden, after which I stood outside on the terrace, listening to a hi-fi playing beautiful Mozart.

But a couple of the guests were to give me indigestion, for in addition to a good group which included Schools Standards Minister Steve Byers, Nick Tate from the Schools Curriculum Authority, Tom Shebbeare from the Prince's Trust, Julia Clavendon from Business in the Community and Michael Barber, who is now in charge of the Standards and Effectiveness Unit, Prince Charles had invited Melanie Phillips of the *Observer* and Chris Woodhead, who came together, sat together and left together. Prince Charles sat at the end of the table with me round the corner on his right and Melanie Phillips round the corner on his left, and Chris Woodhead sitting next to her.

The dinner started off well, with lively talk about the New Deal, the Prince's Trust and Business in the Community. Then we got on to education. Clearly there had been a set-up here. Charles was only interested in the little scheme he has got for schools, centred on initial teacher training. I was quite happy to take this on as one of many experiments, but

I made it clear that we had to monitor it. Melanie Phillips and Chris Woodhead were completely over the top, making what in politics we used to call transitional and impossible demands: whatever you're coming up with, they're looking for something more, and whatever you do and achieve is never enough.

Take school standards. Phillips and Woodhead put forward the belief that there was only teaching and nothing else and certainly no such thing as learning and that, therefore, the learning society was meaningless and a diversion from teaching. We're trying to get across that good teaching, the best teaching methods and structured application in the classroom are exactly what we're about, but that they are not an alternative to the involvement of the family and to adult learning, to inspiring families to want to believe in their own potential and to lift their expectations of it. Those two were just being silly and immature. They are against targets in education and against the learning society, believing that you could only teach, but never learn – a bit like painting a picture by numbers. They could not accept the idea of linking the development of basic tools with creativity and vision. It was all very depressing.

I arrived back in Sheffield at 1.30 a.m., then on Saturday morning went to a constituency environmental clean-up, joining local residents in collecting several hundredweight of garbage from an open space known as Tonge Gutter. This cheered me up no end. It is good to see people doing something about their environment.

August/September 1997

A mixed week, notable for the Uxbridge by-election on Thursday [31 July], which we lost. [The by-election was caused by the death of the sitting Conservative MP, Sir Michael Shersby, a week after the general election. The defeated Labour candidate at the general election was replaced as candidate for the by-election.]

I went to Uxbridge on Tuesday morning and it was self-evident that we weren't going to win it. It was also clear that the decision to remove the previous candidate and impose someone who was deemed to be more suitable was a grave error of judgement. It insulted the electorate by effectively saying that the person they had been asked to vote for by the Labour Party on 1 May, and for whom many had voted, had really been a mistake and there was someone else we would like them to vote for instead.

Secondly, it gave the Conservative Party a cause, which otherwise they would not have had, and allowed them to focus their attack, to paint the local Labour Party as being divided, and to rally latent Tories, some of whom may not have voted at all. John Prescott claims it was a low turn-out, but at 55 per cent it was extremely respectable for a by-election so close to a general election and without any real national media coverage. They didn't even take any opinion-poll ratings.

The affair of Lord Simon, who came in as Industry Minister but has temporarily retained his two million shares in BP, is another highly foreseeable and avoidable mistake. Again it smacks of arrogance, in that we are seen to believe that we can get away with anything and do what we like. It was also indicative of the way in which I think people were seeing the Labour Party and, if they had known what was going on inside, they would certainly have seen it as far too close to business, bending over backwards to compensate for decades of being perceived as the anti-business party.

My reaction at this stage demonstrates two things. Firstly my lack of knowledge about precisely what was happening and the fact that, if anyone who had serious business interests was to be invited into government, they would have to handle their previous investments in a way that didn't bankrupt them.

Secondly, that eight years on I would have to eat my words, not on account of £2 million of holdings but £15,000 of non-disposable investment that was handled with absolute probity but which gave the appearance, thanks to the way the media presented it and to my own insensitivity and arrogance, of there being something unacceptable going on. Had I remembered my own thoughts and in fact my own words, I might not have found myself fighting on too many fronts at once.

This raises another issue of the week. Andrew Smith and I have been working on how much of the New Deal should be offered for competition [which became known as contestability] to the private sector. Initially the proposition was that this should be an opportunity for the private sector, in this particular case Manpower, to be able to deliver one or more of the New Deal employment Pathfinder programmes. We found out about this on the Monday, when it was indicated to us through the normal civil-service channels that Gordon was going to raise it at the Welfare to Work Committee on Tuesday. We made it clear that we were not prepared to have it raised at the committee, but Gordon raised it from the chair by saying that he believed there should be a mixed approach and that different groupings should share the delivery.

It is clear to myself and Andrew that discussions have taken place between other ministers, and I am deeply worried about mingling the delivery of policy with the lobbying of business.

This again is significant because it raises the question as to whether I was naïve at the time or whether later when I appeared to have fallen foul of business dealings myself I had simply lost my old puritanical instincts which had hitherto stood me in such good stead.

In fact, in the committee, I indicated that I am not against, and never have been against, a pluralistic approach with different agencies or sectors leading consortia at local level, but firstly they have to be consortia and not simply delivered by one group of people or the other; and secondly, we need to be absolutely sure about the probity issues or there will be suspicion or suggestion that we are going to hand over profitable activities to people to make money out of.

I think that was probably the most important statement I made in the meeting because Gordon took it on board, saying that there was no question of not adhering to the Treasury rules involving competition, where there was a straight privatisation. He backed off and suggested that he, Andrew and I should meet. He meant Geoffrey Robinson [Paymaster-General] as well – and in fact we did meet, at nine o'clock on Thursday morning at my insistence: I didn't want to give Gordon the opportunity to issue edicts from his vantage point as Chairman of the Welfare to Work Cabinet Committee.

We met at No. 11. Andrew and I had had a session with the employment service and the Permanent Secretary beforehand at 8.30 that morning, and agreed we would make the position clear straight away, which we did. As we went into No. 11 we met the new Joint Deputy Chairman of the Bank of England, Mervyn King, coming out. I shook his hand and said, 'I hope you are committed to saving our manufacturing industry', which rather took him aback.

After the meeting Geoffrey Robinson asked me: 'What can be done? How do you envisage we can help manufacturing industry when we can't get the pound down and we can't talk it down?' I replied that the Treasury could give direct help to manufacturing in a number of ways, to which he responded: 'Not within European rules.' I said: 'Yes, you can. You can

provide credit guarantees, export guarantees and all sorts of other things' –
so a fat lot of effort was going on in there. The whole thing just confirms
what I thought and what I had raised with Gordon right back at the end of
May: we should have raised VAT on luxury goods to 20 per cent and
tackled what is a massive level of expenditure on luxury items, including
luxury cars.

*In retrospect there was a degree of arrogance here on my part. It is strange to
review notes and to realise that whilst instincts may have been correct, the
judgement on timing and ability to act may not.*

We laid down at the meeting that we were prepared to have an additional
Pathfinder district [an experimental initiative to rejuvenate specific areas of
the country] – one not taken over by the private sector, but where the
private sector would act as the lead in the consortium with the employment service, with TECs [Training and Enterprise Councils] and with local
government. It had to be put out to tender and therefore different groups
would be allowed to apply. In addition it would have a defined level of
quality and a defined timescale.

*I am going into detail about this because I think it is important to understand
the way the machinery of government works, the pressures that exist from
outside and the power of the Treasury. Everyone talks about these, but in
reality they have to be experienced to be fully understood. I was deeply
suspicious of anything that smacked of giving favoured groups access to key
services, though sadly the appropriate comment here is perhaps, 'Physician,
heal thyself.' I remember dictating a note for myself: 'Having been responsible
for avoiding anything that smacked of wrongdoing and being as clean as a
whistle in local government, I am damned if I am going to have anything to do
with actions or measures that might be interpreted as corruption or sleaze' –
and we all know where that path paved with good intention led.*

Problems with Alan Howarth, who came to see me. He is complaining that
Andrew Smith is not giving him enough elbow room, or enough work to
do. The truth is that Alan Howarth has been given jobs to do but doesn't
want to do them, so he doesn't. In order to be helpful I said: 'Look, you put
down in writing what it is you think you should be doing, and I will then
call you and Andrew together, and I will also talk to Andrew separately
about it, but don't ask me to provide you with a different job description

from the one you have got.' It is difficult because Alan is pleasant enough but at this meeting he did dither about, taking twenty sentences to say what he could have said in one.

I had a very long meeting with Michael Bichard for the best part of two hours at Thursday lunchtime, going over the past three months, with a list of the positive things that have been achieved and a list of problems that require resolving, including the operation of the Private Office, the diary, and a number of other issues within the Department, including correspondence and briefings which, despite my address to the correspondence section, are still not working properly. To do Michael justice, he was extremely receptive and promised that a number of decisions would be implemented very quickly in the early autumn to put things right.

The good news of the week was that, with the considerable help of Sally Morgan from the Political Unit, it has now been agreed that, as well as Conor Ryan and Sophie Linden, I can have an additional special adviser in Hilary Benn, who will be Andrew Smith's researcher. It helps me enormously – and is a great relief – that Andrew has got someone who can work on the New Deal, and the unemployment and disability side.

At the end of Cabinet, Derry Irvine had a word with me about this room they have offered me in the Lord Chancellor's quarters. I said to him that it was very kind of him and it might work as an interim solution, but it obviously couldn't in the long term. He said, 'Just wait here a minute' and went off, taking Tony to one side. He then came back and said: 'When the new Head of the Home Civil Service and Cabinet Secretary is announced, Tony is going to say to him immediately that one of his jobs is to sort something out on a long-term basis for you. I have told him that Robin Butler is just blocking. He is so conservative that he won't agree it.' I replied: 'We will see.'

I've had phone calls from Stephen Byers's office regarding their view that Sir Anthony Tippett should be the Chairman of the Agency for Schools. I surprised Steve Byers by indicating that I had known Sir Anthony over the years, and that he was a suitable choice which should go down well with No. 10. I then got a letter from Jonathan Powell, who had the cheek to tell me about 'another piece of good news' (the first bit of good news was presumably that the advisers had been sorted out): that Mo Mowlam was moving out of South Eaton Place in November and Tony was happy for me to have it. This is good news indeed, so long as the place is worth having, and I've made a mental note to check with Mo why she decided to leave it.

Two very strange stories have emerged in the papers this week. One is Charlie Whelan describing how unemployed youngsters might be helped to go to university, which was on the front page of the *Guardian* and which is arrant nonsense. The second from Tony Higgins from the UCAS [Universities and Colleges Central Admissions Service] with wild figures about how many students will abandon their deferment of entry into university in order to scramble in before the introduction of fees – an irresponsible piece of silliness. I have set things in train to see what we can do to deal with circumstances where ill-informed individuals are potentially able to wreck the system.

Interest rates up again to 7 per cent. I often wonder whether the decision to give interest rates to the Bank of England and to fail to take into account the manufacturing base of the country in the Monetary Policy Committee of the Bank of England has been the right one. From my point of view the effect is that whereas the DfEE could under a Labour government have pressed for a reduction in interest rates and therefore a stimulant to growth and employment, ensuring that unemployment doesn't start rising and that manufacturing industry isn't badly hit, now no such pressure can be exerted because the link is direct from the Treasury and No. 11 to the Monetary Policy Committee and the Bank of England and not via the Department to the Chancellor.

There is no doubt that at this time I was deeply unhappy with the way in which the independence of the Bank of England was being used. Later I could see that Gordon had been right in allowing separation and therefore independence to the Bank, with the resulting stability and security for the economy (and certainly greater trust from the money markets). Nevertheless I remained unhappy for some considerable time about the make-up of the Monetary Policy Committee.

On a number of occasions, not only in August 1997, I felt that the Bank of England had pushed interest rates up at the wrong moment and had been slow in bringing them down again, given the rate of growth internationally.

A very strange letter from the Prime Minister saying he is very concerned that we aren't developing a childcare strategy and that he would like a senior official to be allocated to it. He asks if we could have a private target of every child under the age of sixteen who needed it having a childcare place. I've had to write back saying that I will take personal charge of getting a childcare strategy off the ground, that we are putting it together, that it will take a little time, but that (a) we shouldn't expect the state to have to provide childcare for everyone as that is simply impossible, and (b) we should expect the private sector and the employers to play a part in this as well in developing partnerships.

October 1997

The Labour Party conference in Brighton has gone very well.

There was some panic on the Sunday from the No. 10 Political Unit and others about whether the vote on higher-education fees would be carried. I was quite surprised because they are pressing me to agree to recommend that Composite Resolution 18 on higher education, which was opposing us, should be remitted (sent back for further consideration, which in essence is neither passed nor defeated), and I had to say no. I said that if they chose to ask to withdraw in the end, that would be their business, but we should go for this to be defeated and do everything between Sunday morning and Wednesday afternoon to get it defeated.

So we set about that, talking to delegates, going round to key fringe meetings, asking delegates to come together to discuss it, speaking on the radio and television, making it clear that persuading people, rather than winning the vote, was the key issue. Of course, in the end, the votes just stacked up and we probably would have won by 90 per cent to 10 per cent anyway, but the movers did in fact ask for a remission.

On the platform, just before I got up to speak, Margaret Beckett was in the Chair and there was Tony Blair, Tom Sawyer [General Secretary of the Labour Party] and me having a discussion about whether I should accept remission. They left it to me – so I did.

As Tom Sawyer said with his parting shot, you've got to consider how it would change the atmosphere if they offer to remit and you refuse. In fact, I'd had to lean over three times to ask Margaret to request someone who was in favour of Composite 18 and against us to come up to the rostrum to speak. She did get somebody from one of the unions, but there was no overwhelming desire from people to speak, and certainly none of the heavyweights such as Ken Livingstone [then Labour MP for Brent East] were interested. Ken did turn up at the conference after his success in getting back on the National Executive Committee in what was clearly a contest with Peter Mandelson for the place that had been vacated by Gordon Brown. Ken, however, has obviously decided that this isn't the issue on which to make his name as the embryo leader of some rump opposition.

The speech itself – and the introduction of eleven-year-old Charlie Nobbs and Liz Fletcher, his headteacher at Patcham High School, to tell us what a difference the first ever summer school had made – has gone down very well and I could not have expected such a warm ovation as the one I received.

I've managed to survive the rest of the week, though virtually every other person I've met – including Tony – has been full of flu, and it is amazing how he has managed to get through it all. It was a strange conference, in the sense that it didn't have any euphoria about it. Tony told me when we were going to the school we visited on Wednesday morning that he has deliberately damped down the excitement, but it has been so low key that, on the Monday, Gordon Brown and Margaret Beckett couldn't raise a standing ovation.

One thing I have discovered during conference week is that the article that appeared in the *Observer* a couple of weeks ago saying that the New Deal proposals for the under-25s aren't taking off and that companies aren't interested – which is not true – has been instigated by a government minister. It is a classic example of colleagues undermining other colleagues' policies, and thereby the government's policies and the government's credibility. Unfortunately I can't find out who the minister was, no matter how hard I try.

Bill Gates [founder of Microsoft] has been over from the USA, and on Tuesday a number of us – Tony, Gordon, Chris Smith [Secretary of State for Culture, Media and Sport], Margaret Beckett, myself and Kim Howells – had to troop up from the conference to London to meet him. There's a chance that Microsoft will help us install new technology in schools, but I'm not sure that anything will come of it.

My son Alastair is back at Liverpool University for his second year. Andrew seems to be doing better at school this year and is much more confident, while Hugh is pulling his socks up for the second year of his A levels, and is taking his driving test shortly. They all seem to be putting up with their dad being Secretary of State for Education and Employment very well indeed.

A story has broken that we are going to join the Single Currency, and even suggesting that Tony Blair is determined to join. I happen to know from a conversation I had with Tony that this is the last thing on his mind. What he said to me was that he is determined not to have his government dislocated and the whole of its future put on the line by the issue of the Single Currency and what he described as 'the wretched referendum'. This is the crux of the matter, because the referendum would have to be carried before entry and would be a divisive issue that could well bring the government to a low point from which we would not recover.

Ironically, the referendum was Gordon's idea when he announced that there would be this 'double locking' device of a referendum and a parliamentary vote. Having sold the party a referendum and having bound us into it, he is now the one using Tony's name as though we are on the verge of agreeing to enter – not in the first wave in January 1999, but shortly afterwards.

We have also had a leak to Sunday's *Observer*, presumably deliberate, that £250 million is going to be made available for the NHS this coming winter, followed by an announcement on Tuesday that it is £300 million and that the money would come from the MoD and the DTI. I am completely in favour of this, but not of the way it has been done. It is interesting how control totals are now for government as a whole, not for individual departments as I had sought to write into the manifesto and the business manifesto during the general election. I have had quite vigorous arguments with Gordon behind the scenes about this.

This week has had its bizarre moments. I went out to dinner with Mike Lee, who works for the political consultancy Westminster Strategy, and Gordon Brown and John Prescott were in the restaurant together, and so was Margaret Beckett with someone else. When we left, Gordon asked me if I had been allocated a house yet and I said I hadn't. He asked what had happened about Mo Mowlam's flat and I replied, 'I'm considering it, but it hasn't got a garden.' I thought no more about all this until Friday afternoon, when I was phoned by Simon Walters from the *Sunday Express* (he subsequently moved to the *Mail on Sunday*), quizzing me about whether I was going to take it. I said, 'I haven't made a decision', and then he began quizzing me about why I wouldn't take it and what a wonderful place it would be, so I said, 'Well, it has no garden and there's nowhere to run the dog, so I have yet to make up my mind.' The *Sunday Express* then ran this story about the house being offered, complete with spokespeople saying that if I wouldn't take it, then someone else would. I wondered afterwards where the story had come from.

It took a long time before I realised how it is necessary to speak very quietly in restaurants.

I went to Paris and stayed in the ambassador's residence at his request. It was very pleasant and interesting to see how the other half lives. I sat at Wellington's desk, a very strange thing to experience over in France, and I got on really well with Martine Auberry, Social Affairs Minister and Deputy Prime Minister. From talking to the major papers – *Figaro*, *Le Monde* and *Libération* – and a number of other weeklies and dailies, it is clear that their journalists deal with things very differently from ours. They are interested in policy and direction rather than trivia, gossip, soundbites and spin, which can sometimes be very depressing.

When I came back from France I had a stinking cold, which knocked me for six at a time when I needed all my wits about me – the continuing pressure to privatise the New Deal programme, and a very stark letter from Tony demanding why Andrew Smith and I hadn't acted on the earlier letters to-ing and fro-ing between No. 10, No. 11 and ourselves in relation to privatising ten of the New Deal districts. I was holding the line on this for the moment, but I did not know for how long I could do it.

I have asked if Tony will defer his final decision until he has seen Peter Davies, Head of the Task Force, who was supposed to be put in place to give advice and who, at least in our company, has agreed with us about not going for wholesale privatisation. We have put forward an alternative which is that we will bring the private sector into play when it is recognised that districts are not coming up with adequate consortium plans and that the private sector will be involved regionally in assessing whether the plans are adequate. You couldn't ask for more than that.

At Cabinet on Thursday we had probably the most mature discussion we have yet had, with heavyweight contributions around the table, not concentrating on the spin or the failure which people took for granted, but on the issues themselves, with a great deal more support for entering the Single Currency than I realised existed within the Cabinet. It is clear, and everybody has to acknowledge it, that we will not be in a position to enter in 1999, and as I pointed out this means effectively that if we aren't to have a referendum a year later, there is no chance of entering before the next general election. In any case, the key issue of being out of the cycle in relation to economic performance means that should we enter early, we will have had a dramatic drop in interest rates which paradoxically will then result in either a massive cut in public expenditure or substantial increases in taxes, both of which would be designed to slow the economy and lead to substantial job losses. Therefore, the choice of joining early is not available, unless we wish to commit political suicide. And sufficient work hasn't been done to ensure that a referendum can be carried out at an early date. The nearer a general election such a referendum is held (and I think everyone is beginning to wish that the commitment by Gordon to a referendum had never been made), the more likely it is to affect the outcome of a general election in 2001 or 2002.

Whatever we do, we should ensure that preparation continues so that, should we decide to join, we won't have to start from scratch either with regard to the economic and business preparation or the political preparation that will be needed. There seems to be a feeling right across the Cabinet that it is inevitable we will join, and therefore the question is one of timing, of politics and of the need to avoid dislocating the life of this government with uncertainty about precisely when that will take place.

It was hard to imagine then that this precursor to the development of the euro would see history repeat itself – the same discussions, the same dilemmas and the same delay over and over again.

On a lighter note this week, I found out that as part of my dictated material being typed up in the Department, an email had gone out which concluded, 'That is all on this tape, thank you very much' – a standard response from me at the end of tapes so that people know not to listen on any further.

On Tuesday [21 October] I spoke at the memorial service at St James's Church, Piccadilly, for Laurie Lee [the author who had died on 13 May]. I had the most dreadful cold and was very lucky that Valda, my assistant in Sheffield, was able to travel down with me that morning. But it was a pleasure to be able to participate in delivering some of Laurie's words from *Cider with Rosie*. For the service I chose the poignant piece about the old couple, the Browns, which I think is some of his best writing.

In 1991 I'd visited Slad, Laurie Lee's famous village in Gloucestershire, as a guest presenter for Radio 4's Down Your Way. *I met him at his home for the allotted forty minutes, and then we adjourned to the Woolpack pub for 'a pint of cider' – which turned into a two-hour lunch that extended into the whole of the evening.*

November 1997

I had arranged to see Tony Blair with Steve Byers and Conor Ryan after Cabinet last Thursday [30 October]. We had an amicable meeting but there was a great deal of anxiety about the whole issue of structures and admissions. A number of very revealing questions were asked, such as: 'Do we really have to go ahead with the issue on changing the rules for grammar schools?' I pointed out that in terms of the politics and the consensus to be gained, we were better off with our proposals than with the old proposals which had local authorities drawing up plans for restructuring their area, and the kind of desultory consultation which would not involve parents. The main thing, however, was Tony's concern about structure and wider admissions. On admissions, his concern was whether we would have to have a code of practice and an admissions policy that made proximity the main issue. I pointed out that we were not doing away with the Greenwich Judgement, we were not stopping people from exercising a preference, and after the agreement which had been reached with them the previous Monday we certainly were not stopping church schools from being able to exercise denominational preference for children, thereby retaining their ethos.

In fact the bishops had welcomed it as a victory for them which suited me fine, because we had won the consensus we wanted by offering to put voluntary controlled schools back in a new church voluntary system rather than into foundation schools, and that had suited them. Promises that we weren't going to take away the right to exercise a filter system in terms of the religious commitment of the families and children had been settled – something that we had never intended to do anyway.

But No. 10 were really jumpy about what they call parental choice. Of course there is no parental choice. There is only parental preference, and the growing dissatisfaction is rooted in two problems. One is the quality of schools generally, which we are trying to do something about, and the second is that for every child who gets into a school where there is over-demand, another one does not get in, and if children get in who live some distance away, then other children close to the school have to travel a much greater distance, passing that school in order to get to another one. The added complication, of course, is that this proximity issue often reinforces social and economic differences and divisions. The only way of over-coming that is to bus children and have catchment areas which bear no resemblance to locality. So although Tony touches on an interesting issue, he does so from a less than egalitarian approach – namely that the school will choose the pupil.

However, it was the structures which concerned me most, particularly the feeling that some thought it was a pity that the issue couldn't be dropped altogether. My response, without any equivocation, was to say: 'But we can't. There is absolutely no question of dropping the structures. They are integral to what we are doing with the rest of the bill, integral to our maintaining some credibility, with everything we have said and done over the last three years, and integral to stopping the party from splitting once again over the issue and therefore causing a massive public diversion from standards and back on to structure.' I realised that although David Miliband the previous week had been very supportive of us and had recognised clearly that we could not separate standards and structure in the way that Derry Irvine, Nick Brown and Ann Taylor had advocated, it was absolutely clear that if Tony had had half a chance, he would have done so.

The debate in the autumn of 2005 was so similar to the debate in the autumn of 1997 that it could have been a re-run of it. My perception at the time (at the end of October 1997), which was that without a resolution of the perceived gross unfairness in the system no radical progressive change would get through the Commons, resurfaced eight years later. It was strange to have been arguing that what we didn't want was the school choosing the pupil, only to find the same arguments emerging all over again in 2005.

This time, of course, the argument was about diverting from the mantra which we, so far as I was concerned quite rightly, had put in place in the build-up to the 1997 election – namely 'Standards not Structures'. The irony was that we had to deal with the structures along with the standards if the radical moves on massive reform were to stand any chance of getting through. Just as we were making very real progress in our third parliamentary term as a government, we began to divert from standards and on to structures, believing that changes in structures would drive up standards. It was strange to find myself in a position with the Secretary of State for Education and her ministers, and with whatever influence I still had in Downing Street, fighting to ensure that we didn't split the party down the middle and allow David Cameron, the new Leader of the Conservative Party, to make mischief.

Hugh and Andrew came down and I introduced them to Paul McCartney, with whom I had lunch to talk about his Liverpool Institute for the Performing Arts. I spoke to him in the office before the lunch, and Hugh and Andrew were able to come in and say hello to him and get autographs. I also managed to show them round No. 10 on Thursday morning. There were some children coming in for a photocall, so the guide who had been hired to do the formalities with the group also showed Hugh and Andrew round a good part of the building, which was really nice for them. We had been to St James's Palace the night before for a reception for the Homestart organisation, so they were able to see the palace as well. I also did *Question Time* from Nottingham on the Thursday evening, which went very well except for the fact that I couldn't add up. I contradicted the electronic counter, which was a very foolish thing to do, and then I mixed up 200,000 with 200,000,000 in talking about further and higher education. Fortunately I have at least learned to laugh at myself, which makes a difference.

The following week there was much of the same theme running – the Tory Party falling apart, no sign of progress at all on the Education Bill, right the way through to Friday 7 November. I have approached both Derry Irvine and Ann Taylor again on these matters and suggested that the higher-education element might be taken in the Lords so that we could move quickly to introduce the Standards and Structures Bill in the Commons, which would take all the public steam out of separating the two. Having suggested an intelligent and sensible division with regard to not having structures separately but keeping them with standards, and separating further and higher education into a separate bill, there is just an overwhelming logic to it. Ann Taylor had the cheek to say that this idea had occurred to her, when actually we had already put it forward – but you just have to smile and let these things ride.

On the issue of the business managers, I am afraid they did get themselves into a bit of a mess over fox-hunting. There were quite legitimate concerns about other bills being bogged down in the Lords and therefore the government's programme being lost, and the way they handled it was very poor and gave the impression of backing off and capitulating.

The Bernie Ecclestone affair is rumbling all around us. The businessman who in effect runs Formula One motor racing has, surprisingly, given a donation of £1 million to the party – and Tessa Jowell has apparently just suggested to EU health ministers that Formula One be exempt from the proposed Europe-wide ban on advertising for cigarettes and tobacco. Bernie Ecclestone obviously has an interest in resisting any such ban.

I'm not putting a lot down here in my diary. All I know is that Tony has not been involved in this at all, although why some people around him didn't see that there would be questions about meetings and pressure on health policy, God only knows.

It looks to me in any case as if we could have resolved the matter via the European discussions – reaching a Europe-wide agreement which would apply in the UK, rather than have us debate it separately.

Frank Dobson seems to have distanced himself from what's going on, which does leave Tessa pretty much in the lurch in dealing with the Health side: she's obviously had nothing to do with donations.

The £1 million was in fact given back to Bernie Ecclestone, so the party never received the benefit of the money, but the affair did not look or feel good.

In dealing with the issue myself when challenged on the *Today* programme on Radio 4, I managed not to drop anybody in it, and later in the week Gordon performed the same tightrope act. *Today* asked me to go on again, and I said I'd appear if 1 could simply say that we'd messed up – but in the event Peter Mandelson did the interview instead.

Now Tony has gone on television and said exactly what I hoped he would: 'Sorry, we made a mess of this.' I'm relieved. It is obviously better that he did it rather than me, which would have looked undermining and presumptive. I simply want to move things on. With the relentless accusations of spin, spin, spin and the danger of looking as if we were getting involved in something sleazy, it really matters to try and draw a line under the whole unfortunate business.

Since then we have tightened the rules on party donations enormously. We changed the law, made everything more transparent, and generally improved scrutiny of politics and public life. Some good came out of the Ecclestone affair in accelerating such processes, but it was a very difficult time for the government, and the allegation of too much spin was spurious. If 'spin' means presenting your policies and your programme as coherently as possible when others have every intention of distorting it, then I'm all for it.

I am having a major tussle over being allowed to spend the money which we have identified within our own budget for further education. I am speaking on 12 November at the Association of Colleges annual conference. They need to know what resources we are going to give them, and where they are going for the coming year, given how badly they have been treated, and I need to be able to announce it. So the problems with the Treasury refusing to clear the announcement, which much to my surprise they have the power to do, is frustrating in the extreme. It appears that they wish, as a result of the first round of the Comprehensive Spending Review, to be able to announce a package of savings and priority changes in expenditure, and they want to do it themselves from the Treasury. They don't want those who have actually done the finding of the resources and the reallocation of priorities to get the credit for it. Anyway we are battling away with the help of No. 10. Again David Miliband and Rob Reed, who used to work in our Department and now is an official at No. 10, are helping us as much as they can, and I am trying to stay as calm as possible in respect of the frustrations – including the fact that the Treasury tried to stop us from making an announcement about the very minor reallocation of resources for specialist schools on 5 November. I managed to get Tony to announce at the end of Prime Minister's Questions that there would be an expansion of seventy, from 260 to 330 schools, which was very helpful as it allowed me to do so in my speech that evening, but it was very much against the will of the Treasury.

Incidentally, Alistair Darling has sent me a letter relating to the argument we are having about resource accounting as opposed to current accounting – so that battle is still to be fought as well.

Week beginning Monday 10 November. I don't know really where to begin. It was a hell of a week: speaking at the CBI conference, launching the Skills Task Force, having forced the Department to create a unit and to take skills seriously. We had the failing schools coming back on stream and those that were making reasonable progress – and I did one of my better contributions on the *Today* programme. That week as well there was a dinner with Robert Reich, the US Secretary of Labour, on the Monday night and a discussion seminar with him on the Tuesday. I started to push the boat out over the absurdity of increasing interest rates only to increase mortgage rates, which pushed up the headline level of interest rates which then led the Bank of England to believe that inflation was rising and pressure needed to be applied. It is not quite as simple as that, as obviously they took account of the underlying rate, but nevertheless there is a kind of truism about the absurdity of actions which, far from helping, actually hinder.

It demonstrates how important the membership of the Monetary Policy Committee would turn out to be.

I managed to avoid voting for this absurd measure on Second Reading by being quite legitimately at the Chief Rabbi's house. This was an interesting experience in itself, not least because he has security guards not only around the house but with him wherever he goes. Maurice Hatter, who had just given £1 million towards next year's summer schools, was there. We had a very friendly and pleasant evening, a nice meal and good conversation, but it was quite intense. They are a very tight community.

Thursday's Education Questions came and went without too much difficulty, much to my relief. I had managed, at the very last minute – thirty-six hours before my speech – to get Alistair Darling to agree to my spending our own money identified within the Department to fund further education: £83 million of new money and well over £100 million from the New Deal for the under-25s, so my speech to the annual conference of the Association of Colleges turned out not to be the fiasco which it would have been.

Week commencing Sunday 16 November. Strange week. I went to Brussels to the Joint Ecofin Social Affairs Council. Finance and employment ministers from the whole of Europe: every one of them turned up and we spent four hours with people making statements round the table, getting absolutely nowhere, not even agreeing the guidelines but suggesting alternative wording for the so-called Employment Summit which took place in Luxembourg at the end of the week. I stayed at the European Union embassy with Stephen Wall and his wife, a great massive place. My impression was of two very lonely people who were just very pleased to see people come through and to put them up.

This was also the week of the Queen's fiftieth wedding anniversary and I went to the lunch. Cabinet that morning was held early because of the commemorative service, and as with the previous time that this happened, when we were discussing the Dome, we were having a really good discussion about Gordon's proposed statement on the Pre-Budget Report when we had to break up. Gordon had presented the scenario that we would have to reduce from the current 4 per cent growth to 1.5 per cent growth in order to avoid inflation rising, and then build growth back again to 2.25 per cent to provide stability. He said interest rates would have to be allowed to rise – well, would rise with the determination of the Bank of England to achieve this. A number of people round the table, including myself, expressed grave concern. I immediately went back to the Department and got the statisticians and the economists to do some calculations. I found out that 1.5 per cent growth in 1999 would result in an increase of 250,000 in unemployment. I then wrote a letter to Gordon spelling out that, while a range of scenarios and possible outcomes might be sensible, if we were even to float the notion that the government believed that 1.5 per cent growth would have to be the norm by 1999 it would be self-fulfilling, in the sense that the markets would respond until that was achieved and economic policy would be judged by it. We would then have a massive hike in interest rates and growth in unemployment, which I would end up having to answer for and to deal with.

It was agreed that I would go to the Treasury on the Saturday when I was down in London speaking at the Trade Union 21 conference and the National Governors' Council. I went across to the Treasury at 1.40 p.m. and did not get away until 3.15. We dealt with two issues, the first of which was that we had found out that Gordon was going to publish an employment paper along with his statement. We only learned this through the officials at the Treasury sharing the fact and trying to get confirmation of what they had put in statistically from our Department – otherwise we would not have known he was going to do it. We got agreement on both the wording and the fact that we would sign the foreword jointly and publish it jointly. After we had dealt with that and my letter, he said he would publish a range of scenarios rather than just the one. He said that it had been his intention all along to suggest that the economy could be saved from having to reduce growth and higher unemployment if all those engaged in the economy would play their part.

Week beginning Monday 24 November. I felt exhausted. Gordon Brown delivered his consultative Budget on the 25th, and took up a suggestion I had made at a supper with Robert Reich a few weeks earlier when I had said that you wouldn't get much credit for tax credits but that you would get quite a lot for Christmas bonuses and the like. He pressed ahead with announcing his interest in carrying through the tax credit but he also announced extra money for pensioners over the winter.

Harriet Harman – who is in very deep political water, so much so that she pulled out of appearing on BBC television's *On the Record* the following Sunday – came with Tony Banks and myself to Bromley-by-Bow Children's Centre. Life does have its funny side. Due to the fact that the press office had not sorted out what was to happen when I arrived, I was sitting down on a very tiny chair with some very tiny children. I slipped my hand on to the shoulder of the 'little one' next to me and said, in what I thought was a gentle voice, 'How old are you?' 'Twenty-four,' said the nursery nurse. I could have limboed under the tiny table.

Thursday saw the publication of the Teaching and Higher Education Bill and a whole range of other initiatives, from the minimum wage submission to Jack Straw's White Paper on youth justice, and from the Welsh Devolution Bill through to the presentation of the Mountford Report on improving government communications – which was quite an irony, seeing the lack of sophistication in sorting out launches for that day. This was partly due to the fact that the 'business managers' seemed to have predominance over any kind of political planning, forethought or management.

We had a good discussion at Cabinet about how to improve the involvement of backbenchers and how to share with each other a little more of what is going on, but it remains to be seen whether anything will change.

We had another spate of silliness from the *Guardian* this week with two articles by Roy Hattersley seeking to try and goad me into what they were describing as a 'feud', to the point where one of their staff rang up the duty press officer on the Friday night to ask if I would respond to letters they were printing on the Saturday morning backing up Roy. One of those letters, from someone who had clearly never read *On a Clear Day*, declared that I could not possibly understand what it was like to live in deprivation as I had gone to a boarding school.

On the Thursday I did not return to London from visits to Manchester and Liverpool – I was opening an exhibition at the Museum of Labour History and new premises at South Trafford College, as well as visiting Alastair in Liverpool – to vote on fox-hunting, partly because I had agreed to open the new premises of the Gremlin Computer Games company who are taking Andrew on work experience next year, and partly because it was futile to rush down to London to vote when there was clearly such an overwhelming majority (it turned out to be 260) and where the business managers were not prepared to allocate government time to allow the bill through anyway. This surely is something where backbenchers can play a significant role in helping.

Spoke at the Institute of Directors' dinner – the first Labour Cabinet member ever to do so – and it seemed to go down OK. I made a speech about how change must be achieved without the victims who have always been sacrificed in the past, and it received a modicum of coverage.

I attended a Privy Council meeting for the swearing in of other Privy Counsellors. I have not been to one before – strange little ceremony, with the Queen being very polite and asking about the dog. I met John Humphrys on the way out as he was coming in as one of the guests for lunch at Buckingham Palace.

December 1997

Gordon is insisting on new compromise on the single-parent supplement. Aggravation is rising, although in the end people will no doubt capitulate. Absurd situation arising about which I have written to No. 10, in respect of single parents who are entitled to the supplement but by taking a job from April next year would lose it if they lost the job. As a consequence this is likely to tighten flexibility rather than loosen it with regard to people's willingness to take part-time or temporary work.

I spoke at the PLP this week on education, including student fees, and received a very good reception, which I was quite relieved about. I also published the Education Standards and Framework Bill. This went down very well, with our being able to target and highlight the things we wanted to get across rather than there being a row about grant-maintained schools or grammar schools.

Launch of the Premier League After-School Centres, for which Pele came to Stamford Bridge with the President of Brazil. Apart from photo-calls and going round to talk to the youngsters there with him, I sat and had a chat with him and the Brazilian President. Pele seemed a very nice man.

I had an interesting meeting with the Governor of the Bank of England, Eddie George, and colleagues over lunch at Threadneedle Street. Fascinating discussion about the balance between skills needs in the economy and the requirement to damp down growth. I discovered that there were fourteen regional advisers who had a network of contacts. They reported back weekly on such issues as wage pressure, skills shortages, industrial and service pressures and orders and other general economic activity. Seemed to be incredibly anecdotal, but they obviously have a profound effect on the decisions taken by the Monetary Policy Committee in terms of raising interest rates, thereby affecting both growth and the rate of the pound. Seemed to be very keen indeed on slowing down exports and it struck me as being the most perverse economy that anyone could imagine, where we want to stop people exporting to prevent overheating, rather than tackling the causes of overheating by strengthening the economy and increasing the skills available. It was agreed that the Bank and the Department should set up a little review group. I suggested that the Bank should be represented on the Skills Task Force. It was interesting, worrying and potentially very important when trying to get this right for the future and overriding the Treasury's absolute caution and the obsession with what happened with

Nigel Lawson in 1988 – which came through at the meeting – as though we were re-running it all over again.

At Cabinet we talked about BSE and Welsh farmers, and Jack Cunningham made an announcement about banning beef on the bone. Even after the explanations I could not be clear as to why the beef that had been cut off the bone was not infected, whereas the beef that remained on the bone and was cooked thoroughly was infected, or potentially so. I could not understand why we had not gone for banning the beef from cattle over twenty-four months old. Jack explained that this was too bureaucratic and administratively difficult.

Formula One was settled at an EU meeting in Brussels in exactly the way that it could have been in the first place if it had never been raised publicly but dealt with by derogation within EU negotiations.

I am about to have two horrendous weeks with early morning trains to London on the Monday, Bonn on the Friday and God knows what the week after, given that Nick Brown and Ann Taylor have tried to stitch me up by moving the agreed date for the Second Reading of the Education Standards and Framework Bill from 16 December to Monday 22nd, with the Christmas recess starting immediately after the ten o'clock vote that day. I have taken this up with Tony and arranged a meeting with Nick Brown and Ann Taylor on Monday afternoon. Clearly internal politics are being played here as they have placed the national minimum wage debate on Tuesday 16th.

I had a dreadful cold and felt so ill that I toyed with the idea of not going to Bonn, but given our pending presidency of the European Union I thought I had better make the effort. I spoke at a number of events in North Rhine Westphalia, including on the Dutch border at a conference which had been arranged at the last moment.

Week beginning Monday 15 December. I had dinner with Bill Morris [General Secretary of the TGWU] on Monday night. I was still full of flu but feeling a lot better in myself. Bill, as ever, knows it all.

There was a 'No' vote on the Northern Ireland Police Bill, as expected. I found out on Friday night, when I was having dinner with Helen Jackson, Ann Coffey and Ann Taylor, that Nick Brown had simply been looking to fill the slot in order to avoid having to give it to me for the Second Reading of the Education Standards and Framework Bill. In other words he was just being completely and utterly bloody-minded, aided and abetted, I believe, by Ann Taylor, who claimed it was nothing to do with her.

Later in the week, when I was having a meeting at lunchtime with Tony Blair, Chris Woodhead, Michael Barber and Stephen Byers, Tony was talking about not having fully understood all the good things that were in the bill. I said I was hoping to promote them, but since it was next Monday there was very little chance of doing so. He reacted very strongly and said, 'Well, I did my best.' I said, 'No, no, I don't deny for a moment that you have.' But it is very clear where power lies, very clear indeed. For instance, Nick Brown and Gordon Brown have put a joint notice out for Monday 22 December inviting all members of the Parliamentary Labour Party who are down for the Education Standards and Framework Bill to come round to open house at No. 11 and No. 12!

I met Charlie Whelan on Tuesday and he was friendly as friendly could be. We had an EAWW [Employment and Welfare to Work] Cabinet Committee, with Gordon in the chair, and he too was friendly and pleasant. Something must be brewing.

Thursday's Cabinet was interesting. I had just had a very good meeting with the Irish Education Minister. We talked about technology and skills investment and the way that they were looking to the future and investing in growth. I therefore arrived slightly late at Cabinet, the first time I have been late. We had a very good and long discussion on Welfare to Work, in which I suggested that we had an Awayday or half a day. By the weekend this was being reported as a crisis Cabinet meeting in at least one of the Sunday newspapers, rather than simply an opportunity to pull together social and economic policy, and to explore with each other what was going to happen.

David Clark, vigorous in his defence of the disabled, was cut off by Tony for going on too long. Ann Taylor went on about the black economy, something I had been trying to get No. 10 (or rather the Leader of the Opposition's office) to look at before the election.

Tony had addressed the Parliamentary Labour Party the day before and had not been as harsh as the previous week's Cabinet had indicated, although I had heard that Ann Taylor's researcher had been going round saying that there ought to be forty-seven heads on poles, which fitted in with Ann's attitude. Tony's speech was OK and he got away with talking about tough choices.

Then on Friday, David Westnall of the *Sunday Telegraph* contacted Conor and during the course of the conversation it became clear that the paper had been leaked the memo about Welfare to Work which I had sent to Gordon Brown dated 9 December. It was a complicated memo dealing with an internal DSS paper on their interim Comprehensive Spending Review, all about whether DLA [Disability Living Allowance] should be devolved to local government and capped so that local authorities would have to do the difficult job of cutting people out, and all about whether incapacity benefit should be treated as an income support/method of providing a lever for getting people back into work, or for direct compensation for provision required and cancellation of industrial injuries. My record on this is unequivocal from *Building from the Bottom* in 1982, all the way through a series of articles in the *Mail* and the *Sunday Times* and other papers, through to the submission to John Smith's Commission on Social Justice in 1993, through to the Julius Silberman Lecture in February 1997 in Birmingham – all of them spelling out the need to get people out of dependence and into self-reliance. Again and again I have talked about it, but this is not how it was in the *Sunday Telegraph*. The upshot was that the idea was floated that I wasn't in favour of a radical review and that somehow I was offside.

No. 10 were given my memo on Friday night, but it seems that Tony didn't see it, and nor did they tell him about it, even though I got the press office on Saturday morning to remind No. 10 that we had passed it across.

At 11.30 on Saturday night, No. 10 contacted me at home and set up a three-way telephone conversation with Alastair Campbell, Tony and myself. It was an odd conversation, in which Tony initially was obviously very suspicious, not surprisingly given that the story had overshadowed his speech that morning from Sedgefield on this very issue. It was a strange juxtaposition, very strange. The whole of Sunday morning and half of Sunday afternoon was a write-off, doing radio and television, a major interview with *The World This Weekend*. I think I came through it all right, but we will have to see what the long-term consequences are with regard to relationships and trust with Tony, and the way in which I was deliberately and calculatingly set up.

It is absolutely clear that this memo was leaked directly. There is no question in my mind that David Westnall actually had the memorandum and that it was done with malice aforethought. The memorandum itself had been initially compiled by Alan Howarth, my junior minister, but I had altered it substantially because it was far too conservative in its outlook. It did, however, make clear, as I did subsequently (and retained this principle all the way through into the third term of our government), that Disability Living

Allowance was quite separate from incapacity benefit and income support, and that industrial injuries, while anomalous in terms of private insurance and exemptions, were not something that we should be tackling. It was not fundamental to the real issue of breaking the cycle of dependency.

I was later given information that a Cabinet minister, who left us towards the end of the first parliament and did not return, was the leaker. As with subsequent leaks of controversial material – and so much of what I dealt with over the years was by its very nature controversial – I could not work out whether the leaking was deeply personal in order to embarrass me, or whether the individual concerned was seeking kudos with the journalists leaked to. One of the twists in politics is that, along with one or two extremely senior members of the subsequent government, I had been guilty of briefing the media in the decade running up to 1997, but like many others did not do so as a government minister in the way that my opponents tried to paint.

We will see more of this later, not least on the controversial issue of ID cards.

Week of 22 December. I took myself across to the drinks that were arranged by the Brown brothers at Nos. 11 and 12. [No. 12 was then the Whips' Office, and thus headquarters of Chief Whip Nick Brown.] I hadn't had an invitation, but I went and was polite and pleasant and wished Gordon and Nick a very happy Christmas.

I have interviewed for the post of Principal Private Secretary because Alun Evans had got the job of Head of Communications and Strategy at No. 10. We had put together a shortlist of five but two didn't want the job, so only three came.

The Cabinet Office were supposed to be preparing a strategy paper on childcare for Tony and myself before Christmas, and produced nothing but a list of notes that could have been prepared back in September. Anyway with the help of Conor Ryan and Hilary Benn, Alan Howarth has produced a memo for Tony. It is overlong, but good in setting out what needs to be done and how it should be done.

A strange end to the first eight months and the run-up to Christmas. I had the deliberate effort to separate Tony and me, and to damage me, followed up by those who were jumping on the bandwagon. It is a good job my writings and speeches make it impossible for them to lay me low on this. Presumably those who did it hadn't done their homework properly, otherwise I would have been scuppered, particularly if I had faltered or done badly over the weekend. Anyway, between them all, they managed to scupper any real publicity on the Education Bill, the first major Education

Bill of any Labour government. The media were more interested in internal strife and warfare than they were in promoting the Bill. I think it speaks volumes.

Some good may have come out of it all – Tony clarifying the principles and where we stand, starting to argue the ethics of the case, rather than the cuts which Gordon had been promoting, ensuring that there are bottom lines and that we know exactly what it is that we are supposed to be doing. Now we have got the Review Group we can begin to get somewhere, but my conclusion in finishing this episode up to Christmas, is that unfortunately there are some people who are more interested in doing others down and preparing for their own future than they are in the success of the government – and that, if anything, will bring us down.

But a good Christmas and New Year. I worked very hard on the second draft of the Lifelong Learning White Paper and caught up on all the correspondence and backlog of papers, but managed to catch up on some sleep, too.

January 1998

Tuesday 6 January. At the North of England education conference Michael Barber spoke without controversy about Education Action Zones, then in interviews afterwards mentioned how at least one EAZ would be 'led and run by business'. This immediately gave rise to an *Evening Standard* headline 'Private Firms to Run Bad Schools', and before I knew it John Prescott was on the phone telling me to fire 'the mad professor'. But I won't.

At the first Cabinet meeting of the year I made the mistake of saying to Gordon that if I could manage to survive on only five hours' sleep a night, I would be well away. He replied, 'Well, how much sleep do you need?', and I realised that five hours was obviously quite a lot for him.

Tony came up to Sheffield to look at the Pathfinder programme for the young unemployed – a good visit because the youngsters at the jobcentre were really positive and full of enthusiasm for the programme, and so were the staff. It was very encouraging.

That jobcentre was used as a location for the filming of The Full Monty, *a film which I have to say I found sad rather than funny, as it depicted not just unemployment but a breakdown in social and family relationships, and a decline in manhood and the standing of craftsmen. What it didn't show was*

the resilience of the community, which went much further than doing a
striptease dance.

But the film included one very funny moment, which for me encapsulated
Sheffield humour. An individual is marooned on the roof of a car slowly
sinking into the canal, and a man walking past with his dog offers a cheery
'Good morning!' (To be frank, for an eloquent cinematic expression of the
difficulties of northern communities in recent years I much prefer Brassed Off
to The Full Monty.*)*

In the Commons, a good Education and Employment Questions day.
David Willetts [Shadow Spokesman on Education and Employment],
whom I have always thought quite an astute politician, revealed in one
of the newspapers that morning that he was going to raise questions about
reductions in the number of Job Clubs (where people were tutored in how
to write a CV, how to prepare for an interview, and so on). As a
consequence I was able to prepare for that very question and deal with
it effectively in the House. I do sometimes wonder about people's political
nous. Had David Willetts not forewarned me in this way, it is certain that
my Department would not have, as I only picked up his comments by
accident from the press cuttings. No one had briefed me on what might
come up and the issues of the moment. This is something I am going to
have to get a grip of and work out how best to deal with. We have been
flying by the seat of our pants and getting away with it until now, but it
can't continue.

   Monetary Policy Committee of the Bank of England: if interest rates
don't go up this month, there is a chance that we might stop the economy
going into near recession. If they do put interest rates up we will be in
trouble, so I've done my best to promote positive messages. This is one
reason why I have gone along with the phasing of the pay reviews, as it is a
very clear signal to the Bank of England that we mean business on pay and
they don't have to think of raising interest rates. I said in Cabinet that if
they do, then in my view we will be in very real trouble. I think Tony is
getting the point.

   Monday 12 January: Mo Mowlam is doing an excellent job in Northern
Ireland but had her Christmas and New Year ruined completely by what
was going on with the killing of Billy Wright, followed by a number of
other killings and the virtual collapse of the peace process, which she had
redeemed. A framework proposal has just been put together with the Irish
government and No. 10, and Mo has pulled the fat out of the fire. I called

her over Christmas and she was obviously exhausted, having only really had one clear day other than Christmas Day. What a mess – but there has been, and still is, universal respect for her.

I have appointed a new Principal Private Secretary: Mike Wardle, from the Further Education Funding Council. We shall see how he gets on.

Tuesday saw the launch of our policy of greater flexibility and responsiveness in the National Curriculum. It seems to have gone down very well, despite the best efforts of the Qualifications and Curriculum Authority to undermine the thrust of what we are doing.

This feeling was confirmed when I had dinner with Professor Bernard Crick on Wednesday evening and talked through the difficulties he is having with his committee on democracy and citizenship and the clear suspicions and strange goings-on at the QCA. Someone had leaked the thrust of the proposals to John Carvel of the *Guardian* last Saturday, but with the emphasis of the story being that we are dropping the rest of the National Curriculum at primary level, when of course we are doing nothing of the sort. We are ensuring that there is much greater flexibility in order to concentrate on the basics.

Anyway, no thanks to the QCA, we have managed to get our approach across, and in his usual artful but incredibly skilful way, Chris Woodhead has made the best of it by not only being very supportive on radio and television, but by writing a detailed rebuttal in the *Daily Telegraph*, giving his support and linking it to my own position. A very clever piece of footwork, I think. You can't help smiling and having admiration for the man. I realise, however, that both the Department and the agencies attached to it are like a sieve when it comes to any kind of private information or security of information. I am seriously going to have to watch everything I do and say.

The Welfare to Work saga continues. I have now formally been appointed to the Welfare Review Body, and have prepared a detailed letter with accompanying papers for Tony, for discussion during a weekend at Chequers on 17–18 January. Nervous of leaks were this to be prepared in the Department, I've had the papers typed up in Sheffield, and will give them personally to Tony.

The letter spells out very clearly my concerns about the fact that unless we change economic policy, and unless the Treasury and the Bank of England are persuaded otherwise, we simply cannot implement the Welfare to Work proposals anyway, so all our efforts will be fruitless.

Sunday 18 January: back from Chequers. I enjoyed it: a different lifestyle altogether, very nice staff from the Navy and RAF. There was a roaring log fire in the main hallway, which was constructed as part of the courtyard and is not one of the ancient parts of the building, the oldest bits of which date back to the sixteenth century.

Fourteen of us sat down to an excellent dinner – good wine, in contrast to Highgrove! – after which I took Lucy for a walk with Eric Anderson, Rector of Lincoln College, Oxford. He used to teach Tony and is obviously a very supportive outside influence for him, and we got on very well. It was lucky we did take Lucy out then because later the wind got up and it started to rain, lashing it down right through the night and beating against the window, which I had to open because the whole building was so hot that you could hardly breathe. I was told that this is because it takes a very long time to get the oil-fired boiler system going and then once they have got it going it takes a long time to ease the temperature down. I presume this indicates that there has been no modernisation of the system for decades. There is a swimming pool, but once it is heated at the beginning of the weekend, it is so expensive that they have to switch it off, so if you don't swim on a Saturday it has gone cold by Sunday.

I had a large bedroom, No. 7. One of the smaller rooms – such as No. 8 next door, a single room with a bathroom – would have been better, but they obviously wanted to put me in a posher one with a four-poster bed, and unfortunately the bathroom was across the corridor. I was a bit thrown at first but then managed fine, and Lucy was superb as ever and found her way around, even learning to find my room.

Just after seven in the morning I was awakened by a terrific banging noise. When I asked one of the staff what was going on, he told me that it was the devil of a job to clean out the fire grate. It really was like something from *Upstairs, Downstairs*. Apparently, when there has been a major log fire the night before, the staff have to clean out the grate, and it was the act of getting the cinders out that made all that noise.

In the morning I had a chance to talk to Tony at breakfast, when it struck me how strange living at Chequers must be, not making even a cup of tea for yourself, or in Cherie's case a cup of hot water at breakfast time and in Tony's a cup of hot water with lemon in it. For myself, I'm afraid I indulged in a large number of cups of tea as well as grapefruit, bacon, scrambled egg, mushrooms and a pile of toast.

After Tony had got ready for church we carried on talking for another twenty minutes in the study, discussing the economy and the paper I had given him. He is really worried about wage levels, an anxiety which Gordon has managed to get across to him, that wage levels were rising and that this would fuel inflation. I said to him that if we created another pool of labour through the New Deal and through skills, we could lessen the pressure on wage inflation.

Then a very busy week, a lot of it in Sheffield with meetings on crime, Lifelong Learning, and a visit to Earl Marshal School.

We've had the launch of the interim report of the Numeracy Group, which seemed to go down very well – except that Steve Byers was asked a mental-arithmetic sum and got his times table wrong. Fortunately when I was faced with the same request I managed to get mine right – buying time by grimacing in the press conference and ensuring that the journalists laughed, which gave me just the two seconds I needed to make sure I got 9 times 8 correct as 72.

The same day there was an anti-bullying launch, so with one thing and another it was pretty hectic – particularly hectic as I had a 7.10 a.m. start on the *Today* programme and worked through until 11.30 at night.

A useful meeting of the Welfare Review Body on Thursday morning. Tony was in the chair, with Harriet Harman, Frank Field [Minister of State at the Department of Social Security], Gordon Brown, Frank Dobson and Hilary Armstrong [Minister for Local Government and Housing] as well as myself around the table. What is absolutely clear from the meeting is that we are really starting from scratch. All the hot air before Christmas, all the hype about rapid savings that Gordon was promoting and the idea from the Treasury that there were immediate savings to be made – that was all just a nonsense. The principles and objectives had not been thought through, although Frank Field did bring what you might call ten subsidiary principles along to the meeting, none of which I could disagree with.

These were later reflected in his Green Paper.

In talking it through with Valda on Friday morning it struck me very clearly that what I need to do is to make a speech about how and why we have a great tranche of our society who see themselves as victims, and who maximise the gain they see they can get by being more ill, more disabled, or more poor than they really are – whereas the welfare state ought to be encouraging them to be healthier, wealthier, more able and more in-dependent. I will endeavour to make a speech about this before long and try not to upset too many people.

I also saw Tony on Thursday evening at his request for half an hour. I thought he wanted to talk about things like the School Teachers' Review Body over which there is a disagreement with the Treasury, who according to Tony want an initial award in April of under 2 per cent, with the rest phased later in the year. I knew this because I had raised it with him at our last meeting. I was expressing the view very strongly that anything less than 2.2 per cent in April – and preferably 2.8 per cent – would be very damaging to teacher morale, to our drive for recruitment, and to the idea that 'Education, education, education' is still at the top of the agenda.

I had a meeting scheduled with Gordon for Monday evening, but discovered that Frank Dobson, who is a wily old bird but who is in this case entirely wrong, has intervened and argued strongly that it would be wrong for nurses to get less than teachers. That came well from him, given that he has appointed Brandon Gough, the man I sacked from the Higher Education Funding Council chairmanship, as Chairman of the GPs' Review Body, which is awarding GPs 5.2 per cent, which is just outrageous. The key difference between more money for teachers and more money for health professionals – as Frank knew well enough – was that at the DfEE we were constructing a major reform of the teaching profession, whereas the NHS was looking for a straightforward pay increase.

But this is a battle for the weeks ahead. Clearly there will have to be phasing, because the amount that the Treasury has put in the supplementary budget in July won't cover a 3.8 per cent increase in April. In any case, Gordon's obsession with holding down wages and the belief that wages and salaries drive inflation upwards is going to make it imperative that he produces a major gesture. I think that, in the end, is what is going to affect the outcome.

In the event, what Tony wanted to talk with me about was the Cabinet, party morale and the aftermath of the fencing with Gordon. I made it clear that while party morale has taken a knocking, this is different from the country outside. I said that what we need to do is to facilitate genuine policy forums at local and regional level where people can feel involved. We need to make clear that they are being listened to and that they have some ownership of the policies we are pursuing. Most importantly, we need to ensure that they understand what is happening – not easy, but involving real political education in the party.

I also said that the Whips' Office has to be absolutely 100 per cent behind him as leader. He said to me, rather endearingly, 'And don't you think they are?' I just looked at him and smiled.

This has also been the week when Jack Straw was given a boost by

Alastair Campbell and the No. 10 briefer who let it be known that Jack is going with Tony to the United States, and is to 'lead' a publicity drive to put across 'the bigger picture' to the public and to the party. It is interesting that they haven't made it more collegiate. Following the disagreement with Gordon, you would have thought they would have done. I think what I probably find most difficult to take is being lumped in a sort of second-rate group of Jack Cunningham [Minister of Agriculture] and Chris Smith, although given Mo's enormous and continuing efforts in Ireland, I don't mind her name being associated with getting out and spelling it out.

One comparatively small thing: I've managed to make some progress in getting a quarter of a million pounds for the RNIB [Royal National Institute for the Blind] and the National Library for the Blind. We have managed to include them in the Year of Reading and the literacy campaign by helping them out.

My sons Alastair and Hugh both had a series of exams this week, which has been pressurising for them. I've kept in touch with them and have kept my fingers crossed. Hugh has not yet got an offer from York University, which is worrying, but Andrew seems to be doing fine and is keeping up his expectations and his self-belief.

Tony has come to Sheffield, and there have been meetings all over the place. I felt rotten on Monday and Tuesday, but have recovered a bit as the week went on.

It has been a very strange week. On Tuesday we had the most peculiar Local Government Cabinet Committee, in which Hilary Armstrong read from a briefing paper on the need to reclaim the money that has been saved by metropolitan education authorities through the discretionary rate relief. Our agreement at the previous committee before Christmas had necessitated the ending of this so-called anomaly on 31 March this year. To say that I am annoyed would be the understatement of the year – annoyed with the DETR [Department for Transport, Environment and the Regions], annoyed with Hilary for bringing up such nonsense rather than dealing with it sensibly behind the scenes, and annoyed with my own officials, who have produced a briefing paper saying that my best option would be to see whether some of the money could be redistributed for local education authorities as a whole, which obviously wouldn't help. If you take from key inner-city education authorities like Birmingham, North Tyneside and Sheffield anything between £40 million and £100 million (depending on whether we went back one, two or three years), then redistribute that amount of money across everyone, they will all get a tiny bit – effectively no good at all. You would have to be a political pygmy to think that a sensible way forward. Fortunately John Prescott, who was chairing the Committee, is not a political pygmy and does grasp the politics of it.

Following that meeting I went off to Windsor for an overnight stay with the Standards Task Force. It was very comfortable at Cumberland Lodge, and lovely to get out in the fresh air. I stayed in what had been the nursery of one of Queen Victoria's daughters, but sad to report there was no rocking horse.

On Wednesday night I had supper with Mo Mowlam, who is feeling beleaguered in the Northern Ireland Office because of the way her civil servants are behaving. She also feels beleaguered by No. 10, because in her opinion she is not being given enough credit – and even excluded, which means that she is having to fight for things. She feels further beleaguered by the people she is trying to deal with outside, and by the sheer pressure. But she is standing up to it all and is remarkably good-humoured.

We talked about the importance of being able to work together with other Cabinet ministers without appearing to form cabals or create groups – to just have supper in a way that wouldn't offend or upset people.

February 1998

The first week of February has been one of the most difficult weeks I have had since coming into government.

On arriving down in London after the weekend I discovered that a note had been received from No. 10 saying that the Lifelong Learning paper was not to be published. It is hard to exaggerate the impact of this decision: it is a major blow. I immediately arranged to see the Prime Minister on Tuesday morning, but knew that I would be starting from a position of weakness. The decision not to publish means that for him to agree to go back to square one would require a loss of face, so I had to try to think of a way of dealing with this that would not lead to a refusal to consider any alternative.

At the meeting itself Tony was worryingly ill-informed about the stage we have reached and the publicity that has already surrounded the expected White Paper. I suggested that we publish a Green Paper for consultation, slightly slimmed down from the proposed White Paper, and that we should look to the major launch of the University for Industry and Individual Learning Accounts rather than giving them pride of place within the paper.

The University for Industry – which became known as Learn Direct – was a joint venture between myself and Gordon when in opposition, its core idea being the use of new technology to reach not just individuals but small and medium-sized businesses, updating skills and promoting enterprise. We considered it a crucial initiative in the urgent need to bridge the productivity gap with competitor nations.

Quite clearly we have to mention these proposals, so Tony and I have reached a compromise whereby we will go ahead with the White Paper but delay its publication by two weeks, from 10 to 25 February. But since the meeting it has gradually dawned on me that Gordon Brown has intervened because he wants to make announcements in the Budget on 17 March, and to be seen to be associated with the idea.

This was a political awakening for me. I had to learn to think ahead and to work out why something might not be flavour of the month at one moment because of other influences being brought to bear, given that there might well be important events coming up or announcements that others wished to make. At this stage of the parliament, I did not have the clout I later had to be able to counteract this, so it was a miracle that my idea of shortening and watering down the White Paper worked.

It is also worth reflecting on why this policy meant so much to me. All my life, firstly gaining my own qualifications at evening class and on day-release courses from work, and then throughout my own time as a tutor in further education and the education of my three eldest sons at Sheffield College, I have been very close indeed to the whole issue of Lifelong Learning. I have been a strong advocate of adult education throughout my time in local government and can still remember the Russell Commission investigating adult education back in the 1970s. I had also been a strong advocate and contributor to the establishment of the Northern Residential Adult Education College (known as the Ruskin of the North) and later, as Education Secretary, saved the college when the civil service could see no good purpose in adult education at all. It is significant that Lifelong Learning has come to the fore again, with the third leader of the Tory Party during the Blair premiership, David Cameron, returning to the issue in 2005.

It is hard to explain the drain on your mental energy and the debilitation that come from having to fight these fights after months of preparation. My special advisers Hilary Benn and Nick Stuart had put in three months of hard work on the project, not to mention the five drafts that I had gone through before, during and after Christmas. Sometimes you just feel like screaming, but you have to pull yourself together and get on with it.

On Thursday I attended a Welfare to Work meeting in Cardiff, one that Harriet Harman had pulled out of. (We'd been having difficulties with public consultation on the welfare reform proposals launched in the autumn, and some Cabinet ministers were being given a hard time.) I was greeted on arrival by a screaming mob, and I chipped one of my teeth on the open car door because the crowd were pressing round and everybody was faffing about. It's a good job that Lucy is a calm and superb guide dog, otherwise I think she would have taken off. It was a miserable meeting – dour, sullen people who are not on the same agenda as us at all when it comes to getting people to work and having some get-up-and-go. There was clearly a bitter resentment about what the government did before Christmas and about the way that the review has been started.

I don't think I shall ever forget that meeting, not just because I had to fill in for Harriet, nor because it was one of the occasions where I was on a hiding to nothing before I stood up, but because of the reaction of the public, as well as those who turned up on the day. On the local radio station, I spoke to a caller who was only forty-two years old and who was complaining that we were forcing him back to work. When I queried what had happened to him, I learned that he had had a heart-bypass operation but was now restored to health. I asked him why he thought it was that, having been operated on at great expense and recovered, he should not then return to work. His answer was bizarre in the extreme – namely that he had been ill and had been receiving benefits, and he saw no reason at all why 'this government' should take them away from him. The fact that we had enabled him to become independent, to take responsibility for his life and to contribute to his own well-being for the rest of his life – when hopefully he had as much of his life ahead of him as behind – seemed to have passed him by.

I found this absolutely staggering. It made such an impression on me that, far from having the impact that he intended, it strengthened my resolve that we were not going to put up with this sort of nonsense.

Monday 9 February: a successful launch of the advertising campaign with Tony Blair on Wednesday, which seemed to go very well, and on Thursday I was involved in the announcement about the first tranche of money for the Class Size Initiative. It is the first time that I have ever been in the key

8.10 slot on the *Today* programme two days running. On Friday we had the opening of the Sheffield Wednesday Homework and After School Centre, which got some good television coverage.

We had all sorts of other things going on during the week. On Tuesday there was a very good meeting at No. 10 at which we discussed the Healthy Schools Initiative – promoting healthy eating, exercise and children generally looking after themselves – and childcare provision. Tony chaired this and managed to pull things together and sum up very effectively. He has a real knack, presumably with only the most minimal time in which to be briefed, of being on top of the issues – in complete contrast to poor Harriet Harman, who came to see me before the meeting and clearly had not even read her own letters and the material that she had sent to me, never mind having read the papers and being on top of them.

The Department is having a tussle with No. 10 about getting more money for the Class Size Initiative. If they want us to accelerate the programme and bring it forward from 2001 to 2000 we need some money with which to do this, and Gordon should announce it in the Budget on 17 March. Gordon has obviously been briefing Tony that there is no money available and that they would have to use the reserve, which is disingenuous because they had lots of cash coming in from better than expected growth over the previous year, the follow-through of Tory tax increases, indirect tax increases and not having a proper spending round for the coming year – thereby avoiding quite a lot of additional expenditure.

Back on the home patch, my constituency report for the meeting on Friday 13th lists all the things that I am still managing to do locally, and I'm really proud of that as those things keep me in touch with the constituency and what is happening.

There's a strange carry-on with the business of the House of Commons. We're ending up with sittings going through until two in the morning, which given our majority is just crazy. We should have been timetabling things differently. Scottish and Welsh Bills in Committee have been taking up masses of time on the floor of the House, which is completely unnecessary. On Tuesday evening Michael Meacher and I had intended to go back to his house for a meal, but the Whips threw a tantrum about it and so that was that.

Despite enormous sensitivity shown by Michael about his position in my team before the election, and the fact that he was now Minister of State and not in the Cabinet, we managed to retain our friendship. But all these years later, not only have we drifted apart but Michael has become further and further alienated from everything that we, as a government, have been doing. I can see from his point of view, given how uneasy he was through all those years, why he felt that once he was out of government he was free to lash out, but it is sad because as Environment Minister he had the most enormous opportunity to take forward the agenda, and he knew the area backwards.

Mind you, I appreciate only too well that once out of government you see things differently, and it can be a rude awakening. When you are inside and you know what is going on, with all the peer pressure and the feeling that you can make a difference, you are swept along on the tide. Once you are out, you are really out.

I had the Joint Education and Health Select Committee on children in care, which took a great deal of preparing for – although the information I brought together is very interesting. There is still so much to be done about the immense underachievement at school of children in care.

While this issue rarely hits the headlines, it remains one of my greatest regrets that we didn't do more. It is strange to think that in the summer of 2005 I was arguing vehemently from the Department of Work and Pensions, of all places, that we ought to give those coming out of care a much bigger boost for their adult life and give special support to sixteen- and seventeen-year-olds. At that time this was all about the issue of pilot programmes for encouraging staying on at school and for learning and employment for those tens of thousands of youngsters who found themselves with neither training nor the chance of a job.

Reflecting on the seven years that had elapsed between my efforts in 1998 and 2005 (and the most enormous effort by David Hinchliffe, then Chairman of the Health Select Committee), one can see just how hard it is to bring about change and how frustrating government can be when those who have responsibility for making a difference to youngsters' lives are so inept in assisting the people who are most vulnerable. Society as a whole loses out, because the problems which afflict youngsters whose lives are blighted by teenage pregnancy, drug addiction and underachievement are carried on from one generation to another and cost dear not only the individual but the community at large.

I've spent quite a bit of time preparing the last phase of what has now become the Lifelong Learning Green Paper before it is printed, and feel deeply disappointed that we haven't been able to live up to expectations.

The good news is that the G8 (G7 large economies plus Russia) finance and employment ministers' summit in London on 21 and 22 February has included Lifelong Learning in the seven principles agreed for future development, and they are very enthusiastic about the concept. The USA was strongly in favour, as were the French and less so the Germans, but we had a good discussion. The Germans are more interested in in-house training than Lifelong Learning, understandably so given their apprenticeship and vocational system, which has stood them in good stead.

Years ago I would have looked on at a G7 or G8 meeting, and if the chief finance and employment ministers had been there I would have thought, 'Well, that's some gathering. They will have some ideas about the way forward.' But when I was there, I found that they had no better ideas than I had.

Dinner was in the room at No. 11 that had got publicity because the floorboards had been polished, costing only £200 and thereby saving money on a new carpet. Presumably Gordon felt that the polished floorboards would look better than a tatty carpet. Not unnaturally this has been contrasted in the press with Derry Irvine's expenditure on the Lord Chancellor's facilities.

The G8 dinner ended in the most ridiculous fashion, when Gordon stood up to say good night to someone who was leaving early, and everyone else got up, quickly shook hands and disappeared before you could say Jack Robinson. They left before the port, the cheese and the coffee, all of which remained to be served and all of which were on the menu. It was a pity that those organising the event on behalf of Gordon and myself didn't intervene quickly to put things right, but the whole place emptied and left Andrew Smith, Gordon, Ed Balls [Gordon Brown's special adviser], Charlie Whelan and myself just having a chat downstairs and being sociable. Talk about a shambles.

One of the things that repeatedly struck me was Gordon's parsimony. As well as the disappearance of the carpets, the wine cellar on which Ken Clarke [Gordon Brown's immediate predecessor as Chancellor of the Exchequer] had been so keen seemed to have disappeared. Instead we drank Australian plonk. I am sure this thrift was extremely good for the UK economy and the Treasury coffers, but I am not entirely sure what our visitors made of it. I doubt if Gordon had paid any attention whatsoever to the issue of the wine – which is, of course, as it should be with a prudent Chancellor. But if I'm completely honest, it was a bit of a disappointment.

Not that I'm a wine snob – at least I like to think I am not – but all those years ago when I was on Sheffield City Council I learned what was and what was not drinkable from the receptions and dinners that we were able to afford back in the 1970s whenever major visitors or conferences came to the city. We always did them proud, not least because Lord Mayor was in those days a prestigious honorary post, held for one year but held with style. In Sheffield we had a Lord Mayor's Secretary, a man named Colin Straw, who was one of the most awkward, obsequious and difficult characters I had to endure at that time, but he certainly knew something about wine. He laid down a cellar which saved the city a fortune so that we could drink decent vintages at the kind of price that people were paying for absolute rubbish over the counter. For good or ill he taught me that a good wine was worth having and, to do justice to good wine, there is no doubt that the head feels far better in the morning after drinking it. Cheap wine is a false economy when you are entertaining people you take seriously.

On Thursday I had a meeting with Gordon to air the issues around the G8 summit, and also around the questions of the Budget. Half the session was taken up with discussing the question of interest rates and the Bank of England, on which he and I disagreed. He didn't try to hide the fact that he thought that interest rates should have risen to 8 per cent rather than 7.5 per cent, and that there had been too much delay already in making the increase. He agreed with the hawks on the Monetary Policy Committee and talked at length about his position, three times mentioning the Lawson boom and the mistakes that were made in 1988 – mistakes he is clearly determined not to repeat.

I am deeply worried about manufacturing and the impact on mortgages, and I am sure Gordon is too, but prudence and stability are paramount.

It is a moot point as to which of us was right. In retrospect, it was critical for Gordon to establish the economic policy of the government as clearly on the side of security and stability first, in order to reduce those historic fears about Labour's economic record. One thing is absolutely certain: all of us are deeply opinionated and I do plead guilty to arrogance. Sometimes the certainty of your own thinking is all that carries you through the bureaucracy, the hot air, the bluster and the inbuilt inertia.

In the Cabinet we had a good discussion on Iraq and on Northern Ireland. I spoke to Mo Mowlam afterwards and she is really feeling the strain. The chance of a settlement in Northern Ireland slipping away and the murders resuming is really wearing her down.

I can get very fed up as well. I'm completely cheesed off with the way that other people are behaving, and have just about had enough.

The launch of *The Learning Age*, the Green Paper on Lifelong Learning, went well enough, despite the best efforts of the departmental press office and the publicity section to mess things up. They couldn't organise a garden fête. But we've been done over, it turns out, by Melanie Phillips in the *Observer*, who while the editor Will Hutton was overseas was given free rein to write the editorial. This reflected her absolutist view (which we'd had at Highgrove) that if what we were doing was not 100 per cent acceptable, that represented a failure. This reminded me of the famous phrase she used on a previous occasion when she didn't agree with me, suggesting that I should be put in a concrete overcoat and dropped down a well. I do get sick of all the whingeing sometimes, particularly in the education journals.

However, the Green Paper was received very warmly by just about everybody else. We got good coverage on BBC television and on radio and a little bit on ITV, which might have been more if the education correspondent had managed to make it to the briefing.

It is at this point that I began to realise just how important press coverage was for me – too important, many might say. However, we were trying to establish a substantial change in policy and embed this, not just in the minds of journalists, but in the minds of the electorate as a whole. In simple terms I was saying to the department that the message and the policy went hand in hand. If the people implementing our policies and those benefiting from them understood what we were trying to do, the chances of success and delivery on the ground were much greater.

This sounds like self-justification for an obsession with what was already becoming known as 'spin', but there is a great and real difference between a government presenting its policy so that people can understand what is going on and what the objective is (and the entitlement of the user of services to what is on offer), and trying to con the electorate into believing that the government is doing something it is not.

We never did establish this difference adequately, so the better we became at putting across the government's point of view, the more we were accused of spinning. The consequence of communicating badly is that you don't communicate at all, and therefore journalists either make up the stories or get their own particular take on them from the people they may have talked to. They are therefore entirely subject to their own perception and not to information they have received, or even the reports or policy documents they have been given.

If I am honest about this, we may well have done ourselves as a government an injustice by our hyping, from the exaggeration of spending plans to the promise of immediate change. This, of course, is in contrast to the fact that while in opposition we did not exaggerate what we were going to be able to do in government – contrary to later perception. In many ways we then played down what would be possible.

We had a Welfare Review meeting where John Denham, Junior Minister in the Department of Social Security, did an excellent presentation – apart from the fact that the Department of Social Security appears to be in the realms of political Noddyland, believing that they could take away people's basic pension when they had paid for it. At the end of the week they tried to say that lone parents who were going to lose out because of the additional allowance for childcare they received would not lose out after all, and that all the dissidents who had voted against need not have worried. And indeed, some of the opponents were now saying, 'Well, if we had known this, we wouldn't have voted against.' The briefing suggested that it was a great victory for Harriet, who had worked so hard on Gordon to pull him round. Next it was claimed that this had been the plan all along, and that Gordon and Harriet had known this but couldn't say so.

By the time we got to Friday, special advisers were briefing that it wasn't just going to be those in work who were going to get childcare or those seeking education and training to get into work, but those on income support too. They must have thought people stark raving mad. Anyway, that was one thing I am certainly not going to tolerate.

There was a bit of a showdown in Cabinet. Gordon did a presentation full of doom and gloom, though there was none of that when it came to giving away public money to one-parent families and childcare. Anything goes then. I challenged his claim that consumer credit and sales were booming because I had met a number of people at the Technology Colleges' Trust dinner on the Wednesday night who made it clear to me that no such thing was going on. The information I had from my own departmental economists was that the mini-boom in January was entirely due to the fact that there hadn't been a surge in the build-up to Christmas, and retailers had cut their prices.

So the battle continues, and I just wish other people would join in more vigorously. There were one or two comments from Donald Dewar

[Secretary of State for Scotland] about public spending, and he endearingly said he hadn't fully understood all that Gordon had said – which I think was a very subtle way of saying that he didn't agree with Gordon, because he had certainly understood it. Jack Straw made some comment or other that I cannot now recall, but most of the other people just sat there. I had to point out that Gordon had failed to mention standards or skills once, and that his intention to further dampen people's expectations would make it even more difficult to deliver what we wanted to deliver. I think Clare Short and Ann Taylor joined in then, presumably remembering that we did have elections to fight.

I have received a circular letter sent from No. 10 to the private offices of all Secretaries of State about the fact that the Treasury is the leader on the Monetary Policy Committee, and direction or policy implications for that committee should come through the Treasury. We replied pointing out that we provided the most sophisticated and detailed information on the labour market and its implications and we would continue to do so.

The weekend saw the 'Countryside March' in London. We have made a mess of things over the last week, giving confused messages on childcare and the impression that we were all over the place, and now we've managed to give confused messages about the countryside as well.

I think Michael Meacher has adopted the right approach by trying to offer some understanding to the protesters rather than alienating them, although you can't help but think: here they are, they don't want us to roam in the countryside, they don't want us to have a home in the countryside, but they do want us to subsidise the countryside.

It is amusing to hear them say that the government has made a mess of BSE. Hell's bells – there have been ten years of complete and utter fiasco over BSE, and we've been in power only ten months. I think John Prescott is going to have to play a bigger part in co-ordinating and dealing with things, otherwise it will all end up on Tony's shoulders.

March/April/May 1998

I cheered up a bit on Monday but since Wednesday I've been feeling overwhelmed again. At the departmental Awayday it was absolutely clear that we had not yet got our Spending Review right. We have three weeks before it is due to be presented to the PX Cabinet Committee (the 'Star Chamber', the Cabinet Committee reviewing public expenditure). Due to an arcane and ridiculous system, this involved the Secretary of State, without his or her officials, having to be on top of every single item in the review, and the performance being judged by the climate it created, the competence of the individual and the credibility of the case being put – which, given the enormous scale of the operation, was patently ridiculous.

Later the system was changed so that officials could be present.

When I appeared before PX previously, I was quite happy with what I did and apparently others were too, but that wasn't the point. The point is that it is a very silly way of making decisions and operating government. Forewarned is forearmed, and we now have a chance of getting the thing together properly.

I've been discussing education and employment issues with Tony, but we also talked about childcare, the Welfare Review and the fiasco of the previous week. He agreed with everything I was saying, and seemed horrified at the idea of providing a dead-weight subsidy to those in or out of work, agreeing that Gordon should run through this with me, although the chances of Gordon wanting to do that are very slim.

It has also become patently obvious that the circular letter in relation to the Monetary Policy Committee and the relationship between departments and the Treasury was principally aimed at me, and we had a light-hearted discussion about the fact that I had 250 statisticians and analysts who could provide up-to-date information. Sadly what is clear is that the Treasury does not want that. They do not want an alternative set of statistics, material or information; effectively, they don't want to be challenged on facts, and are not too keen to be challenged on policy or perspective either.

This is neither as surprising nor as unacceptable as I thought at the time. The truth is that the Treasury had responsibility in this area and I was encroaching on their territory.

In Cabinet I used the story from Roy Hattersley's book *Who Goes Home?* to illustrate that I hadn't really been rocking the boat at the Chamber of Commerce dinner the previous Friday, when airing a bit of 'blue skies thinking' in a speech which had been cleared by Gordon at my request to avoid a major public row. Roy's story was about how he made a speech challenging Denis Healey's economic policy – subtle and subliminal to the point where the audience he had addressed didn't know what he was talking about, but the press did and had picked it up. The following morning when Roy went to Cabinet, he was waiting outside to go into the Cabinet Room and Denis came bouncing in shouting 'Wonderful speech, Roy' and smacking him as hard as he could on the back, cracking him into the coat-stand, making his nose bleed and evoking a jovial, jocular remark from Jim Callaghan to the effect that that would teach him not to cross Denis again.

Fortunately Gordon was unlikely to respond in the same upfront and robust manner, and even Tony jocularly agreed that such behaviour was unlikely to be witnessed from the present Chancellor.

I am still having a struggle getting any extra forward funding to accelerate the class-size pledge. Tony wants us to implement it by 2000, but he will not at this moment order Gordon to give us even a modest amount of additional resources on the capital side. The Treasury keeps saying we should take it from the New Deal for Schools but if we do that we will end up taking it from the hardest-hit authorities and those in the greatest need, in order to fulfil a pledge which would help the leafy suburbs most.

With the Budget due on 17 March, we have been negotiating about some money for skills; for accelerating the class-size pledge, albeit a small amount; for the development of Education Action Zones, so that we could create twenty-five zones during the course of the financial year; and something extra for the University for Industry.

All of this was made slightly more palatable to the Treasury by my managing to get the Department to claim – for the first time ever for a department of the British government – on Objective 4 of the European Union funding, which gave us £160 million over two years for updating of skills, which would help both the University for Industry and the Individual Learning Accounts.

It is amazing to think that for several years the UK missed out on claims on Objective 4 purely because the Conservatives' deep-seated antagonism to Europe had led them to reject rather than engage with the potential of getting back some of our own money. It was therefore doubly satisfying to be able to invest what at that time appeared to be very large sums of money and to demonstrate the advantages of positive engagement with Europe rather than defeatism.

The incompetence of the Department has again been illustrated this week by a revelation on Friday night that the under-fives budget has been underspent by £24 million. Here I am, struggling for peanuts from the Chancellor of the Exchequer, having asked six weeks ago that the department unearth any underspends. I have specifically asked *twice* that we do this so that we can enjoy the maximum benefit and credit for the money spent, and they come up with £24 million and want to distribute it on the priorities they have given me on the previous package of measures in the event of underspend. It just takes my breath away.

It is worth noting that other Cabinet ministers, both then and subsequently, thought that there was something slightly odd about the detailed interest I took in the management of structures within the departments that I headed politically. In all three I did everything I could, not only to provide leadership but to get a grip of the leadership and managerial issues that were arising, as well as the processes for recruitment and for co-ordination between different divisions and sections.

It seems to me that having an interest in delivery and outcomes without understanding the process by which you attain them is like wishing that the world were a better place but being very confused when it comes to doing anything about it. It made me very angry later in my time as a Cabinet minister when newspapers wrote about our lack of willpower without having the first idea of what we were up against in our effort to bring about change. If you are not able to determine appointments, dismissals, promotions or management structures (which is the case wherever there is separation of the political from the official process), then tremendous co-operation is needed from the senior civil service. That was crucially what I had from Michael Bichard and from Leigh Lewis, who ran the employment service and later joined me at the Home Office.

It was a strange week all round because I ended up having to sit in the Commons through the whole evening on Wednesday to deal with grant-maintained schools and the new foundation status. I ended up with some scrambled egg and smoked salmon in the tea room at 10.15 p.m. What a crazy life this is. The sitting has gone through the night twice this week, as on Monday the House did not rise until about 9.15 on Tuesday morning – and this with a majority of 179! This is because those in the Whips' Office won't bring in guillotines, and seem to be finding it difficult to organise the business in a way that doesn't allow the Tories to disrupt everything with just a handful of people.

On top of all this I had the European Union meeting, chairing which was a work of art, particularly with simultaneous translation. I made it to the Barnsley Chamber of Commerce dinner by getting the 5.05 p.m. train from King's Cross to Doncaster and a car across to the Ardsley House Hotel, where I changed into my dinner suit, washed my face and went downstairs and did the dinner.

As I say, all quite crazy.

Having given a picture of the first year in government – the pressures and the challenges, the joys and the disappointments – I will now move rapidly through key events highlighted in the diary, to the run-up to the 2001 general election and the changed world after 11 September 2001.

June 1998

Wednesday 17 June: a speech at the annual conference of the British Chamber of Commerce, chaired by John Humphrys. At the end of the session he and I talked about the ways in which different ministers approached speeches, some simply reading out what they had been given, some relying heavily on the speech but adapting it, and some just having a few notes and speaking to the audience.

He reflected some of this in his entertaining book Lost for Words, *about the use of the English language.*

I've also had a meeting with Alistair Darling, Chief Secretary to the Treasury, about the Spending Review, but we were both really just going through the motions because we know that it will be a meeting with Tony and Gordon that will settle things. I have had to cancel going to the Czech Republic in order to make sure that I am around because I don't think anyone would forgive me, or I myself, if I was out of the country at an absolutely crucial moment like this.

I never did get to the Czech Republic as a minister. Indeed, there were many invitations I turned down which, in retrospect, I probably ought to have accepted, but there are only so many hours in a day.

It is good that we have at last settled the national minimum wage. Although £3 per hour for younger people [aged eighteen to twenty-one] is still going to be a problem, at least it is not linked to anything else such as Individual Learning Accounts, which would have made life extraordinarily difficult. Margaret Beckett has made the announcement to the Commons – and made it very well. All the wrangling that has been going on behind the scenes didn't come through at all, which has to be a winner.

Then one of those mess-ups that occur now and again: No. 10 has requested us to put an article together for the *News of the World*, backing up what was being done on the minimum wage and how important it was. All of us have presumed that different Cabinet ministers with some element of the policy in their brief (mine was training and employment) are being asked to put articles together for the Sundays. Not so simple: Margaret's people have been on the phone. Not only has she not been told, but she has been trying for some time to get an article in under her own name as Secretary of State for Trade and Industry, with responsibility for the minimum wage. I am really sorry. I have certainly had responsibility for developing the policy in opposition and a real long-standing interest, but there was no way that I intended to bounce Margaret.

This was just another example of how easy it is to upset colleagues without intending to. It is very dangerous if you build up a reputation for not working collegiately.

I've been interviewing for a new diary secretary – the fourth since we were elected. There is something about handling the diary that seems to send people into a spin, but the civil service don't rate the job very highly so even the good ones are not graded at a level that makes it worth staying any length of time. It is as though the Private Office is a training scheme for people to dib in and out of, rather than an essential cog in the machinery of delivery.

But at least we are now getting a team together of really good as well as pleasant people who are working with me and the advisers in a way that was not the case a year ago. The problem with the diary is that things are always last-minute. I have invented a new restaurant, given that wherever we are going no one knows where it is or what has been booked. The new restaurant is called 'TBC', which always appears in my diary: to be confirmed.

I devoted the whole of the weekend of 27–8 June to getting to grips with the detail of the budget. I need to be clear what my bottom line will be and what can be done for education by the Revenue Support Grant (separated out and falling under the Department of the Environment, Transport and the Regions, responsible for local-government spending). We have got to make sure that the schools get the money we think we have allocated for them.

John Prescott's absence in China from the 29th couldn't be worse timing, because of his involvement in sorting out the budget for local government and therefore for education. God help the rest of the Cabinet if they are having the difficulty that Frank Dobson (Health) and I are having – and we supposedly have priority when it comes to investment.

We have launched our flagship Education Action Zones with a fanfare of publicity, but the waters were muddied slightly because the original proposals from the local authorities were handed over to David Willetts [Shadow Education and Employment Spokesman] by someone in the Local Government Association. He was therefore able to contrast what had originally been put forward with the financing we now had from the private as well as the public sector. But it is a good programme and it will make a hell of a difference targeting resources on the inner cities and getting business involved.

This programme was the predecessor to the legislation facilitating Education Trusts to oversee the running of schools, which caused so much difficulty and argument in 2006. But nobody argued about Education Action Zones at the time because they were presented in an entirely different light.

I was proud of this policy because it did make a difference, and the partnership with the private sector was not just about money, but about getting people to mentor, to provide management skills and to help with the introduction of information technology, which was coming into the schools – at least many of them – for the first time.

Despite the pressures of preparing for the announcement on the Spending Review, Gordon has been making space to hold receptions at No. 11 for backbenchers. I think his capacity for work is even greater than my own, and that's saying something.

I've begun holding big meetings in Westminster Central Hall for staff from the DfEE's London operation. It seems to me that it is very important to have a regular dialogue with staff, although the beginning of the first of these meetings was pretty frosty. A video had been produced of what the Department was doing and what it was about, but it didn't work properly. However, once we had got the initial short speeches out of the way and people realised that we were prepared to take their questions seriously, things improved.

I adhered to this tenet throughout my time in government. Sometimes the meetings worked better than others, but it seemed to me that it was necessary to ensure that staff at least had an idea of how one set of policies fitted with another, and how what they were doing related to someone else's area. We obviously had to get out into the regions and individual schools in order to reach teachers, but at least we could do it with Employment staff and with the central core civil service at Sanctuary Buildings, our headquarters in London.

Jean Corston, my Parliamentary Private Secretary, had been coming down separately in the main lift on her way to the first of the meetings in Central Hall and heard someone from the Central Briefing Unit saying, 'I'm amazed they haven't asked us to draft something for their speeches.' Later that afternoon I said to the Permanent Secretary that I wouldn't have minded them making quips like that if they had ever come up with one single joke for any speech in the last fourteen months. One of the main questions that came up at the meeting was: why are we so irritated about the quality of correspondence? The answers are very simple. We don't turn correspondence round fast enough; we don't address the issues that people have raised with us; we don't realise what a difference the letters we send out make within the parliamentary party; and above all we don't seem to understand the impact it has on the public if we draft and send letters that we would never send to our own friends and family.

Tom Bentley [special adviser], who has come in to take over from Sophie Linden while she is on maternity leave, is doing well. He seems to have got stuck in straight away.

Tom went on to become Director of DEMOS, a left-of-centre think tank, so at one time he was at DEMOS and Nick Pearce was Director of the Institute of Public Policy Research, while three former special advisers in my department were in 10 Downing Street, one at the Treasury and one at the Cabinet Office. It is remarkable how many of those working with me as special advisers were to find themselves in key positions in years to come – rewarding for them, and also for me.

As ever with July, reshuffle fever has been in full flow, and is causing havoc inside the Parliamentary Labour Party. Those who are worried are jumpy and uncertain and those who are ambitious are desperate and impatient. Coupled with the Spending Review pressure and the fact that people are tired and desperately in need of a holiday, the House is like a tinderbox.

This seemed to happen every July. When pressure built up, the tension grew and the political environment became both fevered and irritable. On this particular occasion, I noted in my diary that Gordon was promoting Alan Milburn very heavily, as well as protecting Geoffrey Robinson – strange to think that no one now would ever have thought of putting in their diary that Gordon and Alan were on the same side.

The meeting with Tony, Gordon and Alistair Darling scheduled for 2 July has had to be postponed because Tony is understandably spending so much time in Northern Ireland dealing with the run-up to the marching season, and generally trying to keep the lid on things. There is so little recognition here of what he is doing over there.

This early part of July sees the fiftieth anniversary of the founding of the National Health Service. To mark the anniversary I visited the Northern General Hospital in my own constituency, and presented a gift to a baby born on the anniversary itself – a really heartwarming occasion. On the same day Alan Milburn [Minister of State at the Department of Health] came to share with us the task of turning the first sod for the new Stone Grove Hospital development in the south of Sheffield.

I have found out that Frank Dobson's bid for health resources is below mine for education and employment. Given that the Health budget is already bigger, this is extraordinary, and makes it very difficult in respect of the final negotiations, when all of us have to give a bit.

I have found time, however, to go to Wimbledon to 'watch' (as I put it) the tennis – I do enjoy the atmosphere there – and then back to watch England being knocked out of the World Cup.

The Welfare Reform Cabinet meeting at the beginning of July produced the curiosity of the three social-security ministers contradicting each other, each one having a different policy. To be fair to Harriet Harman, Secretary of State for Social Security, it must have been impossible prior to the meeting to reach an agreement with Frank Field, Minister of State, because Frank felt that he should have been Secretary of State and knew a lot more about the subject. On this occasion discussion centred on the future of the Child Support Agency and how to handle it.

Little did I know that seven years later I would briefly be responsible for the Child Support Agency, which equalled the Immigration and Nationality Directorate in dysfunctionality but with slightly less public awareness.

A strange little conversation at the Treasury between myself and Geoffrey Robinson, Paymaster-General, at the farewell drinks for David Hill, who was leaving his post as head of the party press office. The exchange went like this:

    Geoffrey: 'Are you and Gordon getting on all right?'

    Me: 'Yes, Geoffrey, we always do.'

    Geoffrey: 'Good. He is a great admirer of yours.'

    Me: 'Geoffrey, you don't have to say things like that.'

    Geoffrey: 'Well, it is very important that you and Gordon are good friends.'

    Me: 'But Geoffrey, I am friends with everyone – or at least I try to be.'

My relations with Gordon were to improve enormously after the Spending Review, but manoeuvring to gain favours has never been one of my failings.

July 1998

What a week! Three meetings with Tony and Gordon together, and one separately with Tony – after Prime Minister's Questions in his room at the Commons – and my first taste of the eyeball-to-eyeball of a Spending Review. The idea that we are about to have a spending bonanza is frankly ridiculous. I have so far managed to win £130 million over and above what was agreed last week, but the draft letter sent across by the Treasury (the last throw before some form of agreement is reached and spending plans signed off) would make people's hair turn: it still includes all the 'demands' which I thought we had negotiated out.

This was all about keeping my nerve, and about not accepting what was clearly unacceptable. There was a trial of strength going on, and although the Treasury held many of the cards, realpolitik meant that a big-spending ministry, particularly if the Prime Minister backed it, could negotiate to reject impossible demands. Even if immediate cash increases were unlikely to be forthcoming, quite a lot could be negotiated for the second and third year of the Spending Review and in particular capital investment – in my case through the windfall levy and an allocation at the beginning of a major building and refurbishment of schools and the introduction of technology.

It was to take years before this became a reality and very often it was taken for granted, but it transformed the environment in which teachers were teaching and students learning across Britain.

The Department of Health has signed up to what are called 'efficiency gains'. I have to say that I laughed when it was suggested that we should impose a 1 per cent efficiency gain on schools. How do you measure it? Strictly theoretically, productivity in schools would go up if you worsened the pupil-teaching ratio and go down if you employed more teachers and teaching assistants. This is one of the perversities of trying to make a judgement about public-sector productivity.

Another meeting with Tony, Gordon and myself – Gordon in very jovial mood – after Cabinet on Thursday. Tony has to deal with Northern Ireland so it was agreed that Gordon and I would speak again during the day. We did so, just after nine on Thursday evening, but we were arguing about £20 million – which, in the greater scheme of things, is peanuts.

Further discussions on Friday between Tony and Gordon led to a greater understanding of how much money had come through the local-government route to schools (an additional £50 million for England), but on Friday evening we were still arguing about the 'Letter of Direction' from the Treasury, the draft of which I had rejected earlier in the week.

The 'Letter of Direction' is what the Treasury set out is their understanding of the agreement with departments on spending, controls on spending and outcomes. At this stage, it was a draft which, given its nature, we were strongly contesting.

This is all extremely wearing and I know that I am letting it get to me but there is nothing I can do about it. If you don't care, you don't care – but if you do, then it really matters. We are also still arguing about how much we can allocate to pilot projects on Education Maintenance Allowances [the embryo programme for payments for post-sixteen education to encourage young people to stay at school or college].

Good news though for the universities. Gordon has come to an agreement with the Wellcome Trust to donate £400 million to science research, which will help enormously. This is Gordon at his best. As I said to Tony at the weekend: 'The Chinese have a proverb. The horse that gets the extra oats will go the extra mile!'

In the midst of all this we've launched the next phase of the numeracy strategy for primary schools. An ITN reporter asked me what 9 times 8 is, and fortunately I gave an immediate and accurate answer. What didn't appear on television (but the *Mail* picked it up the day after) was that in the interview the reporter contradicted me, saying, 'No, it's not.' This, of course, was cut from the broadcast that ran for the rest of the day.

Numeracy strategies are always dodgy. Sue MacGregor on the Today *programme famously once asked me to multiply 12 by 9, and it had taken me, as the* Mirror *timed, fourteen seconds to give the right answer. As with the press conference announcing the numeracy strategy back in January, I had decided to prevaricate. 'Did you say 12 times 9?' I asked. 'Yes, come on, what are twelve nines?' 'Just hold your horses, I'm giving you the answer' – by which time I had done the sum both ways round (9 times 12, 12 times 9) and was sure of 108 as the answer. I decided to take my time getting it right rather than trying to do it quickly and getting it wrong.*

A terrible tragedy in Drumcree, with three small boys killed. No wonder Tony is spending so much time trying to sort out Northern Ireland. Revd William Bingley, standing up and parading religion and the Orange Order as justification for such violence, certainly put into perspective my own irritation on Monday over Polly Toynbee's piece in the *Guardian*. She states that the Treasury is running Sure Start as well as other nonsense about Childcare and Early Years being hived off from the Department for Education (a tale no doubt put about by those who would like to be running it after the reshuffle).

Sure Start was a programme combining the best of childcare and early-years development with support to build the capacity of parents and the talent and commitment within the community to overcome inequality and disadvantage.

We're entering the last phase of the Spending Review, with letters (and a draft of the letter of direction) flying to and fro. Demands are being made which simply cannot be conceded. Early-years and nursery education are still in contention and rigorous discussions are taking place about the amount of the windfall levy that can go to the New Deal for Schools' rebuilding, refurbishment and investment in technology.

While all this is going on, my second son Hugh came down for his eighteenth birthday, and we had dinner with his girlfriend in the House of

Commons – and I then had to attend the late-night debate on the Higher Education Bill.

We reached a last-minute compromise – which was still being contested in the Lords the following day. Gordon made his Statement to the House, and by the time he stood up we had reached agreement, although the final letter of direction remained to be signed off.

Sitting on the front bench next to Gordon before he stood up, I was receiving messages asking if I could come out. Of course, I couldn't. My office indicated to Tessa Blackstone, our minister in the Lords, to hold firm – which she did, with the diplomatic support of Jim Callaghan, who made one of his rare interventions to help us out. The Opposition collapsed and the compromise went through.

Wednesday morning. The usual pre-announcement visit to schools, this time with Tony and Cherie, before making a statement in the House at lunchtime on the education and employment elements of the Spending Review. As ever, I was as nervous as hell about the Statement, but fine on the questions. Tony and Gordon were on the front bench for the early part of the Statement and question-and-answer session.

I gave specific emphasis to Sure Start and the 190,000 additional nursery places (the first real nursery programme that this country has ever had), the money for the capital investment through the New Deal for Schools, and investment in further and higher education.

I remain deeply worried about the way in which we are presenting the three-year funding for both health and education. It exaggerates the level of investment and therefore the expectation of what can be achieved. For the rest of Wednesday, I was in the House for the School Standards and Framework Act: the Bill has returned from the Lords with 420 amendments to deal with.

All the meetings this week have been frayed at the edges. Everyone is tired, desperate to get away on holiday and concerned about the reshuffle on the back of the Spending Review. I am so weary that, having travelled up through the night on Thursday, I was comatose as we drove up to Northumberland to do Radio 4's *Any Questions* on Friday evening. At the hotel before the pre-transmission meal I managed to pull myself round in time to do the programme, and I hope people didn't notice that I was out for the count. Indeed, it was one of my better efforts, even though we had some difficult topics.

And then there is Chris Woodhead, Chief Inspector of Schools, who not only wants his contract renewing but is looking for a substantial hike in his pay. I said to him: 'The Prime Minister and I have agreed to reappoint you but we cannot announce this or your increase in pay in the middle of a major row about controlling public-sector pay and about fat cats in the private sector.' He took the point sufficiently to realise that he should stop rocking the boat until we could establish what needed to be done in the autumn.

On Thursday I had a meeting with Tony about the reshuffle, before I leave for a holiday. I couldn't have predicted that the reshuffle would be right at the end of July, so I'm going to be away during the final decisions. We talked about what needed to be done. There was a silence when I raised the issue of those who had been promoting the idea of hiving off Early Years and Childcare. Sometimes it is not necessary to see someone's face because the face they will keep straight – you just have to listen for the silences.

I found out afterwards that there was enormous pressure on Tony to hive off Early Years – which fitted in with the very high profile on these issues that at least one fellow Cabinet minister had created over the previous weeks but which in the end rebounded.

So having fitted in going to Highgrove to join in the celebration of the Beacon Heads (heads who are judged to be doing such a good job that they can act as beacons and mentors to other heads), I packed my case and went with my family and friends to Majorca.

The reshuffle – which I've been dealing with over the mobile phone – sees Steve Byers moving from my team to become Chief Secretary to the Treasury and No. 2 to Gordon. Alistair Darling has taken over at Social Security from Harriet Harman, who has left the Cabinet. Frank Field has resigned as Social Security Minister as Tony won't put him in the Cabinet, and Charles Clarke – an able bruiser – has joined my team as a Junior Education Minister.

I am not sure whether Charles would like that description of 'able bruiser' these days, but it was meant affectionately in my diary!

Having been fully engaged in the discussions before the reshuffle, my Department has ended up with three changes – more than any other team – and now has more women and more ministers from London and the South East than any other front-bench team. It is truly 'New Labour'.

Nick Brown moved from Chief Whip to become Agriculture Secretary; Ann Taylor has been moved from Leader of the House to Chief Whip; and Estelle [Morris] has been promoted into Steve Byers's job as Schools minister, which is good news as I know we can do the job together.

For some time I have been very supportive of Margaret Hodge, an old friend and someone who has been desperate to show what she could do as a Minister, after doing such a good job as Chair of the Select Committee on Education. Tony said – I thought, quite waggishly – 'If you are so keen on Margaret, you have her in your team.' So I've brought her in to deal with disability and equality issues. I floated the idea of giving Jean Corston, my Parliamentary Private Secretary, a ministerial job, but those around Tony are not keen.

George Mudie, Deputy Chief Whip, has refused to move to Northern Ireland so I've agreed that he can join my team as a Parliamentary Under-Secretary. The problem is that George dislikes the civil service, and dislikes it in a quite different way from my own worry about its failure to deliver. He just doesn't like the civil service – full stop. The difficulty is going to be persuading him that we are not running a local authority.

I had no problem with George being hook, line and sinker 'a Gordon man', and over the eight and a half years that I was in Cabinet took in a number of people who were part of Gordon's entourage. All I asked was loyalty to me while a member of the team, as well as to the government and what we were trying to achieve. Given George's very able performance as former Leader of the City Council in Leeds, one of Britain's biggest cities, I was sorry that his experience and undoubted skill in getting things done turned out to be incompatible with the frustrations of helping to run a department.

August 1998

August has turned out to be much busier than I expected. It is partly my own fault, because while virtually all the Cabinet were away, I was in Britain, and answering not only for quite difficult employment figures in my own area but also for the implications of decisions by the Bank of England on interest rates and the slowdown in the economy. On *Newsnight* I made the mistake of saying that I thought that manufacturing in my own city is on a knife edge, and this was reported in a couple of newspapers as 'the economy is on a knife edge' – which, of course, started all sorts of hares running. There was a time when people understood what words meant and didn't reinterpret them mischievously.

What has really got my goat is the Deputy Governor of the Bank of England, Mervyn King, indicating that he thought that present levels of unemployment were too low in terms of sustainability, and that he expected much higher levels – which to me was a red rag to a bull. I was surprised therefore to read in one Sunday newspaper that Tony 'would deal with conflicting ministers on the economy when he came home from holiday'. There was no 'conflicting minister' to deal with!

I was ready to put the record straight on the Frost programme on Sunday [16 August], but the terrible bombing in Omagh the day before put paid to that. This outrage shocked all of us, and Tony and Mo Mowlam immediately flew back from holiday. All of this underlined the importance that Tony was giving to trying to find peace in Northern Ireland, but the Omagh bombing was by a fringe group and completely regardless of human life.

September 1998

Following the Omagh bomb Parliament was recalled at the beginning of September to pass emergency legislation. How could anybody argue with this? – except that the legislation had never been to Cabinet and was being rushed through in a way that would have very little impact. Strange for the House to sit through the night until 6.40 a.m., when talk all the time has been about 'modernising' the procedures of Parliament and making the House 'family-friendly', especially as we have a woman Leader of the House in Margaret Beckett and a woman Chief Whip in Ann Taylor. So much for all the talk about feminising the process.

But none of us is going to grumble, because making at least some gesture in respect of the horror of Omagh is politically understandable. It remains true that staying up all night would bring nobody back, but questioning the sense of it would look, feel and rightly be interpreted as crass.

So with Bill Clinton over in Ireland and soon to be in the UK, and the party-conference season rapidly approaching, we are moving fast into the autumn.

A Special Cabinet at Chequers on 10 September. Gordon kicked off on the economy and in my usual bumptious way I piled in immediately after him. Apart from Peter Mandelson and Tony himself, no one else commented on the economy.

On 15 September I spoke at the TUC conference but I couldn't reveal the figures which had been given to me by the statisticians, showing a substantial drop in unemployment both in relation to those claiming benefits and on the Labour Force Survey, which is a much more accurate reflection of how the economy is going. In other words, the Bank of England was being far too pessimistic earlier in the summer about what could be achieved. There is a very real chance that we will come through without any form of retrenchment (or what they call these days 'a hard landing').

The day after my TUC speech I launched the Year of Reading.

This increased reading among children but also among parents and grand-parents enormously over the following year. A number of authors such as the Poet Laureate, Andrew Motion, and the children's author Jacqueline Wilson lent their considerable support, but the agents for one or two extremely high-profile authors seemed to think that their job was to get in the way of anything that might look like co-operating with a government policy on literacy.

We've made the announcement on the Office for Standards in Education. We had agreed a new formula with a light-touch approach that would reflect the drive for standards, but also some of the more sensible things that had been raised by heads and teachers.

Then we've had Tony Giddens, Director of the London School of Economics, proclaiming 'The Third Way' – all very entertaining, but the idea that it has just been invented is an insult to everyone who has been working for the last fifteen years to ensure that there genuinely was a 'third way'. Still, it focused attention and gave a sense of purpose and momentum.

In the week running up to the party conference we've had quite a kerfuffle about the announcement on citizenship and democracy being taught in the curriculum.

This was extremely close to my heart. I wanted to announce that we were going to go forward with the idea in principle and ensure that a Working Group could carry it with all-party support. In the end I got my way, but there was a terrific struggle because people were so afraid that it might be interpreted as 'teaching party politics'. Far from it. We were just trying to ignite even the slightest spark of understanding of how democracy works, and how citizenship, identity and cohesion really matter to a civilised society.

This was one of those moments when my not being in this particular post would have been disastrous, and to be there made it possible to do something that ought to have been done years before, and is inherent to the education systems of most major democracies, in one form or another.

On the Wednesday before conference, I spoke at a fundraising dinner for a major international Jewish charity called ORT – Organisation for Research and Technology – which was established almost 100 years ago in the Ukraine. Despite the name, ORT's emphasis is on schooling, with schools and training establishments in around seventy countries across the world.

My friend Maurice Hatter introduced me and the speech itself was fine, but after I'd stopped speaking I couldn't get Lucy's lead from underneath the table leg, where it had become completely entangled. As a consequence, having started to clap at the end of my oration, the audience felt obliged to keep going. I got more and more embarrassed as the clapping went on and I still couldn't get the dog sorted out, with the lead now firmly wound around Lucy's front legs. I tried to get her off the dais on to the floor so that at least everyone would feel comfortable in being able to stop applauding – but she wouldn't move. I wish I had had the presence of mind to hold up my hand and explain what was happening, but I was so keen to get off the platform that I was doing everything I could to speed up the process.

I must have been forgiven, for I was later to work with ORT and Sir Maurice – he and his wife Irene became good friends – after I left the Home Office, offering advice on educational matters and other areas. Though little known to the general public, ORT is an extremely effective charity doing a first-class job across the world.

Immigration has raised its head, thanks to the union representing immigration officials. It's a mess. It is not simply that the lifting of the primary-purpose rule – the test of whether an applicant for immigration on the grounds of marrying a British citizen has a bona-fide claim – has increased the expectation and the pressure. It has also changed the climate in terms of asylum seekers. People think that we are a soft touch because we provide accommodation rather than sending straight back people who are obvious ne'er-do-wells, coming from the Czech Republic, Slovenia and Romania. It is fairly self-evident that they are economic migrants and should be dealt with immediately.

I could not at this stage have known that I was going to be in the eye of the storm three years later, by which time the issues concerning nationality and asylum were at flood tide not only in the UK but right across Europe. Some instinct must have triggered my interest in what was happening, given that I had got enough on my plate with the education and broader employment and equal-opportunities brief. This was the kind of prescience which, on the political front, has always stood me in good stead, even if I have not always had the same foresight in other areas of my life.

October 1998

I've returned from conference and got stuck in over the weekend before having a few days in the Lake District. It was my last conference as a member of the National Executive Committee of the party, as I was stepping down after fifteen years, the rules having changed so that, perfectly reasonably, Cabinet ministers could not stand for the section elected by the rank and file.

I've been working on completing the Green Paper on Special Educational Needs, a paper on revising the formula for distributing grants to local education authorities and schools.

This was particularly important as it was to lead to direct funding to schools, rather than having the money going through the education authority.

I am going through the Admissions Code, trying to bring some fairness to the way in which youngsters and their parents can get something close to their first preference, particularly in the case of secondary schools. The Code is as important as the Act but there is very little attention being paid to it politically or in the media. Once again changes are going to have to be taken a step at a time. Pushing it too far would end up with a major reaction and a row. By avoiding a row we can make progress quietly and effectively.

One major task is to prevent church schools being able to employ such tight criteria that they exclude pupils whom they don't want. Taking on the Anglican and Catholic churches would not be clever, but letting some of the church schools (particularly in the North West of England) continue in the way they do is just not on.

Another task to be addressed before I can get away for a day or two is the

Green Paper on the future of the teaching profession. This is absolutely central to everything we are doing – professional development, new scales to keep good teachers in the classroom rather than in management, training for those who are going to be heads and managers, founding a leadership college, and continuing the drive for recruitment and changing the image of the profession to get the best graduates to think of teaching as a first-choice career.

Getting this to Tony in a form that is acceptable is going to be a real challenge, but, alongside sorting out the teacher training colleges, this could make such a difference to the standards agenda and what we are trying to achieve.

Good news though on Employment Zones – where a row with the Treasury and the Department of Social Security has held everything up. I believe this to be a crucial element in getting people off welfare and into work.

Employment Zones were something I had been pushing for very hard, but were not part of the original New Deal programme and therefore had not received a very favourable reception inside government. The thrust of this public-private partnership was to ensure that imaginative new ways of getting people out of bed and into a job – and pursuing them rigorously when they didn't turn up for work and they dropped out of a job – could achieve the goal of getting to those people who had taken the welfare state for granted for far too long.

In retrospect it would have been better if we had inculcated much more of the radical personalised approach of the Employment Zones into the New Deal programme as a whole, but eventually the development of the role of personal advisers was to go at least some way towards mirroring the success of the better Employment Zones.

We now established that it is possible to move funding from one department to another, and from one heading to another, so that savings in relation to benefits can be applied to saving more benefits by getting people into work and out of dependence. This is really important.

Tony in China, Gordon in the United States, having been to Ottawa, and efforts now going on to prevent a world recession (a little bit on the late side in my view, but who am I to comment?). And here I am, able to enjoy a few days in the Lake District. I suppose that's the difference between being Prime Minister or Chancellor and the Education and Employment Secretary.

I am worried about what the world economy and growth rates will mean for public expenditure and, above all, for employment. I really do want us to be able to get unemployment down below one million. It would be wonderful to be Employment Secretary and achieve that, even though what we can do from the Department has only a marginal effect on the outcome.

Gordon's speech to the IMF has confirmed what he said at a couple of Cabinets, including the Special Cabinet at Chequers on 10 September, namely his projection of very low growth rates for the coming year. On both occasions I queried what he had said, including at Chequers, when he made it clear that he expected growth to be down to 1 per cent. I said at the time that this was very low indeed and the implications were enormous. The idea that higher growth must automatically lead to higher inflation and therefore put at risk our public-expenditure programmes would be a return to the experience of the inter-war years.

The notion that, in a global economy where you can borrow across boundaries, public spending crowds out private investment is laughable, but that is what is being peddled even by those in the very global companies who are quite happy to take advantage of low interest rates wherever and whenever they can.

At the end of the week that I was away, the key-stage education results (the assessment and tests at seven, eleven and fourteen) were leaked both to the *Times Educational Supplement* and to Tim Miles at the Press Association. There have been continuing leaks from both the Qualifications and Curriculum Authority and the Department itself. This is a major problem for us, not because we aren't going to put out the results, but because if someone starts releasing material before we are ready to do so, or before the results have been properly verified, then you can get into a real mess. Presumably that's why it is being done. On this occasion we decided that we might as well release them, thereby accelerating our own timetable in order not to end up with the results farcically being put out twice, once informally and once officially.

The Office for National Statistics has managed to get the figures wrong on the calculation of teachers' pay, so the statistics have had to be reviewed and therefore their publication postponed until they get this sorted. But the Bank of England has cut interest rates by 0.5 per cent, which is not only good news but vindication for those concerned that they had raised them too high at the wrong time – given the long time it takes for them to have any impact.

November 1998

Our departmental Remembrance Day service has reminded me – and everyone else – that this department includes what was once the Department of Labour and National Service. The Department as it was in the Second World War had to organise the recruitment and distribution of labour for the wartime effort, and then undertake the herculean task of employing 4.5 million of those in uniform back in civilian life in the post-1945 era. This is an unsung achievement of the first order by the then Labour government. It strikes me that major Cabinet posts in the late twentieth century combine a range of posts which would have had Cabinet rank with much smaller departments in the past.

We've had a Joint Policy Committee meeting between the Cabinet and the National Executive Committee, looking at how to create an enduring relationship between government and party, and developing the idea of the Policy Forum and Joint Policy Commissions on particular areas of work.

I managed (with considerable support, including from Jack Straw) to get a change to the wording which otherwise would have meant that any resolutions from the National Policy Forum put to our national conference could be amended only if they 'enhanced' the original meaning. We're changing from a party riven and driven by dissent into a party that will tolerate no dissent. This is clearly not only unacceptable but politically inept, given the rows going on in Wales about diktats from the centre, and the furore developing over the mayorship of London.

I also pointed out that it would have been nice if we had all been informed of the outcome of discussions with the Liberal Democrats at national level. (We had all agreed after the election that there could be discussions about joint working on the Constitution.) I said that I had been somewhat taken aback the night before when Don Foster, a Lib Dem spokesman, had said to me as we came out of the Commons, 'Well, with the agreement we've reached, it looks as if we'll all be working together and making decisions jointly.' I'd replied, 'Not as long as there's a bone in my body!', and at the end of the meeting, Tony came round the Cabinet table and put his arm around my shoulder in one of his calming gestures.

I suppose one of my less attractive traits is that if I am left out of the loop, I often become extremely belligerent. While the constitutional discussions behind the scenes had absolutely nothing to do with my departmental brief, I genuinely felt aggrieved because it was well known that the battle with the

Liberal Democrats in Sheffield had run very deep with me, and my antagonism to their duplicity was therefore something that encompassed much more than just our battle at local-government level.

Trying to speak my mind in Cabinet is very difficult, as with 'Well, if we are going to bomb Iraq, what comes afterwards?' I am in danger of becoming the 'awkward squad'.

That night I shot up to Harrogate to do a dinner that Jonathan Powell had asked me to attend, allegedly in lieu of Tony. It was described as a gathering of 'top companies', and turned out to have been organised by someone who had once worked in the Foreign Office. It was a complete waste of time.

It is interesting to reflect that on that Friday night, 13 November, I had been invited to go back to London and join Prince Charles for his fiftieth-birthday bash – and instead had chosen to go to the monthly meeting of my constituency party in Brightside. Whatever the attractions of London, I was still giving priority to my local Labour Party, which was to stand me in very good stead in the years to come.

Hilary Benn had come with me to the Joint Policy Committee – the first time that he'd ever been in the Cabinet Room, and the second Benn to have entered it, after his father Tony.

Hilary, then accompanying me as my special adviser, was to return to that room in 2003 as a Cabinet minister in his own right. Taking him in there for the first time was one of those moments when you feel in your bones that there is more significance than might appear at the time.

I've launched a little booklet on the former Wadsley School and Wadsley community in my constituency, and the sheer warmth and friendship of the people at the Monteney Workshop who were involved in the launch and whom I went to see was lovely. Monteney Workshop is a community printing outfit that also does a range of artistic and basic skills work. They gave me a round of applause as I left, and it was one of those occasions when you feel that it is all worthwhile.

I then went on to Parson Cross Church of England Primary School for the UNICEF 'Put It to Your MP' Campaign. Doug McEvoy, General Secretary of the National Union of Teachers, flew in from Cardiff in an air taxi to Sheffield Tinsley airport – a major gesture by him.

It was a good afternoon. What was staggering was not only the confidence and the clarity of the children but the stories they told about what was happening in their neighbourhood: burglaries down their road, drug dealers, windows being pushed in and cars being burnt out. We are talking here about a primary school, and their tales made a very deep impression on me. There are so many people who haven't got the first idea what others are having to put up with. They remain shielded from it all and yet constantly talk about protecting the rights of those perpetrating rather than those being persecuted by this kind of outrage.

The end of the parliamentary session leading up to the Queen's Speech and the outline of the government programme for the coming session has seen the House of Lords vote five times against the European Bill, which would bring in a list system for regional proportional representation for the European Parliament. The twist is that a majority of our own back-benchers and the Labour Party in the country are rejoicing, because if the Bill doesn't go through (and the use of the Parliament Act is necessary if there is continued blockage by the House of Lords, meaning the Bill has to be reintroduced in the Commons and taken through its sections all over again, not just the controversial item, with a year's delay), there is a chance that the European Union elections in 1999 might take place under the old system. We would do a lot better under the old system than under the new, and fringe parties like the United Kingdom Independence Party and the BNP would do a lot worse.

In fact the list system was introduced, and two of my own former City Council Labour colleagues who were in the European Parliament lost their seats as a consequence, with many other good people falling by the wayside. For those of us against breaking the link between a definable and manageable constituency and the individual representing those electors, this reinforced just what bad news electoral changes of this particular sort were.

I remain exercised by the fact that those around Tony do not understand what we are doing as Cabinet ministers departmentally – and what we have to put up with – compared with what it is like to be the Prime Minister or in the Prime Minister's Office.

Answering correspondence, personally revising policy papers again and again, preventing major upheavals by blocking inept action by civil servants, and so on are not things the PM has to worry about. But Cabinet ministers who are doing their job properly do have to be concerned with such things. This is clearly not understood by Jonathan Powell, and understandably would not even cross the mind of Tony Blair.

Whatever I feel about my timetable, I have to think of Tony. Before Cabinet I went with him to a school in Chiswick. He had got back at 3.30 in the morning from Ireland, joined me at 9 a.m., and was going to St Malo for an Anglo-French summit that afternoon, prior to a European Council meeting in Vienna. We had an interesting talk about European issues but above all about the House of Lords and its make-up. I indicated strongly that I am against giving it legitimacy and such power that whatever we do in the House of Commons can be blocked by a House of Lords claiming the backing and consent of the people.

Criticism of us and the undermining of democracy is not about our doing too much and too quickly, but too little and too late!

That weekend I went, for the first time, to Hillsborough Castle in Northern Ireland, where Mo Mowlam held an entertaining weekend. I was speaking on the Saturday at the Ulster People's College, where leadership skills are being taught to all parts of the community. My sons joined me for the weekend. Chris Smith and his partner were there, as well as Alastair Campbell and Fiona, amongst others, and as ever, I was the first to bed. It meant that I didn't get anything like the amount of work done over the weekend that I had intended to but it was very enjoyable.

Unfortunately I had to be up at six on the Monday morning to attend a conference to deal with the criticism from the Office for Standards in Education that we weren't moving fast enough (after sixteen months) to deliver a particular form of phonics teaching of reading in primary schools. In fact teachers were being pushed way beyond the point of acceptability, and the criticism from the teaching profession, including head teachers, was that we were being dictatorial and far too centralist in demanding that they moved more quickly and in a more focused way.

December 1998

A manic start to the month: six different meetings on the first Friday of the month, five on the Saturday – and, after the previous weekend in Northern Ireland, again great pressure to catch up on routine.

A meeting with Tony, in which I expressed my fear that we are moving into a phase of 'permanent Maoist revolution' as I put it to him – which had all the dangers of instability and overload. We talked in detail about the expansion of specialist schools and the creation of 'beacon schools', a notion which was later to lead to the idea of 'academies'. I was pushing as hard as I could on the foundation of early-years education: the literacy and numeracy programme in primary education and the revision of the school curriculum to be implemented in 2000. I indicated that I would do everything I could to accelerate the reform of secondary education, but there were only so many bricks we could put in the wall if it wasn't to collapse.

Sally Morgan from Downing Street has approached me to ask whether I would talk to Hilary Benn about his becoming Head of Policy for the party, based at Millbank Tower. I can see how the balance between him and Margaret McDonagh, General Secretary, (and David Miliband in Downing Street) would work, but it would be at my expense. I am not sure that it would be good for Hilary, but the decision has to be his.

Hilary chose to stay with me which, in the event of his getting on the shortlist for the vacant seat of Leeds Central, following the death of Derek Fatchett, proved to be a wise decision.

Jack Straw has agreed that General Pinochet, former dictator of Chile, should be extradited. This has been a mess all along. The Foreign Office should never have allowed Pinochet into the country in the first place, and his presence has been a running sore that has been the bane of Jack's life. He told me that he had no choice in any case because of the action of the Spanish courts – which were seeking his extradition there – and the danger of judicial review. But it was a very difficult issue that he handled well.

Two interesting snippets on the domestic front. One is the tussle between Peter Mandelson, Secretary of State at the Department for Trade and Industry, and Gordon over the potential for partial privatisation of the Post Office. There is quite an interesting reversal of roles here in terms of who was pushing for what.

The second is the Department for Culture, Media and Sport pulling a very small grant of £200,000 from the Royal National Institute for the Blind for Braille production. I heard a whisper that they were going to say that this was all the doing of the Department for Education and Employment and that I had been unwilling to help – whereas the truth is that nobody had told me. We've intervened and I've instructed officials to bring me a policy paper – it was necessary to ensure that I did this by the book – to discover whether this was our role and what the justification would be.

We then replaced the £200,000 cut by the DCMS. What an example not only of the government's failure to act collaboratively but of one department being prepared to stitch up another. We would have looked well passing the Disability Rights Commission legislation and extending dramatically the Disability Discrimination Act, only to be blamed for a government decision made by another department.

Wednesday 16 December: bombing raids begin on Iraq ['Operation Desert Fox', in which American and British aircraft attacked specific targets in Baghdad]. Discussion at Cabinet was desultory. We had said it all before. We talked about the need to get across the brutality of the regime, the need to stress that medical aid and food were not being blocked as part of the sanctions, and the fact that we had lost the propaganda war before we started. The media are not lined up, apart from Alastair giving an exclusive to the *Sun*. The BBC have certainly never been on board and the Americans had no communications strategy because of the row that was going on in the House of Representatives and the distraction provided by the efforts of the far right to impeach Bill Clinton [over the Monica Lewinsky episode].

If you had written the script for what is going on at the moment, you would have been laughed at. It is just not credible.

I am afraid I felt this several times during the course of my time in Cabinet. Reality, in politics, is much more bizarre and unpredictable than drama.

What were we achieving with these bombing raids, and on whose behalf? But how can we not act? If we don't, then Saddam Hussein will carry on – to bang the increasingly hollow drum. To act is to be ridiculed, and not to act is to be held in contempt.

But Christmas is upon us, and the drinks parties and Christmas dinners, and the rushing-about to all sorts of events and school carol services, have to carry on.

On the Sunday before Christmas the *Observer* had a headline 'Blunkett fury over Council Tax clawback', a story about a row that had been going on for months about clawing back council-tax benefit from authorities who raised council tax beyond the level projected by the Department for the Environment, Transport and the Regions.

Not only did this come as a surprise to me, as I had had nothing to do with briefing the *Observer*, but I didn't even know about it until Monday morning, when John Prescott, perfectly reasonably in his departmental role as Secretary of State at the DETR, rang me to ask me what the hell I was doing. As the press office had not briefed me on this story on the Sunday, even though it was a headline, I genuinely didn't know what he was talking about.

Another milestone in building up distrust and an example of how those who are not political (those who were supposed to be briefing me on the papers) couldn't spot a highly dangerous political story, and one ripe for inter-departmental dissent.

Later that day – Monday 21 December – I was presented by the Department with a letter on this very issue, sent at the end of the previous week by John Prescott, pointing out that the Public Expenditure Committee had approved this change. My Department, though they knew that I had been arguing vehemently about it, hadn't even bothered to draw down the minutes of this Cabinet Committee to tell me about it. No wonder John thought that this was some sort of buck-passing on my part, dissociating myself from a decision that had been taken.

Thank goodness it's nearly Christmas – but now we've had the *Guardian* revelation that Peter Mandelson has borrowed hundreds of thousands of pounds from Geoffrey Robinson. I am sure it is true when Peter says that he has already 'disentangled himself' from the enquiry into Geoffrey's financial affairs but it feels all wrong.

As I was to learn, perception is all and working out how a situation will look 'down the line', or how others might present it or use it, is all-important.

Wednesday 23 December, a day I shall not forget. At 12.30 p.m. Peter Mandelson resigned. At 3.30 p.m. Geoffrey Robinson resigned. Stephen Byers has become Trade and Industry Secretary and Alan Milburn has become Chief Secretary to the Treasury.

Poem:

> And the spinning of a spider
> Catches flies from out the air,
> And the web the spider spinneth
> Holds you tight within its lair.
> And the spider eats the flies, you see,
> But never are there flies on he!

And so ends 1998.

January 1999

My first major task of the New Year has been trying to sort out appointing the Chief Adjudicator, a new post to deal with a range of disputes over admissions, school amalgamations and closures, and conflict between schools and education authorities. Thanks to the common sense of my Permanent Secretary Michael Bichard, it was agreed that I should see and comment on the shortlist – and a good job too. Officials dealing with this appointment have been favouring a candidate who has been chief executive of an education authority which I know to have massively under-performed.

With the new inspection regime for education authorities I was later to discover just how badly this particular authority had been performing, and Estelle Morris, as Schools Minister, had to take tough decisions about calling in the private sector to help sort it out.

Eventually it was agreed that we should appoint Sir Peter Newsam, but I was flabbergasted that officials didn't initially believe that his experience of running the Inner London Education Authority and his work in France were sufficient experience. Even after a year and a half we are still struggling to link reality outside the Department with decisions inside it. And even at the end of the process there were officials saying that it was their decision and not mine, and that I had no right to overrule them. All I said was, 'Well, go out and tell the world that I have overridden you and I will tell the world why and we will see what the public think.'

A thought on the New Year Honours: the second Deputy Permanent Secretary at the Treasury gets a GCB (knighthood), but Michael Bichard, the Permanent Secretary who has seen the most enormous shift in policy and delivery over the past eighteen months, and whom I had nominated, is not on the list.

Tony was with the family in the Seychelles when a silly story blew up, thanks to the National Association of Headteachers, about his taking his children out of school for one additional day in order to fly back. Much was being made of this, and John Prescott, in charge for the duration, rang me, ostensibly to ensure that we were all clear on the line we were taking, but I think more to find out what Mo Mowlam had been up to, ringing round the Cabinet and phoning Tony in the Seychelles about the activities of Charlie Whelan, Gordon's spin doctor, and his prolonged briefing against other colleagues.

Mo rang me again on Monday to say that she has spoken to Tony, who, wisely in my view, was extremely cautious about discussing anything on the telephone. What he needed was to be left alone.

The same morning reports started coming through on the radio that Charlie Whelan is going to seek another job – a euphemism for 'will be resigning'.

I was quite surprised at the timing. Charlie had been getting up everyone's nose for a very long time, and the clashes between himself and Alastair Campbell had become notorious. Frankly, Charlie was doing great damage to Gordon by being seen to be anti just about everyone, contemptuous of everything and obsessive about internal conflict, rather than promoting the best interests of the government as a whole.

Nevertheless, I had not taken as seriously as I clearly should have done the head of steam which Mo Mowlam's behind-the-scenes activity produced, in terms of the real momentum and pressure that had built up. I was never as good at the internecine warfare as many others, relying instead on reaching out and building support in the party outside Westminster.

I had put on tape my astonishment at how much froth there was in the newspapers at the beginning of the year. I should have remembered just what it was like the year before and how much there was going to be for the subsequent years, whenever journalists and commentators had little to write and speak about. Real political news is so often thin on the ground in the first couple of weeks of January, and journalists are almost bound to be recycling material and issues.

Around this time I noted in the Daily Express *a very strange article by a man named Stephen Pollard – strange because it seemed to be written purely for the* Express *readership, rather than articulating what he himself believed. I wish I had taken a great deal more interest in what he was up to, because I would have been a great deal wiser and, I hope, more cautious about any form of co-operation with him on his subsequent efforts to write an account of my life through to 2004. But being wise after the event, and spotting moments when a signal might have indicated 'Stop', is one of the salutary lessons of a diary.*

In January, apart from looking with increasing incredulity at the way in which the health service was performing (or not performing), I've been continuing an internal battle over toughening up welfare reform. The Department for Social Security is taking through a Bill on welfare issues and this is an opportunity to be stricter with people who are not 'playing the game' when on the New Deal programme. In other words, if they are not turning up for interviews when they should, we need legal powers to force them to come in more often, and to attend training or employment opportunities. Amazingly there is resistance within the DSS, which I think goes back a very long way: that department sees itself as on the side of 'welfare' rather than getting people off it.

In the end, the pros and cons have been put in writing to Tony, who has quietly ruled that we should toughen up – and what once looked as though it was going to be a row has faded away. I just regret that we had to trouble Tony with it at all.

Cabinet on Thursday 14 January is memorable because Gordon gave a presentation on the economy that was much more upbeat than the one we had had in the autumn, accepting that it is possible now to have reduced unemployment, increased employment and low inflation. After Gordon's presentation I talked about what was happening with employment. December saw a 14,000 reduction in those claiming benefits, and the monetarist tendencies of the pundits over the previous summer, advocating the need for higher unemployment, were proved completely wrong.

Education and Employment Questions in the House of Commons on Thursday morning. The new parliamentary timetable is being introduced, with Cabinet followed by Question Time, which would otherwise have been at 2.30 in the afternoon. I am afraid the changes have made no difference to the coverage. We only get Commons occasions written up by the sketch writers these days, except on very rare major occasions. Some of the sketch-writing is very entertaining, but hardly informative at all about what is really going on in Parliament. No wonder people hold the place in contempt.

We have a problem about introducing new pay scales and new requirements for quality and performance from teachers. The nurses have been given a substantial pay increase for those at entry point, and they are now making nursing into a graduate profession. I cannot see any reason at all why young women and men with decent A levels shouldn't go straight into nursing training. There is no reason why someone entering what should be a caring profession should have to have a degree. If feeding a patient or changing a bedpan is going to be beneath nurses, then Lord help all of us when we go into hospital.

More crucially at the moment, how on earth am I to argue with the teaching profession about the new rigour, the idea of 'something for something', and increases in pay levels and promotion opportunities, if the health service are simply handing out the money without any returns in terms of change of practice?

And then a row has blown up about parental choice on the back of an interview which Tony did to do with failing inner-city schools. The focus was on his own choice as a parent, and the *Mail on Sunday* has gone to town. Tony's decision to go to the Press Complaints Commission has kept the story going. What isn't known is that I was due to publish the Admissions Code providing guidance on eliminating selection by schools of the pupil rather than the preference of the parent, and have had to delay it in order not to end up with a clash between Tony's row and the progress we hoped to make with the new Code. It has been one of those moments where public and private get entangled and where, but for very quick footwork, we could have made matters a great deal worse.

Gordon and I are getting on better. We had a very good dinner which he and I hosted for Anglo-American companies whom we wished to encourage to join the employment option for the New Deal, and to use some of their experience from individual states in the US in relation to welfare reform. It went well.

Last week in January, and the education debate is really hotting up. I had agreed, foolishly, to participate in a discussion at the Institute of Education organised by the *Guardian*. This was supposed to be a low-key, sensible debate with the Head of the Institute, Peter Mortimore. I was to speak first, then he was to reflect briefly on what I had said and open the discussion up to question and answer. On arrival at the Institute I stepped out of the car into a pool of water, which saturated my shoes: the start of a wonderful evening! There were over 1,000 people in the lecture theatre, most of them teachers. I gave a speech for twenty minutes, explaining what we were trying to do in terms of standards and improvement and what we were asking of the profession. Peter then rose to his feet and spoke for nearly half an hour, playing entirely to the audience by bringing out every possible prejudice about how unfair we were being to teachers; how standards were unacceptable; and how we were putting schools under too much pressure and demanding too much, too quickly in terms of changing what was on offer in the least competent schools.

Of course, that went down a storm, and as so often, I couldn't help myself. I blew my top. For me, what he had just said had neither coherence nor sensible debating points, and was a wilful misinterpretation of what we were going to do. My response was as vigorous as anyone could have wanted, and the consequence was that I was booed. But I wasn't prepared to put up with the middle-class claptrap which assumes that everything will be well if we would just leave teachers to get on with what they were doing. Of course, if what they had always been doing in every school had been delivering high-quality education, narrowing the equality gap and opening up opportunity, then there wouldn't be a problem. The fact that things are as desperate as they are, and that so many children have been let down, is precisely why we are taking action. It is not some vendetta against teachers (remember: Estelle Morris and I are both trained teachers) but is about trying to raise dramatically expectations and delivery, and putting in the resources to make that possible.

I came out of the meeting absolutely seething. I was shaking with rage.

Whatever impact Peter Mortimore, the organisers of the event and the audience thought they were going to have proved exactly the reverse. I came out more determined than ever that we were going to move faster and more decisively, and that we were not going to put up with self-justifying excuses for years of neglect. Time and time again in my years in government I have seen pressure brought to bear that had exactly the opposite effect of that intended, and in 2006 I was reminded of my experience in early 1999 when Patricia Hewitt addressed the Royal College of Nursing just before the impending reshuffle and was howled down for declaring that the NHS is in a better condition than it has ever been. If the RCN had ever wanted to ensure the security of the Secretary of State and ministers in the Department of Health, they certainly did so that day. It is hard to explain to people who don't understand the consequences of their actions quite what the outcome will be if they don't think through the inevitable response.

If the Institute of Education wanted to influence me and my ministers, they had certainly gone entirely the wrong way about it. I wasn't prepared even to countenance listening to what they had to say. We would turn elsewhere for advice, information and insight, at least for the time being.

Following that maddening 'debate', I changed into my dinner suit in seven minutes, arrived late at the Whitbread Book of the Year Awards, and had to postpone my speech until the end of the dinner in order to calm down and turn to the events of the evening. My job was to give the Children's Prize as part of the Year of Reading, and to remember to give a mention to Chris Smith, Secretary of State for Culture, Media and Sport, who was there as a guest.

The following day saw the opening of the first new secondary school that we, as a government, had opened – and therefore that I had opened. This was the Elthorne Park High School in Ealing, stomping ground of my special adviser and friend, Hilary Benn. Given the time needed for getting a school planned, getting the investment agreed and the buildings put up, this was a remarkable achievement. The new school will be added to as numbers grow, and it's important to stress that this is a new school to accommodate the increased numbers from that part of London, and not a replacement for an existing school. This certainly cheered me up.

Then with Chris Smith to a joint launch in Hounslow, where we were promoting a new fund for reinvigorating music tuition in schools and the purchase of instruments, after which I hurried back to the Atrium restaurant, close to the Commons at Millbank, for a launch I had agreed to do for the Royal National Institute for the Blind. Ten minutes for lunch, followed by the regular meeting of ministers and the Executive Board of the Department.

Cabinet on 28 January was once again dominated by foreign policy, primarily what was happening in Kosovo. But Margaret Beckett and Alistair Darling joined in on the issue of 'something for nothing' in terms of health spending and pay increases. I am glad that other people have noticed and are butting in, otherwise it just looks like sour grapes from me.

February 1999

Chris Woodhead, Chief Inspector of Schools, answers questions at an education session at Exeter University on personal and sexual relationships with students. His answer, recorded by someone there, appears to suggest that he is condoning, in certain circumstances, a relationship between a teacher and student above the age of consent – reopening the controversy that had blown up four years ago about a sixth-form student of his with whom he had subsequently lived for ten years.

This episode took up over two months of my time. Every weekend there were fresh suggestions in Sunday newspapers, and every Saturday I was phoned, and my advisers were phoned, with all sorts of material that we were asked to comment on. There was a tirade from the liberal left, including from broadsheet newspaper reporters, demanding to know why I wasn't prepared to sack Chris Woodhead. These, of course, are the very people who would have been the first to criticise me for breaching equality and fairness in relation to industrial law and fair treatment (and fair hearing) for employees.

This was not, and could not be, about prejudice against an individual or settling other scores. It had to be concerned with what was right, what was provable and what was defendable, should the matter go to an industrial tribunal. I stuck rigidly to my role as Secretary of State and to treating Chris Woodhead as I would any other person, with or without clashes over policy. Only those closest to me know the toll this all took in terms of time and energy, and the diversion it necessarily meant from dealing with serious policy issues.

The one thing I would do differently now would be to ensure that none of my home or personal telephone numbers is known to any journalist, and to make sure of that I would change them. In that way I could have avoided the endless answerphone messages and – when I did pick up the phone – having to deal with the 'accusation' that I was somehow protecting Chris Woodhead from legitimate action. I was not. I found the whole business sordid and degrading for both of us and for those dragged into it as a consequence.

One of the twists in this situation was that Glen Hoddle, the England football coach, had made remarks about disabled people having been 'punished' for wrongdoings in a previous life. Tony had made some remarks on the back of this which had been completely misreported, so when I got in touch with him about Chris Woodhead's situation, he was very keen indeed that we simply stuck to rigid procedure and said as little as possible. His view, which I shared, was that if we didn't, the press would come for someone with some passing relationship with government every week.

Every word now has to be watched, every nuance thought about. This is partly the result of being in government rather than simply commenting from outside, but is also a consequence of a change in the way that reporting is taking place, including people getting extraneous recordings at all sorts of events and then feeding them to the media in a way that never was the case before.

Good news: the Bank of England has reduced interest rates by 0.5 per cent. Is it arrogant to feel that those of us who were worried about the previous hike were justified? But of course this is what is meant by 'independence', and we have to accept the swings with the roundabouts. I just wish that someone would remember remarks made about 'natural rates of unemployment' and how wrong those people were to want more men and women to be dependent, through unemployment, than is absolutely necessary.

And so to the run-up to the March Budget – another to-ing and fro-ing with the Treasury. It is very wearing, and there are times when I despair of the penny-pinching and the fact that although something has been agreed, it is still necessary to come back, and then come back again to defend and protect what was thought now to be policy.

Managed to get a few days in Cyprus with friends and my third son, Andrew. Once again there was to be no Easter break because of the teacher conferences, so it was good to get away for a few days. Although I had no choice but to take work with me, it is always nicer to work outside and away from the daily grind.

There is a fuss over the Macpherson Report into the killing of Stephen Lawrence [the black teenager stabbed to death in April 1993, whose alleged killers had never been charged and whose case became a focus of worries about 'institutional racism' in the Metropolitan Police]. It has been leaked, as everything is these days, and Jack Straw sought an injunction which obviously really put the press's back up (and it doesn't take a lot). It is difficult sometimes to know how to handle leaks when you are not in a position to be able to respond to a report or clarify or correct things before what is only half the truth is halfway round the world.

The publication of the Macpherson Report and the injunction on the *Sunday Telegraph* continue to rumble on. When the report was published, there was a confusion over the names of witnesses printed in the appendices. This understandably led to people asking why Home Office officials, having had the report for some time, had not noticed and done something about it. Macpherson took responsibility.

So it was in this atmosphere that Paul Boateng [Minister of State at the Home Office] had to make the Statement on Friday morning because Jack had gone to the South of France for the weekend – and in normal circumstances, who could blame him? We ought to get away more often, but unfortunately in politics, as I have found once or twice, sometimes it is necessary to stay and do the job. Although it would have cost Jack money to have stayed and joined his wife later, it might have been worth it for him politically. Having said that, I'm sure I would have taken exactly the same decision and gone myself, and I would have been in the firing line just the same. The problem with Jack is that he hyped up the response to the point where anything that went wrong was going to be very much at his door.

Two things strike me. The first is that it was only because of good friends and special advisers that I didn't drop myself in it more often through wanting to press on with what I was doing, rather than adjusting to circumstance. This was true in October 2001, when I dropped going to Egypt and had a day or two in Majorca instead, in preparation for the Statement that I was due to make on counter-terrorism – and I still got flak for taking a day or two out.

Secondly, that Jack did a very good job in implementing the Macpherson Committee Report. He took it very much to heart and by the time I became Home Secretary large aspects had either been implemented or were in train, particularly in relation to the professional development of police officers and the way in which the Metropolitan Police dealt with allegations of racism.

I was never to have the same trusting relationship with Stephen Lawrence's mother Doreen that Jack had built up over two and a half years.

Jack did a robust presentation of Macpherson at the next Cabinet meeting, and I immediately followed him to say that what we mustn't do is to take some of the phraseology and some of the lines of Macpherson and carry them through, because quite a lot of them were made casually and were not investigated well at all, including remarks about the Education Service and what ought to be done about it. We happen to have a report coming out on 10 March which shows that the gap between the races is narrowing quite substantially in terms of achievement, whereas Macpherson was using statistics which showed exactly the opposite. I talked about the anti-racist units of the mid-1980s and not going back to counterproductive measures of showing real angst and middle-class handwringing that made things worse rather than better.

I got enormous support, for once, from around the table – Clare Short, Ann Taylor, Jack Cunningham and a number of other people who joined in. Frank Dobson was the only one who dissented and said that the NHS was riddled with racism. He may be right, but the remedy is going to have to be found step by step rather than by accusing the whole of society of being racist when it is not.

March 1999

The beginning of March was spent in meeting after meeting with Gordon about the Budget, and in drafting and redrafting the document *Excellence in Cities*, a major drive to try to transform education in the inner-city and disadvantaged areas, to which we needed to devote a substantial amount of money and target it carefully, which involved agreement with both Tony and Gordon. No. 10 was very keen to concentrate on London, whereas I was keen to focus on all the main urban centres, not least because, apart from ethos and behaviour, quite a number of the schools we would target in London were doing a damned sight better academically than schools across the country, including some in my own constituency. We do tend to be London-centric.

I abandoned a plan to go to Washington for discussions at the State Department about Bill Clinton's welfare reforms, but did manage to have two days in Germany. Keeping in touch with European Union issues at this moment is very important, and has been emphasised by Tony when I have been speaking with him about the euro.

This was the first time I had stayed at the embassy in Bonn and I knew it would be the last, as it is being relocated to Berlin. I stood on the balcony and listened to the barges going up and down the Rhine, and just across on the hill was where one of Neville Chamberlain's famous meetings with Hitler had taken place. It is ironic that our embassy and the post-war capital of West Germany should have been here.

Back home, 'Peace in our Time' seemed a long way away, not least with the final pre-Budget meeting with Gordon, Alan Milburn, Tony and a couple of Tony's special advisers, Andrew Adonis and James Purnell.

Both Andrew and James were to become ministers in the third-term Labour government – Andrew in the Lords and James in the Commons.

Strange as it may seem, the main bone of contention at the meeting was the development of Learning Centres, equipped with up-to-date computers and providing people with adult learning and computer skills. The suggestion being put to us was that instead of calling them Learning Centres, we should call them 'Computer Access Bureaux' or CABs for short. I suggested that if we wanted to be a laughing stock, that's what we should call them. It is far better to call them what any normal person would call them. The real issue, of course, was how we were going to pay for them, but as with so much in politics, it is often trivia or presentation that gets in the way of substance. On this occasion, common sense prevailed.

We agreed two tranches: first, Learning Centres that would be attached to schools and form part of the Excellence in Cities programme; and secondly, centres for adult learning and new computer access based in the community and integral to the University for Industry (the concept which Gordon and I had agreed when in opposition).

A great deal of this came to fruition, and linked to the investment of information technology in schools there has been a transformation of both access to and knowledge about the use of the Internet, Britain claiming the highest density of computer ownership and usage in the world. The only part that we never fully pulled off was the availability through the University for Industry of computer access for small businesses, but in truth the market won. As the price of computers fell, the individual skills needed to use them dramatically improved, with or without the link with businesses as part of the overall programme.

A hiccup on Saturday 6 March at the Scottish Labour Party conference. The inference has been made that all Scottish teachers will be provided with a personal laptop, and that this will then be extended to England and Wales. Such a move would quickly mop up the entirety of the £400 million that we had allocated for Learning Centres across England.

We did eventually sort this out as well, but it gave a feeling that we were making policy on the back of an envelope, when in fact a great deal of thought, time and energy had gone into ensuring that we got this initiative right.

We haven't, however, sorted out the Individual Learning Accounts. George Mudie has been working on this but we seem to be running into the ground. My original concept of getting people to establish an account through the banks, and to get help either through financial top-ups or some form of incentive, was being subsumed into the Treasury plan to subsidise a 'learn yourself' type of pack, which doesn't add up to a learning account at all.

There were good reasons why the Treasury were reluctant to get involved in the way that we from the Department for Education and Employment had originally envisaged, not least because the major banks wouldn't play ball. This was a great shame, given that in Ireland the banking system had quite independently been instrumental in setting up accounts that grandparents and families contributed to specifically for education purposes.

Nevertheless, a major opportunity was missed and when some five years later the scheme collapsed and there was major criticism of the way in which it had been handled, it was of course the then Department for Education and Skills that received the brickbats.

We have managed this week to wipe out the announcement that at infant level we have reduced the number of youngsters in classes of more than thirty from nearly 500,000 to 200,000 – well on the way to eliminating the number altogether. Unfortunately the announcement was spoiled by the Department for Trade and Industry announcing a clash with the United States over banana imports. The famed control of communication wasn't quite working in the way that the world outside presumed it did.

For the Budget, it has become clear that we have got to present ourselves as competent, coherent and co-ordinated, with policies that are well thought through. The meetings leading up to the Budget demonstrated anything but. Nevertheless, by Saturday evening prior to the Budget day we had got our act together, and no one seeing what came out of these arm-wrestling matches would ever have believed that we had been through the kind of arguments that we had been having. At times the atmosphere was so bitter it could have been cut with a knife.

Twenty minutes on the phone with Tony on Monday evening [8 March] – the day before the Budget – after I had done two major speeches during the day. He was very open and said that he had come to the Budget very late because of the pressure of dealing with Scottish issues and, most importantly, Northern Ireland. He added that he was keen that the capital-investment programme that we had negotiated with Gordon should be used much more flexibly to try and achieve more rapid change in the inner city. It is always amazing how my irritations fade once I get a chance to have these sensible conversations with him – but so often it is close to the wire and all the blood pressure and all the angst and all the unnecessary aggravation have soured the process by the time we get there. When we do get there, there is often a really good outcome, but why can't we do it without the theatricality of a wrestling all-comers' championship? 'It's time to take stock,' Tony said that Monday evening. I couldn't agree more.

And so to the Budget itself, an undoubted triumph for Gordon. Sitting next to him, I cannot but be impressed and carried along, as we all are, by the fervour and commitment – and by the clever presentation of the additional resources of which I am a substantial recipient.

It feels like a radical, innovative and bold Budget, which is the way I described it after opening up after Gordon and Tony in Cabinet, before going on to raise three questions. One was the issue of social policy and how, when we change policy in relation to targeting families and children, we need to take into account the impact this had in France when they deliberately did so to raise the population levels. I said that tackling children in poverty is a critical goal but needs to be seen in a much broader context. I said that we needed the opportunity to debate these issues, because we are not linking social policy with economic policy. Secondly, a query by me in relation to the timing and nature of the 1p off standard-rate income tax: reports that I had opposed this are wrong – and mischievous – though I am the only Cabinet minister to have queried the timing and what the implications would be of trying to move towards a 20p standard rate. It seems to me that we are moving from the accusation of 'tax and spend' to 'indirect tax and spend'.

These were delicate and difficult discussions. Anyone who is against a cut in income tax has to be either in a fringe party with no chance of government, or extraordinarily optimistic that people in the end would vote for the maintenance or expansion of public services. People always say that they will, but the evidence is entirely to the contrary.

My point was somewhat more subtle: are we at this moment in a position to go ahead with this, given the commitments we have made for sustainable improvement in health and education? The subsequent increase in national insurance didn't vindicate me in terms of the very particular arguments that I was raising at the time, but it certainly made my intervention more intelligent than many of my colleagues thought at that moment.

Thirdly, the way we were presenting these increases would have an undue impact on the financial markets, which was completely unwarranted by what was a well-thought-through and very tight public-expenditure settlement for the coming years.

In fact, while the markets did react temporarily in the way that I had suggested, they did not continue to, so my worries proved to be unfounded.

On Budget day I did, it has to be said, go over the top. Having raised difficult issues at Cabinet, I suppose I was psychologically trying to ensure that it was not misunderstood and that my instinct that the Budget was radical and imaginative should be displayed. But I did overdo matters.

I was asked by Gordon to sit next to him, and a combination of wanting to heal the wounds and, I suppose, flattery made me pleased to do so. But slapping him on the back and grabbing his hand as he finished was probably a bit excessive. It is very easy to get carried away, one way or the other, in the House of Commons.

I wasn't too pleased with my speech on the Thursday morning in opening the third day of the Budget debate. I hadn't spent enough time on it and had there been more people in the Commons and had it mattered more, it would have been noticed that I wasn't on form. The truth is that when you are doing too much, it shows.

What the world outside did notice, thanks to the sketch-writers, was that my dog Lucy was sick during David Willetts's speech. David was Shadow Education and Employment Secretary, who revelled in the nickname 'Two Brains', and was making a very cerebral but boring speech. I am afraid my dogs have had a habit of bringing up their dinner at particularly appropriate moments. One of Lucy's predecessors, Offa, was violently sick during Nigel Lawson's giveaway Budget in 1988 which led to the bust, and the Tories' demise, on Black – White for us – Wednesday in September 1992.

Back to the day-to-day battles, notably Harriet Harman trying to persuade us to give away other people's money (over and above more generous maternity and paternity leave) to allow mothers to stay at home for long periods of time. Try that one in my constituency and there would be some of them who would never be in a job ever again. This is nothing more than a kind of woolly-minded liberalism. And who the hell is paying? No one actually putting these ideas forward could possibly have done any work on what the impact would be of a social policy that reinforces idleness rather than rewards thrift and work.

On that Monday (International Women's Day) Harriet had attacked 'male Cabinet ministers'. My reaction at the time in my diary – that I thought people should be judged on competence, not on gender – was exactly the same reaction as I had in the early summer of 2006 when Harriet once again entered the fray, suggesting that the eventual replacement for John Prescott as Deputy Prime Minister should be a woman, on the grounds that if there was a male Prime Minister, the Deputy should be female. I am afraid my worst instinct was also to say out loud, 'And I suppose the Chancellor ought to be disabled and the Foreign Secretary from an ethnic minority.'

This is the sort of nonsense that is nothing to do with equality and everything to do with ring-fencing particular positions. The idea that I should ever have been given a position because I had a recognised disability fills me with horror.

I've just visited a primary school where the territorial team in the Department – the unit dealing with regional visits – has managed to get the name of the school wrong, the name of the head wrong (they had the name of the head who had retired some months before), and the wrong statistics about the key-stage results. I have learned not to believe a word of briefings but to have them double-checked, and in fact undertake a quick surreptitious check myself once I have arrived, to verify or otherwise what I have been given.

At the launch of the Year of Maths by Carol Vorderman [co-presenter of the television programme *Countdown*], Tony was held up with the press outside but I didn't realise this and I asked the audience to welcome him. There was total silence as he didn't appear. I went back to the microphone and said, 'This is one of the problems when you have a Secretary of State who can see a virtual Prime Minister every moment of the day.' They laughed, and at that moment I heard somebody at the side of the platform saying that he was coming through the door, so I was able to say, 'This time you can welcome the real Prime Minister, my good friend, Tony Blair!'

April 1999

Easter – and, yet again, teachers' conferences, year after year. I went to the Association of Teachers and Lecturers and the National Union of Teachers, and Estelle went to the final conference of the season, that of the National Association of Schoolmasters and Union of Women Teachers. We had agreed that Estelle would make positive announcements there because they were being the most positive in terms of the reform agenda, and rewarding screaming and shouting hoodlums is not my idea of sensible politics.

And yes, the NUT lived up to their usual conference reputation. They stamped and they shouted and they booed and the world outside backed me and were horrified at the behaviour of those who were teaching their children in the classroom. It was the most stupid display of turning off the electorate, of turning people against you and persuading them to support the Secretary of State, who would normally be the villain of the piece, to the hilt.

When I heard the Socialist Workers' Party, at this time extremely dominant in the NUT, shouting, 'Bring back the real Tories!' I didn't know whether to laugh or cry. We had just announced the most enormous building and renovation programme, an expansion of teacher numbers, a vast increase in teaching assistants and substantial pay improvement with the new scales, which I had to fight like hell to achieve – and these loonies were shouting, 'Bring back the Tories!' What a bunch of half-bakes!

As Estelle said to me much later when she was Secretary of State, 'You feel ill before you get there, angry when you are there, and exhausted when you leave' – and you do.

I felt physically ill, having had a stinking cold (which often happens to me when stress is high) before the conference. I felt a kind of peculiar release when it was over and went to stay with Tessa Jowell in Warwickshire, going to Stratford for the Royal Shakespeare Company's modern production of *A Midsummer Night's Dream*. It was almost surreal – from the NUT shouting and screaming to the Royal Shakespeare Company in one day.

One of the best things I did in April was visit Exeter University, to address issues around special-needs education with Ted Wragg, Professor of Education there. I like Ted, and despite his being very robust about New Labour, he agrees with many of the reforms we are putting in place.

I was privileged to go to the memorial service for Ted Wragg in 2006. He did a great deal of good for the education of children in our country and for the education service, but he certainly gave all of us a very hard time!

Clare Short [Secretary of State for International Development] is doing a good job on Kosovo. I am not entirely sure what the Foreign and Commonwealth Office and the Ministry of Defence are doing, but Clare has got stuck in, ensuring that there are tents and food for people fleeing over the border.

It is rare for me to be complimentary about Clare, but she must be proud of her efforts in Kosovo. I just wish that others had engaged the same way: it is easy to fly around the world without ever connecting with the squalor of refugees, but the Department for International Development connects all the time.

The trip to the West Country worked miracles. When I went, I felt distracted, almost out of myself, a feeling of drowning – and even though it was very busy in Exeter and Devon and I got through a hell of a lot of speeches, meetings and visits, I felt restored and on top of the job again, able to cope and to focus, and to be a bit more of a human being.

Sometimes you just have to get away from London and get out of the routine. I felt so much better that when I was phoned on the first evening in Exeter, asking whether I would come back the following day, Tuesday, to do an early-morning press conference for the local-government campaign, I simply said: 'No. If you want me there, I will come up on Wednesday morning and be there for 11.30 a.m.' I decided that I wasn't going back on Tuesday for some meaningless breakfast-time press conference which would be old hat by the afternoon. I said that I was very happy to go and do something sensible – and lo and behold, they agreed.

On this occasion it was really a question of helping out John Prescott, who was doing Prime Minister's Questions as Tony was flying to Germany. Not surprisingly John wanted to spend the whole morning (and had probably spent the last two days) preparing for it. He got a terrible press the following morning.

The press conference that had been rearranged didn't add up to a bag of beans, but unfortunately it allowed the media to come back to the issue of Chris Woodhead, his private life and whether he had lied about his relationship with his sixth-form student. The Sunday papers on 18 April went to town on the story, complete with copious quotes from Chris Woodhead's ex-wife Cathy, and accounts of the dossier that she had been sending, bit by bit, to my office. I was criticised for not taking the dossier at face value, but I had already made a written Statement to the Commons about it, and had declared: 'I have considered that material. No evidence has been presented to me that proves that Mr Woodhead had a sexual relationship with Ms Johnston while she was his pupil . . . It is not for me, as Secretary of State, to intervene in the rights and wrongs of a divorce which took place twenty-three years ago, nor to side with either Mr or Mrs Woodhead in a dispute about facts surrounding that divorce. My responsibility is in relation to the role of the Chief Inspector, as a Crown employee, and to apply good management practice fairly and impartially. There is nothing in the papers I have seen that substantiates the allegations made against Chris Woodhead or calls into question his suitability to continue as HM Chief Inspector of Schools.'

I am afraid all this has given me nothing but grief – no thanks from those vehemently supporting Chris Woodhead, and deep acrimony from those who resent the fact that I have not used this private material to get rid of him as Chief Inspector.

Frankly the whole affair has just about finished me off. I didn't come into politics for this. I am not interested in Chris Woodhead's sex life. I can't prove that he lied – and no doubt there will be people saying that we are not concentrating hard enough on the key issues relating to education.

Efforts in Kosovo are a mess. We don't appear to be using satellite or unmanned aircraft for proper surveillance, and the Americans don't seem to have up-to-date maps. We are not getting the credit we deserve for trying to stop the genocide and help people.

It is strange that those who were vehemently against taking action in Iraq because 'it breached international law' were silent as we breached international law and took pre-emptive action in Kosovo without UN sanction. I believe we were right – but talk about double standards.

On 26–7 April I went to Wales to campaign for the Welsh Assembly elections. Visiting a school in Merthyr Tydfil with Peter Hain [Secretary of State for Wales] was an eye-opener. There is such a lot still to be done. It was quite a contrast to Neath, where both the local authority and the schools seemed up for the reform agenda.

What has happened since the establishment of the Welsh Assembly back in 1999 is salutary – a case study in both health and education of New Labour in England and a different approach in Wales, and a taste of what it would be like if we had to rely on the Liberal Democrats. In Scotland, where there was a much more formalised and agreed programme, small minorities within parties have less influence than is the case where a small rump of those vehemently against change can block it. The difficulty, of course, is that the kind of agenda on education and employment, on welfare reform and on security and stability which I espoused was completely alien to a Liberal Democratic Party devoid of reform and denuded of radicalism.

The Cutlers' Feast at Sheffield – the first time I have ever been asked to speak at this great local occasion, and the opportunity for *rapprochement* with the business community after all the years of conflict when I was Leader of the Council.

The Cutlers' Feast is one of the most important events in the Sheffield calendar. The Cutlers' Company is a livery company and one of the very few great prestigious guilds outside London. Doug Liversidge, Master Cutler, had been born and brought up in my constituency, and was later to help enormously on the education front by contributing both to the improvement in secondary education and to the creation of a new and extremely critical sixth-form college.

Well, here I was in white tie and tails, seeking to draw together the whole of the business and civic community and to get across some critical messages about the need to have some continuity and work with a Labour government – in the knowledge that it was quite likely that the Liberal Democrats were about to win the local election in the city.

Although I say it myself, the speech went down very well and I was very pleased to have been able to draw a line under the past. It was helped by the fact that the author and journalist Hugo Young, whose family go back a long way in Sheffield, made a pro-European speech which went down so badly that I was on a winning wicket.

Hugo was a crucial pillar of the Guardian, *and has been sorely missed since his death in 2003.*

And so to local politics and local electioneering in the days immediately afterwards. My main task was to ensure that the proposals for regeneration in the north of Sheffield were successful. So much hung on it in terms of whether we could begin to turn round local communities, not just in relation to the environment and housing but in their self-belief, self-confidence and self-help. Here was a Labour government prepared to put in long-term investment and to take civic renewal seriously.

The first week in May was dominated by the Americans inadvertently bombing the Chinese embassy in Belgrade. As someone put it: 'If they had looked in the telephone directory, they would have been able to locate it.' So much for precision bombing.

The local and Scottish/Welsh elections. The Liberal Democrats won an overall majority of seven in Sheffield, and it felt just like the 1992 general election all over again. To lose my own city, the city I had led for so long, to have felt it slipping away, to know that local people were punishing us for not being radical and reforming enough and for not having made the changes ourselves rather than necessitating a change of power, is heartbreaking.

But there are many lessons to be learned and applied nationally. At least in Scotland we have done relatively well and we have scraped home in Wales, but Llanelli, the Rhondda, and Islwyn have all demonstrated real disaffection. We have the paradox of people wanting Old Labour, but Old Labour being exactly what has failed them in the recent past. How do we persuade people who won't vote that by not doing so they actually damage themselves? And those who do vote that clinging on to a bygone era is the last thing that will bring them employment, decent education and health? Reassurance is the answer, I suppose, and a sense of stability and security while implementing change, and having a few early examples of things working rather than grandiose visions and long-term projects that seem so distant and alien.

But the Lib Dems – who actually came fourth, but because of proportional representation have ended up in coalition with Labour – will be able to start dictating terms on tuition fees and the like.

On Sunday evening, Derek Fatchett, MP for Leeds Central, died. He was a good MP and an excellent minister.

I wasn't to know at the time that I would be losing yet another special adviser, Hilary Benn, who was chosen as candidate for Leeds Central and won the seat at the by-election. Tom Bentley had left me to go and head up the think tank DEMOS, so things were in flux once again.

May 1999

I have discovered that during the election campaign, apart from Donald Dewar in Scotland, Alun Michael in Wales and Gordon with his over-arching role, I had visited more other constituencies than anyone else in the Cabinet. I am pleased about that but I do wonder how much good it does me. One member of the Cabinet had visited precisely none, but which of us is the wiser?

One consolation of all this work was that a *Guardian* opinion poll has me as one of the three most popular Cabinet ministers (along with Gordon and Mo). There are two problems with this. Firstly, such a ranking really gets up the noses of colleagues, and secondly, there is only one way to go and that is down.

Once again reform of the House of Commons has bitten the dust. On Incapacity Benefit we were up until the crack of dawn. I finally left at 4.30 a.m. but others were there until much later. If this is New Labour, a new form of politics, then I'm a Dutchman.

By the time we reached Thursday evening, there were more dissidents on our side than when we had started. What a terrible job the Whips have done. We have a Commons majority in excess of 175, and Andrew Smith is not able to go to the inauguration of his wife as Lord Mayor of Oxford as his presence is demanded in the House. The greatest parliamentary majority in living memory and we couldn't organise a whatsit in a brewery.

In the end we won by forty, but had we exposed the Tories and Liberals for complete duplicity? I think not.

At one of my regular meetings with Tony, he said that his greatest conflict of interest in two years had just arisen because he was going to miss the Manchester United v. Bayern Munich match – the Champions League Final – on Wednesday night as he had to attend the banquet for the opening of the Welsh Assembly. When we had an update meeting a couple of days later we came back to this, and Tony reported that at the Welsh Assembly dinner he was seated next to Rod Richards's wife and Dafyd Wigley, so he had had a wonderful evening.

I wonder just how many wonderful evenings he has had to put up with, sitting between people with whom he has so little in common and whose political views are so opposed to his own: Dafyd Wigley, Leader of the Welsh Nationalists, and Rod Richards, Leader of what passes for the Conservatives in Wales.

The last two weeks in May have been dominated on the education front (in the run-up to the National Association of Head Teachers' conference) by a silly story about whether the Key Stage 2 (for eleven-year-olds) results on literacy and numeracy have been affected by the chopping and changing of the examiners, who had originally set easy questions, realised the mistake in time and withdrew all the questions they considered too easy – then ended up with tests that were so difficult compared with previous years that there are accusations flying around from all angles.

I've decided that we must have a proper independent inquiry to ensure that there is no doubt about the validity, accuracy and comparability of the tests and the results. I asked Jim Rose, Deputy Chief Inspector at the Office for Standards in Education, to conduct an independent inquiry, the real issue being whether we could ever reach the target for literacy and numeracy if the exams were being toughened year by year and the results being questioned.

The Rose Inquiry found precisely what we had expected. The results were valid, the exams had been toughened and there was no question of any kind of 'fiddling' to present improved literacy and numeracy outcomes. Children were being taught better and were learning better, and their outcome measures at eleven years were substantially better.

This was just another diversion, to be seen against the background of the suspicion that whatever improvement government makes has to be question-able. The morale of those of us trying to drive improvement from the centre may not be relevant, but the morale of teachers actually making substantial improvement certainly is.

No one could question the results because we had asked the two main opposition parties to make their own nominations to the inquiry, and I had persuaded the editor of *The Times*, Peter Stothard, to let that paper's education correspondent John O'Leary take part in the inquiry as well, along with one of the best primary-school headteachers in the country. It was absolutely vital that nobody questioned the veracity of the outcome.

June 1999

Early in the week of the European elections I had supper with Tony, and halfway through the meal an urgent phone call came through that the Serbians had at last signed the peace accord. I shook Tony's hand and congratulated him on the leadership he'd shown and the fact that he hadn't wavered, even when people had been saying that it was hopeless and that we would never succeed.

It is interesting how similar the criticism was when it came to Afghanistan and in the early stages with the efforts to bring democracy to Iraq. Obviously in the latter case, the prolonged guerrilla action and destabilisation changed the whole nature of what happened, but the early rhetoric and criticism were very similar in all three instances, with the added factor that people chose to ignore entirely that it was the Islamic community of Kosovo which benefited most from what we did by tackling Milosevic and his regime.

Tony and I spoke more openly that evening than I can ever remember, which is why his trust must be safeguarded.

Nicky came down from doing his homework and I said, 'Give your Dad a big hug because he has saved thousands of people's lives.' And he did.

It was a lovely evening, despite the fact that our meal consisted of a vegetarian spinach dish – and I'm a carnivore of the first order.

I don't think it is giving away any secrets to say that one of the many issues we talked about is how we can support and develop the 'consumer agenda'. This covers the enormous change that has taken place in the purchasing power of people across Britain, as well as the increase in monopoly providers and the disappearance of real choice, while we appear to have the illusion of increased choice.

I don't just mean what fruits we can buy from across the world, but what real difference there is between one store and another, one set of products and

another, and the ability to be able to pop down, as we used to be able to do,
and buy from a hardware store.

Even more important is the issue of quality, of protection from exploitation
and how it links with sustainability and the world's efforts to protect the
environment and our global heritage.

The Euro elections have seen an appalling turn-out in solid Labour areas –
under 10 per cent in Liverpool Riverside, 12 per cent in Barnsley, South
Yorkshire, and only 14 per cent in the area covering my constituency. Who
would be Prime Minister, the loneliest job in politics, when everything that
happens is, in the end, borne upon your shoulders?

Just twenty-nine Labour MEPs have been sent to Strasbourg, seven
fewer than the Tories. Recriminations continued throughout the following
week. All the predictions of the damage that would be done to us under the
regional-list system came to pass. Apart from anything else, we seem to
have been in perpetual election mode for months – which, of course, we
were – and this is a major distraction. I sometimes wonder how the United
States House of Representatives functions at all on a two-year timetable.

I've managed to avoid having to be in the House of Commons after
midnight on four nights by having genuine business in the North West of
England.

While I was in Bolton, I bent down to speak to an eight-year-old boy
who couldn't see, only to discover that nobody had wiped his nose. There
are bizarre occasions, as Education Secretary, when not being able to see
puts me at a distinct disadvantage. I am particularly pernickety about this
sort of thing and, when my own sons needed it, spent half my time with a
tissue in my hand.

I've managed to get the Union Learning Fund off the ground – and with
real money – as I see this not only as critically important for adult
education in the workplace but also as a new role for trade unions,
enhancing the skills and capability of the workforce, helping them through
rapid and enormous global change, and making it possible for them to
accept technological developments and world competition without the
kind of fear that makes people retrench and try to hold on to whatever they
are doing at the time.

On Monday morning I awoke to a *Guardian* leader suggesting that I,
along with Jack Cunningham and Margaret Beckett, could well be dropped
in a reshuffle. (Now, who could possibly have been briefing that!?)

The fact that I even bothered to note this showed how ultra-sensitive I was at the time. Margaret must smile even more. Her demise has been predicted on innumerable occasions by those who never re-examine their notes or their predictions. I don't know for certain, but I imagine that she took a lot less notice of them than I did.

There are times when 21 June turns out to be the longest day of the year in more ways than one. Paddy March, to whom I had given my previous guide dog Offa after his veterinary genius had saved his life, phoned to say that Offa's vital organs had deteriorated so badly that he was going to put him to sleep. How could I say anything other than to thank Paddy for everything he had done?

Shortly afterwards Paddy, who had a wife and children, took his own life. He had always told me that Offa had given him great strength and had become a close companion during the time he had him, since the operation for stomach torsions which had saved Offa's life back during the general election of 1992. After Offa's death Paddy was overwhelmed by depression. What a sad end and what a terrible tragedy for Paddy's family. It was a tremendous shock for me.

I've been to the Millennium Dome. There isn't enough ready to get anything like a feel of whether there is going to be any chance of pulling it off, except that with only six months to go, I thought there would have been a lot more on show. Something a little more imaginative is going to be called for if people are going to flood here in their millions.

I spent a chunk of Wednesday trying to get the policy paper on Lifelong Learning right, as we're having a real tussle with Downing Street about this. I didn't get to bed until 12.30 a.m. and was up again just after six to do a round of broadcast media.

Jack Straw is copping it over the Passport Agency and John Prescott over Transport, but the big issues of the moment (which we discussed at Cabinet) are what is happening in Northern Ireland and the run-up to the launch of a new combined employment and benefits agency.

The advertising agency we had hired had decided that we should call the new agency 'One'. That name didn't last very long – but they still got paid for it!

And the Learning and Skills Council – how do we get across that with a £5 billion budget (and more) we can do a really first-class job, not just on post-sixteen A-level education but on vocational training and on updating the skills of the workforce. This is crucial if we are to get productivity up and prepare people for the competition of the 'Asian Tigers'.

It is damned hard work, though. There are so few people writing these things up who have any experience whatsoever of further education, let alone work-based training or learning.

But for the Statement and the launch, with Jean Corston's considerable help as my Parliamentary Private Secretary, the backbenchers on my side stayed back in force. A lot of our MPs do understand how crucial further education is and have a real feel for it. Like me, many of them actually got their education at further-education college. There were as many as 200 MPs in the House – an unheard-of quantity for a Statement – which daunted Theresa May, on her first outing as Shadow Education and Employment Secretary, having replaced David Willetts.

My reflections at the time on what was happening in government as a whole are revealing. Sometimes you can be so 'hands on' that while you are actually making a difference in the medium and long term, it looks as if you are too closely associated with what's going wrong – whereas being slightly aloof can often ensure that you escape being associated with what is going on, or going wrong, in the agencies and the department you oversee. My notes at the time reflect what I was going to experience in spades – a view of the Home Office . . .

What is going on at the Home Office? The Passport Agency fiasco, immigration, arguments about freedom of information, what happened over the Lawrence Inquiry – it all just brushes off. It must be the most incompetent department and group of agencies of any government department at the moment.

And that was in the summer of 1999.

July 1999

I went to Grimethorpe in South Yorkshire to talk to unemployed young-sters. It was one of those days when I realised how crucial it is to get out and talk to people and not simply be caught up with the material and statistics given to me by officials. I took their cynicism with a pinch of salt, but it was deeply depressing and I was determined not to let this go and to keep in touch with what they were doing. A voluntary organisation called Groundwork was helping enormously, and I was determined that the usual rejection of anything that wasn't a standard delivery mechanism should be set aside.

When I returned to being Employment Secretary in the Department of Work and Pensions six years later, I revisited Grimethorpe at the invitation of a lady to whom I had promised a return visit – this time with BBC cameras. Things had improved, but not enough. Friday afternoon with so many people in the working men's club and obviously so many people retired long before their time was upsetting.

Rejoice! – Alastair's degree ceremony at Liverpool University on Tuesday [6 July]. It was a wonderful day, and a wonderful opportunity to celebrate his achievement. I turned down the official invitation to lunch with the Vice-Chancellor because we had already arranged to have a private lunch – the boys, their mother Ruth, and myself, ensuring that we could share a moment or two as a family. Mind you, I wasn't too proud to accept help from the local police when we arrived at the venue because we had got lost as we got into Liverpool and, without their assistance, I would have been blundering into the ceremony late. A privilege of being Education Secretary!

Then back on the train to London (which broke down) and a whole range of speeches, including to the parliamentary party on the Wednesday before doing a speech in the House. The Tories had chosen education for their Supply Day and it was Theresa May's first 'proper' speech. She made the mistake of talking about a school that I knew something about, claiming that it was a scandal that it had been closed. I got up and asked her how many pupils there were in the school when it was put up for closure. She hadn't a clue, so I intervened again to tell her: only three!

It is this sort of knockabout in the House of Commons that back-benchers really love, and it gains you a reputation for being able to deal with your opponents.

I had a drink with John Reid [Secretary of State for Scotland] – I had a glass of wine and he had a Coke – and discussed how to repair relations with the Scottish Executive. He was pretty robust about what he thought about Donald Dewar, but I pointed out that he was pretty lucky himself to have got out of Transport just before the whatsit hit the fan. Lucky politicians always get out at the right time.

By the time John became Home Secretary in 2006 he had had eight different Cabinet posts, including chairmanship of the party. Ken Clarke was also particularly 'fortunate' in terms of moving. It is a fact in politics that for the benefit of the public, longevity in a post is essential, but for the benefit of the aspirant, longevity is often (in one single post) a distinct disadvantage. I refer, of course, to obtaining another post – and not, as in my case, resignation.

A Home Office classic. A second-hand computer with prison records, including those of one of the IRA Brighton bombers, has been found dumped on a rubbish tip. Given the number of category-A prisoners who escaped under Michael Howard, it is not surprising, but hell's bells – what a bunch of wallies.

What a state we have reached with politics. Mo came out of Cabinet with me saying that she wanted a breath of fresh air, which meant that she had had enough of what was going on. I was going across to Education and Employment Questions. It was only when we stepped outside the front door of No. 10 that she proclaimed – in the way that only Mo could – 'Oh bugger – I've got no shoes on.' The picture appeared on the front page – yes, the front page – of *The Times* the following morning.

Sunday 11 July – the Teachers' Awards, televised for the first time. I thought it all went very well, except that it did feel at times a bit sanctimonious, imbued with a sort of embarrassed guilt about celebrating high-performance success, which led the organisers and the celebrities taking part to be all gooey about special needs – a little less of Kate Adie at a 'special' school in Plymouth and I would have felt much easier.

Everybody loves special needs. Everybody is very keen on special-needs children being boosted, including some of the participants making remarks about how 'we've got to care for these children now, and the more able are getting too much attention'. This was the underlying theme – that we were pushing too hard with literacy, numeracy and the basics.

Most of the people making such assertions have their children in schools which take very few, if any, children with special needs. There was a whole host of people there who send their children to private school, and unless it is a specialist school for things like dyslexia or autism, you won't see a special-needs or disabled child anywhere near them. So I have to confess that my pleasure at seeing the good teachers rewarded was a little tempered by a wish that we wouldn't keep reverting to sentimentality rather than hard-headed practical support and help which, after all, is what everyone would want. The BBC had promised that if I made my words non-political and kept it down to about twenty seconds, they wouldn't cut it out – but they did.

An example of the difficulty of being human and not falling into the trap of appearing to be a staid politician: the *Sun* has carried a piece about the imminent reshuffle, saying that I expect to be moved and am insecure in my job. They quote as evidence the interview with me in the *Sunday Times* the previous Sunday, when I joked about all of us being subject to reshuffle at some time in the future, with the Prime Minister ordering us a taxi from Downing Street when the official car has disappeared. It was so patently a joke when I said it that nobody else has picked it up, but the *Sun* has run it as a serious comment. Of course it has started to take off and people are asking me whether I am in danger, whether I am going to be moved, and whether everything is all right. I think to myself: Am I going mad? Is politics so stupid that we can no longer make a joke, no longer be human beings, no longer have a bit of fun? Do we have to take everything so seriously, including ourselves? It just leads to the kind of politics we now have – miserable, staid, unimaginative, cloned, all the things that make politics boring and irrelevant to people out there, all the things that turn people off politics.

I feel a lot better to have got that rant off my chest.

One entertaining moment in the middle of July was on Bastille Day – it would be – when I went to St James's Palace to talk with Prince Charles. I get on extremely well with HRH and have great respect for his genuine commitment to education, but on this occasion I did find the conversation a trifle surreal.

By late July we are all getting very tired, with tempers beginning to fray inside as well as outside the Department as we wait for the reshuffle.

For me, one diversion has been having three overseas Education Ministers visit within a week. It was a bit like London buses – there's either none or they come in multiples. The Chinese Education Minister, who was clearly high in the hierarchy, told me about how her brothers and sisters had lost out on any kind of formal education during the Cultural Revolution. I also had visits from the Australian Education Minister and a very interesting man struggling to ensure that he could do in South Africa what even we find difficult here – literacy and numeracy for all.

I wish I had taken up his invitation to go to South Africa. I was reluctant to do so because there appeared to be a trail of politicians from around the world arriving there without any idea about what help they were going to give or what value their visit would be – other than for their own benefit.

This was a little bit like my days in Sheffield City Council when the hair shirt appeared to be a badge of honour. To have seen those early post-apartheid days and perhaps to have been able to offer some help, particularly for families of youngsters with a special need, would have been wonderful.

Counting down to holiday. I did the usual radio and television for a pamphlet I was launching at a CBI conference.

I occasionally produced short pamphlets in order to illustrate not simply what we were doing but why we were doing it, and to try and spell out what underpinned the policy announcements so as to explain our direction of travel. I was one of the very few Cabinet ministers who did this – Gordon being one of the others – but it is interesting to note with hindsight that they simply sank without trace.

Lunch at No. 11 with Gordon, and probably the most positive conversation we have ever had while in government. He sounds completely jiggered – as did Tony when I spoke to him on the same day about the reshuffle. I wanted to ensure that as I was going away the following weekend, I wouldn't end up with changes in the ministerial team that I wasn't in favour of. It became clear that it was once again to be a last-minute job in terms of final decisions – simply because of the pressure – which always makes for a difficult time because it is not possible to warn people about what is going to happen.

And so away on holiday to Majorca, this year with a song in my heart. I have done as much as I can. I have completed the jobs I set myself – the announcements, the pamphlets, the speeches – but once again I have ended up being away for the reshuffle, which has been delayed and delayed.

I never did find out why there hadn't been a proper briefing that the Cabinet reshuffle had been held off because of George Robertson's taking the post of NATO Secretary-General, but there must have been some internal reasons to do with that organisation.

In my own team, George Mudie, who had been deeply disaffected, left government and Charles Clarke was promoted to Police Minister in the Home Office. Jacqui Smith and Malcolm Wicks joined my team and additionally, as a special request (from No. 11 through Tony), Michael Wills joined as an additional minister. Negotiations with me had taken place on the Wednesday and as late as the Thursday morning, with Downing Street trying to reach me on a whole range of numbers at 11.30 on Wednesday night, because of difficulties with the reshuffle. This was 12.30 a.m. in Majorca, and I was very glad that my mobile was switched off because that would not have been a good time of night to have engaged in delicate discussions about whether or not I would take any specific individual. Fresh in the morning, it was possible to argue a case with coherence and, it has to be said, less tetchiness, so I was glad to end up with a team I was comfortable with.

I was also pleased not to have this particular holiday ruined, as it was one that was very special to me in terms of genuine relaxation at a time when I was truly balancing work and leisure, serious commitment and happiness. For a variety of reasons that balance was to go out of kilter, which undoubtedly contributed to my difficulties over the subsequent six years.

August 1999

August was one of those frustrating months when the 'silly season' resulted in true political silliness – the idea that we need an increase of half a million unemployed to ensure that the economy will remain stable and that inflation will be held down.

I was extremely angry about this. I went to the training gym of Brendan Ingle, a wonderful man working in my constituency with young people from the most deprived backgrounds who uses boxing not just as a way out of disadvantage but as a way into self-respect and discipline. Putting on gloves and knocking hell out of some punchbags made me feel a lot better.

Perhaps if I had had a punchbag in my departmental office it would have made the lives of my staff much easier, as I could have taken my frustrations out that way rather than on those around me.

The 'non-inflationary accelerating rate of unemployment', as the international financial investors and bankers call it, was rooted in the inter-war financial crises and theoretical monetarism. Given that since this nonsense started a year ago we have improved the job figures by nearly 350,000, those carping were wrong to the tune of 850,000. But nobody will admit to it.

So my riposte on Thursday 12 August when the job figures came out was pretty robust, with pictures at the gym carrying through to the evening television news. Of course, a little bit of mischief was made by those trying to suggest that my commitment to full employment divided me from Tony and Gordon. It didn't.

'Full employment' was exactly the phrase that Gordon was to use in the following two years, but it is amazing in politics how much mischief is made in trying to divide people, and how sometimes we all fall into the trap of allowing them to divide us.

What I want for Yorkshire and the Humber, the North East, the North West and for Scotland and Wales is already happening in the South East, East Anglia, the South West and the Midlands – unemployment (those claiming benefit) down to 3 per cent or below.

One of my lighter moments with the press in August was the fact that, while I had been away, the *Observer* (on the back of Kate Hoey becoming Sports Minister) had been listing those ministers who supported different football teams – and had me down as a supporter of Sheffield United. I wrote a light-hearted letter of correction, at the same time managing to get in a rebuttal of an article by Nick Cohen, one of their main leader writers, which had attacked one of my special advisers, Conor Ryan, for doing his job – 'spinning' – too well. I was able to say in the letter that Conor and I had taken in good part the knockabout which we had come to expect, but what I couldn't take lying down was being called a Sheffield United supporter. For someone who is an ardent Sheffield Wednesday fan, that is rather like finding that you have been listed as an MP for Leeds.

While the bulk of my colleagues were away I launched the first tranche of summer schools. The literacy summer schools have gone very well over the first two years, and we have expanded them dramatically so that there are opportunities for two and sometimes three weeks for youngsters right across England. I am really proud of what we started back in August 1997, and the numeracy programme was intended to give other options so that gradually the summer schools could develop their own ethos and direction and become part of the normal activity of keeping youngsters engaged and interested as they moved from primary to secondary school.

The final touches to the National Curriculum, to be introduced from 2000, have been interesting, not least because of the struggle we have been having to ensure firstly that we give some prominence to history, and secondly that we get the right things in it. I am all for ensuring that we reflect the diversity of our country and its history, but the Qualifications and Curriculum Authority have come up with ideas that frankly are ridiculous, dreaming up figures from the past whom no one had ever heard of.

Getting the balance right is crucial. This is one reason why I have insisted that we should put in the history curriculum much more about Bletchley Park and what happened with the development of computerisation. It is self-evident that if we can get youngsters interested in what happened during the Second World War at Bletchley Park, we will get more of them committed to and interested in science and technology – which we desperately need for the future. There is a story to be told which is both fascinating and relevant today, but it is not part of the curriculum. If I had another year on this I think I could do something really imaginative, but everyone – and I mean everyone – wants it to be very low key and as uncontroversial as possible. Above all, they say, it should give teachers the least possible aggravation, given the reforms in teaching practice and personal development in the classroom that we are promoting at the moment.

During the third week in August, while people are still away, I've received a batch of material in my office from Michael Wills's office, which we are just setting up, which included a very nice letter to him from Gordon. What is especially revealing is other correspondence in the batch, which I have quietly returned to Michael's office. My lips are sealed.

Jack Straw is back from holiday and has been on the radio twice because of the enormous increase in asylum numbers.

It is significant that I made a note of this at the time. It was becoming clear that there were major changes in global movements of people and, of course, we were feeling the impact of refugees from Kosovo and neighbouring countries.

Even so, my prescience didn't stretch to appreciating the absolute enormity of what was beginning, and the inadequacy of government structures and machinery to cope with it.

Because of the fiasco on immigration computer facilities and the difficulties with the Passports Agency, Jack has announced that the Criminal Records Bureau has been put back by two years in order to ensure that concentration can be given to the immediate problems.

September 1999

I've had one of those sad occasions when all my efforts to try to help an individual and their family have come to nothing due to bureaucracy, although individual officials have really tried hard.

This concerned the television sports presenter Helen Rollason, who was dying of cancer and whose one wish was that she could see her daughter Nicky gain the results she needed in her GCSEs and know that she was on the road to a successful future. I had intervened personally, both before going on holiday and when I came back, to ask that very special arrangements were put in place to be able to pick out and give the results to Helen.

I realised, of course, that I was on dodgy ground, but I just felt that if you are the Secretary of State and you simply say, 'I'm sorry, but the rules prevent me from doing this', then you are abrogating any kind of authority in government. If we cannot sometimes help individuals in a one-off, unique situation, then it is a bad job. Universities would certainly do it in relation to degrees, so why not GCSEs? Results are available well in advance, and the weeks up to the announcement are for refining and clarifying, to make sure that there are no mistakes. I suppose people may argue that divulging Nicky's results early would create a precedent, but then every act of kindness doing something outside the rules could create a precedent – if you let it.

On this occasion, my anger was not at those who questioned whether I was doing the right thing – that would have been their job – but at the fact that I was assured that it had been done and that all the mechanisms had been put in place. I thought that everything was going smoothly, but there had been a letter from Helen's sister, saying that given the stress and strain on the family and Mrs Rollason's health, it was best that we didn't do it. So it was devastating to receive in my parliamentary office another letter, very critical of me, from another member of the family. Here I was, stuck in the middle of a disagreement which was not of my making, having originally been told by the Department that it was going to be done – but not having been told that there had been a request from the family not to do it – and with criticism now flooding in from all quarters. This was a classic case of trying to do the right thing for the right reasons and ending up doing nothing.

Helen was obviously so ill at the end that the family felt it was just better to let things be, but I wish I had never received that letter, which was so abusive, so accusing, so convinced that no politician would ever give a damn and that bureaucracy would always win. It will haunt me for a long time.

I know that we are supposed to have thick skins and that criticism is not supposed to matter – but it did. It mattered so much that I dictated extensively into my tape about how I felt. I know that in public life we have to take these brickbats but I believe that the minute the criticism stops hurting and the minute you turn into the caricature of what people believe to be the standard politician, then you are lost. Perversely, the public seems to be quite happy with politicians who keep their heads down and play entirely by the rules – and don't give a damn whether the system or processes hurt individuals – and I find that particularly sad.

My diary notes that Nicky achieved excellent results.

Before the political season began with a vengeance and the party conferences got under way, I wrote a number of what I had come to call billets-doux to Tony. These are notes regarding things that I have been thinking about over the summer, including while on holiday – ideas for change, questions about where we are going and what we need to address for the future – issues which will hit us if we don't start preparing now.

I think these notes must have become a bit of a pain for Tony, although he was always very complimentary and responsive. It seemed to me that putting something in writing before sitting down and talking would make sense, but in retrospect I fear that, given the volume of paperwork and pressure, he could probably have done without them.

I set down such ideas as what in the USA they have started to call 'asset accumulation', to reduce the gap between the haves and have-nots in terms of inheritance and ownership of property, the acquisition of a bank account, the need for some sort of trust fund for children to accumulate a nest egg that they could use as adults, in a way that better-off families do, and my old obsession of civic renewal and non-governmental forms of involving people in participation and decision-making. I also put in material about the need to change radically the parliamentary process and the way in which both Houses of Parliament do business.

The good news on the personal front has been Andrew getting seven A–C grades in his GCSEs but why he didn't get a C in design and technology, goodness knows. The miracle was that he got a C in English Literature. He does so little reading that it makes me wonder about the exam itself, but I am nevertheless very pleased for him and hope that he will start building up his confidence.

Despite the fact that the Department is doing all right, I have to confess that I feel really fed up. I am fed up with politics and completely cheesed off with the thought of having to go back down and start the grind again. I know I shouldn't be. I should be the last person to feel like this. I should be on top of the world, but I just find the whole business shoddy and sordid. It is so hard to get any debate going on forward thinking. I am going to float my ideas in the *Sunday Times* and see if we can start some debate going.

The bad news in September has been the Bank of England putting up interest rates by 0.25 per cent. It seems to be in reaction to the south-east housing market but it is also a kind of reaction to unemployment falling faster than predicted. It will be interesting to see how Ireland performs within the euro, compared with the more cautious approach in terms of growth here. It has to be said, however, that Robin Cook's speech in Tokyo, when he compared employment growth in France favourably with that in the UK, was extraordinary. Employment growth in France is awful. I am going to have to drop Robin a line about this.

I had a lovely visit to Malvern College. I had been promising myself a visit for a long time to look at what they are doing with the International Baccalaureate, and their willingness to reach out and use facilities for state schools across the country, using the Internet for subjects such as Latin. I was also able to enjoy a brisk walk in Elgar country up on the Malvern Hills.

Snapshots from the week beginning Monday 13th : Sheffield Wednesday going down the spout – only one point from seven matches . . . Dinner with the *Daily Telegraph* on Monday . . . Eastbourne on Tuesday, chucking it down with rain, and a nasty wind. Arrived half an hour late at the school I was opening. Went from there to Brighton, where I had a good meeting with all the teacher unions over lunch. Went into the TUC conference and stayed for Tony's speech. Chaired a Joint Policy Commission. Went into the reception for the teacher unions and was very well received there. Went to the TUC dinner. Back to London . . . Got up at 5.30 a.m. Wednesday. Did a pre-record for the *Today* programme at 7 a.m. which they didn't run until after 8.30 a.m., by which time teachers would all be at work so would not hear it. Went to Luton. Did the launch of the key-stage results with Tony and Carol Vorderman: we are having a real push in relation to the maths programme which we are introducing. Then to Chequers. Shared the car with Tony. It was only supposed to take twenty minutes but took forty-five, which gave the chance to talk to him. I congratulated him on Euan's [Tony Blair's oldest son's] GCSE: he had taken French a year early and achieved an A, which I thought very good.

Cabinet was very friendly, if somewhat unfocused. Tony brought Jack

Straw in first, then Robin Cook. Then we went round the table, with me coming in next to last and finally Gordon winding up. In fact we had a little to and fro as to which of us should wind up. We hadn't even mentioned the euro until I mentioned it. We had been talking about direction, definition and delivery and this is very much about definition. The truth is that I'm not sure that anyone is clear now where we are going on that. Over a brief lunch we then had a session on the civil service, with all of the others whingeing along the lines of 'We mustn't be nasty to them, we must be kind, we mustn't allow public criticism'. I said, 'You mean like "pressure and support on teachers"?' – a phrase which had become common when indicating that our job was to both support and encourage teachers to bring about substantial improvement. I was therefore being ironic.

I found it breathtaking. Here we are, struggling to deliver, and we have all got to be as nice as pie. Well, I appreciate that being nasty is not going to help, but being absolutely clear, firm and committed to reform will. The trouble, as ever, is that it is not possible for me to do it on my own, and if those at 'the centre' are not saying the right things to Tony and giving him the right kind of advice on making radical change, how on earth am I going to be able to do it from outside? No matter how lacking in managerial skills or leadership or project management the civil servants are, promotion beckons and security is guaranteed. We the politicians are the ones who are answerable.

The same point was made in October 1965 by Richard Crossman – then Housing Minister – in a diary entry.

I do regret that even though my position was already making me deeply unpopular, I did not follow through more rigorously and more consistently, in terms of badgering Tony and those immediately around him to bring about reform. Even at this very early stage of the government, only two years in, it was obvious that unless we did something pretty drastic we were going to find ourselves in the worst of all worlds. Having committed ourselves to modernisation and radical change, but without the mechanisms to deliver such change, we would get the blame. We would be seen to have put in the resources and to have given the commitment to the public, but we would not have the wherewithal to pull off the very ambitious and genuine policy commitments we were making.

I was lucky because Sir Michael Bichard, along with a substantial number of senior staff, was deeply committed to bringing about those changes, and the development of the Standards and Effectiveness Unit had made a huge Difference in the Department. It is also true that we had the advantage of preparation before the election and of consistency on account of my four years as Education and Employment Secretary. Nothing, however, could prepare me for the difficulties I was to face two years later when I took over at the Home Office.

George Robertson cracked a good joke about there being very few times when a Cabinet minister is able to say farewell to his Cabinet colleagues before he goes – which is true. You've either left for a new post, retired in a general election or you've been sacked. George had become NATO Secretary-General and was to go into the Lords, so was able to make a dignified exit. Would that this were possible for all of us.

I then went to Cambridge to present the Young Writers' Awards and had dinner at Downing College. Tony had raised with me the importance of ensuring that the MIT–Cambridge link went ahead. He had been to Cambridge on the previous Monday and quite obviously this whole issue had been raised with him. He also raised concerns about the new funding streams and how this would work for Oxford and Cambridge. I wasn't unsympathetic. I just don't want to provide historic rationale for funding rather than ideas and developments for the future.

Tony and I talked about his speech for conference, in particular crucial announcements concerning additional administrative and teacher-assistant help in the classroom, not least to give some assistance to primary-school teachers who did not have what is called 'non-contact time' for preparation.

I am having a real tussle with Alan Milburn [Chief Secretary to the Treasury] about releasing money – money that has already been promised – but there is nothing new about this. It appears to be a long-standing Treasury ploy – to make it difficult to spend, and then when you don't spend, to put it about that you are underspending your budget. The trouble is that my Department, and I think it applies to others as well, are so unused to having any money at all to invest that they are finding it difficult to gear themselves up to do so in the timescales we have given them. It is one of those paradoxes that after years and years of starving to death, you give someone an ample meal and they end up choking on it. That's why I am keen that the capital investment that we now have should be projected back to 1997 rather than 1998, so that we can be better prepared.

I then came back to Sheffield, before going on Thursday morning to the Department's site in Runcorn – a good visit – and then to Knowsley to open new facilities at the college, to have dinner and to talk through further-education developments with George Sweeney [head of the college], who, along with Alex Erwin at South Trafford College and Willy Mills, Head of Manchester City College, were meeting regularly with me.

These three were to continue as considerable support in post-sixteen policy over the years, and remained friends when I was no longer Education Secretary.

We came up with the idea that we could have sixth-form colleges within further-education or tertiary colleges, so that there would be administrative and other support but a proper quality-and-standards agenda for sixteen- to nineteen-year-olds.

I was later to experience getting this off the ground with Sheffield College, in the Hillsborough area of my own constituency, but, because of a tussle between the education authority and the local college, we developed a separate college (Longley Park College), comprising the schools, education authority and support of local parents, which took another five years to achieve – and which Tony Blair opened six days before my resignation in December 2004.

I stayed overnight with Ian McCartney [Minister of State at the Cabinet Office]. What a character. He is a mine of information about who is battling with whom and what's happening in the party – but, as during the years in opposition, he is in danger of killing himself. Ian has had to persuade Jack Cunningham to do a slot on the radio instead of him because Jack hasn't been on the broadcast media for two months and, as Ian rightly pointed out, people will be asking where the hell he is.

I then went off to the Wigan by-election, including a visit to a training centre, and then on Saturday to one of the regional conferences in the run-up to the full national party conference. These regional conferences were to give delegates who had never been to conference before a bit of a feel of conference from those with some experience – being told not only how conference worked and didn't work, but also what kind of issues were going to be prominent so that they could consult with their own party executive.

Phew! What a week – and to top it all Sheffield Wednesday were beaten 8–0 by Newcastle on Sunday. How long can manager Danny Wilson last?

So to party conference in Bournemouth. I over-prepared for my speech but hell's bells – when you see Tony preparing for his conference speech (and it was true of Neil Kinnock and John Smith as well), it is a world apart. I have never known so many people involved in trying to help, so many hours consumed and so much scrapping of ideas. It is amazing that the speech is delivered at all, never mind with the aplomb and communication skills that every leader seems to learn.

Tony had really struggled with speechmaking when he was Shadow Employment and then Shadow Home Secretary, but as Leader of the Party and then Prime Minister he blossomed. His speeches grew better and better, both in presentation and in content, as did his mastery of Prime Minister's Questions in the House of Commons.

The week began with a really encouraging headline in the *Observer* – that Gordon believed that we could achieve full employment in the new century. Did I not hear myself having said that and being criticised for it? Thank goodness, we are now singing from the same hymn sheet and I'm back on message.

It is strange being in Bournemouth, fourteen years on from that memorable 1985 conference, famous for Neil Kinnock's speech about taxis scuttling around Liverpool with redundancy notices, and also memorable – at least for me – for my own speech, which made Militant Tendency open up the books and show the world that they were fraudsters in Liverpool.

That 1985 conference led to a financial inquiry into Militant, which in turn, along with its political activities, led to the expulsion from the Labour Party of a large number of its leadership – some of the worst bullies and intimidatory thugs I have ever come across. I am proud that during the six months that followed the 1985 conference, I was able to play my part in getting the Labour Party, under Neil Kinnock, on the right track. Neil did a first-rate job in these difficult years and I am sorry that I was to fall out with him later about the next steps to modernisation and reform.

Strange what is highlighted at conference – Tony's speech, of course, and Gordon's (where Gordon gets the energy to deliver it in the way he does, I don't know), but also silly things such as John Prescott driving a few hundred yards from one part of the complex to the other in his car in order to avoid his wife Pauline's hair being blown about. You can see how these things happen, and I'm sure the position looks quite different at the time the decision is made from how it does when you read about it in the papers the following morning.

Tony's speech was very much to the conference rather than to the nation, which is unusual. I think he felt that he needed to win over people within the party by explaining what it is that he is trying to do. It is always a problem how on earth to get across to people what it is that you are trying to achieve in the long term, rather than just the immediacy of things around you. So much of politics these days is about the immediate, the reaction and the counter-action. How do we get across the narrative about where we want to get to over the next few decades, and how to place ourselves in a position which foils the Tories, protects Achilles' heels and sets and occupies the agenda?

I was relieved that I put one aspect of policy into my speech that may have seemed irrelevant at the time. This was all about greater support for people with disabilities in further and higher education. It turns out that on the Friday efforts were being made to cut back my legislation and shorten the speech by cutting this aspect out – but I had already announced it so it was a *fait accompli*. What a piece of good fortune that I had pressed to keep this in rather than accepting that the speech was already too long.

My usual dinners at conference went well. It is always good to sit down with the leadership of UNISON, the largest trade union in Britain, representing very large swathes of the public service, and with the *Sun* and the *Daily Mail*.

And, for many years, with the Guardian *and* Observer *on the Wednesday.*

The *Sun* – and in particular its editor David Yelland – is really upset at Tony's pro-European stance, while the *Daily Mail* – editor Paul Dacre, with Simon Heffer, Ann Leslie and co. – are deeply unhappy with Tony's anti-conservatism.

In retrospect, I think that Tony himself probably thought that for the conference audience it was fine but for the audience outside there was far too much room for misinterpretation. His attack on conservatism ranged much wider than the Conservative Party and its supporters; rather, it was about the nature of 'the forces of conservatism' within the UK.

October 1999

I was enjoying a few days with friends in the Lake District while the Tory party conference was going its own sweet way, when we heard about the

Paddington rail disaster. There was a genuine sense of shock, and it shook me to the core.

It also meant that the politics changed. Francis Maude, speaking at the Tory conference on the Wednesday, hit entirely the wrong tone by advocating tax cuts at a moment when it was absolutely clear that public investment was going to be needed.

Their 'common-sense revolution' didn't seem to embrace common sense. The headlines earlier in the week had been quite good. It does show that it doesn't matter how good the slogan, if the political antennae are not working then it is possible to score a terrible own goal.

The Tories reacted badly one way. In retrospect we, the government, over-reacted in another. As with so many major rail crashes – and we have too many of them – the tendency was to bring the network almost to a standstill with unrealistic speed restrictions and an increase in general fearfulness, which would never occur over pile-ups on our motorways.

Main post-conference news has been the reshuffle, including Frank Dobson's decision to step down as Health Secretary and being replaced by Alan Milburn. Frank is to go for the mayorship of London.

With the election for the new post of Mayor of London due in May 2000, the matter of who would become Labour candidate for the post soon became a question of how Ken Livingstone, whom the public loved but Tony mistrusted, could be stopped. Frank was making a very brave decision. He had a real love for London, but his candidacy was futile.

There have been rumours all the way along about who will be Labour candidate for mayor. Will Mo Mowlam go for it? Is Downing Street pressing her, and if so what is it that is stopping her? What made Frank Dobson step down? Is it that he was going to lose his job? Is it a brave or a foolhardy decision? And how on earth is he going to get anywhere near Ken Livingstone?

None of us were fully aware then of just how ill Mo Mowlam was, or the machinations that had taken place behind the scenes. If Mo had had a better long-term prognosis health-wise, and had she really wanted to go for it, there is no doubt that Downing Street would have backed her. Whether she would have won is a very moot point. As it was, Frank, who had been deeply committed to London for as long as I can remember, was on a hiding to nothing.

Reshuffle on Monday 11 October. Peter Mandelson is back in as Northern Ireland Secretary and I think he will do a good job. He is wily enough and he is close to Tony, which will give him real salience with both sides. Yvette Cooper has been given a job at the Department of Health and Keith Vaz has been promoted. I'd spoken to Sally Morgan about Andrew Smith's becoming Chief Secretary, and pressed that in that event Tessa Jowell should take over as Minister of State in my department – and this has happened. Tessa has been very much underused at Health, and the Employment and New Deal brief will give her a much higher profile. Clive Betts, MP for Sheffield Attercliffe (and my successor as Leader of Sheffield City Council), is joining the team as a Whip. Together with Tessa and Margaret Hodge, it feels as though I am providing a home for old friends – although how Tessa and Margaret will get on in the same team, goodness knows.

Politics is a strange old world and Clive lost his job as a Whip at the 2001 general election. I have to reflect that it was probably more to do with being on the 'wrong side' than it was to do with competence. It is difficult being a Whip, because if you are not part of the Chief Whip's entourage you are in difficulties, but if you are outside the main departmental team you are working with, you end up looking as though you are offside in terms of policy or modernisation. So much in the political arena is about being in the right job at the right time, and not just the right place at the right time.

I don't know the full truth about what Mo Mowlam was offered or not offered, or what she turned down, and whether the standing ovation at party conference [when she was mentioned in Tony Blair's speech] made any difference – that is, whether she was seen by Downing Street as 'getting above herself'. Politics stinks sometimes. All I do know is that she is clearly very ill and that, after the stint in Northern Ireland, I would have thought that a mainstream departmental job would have suited her. Perhaps she is just so unpredictable that the risk is too great, but if it is, then it would have been as well for the mayorship of London. As for Frank, we can only do our best to help.

Conor Ryan, my key special adviser, stepped down temporarily from his departmental duties in order to head up the promotional and media side of

Frank's campaign. Along with a lot of hard work from those around Frank, Conor was probably responsible for his obtaining the Labour nomineeship, but in the end perhaps this was not such a good thing after all.

It is strange how you can do the right thing for the right reason and end up with the wrong result. One thing is certain, there was little gratitude for the gesture of comradeship.

On Radio 4's *Today* programme on Tuesday, William Hague [Leader of the Conservative Party], responding to Peter Mandelson's return, was doing himself less than justice. In fact it was the worst I have ever heard from him. It wasn't just that what he said wasn't clever: it was that it was pretty vile. He said, 'If Roland Rat were appointed Northern Ireland Secretary, we would still work with him, but we would still call him a rat.'

We have now established the General Teaching Council, and I have decided to make David Puttnam [film producer who in 1997 took his seat in the House of Lords] its first chair. He will do a good job, not only in terms of promoting the General Teaching Council but also, as he has shown with the televised Teachers' Awards, creating an atmosphere of motivation and higher morale. He and Estelle Morris, Minister of State, will be able to do a good job together.

The *Sunday Telegraph* has a leak of a letter sent to Jack Straw by Alan Milburn when he was Chief Secretary to the Treasury. It is all about Jack's announcement on police numbers and his efforts to get police numbers back up again. Lord above, you would think he had committed a cardinal sin. The Treasury is obviously incandescent about what he has done.

It is funny reflecting on this, because the Treasury was equally angry with me at the party conference in 2002, this time about targets for substantial increases in police numbers, having restored the losses that had taken place from Michael Howard's years as Home Secretary.

On Monday 25 October, another meeting with Gordon and his advisers: a good meeting where we agreed that we would use some of the windfall reserve – the money from privatised utilities – to fund the nationwide tightening-up of the pre-employment work with young people and the 18–25 New Deal programme.

At the last Cabinet of the month we had one of those really silly discussions about the fact that the previous debate about the legislative programme had been completely reversed. This was all about whether the

Air Traffic Control Bill or the Learning and Skills Bill should go forward, rather than finding a way to ensure that both of them could proceed, by bringing in extra legal drafters. (The drafting of legislation has always been done by internal experts with what amounts to a kind of medieval guild where the amount of legislation that can be put through in the session is determined by the drafting hours available, rather than determining the volume that needs to be put through and then recruiting the drafting skills to make it possible.)

This did get better as the years went on, but it is strange that there was an assumption that what we wanted to do had to be fitted into the time available to those working for us, rather than the other way round. In the end we agreed that both Bills could go forward – which, given the crucial nature of my Learning and Skills Bill, was a great relief.

We had also had the launch – or should I say relaunch? – of the Equal Opportunities Commission, at which I took the opportunity to say that equal opportunities is not simply about women taking the jobs traditionally occupied by men, but about valuing more strongly in every possible sense the jobs that are predominantly undertaken by women – and giving a new emphasis to equal pay, which Tessa Jowell is very keen on and which seems to me should be central to the work of the EOC over the coming years.

And as October slides into November, we have the Third Reading of the Bill abolishing at least a very large proportion of hereditary peers sitting in the House of Lords.

We've had some amusing moments, including the declaration from one character that 'I wouldn't have sacked my cook in this way', and a pronouncement from Charles Francis Topham de Vere Beauclerk, Earl of Burford, eldest son of the 17th Earl of Oxford, the hereditary Grand Falconer of England, entitled to venison from Richmond Park, descended from the 14th Duke of St Albans, who claims that the 14th Duke was the real Shakespeare.

November 1999

The Pre-Budget Report. We've had a real tussle about what is still in the reserve (that is, the windfall-levy reserve), given that Treasury projections of unemployment are now out by over 300,000. It isn't that they've got them completely wrong. It's that they have deliberately erred on the cautious side in order to ensure that, in projecting how much of the reserve will have to be spent in relation to unemployment, there will not be a substantial addition to the existing reserve (around £400 million). I want a share of this!

For the first time since entering government, the weekend before the Pre-Budget Statement really has felt as though it is detrimental to my health. I woke up in the middle of Saturday night and couldn't get back to sleep again. My heart was pumping away, just as it did when I first had blood-pressure problems back in 1994. I began to wonder what the hell I was doing. The irony is that by Sunday lunchtime, we had begun to get a deal. There was £50 million on the table for New Deal for Schools capital, there was real discussion about using the Capital Modernisation Fund for technology, and it looked as though we might get what we had been asking for in relation to investment in technology in the employment service. What is really galling, because of the Barnett formula [the mathematical formula that determines variations in the level of public spending in Scotland, Wales and Northern Ireland in comparison with England], is that all the efforts that I have put in immediately benefit the Scottish and Welsh secretaries (and the new Scottish Executive) without their having fought the battle at all. The more I get, the more they get – and in the case of Scotland, the more they get is more than I get per head of population.

Having won some of the battles, it is strange to feel that I am at rock bottom. I just feel completely fed up politically for the second time in three months. It is not helped by the fact that I am worried about Alastair, who has still not got a job and is not clear what he wants to do, but I just think that some of the battles we have, and the way that we go to battle internally, are so draining and unnecessary.

Everyone knows in the end there will be a settlement, and everyone knows roughly what the parameters are, but we still go through some sort of war dance. I suppose this has been the case since the beginning of time. Certainly the 'Star Chamber' that the Tories used to operate on a year-by-year basis, without any forward planning, was a lot worse, but I just think that we can do a lot better.

Above all I am being worn down by the internal battling – the battle to get the Department in a shape to deliver, to get those who are really at the sharp end to realise how much rests on them and that if we get the extra resources it is critical that they deliver. We are only two and a half years in but people expect something already. Even though as soon as we were elected we had indicated that there would be a two-year spending constraint, people want to see things happening and things improving around them. When you inherit a system where there are virtually no levers to pull, you have to invent them – and you are then accused of centralism. It does become wearing.

Mind you, I don't know what I've got to be so fed up about. When I think of Chris Smith walking into the lobby outside the Cabinet Office at No. 10 and Gordon telling him about the abolition of the television licence fee for the over-75s – which he was about to tell Cabinet and announce that afternoon (the Pre-Budget afternoon) – I realise that maybe other people are behaving very calmly in the circumstances.

So on the Thursday after the Pre-Budget Statement I launched the £150 million extra capital we had got and went through the usual motions of media events, but you have to go to an enormous amount of trouble to get a meagre amount of coverage – in this case, one photograph in the *Independent*.

I then went off to Shropshire. It was one of those twists of fate that I was going to speak at a youth club that catered substantially for those with special needs, and I had just been having a battle about getting the recommendations of the Disability Rights Task Force into the Special Educational Needs Bill that I had fought very hard to get mentioned in the Queen's Speech.

I think, however, that my general mood was affected by some detailed correspondence I had been having with John Prescott and Andrew Smith, as Chief Secretary, about moving pension fund contributions from our departmental budget into the annually managed expenditure where it belonged, thereby freeing up resources for education. I will not here go into the machinations of the correspondence. Suffice it to say, it was deeply depressing.

I didn't realise it at the time, but the meeting held under Tony's chairmanship about future policy towards the European Union was much more significant than anyone could have predicted. This was because the Portuguese presidency from the beginning of 2000 was to be one of the most effective in the whole of the time I was in government. It wasn't simply that they had a clear idea of how to organise an agenda and, given the size of the country, a remarkable capacity to deliver competently, but also because they really wanted to make a difference and to focus on aspects of policy that could change the way in which the European Union added value to what the nation states were doing.

This led to what became known as the 'Lisbon Agenda', and the meetings that they organised around the more formalised Council meetings of the European Union were extremely interesting and productive.

The European Committee of the Cabinet is normally extremely boring and usually strung out beyond its natural life, but this week the agenda was positive, the ideas on how to support and contribute to the Portuguese presidency were thoughtful, and with the danger of patronising the Portuguese in the back of our minds, it looked as though we might be able to be of real help.

I was glad to be there and to have been able to make my contribution to the employment, social-affairs and social-cohesion agenda, all of which the Portuguese had indicated they were really keen to take forward. This was linked to the whole issue of inclusion – the development of information and communication technology and the importance of skills, both for competitiveness and productivity and for lifting people out of dependence. It is all completely up my street, and just the sort of politics I have been banging on about.

In fact, the general thrust of 'preparing Europe for the knowledge economy' links entirely with our own learning and skills agenda, and the importance of getting Europe as a whole to see that if we are to survive the competition from China and India we are going to have to have what Michael Bichard calls a 'step change', both in attitude and action.

There has been an ICM poll giving a substantial uplift for the Tories and a massive drop in our lead, which seems to have shocked everybody.

Looking back, it is ironic to think the shock was because our poll lead had dropped to only 10 per cent. It was amazing, however, how people panicked, and when we ran into real difficulties, both at the 2005 general election and particularly in 2006, I had to think back on those days.

Luck has been with us. In the 1980s luck was against us and with the Conservatives, and now it is the other way round. But how long will it last?

And then there was an example of how I must not go over the top without pausing and sorting things out. This was all about whether the Sure Start programme was going to be transferred to the Department of Health. I was quite happy to oversee policy and for it to be run jointly, but an idea had been floated within Downing Street that the lead should be taken by Health. What I did was to offer to transfer the whole of the

£452 million spend to the Health Department. This would have appeared on their budget, but perversely it would have also reduced my budget and the percentage of GDP spent on education by an equivalent amount. As a consequence, given our commitment to raising the proportion of national income spent on education in comparison with our European partners, there would have to have been a major boost in additional funding to the Department for Education and Employment.

Of course, it was game, set and match. The necessary alterations to the proposals were made and all was sweetness and light again, but it did demonstrate how you need to be pretty quick on your feet.

The Tories chose 23 November for the debate on the Queen's Speech and – surprise, surprise – they made education and employment the second part of the debate so that I would have to wind up. This meant that I couldn't go to the Association of Colleges' conference in Harrogate to announce the record 10 per cent increase in funding for further education – the largest ever in our history. Of course, given the system, I can't blame the Tories for making mischief and ensuring that they cause maximum difficulty for the government, but it is all a game.

I am informed by officials that this is the first time ever that the Secretary of State has personally taken an interest in the Letter of Direction to both the Further Education Funding Council [later amalgamated into the Learning and Skills Council] and the Higher Education Funding Council (university funding). Apparently not only have Secretaries of State not gone through it in absolute detail, but nor have they signed it off themselves. I find this staggering. The Letter of Direction is crucial to how the money is used and to what priorities the Council will address itself.

It is worth noting that Don Foster, Liberal Democrat spokesman on education, has raised the way in which correspondence is dealt with by departments. This is something I have been having a go at for the past two and a half years, stressing how important it is that letters should reflect the new government's policy and the way in which we have changed things. I don't mean just personable letters that address the issues, but ones that are relevant to this particular government, not just any government. Here we had Don Foster reading out a letter from the Deputy Prime Minister and then contrasting it with a letter he had received before the 1997 election from the Conservative minister – and the two letters were word for word the same! This is what we are up against.

But there was good news on 27 November because David Trimble [Leader of the Ulster Unionist Party] has persuaded his party, albeit narrowly, to go along with the further steps on the peace process. Let's hope to God that it turns out to be successful.

I went to the Guildhall, where Tony was speaking at the Lord Mayor's Banquet. One really amusing aspect of the evening was that, on account of the beef ban that the French are still holding to [in the wake of the BSE crisis], the French ambassador refused to eat his beef – but his wife ate hers. I had that old nursery rhyme about Jack Sprat, who would eat no fat while his wife would eat no lean, going through my head over and over again – except that this time it was in reverse.

In Cabinet at the end of November, John Prescott said to me, 'Are you running your own economic strategy?'

I replied: 'I'm doing my best. You used to have one in the 1980s.'

John said: 'Yeah, but this is the alternative economic strategy you are running.'

I said: 'Well, John, it's the economic strategy that works that we are all in favour of.'

A really pleasant supper with Pat Seyd and his wife Ros, and Alan Walker and his wife Carol. Pat was a young lecturer when I was a student at Sheffield University and later became Professor of Politics, Alan is Professor of Social Policy at Sheffield University, and Carol at the University of Lincoln.

We were talking about how Mo Mowlam had fallen from grace – and how, if she could, then anybody could. I recounted to them what had happened to her at party conference on the Monday afternoon, how the Downing Street entourage had frozen her out, almost put ice packs round her – and none of the supper guests who had been at the conference had noticed that. It is very interesting how people, even those deeply involved in politics, don't take such things on board.

I went to a reception that Richard Wilson, Secretary of the Cabinet, had laid on for organisations working on behalf of deaf people, where he had a genuine interest. He said to me, 'I just want to say that you are the best in-fighter in the Cabinet in terms of fighting battles and getting your way.' The following day I reported this to Michael Bichard, who said that perhaps he should decode it for me: 'It means that you are far too pushy, you are getting your way too often, and you ought to ease off a bit.' I replied: 'There's nothing I can do about it. I don't know any other way except to just keep going and to battle away and keep at it.'

The big news the same day was that Tony Blair had now ruled absolutely that the Disability Rights Task Force material can be incorporated into our legislation this winter. So he has overridden Margaret Beckett, as Leader of the House, and those who were against extending the legislation – but what a battle.

Perhaps I'm beginning to learn. I've abandoned sending a real stinker of a letter round Cabinet about the Welfare Reform Bill and the danger that we are about to abandon tough sanctions for those who breach the rules three times by not either attending a job interview or taking up a training place under the New Deal proposals. Instead I spoke to Alistair Darling [Secretary of State for Social Security] personally. This issue is all about strengthening people's arms because of the threats of votes against, and of the lawyers for the Foreign Office saying that such a move is likely to breach people's human rights. I have never heard such nonsense.

Fortunately our own departmental lawyers think differently, but what a silliness, having to intervene and argue, with all of us getting uptight with each other. All I know is that if we don't get tough now and send out the right signals, then we will be a laughing stock. If people know that all they need to do is to prevaricate long enough and we won't sanction them, then they will just do what they like. There has got to be something for something. It has got to be tough love.

One of the diverting moments of November was Prime Minister's Questions when John Prescott flew back from India and arrived at dawn to substitute for Tony at noon. John didn't do too bad a job, but what was amusing was when he used the word 'dentistry' instead of 'density' when talking about the redwood tree (because John Redwood was standing in for William Hague). Given my own propensity to dyslexia I am normally sympathetic, but on this occasion it was just extraordinarily funny.

On the family side, it was good to be able to invite Hugh to lunch with the Queen for the opening of the Jubilee Campus at Nottingham University, which incorporates a computer-science block in which Hugh is doing his degree. It was one of those very pleasant occasions and one of those rare lunches when, given the quality of the St Emilion, I decided I would have a glass of wine.

Later in the day I went on to a city technology college in Nottingham, one of the original fifteen that the Conservatives had established. An eleven-year-old had emailed me when I had previously had to pull out of a proposed visit on account of traffic jams on the M1 and shortage of time, very angrily saying that I was a disgrace as I had promised to come and hadn't done so. After that, I didn't think I had any choice but to go!

I insisted on meeting this girl, which was a bit unfair because it took her aback completely that I had not only remembered the letter but knew her name.

I can chat to youngsters now. I never used to be able to but over the time I have been doing the education brief I have been able to relax and talk with them on equal terms, rather than patronising or talking down to them. It feels much easier and the youngsters warm to it. So some good is coming out of the grind and the impact that it is clearly having on my personality.

That evening I went on to the awards presentation at Chaucer Comprehensive School in my constituency. I asked a young woman who had just achieved eight Grade As at GCSE what she was intending to do from now on and she replied that she wanted to become a trainee hairdresser. What do you say to that? You don't want to denigrate. Hairdressing is a good profession, but I wanted to say to her, given that so few youngsters have aspirations: 'Why don't you go on to college? Have you thought of doing A levels or a vocational equivalent?' But in the moment of giving her the certificate, there was nothing I could say except tell her to keep studying as it would be worth it.

December 1999

It is cold and miserable, and having to go to Eastbourne for a National Policy Forum – these are the new forums we had set up for policy-making, to report to party conference – wasn't exactly a bundle of fun, although the entertainment after the evening supper was Tony Robinson (of Baldrick fame but also a long-standing Labour Party activist), along with an entertaining speech from John Prescott.

A strange little incident with Clare Short [Secretary of State for International Development] occurred while I was down in Eastbourne. There are real problems in non-governmental organisations trying to continue delivering provisions in the outlying areas of Pakistan – because we are putting in place agreed sanctions against the Pakistan government because of the reversion to military rule.

I have to say that I didn't argue against the policy in general, although looking back in relation to the build-up of the Taliban (funded and supported from dissidents in Pakistan, as well as Saudi Arabia) and subsequent events, there is at least a prima-facie case for arguing that we might have been more circumspect in the circumstances.

I have been lobbied about the cutting of funds to basic education programmes in the hill villages, not least by an old friend of mine, Tony Tigwell, who worked in an inner-city school in Sheffield and spent a lot of time in India, including as a volunteer. So I spoke to Clare on Saturday evening and said that I was going to drop her a line with some material from a friend of mine who had been in Pakistan and had seen the terrible impact of the sanctions on education in the mountain villages.

She just flew off the handle and said she didn't want to be lobbied. I said that I wasn't lobbying her, I was simply talking to her as a Cabinet colleague. She said that it was the government we were tackling and if they wanted to change things, they could change them. I said, 'I am simply talking to you about children who are affected by our actions', but she just stormed off saying that I could send her the material if I wanted to. I said that I would do so, but that there was very little point if she was not prepared to listen. What a contrast, I thought to myself. I am prepared to listen to Alan Simpson, Chairman of the Socialist Campaign Group of left-wing Labour MPs, over the funding of maintenance in further education for art and drama students from the poorest backgrounds who have never had a chance before, and to change the policy completely to make it possible for them to have some help. Yet Clare won't even listen to a Cabinet colleague about what is happening on the ground. It is just bizarre.

Rumour has it that Mo has done a deal with HarperCollins for £375,000 for her book on her experiences in Northern Ireland. It must mean that she has made a decision to step down.

We have a little dispute running now with the Department of Health and the Treasury about the exact nature of the Sure Start programme. There is a danger that it is just going to become an adjunct of childcare, aimed purely at the disadvantaged in the old-fashioned, professional way. But the intention of Tessa Jowell and myself all along was that Sure Start would engage the community and ensure that it was as much about self-help as professional delivery, and that getting the wider community involved would mean that inevitably it would not simply focus on disadvantage.

The notes on my tape are significant, because ironically the criticism a few years later, when Sure Start underwent evaluation, was precisely that it wasn't concentrating sufficiently on the core disadvantaged elements of the community. Clearly the outline for those undertaking the monitoring had been on the basis that it was purely for the disadvantaged and was about delivering to them, rather than engaging the wider community to uplift them.

I wish now that we had been much clearer. At the time I thought I had won the battle but clearly I hadn't, and therefore we end up with a criticism of the Sure Start programme that arises out of a misconception about what the original local programmes were all about. Of course the outcome measures have to be robust in terms of reducing teenage pregnancy and bringing about a substantial drop in infant mortality, but they were objectives for services as a whole and not purely for the measure of whether Sure Start had achieved its goals – which were very much wider, and about building social capital and not simply improving health care, which should be the measure of improved prevention, primary and broader health-care policy.

Cheery news. A MORI poll in *The Times* on 17 December showed that the three Es were top of people's list in terms of government successes – the economy, education and employment. I was really pleased about that because it shows that people do see progress being made in these crucial areas.

George Wilson, my old sparring partner and former Leader of Sheffield City Council, has died. It is very much like the end of an era. I took over from George as leader in 1980 when he left the Labour Party in a huff to join the SDP. He then rejoined Labour in the 1990s. We had enjoyed a true *rapprochement*, so speaking at his funeral service seemed perfectly natural – although it was one of those dark, gloomy, miserable winter days when depression drags you down. So 22 December was a black way to start the Christmas break.

After a terrible bout of flu – and I admit I am mardy on these occasions – Christmas and the week leading up to the millennium passed without anything traumatic.

January 2000

I didn't go to the opening of the Dome and the New Year celebrations. Instead I spent New Year's Eve quietly and enjoyably with friends, probably the last contentment for quite a time.

I didn't go because I didn't fancy the razzmatazz and having to be in London rather than with those I am easiest and happiest with. Thank God I didn't go. I would have hated it. From talking to those who did go, I was well out of it. The security and the way in which the media were handled probably finished off what was left of any chance of the Dome being seen as a success, and the actual ceremony itself sounded just the sort of dreary event that would have finished me off as well. Cabinet members were lucky as they were at least looked after with getting something to eat and drink and being able to get in and out of the event in some comfort, but Lord help everyone else.

I feel a black hole coming up. I don't know where I am going. Up to now the sheer momentum, the planning and the delivery, have carried me forward, and I've been able to balance these with family and with sufficient leisure activity to keep me sane. I'm not sure now whether this balance is going to be sustainable, and with the boys having effectively left home I'm going to have to decide how to manage my life in a more sensible way.

Not an auspicious start to the year 2000, and I think at this point I probably should have said to Tony: 'I'm going to take a fortnight's holiday abroad. I hope you don't mind, but it will do me the world of good and when I come back I will be a lot better.' I wish I had done that on two or three occasions over the eight years I was in Cabinet.

And so to the end of a century – two world wars, the development of nuclear weapons, the Holocaust, the gulags, the development of television and the Internet, the mass use of electricity, revolutionary changes in media, the familiar use of flight, satellite, 24-hour, seven-day-a-week communication, including television. What a change in a century, and what will become of us in the century ahead? But we have in our hands the chance to change the world for the better, to use technology and advances in science, to be able to use our knowledge to draw lessons from history, to be able to make a difference. The question is: are we up to it?

I am very lucky to be a Cabinet minister with a really good job at the turn of this millennium, being there where others would want to be and sometimes, when I am feeling down and fed up, forgetting that. So why do I feel as though I am in a black tunnel?

Back in harness, the North of England education conference in Wigan went well – or rather, as well as it could, given that the education service are still very grumpy. What was really nice was visiting a school and talking to the youngsters, who were so sparky, full of beans and hope, and enjoying what they are doing. When I meet confident youngsters who are pleased to see me, without an ounce of cynicism or side, it makes such a difference. It is so uplifting.

I was trying to set out a vision of a much broader education service, not just the foundation of literacy and numeracy, crucial as they are, but about creativity, about the world of tomorrow, about preparing youngsters for such rapid change in a global environment. I published a pamphlet about creativity that had taken so much writing, so much effort – and for what? So little reach into the public, so little impact through the media. Why do I waste my time on producing this material? Why set out these visions if no one reads or understands them?

In retrospect I would do the same again. It was worth publishing the pamphlets, trying to broaden the debate and get people to address long-term issues. But it was exceedingly hard work, not just producing the material and constantly having to update and proofread it, but also trying to carry the officials with me, and attempting to get some publicity for it so that it had an impact – not just on the wider public but on the education service, so that teachers would understand, and so that commentators would appreciate what it was we were trying to do. On this, I am afraid I can only give myself five out of ten.

In the *Observer* on Sunday 9 January the 'One Foot in the Grave' column by Richard Ingrams, one of the grumpiest old men I have ever come across, attacked the pamphlet. He seems to think that all we are arguing for is a kind of utilitarianism and preparing people for the world of work, whereas what we are saying is that we need to provide scholarship and a broader education, but that unless people can get a job, then all the paternalism, all the patting on the head, all the being in favour of a great liberal education, is a complete waste of time.

Of course, my own experience at school affected the way I saw this. I was very much in favour of the kind of broad education that I had but it would have been very nice to have had qualifications when I left rather than having to go through evening classes, day-release from work, and six years of grind to get to university.

I wondered, in a kind of benevolent way, whether Richard Ingrams would have survived for a moment the kind of experiences I had.

The pamphlet had been about the broadest possible rounded education for citizenship, for self-fulfilment, for culture, and for broader, advanced thinking skills – so to find it attacked by Ingrams in that way was really lowering.

The papers tell us that we have an attack on special advisers coming up from the Neill Committee. I think those who attack special advisers haven't got the first idea what they are talking about. They have no understanding of what is going on inside departments and how crucial special advisers are to making a difference, to carrying through government policy (as opposed to previous policy) and to monitoring what is taking place.

As I learned to my cost later, it was crucial to have a monitoring capacity, and I should have taken this on board much more centrally within the civil service. I am afraid that I wasn't alone in this. Nobody else did either.

I am having a real up-and-downer about what is known as psychometric testing for the promotion of officials into managerial positions. I am wholly against these tests. Anything that doesn't address what people have done in practice, their ability to manage people, to manage projects and to be able to deliver, is just meaningless. You can have as many psychometric tests as you like. They can fit pieces into squares or triangles, they can match or spot the mismatch on anything theoretical, but the truth is that if people can't manage, they can't manage.

What we seem to have is a method of dealing with promotion and personal development which is about twenty years out of date, still clinging to meaningless experiments that took place in the private sector donkeys' years ago. But, of course, I am not in charge of management or the civil service, so all I can do is try to influence the people who believe that their job is merely to influence me. Power lies in being able to make change, not simply to make policy.

We had a spat about figures that Theresa May, Shadow Education Spokesperson, had used in Parliament about the funding of higher education. I couldn't understand what figures she was using and said so. I then initiated an inquiry within the Department and found that she was using figures that had been put in the annual report, except that they had missed out the fee element that the universities themselves were now collecting and therefore could keep. This was, of course, the crucial element of additional higher-education funding, but the Department had missed it.

We were therefore in a situation where the Tories were claiming that we were investing a lot less than we were – and on the statistics they had, they were right! The problem is that they were wrong. I just despair. How on earth can we deal with a situation where basic statistics are wrong because those compiling and collating them fail to understand that there has been a change?

This is an example which demonstrates the problem that both Charles Clarke and John Reid had at the Home Office in 2005 and 2006. It is pretty basic management and administration to check statistics before they are published – and absolutely crucial in not making the politicians look complete prats.

On Tuesday [11 January] I had dinner with Mo Mowlam in the Churchill Room at the House of Commons. She is deeply depressed. I managed to cheer her up during the course of the evening, and she thanked me when I saw her at Cabinet on Thursday and said she felt a lot better.

But she is obviously in a real pickle. She is fed up with being bad-mouthed and done over and resents it bitterly. She thinks it is because they want to cut her down to size and make sure that she doesn't become any sort of threat, but I think it's because there is a recognition that she is becoming more ill and less reliable by the day. That being the case, it would be really nice if someone were to help her.

Jon, her husband, has lost his job and ironically the only bit of work he has got at the moment is advising Sheffield on how to deal with the historic arrangements for debt from the World Student Games in 1991, which Jon himself had been involved in on the other side when he was working for the bank and the consortium that provided funding for the Games. He and Mo are obviously having to reassess their lives and their funding.

As I know, this brings the most enormous strain. For all of us, whatever our income and whatever our background, stability and security are absolutely crucial to our well-being.

They need to sell their house, but Mo can't get a mortgage because of her brain tumour, and Jon is out of work so he can't get one either. They need to get rid of the existing mortgage that they can't afford to pay, and then, using any residual income and collateral from the advance on the proposed book about her experiences in Northern Ireland, they would be able to get a place of their own. She has had to tell Tony that, come hell or high water, she is only accepting the Cabinet Office job if he gives her the flat in Admiralty House.

Over dinner Mo told me what had happened about the mayorship of London, which is, of course, just water under the bridge now. That story is one for Tony to write in his memoirs.

January was a bitty month in which I made a record of things which, although of consequence to me, are inconsequential for this diary. I include therefore only two or three reflections before moving on to the spring and summer.

I am disturbed by what is being said and written about Mo Mowlam. It is clear that she is in no state whatsoever to take the kind of drubbing she is getting, and I don't understand why they are messing about with her security. I don't know whether it is true that she asked for it to be withdrawn and then changed her mind. All I know is that here is someone who is clearly in a state and needs support. What support are we giving her?

On 24 January I went with Mo to speak for Frank Dobson at a party gathering as part of the campaign for his nomination [as Labour candidate for London mayor]. The reasons I mention this are twofold. Firstly, the day before, Tessa Jowell and Margaret McDonagh, General Secretary of the party, had been to talk to Frank about the campaign, where he was going and what was happening. He had decided to fight on – though he knows, as does everyone else, that defeating Ken Livingstone is a hopeless cause. It was strange therefore for Mo and I to be there the day after, knowing this and battling away to help him against all the forces ranged against him.

Secondly – and a matter which made me much less sympathetic to his cause – was the way Frank patronised me about not being able to see. If there is anything that absolutely gets my goat, it is other people pretending to be nice while being deeply offensive. Give me someone who is clearly just deeply offensive any day and I can deal with them, but save me from paternalism. Frank will never know – or perhaps he will – just how offensive his introduction of me as 'my blind friend' was. He went on: 'What a remarkable achievement it is for someone who can't see to have made the progress that my friend has made' – perhaps the kind of remark that some well-meaning but ill-informed distant acquaintance may make, but not a fellow Cabinet minister of two and a half years' standing. I could at that moment have walked out of the room and finished Frank's campaign there and then, but I managed to get a grip of myself, and, as so often, I let it go.

We launched Maths Year 2000 on 25 January with all the usual razzmatazz, but at least it gets the message across and creates a real interest that otherwise wouldn't occur.

Conor Ryan was rushed off to hospital to have his appendix out. I knew the effort he was putting in on the nomination for Mayor of London was difficult, but I hadn't realised that it was going to have such a dramatic impact. I shall be very glad to have him back, but my remaining special advisers have been doing a good job and I have been throwing myself into communication and press work; however, the effort is, as ever, at a price.

Alastair Campbell rang me and asked me if I would do radio and television on 'A Thousand Days' of this government. Goodness me, it feels a lot more than that! So after the conversation with Alastair, I used the Anglo-German Chamber of Commerce speech that I had already prepared as a platform for my account of 'The First Thousand Days'. I thought this sounded a bit like the German Reich but Downing Street seemed very keen, so I agreed that I would do the *Today* programme and other events to highlight the achievements and challenges so far.

One of those challenges was the issue of what had come to be known as Section 28 – whether, in schools and youth clubs, there could be mention of issues around homosexuality and lesbianism. This had become controversial when David Wilshire, a Tory backbencher, had moved an amendment to a previous Local Government Bill to outlaw such discussion or teaching. Frankly it was a storm in a teacup. Nobody took any notice of the amendment and in any case there were only a few quirky instances where anyone could suggest that proselytising had taken place. Given that in 1994 I had taken a very firm stand to protect from such proselytisation young people who were in vulnerable circumstances, such as residential homes or boarding schools, it was one of those paradoxes that led Tony to want me to try and find a way through. That way through was to use the new sex and relationship guidance, which I had the job of producing – negotiating with a whole range of interested parties, including the churches – to take the steam out of the issue.

In the end, Section 28 was to go in 2003 after the extensive shadow boxing, but the task of producing the sex and relationship guidance and placing adherence to the code in the Teaching and Higher Education Act was to prove one of my most enduring, if little known, successes. The area was nothing short of a minefield in terms of not being able to satisfy everybody. On one side, my most liberal colleagues opposed any kind of presumption about the primacy of marriage, while on the other side conservative pressure groups saw anything which suggested value in stable non-married relationships as being akin to Sodom and Gomorrah. My negotiating skills were tested to the ultimate, not least in reaching agreement with the representatives of the Christian churches, whose political skills and use of both public and private pressure points constituted a masterclass in political manoeuvring.

I had written round in December warning everyone that Section 28 was going to blow up and that we needed an alternative strategy to deal with this, including the potential for our own amendments to the original amendment, rather than simply its deletion. As so often, everyone is keen to get on with the immediate business in hand and to let the future take care of itself.

I recorded GMTV on the Friday, and thanks to a briefing after Cabinet that I was taking on the issue of Section 28, it dominated the discussion.

On Saturday night, I spoke at the centenary dinner for the Labour Party in Leeds, 100 years after the establishment of the Labour Representation Committee. It is strange to think what has happened over the intervening century.

It is a long time since I have had so much work over a weekend, because as well as the speaking engagements and constituency work, I had twenty-three tapes from the London office and four from the constituency and parliamentary offices combined. This is a record – so far. There is only so much that I can take, and I am getting very close to the boundaries.

I had a meeting with Tony and Gordon on 25 January to go through (yet again) the run-up to the next review of spending.

No sooner had we dealt with one Spending Review than we were arm-wrestling over the next, and if it wasn't the Spending Review it was either the Pre-Budget Statement or the Budget itself.

We were talking about education maintenance allowances. We are all in favour and we want to do something to encourage young people to stay on and to help lower-income families to be able to cope, but we are also concerned (and David Miliband, as Policy Officer, was very coherent on this) to avoid deadweight costs where we are paying people to do something that they already intended to do and could afford.

This is a perennial problem and was true not only in respect of education maintenance allowances but of a whole range of policies where universalism, while seemingly the right approach, would lead to our simply moving money around (cash transfer, as I call it), taking from people only to give them back their own money.

At the LSE on the Wednesday I took part in Professor Royden Harrison's launch of the first volume of his biography of Beatrice and Sidney Webb.

Those present included Michael Foot, Professor Eric Hobsbawm, and Anthony Giddens, Director of the London School of Economics. Sidney Webb had helped set up the London School of Economics at the beginning of the twentieth century, so it was appropriate that we were able to launch the book there.

Afterwards, together with Professor Michael Barrett Brown, who had been Principal of the Northern Adult College, we had dinner in the House of Commons. It was a pleasant occasion and a pleasure to be able to do it. Professor Pauline Harrison, Royden's patient wife, who is an internationally renowned scientist, was also there and was able to help Royden, who is now very ill. Listening to people talking about George Orwell and H.G. Wells from personal knowledge was one of those remarkable occasions where we are touching history. I wonder who, in fifty years' time, people will talk about in the same reverent way.

That week we also had to put up with one of those stupid all-night sittings that went through the following day all the way into the Wednesday evening. I was lucky that, because of the activity I was involved in publicly, I didn't have to suffer as our backbenchers did, sleeping in their offices.

This used to be a feature of the macho politics which some colleagues still hanker for. There is a kind of reverence for self-flagellation which has absolutely nothing to do with delivery of services nor sensible policy debate, and everything to do with people playing silly games.

Unfortunately the modernisation and reform of Parliament which took a few tentative steps forward was then set back, and the forces of reaction reasserted themselves. There seems to be a view in some quarters that if you revert to bygone days, no matter how irrelevant they are, then Parliament will regain respect and relevance. Of course, the opposite is true.

February 2000

A Tory reshuffle, with Michael Portillo (my old adversary when he was Local Government Minister) becoming Shadow Chancellor. Would there ever be a time again when he and I would cross swords across the Dispatch Box?

I had a good supper with David Miliband, talking about everything from asset accumulation to the way in which we need to reach out to those who don't vote, and to hold on to those who do vote and whose decision determines who wins the next general election. We both agreed that the paradox is that those who need us most are least likely to vote, and we therefore most need to win the votes of those who have least to gain. The core cities are absolutely crucial to regeneration, acting as a magnet for development economically but also culturally, and we both feel that the regional strategy that John Prescott is laying out is unlikely to go anywhere and that there has to be an alternative.

I just wish we had pushed this much harder. It is clear now that the old-fashioned 1980s view of regionalism had had its day long ago, and what we needed was to be able to build on the major cities in a way that wasn't detrimental to the rural economy or the life and well-being of what I came to know myself as being old-fashioned community. There needed to be a kind of dynamic that provided for a very large hinterland, a driving force and engine for regeneration that otherwise would not exist.

Peter Kilfoyle has resigned [as junior minister at the Ministry of Defence]. We have come fourth in the Ceredigion by-election. When people have a clear alternative and when they feel that we are no longer speaking their language, then they use their votes accordingly. This is the new politics and we have to get used to it. I recorded an appearance on the Michael Parkinson chat show for BBC television, but didn't get to see it as I was up at the local-government conference at Blackpool. I enjoyed doing it – I'm not sure why, because it was the same old stuff, going over the same background and history and what I feel – but I got on with Michael very well. Apart from stumbling down the steps on to the platform and sitting on Martin Kemp's knee instead of the chair provided, I enjoyed the programme.

Tony told me afterwards that he had been flicking through stations trying to find a football game and he had stumbled upon Parkinson *– a riposte to anyone who believes that Downing Street was monitoring our every move when it came to media appearances. He was good enough to say that he thought I communicated with the audience very well. But these occasions are only a performance, like being in the theatre. Although appearing on such a programme is extremely nerve-racking and stressful, I suppose it is necessary because it gives us the chance to talk to people in a way and through a channel that otherwise would not be available. Those people who never see politicians or tune into the news might at least be watching such a show. But too many such appearances and you end up being just a performer.*

Tony has sent me a really nice note thanking me for the work that I have put in and the presentations I have done in January. Such recognition shouldn't matter that much but it does. I really appreciated it. Anji Hunter also rang Julia Simpson [in the departmental press office] to say how pleased all of them at No. 10 are with what we've been doing. If we got little notes and phone calls like that more often, I think it would motivate everybody and I could pass on the thanks to the ministerial team – because all of us have been batting away, not just me.

We have launched the professional-development document for teachers and the new pay scales, including the £2,000 increase for those who demonstrate high competence, the new threshold payments and the advanced-skills teacher posts, all of which is designed not just for recruitment but to hold good teachers in the classroom rather than seeking management posts.

In June 2006 I went to an inner-city comprehensive school in Westminster, and in the course of taking a class for poetry chatted to an extremely able and experienced teacher who had taught in the school, including the sixth form, for ten years. I asked her if she was an advanced-skills teacher. She said she was about to apply, and then revealed that she didn't know that I had had anything to do with the threshold payments, the new scales or the advanced-skills teacher posts. I wasn't aggrieved, just deeply concerned that what we had done six years earlier had obviously had no impact whatsoever in terms of recognition that this was by choice not by chance, that it was politics and politicians who had made the decisions, and that the opportunities now available were only there because of the decisions we had taken.

On the Thursday evening I did *Question Time* on BBC1. God, what a combination of questions. Alun Michael had resigned as Leader of the Welsh Assembly; we had the hijackers of the plane from Afghanistan that had landed at Stansted; we had Section 28 rumbling on; and the Northern Ireland peace process falling apart, with the suspension of the process of power-sharing for the Northern Ireland Executive.

Peter Riddell has done a good article for his column in *The Times* following his visit to Sheffield.

I had invited Peter to come to Sheffield when he had written an article about parents taking over schools. I pointed out that I was all in favour of parents having much greater influence, but said that frankly getting them engaged at all was the issue in my constituency, never mind becoming involved in running the schools.

When he came up, he had an extraordinarily good day, meeting heads and teachers, parents and young people. Afterwards he was sufficiently generous of spirit to say that it had been an eye-opener, and that he had gained a great deal from seeing just what was happening, the enormity of the challenge and the way that people were taking it on.

In the Open Forum that morning at the City Hall, a youngster aged eleven had challenged me in a way that demonstrated, I think, just how open our politics had become in Sheffield. It wasn't just that the young man was confident enough to raise the question with me but the way in which he did it and the fact that he felt easy, in a large audience, to be able to challenge the Secretary of State for Education and Employment.

I had one of those extraordinary instances when consultants are drawn in to provide advice on advertising. This was all about age and diversity as part of equal opportunities, and I had to veto a poster that was going to have a youngster pointing at an elderly man and calling him an 'old fart'. I found it so offensive that I asked them whether they had lost their marbles.

It isn't the job of the Secretary of State to have to deal with all this, but if I don't, then it rebounds on me. I end up having to keep an eye on minutiae, because if I don't, I know that days will be spent picking up the pieces. Of course, no one would ask who produced this garbage in the first place, but they would immediately ask which politician allowed it to happen.

Good news. The Order we had laid in Parliament to bring citizenship and democracy into the curriculum has now gone through. We will be able to do it at last, and I just pray that it works in practice.

I spent the weekend doing my advice surgery, preparing a pamphlet on higher education and a speech on further education that I was to make the following week.

The higher-education pamphlet was really important – outside Parliament, where I had made several speeches on higher education, the most important contribution I had made to forward thinking on this issue. The pamphlet was about how we could develop technology in order to share resources across the UK and link with Europe and North America, and how we could share research facilities with major North American universities and the development of vocational as well as more traditional academic learning. This would include foundation degrees and how they might be organised with employers so that people could undertake them, as with MBAs, while still working rather than having to take on full-time courses.

My intention was that we should develop the concept of the Open University in an imaginative way, but I have to say that although the pamphlet went down very well, the kind of changes I envisaged back in 2000 were never really implemented, and the universities as a whole have been more interested in gaining changes in formalised funding through the new flat-rate fee contribution than in seeking a forward-looking appraisal of where they were going and how they would get there.

And then, in the *Independent* on the Saturday morning, I find that the Higher Education Funding Council have simply blabbed, giving the content of my speech to their education correspondent Lucy Hodges. The speech has been blown before I have made it. This is the kind of leak that causes complete havoc. It disrupts any strategy for getting the message across and being able to present it in the way that we want – and for what purpose? Presumably for someone inside the Higher Education Funding Council to get a thank-you or accolade from an individual journalist. What on earth do these people think they are doing?

March 2000

On to the big task of moving from the initial efforts to change dramatically the standard of education in primary schools to the daunting task of changing the appalling state of affairs in some of our secondary schools. The goal now is to tackle those where 25 per cent or less of pupils get five or more A–C grades at GCSE.

This was to become a key task over the fifteen months that remained to me as Education and Employment Secretary and continued, for the succeeding years, to be one of the biggest challenges of the Labour government. At the time we were starting the drive for improvement in secondary education we did not yet enjoy the advantage of youngsters who had benefited from the literacy and numeracy strategy moving through to secondary school. And the whole of secondary education was bedevilled by low aspiration and low expectation, particularly worrying in the most disadvantaged areas that most needed high standards of education.

Cabinet on Thursday 2 March produced one of those bizarre occasions where things had not been settled behind the scenes and open warfare broke out. This was all to do with who was going to pay for the military aircraft that had been used to help with the aid effort in Mozambique [where there had been catastrophic floods]. Clare Short began to rant about how the Ministry of Defence had sent the Department for International Development a bill and had declared that they would not continue to supply the aircraft unless DfID agreed to pay.

It was clear that Tony had not been approached on this matter, and as far as I could see Gordon hadn't either. My intervention was to point out that under the new rules which Gordon had brought in there was 'end-year flexibility' which would allow transferring from one financial year to another, particularly where there was an underspend, and therefore it was possible for the Department for International Development to go ahead and to be able to afford the planes if it was agreed that behind the scenes there would be a clear sorting-out as to whether the MoD were in order in charging for them.

Clare won her point. It was clear that Cabinet wanted to sort this out and thought that there could be a sensible approach in a situation where the MoD had already got the aircraft and their crews, and the question was about the marginal cost and who should meet it.

However, Clare had obviously decided that this was a *cause célèbre*, and appeared on the *Today* programme on Radio 4 the following morning and repeated all the things that she had said at Cabinet, even though in the intervening twenty-four hours things had moved on. As a consequence she didn't achieve anything more, but she achieved a great deal less by irritating Cabinet colleagues, the Treasury and the MoD, and by confusing the public who, instead of believing that we were doing an excellent job of relief work, now thought that there was a terrible row going on, that we weren't doing it, and that if we were, we were doing it grudgingly and were in a muddle.

This has to be an example of how to win a point and then lose it within twenty-four hours, and how to ensure that petulance gets in the way of achieving the objective.

The important thing is that we are providing substantial aid to Mozambique. The internecine squabble is being sorted out, but it illustrates just how silly departmentalism can be and how too often we can all fall into it, fighting battles where really we are dealing with paper tigers rather than substantive issues of principle.

Dinner with Greg Dyke [Director-General of the BBC] was both interesting and informative. He clearly thinks the Corporation can manage with the rise in the licence fee, but more importantly that we can do business on educational programming and the new digital and teacher Internet arrangements, so that we can share across schools and colleges the best that any teacher has to offer. Deploying new technology, the possibilities here are enormous.

We are still arguing about the sex and relationship guidance. Alan Milburn approached me and said that he and Yvette Cooper [Minister for Public Health] had been talking in the Department and they were very worried that we might initiate a 'Back to Basics' campaign by the media. I said, 'Well, Alan, if they do, it will be me they will be targeting, not you.' Chris Smith and Mo Mowlam have both phoned me on the same tack, so there is quite a little campaign going.

We published the guidance on Wednesday 15 March and it was extremely well received everywhere, except by the Daily Mail, *who managed to put the name of a former Chief Rabbi to an article suggesting that what we were doing was tantamount to going back to an orgy in ancient Rome. But after an enormous amount of work, we pulled it off. We got the balance right and a lasting solution, although one of my special advisers, Sophie Linden, had had the most terrible time with the House of Lords, with elderly peers ringing her up and in one case reading from the most disgusting pamphlet that he had managed to dig out – doing so deliberately and looking for her reaction. She had to persuade me not to take the matter further. If I had, it would have become a* cause célèbre.

I visited Cornwall where I was opening the extension to a school where my ex-wife Ruth's sister, Ann, was Head of Maths. I stayed overnight with Ann and her husband, Steve, and we had an extremely enjoyable supper – so enjoyable that we were all slightly the worse for wear when we set off the following morning. In Plymouth I stopped in a park to run my dog Lucy and met three girls sitting on a bench, skiving from school. I persuaded them to go back to school (and to stop smoking) and then went to the reception for headteachers in the city – only to find that I was talking to the headteacher of their school: I was able to pronounce that I had managed to get three truants back into class.

In the afternoon I flew back from Plymouth to London and just made it in time for a meeting with Tony. This was originally supposed to be with Alan Milburn, Jack Straw and myself, but Alan couldn't make it. It was all about how we should, as major spending departments, approach the Budget, which is only a couple of weeks away. Not least of our concerns was that while the Spending Review was going to examine every million pounds of departmental budget, the new Annually Managed Expenditure, tax credits and benefit increases would not be scrutinised at all. Jack and I were very strong on this because quite clearly every pound that went somewhere else was a pound that couldn't be spent either on education or the police service – what I always describe as the 'displacement factor'.

I then shot off to the Treasury for a late-evening meeting with Gordon. Things were so hectic that I had to feed Lucy in the courtyard of the Treasury before going in and then have her taken for a walk. I had sent Gordon a private letter of my own, and we had one of those 'round the houses' discussions where we concluded absolutely nothing, though it was clear that a lot of the ideas on employment and targeting the 'blackspots' were going to be taken up by him. In fact the main task was to get the Department to understand the coherence of including Employment Zones and European-funded Objective 1 Areas in the 'blackspot' list, where unemployment was high and prospects of employment low.

Objective 1 is the European regional programme designed for those sub-regions with the highest level of unemployment and deprivation, four of which were designated in Britain.

In fact Gordon did use my ideas in the Budget, which I was very pleased about, as it meant that we were able to make real progress in the year ahead.

We've also been discussing the amalgamated employment service and benefits-service agency which was to be announced the following week. There was very little interest in this, except by Jill Sherman, Whitehall correspondent of *The Times*. She had clearly been fed the idea that when the agency was completed, there would be an entirely new department.

I had pooh-poohed the idea and was very keen indeed to keep the education and employment service together, linking as it did the skills needs of the nation with the employment prospects of the individual, but I was to lose out on this and Jill Sherman proved to be right. She had obviously been correctly briefed from within government.

On Saturday I made one of my mistakes. I answered the phone just before going to do my constituency advice surgery. It was Martin Bentham, then of the *Sunday Telegraph*, who asked me about the issue of ballots being held (in Kent and Trafford) about whether there should be a separate vote on the abolition of the Eleven Plus, a deep-seated and long-standing irritation to the bulk of the Labour Party and something on which we had had to compromise in the run-up to the 1997 election in order not to be distracted from the agenda of standards and improvement for all children.

Bentham asked me about my 1995 commitment, 'Read my lips, no selection under a Labour government.' I explained for the umpteenth time that I had done seventeen interviews on the day explaining that I meant 'no further' – that is, no more – selection than existed, and crucially that 'Read my lips' was a playful echo of George Bush senior, who had used the same terminology in relation to tax increases in the United States. Back in 1995 the audience had laughed and had understood perfectly well that I intended a parody. Bentham said: 'So it was a joke.' I said: 'No, a parody is not a joke; it is a way of providing a light-hearted quip which everyone understands.' But he wrote up that I was now saying that that part of my speech to conference in 1995 had been intended as a joke.

The following week Bentham left me an answerphone message apologising, but of course the damage had been done by then. Roy Hattersley cancelled a proposed visit to Sweden to speak at the spring conference in order to return to the attack in which he had enjoyed indulging over the previous four and a half years. Roy knew perfectly well what I had said, and all about the debate that he and I had had both at conference and in the media, that year and since. He knew what the arguments were about, but he simply couldn't resist appearing on radio and television and writing in the newspapers.

It is very interesting that once a half-truth has got its boots on, there is nothing to be done about it except hold your breath. Broadcast and print journalists just keep on running the calumny. Politicians are seen as liars, journalists back journalists, and there is very little you can do about it. There is a lesson in life and that lesson is: don't pick up the phone on your way out to do your advice surgery – and if you do, certainly don't answer questions in an open and reasonable fashion, but close everything down and remember that politicians in the twenty-first century must be the most boring of the species, must have no private life and must have nothing to say, because if they do, it will be distorted and thrown back at them. Therefore we get the politicians and the politics we deserve. I suppose the worst thing was that the Parliamentary Labour Party and the party were upset, not only at the accusations and the damage to my credibility, but also about the grammar schools. They were hurt by the ballot – as I was – but whereas I just recognise the reality of what a 2–1 majority means and what it says for us, they just get resentful that I should even pose the question of not making grammar schools a big issue.

The Tories called a Private Notice Question on Wednesday which Betty Boothroyd, the Speaker, amazingly, granted, following the success by five votes of Baroness Emily Blatch of the Lords on Tuesday night in passing an amendment to abolish the ballots. It didn't get mass publicity and the Private Notice Question in the House only got a small amount of notice, which allowed me to sell the policy I was speaking on that evening at the Social Market Foundation, the pamphlet I was publishing on tackling failure, the idea of city academies, and a range of other policies.

I got on the ITN news from the Commons so Theresa May, Shadow Education Spokesperson, did a first-rate job there in allowing me to put on record what my position was. It also helped me to rally the backbenchers and to be able to lay out exactly where we were.

So the ides of March weren't quite so bad after all. What an example from the Tories of how not to use Parliament.

I have seen this time and time again, including when we were in opposition, where something is running and the best thing is just to let it run – a bit like in football with the advantage rule. But the belief that Parliament will be the cockpit for further assault leads people to think that they are best getting up at the Dispatch Box. The real art is to be able to distinguish when it would be advantageous and when it wouldn't, and it is quite likely that those who are least experienced (those advising as opposed to those with parliamentary experience) will advocate one thing while in reality the politician should be doing the other.

Down on the first train out of Sheffield on the Monday morning for further meetings with Gordon and Tony (two on Monday 20 March alone). Health will get a four-year spending settlement, while we will get an immediate increase of £1 billion for education and then the follow-through of the Spending Review later in the year. This is clearly the best of both worlds – a massive announcement and boost now that will give schools and colleges time to plan, and a further bite of the cherry in July for following years.

It didn't take a genius to work out very quickly that as education was Tony's top priority, and as health would be competing in the Spending Review for resources, this two-stage arrangement was going to be beneficial all round. It had political advantages for the public and those working in the service, and the economic advantage of giving time to work out priorities across government and reallocate resources from lesser priorities and from savings.

Although it had been an enormous eyeball-to-eyeball once again, this time the two parts of Downing Street had been working together for longer and in a more engaged fashion than was customary. So while the process for any departmental-spending Cabinet minister remained as frustrating as ever (particularly, on this Budget, for Health, with very last-minute decisions), for me it was extremely satisfactory. Unfortunately, given what I was to inherit, the same couldn't be said of the Home Office.

The only remaining battle on the education side was the distribution of resources that we were now going to allocate direct to schools. Schools would be given a specific budget depending on their size and type – primary or secondary – and whether they had a nursery and infant school attached.

This was an enormous change, which I had argued strongly for, but it had to be done in a way that wasn't detrimental to local government – bridging the gulf between on the one hand Tony's advisers, who wanted a complete change in the process, and on the other John Prescott, who was deeply aggrieved. It was pretty clear that Gordon knew that he couldn't lose on this one. He was going to get the credit either way – one of the advantages, of course, of being Chancellor.

For my own part, I was just pleased that I was achieving what I wanted – money direct to schools and setting aside the complex and deeply unfair Spending Assessment, which so disadvantaged schools in deprived areas outside London.

The schools were going to love it, but we had to settle one last debate – namely how much primary would get as opposed to secondary. The starting point was so low for primary that I said we would be laughed out of court, and all the great gains for the service and for standards, and the political gain in terms of applause for what we were doing, would be cancelled out by the understandable and justified grumbles of the primary sector – not least when we were demanding so much from them in terms of a rise in literacy and numeracy. On this one, I was prepared to go to the wall, but I didn't have to. We reached agreement.

With 18,000 primary schools, it was self-evident that we were going to have to balance the distribution in a way that benefited the more expensive secondary-school education – and this is what we did.

One final twist, however. Neither my Department nor Nos 10 and 11 Downing Street had taken account of schools catering solely for children with special needs. Had I not attended one myself, I might have overlooked it as well! What a catastrophe that would have been. I chipped in at the end of the discussion: 'And what about special-needs education?' There was total silence. It was one of those occasions when it really was worth being the person in the post rather than just the post-holder.

But the announcement in the Budget went extremely well, and on the Thursday, when I did the debate in the Commons, I was able to get a second day's publicity alongside the 'good-news story' for health.

April 2000

A busy period, but understandably much calmer than March.

I had dinner with Delia Smith and her husband to talk about how we might radically improve nutrition and school meals.

I wish I had pressed the agenda harder. I had introduced minimal nutritional standards back into school meals but, with the entertaining support of Delia and Ainsley Harriott, whom I found to be absolutely superb with children, we could have done more long before Jamie Oliver managed to get school food elevated to a major political issue.

We launched the extra package for teachers – golden hellos – to attract recruits into the most difficult specialist areas.

All of this was to have the most dramatic impact on what until then had been a real problem of recruitment to the teaching profession and was in subsequent years to be set aside completely with regard to graduates wanting to enter the profession. There were more teachers than we could manage to find places for.

At the Local Government Committee of the Cabinet, I found myself united with Jack Straw in arguing about the Local Strategic Partnerships. This is the latest idea for co-ordinating what goes on within and outside local government, but it is very top-down. We both made the point that these 'arm's length' organisations are becoming a feature of everything we are doing. No one is clear about who to hold to account for anything. If local government isn't performing, we should do something about the issue, rather than just inventing a new tier.

I made the point that it is often the same people with different hats on, in terms of their particular background or responsibility, attending different meetings – but it is still the same people. Who represents the experience or the voice of those who are not in the professions, who do not know each other, or eat with each other at lunch or over dinner? Jack made the point that there were somewhere between fifty and a hundred people who were now virtually running towns and cities across the country – in different ways – but very few of them emerged from the democratic process.

The Department for the Environment, Transport and the Regions is launching its revamped regeneration package, and there is no clarity about who is taking responsibility for delivery or who will be held to account for failure.

I had the interesting experience of addressing the annual conference of the Chambers of Commerce – with John Humphrys in the chair. They had had a ballot of those attending about who they thought should be Mayor of London, and Frank Dobson had come fourth. All I could think of saying when I moved to the rostrum was, 'Well, having voted Ken as top, it is clear that the Chambers of Commerce have great nostalgia for the return of Old Labour.' Actually, of course, they were voting to stop Old Labour.

But I am in danger of putting off all my closest friends and political colleagues whom I need for the future. All I seem to be doing is grumbling and making myself grumpy and unpopular, as well as deeply unhappy. I have just got to keep doing the job as well as I can, pull myself round and try to give myself space.

At Easter my sons Alastair, Hugh and Andrew went with me to see my cousin Pauline and her husband Minolo at their house in southern Spain. It was a really good break, and excellent to be able to enjoy some of Easter, even though I had to share the ministerial presence at the teachers' conferences, and therefore give Estelle Morris more than I would have wished to do over the holiday period. But even grabbing four days felt like real liberation.

Estelle said to me when I came back from holiday that she was pleased she had had a baptism of fire with her first throw at the NUT: she has come out of it with flying colours. It is important for her own future and for building her confidence – and good for me to be able to give it a miss for a change. As I was refreshed from my break, I found doing the National Association of Schoolmasters and Union of Women Teachers' conference much easier than usual. They are more constructive than some of the other teaching unions – albeit pretty grumpy – but addressing them is a challenge, one which I am happy to take on. My message was about discipline and the importance of the ethos of a school.

This is often more important to parents than differences in academic achievement within a school, because bullying, thuggery and the generally anarchic atmosphere in some secondary schools are the primary reasons why parents choose to scrape money together to send their children to private school.

May 2000

Sheffield Wednesday have lost against Sunderland, and to Leeds at home, and with Bradford having won, we are on our way down, which was so predictable all those months ago, from the 8–0 defeat at Newcastle to the sentimentality about hanging on to the manager.

It is amazing how football and politics have so much in common, with two notable exceptions: in football at least there is usually some big contractual golden handshake, and there is often a great deal more loyalty than you get in politics. On the left of politics we always preach mutuality, solidarity and comradeship, which is hard to reconcile with the way in which some people then perform.

Local-election week. I forgot completely – it just went out of my head until the Thursday night – that it is the thirtieth anniversary of my election to Sheffield City Council.

The night before the election I came back to the House of Commons after the centenary reception for the *Daily Express*, where Esther Rantzen had been having a little bit of a go at me about providing even more funding for Childline. I decided not to go into the dining room but to go into the tea room and have something light, so I ordered scrambled egg and smoked salmon and a pot of tea. Hilary and Tony Benn were in there.

Tony had announced that he would not be standing at the next general election, claiming that he wanted to spend more time in politics. He had first entered the House of Commons in 1950.

Tony was reminiscing and Hilary was being Hilary – listening and being pleasant, as ever. His dad was saying how he was going to miss everything, and both Hilary and I said that he wouldn't have to, that we would find a way of dealing with this. I rather foolishly said, 'We could always put you in the Lords again.' (Tony had inherited a peerage and had renounced it back in the 1960s as he wanted to stand for Parliament.) He said he wouldn't want to go to the Lords and had no intention of doing that, but that he did hope that they would find some way of enabling him to be able to use the library and see people.

I realised then just how much Tony was going to miss the House of Commons and the Palace of Westminster in general. Whatever he might think or say, he was now thoroughly a parliamentarian, and I knew that we had to do something to help. In fact something was done, and he was given access for life to the facilities of the House. I thought it was a fitting gesture, which showed the nicer side of politics, that ways were found to ensure that Tony was not left out in the cold.

Tony told me the story that he had related many times before but that I had never heard, of the salutary lesson of George Brown who took to the bottle in a big way when he was Deputy Leader and Foreign Secretary in the 1960s. He was in Peru at a reception. The evening was growing late when the music struck up, and he got up and asked a nearby diner in a flowing purple ballgown whether they would like to dance. The reply was a firm 'No'. Then George belligerently asked, in the way that only George could, 'Why not?' The answer came very quickly: 'Firstly, sir, this is the Peruvian national anthem. Secondly, you are exceedingly drunk. And thirdly, I am the Bishop of Lima.' Tony swears that this is true – but true or otherwise, it is a damn good story.

The other story that Tony told about George Brown was when again he had been at a reception prior to a dinner. They sat down to eat and George was next to the French ambassador's wife. George began to get very flirtatious and asked her whether she would like to have dinner with him again. She said, 'No, thank you.' When George asked her why not, she said, 'I never accept any invitations before the soup.'

Local-election day itself had Cabinet, followed by Education and Employment Questions, followed by a mad dash by train up to Sheffield to vote and to go round the committee rooms, and then back down on the train for something to eat with Conor Ryan before doing the round of television studios. Tony had asked me to play a specific role in the elections but it was a poisoned chalice, given that we were fighting seats that we had never won until the previous election. The evening was only saved politically by the fact that the Tories lost the Romsey by-election to the Liberal Democrats.

I called a meeting the following Wednesday to see what our backbenchers thought of the results, and what lessons we should learn. It seems to me that testing the water and giving those closest to it on the ground the chance to have a say is much more sensible than the usual way in which we deal with post-mortems on elections. Much to my amazement, over 100 of them turned up, and most of them lasted the hour and a half of the meeting. It was very instructive and much more worthwhile than I could ever have imagined. Hazel Blears [MP for Salford] chaired it and members of my own team, including Tessa Jowell and Jean Corston, were there, along with Keith Bradley from the Whips' Office [now in the Lords] and one or two of the parliamentary private secretaries. I was disappointed that so few ministers attended. It is so easy to get out of touch when in government.

I produced a paper for both Tony and the General Secretary [Margaret McDonagh], indicating that I thought we had lost the focus of the three Ds – direction, definition and delivery – that we had talked about.

Part of the problem of the years in government was the way in which we would start a particular theme running and then drop it. It was as though people got tired or became bored with what we had agreed as being absolutely key benchmarks to guide us and to keep coming back to. The same happened with the Big Conversation and, for that matter, with the concept of the Third Way. I have to say I was relieved when the constant repetition of 'stakeholder democracy' died a death.

The 'stakeholder' theme arose at a weekend conference in Lisbon, part of the informal arrangements made by the Portuguese presidency and one of the more interesting discussion groups. I was speaking alongside Tony Giddens, Director of the London School of Economics. David Miliband was there, along with a very enthusiastic group of people from across the European Union. I had the pleasure of sitting next to the President of

Portugal for dinner in the evening, and he was kind enough to give me three bottles of Portuguese red wine – excellent bottles, but not expensive enough for me to have to log them in the Register of Members' Interests. The President's English was impeccable and his grasp of UK politics better than most of the people I talk to back in Britain. He was, it has to be said, critical from a left-wing standpoint of both his own Social Democratic Party in government and ourselves.

On 4 May, the same day as the local elections, Ken Livingstone had been elected London Mayor. Frank Dobson came third in the first ballot, with only 13 per cent of the vote.

I ended up as the first Cabinet minister to have to share a platform with Ken Livingstone as the new Mayor. It wasn't difficult at all as we were talking about skills for the city, and I have known Ken long enough and crossed swords with him enough times to be able to handle any banter. There is no point in falling out with him anyway. We have got to just do what is right for the people of London: they have elected him.

In mid-May, another of our trips to Highgrove, this time for a reception for headteachers. It was very pleasant indeed, except that Lucy rolled in something extremely foul, probably fox dung. We went into the bathroom and did everything we could to get it washed off, but by the time we appeared at the formal event there was still a strong and lingering aroma. I joked with Prince Charles about it, and he said he was very familiar with fox dung – so all was well. Except of course that I had to endure the smell all the way back in the car and it was a day or two before we were free of it.

While I was Education and Employment Secretary, as well as when I was Home Secretary and had responsibility for the issues around enforcement of policing, I voted for the 'third way' compromise option in relation to hunting with hounds. I was against the cruelty of unregulated hunting, but also deeply concerned about the expansion in numbers of foxes and the undoubted damage they were doing. I also presciently perceived that we would either pass a law and then turn a blind eye to it, or we would pass a law and then rigorously enforce it with all the difficulty that that would bring in terms of diverting police resources. In fact, of course, we managed in the immediate post-legislative era on hunting with hounds to find an even more subtle compromise – letting people carry on hunting but accepting their word that they hadn't started out to chase foxes!

Prince Charles was very nice, as ever. He asked about my sons and I asked about his. In his speech, he was very warm and effusive, but managed to point out that I had 'only missed one of these events in four years', which indicated that he had been counting.

Saturday 20 May: Leo Blair is born to the world. What will things look like when he is twenty-one? It is lovely for Cherie and Tony and I think it will give both of them a new lease of life, although – hell's bells – what a responsibility. It is also good for Downing Street to have a baby on the premises. It will certainly be very different from anything that staff there have experienced before.

Sunday 21 May: I stayed with Jonathan Dimbleby and Bel Mooney and went to the Bath Festival. We had an interesting supper afterwards with poetry reading, and then on Monday morning I went to a local school where the children were more interested in the Harley-Davidson motor-bike on which I arrived (and which belonged to Bel) than they were in either me or the dog. One or two newspapers picked up the pictures, but I was primarily there to see what difference we were making to rural schools, given my own obsession with urban education.

I just made it back to London for lunchtime to launch Adult Learners' Week, then later in the day had dinner with Alan Wilson, Vice-Chancellor of Leeds University, and Robert Ogden, my friend from North Yorkshire, who was putting up substantial sums of money for the scheme to get youngsters from the South Yorkshire coalfield to go to Leeds University. The scheme had started very well and was a forerunner to the Education Maintenance Allowances.

At Cabinet on 25 May Gordon mentioned to me that he was making a big speech at a TUC conference. He asked if I minded his mentioning a couple of things to do with my Department. One was on the equal-opportunities front and the gap between men's and women's pay, but he said that he didn't feel that that was a sufficient story and wondered whether he could give mention to a speech I had made a couple of weeks ago: the AUT speech at Eastbourne about access to higher education. I was happy to agree, so Gordon went off and made his speech – and hell broke loose because the example of unfairness in selection that he had used was of one specific student.

We didn't know anything about her, but the media were determined they were going to find out. I wasn't surprised that this whole issue had been picked up, because Charlie Whelan has been doing some low-level advising to the Association of University Teachers – where, of course, I had made the original speech.

The student in question was Laura Spence, a pupil at a comprehensive school in North Tyneside who had been turned down for a place to read medicine at Magdalen College, Oxford, despite having achieved five A grades at A level. She had subsequently accepted a place at Harvard.

Laura Spence was clearly a very able young woman. The difficulty here was not the issue itself but the fact that we had not co-ordinated and prepared to deal with the wider implications of raising an issue I had been dealing with behind the scenes (particularly with Oxford, where I had been working with Colin Lucas, the Vice-Chancellor, on dramatic improvements in the way in which colleges undertook their selection process and overcame the deep unfairness of the interview system).

The story was even more strange in the sense that Laura came from the same school as a girl called Lara, who the previous year had failed to get into Oxford and had also been offered a place at Harvard, so there seemed to me to be a pretty direct line to one of the world's most prestigious universities.

So when I discussed the issue with Colin Lucas on the *Today* programme on the Friday morning I had to go out of my way to indicate that I had recently been to Magdalen College and knew the efforts that were being put in to improve the selection process. But I agreed with Gordon that there were broader implications and that we all needed to look at how we might break down the historic barriers that prevented children from disadvantaged backgrounds and from many state schools from even thinking about going to Oxford or Cambridge, never mind the difficulties of getting accepted.

We were to work with Peter Lampl of the Sutton Trust, a philanthropic organisation that promoted high standards in education, and with schools and universities on how to develop summer schools and work on preparation, not simply for the passing of appropriate A levels but also in terms of the approach to university itself – learning how to study, as well as how to present yourself.

I am afraid all of this really did undermine completely my efforts to get across our anti-bureaucracy drive when speaking to the National Association of Head Teachers over spring bank holiday. I know I shouldn't be irritated because there have been occasions when I have done the same thing to other colleagues but it is the only story in town in relation to education and getting any others up and running is now impossible.

Michael Bichard has gone into hospital for a very major operation, and just before he left the Department we had a discussion about the way ahead in the next year, with a general election almost certainly looming. He talked about the 'dead-duck-president year', and how he had said to the Board that we simply couldn't have a situation where they are anticipating a general election and things grind to a standstill. I said it was funny because I had been thinking about exactly the same thing the previous weekend and the importance of momentum. At all costs, we have to avoid the doldrums, where everything runs down and the energy and the drive and the appreciation by the civil service that the continuity will be there, and that we mean business, somehow becomes diminished.

We are still having major problems getting statistical detail and getting it accurately and quickly. There appears to be no proper database, and despite the fact that we have a very large statistical section, it is a major struggle to get figures that we might confidently expect to be reliable. For instance, it took days to get the breakdown on which particular sectors of the education system – private, comprehensive, selective – got what percentage of grade As at A level. Even after three years in government and the enormous efforts that Hilary Benn made when he was an adviser, we are still struggling with the supply of statistics.

This illustrates how the government scores own goals and is not able to handle extraneous issues quickly. Education and Employment is one of the better departments at rebuttal (in fact we are the best), which doesn't say a lot for the others. I am just surprised that nobody has written about this before. I think it is partly that people have not been close enough, as politicians, to the system. There is a kind of lethargy in the system. Things have always been done a particular way, and if they have always been done that way then the system works reasonably well, but the minute you try to get them to change anything they are in a terrible mess.

It's a bit like the new process for dealing with correspondence in the Department, which is total chaos. Letters are being lost. I am noticing one about every ten days that is going missing – sometimes more – so what is happening across the board, God only knows. Sometimes I only find out that they have gone missing when people take the trouble to demand why they haven't had a reply. Others just go away disgruntled.

What won't go away is the issue of access to higher education. I am very lucky because Andrew Adonis, using the clout of Downing Street, has managed to pull off an extremely helpful intervention – persuading Peter Lampl of the Sutton Trust to postpone the launch of the findings of the

Trust about the breakdown of different types of school and their access to different types of university. Postponement is critical because it was originally due to take place on Thursday 1 June, the day I am addressing the National Association of Head Teachers. We have worked for weeks on the announcement of tackling bureaucracy and lifting 'burdens' from headteachers, and it is staggering that nobody in the Department seems to know about the launch. All the mechanisms that we put in place to ensure that we knew what was happening externally, and not just what other departments were about to announce [what became known as 'the grid'], don't seem to function. The political antennae are not working.

Since I've spoken to Andrew Adonis about it he's pulled out all the stops and we've been able to agree that the Trust's launch will be on 5 June and I could make my speech as planned on the 1st. This was to be in Jersey and publicity was therefore going to be difficult logistically at the best of times.

In the event the launch went extremely well. Apart from Radio 4's Today *programme, which wanted to run an entirely different story of their own rather than covering the news, the media generally were very sympathetic and we received extensive coverage. But it was a close-run thing.*

June 2000

Friday 2 June: Gordon rang to apologise for the way in which things had emerged and the agenda had run publicly over the past couple of weeks. It was a generous gesture and one which I appreciated greatly. Our discussion on the phone was about how to implement broader radical policies in relation to higher education, but also how we could build up to the Spending Review without the usual clash of personalities. I was very keen indeed, as I had been at the Head Teachers' conference, to get the whole agenda back on aspiration and expectation and on how we could turn things round both in the school and within the family – not just tweaking the arrangements for access once, for many children, it was too late.

I was also in the middle of writing and rewriting my welfare-reform paper for the Institute for Public Policy Research conference the following week, under the heading of 'On Your Side'. I had spent a lot of time putting this together, laying out what a welfare agenda would be – the something-for-something approach – that would win over those who were having to contribute to the welfare state, as well as providing a different perspective for those reliant on it.

This was an agenda to which I was to return five years later when formulating the Green Paper on welfare reform. Although a great deal of progress had been made in the intervening five years – with pilot programmes and experiments – the Green Paper was substantially picking up the themes of the pamphlet that I had published in June 2000.

Unfortunately Wednesday 7 June, when the pamphlet and the speech were to hit the media, turned out to be the day that Tony was addressing the Women's Institute conference at Wembley Arena. I hadn't realised this until I spoke to him the previous weekend and he had asked me to put a few notes together for Monday to contribute towards his speech.

I did do this but he wasn't able to slot in the ideas I had put forward. He had consulted a number of other people and, of course, the record speaks for itself. While it was only a small number of the audience who heckled and slow-handclapped, and only one or two who walked out, the speech had a profound impact, both on Downing Street and in terms of general perception.

The address to the WI, uniquely in my experience of Tony Blair, hit the wrong note. Those advising him had not understood the nature of the audience and the very fine but crucial line between rhetoric and vacuousness, and the danger of speaking too politically to this type of audience or stating such banalities that they would become irritated. It is clear that someone within the WI had set out to have a go at the Prime Minister, and whatever he said would have received a raspberry. In retrospect, it may have done some good because, as I found when I was going round in subsequent weeks, people out in the country were as annoyed by the way that some of the members of the WI had behaved as they were by the unwillingness of people to listen to something serious. (In this case, the Prime Minister was talking about the health service.)

And the speech had another consequence. It shook people in the party out of complacency at a time when we had dropped to just a 3 per cent lead in one opinion poll – something often forgotten.

In my usual petulant way, I was grumpy about the fact that none of us, including myself, had reckoned on a clash with the Women's Institute. Self-evidently my speech was going to receive much less coverage!

Actually something deeper has been going on. Anji Hunter, long-standing aide to Tony, had clearly had an up-and-downer with Alastair Campbell during the previous week, and she was more shaken by the Women's Institute than anyone else, given that it coincided with the atmosphere which, following Gordon's outburst against Oxford and Cambridge, had been created in the kind of contact groups that she was in touch with. We seemed to be tilting towards Old Labour and Anji's job is to warn Tony about it.

We also have the Ministry of Defence briefing heavily that they are so short of money that their rifles and radios don't work. Nothing to do with a complete failure of maintenance, of course – just give us more money. Now what could have occasioned this? Oh yes, the pending Spending Review! We have this every single time from the MoD – not only leaks and innuendo but people from the senior echelons of the services briefing the papers. It surely must be time to ask them whether or not it would be a good idea for them to do the job more thoroughly themselves and spend less time at major functions, usually flying there with a large entourage and with no expense spared.

The curious thing is that we have an economy that is working – unemployment down, employment up, education working, people feeling better, with more money in their pockets – and we are getting a drubbing for it. It is a really strange moment in politics. I suppose we are fair game. When things are going well, as they have for three years, we have got used to everybody being nice and on side. Now suddenly it is becoming respectable again to be a Tory, and the implications of that are very substantial in terms of people being prepared to co-operate with us. We will just have to hold our nerve and see how it goes.

William Hague has tried joining in on education. He has obviously dropped what he was going to say about funding, because I've already done that at the NHT conference, and picked up what I had already done at the NASUWT conference, specifically with the encouragement and help of Nigel de Gruchy [General Secretary of the NASUWT] in respect of children excluded from school. We had already made enormous changes and announcements at Easter and I had backed that up at the Head Teachers' conference at the spring bank-holiday weekend in terms of exclusions and the tribunal hearings, but that didn't daunt William Hague. He just picked up the issue and ran with it. What was interesting was how little the columnists, particularly the political commentators, know about what has already been announced and what government policy is.

I had picked up this issue from a number of individual cases that had been drawn to my attention – including some in Sheffield, where perverse decisions had been made that were clearly dangerous to youngsters who had been assaulted or bullied by those who should have been excluded.

We were in the middle of creating Learning Support Units so that we could put the individuals who were causing difficulty out of the classroom but not on to the street, and, critically, locating the Pupil Support Units off site so that we could get out of the school altogether those youngsters who were very disruptive or even in need of substantial psychiatric support. Despite spending over a couple of years somewhere in the range of £500 million, it was taking the most enormous length of time to get anything changed and to get the momentum at local level to ensure that we reversed what had been a scandalous position where those excluded usually got something in the region of two to three hours' tuition a week rather than a full timetable – which, of course, would have literally kept them off the street.

Gordon gave me a birthday cake when I went across to the Treasury on the evening of my birthday [6 June] for discussions on the Spending Review. I managed to make him laugh by suggesting that by the time I had left the room, a third of it would have disappeared.

Visit to China – to Beijing and Shanghai. A meeting with Vice-Premier Li, one of the five Vice-Premiers, as well as with the Education Minister, who is very close to the President. The most enjoyable part of this visit was speaking to young people at one of the main universities in Beijing. Over 300 youngsters, all involved in teacher training, who were sparky, amusing, able to get even my clumsy jokes, hissing the President of the University when he was slightly patronising towards me – what a contrast with my visit to China seventeen years earlier. On to Shanghai, where we could have been anywhere in any major Western city, but there were two things that struck me most: firstly, absolute dynamism and commitment to education and re-skilling; and secondly, a major problem in protecting the integrity of the city and the ability to provide health and education to the citizens without being overwhelmed from the countryside. Their solution is what I suppose you would call a form of identity card, where only those who can show that they are legitimately resident in Shanghai are entitled to the full range of services.

The other thing that has struck me is just how hard the leader of the delegation (in this case, me) has to work on these overseas visits compared with anyone else. It is not just the speeches to be delivered and the interviews to be undertaken, but also the discussion over every meal, the formalities for getting things right, always being on show and always needing to be on the ball. This is true particularly in China, where the main players are the ones who converse, even at mealtimes.

But it was certainly worth going, and I came away determined that we were going to develop much better contacts on the education and skills front, and to help the universities (members of which had come with us on the trip in the form of the Higher Education Funding Council) to make more of the links that are being already forged. I also believe that we need to teach Chinese much more in our schools. This is clearly going to be an important subject for the future.

I made some progress while I was Education and Employment Secretary with stepping up contacts, facilitating exchanges and getting far more Chinese students into our universities to learn English. But in all honesty, I failed to make a real impact in getting Chinese taught in our schools, even with the advantage of having the Internet and the ability to use Chinese teachers more extensively than would ever have otherwise been possible. There was just so much on the agenda and so much to do that having set something in motion, it was virtually impossible to follow through and to monitor – day in, day out – whether people were doing it.

Two other things struck me about my visit. The first was the way in which the students always reacted well to the idea that English was the language of the Internet and the most understood but Chinese was the most spoken, and secondly that they were completely pragmatic. The idea of balking at all at ensuring that the brightest students had what we would describe as access to specialist facilities and specialist schools struck them as ridiculous. They just took it for granted. If someone has an aptitude for music, that person would be offered the very best tuition. It was strange to come back and debate these issues in the Parliamentary Labour Party.

Another very good thing came out of the visit. Jessica Rawson from Oxford University, a Chinese speaker and greatly knowledgeable about Chinese life and antiquities, was superb. She told me about a student who was profoundly deaf and had made her way to Britain to earn her own living and get her A levels because her father had died and her mother was in no position to help her within China. She was staying with a distant cousin but earning her way, and in just two years she had achieved the necessary A levels to get into Oxford. She had no funding and no prospects and I was able to help.

In this case, I was able to make contact with someone I knew who was deeply committed to education prospects, not just of those most vulnerable or where there was greatest inequality, but also where there was greatest tenacity. This seemed to me to fit the bill – and funding to help her through was agreed in circumstances where public funds would clearly have been outside policy and out of the question.

This was one of those rare occasions when it isn't your formal office but your contacts who can make a difference – even though I don't have an old-school tie!

I have been thinking over the past few days about how you are sometimes up and sometimes down, sometimes in and sometimes out of favour. The outside view doesn't always bear any resemblance to how it feels inside but it affects other people's view, and that in turn affects the way that people perceive and see you. It is a really strange merry-go-round where, if the parliamentary party think that you are in, then they are much more likely to take notice of what you are doing and support you. On the other hand, some judicious briefing by those who are aggrieved (and by hell, you only need a bit of good publicity to get people aggrieved) can end up with stories being written that you are somehow on the slide, or that you are not in favour. At the moment I appear to be in favour.

We have Harriet Harman still banging on about how 'if only there were more women in charge, then all would be well'. Well, there are five women in my team and all feels well but it has absolutely nothing whatsoever to do with gender and everything to do with commitment, political skill, intelligence and damned hard work.

Harriet was making the same old points six years later when arguing that the Deputy Leader (or a deputy leader if there were to be more than one) of the Labour Party should be a woman. Over those six years a very large number of women have gone through key Cabinet responsibilities and, thank God – not least for them – they weren't judged on being a woman – although it has to be said that even now I do think it is harder for a woman to succeed because there remains an underlying misogyny in many of the commentators on national newspapers.

Harriet's suggestion is a complete diversion. By the same token someone might claim that I am in the Cabinet because I have what others think of as a disability, which is clearly arrant nonsense.

Andrew has finished his first year of A levels and Hugh is awaiting the next batch of results before going on to his final year. I have been talking to Alastair about the Human Genome Project, and because he has done marine biology he knows more about it than I ever will. But the results of the project are coming up next week and it is probably the most significant scientific breakthrough for donkeys' years. I am really intrigued by this: the human code, what makes us special. What are the implications for policy? Where will it take us in years to come?

I had no idea then how significant my thoughts were in relation to my work as Home Secretary, not least in relation to the extensive and rapid development of forensic science, biometric technology and the like. The world is changing so quickly but the political process and the way in which it is reported changes very slowly.

At Cabinet on 23 June there was one of those slightly amusing moments. I had left my papers on the Cabinet table, and Jack Straw helped me pick them up, saying as he did so, 'You do terribly well.' I replied: 'Given that you have a real problem with hearing in one ear, you do remarkably well too.' We both laughed, but it was one of those moments which could have gone so badly wrong. Jack then told me that his protection team had saved him on one occasion when a car had been coming towards him on his bad-hearing side and they literally dragged him back from stepping under it.

It was going to be another year before I had the support systems that are so difficult to incorporate into your life and then very difficult to contemplate living without, given your public profile.

When, soon after my return from China, I popped into No. 10 to see Tony, his pollster and close confidant Philip Gould told me that his children were learning Mandarin at school. I said to him: 'Given the number of leaks of confidential material, including your own submissions to Tony, it might be sensible if in future you wrote them in Mandarin – then it would be pretty difficult for people to leak them.'

The Third Reading of the Teaching and Higher Education Bill provided an unwelcome example of the perversity of the parliamentary process. I had twice requested in writing that we should have a guillotine to limit the time allotted to the debate, but Ann Taylor [Chief Whip] wouldn't agree to it.

This was related to the old-fashioned view that we needed to have ample time to debate an issue, but we needed to avoid people being able to filibuster. For those who love the theatre of Parliament, filibustering is just part of the game. But for those of us who want to ensure that legislation gets through in at least a reasonable form, and that MPs don't have to sit through the night, it's not fun at all.

All day Ann snarled and growled and abused Clive Betts and, as everybody said, gave me the foullest looks. It was self-evident that we weren't going to finish by eleven or midnight. I was going to pull stumps at midnight but Jean Corston pointed out to me that under the rules of the House they could debate the damned motion of closure for another hour, so there was no point in my doing it. I confirmed this with Dennis Skinner when I had a meeting with him behind the Speaker's Chair. His view, as an expert on parliamentary procedure, was that Jean was correct, so we just had to plough on.

We dealt with city academies. I saw that off. We dealt with grammar schools. I saw that off. I then handed over while I went to meet the principals of FE colleges for a very quick supper. Jacqui Smith did sexual relationships and education, and then Malcolm Wicks (who had joined the team at the reshuffle) did great chunks of the rest of the evening. When I wound up the Third Reading at 1.25 a.m. I thanked everybody for staying, and I thanked Peter Brooke – Tory backbencher who had been Secretary of State for Northern Ireland – for his courtesy in thanking Malcolm and colleagues and myself.

I then picked up on the rambling and irrelevant speech of Ian Bruce, the Tory MP for Dorset South who had blatantly been wasting time since about 12.45 a.m. I said that if I had known that the Hon. Gentleman was going to make the speech he made at this time of the morning, I would have personally carried 78 people to the polling booths on 1 May 1997. The House erupted. People cottoned on really quickly that he had only been elected by 77 votes. I never expected the quip to be seen as being so funny, but they were all rolling about. It was one of those occasions when you just touch the mood. I then said: 'But as my friends know, I am deeply committed to timetabling every major piece of legislation in order to provide a legislature fit for a modern century.' Ann Taylor stormed out. She was in her car before I was and Barry, my driver, said that her face was like thunder. And they didn't call a vote on Third Reading.

All of this reminds me of the 1964–70 Labour government and, for that matter, the 1974–9. Richard Crossman in his diaries refers to these all-night

*sittings and late votes and the impact on the health and decision-making
capabilities of Cabinet ministers. Why, I ask myself, had we not learned the
lessons by the new millennium?*

*Evidently we were so bound into our history, to parliamentarianism, to
playing the game, that we as a radical party couldn't break the traditions –
and as soon as we had, we started to return to them, so that even the reforms
that were made from 2001 onwards were rapidly reversed. My own view is that
until Parliament has procedures that accord with the normal common-sense
view of men and women across the country and behaves in a way that
everyone else would expect, then we really cannot expect to receive the respect
we seek.*

So the Teaching and Higher Education Bill with all the additions in relation
to sex and relationship guidance and academies is through, and it will now
go to the House of Lords.

At Cabinet, Jack Straw reported on the hunting issue, saying that we
should be very careful not to over-commit ourselves to one solution
because hunting on foot in the uplands was a different matter from
hunting with dogs. I said, 'Do you mean the John Peel amendment?' There
was a murmur round the table and Tony said to Richard Wilson [Cabinet
Secretary]: 'Does he mean the disc jockey?' Everybody said, 'Noooooo, he
means "D'ye ken John Peel?".' John Prescott said, 'There is a generation
gap here, I think.'

Next week I pass Margaret Thatcher as the third-longest-serving
Education Secretary since the Second World War. Continuity is so
important. To have been here for three years makes such a difference.

A good piece of news at the beginning of July is that the Modernisation
and Reform Committee of the House of Commons is about to report, and
rumour has it that we might make some progress over getting a grip on the
absurd hours. If ever there was a reason for people, even with our big
majority, to understand what it must have been like to have a narrow
majority, it has been the recent weeks of all-night sittings! While the world
sleeps, we waffle on.

My Parliamentary Private Secretary and friend Jean Corston has told me
that she was thinking of stepping down from her seat in Bristol at the next
election, but Ann Taylor has suggested to her that she might chair the Joint
Human Rights Committee of the Commons and Lords and she seems
quite keen to do that. It will mean, however, that she steps down as my
PPS. She has done a phenomenal job and I am just so sorry that I have been

unable to do more for her. It will be quite a task to find someone to match her political nous and contacts on the back benches.

I was very fortunate that Paul Goggins, who was later to become a Junior Minister in the Home Office and Northern Ireland, agreed to take on the role. He was superb – and followed as he was by Andy Burnham (who also became a Minister in the Home Office, then a Minister of State in the Department of Health in 2006) and, for a short time, Laura Moffatt at the Department of Work and Pensions, I was extremely lucky to have such able, likeable and dedicated colleagues to help me.

July 2000

On the second Tuesday in July I met Chris Woodhead, who is getting more and more grumpy. This time he was grumbling about teachers' performance-related pay, not because we weren't being generous but because he believed we were being too generous in not reducing people's pay as well as increasing it. Well, I have enough on in terms of trying to win over the teaching profession to accept the enormity of the change we are introducing – in professional development, standards in the classroom, discipline and expectation. The idea that I should start threatening to reduce people's pay is just off the wall.

I indicated to Chris that I had read Melanie Phillips's article in the *Sunday Times* – which attacked us for not being radical enough and going further to create a market economy in education – and that I would be seeking a right of reply. I just thought that Chris needed to know that I am more than aware as to where stories emanate from, and that I do take note of them.

My friend Mike Lee has told me that he has just landed the plum job of Director of Communications for UEFA [the governing body of European football], with a house in Switzerland and frequent travel back to London to see his young son.

Mike had been my researcher when we were in opposition, before moving on to a consultancy. After his success at UEFA, he took on the daunting task of Head of Communications for London's bid to stage the 2012 Olympic Games, which by anyone's standards was a risk – but in Mike's case one worth taking, because the success of the London bid led to him setting up his own consultancy.

I feel proud of the fact that so many people who have worked with me, or been associated with me, have done well – and unlike those who spend their lives denigrating and pulling down politicians, all of those I respect who have done well in life have done so not at my expense but to my benefit.

Tony has done a special edition of *Question Time* in Brighton, and on the way back into London dropped into a pub to talk with the regulars. I wish he would do that more often. It seems to me that he is so good with people that if he could just be seen informally and spontaneously, just dropping in and meeting people, it would be so beneficial to the party – but I suppose it is just finding the time that makes it impossible.

This was a bit of a recurrent theme with me, and one which I kept on raising with Tony and the people around him. But of course after 11 September 2001 security issues kicked in, making things a lot more difficult and ruling out the kind of informality of 'dropping in'. It was a great pity and little understood, I think, by the public as a whole.

The final throes of the Comprehensive Spending Review. On the Tuesday afternoon I spent an hour and twenty minutes with Tony and Gordon in what the Secretary to the Cabinet, Sir Richard Wilson, later described as 'the feistiest' of the sessions. All the work of the cross-cutting reviews that had been set up the previous year (inter-departmental and trying to draw across traditional boundaries) may as well never have existed. What we had in front of us was what we had thought of in the first place. I am afraid it confirmed my view that quite a lot of what we do behind the scenes, in what the Tories used to call the 'Star Chamber', is pure theatre. In the end the question is – how much money is available and what priorities are we prepared to give to particular areas? The Children's Fund was the newest item on the agenda.

The Children's Fund was established to provide investment across departments, rather than for one particular purpose, and was established in two parts: one for investment that would be undertaken by government, using local government as the conduit; and the second tranche which would be for the voluntary sector.
I was supportive of the initiative but wanted to make sure that it was linked to what we were doing on education and standards, and not just an extension of childcare into the older age bracket – in simple terms, to develop what later

became known as the Every Child Matters agenda, which eventually led to the Children's Minister and a defined area and role for that ministry within the Department for Education and Skills. The task therefore was to link the Early Years agenda, on which we had done so much work, with the Out of School agenda and extended homework classes and support for parents and parenting.

It may be hard to understand why the nuances mattered but they really did, because while I was deeply supportive of broader efforts to reduce child poverty, I saw this initiative as being much more about trying to help people help themselves, rather than simply bailing them out. I was also deeply worried in case the money was going to be given to completely unaccountable and non-representative quangos, nationally and locally, who would then fritter it away on pet projects rather than getting into the major issues of changing the way in which families worked – overcoming dysfunctionality – and the aspiration and expectation that would transform the lives of children for the future.

Transferring the prison education service from the Home Office to us at the Department for Education and Employment is something I have been battling for, and something I would have liked to have worked on earlier. Jack is not being defensive about this, but I have made the point that the money that the Home Office is currently spending on education and skills within prisons is so poor that we are going to need substantial additional resources to make the service work. And we have to link it with the basic-skills agenda, so that the targets we have set to overcome adult illiteracy and innumeracy can take account of the largest population of innumerate and illiterate men and women – those in jail.

In any case, it is the only way in which we will turn round their offending behaviour. It is the only way in which we will be able to rehabilitate them and get them into a job. But it is yet another call on the funding, and as all the pressure is perfectly reasonably on increasing the funds direct to schools, anything that isn't funded properly now will end up being either cobbled together or simply managed on an ever-decreasing shoestring. Then when things go wrong, everybody will demand to know why what they had expected has failed to materialise.

And then I wrote this in my diary:

I wouldn't even mind getting the Home Secretary's job so long as we could really make a difference.

It was a funny thing to write at that particular time, because I wasn't pushing for the job, and in any case it looked horrendous from outside: police numbers still not back to 1997 levels, asylum and immigration taking off as major issues, and the prison population rising exponentially. But I think my philosophical predilection that we needed to create stability and security in order to reduce fear and to develop the agenda around citizenship and a sense of belonging must all have clicked in at the same time.

Tony backed me extremely hard on something that was crucial to the whole delivery of my policies, namely that the £1 billion announced in the March Budget should actually be incorporated into the baseline of the Department's existing budget, rather than counting as part of the newly announced expansion of funding for this Spending Review: in simple terms, to avoid announcing the £1 billion twice and to avoid a situation where the announcement in the Budget may as well never have taken place.

Therefore the political pressure to ensure matching what Health had got, and a really good announcement for the Spending Review, would have diminished. It was one of those absolutely key moments where fighting the battle to the bitter end was absolutely essential, even if the outside world didn't know what the hell I was doing. So I carried on fighting until the battle was won, but once again it was at a terrific price in terms of using up my political clout and trying to avoid my blood pressure going through the roof.

What is interesting about the contrast between my time in local government and now here in central government is that when you were dealing with the budget at local level, your baseline included an automatic update for an agreed basis of inflation, plus the consequences of any decisions you had already announced. You then started from there in terms of any new money to deliver new initiatives or build on what you were already doing. But not in central government, where the baseline did not include inflation, nor the announcements already made (unless you insisted) and therefore anything announced had to take account of the already agreed and automatic increase in spending.

We went round and round the houses on this, with officials from the Treasury and Sir Richard Wilson doing everything they could to argue that my own calculations were wrong. Gordon was very revealing because he sat there looking through his papers but only joined in at very crucial moments, rather than becoming involved in the affray. I thought this an excellent and very effective technique.

I won the argument in the end but it took another twenty-four hours before people accepted that the way I was calculating the impact was correct, even if I didn't get all the money that I had set out to obtain.

What we have agreed is the longest sustained run of increase in expenditure on education in Britain's history. It doesn't buy anything like as much as people outside think, but it is a manageable agreement and a hell of a sight better than I could ever have expected back at the beginning of the year. This makes being in government worthwhile. This is what I came in to do – to put in the investment that our opponents would never even have dreamt of, and to be able to do so on a long-term basis so that it really makes a difference. But we have to make it deliver, we have to continue the reform and modernisation in order to make it happen, to change practice, to raise expectations and standards, to make sure that the literacy and numeracy programme doesn't dip and that the pressure isn't off the accelerator.

In other words, we have to keep on banging away and making the increased spending the oil to lubricate the machine – and it is not doing so yet. A one-third increase over five years – and that includes the two frugal years at the beginning of this parliament – and a true transformation in the buildings and equipment we inherited will eventually make a difference.

Wednesday morning: we have been able to announce that we have created one million jobs. The press conference with Tony has gone extremely well and he is uplifted. Prime Minister's Questions today was one of the best he has ever done. We are beginning to deliver, and with the money in the Spending Review I can expand Sure Start, accelerate the literacy and numeracy programme, recruit teachers and repair the buildings – and Gordon will always ensure that the New Deal programme doesn't suffer so the employment side of the brief is almost taking care of itself.

And then the Annual Government Report – what a disaster.

This was a review of the activity and delivery of departments, particularly focusing on the targets that had been set. Even though we had good news, the report looked as if the government was being triumphalist – it was a gift to anybody who wanted to say, 'Well, they would say that, wouldn't they?' – and I was not sorry that the idea was quietly dropped after a couple of years.

God knows who invented this idea. We had done everything we could, given the pressures that were on with the Spending Review and everything else, to proof-read the document so far as our bit was concerned, but the press and Opposition were able to have a field day as it became quite clear that some people hadn't proof-read theirs at all – and in any case, a lot of it is out of date. We had pictures and nobody could explain why they were there. We had Culture, Media and Sport saying that the Institute for Sport had been established when nothing of the sort had happened. Talk about an own goal! This is where we get stuck on some idea of a way of presenting our achievements, but one that has not been thought through and goes badly wrong.

Meanwhile, before Gordon's final presentation of the Spending Review to the House of Commons, I was battling away over a legal action taken by the National Union of Teachers. Bizarre as it may seem, they were fighting to stop me from introducing performance-related pay (the increase in teachers' pay so that they would be paid more for staying in the classroom, but they would have to go through a threshold of quality before entering the new scales). In fact the NUT won on a technicality – that we hadn't properly used the School Teachers' Review Body to appraise fully what we were doing rather than seeking to implement the new structures in addition to the annual pay increase for which the review body was primarily responsible. It transpired that the legal advice that had been taken from outside government had warned us on this point, but it had been drawn to the attention of Estelle Morris too late and had never been drawn to mine at all. Of course, in characteristic Blunkett fashion, I overreacted. I was so angry that we should have had a presentational loss that looked as though the government itself had been defeated on performance-related pay that I blew my top.

Years on, it all looks trivial, but at the time there was a major propaganda battle going on to convince teachers that what we were doing was good for them – as, of course, it turned out to be.

The NUT were suggesting that we were scurrilously going to link everyone's pay to their immediate performance, and so the merry-go-round went on. The defeat was overturned and we did introduce the new threshold payments, the new scales and the concept of the advanced-skills teacher, but when you get defeated in court it does look messy. It looks as though the government has suffered a setback, or even that we didn't know what we were doing – when we did.

The Spending Review presentation is a triumph for Gordon. I am just relieved that we managed to sort out the final details, including avoiding a clash over what was to happen to child benefit for sixteen- to nineteen-year-olds with the introduction of education maintenance allowances.

The good news of the week was that we got the Learning and Skills Bill through the House of Lords and the key element on sex and relationship guidance went through by only fourteen votes, with eleven bishops voting for us. Had they not, we would have lost it. So much for those who continue to snipe at me for making an agreement with the churches. They obviously thought that somehow their belief in libertarianism would carry the day, whereas of course it was the exact opposite. It was those who were aggravated that we were being too 'liberal' who were the key, and only because the people we had been talking to, negotiating with, reaching agreement with, knew precisely what it was we were doing in achieving a balance and then voting for it did we get the thing through at all.

This is a classic case of self-delusion, where the liberal left believe that if they think hard enough that the world is with them, then somehow it is, whereas the very opposite is true. Britain is an innately conservative country and we need to win people over to progressive policies – and not just assume that they are automatically with us because we believe it.

We have succeeded – so everybody just takes it for granted. It feels rather like being a very good goalkeeper when you save an almost certain own goal and everybody presumes that it was dead easy because you pulled it off.

One of the problems of not being able to see is drinking orange juice when there is a wasp in it. This happened to me. I had it in my mouth and was about to chew it when something told me to spit it out. I did so, but it stung me and my mouth, face, arms and hands all started to swell. It was one of those frightening experiences when you think, 'There's no one around, what do I do?' Living on my own is sometimes quite frightening.

What was worse was that I was due to speak at the memorial service of the wife of a dear friend of mine, Councillor Peter Price. Janet, who had struggled against cancer for six years, was being commemorated in the cathedral in Sheffield. How I got through speaking my words and being able to read the Braille when my hand was swollen, God only knows.

The NHS Plan, when published, was a lot better than I thought it would be. Tony Blair and Alan Milburn did very well and I said in Cabinet that it was a good plan and they needed congratulating. I said that if anybody thinks dealing with the education service and professionals is difficult, they should try dealing with the NHS. I remember the difficulties only too well from the two years I was Shadow Secretary. What a challenge.

I think I would have gone even further than the Plan, with a massive programme of walk-in centres. We have got 500 health centres coming up, but they have got to be able to treat people. They have got to be able to do what the private sector is doing on cataracts and similar minor elective surgery (hips, knees and the things you can plan to do). It is the sort of thing that people really notice: if they were better off, they would be able to go into the private sector to be treated very quickly. If we can do it – and we should be able to – it will make a big difference to people's perceptions.

August 2000

Dinner at Andrew Adonis's home with Roy and Jennifer Jenkins and Peter Riddell and his wife Avril. A fascinating evening – intellectually stimulating and historically interesting, but slightly chauvinistic. I had to make a proper effort to ensure that the wives weren't left out. Roy had picked up that there was a real possibility of my being Home Secretary in the future, and said: 'Let me give you a piece of advice. Don't try and pretend that you can reduce crime. There is no way in which the Home Secretary can change the trends on crime because it is down to social policy.' So I said: 'Well, there's not a lot of point in being Home Secretary unless you accept that what you are doing on social policy from within the Department is going to have an impact, and that what you do with the police and the criminal justice service can change things.' He replied: 'Well, good luck. You will only get the blame and it is much better to hover above it than to try – and fail.'

I am horrified by this view. If we are not here to change things, to do whatever we can to adapt the tools we have at our disposal to change the lives of those we represent, then we may as well give up.

Both intellectually and in terms of his contribution to politics, Roy Jenkins was a very substantial figure. As Home Secretary he benefited from very progressive Private Members' Bills, but he also benefited from the respecting of privacy.

Roy is not unique in being one of those politicians of his era who would not have survived for five minutes in the very late twentieth and early twenty-first century, as intrusion into every element of our lives destroys the separation of the public and private, and the reverence in which those who were able to be 'aloof' could protect themselves. There are, of course, benefits in terms of transparency and openness, but it is also devastating with regard to people being able to live out their lives in their own way and in private, rather than having every aspect of their failings highlighted as though we live in a goldfish bowl.

Listening to Roy, it struck me how the 1964–70 Labour government was full of people of very great stature. Roy himself, Jim Callaghan, Barbara Castle, Richard Crossman, Anthony Crosland, Tony Benn: they did not necessarily form a highly successful administration, but they were all substantial figures.

Yet how would they fare today with the light shone upon them by 24-hours-a-day, seven-days-a-week scrutiny; with the necessity of coming up with immediate answers all the time; with all the attention on how successfully they were delivering; and of course with the necessity to keep winning elections?

How unfair will history be to the politicians of today, dealing with an entirely different political environment, one dominated by globalisation and rapidly changing technology? I suspect that what will be remembered from our government will be much more substantial than anything from 1964–70 or 1974–9 – or am I being arrogant and unfair?

Roy, who of course is Chancellor of Oxford University, told me at that dinner that I am a 'relative hero' at Oxford – referring to the spat between the university and Gordon over Laura Spence. I wasn't sure whether that was a compliment or an insult, but we parted on good terms.

Holiday in Majorca with Andrew and Hugh. (Alastair is having a separate holiday this year.) They are stars for coming with me, taking it in turns to look after their dad. The sun shines bright, but you have to feel it in your heart to be truly warmed.

Wednesday 16 August: the *Daily Express* has had a real go at those of us who have government accommodation.

I should have foreseen that this was going to be a continuing theme throughout my ministerial career, and had I done so I would have ensured that I had found a way of getting out of the government house sooner, whatever the consequences to me. It is hard to put your finger on what it is that irritates editors and journalists so much about government property, given how well senior journalists look after themselves, but it is a fact a life and one which I personally should have taken cognisance of a lot earlier.

And then I put in my diary something that was prescient with regard to what would be happening years later.

While I was away in Majorca there were riots, with mobs wrecking people's houses and killing their pets over the issue of paedophiles. Just reading about it was breathtaking. They had got the wrong people; they had trouble with names; they targeted houses where they thought paedophiles were lurking; they got kids out on the streets. It was all disgusting. Fortunately it has very quickly died down, but what a state of affairs, what a level of intellect and maturity. Thank God we are introducing citizenship and democracy into schools.

Years later I was to toughen the rules through the Sex Offenders Act, bringing in new measures to protect people by ensuring proper registration and supervision. I was also to resist what was known as Megan's Law from the United States, where paedophiles were named and exposed when they moved into local communities, rather than being tagged and properly supervised and treated.

Given the number of vigilante murders that occurred in the US once people knew that a paedophile was in the area, and given that in my time as Home Secretary attacks were launched on the homes of paediatricians because people misunderstood the difference between paedophile and paediatrician, I was glad that all those years earlier I had been revolted by the idea of lynch mobs instead of rational, clearly thought-through and effective policy.

While I was away I received an interesting 'Principal Private Secretary to Private Secretary' letter from Jeremy Heywood at No. 10, about our project to examine the impact of the euro on employment and unemployment and the lessons for Britain. At the moment we are examining the literature and we have gone so far down the road that they are not able to stop us, but the letter clearly implies (and it has Treasury fingerprints all over it, not least because of Jeremy's history as a Treasury official) that we really shouldn't have done this. It implies that this was out of order, and that before taking any further steps we should gain clearance from Downing Street. Also, that we should look at the potential for how the euro has affected employment in the eleven countries that have adopted it, rather than doing the work we are doing, which relates to the direct implications for and against entry for Britain.

Of course, the heart is with the manufacturing sector and whether it would be a good idea to join, but the head is entirely different in terms of what the implications would be for public expenditure and the future, for the next spending round and for our broader policies.

September 2000

And so to the autumn of oil-price rises; of blockades at fuel depots and consumer raids on hypermarkets for stocking food; of enormous political pressure; and of Labour dropping behind in the opinion polls for the first time since 1992.

The TUC came out strongly, backing the government in demanding that oil companies should deliver the oil that they have at the refineries and distribution depots. But the police seem incapable of acting – or unwilling. It had a peculiar ring about it to hear John Monks, General Secretary of the TUC, genuinely and really helpfully – but ironically in one sense – saying that the country could not be held to ransom.

I ended up on the *Today* programme on Wednesday morning doing the launch of the parenting guides, and ended up having to deal with the oil issue as well. On the same day I was in the middle of a live down-the-line interview with Radio 5 Live when the news came through that the Japanese bank Nomura had pulled out of buying the Millennium Dome. After Radio 5 had gone across to a reporter to hear this news they asked me what I thought, and I replied that it never rains but it pours – at which the interviewer said, 'Well, yeah, what about the oil crisis, seeing as you are talking about raining and pouring?' So I had to answer about that again.

This was clearly going to be a crisis if we didn't get a grip of it. It was also clear that we were going to have to reverse the decision to continue Norman Lamont's move, as former Chancellor, to have an automatic increase in fuel duty on what was called an 'escalator', which in simple terms means greater than inflation, linked to a particular formula. You can't help but wonder what the agenda of the oil companies has been in sitting on the supplies and being so very reluctant to breach the blockades, or picket lines as we used to call them.

TUC conference in Glasgow. Tony has been in Hull, where a dinner for John Prescott's thirtieth anniversary as an MP has been disrupted by the hauliers who, using mobile phones and new technology, have got themselves extremely well organised.

The fuel-protest episode was probably the first time the new forms of mobile technology were used in this way outside the military, and I think it came as a very big shock to the government. Later my attitude as Home Secretary was certainly influenced by it with regard to contingency planning for any events of this sort in the future.

I was surprised when taking on responsibility for these issues in 2001 to find that before the autumn of 2000 very little thought had been given to what the implications of new technology might be, and the way in which people would be able to use it so effectively. Animal-rights activists (as they call themselves) were already becoming familiar with these tactics, which were used first by those youngsters organising impromptu raves – which might have given a bit of a clue as to what to expect from more serious opponents.

Tony was due to open the rebuilt Firth Park Community College in my constituency on the Tuesday morning. Over the weekend and throughout Monday it became clear that the fuel situation was a great deal more serious than had originally been thought – more on account of inaction rather than the action that was being taken.

What appears to have happened is that people thought that the blockades on Saturday 9 September were tantamount to a gesture, almost a shot across the bows, rather than the beginning of something more serious, and it may well be that the organisers were taken by surprise themselves at the kind of response they got. We certainly were.

One of the other twists of new technology is the computerised 'just in time' delivery system, so that the kind of stocks which would have been available in the past, and the ability to distribute those stocks, were no longer there. So technological change was both a cause of deepening the problem and of enabling others to make it worse. The situation was considerably exacerbated by panic buying (including the panic buying of things like bread, which imparted a sense of impending doom). What strikes me as very curious is that the haulier drivers and the taxi drivers who have joined the blockades have no problems at all in getting fuel.

By Tuesday morning – the day Tony was due to visit Firth Park Community College – it was clear that the Prime Minister was going to have to take charge. I rang the Hilton Hotel in Sheffield, where Tony had stayed overnight – half a mile down the road from where I live – and spoke to Alastair Campbell, who put me on to Anji Hunter, and I then spoke to Tony. The message was very clear. There was no way they were going to be able to come to the school – not only because they didn't want to face some sort of spontaneous blockade (which I thought was a daft worry), but because it was felt that Tony needed to act and to be seen to act decisively, and therefore needed to go straight back down to London. How on earth could anyone argue with this?

It was awful for me to have to go to the school and explain to them that the Prime Minister had been within three miles of the school gates but was now unable to make it.

So I took myself off to the school and explained why Tony simply couldn't be with them, adding that he had promised to come back and do the official opening (his name being on the plaque).

He did so, in style, some time later.

There were no protesters at the school. I know my own community and they know me. They would have seen off those trying to blockade or block in Tony – which seemed to be the main fear of those around him – because my community had invited him as a guest, and although we may have our fair share of hoodlums we do still have some of those basic values that make Sheffield the city it is.

A phone call on Wednesday afternoon [13 September] to say that there is an Emergency Cabinet on Thursday morning. I was due to speak at the Vice-Chancellors' meeting so Tessa Blackstone will have to step in.

Tessa Blackstone was Minister of State for Higher Education throughout the time I was Education and Employment Secretary and handled all the departmental business in the House of Lords.

Estelle has been over to an emergency meeting on Wednesday that I couldn't get to. John Prescott was in the chair. She said that Jack Straw was being very calm and very strong but that he got very little support for decisive action.

One thing I discovered in government was that at all costs you had to be able to make decisions, to act decisively and not dither about, seeking refuge in 'further information' or allowing events simply to overtake you. I like to believe that if I had been in Jack's situation as Home Secretary I would have taken the same stance, but I would have had one advantage: as Home Secretary I took over chairing what became known as the Resilience Committee. I suspect that Tony's decision in 2001 to appoint me to do this, as well as chair the Counter-terrorism Cabinet Committee, was in part a result of his experience the previous autumn.

The Queen had signed the Emergency Order over Monday evening so the powers to declare a State of Emergency were available. The question was clearly – were we to use them?

It is worth mentioning that this was all supposed to be hush-hush in order not to heighten tensions still further, but no one had noticed that the Court Circular went out every day with Orders approved by the Queen, and so *The Times* printed it. It would be funny if it weren't so serious.

Downing Street asked me whether there was any pressure to be brought to bear in influencing public opinion by schools being closed and children not being able to attend, and what impact that would have. I said: 'My job is to keep the schools open, to move heaven and earth to ensure that there is as little impact as possible, rather than to highlight the impact that these people are having.' I know this isn't helpful in terms of putting pressure on the blockaders, but they are doing what they are doing simply because we are not taking decisive action. I don't want any excuse for anyone to be sending children home from school.

I've seen it all before. One fall of snow and teachers can't get to school, kids can't get to school and schools are too cold, etc., etc. Well, it's only September, it's not cold, people can share cars, and in most cases children can walk to school and teachers can do what I did in the 1978/9 winter, when I was a tutor at Barnsley College of Technology – which was to walk four miles through the snow to a railway station because there were no buses!

At least the fuel dispute has reduced to insignificance the serialisation in the *Mail on Sunday* of Julia Langdon's book on Mo Mowlam – complete with back-up pieces about Mo's sex life. This has been pulled forward because Mo has announced that she is standing down at the next general election. I don't think any of us are surprised.

Thank the Lord the Tories are so useless. They have not exposed the fact that in the eyes of the public we have been unsympathetic to the issue of fuel prices, and uncertain what to do. In fact they have published their own ridiculous proposals as an alternative to university fees – an endowment to give universities complete independence. God knows where they think they would get the money in order to provide a lump sum, on which students would then be able to draw down on the interest. You could not have invented a dafter proposal in a month of Sundays.

Charles Clarke has made the point that Andrew Miller, the local MP at the Cheshire depot, has been along and talked to those picketing, and what a good idea it might be for more of us to do so. It probably would be if only we had a decisive strategy alongside it.

Sunday 17 September: the opinion polls say it all. Here we are, with inflation down below 2 per cent [on the old RPI measure], unemployment down to 1979 levels, a wonderfully quiet August during which our opinion poll ratings went up in inverse proportion to our political appearances, and just weeks later we appear to be losing touch again. And while all this high politics is going on, I am trying to sort out what is happening with housing in my constituency. The Lib Dem council are creating absolute havoc in terms of demolition. It's not that I am against the plans for mixed housing, but the way it is being done is creating complete chaos, with tenants and community groups up in arms (and at the same time one of my local councillors has been arrested on a pornography charge).

A thousand people have turned out at one meeting about local housing and 600 at another, and this in an area where getting six people out is a considerable achievement. Not a word about oil prices: this is about their homes and their future.

I loved a column in the *Sun* by Richard Littlejohn, who obviously skipped history when he was at school, as he wrote that 'unlike this Labour government, Margaret Thatcher and Winston Churchill would never have attacked their own people'. So much for Tonypandy and Orgreave.

Here we are in September, a time when the media usually report that MPs are on an extended holiday, and all senior members of the Cabinet are appearing on radio and television almost hourly and the pressure is as great as at any time when Parliament is sitting. I am thinking of saying something along these lines at my next interview but I would probably get pulled to pieces for doing it.

We have all taken to walking to Cabinet. It is one of those spontaneous gestures that is about political survival. Jack was sneezing his head off and said that it was because there was 'no air in the bunker', the bunker being the room under the Cabinet Office used for the emergency meetings.

I was to become very familiar with the bunker as Home Secretary, not least after 11 September 2001, and it is certainly true that if you wanted to ensure that you cut people off from a sense of reality and end up with everybody having chest infections, then you couldn't have invented a more claustrophobic environment.

One thing that has really got up my nose is to hear Jonathan Porritt, high-profile environmentalist, interviewed on the radio and making none of the arguments about the use of energy and the impact on climate change and the environment that they are always banging on about. But it is perhaps not surprising, given that his Environmental Forum is at least partly funded by big business – including oil companies.

When the flak starts flying, the politicians find themselves alone.

I had talked to Tony about this on a more general front in terms of politics – namely that when taking on difficult issues, it is always worth having a look at which troops will still be alongside you when the real battle begins. In other words, you have to weigh up who is on your side and who is against you, and who will remain on your side when it is no longer fashionable. It is, of course, true as much in internal political circles as it is in terms of carrying policy and winning people over publicly. In September 2000 the vehemence against Tony (because, of course, as ever the focus was on the Prime Minister – whoever was Prime Minister) was palpable. When times are good, everyone benefits. When times are bad, it is the Prime Minister who feels the heat.

The TUC have remained stalwart. Bill Morris, General Secretary of the Transport and General Workers' Union, has bravely gone up himself to see his members in Scotland. This is a formerly unheard-of piece of solidarity and shows how seriously the trade unions are taking the situation. Who could have believed it?

A lighter moment of the week came when I was at Herdings School in Sheffield. I popped into a classroom unannounced and put my arm round a little fellow who had jumped up to say hello to Lucy, my guide dog. Unfortunately there was catarrh all down his front and I got it all over my arm and hand! There was chaos in the classroom so why the teacher didn't get some order and wipe their noses, Lord only knows. I thought to myself: 'Well, my job is snotty noses one minute, opening a school the next, unemployment figures the next and Emergency Cabinet the next – and it all makes for a very interesting, if somewhat fraught, life.'

Thursday before the party conference: the Key Stage 2 results (the results on literacy, numeracy and science for eleven-year-olds) are published, and they are up on the previous year. The programme is working, even though these youngsters have only had a couple of years of the new programme rather than having it all the way through from infant school. So all the effort and all the planning and resources and in-service training are beginning to be effective.

Tony and I have visited a school in Tower Hamlets where they got 80 per cent of the youngsters up to the expected level 4 in English and 75 per cent in maths. It is a phenomenal achievement in an area with a very high influx of recent immigrants from Bangladesh, and demonstrates that it can be done and that those who constantly say that it can't because 'this is too disadvantaged an area' are completely wrong.

Before going to conference I was listening to a cassette that had been sent up by the department, and it reminded me of some of the wonderful phraseology of the civil service. 'Stand ready' means sitting down doing nothing; 'content' means deeply irritated by what they have produced but not able at this point to devote the time to doing something about it; 'delighted' means 'I am begrudgingly agreeing to do this'; 'take your mind' means 'suck out any remaining semblance of initiative or innovation that you may have come in with' – like a space odyssey where your free will is taken away while the aliens occupy your mind.

Suddenly, despite the party conference starting tomorrow in Brighton, I feel so much more cheerful. It is amazing how up and down I go, and sometimes it is not at the moments you would expect.

The weather is the foulest that I remember it at conference. At least having had a cold during the past fortnight, I am unlikely to get another. If you don't get one before conference, you are certain to have one pretty soon – in and out of the heated, stuffy buildings, almost blown away along the prom, and too little sleep.

Monday saw another powerful speech from Gordon, but the issue of the week is pensions and there is no give there.

I upset the applecart on the Wednesday evening when I went to the reception hosted by UNISON, the union I have belonged to since the early 1970s. All the big unions hold drinks receptions and Tony, Gordon, John Prescott, Jack Straw and myself attend at least some of them. This is the final year for Rodney Bickerstaffe as General Secretary of UNISON, and therefore his last conference in the post: he had argued strongly for restoring the earnings link for pension updating. John Prescott pushed the microphone into my hand and said, 'Say something – you're a UNISON member.' So I did. I said that I thought that Rodney had made a powerful speech on pensions; that no one could have expected him, given his stance over the years, to have withdrawn the motion; and that we needed to respect each other and our right to differ. Unbeknown to me, *Newsnight* cameras were there, although it wouldn't have made any difference as I would have said the same anyway, but my words appeared not just on *Newsnight* but on the main BBC television news and were picked up by *The Times*. In this way was created one of those minor internal storms that are completely irrelevant to the world outside but cause enormous aggravation internally. I am going to be out of favour with Gordon and his entourage for some time, but a rift wasn't intended. I was merely speaking my mind. In any case, it is important to heal the wounds.

Who could have thought that six years later, the aggravations of con-
ference 2000 could have been so decisively put behind us when we adopted
the package of measures on pensions which I myself had worked on as
Secretary of State in 2005. As Margaret Thatcher once said, 'It's a funny
old world.'

Humdinger of the week: I asked the civil servants a simple question: is the Children's Fund a separate budget head, or have we missed it somewhere, because in trawling over how we are finally going to distribute the Spending Review starting in April next year and how we are going to determine priorities, I couldn't see where the Children's Fund was? I've been phoned and told: 'This is deeply embarrassing and we are very, very sorry but we have missed it.' Apparently this is because of the way in which the Letter of Direction is set out, and the way in which we have responded. One hundred million pounds, £150 million, £200 million to be found over the three years, while maintaining all the priorities and commitments that we have, believing that we have that £100 million, £150 million, £200 million in the bank for delivering the other services. It beggars belief. It is so breathtaking that it is too hard to contemplate. I haven't lost my temper. I haven't even got angry. I'm just so flabbergasted. What is amazing, of course, is that when they are to blame the Department can then cobble together money that would never have been available for spending had they not themselves made a total mess of it. In simple terms, they know they have to dig me out, and to do so they have examined every single budget again. The main challenge is to find the £100 million for next year because at least we then have time to put together the totals for the following years.

Amazingly they managed it. It took some weeks but it was achieved. Of course
I was pleased. I thought they had worked a minor miracle, by scrutinising
every £100,000 in every budget and scraping together the money.
  The downside, of course, was that the Treasury were rubbing their hands.
Quite understandably, they felt that if we could find that sort of money, then of

course we would not need a generous settlement, as things must be nowhere near as tight as I had been saying. But in reality they were now as tight as a drum! There was no room for manoeuvre, no reserve to draw on. We had to find money for the Children's Fund, even though it was not directly spendable on all the priorities that I wanted, given that it was a cross-government initiative.

October 2000

The other significant news is that, at my request, Andrew Adonis has faced down Chris Woodhead. Rumours have been rife for weeks that Chris has been seeking another job, either setting up his own company or writing for newspapers: we have proof that he has been making approaches. We have been building up to this for the past two years but we are not having him deciding he has to go, and delivering a last-minute denunciation of the government, just as Tony calls a general election. Chris Woodhead is so negative that I think he hates us all, in a quite personal way. Funnily enough it means that he doesn't even get credit for what he has done because he denounces everything around him, including of course his own contribution. He has been boasting about 'big money' columns for the *Telegraph* or *Mail*.

It transpired that Chris Woodhead had approached the Daily Mail, *who took offence when they discovered that he was already considering an offer from the* Daily Telegraph *and declined to offer the sum he had in mind. His* Telegraph *column proved not to be the success that either he or they had predicted.*

Andrew Adonis phoned me at breakfast time on Friday morning, 6 October – when I was temporarily distracted by the fact that I had no hot water in the house. I was trying to sort out getting someone to come and look at what had happened to my boiler so that I was able to have a shower and wash my hair. I listened to Andrew's message and rang him back, telling him that my view was that we should let Woodhead go as quickly as possible, that we have a file and that we are prepared anyway, and that I am prepared to stand up and support my policies. Andrew agreed that if Chris does go now, he shouldn't serve out the three months' notice, which is what he wants to do. He must go immediately. Andrew had said to him that he knew he was a Tory and that Hague had clearly offered him something, and Woodhead confirmed that he had been offered a peerage. Andrew said: 'Well, he can't offer you one immediately, so there is no question of that.' But clearly Woodhead would like to become a Tory peer and enter the political fray in a more overt way than he has been able to so far. Whether he ends up writing for the *Mail* or the *Telegraph*, he is going to attack us and is going to be unpleasant. I have checked the law and we have restrictions in relation to his outsourcing and working for companies but not with regard to his leaving and writing.

But even Chris Woodhead pales into insignificance against international news – the fall of Milosevic and the potential for sorting out the Balkans; and the opposite in Israel, with Sharon being deliberately provocative and undermining any chance of moving forward on the plans for peace. I rang my friend Alan Billings.

Alan Billings, who had been my deputy at Sheffield City Council, had built up a real expertise in international religions and their impact on civil society, and established a unit at Lancaster University that acted as a conduit for discussion and debate.

Alan's view reinforced my own instinctive feeling that what Sharon was doing was an absolute disaster – a calculated way of dividing, of reinforcing suspicion and bitterness and making it more difficult for the moderate Palestinian leadership to be able to do anything that would take the peace process forward.

A more positive note in relation to the Office for Standards in Education: the inspection results are very good. There has been a tremendous improvement over the last year in teaching quality, in the gap between successful and unsuccessful schools with regard to literacy and numeracy programmes and, particularly at primary level, it does look as if we are succeeding. I just wish that Ofsted had not tried to claim credit for what they were inspecting rather than changing.

My diary then has the following remark, which related to the introduction earlier in the week (2 October 2000) of the Human Rights Act, which incorporated the European Convention on Human Rights – nothing to do with the European Union but a separate cross-Europe convention which had been in operation for fifty years.

Now we have got the Human Rights Act in, everything will be all right for everybody – ho, ho, ho! It is probably the most hyped and overrated change in a very long time.

Sunday evening, 8 October: Andrew Adonis rang me to say that Chris Woodhead was in principle agreeable to going, but that the phone call had been recorded by Chris and that I needed to be very careful in taking things forward over the coming fortnight. He said that he (Andrew) had the impression that Chris Woodhead may change his mind. He also said he had never had a more difficult and distressing phone call in his life.

On Tuesday morning, 10 October, we had a meeting at Downing Street to work out how to handle the situation in which Chris Woodhead was playing all sides against the middle to get what he wanted – that is, to delay his departure and then take up a new role immediately after having left.

By Wednesday afternoon things had become so fraught that Tony and I had one of our least friendly conversations on the telephone, and in the end it was agreed that he would trust me to handle the situation and back whatever I did. Subsequently I had a face-to-face meeting with Chris Woodhead which was as unpleasant as Andrew Adonis's phone call – and in spades.

Suffice it to say, this wasn't the end of the matter. Chris Woodhead immediately rang Andrew Adonis, but Andrew told him that it was all now in my hands. We exchanged letters by courier on Wednesday night and then Chris insisted on seeing Sir Richard Wilson on Thursday morning. There was still some equivocation but it was all over bar the shouting.

The *New Statesman*, which never misses an opportunity to have a go at Andrew Adonis, carried an article by Francis Beckett trying to stir things up by suggesting that the policies we were following were those of Andrew rather than those of myself and my ministers.

The fact that I recorded this in my diary illustrates that Beckett managed to hit the bull's eye by irritating me.

In fact all our major policies can be traced back from the autumn of 1994 through Diversity and Excellence, Excellence for Everyone, the Excellence in Schools White Paper as soon as we got in. The fact that Andrew Adonis didn't come into No. 10 until 1998 has obviously escaped Beckett – and deliberately so.

In fact we have carried out almost to the letter what we had set out in detail, building on it with the Excellence in Cities programme alongside the reform of the teaching profession and the investment in professional development. Unfortunately it is usually from the left that we get the sniping, which is rather odd, because I would have thought that the children who have benefited the most would be those closest to their hearts.

Donald Dewar, First Minister in Scotland and a former Cabinet colleague, has died. He had seemed ill to me for a long time and then he'd had a fall, but clearly whatever was wrong had not been treated well. As ever, when you are dead people say the most wonderful things about you – quite the opposite to what they have said when you were alive. But that's the way it goes.

Donald was such a sad and lonely man. After his wife had left him to live with Derry Irvine he never seemed to recover, but it seems he had been lonely when he was young too. I am struck most by a quote of his which describes when he left school: 'I left school alone, and they left me alone.'

We flew up to Scotland for Donald's funeral, which was a dignified but very sad affair, with many people speaking who themselves must have had deep regrets about how much time they had been able to spend with him or spare to help him on those lonely Sundays and lonely Christmases. It made me feel very sad.

Thursday's article in the *Daily Telegraph* by Rachel Sylvester has an unnamed colleague who apparently 'would rather blow themselves up' than allow me to become Home Secretary. Who is it who keeps putting it about that I am going to be?

On Sunday evening, 15 October, it started to look as if Chris Woodhead would not resign after all. On Monday morning he and I had the most enormous up-and-downer, most of it conducted on the telephone – though I did see him briefly. But I stood my ground, and by Tuesday evening it was agreed with No. 10 that what I had been doing, and what I am doing, is right.

Not to exaggerate, we had had forty-eight hours when we feared that Chris Woodhead might call the bluff of the government and suggest that, on his departure, he was going to attack us so vehemently that it would be damaging. My line was that of Wellington: 'Publish and be damned.' I said that we had nothing to worry about: our record spoke for itself and the teaching profession would breathe a collective sigh of relief at his departure.

Here is a man who has made a really important contribution to rigour and to standards but who found it impossible to accord anyone else a difference of opinion or even a minute piece of credit. Now I had to handle it with dignity – which I did when, on his departure, he launched his most vehement attack. But being aloof, refusing to be aggravated, and not responding worked. For once in my life I didn't allow my own personal emotions to overwhelm the logical, rational way of dealing with what had become a very personal matter.

We were all united – Michael Bichard as Permanent Secretary, David Normington as Director-General of Schools, Michael Barber as Head of the Standards Unit, Conor Ryan as my key special adviser – all of us, and everyone around us. It is on such occasions that you know that you have pulled a team together, that people are working with each other, that the civil service, special advisers, and those from outside the Department are all on the same side, wanting you to succeed.

Another three-quarters of an hour with Chris Woodhead on the Wednesday – much more difficult than last time. He wriggled and wriggled about whether he would go voluntarily, but eventually agreed that he would. It was probably one of the most difficult discussions I have ever had and, I have to say, one of the better ways in which I managed to conduct a dialogue: I knew that he himself had to agree to go, and he knew that the best outcome for him would be for me to sack him. I have never played a hand of cards like it but it worked, and in the end he decided that he would fall on his sword.

I gave him a week to be able to determine and announce his decision – a way of setting a deadline without formally dismissing him. None of us was sure that this would work, but it did.

We've had one of those strange events in Parliament: a photograph of all MPs present at 2.30 p.m. on Monday 23 October 2000. I think I would rather be remembered for what I did or what I tried to do than for whether I was present, but the Whips were very keen indeed that we were all there.

I am not sure what happened to this photograph or what its relevance might be in future, but I do know that I thought it had little relevance to me at the time.

I spoke at Toynbee Hall, returning to my old themes of building from the bottom and enabling government. Jack Profumo had asked me to speak. He is eighty-five years old and a magnificent figure, a man who has devoted his life since the early 1960s to the improvement of the lot of others. If anyone who has erred has ever paid their debt to society, it is Jack Profumo.

Nick Brown, Secretary of State for Agriculture, Food and Fisheries, has made a Statement arising from the Phillips Inquiry into BSE [the crisis in farming over whether humans could contract 'mad-cow disease'], a Statement carefully drawn up by the civil service, a Statement defending a previous government, a Statement that mirrored the kind of words used by the inquiry report, describing the failure of MAFF to work with the Department of Health as 'inter-departmental reservation' – meaning that they hadn't passed information across and they hadn't thought that the implications might be somewhat greater than those being experienced by the farming community. I sat on the front bench for that Statement, which is one reason why it will stick in my mind for a very long time.

Never have we been kinder to our predecessors, especially in picking up the billions of pounds which the BSE crisis has cost all of us. Taken together with the cost of the poll tax and the mis-selling of pensions, we are displaying political benevolence on a grand scale.

It was only to be a matter of months before another catastrophe was to hit the Ministry of Agriculture, Food and Fisheries – namely foot-and-mouth disease, for which that ministry appeared equally ill-prepared.

Another phrase struck me from the report into BSE. This was about those clearly culpable in relation to what had been put into animal feed. 'It could be said that the animal-feed industry has not come out of the BSE affair with great credit.' Talk about the understatement of the year – words reminiscent of the way that Richard Scott had phrased his report into arms to Iraq.

I went back to the harsh reality of one of those things that don't touch the public mind, things so Byzantine in their complexity that they are rarely explained in any debate, column or commentary: the Standard Spending Assessment for local-authority grant distribution. Complex as it might be, this is absolutely vital, as it means money for education, for social services, for libraries, for roads and for all the things that people on a day-to-day basis naturally take for granted. But the proposals drawn up by the Department for the Environment, Transport and the Regions would suck money out of the very inner cities and northern counties into which we have been putting money through the Excellence in Cities programme for education, the regeneration programmes from the Department itself and the effort to try to restore police numbers.

The announcement on distribution of grant is always made towards the end of November or early December, and for the last half century there has always been a major problem in determining how the grant should be distributed. On this occasion, the way the formula was drawn up by officials – reflecting pay levels in London and the South East outside the public sector, but then skewing the grant as though public-sector workers were paid substantially more, plus the issue of population drift into the South East – was potentially disastrous for most of the northern cities, and counties such as Derbyshire and Staffordshire.

As ever the politics were contradictory, because while our programme of regeneration was aimed at lifting the most disadvantaged and deprived, the general election was going to be won in the Midlands and South of England and not least in London, where funding for education was on a scale undreamt of in equivalent northern urban conurbations.

If we are not careful we are going to end up with a system where we are pouring money in from several pots designed to help with deprivation, with the money pouring out at the other end in the redistribution of grant. All my experience in local government – notably the task during my time as Leader of Sheffield of trying to balance the books in the teeth of the massive withdrawal of central-government grant in the early 1980s – means that I do have some grasp of what I am talking about, but admittedly it does have the tendency to make me look like a know-all. It certainly gets up John Prescott's nose, that's for sure. John and I had words – not belligerent, but 'words' – as we went through the Lobby on Wednesday. But this one is going to run and run.

The foul weather seems to have caught the rail industry off guard, so here we are again with rail services grinding to a standstill, with everybody blaming everybody but themselves. I have a feeling that public transport in this country is disintegrating – another wonderful legacy from the Tories' privatisation and fragmentation. But someone is going to have to get a grip of Railtrack, and of the operating companies.

In South Eaton Place the central heating and the water heating has gone again. That makes three times this year.

I had to go into the department to have a shower on the Wednesday morning. I have always been pernickety in the extreme, and don't feel properly alive until I have had a shower and washed my hair in the morning, so the heating going off once again was more than an inconvenience. It was a major irritation.

November/December 2000

I've been trying to get some publicity for the fact that we are now down to 30,000 youngsters in infant schools with more than thirty in a class, compared with 485,000 two years ago. It is just amazing how difficult it is to get good news across.

We thought we had got ITV to cover a visit to a school to highlight the improvement in pupil-teacher ratio, but when they found out that the BBC were not going to run it, they dropped it as well!

I had a really nice supper on Wednesday evening with Cherie and Tony. It was one of the most relaxed I have ever had with them, and it was lovely to see Leo and Tony so close to each other. We talked through what I call 'the Balkanisation' of government, the breakdown of departments into tiny units and the splitting within departments, the fact that it changes the whole power balance within the Cabinet and the government as a whole. We talked over the oil blockade and the difficulties and where things had gone wrong, about pensions and what the possibilities might be, and about the Pre-Budget Report the following week.

I left behind material for Tony to look at on the slow progress of the combined employment and benefits agency. Understandably he doesn't get to see all these documents, and had never seen the correspondence in relation to the adverts for teenage pregnancy where I had taken out some of the most offensive words and had a major argument across departments about it (teenage pregnancy not being the direct responsibility of the DfEE). He was horrified when I told him that the government were about to put out adverts which included the word 'shag' prominently in them. It may be trendy and it may get the message across, but it is not acceptable for government to be using such language – at least I don't think so, and Tony agreed.

I have to remember that Tony's workload means that he has a pile of papers to get through before going to bed, and I think I may have overstayed my welcome by about a quarter of an hour. We do need to be sensitive to these things because at this time of night there is no civil servant to knock on the door and remind you gently, often without a word, that it is time to go.

This November has been dominated by the US presidential election result. To get more votes and to lose, to have votes disqualified spuriously in Florida because a machine didn't work properly, to have people denied the right to vote in the first place, overwhelmingly from the disadvantaged and black areas, to have judges ruling on the result in circumstances where the practical, technical election abuse is undeniable, just strikes me as staggering – coming as it does from the world's most powerful democracy. I am always preaching that order and stability are critical, by which token Al Gore's disputing the outcome is destabilising. But the argument that is now being put, that it is better to leave things alone, is an argument which those who manipulate or seek to corrupt the system could use any time, anywhere. One standard in Pakistan, another in America.

Voting in the US presidential election had taken place on 7 November, but after all the to-ing and fro-ing about the validity of the Florida result – dimpled chads, hanging chads and the rest – and recourse to the Supreme Court, Al Gore did not finally concede victory to George W. Bush until 15 December.

The initial results of the US election came through while we were on a DfEE Ministerial and Executive Board Awayday at Chevening, the Foreign Secretary's residence. It is the first time that I have been and it is a lovely place – if you can stand the clock chiming on the hour, every hour, throughout the night.

I played an episode of *Yes, Minister* as a stimulant to discussion after dinner. This series was so realistic – as well as extremely funny – that it is frightening.

Then in the morning, up for the Special Cabinet for the Pre-Budget Report. Gordon has agreed to £200 million extra for devolved investment for school buildings and equipment – known as capital spending. The argument has been about whether we should spend it from our own resources, but it has been taken from the windfall levy instead and will really make a difference in kickstarting the next round of improvements, rebuilding and renovation.

We were now really motoring on a transformation of the whole of our school system, an initiative that was to be complemented three years later in 2003, with a further boost in 2005. By the time I left the Department for Education and Employment we had quadrupled the amount of money being invested in new building, repair and improvement in equipment, and over the subsequent five years this amount was to be trebled again.

As with so much of government action, the actual decisions are made two or three years before the results start to become visible because of the time it takes to agree the plans, get planning consent, start the building and complete and occupy. In 2000 we were only just beginning to see the results of decisions taken back in 1998 with money allocated in 1999, but I am very proud indeed of what we were able to start in those early years, reversing the neglect of two decades of Conservative government.

Gordon did well again with the Pre-Budget Statement, getting the balance right in dealing with the truckers and ensuring that further threats of blockade came to nothing. It is amazing to think back two months – how quickly the atmosphere changes, and the political outlook with it.

The increase in the winter fuel allowance from £150 to £200 a year for retired people is a clever move. The psychology is obviously very good and something needed to be done, not just to reassure people in relation to their worries on the fuel front, but more critically in relation to their anger about the pension increase.

Thursday 16 November saw publication of the school performance tables. They not only show that things are really improving, but just for once the publicity reflected that. People are just beginning to see that things are changing, and it is still very early days in terms of what can be done and must be done.

Sunday 26 November: I have been feeling rough for about two weeks, but suddenly am a great deal better and able to face the run-up to Christmas – as well as some of the continuing battles over local government funding and the like. The Department for the Environment, Transport and the Regions has discovered that their statistics were 0.6 per cent out, which doesn't sound a lot but is a hell of an amount of money with respect to what is available for distribution and what the floors and ceilings for each category of local authority should be.

This mattered a great deal, because if we were going to have an amount below which no authority would fall in terms of the uplift of spending – taking account of inflation and wage increases – then obviously this would mean less at the top for those authorities that were the great gainers from the distribution of the funds.

As it was the less advantaged areas on the whole that were going to rely on the guaranteed safety-net increase, it was crucial to reduce the enormous gains that some authorities were making under the formula for distributing the grant.

Whatever the opinion polls had been saying, a better measure of the government's standing towards the end of 2000 was the three by-elections held

*on 23 November: at Glasgow Anniesland (Donald Dewar's seat); Preston
(made vacant by the death of Audrey Wise in September 2000); and West
Bromwich West (which had been won in 1997 by the then Speaker, Betty
Boothroyd, and so had not been contested by the major parties: the by-election
followed Betty's moving to the House of Lords in October 2000).*

Supporting our campaign in the West Brom by-election, I visited a school
where the children had been told that I was going to tell them a story. The
local radio station also believed that I was going to tell them a story, except
that nobody had told me. So I had to make one up on the spur of the
moment, and I asked if any of the children had a rabbit. One little girl –
these were four-year-olds – told me she had a rabbit called Lucy and an
uncle named Kevin, so I was able to explain that my dog was also called
Lucy and went on to invent a little story about the dog saving the rabbit
from the fox which was getting into the garden and threatening the rabbit
hutch. Lucy was nearly shot by Uncle Kevin who lived down the road and
had heard the kerfuffle, seen the fox and had a rifle from the Second World
War. But having mistaken Lucy for the fox, it was only the intervention of
the little girl running out to shout, 'No, uncle, no!' that saved Lucy from
being the victim rather than the victor. All this went down a bomb with the
four-year-olds, but when I was coming out of the classroom I met the little
girl's mother, sister of Uncle Kevin. I said: 'Please let me apologise if I have
embarrassed your brother. Tell him I was only pulling everyone's leg.' She
replied: 'Kevin had one of his legs amputated two weeks ago.' I wished the
ground could have swallowed me up.

We are having difficulty again in relation to answering parliamentary
questions. I don't know whether there has been a hiccup in the section that
deals with this area, whether people have changed or whether they have
just lost interest, but if we put down some of the answers they send through
and if my special advisers weren't on the ball, we would have a constant
storm.

Take an answer to a parliamentary question (hostile) about how much
money has been donated by the private sector in Education Action Zones.
The answer has come up on the figures for two years ago, on the grounds
that they are the only ones that have been audited. The up-to-date figures
that are available are very good, but two years ago the Education Action
Zones had only just started. If I had put down the figure as given to us by
officials, there would have been a real row about 'failure' and 'another
initiative bites the dust'. We would have then spent forty-eight hours on

the defensive trying to say that the better figures were the ones that we hadn't put down. In the end we put the whole of the figures down, not just the audited ones.

In answering parliamentary questions, or under the new system of laying written statements, it is absolutely vital that the whole of the story is outlined, rather than just the specific question itself answered. Very often a clever question asks for a very limited amount of information, information that is then re-presented by our opponents to demonstrate whatever point they are trying to make. It would be quite wrong not to answer the question, but to answer it more fully makes a great deal more sense politically. This is where the politics of the real world clash with the apolitical stance of the civil service, who often think that doing more than simply going through the motions is somehow to be politicised.

I commented on this in my written and verbal evidence to the Public Administration Select Committee at the end of June 2006. The way the process works does explain why, on many occasions, there are strange results from the answers given to parliamentary questions and why it is that governments, despite their resources, so often score own goals.

To Harrogate for the Association of Colleges' annual conference and the launch of the pamphlet setting out a way forward on vocational education and excellence in the further-education sector – Centres of Vocational Excellence, as they were to be known. A new beginning for sixth forms, sixth-form colleges and further education. The 4 million people a year who go through further-education courses, in addition to sixth-formers, are so often forgotten, and yet it is absolutely vital for our economy and prosperity. It is just not something that touches the public arena. It is not something that you win or lose elections over. So it is quite a battle to keep a focus on it.

I seem to be speaking better at the moment. It was true of the leadership conference on the Thursday morning that I did with Tony: leadership, so absolutely vital to standards and to transforming schools but so difficult. There has been so little attention paid to leadership in the past, and it is so important to get the National College for School Leadership off the ground and above all retrain the 24,000 heads already in the system. All Tony and I can do is try to inspire and encourage, and indicate that we do really care. The New Year and Birthday Honours will help but they are only a gesture.

At least heads will be getting damehoods and knighthoods for the first time ever, and good heads may well inspire others. We will see.

But what a Thursday on the 23rd: Cabinet, oral questions in the House, the leadership conference and then a flight up to Leeds (again), this time for *Question Time* on BBC1. Leeds Bradford airport was in danger of closing because of fog and we thought we were going to have to fly to Manchester and a great kerfuffle ensued about getting a car there. But in the end the scheduled flight to Leeds Bradford was able to take off after all.

And surprise, surprise, after everything that has been happening, we won all three by-elections.

January 2001

The year 2000 has been really strange, and I am hoping that 2001 will perhaps be the true beginning of the new millennium. Who knows what will happen politically? I can't help but be apprehensive. We will have the general election and its result and then the reshuffle, when you find out where you are and what you have to do with no notice, no time to prepare and no handover period. Not for us the luxury of having a week or two to get to grips with the issues and policies. There is the Queen's Speech followed by the Second Reading debates. And at the precise moment when a Labour government wins a full second term, the Opposition will delay any reshuffle and so will have people in place who, just for a short time, are likely to know more than a government minister at the Dispatch Box about the subject under discussion, particularly if the Bills have been debated more than once in the previous session and then fallen at the general election.

It is the protocol that when a general election is called, those Bills that have nearly completed their stages are negotiated between government and opposition parties so that the whole of the legislative programme started in that particular session (in this case over the winter) does not fall. However, many Bills that are only part-way through are blocked by the Opposition, who at this moment have the whip hand. A Bill could have gone through all its House of Commons stages and just entered the Lords or vice versa and still fallen. The process then has to start all over again if, of course, the government wins the general election and reintroduces the legislation. Even within a political party there will be differences between ministers, so a new ministerial team coming into a department may decide to change the legislation that they inherit. The direction – and for that matter the values – of the government can remain the same but the approach to policy and delivery can be very different.

I went to see Enid Hattersley, Roy's mother, at her home in Sheffield. At ninety-six she's in very poor health, and this made me reflect on how sad it can be to grow old. People said to me when I spoke of her, 'Oh, is she still alive?' and I know that one day perhaps, if I live too long, people will say the same about me. They will ask who I was – or more importantly, what I was.

I had a session with Tony on the Tuesday about the Knowledge Economy White Paper and just went round the houses a bit. The fact that Steve Byers and I had not read it until Tony had got it didn't help, and I have to say that we all agreed that it was pretty useless and needed a lot of work doing to it. It is not good when Tony sees things before we have had a chance to look at them because he must think that we have approved them.

It was highly unusual for raw material to be passed across to Downing Street without my having crawled all over it, but on this occasion we were running out of time – a general election was imminent – and Tony's staff had specifically and unequivocally requested that they saw the material emerging from the Department at the same time as we were getting to grips with it. Of course we had had the discussions and seen the 'submissions' [the term for component parts before they are put together into something more coherent], but simply seeing the parts does not constitute seeing the whole of a co-ordinated and well-thought-through policy paper.

In fact many such papers emerge without proper co-ordination or are supported by bland statements rather than clear principles and values that make sense of the individual propositions. This is why I spent so much time in government going over, again and again, anything that was to emerge publicly.

I saw Tony later and he asked me what I thought about William Hague's little forays on issues relating to policing and immigration. I said that I thought Hague knew what audience he was playing to and that it was calculated, and that if it had been anyone with greater credibility than William Hague it would have damaged us. Tony said that he agreed entirely and was really worried about it. I also took the opportunity to ask him about the Working Age Agency [the combined employment and benefit agency that became known as Jobcentre Plus] and said that I had just one request – which was that he talk to Andrew Smith. He said, 'Andrew?' and I said, 'Yes, you gave him the job of chairing the working group and seeing it through from the Treasury.' He said, 'I perhaps take a different view but Alistair [Darling] is a good bloke,' and I said, 'Yes, he's a very good bloke, Tony, but that's not the point. I can see the problem you have got but this is a total mess. We do have to resolve whether to amalgamate the two agencies (benefits and employment) and which department is to be in charge. What do we say to people?' He said, 'Well, that is the issue.' I said that Richard Wilson would be writing to him – and he did.

I include this only to show how difficult it is when dealing with structural change. The Working Age Agency had been thought by myself and Michael Bichard to be the way to pull together the benefits and employment system, not merely structurally – jobcentres and Benefits Agency offices – but as an end-to-end process. It was, in fact, to prove a great deal more difficult to achieve this than either of us had envisaged, not merely in getting the agencies together (that proved to be the least of our problems) but rather the major issue of adopting modern technology while trying to make enormous savings and deliver results at the same time.

Had we not had a continuing reduction in unemployment, we would have been in very deep trouble. When I eventually became the Work and Pensions Secretary, inheriting the new agency along with a great deal else, I realised just what had happened in the intervening years. The plot had been lost somewhere along the line. In simple terms, we were delivering mechanistically rather than in a way tailored to the requirements of particular individuals or groups of individuals with specific needs. The upheavals of 2005 and through into 2006 in relation to the introduction of new phases of technology should have been predictable but were not.

It still does not mean, of course, that the original concept was wrong. Alistair Darling had been Social Security Secretary at the time and Andrew Smith (taking the job that Alistair had had in the early period of the parliament) was Chief Secretary. It was in this 'independent' role that Tony had asked Andrew to try and knock our heads together. The Permanent Secretary at the Department of Social Security was vehemently opposed to the new agency, but I ask myself now why on earth did I spend so much political energy and personal goodwill on the idea of a major change in the machinery of government?

It says something for Alistair Darling that he and I never referred back to this period, nor did either of us feel any form of personal antagonism because of this incident. I shall not go into detail here about the nature of the correspondence or the leadership shown by Richard Wilson. Suffice it to say that in private enterprise, something very different would have been expected – in fact required.

The Dome ended the year as it had begun it – under attack. Everyone who had given any money or support to the Labour Party was now under scrutiny, I am afraid, but that was something we just had to expect and deal with.

It has become very clear that the tactics of the right are now to discredit me and everything we have done on education. When they can't discredit what we've done, they claim that we're acting fraudulently, that we were fiddling the figures. They're so deeply sneering and cynical, especially Melanie Phillips in the *Sunday Times* and Peter Hitchens.

Getting into the swing of things after the New Year was very difficult, even though I had been working at home. On Thursday I went to an IPPR [Institute for Public Policy Research] seminar and was called out because there was going to be a meeting on local-government finance, and was then told when I got in the car that the meeting was cancelled; so I returned to Cabinet; then went to Education and Employment Questions; then rushed to Paddington and got the train to Heathrow; sat on the tarmac for forty-five minutes and arrived late in Manchester; went to St Edward's School; went to Crosby to a jobcentre; then crossed the Wirral to attend a dinner for fellow MPs Steve Hesford and Ben Chapman. Steve is in the most marginal seat we have. I had a really good reception at the dinner, which was at the Tranmere FC ground, but was I tired. I didn't get away until 10.30 p.m. and got home at 12.30 a.m. exhausted, as I had also tried to get through some work during the day. The following day, Friday, was busy in the constituency. I visited Hinde House School, Northern General Hospital, and Hucklow School, then went into the office in the city centre and back home before going to the constituency monthly meeting in the evening.

I then had my constituency surgery on Saturday morning followed by community meetings afterwards. I spent the remainder of the weekend dealing with the Royal Society of Arts speech, with the draft pamphlet for the Institute of Economic Affairs for the week after, with the Knowledge Economy White Paper (which was absolute garbage), which I had to go through, plus correspondence, plus policy papers, plus trying to write speeches for the Tory half-Supply Day on recruitment that they called for Thursday 18 January. I had to make notes on that, and also to prepare speeches for the Spanish/UK seminar in Birmingham (I had to speak in the afternoon and again at the dinner).

Two thoughts strike me about what was a typically pressurised period. The first is that there is only so much of this that anyone can take without losing a sense of reality. The second is just how much punishment it is possible to take when the adrenalin is running and it is felt to be worthwhile. That's what I miss most now that I am not in the Cabinet: working at the front line. At times when I was extremely busy, I used to yearn for the opportunity to have a chunk of the weekend off, to be able to walk and think and play music and eat with friends. Of course, when the pressure is off and it is possible at last to do all those things, I just wish I was back in the thick of it.

I have never met a politician yet, at least not one with any ambition, who does not think, other than on very rare occasions, that they can do better than the people they see in the thick of things. As for Tony and Gordon, I have to say, to be fair to them and to myself, that there have been many occasions when I've thought, 'I don't think I could have done better than that.' There have even been occasions when I have thought that, quite frankly, 'I could not have done that anywhere near as well.' If you are to survive at the cutting edge, and if you are to have any influence at all, then you do not admit to such modest thoughts in the hearing of fellow MPs (and particularly not journalists). Taking comfort with friends is a rare and treasured aspect of holding on to those long-standing relationships that don't let you down when things go wrong. I am afraid, though, that too often we use the term 'friend' when we mean 'acquaintance' – and in politics even long-standing acquaintances do go to parties and to dinners, do mix with journalists, do sometimes forget what is private and what is public, and what is to their benefit and what might be to yours.

The next week I tried to get some movement on the Working Age Agency. I thought I had reached agreement with Andrew Smith but he discovered that we were talking about Appendix C to the original papers that Richard Wilson had put to Tony, whereas Alistair Darling was talking about Appendix B. So having thought that we had reached a compromise, we ended up back at square one.

Any hope of success for the department in the local-government finance settlement started to slip away, as in the words of Jeremy Heywood [Tony Blair's Principal Private Secretary] to Mike Wardle, Gordon and Tony had not so much a discussion as a slanging match. The Treasury apparently felt that the settlement was fine and that it was the way that we were spending the money that was the problem – presumably on things such as discipline, literacy and numeracy, reducing class sizes, etc. I put forward some proposals that I hoped would allow us to free up £50 million for a special grant. What we really needed was for John Prescott not to have to find housing money from the regeneration budget, but real new money.

Went to Wolverhampton to see Winifred Golding, who was alert and bright.

Winifred was a councillor when, at the age of twenty-two, I was catapulted into the local council seat in Southey Green, where I was living with my mother at the time. With just a few weeks to go before the election, the local branch took a big risk and decided to put forward a 22-year-old blind man. Winifred acted as a mentor, taking me under her wing, sometimes clipping my own wings but mainly showing me how to use them. To be honest I think we forget too easily the contribution that people have made. In politics, when you're gone, you're gone, and if you are lucky you are left with your close family and those really good friends who wanted to know you before you were 'somebody' and still want to know you when you are a 'nobody'.

I had meetings about Welfare to Work on the Tuesday. I saw Tony first about the local-government finance and met him again after Prime Minister's Questions.

I was trying to get hold of John Prescott. I gave him a ring at the weekend as I learned that his dad had died, but he had already left for London, and I didn't trouble him on the journey as it is useless trying to talk to people on mobile phones that keep cutting off.

It is sad that John and I had continuing difficulties and that a rift gradually opened between us. We both reflect a particular northern background and a propensity for straight speaking – and sometimes shooting from the hip. I shall never know what particularly triggered the antagonism and suspicion he showed towards me, but one thing is for sure – it reached the point where it was virtually impossible for John and myself to have a civil word together, and where if there was the possibility of believing something unpleasant about me, he would believe it.

We then had the Welfare to Work conditionality meeting. Gordon came in late and spoke briefly but what he did say was reflected entirely in the minutes.

We had a constant tussle over conditionality (you only got the funding if you were prepared to follow the rules). People blew hot and cold. Sometimes we

were going to get really tough and then at the vital moment we would waver.
The timing never seemed to be appropriate, and during the run-up to a general
election it is doubly tricky to get it right.

I do think it a great pity that we didn't try harder, so that a great deal of
what was presented five years later in the Welfare Green Paper of January
2006 might already have been achieved. But the truth is that in politics, as in
so much else, you set down one building block and wait until the right political
moment when you can place another block on top of it. It is a gradual process
of changing minds, pushing out the boundaries and establishing a foothold. It
is painful and it is slow – but it is the reality. Try and do something at the
wrong moment, in the wrong way, and you can be set back sometimes for
years. It was of course Lenin – who, languishing in Switzerland, waited until
the appropriate moment had come to cross in a train to revolutionary Russia –
who remarked, 'Timing is all in politics.'

I think part of the problem was that I was trying to deal with the education-
strategy document, contributing to the Knowledge Economy White Paper,
writing a pamphlet for the Institute of Economic Affairs and dealing with the
media, as well as the continuing silliness over teacher recruitment. I grew sick
and tired of the word 'crisis', a word that was continually being bandied about,
and felt that it would simply serve to put off would-be teachers all the more.

Looking back, it is clear that I was far too focused on – and irritated by – what
the media were saying about teacher recruitment. If I had my time again, I
would recognise that some things pass in the night as the measures you have
taken begin to bite. Of course, making a judgement on what will and what will
not go away is a particular art – one that I think I was reasonably good at
politically, but obviously not as far as my own personal well-being was
concerned, as I was to find later.

On Sunday lunchtime I aired general public-service issues on *The World*
This Weekend on Radio 4. It wasn't very sparkling because I was just not
feeling sparkling. I was under-performing, not with regard to turning
things round, just as far as general activity was concerned; I was feeling a
bit down. Not surprising, I suppose, bearing in mind the amount of time I
was spending working at weekends.

I have rarely done interviews about – and even more rarely written about – the
way I work and the challenge of overcoming blindness. But it seems appro-

priate at this juncture, as I enter what I consider to be a new phase of my life, to reflect a little and perhaps to offer a better understanding of what it has been like to deal with avalanches of paper, to have all print material read on to tape, to ensure that people stayed long enough in the Private Office to become competent in summarising and presenting material in a truncated form – and, of course, of the time I needed to take to absorb, to listen to and to be on top of the material in a way that would never allow people to be able to say, 'If only he could see, he would have understood that better.' I haven't been able to prevent completely their speaking in such terms, but I hope I have proved that such a suggestion is quite untrue.

When I first entered Parliament I struggled to get some additional equipment (for Brailling) and additional staffing hours for reading, and will never forget a remark made to me by one colleague who became a very senior Cabinet minister when we came to power in 1997: 'It's all right for you with the extra resources you get. No wonder you can churn out the press releases.' My reply was fairly succinct: 'I'll swap with you any time.'

To be fair, most people around me were very understanding, and I know that colleagues were careful to ensure that their own offices provided material in a format and within a time period suitable for translation into Braille or putting on to tape, for which I have always been grateful. But there are always one or two people who seem to resent the fact that despite lack of sight, it is possible for me to work on equal terms with them.

It is an attitude I have encountered throughout my parliamentary career. When I first entered the House of Commons in 1987 I came across many who were patronising, even if they meant well. Of course I was very sensitive about people being indulgent to me, and my pigheadedness, my inherent independence and sometimes my unintentional rudeness soon put paid to any do-gooding. I didn't want to be promoted out of sympathy, though it was never easy to pull off the feat of being seen to be effortlessly on top of things. Sometimes I have thought of nothing else but how I was going to get through the masses of tapes that arrived in the box each weekend or the nightly tapes that had to be done either that evening or at least first thing in the morning. And caring for my three eldest sons each weekend and wanting to keep their own commitment to see me and to spend time with me also took up an enormous amount of time while I was in opposition and at the beginning of my eight and a half years as a Cabinet minister.

In these early years of government the sheer volume of work left no time for 'gallivanting around in London', as my mother would have called it. I was at that time very much what the press saw (and wanted me always to be): the *dedicated, workaholic, almost obsessive, dour northerner. For me those days of commitment and dedication were good years, productive years and protected years. The only way I knew to stay on top of the job was to give it 150 per cent. This often made me seem aloof, distant and anti-social. I got to a stage where even talking to friends on the telephone seemed to be getting in the way of being on top of the job. What a terrible thing to admit – that sometimes I just wanted to curtail the conversation because I knew I had so much to do and it would not wait. I now ask myself: what sort of life was it, what sort of management of my own time and priorities, and could I have done it better? Getting up earlier and earlier in the morning was one solution. When I was in opposition, I used to be able to stay in bed until 7.30 a.m. What luxury! By the time I left the Home Office I was regularly awake just after 6 a.m. Putting a cassette on to my machine and listening to it while I made breakfast, while I was on my exercise bike and even, when things were pretty desperate, trying to listen to it while I was in the shower, became a normal part of life.*

The difficulty of being able to dictate notes at the same time as doing two other things was a juggling act that I didn't always manage, though I could get out my mobile phone and leave answerphone messages on the specially constructed series of answerphones that we had in the office. When I was at the Home Office, answerphones filled up so quickly that we had two or three so that I always had a back-up. This was in lieu of email, because using a computer and tapping into the world-wide web was something that was going to have to wait until I left office in 2005. With staff available and with the daunting task of having to go through the training and learn how to cope with the synthetic voice (and the enormous time that it would take to access information), it made sense at that time simply to use support that was available from the civil service. So answerphones and the tapes I handed in were my method of communication.

If I was handed a printed document or a letter from outside the Department, I would dictate a note relevant to its content and enclose it with the tape, or I would just wait and hand it in to the office, explaining what it was and what I wanted doing. My speed of working, my method of working and sometimes my lack of appreciation of the importance of carefully filing printed material (which to me was, of course, secondary) does not explain why in 2003 I found myself handing in a departmental standard letter on visa renewals without giving a second thought to the personal danger in which it might place me at a later date.

Feeding and grooming a guide dog, and of course making sure that it is exercised and has a chance to do what the Guide Dogs for the Blind

Association call its 'spend', are all-important. So each morning my dog and I would set off walking (having handed over to my driver official material and any other bulky or cumbersome items that needed to be taken into the office). We would have a decent walk and the car would collect us. We would then run the dog properly (often but not always in New Palace Yard at the House of Commons) before going into the office. I did not, in fact, get to the office as early as some of my colleagues. I preferred to work at home in peace and quiet where I could clear the backlog.

Each morning I would, however, have had a phone call from the press office. They were lovely young – forgive me if I call them that – people who volunteered to do a rota for what increasingly over the years became an extremely grumpy man. The more difficult the coverage we received, the grumpier and more bad-tempered I became.

It is a tribute to the tolerance and dedication of those working in the press office that they were prepared to put up with me: reading over the headlines and the key items, taking down what I wanted to have read in full on to tape, reacting as quickly as they could to my bark of 'For God's sake, get that to . . .' when I came across something which I knew the civil service themselves would not have picked up – or if they had, would have done nothing about it. It always staggered me that even with some ministers, it was necessary to pick out items from the daily press or from the early-morning bulletins and ensure that action was taken either to find out the truth of the matter or urgently to put something right. Those less prone to reach for the whip and to want something done immediately seem to have a more relaxed time – and, it has to be said, in some cases were no less effective. But this was part of my insistence on doing things the only way I knew – thoroughly.

Once in the office (where I would have agendas Brailled so that I could chair meetings, as well as a daily diary) I would set about working through the internal discussions, the meetings with external partners, organisations or MPs who were wishing to lobby; or, on many occasions, turn things round very quickly, pick up new material and then head off for either a conference or a visit, taking things with me to work on in the train or in the car. We had to swap the first car I had (inherited from Roger Freeman, the former Transport Secretary, as it was suitably stretched to allow the dog space to lie down) because the road noise was so great that I simply could not hear a word that was being said, and staff listening to tapes that I had made in the car could not hear the dictation. It was therefore necessary (and I got some ribbing for this) to get a better car, with much better soundproofing, less road noise and a quieter engine.

All the time I spent travelling would otherwise have been dead time, and working while travelling was the only way in which I could possibly turn the work round. Every minute of every travelling hour had to be spent working. It was the only way. I kept a Braille machine of my own on my desk so that I could make notes (and keep a record of things that I had asked to be done) which always caused people some disquiet, as I think it is common practice to believe (not just in politics) that when someone asks for something to be done, there is always a fair chance that they will forget all about it. Contrary to common assumption, I didn't always rely on my memory, although I did try to develop it, much in the way that one develops a muscle, to ensure that with particular aspects of the job it was possible to achieve better recall than would normally be the case.

It is worth saying at this point that my broader recall is no better than anyone else's who has a good memory. I cannot recall a sonnet any more clearly than the next man or woman – but I can recall facts and figures, I can recall dates and, above all, what people said and the context in which they said it, purely because I trained my memory specifically to cope with the job.

The same is true of my hearing and my ability to be able to sense what is going on around me. I am still learning, and I still sometimes get it wrong. When I am chairing a meeting I often ask people to indicate to me when they want to speak with a quiet word or cough, or make some other sound to show that they would like to come in on the discussion. Of course, this can go drastically wrong. Someone may genuinely have a cough, for instance. Others may simply be making an aside to someone sitting next to them. Someone may want to interject inappropriately.

And I also have to be careful not to blunder in. This is a particular issue for blind people. Speaking at the wrong moment, intervening just when someone else has their hand up and is about to be called, or failing to recognise a visual indication (which often can be discernible body language) that this is not the moment to speak out, is something that has been difficult, to say the least.

Honesty is a mixed blessing. Saying what you think, you cannot see the thunder in the faces around you. It does lead to honest, plain speaking, but it also undoubtedly sometimes makes you a pain in the rump.

I often thought that it would have been a great deal harder for me to have been a minister of state or a parliamentary under-secretary, because I would have had to deal with so much paperwork and routine that I would not have been able to deal with policy and communication, which is my forte. (I could easily have entered government as a minister of state had we won the 1992 general election. God knows how the secretary of state for that department would have coped with me, or me with him/her.) But the nuances mattered most in Cabinet and in very large meetings and conferences, where it was necessary to feel the atmosphere and judge it correctly.

Using tape machines which allowed me to speed up the sound has helped, but even with recordings half as fast again as the normal reading speed, it is still substantially slower than anyone who is a reasonable speed-reader of print. What is more significant, however, is the fact that I cannot skip-read. What I have on tape, I have to go through because at no moment can I scan the page to decide what is and what is not relevant. I certainly cannot do that with figures, so I have to go through them in detail.

This does, of course, have an upside. It means that things are done very thoroughly. If I am not skipping, then I am not missing anything. But the time constraints are such that it adds literally hours a day to the task of going through the voluminous material.

Since I do not have immediate access to written sources (and one of my greatest regrets is not being able to browse through a library), it is necessary for those who are supporting and working with me to know exactly what I need and to be able to deliver it in a format and fashion that meets that need. The general propensity of all ministers to play musical chairs following reshuffles made my situation worse.

Which brings me to what I am good at: absorbing facts quickly, discerning the big picture or the essential facts, and communicating them in a way that relates to people's lives. When you are interviewed you have to answer the questions put to you, rather than first peddle your own agenda, and you are therefore dependent on the competence, clarity and focus of the interviewer, as well as your own wits. But the development of policy, the ability to communicate it and an emphasis on delivery were all extremely close to my heart and still are.

Speaking in the House was never a problem, though it was certainly challenging when I first came into Parliament, when I thought I knew it all. As a member of the Labour Party National Executive Committee, as Leader of Sheffield City Council, as Deputy Chairman of the Association of Metropolitan Authorities, I had already been on the public stage and had substantial media exposure, but the House of Commons was different from anything else I had ever experienced. In the space of a few sentences the atmosphere can change from positive, uplifting support to resentful animosity. Being aggressive or bumptious at the wrong time can change not only the attitude of the Opposition but that of your own side, and so can being obsequious. In many ways, not being able to see required me to be much more alert and alive to

*what was going on around me, as well as knowing when people wanted to
intervene and being ready to sit down and allow them to raise a question or
make a point. It is possible to work out where someone is most likely to be
sitting. It is possible to know from their voice who they are.*

*Question time, which for departmental questions is once a month and lasts
for an hour, I always found easy. After all, the Secretary of State has the last
word and, with the exception of the main opposition spokesman, only one
question can be put by other members supplementary to the original question
down on the Order Paper. (Questions have to be submitted in advance and are
selected at random and then printed up in the agenda for the day.)*

*But I found delivering written – what are known as 'oral' – Statements very
difficult. They are oral in the sense that they are delivered to the House, but
they are written and have to be read verbatim. Written Statements (a more
modern version of 'planted questions', which used to involve members of your
side putting down questions which you would then answer in writing at
length) are now used regularly to brief the House, so the minister does not have
to come to the Dispatch Box to do it in person. Again, it was not answering the
questions that followed the delivery of the Statement that I found difficult, it
was the reading of the Statement itself.*

So back to the day-to-day grind of January 2001 . . .

John Prescott took Cabinet on Thursday – a horrendous day when I had to
jiggle things around to get from the Commons to do the phone-in for
young people on *Westminster Live* on BBC2, then go back for the wind-up
speeches, then do *Hard Talk* on BBC News 24, then go back to the office to
see Greg Dyke and Michael Stevens [respectively Director-General and
Head of Public Affairs at the BBC] about the Digital Curriculum, which
was a nightmare to sort out. I then had a meal on the train on the journey
home. I'm going to end up being run ragged if I'm not careful.

To a Fabian conference, which went very well – nearly 700 people there
– but which, because of everything else going on, got very little publicity.
There was something in the *Financial Times* and the *Guardian*, but the *FT*
was better. There was a good reception and a lot of discussion about ideas
and the things I really wanted to talk about.

My pamphlet on employment and employability and the role of the
DfEE, which we published at the Institute of Economic Affairs on
Wednesday, got reasonable publicity on the vocational educational material despite everything else going on. The *Today* programme refused to
have anything to do with it, but the papers on Wednesday and Thursday

covered it pretty well. There were a couple of leaders, including one in the *Guardian* on the Thursday – which was nothing short of a miracle, given Peter Mandelson's demise, which overshadowed almost everything.

This was Peter's second resignation from Cabinet. His borrowing a loan for his flat from fellow MP Geoffrey Robinson, which precipitated his departure from the DTI in December 1998, should not have been a resignation issue, and now he was again being forced out after allegations that he had intervened improperly over the Hinduja brothers' applications for British citizenship. The Hindujas had donated £1 million towards the Faith Zone in the Millennium Dome, which at the time had come within Peter's ministerial responsibility.

In many ways the distrust of Peter in political circles was a critical factor in his fall. I would describe him as an enigma: brilliant at his departmental jobs and at advising Tony, but with a self-destructive streak that in a way makes him a more endearing person than people give him credit for.

The papers, of course, have been absolutely full of Peter's departure. What a mess. It will be a long time before we get to the truth of precisely what has happened with Peter, but whatever it is, it's certainly a deeply mixed-up affair.

Four and a half years later, I was to experience a not dissimilar set of circumstances, but over two events rather than one. Visas, Asian businessmen, complete confusion over the facts, massive media pressure and danger to the Prime Minister and the government at a crucial moment: I was not to know then just how many of these ingredients would confront me on my own return to Cabinet on 6 May 2005. For very different reasons, neither Peter nor myself were flavour of the month with our own immediate colleagues, and both of us experienced the determination of certain elements of the British media to deal the Prime Minister, as well as us as individuals, a fatal blow. In both cases, the cry was: 'How dare the Prime Minister bring you back so soon?'

When I went into the Commons, Peter was sitting beside Geoff Hoon, who eventually moved to allow Gordon to go and sit where he usually sits, up by Tony, and therefore by Peter. In any event, I tried to be nice to Peter and leant over and touched his arm.

The following morning said it all. Everybody started to be very silly, with smirking faces all round. So Peter had gone – but there was nothing to smile about. Who has lost? Not those smiling, not me, but probably those in the marginal seats.

Anyway, I did my best, and in a large number of interviews – including the *PM* programme on Radio 4 and a big interview on *Newsnight* – I tried to get things back on track a bit.

Strange to think of me defending Peter Mandelson so assiduously, trying to get things going again. There must have been some premonition . . .

The pressure was no less. Apart from dealing with Welfare to Work issues and trying to get material together for the Budget, I had to try and settle sufficient money on local authorities on the back of John Prescott's regeneration allocation, which took place on the Wednesday when Peter Mandelson went. Apart from two sentences in *The Times* it got no coverage at all, but I managed to find £52 million to allocate specifically to local authorities. As part of this I was trying to arrange things so that those that received regeneration funding were not disqualified and we specifically helped those who had lost out through the change in the adult-education and pension payments after the creation of the Learning and Skills Council.

I said every authority that had no regeneration must get a minimum of £100,000, so at least there was some good news for authorities. I tried to help authorities like the Wirral with £1 million. It was definitely one of those occasions when being there made a difference. Anyway I did my best to give everybody a boost. It should have all been packaged together and Gordon should have doubled it. We would have been all right then. Everything would have been satisfactory and the problem would have been resolved. But it wasn't to be.

The allocation of regeneration funding was a deliberate effort between all of us to try to compensate for the fact that we were unable substantially to change the formula by which grants to local government (and through to education) operated.

It is a complex issue that, going back to my days as Leader of Sheffield City Council and my role in the Association of Metropolitan Authorities, used to drive me crackers, but it did help now to understand what was going on. I do not believe it arrogant to say (because I was one of the very few who had that kind of senior local-government experience) that I knew more about local-government finance structure and its impact than just about anyone else in the Cabinet.

Finding additional resources out of my own budget was a major problem, but necessary as a way of avoiding flashpoints. I had seen Gillian Shephard struggling in 1995 when Ken Clarke, that great swashbuckler and populist, had refused to help her out when he was Chancellor. As a consequence, in her case an already poor situation was made much worse by allowing particular hotspots to emerge that the press could focus on and that would become easy for us in opposition to highlight. I was determined that we were not going to meet a similar fate.

It was neither the first nor the last time that imagination and personal knowledge helped in delivering politically, rather than simply accepting what officials put in front of us. In my experience of government, not enough ministers actually act as politicians, think as politicians and insist on delivering as politicians. If simply signing off recommendations is what ministers are all about, then there is no point in having them there.

Then, on the back of Peter Mandelson's demise, we had Keith Vaz (or Vazeltine as the *Sun* calls him) [also implicated in the Hinduja affair]. I was worried that there was more there than there was with Peter, far more.

Other news of the last week of January. Good about Nissan and the plant being saved. Had a meeting on Corus [the steel giant that had taken over the British Steel Corporation some years earlier] on the Tuesday morning at No. 10, pretty desperate stuff – again, with no chance of funding from the Treasury, it was all going to be very difficult.

This was all about job losses in the steel industry, not only close to my heart because of Sheffield and Rotherham being the UK heart of special steels and engineering, but also because in the run-up to a general election, as we found with Rover in 2005, large-scale job losses and deterioration in manufacturing have serious repercussions in the media and with the public, even when individuals themselves are not directly affected.

February 2001

When I returned to South Eaton Place there were twenty-five messages on my answering machine. One of them was from Peter Mandelson, who said he had now come back to London and would like to get together, perhaps for a meal. He stressed that he had no intention of causing any waves but that he did have a real story to tell that he would be offering to the inquiry [the Hammond Inquiry into what had happened].

The Peter Mandelson saga continued, the 'Vazeltine' saga continued, and our efforts to get real politics back on the agenda continued.

Had a decent lunch with Dominic Lawson [editor of the *Sunday Telegraph*] and his colleagues. It was interesting to learn that he had a daughter with Down's syndrome, about whom he was deeply concerned. I also had lunch with Brian Groom and Phil Stevens of the *Financial Times*, with Phil going on about the government, its duplicity and its timorousness.

I suppose the success of the week had to be Tony's decision, when I met him before Cabinet on the Thursday, to agree that I could rule out top-up fees for university students for the next parliament. I was so relieved about this and it had taken almost a year.

In the end, of course, we adopted something not dissimilar to the Scottish system, where admittedly much larger fees were deferred, rather than making the better-off families pay in advance. This had been the only way of getting resources directly into the universities very quickly. I would therefore have done exactly the same again and I certainly would have pressed for the ruling-out of top-up fees, which would have provided considerable variation across the country, deep inequity and, as originally envisaged, no proper support or amelioration for the worse off (which my own scheme provided in spades).

What I did find strange over the subsequent two years was how little anyone seemed to know about what we had done, why we had done it or even about the introduction of measures to help the less well-off families.

I had a couple of interesting evenings, one at the Hilton Hotel, replying to Michael Dell, Head of Dell Computers, who gave the Fulbright Lecture on Wednesday night. 'Please be brief', they kept saying to me, so I was. At one point I said it was a good job that the W's hadn't been taken off the computers at the Pentagon otherwise what on earth would this have made of Star Wars? The ambassador and his wife absolutely loved it, but it took half the audience a couple of minutes before they got the joke. I think they were probably punch-drunk from Michael Dell selling them his wireless or infra-red new computer generation. I was referring, of course, to the rumour that Clinton aides had messed about with the White House computer system.

The following night I went first to Trent University, arriving late to a demonstration outside but a good reception inside, and then on to a most remarkable reception from 300 students at the University of Nottingham.

Nobody booed, nobody demonstrated, nobody heckled. They all listened, they asked polite but difficult questions, then politely applauded at the end. It was a great relief to my son Hugh, who of course is a student at Nottingham.

Politically speaking, my bright spot of the first week of the month was at Education and Employment Questions. When the Lib Dem MP David Heath asked me in the most melodramatic fashion (which really helped me) whether I would agree to rule out top-up fees for the next parliament, 'Yes or no?', I was able to stand up and say, 'I am sorry to disappoint the Honourable Gentleman, but I have made my position clear on top-up fees over the last year and I am very pleased to say that I can now make the position clear on behalf of the government. There will be no top-up fees in the next parliament should we be re-elected.' Those who were in the Chamber on our side just went wild. I really enjoyed that.

I was being careful not to provide any hostages to fortune here. The top-up fees were not in the next parliament, but the legislation was.

I did not enjoy trying to put together the Education Green Paper.

It wasn't so much a Green Paper as a White Paper, the distinction being between quite open consultation and a set of propositions that you really want to carry through.

I did not enjoy the continuous rewrites and reading it through over the weekend. It was such a shame that we seemed to have nobody in the Department who could write in short sentences that didn't go on, line after line after line. It was a document for the professionals, but having tried five or six weeks running to rewrite the crucial political element and get the nuances right, I just could not rewrite the whole damned document myself. I was looking at it on Saturday night and 'as' and 'so' were transposed in a way that made one part in the teacher-recruitment section sound like Japanese.

More important was the disagreement we had about whether we would write off the debt for trainee teachers to assist with retention. The truth of the matter was that it was not my idea to have a 'gradual write-off', but I was warming to it. It was first mooted for all teachers but was rejected by Gordon, who said he would wear only secondary-school teachers. I said that would not do as it would split the profession if we simply said we were doing it for secondary but not for primary. The Treasury came back and said it could only be done for secondary on value-for-money grounds. I said: 'Sod value for money. Do we want an industrial dispute?' It started on Tuesday and built up to a crescendo on Thursday, when we thought we had an agreement. Late Thursday night, the Treasury simply said they weren't going to do it and they weren't going to pay for it. We didn't have the money to be able to do it in the long term, and we couldn't commit past the end of the Spending Review.

So we got Tony involved. I spoke to him very briefly at 7.15 a.m. on Friday when he was in the car, waiting on the tarmac to go to France. As I said to him when he rang me just after 8 a.m. on Sunday, had he been in London on the Friday, we would have been able to sort it out, but he was in meetings literally all day, with very short breaks. We tried in the breaks to reach agreement but we couldn't as the Treasury wouldn't budge. So I said in the end that we would have to provide for shortage subjects only (for instance, maths and science) – so that is what we have put in the document.

About that phone call on Sunday morning: I picked up the phone and heard 'It's No. 10.' I said, 'Whoever it is, I'm making my porridge,' and she said, 'It is the Prime Minister' – then she laughed and said, 'I'll get him in five minutes.' I rang back when I had eaten my porridge, as you can't leave porridge half cooked, even for the Prime Minister.

I managed to get the Pupil Learning Credits up and running, though, in the *Observer*.

This was an idea to provide additional targeted funding specifically earmarked for the individuals in schools in the poorest areas who came from the most deprived families (based on free school meals and the like). It did a lot of good in providing extracurricular activities that other parents could afford to pay for, including Outward Bound activities, sport, theatre and music lessons. The idea was dropped in the following parliament when all specific funding of this sort was incorporated into the general schools budget. To be honest, as a Cabinet minister overwhelmed with the affairs of the Home Office, I did not even find out that it had happened until afterwards.

It is hard to describe what the Thursday and Friday were like, dealing with the last phases of the document and in particular the rows; it virtually wiped out Friday altogether. From 7.15 a.m. until 11.15 a.m. I was on the phone for all but twenty minutes. I got my shower at 11.30 a.m., had a cup of coffee, took Lucy out and then spent most of the afternoon on the phone, apart from a visit to the bank to try to sort out my financial affairs.

I then had the constituency meeting on Friday night in a freezing hall with no heating on, my surgery on Saturday morning, which consisted mostly of immigration cases, and then on to the UNISON forum in Leeds – where no one was there to meet us, which meant that we could not get into the civic centre. It was farcical – pouring down with rain, absolutely freezing, and to cap it all it was a complete waste of time. I was sticking to something I had previously agreed to do, but sometimes I think I must be crackers, as it was three hours down the drain. Nobody else seemed to make the effort. Of the UNISON MPs, only Alice Mahon [Labour MP for Halifax] and myself turned up.

On the Sunday morning I did *Breakfast with Frost* and Adam Boulton's politics programme on Sky, travelled to Blackburn cathedral, and then back home. Thank God for my Sunday dinner – but then down to London for the launch of the Green Paper on the Monday, God help us!

After my television interviews on Sunday morning I got a phone call from Mike Wardle to say that he had learned that a script had been prepared for Tony that included the term 'post-comprehensive era'. Having argued about this all week, having seen Tony immediately after Prime Minister's Questions in his room and got him to agree that the most he would refer to would be 'post-comprehensive argument', it seemed we were now back to square one. I was not pleased, to say the least, because it took no account of the impact on the party and the teaching profession, both of which I had to keep on board.

The party's commitment to the comprehensive principle meant that the words used and the way they were interpreted assumed enormous significance. Many suspected that we were going to abandon comprehensive education altogether. 'Era' suggests a time in the past, whereas 'argument' is about work in progress.

To Mansfield College, Oxford, to give a lecture that among other things took a look back to the Friendly Societies of the nineteenth century and the lessons we might learn in relation not only to Welfare to Work but also civic society and the involvement of men and women in taking responsibility and giving to others. I enjoyed meeting the young people, including the deaf Chinese girl whom I was going to try to help in finding some cash to keep her going because her dad had died and her mum was trying to support her from Beijing. She was a remarkable young woman. I liked meeting the students and the staff, but what about this? My Principal Private Secretary had told the college not to do anything for the dinner that they wouldn't do for anyone else – so they cut the meat up into tiny little chunks. This just ruins it for me. I am quite capable of cutting my own meat. I don't want it in tiny little chunks. They also smothered the dinner in gravy, which just leads to a lot of splashing and spilling. Sometimes I feel like commenting, because it does feel a little patronising, but I just have to stop myself. Mike Wardle, sitting next to me at the dinner, touched my arm as his way of indicating, 'Don't say anything' – so I didn't.

All this may seem rather petty, but this sort of thing has bedevilled me all my life. Once, when I was Leader of Sheffield City Council, the Queen and the Duke of Edinburgh came to Sheffield for an official visit and I was hosting lunch. It was one of those very pleasant occasions when it was possible to sit next to Her Majesty and have a genuine conversation, but (and I know she will forgive me for recalling it) it was strange when twice she asked me if I would like my meat cutting up – strange not because it was not a kind and thoughtful question, but because of the comment she made when I politely declined: 'You know, I often do it for the corgis.' Well, well, well.

Conor and I had a good dinner with Paul Dacre and Simon Heffer from the *Daily Mail*, keeping the wheels on the cart. Paul Dacre said that Chris Woodhead had tried to get a job with the *Mail* and had been touting himself around for a long time. Paul had weighed it up and decided it wasn't worth taking Chris on, which I thought was very revealing.

One person I certainly don't want to lose is Michael Bichard, and I am mortified that he has confirmed he is leaving the Department at the end of May to head the London Institute. I am very sorry, but I can understand why he is going. His can be a wearing job at the best of times.

I flew down to London for the seminar at No. 10, bringing together people who have a real interest in education. I spoke, then Tony did. He had in his script the phrase 'post-comprehensive argument', which he used. The BBC later in the day asked me about the 'post-comprehensive era'. Two papers at least, the *Telegraph* and *Mail*, quoted the phrase as 'post-comprehensive era', while others quoted what he had actually said. There were those around Tony (not, it has to be said, on this occasion, Alastair Campbell) who wanted what might be described as a 'big bang', with a story that would provide a peg for real debate. Alastair quite separately and unexpectedly (including for him) gave them more than they had bargained for.

My notes tell me that one aide to Tony said to Michael Barber on the Wednesday, 'Mission accomplished.' Michael Barber replied: 'It didn't feel like that talking to heads and teachers in comprehensive schools in Brighton that day.'

So, what created this storm? There had been a full speech and a question-and-answer session in the morning at No. 10 that had been carried live on Sky television, and what did Alastair say? He used the term 'bog-standard comprehensive', and the world just erupted. It was like pulling a pin out of a hand grenade. The Parliamentary Labour Party, the Labour Party, the teaching profession, those working in comprehensives, every Old Labour-ite, everyone with a grudge, everyone who didn't like every other bit or one tiny part of the policy paper *Schools Building on Success* – all were unleashed. It was like turning a key, opening a door and letting out the mob.

What was really interesting was that even people who weren't political kept saying to me 'Why did you say that?', to which I replied: 'Don't be stupid. It says that the Prime Minister's official spokesman said it, and I am not the Prime Minister's official spokesman.'

This nonsense carried through to Thursday night and *Question Time* on BBC1, on which Glenys Kinnock was frankly outrageous. She suggested that specialist schools were private schools. The programme also repeated allegations that I had used the term 'bog standard', when I had said nothing of the sort.

I'd written to Alastair Campbell on the Monday evening – the day of the notorious remark – and the following week received an apology (handsomely so from Alastair, who, I think he would agree, is not generally minded to apologise for anything). Tony then phoned me when I was at the Queen's Awards for Higher Education dinner. I had tried to get out of it three times but Michael Bichard had persuaded me that my absence would be taken as a slur. Tony got me out of the dinner to ask if there was anything that he could immediately do to help, and I said that it would certainly help if he were able to say something in his speech at the spring conference in Glasgow the following Sunday.

Bruce Grocott, who at the time was a parliamentary aide to Tony and in the 2005 parliament Chief Whip in the Lords, told me that it was Peter Hyman who kept repeating the phrase 'bog standard' to Alastair Campbell before he went into his briefing.

Peter Hyman left Downing Street to become a teacher in an inner-city school, and has written about his teaching experiences. He changed his mind about comprehensives to the point where the all-party House of Commons Education Select Committee took his evidence in relation to the Education White Paper published in autumn 2005, in which I played my own part in finding a way forward between Downing Street and a very large number of Labour back-benchers. It astonished me how many of the arguments taking place through to the publication of the Education Bill in 2006 were the same as those that had occupied a great deal of my time in autumn 1997 and the early part of 1998 (and again, as can be seen here, in the run-up to the 2001 general election).

So, I delivered my Statement to the House on the Education Green Paper. I hated doing it but I was fine on questions.

I have already mentioned my dislike of having to read the Statement, but when things are very difficult on your own back benches, reading the Statement is like walking the plank. This is particularly true when you have a great deal to set out and therefore the Statement is longer than you would wish, and in my case the number of Braille sheets are such that it is not easy to handle them. I had taken to dusting them with talcum powder so that they didn't stick together.

Thinking back, and with experience, I wish that I had simply trained myself to remember the Statement so that reading it became an irrelevance. The problem is the messing about that takes place leading up to the statement itself. We always tried to give the Opposition the Statement at least half an hour and preferably an hour before it was delivered, so that they could respond in a meaningful fashion if they chose to do so. This is a courtesy that the two main parties have always maintained, and where there are very lengthy reports going alongside a Statement the material is given to them much further in advance.

Difficulties arise, though, when both No. 10 and No. 11 Downing Street want to see the Statement and want a hand in its final shaping. I was less subject to this than most, but for absolutely crucial Statements it was understandable that they would want to ensure that the nuances were right. The hardest part was getting the Braille run off in time for me to have a look at it before delivering it. And here is the rub: I am not a good reader. Very few people appreciate just what a nightmare it is in such circumstances to use Braille, where there are no capital letters as there are in print, no highlighting, no underlining and, given that Braille is so bulky, masses of paper. Even a short Statement requires a large number of sheets.

Delivering a Statement to the House of Commons was my worst nightmare. When people asked me if there was any chance that I might ever be Prime Minister (as they did on occasion, though it seems a long time ago now), my immediate thoughts before answering were not all the normal niceties but, 'Would I ever be able to deliver a Statement in the way that Tony manages to do it?' And I am afraid the answer was very simple: I would not. There are blind people (not many, but there are some) who can read Braille almost as well as a sighted person reading print. If it had been possible to agree a Statement the day before delivering it, it might have just been feasible for me to memorise it. But it is not possible less than an hour before delivery (and in one case, ten minutes before) to convey to memory what has to be delivered verbatim.

If I had my time again, I would do two things. First, I would look after my fingers a great deal better than I have, because the skin was burnt from cooking and toughened by manual chores, resulting in clumsiness. I would also have made sure that they were cared for, using whatever ointments or creams were necessary (even if that did make me a big girl's blouse). Secondly, I would have practised Braille over and over again. The only excuse I have is the lack of time. Just as I was not able to use a computer and access the Internet until I left office, so it was with anything else that didn't immediately have to be attended to: it went by the board. I do regret that now, because it was certainly an Achilles' heel noticeable not simply in my awkward and sometimes stumbling delivery of the Statement (in contrast to answering questions, where I was easy, confident and articulate) but in my whole body language – the tension, the hunched shoulders, the unrelaxed facial muscles, which came from what inside was frankly downright fear.

We have found out from Ann Taylor, the Chief Whip, that a general election on 3 May will have to be called by Thursday 4 April, because Maundy Thursday, Good Friday and Easter Monday would not be included in the seventeen working days' notice demanded by electoral law.

The bombing raids on Iraq have started, though I was not told about them in advance. I spent some time with John Prescott on Saturday morning, doing a photocall for his yellow-bus transport scheme for children. In the course of talking to him I found out that he had not been told about the bombing raids either, any more than the rest of us had: I learned about them from Michael Prescott of the *Sunday Times*. I did not expect to be consulted because I am not on the Cabinet Committee, but it would have been nice if No. 10 had tried to contact Cabinet ministers to tell them what they had agreed and that it was happening. It would have been even nicer if they had told the Deputy Prime Minister, who found out by watching Sky television. John said to me that he had phoned Tony and he had been absolutely livid with him. Tony had apologised and said that it was a mistake and that he had been busy writing his speech. Prescott said to me: 'When I say what I am going to say this afternoon about bog-standard comprehensives, and anyone asks why I didn't clear it, I am going to say that it was the Baghdad factor.'

I had dinner with Peter Mandelson on the Wednesday night – and a phone call subsequently from the *Daily Telegraph*, the same *Daily Telegraph* that followed me about to find out what I was buying at Christmas, the *Daily Telegraph* that wanted to know why I was eating with Peter Mandelson and what our conversation was about, the same *Daily Telegraph* that let Chris Woodhead loose in print on Thursday 1 March.

In this article Chris made the fundamental error of going over the top, of being personally abusive and using too much vitriol. I have never seen more contradictory claptrap – the great utilitarian accusing other people of being utilitarian, the great believer in absolutely targeted focus on literacy and numeracy saying that education should be something broader. I managed to rise above it and stay calm and deal with the accusations in a way that won support and deflected his attack, but there was no doubt it would make a difference: if you throw enough mud, some of it sticks. He knew that and I knew that.

I thought it amusing that Charles Moore [editor of the *Daily Telegraph*] appeared on *Any Questions* and tried to infer that we and our advisers had started using terms like *learnacy*. I don't think I remember anybody ever using it in my presence. This all stemmed from Chris Woodhead claiming that someone in the Standards Task Force had used the term *learning professional* to talk about teachers and that ministers hadn't slapped him down, as though we were the damn thought police to go around telling people that they can't use such terms and phrases. It was just such trivia, and typical of Charles Moore and the *Telegraph*.

What strikes me about these passages from my tapes is once again that I was taking far too much notice of what people were writing. It didn't really matter a jot what Charles Moore wrote, except to Charles Moore and his friends, and just as I had forgotten the incident, so, of course, has everyone else. I give very little advice to others in this book, but one thing I would say to both existing and budding politicians: take a good deal less notice of what people – other than your friends – write, speak and think of you than I did.

Our representative on *Any Questions* was Patricia Hewitt, who was less than fully briefed. She had no idea of the number of teacher vacancies and no idea what we were doing on class size. We had Malcolm Bruce [Liberal Democrat MP] saying that we appeared on the *Today* programme spinning too much. I have only been on the *Today* programme three times in the whole of the first two months of the year: one of those appearances was answering Woodhead on Thursday morning, while another was launching our own Green Paper.

I saw Helen Boaden, head of Radio 4, on the Wednesday night when I popped into the celebration at St James's Palace for the fiftieth anniversary of *The Archers*. I said that after the election I would get together with her and see what could be done about *Today*. They had somebody tapping away at a word processor during my interview on Thursday morning with John Humphrys. I had to stop the interview in its tracks – live – and ask if they could stop the individual typing as it was deeply distracting.

I am afraid I didn't manage it after the election but I did after the following one. Editing the Today *programme on 30 December 2005 was one of those events I shall remember with great affection, not least for my interviewing John Humphrys rather than his interviewing me. I found myself interrupting him more often than I had intended, which shows that it's not so easy after all.*

It is history now, but at the beginning of March 2001, my tapes show that Peter Mandelson was understandably depressed and bitter about what had happened to him. He was angry with the role that the Home Office had played in his demise, and having seen how Bev Hughes was so badly let down by officials three years later, my instincts are to believe that Peter's version of events was very close to the truth. I did my utmost to stop him turning all this against Tony. I said I would come and speak for him in Hartlepool. Somehow, I had to help him.

Michael White from the *Guardian* told me that on Friday night, the day after Peter had lost his job and while he still had his official car, he had just got into it in New Palace Yard when a figure moved through the rain and tapped on the window. He rolled the window down and the figure said, 'I am very sorry indeed that this has ended with your removal from Cabinet.' I wonder who it could have been.

After the general election it fell to me as Home Secretary to allow Peter to keep the car – on security grounds, after his time in Northern Ireland, but also because few people really understand the terrible price that a handful of politicians pay for notoriety.

The run-up to the Budget – always a terrible trial for spending ministers. You pick up little hints here and there about the direction it's going, enough to rewrite what you are asking for and to get it across and press it upon Tony so that he has got it clearly spelled out – such as what it would have cost for a reasonable degree of devolved revenue funding (in addition to capital for repair and buildings) to schools rather than through education authorities, and a really imaginative recruitment programme for teachers, but it is really hard work.

Special Cabinet on Tuesday about foot-and-mouth disease. We have had a number of disasters – three major rail crashes now, the floods, the aftermath of BSE, and now foot-and-mouth disease. Cabinet was interesting because we had a proper discussion, and I joined in for once on this issue about the terms of compensation payments for farmers affected by the foot-and-mouth crisis. As the only one who had joined Nick Brown in arguing for them, I said that I thought people were horrified by what was happening. The awful pictures on television of cattle being led to slaughter and burning carcasses were deeply distressing. Although there was no money on the table to begin with, three hours later Tony had pulled Gordon round and indeed insisted, and as a result we had a package of £170 million – so some good was done at that Cabinet meeting, thank goodness.

Looking back, I wish that we had had an argument not just about compensation but about how it was to be delivered. In retrospect it was right, and politically essential, to provide compensation. It is amazing that it wasn't self-evident there and then. What does strike me is how poorly the plans were prepared, how much public money went not to those who really lost out (the small businesses, the little men and women in the rural areas) but to people who did very well from what was effectively a tragedy not just for all caring people but for the economy of great swathes of our country. Regrettably there are always those who will exploit a situation, no matter how desperate, and of course fortunes have always been made in times of war.

Launch of the Adult Literacy Strategy at No. 11, to which Tony came along.

I had to address both the Parliamentary Labour Party and the Labour Lords on education policy: a moderate response at the PLP, not enthusiastic, but I managed to get over the problems. Funnily enough, the Lords were much more supportive by the time I had finished.

On the Tuesday I spoke at the Parliamentary and Scientific Committee lunch at the Savoy and to the Adam Smith Institute, and I was trying in between to deal with No. 10 and No. 11. I saw Gordon in the morning as well as speaking to him three times on the telephone. Over the rest of the day I spoke to Andrew Smith twice about the New Deal for the un-employed, and I was in constant communication with No. 10. In the end I got an appointment with Tony. Tony was detached – understandably so, with Northern Ireland, with foot-and-mouth, and with the Hammond Report on Peter Mandelson coming up.

The problem was not so much the result as the process. Alan Milburn was particularly angry as his budget for Health was not dealt with until late on the Tuesday night, during phone calls to him in the West Country, and I understand that argument continued all day and through the rest of the evening. I didn't have a row, but I was talking to Gordon on the telephone at ten o'clock on the Tuesday night, having come out of the Marx Club, where I had given my old school friend Bob Jones and his wife dinner. I saw Tony before Cabinet and said: 'We can't carry on like this. The process is hopeless.' There was simply not enough consultation before decisions were made.

Talked to Peter Mandelson later in the week. When I rang him after the publication of the Hammond Report, he repeated what he said to me over dinner. Tony is very down, detached and depressed – and I can feel it.

The Budget went well despite the fact that it was about cash transfers and that forty- and fifty-year-olds didn't really gain anything. I raised all this again at Cabinet and several people approached me afterwards, including Ann Taylor, who said the points I had raised were exactly the ones she had got down. A lot of people said that I was right about the cracks opening up in relation to the Barnett Formula with Scotland and Northern Ireland. John Prescott, leaning back on his chair, said, 'Wow, there we have it!' when I had finished speaking.

The Barnett Formula was put together by the then Chief Secretary to the Treasury, Joel Barnett, back in the late 1970s, and was designed (on the back of the surge of nationalism which had elected twelve Scottish Nationalist MPs in the 1974 general election and the failure of the referendum on devolution) with great sensitivity to keep the United Kingdom together by varying amounts of funding going to England, Wales, Scotland and Northern Ireland.

However, the consequences (diminished since but still there) were that Scotland did extremely well per head of population on investment in public services (particularly in areas such as education and health), compared with England and Wales. Northern Ireland had a very separate arrangement. Of course, the argument was affected at the time by the emergence from 1975 onwards of North Sea oil and the fact that so much of that oil came in from rigs off the Scottish coast.

I talked at Cabinet about the people whose children had grown up, or who did not have children, who were not gaining, and the pensioners who were just above benefit levels and did not understand the tax credits but ended up paying tax. But nobody would join in.

Gordon rang me afterwards, even though he was leading up to the Budget in the afternoon, and said, 'I can't do anything about the Barnett Formula before the election,' and I replied: 'No, I don't expect you can. I want to win seats in Scotland and Wales as well.' An interesting man is Gordon – very bright, very intelligent, and driven.

In the Budget we got for the UK £330 million a year. For England, by the time we had sorted it out, it was just under £270 million a year. It was enough to do something on recruitment and retention, enough to do devolved funding to schools, split between capital and revenue, which was good news. It could have been even better news if it had been better thought through.

March 2001

Dinner with Charles Clarke on Monday [5 March] was an eye-opener. It is not what he said, but what he didn't say. He was vehement about the Home Office, vehement about what the Treasury are up to. He too thought that Tony was down in the dumps. Another interesting man is Charles, a real bruiser.

Monday 12 March: I went with Tony to Southfields Community College, a comprehensive school struggling with selective schools around, but a good school with a positive head. It turned out to be a worthwhile visit because I was able to spend the best part of half an hour in the car with Tony, talking to him. I tried to get across some really important messages about not fragmenting government, and about the balance of power. I did my best, as gently as I could, but I had to follow it up vigorously during the week. I saw Richard Wilson on the Thursday afternoon as it had already become clear from my earlier conversation with Charles Clarke that things were afoot.

A lot of jumpiness in the run-up to the general election, both about whether we will hold the number of seats we have and what will happen in the reshuffle afterwards. I am not the only one who has raised vigorously with Tony and with those around him the need for time to be made available by Tony to see MPs and to make more effort to get across that people are 'loved and cherished'.

Tony let me have a draft of the full manifesto, which Sophie Linden read on to tape for me. I spent a great chunk of the weekend of 17–18 March reading and annotating it and doing my best to try and upgrade it. It was far too provider-orientated and not sufficiently geared to the consumer, to the people, as opposed to the providers – so I had a go at it.

The manifesto itself was to turn out to be very different when we eventually launched it in May – though some of my input was retained.

So Monday was an interesting day. I had to speak in the House on the Monday afternoon [12 March] – probably my last set speech on education and employment and very low key, but it went OK. Halfway through I joked that I was having difficulty staying awake myself. But there is no point in trying to do a barnstorming, tub-thumping speech when there is hardly anyone in the Chamber. It just doesn't work.

Education and Employment Questions on the Thursday – followed by sarcastic pieces from the sketch-writers, as ever. The foot-and-mouth-disease issue went grinding on, with the broadcast media doing everything except seriously presenting the issues and the options. The imagery was so powerful and made such a difference to people's perceptions and to the build-up of pressure to delay the local and general elections.

Personally, it would have helped me to delay the general election because apart from the Association of Teachers and Lecturers' and National Union of Teachers' conferences, it would have meant I could have a really sane April. Tony would not delay the elections though, because the civil service had run right down and government had virtually stopped. Everything was in train for polling day on 3 May and it would take an earthquake to change it.

How wrong can you be? Of course, Tony took the right decision when postponing the general election to 7 June, although I have to say that I was not one of those pressing a delay on him. I wish that I was able to say how wise I was – but I wasn't.

We had Cabinet on Wednesday morning as Tony was away from London on Thursday. The best event of the week, after the most enormous struggle, was the labour-market statistics and getting unemployment below 1 million for the first time since 1975. Both the rate and the number of vacancies went up, and earnings stabilised – so it was a good day. It reminded me that David Hunt had become Employment Minister in 1993 on 3 million unemployed and rising. I am so very lucky to have been the Employment Secretary when employment dropped below a million.

The day of the announcement of the reduction in unemployment to below 1 million was one of those very special days when everyone around me was celebrating and saying, 'This is what we came into the party to achieve.'

As soon as Cabinet was over, I shot off to the British Museum to open the Clore Education Centre, then shot back for backbenchers' lunch, the last one for Education and Employment.

From 1997 through to 2005, I held regular lunches every few weeks for backbenchers from different regions of the country (we held separate ones for the opposition parties), so that people could raise their constituency and local concerns, as well as question us on broader policy. In retrospect I wish I had done more of these – more regularly – because they were valuable not only to those who bothered to come (and not everybody did) but to us as ministers.

Dinner in Sheffield with Paul Potts, Chief Executive of the Press Association. Paul and I have known each other since 1970, when he was a cub reporter on the *Sheffield Star* and I was wet behind the ears as a junior councillor. We were both learning about how pre-emptive briefings and what has become known as 'spin' could be beneficial to all sides.

I went to see Enid Hattersley, who has been taken into the dementia ward at the Northern General Hospital. Roy had not let me know but I had got the news from Paul Potts. After seeing Enid I left Roy a message, and he rang me back on Sunday with a really nice message in return.

I was trying to keep some perspective on foot-and-mouth disease, but the situation was absolutely devastating. What on earth were we to do with the media? I was also trying to write the speech for the Second Reading of the Special Educational Needs and Disability Bill and to make sure that I was on top of all the facts – as well as preparing for the massive number of visits I was making on Wednesday and Thursday, followed by the Secondary Heads' conference in South Wales on Friday, a big speech and probably my last before Parliament was prorogued. I didn't expect the ATL and NUT conferences to be covered but I wanted to go and try to protect Estelle from the worst of it. I might as well go out with a bang.

I had the Second Reading of the Special Educational Needs and Disability Bill, and a very pleasant dinner with John Monks. On Wednesday I had a visit to Southampton and Portsmouth, then back to London. At Cabinet on Thursday we discussed foot-and-mouth, and I then had a meeting with Phil Redmond about what he could do in the election.

Phil was well known through his production company, and in particular the Brookside *soap opera on Channel 4. He had been extremely helpful, not only because of commitment to education (and some of the important initiatives such as the Year of Reading), but also in trying to ensure that the series itself took a socially responsible approach.*

I then shot off to Romford and I was very late because of traffic, then on to Braintree to a school there – where I was also very late (but a lot earlier than those from the press office who had taken a taxi, paid £71 and arrived half an hour after I did). Then I went on to Norwich and caught up a bit of time, spoke to heads and governors, and did a fundraising dinner. On Friday morning I went to a Sure Start premises and flew to Bristol, where I attended the Secondary Heads' conference. I went on to a school in Abergavenny and then to a fundraising dinner. Each of the Thursday and Friday night events turned out to be buffets rather than dinners – and I hate buffets for obvious reasons.

Perhaps my hatred of buffets merits a little more explanation. In order to get the true picture, close your eyes and imagine you are in a very noisy room, with everyone standing about with glasses in their hands, normally at an angle just right for tipping over if you happen to bang an elbow. People are milling about and someone (you've no idea who) approaches you and begins to talk – and talk, and talk. In order to break away, you suggest that perhaps they might be good enough to help locate the gents' toilet. They say, 'Of course,' and when you come out they are waiting for you. There is someone somewhere in the room that you would really like to talk to but unfortunately, because your eyes are closed, you cannot see them. You are desperately trying to avoid being rude because, God knows, you might need help in the future. You can't easily move about, even with the aid of the dog, because knocking into people at a reception is not likely to make you very popular.

So you try just to pop in, show your face, hope that someone really interesting will 'take pity on you', and eat what you can. It has to be said here that this is usually a plate of food collected for you by someone else and which understandably reflects their taste in food but not necessarily yours. You make your speech if you've been asked to do so, and do your best to get round the room and shake hands, particularly at party events, with people who are giving up their free time and providing voluntarily all the energy and commitment to get you and 'your kind' elected.

If it is not that sort of event but just one of those tedious occasions that has to be done as Secretary of State, then you try to get off home as fast as you can.

April/May/June 2001

The Secondary Heads' conference went all right but my speech had a strange conclusion. I got to the point, very close to the end, where I said 'In the words of the song' – although it wasn't really a song, I had made it up – 'You may not love me, but be with me for one more time.' They all started to clap, and the President came across, grabbed me and pulled me away from the lectern – so that I had no choice but to stop my speech there rather than using the ending that I had intended.

That's the first time that the applause and the actions of the person chairing were such that I had absolutely no choice but to give up the rest of my speech. It was bizarre, absolutely bizarre.

A fundraising dinner on Sunday night for Chris Smith at Frederick's restaurant in Camden Passage – £100 a head. How the hell do you speak with people paying that amount of money? Lord above.

Watched the six o'clock news on BBC television – a dreadful broadcast from every point of view. An attempt appeared to be made to blame Tony for reconsidering the date of the general election, when the week before the BBC had been running footage of farmers crying and asking us not to cull the sheep and pigs within a three-mile radius of their farms. They had completely changed their tune after hammering the government for not acting – although it has to be said that David King, the new Chief Scientific Adviser, and Nick Brown were all over the place. They were talking from entirely different scripts, so the BBC were right to say it was a mess – but the rest of it was absolutely scurrilous. We even had slogans on the side of cattle trucks saying 'Tony Blair – fortunate for you, cattle don't vote', which was pathetic. It is very difficult trying to organise a policy with that level of emotion running; in fact it is impossible.

Michael Bichard phoned me on Saturday night to say that all the signs were that the co-ordinating central body that has been reconvened for the foot-and-mouth situation, as it was in the oil crisis, is going nowhere. It seemed nobody had a grip of anything and no one was responsible or accountable – just like last time.

The first time I had a proper conversation with Tony on something like this that was outside my area was at the weekend, and then Alastair Campbell came on the line and so I ended up in a conversation with the two of them that lasted half an hour. Tony said his instincts were to postpone both the county elections and general election until 7 June, but he would not make his mind up for a couple of days. It was a really hard decision, as everything had clearly wound down in anticipation of the May polling day.

We had a meeting at No. 10 on Tuesday morning – quite a long one, firstly with Jack Straw, Margaret Beckett, Alan Milburn and myself, and then just Alan Milburn and me.

The first one was about the manifesto and the fact that we needed a thematic approach. This was very encouraging. Tony was talking about an enabling government – on your side, helping people to cope with change. I was pleased about that, because these were the themes I had been pushing for. There was a long way to go before the manifesto was right, though we were getting there on asset accumulation. There appeared to have been a paper agreed, although the Treasury was interfering because they were worried about the impact on savings and pensions in other areas. A compromise was beginning to emerge.

The meeting after that with just Alan Milburn and myself was very significant because I put my head on the block and hoped to God that Alan would support me – and to be fair, he did. I just told Tony the truth, that he needed to be seen to be responding to the junior ministers and backbenchers who were on his side, and to be giving them a lead. Alan Milburn was much tougher, much more straightforward than I have ever known him before. It was quite an eye-opener. I thought it was a worthwhile meeting, telling Tony the truth over and over that he just needed to signal to those who were backing him that they could rely on him, that he would support them, and that he intended to keep in touch. The difficult thing – and this arose from a meeting I had on Monday night with a group of close advisers, including Jonathan Powell and Sally Morgan – was that he wanted to reorganise No. 10, effectively putting just Jonathan and Anji in charge, taking all the politics out and relying heavily on John Birt, God help us. This would effectively have pushed Sally out and would mean no liaison with the PLP and the party. So we made progress in one direction and lost it in another.

I am afraid I laid down the law and said that fragmenting departments, creating a Department of Justice, breaking up the Home Office or the DETR was just crazy. I spoke to Jack Straw about this immediately after Cabinet and he was entirely in agreement. Charles Clarke told me in Norwich that Jack would really like to do the DETR but he wouldn't do it if it was split up. I agreed that I would have a bit of supper with Jack in his room in the Commons on Wednesday night: God knew what food he would be getting in, but it would be a chance to talk privately with him. I was also arranging to see the Acting Permanent Secretary in the Home Office. It was clear, from the hints I'd been given from Downing Street, that if there was still a Home Office and if we won, I'd be going to it – a really daunting task.

In the event Jack and I ate food brought in from the tea room, and we had a very good talk. He was very honest and open and indicated that he thought that at the reshuffle he would be moving and I would be moving. We talked through a number of things to do with policy and the Home Office and security. Jack has static security, which means he literally has protection round the clock, twenty-four hours a day, when he is at his country home in Oxfordshire. It sounds incredibly restrictive. He told me that he had managed to escape one morning without anybody noticing, going down the road to buy a newspaper. It's like being permanently under surveillance. It was generous of him to talk so frankly to me, and I appreciated it.

I was sorry, three years later, that I had been less than generous to him in return. Whatever our differences of style and approach, he did not have to talk to me openly in the way he did at that time, and although some of the published comments in relation to what I did or did not think of the Home Office when I inherited it were distinctly not of my making, my later 'on the record' comments were and they were unworthy of me.

And so the election campaign.

It wasn't an auspicious start. I had been having a long weekend – May Day weekend – with Margaret and Henry Hodge in Norfolk, but had to leave on the bank-holiday Monday morning because Tony had called a Special Cabinet for that afternoon. This was a desultory affair. None of us wanted to be there, and although on a slack media day it did get attention, I am not entirely sure whether performances of this sort win a single vote. It wasn't the launch of the campaign; it was the launch of the phoney war before the campaign. We all trooped out to try and be as cheerful as possible as the House of Commons went into its final throes of agony at the end of parliament.

There are occasions in politics when you know you will never do the same thing again (and be glad). One such occasion was the launch of our 2001 general-election campaign. As education was at the top of the agenda, Tony had asked me if I would join him in the key visit and televised formal launch, which he was to do from a school. What none of us had realised until we got there was that we were literally doing it to the schoolchildren – not parents, not even teaching and non-teaching staff and not the local community, but the girls themselves.

So there we were, sitting in the front row, and Tony comes in with the live broadcasts, filming not just his speech but, of course, the reaction of the audience. No wonder the young people present were bewildered, because the speech itself had to address the adult audience across the country and what was necessary for the media. But for teenagers, all of this was a bit too much – as the press the following morning demonstrated with photographs of bewildered looks on young faces, the nudging and the closed eyes. In retrospect, perhaps even a mention of young people would not have come amiss, but of course the speech had been written for a wider audience.

After that misjudged start I began to trudge my way around the country. I had reasonable visits to Saddleworth and Colne Valley and managed to get home in the evening, then on Tuesday made my weary way to launch the county-council election campaign with Hilary Armstrong in Derbyshire, and then went down to London.

Press-wise, it was a complete fiasco. They had intended to have John Prescott in Derby at the same time as Hilary and I were in Derbyshire launching the Shire County campaign – which was crazy. In the end they pulled John Prescott out.

The whole week was like that. People were being pulled so frequently that candidates didn't know whether or not someone would turn up. It culminated on the Saturday with two different cars arriving to pick me up to take me to Leeds to a pensioners' rally. This was very entertaining, featuring Rodney Bickerstaffe, Dickie Bird [fabled cricket umpire] and Tom Owen, son of Bill Owen [actor best known for playing Comp in *Last of the Summer Wine*], but a complete waste of time as we were only talking to the converted.

The press releases being produced were garbage. There was no co-ordination between Millbank [Labour Party headquarters in London] and the regions, and as I have said, often MPs didn't know – as Judy Mallaber (candidate in Amber Valley, Derbyshire, one of our key marginals) didn't on Tuesday – that somebody would be coming until the night before. So it was all real hand-to-mouth stuff that should have been sorted out weeks, if not months, in advance. There was no point in either visiting or speaking if we were not getting across to the public, either reinforcing or winning the vote. The whole thing was a shambles. We were just staggering along. Thankfully it didn't seem to be affecting the opinion polls.

I have often thought that we would probably have done a lot better if we did a lot less. If we had a day or two off and hadn't harangued the public at all, we would probably have shot up in the opinion polls. This was borne out by the fact that, when we made less fuss in the recess in August, we did extremely well and did better in the opinion polls, whereas when we were hyperactive, we did badly.

We had a remarkable day on the Wednesday. I got up at the crack of dawn. The plan was that I would meet Tony at Euston station. I knew I had to run Lucy before I got on the train and the driver who had come for me said he knew of a grassy area near the station that would be open for her – but it turned out to be locked up. Then he couldn't find where we were supposed to be on platform 18 at Euston because nobody had given him any instructions on where to go, so I missed Tony and arrived after he had got on the train (whereas I was supposed to be welcoming him on to the train with Gordon). I sat with Tony and Gordon and the entourage. The other Cabinet ministers were in a different carriage, with the press in another.

The front page of the *Sun* was full of my becoming Home Secretary. I said to Tony: 'What the hell's this? It doesn't do me any good at all.' He said that he was sorry, that it was their fault. Alastair Campbell, because he thought the *Sun* were going to run a story they didn't want, had apparently given them a bit of something else to get their teeth into. But it was far more than 'a bit of something'. It was a huge splash with an interview inside that I had done a month before, hyped up and embellished by drawing heavily on my first book *On a Clear Day*, and also an editorial and a piece by Trevor Kavanagh [*Sun* political editor] in addition to the front-page story. I said to Tony that he would need to explain the situation to Jack.

I was genuinely worried, as Jack had been so generous to me in predicting what might happen, and to have his nose rubbed in it was unacceptable. Effectively, his job was disappearing without a firm promise of his next destination. The problem was that I felt in my bones that Jack would think it was me who was responsible – and even if Jack didn't, John Prescott certainly would – and therefore there would be bad blood all round. Who could blame anyone who wasn't in the know for thinking the worst? I did hope that Alastair at least would brief Jack, but I am not sure what happened.

Jack was in the middle of a hell of a day of his own because he had to address the Police Federation, where he got a poor response, and Tony had a really bad day at the Queen Elizabeth Hospital in Birmingham, where he was harangued by an irate resident whose husband was suffering from cancer. It was one of those impossible situations where you just couldn't win. Tony handled it well but it diverted attention away from the manifesto.

Meanwhile John Prescott went over to Wales and delivered the famous Prescott 'kiss' with his left hook. The whole day seemed to be imploding.

We arrived in Birmingham. We went round, and round, and round several roundabouts to allow the press to be organised. Talk about silliness.

John's exploits in North Wales livened the election up and provided a diversion – but there were those who liked it and those who didn't, men on the one hand and women, middle-class women in particular, on the other. But on the whole I would say that it did us more good than harm, though not to be condoned, of course.

To Estelle Morris's constituency, Birmingham Yardley. I was pleased to be able to help Estelle, who I fear might have some difficulty retaining her seat. When I visited a school there, I said to a class of children: 'I bet nobody knows what the big event is to be on Thursday 7 June.' There was a deathly silence. Then a little lad put up his hand and said: 'We're getting Sky TV at our house on 7 June.' We all completely doubled up and it made my day. It was a bit of light in the darkness – and I was able to use it to make people laugh during the campaign, which was really helpful. I'm afraid there has been little to laugh about in this election.

I then came back and had a chat with the security people from the Home Office and Special Branch about security at Clifton Crescent, my home in Sheffield. I managed to persuade them that while I would put up with electronic security, I was not prepared to have intrusive personal surveillance. They appear to have already had a discussion behind the scenes and decided that they would have to concede that there would not be permanent surveillance in my garden – which was a major step forward – and secondly that there would not be surveillance and personnel on permanent duty with me at social events, another breakthrough. I agreed that we would step up the electronic security and carry out some work at the bottom and side of my garden, and they are coming back to take another look at that. I didn't want people parked in my garden or in the shed, like Jack Straw had.

While I could not of course be 100 per cent certain that I would become Home Secretary after the election – Tony had to confirm it, and in any case the electorate had not yet voted us in – there were certain practicalities to be considered. Because of the nature of the job, Home Secretary was one of four offices of state for which, at that time, stringent security arrangements were essential.

I had another meeting on Thursday with David Veness, Assistant Commissioner, Scotland Yard, in charge of security and that side of things, together with John Gieve, the new Permanent Secretary at the Home Office, and Bob Whalley, Head of the Terrorism Unit. We reaffirmed what we had agreed for Sheffield and for social events in London, then got down to the harder issues.

I am afraid that David Veness and I were talking a slightly different language, as John Gieve pointed out to me afterwards. I was indicating what I was prepared to do to be helpful to him, but it wasn't quite what he wanted. We agreed that we would restore the alarm system and upgrade security at South Eaton Place. I made it clear that I was not prepared to have a policeman in the room in the basement, nor was I willing to have to enter the house by the rear. David Veness didn't argue, but John Gieve indicated to me that that was what he had wanted.

We then argued about cars. I made it clear that I wasn't prepared to travel around in a police car and they conceded that, as apparently neither

APRIL/MAY/JUNE 2001   *263*

does Jack in Blackburn, although he does have a police driver. I said that I wasn't prepared to travel round in a bullet-proof vehicle in London either. They agreed that I could keep my existing car. They then tried to argue that there should always be a security man for diaried official events. I said that I would be happy to go along with that so long as it didn't involve someone having to travel with me, and that is where we reached a sticking point. I was quite happy for them to come and meet me there, but they wanted to travel with me. So we left this one for another discussion, because I pointed out that if I had a private secretary in the car and Lucy the dog and the security man, we couldn't manage. They suggested that I use a people carrier but I said that I wasn't prepared to have a people carrier. I can't work in a people carrier: the road noise is too great on fast, long journeys, and it is not possible to fit a cassette machine in the rear, and as the security men insist on sitting in the front, it would be just hopeless for me. Barry, the driver, said that we could have a BMW specially extended with extra width – because to have a wider car was the other suggestion. Barry had seen a BMW and a Mercedes, but I said that we didn't want something that drew attention to us: a Jaguar is quite obvious enough.

I went to Southampton on the Wednesday after the morning press conference, joined up with Tony and did the live press event, then went across country to Swindon, ending up two and a half hours late back in London because the line buckled.

One train was cancelled, which turned out to be fortuitous, because I met my second cousin Emma Blunkett for the first time, as I was waiting on the platform as she got off a train from London. She told me she was getting married at the end of June and I took her address. She is the daughter of David Blunkett: we used to laugh when I was young about the fact that my uncle Reg had called his son David, even though there was a David Blunkett in the family already. I remembered that David had been a policeman and learned from Emma that he still was – which might be rather embarrassing for him after 7 June if everything goes according to plan. Emma was a really nice girl and it was good to have met her.

This week Donald McIntyre of the *Independent* came with me for a day and wrote a really good piece on Thursday morning. There was also a nicely balanced piece by Kevin Maguire in the *Guardian*. I had not done badly with national items during the week. Margaret Hodge said to me on the phone that I was having a much better election than some, which pleased me.

I did *Any Questions?* on Friday night – one of my better ones. I had earlier joined Roy Hattersley for coffee at the end of the lunch that he had organised following the death of his mother Enid. I had declined to go for lunch and said I would just have a coffee with them before going on to the crematorium, where we were to send Enid to her rest – no service, no memorial, which was apparently her wish. Roy genuinely seemed to want me to be there and I was pleased to be able to pay my last respects to her. Tony Howard [journalist and political commentator], who is a good friend of Roy Hattersley's, was at the dinner prior to *Any Questions?* and I talked to him about Roy's dog Buster, who appears to be basically a killer. He has killed not only a goose in St James's Park but a pet guinea pig and even the poor old cat that Roy and his partner Maggie had at their house in Derbyshire. The cat was twenty years old and Buster gave it a shake, and that was the end of it. Buster sounds a particularly unpleasant character, but he has earned Roy a lot of money through his writing about him.

Sunday night's party political broadcast – the Tony one – was not as over the top as I expected. The only Cabinet ministers to be shown in the broadcast were Gordon and myself, pictured but neither of us speaking.

Peter Mandelson rang me in advance of my going up to Hartlepool on Tuesday: he said Tony was just taking control of his own schedule and his own campaign.

So to the North East of England: Stockton-on-Tees once more, and Hartlepool Community Centre, where there was a good turn-out and Peter made speeches about crime, which gave me an uneasy feeling, really weird. (Does he want to be Home Secretary?) Both visits were a waste of time, really, other than to keep in touch with Peter. I don't know what he is up to. Who can know? Who does?

I had a strange phone call from Jack Straw on Wednesday night. I don't know whether an *Evening Standard* diary piece about creating a kennel for the dog at the Home Office had got to him, but something certainly had. He told me that his press officer wasn't going to move with him and asked me what was going to happen to her. I said that I didn't mind what happened to her so long as Julia Simpson could move across, because I needed someone whom I knew I could work with and whom I could trust. He gave me a great talking-to about his press officer being very good and having been there for years – which is precisely the wrong thing to say to me. He then went on to say that all the speculation about my becoming Home Secretary was embarrassing and difficult for him, and he had always done his best to be nice to me. It was not my fault that Alastair Campbell did the front page in the *Sun* and that everybody else used the cuttings.

I did the *Today* programme on education on the radio on Thursday morning and *Newsnight* on television on Thursday night, but I didn't feel as if I was playing to my strengths. They did not put me up for doing one of the Radio 4 *Election Call* programmes, which I would have liked to do. Andrew Marr wrote at the beginning of the week that the reason that I wasn't so visible in the campaign was because I had been given the green light to read and prepare for the new brief. What rubbish – I was going all round the UK. Skegness, Louth, London, St Albans, Stevenage, Sheffield again, then Wales, London, the West Country, the final rally with Tony in Derby on Tuesday night, and of course canvassing – no wonder I was jiggered.

The bizarre campaign continued. I had one of those wonderful days when I went to Boston and Skegness, where I had strong family links as my father and his brothers and sisters were brought up there at the turn of the last century.

Now it is a marginal seat that in the end we lost by just over 600 votes.

This was followed by visits in Peterborough and London, and a phone call on the train, asking whether I would go to Manchester to join Tony in Salford.

I said farewell to Conor and gave him his present, then tidied up in the office, which has been repainted and recarpeted in dark green carpet tiles (which I understand look very gloomy). It didn't feel like my office any more and Lucy didn't want to stay in it, but I still felt desperately nostalgic as I walked out and went down in the lift and out of the Department for the last time as Secretary of State. The Department is shortly to be dismembered and Gillian and I will remain the only ones who have held the post of Secretary of State for education and employment. It felt very strange.

I went back to the house and picked up a shirt and some food for Lucy, put a little sponge bag in my briefcase, then was driven 220 miles up to Manchester, arriving just before 1 a.m. at the Lowry Hotel. Anji Hunter was there, and after a wide-ranging conversation she kindly agreed to take Lucy out for a walk. Eventually I had to go to bed as I was absolutely exhausted. The next morning I had breakfast with Paul Goggins, and then I went up to Tony's room. Cherie was still in her pyjamas and Alastair Campbell was hanging about, full of cold. Tony bizarrely drank the cup of tea they had brought for me. We did a press conference, which went well. When we were on the road in the campaign bus I was able to talk to Tony about various possibilities. For instance, he was still toying with the idea of

Jack having the Foreign Secretary's job instead of Robin. Tony felt nostalgic because Robin had been on his side and supportive over the euro – and presumably, although they didn't say this, a bulwark against Gordon. But Robin had lost it all – both Tony's support and the following on which he relied across the party. But I thought Rural Affairs, which is what they were toying with, would be a bit much for Robin to take.

The *Times* piece about my visit to Aberdeen was fine, and there was a piece in the *Sunday Times* about good campaigns and bad campaigns, saying that Gordon's was bad but citing my dealing with Jeremy Paxman on the *Newsnight* programme on Thursday night as being good – another piece of mischief, setting Gordon and me against each other.

It was a lot better campaigning out in the real world. I had tried from the very beginning to get them to do press conferences away from Millbank every other day. It would have been a lot better if it had been done from the start – but better late than never, I suppose.

The last few days were frenetic – for Tony and for all of us. After Salford and Shipley, I joined him in Harlow because they provided me with the plane. As I have said, I felt we were all a lot better out of Millbank, having dropped the anodyne press conferences in which we weren't reaching people, nor getting across the core messages about where we were going and what we stood for. It was all about 'what' but not about 'why'. The Liberal Democrats got away with murder with both their spending proposals and the abolition of tuition fees – utter nonsense – but they have targeted their audience very well and that is something I felt we weren't doing. We weren't identifying, targeting, and then following through.

I got home for my birthday on the eve of polling day and Andrew and Hugh came. It was a fine evening and I had had a few laughs during the day – but I felt so depressed on Thursday, election day itself. I was talking to Sally Morgan as Tony was too distracted to concentrate on the reshuffle and restructuring.

We were returned with another thumping overall majority – 165 – and the Tories won just one more seat than in 1997. In Sheffield Brightside (which, incidentally, has the smallest number of eligible voters of any constituency in England) my percentage of the vote went up.

What a four years. I just feel shaken to the bones. I should have been elated, on account of the result for the party and the new challenge for me. But I was not.

2

HOME SECRETARY

2001–2004

I knew that the new job was going to be very different. The pleasure and personal motivation of dealing with schools and young people was no longer going to be one of the great rewards of my job, and I would miss that greatly. But I was also aware that my performance at the Home Office was going to be critically important to the future of the country, and to the continuing survival of our government as we worked towards a third successive general-election victory.

What daunted me in particular was the realisation of just how many challenges my own constituency would reflect with regard to Home Office issues – whether issues around basic crime and the despair that drug abuse had brought, or the increasing and very visible problem of asylum. Home secretaries find that their advice surgeries are dominated by nationality and immigration, as people learn that if they have an address in that constituency they can get personal treatment.

These feelings lay behind my feeling of flatness, rather than any euphoria, on the morning of Friday 8 June 2001.

June/July/August 2001

Strange to feel once again a kind of detachment as the votes and seats miraculously piled up. Because I could not resist a challenge I had agreed beforehand to be the party spokesman at 7.30 a.m. on the *Today* programme, and surprised Jim Naughtie [presenter] by saying that I was worried rather than euphoric, on account of the turn-out and the disillusionment with politics and politicians. I was just getting into my stride about how to reconnect with voters when we were interrupted to go live for William Hague's snap decision to resign as Tory leader. All I could do was wish him well as a fellow South Yorkshireman.

And so we now have the new Cabinet. Ann Taylor and Chris Smith have gone, and there are now seven women – one of whom is Estelle, who, thank God, has held her seat and has replaced me as Secretary of State at what is now called the Department for Education and Skills. Tessa Jowell has made it [replacing Chris Smith as Secretary of State for Culture, Media and Sport] and Patricia Hewitt [replacing Alan Milburn as Secretary of State for Health]. And we have Charles Clarke, the Party Chairman – subject to the party ratifying him – with no department. Well, well.

It took until 4.30 p.m. on Friday before I got in to see the Prime Minister. I was due in firstly at 3.30, then 3.45 and then 4.15, and I eventually went in after John Prescott and Derry Irvine. I met Robin and Jack when I was just going into No. 10, and I had a shrewd idea what was going to happen because of my trip on the campaign bus between Salford and Shipley, but I couldn't have said anything to anybody.

My special advisers came with me to the Home Office – plus Nicky Roche, Julia Simpson and Tricia Jones, my personal assistant. Thank goodness they were there because it was very different from last time – different department, different reception. It is going to be very strange. One of the press officers at No. 10 rang across to complain that cameras had filmed me going into the Home Office, as though, having seen me come out of No. 10 smiling, get in my car and drive away, they couldn't have anticipated this. Of course the cameras would be there waiting for me. Some people around Tony got in a huff about it – presumably they wanted to make the announcement themselves – but I just ignored them.

I got things moving with articles in the *Sunday Times* and *News of the World*, cobbled together from the press statement and briefing I did on the Saturday.

The Sunday Times *article was almost a position statement, setting out what I was determined to do. It had been thought through before election day but written while waiting to go across to Downing Street, and I still think it was the kind of flying start we needed, given that we had not been able to do the groundwork and the preparation that I had been able to do in the build-up to the 1997 election.*

I also did *The World This Weekend* on Radio 4, where I was able to talk about the Police Standards Unit and what we were doing about work permits.

There was so much to reflect on about the Department and the behaviour of some of the senior civil servants, who were clearly not used to implementing anything, just legislating. It was really strange to be without any other ministers, just to be on my own, with only the support of those I brought across.

And what a wait I had for those ministers. I talked to Tony on Sunday morning and he promised me that he would finally clear with Derry Irvine who was going to be responsible for the court services, as this had been going on since Friday afternoon when he had told Derry that he was minded to transfer them to the Home Office from the Lord Chancellor's

Department. The No. 10 press office put out late on Friday night a list of those minor functions that were going to leave the Home Office, but not what we were taking on. But, as I have said, I talked to Tony on Sunday morning, to Jonathan Powell on Sunday teatime and to Sally Morgan at 10.30 on Sunday night and I couldn't get any sense out of them. I made it clear that I would like to see Tony rather than just talk on the telephone.

There was a really stupid article by Richard Ingrams in the *Observer*, a nasty piece questioning whether someone who can't see can possibly do the job of Home Secretary. Unbelievable.

I'm feeling apprehensive, not only about the job but also about my reactions to things like Tony's proposals on my team and my reaction to the way that the Department behaves. I've just got to get a grip on myself.

Saturday 16 June: the end of my first full week at the Home Office. This has turned out to be a Department that has been running on fresh air for a very long time: no systems, no way in which Private Secretaries take down detailed notes and work out an action plan as to who needs to do what, what instructions need to be given and on what timetable. It is just as if I've gone back four years and I am starting all over again; or like having reached the peak of one mountain, sliding back down to the bottom again and being told that there is a much higher mountain to climb and you will get much more prestige out of managing to scale that one, over the moraines and glaciers and chasms.

I feel fairly hairy, and I've been having to calm down certain of my special advisers. Sophie and Katharine have stayed a bit calmer, and Tricia, although staying calm, says she is at the end of her tether and has just about had enough. There are no systems for dealing with correspondence: no one in the office deals with it and private secretaries have been trying to deal with it themselves. The diary secretary has no briefing officer working with her and no system of dealing with invitations in a filtered way, a practice we managed to put together in the DfEE, so that I would have to deal only with the ones that obviously needed my consideration rather than absolutely everything. They are also trying to push me into putting things into the diary that are not worth doing, but then not spotting things that ought to be in the press diary that are really important. So far as the Halliday Report, which dealt with sentencing policy, is concerned they have no idea what to do about a Home Secretary who has ideas about which bits he is in favour of, which bits we are consulting on and which bits to rule out. They're just used to publishing things, and then waiting for the world to hit them.

We had a ministers' gathering and I tried to pull everybody together. I had to deal with the disturbances in Oldham and chaired a meeting for which there had been no preparation. Apparently when I was chasing up why they hadn't got me the statistics on New Deal placements in Oldham, they said, 'What is the New Deal?' Just breathtaking. They kept coming forward with even more legislation, and they jumped every time No. 10 spoke. If No. 10 said they thought priority should be given to something (No. 10 being Jeremy Heywood and the advisers around him, or even any junior spokesmen ringing across), they panicked. They had obviously been completely programmed by, and under the control of, No. 10, including on legislation and press work. So it was difficult to get some sense out of the legislative programme and what was going to go in on the back of the Queen's Speech. The senior staff had got no action plans, no way of implementing. There was a lot of legislation where the Orders had still not been laid, and it had still not been put into practice.

For very practical and sensible reasons, large swathes of legislation rely on the laying of Orders before the two Houses of Parliament before a particular set of clauses comes into operation. The Orders will spell out the detail of how the legislative framework is to be implemented and where the original legislation has indicated it to be necessary, and also give the House another opportunity to deal with a very specific issue that otherwise would prolong an already lengthy piece of legislation. It is a democratic safeguard. Unfortunately it obviously had become a habit for Home Office legislation to be left for up to two years before Orders were laid.

I had to prepare the material for the parole hearings of Venables and Thompson, the boys who killed the toddler James Bulger. I placed emphasis on holding them in secure accommodation rather than what had been proposed – that they be released. I took on the Parole Board about this, but the publicity was hotting up and becoming nastier.

These were not crises or unforeseen eventualities. They were just part of the job, but they were built up into major issues.

I lost the battle with Derry Irvine. It was a major constitutional issue, and he was very much against transferring court services to the Home Office. Derry was being just Derry. I suggested that we should have a commission into the role of the Lord Chancellor's Office and in particular the appointment of judges, and he nearly fell off his chair. Tony came in and said that it was an idea worth considering, but then he made the fatal error of agreeing to see Harry Woolf [Lord Chief Justice] and Lord Bingham, Master of the Rolls – which he did on the Wednesday on his return from a trip to Brussels. They threatened to resign and he believed them, and therefore, instead of passing the court-services administration to us to get on with, we compromised by appointing a specialist to oversee the installation of the technology necessary to allow the courts to be able to communicate electronically (they didn't even have email): the National Criminal Justice committee, which I was to chair, with Derry and members of the judiciary sitting on it. This committee would oversee ideas for reforming the court services, but Derry would have the responsibility for carrying these reforms out. In one sense, it could have been a lot worse, because he was then responsible for what happened, and if it didn't happen, it didn't happen. This was not a coherent solution and it didn't make sense, but it might work in my favour.

I went down to Brixton on Tuesday and met Commander Brian Paddick.

Funny that in January 2006 he denounced the reclassification of cannabis, which would have a very similar effect to the changes he himself had introduced in Brixton in 2001.

He is an interesting man who came to the fore later in the week when he announced formally that they were going to concentrate on Class A drugs and just warn people whom they found with cannabis rather than going through the extraordinarily lengthy process of arrest and charging. In the flats on the Cowley Estate in Brixton they had done a very good job, the community coming together with the police to rid themselves of crime and drugs and needles and violence. But the police station in Brixton was something else. It was terribly hot because the air-conditioning wasn't working, except in the rest-room, where it wasn't functioning properly but was still managing to make the most tremendous noise. In the canteen two officers were writing up notes from an arrest at 8.10 a.m., and they were still writing them up after 11.00 – and then they were going to put the notes into a computer, rather than having a laptop at the point of arrest and charge so that they could just tap in all the details on a set format. What a farce. No wonder they don't want to charge people for things like cannabis.

Paddick is trying this experiment and I said to him on Tuesday that my priorities are tackling Class A drugs and violent crime. It is the traffickers and pushers we need to nail. So that fitted in extremely well but it was a good job that I had seen him. The Department hadn't told me what he was intending to do, and if I hadn't had a conversation with him, they wouldn't have known.

After Cabinet I saw Tony about Derry Irvine and the court services. 'You are not pleased,' he said. 'I can tell when you are not pleased.' I said, 'Of course I am not pleased. I think we have been all over the place.' The previous Friday we were going to do it, Saturday we weren't, Sunday we were definitely going to do it, by Monday it was in doubt, Tuesday we were definitely going to get a grip of it, Wednesday he sees them, Thursday it is off. What a joke! Uncle Derry wins again and somebody leaks it. Well, well, well.

The other news of the week was the reshuffle. I didn't have very much choice in negotiating with Tony. Having vetoed one suggestion, I agreed to take Angela Eagle as a junior minister. All my DfEE team got promoted, not just Estelle and Tessa. Jacqui Smith became a Minister of State at the Department of Health, and Margaret Hodge was over the moon at getting the Minister of State's job for Higher Education and Lifelong Learning. We also had all the messing-about for Anji to stay. Sally Morgan is made Minister of State and put into the Lords and the Cabinet Office. Jean Corston is very upset and Hilary Armstrong, Chief Whip, said that it was a very close-run thing and that she had argued for her. I said that she had obviously not argued strongly enough. Otherwise everybody who has worked for me has done well and that is a plus. I was very surprised that Mike O'Brien got the sack – there had been no suggestion that he had behaved improperly over the Hinduja-brothers affair.

Mike was later reinstated, becoming Solicitor-General after the 2005 general election.

A whole range of people got the sack, including Clive Betts, but Richard Caborn has been made Minister of Sport.

Richard turned out to be a great success, even though at the time it looked like a leg-up from John Prescott, to whom he was very close.

I am finding out some staggering things. The Crime Reduction Programme was underspent massively in 1999–2000 and 2000–2001. In the financial year 2000–2001 they only spent half of the £160 million budgeted, and the Treasury has clawed it back. They didn't get agreement to carry it over into the new financial year, as we did in the DfEE with Sure Start, so they have given it up. They have obviously just capitulated to the Treasury on everything.

This theme of financial mismanagement and ineptitude was to carry on throughout the four years that I was in the Home Office, and was reflected in a National Audit Office report in late January 2006. I thought by the time that I left we had got a real grip, but things have deteriorated again since.

I am doing quite a lot of work in preparation for the Parole Board announcement on Thompson and Venables, and also in support of Alan Milburn's Mental Health Bill, which includes issues concerning Michael Stone [jailed in 2001 for killing Lin Russell and her daughter Megan] and now Barry George, who killed Jill Dando [television presenter murdered in 1999]. Both Stone and George were released from secure institutions because they weren't treatable, even though they were clearly criminally insane. I have raised it at Cabinet and got quite a lot of verbal support, for once, although it didn't seem to make any difference to Robin and Tony. Robin completely misunderstood and thought it was my Bill. Even when I had explained, he obviously had no idea who Michael Stone was. So it doesn't bode well, I am afraid.

One other thing worth noting is the fuss about whether I am capable of signing off the warrants for security, part of an elaborate protection of our civil liberties, when phone taps and surveillance are requested by the security and intelligence services. I managed to deal with that by having a regular daily verbal update, where I questioned any that were patently suspect. It is very strange to have Stephen Lander [Director-General of MI5] with me and to be dealing with such things.

Week beginning Monday 18 June: Tuesday night and Wednesday, I nearly blew my top. It was a very close-run thing as to whether I flipped altogether. John Gieve, my Permanent Secretary, took a hand in rewriting my original version of the aims-and-objectives document in such a way that reflected how the senior civil service seek to interfere if the Secretary of state is prepared to let them – but I soon dealt with that.

The correspondence system seems to be non-existent. I made a particular point about that at our first Awayday when I did my introduction. I had found out from Estelle Morris that John Gieve had said to David Normington, when asked how he was getting on, that he was 'standing up to' me. So I made a point of indicating that we were standing up for the people, not standing up to each other, and John Gieve made a kind of wincing sound. The Awayday was useful – pulling people together and going through things and finding out that at least the team agreed with each other, surprisingly so on immigration.

I have got clearance for all the advisers now. Huw Evans is going to start on two days a week as my new special adviser dealing with the media. Jack's former adviser Justin Russell has been made adviser at No 10. Michael Barber, previously head of the School Standards Unit, has got the job of Head of Implementation and Delivery at No. 10, and Andrew Adonis is the second-in-command to Jeremy Heywood, Principal Private Secretary to Tony, on the policy side.

The big event of the week was the Thompson and Venables Parole Board and release. I had another visit that day from the security people about my house in Sheffield. If anyone was going to threaten me, it would be on the weekend of the Thompson and Venables release. I made a written Statement to the House on Friday the 22nd, very carefully worded. I spent a lot of time the previous two days getting it right.

I also had to prepare to deal with the Chief Constable of Sussex, Paul Whitehouse, who promoted the officers who shot a naked unarmed man dead in Brighton and backdated the promotion. There were a whole range of things that I went through which caused me concern. The Assistant Chief Constable has really taken over and started to do the business. It also showed the Police Complaints Authority to be absolutely useless.

On the personal front, my son Hugh got a 2.2, and has had a good interview for a job with Electronic Data Sources. Andrew has sat his last two A-level exams, and we will just have to pray for success.

I had dinner with Peter Mandelson, who is deeply hurt and upset because he thought he had been promised a small role working with people in Brussels on the expansion of the European Union, only to find that it had been vetoed by others. I did mention this to Tony in a private session at the end of a very long meeting from 3.00 to 4.45 on Tuesday afternoon, at which we talked about a whole range of Home Office activities. Tony wants no asylum seekers entering the country and all those who have failed their appeals to be deported. I had to point out to him that we were £430 million overspent on the asylum seekers' support system and that I cannot turn things round in that sort of time. I have never seen a budget like it. One hundred and sixty-nine million pounds overspent on other areas, most of which is because they allowed money to be clawed back rather than carrying the underspend into the new financial year. What a set-up.

The Venables and Thompson issue has calmed down. My letter to the Police Authority in Sussex on Friday was released by me on Tuesday, and Paul Whitehouse, the Chief Constable, immediately resigned, which made it look as if I had either waved a magic wand or got really tough – which in one sense I had, trying to reverse the effects of three and a half years of people doing nothing. The same approach will be needed for the Afghan hijackers as well.

This was a long-standing case concerning a hijacked plane that in February 2000 had landed at Stansted airport, where the hijackers (and those claiming to have been passengers) claimed asylum. There was, of course, a major complication here, because these individuals were fleeing from the Taliban, and Britain had to fulfil its obligations: under our law (and the conventions) we had to deal with each individual case. This meant trying to disentangle those who were genuinely fleeing and those who were not, and those who had deliberately taken part in the hijacking and those who just happened to find themselves aboard the plane and were not originally intending to claim asylum at all. For the press, the fact that these people were permanently housed in a reasonable hotel had become and continued to be a cause célèbre.

The number of warrants I was signing with regard to telephone interception and surveillance had reached an annual total of over 2,500 by the time I left the Home Office. I took these extremely seriously. We have the most stringent rules in the world for telephone-tapping and surveillance, but they are still difficult to square with civil-liberties concerns. These operations are necessary for our protection on a wide range of fronts with regard to terrorism and organised crime, but sensitivity has to be applied. I was particularly keen to ensure that we didn't get the security and intelligence services embroiled in the political arena.

The big event on Thursday, my speech to the National Probation Conference, on sentencing, went remarkably well.

This was the first ever National Probation Conference, because the service had been drawn together on a national basis for the first time, and the main point of the conference was to debate the sentencing report. I set out alongside it in my speech my ideas about balancing improved, more robust but much more extensive community sentencing with much tougher sentences for heinous crimes. It took me another two years to get this into legislation but the balance between the two seemed to be crucial. I believed that people would accept more sensitive and sensible sentencing for non-violent and less heinous crimes (reducing the pressure on the prison population and doing more remedial and rehabilitative work) if they knew that we were really getting serious about those crimes that hurt, distress and anger people the most.

Some of the papers picked up on my remarks in relation to the judiciary and sentencing guidelines and the way in which Parliament and senior judiciary interrelate in the wake of the Human Rights Act. It is something we talked about at No. 10 on Monday night when I went for dinner with Tony and Cherie. Steve Byers, Alan Milburn and Estelle were also there. It was an odd evening because I don't think people were talking as freely as they might have wanted to. We went round the houses on what the difficulties would be and what was happening with public services. I discovered that Steve, Alan, John Reid and Tessa Jowell were meeting after Cabinet and I will be keeping a close eye on things to see what they are up to. I had a very useful discussion with Tessa over dinner on Tuesday night. She knows more about what's going on between the colleagues than anyone else. It is useful to be just slightly out of it – one step removed, as it were – because that allows me to be more of a free agent.

My appearances on television on the Sunday resulted in extensive coverage of my comments on the Bradford riots.

It is hard now to remember just how profound an impact the disturbances in Bradford had, taken together with the situation in Oldham and Burnley and the smaller disturbances in Leeds and elsewhere. This was a real test, not only of whether I was going to be able to get a grip and stop any further flare-ups, but also of whether the backbenchers would support me in getting tough. This meant condemning not only the fascists who had stirred up the troubles and used every opportunity as a tinderbox for their own purposes, but also the Socialist Workers' Party and hangers-on who made matters worse and played directly into the hands of the far right.

The fact that I was dealing with a number of issues at the same time became par for the course over the years ahead – juggling several balls. Sometimes those dealing with the media at Downing Street (with the exception of Alastair Campbell) didn't seem to understand that if you have a major calamity to deal with you should calm down rather than going on the defensive, being negative or unnecessarily aggressive.

On the Wednesday night, prior to the speech on sentencing, I had a bizarre conversation with Hilary Jackson, my new Principal Private Secretary, who inherited me when I took over as Home Secretary. Apparently she had been phoned by 'No. 10' trying to take out bits of my speech about what I call 'sentencing minus'. This is a custodial sentence that becomes a community sentence instead unless the person breaches it, in order to give them a chance of rehabilitation. I told her to get lost, saying that if an ex-civil servant (John Halliday, who wrote the sentencing policy document) can come up with a range of ideas that I publish and we can debate, it is pretty pathetic if the Home Secretary himself can't come up with ideas and include them in the speech and have them discussed.

That is the sort of attitude we get. Even in this second term, with this new parliament and with this massive majority, we have people in No. 10 trying to use Tony Blair's name to preclude senior Cabinet ministers from contributing their own thoughts and ideas. But they got short shrift from me, and that was the end of that. I said I would speak to Tony if they felt strongly about it, but they never came back to me – so that was one occasion at least where I had called their bluff.

There was too much of this interference at that stage of the government, where juniors were using the Prime Minister's name in a way that was inconsistent with what the Prime Minister himself would have wanted. There are times, of course, when it is convenient for any Prime Minister (or for that matter any senior politician) to use junior staff to test things out and to see where the boundaries can be probed or drawn in. But on the whole I found that people were using their position either very defensively or to promote an interest of their own. The most successful politicians are those who call such people's bluff. (In fairness, people like Justin Russell and Jeremy Heywood at No. 10 worked closely with my advisers and added value in a number of areas. It struck me, though, that No. 10 advisers have time to think, a luxury not afforded to people running departments.)

All of this was a distraction at a time when trouble was brewing in the North. During the build-up to the Bradford disturbances it had become clear to me (bearing in mind that this was two months before the attacks on the World Trade Center and Pentagon) that insecurity, instability and a fear of difference would be reinforced by the clashes that had taken place in what euphemistically became known as the 'northern towns'. I had the feeling that the media thought that, given the distance from London, all of this was some sort of aberration. Simplistic views were aired and demands for government action were plentiful, but few insights emerged. The truth was that we were dealing with a variety of deep-seated structural problems relating to housing and broader geopolitical issues, as well as economic, social and educational segregation. Regeneration programmes had been badly tailored to areas which were 'divided', sometimes simply by a main road, on ethnic grounds. As ever, the British National Party thrived just outside areas of diverse ethnicity. It is in the deeply deprived working-class and lower-middle-class areas where their message is most salient, and we saw this in the seats that they won in Burnley, including on the edge of the town.

What was encouraging at the time, including from my own backbenchers, was the realisation that paternalistic patting on the head was a thing of the past. Thugs are thugs, from whatever community, ethnic or faith background. The problems that they articulate need to be addressed, but their methods need to be crushed. That was the message that I promoted, both on the GMTV programme on the Sunday morning and in my Statement in the house. The reaction from the police was remarkable. The fact that I had stood up for law and order and for tough – though fair – action in dealing with the self-destruction of home and community was widely welcomed. In other words, I had established a very clear message, that we were not prepared to tolerate mindless violence and the counterproductive undermining of all our efforts, and that we would take any action necessary to stop it.

And it stopped. Nothing irritated me more in my time as Home Secretary than people who not only failed to understand history but believed that a kind of woolly benevolence could replace clear public policy. Priority had to be given to restoring security and safety for those living in and around the areas affected and setting in train nationally the local mechanisms for pulling people together to restore a sense of identity and a way forward for the future.

Good news of the week is that Alastair started his traineeship in environmental health at Hull. Hugh had his twenty-first birthday on the Friday [13 July], and we all went out for a meal on Thursday night. Hugh also had the use of the house in London to celebrate with his friends. Andrew started his volunteering at Denford's Engineering near Huddersfield and we await his A-level results.

A mixed week one way and another. Things weren't getting any easier, but the *Guardian* had a complimentary leader about me on Saturday morning. I don't recall ever before having a complimentary leader in the *Guardian*. The trouble was that it was double-edged, because it attacked Jack. It is really annoying when people do that. Then during the week there was the meeting with Stephen Lander, Head of MI5, who came to talk to me about the general issues around security, the international side of things and the liaison with MI6. He was obviously deeply upset about a warrant that I had declined. I just spread my hands apart and said, 'I am so sorry, Stephen, I won't do it again.' Everybody had to laugh because it got the point across pretty starkly. I said: 'Look, in future, if I am minded to turn down a warrant relating to the service, I will come back to you and give you the chance to talk to me before doing so – but there wasn't a leg to stand on on this one.'

I had two meetings with Tony, one a catch-up meeting on Tuesday. I had only got three-quarters of an hour so there was not a lot we could do, but I managed to bring him up to date. The second meeting was on the Thursday with Derry Irvine and Peter Goldsmith, and concerned the Criminal Justice Bills. This was a constructive session because in the end I think we got them to understand that we couldn't just plough ahead, particularly with the wholesale disclosure of information and the admissibility of previous convictions, without thinking it all through carefully, on the grounds that we could lose either the first Criminal Justice or the big second Criminal Justice Bill, or rather have to introduce the Parliament Act, which means one or other of them would be pushed back by a year, which would be crazy just for one measure. I suggested that if we do decide to go ahead we should have either a separate Bill or include it with victims' rights in order to ensure that we do not end up with the House of Lords holding everything up so that we would have to drop it in the end. There is nothing worse than going ahead with something and then dropping it, causing havoc and ill will at the cost of enormous amounts of money, time and energy.

The problems about financing that I had found when entering the Home Office – the fact that they had 'given back' money that they could have held on to through what is known as 'end-year flexibility' – were getting resolved. Andrew Smith [Chief Secretary to the Treasury] came across to say that they would agree to reinstate the end-year flexibility but they wanted a say in spending on the criminal justice system, as it affected the Lord Chancellor and the Attorney-General. It was good not only to have agreement but also to have had a discussion with Gordon about how we might link additional funding through regeneration for local warden schemes with recruitment of civilian staff, and put the whole of this agenda (developing the role of civil society and community action) together.

This was to prove prescient, as we were later to be able to develop community support officers with substantial additional funding and to link these in with the street wardens funded through the Office of the Deputy Prime Minister. It was therefore at this very early juncture in July 2001 that we began to move on to what would become the new Community Beat Teams and a return to genuine neighbourhood security and policing.

I met Harry Woolf, the Lord Chief Justice, and was as nice as pie to him. He said he thought my concept of custody minus an excellent idea. I smiled, because everybody in the Department and, subsequently, the minions at No. 10 were trying to stop me from announcing it and making it part of the consultation and the speech. So that was one of the twists. He could see straight away that it was a way in which the new system would avoid a huge increase in the prison population and would get people into intensive supervision and reparation rather than a month, six weeks or even three months in jail, which would simply make matters worse.

I got on with him quite well, and mischievously drew his attention to Lord Bingham's interview in *The Times* on Monday about the Supreme Court.

Lord Bingham was suggesting complete independence for the Law Lords, overseeing our unwritten Constitution but without the political element of the US Supreme Court's membership, who are nominated by the President.

He had a fairly good explanation – that he did not want to set up a Supreme Court in the American style but only to separate the Law Lords from the Lords, which he (Harry Woolf) said he was not keen on. But we are going to have an up-and-downer about the Guidelines Body and what happens to the current Advisory Panel.

This was the idea of giving Parliament and the public a much bigger say in sentencing. Eventually it was to become the Sentencing Guidelines Council and I would eventually compromise by agreeing that the Lord Chief Justice could chair it but that there would be a substantial widening of those involved in advice and guidance on sentencing policy in addition to judges. It was going to take two years before we were able to get this passed in the Criminal Justice Act, an illustration of how long it takes to develop an idea through to legislation – never mind implementing it.

There are so many offshoots of the Home Office, so many advisory groups, special and service agencies, so many bodies that nobody has any control over – and virtually accountable to nobody at all. This is something I do want to get a grip of over the next two years. Everybody seems to be doing their own thing – from the Association of Chief Police Officers to the National Criminal Intelligence Service and the National Crime Squad. No one is in control of anything. As far as ACPO is concerned, they did themselves enormous harm because Colin Phillips, Chief Constable of Cumbria, appeared on the *Today* programme and was asked two questions. The first concerned what, in his opinion, would be the most significant way of reducing crime and improving detection – to which he replied that the problem was really about unemployment and education. In other words, he said that there was nothing we could do in the short term. Then he was asked about the Standards Unit, and he said that he was against it because you couldn't compare policing anywhere else with what he was doing in Cumbria. This was just breathtaking: of course you could compare what they were doing with detection in Cumbria with Derbyshire or Cheshire or Staffordshire. What nonsense.

On Tuesday night I had dinner with the *Daily Mail*. In the Tory leadership election, Iain Duncan Smith had, as it were, unseated Michael Portillo, while the *Mail*'s favourite was Ken Clarke. All this made for a lively discussion. Sophie Linden and Julia Simpson came along and Paul Dacre, David Hughes [then political editor of the *Daily Mail*], Stephen Glover and Edward Heathcoat-Amory were quite affable.

At Cabinet we discussed the missile defence system – briefly, but at least we discussed it. I had my little say about how the money could be better spent elsewhere and about other more relevant forms of defence that could be put in place. That went down like a lead balloon. I couldn't remember the name of Menwith Hill, the tracking station in Yorkshire. I had got Fylingdales on my mind and said, 'What's the other place?', and they all said, 'Menwith Hill'. I said, 'I ought to remember that' – recalling my days as a CND activist – 'I was there in the 1980s.' Geoff Hoon [Secretary of State for defence], who was supporting the defence system, said, 'I was there last week.' I said, 'What, climbing through the fence?'

In the absence of Steve Byers [Secretary of State for the Environment, Transport and the Regions] I had to deal with John Spellar, a junior transport minister, on speed cameras, which involved a whole range of issues that the DETR had not bothered to consider properly – issues like the enormous use of police time spent on the cameras, and the problem of catching people transgressing as opposed to deterring them in the first place. He had a variety of practical questions that should have been dealt with and answered long before his Department got to the point of wanting to make the announcement. But John was desperate. It had been put in the media diary so I agreed to announce it so long as we indicated the following: that we were going to review and get a grip of these other issues; that we made it clear that we were extending the scheme to four counties and not trebling it; and that the speed cameras were visible. I insisted that this was made clear so that it wasn't seen as a surreptitious exercise in pursuing the motorist. So that's what we did. They didn't want to announce the review of the speed limit on motorways until Tony was back and had cleared it, so I still had that to deal with.

I never did get agreement to a review of motorway speed limits because other events overtook it. It had been my intention to see if we could put the speed limit up to 80 m.p.h. while increasing enforcement.

We had meetings on asylum and the fiasco of the manual count and what we were to do with it.

Figures on asylum that had been produced previously were simply inaccurate. I had initiated what was known as a 'manual count' because this went through every particular source (port and airport of entry) rather than the ad hoc computer account, which did not include all those coming into the country and claiming asylum.

On the personal front, I went to the Northern General Hospital and had a gastroscopy, which showed that I have Barrett's Oesophagus, a condition of the gullet. It was very lucky I went because it is pretty clear that had I not done so, the acid and reflux would have permanently damaged my oesophagus and could have led to cancer – never mind the discomfort and inability to eat properly. I was in a complete state about going to the hospital and having the test, and I started to sweat when they began taking samples. The staff were lovely and those in the waiting-room said that they didn't expect to see me there with the rest of them, and that it couldn't be all that bad in there if I was there. They don't expect you to be a normal citizen, a normal human being.

The week beginning 20 August proved busier than ever – I have never known an August like it. I went down to London on Tuesday and Wednesday and saw John Monks about the TUC conference and the worries that he has about public services. I then went to Tessa Jowell's for the evening and ended up in an argument with her husband David about legalising drugs: I think he was taking a determinedly libertarian stance to make for a good debate. It was a shame, because I had gone to dinner full of sympathy because a sixteen-year-old friend of their children Matthew and Jessica had been tragically killed in South Africa in an accident.

The most bizarre part of the day was a conversation with Jack Straw [Foreign Secretary], ostensibly about reinstating the immigration checks at Prague airport, about which he has been very helpful. But he then asked if officials could put their telephones down – civil servants routinely listen in to conversations between ministers regarding formal government business – so that we could talk privately. He then launched into this tirade about my having wanted his job and what had happened on the day of the launch of the manifesto. I said: 'Hang on, Jack, you know perfectly well that it was No. 10 – it was nothing to do with me.' In fact Estelle Morris had had the same treatment, so I suppose he could blame her for wanting my job. He then said, 'You have drawn a line. It is year zero from 7 June. You are overturning everything.' I wondered who on earth had been winding him up. There was one article written by Anne McElvoy in which she had hinted that people were saying that I had started afresh. I suspect that this may have been drawn to Jack's attention and he had got himself into a right old pickle over it, which is really sad.

I spoke to Charles Clarke the following week. He was, to say the least, outspoken about his time in the Home Office, and it was certainly illuminating to hear what he had to say. It is not going to be easy if both Jack and Derry Irvine are offside with me.

I don't think that the relationship between Jack and myself ever recovered. Although it was absolutely true that I had not been briefing journalists or saying anything publicly, at a distance I can now see what it must have looked like: I was coming in like a steamroller over the way the Department worked and its wider policies. I know now that I should have been more diplomatic and briefed Jack about what I was doing and why.

It was undoubtedly a general failing of mine that I should have been much more diplomatic with my colleagues, and it is something that I genuinely regret. However, the changes needed to be made because on so many fronts I was about to be swept away if I did not introduce major reforms. Over a longer timescale I have had to live with the same kind of changes to my own policies, firstly at Education and subsequently following my resignation as Home Secretary.

I have received some really very silly letters from Derry Irvine, one suggesting that we should publish Robin Auld's report on the criminal-justice system and the courts before the end of September. We haven't even received it yet. It was due at the end of July/beginning of August and now it is due during the first week in September – and he wants to try and publish it in a fortnight, without any commentary or comment. He has also sent me a stupid letter about Remembrance Day, because he has taken over some of the Home Office responsibilities for organising events in which the Queen is involved. Talk about pomposity. He sent me yet another letter which asks why his Department has not been involved in the asylum reviews. I have written back to him, saying that the voucher review was initiated a year ago at the Labour Party conference. If he has been a political hermit for a year, that's hardly my look-out.

And asylum goes on, and on and on. It's getting to absurd proportions now, with what is happening at Sangatte, the refugee camp outside Calais. We have silly articles about orphans crossing Europe specifically to reach the tunnel and claim asylum in the UK. One such story appeared in the *Sunday Express* on 26 August – as if anyone seriously believes that no one is trafficking them and taking money from them. I found out from teachers who wrote to me that in schools up and down the country they have asylum seekers claiming to be fifteen years old who are much, much older. Meanwhile the Australians are holding off shiploads of Afghans. The whole thing is just getting out of hand.

September 2001

I went to Munich for the Germany v. England game on Saturday [1 September] and had a wonderful time, with a wonderful result – a historic 5–1 to England. Apart from the dreadful weather and oppressive security for me personally, it was a lovely weekend and it really did me good.

I recall with pleasure sitting next to a man who became a genuine political friend, the Interior Minister and Sports Minister of Germany, Otto Schily. He was over the moon when Germany scored the first goal – and then one by one, as England's five goals overwhelmed the German team, he had his head in his hands and kept saying, 'Oh no, oh no!' At the end of the game I gave him a hug. We were supposed to be having a formal discussion afterwards about interior matters (about the joint action on hooliganism taken between ourselves and the German authorities, which had worked extremely well), but quite understandably he was in no mood for it.

I did not, on the whole, take part in jaunts. There were visits to a number of countries that I really ought to have made, including South Africa, but that

*short weekend in Munich was one of the genuine perks of being Home
Secretary.*

I now have to get a grip on asylum. I wrote a very long personal memo to
Tony and spoke to him on the telephone on Monday 3 September, because
the material that was produced by the Immigration and Nationality
Directorate and the Home Office was absolutely useless. The Home Office
tend to give up on doing this altogether and just hand it over to IND – as
they do with the prison service, the police and everything else. I have
therefore done a long and detailed chronology of what needs to be done,
and I have agreed to go to Paris on 12 September to see the French Interior
Minister. I should have done this before but the French were away in
August, which was a problem.

There was a very interesting front page of the *Sunday Telegraph* saying
that I had already been in touch with my opposite number in France about
closing Sangatte. I had said to officials that I wanted to raise it with him,
but I had not raised it with anyone who could have told the *Sunday
Telegraph*. The Home Office is a bit of a sieve.

I've had an absolute hell of a week. I rewrote completely what the
officials produced for the meeting with Tony Blair on the 12th – rewrote it
myself as my memorandum, setting out where we are going. They couldn't
come up with the figures, even though they have had more than two
months to do so after I told them in June what I was going to do. All the
papers are asking: where's the policy? I then find out on Friday night that
the Immigration and Nationality Directorate think that their request to the
Treasury for a supplementary allocation of cash of £450 million is
£300 million short. I found it so staggering that I could have wept.
The whole thing is out of hand.

I went to Nick Stewart's farewell do at Moorfoot, the education headquarters in Sheffield: he's finishing as deputy at the DfEE. Nick told me
what John Gieve had told me when we met for the first time after the
holidays on Tuesday, and in pretty much the same words – namely that he
had met officials who said that they were in shell-shock, reeling and
knocked sideways. Nick said that the official he had spoken to said that she
had found my arrival invigorating, but that others had gone into a sulk.
Well, they can come out of the damned sulk pretty fast, otherwise I think
they are going to find that they will be sulking elsewhere.

John Gieve has come back from his holiday a lot more vigorous, a lot
clearer, a lot more onside than he was – so that has got to be a plus.

And then, on Friday, the *coup de grâce*. Justice Andrew Collins ruled in favour of the appellants that we are infringing the European Convention on Human Rights by keeping people in the fast-track centre at Oakington in Cambridgeshire. We intend to appeal to the House of Lords immediately. The ridiculous thing is that I am not in a position to do interviews or say anything about the ruling if I am to stand any chance of winning on appeal. This is because what I have to say would not only infringe the normal legal conventions but would completely get up the noses of the Law Lords. All I can do is to change the wording of my statement from 'I am disappointed' (which is what the officials asked me to say) to 'I am deeply disturbed and concerned.' I feel so frustrated. I started all this rolling on 11 June and have been working on it for three months. I have got some way there, but then what I have managed to do gets knocked sideways by judges who are completely out of touch with reality.

I'm afraid the whole asylum issue is now out of hand. The pictures from Coquelle freight depot have blown everything sky high. Asylum seekers were shown breaking through the fence and mounting the freight trucks in their hundreds. Jeff Rooker went to Coquelle on Monday night and said that there were more cameramen than there were people trying to get on the train.

All the ideas I had had earlier in the summer about being able to have a sensible rethink over August and come out with policies in the autumn had gone by the board. Almost nightly, the early-evening news broadcasts on both BBC and ITV were running footage of events at Sangatte. There were even journalists posing as asylum seekers, going out to France to show how easy it was to get back into the country. All I knew at the time was that I really did need to make some progress and unfortunately, given the French politicians I was dealing with (although they were politically sympathetic), we were getting nowhere. They just wouldn't make decisions.

I have been dealing with the difficult case of a former civil servant who murdered his wife with an axe and then presented himself as mentally ill. The advice I was given was just extraordinary – that we would lose and so we might as well give in because the review of his case by psychiatrists had strengthened the hand of those wanting him out and the panel would almost certainly let him out. I told them to do everything possible to stop him getting out. I think it is disgraceful.

This man had substantial support (and I will put it no stronger than this) in some highly placed quarters, as he had been a Grade 5 civil servant in the Treasury. But the real issue here was the operation of the panel. What I came to realise was that those who claimed mental illness in order to circumvent the normal criminal justice system could be dealt with outside the sentencing policy for murder and then be released once the claim to mental illness had disappeared and the psychiatrist judged that such an individual was no longer a threat. As a consequence, someone who would otherwise have gone down for thirty years was out in under three, and at the same time had treatment, visits and facilities – completely different from someone who had been convicted of murder. During my time as Home Secretary I did manage to get this system tightened up, just as I tried to toughen up the operation of the Parole Board, but in retrospect I believe I still did not do enough.

Friday was an odd day, not least in terms of funny incidents relating to my blindness. A man who rang in to Radio Sheffield said in all seriousness that I had flown over part of the city in a helicopter when I was Leader in order to see the devastation of industry – a fat lot of good that would have done me. Then in the evening I went to a fundraising dinner for the Labour Party in Sheffield and a woman said to me, 'I hope you don't mind my being personal but how can you tell when it is morning and night?' I said, 'Well, I just look at my watch.'

The big issue of next week is Tony Blair's speech to the TUC. Tony's 'row' with the public services is the great drum being beaten by the TUC – foolishly, in my view. And the tension over immigration, fuelled by the human-rights pundits who paraded the likelihood of £100 million of compensation, is palpable. You can feel it and it is very dangerous.

These were the civil-liberties lawyers who were dancing for joy at the victory of the asylum seekers over the government. They had announced their intention to go for mass compensation for those who had been put through the system.

But all of this paled into complete insignificance as the events of Tuesday 11 September unfolded. The day started as usual with my own very minor problems that morning getting to the Police Superintendents' Association annual conference in Warwickshire. In the end, my driver Barbara had to follow the Special Branch escort, using the flashers and the siren, down the hard shoulder of the motorway. I delivered the speech, then did *World at One* and the *Jimmy Young Show*. (It had just been announced that Jimmy was being retired, and he rang me later in the week to see if I could help with saving his job. I did in fact put in a word for him.)

At about 2.10 p.m., as I was on the train coming back from Coventry, the news started to come in about the suicide attacks and the planes that had flown into the twin towers of the World Trade Center in New York and the Pentagon in Washington, DC. News was also coming in about the plane that had come down in Pennsylvania, which had presumably been aimed at killing thousands more people: it appeared that some of the passengers had been told to ring their loved ones and tell them that they were going to die. What a terrible, wicked thing to do. It seems that one of the passengers had told a member of their family over the telephone that they were going to try and tackle the hijackers and attempt to bring the plane down away from populated areas. What tremendous bravery and presence of mind at a time when they must have been numbed into fatalism and acquiescence. It was such a wicked act.

How do we deal with suicide bombers? The World Trade Center was not a symbol of capitalism. Of course, many of the people working in there, attending meetings and conferences, were well-off, but it was a symbol of international commerce, which those who sneer at most live off most. The people most damaged by the attack in terms of the undermining of the world economy are the poorest, those who always suffer when there is a downturn in the world economy, and when money is cut from essential international aid, public service, investment and renewal.

We had a hastily convened COBR meeting on Tuesday teatime, which Tony chaired – and chaired very well (though for normal civil contingencies or minor issues, the Home Secretary is the chair). Sir John Stevens was talking about the Metropolitan Police Special Branch. I pointed out that there were major cities across the whole of Britain – Edinburgh, Glasgow, Sheffield, Liverpool, Manchester, Birmingham – and that all of them matter. Geoff Hoon was gung ho. 'We are ready,' he said to Tony, 'to put our Air Force and our facilities at the disposal of the intelligence services.' I said, 'I think we need a moment's pause on this.' I could tell they were getting carried away. Gordon was very good, not only in terms of his confidence about the economy but also sharing my view that vacating both the Stock Exchange and Canary Wharf gave a very bad signal. We all know about the dangers. Later in the week the *Sunday Telegraph* was going to run a story about the chemical and biological infiltration of the water supply. I said that they must not do that and that of course we had the filtration and the stations covered and the press must not scare people. We need to keep calm.

I think in retrospect that all of us were in shock that Tuesday teatime. Gradually the sheer horror of what had happened and the enormity and scale of it began to filter through. When I had first received the information on the train (two of my sons rang me during the course of the short journey) what had happened was so surreal that many people in the carriage could not believe what they were hearing. Jonathan Powell rang me from Downing Street to arrange the COBR (civil contingencies) committee meeting and, of course, Tony abandoned his speech to the TUC and immediately returned to London. All I could think about on the train journey and in the car to Downing Street was what measures would be meaningful in terms of practical security, how we could avoid panic and what the consequences would be in the long term. The immediate evacuation at Canary Wharf had been an example of how important it was to persuade people that they were not immediately at risk of the same thing happening here. But to ensure stability and avoid such panic it was necessary to be clear about what it was we were able to do and were prepared to do – such as establish a no-fly zone over the centre of London. I knew that attention would immediately be paid to our border controls: who was coming in and out of the country and with what background. My discussions with the Interior Minister in France had been cordial but not very productive, and the next day I flew in an RAF plane over Paris with a no-fly zone in operation there. We were the only aircraft in the air and those accompanying me had a rare view of the city centre and its lights. It felt slightly surreal.

The issue that was to emerge, linking the riots, 11 September and a clearly insecure world was the fear and instability that the new atmosphere created for people in their day-to-day lives. People coped in stalwart fashion outwardly, but undoubtedly were affected internally. In the months ahead I constantly returned to the business of providing security and stability in the community, nationally in relation to terrorism and internationally in terms of a more stable and rational world. Alongside the security and stability created from 1997 under the tutelage of Gordon Brown in our economy, Tony was driving an agenda of providing much greater reassurance and stability in a world of ever more rapid change – an agenda I was attempting to pursue domestically. Helping people through that change became central to everything I was trying to do.

Part of the machinery of government developed during the Blair premiership was the regular 'stocktake meeting' for updates with appropriate ministers and officials (policy officers from Downing Street and the Treasury) round the table. This was not one of the 'chats on the sofa' referred to some years later by the former Secretary of the Cabinet, Sir Robin Butler, but formal meetings that were much more useful than traditional Cabinet Committees, which tended merely to confirm a set of agenda items with predictable reports from departmental officials. Stocktakes were very much more about investigating what had gone right or wrong and determining the next steps to be taken while ensuring both prime ministerial and Treasury support.

I cancelled the main stocktake meeting this week but saw Tony privately on Thursday. He gave me the principled agreement to go ahead with the changes on asylum but wanted a lot more information – though getting information out of the Department is the killer. I have told them to revise everything. We need to look radically at what we are going to do, at the numbers coming in, how we are processing them and what happens to them. I talked to Tony about the internal situation and I talked to him again on Saturday at length on the telephone. He really wants radical change.

I have written a detailed memo to John Gieve, setting out what I think we need to do on the back of that conversation – a whole range of measures, trying to tackle the issues around the ECHR [European Convention on Human Rights] and the Human Rights Act, as well as practical measures for extradition and for securing ourselves. A lot will depend on the actions of the US. As Tony said, if he hadn't embraced the US and been really positive, they wouldn't have taken any notice of us at all and at least they are doing so now, as I dictate this note on Sunday 16 September.

Parliament is being recalled, which I do not think a good idea. Tony did extraordinarily well, as he had done all week, but Bush was completely naff, flying to Nebraska to go into the bunker before realising that he had made a mistake and flying to Washington. Bill Clinton got to New York and to the victims before he did.

At noon on Friday I went to St Paul's Cathedral for the service to commemorate the victims of the attacks, and felt very emotional. Never mind all the sneering and cynicism and what the US policy has been in Afghanistan and the Middle East. We know all about that, but it is not the point at this moment. I did as little media as I could whereas Jack Straw did a great deal. It's funny what happens to people when they become Foreign Secretary – the role just seems to take them over. I did the *Today* programme on Friday morning and pointed out that we needed to debate how to protect freedom and democracy, while at the same time maintaining them. I don't think that John Humphrys fully appreciated the broader argument that I was trying to make. I was trying to reflect on the Weimar Republic and the Spanish Civil War – and I let forth on Oakington and the human-rights fanatics who evoke exactly the wrong reactions.

One of the ironies of this time was the fact that I was arguing very strongly that we should not believe that identity cards were a panacea for all our ills in terms of terrorism. (I was talking about entitlement cards at the time to try and get across that they were about beneficial gains for the individuals and not just for the state.) On that programme and in two further Today *interviews in subsequent weeks I stressed again and again that I believed strongly that we would need biometric identification and security, but I also stressed that this was to ensure that we knew who was in the country and who was entitled to services; that we could tackle organised crime and fraudulent working; and that while this in itself would contribute to intelligence and security measures, that was not the reason I was putting forward the proposition.*

Opponents of ID cards, understandably from their point of view, continued for the following four years to try to present those in favour of them as being obsessed with the idea that this would protect us from terrorism. This had never been the case and was a complete distortion. In every subsequent document we issued (starting with the serious internal discussions in the early New Year of 2002) we stressed the broad approach. But having a serious debate about anything became harder and harder over those years, partly because, almost imperceptibly, the British print media (and gradually the broadcast media) had moved away from reporting fact and moved instead into opinion – so much so that the editor of the Independent *newspaper could boast that his was 'more a viewspaper than a newspaper'. I am afraid democracy is the worse for it, although of course one of the world's paradoxes is that sometimes the things we like the least help us personally in times of need: when I became a columnist for the* Sun *in the late autumn of 2005, I did so in the knowledge that here was someone else providing 'views' and not 'news'.*

One or two remarkable things over the past extraordinary week. The *Sun* was so positive and helpful in trying to damp down anti-Islamic feeling, a really important message, while Israel was extremely unhelpful, taking the opportunity to go on the offensive rather than find peace. My grandfather used to say that the Middle East would be the tinderbox that would ignite global conflagration – God help us.

My job now is to sort out security measures and get the law changed to try to protect ourselves, and to reorganise the extradition laws. I have to make sure that we are on top of what needs to be done but to say as little as possible unless it needs to be said.

Given the febrile mood of that week, it is perhaps not surprising, but is none the less curious, that my diary made no mention of the fact that on the Friday – three days after the attacks on New York and Washington – the Tories finally elected yet another new leader in the shape of Iain Duncan Smith.

On Saturday I went to a community group at Shiregreen, a large rented-housing estate in my constituency, just for half an hour. Their pleasure that I had turned up made it worth the effort, despite everything else going on. That evening my sons came round and we had a nice dinner, but they are all going their separate ways from here on. Before the end of the month Hugh is starting his job, Alastair is getting his retake results, and Andrew is going to his freshers' week. It is a strange sort of watershed for all of us.

It is funny that I didn't even notice that George Bush had used the term 'crusade', but it has been pointed out that it was a very unfortunate word in respect of the Middle East. We have to be so careful.

In Sheffield for the weekend, I have been reflecting on changed relationships. I took a call from Gordon prior to his speaking to the US Treasury about money-laundering, underground banking and a variety of other issues. We had a very positive conversation, talking the same language.

Jack Straw has called his press conference for 8 a.m. tomorrow and everybody is wanting me to come down to London for more meetings, whereas I just want the time to get on with things.

Tony rang me on his way down to Chequers on Monday night. He is going to have a hell of a schedule – Germany, France, Washington, New York, then back for the European summit on Friday. God knows what party conference is going to be like or what sort of speeches we will all be making. It will be chaotic.

Monday, and we still have not got Alastair's results, although his girlfriend Clare has failed her retakes, so there is misery all round. Hugh is not now starting his job until next Monday because they didn't sort out his training placement at EDS and Andrew has gone to Huddersfield. So it is rather weird on the family front.

What a strange week this last week has been, culminating in a detailed and most rigorous interview, of almost twenty-five minutes, with John Humphrys for *On the Record* on BBC1, after which I went straight off to do *The World This Weekend* on Radio 4. The interviews covered what internal measures we might take, our stance and how we deal with those who are most concerned about human rights. I floated the idea that it is Parliament and accountable elected representatives who, in a democracy, must safeguard that democracy, and that we cannot rely on the judiciary.

I had to take the decision about whether to carry on with the launch of my book *Politics and Progress* on Wednesday. It is in danger of sinking without trace but there is little I can do about it. I think if we don't launch it now, it will just dither about and disappear into oblivion, so we might as well just get on with it.

Tony has been absolutely superb. He has stood out as a real world leader and got great credit from everyone, including his enemies. How he coped, I just don't know. I had a conversation with him for about forty minutes on Saturday when he got back.

I have had a lot of silliness from the Treasury over my revamping nationality and asylum policy, including a letter from Andrew Smith that had clearly been drafted for him. This claimed firstly that they got there first, before I put my proposals to the Prime Minister, and secondly that this should be left to the Spending Review 2002, by which time the world in relation to immigration, asylum and border security will have imploded. They also said that I should spend the money on upgrading accommodation. They have missed the point completely. I was saddened that an officially drafted letter had been sent across with arguments that bore no resemblance to what I was trying to do on immigration and asylum.

On Wednesday night I went to Brussels and had supper with the Belgian Interior Minister, who was co-chairing the Justice and Home Affairs Council, and the following day managed to get quite substantial change to the declaration before leaving the Council session after four and a half hours when, as ever, they were starting to argue about complete minutiae. The small countries were really awkward, more interested in defending the ECHR and the judges than their country – but as Tony said to me on Saturday, they don't feel at risk so they aren't bothered by it.

We got included: EU action and report-back on people movements and what will happen with people flooding across from Pakistan, and examining the balance between broader judicial rights and the need to protect ourselves (although they wouldn't put the words European Convention on Human

Rights in). Denmark, Sweden, Finland and the Netherlands had a fit about it.
We managed to include the need to speed everything up.

They work at a snail's pace – in fact, it's a technique. This time it is not the fault of the Commission, rather of the officials behind the justice ministers who, as I have discovered from the Home Office, are so cautious that it is a wonder they get out of bed in the morning.

I am at the moment working an eighteen-hour day and it is taking its toll. It is not good for any of us as we don't necessarily think as calmly and as brightly as we might otherwise do. The ID-card idea has taken off in a big way. I am not damping it down but not confirming it either until we have got something clearer.

After getting back from Brussels I spent Thursday night in London, trying to sort out asylum and immigration. During a $2\frac{1}{2}$-hour meeting with the head of the Immigration and Nationality Directorate, it was unbelievable to discover that he did not know the figures for the running costs of his department, nor how much was being spent on asylum support. The lack of knowledge and detail is quite breathtaking.

I had found out quite a lot when on the Wednesday I went down to Dover, where I made an announcement about a package of measures on security X-ray, acoustic heartbeat equipment and CCTV for airports, stepping up removals and the protocol with the police.

On a lighter note, the No. 10 switchboard rang me on Saturday evening – Hugh was with me – and announced a conference call at 9 p.m. with Alastair Campbell, and other ministers doing broadcasts the following day.

I said, 'Well, there isn't for me.'

The switchboard lady said, 'Pardon?'

I said, 'I am not doing it. Tell Alastair I will ring him in the morning.'

Hugh said, 'Was that No. 10?'

I said, 'Yes, it was.'

He said, 'Did I hear you tell them that you weren't doing it?'

I said, 'Yes, but I had a good reason.' I knew perfectly well that Alastair would be on the train coming back from Norwich, where he'd gone to watch his team Burnley playing. As first editions are not usually out until after 10 p.m., I knew that the 9 p.m. timing was designed to ensure that we knew precisely what would be in the Sunday papers. I put a message on my answerphone saying that it was Saturday night and that I should be grateful if callers would ring me in the morning.

Next Monday afternoon we have the meeting on the terrorism package, the other big collection of measures for which I'm responsible; both that and the asylum and immigration paper have to be done with advisers. In fact on Friday Nick Pearce and I wrote for Tony the latest update of the asylum and immigration paper, which clarified and refined what we are proposing.

The IND statistics on the backlog of asylum seekers were all wrong, as were the figures on the number of people who came in last year. The main thing I was keen to do was get the statistics on a quarterly basis so that we could verify them and clean them up, and we have managed to do that.

Officials were better on the terrorism and legal-change measures, which we had to spend a good chunk of the week revising and refining, but that is par for the course. Nick was virtually left to do the asylum paper himself. The meeting on Monday afternoon will deal with both areas, so it is going to be quite a task to get the papers ready – and meanwhile Derry Irvine is ringing me up and wittering on about when we are going to publish the Auld Report, asking when he can appear in front of the Select Committee and whether we can publish before he appears so that he can be the one who answers on Auld at the Committee.

Alastair failed just one exam – food technology. Andrew is obviously settled at Huddersfield because he has not even been in touch. Hugh says he is fine and starts work next week.

On Monday I had to go down to London early for emergency meetings on pulling everything together, and to see Tony about the asylum and immigration package. Gordon wasn't scheduled to be at the meeting but he turned up, and we had the most incredible up-and-downer. For the first and only time in my political life, I was so angry that I broke a pen in half and threw it across the table – at which Tony exclaimed 'David!!' in a shocked voice. But I had to get really tough – partly because so few people seemed to grasp what the scheme is about.

In the end I agreed that so long as I could announce a package to the House of Commons at the end of October, I would not press to have to make a full statement to party conference on the Wednesday. In any case, I wouldn't have been able to, given what else is going on. It would have been inappropriate, but at least it was some sort of concession.

We got a date but we didn't get the clarity that we wanted, so we are going to have to come back to it. Michael Barber has been extremely helpful, but Richard Wilson is unhelpful on every occasion by just being himself.

I have long been troubled by the difficulty of telling the truth on the vexed question of civil-service reform, and tried to tell the truth – or at least my version of it – to the senior civil servants' conference for the Home Office on the Tuesday morning. But I went slightly further than intended and talked about the episode of *Yes, Minister* where the hospital was running without patients. I said that I thought the Home Office would be very glad if it were run without ministers. I told them that productivity was appalling, and that while they were good in crises, what we needed to do was to deliver to people outside. That's what really mattered. I think they were shell-shocked, but it seems that they were nowhere near as horrified as I had thought they would be. I may have been going over the top, but I thought it needed to be said. There can only be one Home Office: there couldn't be ministers and a separate Home Office. I hope that message got through because I think that is the real crux of it. We are not two universes.

We have had a terrible time – and this is not the fault of the Home Office – trying to pull together both the information about, and presentation of, what is happening on the security-service side but, even worse, on the civil-contingencies side.

This is what became known as 'resilience' – or, in anyone else's speak, old-fashioned civil defence and protective measures for major potential targets. This is different from intelligence and security and the screening that goes with it, because civil contingencies were also linked to non-terrorist threats such as flooding or major explosions.

As it was unified in the Cabinet Office, there is no clear line of official reporting and accountability to me, as the politician who is in charge of civil contingencies under the Prime Minister. So if COBR is not meeting – which it isn't – then civil contingencies fall to me. But getting the civil-contingencies and security services to work together has been virtually impossible, and I called everybody together late on the Thursday, after my meeting with Tony.

I have nominated Nick Raynsford to take over co-ordination in London. I have talked to David Veness, Assistant Commissioner at the Met, and to Toby Harris at the Metropolitan Police Authority because we are trying to make sure that we get a grip of what Ken Livingstone is up to. Toby Harris told me that Ken has made it clear that if anything does happen he would like to be like Rudi Giuliani, charismatic Mayor of New York. Well, there's just no answer to that at all.

I have warned everybody and tried to co-ordinate everybody. Nick will take over pulling together the London elements so nobody can say, as the *Evening Standard* has been doing, that dear old London is not being properly protected. God help us, we are doing everything we can.

I have made it clear that on the civil-contingencies side we need proper lines of reporting, a sense of pulling together, and a much more robust approach. It is clear already that we have not got things in hand in the way that we are having to reassure the public that we have.

I am afraid I am having to be two-faced. On the one hand, I have to tell the public that we have things in hand, that we know what is happening and that everything is being done, in order to damp down fear and prevent what otherwise could become hysteria and the major erosion of our economy and social well-being. On the other hand, I am having to get to grips with these people and make sure that they are doing what needs to be done, while at the same time preparing for the major legislative programme, answering in the media, day after day, trying to liaise with other colleagues, linking with Tony and trying to make sure that the nationality and asylum proposals go forward as well as police reform.

I had Tony Burdon [Chief Constable of South Wales] and David Phillips [Chief Constable of Kent] in and they brought with them a staff officer with a great stack of papers to show what codes of practice would mean, how difficult it all was, how they were working on it, how important they were and how they ought to be the channel for deciding, disseminating and reviewing all policies, operational matters and anything to do with codes. In other words, they wanted me to put them in charge of everything and just leave them to it because they are the police and we have no business with it. I did everything I could just to keep calm and hold my temper. The superintendents, on the other hand, sent me a very nice letter after the conference because of the way in which it was wiped out because of the calamity at the World Trade Center, and were really trying to be helpful.

As well as police reform, I have had to ask John Denham [Minister of State at the Home Office] to deal with the issues concerning biological and chemical warfare, and he is horrified at the state of play. So between him and Nick Raynsford we are going to have to coral everything with Chris Leslie, the Parliamentary Under-Secretary at the Cabinet Office.

In the middle of all this I went to Brussels, where I had supper with the Spanish Interior Minister and attended the Home Affairs Council. I saw Neil Kinnock at breakfast. He hasn't changed a bit, and remembered what we were talking about in terms of trying to get a values paper together in 1987–8 as though it were yesterday.

I am meeting Greg Dyke [Director-General of the BBC] next week to see if I can save Jimmy Young's bacon. Jimmy did a good interview with me and promoted my book (also, Edward Heathcoat-Amory wrote a piece in the *Daily Mail* on Friday, which partly alleviated the disappointment of the *Mail* not taking extracts).

The book launch, at a community centre in Great Smith Street, was a very pleasant, friendly affair and a lot of people turned up, including Steve Byers, Alan Milburn and Estelle Morris – God bless them. They put themselves out because they were not going to come, then said on Monday night that they would after all. My own ministers turned up, as well as people like Margaret Hodge and past ministers from the old team. Geoff Green, who had previously worked with me in Sheffield, was there, and David Jackson came on behalf of his mum (Helen Jackson MP) and dad. David Yelland, editor of the *Sun*, came, with two of his senior journalists, but no one came from the *Daily Mirror*, surprise, surprise.

While Gordon didn't make the launch party, he had read some of the book. I know this because when I went to see him privately the same afternoon to discuss whether we could square things on the asylum front, he referred to my remarks about Robert Reich and my sideswipe at what tax credits meant.

I still have the problem of how to deal with Derry Irvine and the publication of the Auld Report. I told Derry: 'If you want to publish it on 8 October so that you can appear on the Select Committee on the 16th, then get on with it' – and I'll make sure that we brief before publication, otherwise Derry will pretend that the Auld Report is only to do with him.

On Tuesday night I had dinner with Robin Cook. Gaynor was supposed to come but in the end didn't. Robin was understandably bitter about losing his job [as Foreign Secretary], having believed that his position was secure. It is a rotten world sometimes, is politics.

Leading articles in two newspapers on Saturday, *The Times* and the *Independent*, illustrate the utter contradiction, diversity and confusion that I am trying to pick my way through. They are entirely opposites in terms of every element of what we are doing. And, of course, the press are juxtaposing everybody's comments, picking over words and nuances. We have to be so careful to get it right, as Jack Straw found from the way the Israelis reacted when he referred in an article to the Palestinian state rather than the Palestinian Authority. What a mess we get into. We had the same at the end of the week over innocuous remarks from Peter Hain and Jack in relation to the likely threat. It is just too silly for words.

Journalists and leader-writers on papers like *The Times* know perfectly well that it takes weeks to draft legislation that would stand up to scrutiny and last more than a week or two in the courts, but they just ignore that.

One of the meetings I held during this last week was on Labour Party conference security. It was put to me that there should be a battleship off the coast that would have capacity for ground-to-air missiles in case unauthorised planes looked as if they were going to attack the conference centre or hotel. When I said that I thought this was way over the top, the MoD came back with a suggestion that they could have missiles mounted either on the roof or in a series of lorries near by. I vetoed that as well and said that we would have whatever would be available to other people holding conferences or events.

So while they put up barriers to prevent people crash-bombing the facilities, we are trying to calm it all down. But, of course, these are exactly the sort of things that I can't tell people about. Nor can I tell people about the fact that long before the 11 September attacks I authorised surveillance on a number of people, including the man who has just been picked up in Leicester and transferred back to France. Having arrested him under the Terrorism Act, we got round the problems of human rights and extradition by releasing him and then detaining him on immigration grounds – namely that he had a false passport. We then reached agreement with the French that we would transfer him under immigration rules back to France, from where he had come, so that they could in turn arrest him and take him through. Nobody knows any of the detail of this. They don't know that this came from surveillance and that we had staved off the bombing of the American embassy in Paris.

October 2001

Party conference – and what a week. I spent a great chunk of Monday and Tuesday having to deal with Bill Morris's prima-donna antics over asylum, immigration vouchers and detention centres. We had to pull in Dave Prentis, General Secretary of UNISON, Tony Dubbins from the GMPU, Bill Connors from USDAW, John Monks [General Secretary of the Trades Union Congress] and numerous other people, all of whom we got involved in helping. Tony had to see Bill Morris, and these are things that every one of us could have done without. In the end Bill Morris remitted his resolution with a great fanfare of trumpets, pretending that I had said

'Trust me'. I just burst into laughter and treated it as a joke – which it was because I had said nothing of the sort. Having seen him the previous Thursday and then seen him twice before the debate on Wednesday morning, I could have throttled him.

Gordon made quite a good speech on Monday afternoon but it obviously got subsumed. The whole conference was as dead as a dodo – really flat. We curtailed it on Wednesday lunchtime and I made my speech at the end of the debate, between 11.30 a.m. and noon.

As part of my speech setting out in more detail what we would be doing in protecting the nation – and spelling out how historically crucial it has been to the maintenance of centre-left governments to put stability and security at the very heart of the agenda – I introduced the idea that we should extend race hate to 'incitement to religious hatred'. This was extremely popular at the time. Could any of us know that four and a half years later in February 2006 we would still be arguing about it, and that the Conservatives would be cheering as they defeated the third-term Labour government on two quite minor amendments that weaken still further an already weakened Bill? Could I have known at the time that I would have to jettison a key clause of the Anti-Terrorism, Crime and Security Act in order to get the core of the Act through Parliament because of the opposition of the House of Lords? Could those opposing the legislation all the way through to 2006 have understood the significance of what terrorists like Abu Hamza really meant until his conviction and the revelations which were then permitted in our media on 7 February 2006?

I made one of my better-constructed speeches – not badly delivered, clear and with some good phrases about the fact that we seek justice, not the primacy of jurisprudence, and that our judicial system is intended to protect the majority from the minority as well as the minority from the majority.

There is terrific speculation that ID cards are going to be dropped, including a ridiculous article in the *Mirror* saying that I have been overruled. I expect such treatment from Paul Routledge, who two weeks running attacked me in the *New Statesman*. He has this wonderful phrase reminiscent of what Winston Churchill said about Attlee – that I published a modest book immodestly promoted. Wrong on both counts.

Little did I know the personal difficulty which the issue of ID cards was going to cause me, and the long-drawn-out agonies it was going to cause the govern-

ment. I felt acute pain when, with the power of the House of Lords at its greatest, the government had to abandon legislation in the run-up to the 2005 general election. Then, in February 2006, it took the extraordinary decision to abandon retaining in primary legislation the compulsion that was so crucial to making the programme work, accepting the Lords' amendment that primary legislation would have to be introduced in order to have a mandatory scheme. I have never seen a surer way of keeping the issue alive during the next general election, nor a more certain opening for legal challenge. But this is one of the weaknesses of being out of government as opposed to being at the heart of government, and I have only myself to blame for not being there at the final stages of fighting through something that I believed to be fundamental to the very well-being of our nation.

The Civil Contingencies Committee that I chaired on Wednesday was well attended. John Prescott sat next to me, seething that Jim Wallace, from the Liberal Democrats in Scotland, was there as the Justice Minister and Deputy Leader of the Executive. It was a curious meeting because of the complete irrelevance of some of the things that were on the agenda, particularly the failure of Mike Granatt to understand the likely impact of sending out to local authorities and outside bodies inflammatory material. It is just bizarre what these people come up with. Having carried out a review of civil defence they think they have got to send out a booklet with the findings. We had a discussion about biochemical warfare. It would frighten me to death if I believed that it was going to happen. In fact I think people are frightening themselves. The last thing we need is a panic.

Tony went off to Russia, Pakistan and India. I had quite an entertaining description from Alastair Campbell on Saturday evening on the telephone about their visit to India and how he couldn't get rid of the valet who had been assigned to him, day and night. He said that he followed him round – to the gymnasium and back to his room. He then sat outside his room, and followed him to Tony's room. In the end Alastair lost his cool and said, 'Please sod off. I am not prepared to be followed around as though you fancy me!'

On Sunday I spoke to Tony at some length. He seemed very bright and cheerful, given that he had had no sleep, and said that he would talk to Gordon about the alternative nationality and asylum programme. I shall just hold my breath on this one.

Sir John Kerr, Permanent Secretary at the Foreign Office, has got Jack to sign up to a letter saying that there was no point whatsoever in going for bilateral agreements with certain countries on transfer of potential terrorists or extradition claims, because it had been tried before and wouldn't work, and neither would the ideas on third-country safe transfer. This arose from the fact that I had suggested that we might get people out of the country by thinking laterally and moving people to Gibraltar. Someone said that we couldn't do it with Gibraltar because it is too easy to escape from, and anyway it is too close to Morocco, so what about Ascension Island? We went round the houses on that, but the Foreign Office were apparently unhappy so I said, 'Well, we could send them to the Falklands!'

I visited the mosque on Industry Road in Sheffield on Friday – quite an experience. They were very friendly to me and to the government and Tony, but they were asking all sorts of questions that indicated what worries exist. There is certainly an underlying tension there.

As predicted, the Afghanistan strike took place at the weekend, on Sunday evening. It mostly involved the Americans, with us assisting from our submarine missile sites. Everybody's getting really worked up about it.

I am still hoping to go away on Tuesday. I can do loads of work while I am out of the country and keep in touch on the telephone, and I desperately need a break. I have started to do silly things, one of which is getting angry – which shows that I am beginning to feel the strain.

On Sunday morning I appeared on *Breakfast with Frost*, and wasn't bad. There are currently all sorts of leaks from the Home Office, particularly from the Immigration and Nationality Directorate. Someone has given a story to the *Mail on Sunday* about our provision of reception centres. It was slightly muddled but, had the attack on the Taliban and the debacle of Railtrack not taken place on the Sunday, it might well have BEEN carried and there would have been real difficulties. There are several people in the Home Office who are clearly out to cause maximum damage.

This was the beginning of a serious and perpetual problem of leaks, which caused havoc inside the political arena, as well as in the development of policy.

I don't know whether they have linked up with people in the Treasury, who have every reason to try and scupper the reception-centres scheme. I told Nick Pearce to go to Croydon [the Immigration and Nationality Directorate] and sort out where they are spending the money that doesn't go on vouchers and cash payments, so that we can bottom the difference between that and the £1.1 billion being spent on asylum support.

Further reflections on the conference: Tony's speech was superb – long but very good. The low part of the week was the prediction of a change in the contribution by students towards university funding, made in Gordon's speech on Monday, and then by Tony, and Estelle Morris (who appeared to have heard it first in Gordon's speech). I had predicted that there would be an effort to change the existing scheme, but given that we had won such an overwhelming majority and that I had not found this a contentious issue when visiting constituencies across the country during the general election, I was surprised at the impact that the campaign against student loans had had on senior members of the party. After all, we were now raising the money and therefore reinvesting it, protecting the worst off and avoiding everyone, including the very poor, having to pay for the rest of their lives. Those in favour of change appear to have forgotten that Opportunity Bursaries started at the beginning of this term, and a third of the country have students eligible for them under Excellence in Cities and EAZs [Education Action Zones]. It's a funny old world: on the one hand we have a scheme that is working but which people want to change, while on the other we have a programme on nationality and asylum that is doing anything but working, which people want to stop me from changing.

Hugh has had his first week at work, and apart from the fact that he doesn't yet have a computer, he seems to be going on all right. Andrew is clearly enjoying himself, while Alastair is overcoming the exam problem and beginning to get his head round things.

Parliament has been recalled for Monday evening. I found out that there was to be a Cabinet at 4 p.m. and Parliament recalled for 6 p.m. only when Valda phoned me because she had seen it on Ceefax. What a laugh – nobody at the department has told me. Unbelievable.

My Principal Private Secretary is to be replaced, and this week I got agreement that we would advertise her job. She talked to me on Friday night and started giving me a lecture about whether or not I ought to go away for my break – and she is going away herself. These people are so audacious. They really do think that they run the show, and we ministers are just the passing flotsam and jetsam.

We are publishing the Auld Report on 8 October, and it will sink without trace. Derry Irvine wanted it published early, so it is published early. Even with that, the Lord Chancellor's Department attempted to cut out great chunks of the press release and statement, including trying to alter my quotes, cutting out the material about specialist courts – which was in the election manifesto – as well as comments on the ridiculous distortion of juries by ethnicity.

In the middle of everything else that was going on, Geoff Hoon rang me about a row between Derbyshire County Council and the Home Office about how much money the Home Office should provide to pay for Derbyshire Special Branch to protect Geoff's home in Derbyshire. I just couldn't believe it, and told Geoff I would sort it out.

The world has gone crackers, and the *cause célèbre* of the week has been the débâcle over Jo Moore, which is going on and on. She is Steve Byers's special adviser on press work at the Department of Transport, and did the most ridiculous (or what I described on the *Today* programme as 'stupid') thing on 11 September by emailing two civil servants, one of them Alun Evans [Head of Communications at the Department for Transport, Local Government and the Regions], at 2.55 p.m., while the Twin Towers were on fire but had not yet collapsed, with the suggestion that this would be a good time to get out unpopular messages. It is hard to make any comment on this, except to say that I did make it clear on the *Today* programme that all of us in government thought and felt the same about it as everyone else did.

Steve was intending to sack Jo Moore, but by early afternoon it had all changed and apparently it was because, quite rightly, Tony had perceived that this was a try-on by the civil service. It was felt that they were the ones who had received the email and leaked it, and no matter how appalling the email, the declaration of war by the civil service and their ability to leak emails and thereby bring down special advisers had to be countered.

Unfortunately life is not as simple as that. Tony's interpretation of the situation is right, but Steve's initial decision to sack Jo Moore for the content of the email was also right because this story has run and run and run. She would have been better going on the day, when at least we would have got some credit for it as a government, whereas if she goes now we get no credit at all, and the acrimony and bitterness continues.

In dictating this at the time, I had no idea just how catastrophic it was going to be for Steve Byers. I think those advising really did mean well, and it was a difficult situation to call. There is no doubt that Jo Moore paid the price, but what price Steve Byers paid can only be judged by appreciating the pressure he was under at the time – all the way through to his dignified apology to the House of Commons in February 2006 for a quite separate issue relating to his role as Secretary of State for Transport.

Politics in the twenty-first century is very different from anything that anyone experienced over the last 250 years. There can be no comparison with any other era of our political life, either in terms of the chain-reaction effect of events or the way in which media impact makes such a difference to perception – and therefore, in the end, the outcome.

One further reflection. I later learned that Jo Moore herself was keen to draw a line under this affair and leave Steve's employ, which was hardly surprising, given the drubbing she was getting. She had worked loyally for the Labour Party for many years and did not want to see it damaged further. Her whole life was going to have to be restarted – another reminder of how one mistake can make such a difference to the life of an individual, as well as to those around them.

The Tories have put down to raise the Jo Moore issue in a Supply Day debate for Tuesday 23 October. What a terrible mess for Steve: he has been under enormous pressure because the Treasury have been briefing against him on his decisions announced about Railtrack on Sunday.

I had avoided dropping Steve or anyone else in it on *Breakfast with Frost* that day, but then it all started to go wrong, and instead of its being a good-news story about taking on Railtrack and sorting it out, it all started to go astray – and it particularly went astray over Jo Moore.

I was still determined to have a break, but had to postpone going to Majorca until Wednesday – rather than Tuesday, as I'd originally intended – and then we had a farce of all farces. When I got off the plane in Palma, someone, presumably on the aircraft, working with or for the *Majorcan Bulletin*, contacted *The Times* and *Daily Mail* to tell them that I was out of the country.

Apparently both the *Mail* and *The Times* contacted the press office, and Huw and Julia between them came up with the decision to offer the story to the *Sun*, which then produced a front-page story and a supportive, if patronising, leader. Unfortunately this decision proved to be a miscalculation because *The Times* and the *Mail* both took editorial decisions not to cover the fact that I had gone away for four days. But, of course, the *Sun* using it meant that every other single newspaper all the way through to the Sundays used it as well – very few critically but nevertheless giving the implication that I shouldn't have gone away. They even had the cheek to say that I had been away for four days when two of those were at the weekend. Although I do work through 80 or 90 per cent of weekends, it is good to have some assumption that weekends are not weekdays. The fuss ended up giving me a lot of worry as well as disrupting my evening and causing me to sleep badly, which was not ideal as I had taken a few days' holiday in order to try to relax. It could have been avoided if the press office had just kept calm, but to be fair I suppose it was a good idea at the time that went drastically wrong.

But I enjoyed the rest of my break. Although I did a lot of work, I also got in some swimming, some bicycling on a tandem, some sunshine, some reading and some good eating and drinking. It did matter to me just to get away for those few days, having previously cancelled my week's holiday.

I came back to it all, including doing the Statement in the House on Monday [15 October], which went a lot better than I could have hoped. As with the Bradford Statement I seem to be better now that I am in the Home Secretary's job than I was when doing Education and Employment. This is strange, as I knew the Education and Employment brief much better. But it is at a price: I feel so exhausted, and on Tuesday and Wednesday of that week was really down in the dumps. It's not usual for me to be depressed but I was. If I hadn't had the benefit of going away, God knows where I'd have been.

On Saturday 20 October I did a $2\frac{3}{4}$-hour surgery, which was a pretty killing experience. Most of the people who came were asylum seekers and quite a number of them were brought along by a white, middle-class woman, a real do-gooder. A number of those she brought weren't even my constituents, and she couldn't even grasp that I expected other MPs to do their job. She obviously just thought she would roll all these people up from the dispersal centre and present them to the Home Secretary! The upshot was that I got home, very quickly cooked myself some fresh tuna and within an hour I'd got a roaring temperature, blinding headache and was starting to get stomach pains. I had to go to bed, which not only knocked me out but stopped me working. This then put me behind for the rest of the week, which is a real bind.

So I did the Statement and got that out of the way. It was better received than I thought it would be, except for the clause outlawing incitement to religious hatred. It all got a bit silly during the week, with Rowan Atkinson appearing to think that ruling out incitement to religious hatred would rule out telling religious jokes. I wrote a letter to *The Times* [Friday 19 October] in an effort to calm things down.

This initiative has done a lot of good within the Islamic community in Britain and in the wider Arab world. I did an interview for one of the main Arab satellite television stations operating out of Dubai, and they were very interested in our seeking to protect people from incitement on grounds of religious hatred.

I had no idea at the time that the clause concerning religious hatred would cause us so much grief, all the way through to autumn 2005. I still believe it was the right thing to do – and, as will be seen, it did give me the opportunity of being able to compromise in December 2001 in a way that allowed the House of Lords to feel that they had made a significant change to the Anti-Terrorism, Crime and Security Bill proposals without affecting the main proposals at all.

There is a lot of leaking going on about proposals in relation to immigration and asylum. On Thursday 19th we had the long-awaited Cabinet meeting on asylum, which lasted longer than any meeting I've had other than Awayday Cabinets and informals or dinners at Chequers – an hour and three-quarters that Tony could ill afford to give, with Derry Irvine acting like one of the characters from *One Foot in the Grave*. He was intervening inappropriately, misunderstanding and saying the most crass things at the wrong moment. The Treasury team present was not very helpful, notably Nick McPherson. I suggested that he should come and work for us for six months at the Immigration and Nationality Directorate in Croydon, which got Richard Wilson and the Cabinet Office people laughing – but not the Treasury officials! I suggested that if Gordon thought he could run this so well, I would transfer IND to him. At one point he said, 'You only want this new structure in order to abolish vouchers,' and I replied: 'Oh no, you don't catch me that way, Gordon. I'm going to abolish vouchers whether you agree to this scheme or not.'

I spoke to Tony on Sunday night [21 October]. He said he was going to settle the matter once and for all at a further meeting. I hope he's right. We really do need to. I've been ringing round trying to sort everything else out, including the announcement that I want to make to the Home Affairs Select Committee on Tuesday, about reclassifying cannabis from a Class B drug to Class C.

It was later claimed that Cabinet colleagues had not been consulted about this, which I am afraid is a rewrite of history.

I also spoke to Chris Mullin, Chair of the Select Committee, and had spoken last week to Michael Rawlins, the professor who chairs the Advisory Council on the Misuse of Drugs, and to Keith Hellawell, who is going to give international advice on drugs issues – and all have kept 'mum'.

This silence was unheard of in my time in government, when everything we did was likely to be leaked, usually with malice aforethought.

I've got to send a note round on Monday to members of the Cabinet Domestic Affairs Committee, so I have already told Alan and Estelle and they have also kept 'mum'. It is just a miracle. Nothing else I have been doing in the Home Office has been kept under such wraps and the IND and asylum stuff will be the last thing I'll be able to keep quiet next weekend, but I can only do my best.

I am genuinely concerned about the civil-contingencies measures and the importance of getting this issue right. This was really brought home to me on Sunday when I spoke to my old school friend, Graeme and his wife Christine, who live in Vancouver. Christine said that someone had come into her physiotherapy clinic who had a relative who had been in London and had found someone's wallet and had returned it to them. They had been offered money as a reward, which they refused, so the owner of the wallet, who was an Arab, said, 'Well, I've got to do something for you. Don't be in London on 11 November.' I immediately registered the significance of this: 11 November is Armistice Day, the one time in the year when all leading politicians from the three parties, the Queen and other members of the royal family, and the leading personnel of the armed forces are all in the same place, at the same time – a known time – in central London.

I decided that I should at least tell Tony, as it was absolutely clear that nobody had thought of it. We agreed that there was no way we could cancel Armistice Day, but we are certainly going to have to take some precautions. With so many people coming into the centre of the city I'm not sure what we can manage to do, and I feel both scared and slightly overwhelmed – and perhaps a little proud as well that we may have picked something up. If they are going to go for us, at least we stand a fighting chance if we have thought it through and in time.

Both at the Monday morning so-called War Cabinet and at the Cabinet meeting on Thursday it was pretty clear:

a) that there was no co-ordinated strategy between the US and Britain;
b) that the military were unsure what strategy should be in terms of the Afghan Northern Alliance in particular;
c) that while they were going to take Mazar-i-Sharif or, rather, open up the lines for the anti-Taliban forces to be able to get there, they were highly reluctant to do so for Kabul;

d) that Geoff Hoon had been sold a complete pup about how 50,000 people had been massacred last time the Northern Alliance had been in Kabul, and therefore we couldn't possibly allow that to happen again; and

e) that the strategy that Tony Blair was laying out – and he was incredibly vigorous and clear about it – was something that had not yet been implemented. He kept on saying to the Chief of the General Staff: 'But I am giving you an instruction. This is what I want you to talk to the Americans about. This is what I want you to do' – and it struck me that it was falling on deaf ears, and the Chief of the General Staff was less than convinced. The military had clearly been waiting for an absolute instruction rather than already taking the initiative. I intervened vigorously, saying that I thought that if people outside could hear the discussion, they would be incredulous, and that it was absolutely crucial that Tony's clear enunciation of the way forward should be backed.

You can see the same sort of problems that we are having with the Civil Contingencies Committee and the inability of people to rise to the occasion. I am praying that all the effort that Tony is putting in will bear fruit, but he will tire himself out flying all over the place. Just after we had the meeting the week before, he flew to Switzerland to see the UAE sheikh, then to Amman. He's all over the place. Then, of course, at home he's got to deal with all the stupidities – on asylum, the Jo Moore affair, and now the Department for Environment, Food and Rural Affairs and the fact that they had not been testing sheep brains at all but cow brains for BSE, and the fact that DEFRA's press office put out a press release and tried to hide it at 10.30 p.m. They must be out of their minds, and it just undermines trust. People think we are all spin, no substance, no trust, and no credibility, and everything else we're doing then is damaged by this.

Week beginning Monday 22 October: I got down to London very early for a series of meetings that were unavoidable, and then I had the speech to the National Family and Parenting Institute's Parents' Week.

After Home Office Questions came the Civil Contingencies Committee, which I had to chair and which was a much better meeting than the last one. I think we are getting somewhere at last now. We have clearer lines of accountability and clearer co-ordination. Thank God nothing's happened in the meantime. We are not entirely there yet, but the Department of Health wanted to spend £150 million on serums and antibiotics just in case. It is absolutely crackers to be spending that sort of money, displacing everything else that they need to do, causing aggravation and community havoc on top of the problems we've got in the propaganda war as it is.

It is worth noting here that it would be sensible and necessary to make vaccine available for health workers and key workers who would have to provide immediate intervention in an area or group of people affected. The problem, however, was the deep reluctance of the key workers to be vaccinated, given the very high risk and danger to them of this form of vaccine.

Then we had another meeting with Gordon, Andrew Smith, Derry Irvine, Tony and myself. We had a private session before going back into the main meeting with officials, and I ended up having to compromise. I got my 3,000 places for contracting for next year, but I did not get a commitment to being able to go ahead with it as a Pathfinder, rather than a trial. Tony thought that he had given me what I wanted.

But in my usual way, I felt deeply grumpy that I had not received everything I had set out to get. The difference is significant because nothing more could be agreed until the 'trial' had been evaluated. As it happened, the measures we took across the board made my original concept of accommodation centres less critical, but no less important to avoiding administrative chaos and bewilderingly lengthy processes.

Big event of the week was the IRA at least prima facie reaching agreement with John de Chastelain [head of the international arms-decommissioning body] on the issue of decommissioning and starting to put their weapons into concrete bunkers. It was sufficient to get David Trimble and his ministers back on to the Northern Ireland Executive and to have genuinely made some progress. Not that we have made any progress with the Real IRA or the splinter group, the Continuity IRA, but at least we have made some progress, which is a terrific feather in Tony Blair's cap.

I'd been saying for weeks and had arranged for weeks – including with Chris Mullin and with those who needed to be in the know – that I was going to announce a package of measures on drugs and the recategorisation of cannabis on that evening – Tuesday 23rd – when the IRA announced what they were doing. Despite the fact that I'd spoken in the afternoon to David Yelland, editor of the *Sun*, he still wrote, and so did Trevor Kavanagh, and published the inference that this was a carefully planned piece of spin and that it all fitted in with the Jo Moore approach. They even carried a photo of Jo Moore and me, which I consider a deep insult. So there we were, supposedly having fixed it with Gerry Adams and Martin McGuinness so that we would know precisely when they were going to make the announcement. Even though we'd briefed Professor Michael Rawlins, Chairman of the Advisory Council on the Misuse of Drugs, and Keith Hellawell (Drugs Tsar) a good deal in advance (and, to be fair, they had kept it under wraps), it was still implied that somehow I had spun this and tried to cover the announcement up.

John Humphrys raised it with me on the *Today* programme on Wednesday morning, and although I ridiculed the idea I made an error by engaging in irony. I said: 'And what's more, this is the first time, since I came into the Home Office, that something of mine has not been leaked on my behalf.' So what do three newspapers do? They assume that, on every other occasion, I'd leaked my own papers and my own announcements. In truth the Select Committee hearing had been planned for a long time; their upcoming inquiry was precisely why I wanted to get the issue on the table rather than being pushed and shoved.

But everybody's looking for spin, everybody's looking for corruption, everybody's looking for everything except the truth. The announcement itself went off fine and, with the obvious provisos of those who are genuinely worried, was widely welcomed.

I did *Any Questions?* in Kent on Friday: what a journey, down there from London then back up to Sheffield. We had plenty of things to go at because in addition to the drugs announcement there was stuff in the *Guardian* that morning from my book about citizenship and asylum. Then we had the IRA stuff. We didn't get asked about the British Crime Survey figures, published the day before, because they were very good.

Unbeknown to me, a very senior civil servant has left his briefcase in a pub, from where it was subsequently stolen with masses of highly confidential and restricted papers in it. This then all appeared in the *Observer*. Part of the twist was that it wasn't until Saturday, when Huw Evans and then Julia Simpson phoned me to let me know what was happening, that anyone had bothered to tell me that he had lost his briefcase and papers, even though it had happened ten days earlier. And we're trying to prepare the legislation for the Bill on anti-terrorism and get the other things right at the same time as dealing with the Department.

We had this joint permanent secretaries' Cabinet meeting on the Tuesday morning and I think it was pretty much a waste of time. Clare Short said that we shouldn't bring people in from outside because it demoralises the civil service. When I attacked the Civil Service Commission, Richard Wilson said: 'But we've improved it, David. We've brought in Ushar Prushar as chairman and Julia Neuberger as a member.' I just looked at him in utter contempt. These people have done the rounds on quangos and appointees since the early 1980s – they might justifiably be described as 're-treads'. If that's modernising the Civil Service Commission, then God save us all. I made some pretty trenchant remarks about the best way of dealing with someone who is incompetent being to get them promoted. Sue Street, who was invited there as the new DCMS [Department for Culture, Media and Sport] Permanent Secretary, said, 'I don't know whether the Home Secretary was referring to me', and I just lifted my eyebrows.

I put some notes on file, including one to John Gieve, telling him what he needed to do to get a grip of the Immigration and Nationality Directorate. He doesn't like the note at all, but he has not grasped the scale of the problem. Those working in Work Permits UK, who can turn things round within two or three days, are bewildered when reading papers from the IND indicating that they want to do a similar job in relation to their bit of economic migration in up to sixty days.

I've been in touch with the Archbishop of Canterbury, George Carey, trying to see if I can get agreement on abolishing the blasphemy law. He wasn't too keen and I don't think Tony will be happy to do it unless I can get George Carey to agree, so I may have to drop that one, but I would have liked to do it. I'd have liked to clear up a whole range of things while I can, which is why I'm so frustrated with the current drafts of the Police White Paper, which is really poor.

The war against the Al Qaeda and Bin Laden group is not going well, and War Cabinet on Thursday morning wasn't good. It's clear that quite a lot of what is being said about whether the Americans and ourselves know what we're doing is true – and we're losing the propaganda war. That's why I had got so irritated on *Any Questions?* with the appeaseniks. They really are getting up my nose. They want us to do something, but they don't want us to do anything. They want to be safe, but they don't want us to make them safe. They don't want us to go after the people who committed the crime, but say something has to be done. It's just pathetic – and the papers are really stoking it. I've got a recording of the Jimmy Young programme the week before when I made a reference to Lord Haw-Haw and whether he would have had a mainline slot on the BBC today. That's how I feel.

I didn't mention, at the beginning of the week, the saga about the fire alarm and the sensor on the top landing of my home in Sheffield going off when I was using the shower. The steam set it off and there was me, running about with nothing on, and the fire brigade arriving and banging on my door. I had to open the front door before they broke it down – this is the new front door that had just been varnished on Monday morning.

On 29 October I went down to London early and delivered the Statement on asylum, migration and nationality, which I'd finished off in the car from the station. The weird thing was I was so nervous. As I had done the anti-terrorism Statement two weeks earlier better than I'd done others and been much more relaxed, I thought I'd got over the nerves, but I hadn't. I felt physically poorly and, when I was delivering the Statement, it wasn't the barracking that got to me – though there was a lot of it – but rather the fact that my mouth had gone dry before I stood up. I got a drink of water when I was answering the questions but my mouth stayed so dry that I could hardly speak. I had to build up my confidence and clarity, and one of the techniques I adopted was that if I was interrupted by barracking, I would simply go back and read the sentence or the paragraph again. This made sure that my own side could hear what I was saying, and if there was a clip taken out for TV or radio, they are so tight these days in terms of time that it's unlikely that they would use up four or five seconds replaying me being barracked and then re-reading it: they're more likely to clip the full paragraph, even if it catches the end of the barracking.

I don't want to over-egg the problems that I have already outlined about delivering a Statement, but it is certain that if I had my time again I would adopt an entirely different strategy: either, as I have already reflected, memorising the Statement – given time to do so – or reading it so slowly that my method of delivery became my usual pattern. That way people would not notice that I was reading carefully one sentence at a time. George Bush adopts this very strategy. He reads so slowly that it is absolutely impossible for him to get it wrong – though I should qualify that, having heard him early in 2006 talking about a 'liberty tower' in California when it should have been 'library tower'. But the technique is a clever one.

In the political bear pit I cannot, of course, explain to people that my fingers have toughened up, that Braille is bulky and that I can't turn the pages properly without real difficulty. If I made a fuss I wouldn't last five minutes, because no matter how generous people are in appreciating that there may be obstacles in our way which we have to deal with, when push comes to shove, a knife is a knife – whether from an opponent in front or behind you.

A lot of work went into contacting organisations and key MPs – not the hard untouchable ones but those who have a genuine concern in this area – just to make sure they knew what we were doing and got the right end of the stick.

On the whole the reception from the newspapers, the Parliamentary Labour Party and elsewhere was good, given that this was a tremendous balancing act. The *Daily Mail* quite rightly picked up on Tuesday morning that I had only got resources and commitment to 3,000 accommodation places at any one time, which is indeed the nub. One untoward consequence of all this activity was a couple of silly articles asking whether I was challenging Gordon for the future leadership of the party!

I fear Tony is killing himself. He went to Saudi Arabia, to Syria, to Jordan, to Israel and next week he's going to Washington. He's just completely doing himself in – it's frightening. At last, they're starting to bomb the Taliban front lines. It's a bit late in my view. I understand about Pakistan and the balance and whether Pakistan would tolerate it but, honestly, what a state of affairs.

November 2001

I'm very, very tired but in myself I'm better than I've been for a long time – comfortable and hopeful that I can get some holiday at Christmas or New Year. I don't know how Tony does it. I just couldn't put up with the travelling he does. It must be exhausting.

I've been making sure I have not neglected the constituency. I went to an event on Friday – eighty mums getting certificates for involvement in the breast-feeding campaign. It was really warm and friendly, as were the two events I went to on the Saturday – just good to be in touch. This was apart from dealing with the Red Box and everything else that's coming through on the anti-terrorism material, because we're still building up the legislation, still having to prove everything, to go through everything and be on top of everything.

I've got to do the draft again this weekend of the Police White Paper. Again, it's just the same as I was commenting on in the former DfEE, where people think that the civil service write the White Papers or the Statements and that all we ministers have to do is tidy them up a bit. Would that that were the case. I have to write and rewrite everything. In the case of nationality and asylum, it was Nick Pearce and myself writing and rewriting and even now making sure the policy is understood, because it's quite clear that the Head of the Immigration and Nationality Directorate doesn't understand. We've had to tell them how to develop project management and to start carrying it through, and likewise with the Police White Paper. I am having to tell them how to write a White Paper, as the first drafts were just appalling.

We are making some progress, however, on identity cards. Steven Harrison [former Private Secretary] is doing a good job in pulling together the material and John Prescott is being helpful on that as well, so we might get somewhere.

I received an apology from Geoff Hoon this week, about the jubilee medal for the police. There had been a dispute as to whether such a medal could be struck and who would pay for it, at a cost of £3 million. We were prepared to pay for it from the Home Office, but a junior defence minister sent me a letter saying that I was out of order and that they would block it. Geoff had the decency to deal with this swiftly and put the record straight.

Saturday night there was a bomb placed in a car by the Real IRA in Birmingham. Fortunately, it didn't detonate properly, so there was not the calamity that otherwise would have been the case. But we were very lucky. I've kept a very low profile, not doing any broadcasts or saying anything inflammatory.

I'm trying to keep a low profile generally at the moment. I've turned down the *Today* programme four times in the last eight days, but of course the world outside doesn't know that.

We are still getting reverberations, including in the *Daily Express* on Monday [5 November], about the lost briefcase and all the papers. The material keeps emerging as leaks – most of it straightforward stuff that's been revealed already, but it's still a damned nuisance and the Jo Moore thing keeps resounding because everything is now interpreted as spin. They allege that I revealed to the Select Committee on 23 October that we weren't going to make the removals target this year for asylum seekers in order to hide it away while I was doing the cannabis announcement. The fact that I'd announced exactly the same thing at the end of June in the Queen's Speech debate has obviously passed people by.

Good news of the week is that Mazar-i-Sharif fell in Afghanistan. This has lifted optimism about making progress, after the early meetings when everybody was reluctant to do anything that might put the Northern Alliance in a strong position, in order not to upset Pakistan. I noticed that they started to make warnings straight away on the Saturday [10

November] about that but we had to make some progress and open up some of the routes for aid and food as well as for military support.

My constituency meeting on Friday the 9th was very difficult, with a tremendous amount of suspicion and anti-war feeling, and I had to be quite robust. It's amazing how quickly people back off and lose heart.

I chaired the Civil Contingencies Committee and we are beginning to see the light of day on that, though Tony's asked me to chair a new sub-committee, DOPIT, about assessing risk and trying to balance the actions we take. This committee has been formed so that the Head of the Security Services and the anti-terrorist branch SO13 can present the options to us. We will then make the decisions, although we have to recognise that they (the services) retain operational responsibility. We have accountability but we don't carry the day-to-day responsibility for decision-taking. This is a difficult balance, because when things go wrong it is the politicians who have to stand at the Dispatch Box and be answerable.

So I shall have to get a grip of that, on top of the Anti-Terrorism Bill that we're publishing on Tuesday 13th and all the internal security measures, never mind civil contingencies. I have a pile of work which I need to get through because I have to address the Ethnic Minority Network [Home Office organisation for staff from ethnic minorities or interested in diversity], which was obviously counted as a very big thing. Jack spent a day with them last year. Personally I think they just need to see themselves as part of the Department and not separate from it. I've got to try and say so in a non-offensive way, otherwise I suppose the blooming roof will come down. I am also addressing magistrates and labour lawyers. I have got a Refugee Council AGM and I've got to address all the staff of the Immigration and Nationality Directorate at Gatwick airport, where there are facilities not available in Croydon itself. There are virtually no notes for me, and no preparation done. Advisers are not to blame because it is the job of officials. Advisers are claiming that their last-minute efforts to put matters right were thwarted by the complete breakdown of the computer and email system in the Department. I have told John Gieve that we have to either get this sorted in weeks or we sack ICL and Sirius, the subsidiary which is supposed to be overseeing the system. He said that the contract, as drawn up, was not specific enough. I said it had to be specific enough for things to work, for God's sake.

I am afraid the system continued to break down on a regular basis – just as bits of concrete fell off the Home Office building and the lifts failed to work one day out of three. If I had not lived through it, I would not believe it.

Having appointed Jonathan Sedgwick as my Principal Private Secretary, I am hoping very much that when he starts on 3 December we will manage to get things organised in the office pretty rapidly. The problem is that if the computer systems go down then everything stops, because people are now dependent on email. They used to be dependent on sensible things like telephones, typewriters, faxes, or even using a pen – but not any more.

The major problem I've had is the budget. I cannot find out what the underspends/overspends are in each area. I get some round totals but no detail, virtually no preparation for the Spending Review, and no real effort or proper links in co-ordination for the Pre-Budget Report, despite John Gieve having come from the Treasury.

What the advisers say, and I believe them, is that in the DfEE the staff dealing with budget matters and with the Treasury were committed to us personally, to our agenda, and to the way it would improve things, whereas the staff in the Home Office seem to have no connection with the fact that what they do, how they re-use the money and how imaginative they are, will make a difference to people's lives. So presumably they think that making a difference, delivering and improving things is somebody else's job and their job is just to go through the motions. In that case, presumably my job is to conjure up money out of nowhere.

We are starting from square one, which is really bad news.

It is worth reflecting here what will become clear later – that it was possible to build a first-class team of people who were committed in every fibre. That is what I had in my Private Office by the time I left the post of Home Secretary in December 2004. At senior level, the officials became engrained in and deeply committed to bringing about change, even though the mechanisms for doing so were so rusty and out of date (as we have already seen in relation to the computer system) that it made their jobs very much more difficult. At this stage, my task was to convince senior officials that there were real problems with the financial administration, the forward budgetary planning and the grasp of basic audit detail. I had raised this back in July when I started to feel, instinctively, that all was not well. I had already learned – and Jack had confirmed this – that the process for the Spending Review in 2000 had been awful. In the end, they had had to bring people in from outside to help, but the basic structures had not been changed.

The 'financial settlement', as it is called, for 2000 was very tight indeed for the Home Office, and I was determined that we were going to have much greater leeway as we strove to expand police numbers, bring in the new community support officers and implement the reform agenda right across the board. Resources for counter-terrorism (while not easy) were undeniably required, and therefore that battle was one on which I would receive substantial support in Downing Street. But other aspects of the Home Office were seen as inefficient and ineffective, and this formed an appalling base for persuading colleagues that more rather than less resource was needed.

It is also a simple fact that the Labour Party historically has been suspicious of the whole issue of investment in law and order. Tony had started to turn this round when he was Shadow Home Secretary in the early Major years and progress had been made under Jack, but it was still a niggling irritant that people had not grasped that so much of the agenda of security and stability and the reduction in fear was a Labour agenda. It was all about ensuring that people experienced not just the economic security that we were giving them, but the ability to live peacefully in their homes, to walk safely on their streets and to see the world as an opportunity rather than a fearful place of continuing challenge. In that way, as I tried to prove over subsequent months and years, we could win people over to a progressive agenda, learning the lessons of history whether from Germany, Spain or elsewhere – and at the time learning the lessons of what was happening right across Europe with regard to the far right, racism and a reaction against a kind of flabby liberalism. This was to be seen in months to come, from Holland to Austria, and from France to Denmark.

Dinner with John Birt. He's a strange man but did give me some food for thought about going back to the policing and crime agenda he was dealing with before the election. So I was able to pick up some useful stuff.

Tony's still on his travels. On Wednesday after Prime Minister's Questions he went to the USA on Concorde. He saw George Bush, got something to eat and then returned home on the overnight flight. He then took Cabinet, slightly delayed, but nevertheless he took it. I'm afraid he will finish himself off if he carries on like this.

Two political insider stories. Henry McLeish has to step down as First Minister in Scotland because of the subletting of his offices, and the *Daily Record* has said that they will trawl over the lives and families of those standing to replace him. It was foolish of Henry, but that's all: I don't believe he is a dishonest man. And Anji Hunter goes to BP with a £200,000-plus salary, while Sally Morgan moves back into No. 10, giving up her ministerial post.

Sunday 11 November, and we've come through Remembrance Sunday safely. All the worry was for nothing, thank God. Gordon seemed to be in a bad mood and didn't even say good morning, and I found out later in the day why. John Reid rang me to tell me that Wendy Alexander had been forced to pull out of the race for Scottish First Minister, because of lack of support and because the unions refused to back her, even though Gordon had tried to get them to override the one-member-one-vote ballot and just nominate her. John Reid is very funny. He's obviously decided to hook on to me, and talked about the fact that they didn't want a 'phone a friend' First Minister.

Monday morning's papers [on 12 November] carried wonderful tirades about taking away civil liberties. The *Telegraph* leader is the best because it puts the contradiction beautifully, criticising me heavily for taking away civil liberties by being prepared to detain people and then declaring that what we ought to be doing is pulling out of the ECHR [European Convention on Human Rights] and then we could send people back to these countries – that is, to death and torture. What these people don't know is how much I've been resisting completely over-the-top action – to pull out of the ECHR, to have a certification system so I could send people back to their death. I have resisted all that – and then I get tirades about how brutal I am and how I don't give a damn about human rights or civil liberties. What a joke.

At Cabinet I did a presentation on the Anti-Terrorism, Crime and Security Bill so that people would know exactly what was in it. The response was almost unanimously favourable – the one exception being someone who asked an oblique question. A number of us felt afterwards that this had probably been done in order to be able to say, in the future, that he/she – who had a strong civil-liberties background – had raised an objection.

Then another horrendous week. I was supposed to be going down to London on the train, but when I got to Doncaster station we found that the power lines were down. Barbara had to drive me down the A1M and Barry met us just north of the M25.

Barbara Smith was then my driver in the North, with Barry Brazier driving me in the South – as he still does.

I saw the Indian Prime Minister, Atal Behari Vajpayee, who is not easy to talk to.
    I said, 'Hello' and he said, 'Hello' – then silence.
    I said, 'It's good to meet you' – then more silence.

I said, 'We've got a real challenge together on issues of security.'

He replied, 'Yes, we have' – then silence.

I said, 'I'm taking a Bill through at the moment' – silence.

Then from him: 'Our measures don't go anywhere near as far as yours, but we're getting a terrific hammering.'

I said, 'That's very interesting' – then silence.

Then he said, 'I hope you're going to assist us with terrorists based in your country.'

I said, 'I think you know that the Prime Minister is very keen to assist and we are doing our best to ensure that we do, and our officials will co-operate' – then silence.

And so it went on like this, for what felt like an age. John Prescott told me later on, when he was having a laugh with me, that Tony had had the Indian Prime Minister to lunch and it hadn't been quite so bad then because other people had helped out, but apparently John had seen him three times, and the first time had been just like that. But it did get better subsequently.

It is particularly difficult on occasions like this when you can't see, as it is not possible to make eye contact, and if there is no verbal interchange it is not easy to get the measure of the person – whether they are interested, or in the case of the then Indian Prime Minister, notorious for reflecting in this way, even when being interviewed on television. Apparently his supporters thought that this made him extremely intellectual and thoughtful, whereas for me it made it very difficult indeed to have a simple conversation. On this particular occasion, although my notes don't reflect it, at one stage I asked if he would like a cup of tea. We then had a palaver about which tea and whether we had it. It took a moment or two for me to realise that the tea had arrived and been placed in front of me. Sometimes in my official duties, I have had this problem, where I wanted to put out my hand and search for the tea but was quite concerned as to where the tea had been placed and the fact that I might send it flying. To do so would not only have been an embarrassment but would have been to place myself at somewhat of a disadvantage. In other words, I would become the object of concern (not pity but concern), which in the political world is not something that anyone would wish to be.

There was an awful leader in the *Observer* about the Anti-Terrorism Bill, and I'm having a lot of trouble now because people are misinterpreting what is happening. The former Master of the Rolls, Lord Donaldson, clearly didn't understand it when he went on the *Today* programme, and it doesn't help when people haven't got a clue what you're talking about. The Joint Committee on Human Rights was not helpful. I gave evidence to it on the Wednesday night and was asked some very bizarre questions that made it impossible to have an in-depth conversation. Even though Jean Corston – who had been made the chair of this new committee – did her best, it was very clear that the committee itself was extremely biased in favour of individual rights as opposed to our mutual rights (which is not surprising, given that people opted to be on it).

It was going to be a continuing theme of mine to try to get the balance right, to achieve proportionality between our historic heritage in defending the rights of the individual and our necessity to protect ourselves as a people and a nation, and our way of life.

I also gave evidence to the Home Affairs Select Committee, which was more helpful. The two committees cancelled each other out on incitement to religious hatred: Joint Committee on Human Rights in favour, Home Affairs Select Committee against, the exact opposite of how they had come down on the main issue of detention. We have silliness now that we've cleared two-thirds of Afghanistan from the Taliban. The very people who were against taking action in the first place are now saying that despite the fact that it wasn't the Taliban we were after, more the fact that they were hosting Bin Laden and the Al Qaeda group, they now believe that there is no risk any more and the Bill is no longer necessary. That was the thrust of the *Observer* leader.

However, it is getting a bit hairy and our backbenchers are getting really jumpy – there'll be a fair revolt against, no doubt about that. So I've just got to see it through. We've got Committee Stage on Wednesday, which will be particularly difficult and then the final stage on the 26th. I had to see Lord Strathclyde and Oliver Letwin [Shadow Home Secretary] with some of our people from the Lords on Thursday because they've got their knickers in a twist. The Lords were going to stymie the timetable by refusing to accept the eight days of debate they've been offered by Dennis Carter, Government Whip in the House of Lords. I am afraid I had to do one of my 'not losing temper but going rigid' scenes with him. He had begun by saying that unless we were prepared to concede some changes, they couldn't guarantee the Bill going through, at which stage I said that I was certainly not going to be blackmailed in that way. I said that I would be very happy to meet him on prime-time TV to explain what I was trying to do and why he was trying to play party politics by preventing it going through before Christmas. I also said that he'd brought out my working-class instincts with the way he was performing – which everyone said physically deflated him. They did get the agreement on the eight days, then started messing about with the Derogation Order and the fact that they did not want to pass it in the Lords until after the Bill had received Royal Assent – which is ridiculous as the damned thing can't come into operation unless we pass the measures on detention. So it's just a piece of jiggerypokery. I talked to Tony on Saturday and I've written to them about it and we will see where we get to. It's not a big issue for the world outside – it's just a piece of silliness.

I had promised to speak to the senior management of the Immigration and Nationality Directorate meeting at the Gatwick airport conference facility first thing on Thursday morning. Before full Cabinet that day there was scheduled a meeting of the War Cabinet, but I had taken a conscious decision that, given the progress that was being made, it was worth sticking to trying to motivate and direct the senior IND staff, so I decided to stick to the plan of going down to Gatwick, thereby missing War Cabinet. I went down on the train and there was no problem with that, but when we got back to the station for the return journey it was announced that it was going to take over half an hour longer to get back into London. So we got in a police car and just hared it. We set off from Gatwick at 9.55, the outriders met us in Brixton, and we reached No. 10 at 10.29. When I got out of the car the brakes and the tyres were giving off smoke. This was the only time that a War Cabinet has ever been filmed – for a Michael Cockerell film for BBC2 about how the Cabinet is run. So I didn't appear in the War Cabinet's only ever film – but in going down to Gatwick I think I probably made the right decision.

Three snippets relating to the Anti-Terrorism, Crime and Security Bill: one is that it was pointed out to me that I was asking the Parliamentary Labour Party to go a long way down the road of the Prevention of Terrorism Act that they'd been whipped regularly to vote against throughout the early 1980s and 1990s. I was therefore trying to overturn deep-rooted antagonism. The second was that the Joint Committee on Human Rights agreed their report immediately after I'd left the room after giving evidence, with at least two and possibly three Labour members missing. The report had been pretty well written by the clerks and advisers before I'd even given my evidence. The third was that Chris Mullin in the Home Affairs Select Committee report in relation to the Justice and Home Affairs

Council material had misunderstood (a) that the arrest warrant was going to go through the main Extradition Bill and (b) that we'd already been negotiating particular types of measure that would fall under the mutual recognition, and therefore, the affirmation under the affirmative order secondary legislation. So having misunderstood that, he then got the Committee to come out against it.

The Second Reading debate was more than gruelling. I was on my feet for an hour and twenty minutes and it was a pretty rough time. I got some brownie points for giving way and being prepared to let just about everybody who wanted to, have their say and respond to them, and more for having a clue what I was talking about.

An amusing moment came when Kevin Hughes from Doncaster intervened to ask me whether I would agree that the people who were against this Bill were the yoghurt-eating, muesli-consuming, *Guardian*-reading civil libertarians. I said, 'Well, I have been known to eat yoghurt myself and I sometimes have muesli for breakfast – and I even wear sandals in the summer.'

It's been a very difficult run-up to the Pre-Budget Report this year, and because Tony has been so heavily distracted with other things it wasn't until Sunday [25 November] that he really got round to talking to Gordon seriously. Jeremy Heywood had been on paternity leave, returning on the Monday before the report, and with David Miliband having become an MP [for South Shields] there was no one else there who had got a grip of these things. Tony desperately needs someone who knows something about public finance.

We'd had a meeting of the new Cabinet Committee on prioritising security measures on Thursday morning, when it struck me – as I had said to Gordon when I met him earlier in the morning – that we really do need a formula for being able to meet the security funding, otherwise departments, and particularly mine, will end up having to destroy other services purely to meet the cost of security measures. The problem for me is that everybody is parading what needs to be done but nobody is willing to take responsibility for the funding.

So I went off to Spain to sign the bilateral extradition agreement, have discussions with ministers there in the run-up to their presidency of the EU, speak at the European University in Madrid and then stay overnight with Pauline and Minolo, my cousin and her husband who live just outside Madrid. Although it was cold and very crisp, the sun shone. I was glad to get back to London though, because I'd got so much to do – notably the

Police Reform White Paper to rewrite for the third or fourth time. We are now getting very close to D-Day with that so I had to go through it in detail, literally rewriting clause by clause, as well as trying to catch up on the enormous pile of material, including preparing for the next round of the debate on incitement to religious hatred, which is to be taken early on the afternoon of Monday 26th. (The debate goes through until midnight, when we vote on the Third Reading – so that's going to be a hell of a week again.) We've got a UK/French summit on Thursday and I'll have to prepare for that as well.

Gordon's Pre-Budget Statement on Tuesday [27 November] was, with its provider-driven agenda, viewed as a return to Old Labour. It certainly seemed like that to me.

I can't describe how much of the week I've spent going back through the material on the White Paper, item after item, reaching compromises with No. 10. Tony did me the honour on the Thursday morning of saying once again that he trusted my judgement, and that I could go ahead if I wanted on the issues of taking powers to deal with chief constables. I've reworded it slightly to say the same thing in less aggressive terms, but his words were very touching.

Steve Byers did himself enormous harm with the release of the notes of a meeting with Railtrack on the afternoon of Gordon's Pre-Budget State-ment, and in Cabinet I asked him why on earth he had done it. He said: 'It was the deadline for the Select Committee.' So presumably somebody did it and he didn't know they were doing it at that particular time – but it was pretty basic, and given what had happened it damaged him more than I expected, as I had thought he was getting over the previous problems caused by Jo Moore.

It's hard to remember that it was only on Monday that in the Commons we went through until midnight on the final stages of the Anti-Terrorism Bill. On Thursday the Tories passed an amendment that purported to take out the international terrorists – it's this esoteric debate about Northern Ireland and internal terrorism. I can't get worked up about it – I mean the whole point of it being international terrorism was to be able to derogate from Article 5 [of the European Convention on Human Rights] but in view of the way in which they've passed the amendment, we might just accept it and let it ride. There'll be a lot more amendments passed before it comes back to the Commons and people are panicking. I'm busy trying to make sure I can do the things I've indicated, like finding a compromise with Brian Mawhinney [Conservative MP for Cambridgeshire North West], to whom I responded very positively.

In fact, he thanked me – as did Oliver Letwin. Ian Paisley came across and shook my hand – a frightening experience for anybody.

At this stage, we thought we were on the verge of agreement. In fact it was going to be another four years before a version of this clause was passed by both Houses of Parliament. This is the strangeness of politics and demonstrates how close you can get to success and yet still be so far away.

War Cabinet this week was pretty desultory and didn't take us much further. I went to the service at St Paul's for British victims of the World Trade Center attack, which was very moving. When Judi Dench read Christina Rossetti I could feel tears welling up.

December 2001

This week I had to start the process of going through the detail of those whom I might certificate and who would then appeal to the Special Immigration Appeals Commission. I have to go through the detail firstly of the broad general themes, then of the individual's background, then a two-hour meeting going through point by point with the security services and the lawyers. I weeded out one that I didn't think was acceptable, and asked for further information on two out of the six. What a process – and I've got to return to this in the coming week for another eight or nine.

I did an interview on *The World This Weekend* on Radio 4 that went fine, except that we had one of these ex-Law Lords, Lord Ackner, patronising me by saying that it was a matter of intelligence and that if only someone would explain it to me, everything would all be all right. What a cheek! But the Lords made a very big mistake on Thursday night [6 December] by savaging the whole Bill and effectively taking out four major parts, seven amendments. That was overdoing it, and I will restore all of those. And I will amend the Bill in other areas, providing a review by Privy Counsellors within two years of the whole Bill, but not a sunset clause [time limit]; putting on the face of the Bill that there will be guidance issued by the Attorney-General in relation to incitement to religious hate (this is probably the one clause that I can't be certain of holding on to, but we will see); and a new idea for making SIAC a Court of Final Record – and that's no problem at all if it gets off the hook Lord Donaldson and some of the other old codgers who clearly misunderstood what was going on.

*This was really important, because it gave the Special Immigration Appeals
Commission the status of a Court of Superior Record – in essence High Court
status – and therefore was not just a technical change but a significant move.
In retrospect, I was unfair to Lord Donaldson, because he was extremely
helpful in trying to find a way forward, but my notes at the time reflect my
growing frustration.*

Credit needs to be given to the thought and persuasion of Lord (Peter)
Goldsmith, As Attorney-General, in helping to broker a way through, in
what was a good example of people working together to find a solution
rather than accepting that prevailing practice offered no way forward. But
we do now need to draw a line. We need to say that we have amended and
amended this Bill and we've listened and responded – but enough is
enough.

I wrote an article in *The Times* on Monday [10 December] that spells out
where we are and the way in which we are moving forward. I am in the
middle of what is turning out to be one of the most difficult times in my
political life. I did an interview with Colin Brown of the *Independent on
Sunday* and the piece, although truncated, was accurate – but the headline
and the front-page story was a distortion, and a leader in the same paper
was just breathtaking. It listed the things I was doing and said I was too
hyperactive, asking me to 'lay off' – as though I could lay off the anti-
terrorism and civil contingencies, as though I could lay off asylum and
immigration which had blown up over the summer, as though I could lay
off the disturbances and the reports we'd set up in their wake, as though I
could lay off police reform even though it was in the Queen's Speech and
there is a slot for it in the legislative timetable. It's as if they think I could
just 'lay off' anything I liked despite everything going on around me or, as I
suspect they would prefer, just come out with bland platitudes, say
nothing, do nothing – and then presumably be criticised for that. It's a
very strange political world we are living in at the moment and there are
some very odd leader-writers, some very odd editors and some very strange
columnists. If I am honest, I just feel at the moment that I've almost bitten
off more than I can chew!

I'm trying to get people to debate things. There has been a terrific
reaction in favour of what I've been saying within the community, and
terrific reaction against within the glitterati, the media, the do-gooders, the
conscience-wringers – what a strange world.

And Paul Marsden, MP for Shrewsbury, whom I helped so much, over and over again – not least when we at the DfEE assisted with a one-off special allocation of capital investment for schools after the River Severn in his constituency had broken its banks – has defected to the Liberal Democrats and said that nobody helped him to get elected. What a nerve.

In the middle of all this I finally published the White Paper on police reform, which everybody agrees is the most radical for forty years, and goes a lot further than the Sheehy Inquiry in the early 1990s, which had triggered a mass rally of 10,000 police in the Wembley Arena. It's just amazing how something like that can be absorbed: the amount of time that we spent on it, and the frustration as officials simply refused, at one point, to do as they were instructed in putting in changes. It was breathtaking the way that one official in particular behaved, refusing to make the changes in the text that myself and my special adviser had directed him to do.

Once again we ran up against the way in which some – but only some – civil servants saw ministers in the Home Office as kind of advisers, rather than the other way round. It is fair to say that these early months were difficult because I was establishing not only the way I wanted to work but the way that the whole of my ministerial team approached issues. As time went on we did bring about substantial change, not simply in the personnel but in the way in which people were prepared to work together and to see that while traditional civil-service rules were there for a purpose (to protect the neutral civil-service from political interference), political interference was not the same thing as co-operation in relation to the development of policy and, crucially, to ensuring that it was delivered.

Having got the Police Reform White Paper up and running, I made the Statement to the House. I even managed to make people laugh a little and with everything else that's going on, I'm just amazed that I'm managing to survive at all.

I abandoned going to the Justice and Home Affairs Council in Brussels, which I wasn't sorry about. There were major delays because Silvio Berlusconi vetoed going ahead at this stage with the European arrest warrant because he himself was in danger of being extradited to Spain – which speaks volumes!

On Thursday [13 December] I held a series of meetings, negotiated my way round the difficulties, and made sure that Dennis Carter was clear this time as to what was required. I think Jeff Rooker did his best in really difficult circumstances. I stood at the bar of the House and listened to part of the Lords debate: some of those peers are just off the wall.

But using Huw Evans as an intermediary, we were getting somewhere with the Tories, separating them out from the Lib Dems in the Commons, and with Oliver Letwin, despite his silly article in the *Guardian* the previous Friday when he told an untruth about European arrest warrants. Everybody is telling untruths about that. There is a massive campaign in the *Mail* and the *Telegraph*, and I am going to have to deal with the issue in the New Year. But just at the moment, having done police reform, social cohesion and the Anti-Terrorism Bill, and having to deal with the aftermath of Sarah Payne's death and Roy Whiting's trial, I think I've got enough on for the time being.

Eight-year-old Sarah Payne was murdered in July 2000 by the paedophile Roy Whiting, who was sentenced to life imprisonment – on which I imposed a tariff of fifty years.

But I got amendments sorted which got all the things that I wanted – the police powers, communications data, disclosure, and the avoidance of a sunset clause on the whole of the Bill, which the Liberal Democrats pressed to the very last limit.

The sunset clause that was agreed was on Section 4 of the Bill only, although (and this was a given) derogation from the European Convention on Human Rights had to be affirmed annually.

They took it back to the House of Lords at midnight on Thursday night when everyone else had agreed, which is why I was so irritated and angry. They wouldn't give an inch. I was furious by the time we got the Bill back at 9.30 p.m. because it had come out of the Lords by 7.45. The House authorities are just so inefficient: they couldn't get the material photocopied, which was maddening. I thought there was a bit of collusion from our side as well, with people taking their time over dinner, while I'd had my dinner in five minutes in the cafeteria in Portcullis House with Paul Goggins and Huw Evans. I was absolutely livid, which didn't help. I managed to deal with the Liberals firstly on their police powers, and got everybody laughing about their having to put amendments down to restore what the police already had in the way of powers and the extension of British Transport Police and the MoD, never mind helping to increase and improve them. And secondly on holding communications data: we have to hold such data for the purpose of accessing it for anti-terrorism, so their amendment that said we can only hold it for that purpose was completely irrelevant, and I said so. Then I announced that we were having to drop the incitement to religious hatred because we'd discovered that if an individual clause is refused more than twice – and that's not just by one House but by either House – then the whole Bill falls.

This was known by very few people then, and I have discovered over the years since that it is still rarely understood, including by those covering parliamentary activity for the media.

So I announced that in order to save the Bill, we were going to drop incitement because the House of Lords had rejected it twice already and if it went back and they rejected again, the Bill would be dead. So they cheered. The Tories and Liberals cheered at the top of their voices, and some of our side joined in. I was so taken aback that I let myself go and declared: 'Go on, cheer, have your moment of glory.' This was churlish, and I regretted it immediately.

When I looked back a day or two later, I was very angry with myself, because we had done so well and by rising to the bait I played into the opponents' hands by allowing them one small moment of victory. It was so irritating to hear people dealing with such sensitive issues, believing that they were at a football match and their side had scored. I learned my lesson – but it should not have been necessary.

I got up at the end of the debate and pulled a few words together to finish on the right note. I've done Oliver Letwin a big favour because I've boosted his standing, but it doesn't matter. If I have to attack him then people will at least know that I've respected the fact that I can trust his word – unlike that of Simon Hughes [Liberal Democrat Home Affairs Spokesman].

I got an article on the Anti-Terrorism Bill in *The Times* on the Monday [10 December] and one about social cohesion in the *Guardian* on the Friday [14 December]. I also had an article in the *News of the World* about the Roy Whiting conviction. We had a terrible time on Friday night and the Saturday, and in the end I had to speak to Rebekah Wade, editor of the *News of the World*, to persuade her not to go completely over the top, and to make sure that I wasn't screwed and that what we did was seen as rational.

This was more crucial than anyone may have understood at the time, not simply because I didn't want the News of the World *whipping up hysteria. As noted earlier in this book, we'd had the bizarre situation of someone being attacked as a paedophile in the West Country, when he was a paediatrician, and we had already seen in Portsmouth what happens when the mob is let loose. But also because as Home Secretary I was trying to deal with the issue of Roy Whiting, his trial and subsequent conviction in a way that would allow me to hold on to the right to determine the tariff – i.e. the period to be spent in jail – before that power was taken away from me, a move which was imminent under a challenge through the Lords and the European Court of Justice. At this stage anything that I had said which would interfere with the judicial process would have made it impossible for me then to handle the case. As it happened, I was proved to be all too right, in that as late as March 2006 a challenge was launched on technical grounds to my decision to enforce a tariff of fifty years on Roy Whiting just before my powers were withdrawn.*

Special Branch have started to brief about what I'm going to do this coming week on having picked up people whose asylum appeals have been turned down. I spent a great chunk of last week going through the cases again, and have now got them down to ten. I've rejected two outright, one has fallen because they cannot find him, and another has fallen because it's better to take him on a series of other minor charges adding up to a decent period in jail rather than having to go through SIAC. We got an excellent agreement on SIAC in the end with the Court of Superior Record avoiding judicial review but satisfying people. Peter Goldsmith did a really good job on that.

In the middle of everything else that was going on on Thursday I had a bizarre conversation with Derry Irvine, who wanted to tell me that the judges had told him off for not being a proper protector of and not acting as an intermediary for them. They felt that I was going over the top in attacking them and they didn't like it. I said, 'I know they don't like it, Derry, but I'm representing the public.'

When I got back to Sheffield, I went to the first ever Christmas illuminations in the Firth Park district of my constituency: 300 people turned up and it was a lovely, happy occasion. Then I get called a populist for this – because I try and represent the public, to speak it as it is, to tell the truth and not be mealy-mouthed.

Just one other thought from the week. I saw Bill Clinton coming out from having a coffee with Tony, on Thursday morning before the War

Cabinet. Again, I noticed that Tony's having a right job to get the MoD top brass and the Foreign Office to do what he wants in relation to Afghanistan, which is still going extraordinarily well. There are threats, however, and we have Stephen Lander constantly repeating the nature of the threats. But then he withdraws and says that of course they cannot say that all the intelligence is reliable, so we get a contradictory set of arguments. It's very strange the way MI5 operates. Then we had a very decent Cabinet meeting, with the Political Cabinet just for an hour and a quarter after the normal Cabinet. It was good because everyone joined in really positively, particularly on social cohesion, and Tony said it was very important because social policy had been shown to be crucial in the Australian and Danish elections. I said, 'Yes, asylum particularly.' I got the feeling he was making a point to Gordon that, while the economy mattered, other things mattered as well. I made the point that trust counted for a very great deal. Lose the trust and you've lost the war. One funny bit was when Gordon was talking about the *Daily Mail* being against us. I said: 'Well, the *Daily Mail* is fine with me but horrible to other people, whereas the *Daily Mirror* is fine with you, Gordon, and horrible to me, and the *Sun* is horrible to John and some papers are horrible to everybody. That's life.'

On Monday 17 December I had to go down early for a meeting with Tony Blair and Stephen Lander which was really quite weird, because Tony was distracted and Stephen Lander does not explain clearly what is going on or what he is doing. I don't know whether it's part of the pattern that he's developed over the years in dealing with MI5, but it's almost as though he talks in riddles, which makes it very difficult to pin him down. We had the promise, having signed the certificates that I had, that ten people would be picked up on Wednesday morning, and Tony agreed to all this.

I then went to St Margaret's Church for the Christmas carol service run by the DfES, because none of the other departments have Christmas carols. It was freezing in the church so it's a wonder I didn't get pneumonia.

Home Office Questions that afternoon went off fine, then came the ministerial Christmas dinner on the Monday night.

I had a visit from Sarah Payne's mum and dad, Sara and Michael – a very sad meeting. I tentatively suggested that they should consider how best to help their other three children, Sarah's older brothers Luke and Lee, and Charlotte, who is only seven. I feared they might think that it was not my business to intrude on how they should be handling the tragedy and their feelings but they responded very well.

I couldn't help myself at the time. I was so worried about their other children and the fact that, while there was nothing that could be done to bring Sarah back, the family as a whole needed support, love and attention. It is a problem, not being the official politician all the time and playing the role, but slipping back into what I would say and do in my own constituency – sometimes to my own detriment.

These are very painful meetings – like with the father of James Bulger [the toddler who had been abducted and murdered in 1993]. I'm doing the tariffs all the time – easy with people like Harold Shipman [the doctor convicted in January 2000 of murdering fifteen of his patients, though it was estimated that he had in fact murdered in excess of 230], but not so easy with others.

A farce on the Wednesday [19 December]. I was due to chair a Cabinet Committee on crime, but had to hand over to John Denham because I discovered that eight of the ten terrorist suspects had been picked up but not Abu Qatada [radical cleric] or another leading dissident. It seemed that Special Branch had just lost track of them. In the case of Abu Qatada they were watching his home at ten on Monday evening and then had lost him when he went out. When I asked how they could have lost him, they said that there were lots of press waiting up the road and by the time they'd picked up that he'd left home, they weren't close enough to keep in touch. I was flabbergasted and said so. They then said that they thought they'd got him as his car was parked outside a known address and they had raided it first thing Wednesday morning, but he wasn't there. I said, 'Well, he wouldn't be, would he?'

They then said that they wanted to raid his home at 11.30 that morning in the hope of finding something that would give them a clue. I said, 'Do you mean he might have left a little note saying that he was round at Uncle Joe's and here's the address?' I also said: 'If the press are outside, with all the cameras and paraphernalia, what do you think would be the consequence of your raiding his house? You know he's not there and so you come out without him. What will the media do?' Total silence. I said, 'They'll splash it across every TV channel and every front page that we've lost Abu Qatada.'

I said that the Prime Minister would be up in the House for Prime Minister's Questions at noon and that, if we didn't raid the house, we would at least have bought ourselves some time. I didn't know how true that was because, as it turned out, we had got as much time as we needed because there was so much confusion about whether or not Abu Qatada was one of the eight people who had been picked up. We had already agreed on my instructions that we would not issue a list but if anyone – the family or the solicitors – put the name out, then we would confirm they were there – but of course most of them don't want to do that. Only one did so, and he was a Tunisian who wanted to go back to Tunisia, which leaves us with seven. This was at 11.25 a.m., by 11.28 a.m. I'd got the picture. I said: 'Well, I'm not in operational control, you are, but I'm instructing you nevertheless to abort the invasion of Abu Qatada's house' – and they rushed out and phoned. So with ninety seconds to spare, they cancelled the raid. What a carry-on – more like 000 than 007. MI5 claim it was their job to put the case together, but the Metropolitan Special Branch should be in charge of tracking and picking up. The immigration service were involved and I had to instruct them not to put out separate press releases.

And we've got the Special Branch involved in the next incident, which was the ship containing sugar. This happened on Thursday evening, after I'd arrived home in Sheffield rather belatedly because tragically two people had committed suicide on the East Coast main line. When I was told about a ship that allegedly contained materials for a chemical attack I swiftly abandoned the idea of going to the carol service at the Black Bull in Ecclesfield, which is what I was supposed to be doing with Helen Jackson. Instead I spent most of the night on the telephone, dealing with this ship affair. I was told it had left the Yemen, moored off Somalia, and was a danger. Apparently someone in Islamabad had given the security services a tip-off that a ship carrying chemical-warfare material was going to Bristol, whereas this ship was in fact going to the Tate & Lyle refinery in London.

But that didn't worry the security services. They asked if I would agree that the Special Boat Squad could attack the ship and stop it. I said, 'Can't we just ask them to stop?' They said, 'Well, they just might discharge the dangerous materials into the air.' I said that they had to have a method of delivering the chemicals, and asked which way the wind was blowing. 'Towards France' was the reply. I said: 'You think they're coming to Britain to attack Britain, but are prepared to put something into the wind which is blowing over France.' What a farce. I said: 'The consequence of stopping the ship by force would be the accusation of piracy on the high seas, a massive compensation claim, world attention, and egg all over our face if there is nothing on the ship. You must consult Peter Goldsmith' – which they did, and discovered that he agreed with me.

I then phoned Tony, who was at his constituency-party Christmas dinner in Sedgefield. I got him out and put him in the picture. He said that he didn't want anybody killed and I said that there would not be anybody killed if we did this sensibly. He then said, 'Well, what's the position?' I said that Geoff Hoon had already authorised the Special Boat Squad to go in, but my view was that we should calm it all down. We should ask the ship to stop, but should do so in the morning when it was light and there would be no risk to anyone. If they didn't comply then we would have every justification for going in and using force. Tony said, 'OK – I'll take your judgement.' So I told our people that that is what they should do. They then rang back saying that they agreed. I said, 'I'm very glad you do, because if I say something with the Prime Minister's support, then I expect it to be done.' John Warne, Head of the Organised and International Crime Directorate, asked me, 'Ought you to phone Jack Straw and Geoff Hoon?' I said: 'No. This is a decision taken because it is a possible risk to the United Kingdom, and it is therefore my responsibility.'

I should have informed Jack and Geoff. One of the things that I failed to do in Cabinet was to realise that even when it was my responsibility and there was no obligation, consulting colleagues and keeping people involved were crucial contributions to ensuring that I didn't rub people up the wrong way or cause resentment. I much regret what in retrospect was a form of arrogance, born of determination simply to get on with the job. I have never been any good at ringing round and networking and there is a price to be paid for that failing – as Denis Healey had found out.

The ship was apprehended off the Isle of Wight, and samples taken from material in the hold and sent to the chemical-weapons research centre at Porton Down.

It all worked out fine and by Monday, Christmas Eve, it was pretty clear to me that the security services had not found a thing and there was no risk. So I told them to get off the case. I'd spoken to Tony on Sunday night at Chequers and got his agreement that I could stand them down, subject to the clearance of the materials by Porton Down. We needed to get off the ship and get off quickly, firstly for the sake of the people on the Isle of Wight who were scared stiff about its being moored offshore, and secondly because the sooner we got off it, the less likely we were to be taken for compensation.

And then we had Richard Reid, the man with explosives in his shoe who had managed to get on an American Airlines plane from Paris to Boston –

but was thwarted after a fellow passenger had seen him behaving erratically as he tried to take off his shoe and detonate the explosive.

We also had the 'invasion' from the Sangatte refugee camp in France on Christmas Day, when 450 people tried to get through to Britain by climbing on to trains about to enter the Channel Tunnel. They were stopped and nobody made it across, but that didn't prevent newspapers pretending that this was a great catastrophe. I have not yet had the chance to implement my announcement of 29 October. I've got a White Paper and a Bill coming and I am getting a grip of it all, but that doesn't stop people being cynical and slagging us off.

The other thing I ought to mention from Christmas week was the meeting on ID cards chaired by John Prescott, who was very helpful. We're having a further meeting because we have not yet reached agreement.

I smile now at the idea that we might have reached agreement way back in 2002. It was in fact 2005 before we came to agree as a government, and March 2006 before the slightly watered-down proposals were to gain approval through Parliament.

The good news of the 27th is that we've reached a pay agreement with the Police Federation, ACPO [Association of Chief Police Officers], and the Superintendents through the Police Negotiating Board. John Denham kept me in touch during the evening, after I'd given a bit more by authorising that we reduce, from fourteen to eleven and then to ten, the incremental points on the scale for constables, plus a new scale on competence that would add in an extra amount. We've accelerated the scales and made good progress, and by holding firm and holding my nerve while others, it has to be said, were dithering and flailing about all over, I've managed an agreement, and I am really pleased about that.

As Police Minister, John Denham was overseeing the tripartite negotiations between ourselves, the police authorities and the police service.

Christmas itself, and this is the message – complete with suitable background music – on my telephone answering machine: 'We wish you a happy Christmas and a lovely and restful holiday. If you are friends or family, leave me a message. If you are the press, then please leave me alone. God bless and have a wonderful Christmas, and that was the Mormon Tabernacle Choir from 1959 singing the Lord's Prayer.'

The sons and I had a Christmas Eve goose because they were spending Christmas Day with their mum, and we were a bit disappointed because there seemed to be a lot of stuffing but not enough goose! The boys stayed with me on Christmas Eve and on Christmas Day morning we went for a walk. I had agreed with the *Mail on Sunday* that we would take some photographs and they would then make a donation on my behalf to the new hospice to be created at the Northern General Hospital in Sheffield.

Sod's Law: the camera didn't work and the photographs didn't come out, so we don't have a memory of that Christmas. But to do the Mail on Sunday *justice, they did stick to their side of the agreement and made the donation anyway.*

Friday 28 December: Sarah and Gordon's baby girl has arrived. The poor little thing is only 2lb 4oz and had to be delivered seven weeks prematurely by Caesarean, so I think we're all praying that she will thrive and survive. I understand the birth was brought forward because she wasn't growing. Anyway, I've left a message for Gordon and Sarah, congratulating them and wishing them well.

And so we come to the end of the year. We have the Indians and Pakistanis with a stand-off on the border, Palestine and Israel more difficult than ever, Afghanistan virtually clear of the Taliban – and me still worried about Andrew, Hugh and particularly Alastair and his illness: he's going in for tests. I worry for the New Year. It feels a little bit like walking with friends into an abyss.

How prescient this was. In my private life I was walking on the edge of a cliff, but sadly not with my friends.

As for the New Year, my resolution will be not to be the Home Secretary who sends out letters, delivers speeches and makes responses that are the standard fare produced by the civil service year after year. It is important not to be the same, but when you're not, you're criticised – and if you are in the usual mould, you are still criticised. What a world!

And we move towards the euro – twelve countries joining on the stroke of midnight: Greece at ten o'clock our time because they are two hours ahead, the rest of continental Europe at eleven o'clock and Ireland at twelve o'clock our time. What a strange carry-on, with all those currencies merged into one. What will the UK do?

January 2002

New Year's Day 2002. Worked on the Asylum White Paper, reshaping it so that it is a Nationality, Asylum and Immigration White Paper. I have rewritten much of it because it just had entirely the wrong tone. The draft, which I know Nick Pearce has spent a lot of time on as well, was far too middle-class London liberal. It is going to be hard work getting the tone of this right. They don't understand that unless people feel secure and trust us, there's no way we can have integration with diversity, no way we can do what we want to do on the wider front. But above all they have no answers. They are still repeating what I wrote and put in the Statement on 29 October. Nobody ever takes a further step forward, and it is really frustrating. Anyway, I'm off to the Lake District for a few days. I'm going to get some fresh air before going back into the maelstrom again.

The *Guardian* interview with Estelle on 2 January reveals that members of the Department for Education and Skills have been offering counselling to Home Office staff since I took over, because of the impact I'm having on them. Well, well, well.

I had a lovely break in the Lake District despite having caught this rotten chest cold that's been going round. Thursday and Friday were beautiful days – cold, snowy and crisp underfoot but sunny and bright. The air was so clear and fresh.

I'm having a real problem with correspondence concerning Keith Bennett, who was killed by Ian Brady [convicted, with Myra Hindley, for the notorious Moors Murders in the mid 1960s]. His brother Alan had written and it had taken two months for the letter to come through to me. I replied to him personally, and now find that Mrs Johnson, Keith Bennett's mum, had written on 15 November and her letter has just floated round until Christmas, with no one taking responsibility for it. I've written a robust letter to John Gieve about this as I feel it was just grossly incompetent and insensitive. How they could possibly have missed that this was a significant and sensitive letter I can't imagine, bearing in mind that the letter began: 'Dear Mr Blunkett, My son Keith was murdered by Ian Brady and Myra Hindley. My life ended then . . .' It should have been clear to anyone that this was a matter which should have come direct to me, rather than into the Correspondence Unit. But there we are – that's how it is, I'm afraid, and I can't keep going on about it.

Poor Gordon and Sarah have revealed that their baby girl – whom they have called Jennifer Jane – has had a brain haemorrhage, and it seems she has been in difficulties since she was born. I understand that Gordon and Sarah have known for some time that things were desperate. My heart just goes out to them – as does everybody's, as it's just so terrible for them. I've tried communicating with Gordon but obviously he won't want to talk to anybody. I wouldn't if I were in his place.

Monday 7 January, 5.20 p.m.: Little Jennifer Jane has died. Sue Nye [Gordon Brown's closest aide] had phoned me just before I heard this awful news, to say thank you from Gordon for my messages.

And Jeff Rooker's wife Angela is going back into hospital tomorrow, I think for the last time. I am surrounded by terrible sadness.

After Thursday's Cabinet I had a conversation with Jack Straw, who had asked to speak with me. Again he talked to me about how he was being undermined by my setting aside everything he'd done. He also said that he had heard from those in the Home Office that I was putting him down. I said: 'Well, I cannot really deal with things like that without any names or knowing what people are saying. All I know is that on every public occasion – broadcasts, speeches, what I have written, debates in the House – I've given you absolute credit.'

He replied: 'I don't deny that. It's just this constant drip, drip of you trying to establish yourself.'

I said: 'It's nothing to do with establishing myself, it's to do with trying to do the job, in the same way that you've got to do in the Foreign Office and Estelle's got to do in Education. We've all got to deal with it from the point where we pick up and run, otherwise all we would do is have one term in government, which is what happened to previous Labour governments.' However, it did make me think about what I do when I take over something. It was the same with the leadership of Sheffield City Council; it was the same when I got on to the front bench; and it was the same when I took over the Shadow Health job, when I had to rebuild a policy because Robin [Cook] had got a very good attack mechanism but no policy. It was the same when I took over from Ann Taylor on Education, and I suppose it's the same now. So that talk with Jack did make me wonder about the way in which I obviously see a challenge and have to go for it. But I don't see any other way of doing it.

It was too late to learn the lessons for the Home Office, but not too late when I took over Work and Pensions in 2005. Although my sojourn there was brief I did adopt a different strategy, which was not simply due to the fact that I had been humbled but to the fact that I had learned a lesson or two. I have much

more understanding now than was the case all those years ago. I noticed in
March 2006, when issues of asylum once again bubbled to the surface after a
period of calm, that I was jumpy about suggestions that 'measures were just
being taken' in the words of the then Immigration Minister, when anyone
studying what was the most enormous mountain to climb in 2002–3 would
have had some grasp of just how much progress had been made.

And then I stopped myself and thought: 'Just a moment, David, can you not
now see how others perceived what you said and did?'

Constituency surgery on Saturday morning [12 January]: the surgery was
very weird because the cases were so horrendous and difficult. I had one
man who was completely round the twist and who came to tell me that all
the recent deaths and fires had been caused by debris from outer space –
and then stumped off in a huff because I wouldn't initiate an investigation
for him. There were two further cases – one man and one woman – where
the child had been taken away and they wanted me to do something about
it. Then I had the usual high number of immigration matters, and one
appalling case where neighbours had been trying to look after a woman
who had been mentally ill for twenty years and had lived alone since the
death of her parents. No one would take responsibility and she had set fire
to her home by using candles, virtually gutting the house. These are just
terrible cases where people are struggling to help others but are not getting
any assistance.

We are still dealing with the Anti-Terrorism Bill, and I've been trying all
week to get Special Branch to pull their finger out in finding Abu Qatada. I
had a long round-table meeting about that and where they're going from
here on other measures. It's still taking quite a long time to get it sorted.

There was a pre-Cabinet meeting on the Afghanistan situation. It's very
strange: the difference between our approach and that of the Americans is
beginning to show quite starkly. We want to reconstruct and get aid and
coherence in there, and they are only interested in going after the Al Qaeda
group and Bin Laden.

The transport dispute [when Railtrack was wound up and replaced by
Network Rail] has been continuing all week and has been a nightmare. I
think things are beginning to calm down now for Steve Byers but it's been a
terrible time for him, particularly with all the criticism he got in the press
for being on holiday just after Christmas.

It was little Jennifer Brown's funeral on the Friday. I didn't attend but
spoke to Gordon on the telephone on Thursday. I felt it was a private thing,

absolutely private. I understand why Tony and Cherie went, of course, and perhaps John Prescott and Pauline, but I was amazed at some of the others who attended, including leading members of the press.

I had a meeting about the Police Reform Bill which was just appalling. Some of these Home Office officials are the worst, most obstructive, miserable, disengaged and disinterested group of people I have ever come across, which indicates a degree of demoralisation and complete lack of leadership. In the end I said that I was not putting up with the atmosphere any longer, and brought the meeting to a hasty and premature close.

Someone leaked to Frances Gibb on *The Times* the meeting between Derry, Peter Goldsmith and myself, and I am absolutely livid about it. No sooner are we in a discussion with Tony and all these people around the table than someone starts leaking. The problem is that it could be anybody. There were a lot of people there when we met on Thursday and it could have come from any one of them. It's just hopeless. You can't have a conversation, you can't float an idea. You can't do anything without its being leaked.

I spoke to Gordon on Sunday [20 January] and asked him and Sarah out to dinner, but he said that Sarah didn't want to go out just yet. She just wanted to be quiet and away from things. He asked instead that I go and have dinner with them – which I will.

We are still having a battle internally. The officials jumped on something that Robin Cook said to me about splitting the Nationality and Asylum Bill. I said I am not splitting it: it stands or falls as a single entity. We are not having bits any more. But they can't grasp that, and I am now getting beyond the point of frustration with the officials.

Monday papers [21 January] – *Times* and *Guardian* – were not good. They made it look as though I had leaked the fact that we were going to change the mode-of-trial proposals. [This was the issue about whether we would reduce the scope for jury trial and effectively abandon attempts that had been made in the previous parliament which had caused so much aggravation and diversion of time and effort.] This was worrying because Tony has not agreed them yet. Somebody is doing me a disservice.

And I have not felt good in myself this week. I feel sharp-brained but brittle – like they describe people who have been fasting. Really weird. It's a bit like when you have one of those dreams and you wake up with some earth-shattering idea, and it starts to fade and then disappears entirely.

I have been trying to reshape the whole of what we are going to do about the prison service. There is such poor thinking. We have got a nineteenth-century system and we are just adding to it, trying to improve the same system rather than thinking radically about what we do for people on remand, how we mix tagging with open prisons, and how we have a home/ domestic curfew before people are sentenced and not just as an early-release scheme. I am trying to think the same way about other services as well, rather than just going through the motions.

The leaks on the mode of trial don't appear to have done any terrible harm. Whoever decided to give it to Frances Gibb on _The Times_ and Alan Travis on the _Guardian_ (who I think already had it but had been asked not to use it until it emerged elsewhere) might be slightly closer to my office than I find comfortable. As Mary Ann Sieghart put it in her column in _The Times_ on Wednesday, I had wanted to do a three-point turn and was forced to do a U-turn. I had wanted to get it all right, I had wanted ideas from Derry and Peter for having an alternative to the mode-of-trial proposals so that the package stood up and was coherent. Instead it was leaked deliberately and just dribbled out, and was intended to jump the Prime Minister. Fortunately Tony believed that it wasn't me. I got a message from him on Monday night saying that he had no doubt whatsoever.

Tony, Cherie, Michael Barber and Sally Morgan came round to South Eaton Place for dinner on Wednesday night. It was a very enjoyable evening, although I had a blinding headache unfortunately. Tony was very relaxed and the chef who was doing the food did it really well. During dinner I did go a bit far in saying to Tony that it was important that he didn't introduce top-up fees and that it was a matter of trust. There was a slight pause and a moment's awkwardness. I also talked to him about radically revising the civil service.

I had an entertaining dinner on Tuesday night with Ken Clarke, who is a real character, and who had clearly had the same problems in his brief sojourn at the Home Office [1992–3] as I am having. He remembered the David Waddington problems very well indeed. David Waddington was Home Secretary in the late 1980s when a spate of prison riots (and a failure to deal with them swiftly) incurred the wrath of Margaret Thatcher, as well as being a disaster for the Prison Service as a whole. Ken said that David had told him firstly what the civil service had not told him about the Prison Service going haywire, secondly that they had overridden the Governor of Strangeways and thirdly that they had told the Home Secretary that it wasn't his job, it was operational. But he was the one who had to take the rap for it because the civil service are never ever held accountable for what they do.

This conversation with Ken had an impact on me because it was to be recalled rather vividly later in my time as Home Secretary when a riot broke out at Lincoln Prison.

I am still struggling with the Nationality and Asylum White Paper. I find it breathtaking that the Department should think that we could delay getting rid of vouchers until spring 2003. I've just had to blow my top about that, ramming home the point that the timescales they work on are completely different from anything I've ever been used to.

Astonishing as it may seem, the proposition had been put to me that we should continue paying 'back money' to those granted formal immigration status on the grounds that they had 'lost out' because the voucher had only been 70 per cent of total social security, reflecting the fact that housing and other costs were met direct!

This is what we are having to put up with all the time – delay, prevarication, ineptitude. Nick Pearce came to me and said that they were saying that because of a European Court ruling and the ECHR I couldn't automatically send people back to other countries in Europe because it had been ruled that there shouldn't be a presumption. I said, 'OK, I'll certificate them,' and worked out with him there and then a scheme that he wrote down. I then told him to go away and tell the officials who had told him it couldn't be done, to do it this way. I was only able to do that because of the discussions, and the background knowledge and all the work we had done on the Anti-Terrorism Act.

It was astonishing to be told that there was a danger that returning people to other European countries who had signed up to the European Convention on Human Rights was 'unsafe'. In the end it wasn't an issue at all, but it was the kind of thing that not only caused irritation but took up enormous time in arguing through a case that was irrelevant to the central issues.

There's something about January – the cold and the dark – which affects me. Roll on spring.

A harrowing weekend – the Holocaust memorial service in Manchester, where I dropped my notes and just spoke off the cuff – followed by meetings, meetings all week, including a police-reform meeting on the Tuesday with Bill Bratton, ex-Commissioner of the New York Police

Department. It was good to have him across – a positive gesture when dealing with those who are only interested in the tripartite approach of Home Office, National Association of Police Authorities (councillors and lay members) and ACPO.

The National Association of Police Authorities didn't mention crime reduction once. They just whined on about their position, as though the constitutional protection from action was more important than anything they had to do to protect the people.

This dispute was sad for me, as I got on very well with Ruth Henig, Chairman of the National Association of Police Authorities and later a baroness.

We had an early-morning meeting on the Thursday all about public services and the agenda for reform. I finally joined in towards the end, but it was a good discussion on the back of some very strange things that have been going on.

We've had the Post Office regulator virtually announcing that there will not be any rural postal services by 2006, something that I raised vigorously in the meeting before Cabinet.

Thank goodness this did not come to pass, but the withdrawal by 2010 of the Post Office card account – the payment of pensions – ensured that the issue of keeping open small businesses that were also post offices was not going to go away.

And then the farce of what happened in the press office on Friday night. They were apparently faxing something completely trivial to the Press Association, and at the same time were printing off sensitive material in relation to asylum costs. They then faxed the sensitive material to the PA along with the trivia – and it made the front page of the *Sunday Express!* At least the press office owned up and didn't try to pretend that it had been a leak, but it does make me wonder just how many leaks have been leaks and not just things that people have simply messed up.

All of this comes on top of trying to sort out the various announcements for prisons, and to add to the pressure, on top of Home Office Questions on Monday 4 February, the Tories have chosen asylum and our relations with France as the first part of their Supply Day. So I have now got to deal with that, because I can't just walk out of Home Office Questions and leave it to Angela Eagle [junior minister in the Home Office], because Jeff Rooker is Immigration Minister in the Lords.

February 2002

The first week of February must have been one of the most challenging, difficult and overcrowded – and in political terms one of the most successful – single weeks I've ever had. On Monday I did the *Today* programme, and the speech to the prison officers went well, as did the television and reporting about the proposals for thinking imaginatively about prison and correction policy. Home Office Questions were fine, if dull. The debate around the Tory motion about sending people back to France also went smoothly. I'd learned enough to be able to answer perfectly reasonably. It was a civilised debate – to the irritation, I think, of the Tory benches, and there were responsible reports of it.

Tuesday was busy. I am still having enormous problems with trying to get things sorted out for the Spending Review and some preparation for approaches to Gordon on what might be achieved in the forthcoming Budget. We were doing the final touches to the Statement and the proof copies of the White Paper on nationality and immigration. The Department failed to do what had been required of them on the habitual residents' test. This, as I have mentioned before, is where people get their asylum claim accepted but not nationality in other European countries, and then come over here and survive for long enough for them to claim that they are entitled to be supported by the state. Somalians in particular are doing it. I had said that we would issue a very clear guidance note ruling out giving them support – and the Department just failed to do it. I didn't find out until the Tuesday. They are doing this all the time, and if Nick Pearce and I hadn't chased them there would have been loads of aspects of policy that would never have appeared in the White Paper. My adviser Sophie Linden had the same problem with the Police Reform White Paper. It is obviously a tactic they have adopted over the years: they are told to do something and they don't argue; they just don't do it.

It looks as if Andrew Adonis has won on the one thing that Tony and I really fell out about in the last parliament (on the education front, that is, as opposed to other things): the super A level, which I'd blocked against pressure applied in conversations with both Tony and Andrew Adonis. Two years later, and the same debates are taking place.

The reason I was against a special A level over and above the grade-A A level was very simple. Every time we do this, we effectively downgrade the qualification that originally was the gold standard. In simple terms, we should be getting tougher with regard to people getting high grades, whether at GCSE, A level (or diploma) and university-degree level. The way to ensure that standards are upheld is to make the qualification being taken robust, reliable and comparable – not to invent some new qualification that only a few people will take.

Derry Irvine has gone ballistic, saying that I hadn't properly cleared the fixing of a date by which those cases, prior to the introduction of the Human Rights Act on 2 October 2000, can claim on human-rights grounds even when they've been turned down for asylum. I want to set a date by which anyone, pre-2 October 2000, who hadn't claimed on human-rights grounds, can't claim it. It's very strange, because Derry was initially arguing against the refusal of automatic bail for those whose appeal had been turned down. This of course meant that we wouldn't have been able to hold them in the removal centres, which just made a farce of everything.

Anyway, we made it to Thursday and the launch went well. I did the *Today* programme and Radio 5 Live, and have got sufficient coverage with an article in the *Sun* and an interview with the *Mail.* I did the Statement as well as I can manage Statements. My problem is that I still end up with long complicated sentences rather than simplifying it and making it easy to read. The questions went fine and the newspapers for the week tell the story.

This Statement and the White Paper provided the most carefully crafted overview of nationality and immigration that I could manage. Reflecting on the document now, I am proud of it. It set the scene for what we were to do over subsequent years, and placed asylum where it belonged – as a small part of a much bigger nationality, immigration and citizenship debate, including my subsequent actions in bringing in new preparation for, and celebration of, citizenship when people sought naturalisation.

What remains a simple fact, however, is how few people ever read either the Statement or the White Paper. Time and time again over subsequent years, I found that people had not got the first idea what we put in a document that was carefully entitled Secure Borders, Safe Haven. *I judged everything I did subsequently against whether it fitted in with the values and the framework laid out in that document, which again formed the basis of the five-year strategy I had been drawing up in autumn 2004, with the announcement subsequently made in February 2005 leading to the further update in March 2006. (The points system that was announced then was the formula we agreed in October/November 2004 in rigorous discussions, but because of my resignation everything was understandably delayed.) The lesson in relation to people not having read the White Paper is that we ourselves should have published a small, easy-to-read pamphlet that even the most dilatory correspondent or media pundit would have understood, and the contents of which they perhaps – just perhaps – would have remembered.*

Quentin Letts in the *Daily Mail* on Friday was very funny about my own side. Having had the White Paper for two and a half hours, the Tories had clearly decided as a matter of policy that they should cheer at the things they liked, which totally threw our side, who in Quentin Letts's words 'folded their arms and hugged themselves like naked men in a snowstorm'.

David Cameron's performance in relation to the Education White Paper and subsequent Bill in 2005–6 was reminiscent of this. It is an old tactic but it seems to catch our side out every time.

My request to the ethnic-minority cultures concerning arranged marriages got a hell of a lot of publicity – mostly misinterpreted, mostly distorted, as was what I said about the teaching of English and the taking of an oath of allegiance.

This was about asking ethnic minorities to consider marriages within this country rather than pulling in spouses from – for example – rural villages in South-East Asia.

It all went as well as I could ever have hoped. It is implementing it now that is the problem.

Val Woolrich from the Guide Dogs for the Blind Association phoned to say they thought they had found a suitable dog for me, called Sadie. I said that Lucy wasn't ready to retire yet and that I thought she had got another year in her.

Surgery on Saturday the 9th was the worst I've ever had. Two and a half hours, and there were still five people I didn't have time to see. I've arranged to hold an additional surgery and had to ask them to come back. It's getting worse and worse. The workload is getting overwhelming in the constituency office as well as in the Department. How much more can we take?

The workload did in fact get a great deal worse, because not only was I Home Secretary, I also had an urban 'dispersal' centre in the constituency for asylum cases. Those in the know (and those determined that they should be in the know) simply sent asylum cases along to my advice surgery. Margaret Beckett made a brave stand over this by insisting that asylum complainants complete and submit a form, rather than take up surgery time that should have been spent with her own constituents. For myself, I established a new system, which protected the voting population from being put off coming to surgeries because they would have to wait so long in a queue, and because of the feeling that they were themselves becoming second-class citizens. I understood all too well, from the experience of my advice surgeries, just how easy it was for the BNP to recruit in white working-class areas.

A meeting with Rudi Giuliani, mayor of New York, who has had enormous success with a basic statistical information system known as CONSTAT that Bill Bratton, the most successful of his police commissioners, had been telling me about in January. There was a lot of publicity around that, not least because on Monday night when I had dinner with the Met Commissioner – a social dinner – we arranged that we'd have a photo with Giuliani, alongside which we'd publish the latest figures on the Met's street sweep that I've been pressing them to do since November.

Then on the following day, we found they'd already published them, and I was left on Wednesday with an interview lined up with the *Evening Standard* and photo with Giuliani – but no story. So in the interview I extended to six months the eight weeks that the Met had given themselves to slow down the inexorable rise in street crime before starting to turn it round, thereby giving the Commissioner six months to stabilise it and two years really to turn it round – and this became the story.

All hell broke loose. The Commissioner was going to resign, everyone was up in arms, and the President of the Association of Chief Police Officers wrote to me in high dudgeon. People – including John Stevens himself – were briefing that this was an outrage, and how dare I interfere? All this took off and the story ran and ran, aided and abetted by the fact that the Police Federation ballot went nine to one against me with regard to their acceptance of the proposition on police reform and the radical change in outdated regulations: it wasn't exactly helpful to find that so few of the police officers understood what was going on.

I thought at the time that this episode was no more than a spat between myself and the police, but it went much deeper than that. The reason I have given some space to reflecting here on what happened in 2002 is because of the significance it took on three and a half years later in early September 2005 in the context of publication of a book by John (by then Lord) Stevens.

The reality is very simple. I made one mistake. I did not warn John Stevens that I was going to spell out in words of one syllable in the Evening Standard *interview that we were going to have a major drive against street crime, which for several weeks had nightly been appearing on our television screens, as well as providing front-page stories in national newspapers. Tony Blair and I had already decided that in March we were going to deploy substantial resources, but at this time I was under enormous pressure to say precisely what we were going to do, and I was not going to respond with, 'I don't know, ask the Met Commissioner.' As Home Secretary I was ultimately responsible for what happened in relation to law and order in England and Wales, irrespective of the responsibilities of police authorities.*

My not telling John Stevens was an error of judgement and a discourtesy. I did apologise to him privately at the time, and he in turn apologised for his 'mistake' in pre-empting the agreement we had about how to handle these matters together.

In my view (and it remains my view) we were indeed both mistaken. I did not, as his book describes, brief Trevor Kavanagh on the Sun: *I did an open interview with the home-affairs correspondent of the* Evening Standard *which appeared on that paper's front page and was subsequently picked up. This is a matter of record, not of reflection. However, John Stevens's vitriolic attack on me all those years later happened to come at a moment when I was particularly vulnerable, given the lies that were being told about my private life and the sustained attempt by some branches of the British media to dislodge me from Cabinet a second time, as they had done with Peter Mandelson.*

I could not see at the time, but clearly should have seen, that someone could be so petty and vindictive and at the same time – to use one of his own words – spend the next two years working hand in hand with me and appearing time and time again with me. We even shared platforms on his stepping down as Commissioner, even after I had myself ceased to be Home Secretary. This is a lesson in life which I will not forget.

But back to the daily routine and reality of fighting for reform at the time . . .

While I was at the Justice and Home Affairs Council in Santiago de Compostela, the removal centre at Yarlswood in Bedfordshire was burnt down – or rather, half of it was – by those awaiting deportation from the country.

This story is unbelievable. Those in charge – the private operators Group 4, who had been given the contract back in 2000 to run the centre – just hung around as things turned nasty and were incapable of taking decisive action, though I had told them twice that if there was ever any hint of trouble they were to clamp down immediately. Instead they dithered, while some of the staff were so terrified that they barricaded themselves inside rooms: self-made hostages.

When the police were eventually called very few turned up, and those who did arrived too late to be of much use. When the fires started, the fire brigade decided they wouldn't go into the main building unless there was adequate protection for them, so the building burnt down.

Then the insurers put it to the Lloyd's underwriters, who decided that they were going to sue the Bedfordshire police for £40 million. So Group 4 don't have to meet the insurance claim, on the grounds that it constituted a riot under the 1886 Act. Sprinklers hadn't been installed because the previous ministerial team had decided that they would cut the building costs, having taken advice on a national basis in relation to the fire service and the balance of risk.

Immediate action wasn't taken at the other centres, so more of the immigrants escaped from Harmondsworth. It is a testament to incompetence and dithering, and I'm just totally bewildered by it.

Fortunately for me Parliament wasn't sitting the following week, otherwise I'd have had to fly back from Spain rather than going down to the south to stay with my cousin Pauline and her husband Minolo. Although it was not sunny and in fact was cloudy and cold, it was still a very nice break and did me the world of good.

I must now get a grip of the police reform agenda. I think what we need to do is implement parts of it, on a sort of phased basis, a bit like we did with the teachers. The teachers would have voted against it if they'd had a ballot, but we were able to go over the heads of the unions and do it direct.

Steve Byers is in the mire because he's got rid of Jo Moore and Martin Sixsmith [Director of Communications at the DETR], and Sixsmith is saying that he never agreed to go. In the *Sunday Times* [24 February] in the review section, a piece by Sixsmith is a clear example of the kind of betrayal we're now getting from the civil service, where they take detailed notes and then use them against us in what I consider to be quite an immoral way. Everyone eulogises about our free, independent, apolitical civil service. They are apolitical all right – an island within an island, a government within a government. They have clearly declared war on special advisers and on some ministers, and they are determined to pull Steve Byers down.

It is absolutely appalling but it's impossible to hit back when you are in government – so I'm going to have to tell the truth once I'm out. And it won't be politics, it won't be the difficulties, it won't be the great challenges and the awkward questions that will have me out, I think.

Lord, what foresight! If only I had reflected on my own words later, who knows what might have happened? Ironically, I cannot hold the civil service responsible for my demise – at least not on the first occasion. The people around me could not have been more supportive. But on neither occasion was the outcome anything to do with the big challenges of government, the handling of policy, communication or delivery.

I had a bizarre message left for me by Sally Morgan when I was in Spain. I rang her back and she said that Tony just wanted to tell me that he was worried that I was too exposed, and that I was taking on too many people at once. I said, 'Yes, I know all about the white charger riding out without anybody behind, but tell him not to worry.' When I came back, he'd left a message asking if I would talk to him – which I did. It turned out to be a non-conversation. I said: 'I know you're going to say that I'm taking too many people on, but I can't do what you want me to do and set about seeing through the reform agenda, and then in the next breath back off. We can't have it both ways. Either we get on with it at this stage of the parliament, we take on the difficulties and we see them through, or we dither about, backing off and going off into a nervous fret every time something happens.' Anyway, he didn't pursue the matter, and we finished the conversation in a very friendly fashion.

The Liberals have been whining about the conditions at Yarlswood being too harsh – £100 million worth of specially built accommodation with all the facilities anyone could want, and they say it's too harsh, just because we locked the people in so that they wouldn't run away. God help us. It's pretty clear that some of the people who were put in both Yarlswood and Harmondsworth should have been kept in jail anyway, because they were criminals and some had committed violent offences. And the prison population has gone up by 3,000 in six weeks, which is just incredible.

I am desperately trying to stay one step ahead of everything. Am I getting any suggestions out of the Department? Am I, hell!

A phone call on Sunday stopped me in my tracks. 'Hello, Mr Blunkett,' said a deep voice, 'this is the Police Federation. We're just ringing to say we know where you live.' Then a more familiar voice: 'Hello, Dad, it's me, Hugh, sorry . . .' At least it made me laugh.

The Statement to the House about Yarlswood went much better than I thought it would – and better than we deserve, given the way in which the incident had been handled by the Immigration and Nationality Directorate. Over the lunchtime before I went across to the Commons we delved further into what had happened, and the more I discovered the more horrified I became. It had taken them days and they still hadn't got the search dogs in or the equipment to hold the roof up so they could do a proper search for human remains. As I said, there were clearly people in the centre who shouldn't have been there and should have been kept in prison. We transferred twenty-five back into prison, one of whom was under surveillance by the Security Services and would have been picked up under the Anti-Terrorism, Crime and Security Act had he not been in the process of being removed from the country under immigration powers. I've agreed to go to Yarlswood on 18 March so I shall talk to local people who had been warning Group 4 of the difficulties, and I will find out what's going on.

I then had another series of meetings and a conversation with Tony about the Police Reform Bill. Again it was a perfectly reasonable conversation, but still with an undertone of 'Are you taking too much on?' and 'Shouldn't you compromise?' and in particular 'Couldn't you abandon the cuts in overtime?' I said: 'Tony, I do know that overtime is the big issue for the police and I have got plans to try and do something about this, but I've got to achieve the goal of reducing overtime as a method of managing the service, and I've got to find reductions in other parts of the package to compensate if we can't cut it.' These are the real decisions that have to be taken and lived with.

The Tories have upped the ante on the Bill as well as trying to exploit our difference with the police, and they gave Jeff Rooker a really hard time in the Lords. Oliver Letwin and Iain Duncan Smith have been writing silly things, trying to pretend that we're taking over operational responsibility. I think we need a much more sophisticated approach to how we rebut this but it's very difficult, because anybody who's got anything about them, including the special advisers, are constantly under pressure and, of course, special advisers are now *personae non grata* in the wake of the Byers/Jo Moore/Sixsmith affair. Ludicrous.

We talked about special advisers at Cabinet. Steve said his bit and John Reid said one or two sensible things about the dangers, but the discussion wasn't going anywhere so I just launched in. I know Richard Wilson will not forgive me for this but it's too bad – because apparently he went grey and looked daggers at me. I said 'Well, I think if we're going to have legislation that protects the civil service from the government, could we build into it protection for the government from the civil service?' I continued: 'We have a situation in my Department where virtually anything of any importance is leaked. The Immigration and Nationality Directorate is a complete shambles. The only reason we got a Police Reform White Paper and the reform of immigration, nationality and asylum was because the two respective advisers worked extremely closely with me on them.' I said that there were 153 Grade 7s in IND and God knows how many above that grade, and not one of them could have managed to do this work – hence the reason why previously we did not have a policy that added up to anything. I carried on in this vein: 'I was very lucky when I was at the DfEE, and I am now, that I get on with the Permanent Secretary, but what if I didn't? The civil service are very lucky that we can't sack them, that no one can sack them' – with the implication that they damn well would be sacked if I had my way, and they would be. At the end of all this diatribe Tony said: 'Well, I think Richard Wilson's got the message. You really love the civil service, David. You've got a lot of time for them and you believe they're doing a first-class job' – and everybody just doubled up.

Not one of my finest hours. The pressure was obviously building and this was a safety valve, but that is not the way to behave in Cabinet. Nor is it sensible to take the civil service head on, not least because the message gets back, and it affects the morale and motivation of very good civil servants, while those who are incompetent don't give a damn anyway and just resented me even more. One of the lessons I learned was firstly to stay calm, and secondly to think through the best way of achieving change, rather than simply making myself feel better by letting off steam. But by the time I had fully learned this lesson, I was back for only six months – when I was more patient, more supportive and more aware of the dangers than ever before. Most of life is about learning lessons when it is too late to implement them.

Strangely (but not wholly unexpectedly) Professor Peter Hennessy, the historian and commentator on civil-service matters, had a full write-up of the

Cabinet exchange – with me, it has to be said, not portrayed in a favourable light.

I had already blotted my copybook at that Cabinet meeting by raising the issue of Iraq and the need to talk through any future scenarios, though Jack Straw wasn't there so it was difficult to have a discussion. It was a very funny Cabinet. Robin Cook joined in on Iraq and said how important it was that we had the discussion in order to look at where we were going. He approached me afterwards and thanked me for raising it.

But just to reflect how focused I was at the time on the need for civil-service reform, it is worth recording a further passage from my notes from the time which gives a measure of why I think (and thought then) that government was struggling to provide both clarity of purpose and competence in delivery.

Every time I want to do something, the Department argues with it. Everything I've done of any worth on immigration and nationality has been in spite of the Department rather than with their support. No wonder the Tories didn't sort it out, because they didn't use their special advisers effectively at all.

And that is why government has worked so badly. The civil service have a particular line that they've developed well over the years. First, if they don't want you to do something, they produce the lengthiest, most obscurantist document, with no clear recommendations but in the text itself all the so-called pluses and minuses, except with the minuses (which avoid their having to do what it is they do not wish to do) highlighted. Alternative ways forward are either not laid out in detail or simply ignored, because the civil servants don't go outside the civil service to find out if there are alternative ways of doing things. Not least, they don't look at what's taking place in the rest of the world: so, for example, I get told that it's not possible to return people to Afghanistan, but then find that the Dutch and the Germans have already been doing it in the early part of 2002.

The second element is to put up costings that make it impossible even to contemplate arguing with the Treasury, so everything is inflated beyond belief and you have to go through the figures again and again to pare them down. We had this with the accommodation centres, where I could have built a pretty reasonable four-bedroom house for every two asylum seekers who were going to be housed there, before we got some sense into the system.

On the nationality side we've had costings for language tuition put up, which they claim they had got from the Learning and Skills Council, which would have paid for a sixth-former for a full course for a full year.

The other element is to prevaricate and not produce a report at all until you force them to.

I am really worried about the Criminal Records Bureau. It is a big organisation funded with very large sums of money, but it is not touching areas such as European citizens coming in, nor is it touching those organisations which don't register and therefore don't use the service. It is a mess all round.

Little did I know what havoc this was going to cause later in the year. My visit to the CRB had alerted me to the fact that all was not well, but there are only so many hours in the day and, having written down my concerns, I had asked the civil service to check whether the plan that had been devised prior to the 2001 general election was likely to work, and whether or not we should phase in more cautiously the administration of the Bureau. Not for the first or last time, I wish I had followed my instincts more rigorously in instructing the civil service rather than seeking advice from them. We were in the end able to sort out the Criminal Records Bureau but, as with so much of the introduction of new technology and modernisation, it was to be at the price of damaging the credibility of government (and particularly the Home Office) in carrying through such very high-profile and critical but complex technological developments.

March 2002

The frenzy about special advisers is getting to absurd proportions. On Monday [4 March], following an interview with the *Daily Telegraph* on Saturday, Sir Nigel Wickes said that as Chairman of the Committee on Standards in Public Life he is going to investigate the relationship between advisers, ministers and the civil service. Sir Nigel had been a civil servant in the Callaghan government: in the words of the Monty Python sketch, 'Say no more.' He said that he thought that it was the job of ministers who had been party political when in opposition to represent the wider general interest, and therefore it was the job of advisers (or at least he inferred that it was the job of advisers) to follow suit – as though ministers leave their politics behind when they become ministers.

Of course ministers should govern for the general good and we govern for all the people, but we don't govern in a vacuum, without values or philosophy or the intention of delivering what we came in for. It is just extraordinary. I don't govern for the Duke of Westminster; I govern for the people of Sheffield Brightside. So we are on a hiding to nothing here if we are all supposed to be neutral, as well as the civil service being neutral.

A silly situation with regard to Stop and Search has really got to me. The editor of the *Voice* magazine, read widely in the Caribbean community, has stated that Stop and Search is justified and would have to be stepped up. I did an interview for the paper on Thursday and indicated that I was backing him and that the way we were going to implement the Stephen Lawrence report (the MacPherson Report) recommendation 61 on Stop and Search would be with a light touch, which would increase confidence in the police force using it, and would increase co-operation and support from the community. We all agreed that that was the case. I had given him an outline of Code A (the update of what we were going to do) and had then asked that those most affected should be contacted – specifically John Gieve as Permanent Secretary so that he knew what we were doing, and Sir Ian Blair, the Deputy Commissioner of the Metropolitan Police, who had been closely involved with the discussions internally with the police service about a new, sensitive and less bureaucratic way of dealing with stop, as well as search, powers.

Instead a junior press officer rang the Met press office for a quote! Given the enormous sensitivity of these issues and the way in which it could be misinterpreted, this was the last thing we needed. Within fifteen minutes the *Daily Telegraph* crime correspondent rang, and then a host of others started to ring. The *Telegraph* then ran it on the front page on Saturday morning, with Glyn Smythe from the Police Federation attacking me. It changed the whole context of what was supposed to be a presentation of all this on the Monday morning to coincide with the publication of the *Voice*.

I went ballistic. I can't remember when I had ever shouted down the telephone in this way, but I was incandescent, because I had stressed again and again how crucial this was, not merely in its own right but because of the atmosphere we are in. The *Sun* editorial on the same day [9 March] ended up by saying that if the Tories get their act together on crime, they will win the next general election. What a warning. This followed days and days of the *Sun* providing pages of support for Sir John Stevens's attack on the criminal justice system.

I mention all this because, instead of Stop and Search being seen as a positive inclusion measure that would gain the backing of ethnic-minority communities and therefore their engagement with fighting crime (not least terrorism), it was turned into a bad-news story which played into the idea that bureaucracy was getting in the way of everything. Little slips can make such a difference in the 24-hour seven-day-week news era, where everything is picked up and analysed and every sentence weighed, and where there is instant recounting of what has been said and written. I have also related this story to show that just once or twice I really did lose my rag. If I have a criticism of myself, it is that so often I felt too strongly, too emotionally, too closely engaged with everything that was going on.

Although in my book Politics and Progress *the previous autumn I had been able to step back and take a wider look at what we were doing and the values that underpinned it (and apart from Gordon, this was unique in government in modern times), it is still the case that I was too close to detail and too often intolerant of incompetence and failure. My only justification is that when people did a good job, they knew that they would get my full backing and appreciation and that I would build teams of people who would genuinely deliver and who would also care. The downside is that those who for one reason or another felt resentment and became my opponents were to prove very dangerous indeed.*

I launched the Sentencing Review in July and called upon the Opposition to provide some long-term continuity. Sir John Stevens, who is a great self-publicist, was able to use the kind of language that I couldn't possibly use as Home Secretary, and got a huge amount of coverage for his attack on the criminal justice system and his sideswipe at the government for not acting fast enough. The whole atmosphere is rotten – and rotten in Rotterdam as well because on Thursday, the fascists got 34 per cent of the vote in the city-council elections, becoming the largest party, using straight crime and anti-immigration campaigning. They are expected to do very well in the Netherlands' general election. The whole picture across Europe is desperate.

I was trying to get across publicly that the agenda of stability and security that we were following was precisely to avoid the tide running across Europe at the time. It is strange how the tide comes in and then recedes, which was to lead to the defeat of the socialists in France as well as the liberals in the Netherlands. It was, however, extremely hard work. There seemed to be a view that if only we ignored the fears and worries of those who were inclined to vote for the far right, they would somehow go away. This was to misunderstand, as the leaders of the European Union did in the run-up to the ballot on the so-called constitution, the deep-seated feeling and resentment that existed (and still does) about ever more rapid economic and social change. It raised the issue which had become a theme of mine – namely reshaping government to help people through that change and the challenges of modernity and globalisation.

The initiatives I was to take on citizenship, nationality, identity and sense of belonging were all based on my stated view, both in writing and in speeches, that we had to take seriously the resentment of so many people (sometimes affected by false nostalgia) that the world was not what it used to be, and that the breakdown of respect and decency was something to do with the failure of national government to hear their concerns and respond to them.

The polling evidence that we had at our Home Office Awayday – and repeated by Tony at the Cabinet Awayday at Chequers – is that all the polling for the local-government elections shows that crime is the main issue, followed by asylum. In national polling, health is the issue, followed by crime, asylum and education.

At Cabinet [on 7 March] we had a very good discussion about Iraq, which lasted for the best part of an hour, during which we all said our bit. I talked about social cohesion at home and the obvious issues that had arisen over 11 September, where the real message was: Why aren't you doing something about the Middle East and the Palestine-Israeli conflict? Why are you just backing the Americans? I also drew on the steel-industry problems and how this had changed the climate of our automatically backing the Americans.

At this time the USA was tightening restrictions on steel imports and making it very difficult for even the most competitive and excellent companies to be able to sell their products into US markets – as I was only too well aware from my own city of Sheffield. It struck me that a bit of reciprocity wouldn't come amiss.

Apart from Jack Straw and Geoff Hoon who had clearly got the message to be gung ho, everyone else was drawing the conclusion that we needed to go into depth with this. In the end Tony said: 'Look, the management hasn't lost its marbles. We do know these things. We are not going to rush in.' But we all fear that they will.

Then, as ever, somebody talked too much and it appeared in Friday's papers as a big Cabinet split, with people threatening to resign. It also said that Clare Short was saying this, that and the other, when in fact she wasn't even there.

I had dinner with Rupert Murdoch at the Hampstead home of Les Hinton [CEO of News International UK], with Paul and Judith Potts. Murdoch was perfectly decent to deal with – very reasonable, although I accept that he may not be so in business matters. I didn't put on a show for him and it was a better evening for it.

I had dinner with Gordon and Sarah on Thursday night, and we didn't talk about the Budget or the Spending Review. I had never been in the flat at No. 10 before: up in the lift, then six steps up. The flat is quite small, so no wonder Tony and Cherie decided to live in No. 11.

Then the Awayday at Chequers: a lot of waffle, but at least we talked.

I have got the Spending Review proposals ready – three weeks later than everybody else but I desperately needed to get them right. The next job is to write the White Paper on criminal justice and law reform. I saw Robin [who as Leader of the House of Commons was responsible for timetabling government business] and told him that there was no way that we are going to have fox-hunting rather than law reform.

I've been resisting a massive effort by the management of the prison service to get me to agree to Executive Release – that is, releasing all prisoners within a certain period of their due time to be let out.

We were reaching the point where we no longer had enough cells to cope with the exponential rise in prison sentences that were coming out of the court system.

I just dug my heels in and told them to go back, find out how many places there were in Scotland and Northern Ireland, work out what other steps could be taken, and look at emergency construction measures so that we could find places across the country. We got agreement with Harry Woolf and the other senior judges that they would help out strongly in relation to non-violent, non-sexual offences, and what magistrates and district judges were doing in providing tough community sentences while maintaining consistency in sentencing. I backed that immediately.

We've had three meetings during the course of the week on the rising prison population, but I've just got to hold my nerve and not allow myself to be pushed about by officials who always manage to get ministers to end up being the fall guys – because managing the prison service in difficult circumstances falls to the managers, but Executive Release, which releases them from having to manage it in that way and lets the safety valve go, that's down to ministers.

I think the week beginning Monday 11 March should go down in my diary as one of the worst weeks that I have had since I came into government – and that's saying something. It wasn't an all-out assault in the press – it was just a sour erosion of the general support and backing that I have been receiving. I've had a false sense of security, a false sense of invulnerability which has been effectively kicked away.

As things improved, so my false sense of security returned.

I enjoyed staying with Jonathan Dimbleby and Bel Mooney. It was nice to go to the Bath Literature Festival and escape for an hour or two. I always like their farm and the peace and quiet.

But Monday in Bristol was a total fiasco. The visit – to view a community project and see the work of the local police – hadn't been properly planned, and there was no organisation at all. There were local residents chanting when I arrived, and I was told they were anarchists. Why can't people understand the difference between aggrieved local residents and anarchists? It turned out they were local residents: if I had known that, I would have gone across and spoken to them. The press office hadn't arranged to wipe out the horrible graffiti and the alteration of posters to abuse me, as with the chants. This was all a publicity stunt. They even managed to get me in the photographs in the national papers. They fitted me up with the main photograph, sitting with a local resident who turned out to be the Liberal Democrat candidate for the area. He was apparently standing against my own colleague (who hadn't been invited but had turned up). Even the Lord Mayor, who was a local councillor, had not been invited. It was breathtaking. I pulled in Jean Corston MP and the local inspector who was going round with me, to join me in the photo-graph, otherwise there would just have been me and the Liberal Democrat candidate! I don't know whether somebody was trying to be funny or what but it was a total fiasco from beginning to end.

From that moment on, I determined that we would have a proper skilled official working on planning visits and organising at local level what was to take place and on what basis – not just leaving it to a press officer who could only manage to get up there the night before and whose job was all about communication, not organisation.

Tony called me that evening and I thought he was going to tell me off, because I'd been on the *Today* programme from Jonathan Dimbleby's place, and when I'd been asked about Iraq I'd given a fairly robust answer about the importance of getting this right for social cohesion. I had also talked about the Middle East.

But Tony wasn't concerned about that. He wanted to talk about launching a major drive on street robbery and criminal justice. As it happened we have been preparing for July a major initiative on street robbery in ten police-force areas. I've managed to get South Yorkshire in this time because in the past they've always missed South Yorkshire out as a metropolitan county. It is astonishing what the Home Office can do: they think there are only five metropolitan areas in Britain. But there are ten in this initiative and I'm pulling it forward to April, together with the ones that we were going to run in April anyway – Hackney and South Manchester.

On Wednesday we had the demonstration at Parliament against our reform measures by the Police Federation, which could have been worse. They were very abusive to backbenchers, which has frightened many of them: Alan Milburn told me that he had got quite tough with some members in the tea room who were dithering about the need to give way.

We are still desperately trying to sort out the Nationality and Asylum Bill which cannot be left to the officials to do, and I've now signed off the Spending Review proposals, a month late but in a much better condition than before. The Treasury have been briefing against me: I know we are late but nothing can be done about that.

When I launch something like this street-robbery initiative, it wipes out great chunks of the week, as did the preparations for conciliation on the police negotiations, because I had three meetings on that in two days and four meetings on street robbery. People are really struggling now in the press office and with all the speeches. I don't know, I seem to be making a terrible mess of things all round, while trying to keep the public profile and maintaining a grip of myself and everything else that's going on.

I did the David Frost programme on BBC1 on Sunday morning. It was a long and decent interview from my point of view, but he seemed not interested at all. He was off to Andrew Lloyd Webber's castle in Ireland for the Easter holiday, and I think that mentally he was already there. I then did the photos for the local-government elections [coming up in May] in London, and the local councillors were telling me the truth about what was going to happen. Charles Clarke won't accept it but sadly it will happen: we are going to lose quite heavily.

I then had a briefing in my office in the Commons for the lobby and home-affairs journalists. Fancy my being in the Commons on a Sunday morning! Then throughout the week in the *Financial Times*, the *Sun* and even the *Guardian* there were wonderful bits that picked up the myth being peddled that somehow I'd set all this up. There were front-page stories day after day in the *Mail*, the *Mirror* and the *Sun* about 4,000 extra prisoners, street robbery and eleven-year-olds putting bricks through windows – pages and pages of it. And the spin was that this was all a conspiracy by me to bring pressure to bear for the Budget and Spending Review.

When I was interviewed both coming out of Downing Street with Sir John Stevens on Wednesday morning and on the *Today* programme on Thursday, I went out of my way to say (a) that this wasn't a gladiatorial contest and that we were all in this together, and (b) that I wouldn't be the loser if the resources weren't made available to fund what we were talking about – the losers would be the British people. Furthermore, in my lengthy interview on the *Today* programme I said that having a strong and stable economy that provided the resources to invest in public services was the business of all of us, and the priorities we adopted as a government were the business of all of us.

Gordon has asked me to come in for the first PSX (public services and expenditure) meeting following the submission of the Budget proposals in detail this Wednesday, and he's asked to see me privately in the afternoon: very interesting . . .

I went to Yarlswood on Monday. The building is full of wood – all the corridors and the stairs. Barbara Roche, who was Immigration Minister at the time the centre was constructed, had clearly been right: sprinklers were needed and should have been provided. They said that they still thought it was likely that they might find human remains but as they have not done so all week, I suppose the longer it goes on, the better chance there is that they will find none.

And then there was a row about armed-forces jobs (again in the run-up to the Spending Review), with Jack Dromey [Deputy General Secretary of the Transport and General Workers' Union] way over the top in his criticism. I've never heard anybody bad-mouth the government in these circumstances as much as Dromey did. There is also Stephen Byers and compensation for the former Railtrack shareholders – it's an extra pound that is being allocated again. Treasury-driven because the Treasury wanted a settlement that would satisfy the City but it is Stephen Byers who has to take the rap. There are 11,000 job losses to be announced and a lot more still to come.

Monday night [18 March] saw the vote on fox-hunting. I voted for the middle way and then for abolition, as I did last time. When I was going through the lobby for the middle-way option, Peter Mandelson said, 'Don't let Tony down on Iraq.' I said: 'I beg your pardon. I'm not letting anybody down. I'm simply saying what I believe to be sensible.'

Peter misunderstood my position. As will be seen later, we came to a point where I believed we had absolutely no choice but to take on Saddam Hussein, who had called the world's bluff (and my view was nothing to do with weapons of mass destruction). But at this stage of the discussions, that was not the agenda. We were way off such an eventuality, and it seemed to me that clear and open discussion was not something to fear but rather a prerequisite to winning people over to an agreed stance.

There was the PSX meeting on Wednesday and a private meeting with Gordon, plus an additional Cabinet Round Table on the street-robbery issue. There's a big effort now to sort out the anti-terrorism money that has still not been sorted – and it's got to be if the police aren't to pull the plug.

April 2002

Back from a short holiday in St Lucia. Why is it that every time I go away something happens? Either there's a reshuffle, or there's pressure at the very end of the week before I go, which means I take ages to wind down, or there's something else – in this case the death of the Queen Mother just two days after I arrived in St Lucia. Parliament was recalled but I could not get back and the Palace resented it. Peter Oborne in the *Spectator* wrote that this was an insult. The Palace officials then sat me way out of the way for the service in Westminster Abbey, rather than with Gordon and Jack. They said patronisingly that it was because they thought it would be a better place for me and Lucy and more easily accessible, but other opinion has it that it may well have been because I didn't make it back for the recall of Parliament. How the hell could I, what with a twelve-hour flight, a five-hour time change, abandoning my sons and chucking £8,000 down the drain? There was an upsurge of feeling for the Queen Mother, even though she was 101, and 150,000 people passed her coffin. It was a remarkable expression of Britain past – a bygone Britain, a Britain from long ago.

Having had a couple of meetings with Gordon before going away, I had another as soon as I got back. The first one didn't touch on the Budget – it was more about where we were going and the voluntary sector – and the second, about the Budget, was very short. All the vibes from Gordon are that he doesn't want to be seen to bow the knee to Tony and myself on street robbery. He will have to give something on remand facilities, prisons and counter-terrorism, and I can use both as part of the overall policy.

The interim report on Yarlswood came through while I was away, and it is devastating, with just about everybody having mishandled the situation on 14 February. It's going to be awful when the full report comes out, pulling together the other reports. What a mess. And talking of asylum, we published the Nationality, Immigration and Asylum Bill on Friday 12 April. The BBC chose to run garbage about insurance cover for Yarlswood rather than the Bill, but there was reasonable coverage on the Saturday. The same day there was John Lloyd's so-called biographical article about me in the *Financial Times*, which started off with complete trivia about whether my trousers were too long!

Derry Irvine has done a series of interviews in which he tries to claim credit for the dropping of the mode-of-trial proposals, trying his best to discredit me over what happened immediately after the general election and saying that it was he and not the judges who saved the court system from being transferred to the Home Office. I don't know what he thinks he's playing at.

This was all about whether the court system was going to come under the Home Secretary, who already had responsibility for the wider criminal-justice reforms and chaired the National Criminal Justice Board, and who had pressed for a change in the previous efforts to get the mode-of-trial (jury trial) proposals substantially revised. Looking back, I don't know what possessed me to want to take over the court system. Before 11 September 2001 I believed that coherence in gaining radical reform and being able to persuade (or arm-twist) the judiciary into substantial improvement and modernisation went hand in hand with the other responsibilities. Of course it did, but the workload was such that in all honesty it would have been unmanageable. It is strange to look back now on things that seemed so important at the time, but it has to be remembered that there was a massive push by some colleagues to create a 'Department of Justice', which in effect would have been a human-rights department, and which, whether future administrations create it or not, I am convinced would create the kind of gridlock that I have seen in other systems across Europe, where the Interior Minister attempts to provide justice for the community and the Justice Ministry provides 'justice' for the perpetrator.

Various annoyances. An article in the *Financial Times* bears all the hall-marks of the Treasury trying to stuff me with regard to the Budget. Mo Mowlam out on manoeuvres, slagging everybody off in a Channel 4 programme linked to her autobiography. Accusations of sleaze in relation to contracts going to businesses or businessmen who have given something to the Labour Party. I think we're going to have to introduce state funding for political parties now because it's getting beyond a joke. If anybody who has given anything is going to be fingered for getting any kind of contract, then I think everybody's had it.

Four years later almost to the week, we had the major row about loans to political parties in the run-up to the 2005 general election. (It turned out that the Conservatives had received more loans – and much bigger loans – than Labour.) The storm in 2006 was of a different order entirely, but it is interesting to look back on my diary now and to recognise the signals. Part of what I tried to do in the departments for which I had responsibility was to be prescient about what was coming up. I have to admit that I did not return to these issues in Cabinet or with colleagues. I wish I had.

Dinner with Peter Mandelson: I think he wants the job of ambassador to the USA – a job which a good friend of mine while we were away on holiday together, suggested mischieviously that I might take! Peter had one or two further trenchant remarks to make about those who had affected his survival in Cabinet, and quizzed me about my attitude to Iraq and issues of that sort. He suggested to me that prime ministers were able to travel in greater comfort than the rest of us when travelling around the world and asked me if I was really put off, then remarked that people say that I get tired. I said: 'That's the second time I've had that from someone recently but yes, I do get tired. I get tired because I work damned hard.' This was exactly what Fiona Millar had said to somebody.

In politics, it is important to hear not only what people are saying but what people are not saying. It is called 'reading between the words' rather than between the lines, and trying to interpret what is behind them. I have never found this easy, because although I am no saint I do tend to call a spade a spade, and therefore if I have something to say to someone, I say it. This is a trait that has not always endeared me to people, as is evident. But I have had to learn, from just sitting in the tea room or talking to colleagues in a corridor, to go back and think about what was said and try and work out the code. In other words, work out what the message was.

Some colleagues send you a message via the papers (usually the Sundays), organised by their press office, or more likely by their special advisers. This particular message seemed to be asking: 'If you were to take on a different role, would you be up to it? Do you really dislike travelling so much? Can you cope with the workload?' Certainly I could, as even Jack, with the pressure which undoubtedly was greater in peacetime than ever before because of Iraq, indicated to me that the sheer volume of issues, paperwork and the like was much less in the Foreign Office than in the Home Office. Peter would know this. So I had to work out what question he was raising with me. It is funny to think of those times (and it also occurred when I was heading Education and Employment) when promotion rather than 'resignation' was on the agenda.

But I never thought it conceivable that I could be Prime Minister. I do not believe, and I have said so a couple of times in interviews, that the United Kingdom is yet ready for a Prime Minister who cannot see. Nor was I ready to take that further step, even with the massive resources available to a Prime Minister (not to mention the patronage), because the sheer volume of work which a twenty-first-century premier has to face would be daunting for anyone, even without the challenge of working through an avalanche of paper.

In addition, I had Tessa Jowell on Monday morning telling me that I'd upset people enormously by being too pushy on the issue of street robbery and trying to get money out of people, and how upset the MoD and Lewis Moonie [Minister of State at Defence] were. She said that I should be nicer to people. I know I should, but I just don't have time to mess about with the niceties, in the face of the prima-donna-like behaviour of some of my colleagues. But I will think about it because I do need to be more diplomatic.

I should have heeded Tessa more strongly and, pressure or no pressure, have forced myself to be less arrogant. Tessa's words reverberated not only at the time of my own case years later, but in early 2006 when she was under pressure herself, and it was soon clear that she had practised what she had preached and it had paid off.

The first round of the French presidential election has been absolutely catastrophic, with the fascists doing so incredibly well. This relates to the gut feeling I've been getting in my own constituency office, from people ringing up to see if there is a BNP candidate, and from the messages around the country. It just underlines what I've been trying to say and the importance of both asylum and crime.

The other major issue has been the Budget, with Gordon putting up National Insurance for everyone, including those above the current threshold, by 1 per cent. When this takes effect in 2003 it may prove to be a real killer in the Welsh and Scottish elections and with regard to employment, so we'll need to watch that. But the Budget was a great triumph for Gordon. The speech was well put together, he delivered it well, and he rallied the backbenchers. At the moment Gordon is riding high.

Another triumph for Gordon is the news that Andrew Turnbull, his Permanent secretary, has been confirmed as the new Secretary to the Cabinet.

The Budget itself was fine for me. I got £180 million of new money and £100 million drawdown from the criminal justice reserve, and £60 million I will then have to find from inside the Budget for counter-terrorism, for street crime and for the creation of remand and prison places (2,300 of them).

No other department got new money for this year. The health service had already announced a five-year budget settlement to 2008, Education has reassigned its money to pay for the direct payments to schools, and nobody else got a bean. So I was quite pleased that, with Tony's considerable help, I got £180 million, £110 million of which comes from the reserve, which the Treasury officials had opposed vehemently.

A footnote on the Budget. It did occur to me in contributing at the Special Cabinet on the Wednesday morning to say that I was in favour of hypothecation and always had been, so was very supportive of this measure. But then I reflected that I had been bad-mouthed by Gordon's people for querying the further reduction of 1p in income tax, which of course Gordon had brought in a year ago, when everyone knew that we were going to have to raise more money. It's a funny old world, especially as I had told Gordon and Tony that I thought the NHS was £2 billion short of what they had previously decided to put into it on the back of the Health Plan. I think we are probably just about back on stream with that £2 billion now – £40 billion over five years, rather than £21 billion over three years.

Reading this again does make me think, 'What a big-head you were, Blunkett.' No wonder I got up people's noses.

The Israelis have started to withdraw from the encampments and from Nablus. There's been the most terrible slaughter and now there's a UN investigation into it.

On Monday night I gave a speech to the Community Security Trust, which involved addressing about 1,200 of the wealthiest and I suppose the most influential Jews in Britain. I had to tread a tightrope, because I didn't want to say that we weren't absolutely devastated by what the Israeli government was doing, but I did want to indicate that I understood the insecurity, there and for Jewish people in Britain. It became evident when I was talking to people during the evening before I spoke just how desperately uneasy they feel, so I made reference to what was happening in France in Marseilles and Paris, and gave them reassurance that we were behind them and we would secure their protection. I got a standing ovation and I was absolutely staggered by it.

A stocktake meeting with the Prime Minister first thing Tuesday morning [16 April]: I've adopted a new strategy, which is to be more extreme than Tony so that he has to then pull me back. I said: 'We've got a major problem on nationality and asylum and I'm going to have to get really tough with the French after their election.' He asked how tough, and I said: 'We may well have to use troops.' This was a shock tactic, so Tony then becomes more cautious, just as he has been in advising me in relation to police reform. Anyway I think it's working because it means that if I can get very tough policies, then I can see them through because he has to back me and the diplomacies around it have to work, and if he doesn't want them then he will have to be the one who vetoes them.

The week beginning Monday 22 April was one that I will not forget for a very long time. I know I always say that, but this one was particularly special. By the time I reached Friday night, Home Office Questions on Monday afternoon seemed like a month away. It's really hard to reflect on the enormity of what happened.

I had worked very hard on what was coming up this week – the Police Reform Bill in the Lords and the likelihood of defeat on the Third Reading on Thursday. The Lords amended four elements of the proposals on community support officers, on civilianisation [using civilians for administrative duties] and powers, all of which we will reverse. But that was the insignificant bit of the week. The real week was only just beginning.

I had interviews about Le Pen's success over Jospin in coming second, including a very lengthy pre-record for *The World at One*, which I had to fit in between all the normal diary items, such as a speech to the British Chamber of Commerce conference, another early-morning stocktake meeting with the Prime Minister, dinner in the evening with the Chief Rabbi and his wife and a meeting with Conrad Black [proprietor of the

Daily Telegraph group of newspapers] and his wife Barbara Amiel [*Telegraph* journalist]. It was a very, very strange evening. Initially Conrad Black played no part, eventually bringing himself into the conversation after the rest of us had been talking for a long time. His wife, who reminded me of Hillary Clinton, was much more forthcoming but I am afraid not a woman of much warmth. It was interesting to have met them for the first time, and they are very taken with Gordon.

Subsequently Conrad Black was embroiled in considerable financial controversy, and relinquished his ownership of the Telegraph Group.

And then, on Wednesday morning, the saga of the interview on the *Today* programme about the Nationality, Immigration and Asylum Bill, as well as Le Pen and other issues. Here we had the great fuss over my use of the word 'swamping' in relation to schools and GPs' surgeries that are either very close to major dispersal centres for asylum seekers under the Dispersal Policy, or would be very close to accommodation centres – and therefore would indeed be swamped, the dictionary definition being 'overwhelmed' or 'burdened with work or correspondence'.

That afternoon Alastair Campbell phoned me in my House of Commons office to say that the 'swamping' reference was playing badly – which we had already grasped. Huw has recalled that I hurled the phone across the room in rage, with Rebecca and him taking rapid evasive action!

What I had not realised until some days later was that the day before my interview with John Humphrys on Today, *the* Guardian *had had a reflection in a piece that had not been drawn to my attention (and no reason why it should have been) that referred specifically to Margaret Thatcher having used the word 'swamped' in regard to immigration generally and in a completely different context from the response that I was giving. I do use words carefully and therefore it was not a slip, but the deliberate use of the word 'swamped'. It was not, however, in any way designed to create a furore but to get across the enormity of what I was being presented with, including an instance in my own constituency where one GP practice had a third of its total registered patients speaking not English as a second language but no English at all.*

I have thought about this interview since, and the issue came up when I had the opportunity of interviewing John Humphrys in December 2005 when I edited the Today *programme. As I said to him then, I came to the conclusion that had I seen the* Guardian *piece and therefore understood the link that would be made to Margaret Thatcher's comment, I would have used the word 'overwhelmed' instead. I reflect on this at some length to indicate how easy it is to get yourself into controversy and how difficult it is to deal with not just broadcast but new forms of news media that politicians from even a few years ago did not have to engage with. Would the great political figures of the past be able to cope with this today with the same dignity with which they were able to handle the occasional newspaper interview and a radio interview perhaps once a month?*

On Sunday I rang Alan Rusbridger, editor of the *Guardian*, but I got nowhere with him at all. He tried to say that there had been an editorial discussion and that in the end they'd decided that they would back the suggestion that I was attempting to speak to more than one audience at once. Well, in the sense that I'm trying to square the circle on nationality and asylum I suppose I am. I'm doing what I've done all the way back from the early 1980s. John Spencer, whom I had dinner with on Friday night, was reminding me that when he was the municipal correspondent on the local newspaper in Sheffield he dealt with the issue of my stopping people ruling out the use of the word 'black'. He reminded me how I'd intervened immediately to stop the silliness and had prevented a real fiasco. As far as I could, I have always tried to speak the language of people who want to hear that something sensible is being said and done. I know this because I've been out canvassing four times in the last six weeks, knocking on doors as well as doing the shopping-centre visits. I think I've done three in Sheffield alone as well as elsewhere, and visits to Enfield this week and Croydon last week.

The party-political broadcast that I recorded in Sheffield last Saturday was with just those people – people who want answers to questions and expect me to come up with them, to speak their language but also to give leadership, to be rational but also to be sensitive. But I can't get this across to those in the media who have never made a difficult decision in their lives, never had to take a difficult choice or find a way to square what they themselves often call 'unsquarable circles' like grant-maintained schools, grammar schools, or student funding. It is up to us politicians to find solutions.

On Saturday I went to Hull for John Prescott. I learned he was suffering from diabetes, which he said had resulted in his changing his diet and having to calm everything down, which explains quite a lot. I then presented the awards for the golden jubilee of the Girls' Brigade, with their band – complete with bugles and drums and everything – just a yard behind me on the platform. Twenty-four hours later I still can't get the sound out of my head.

We've also had a palaver over street robbery, because in PMQ Tony inadvertently gave a date of September for turning things round. I'd already given a six-month deadline in the *Evening Standard* interview in February, but it seems that the lobby journalists don't know anything. The corporate amnesia is just unbelievable. So a great kerfuffle arose. Tony had set this target – what was it for, did it mean that we'd stop street crime, did it mean we'd cut it, did it mean we'd stabilise it, would we reverse the upward trend? Of course, it meant the latter because I'd said it did, and I'd given them six months, which would have taken us to August rather than September. But the story ran for three days, going over and over what it meant and whether Tony was setting a target and asking if it was a gimmick. The Tories suggested that we knew that the mobile-phone industry was going to take action in any case by blocking all phones that were stolen and making it difficult for the phones to be reprogrammed. We certainly did know that, because we were responsible for doing it. Jack Straw had started it and John Denham and I had completed it, including getting a short single Bill ready. The problem is that No. 10's operation is less than slick. Instead of just being calm and saying that this is entirely in line with what has already been said, they just go into overdrive, and as a consequence it adds to a sense of bewilderment and confusion. And they didn't back me up strongly enough in relation to using the word 'swamp'. Had they done so, we could have dealt with that much more decisively as well.

At least I can celebrate that I've reached agreement through the Police Negotiating Board; celebrate that the House of Lords overturning parts of our Police Reform Bill on Third Reading did so in such a cackhanded way that we were able to make something of the stupidity of the Tories and Liberals; and celebrate that the debate itself in the Commons on Wednesday was a good one.

But I feel quite ill. I'm not at all sure I haven't got something wrong with my throat – something that's a bit worse than last year's gastroscopy led me to believe.

Following an article by Mary Ann Sieghart in *The Times* [26 April], the Sunday papers went wild about the idea of taking away child benefit from parents who would not keep their kids in order. It's an idea on which the Prime Minister was going to ask me to chair a working group, and I was in the process of explaining that, with all that I've got on, I needed another lead role on a controversial issue like a hole in the head as it would finish me off altogether as the bogey man.

Very good results in Sheffield in the local elections, thank the Lord. There was a lot of support for what I said and did and what I'm trying to do on both crime and nationality and asylum, so that's cheered me. An exhausting week, though. I've been struggling to sort out with Derry Irvine and the Lord Chancellor's Office about the appeals system for asylum. Sometimes it feels a bit like being in a skittle alley – get tough, give in, stand up, lay down, speak out, shut up. It is rather like crewing a small dinghy not knowing where the wind will come from next, and not knowing whether you should prepare for 'ready about' – when in actual fact you should be crewing a super-catamaran.

In the end I didn't go to Mo Mowlam's book launch because I voted on the national-insurance changes instead. I think if I'd turned up and been seen at the launch and had missed the national-insurance vote, I'd have been rather foolish. I'm feeling a bit beleaguered at the moment and a little bit isolated. I have a very funny letter that I've got on file from Peter Mandelson that really says Tony won't expose himself so don't overdo it, don't demand too much, don't head for a fall – which is fine except that I've got to do the Spending Review for the next three years and if I don't get the money I fall, and apparently if I fight and lose, I fall.

The Queen's presentation in Westminster Hall on Tuesday morning was one of those theatrical occasions again which mean nothing to anybody afterwards. Then there was the discussion with Oliver Letwin at the *Daily Telegraph* Free Country debate at the British Museum, about mutual versus individual rights. He'd bet Charles Moore a bottle of champagne that I wouldn't turn up, but I did.

There was very good policing of the May Day marches and the anarchists by the Met. I saw Jacques Lang [French Culture Minister] and the Mayor of Sangatte, to try and give them something on which we could agree about stopping the flow of immigrants. It was an interesting meeting. The Home Office didn't want me to hold it but quite obviously I had to go ahead; it would have been daft not to. So we'll see what comes of that.

Fred Broughton, Chairman of the Police Federation, is either very cunning or not very quick or both, because he's not pushing through the negotiated settlement, which is a very good one, but allowing his people to run him ragged. The letter I had sent to him following a conversation on Wednesday night has found its way into *The Times*.

The Criminal Justice White Paper is a shambles. We are a month on from my original version and a week on from a massive effort to revise it – and, if anything, they've made it worse.

There were accusations at the local-election press conference that I'd broken purdah by announcing the amounts for the police on street crime and counter-terrorism and on custody and the prison service. It was well worth the risk because it was a good story and we got it across. I've just got to hold my nerve, that's the main thing.

The local-election results in Sheffield meant that we became the largest single group with forty-three seats, the Liberal Democrats with forty-two and the Tories just two – one of which was a defector from the Lib Dems. We will take control of the council but with some real difficulty, being in a minority, but it was a really good night to have won seven seats. I phoned Jan Wilson, the Leader of the Labour Group, and talked to her about it. I also phoned Tony and very interestingly he took the phone call at midnight, whereas of course when earlier in the week he knew that I was going to badger him about the argument with Derry Irvine he declined to take the phone call – which speaks volumes.

Anyway he genuinely sounded pleased that we'd done so well in Sheffield. The Tories won the mayoral contest in Steve Byers's area.

It's very strange. None of us is having any real influence – at least I don't think we are – but at least it was good news here in Sheffield. And the Liberal Democrats did quite well in Hull, where my son Alastair works as an environmental health officer, and it just confirms what Alastair has said to me about what was going on there. It could have been a lot worse across the country. I was pessimistic, but that's because I've been to places like Enfield, which we did lose.

I went to Bristol to see Dan Gallamore, the young man who got blinded trying to save another kid from being beaten up. I was glad I went. I think it did some good. I've got a number of things to follow through – for mobility, for training, for potential for a job, for the whole area of access to work – so I hope that was helpful. Then I went to Jean Corston's sixtieth-birthday lunch. She was feeling very poorly so it was all a bit downbeat. It was a good occasion because I sat with Michael Meacher and Peter Hain and their wives and partners. It was pleasant to talk but Gloucestershire is a long way to go for lunch.

I'd spent great chunks of the weekend going through the White Paper with the overview, summary and everything else: ten tapes but I went through it page by page, blow by blow, again. Having done it previously on the way out to St Lucia, I knew what I was doing. I know what needs to be changed, so every time Derry Irvine is really awkward, every time he raises something in his usual way, as though he wants to try to destroy any chance of progressing and making something of the White Paper, I counter it and weave through it – and the result is that we're through to the next round.

I think they're going to win on when it should be published though. I wanted it published in June, but I think they're going to force a hold until after the Spending Review, and I may have to give in on that. I do find it really difficult to give in, and that's a plus in the sense that I care, I'm tenacious, I push things through; but it's an absolute disaster politically in terms of always wanting my own way and always pushing it to the very end. And in the end some things matter more than others, and I ask myself does it really matter if it's published after the Spending Review other than it delaying drafting the legislation?

Every Leader of the House has been the same. They see the length of the Bill, they try and cut things out and then we have to legislate again the year after. The Home Office have done it year after year, instead of having coherent legislation that really achieves what you are setting out to do.

We had a very productive meeting on civil society, which Tony wanted to turn into a meeting on anti-social behaviour. I was asking: what is the role of government and how do we relate to people in the community?

Steve Byers had to come back to the House for the umpteenth time to make a Statement about the events around Martin Sixsmith's departure. God, it's a fiasco. He must have nerves of steel to keep going, given the history behind it.

To Cardiff on Tuesday [30 April] to the justices' clerks' conference. I went because the prison service is on the edge of meltdown, with the prison population having gone up by 480 the week before. I got a slight drubbing in the Commons for not being there for the Second Reading of the Police Reform Bill that had come back from the Lords, though I'd agreed ages ago that John Denham would do it. Charles Clarke had done the same when in Jack's team. It's good for other people to move it. John's been handling the damn thing after all, and I needed to be at the justices' clerks' conference because I needed to get the message across about the coherence of what we're asking them to do on sentencing and why it matters, and why variation needs to be dramatically reduced.

Unfortunately there are occasional hiccups. One such was when the *Guardian* and *The Times* covered material that I had had to drop from my speech because of time constraints. On this occasion I had not received a

Braille copy of the press release, which is always helpful to me in checking what it is crucial that I say and what I can cut if the speech is too long. I had spoken about this at Cardiff, but of course, Cardiff being Cardiff, only the Welsh media were present. So they covered the stuff about collecting fines and the amount of money that is outstanding when I hadn't said it, I'd dropped it because I'd already exceeded the time and needed to answer questions and get back on a train. It is difficult to get across, even to those working closely with me, how difficult it is when making speeches not to be able to take advantage of highlighting, capital letters, underlining or bold. It's not necessarily more difficult because I've learned to do it, but they don't understand how different it is in making a speech and organising myself.

Obviously this was something that I had to learn to deal with by ensuring that my own notes did have, on a separate sheet, any absolutely key announcement. (I only spoke from notes rather than reading out speeches.) It was worse at party conference because there were a number of key announcements or important points to be made, and all of my special advisers dealing with media got very frustrated with me when I might just have missed a word. Thank the Lord none of this happened too often, but I can now see that I should have organised myself more carefully, rather than expecting other people to organise around me. Again it is easy to do when making only the occasional speech. It is much harder when running the Home Office.

May 2002

Big news of the week was the assassination of Pim Fortuyn, the head of a very strange right-wing, racist, pro-drugs party in the Netherlands. In France, Chirac was massively re-elected as President after the fiasco a fortnight before. Now we have a right-wing French government until the National Assembly elections, and probably for a long time afterwards.

Fortuyn's lot are likely to do very well in the Netherlands elections this coming week. They had toyed with cancelling the poll, but the whole government in the Netherlands had resigned – another act of stupidity – over some domestic issue a few weeks before, so I suppose they had to go ahead with it. But it's certainly put the cat amongst the pigeons.

At Cabinet I was saying that in the local elections I felt we'd done a lot better than I thought we would but not as well as we'd claimed afterwards.

We'd talked it up and done very well at presenting something which really wasn't a victory. Signs across the country are that people are not prepared to put up with things. But at least in Sheffield we acted as a kind of beacon, even though we hadn't taken overall control.

Week beginning Monday 13 May: ACPO conference went fine. David Phillips [President of ACPO] made a complete idiot of himself by attacking community policing – the beat, as he called it. Michael Gove wrote a really clever piece in *The Times* the following morning because Phillips had suggested that those who were in favour of beat officers were nostalgic for Enid Blyton. Michael Gove wrote: 'Give me Enid Blyton any day if the choice is between David Phillips and Enid Blyton.' Phillips also attacked community support officers, and Ian Blair from the Met went down the following day and dealt with that, getting ACPO to say they weren't really against community support officers after all. It is surprising how they all back off when somebody stands up to them.

I've given up wine on Sundays, Mondays and Tuesdays, which is a good job because I am in a reasonably fit state and not too tired for my speech to the Police Federation conference on Wednesday.

All the papers and all the broadcast media had it that I was going to be done over at the conference, and I was asked about it in the *Today* programme on Wednesday morning. I did suspect that I was going to be attacked, but I crafted the speech very carefully, not apologising but saying that we had made mistakes and spelling out what our agenda was, stressing that I wasn't going to pull back from the reform agenda, from the negotiations that we had concluded, or the legislation, but admitting that there had been mistakes and we needed to go forward. Unbeknown to me, Sky were broadcasting it live. And once they'd started to clap and once they'd laughed, I had won them over: no booing, no hissing, no slow handclapping, no sitting in silence. *The Times* the following morning carried a checklist of home secretaries and how they'd done at previous conferences, with me at the top of their marking scale – so that was some going.

I think my pride at the time was simply because other home secretaries had had such a hell of a drubbing and that the circumstances of this particular conference followed the mass march on London and the great fears of fellow MPs that I was pushing the reform agenda too far. I was more worried that there might be a walk-out than a slow handclap because when Education Secretary I had got used to that kind of nonsense at NUT conferences. I was greatly aided in the preparation by Gareth Hills, a young man in my Private

Office who had taken detailed notes and notice of what had happened the previous year during the general election. He was able to advise me about how to avoid provoking, and in the early part of the speech lecturing, the audience.

Gareth also pointed out that I had the advantage of speaking in the morning, and that early afternoon was the worst possible time to speak at the Police Fed conference. Since those days, the leadership has changed and adopted a very different and much more effective strategy of working with the government and scaling down the belligerence. Maybe I'm deluding myself, but I like to think that I made some contribution to persuading the membership that they would get a better response if their attitude was more rational and in keeping with the twenty-first century.

My cousin David Blunkett, who is a police officer, rang me the previous weekend and told me he was going to the conference and would like to meet up.

My dad's brother and his wife chose to christen their own son David. Of course, they were not to know at the time the embarrassment this was likely to cause him later in life.

We talked about having a photograph taken together and I rang him again to make sure that he understood what the implications were of meeting publicly and being photographed with me. Sophie Linden, my special adviser, in fact rang him three times. But it all worked out very well. The *Mail on Sunday* offered him money for an interview, and he asked if I had any objections. I said I can't object and that it was his decision, but he should just be aware that the *MoS* would try to extract a story from him that's detrimental to me. In the end they went ahead with the interview but didn't run it, because he wouldn't give them what they wanted: a minor triumph in the circumstances.

One of the silliest things of the week was when my office received a phone call from the Foreign Office, asking whether we would accept two of the Palestinian terrorists from the siege of the church in Bethlehem. I sent a message back saying I couldn't believe they were asking this. We have got nine people going through the Special Immigration Appeals Commission; we are being challenged on derogation by the Council of Europe and by the Joint Committee (of both Houses) on Human Rights; we are desperately trying to hold on to making the case – and the Foreign Office was asking us to take two terrorists. We heard nothing more about it.

The weekend papers were full of asylum and nationality, most of it totally irrational. Right-wing papers want asylum centres but they don't want them in rural areas, they want them in the middle of urban decay, which means that those areas would be wiped out altogether. It is irritating. We've got people demonstrating in Worcestershire, including pop figures like Toyah Wilcox. Some might call this hypocrisy: 'Not here, mate – build the centre somewhere where the working-class can put up with it.'

Despite all this, I felt a lot better going down on Monday 20 May than I have for a long time, even though I'm told I am going grey – and I'm not surprised!

Week beginning Monday 20 May: Bush and Putin reach an agreement on cutting by two-thirds their nuclear weapons. Unfortunately, it's those surrounding them who are the big problem, both internally and the former Soviet Union states. Pakistan and India are on the verge of nuclear war: Pakistan is testing missiles, and India has half a million men on the border.

A big storm about Sangatte. A Catholic weekly did an interview with the Italian Social Affairs Minister, who mentioned that one of the ways in which Sangatte might be able to close is if we agreed to take the people in it. The asylum issue, particularly Sangatte, has reached a point of hysteria but we did agree, at the recalled meeting under Tony's chairmanship, to go ahead with my proposal on what are called non-suspensive appeals, which effectively means that we can turn people round if we can get the administration to manage to do it – literally just turn them round and send them back. They then make their appeal from their country of origin, and I have to certify that they are not at risk.

The prison population is now over 71,000: it went up by another 400 again last week. We are still struggling to get a grip both of crime and of the Criminal Justice White Paper, and I'm afraid we are not getting on anywhere near as fast as I would wish. Anyway, the big issue around the meeting with Tony was the fact that Clare Short had leaked to the *Guardian* the report that we'd received the week before, with the idea of encouraging countries to take people back if we were giving those countries aid. Clare is vehemently opposed. Of course, as we are giving them aid, there is a presumption that these are countries fit to give aid to, which Clare seems to have missed.

Dinner with Tony on Monday night. It was Leo's birthday, so I took him a little present and he seemed to like it. Sally Morgan was there and as ever these days we got back to talking about the euro – a robust discussion. I am deeply worried about the impact on public spending and the cuts that would follow if we were to enter at anything like the present rate of sterling. There are so many people pressing Tony to see this as his legacy and I see so many things that could make up his legacy that would not put everything else at risk. I said as much, including the fact that a referendum would give the British people an ideal opportunity to give us a bloody nose without having to change the government.

Just as it was impossible in the earlier part of this book to cover every aspect of my time at the Department for Education and Employment, so after giving a flavour of my first year at the Home Office it is appropriate now to skim over much of the daily business and pick out some highlights of the months ahead.

June/July 2002

It was one of those nights that I have started to have, waking up at 4.30 a.m. By 5.30 I was still tossing and turning, so I tapped into my mobile to see if there were any messages. Huw Evans had left me a message and my heart sank. Once again, we have been subject to what is clearly a deliberate and calculated leak, this time of the whole of the Criminal Justice White Paper. We have kept the draft under wraps and we have a planned programme for communication and presentation, agreed with all involved in developing and delivering the criminal justice system, including the Lord Chancellor and the Attorney-General. The leak clearly hasn't come from either of them. Whatever disagreements we may have had, I have no reason to believe that there has been deliberate passing-over of papers and documents either from them or from their advisers. The same cannot be said of more junior players.

I am pretty certain who did this and why, but it is inappropriate to identify them, even at this distance from events. One of the most effective ways for a minister to damage a fellow minister, or for a senior civil servant to undermine a politician, is to create the impression that everything they do is either leaking or has been deliberately passed to the press either by their advisers or themselves. The higher-profile the issue, the more likely this is to happen – for the very simple reason that there would be more point in doing it.

It immediately crossed my mind that there was a relationship here with what had happened with leaks to the *Observer* and arguments I had been having about the prison service. Of course, the early hours of the morning are not a good time to reflect on anything.

It is a lesson that I am still learning that the sharpness of thought in the early hours is often beneficial, but the rationality of how those thoughts come together is not. To make decisions at that moment or to rely on your interpretation when your mind is at the point of re-entering the day can be very dangerous indeed.

Huw reported that this wasn't just one newspaper but the *Independent, Mirror* and *Times* – a nap hand, as you might say. He didn't allude to this, but I recalled at that moment the eleven pages that the *Mirror* had devoted to the crime statistics: not to covering them accurately but to highlighting every possible disadvantage or downside. It doesn't take a genius to see that what has been done has almost wiped out the very positive story that we had planned about the closure of Sangatte.

So here we had two major stories with a careful media-presentation plan, both undermined by a deliberate act of sabotage.

There were times when I clearly felt issues more strongly than the reality deserved, but this was not one of them. The desperate feelings I had in the early hours of that morning were fully justified. This was one of those occasions when being paranoid did not mean that I had no justification for believing that I was being systematically undermined. I have been as tough as the next man or woman in politics. I have had to be throughout my life, but I can never imagine when I would have deliberately used the media to undermine a colleague by leaking a major document in the full knowledge that it would wipe out a substantial triumph – in this case with regard to the enormous task we faced on immigration.

When I rang Huw Evans, he also brought me news of the first major intrusion into my private life by the British media since I had become a Member of Parliament. A former girlfriend of mine, Pamela Edwards, who now lived in France, had (inadvertently) done an interview for the *Daily Mail*, which they had printed on page three.

I should have clocked at the time that the almost desperate desire of the British media to get into my private life would continue. As I reflected much later, the fact that I had kept my private life so private was a source of irritation for some journalists – and a challenge to others.

Underpinning all this was my continuing worry about the Spending Review. Not a day went by when I didn't return to it in my mind.

We have had no debate at all about benefits and tax credits, and then we end up arguing about £50 million here, £100 million there, and even £25 million somewhere else. The whole style of this Spending Review has been just the same as it has always been, and Tony still hasn't got himself a public-sector economist who can plan ahead and help him through, rather than resorting to last-minute engagement with the review.

Thursday night was a classic: Gordon and I together, him saying he could do nothing, me saying that he had to, his senior officials chipping in, and me losing my rag. I told his officials that being clever wasn't enough. It was delivering services to people that was important.

At this meeting the future Permanent Secretary to the Treasury, Nick McPherson, was (as I had it described to me) sartorially elegant and, as befits a senior mandarin, extremely calm and cool. I should have been equally calm and cool, but as so often my emotions and the sheer fervour of my desire to look ahead and enable us to make progress got the better of me – tactically a mistake.

At this meeting with Tony, I had told Nick that I would buy him a bottle of Burgundy if his figures turned out to be correct in the final analysis. I never had to deliver that bottle.

The idea of a tax on household rubbish has emerged. I was staggered when I heard this, given our commitment to the environment, and Tony had to intervene to ensure that whoever put this out as an idea understood that it wasn't policy and it wasn't going to be policy. Those of us doing regular advice surgeries are all too familiar with the problem of people dumping their rubbish, even when they are not charged for taking it to the tip – never mind having to pay a tax on it. When I went to my constituency meeting on Friday night, everybody was up in arms about this.

Reality soon returns when I hold my surgery – and on Saturday 13 July (my son Hugh's birthday) I also went along to the Parson Cross Festival and had a meeting with governors of Concord School in my constituency. This is the real world and these are the realities.

And so it continues. The joy of being welcomed back into the constituency at the weekend, the pressure of wanting always to succeed and, as with every July that I experienced in government, the absolute desire to see the end of the month and to get away on holiday.

July always ended up being a period of pressure, not simply because this was the time of year for the Spending Review, but because the civil service were winding down for the August break. As a consequence, unfinished business was placed in the Red Boxes and outstanding reports were rushed through. Even dealing with correspondence became a nightmare, as efforts were made to try and clear the decks before the recess began. And for junior ministers, this was equally true of parliamentary questions, so my advisers who were scrutinising them had to watch for political googlies, while my Private Office were having to ensure that we co-ordinated what was taking place.

Everyone was under the most enormous stress, which has a knock-on effect with your own reactions. A combination of deadlines and real heavyweight policy decisions come together to make for what has often been described as the 'hothouse'. All you need is a very hot and muggy July, with pollution levels in central London hurting even those who don't suffer from either asthma or bronchial problems, and it is an unholy combination.

I do need to keep cool. I had dinner with Peter Mandelson on Monday night. The last time we met he had said that my problem was that I cared too much and let my emotions show. I certainly did. I got hold of Paul Boateng's lapels on the way out of Gordon's office on Thursday night. As Chief Secretary, he wasn't to blame. He was doing what was expected, but my fuse blew. To do Paul justice, he kept really calm.

I recall that we shook hands and it was never mentioned again, and I can honestly say that this was the only time in my life that I have threatened violence, and that against someone for whom I had much less reason to be antagonistic than many on whom I could cheerfully have planted a socking left hook.

On Saturday I spoke to Tony about the way in which the press were commenting on the Spending Review – the *Daily Mail* claiming that I had tripled my demands, the speculation in the *Guardian* in relation to investment in the prison service, and the 'rows' which the papers were generally presenting as some sort of battleground.

As I said to Tony, it was hardly likely to be me as I knew what I was going to get, pretty roughly, and therefore I was likely to talk down the amounts of money rather than talking them up, given who would get the credit for what and how it would be perceived when the announcements were made. It appears from preliminary investigation that Downing Street had conducted that it was the Independent *newspaper that had been given the full version of the Criminal Justice White Paper – an interesting outlet to be given it, with all the possibilities of launching an assault on my being the 'draconian' Home Secretary. Tony and I both agreed at least about the particular political stance of those who had leaked it, even if we couldn't agree on the likely source. He did promise, however, that there would be a proper inquiry so that we could stop the kind of nonsense speculation that it had anything to do with ministers in the Home Office or, for that matter, civil servants there.*

We were still negotiating the final criminal-justice budget that related directly to the White Paper, so this particular weekend was very difficult all round – and I was trying to make sure that my son Hugh had a decent birthday. Some years later I was reading Edna Healey's autobiography, in which she tells the story of one of her daughters who had said to her dad, 'I've fallen out of a tree and broken my leg today, Dad' – and her dad said, 'Well done' as he abstractedly dealt with his Red Box. I am sure all of us who have been in government have had that sort of situation with our own children. The trouble is that you can never get to witness, and to take a full enough role in, their childhood, because of the sheer external pressure on you.

I said to Tony that we were in a real difficulty because there was not a proper conjunction of the Spending Review with long-term policy thinking and strategy. The Prison Service and the National Probation Service were classic examples of where a plan was needed for five years or more, but the Spending Review was effectively (discounting the last year of the existing Review) for two years. This was not a timescale with which we could work, nor was it one that applied to policies that were not constrained by departmental budget limits.

It has to be remembered that a great deal of public expenditure is not constrained or confined within departmental expenditure limits, and it is this very large and substantial uncapped element of public expenditure which receives the least scrutiny during the Spending Review periods. We were to introduce five-year strategies, but again they were not in line with five-year budgets as a whole (although Gordon had moved towards the five-year health budget and later towards providing much greater certainty for capital investment for education).

The decision to wipe out the 2007 Spending Review for a substantial number of departments was effectively to give them a long-term budget –

frozen, other than for inflation, for the Home Office and a cut of up to 5 per cent for other departments, hardly the long-term Spending Review that I was arguing for in 2002.

One of the gains that weekend was to get agreement for the Spending Review to include gaining assets through the new Asset Recovery Agency and the legislation that had taken months to get through Parliament. Being able to 'keep' some of the money does not sound much of a victory, but it was. It meant that there was potential for very large sums of money to come back into the budget for policing and crime reduction and, in the early stages, an agreement that there would be an assumed gain that allowed me to plan ahead and for which the budget heading would be Asset Recovery. But the Treasury would underwrite the first tranche until we had the opportunity of really getting progress, including through the courts. I had also got agreement on a review of prison and probation which would keep the spending issue alive – although it wasn't quite presented like that in the Sunday papers.

The morning broadcast on Monday drove me bonkers. It once again presented a '£90 billion' spend. This was, of course, as we had seen from 1998 onwards, a combining of the spending run for three years, not an annual increase, and in any case raised expectations once again beyond the ability to deliver them. If I have a criticism which has been with me since 1997, it is that we make the mistake of offering, to those who believe strongly in public expenditure, far too rosy a view of what we are doing in reality. I fear that the chickens will come home to roost.

The chickens certainly did. It is not merely that it is difficult to translate cash into delivery on the ground, but that people do believe that there is so much money swilling about that they expect dramatic change. There were never large sums of money and, as we did in the build-up to 1997 and in the first year in government, it would have been better if we had played down the expectations to a point where people were genuinely pleased when they saw the results of essential investment in public services.

I came home on Saturday [20 July] to find twenty messages waiting for me on the answerphone. I am my own worst enemy here, as I would be better not to have an answerphone at home at all and route all but the most private calls through the Department. But I just can't bring myself to do it. It would be too pompous.

Time to move on, away from the Spending Review, to think of holidays, to prepare for the autumn and to spare readers the agonising of those weeks leading up to getting away to the sunshine. After three oral Statements to the House in as many weeks, the Criminal Justice White Paper and the Spending Review, and reading in the Daily Telegraph *on 23 July that my star was waning, I thought that I deserved a holiday.*

August 2002

When I returned from holiday, I remained concerned about what was going to happen when the Special Immigration Appeals Commission made their judgement on the continuing saga of the legality of our certifying the Al Qaeda terrorists whom we had secure under Section 4 of the Anti-Terrorism, Crime and Security Act: they were placed in Belmarsh Prison and Woodhill. So much rested on this and, given that Judge Andrew Collins took an extremely liberal (with a capital L as well as a small one) view of the Act, it was by no means certain that we would win. So much credibility at this stage rested on ensuring that we were secure, both with regard to protection from the individuals and the organised network behind them, and as regards public confidence in what we were doing.

This had now been rumbling on for some months and formed a backcloth (and certainly within my own mind, a subconscious niggling) week after week.

The forces of very right-wing darkness are mustering with a tinpot one-man organisation called Immigration Watch. There are a number of these right-wing think-tanks that have perhaps at most two or three people in them but get very wide publicity. Immigration Watch is one of them and it should have been foreseen by the Department. But it hadn't, so there was no plan for dealing with their attack on migration generally. It is clear now that there is a very substantial effort going on across the right, including in the media, to muddy the waters by not distinguishing between legitimate economic migration and clandestine illegal migration.

While I was away SIAC had delivered a verdict, with our winning two of the three key points. I had already prepared our response with varying elements to take account of the likely outcome. The two points we won on were those of the ability to derogate from the European Convention on Human Rights, and that there was a State of Emergency arising from a terrorist act.

At this stage we lost on the issue we were to lose on in the House of Lords in December 2004 – winning, as we did, at the Court of Appeal under the Lord Chief Justice, Harry Woolf: namely, that we had been discriminatory because we had used immigration law to deal with the holding and removal of those who were not British citizens and who therefore (if the country of origin was safe) could be removed as non-conducive to the public good. Of course, this was the crucial issue because, as we saw two and a half years later, to lose on this point was to lose Section 4 of the Anti-Terrorism, Crime and Security Act itself.

In his judgement, Andrew Collins also threw away the *obiter dicta* that he believed our actions were disproportionate – not something that was pursued through to the House of Lords.

I fear that by this time the impact of what had happened on 11 September was dwindling. Terms such as 'so-called' war on terror were being used by the BBC as well as liberal journalists. Once again I reflected on how the liberal left had responded to the rise of the Nazis, through to Hitler occupying the Reichstag in January 1933. The issue at the centre of the argument – discrimination – was something we had debated at considerable length, to-ing and fro-ing between the Commons and the Lords in the autumn of the previous year. The will of Parliament was very clear, but the judgement of the democratic assembly of the UK was questioned by a section of the legal profession and a small number of the judiciary who found themselves in significant positions at a time of historic moment.

Despite having given lines to take, I am afraid I was foolish enough to spend far too much time on the telephone to the Department when I was on holiday. Were I to be able to rerun this period of my ministerial life, I would certainly not behave in the same manner again. Having thought through in advance what we would do, I should have left it to junior ministers. I was aware of this the moment I came back, reflecting on how much I had been disrupted during what should have been a family holiday.

We also had a media frenzy around the Al Mahdi family, who had claimed refuge in Germany, didn't much like being there, and had come to Britain. Even under very feeble European jurisdiction, we had every right to transfer them back to the country in which they had originally made their claim – otherwise people would simply move about Europe depending on where they could obtain the best deal. But, as ever, there were lawyers prepared to have a go and sections of the public who were ready to back them, claiming that we were acting unfairly. Unfortunately we had to remove them from a mosque where they had taken refuge. Although authorisation to do so was clearly given by ministers, the handling of it by the West Midlands Police left a great deal to be desired – 'clumsy' would be the understatement of the year. As a consequence we had to deal with the backwash.

This went on for month after month, demonstrating very clearly the tremendous cleft stick in which we were always to find ourselves. Day after day in the Guardian *we had stories about the children and how unfair it was. We had the Liberal Democrats joining in, even though they had always claimed that they wanted a European-wide asylum policy, which is precisely what we had got.*

Bev Hughes had done a first-rate job on dealing with the public campaign, but I was astonished on my return from holiday to find the BBC joining in as though their job was to act as an advocate rather than an information service. We even had BBC Radio 4 presenting an item attempting to demonstrate that Germany was not a good place for asylum seekers to be returned to. But what really took the biscuit was the Community Fund of the National Lottery, which had given a grant to an organisation described as the 'Coalition Against Deportation', who had been involved in threatening to lie down in front of the planes to prevent them taking asylum seekers out of the country. This, of course, was very different from the Refugee Council and those organisations working with and supporting asylum seekers – a perfectly legitimate activity. The idea that an organisation campaigning to prevent any asylum seekers being removed from our soil was deserving of a lottery grant was just bizarre.

In August 2002 Holly Wells and Jessica Chapman were murdered in Soham, Cambridgeshire. This was a terrible tragedy, and was to lead to a major inquiry (chaired by Sir Michael Bichard, my former Permanent Secretary at the DfEE) and a clash with the Chief Constable of Humberside two years later. What, I asked myself, were some national newspapers doing claiming that there had been insufficient vigilance in letting Ian Huntley – who was convicted of the murders – be appointed school caretaker, given his previous encounters with the police in relation to crimes against children, when the year before they had ridiculed ministers in relation to their attitude towards the Brass Eye *programme, when we tried to suggest that mocking those concerned about paedophilia was a road to disaster. But no one is held to account; no one has to answer for these contradictions. They say one thing one week, and say the opposite the next and hope that nobody notices.*

It is amazing what an impact murders of this sort have on you inside your head. I needed to keep a low profile in order not to intrude and to get on with the job behind the scenes. I needed to get the then Chief Constable of Cambridgeshire back from holiday, and to ensure that at an appropriate moment the Metropolitan Police lent a hand.

We had to deal with Ian Huntley's solicitors trying to go down the mental-health route – taking it out of the legal process altogether, as I had seen so vividly with the Grade 5 civil servant a year earlier. We had to deal with the issues of explaining how we had already acted decisively in respect of chat rooms and the Internet but what we needed was co-operation from all the service providers involved in delivering.

As I was dealing with this, little did I know that I would have to deal with Ian Huntley's girlfriend Maxine Carr, whose case was to run and run. I deeply regretted the News of the World *using the photos of Holly and Jessica on 18 August to relaunch their 'Sarah's Law' campaign against me with a banner headline – 'Only More Broken Hearts, Mr Blunkett' – attempting to make me personally responsible. These are the pressures that home secretaries have to bear in a way that no one else in government can imagine, other than the Prime Minister.*

My immediate thought was: 'When people accuse us of being driven by the press and we stand up to the press, why don't they ever remember?' And in the midst of all this and the heartache of learning from the Police Family Liaison Officer of the trauma of the families, we were also trying to deal with the outcome of the first few months of the Street Crime Initiative, which was going extremely well.

On the Thursday after returning from holiday, I attended my local hospital for a gastroscopy. By this time the problems I was having with my digestive system were becoming chronic: I could not eat at night, I couldn't sleep without being propped up and I felt constantly ill. The tablets that I had been prescribed were clearly not working, and often made me feel worse. The result of the test was that while cancerous cells had not yet appeared on my oesophagus, there was such damage to the surface that action had to be taken, given the prospect of the growth reaching dangerous proportions if unchecked. Doubling the dose of medication didn't seem to me to be the right thing to do, but at that moment it was all that was on offer.

So I was fortunate a few days later to encounter the Chairman of a small Sheffield company, and a former Master Cutler, whom I had known for some time. A friend of his was a leading consultant at the Leeds Royal Infirmary and Nuffield Hospital, at the time one of only a few surgeons who undertook the necessary operation to deal with Barrett's Oesophagus – which is what I was diagnosed as having – on a regular basis. After a consultation an early date was set for surgery.

Charles Clarke is being well and truly done over in certain sections of the media for his performance as Party Chairman. It is hardly his fault that the party is in such financial difficulty. Someone has certainly got it in for him, judging from all the briefings taking place against him. Sometimes politics really does stink.

And so through to the party conference, with visits to mosques and a meeting with the Deputy Prime Minister of India (who is also the Interior Minister), who was pressing me to make a visit. We also had the terrible mess over the Criminal Records Bureau that did so much damage to Estelle when the head of the DfEE press office made a mistake – giving out information which had not been cleared with ministers and then trying to get ministers to stand up and justify the erroneous material. It led to the most horrendous row about clearance of teachers for working in schools and a palaver about a four-day week in schools if teachers were not cleared in time, and a host of completely exaggerated nonsense which, as ever, was aimed at destabilisation – and went quite a long way to achieving it.

But before moving rapidly on into the autumn, it is worth reflecting that at this time I was reading a book (Lord knows how I found the time) about a major gathering at the Queen Elizabeth II Conference Centre in Westminster and a threat to assassinate the Home Secretary. It was about the Home Secretary having the power to do this, that and the other, and I thought to myself: 'Is this really what people believe is the power of my post?' It really was strange to see in print a perception of the job I was doing and to realise that others would see not only me as an individual but the role I played in a quite different way from how it appeared to me. I have done everything in my power not to see myself as 'the Home Secretary', because once you become the position, rather than the position enabling you as an individual to do the job you need to do, I think you are finished.

September 2002

The prospect of our getting involved in military action in Iraq is damaging the economy. Capital markets have been affected and PEPs and ISAs are going down the pan. I am amazed that we are not getting a bigger drubbing for it, not because it is our fault but because people really do feel the impact in their purses and bank accounts. I have raised with Sally Morgan (and with Tony when I spoke to him earlier in the month) the issue of pensions. I am really worried about the future. I think we could win over trade-union leaders if we had a much clearer idea what we were doing and where we were going. Andrew Smith [Secretary of State for Work and Pensions] is doing a good job on fighting for those who have lost their pensions, but we are not saying enough about it as a government as a whole.

What strikes me as we approach conference is the pincer movement against Tony, involving Piers Morgan (who had done an interview with the *Spectator* earlier in the summer) and Paul Dacre, who did an interview in the media section of the *Guardian*. Each is coming from a different angle – a kind of contempt in Piers Morgan's attitude and a kind of hatred from Paul Dacre.

I encountered Piers Morgan at a *GQ* magazine award event when I was named Politician of the Year (which my sons enjoyed enormously). He approached me during the evening and said, 'Plan B is in operation.' Plan B, as he had explained to me earlier in the year, was the destabilisation of Tony Blair.

Just before conference, I sent a detailed note to Tony with ideas on radical reform of the civil service. It was intended to try to get some momentum going in radical reform five years in.

I probably chose entirely the wrong moment in the run-up to conference. The strains and stresses on any party leader in the build-up to his or her conference speech are enormous. It is bad enough speaking from the platform (which I had done myself from 1984 onwards), without having the world's media attending every word.

I also raised my concerns with Gordon when I stayed over in the middle of September with Sarah and himself after flying back from the Justice and Home Affairs Council meeting in Denmark. Copenhagen is a much nicer place than I had expected. I managed to get out of some of the meetings and take myself on to the waterways.

We all visited Jennifer's grave, a truly touching moment. We also had a lovely walk on the beach, which gave me the opportunity to talk to Gordon and reflect on where we were, and to hear his perspective on the immediate future. It also helped to settle the tensions that had built up during the fraught period of the Spending Review. Once again I found Sarah and Gordon to be excellent hosts.

Perhaps we ought to move the UK Parliament to Edinburgh . . .

Murray Elder came to stay over and eat with us. Murray is now in the Lords and runs the Smith Institute, named after John Smith. I have to say, enjoyable as it was, the conversation at dinner was very much about figures from the past and I thought to myself, 'Well, this is Scotland.' On Sunday morning, we went to the local kirk, which brought back all the memories of my teens and early twenties in the Methodist church.

At this point it is worth reflecting that other than my annual holiday, I was out of Sheffield for a longer period during this September than I can ever remember. I rarely made notes in my diary when I was away, so on this occasion I was doing the odd taped note either when I was travelling or in London, but less systematically.

Before party conference I was interrogated by the Home Affairs Select Committee. This is the investigatory, all-party committee that scrutinises the work of the Home Office, as opposed to the Standing Committee that takes through legislation once it has received its main Second Reading. On this occasion there were a number of ticklish issues to be aired, from what was happening with the Criminal Records Bureau through to an essay that I had produced in a booklet published by the Foreign Policy Centre earlier in the month. This started the debate about migrant families learning English and, as well as speaking their mother tongue, learning to speak English to their children at home.

I was to come back to this with a vengeance later in the year. I seemed to be courting controversy, but although what I did was deliberate and thought through, it was not consciously aimed at stirring the pot. The fuss resulted, as so often, because the issues with which I was dealing were by their very nature high-profile, controversial and critical to the future well-being of the country. Nothing would have been easier than to duck them and to simply tick along dealing with issues as they arose, avoiding looking to the future and trying to close down challenges that would come back to bite us. Instead I was more positively trying to ensure that there was a clear government programme, step by step, to ensure that in years to come society would be more cohesive, more confident and more content.

This particular day ended up with a late-night response to the BBC's 'Crime Day' which, as we had predicted, ended up raising fears and creating concern, without either the facility or the space to have sensible debates about the issues raised. Thank the Lord that Oliver Letwin was so useless. On this occasion he played the soft liberal card, which was a gift to me. Long may he remain Shadow Home Secretary.

My son Alastair and his girlfriend Sarah came down to stay with me in London on the weekend [of 20–22 September], and we were able to celebrate that he had got his Master's degree and started his new job in Nottinghamshire.

During the following week, controversy increased about A-level results and whether the marking system had been correct. This, and the Criminal Records Bureau row, had increased pressure on Estelle. All I could do was to tell her to stay strong, but I realise that it is easier said than done.

Then there was the recall of Parliament over what we might do with regard to Iraq. As ever on these occasions, Tony was outstanding and gave a magnificent performance – especially as the pressure on him during the build-up to conference must have been enormous. This was the first really big parliamentary round on Iraq and Tony's clear determination to back George Bush in facing down Saddam Hussein.

My diary says: 'Iraq, Iraq, Iraq – that's all we are getting in the broadcast media – Iraq.'

Within the Department, and with Andrew Turnbull having taken over from Sir Richard Wilson as Secretary of the Cabinet, there now does seem to be some real momentum for reform within the Home Office. John Gieve has embraced this strongly, which has suddenly made it much easier to push through changes that I have been desperate to see for the last fifteen months.

John Gieve and I called a meeting of the ministers with the Department's Executive Board: it had been my practice to have regular meetings of this sort, which I chaired. I simply said that we had a choice. We either embraced change enthusiastically or it would be forced upon us through the Delivery Unit at Downing Street. That did the trick.

On Thursday [26 September], just before conference, I had a success. Nicolas Sarkozy agreed a date for blocking people entering Sangatte, with the prospect of closing it by Christmas. We had already agreed the principle, as I have spelled out previously, but it was important to have got some deadlines and real measures in place to make it happen. At this stage, Sarkozy was still talking about 'by April' for the closure, but I had made it clear that they couldn't possibly go through the winter with people on the streets of Calais, as this would be a public-relations disaster as much for them as it would be for us. Getting the security and intelligence controls on French soil and getting the freight depot at Coquelle sorted out so that people can't jump the trains is all proving to be really important.

As it happened we were having a meeting in Zeebrugge with the Belgian Interior Minister and signing a future agreement for similar action with the Belgians, and then Nicolas Sarkozy laid on a helicopter from Calais, where we had done the formal handshaking and the announcement, to Zeebrugge.

What struck me then and certainly strikes me since is the way in which other European (and North American) governments make life much easier for their ministers than we do. It isn't simply that we are (in many ways very sensibly) hair-shirted and frugal. It is almost a fear of acknowledging that people doing extremely busy and stressful jobs need slightly more support than people who are going home at 5.30 in the evening. To say so, as a front-line politician, is to sound like I'm whingeing and asking for special treatment. Of course, nobody blinks an eye if the chief executive or managing director of a major company gets into a plane in order to fly from place from place as quickly and as easily as possible. But even in the twenty-first century, there are constant gripes in newspapers about Tony making life tolerable by flying by charter plane or the Queen's Flight. It is almost a feeling that we should be in Ruritania.

So at least with the Street Crime Initiative working and an accord with the Metropolitan Commissioner, we are on track to make a real dent in the problems of law and order, at the same time as getting a grip of nationality and immigration.

There have been many times when I have thought that party conference was going to be destabilised by the build-up, but this week [Monday 23 September to Saturday 28 September] has been one of the strangest of the lot. The recall of Parliament had upped the ante, and all the media coverage around it had encouraged posturing on the issue of Iraq and what position we were going to take *vis-à-vis* the Americans. It was like a formulaic romantic novel, but without the romance. Robin Cook and Clare Short were going a long way publicly to putting themselves out on a limb – particularly Clare on GMTV – and then climbing back down again when we reached Cabinet on Tuesday, prior to the recall. As Robin put it, 'Tony, you've played a blinder' – with reference to pushing George Bush towards getting a unifying UN resolution to the Security Council. I can't understand why Clare cancelled her pre-arranged overseas trip in order to be around, unless she was going to go all the way in separating herself out from the government.

There was a lighter moment at the end of Cabinet, when John Reid in one of his more sarcastic modes said that so many people had praised Tony that it was difficult to find words to match them, and as he was sitting next to me he felt it was inappropriate to use the term 'blinder' again. It lightened the mood and everyone (well, it seemed like everyone) chortled.

When I had dinner with Hilary Armstrong and her husband Paul Corrigan we talked about whether it would be wise for Tony to offer Robin some plum overseas job, as the Tories almost certainly would have done in a similar situation – although I don't know whether Robin would take it. I said to Hilary that I thought that we should have looked after Frank Dobson and given him a positive role after the débâcle of the London mayoral elections. To top it all, in his Channel 4 programme Charlie Whelan [former press adviser to Gordon Brown] was promoting Clare as a likely Deputy Leader.

The weekend saw me speaking at the annual conference of the Law Society – a bit like Daniel in the lions' den, except that the lawyers were extremely positive and received my message very well indeed. It is clear that when there is the opportunity to talk to people and get feedback from them, they begin to understand what it is I am trying to do and why.

The beginning of conference week was temporarily diverted by the revelations about John Major and Edwina Currie. The only comment I thought worth remembering was that of Mary Archer, of all people, who in true Dorothy Parker style said: 'I was not a bit surprised about the indiscretion of Edwina Currie, but was surprised and shocked at John's lapse in taste.' I had to smile at the *Mail on Sunday*, who having devoted pages and pages to the story had the cheek to say that they thought that the BBC had made a mountain out of a molehill.

On Saturday evening, Professor Peter Hennessy appeared on a Channel 4 programme compered by Martin Sixsmith and declared chapter and verse on what I had said in Cabinet about the civil service earlier in the year. I knew that the message had been passed on to the other permanent secretaries in respect of my outburst in relation to the activities of the civil service. As Tony had warned me, I should have expected that this would be passed on verbatim.

And so to Blackpool, where Tony's speech was the highlight of the conference. I think it is the first leader's speech in all the years I have been attending conference where I didn't drift off halfway through into thoughts of my own. Mind you, it did have an enormous number of references to the things that matter most to me – enabling government, developing civil society, and being 'on your side'.

By contrast, at the end of the week I can't remember a single thing that Gordon said in his speech, but I do remember that it was a magnificent barnstorming performance. Given that he had flown back from the USA to Manchester and driven straight across to Blackpool to deliver it, you have to admire not just the strength and commitment but the sheer focus – which is, of course, what will carry him through into the job of Prime Minister.

Bill Clinton's speech wiped out the public message on health and education, which I thought was deeply unfortunate for the party and for Alan Milburn and Estelle Morris. It didn't do too much either for my efforts to get across our policy on law and order and criminal justice – but there we go.

I am afraid, however, that I shall remember this conference most for the irritation of other colleagues when Tony, in his platform speech, declared that I had the most difficult job in government. Given the issues, it is true that the Home Secretary of this moment has the hardest job after the Prime Minister's – but, goodness me, his comment didn't half get up some people's noses.

As ever, I had a stinking cold that week: going to conference is guaranteed to give me a cold if I haven't got one already. I suppose it is because we are all cooped up in fringe meetings every evening, as well as in conference itself, and bugs are passed round.

I have to say that what I used to find a pleasure as a young activist has now become a real grind. But fringe meetings do have their moments. The

Observer had organised a session with me in which they had done a special video and promoted the meeting on a couple of Sundays. Andrew Rawnsley chaired it extremely well and the meeting was one of the most successful fringe events I have ever done at conference.

I was to do an equally successful one with David Aaronovitch of The Times *a couple of years later.*

It was another of those occasions when I had the opportunity genuinely to explain the policy and get feedback and questions from the audience. It lasted an hour and a half, not like the meeting organised through *Tribune* magazine, where the atmosphere could have been cut with a knife.

In the 1970s and 1980s I would speak at the Tribune *rally which in those days attracted a couple of thousand people rather than a couple of hundred, and used to be the rallying point for the sane left of the party. But those days have long gone. This meeting was held in a seedy night-club where there was so much filth, stale beer and what appeared to be a coating of glue on the floor that I could not let my dog lie down.*

This was Old Labour at its worst – with the then General Secretary of the T&G Union launching a vitriolic attack on me, ranging from immigration through to drugs. (The T&G published a dossier to coincide with conference, attacking the fast-tracking process and accommodation centres for asylum seekers.)

The only other thing of note from this conference was where I stayed – in the room that Ted Heath had occupied, year after year, including when he was Prime Minister. It was a nice venue – Skipple Creek – and gave room for me to run my guide dog Lucy along the water's edge where boats were moored. The food was excellent but the room itself was extremely poky. There was just about room for Lucy to lie down.

I never liked going to Blackpool. As a northerner I should have really enjoyed being there, with the rawness and sense of history, but frankly I found it run-down to the point of seediness. At least this conference week, unusually the sun shone.

October 2002

When I wasn't doing numerous fringe meetings, I spent a good chunk of the week in Blackpool holding meetings and preparing for the announcement on immigration and asylum on Monday 7 October, which will cause a great deal of anguish and recrimination. I am trying to put asylum seekers on the same basis as everyone else with regard to entitlement to benefits and support, closing down on exceptional leave to remain, and effectively ruling out asylum from the ten accession-candidate countries coming into the European Union. It is just ludicrous that the Czech Romas should be able to come here and claim asylum. People are not going to like it, but I have to see these things through.

Alastair Campbell has asked me if I will do the first Cabinet ministers' live press conference of the new session on Monday the 14th, as Parliament resumes. It's a follow-through from Tony's open lobby briefings.

Odd little snippet from conference: I don't think I recorded the weird little paradox about the *Tribune* meeting and the fact that they'd made a terrible blunder by inviting Christopher Hitchens, who they believed to be a left-wing journalist – which he has been, but he is vehemently anti-Saddam Hussein and gave the most brilliant lecture about the background and the detail of the individuals and why taking on Saddam Hussein was so important. Everybody sat there in absolute silence, and the next person to get up to give fraternal greetings from the government was me! I think that was a lovely piece that the newspaper diaries never picked up. Bill Morris, needless to say, published further material on the Friday after the conference and ran it into the Monday, attacking the Nationality and Immigration Bill and accommodation centres – including engaging the Bishop of Portsmouth, of all people. So it's been a very funny time. Anyway, we will see what the week ahead brings. I've got several weeks of real tension coming up now, private as well as public.

The major internal issue during the week beginning Monday 7 October was the reorganisation of the Department and the all-day meeting of the Executive Board with the ministerial team. It was useful and revealing: everybody agrees on the analysis of the 'what' we ought to be looking to as well as the 'when' of doing it now, but not the 'how'. I had to get really tough and said that there needs to be a completely new revamp. If the Permanent Secretary is not to go – and it's quite possible that that might have to be the solution – then we probably need a second Permanent Secretary who is properly in charge of management change and delivery, while the current one does what he is good at, which is networking and the internal civil service. I've called a further meeting for a fortnight's time, at which we need absolute clarity about where we are going, what we are doing, those who have got to be shifted, bringing in new people, and a new personnel and human-resource element – because none exists at present. Ministers have just about had enough now, so something has got to give.

Given the Peter Hennessy stuff at the beginning of the Martin Sixsmith Channel 4 programme, it's very interesting to see just how much everybody now agrees entirely with my analysis, and I'm the one having to restrain them from doing something completely over the top. The sacking of a Permanent Secretary is, well, a nuclear option: they'd certainly get their own back on me, that's for sure. And I would need absolute backing from Tony.

There's no doubt that John [Gieve] had the most difficult Permanent Secretary's post in government. I did not always recognise this, but while I always liked him, I came to respect his professionalism, his loyalty and his ever-growing commitment to improving the delivery of our policies on the ground.

As I indicated on the Today *programme at the end of May 2006, I had weighed up the pros and cons of further change (because we had already made a great many changes), but apart from the fact that the disruption would have dislocated the progress we were making in reform and delivery, I saw no potential candidate – and the resistance to bringing in someone from outside would have been enormous – who could manage change better, and in any case the Permanent Secretary supported the reform agenda. Our problem was finding excellent people within the service who could be put in charge of key directorates, or persuading people from outside the service to come in, with all the risks to them, given the reputation of the Home Office. The more you talked the truth about the state of administration and management, the less likely you were to get good people to come. Again this was a point I made to Jim Naughtie on the* Today *programme when talking about the challenge facing the incoming Home Secretary, John Reid, following the reshuffle in May 2006.*

The week was all end-on meetings, starting with one on asylum with Tony, which went well. We got agreement to our way forward – which was very important because we had just announced it in the morning, though the *Today* programme didn't realise the significance of it, and did only a very brief factual interview with me. It took two days before the *Guardian* bit back with a leader attacking me, but otherwise coverage was very sensible.

We've had some stupid votes in the Lords, and the Whips are not doing a very good job. I had expected an attack on accommodation centres, but the idea that the Tories would get away with voting us down on our approach to removing from the country serious criminals who were claiming asylum was breathtaking. I don't know what the Tory Party think they are up to. There was another vote that went down by one.

I remain staggered that the Conservative Party got away with opposing our measures for dealing with serious criminals. The media would have utterly slain the Labour Party in such circumstances. The utter cheek of David Cameron and his front bench in spring 2006 over related issues is staggering, not least because the 'Notting Hill set' of Conservatives are more, not less, liberal than their predecessors. The collective memory of those reporting events – the broadcast as well as the print media – is so short, and departmental records are so poor, that you end up in a situation where only a handful of people ever remember what has been said or done. You would imagine that new technology would have made it easier and quicker to look back and access records. On the contrary, it has made 'moving on' and ignoring the past easier, as people deal only with the instant they are living in, rather than drawing on any kind of history or knowledge of the detail and background to a particular issue. I consider this very sad.

We had a Public Service Select Committee meeting on Thursday morning, at which I let rip about the accountability of trusts and agencies and NDPBs [non-departmental public bodies] separate from the Department, saying that the Treasury was obsessed with them. Alistair Darling is funny. At this meeting I said to him: 'Didn't you have trouble with the Benefits Agency when you were Social Security Secretary, and they were attempting to make policy themselves?' He replied that it was only a personality problem, and simply a matter of removing people. It was nothing of the sort.

Paul Boateng, Chief Secretary to the Treasury, has refused to meet Charlie Falconer [Minister of State for Criminal Justice] on the issue of the Criminal Injuries Compensation Scheme and the old scheme deficit – a massive £220 million. Firstly he said he would meet him on 31 October, after the deadline for the money running out; then said he would talk to him on the phone for quarter of an hour; and then pulled out of doing that altogether, so I'm just going to refer the issue to Tony. If the Chief Secretary won't talk to Charlie, that speaks volumes.

The really bad news of the week is the unravelling of the Northern Ireland Accord. I'm hoping that Tony will manage to find a way through it, but we will have to suspend the Executive. Tony has flown to Russia to see President Putin on Iraq, and there's a good deal of tension about that as well.

I went to the doctor on Saturday morning and got some antibiotics to keep me going. I am filling myself with pills at the moment.

An awful advice surgery, with 80 per cent of the people there about asylum or immigration cases, which wore me down. Then I had a lobby of so-called teachers claiming that they had 100 signatures of teachers asking for asylum-seeker children to be placed in school rather than our accommodation centres. What a bunch.

I've put on file a letter from Bernard Herden, the head of the UK Passport Service and the Criminal Records Bureau, because until I raised the issue of how a *Sunday Times* journalist infiltrated their organisation they'd still been employing temporary and agency staff without doing a proper vetting or even checking the last employment listed on their CVs, even though they'd been checking full-time staff through the whole vetting process.

Tony made a very powerful speech in Ireland on Thursday [17 October], challenging Sinn Fein and the IRA on the issue of decommissioning weapons. The clumsy raid on the Sinn Fein offices seems a fiasco – not the raid itself, but who authorised it, and why, and who knew in advance? The Chief Constable of Northern Ireland claims he didn't know about it. Everybody thinks that it was political. So there are some real shenanigans here that John Reid [Secretary of State for Northern Ireland] has managed to keep the lid on, though it must have been damned difficult. On Monday the Executive and Assembly were suspended and direct rule reimposed.

Also on the Monday I had the dubious honour of starting the new lobby press briefings with Cabinet ministers. As I said to Alastair Campbell, he really owes me one because they set me up as the damned guinea-pig. The briefing was held at the Foreign Press Association building, which used to be Gladstone's house. It was too small for the number turning up, and there was no direct lead for television. I thought I was addressing television via Sky and BBC News 24, and it turned out that I wasn't. If I had known that, I would have done it differently. The press didn't want to be there and were really grumpy about the new lobby system being imposed on them. But the *Financial*

Times covered it well on the Tuesday, and Andrew Marr [political editor of the BBC] did a sketch piece in the *Telegraph.*

Could I intervene on top-up fees? I've got to talk to Tony about that, as it is clear that he has been persuaded to go ahead and, what's more, to try and go ahead this session of Parliament – perhaps even without taking it through Parliament, which is an absolute commitment.

Estelle had a good week, with the Tories putting a Supply Day down, and she came out of it better. Tony did a really good Prime Minister's Questions on Wednesday [16 October], slaying Iain Duncan Smith on whether A levels have got easier – and he did so, it has to be said, with information that had been gathered not by the DfES but by Conor Ryan in his role as a freelance education specialist. Conor and I had talked on the telephone and unearthed the fact that all this had started with Gillian Shephard and Ron Dearing's committee, which seemed to have passed the DfES by completely. They just didn't seem to have grasped that crucial fact, and had Estelle had it at her fingertips earlier she'd have been in much less trouble. Anyway, she came out a lot better than she went in, thank goodness, but it is difficult to understand why Tony should want to put her at risk and expose her in this way on top-up fees, as it would be disastrous for her.

During the week the antibiotics that I got at the doctor's on Saturday began to work, but it is a bit wearing at the moment. I missed very greatly not having the break after party conference – but Tony is full of beans and taking on all comers.

It was encouraging on the Wednesday that the big staff meeting – 1,500 people – warmed to what I was saying. They genuinely appeared up for listening and for feeling part of the team, which is more than can be said for the Grade 3s that I addressed on Monday evening. We've got the most enormous struggle with motivating staff. One young woman, a graduate working at Croydon, said that the only work she had had in a month was two pieces of photocopying.

At the farewell reception for winding up the Criminal Justice Area Committees, I got on well with John Kay [Lord Justice Kay]. I met Harry Woolf coming in, and he had no idea what I was talking about when I said that I hoped that the Millwall football rioters wouldn't get treated any less favourably than the Bradford rioters. They just don't think of the race and community-relations aspects of these things, nor the public perception and policy elements. We've got a lot of court cases coming up and I just hope we win some of them – the SIAC hearing and the Oakington [asylum] case in particular.

I went to Margate to unveil, with Michael Winner, a plaque in memory of a dead policeman, then flew to Luxembourg where I at least managed a success. I got them to agree to the ten accession countries being declared safe, plus Austria; that we were able to add other safe countries as a European-wide agenda, and that they would change the reception directive to accommodate our new legislation on in-country claims [people who had been in the country for some time belatedly claiming asylum in order to get benefits] and withdrawal of benefit.

The Tories have made a right pig's ear of things in the Lords by voting down my tougher laws about those who commit criminal acts disqualifying themselves from asylum, so I'll be able to use that quite effectively.

I think the Lords is backing off a bit, because at the Committee Stage they didn't block our putting down the new measures, and the meeting with backbenchers had gone well, which was a good sign. No doubt Vera Baird and Jean Corston's Joint Committee on Human Rights is going to give us a hard time, but I am just going to go hell for leather and accept no less of asylum seekers than we ask of the indigenous population.

I spent a great chunk of the weekend going through the sex-offenders/sex-offences paper. I had to alter it quite drastically with regard to how it would be interpreted, or we would get wiped clean by the media.

The week starting Monday 21 October was an extraordinary one. (I know I say quite often that it has been an extraordinary week, but this truly was one of them.)

Most extraordinary of all – just totally out of the blue – was the resignation of Estelle Morris as Secretary of State for Education and Skills. She decided to do it on Tuesday, went to see Tony, and then confirmed it on Wednesday. None of us knew until early evening on Wednesday. She didn't contact me because, as she said to me afterwards, she thought that I would try to persuade her not to resign and she had decided she had to. She said that it was an accumulation of events, from the Criminal Records Bureau furore (which was D.J. Collins's fiasco, not hers – as head of the press office at the DfES he had briefed without getting ministerial clearance) through the A levels (which was the Qualifications and Curriculum Authority's fiasco), through the various trivial problems that were besetting the Department, to the point where the Tories accused her of having lied because she'd been on the record talking about resignation over the literacy and numeracy programme back in 1999. She'd meant that comment ironically, but it was interpreted as a serious comment and I believe she got in a panic. She was also worried about the Individual Learning Accounts audit report, which was entirely the fault of the Treasury for switching from Individual Learning Accounts to straight subsidy.

None of these added up to a bag of beans and all were perfectly manageable, and with decent advisers and a decent press office all of it could have been handled perfectly well. The worst thing was that she just declared herself as not being up to the job. I can understand her not being happy in the job. Lord knows, there have been times when I've been deeply unhappy and I've wanted out, but you realise that three months, three weeks, even three days later, you'd regret leaving. But sadly Estelle has done it, and has become the heroine of the moment – the honest politician, the person who says 'I'm not up to it', the person who says, 'I liked my previous job but I don't have the strategic approach to manage this Department.'

I fear that Estelle's resignation has done damage to the cause of women being promoted – to those who are not macho being promoted, and those who are not part of the metropolitan élite and glitterati being promoted – and even to Tony being prepared to take risks. All of this has been damaged.

But how can you not feel sorry for her, how can your heart not go out to her and want to support her, as some of us have tried to do for the last two months, desperately trying to bolster her and having more confidence in her than she has in herself?

Gordon and I did a press conference on terrorism and terrorist financing on Thursday [24 October] and I was asked about Estelle. I said that we had more confidence in her than she had in herself, but the dividing line between lack of confidence and over-confidence is a really fine one that we all tread with trepidation – and we do, because when you've gone, you've gone. It's like suicide. So it's all very sad, and sad for me in particular, because I pushed her really hard and got her into Cabinet. But what do you say?

Charles Clarke is now Education and Skills Secretary; John Reid has taken over as Chair of the Party; Paul Murphy has moved to Northern Ireland (which is sensible), and Peter Hain to Wales. Peter took the trouble to turn up to a drugs seminar and consultation with parents and community that I did in Aberdare on Friday [25 October].

I did the Rhondda fundraising dinner in the evening. It all went extremely well and they were very friendly and pleasant. But I realised that I'm getting old, because I did the drive to Wales, then drove back to Sheffield, getting home at 1 a.m., and it took me the whole weekend to get over it. I felt as if I had jetlag. Mind you, I was dealing with the further rewrite of the sex-offences/sex-offenders paper.

The civil service are resisting the Mental Health Bill in the Department of Health. Alan Milburn is in America but I raised it at Cabinet. Then in the *Independent on Sunday* appears a piece of silliness suggesting that conflict has taken place and that I'm interested in all this 'to reduce anti-social behaviour', whereas what I'm trying to do is to stop murder. It is unbelievable.

Wednesday was a particularly strange day. I was on my way to a dinner with Sir John Stevens, Keith Povey (Chief Inspector) and John Gieve when I learned about Estelle's resignation. It was an enjoyable dinner: good wine, good food, good argument. I'd already authorised the arresting of Abu Qatada, and halfway through the dinner John Stevens was rung by David Veness to say they'd picked him up. The security services – MI5 – had found him again, 500 metres from their headquarters. I had reauthorised the certification, but it was up to the Special Branch to pick him up as it was Special Branch who'd lost him.

When I got home on Wednesday evening, I was immediately phoned to say that Lincoln Prison had been seized by the prisoners. There wasn't a single prison officer left inside. The prison service started to equivocate about negotiations and what to do. First I spoke to Jonathan Sedgwick, then to my special adviser Kath Raymond, and to Martin Narey, in overall charge of correctional services. I said to Martin: 'I'm sorry but there's absolutely no question of dithering. If I have to ring Geoff Hoon and bring in the army so be it, but by dawn I want the prison retaken and I want order restored.' I said that I had read what happened twenty years ago to David Waddington, then Home Secretary, and that I was fully aware of what would happen if we dithered. There would be a chain reaction: other prisons would go, and the public would think we'd lost control. The television cameras from 24-hour rolling news, which didn't exist twenty years ago, would be there hour after hour, communicating with the prisoners and making a mockery of order. I said: 'Just get in there, and whatever it takes, do it.' By 5 a.m. they had retaken the prison; by 6.30 a.m., when I talked to Martin Narey, we'd got full control, and by the end of the day the situation was just a small item on the news. But we were within a whisker of having on our hands a total and utter catastrophe – and the difference between success and failure in these situations is just that: a whisker.

I believe that this was one of those occasions when my being there made a difference. It made a difference because I had read history; it made a difference because my instincts were that this was one that could be dealt with decisively; and it made a difference because I was able to strengthen the arm of those who were prepared to act and were prepared to override those who were dithering.

The worst ministers are those who won't make decisions, who want further information, who equivocate. The best are those who show leadership and are prepared, within reason, to take risks and be bold. The prison riots when David Waddington was Home Secretary lasted for weeks, with the most catastrophic breakdown of order within the prison service that we have ever seen in modern times. I was absolutely determined that we were not going to start that firestorm catching hold.

However, we had a really good piece of news on the Friday. We won the Appeal Court judgement on the Special Immigration Appeals Commission, which we'd lost when I was on holiday at the beginning of August. All three judges, including Lord Chief Justice Harry Woolf in the chair, ruled in our favour. But what silly nonsense we had from Liberty, from a lawyer who used to work for the Home Office and now works for Liberty – as though this was an outrage because Parliament's decision had been upheld. The democratic Parliament, the elected representatives of our country had won a judgement – and she declared how outrageous this was and entirely contrary to what Harry Woolf had said in a lecture a week earlier. And I thought: these people have no sense of understanding of public policy and the critical nature of democracy itself. Democracy does not rest on judges constantly overturning the democratic assembly.

What's interesting about this job is how little credit, knowledge or weight is given to the amount of time spent on security issues. People neither know nor care, and the media don't report on it because they've no real interest except when you are defeated. This is a substantial part of the Home Secretary's job now, not least after 11 September 2001, and yet the interest in it is partial. The security debate on 11 July generated no interest at all.

This week I've been working with John Gieve and Jonathan Sedgwick on the reorganisation of the department. It's proving to be hard work. I'm encouraging John Gieve, step by step, into reform and change. It is real hard work just getting across the enormity of what has to be done, particularly in immigration and nationality, but also across the board.

I had an early start on Wednesday morning because we had a security meeting at No. 10, looking at the aftermath of Bali and what that outrage meant. I had an equally early start on Thursday morning after the night to remember on the prison front, with a meeting about the Local Government Revenue Support Grant and the fact that the Office of the Deputy Prime Minister had put up a proposal that withdrew something between £40 million and £50 million from police authorities and redistributed it, including to district councils. What a joke. I really have to be on the ball. John Denham and I had had three meetings on all this before we got our own officials to pull their finger out. They'd just looked at it as though it was an ODPM matter and nothing to do with them. And if I hadn't had the background, as Leader of Sheffield, if I hadn't known it backwards from being on a local authority, we would never have delved into it and we would never have got it right.

So often, having been Leader of Sheffield proves outstandingly important in knowing how to reorganise the Department, how to take on the civil service, what questions to ask and where to go, and having the confidence and the ability to take on the challenge.

I spoke to Estelle, who's going to Aix-en-Provence for a few days. She said her worst fear was that she would have an empty diary, and asked if I could think of things that I could find for her to do. Of course, the empty diary is precisely what worries all of us. When our diary is too full, it puts us under pressure and makes life difficult, but the empty diary is like walking off the edge of a cliff.

I also spoke to Charles Clarke and he's going to have another go at Tony. He asked me what was driving Tony on top-up fees. I said that Tony has been heavily influenced by Oxford and Cambridge, but there's more to it than that. It goes back to Roy Jenkins and the desire to try to match the North American universities. I said to Charles that I had put forward the idea of trying to link with the more prestigious North American universities so that both research and teaching could be joint, but there is no way that we could ever compete with them. The issue of top-up fees has emerged again in the weekend papers, so good luck to Charles.

The siege by the Chechens in the Moscow theatre has been a complete catastrophe, with the gas they've used killing very large numbers of the hostages. We are still talking about having saved two-thirds of the hostages, but what a terrible state of affairs.

Monday 28 October: had dinner with Sarah and Conor and who should be there with Tim Brighouse and a colleague but Estelle? She was going off to Aix-en-Provence the following morning, but we were able to have a chat.

All sorts of odd things this week – like having to ring Nicolas Sarkozy to keep the wheels on the cart after Tony and Chirac had fallen out at the European summit meeting over the Common Agricultural Policy. The version at Cabinet was that it was Chirac who had been rude – and I believe it because Tony has never been rude in his life. Chirac had been rude to him because he was not used to people standing up to him. I restored relations with Sarkozy, who is easy to get on with, and he is still coming across even though the French summit has been cancelled. I said to him: 'All that's left of the summit is you and me, Nicolas.' He liked that.

They are going to close Sangatte to new entrants a fortnight early, which will help from the point of view of presentation, because we've had the Bill going through and the Tories enjoying giving us a hammering. They defeated us four times on Thursday [31 October].

But we will sort out the Bill, which, given what we've piled in at the last minute and the enormity of the changes we are making, is nothing short of a miracle. Nobody's really got across the seismic shift that we've brought about in this Bill.

We had the trial of Paul Burrell [former butler to the late Diana, Princess of Wales, who had been charged with the theft of some of her possessions] collapsing because the Queen had just remembered that he had had a conversation with her and she didn't want to give evidence. I knew about that forty-eight hours before it happened. We had the events around Iain Duncan Smith and people trying to pull him down. He made a better performance at Prime Minister's Questions.

But the Tories missed a trick by not doing Criminal Records Bureau on their Supply Day and messing about instead with Sinn Fein officers and human rights. I got Bev Hughes and Yvette Cooper [junior ministers at the Home Office and Department of Constitutional Affairs, respectively] to handle that, so Oliver Letwin pulled out. But I did the Order on Wednesday on banning the organisations. It was interesting because it stimulated my thinking after meeting the Yugoslav Federation Foreign Minister about border controls and what we are doing with NCIS

[National Criminal Intelligence Service] and NCS [National Crime Squad].

NCIS and NCS were subsequently combined into the Serious Organised Crime Agency.

I've been banging on about this for a year now but with everything else going on – police reform, nationality and immigration, criminal justice, drugs and everything else, including terrorism – I've not really had time to get a grip. But I am getting a grip now.

As so often, the decision simply to reshuffle the cards at the top of the Department is not working. I know I am impatient but it is possible to spot very quickly whether someone is performing or not. I need to kick some vitality into what is going on. For instance, on immigration and nationality, it is utterly useless: the Immigration and Nationality Directorate (IND) head Bill Jeffrey, six weeks on, has still not got a clear plan for getting rid of the dead wood and the sheer, incompetent lethargy going on in there. So on the back of a meeting after Cabinet on anti-social behaviour, where all of us agreed that we have to have a major push, I was asked to take charge of this, pulling across departmental agencies grouped together to work as a unit [the Anti-Social Behaviour Unit], along with people from outside. I have appointed Louise Casey because the Department has been messing about. She is the woman who ran the Rough Sleepers' Unit and had to take a hell of a lot of threats and intimidation.

Louise was later to run into a great deal of flak but I never regretted her taking on the Anti-Social Behaviour Unit. In this job, her failings (not being in any way a traditional civil servant and not always behaving in the way that all of us would wish) were a strength. It meant that the whole operation was going to be pushed really hard and that a spade would be called a spade. Above all, it meant that Louise would get out there and do the job on the ground, working with people and if necessary really pushing people at local level to believe that they could do it and translate good practice in one area into self-belief and reality in another. It was the 'It can't be done, nothing can be changed' attitude that I was trying to counter.

We had an impromptu meeting with the Secretary of the Cabinet and with Tony's PPS Jeremy Heywood at the conclusion of the anti-social behaviour meeting. We then somehow got on to organised crime and security, and

Jeremy volunteered that he had offered to do the Home Office job on serious organised crime. I said that my Permanent Secretary had not told me that, and had in fact moved the Head of Immigration into the job instead. I said that I would sort it all out, and since then my relations with my Permanent Secretary have become slightly frosty.

I am determined to get movement and change as rapidly as possible, because the presentations at the joint meeting with the Board were very reasonable and there was a good spirit. But it is carrying this through into practice that is important, particularly with IND, who are driving me bonkers. They have currently got only 1,600 removal places, taking into account that we lost Yarlswood. We were supposed to have 4,000, so if we take the 900 out of Yarlswood and take half of the Harmondsworth places (as it is being refurbished, with sprinklers, and is taking an inordinate length of time), we should still have at least 2,500 places but have only got 1,600. This is just incompetence. The IND are incapable of carrying through programmes rapidly. As far as Harmondsworth is concerned, they were proposing to finish it in spring 2004, which I am immediately doing something about. The ARC [asylum seekers' Application Registration Card], the new entitlement/identity measure for asylum seekers, was supposed to be in for this autumn and they are now talking about having 85 per cent coverage by next spring, so I am doing something about that as well.

Sometimes you do get a moment when people remember what you have done. It was really nice when I was giving a speech about the Mental Health Bill [finally dropped in March 2006], which was led by the Department of Health. This was intended to help with the situation in which severely mentally ill men or women could not be treated but were not therefore held in secure accommodation either but let out on to the streets. In the question-and-answer session, Judith Baptiste stood up and said that ten years ago her schizophrenic husband had tried to commit suicide, failed and was so badly injured that he was now a paraplegic. She recalled that I had gone in a taxi to see him in a run-down flat when he was on the edge of desperation, after she had gone on the radio to say that nobody cared. I thought it was really pleasing that she should have remembered that. I have always wanted to help those crying out for assistance.

Her husband had jumped from a building to try to take his life, and the attempt failed. I had heard her speak about it on the radio and got in touch just in case there was anything that could be done to lift his spirits.

We had an interesting meeting on the Budget, another area on which I have been heavily intervening. Philip Nye, a senior official in the Treasury, has been appointed by us and he is working miracles. He has already found how to route some of the funds that need to go into the old scheme for criminal-injuries compensation back to earlier years when the accounts have not been closed and where there were underspends. So instead of the proposition that had been put to me to find money by cutting other parts of the Department's programme, I have been able to deal with the enormous backlog in an imaginative way, just like when I was Leader of Sheffield City Council. He has also found a re-interpretation of the Treasury agreement at the time of the Spending Review that will release somewhere between £50 million and £100 million for Year 2 of the three-year programme, which is no mean feat and will help us enormously, including in expanding the police budget, which I am really worried about.

There was a continuing battle about police numbers. I was very keen indeed to expand them as part of the quid pro quo for the pressure we were bringing to bear on the police service, and this was to become even more important when I began to introduce community support officers and needed to avoid the fear that was expressed at the time (but has thankfully proved unfounded) that we were going to replace uniformed and fully trained police officers with CSOs rather than making the two complementary.

November 2002

It was good to celebrate Andrew's twentieth birthday and, on Friday [1 November], to get through the tests needed for the build-up to my throat surgery in a few weeks' time. It is deeply unpleasant to have tubes up your nose and down into your stomach, but it's a damn sight better than risking cancer.

On Saturday [2 November] I had agreed to speak at a fundraising charitable dinner in London for the MACS charity. This is a self-help group for youngsters born with no eyes and other disabilities, and provides support to parents as well as to the children themselves. Organising such a major event had clearly stretched this small charity's administration, and Valda Waterfield, my PA, offered to help them get sponsors and persuade companies to buy tables for the dinner. We contacted a large number of people, well known and not so well known. Richard Branson agreed to give two first-class return tickets to either Los Angeles or New York as a raffle prize, and with Huw Evans's help we got the *Sun* to do a piece about the dinner on Friday, inviting people to ring in and pledge £5 in order to be part of the draw for the tickets. I was just glad to have been able to help.

Back north on Sunday to get to a chiropractor appointment on Monday morning. I wish I hadn't made that appointment. As I was on my way up to the clinic, a member of my protection team let the door swing to just as my left hand was in the jamb between the hinges. I returned to London as planned, but my finger was very painful all day and in the end I had to go to St Thomas's Hospital, along with my friend Alan Billings, at about 9.30 in the evening. It was found that the finger was broken quite badly: 'shattered' was how it was described in the hospital.

The poor chap responsible for the accident never lived down the fact that it was a protection officer who injured me and not Al Qaeda, and it took about eighteen months before I could use my left hand with anything approaching normality, which made reading extremely difficult.

When I was in the Commons voting on the Adoption Bill, colleagues had advised me to find a walk-in health centre. Unfortunately they close at 9 p.m., which is why I had to go to St Thomas's A&E. They were really very helpful, but the place was full of drunks: goodness knows how the doctors and nurses survive.

My broken finger was a talking point at the launch of the new edition of my book *On a Clear Day* on Wednesday, which went very well: Alastair and Sarah came down. I did *Woman's Hour* on Radio 4, and in *The Times* on Thursday morning Melissa Kite wrote about my being a chauvinist. Talk about stereotyping: just because I said on the radio that men should be men and women should be women. I also did *Richard and Judy*, and they dug out the clip from 1968 when I clashed with David Dimbleby on the *Feedback* programme on BBC television. This was only my second ever television appearance, and was about my objecting strongly to naked bodies being shown in a morgue. It was the combination of the naked bodies and the idea of showing people in the morgue that had got me going. To do the BBC justice, they handled very well the discovery that they had on the programme a man who couldn't see, not having realised before I got there that this was the case. I was then pursued for months by Mary Whitehouse's National Listeners' and Viewers' Association, who saw me as a suitable recruit. It was strange to see a rerun of that programme – a very bumptious, self-opinionated young man, completely undaunted by having to deal with visual concepts. The sports presenter David Coleman chaired the programme and David Dimbleby (then a very young Dimbleby) was the maker of the film under discussion.

On a Clear Day was unlikely to – and indeed did not – make the bestseller list.

A normal Cabinet on Thursday [7 November]. Big news of the week is the unanimous vote of the Security Council on Iraq [the passing of Resolution 1441, which returned weapons inspectors to Iraq]. This is a very substantial victory for Tony's tremendous diplomacy and efforts with George Bush. Let's hope that the Iraqis respond so that we can reduce the threat of war.

We were not able to discuss this at Cabinet on Thursday, but we had a Cabinet Awayday on the Friday. I took the view then, and do still, that the vote of the Security Council was the watershed, the seminal moment. Everything else that happened afterwards sprang from the decision freely entered into by all those who later were to attempt to rewrite history, in which they agreed to lay down terms to Saddam Hussein – and if he did not comply fully, then the necessary action would be taken. This was the whole thrust of Resolution 1441 and for me compliance with that resolution was the crux of the matter, and not whether, in the end, weapons of mass destruction were to be found. The bluff of the international community was being called by Saddam Hussein, and failure to act would lead not merely to the diminution of the United Nations but to the aggrandisement and increased authority – and therefore power – of Saddam Hussein. Eleven years on from the first Gulf War, we were faced with the stark choice, and at that moment – whatever people felt later – it was clear to all of us that we meant business.

It was a very good Cabinet Awayday on the Friday, a three-hour meeting that I had to leave slightly early, just after Gordon had done his homily about the economy and the difficulties of trawling in revenue from the corporate sector and VAT (although VAT will be pretty good because sales are the one thing keeping the economy going).

The state of the Conservative Party at this time was such that their behaviour rarely featured in my diary, but in early November 2002 I did make a note about the antics of Iain Duncan Smith, and wondered who on earth was advising him.

Theresa May's remarks at the Tory conference about their being 'the Nasty Party' have been followed by Iain Duncan Smith's 'Unite or Die' plea. But they are so bizarre. They refused to have a free vote on the Adoption Bill (which we were having); they then got John Bercow [Conservative MP for Buckingham], of all people, resigning; and they had Shadow Cabinet members abstaining. They then had a tantrum and Iain Duncan Smith did these amateur dramatics on the television on Tuesday morning, which were so naff it was unbelievable, with other Shadow Cabinet members such as Theresa May, Oliver Letwin and Michael Ancram coming out on the platform and then Iain Duncan Smith emerging, pronouncing 'Unite or Die', and then disappearing without any questions. During the day when we had the six-hour debate on the Lords' amendments to the Nationality, Immigration and Asylum Act, we had the bizarre spectacle of Humfrey Malins [Conservative MP for Woking] talking to one of our propositions and saying, 'My Honourable Friend behind me . . .' – at which point he turned round and there was not a single Honourable Friend behind him. Everybody was hooting: there was nobody, but nobody, on the Tory benches.

Anyway we got the Nationality, Immigration and Asylum Bill through. The Tories had one last go at trying to make us avoid putting any accommodation centres in the rural areas at all. I moved a very carefully worded amendment. I had had amendments put to me and I devised one which the officials slightly altered but that was effectively mine, which talked about monitoring the need – that is, the need of an individual and whether it was being met by any accommodation centre – rather than monitoring the actual location of centres. Oliver Letwin managed to persuade his backbenchers that they had got what they wanted.

When I think of the struggle firstly to get internal agreement on investment for accommodation centres, and secondly to get this through Parliament, only to find that the other measures that I had taken and the change in the political environment no longer necessitated them, it makes me smile. I still believe that it would have been the right thing to do. It would have speeded up the process; it would have allowed for immediate removal of those who failed; and it would have lessened the pressure on inner-city communities that had enough to put up with already, with failed asylum seekers who could not be removed to countries where risk existed to their life and liberty, who were not in removal centres and not removable at that moment. This became an issue on which I can fairly say that, while I was obsessive, I was certainly right to be.

Tom Ridge, Homeland Security Secretary in the USA, has been over. I had two meetings with him, one a formal session in the House of Commons and another over dinner at Carlton House Terrace on Thursday night. As ever on these occasions there has to be something to say publicly afterwards, so we put together material for publication, partly to keep the public updated on what was happening and partly to ensure that the visit was not seen as a one-way street (with the USA in the driving seat). I had virtually lost my voice due to a very bad chest cold.

We have a word up North: 'mardy'. It is a very expressive word because it sums up what I am when I have a cold. In essence, it means feeling sorry for yourself or being self-indulgent and, above all in my case, going on about it. I fear I may have picked up this trait when seeking attention from the young housemothers when I was at boarding school at the age of four or five and needed a bit of tender loving care. These days they describe mardy men as having 'man flu'.

We are very jumpy about the activities of Al Qaeda. We have had no specific and therefore pinpointed warning, and given that general concerns are raised with me regularly, we've decided that unless we have clear and specific knowledge or something very focused to say, we won't put anything out that might scare the public. On this occasion, our real worry has been the London Underground.

And yet, by the Thursday, the heightened state of alertness had once again been stepped down. It is like the tide coming in and going out. We are getting this all the time now – an alert followed by stepping down, a worry followed by reassurance – all of which it is necessary to balance in order to ensure that the public do not feel these ups and downs, which would frighten them to death. Quite a lot of worry in the USA is about the way in which information is put out, but we have to balance that by ensuring that people do know what is taking place and that we are not hiding things that we should be putting into the public arena. Half the difficulty is knowing whether the security, intelligence and policing services are aware enough and have sufficient robustness to be able to stand up to the worries. It does take its toll, combined as it is with the daily grind of doing the warrants for tapping and surveillance.

I am making a lot of judgements by instinct, just by feeling in my guts whether the information being given to me stands up. Much of politics is like this. People expect it to be scientific and clinical – but it isn't.

There were occasions when I felt that people were running round in circles, when it was necessary to reduce the hype in order to be able to get at the nitty-gritty of what people knew, rather than what they were speculating about. And I had to make judgements about major events – for example, at this time, the approach of another Remembrance Sunday. This is an element of the job that didn't exist before September 2001. Even in the darkest days of Irish terrorism, MI5 had substantial intelligence and could expect warnings to be given.

A paper on threat levels and likely public reaction has been produced by fairly junior officials, and the original draft was so full of stuff about risk on various forms of travel that it made me start singing the great Burt Bacharach song 'Trains and Boats and Planes'. The paper's first version had the over-arching 'likely to be a threat' just about everywhere, and it is sometimes necessary to lighten the load in order not to go completely mad. We also had a problem in the original paper with reference to a 'dirty bomb' – just something calculated to get the media going in a big way. (A dirty bomb was a low-level nuclear device, but the term didn't really mean anything in practice.) I knew nothing about the fact that there was a minor error of a date being wrong but the paper had been sent back for this to be corrected. There appeared to be no proper system for proofreading, or for ensuring that early copies were eliminated, which I suspect was something to do with the way in which the computer system holds things. Anyway, it was the previous version which then got put out, rather than the revised and updated one. Immediately – and predictably – the hysteria started because the original referred to a 'dirty bomb'. We had to withdraw it and publish the updated one, with all the accusations of incompetence that are always coupled with whether we had something to hide and whether there was a plot that we weren't coming clean about, and whose fault was it? But clearly the youngster who was doing her best was not the one to have a go at, especially as I understood that the person in question had become a nervous wreck almost immediately and was in floods of tears and fearing for her job. So I sent a note there and then saying that all of us make mistakes and we expect others to put in place systems that help us to avoid them and to support and supervise.

I gathered later that this had an enormous impact, not just on the individual member of staff but on all those working at that kind of level in the Department, who realised that they would not always be jumped on from a great height and made the scapegoat. But I did think that the Terrorism and

Protection Unit might be just one place in the Home Office where triple care would be taken to make sure that we got things right, and that what went out was the final version rather than an earlier draft.

The first week in November concluded with my signing off the first ever National Policing Plan, and I had my constituency meeting on the Friday night and my advice surgery on the Saturday and then went down to London for *Breakfast with Frost* on BBC1 and the Remembrance Day service. This is two weekends running that I have been in London, which is very unusual for me.

One thing worth reflecting on from this week is the issue of the introduction of visas for those travelling from Jamaica. We have had enormous problems for the last two years with drug-running and gun-related crime, but the Home Office (and the Foreign Office) have been deeply opposed to the introduction of visas, and have come up with all sorts of costings and obstacles. In the end I just decided to take a political decision, knowing the flak that I would get, but believing that in the end it would be beneficial to the substantial Jamaican community in Britain – as well as to Britain as a whole – to have a system that works and to filter out the so-called 'mules', who risk their lives for very little reward in carrying drugs in the most dangerous ways possible – often having swallowed the bizarre containers – and then end up in our prison system.

This is certainly another example of where a political decision had to be taken which overrode the official advice and deep-seated worries – and where it worked.

I remain worried about Estelle. I have invited her round to dinner with other Cabinet ministers.

My abiding memory of the Queen's Speech was walking from the Commons to the Lords and being hit by an overwhelming smell of mothballs. I presume that the ermine had been retrieved from the back of the wardrobes.

On Friday 15 November Myra Hindley died. For once I agreed with Michael Howard when he appeared on the *Today* programme the following morning, when he said that we had to see her continued incarceration in the light of the abolition of capital punishment. That is precisely how I see it, but it is going to take some persuading to get people to agree. Hilary Benn and I have been dealing with a number of tariffs.

*We still had the power then, which we lost because of challenges through the
courts and by the European Court of Justice.*

So if we want to make 'life' mean life we have to give them a definite fifty
years, otherwise they will be let out God knows how much earlier. My
article in the *Daily Telegraph* on Tuesday was one of the best that I have
done while in government – though naturally the comment column
attacked it from a libertarian angle. The Tories really are going to have
to decide whether they are following a traditional or libertarian stance on
these matters, ranging from criminal justice and anti-social behaviour
through to counter-terrorism and threat to the nation.

   We have had another Cabinet photograph. This always makes me
jumpy, as it reflects another Cabinet reshuffle. How many more before
it's me?

*I was now endeavouring to get as much sorted as I could before going into
hospital on 8 December, including the difficult policy on sex offenders and sex
offences. Sex offences had not been modernised and reformed for 100 years
because it was such a difficult and sensitive subject. Jack Straw had begun to
tackle it in the first parliament, but it was necessary to find a formula which
balanced public decency with a recognition of private reality, protecting
children and coming down like a ton of bricks on paedophilia while reflecting
David Steel's Private Member's legislation of the late 1960s. Getting the
wording right was going to be crucial, and my diaries at this point reflect the
agony of having to consider the detail over and over again to ensure that the
balance was right.*

   *In essence I felt myself doing a Richard Nixon (when he recognised China)
from the standpoint of someone who, in the eyes of the liberal left, would have
been the last person to have brought in such radical measures. Newspapers like
the* Independent *reflected this schizophrenia, with compliments about the
changes and then scepticism that this could possibly have had anything to do
with me.*

So I published the proposals on sex offenders and sex offences, which got a
better and more rational response than I had expected – the *Independent*
grudgingly applauding and the *Daily Mail* covering them with balanced
reporting and no leader comment. I was really pleased, not least for Bev
Hughes and Hilary Benn, who had worked really hard on this over the
previous eighteen months. For me the Statement in the House went well,

with the Tories once again agonising about which way to jump and therefore being much more reasonable than I had anticipated.

One amusing moment came out of that most common of frustrations, a London traffic jam. I'd written to Alistair Darling, updating him on the most horrendous journey I had had coming into London on Sunday evening, and he had read from my letter when speaking at a conference a day or two later. *The Times* offered a bottle of champagne for the identification of who his correspondent had been – and the London *Evening Standard* speculated that it was me.

I never did claim the bottle of champagne. My digestive system would not have taken it.

The asylum figures published on Friday [29 November] were awful. The *Daily Mail* had got them the day before, virtually accurately – which is interesting given that they are official statistics. I had to insist that to coincide with them we completely changed the exceptional leave to remain, which is just an open door for everybody to claim that they cannot go back. We really do need to get a grip now. It doesn't matter what the liberals say – and they seem to cover the Tory Party as well as the Liberal Democrats and some of my own backbenchers. We have to address this if we are to have any kind of managed migration policy, any kind of considered, balanced cohesion policy for integration. Why can't people see what has happened across Europe?

Someone inside the immigration service is clearly deeply opposed to my agreement with Nicolas Sarkozy on the closure of Sangatte. The briefing on how people would come and where they would come, the follow-through from the Kent police – God knows what they think they are playing at. It surely has to be in the interests of the immigration service and the police for me to be able to settle this and to stop the magnet of Sangatte and the flow. It is like a dam that rests there with the floodgates opened every night. So come hell or high water and whatever the criticism, I am going to deal with this once and for all. I just wish there were more people on my side. I just wish that I didn't have the criticism from all angles – either I'm not doing enough or doing too much, either I'm unsympathetic or far too sympathetic, or I'm too strong-willed or don't have the will. And, of course, as a politician I am bound to have some hidden agenda.

December 2002

Discussions with Nicolas Sarkozy on Monday [1 December], and again on Tuesday morning. A lot of work had gone into the Monday evening meeting prior to dinner. I wanted it to be a nice social evening because Nicolas was not only bringing his wife Cecelia but her daughter Judith, who was coming down from the University of Sheffield for the dinner. Nicolas wanted Peter Mandelson to be there as he had known him from way back, but obviously the meeting between ourselves was private. What became clear the moment we began to talk was that Nicolas knew entirely what my strategy was. He knew the maximum numbers that I was prepared to take and he knew the detail of the transmissions between my Department and the British Embassy in Paris.

It is not at this stage in the best interests of either country for me to speculate on how he had this information. That will be for another day. Suffice it to say that it took me about five minutes to realise that my bottom line was his top line. In order to get agreement on long-term security and immigration posts along the French coast as well as the early closure of Sangatte and good and strong security at the freight depots, I was going to have to give on numbers – specifically the Iraqi Kurds who were congregated in Sangatte. This is the worst of all worlds: having to agree my bottom line in a public environment where briefings have been purely about what it is that I am having to give and nothing about what it is that I have gained. It feels like sabotage. Gordon and I had agreed that part of the Autumn Statement [now usually known as the Pre-Budget Statement] highlighting the importance of managed, legal economic migration, but Andrew Green, the ex-diplomat who constituted an organisation called Migration Watch, was able to have a field day with the juxtaposition of agreed increases in legal migration on the one hand and the presentation of 'capitulation' to the French on the other.

It was from this time that the BBC started to take seriously one-man organisations such as Migration Watch and give them air space. The Daily Mail *and the* Daily Telegraph, *for obvious reasons, had been quite prepared to take articles or stories on the back of short reports (often drawn straight from the statisticians in government), but it was new for the broadcast media to take them seriously. There appeared to be then, and still appears to be, no editorial control over the weight to be given to one organisation as opposed to another – in simple terms, whether an organisation had substantial research capacity, whether the work being undertaken was truly value-added, and whether there was an organisation behind the individual being presented under the banner of some fancy name or other. (Privacy International was another that was to emerge in a similar vein.) Having been in the Diplomatic Service, Andrew Green also had the benefit of a knighthood which, like the term 'doctor', always adds a bit of weight to the otherwise spurious or low-level.*

My mood hasn't been helped by the fact that I have had fifteen cassettes to clear over the weekend, and then the trip back down to London for the dinner at the French embassy on the Sunday evening. Mind you, even in my grumpiest moments I do sometimes get a laugh. On the Friday night when I was travelling to West Yorkshire to speak at a fundraising event in Yvette Cooper's Pontefract constituency, I received a phone call from my office to clear a security warrant. Nothing exceptional about that. However, when I got back home, I found two messages relating to this on my answerphone – one ringing me when I was clearly on my way to West Yorkshire, which was in the diary, and one ringing back saying: 'Please ignore the previous message, because I have just spoken to you on your mobile and therefore we have dealt with it.' I have to say that instead of being angry at the stupidity of it, I just burst into laughter. The fact that this official had dealt with it via me did not seem to have occurred to him when then telling me on my answerphone that he had already dealt with me!

Nevertheless, despite the fact that here we have people who would not be alive today, never mind here in the UK, had they not passed through safe countries to get here, those with a Jewish heritage attack me. I find this really difficult to take, and it makes me very angry.

The proof will be in the eating of the pudding – if we can get asylum and immigration down, if what I've done accomplishing the closure of Sangatte shows that economic migration not asylum was behind it, and if we can begin to improve the competence of the Immigration and Nationality Directorate. Contrary to what my accusers say, I did make the situation clear in the Statement to the House on Monday [2 December]. That morning I had already met the MPs from northern France, the mayors of all the localities (including the Communist mayor of Calais) and the Prefect of the region, all of them committed to cleaning the area up, to new security measures, and to overcoming the tolerated illegal presence – because they need to for their own purposes.

The *Guardian* got it right for once in their leader on Tuesday morning when they said that the newspapers that had campaigned most for the closure of Sangatte would be the ones who would be most opposed to what I'd done – and it was true.

Meanwhile I published the updated drugs strategy which, it has to be said, was pretty widely welcomed on the Tuesday. I had to do the Criminal Justice and Sentencing Second Reading on the Wednesday together with the launch of the volunteering and giving paper with Gordon. Then I had to sort out the police grant and the funding for police for the coming year, which the chief constables savaged even though it was 6.2 per cent, as against 2 per cent inflation.

All these things in a week when I am under enormous personal and emotional pressure coming up to going into hospital. I am trying to sort things out but am feeling the sword of Damocles hanging over my head. I am also dealing with all sorts of other things that are going on behind the scenes. I had meetings in No. 10 on the catastrophe of the IND, firstly round-table Cabinet Room meetings and with Tony, John Gieve and Andrew Turnbull privately in Tony's study. We discussed the changes within the Department and the need for much, much more radical reform. I had private meetings with Bill Jeffrey [Head of the Immigration and Nationality Directorate] and Bev Hughes about IND and about the failure to implement the ARC card in place of the corrupt letter.

I have already explained that the ARC card was the forerunner to the ID card, but solely for asylum seekers. This replaced a simple letter that was sent out without any security or personalisation so that when it was duplicated (and sold) to other illegal immigrants, they could then claim, using the letter as proof of identity. It was a crazy system and its replacement took far too long, to the point where we had lost some of the momentum and credit for having made the change. It did, however, help us dramatically clean up abuse of the system, not only the false claims but also where people continued to claim long after their entitlement had ceased, and in finding out the true nature of the claims made by local authorities (where, before the National Asylum Support Service was established, local authorities were responsible), which was mopping up hundreds of millions of pounds in rent on accommodation.

We also discussed the correspondence system, where the civil servants had claimed to have eliminated the backlog of ministers' correspondence –

literally thousands of letters. It turned out that they had eliminated the backlog by setting a date of 30 June as the cut-off point for catching up – except that the backlog in July, August, September, October and November still existed. They had eliminated a backlog by cutting out four months! This is the Department I have to oversee, where I have no power, as I said in the Commons on Monday, to sack or to appoint.

But the criminal justice and sentencing debate on Wednesday went well. I spoke for an hour and ten minutes, taking all the interventions, and it felt good. I was pleased with that performance – it redeemed a poorer showing on Monday.

It is interesting looking at my diary to see how little I recorded of that day, bearing in mind the significance of the Bill that we were introducing, the most radical reform of the criminal justice system for as long as anyone could remember. Much of its impact we knew would not be felt for years, with the exception of minor misdemeanours and the introduction of automatic supervision of prisoners on release, which were being brought in immediately.

On the other hand, a revision of the rules of admissibility and the use of forensic and scientific evidence would reform a system that was effectively rooted in the late Middle Ages: double jeopardy. Each stage of this Bill, including aspects which the legal profession made it clear they would never allow to rest (such as life meaning life and new terms for judges to follow more generally in relation to murder), was fiercely fought. Taken together with the forthcoming anti-social behaviour legislation and the passage of the Nationality, Immigration and Asylum Act (and the work on the forthcoming sex-offenders/sex-offences legislation) this has to be one of those seminal periods in rebalancing and modernising the law in which I take greater pride in retrospect than I was ever able to do when I was battling away, clause by clause, to get through what in general now is accepted as unexceptional but which at the time was denounced in vehement terms.

It struck me that I have to come up all the time with alternative ideas, otherwise I'd be finished. That's what it's been like all week – manoeuvring, thinking, working through. But nobody sees that, nobody sees the background, the preparation, the complete revision of papers, the detail that has to be gone through, as with the debate on criminal justice, so that you are not caught out, so that your words are clear, so that you understand each and every section and clause. And what credit do you get?

I often wonder when I do let my emotions show whether something clicks politically in my head, because I had been thinking about letting in these Iraqi Kurds and the publicity around the closure of Sangatte, and wondering whether it would give a real opportunity to Migration Watch and organisations like it which are now getting a higher and higher profile, as I predicted they would, for their goal of what amounts to no immigration at all. It is a ridiculous policy that could never be implemented, and in any case, as American evidence has shown over the last fortnight, it would be catastrophic economically, not least because of the demographics and profile of the work-force. So I have decided, consciously or subconsciously, to up the ante by trying to stop the tide coming up the beach before it gathers momentum. The critics are really in a cleft stick, because I'm the one who's raised all the difficult issues over the last year without saying that we should adopt a right-wing policy, and yet they had to attack me, and by doing so they were diverted from what otherwise would have been a barrage of criticism against the policy itself, which would be extremely dangerous for community and race relations as well as for the government. So it's funny how you do something and temporarily people gasp and think, 'Oh God, he's blown it, he's let his temper show' – but a lot of people like your temper showing sometimes. In any case, it pushes other people back so they have to pause, and if they pause long enough the moment and the momentum have passed.

I was busy on Friday and Saturday in the constituency. I visited Brendan Ingle's gym; I met with representatives of UNISON; I had meetings in the town hall; held my surgery; opened the new Sure Start facility at Shiregreen and Firth Park and the North Sheffield Forum community building; and switched on the Christmas lights at Firth Park. I did all this as well as trying to finish all the correspondence and tidy things up so there are as few loose ends as possible before I go into hospital.

Just a little thought: if any of the senior civil servants had to do my advice surgery, if any of them heard what was going on in the real world and could see how the administration and its incompetence affected people and how people saw the Home Office in all its guises, they would surely be motivated to do something about it. But they're completely cocooned; they're isolated and protected from it all. That's why they don't have a clue.

As I have said before, things did begin to change and there were many people in the service (as there had been in Education and Employment) who warmed to the idea of really changing people's lives. I put this down to two things: firstly, I was driving people mad by constantly drawing attention to failures and to the

With my mother in Skegness, aged eighteen

At Albrighton College, aged nineteen, 1966

With Ruby, 1972

Councillors training for the Sheffield Marathon: Sam Wall, Peter Price,
Mike Bower, myself and Clive Betts

Elected as MP for Sheffield Brightside, with friends Joan Barton
and Peter Price, June 1987

Tony Blair and members of his Shadow Cabinet (*from left*: Gordon Brown, Margaret Beckett and myself) pose at a news conference on the first day of the election campaign, February 1997

Leaving 10 Downing Street as the new Secretary of State for Education and Employment following Tony Blair's public announcement of Cabinet appointees in his new government, May 1997

Budget Day: Jack Straw, Geoffrey Robertson and myself, March 1998

Visit to Firth Park Summer School for Gifted Children, Sheffield, September 1999

Tony Blair playing guitar and myself on drums at Firth Park Community College, Sheffield, February 2003

At Lewes Prison, East Sussex, where the first touch-screen computers giving inmates access to all job vacancies across the country and Europe have been installed, August 2002

Meeting police officers maintaining security during the week of the Labour Party conference in Bournemouth, October 2003

Standing with the Queen at Horse Guards awaiting the arrival of Russia's President Vladimir Putin, June 2003

With HRH Prince Charles at the first citizenship ceremony for immigrants seeking British naturalisation, London, February 2004

Walking beside Margaret Beckett through the Central Lobby of the Palace of Westminster to listen to the Queen's speech during the State Opening of Parliament, May 2005

Wearing a ceremonial *tilak* in the Shree
Ram Mandir temple in Southall, south-west
London, September 2003

Wearing a Sheffield Wednesday scarf leaving
Downing Street, November 2003

Left to right: Italian Interior Minister Giuseppe Pisanu, Spanish Interior Minister
Angel Acebes, French Interior Minister Nicolas Sarkozy and I
take a rest after meeting in Jerez, May 2003

Sitting on stage as my guide dog Sadie rolls over at the Labour Party conference, September 2005

Tony Blair listening to my keynote speech to the Labour Party conference in Bournemouth, October 2003

Reading braille notes at the Labour Party conference, October 2002

Meeting students from Bishop Thomas Grant School in Lambeth, south London, while attending the launch of a video intended to educate children away from crime, December 2004

Asylum seekers demonstrate at Calais harbour as French Interior Minister Dominique de Villepin and I inspect new detection technology at the ferry terminal. Two years after the closure of Sangatte refugee camp we agreed to build on recent successful co-operation between services tackling illegal migration networks, November 2004

With singer Andrea
Bocelli and Tony Blair in
Tuscany, August 2004

Sadie, my guide dog, rests
her paws on the shoes of
Tony Blair as we visit the
asylum screening unit in
Croydon, south London,
August 2003

With singer Katie
Melua the day after my
reappointment to the
Cabinet after a private
concert, May 2005

At St Paul's Cathedral for the National Memorial Service dedicated to victims of the 7 July bombings. Victims' families, emergency service workers and survivors joined dignitaries including Tony Blair for the one-hour-long service, November 2005

Transport Secretary Alistair Darling and I talk to resident Betty Chirray during a pre-election tour of a housing estate in the Broomhouse area of Edinburgh, April 2005

Arriving home in Sheffield following my resignation as Home Secretary, December 2004

Leaving home in the run-up to my departure from government, November 2005

consequence of failures out in the field where it mattered; and secondly, and more positively, I think my own commitment and enthusiasm for improvement and change rubbed off on some of the best people in the civil service. They pulled together and began to believe that what they did was really worthwhile in ameliorating the lives of those at the sharp end.

I am now out of hospital safely. Professor Michael McMahon and his fellow consultant Simon Dexter were wonderful. They couldn't have done more and they couldn't have been nicer, and now I've got to learn to digest again. I've got to learn like a baby to move from sloppy food to solids, from eating tiny amounts very often to eating more substantial things infrequently – in other words, to regain the art of eating, digesting and enjoying. It's funny how both the anaesthetic and the air that was pumped into me – because they have to make you into some kind of tent in order to use the instruments safely and to have space inside you – both take a very long, long time to disperse (highly embarrassingly, in the case of the wind), and they don't add to the ease of taking in food. But what a wonderful thought that if this works the chances of oesophagus cancer lessen enormously. They don't disappear altogether – they can't – but the chances of my getting cancer are now lower than in the population as a whole, rather than a threat lurking at the back of my mind.

People have been very warm, and I've had lots of goodwill messages. I'm very anti-social at the moment and I only want those people to visit me who will make me feel better. But it's good to have good friends and you know who they are when they care for you even when the heart is heavy, when they look after you and feed you and make sure you're comfortable. A man is very lucky to have friends like that.

To give them credit for once, the press have left me alone, mind you. On 10 December there was quite a lot in the papers about my operation – including a very good piece in *The Times* about what was involved. There was a strange little statement by Jack Straw on the back of the Intelligence and Security Committee report about the Bali bombing, where he described my operation as a minor one: goodness knows it wasn't and it certainly doesn't feel minor!

Cherie Blair has been having a really rough time, one way or another, and I have kept in touch with her to offer support.

The Treasury has fallen out with us again because we insist that the Green Paper, their element on pensions, should specifically rule out taking away the lump sum from the police because, if we don't, there's no doubt whatsoever we will have a mass exodus of people getting out while the going's good and it'll completely jigger our numbers.

On *The Westminster Hour* on Radio 4 on Sunday evening I heard the Treasury being applauded as the only truly efficient department in Whitehall. But they don't run anything – they just try to run everyone else. They don't run monetary policy; they're responsible for fiscal policy but that's not running something, that's not administering, that's not delivering, that's not having to make changes, managerial or otherwise.

Everyone at the Department agrees that while I have been away from my desk Nick Pearce has been doing a fantastic job, working with Bev Hughes on sorting out the aftermath of the Sangatte decision. Bev has held the fort magnificently and is having the most enormous struggle with her own officials to try and get them to use any kind of initiative. But we will have Sangatte closed by the end of this week, and then we need to see what the figures are for December, and then what they are for the New Year.

It is interesting to see which newspaper editors got in touch while I was recuperating. Rebekah Wade sent me a massive basket of fruit from her and Ross Kemp. Paul Dacre sent me champagne and flowers and a little cryptic note – and I have sent him a cryptic one back! David Yelland sent his best wishes via Paul Potts, who has been very helpful.

I'm getting back to work by chairing meetings on the Immigration and Nationality Directorate, on the Criminal Records Bureau, on anti-social behaviour and on departmental change. I have just got to get these things moving and give them a shove and make sure that I have got the policy material on prostitution, on entitlement cards and on anti-social behaviour, which I need to push on with really hard – as well as the paper on domestic violence. I must have these prepared for the New Year so that we don't end up with a last-minute rush – but I do need also to find time to take it easy. I keep falling asleep still.

We were still calling ID cards entitlement cards at this stage, as we had not yet had the polling evidence that showed that people much preferred to simply call them ID cards. I always felt that entitlement was what this was all about, but sometimes you just have to ride with what people are easiest with.

I have spoken at length to Margaret Hodge [Minister for Lifelong Learning and Higher Education] about top-up fees. We are getting ourselves into a terrible mess. Just before I went into hospital, Tony looked as if he had backed off them when he hadn't, but they are going to go for a system where, in my view, they simply increase the fee that is paid and remove the subsidised interest rates, extend slightly the Opportunity Bursaries and call this a grant, and allow people to defer paying.

I've just heard that a television programme in January is going to reveal that fraudsters managed to obtain a driving licence in my name, and one in the name of Frederick Forsyth. They also used Frederick Forsyth's name to obtain a fraudulent credit card.

Iraq is still dominating the news, and together with the continuing friction, fractions and disintegration of the Conservative Party, we move towards Christmas.

I have been supported and helped towards Christmas by Alastair, Hugh and Andrew and good friends, and I shall do my best to enjoy it although I can't eat very well. I am taking soup and porridge and trying to mash everything down, so it is going to be the smallest, longest and most chewing Christmas lunch I have ever had! I have had to keep checking with the hospital whether what is happening to me – not being able to swallow things and feeling absolutely dreadful – is normal. Apparently it is. But I am not letting on to the world how bad I feel.

Christmas 2002

Well, I survived Christmas. Alastair did a first-rate job of entertaining everybody with helium balloons at the Cavendish Hotel, where we had a family lunch on Christmas afternoon. It worked out well and was much better than if we had tried to cook and wash up. The good news is that I am gradually getting more and more food down. The bad time that I had leading up to Christmas seems to have eased, and I was able to eat some Christmas lunch – a little bit of turkey and mashed potato. I am doing better now and getting there, bit by bit, thank the Lord.

Estelle came on Boxing Day, and Val Woolrich from the Guide Dogs for the Blind Association brought Sadie, who is to replace Lucy, to see me. It was very strange. Val rang me and said that she was in Sheffield. I needed Sadie to know where to go on our walk from the cottage and how to get back, and she brought her out to Derbyshire, which was helpful.

In addition to my house in Sheffield, which I'd bought back in 1988, I had for some time rented a cottage on the Duke of Devonshire's Chatsworth estate in Derbyshire.

So we had Lucy, Barney (Val's dog) and Sadie all running together. We then fixed for the end of January for Lucy to retire. It is going to be a very strange year. I have got to steel myself to see through whatever hits me.

I also worked very hard over the Christmas break. I revised the paper on prostitution, and completely ripped apart the first draft of the Anti-Social Behaviour White Paper. I spoke to Louise Casey on New Year's Eve about rough sleepers in London, just before she started full-time with us on heading the Anti-Social Behaviour Unit. In addition I completely rewrote the race equality paper, which might well have been written by someone with no knowledge whatsoever, apart from some feel for the gesturism of the 1980s. I also did some work on the future of the Criminal Records Bureau, and I have got to set about looking at entitlement cards and the question of access to communications data and RIPA (Regulation of Investigatory Powers Act).

This issue, catching up on a delay of two years in laying the regulations, was to cause me considerable grief.

January 2003

I got a message from Gareth Redmond, the new PS who has taken over from Gareth Hills, saying that officials claim that they can't manage to get the material on gun crime together and have a proper paper to publish next week on the decision taken in December. This is that anyone found guilty of carrying a gun would automatically get five years or more in prison. Just after I had told him to go back to them and say that if they couldn't do it, they should resign, the *World at One* programme came on and was absolutely full of gun crime: killings in Birmingham and the siege in Hackney. The whole thing is gearing up again, I can just feel it.

I've sent Tony a note on his return from his holiday in Egypt because I didn't think much of his New Year message. I thought it was Harold Wilson all over again, where we put doom and gloom on everybody. People just don't like that. They don't want doom and gloom from the government: realism, yes, but not doom and gloom.

I then received a phone call in relation to the approach to the Foreign Office by the USA, requesting that I allow several thousand so-called Iraqi oppositionists whom the Americans want to nominate, to come to this country to be trained. I said: 'Tell them to train them in America. We are not taking them, not after the decision on Sangatte.' I am not having the Iraqis here in large numbers. The public just wouldn't stand for it. I did a note to Jack in his capacity as Foreign Secretary saying that we don't owe the Americans anything on Iraq – and we don't, they owe us.

But the Home Office is a weird department, and no mistake. There is no sense or feel for the rhythm of politics, how the tide is flowing and the need to be ahead of things rather than trailing behind.

I still feel tired. I am not really ready to go back to work but I have got to. I have had to deal with the gun-crime issue, which was going to be big anyway on account of the statistics that are to be released on 9 January, but has now really blown up because of the killing of two teenage girls in Birmingham by gun gangs. I had worked very hard indeed in November to get the Street-Crime Group to agree the five-year minimum sentence for carrying a gun. With the assistance of John Stevens and John Denham – John Stevens to raise the issue, John Denham to ask the Prime Minister whether he would approve it going ahead – I'd managed to manoeuvre so that we wouldn't get blocked by Robin Cook in the Legislative Programme Committee.

I also had the preparation on air guns and replica weapons which I will put into the anti-social behaviour legislation. All of that took long, long preparation – but I then get accused of knee-jerk reactions and gimmicks. I have agreed to pull everybody together for a round-table discussion, which is the least I could do, on the back of the statistics – never mind the fuss in the press.

It is an odd world where if a government doesn't have the drive and momentum – and, it has to be said, the energy – to be dealing with real issues in real time, they are accused of having lost the plot or having run out of steam. If they do have genuine policies, albeit a range of different policies to deal with different issues, the government is accused of 'gimmicks' or 'knee-jerk reactions' and – even worse – 'populism'. Of course, a democracy that doesn't respond to the fears and concerns of men and women across the country is one that fails. So it is not surprising that opposition parties are quick to cry 'gimmick', but it is a bit odd when others who should know better will on one day use this stick to beat the government and on the next day do the very opposite.

So we have known all this was coming and we just have to get stuck in – but I know inside myself that when all this has gone, the public profile, the ability to intervene, the chance of changing policy, of saving, never mind improving, people's lives – when all of it has gone, there will be a vacuum. And if that vacuum is not filled by what Denis Healey called 'the hinterland', then you really are as good as dead.

A further thought on the first few days of January: the number of times I have heard Louise Christian, human-rights lawyer, on the radio presented as 'the lawyer', not as 'a political activist', not as someone who has been politically active for the past twenty-five years, firstly as a member of Militant Tendency and a fellow traveller. It is clear that the political correspondents don't know because, with the exception of people like Michael White and Andrew Marr, their collective memory only goes back about five years at the most. They have no idea who she is.

I think the best way of describing the first full week back in politics – at least external politics, having done all the policy and paperwork over Christmas and New Year – is just to say that for the first time in six years as a minister I had to go to a London chiropractor – not once, but twice. On Tuesday I could hardly move my neck and shoulders. I could barely manage to get out of bed, and had to roll on to the floor. It is a combination of personal and political pressure, but there is no doubt whatsoever that a month doing background work but not front-line politics is not a good preparation for the sort of week that I had. When you are away from the front line, your whole system runs down and goes into a different gear, and it takes a hell of a lot of strength and will-power to get back up again. I don't just mean in terms of productivity – I was doing the interviews for the chairmanship of the Commission for Racial Equality and for the Head of the National Criminal Intelligence Service, and all the usual meetings and preparation for major speeches – but the sheer grind of having to deal with issues that come flying at you from all angles, many of them entirely not of my own making – nor, it has to be said, of the Home Office's.

An example would be Derry Irvine's lengthy pre-recorded interview with Jim Naughtie, conducted at the end of the previous week. They didn't warn us what he had said, they made no effort whatsoever to prepare and they had no handling strategy. When he did the interview, Derry knew perfectly well what he was saying in relation to burglary and his backing of the Lord Chief Justice against our very tough line. If he had the slightest touch of political nous, he would have known that there was going to be a storm. And it certainly did cause a storm – a donkey brought by the *Sun* to Downing Street and on to the Lords, and sheer ridicule from all the tabloids and some of the broadsheets. Combine this with smaller things such as trying to handle the fact that, because the Prime Minister's Office had said Tony was going to do the announcement on replica and conversion guns and air pistols, we didn't announce it at the same time as the introduction of the five-year mandatory sentence. Now Tony, having come back from his holiday, has decided that he is not doing it after all, so we are left having to do it later in the week, making us look incompetent.

This was the beginning of a very bumpy ride indeed. A whole range of circumstances combined to make the following three months extraordinarily difficult – but more than that, to undo some of the good work that had been done by ministers and officials across the board (involving all the departments engaged with criminal justice) over the previous year, including the great success in reducing street crime. From time to time, every government hits a difficult period domestically, although in the case of the Labour government from 1997 it has generally been foreign policy which has given us the greatest grief. It is rare, however, for an own goal to have such ramifications as this episode did, and it reinforced in my own mind how important it is, ridiculed as elected MPs might be, for us to remember that those who are elected learn a great deal over the years about the likely reaction to what they say and do. That is the difference between good politicians and those who should be in administration.

Then there was Kim Howells, who, in dealing with the issue of gun and black-on-black crime, decides to attack the world of rap. I therefore get asked about it on the first ever Jeremy Vine programme (which has replaced the Jimmy Young programme), and on Monday John Denham gets asked about nothing but that on *The World at One*. What Kim Howells has said has been interpreted as what I have said. For instance, in the *Sun* a young man wrote a whole article predicated on what I am allegedly saying about rap, when it wasn't me who said it.

Then *The Times* ran a story saying that there wasn't going to be a five-year minimum sentence and that I had had to back down. We therefore got all the usual business about U-turn, backing down, weakness, semi-incompetence, etc., which was enormously damaging. It completely undermined the message and the credibility of what we were doing, and allowed people to accuse us of confusion. So with the Kim Howells business added to the delays about what announcements we were going to make and added to Derry Irvine and the burglary business, we had a real porridge on our hands. All this was followed by the emergence of the statistics on recorded crime and British Crime Survey figures on Thursday, which we knew were coming.

There are lies, damned lies and statistics, but the saga of the difference between recorded crime and the British Crime Survey is one sufficiently labyrinthine to finish off even the most dedicated reader. Suffice it to say that the refined and expanded British Crime Survey had lasted for twenty years under all political parties and was seen as the most reliable measure of how crime was moving.

On the other hand, recorded crime was affected by the new recording standard brought in by the Association of Chief Police Officers before I took over. This recorded all sorts of things, including the most minor incidents such as pushing and shoving (recorded as violence) and things like an egg being thrown at the wall of someone's house. Not surprisingly when police numbers had been cut in the era of Michael Howard as Home Secretary, recorded crime had gone down while British Crime Survey statistics had shown a rise in crime. Now we had a drop in British Crime Survey figures of substantial proportions, but a rise (which was reversed) in recorded crime as police numbers started to rocket.

I mention this only to show how perverse what otherwise would appear to be straightforward statistical reporting can be. No wonder the British people are confused as to who is telling the truth about what, when and how.

The other big accusation of the week is that of 'knee-jerk reaction'. I have said to John Denham that he should use ridicule to dismiss this when he is on the radio. We need to say that it is ludicrous to believe that when youngsters are killed in Birmingham on New Year's Eve, I have policy clearance to add a new measure to the Criminal Justice and Sentencing Bill by Friday morning – which is when we first confirmed it to *The Times*. Phil Webster of *The Times* had picked up, in a way that those in the Department hadn't, that we had raised and mentioned this issue before. The following week, not one of his colleagues writing leaders acknowledged that fact: instead we get 'knee-jerk reaction', we get 'too little, too late', we get 'piecemeal', we get 'panic', and then, of course, we get 'U-turn'. And on top of everything else, with Derry we get 'confusion' – and Tony ridiculed as well as me on the 'tough on crime, tough on the causes of crime' pledge.

Tony called Derry in with Charlie Falconer and myself on Tuesday morning, and I have never witnessed him so angry with Derry. I couldn't resist saying part way through the meeting: 'You see, Derry, you wouldn't be in this job at all if there wasn't a Labour majority and a Labour government. It would be a Tory Lord Chancellor.' It was just as though he had no feel for the fact that he was in politics. He sees his job as representing the judges, not representing government to the judges, so he sees his role as not only defending but promoting what the judges do, as though they are his constituency.

All of this had been generated by the interview, split over two days, with Jim Naughtie on the Today *programme. Essentially this was about how to handle low-level crime and specifically burglary, but it generated all the usual froth about everything else that was going on at the time, including arguments about what the statistics meant.*

The statistics themselves were really seen in the light of both the gun-crime issue and the way in which the recorded crime statistics are now showing massive increases because of the change in formulae. It is just bizarre. What really got my goat was not Iain Duncan Smith blatantly lying on the radio on Friday lunchtime – and I mean lying – by saying that all crime had gone up, but interviewers picking up the line as though it were fact that because recorded crime is recording more of the crime that exists, it means that crime has gone up. *The Times* on Friday morning really infuriated me with a leader that accused us of deliberately putting out both sets of statistics to confuse everybody, followed by the *Sunday Times* picking up the same theme. I rang Robert Thomson and he agreed to take an article from our Head of Research, Professor Paul Wiles. We had put out both sets of statistics to try and be as transparent as possible, and so that people could see the two running alongside each other. In an ideal world, there would be one set of statistics, but there were two different statistical databases and two different methodologies for collecting the statistics. That is just a fact.

Apart from the obvious area of more police equalling more reporting equalling more recording, alongside the new recording methodology there has also been the introduction of CCTV, which picked up previously unrecorded (and unnoticed) crime. This means that we are in the strange situation of having invested heavily in CCTV and are now getting blamed for the consequences of picking up the crimes that the cameras have revealed. What I find really galling is that *The Times* itself has been running for months that we should publish both sets of statistics alongside each other and has been saying that the British Crime Survey is the only truly reliable guide. We then end up with the newspaper doing a double somersault.

Admittedly politicians do this all the time, and it would be churlish simply to blame the media for a misinterpretation of the message. But sometimes I do wonder how we survive together when both those reporting and those being reported end up disagreeing about the very basis on which the debate is taking place. No wonder people become disillusioned with politics and politicians. But unlike those reporting on them, politicians are accountable.

Running alongside all this we have the uncovering of the plot involving Algerian terrorists and ricin – the chemical made out of castor-oil beans, easily produced but difficult to distribute and use. Two of them were asylum seekers, which started a real furore in some of the newspapers, including the *Evening Standard*. I managed to get an article in the *Standard* on Friday [10 January], in order to put the record straight. There were some bad articles in the Sundays – burglary, gun crime, terrorism, asylum, the lot.

Officials (not just Special Branch, MI5 and our own Terrorism and Protection Unit but also the Department of Health) came out of COBR in a right old panic, wanting to do a fully fledged press conference about all the people who had been picked up. I managed to calm things down. Initially I was going to put out a statement in my name but it was decided that this would set a precedent, so we put it out in the name of the Deputy Chief Medical Officer and David Veness from the Anti-Terrorism Unit at the Met.

The highlight of that Saturday was Sheffield Wednesday v. Reading, when my schoolfriends Tony and Irene came up to Sheffield with their daughter Alex and son-in-law Lee. I accommodated them at the cottage. Wednesday were 2–0 down at half-time. It was like Sunday-league stuff, terrible. When we came out for the second half I borrowed a Junior Owls baseball cap because I had left my hat at home and it was absolutely freezing – and it must have brought us good luck because Wednesday started to play well. They pulled one goal back, then equalised at 2–2, and then a third goal and we were winning. We were going absolutely wild. We were the only ones in the directors' box who were cheering. I saw Roy Hattersley, and he said: 'It's a good job we won or I would have had to have written in my Monday column in the *Guardian* that it was your fault for coming.' I said, 'Quite right, Roy' – then he declared, 'Of course, I blame you for everything else.' It was interesting banter in which his partner, Maggie, is always very nice to me.

The atmosphere at the ground was just like the old days. It was wonderful: the crowd rose to their feet, the band played, and the lads were full of it. It was just one of those lovely occasions.

Sunday 12 January: having visitors has made it quite a pressured weekend, because I obviously had to drop doing any work on Saturday night. So after my friends' departure I've had a whole week's preparation to do, including the speech on the Supply Day which, quite rightly from the Tories' point of view, Oliver Letwin has called for tomorrow afternoon [13 January] on criminal justice and crime. I have the Ethnic Network speech on Tuesday, entitlement cards on Wednesday, and a press reception at which I have to have an entirely different approach from the one I feel inside myself.

I am afraid that this was par for the course at the time: hardly having time for friends, never mind myself. It is an absolute wonder to me now that I managed to hold on to so many of my friends and that they were so understanding. Even speaking on the telephone for any length of time became difficult, as I began to think about the work I ought to be doing. My best friends commented later that they had seen me drift off at particular moments in time, which must have been absolutely awful – and then people wonder why we get out of touch and disconnected from the day-to-day lives of those we represent.

To be honest, it is a miracle that it is not even worse than it is. Perhaps colleagues who took a different view were right after all in being much more laid back and less obsessed with detail.

Week beginning Monday 13 January. the most important event that I had anything to do with was on Tuesday, when I signed two warrants for the arrest of suspected terrorists under the Anti-Terrorism, Crime and Security Act – one in London, which was straightforward, and one in the Crumpsall district of Manchester. They didn't do the raids early in the morning, which is what they usually do, but waited until the late afternoon. The police, wearing body armour, entered the suspects' flat, where they found three men whom they secured with handcuffs – and one of them was the one I had certificated. Special Branch came in and recognised one of the others as being connected with the Wood Green ricin 'laboratory'. They moved the other two, including the one I had certificated, and decided that they would try to secure any forensic evidence on the one they believed was from the cell in London. In order to put him in protective clothing, they took off his handcuffs – without putting on any body armour or calling up the Armed Unit, which had remained outside – and he stabbed to death DC Stephen Oake.

One national newspaper claimed, among other things, that it was because people were politically correct: that is, the top brass allegedly didn't allow the police to carry guns when going in to apprehend foreigners, which is just ridiculous. The same paper also claimed that France had pulled out of the European Convention on Human Rights, whereas they have done nothing of the sort. It is not possible to derogate from Article 3 of the Convention, so a lot of rubbish is being written.

The death of Stephen Oake was a tragedy. I had to go through the formality of making a Statement to the Commons on Wednesday, but in personal terms I am just so deeply sorry: it is the worst moment of my time as Home Secretary. Paul Goggins was with me when on Tuesday night I found out what had happened, and he said that he could see from my face the sheer horror that a process which I had commenced, perfectly reasonably, had ended up with an officer losing his life. But I have to do my job, I can't be blamed for the way they did theirs. Mind you, Robert Kilroy-Silk [former Labour MP and then television-show presenter] thought I should shoulder the blame, and said so in the *Sunday Express* [on 19 January], demanding that I should resign because Stephen Oake's death was my fault. When people write things like that, they don't realise how much hurt they cause to those doing a virtually impossible job in very difficult circumstances.

I was talking this week to more than one person about how the job of Home Secretary is so much different since 11 September 2001 – so much broader, so much more burdensome, so much closer to the security services and the anti-terrorism action and having to carry the responsibility, as John Prescott rightly indicated when he handed the responsibility back to me when I returned to the Home Office.

John, Deputy Prime Minister, had taken over responsibility for security warrants from me during my time in hospital – and I don't think he particularly relished the experience.

What has happened since Tuesday night is the most enormous upsurge of hatred and bitterness against asylum seekers in particular and against foreigners in general.

Rebekah Wade, whom I know very well, has taken over editorship of the *Sun*. She was very honest with me about the situation when I spoke to her on the telephone, saying that whatever the *Sun* readership want to hear and believe is what they will get.

This is very important because it explains a massive fall-out I had with Rebekah and the Sun, which lasted several months. Revisiting my tapes, it is clear now that the build-up to the Holocaust Memorial Day (which triggered my argument with the paper) contributed greatly to my own state of mind and my reaction to unfolding events.

The Sundays were naturally full of the death of Stephen Oake. I did a long interview on *The World This Weekend* on Sunday [19 January], which went well, I think. I tried to put things into context – that of course we are worried and that everyone understands the fear and concern, but that we have to find a balanced and proportionate way through.

But the debate on Monday was not good, with Oliver Letwin confessing that he had changed his mind about what to do with burglars: he had changed it between 21 December and 9 January! He had obviously been ordered into action, as he had been again in the Statement on Wednesday.

I know I am still getting too angry in the Commons. My body language is all wrong. I can stay calm in my voice but I look very angry, and that won't do at all.

There was also a drugs debate in the evening so I had something to eat with Chris Mullin, who (I had forgotten entirely) had finished third, behind me when I was the runner-up to Alan McKay in the selection conference for Penistone in 1978. What a small world. Bob Ainsworth and Hazel Blears did the drugs debate.

I was consulted on, and agreed to, the high-risk strategy of the raid on the Finsbury Park mosque which took place at around two a.m. on Monday 20 January. We had been talking about it during the latter part of the previous week, discussing what to do and how to do it and taking advice on handling it from the Anti-Terrorist Branch. Huw said he feared that in my interview on *The World This Weekend* I was going to give the game away – which I didn't, but I did indicate that we would do whatever was necessary, without fear or favour. I also attacked Abu Hamza [imam at the Finsbury Park mosque] and all his works when answering questions on the Statement on the previous Wednesday lunchtime. We had been to-ing and fro-ing on this for months and I had been desperate to get across that political backing was there for any action that was needed. There was going to be no political correctness.

In replaying my tapes, this all seems so close to home. In February 2006 Abu Hamza was convicted of inciting racial hatred and soliciting murder, and many questions were asked about how long he had been active in our country, what had happened over the years from the mid-1990s, what advice had been received and what support had been given by politicians.

Much has to remain private. Suffice it to say that there were occasions, like any human being, when I got it wrong. With Abu Hamza, I did not. On the one hand I was defending the security services and SO13 – which any Home Secretary would do – and on the other I was creating mayhem inside the system to see if we could get something done (with Tony's wholehearted support). As will be seen, we were to change the law to withdraw citizenship from those with dual citizenship in order to ensure that we could remove them from the country – judges permitting – and three years on, Abu Hamza had managed to manipulate the legal system to continue appealing against my decision at the time he was convicted in the British courts.

Running alongside all this was the Domestic Affairs Committee debate about the future of higher-education funding, which is a story in itself.

I had a chat with Tony for half an hour about issues, including getting our act together on crime – where the trends are and what we need to do – and putting together material on asylum and nationality. Anybody would think that we hadn't done anything – and we have done more than anybody could ever have expected. He asked me how things were going on the non-political front. The two full weeks back after New Year have felt like three months. It's been unbelievable.

Week beginning Monday 20 January: it is just relentless. I have never known the beginning of a year like it. The light touch of the week – not light in terms of emotion but light in terms of issues – was Lucy retiring and Sadie arriving. Lucy just went off thinking she was going on holiday, all bouncy and full of beans, with not a care in the world. It was all the rest of us who were feeling emotional. We did a photo for her on Friday after the Special Cabinet. We had talked about what to do, and given that there was real press interest and they wanted photos, and the fact that I certainly didn't want to be followed around, it seemed sensible just to have a formal photo – which is what we did, with both Lucy and Sadie together, and then just me with Sadie. Even then the *Evening Standard* diary had a go at me for hyping the retirement of the dog. It wasn't me who had hyped it up: it was the press. They had even said that they would pay people money to find out in advance the name of my new dog. I really cannot win on these occasions.

Sadie is a very well-trained, affectionate dog. She took to me immediately, thank goodness, and I am comfortable with her. And Lucy just trotted off into the sunset, wagging her tail. I shall miss her. She has given me nine years of excellent work and companionship, a wonderful dog, through thick and thin – and through opposition, from the time when I was Chairman of the Party when John Smith died. I got her during the European elections, and now here is Sadie, her half-sister and the spitting image, although thicker set, broader and slightly more muscular – and only two years old and full of bounce.

Funny to think back on it because Lucy managed the feat of trotting vigorously to the Dispatch Box back in 1994 almost as though she thought because we had done so well in the European elections, we had just taken over government – and here was Sadie, in government, having to learn how to cope with Prime Minister's Questions, even allowing for the fact that Val Woolrich had been spending the last few weeks ensuring that she got used to the Palace of Westminster and surreptitiously sneaking her in, with agreement, behind the Speaker's Chair to make sure that she was comfortable with the noise.

The changeover from Lucy to Sadie has come at an unfortunate moment both emotionally and in terms of time and commitment, because it will take months before I can relax with her in view of all the things that are happening politically, plus my own emotional and personal problems.

Home Office Questions were awful. I got very angry and denounced the Department for incompetence, because we had just had a major incident at Sittingbourne [where there was fierce opposition to plans to convert a hotel into a reception centre for asylum seekers]; and over the issue of induction centres, which we had told them to do a year before and they had opened just one.

We had agreed to have a much clearer process of induction for everyone claiming asylum, which would have a set process and would set them on the road to continued monitoring. Months had gone by and we had ended up with just the one centre.

We had gone ballistic, and Bev Hughes had ordered them to find places and so they went round seeing if they could buy up hotels through another company. As ever, they acted so incompetently. They hadn't consulted the local community, and Derek Wyatt, the local Labour MP, was very unpleasant to Bev, who had to leave London first thing on Tuesday morning and abandon the Home Affairs Select Committee hearing into asylum as her mum was very ill – so ill that Bev was at her bedside for the following four nights. So all of these things conjoin with accusations of ineptitude and stories about asylum seekers being members of the Taliban and getting asylum because they were at risk if they went back.

On the Taliban story, which has been running heavily in the press, they did in the end get round to making sure that we had fast-tracked and refused asylum to the man whose story Jon Owen Jones MP had raised which had started it all. But the story ran and ran, appearing in articles and on television. Even David Frost raised it in his Sunday morning [26 January] television interview with Tony. The reason I hadn't been able to get out on Friday that it was all lies was because they went to pick him up and they lost him. He absconded. I daren't say anything about it to the press because it just fulfils every possible nightmare of their view of how incompetent and awful we are.

So they had just dropped another clanger on top of everything else – everything they did, even the searching for premises for induction or screening centres (as I had told them to call them, because it had all got mixed up in the press with accommodation centres and removal centres). They talked about searching for country houses, which was a complete muddle because it was the Angel Group [an organisation that operated asylum centres] who were looking for property in Lincolnshire, on speculative grounds, as they have been for the last two years. But that all got fed into the idea of hotels. Bev had never approved this, even though the Department claimed that she had. One removal centre was reported to have lost forty-three people in a year and it turned out to be four, and only one of those had not been recaptured.

I did an interview with the *New Statesman* that was picked up on television all day on Thursday, with people wondering why I had talked about the nation being a coiled spring. Then the BNP won a local by-election in Halifax that very day. I didn't know that this was on the cards. Nobody had warned us. The party hadn't. Alice Mahon as the local MP hadn't. The media had not picked it up. It was just like a bolt out of the blue – partly because a dissident Labour Party member had stood and got 140 votes, which did it – but nevertheless it was a shock.

But I was ahead of the game. I had predicted that there was a real problem and that got a lot of publicity. I am just trying to pull things back and steady the ship and then go for a major reorganisation. I have got to sort the Department out, and I said so to Tony on Friday night when I rang him. He phoned me back on Saturday night to tell me what he was going to say on *Frost*. I counselled caution because he was talking about pulling out of the European Convention on Human Rights. He did mention it on *Frost* but only as a last resort if everything else that we were doing failed. But the papers are just horrendous. Everything is just awful and it is funny how once you get into that position, everything atrophies, people panic and get into a terrible flap, and then it is very difficult getting them out of it.

We had a departmental Awayday on Wednesday: a complete waste of time. It did confirm in my mind that we had to have a megadrive and solution. In other words, it did reinforce that we couldn't just drift along any further. They talk the language, but they don't do anything. So now is the moment.

Special Cabinet on Friday morning. Given that I felt lousy and had a cold coming on, just to add to the problems, I had a really good response and support round the table. I think a little bit of the support was rather like dealing with a poorly man who needed some grapes and attention, but a lot of it was good, genuine backing. I spelt out the usual message about stability, order and security being the prerequisite for everything else, but at that meeting it was clear that if I didn't do something pretty profound, we had had it. I pointed out that last year everything I was doing was a step too far, and now it looked as if it was a step too little – which is a classic. And I pointed out that I didn't want the same on the Anti-Social Behaviour White Paper and legislation, and I got quite a lot of support for that as well. I said that there is a lot of pressure around Whitehall against doing radical things, and they all agreed with that. I don't want a scattergun, but by God it's got to work. I said to them that there was no point in my producing the White Paper or doing anything on anti-social behaviour unless we do it properly.

On Monday night I had Tony and Cherie, Michael Barber and his wife Karen, Alastair Campbell and Fiona, and Sally Morgan and her husband John round for dinner at South Eaton Place. A very pleasant evening, although Tony and Cherie were very late arriving. I had two messages to deliver – one is that we have really got to sort out what we are doing about public service versus the market, and the second is that Tony has got to reward people who have put their heads on the block.

I had a good evening out on Tuesday at Rhodes in Dolphin Square, which had offered me a free meal because of a complete mess-up that had occurred a few months before.

Two years later, this would have been a cause célèbre!

On Wednesday night I was at home and nearly choked to death. It is alarming how sometimes the digestive system seems to go chronically wrong again. I have also had the physiotherapist in to see if we can do something about my broken finger, which is not healing.

Farce of the week concerned my telephones at South Eaton Place, which were completely put out of action for two days, including when Tony was with me. The system was out from Monday morning to Wednesday afternoon due to the incompetence of those who were supposed to be fixing up new links between a camera on the roof and the local police station, and they disabled the lot. They screwed it up on Monday night, came to fix it on Tuesday, then messed it up all over again, so that the telephone started to ring – not the ones that I had had installed but the original ones that Mo Mowlam had had. Every time I pulled out the plug on the phone that was ringing, another phone began ringing elsewhere. It was just bizarre. In the end, the only one I couldn't pull out was the one in the empty police office in the basement of the house. I couldn't get in there because the door was locked. Fortunately my bedroom is at the top of the house and I couldn't hear it ringing all night, so it didn't stop me from getting to sleep. But it was the most crazy experience imaginable: just picture me running from floor to floor, and room to room, first the hall, then one of the bedrooms downstairs, then just inside the garage, and then finally not being able to get into the police office. In the end I rang my Principal Private Secretary and let his answerphone listen to first one telephone switching off and then another starting in another part of the house. It was like a Brian Rix farce. You couldn't make it up – and this all connected to supposed security. What security? I ask myself. I have to laugh.

And alongside it all, discussions on Iraq, with 34,000 troops deployed on the borders of that country, not all of whom have the proper clothing. Geoff Hoon had already announced that we were going to co-operate with the Americans on Fylingdale becoming part of the Star Wars project – with no discussion in Cabinet. This is something I am vehemently against.

Monday 27 January was Holocaust Memorial Day. I spoke in the afternoon at an ecumenical church meeting in Derbyshire before flying to Edinburgh for the Holocaust Memorial event in the evening. On this day of all days, we had the *Sun* – and Trevor Kavanagh, for whom I have a lot of respect – blatantly using words that can only be described as racist. And it is racism.

For example: 'The betrayal of the British people is irreversible. The flood of cheap labour was encouraged by Chancellor Gordon Brown to boost his "economic miracle". It has brought with it alarming levels of infectious TB, Hepatitis B, incurable Aids – and a horrific knife culture.'

There is no point Trevor saying, 'If I say this I will be accused of being a racist,' because anyone who uses those words is a racist. And I'm no gesturist. God help me, I have done my best in trying to sort things out in taking on the glitterati and everyone else.

I've not had a decent word said about me in the *Independent* and very little in the *Guardian*. But how could I not condemn Trevor Kavanagh? How could I say what I said in the opening short speech which I made at the beginning of the event in Edinburgh, that we need to remind ourselves that for evil to conquer takes only that men and women remain silent – paraphrased but none the less the point – and then not denounce what he said? But I have taken on the most enormous tide against myself. Brave, said the *Mirror*, a word that all of us love but forget. But we will see. We will see what they do to me. But it's far better to stand up and be counted than to crawl under a stone.

I didn't crawl under a stone but it is one of those twists of fate that I should end up as a columnist for the Sun. *I am not entirely sure who would believe that 'forgiveness is the greatest gift of all' – me or Rebekah Wade and Trevor Kavanagh. As we shall see, I did settle my differences some months later, but as no* Guardian *or* Independent *readers ever read the* Sun, *it was interesting during the course of the coming year to find how few people knew that I had had this battle. And if any of them wished to criticise me for taking on a column in the* Sun *in which I can speak my mind, they might reflect on how little support they gave me at the time I was battling to ensure that moderation and proportionality prevailed all those years ago.*

Meetings, meetings, meetings: meetings with my Permanent Secretary and meetings on asylum, as well as a meeting on drugs that I chaired. At the same time I am trying very hard to make time for Sadie and for teaching her what needs to be done, and slowing things down so that they could be done. But it is a hell of a busy time.

The Tories launched their alternative policy on immigration and asylum on Tuesday [28 January]. It was pathetic.

Tuesday also saw John Prescott's announcement to the Commons (we hadn't agreed this in Cabinet, except in general terms about a month earlier) about invoking a defunct law in the hope that it will force the Fire Brigades Union [then in the middle of a dispute with the employers] to pull together and get a settlement rather than having to put the law through Parliament.

In between everything that was going on, I've had the lunch for the Newspaper Society, who certainly know how to look after themselves. Sadie is doing a wonderful job, but I do need to make sure she is all right and feels wanted. She survived her first Prime Minister's Questions [on Wednesday 29 January]. She was very good, except that halfway through she rolled on to her back and spent the rest of the time kicking her legs in the air – which is sometimes what the rest of us feel like doing.

We had an hour and three-quarters in Cabinet, partly on Iraq but mostly on the idea of bidding for the Olympics. I declared myself a positive sceptic: No, but willing to be persuaded. Most people were 'Yes, but . . .'

After that I spent most of Thursday working on the reorganisation of the department, talking to Leigh Lewis on the telephone, and to Andrew Turnbull.

Tony has flown to Madrid and then on to Camp David, so we will see what comes out of that. It is all getting very nasty now.

February 2003

I am so glad January has gone. It was a dreadful month that destabilised and reversed all the big wins that we had had on crime, on stability, on anti-terrorism, and on nationality and asylum. It was all just swept away in a month and our opinion-poll position on all these issues just disintegrated, and with it the popularity of the government. It was just unbelievable. But if we can sort out the Department and get back on track and quieten things, we will make progress.

I had a dinner with Paul Dacre on Monday night, with Edward Heathcoat-Amory and Huw Evans. It was a genuinely pleasant evening and we talked sense, as well as having a laugh. I thought it was well worth doing.

On Tuesday, I went to Croydon to speak to the middle and senior management of the Immigration and Nationality Directorate. It wasn't a very good speech, but I think it got the message across that it is change or die. I used the example of the young woman at the staff meeting held in

Westminster Central Hall in the autumn and how she had been there for a month and still had nothing to do. I said that we were not going to put up with this any longer.

I then flew to Le Touquet for the meeting of the Anglo-French Summit. It was interesting to meet Jacques Chirac, who is a much more impressive character in person than comes over from outside. Also there were the French Prime Minister and Nicolas Sarkozy. Sarkozy and I were the only ones who walked from the lunch to the main conference venue, and he was really warmly applauded by the groups of people who had gathered. It was very revealing. We had decent discussions, and Tony came out of it with some dignity. We then flew back for the vote on the future of the House of Lords.

I had been on the *Today* programme on Tuesday morning to put my point of view that, with regard to a nominated secondary democracy, there were alternatives to the nonsenses that had been put up. We made it back with thirty seconds to spare, flying into Northolt on Tony's A146, followed by outriders for the journey back to the Commons. We walked into the lobby to some cheers from the troops, who were against what Robin had been putting forward, and just made it. I thought I had put a pretty good case in the morning that with devolution to Scotland and Wales and now to the regions, to Northern Ireland, to the European Parliament, with the judges having invented judicial review, with people having power in their own hands and global power and the economic power of transnationals, the world has changed totally. I said that to add a further gridlock of an elected Second Chamber is just suicidal, and that people weren't aggravated by politicians acting swiftly and decisively: they were aggravated by politicians not acting at all.

I found myself writing in my column in the Sun *on exactly the same lines just over three years later at the beginning of April 2006.*

We managed to defeat all the options – just – and I hope that we can start asking the questions that I raised and that others raised: what is the purpose of the Lords, followed by what should the make-up be, and then how do we get that make-up in place and make sure that it has a degree of accountability? Above all, what is its place in what is a very crowded checks-and-balances constitution? It was unfortunate that Robin made it a personal battle with Tony. I think it was the Liberal Democrat Whip who compared Robin to Terry Venables, the Leeds United manager, with regard to the position in which he found himself after Leeds had transferred Woodgate and a load of other players. He couldn't go, but he didn't want to stay.

By Wednesday we were ready to announce the changes at the top of the Department – following months and months of work. We were able to get out the top changes, with Leigh Lewis coming in, Martin Narey's new position, and the way in which we would be reconfiguring the top responsibilities. John Gieve and I went to address the senior staff at the Institute of Directors on Wednesday afternoon. We have just got to ensure now that we follow through so that, layer on layer and with a clear timetable, the consequent changes are put in place.

Following Tony's appearance on *Newsnight*, *The Times* completely mixed up the changes in management and Tony's answer to the question on immigration, thereby making out that No. 10 had forced us into making radical changes in the Home Office, whereas the reality was that I had been fighting for twenty months to bring about change, with only spasmodic support. What matters is not what is perceived in *The Times* but whether I can get it done, particularly the changes that I want in the Immigration and Nationality Directorate. I saw the three non-executive members of the IND Supervisory Board during the week, together with Bev Hughes, about what needs to be done and how we can get on with it.

As for the rest of the week: I went to Wormwood Scrubs on Thursday – God, what an experience. The Cabinet discussed Iraq again, and we are going to talk about the Olympics next week. I saw the South African Crime and Safety Minister, who was a real character; I liked him a lot.

This week I've seen my surgeon Michael McMahon, who was very pleased with my progress after eight weeks and said I was doing extremely well. I had my finger X-rayed and found that at last, after well over three months, it is beginning to heal. They confirmed by an X-ray on my other hand that my forefinger has got a real problem at the joint. The physiotherapist is helping with that but I am in a pretty decrepit state at the moment. I feel better for having lost some weight and I intend to keep down to around twelve stone.

This week dear Winifred Golding, the ex-Sheffield councillor mentioned earlier in my notes, died. I shall go to her funeral on the 17th, whatever else happens. Dear Winifred.

We are still struggling with the White Paper on Anti-Social Behaviour. We seem to have taken a massive step backwards in six weeks rather than forward, so what I did over Christmas and New Year was a complete waste of time. I then wake up in the morning to find that the police national computer is not being inputted properly – but the Home Office gets the blame, not the police.

A meeting at Downing Street on Monday morning to assess the threat of an attack on Heathrow, which had been rumbling around for the previous two or three weeks – specific to Heathrow but not verified in any sense. I found this extremely dubious and said so. I thought it was a double bluff and I didn't like it. I didn't like the gathering either: there were far too many people there, and we weren't addressing the real issues, but rather were allowing the momentum to carry people away. I raised a number of questions: where were we going to deploy police and why so many; why they wanted to bring the armed services in; where they were going to deploy them, at car parks or at junctions; and why the Special Forces? Nobody had got an answer to any of these questions, and although we managed to get them to agree a statement to go out at 6 a.m. on Tuesday, they immediately started to brief.

By the afternoon people had got the story about rocket launchers and they had moved armed vehicles into Heathrow. They'd moved armoured personnel carriers – the equivalent of tanks as far as the public were concerned – and of course all this frightened people to death, particularly women. You could feel that: the minute it was described to me, I knew it was a mistake. It was way over the top and worried people enormously, but we are not operationally responsible and apparently governments in the past, particularly when Michael Howard was Home Secretary, didn't even engage in a way we've engaged all week in trying to get a grip of things. We did try to wind things down and stop SO13 doing things that would cause panic.

Sophie Linden, one of my advisers, described to me in detail, having watched the television, exactly how it looked as the armoured vehicles were placed right in front of one of the terminals at Heathrow. I spoke to David Veness (in charge of SO13) and to be fair to him, he did get the point. I also spoke to John Stevens but, as he says in his autobiography, he wasn't in charge of the operation.

In retrospect, there is no doubt that there was a genuine threat of some kind, but the way in which it was dealt with created an atmosphere of immediate fear. The upside was that if there had been a plot, it would certainly have been substantially discouraged by the visibility of what was taking place, but I really worried about the economy and social life of London. Al Qaeda would have liked nothing better than to have damaged the economy of the capital and the willingness of people to travel to work and to leisure, never mind the tourist industry.

Later in the week a hand grenade was found on an incoming flight at Gatwick, so instead of just dealing with the specific incident they closed Terminal 3 for hours. They also closed Terminal 2 at Heathrow over a scare that turned out to be nothing on the Friday [14 February]. I had to make a Statement to the House on Thursday when the Tories put in a Private Notice Question. I think the Speaker probably regretted it because they didn't use it for the specific issue at all. They simply wanted to have a go in general at so-called lack of preparedness and resilience issues, and *Hansard* will show that very clearly. I couldn't say anything in my Statement about the operational issues and the security background, for obvious reasons, but because I couldn't, I did get criticised. Why can't the House be told more? Answer: because the House cannot be told more. As we said, in the Statement and in answering questions, when we were in opposition we never demanded operational details in dealing with the IRA. But it seems to have all become a game now for the press – for instance, Tony plays the guitar and I play the drums on a visit to Firth Park School in my constituency and the *Daily Mail* try to make something of the fact, as did Radio Sheffield all day, that Tony and I shouldn't be in Sheffield doing this – relating to youngsters and boosting kids – but rather should be in London, hanging about waiting for the next terrorist threat and expected to be overseeing operationally what we are not permitted constitutionally to oversee.

Tony and I had a very strange time during the early part of the week because of his remarks on the target of a 50 per cent drop in asylum. It is not clear that it is understood that it's a drop in people coming in and claiming. That's the crunch.

The upshot was that the Monday papers were very bad. When I'd spoken to Tony late on Monday night I didn't know that No. 10 had been briefing, and we'd had a very pleasant and sensible conversation. When he rang me, it seemed to me that it was a deliberate move to try to heal the breach – and I thought we had. Then I opened the papers on Tuesday morning, particularly the *Daily Express*, and we had Andrew Adonis writ large. He was in No. 10 later in the day and I just told him to lay off, that I wasn't prepared to have any more of it.

At Prime Minister's Questions, Tony said that it was a firm commitment. I think we got away with it pretty lightly then. But what a week – with terrorism and security, with asylum still running and with the *Sun* continuing to have a go; they are determined to wear me down. Tony said that he had spoken at length to Rupert Murdoch [proprietor of the *Sun*] on Thursday morning and thought he'd pulled things round – but it certainly hadn't made any difference by Friday.

And one of those twists of fate. This time last year at the spring conference of the Labour Party in Cardiff, the press office faxed to the Press Association details of the spring estimates on asylum and the necessary uplift to cover the costs. What happened this time? This week the *Daily Mirror* on 14 February had a piece which arose from a senior official who has moved over to be the Finance Director in the Immigration and Nationality Directorate and who had left his papers on a train. Again, it was the spring estimates and the claim for the Treasury in relation to asylum. Brilliant! What the hell do I do with this Department, except plough on? I saw Leigh Lewis and Martin Narey with John Gieve this week, and I told them to get on with the changes and the update.

I am also struggling with the Anti-Social Behaviour Bill. I have gone through it twice but they have still failed to produce a satisfactory version for this weekend.

Domestic Affairs Committee which went very well, simply talking through the wider issues. Then we had a Cabinet Committee on nationality and asylum, trying particularly to get to grips with the health screening, housing and education issues.

Hans Blix and his team of weapons inspectors in Iraq are reporting back to the UN on Friday 14 March. It does not look good. This is not going to be an easy time, with three-quarters of a million people expected to demonstrate over Iraq on the streets of London on Saturday.

I'm doing too many internal meetings and too many speeches, rather than a few really good ones that get the message across. I've been listening to the letters coming in to the *Today* programme on Radio 4 on Saturday 15th. We've had the case of Mary Martin, who has been in the country for fifty-two years from the age of two and who has been told by one of the Immigration and Nationality Directorate staff that she would have to leave the country because she was here illegally. I rang the office the moment I heard this: Bev Hughes has intervened and put it right.

I was the warm-up act for the Labour Party spring conference in Glasgow, setting up Tony's speech by just keeping the audience in tune.

I think I did a good job. I'd like to believe I did anyway, in kicking it off and setting the scene and using the idea of the family – where families fall out but don't lash out – and Tony picked up the same theme. He did very well, but my speech just got wiped out by events and circumstances. How do you counter a march like the one in London and Charles Kennedy playing to the gallery?

Looking back at that momentous period, it is amazing just how calmly my notes reflect on it. There we had well in excess of a million people on the streets of London and the Labour Party rent down the middle, and somehow life just went on. Although we understood the tremendously deep and passionate feelings generated by the Iraq issue, I don't think that at that stage we fully appreciated just how long and how deep the split would be, not just in the party but in the country.

On a lighter note, I had flown up to Scotland with Tony, and the aircraft was so small and noisy that Tony said that Sadie had gone to the rear of the plane and was putting on her parachute! I gather that Morgan Freeman and Bob Hoskins were making a film in Glasgow and were staying at the same hotel as I was. The film, called *Danny the Dog,* was about a blind man, and I said to the hotel manager 'You ought to give me a go at showing Bob how it should be done.'

When I was travelling in the car with Tony I was privileged to hear him dealing with international leaders over the phone. I could only hear one side of the conversations, of course, but José María Aznar [Prime Minister of Spain], for one, is clearly with him totally and very supportive.

I think Tony has stood up very well to the enormous pressure of such a large turn-out in London – frighteningly intimidatory, and people so bellicose.

More silly stories about Afghan fighters for the Taliban. They all turn out to be mythical but by the time I've got our lot to pull their finger out, it's too late. We've got the publicity about Holloway women's prison and even though I'd intervened three weeks before to make sure that pregnant women had showers, none of that appeared. I am afraid that the press office are not doing too well at the moment.

I went to Winifred Golding's funeral on Monday – a gloriously sunny, brilliantly cold day. It took up one of the days of my tiny break, but I was glad I went. I stayed in Derbyshire on Tuesday morning and had a really nice walk, except that Sadie got into a hen coop: God knows what happened, but a hen came flying past me with Sadie after it. I managed to get her back but I imagine she's frightened the chickens to death, and whoever they belong to will think it's a fox. It will only reinforce the hunters and their desire to get out there.

Finished Roy Jenkins's book *Churchill*, which is fascinating. In the run-up to the 1951 election, Churchill attacked Attlee by saying that he had neglected to develop the atom bomb and that it was his fault that we hadn't got one. Of course we had got one – but on security grounds, this fact hadn't been released, and so Attlee couldn't attack him back. If he had been able to do so he would have destroyed Churchill completely, but he just stuck entirely to his guns. I thought to myself: that it is not quite the same as with me, but similar. We have to try to tell people the truth and tell them what's going on and yet keep security issues secret – and we get slagged off for it. In Attlee's case it was a disaster. Labour might not necessarily have won the election, but it would certainly have helped if Churchill had been made to look a complete idiot.

The workload continues to drive me crackers. Part of it was revising for the umpteenth time the Anti-Social Behaviour White Paper – another last-minute job after seven weeks, everybody panicking. And I had to see Gordon first thing Wednesday morning about the spring estimates and the asylum budget. We compromised on £40 million, which will keep the Criminal Injuries Compensation Scheme going and allow us to manage the budget. I have always to make a judgement about whether the officials are trying to squeeze that bit extra by sending me in with arms flailing, or whether the figures they give me are genuine. I have to make a judgement on what I feel I can get away with. When I came back and Gordon got in touch a couple of hours later, they certainly thought that I'd done a damned good deal – and for them to be really cheerful about it means that I must have done a good deal. It was a strange conversation, because Gordon was probing me about what I thought about the party and the present situation.

Supper with Tessa Jowell and her husband David Mills. David is having a hard time because of the Italian magistrates investigating his links with Berlusconi.

I had a large number of meetings with officials over the Wednesday and Thursday about security – a move to make a deal with Sir David Omand (who had taken over as Head of Resilience and Counter-Terrorism) at the Cabinet Office, for a different way of carrying on so that we can get things sorted a lot better than we have been able to do so far. I would be very pleased if we can. We also had a round-up of what had happened the previous week. I think they have got the message that the armoured vehicles were not a good idea.

I am now preparing for the speech on 3 March on the Anti-Terrorism Crime and Security Act Part 4 Renewal, and with it the publication of a major paper on protection and civil renewal. I have come up with the idea of a security website, that will have everything on it – anything that is public and publishable will be on it so that people can access and look for themselves for advice and assessment, what is operational and what isn't, and try to overcome the silliness that we have had. I am determined that we are going to go on the offensive, that we are going to get the initiative back on a whole range of areas that, post-Derry Irvine, we lost.

We also had the judgement on the judicial review on withdrawal of benefits and housing for asylum seekers who do not claim when they first arrive in the country. The judgement was handed down by Judge Collins: Andrew Collins, the man who turned over Michael Howard in 1996; the man who tried to scupper Oakington; the man who ruled against us on the Special Immigration Appeals Commission on the very purpose of SIAC even though he chairs it; the man who sat next to Derry Irvine arguing with me about what should go in the Bill in relation to the Lord Chancellor's elements on the appeals process. No. 10 now want us to be gung ho but there are times when backing me would help a great deal. Although Huw Evans is ambivalent, I think that the response I gave was a suitable way of getting back on the offensive and winning back some of the support of the tabloids and certainly that of the people, just by using television and radio.

What is very sad is that in court we didn't necessarily put our best case forward. But the outcome suits me, because losing gained us the initiative and enabled us to get back at these people – so long as we win on appeal. But nevertheless it is disheartening to say the least.

Apart from Andrew Collins's judgement, the most bizarre thing of the week was the proposal – submission as they call it – on the sentencing of murderers. I had been through this again and again. I'd had a definitive meeting in the room off my office where I decided what the terms should be that we lay down in the Criminal Justice and Sentencing Bill. They then come back, having been gone over by the Lord Chancellor's Department and the judiciary, recommending far lower sentences to the fixed terms that I had already determined we should stick to. If I didn't care about it and had not kept notes myself and had not got a good memory, we would be up the spout. They were proposing three tariffs: life (because I'd indicated life meant life so there was nothing they could do about that) for absolutely horrendous crimes; twenty years for things like killing a policeman or even a second murder that wasn't judged to be horrendous; and twelve years for other murders, which I've now upped to thirty years and twenty years respectively. This was based on the fact that previous tariffs given by home secretaries had been in the lower range and that judges would try to lower the figure, whereas if we set a low figure as the commencement, they would raise the figure. You have to be beyond naïvety to believe that what you need to do is to set a low figure so that the judges will increase it. I have overturned that, but it just shows what goes on. Nobody knows these things. The public don't know and neither do the journalists, who take us apart without ever having had such responsibility.

This half-term last year I was in Spain enjoying a break, but this year I am going to the cottage on Friday 21st and Bev Hughes and her husband Tom are coming across. My sons are coming over on Saturday and then I am going to go back down to London on Sunday afternoon because I am making a contribution to the major launch of the Asset Recovery Agency on Monday 24th.

I have received an outrageous letter from Harry Woolf. The sheer gall of it was quite breathtaking. I think we have now reached the point where the judges really do believe their own rhetoric. Anthony Scrivener wrote a piece in one of the Sundays asking, 'Who will save us from David Blunkett?' It has to be them, the liberal élite riding out on a white charger, saving the world from democracy, from totalitarian parliamentarianism, from elected dictatorships, from the terrible breach of a twenty-year-old rule called 'judicial review' that they themselves have invented and pushed into our constitution. And helped by Liberal Democrats like Anthony Lester in the Lords, who compared what I was doing in challenging the judges with Zimbabwe. What a bunch!

There are those now on the left who are accusing me of giving up the struggle on racism, but I am in somewhat of a cleft stick. I have got them talking garbage, and at the same time I have leader after leader appearing in the *Sun* attacking me. I also have the ultras outside the *Sun* exhorting us to cease all immigration and stop all work permits – and in between I am just trying desperately to set a course that is moral, rational, and practicable. It is very hard work.

Week beginning Monday 24 February: there was a strange little piece in the *Mail on Sunday* [on 23 February] about Alan Milburn gearing up to attack Gordon – or was it Gordon's people doing a pre-emptive strike? Who knows? I went to the farewell do for David Yelland [editor of the *Sun*]. He was very positive with us all. Tony and Cherie came as well as Gordon, Sarah and myself, but no other Cabinet ministers had arrived by the time I left. Rebekah Wade came and made it clear that she thought we were having dinner with Les Hinton and Trevor Kavanagh in a private room somewhere so we could talk. I said: 'Oh good, we have it in hand.' We had nothing of the sort in hand, but I said to Huw that if it was supposed to be an olive branch, let's accept it and let's get on with it.

On Iraq, we've got a Statement by Tony at lunchtime on Tuesday and a debate in the House on Wednesday. It's all hotting up now.

It was inevitable that my attention would be focused on domestic security rather than a deep involvement with the detail of foreign policy. Nevertheless, with the ever-present benefit of hindsight, I would now have spent more time intervening on the presentation and justification of the case for our taking military action in Iraq, and not just, as I did later, the arguments as to how win the peace.

The week was undoubtedly dominated by the 122 Labour backbenchers who voted against the government, or voted for an amendment moved by Chris Smith that basically endeavoured to stop the government being able to back the Americans in any circumstances. The government motion was perfectly reasonable and straightforward, and the amendment was designed effectively to scupper everything. What is clear now is that people really did not want Resolution 1441 [UN Security Council Resolution calling upon Iraq to comply with its disarmament obligations], and they have no intention that its terms should be carried through. It is a mess caused in part by Hans Blix being so naïve. He comes out with a report saying there was very limited compliance and this relates to chemical and biological and potential nuclear development and the holding of chemical and biological components and material – and then the moment that Iraq says, after prevaricating, that it will after all destroy some very low-grade missiles, Hans Blix says that this is a very significant move. This has clearly not helped at all with regard to the overall climate: after a million people demonstrating on the streets of London, and now this vote, we have got a real uphill struggle on our hands.

I certainly had a struggle on Friday's *Any Questions?* in Hereford, at the

Royal National College for the Blind which, when I was at Shrewsbury, I had attended in my teenage years. Everything was dominated by Iraq, and it was really hard work to win the audience round. The issue is obsessing everyone and permeating everything. It is affecting the world economy and creating a degree of insecurity and tension that everything else is feeding into.

What is interesting looking back is how little the so-called dossiers impacted on my own perception and thinking. This is partly because the information in the dossiers did not affect my judgement one way or the other in relation to Iraq because, as I have already indicated earlier, it was in my view Resolution 1441 on the previous 7 November that was truly significant, and we were dealing with the aftermath of and Iraqi compliance with that resolution, not with dossiers cobbled together as part of the 'winning minds' approach, important as that was.

When interviewed much later by Sir Robin Butler (former Secretary of the Cabinet) and Ann Taylor (at that time Chair of the Intelligence and Security Committee), I was to indicate that part of the reason why I didn't take a great deal of notice of the dossier was that I didn't think it would be used or seen as significant in the way that it was. It seemed very low level and lightweight then – as indeed it did later. I wish I had taken its likely use more seriously and intervened more heavily by suggesting that it didn't add up to very much and (certainly in the case of the second dossier) required a great deal more work. Frankly, those who were much closer to it than I was – and I was after all in the inner Cabinet – were so pressed at the time that it is not surprising that they didn't go through it with a fine-tooth comb. Once again, we relied on others to do the job. As I have indicated on numerous occasions, going through documents over and over again is not something that is anticipated or seen as necessary – but it is essential. That was one of the profound lessons of government which, in my own sphere of influence, I took very seriously indeed.

We've had the asylum statistics for 2002, with the final quarter completing the year. They are very high indeed: 85,000, but 110,000 when dependants are included. The news media have seized upon our transparency about family members and insist on making them sound as though they were all individual asylum seekers. In previous years, before I took over, only the head of the family – the actual applicant – had been counted. I try to give transparency but it is then distorted.

We had a news briefing. I did the *Today* programme on Friday morning and then Bev Hughes and I did an on-camera lobby briefing. It's been a really tiring week.

On Saturday I went to the home of my Permanent Secretary John Gieve for dinner – the first time that I have done that.

On Sunday I presented the awards for the Worthington Cup at the Millennium Stadium in Cardiff. There was a lot going on that weekend, including the installation of the Archbishop of Canterbury, Rowan Williams. I had met him earlier in the week when I'd popped in to give a little speech and say farewell at the reception for the Bishop of Blackburn, who had worked with me on the Sex and Relationship Guidance three years earlier when he was in charge of the Education Department of the Church of England. I was able to have a chat with Rowan Williams and he is a very able and impressive man.

The measure of the man is that he took no umbrage at the disagreement in writing we had had when I wrote an article in the Spectator *at the turn of the year. And his installation will always be memorable for me on account of the behaviour of my guide dog Sadie, who took great exception to the sound of the African drums and kept up a low growling throughout that part of the ceremony*

We had a real mess on Wednesday morning. *The Times* carried an article about prison funding – it was really about capital modernisation – following a row between Tony and Gordon, but the way it was presented left me absolutely livid. I spoke to Tony about this while I was clearing the last vestiges of silliness about the anti-social behaviour legislation. We had an LP [Legislative Programme] Committee to clear that, and we also had a Civic Society meeting that Tony chaired on Thursday. It's amazing how much blockage there is. I got annoyed with Tessa Jowell over a disagreement we were having over the Licensing Bill and irritated with Kim Howells.

It is difficult getting annoyed with friends and much easier to fall out with political opponents.

March 2003

The row rumbles on with the judiciary and Derry Irvine about the antics of Andrew Collins. Peter Goldsmith, as Attorney General, is taking the case this Monday [3 March], and Harry Woolf, the Lord Chief Justice, is taking the battle to me on Thursday. I am speaking at a fundraising gala dinner for the Labour Party in the South West of England in Bristol, sponsored by law firms on Thursday evening, and Harry Woolf is speaking in Oxford on human rights, so that should be an interesting day.

On Monday I've got the renewal of the Part-4 Order on the Anti-Terrorism, Crime and Security Act, and the derogation from Article Five of the ECHR.

Tony phoned me on Saturday evening just before I went for dinner to thank me and Bev for what we'd done on the Friday on the asylum front – which I think was a gesture of goodwill. He did sound dreadful but he's kept going, spending Monday and Tuesday in Northern Ireland, pushing the settlement forward. He gets no credit for it and he's doing a fantastic job.

A very strange dinner on the Wednesday night to accord Paul Dacre his award at the Media Society, but I thought it was worth doing – taking pains to speak very, very carefully. Gordon appeared courtesy of a video recording. He and I appear to be the only Cabinet members who still have some form of dialogue going with Paul Dacre and the *Daily Mail.*

A great chunk of the week has been spent on counter-terrorism and resilience, and the Order on Monday publishing the civil-contingencies/resilience paper and quite a lot of media around that. There were five meetings in all on counter-terrorism and resilience, two major Cabinet Committees, with three meetings to prepare for that, and the usual Criminal Justice System Cabinet Committee that I chair. I had more meetings with Tony on asylum, meetings with the Association of Chief Police Officers and with the Met Commissioner, and a whole range of things that were simply bitty and irritating. I sometimes just wonder how much good I'm doing and whether I am getting anywhere.

A short meeting with Tony first thing on Thursday morning [6 March]. We just touched on one or two issues about better relations between my staff and his, because it's all got a bit edgy lately. We talked about whether there should be an extra Bill on asylum. We need some extra powers on terrorism – small measures but we need them, even if they have to be in other Acts. We then had the asylum meeting, which was quite good-natured, and Cabinet, where we talked about Iraq. It turns out that the material that appeared in the newspapers on so-called intimidation of third nations over the Iraq issue had been doctored and leaked by a woman at GCHQ. She is apparently married to a Kurdish asylum seeker who's been thrown out of the country, and she should never have been at GCHQ in the first place. So God knows what the Foreign Office and MI6 were playing at.

We discussed the way in which France in particular was intimidating Eastern European countries – the ones that have still got aspirations to join the EU in the next round of accession countries. I think there is a general feeling that France is behaving absolutely abominably and that Russia, for its own reasons, is not behaving much better. Germany is just tagging along. But we are not too worried about that. It was interesting though to be able to talk to Tony at that private meeting about Iraq. I think he's optimistic about getting a majority in the Security Council but not about whether the French in the end will veto. The strain is really telling on him. He came back from Ireland at 3.15 a.m. on Wednesday, saw the Russian Prime Minister at 8.30 a.m. and did Prime Minister's Questions in the House at noon. He really cannot keep up that sort of schedule.

The end of the week was dominated entirely by the Security Council and Hans Blix's report. As Tony had suspected when we discussed it at the private meeting I had with him before Cabinet, and had also hinted in Cabinet itself, Hans Blix was just terrified of being blamed for starting the war. So all of what he did was bound by obfuscation with regard to the actual biological and chemical capacity of Iraq, which is the real issue. But it does make it very difficult because France, Russia and Germany – and it's France that is the key here – have a kind of spurious logic on their side. They have a situation where what they say is simple and easy, and the simple and easy is what people hear most. It is very hard to cut through that and say that in the report there's an indication that Saddam has now re-established capacity to create biological and chemical weaponry that was destroyed back in 1991 through to 1995 – yet people are still deluded.

We also have really stupid stories appearing on asylum from Eben Black, the assistant political editor of the *Sunday Times* who is standing in because David Cracknell [political editor] is off sick.

Message on answering machine: 'David – Hi, it's Eben here again. Sorry about phoning you at nine o'clock on Saturday night. It's just that I thought if you were around, I wanted to bounce a *Sunday Telegraph* story off you, which is saying you are planning to send all asylum seekers who arrive in Britain to Albania.'

Iain Duncan Smith was making a speech at the Conservative local-government conference in Coventry in which he put up the idea of floating asylum seekers off on a boat or on to an island somewhere – an idea picked up by Oliver Letwin, much to his regret. So someone somewhere in the labyrinthine communications network of government must have had the smart idea that knocking down an idea like this was a bad idea – but I'm afraid I had to knock it down anyway. On the other hand, we had some inter-departmental briefings in the run-up to the Seville European Council (Heads of State) that bore the stamp of internecine differences within government – and this could be part of it. It's all mixed up with the safe zones and the work we are putting through the Justice and Home Affairs Council and the UN, and have been doing for some time now.

Still preparing the Anti-Social Behaviour White Paper – still revising the wording, and I was also working on the Statement. We finally got there on Wednesday morning [12 March]. I did the *Today* programme and the Statement to Parliament, which was pretty well received. Unfortunately the press office didn't contact and talk through the issues with the crime correspondents, so the *Sun* crime correspondent hit back on Friday morning. We didn't do too badly with the home-affairs correspondents, but the press office are one-dimensional: they can't see that there's a whole range of people who have to be soothed and nurtured.

Lord knows, the press office were one of the best sets of people I have ever come across. When things got really rough for me the following year they were fantastic, and no one could have asked for more from them. I feel rather rueful therefore about my gripes at the time.

Talking of soothing and nurturing, I had to suffer Piers Morgan with his chairman, Victor Blank, at Thursday lunchtime, which was an extraordinary experience. It became very clear that Piers Morgan just hates some people and then they've had it. Jack Straw is one of these. Other people he loves – such as Gordon, who in Morgan's eyes can do no wrong. On the night that I'd done the Media Society awards with Paul Dacre, Piers and Gordon had an absolute knees-up – a big dinner party at No. 11, followed by going up to the flat at No. 10. They then had what can only be described as a knock-about in the Cabinet Room, where apparently Piers sat in Tony's chair and pretended to sack Gordon. It all sounds very silly – but it was even sillier that Piers Morgan was telling us about it.

Dinner with Andrew Marr and Jackie Ashley on Thursday night at Christopher's restaurant in Covent Garden, owned by the son of former Tory cabinet minister and 'wet' Ian Gilmour. Jackie had written a really nice piece about me in the *Guardian* that morning, and the day before Patrick Wintour had done a nice interview on anti-social behaviour. It was an enjoyable dinner as far as the company was concerned, but the food was awful: apparently they couldn't tell the difference between swordfish and tuna. Fortunately Jackie Ashley backed me up on this.

The early part of the week was full of Clare Short having rung Andrew Rawnsley to ask if she could come on *The Westminster Hour*, the Sunday evening Radio 4 programme he presents. On the programme she pronounced that Tony had been reckless, that she would resign from the Cabinet if we didn't get a second resolution, etc. etc. – and the whole thing took off from there. Then she had the cheek to come to Cabinet on Thursday and start talking and intervening as if nothing had happened. I just couldn't resist saying (and the *Guardian* reported this on Friday morning), 'Well, I think we could all agree that Jacques Chirac has been completely reckless.'

I told the story about the demonstration outside my constituency surgery by the Iraqi Kurds. When I asked them why they were here, they replied that they had come to tell me not to bomb their country. I said: 'No, I don't mean why are you here demonstrating outside my surgery. I mean why are you here in Britain?' They said they were here because they were being persecuted in Iraq. I said, 'Precisely, and that's exactly why we are trying to take Saddam Hussein out' – and, incidentally, why we have 18,000 asylum seekers from Iraq.

It looks as though Robin Cook will resign, although anything's possible. Both Robin and Clare have had it, anyway. They've burnt their boats. It was important to be really supportive of Tony at Cabinet, and when I saw him privately afterwards he was very grateful. Gordon had decided he was coming on board. I think Clare's intervention, plus the bizarre statement by Jacques Chirac saying that he would veto any second resolution and in fact would veto anything that resulted in taking military action, have solidified great chunks of our backbenchers. This became clear at Prime Minister's Questions on Wednesday, and it has given us at least some perspective on what we might do as we come to the weekend and Tony meets Bush and Aznar.

Tony's work on Palestine has yielded fruit, with Bush on Friday [14 March] making a speech indicating that he's prepared to go for an independent Palestinian state and to forward what is called the road map to achieve that with the new Palestinian Prime Minister, Mahmoud Abbas, who has now been nominated. So there is some progress, even if it is only nominal and at the moment only on paper. This does make a difference to Tony's position, which looked disastrous at the beginning of the week, and we all just had to strengthen his arm. I'd talked to him on the telephone on Monday morning. I was all for sacking Clare Short but he decided to play it down, purely on the grounds that splits and weakness together are the two things that really kill governments. I think his judgement was probably better than mine: it would have been precipitate to sack her – and as it happens, the way he's handled it has strengthened his position rather than weakened it. But it has weakened Clare's position.

We are getting demos all over the place, including in West Yorkshire, where I was on Friday, and at my constituency meeting that evening. I'm jiggered. There are so many things to go through, dealing with the security side as well as the shambles that keeps emerging in relation to asylum and the difficulties I have on the civil resilience front. The UNHCR has produced its annual report with its world-wide figures, and the IND and the Home Office centrally knew nothing about it. I picked it up on the six o'clock Radio 4 news when I got back from West Yorkshire on Friday evening before going to the constituency meeting.

Looking back I ask myself whether there was anything more that I could have done halfway through my period as Home Secretary to change the nature of the bureaucracy, the effectiveness of the way that different parts of the Home Office worked together, and the service given to ministers. It is not possible, as a serving Cabinet minister, to blame officials publicly, not merely by long-standing convention but because of the likely reaction and the damage that would be then done to you. As I have indicated already, it is not possible to sack or move them without the agreement of the Permanent Secretary and Executive Board. We had by this time changed the whole of the upper echelons of the Home Office, with the exception of the main Permanent Secretary, John Gieve, who had been appointed by Jack and Tony only six weeks before I came into office.

It is interesting to reflect that three years later, during the difficulties that Charles Clarke experienced in late April 2006, his own instincts were not only to follow the convention but to do so in spades. This, as with the difficulties Rab Butler had in the five years when he was Home Secretary between 1957 and 1962, may have sprung from their mutual experience of having had a father at the top of the civil service.

For me, it was much more simple. Had I had managerial control, I would have undoubtedly taken steps to recruit directly from outside the civil service in the way that we had in the Education and Employment Department, with the full commitment of the then Permanent Secretary, Sir Michael Bichard. But given the changes that John Gieve had agreed and that we had made, with the pressure of work around us it was unthinkable to have an earth-shattering, government-rocking row about the nature of civil-service recruitment and promotion. All our minds were on the job, on spotting the googlies, on thinking ahead and on taking the policy decisions that would in time yield fruit, but required the managerial commitment to make them work in an acceptable time frame.

One such decision at this time was to introduce into the Criminal Justice and Sentencing Act amendments relating to the measures that I had taken just a few months earlier in passing the Nationality, Immigration and Asylum Act, which we were gradually introducing as regulations were laid following its stormy passage in the autumn 2002. The Tories and Liberals had voted against the measures, and many on our own side had argued that we were being too draconian, not only in laying down that all asylum seekers who committed an offence would no longer be entitled to protection under Article 33(2) of the Refugee Convention, but that they would be immediately deportable from the country either during or at the end of their sentence. The argument that went on through to July 2004 about the schedule of lesser offences that would fall into the same category was a vigorous one, as I had wanted all those who had committed a crime that in any way would warrant a prison sentence to be removable. We needed to change the criminal-justice procedure in the new Bill to permit removal during sentence and start the process earlier, and to gel the two pieces of legislation together.

I only wish that I had gone further and applied this to all non-British citizens, but the atmosphere at the time was frenetic, and even getting the withdrawal of Abu Hamza's dual citizenship was to take three years, amid accusations that I was the most vicious and draconian Home Secretary in our history.

Three years later when Charles Clarke was experiencing such enormous pressure in the run-up to the May local elections of 2006, I wondered where everyone had been three years earlier when I had been battling away to get what I considered to be balanced and rational changes. We were acting on the growing number of foreign prisoners, which was rising exponentially as we took action against 'drug mules' and organised crime. As the prison population rose so did the number of foreign prisoners, but at a much faster rate. Catching them and imprisoning them would normally be considered to be a success story, and my drive to get them returned home during their sentence and to complete their punishment in their home country was only just starting. Again I wish that I had accelerated this, but the outcry about transferring people back to countries where they were considered to be at risk (not least because they had committed a crime) was astonishing.

I had one of my regular meetings with the Executive Board and Ministers of State. We are beginning to change things within the Department, and are getting new senior staff in. Things are not moving anywhere near as fast in Immigration as they ought to be so I am having to keep up the pressure, but I think gradually we will begin to turn things round and make things work. I have now got the anti-social behaviour policy agreed. I can't always say this but on this occasion I know that it's true: if I hadn't been involved, great chunks of it would not have been in there, including the clampdown in relation to housing and private landlords and tenants, and all the environmental-health material. None of that would have been in there, so it's worth my having been Home Secretary for this alone.

But having got that out of the way, I've now got to try to concentrate on winning a much more difficult battle: entitlement cards. I need to start on that as soon as the Iraq situation is resolved – God willing.

And so to the week beginning Monday 17 March 2003, the week when Parliament voted to go to war: this is something I would have considered unthinkable and unbelievable when I first entered politics, when I came into Parliament, and when I entered government.

Robin Cook saw Tony on Monday morning and resigned. Letters were exchanged that were published as Cabinet was meeting that afternoon, and Jack Straw made a Statement to the House that evening about there being no other conclusion than that we would have to declare war. Ben Bradshaw, as Robin's deputy, did a Business Statement for the debate on the Tuesday and then Robin made his Statement. I didn't go in for it. I think crucifying myself by sitting there listening to and witnessing chunks of our backbenchers not only rising to their feet but clapping (which is totally unheard of) would have been the last straw.

It certainly was for John Denham [Minister of State in the Home Office]. I'd spoken to him twice and was pretty reassured that he was going to stand firm and was not going to resign. But he listened to Robin and I suspect that there were also personal pressures on him, and at 7.15 on Tuesday morning he rang me up to tell me that he couldn't vote with us and was resigning. I immediately got hold of Tony, who agreed to see him – but, as Tony told me later, it was too late: there simply wasn't enough time to get John to change his mind. Tony thought that if there had been time he might have managed it – which is perhaps why, as with so many occasions like this, as with Estelle resigning, John didn't give me time and he didn't give Tony time. I think it's such a great shame because he was doing well and was on top of things. He was dealing with civil contingencies and resilience. John sometimes drove me to distraction because he took everything to heart too much and sometimes went over the top, but he did the business. (And yes: who am I to talk?!) But he's gone and I owe Andrew Marr a bottle of whisky, because at dinner the previous Thursday I'd said to Andrew that I didn't think that ministers would resign, and we'd had a bet on it. Philip Hunt, Health Minister in the Lords, resigned on the *Today* programme without telling Alan or Tony. At least, John Denham had the decency to resign in the proper way.

I was very shocked by John's resignation. It made a big impact on me: I felt emotionally drained, and really upset by what he'd done, and I felt shaken for the whole day. In the Commons, Tony made the most brilliant speech, interrupted all the time by Glenda Jackson [MP for Hampstead], who knew exactly what she was doing: as a brilliant actress, she appreciated perfectly well that he was coming to the end of his speech. Even Mike Gapes, one of our own side, managed to intervene at completely the wrong moment, just as Tony was explaining that we were going to put Iraqi oil revenue into a UN trust fund to rebuild Iraq. Talk about ineptitude – just amazing.

The other speeches seemed second rate after Tony's. Iain Duncan Smith hadn't constructed his at all: I was sitting next to Gordon, and we did nothing but chunter about it.

I saw Sally Morgan in the evening to try to sort out what I was going to do with ministerial responsibilities following John's resignation, and had got angry with her because she said Tony was too busy. I said: 'He can't be too busy. I've just lost a senior minister and I've got to see him' – which I did the following day. He said he was too tired to do a reshuffle, to which I replied that I needed to know whether he was planning to do one immediately or whether he was going to leave it. I said: 'I can live with having one minister of state less, until immediately after the Scottish and Welsh elections, but I cannot live until July without a full complement – certainly of ministers of state – because of the amount of legislation that's coming through, including stuff coming from the Lords.' I said that I would be under incredible pressure.

There's a separate issue about my Permanent Secretary and the fact that he is trying to reduce the number of ministers. He wants to get rid of a minister and I got angry with him in the end and said: 'You know and I know that civil servants have enormous influence over who becomes a minister and who stays a minister, but I am not prepared to have a situation where pressure is increased on me to make your life easier.'

The upshot was that Tony said that he would think about it over the weekend, and would either do something modest now or leave it until the beginning of May, but wouldn't leave it until July. I said, 'Fine, I'll reallocate the portfolios,' and Sally Morgan said, 'Couldn't we up Hilary Benn to Minister of State?' I said, 'You can if everybody's forgotten what Margaret Beckett did when she took Joan Lestor's job after Joan had resigned in the 1970s' – which rather took Sally aback. I am keen to get Hilary promoted to Minister of State, but I think it will have to be on a slightly different basis from taking John Denham's job.

Gordon has made a real effort to bat in this week and I think there's been a realisation by him that Tony isn't going and that he's got a choice. He either bats in and holds on to the Chancellor's job or he fails to bat in and Tony will take him out when the military action is finished. Michael White's *Guardian* piece on Tuesday morning reflected quite well how Gordon and I had heavily supported Tony at the Special Cabinet on Monday afternoon.

Then there's Clare Short's demise. As the weeks have gone on I have appreciated more clearly in just how much contempt she was held for having announced on television that she was going to resign and then having completely reneged on it and decided that she'd like to stay. Clare has a view, I think, that she and she alone can deal with the reconstruction and post-conflict side of Iraq. Of course the war has been conducted very differently from what people expected. I've been saying to everyone that it is modern warfare with very, very carefully targeted action to demoralise and destroy the regime without blanket bombing and without destruction of the infrastructure. Even so, all the anti-war people still carry on saying exactly the same things – that we are destroying the whole infrastructure, that there will be 10 million refugees, that women and children are being targeted, that Iraq has been destroyed – but they are not cutting off the electricity supply, they are not bombing bridges, they are not bombing hospitals and they are bypassing, wherever they can, towns and cities and just cutting them off. They are telling the Iraqi troops that if they move away from their armaments, they will let them go, rather than taking mass prisoners of war. By Saturday a whole brigade of 8,000 men had laid down their arms.

It is worth reflecting that throughout this period there were some of us who were raising, both in the War Cabinet and privately, the questions that I think Tony was raising personally with George Bush but which were never satisfactorily answered – namely, how we were going to win the peace. In particular there was the question of the complete disbandment of the Iraqi army: allowing them to go home was one thing, but not reconvening them and formulating them into a fighting force was quite another – as well as the complete disbanding of the administrative and bureaucratic structures run by the Ba'ath Party under Saddam Hussein. These included all the mechanisms of law and order, but also local government and other key structures of running a functioning modern society. It seems to me that, as Condoleezza Rice admitted herself on her visit to the UK in March 2006, these were the big mistakes following the initial attack on Iraq.

It wasn't just Tony's performance in the House that was brilliant. He was also brilliant with the Parliamentary Labour Party, saying: 'Don't vote with me out of loyalty, vote with me because you believe in the argument. You may be worried, you may be concerned, you may agonise, but it's the argument now at this moment, with what's happened and the French veto.' I think that's what's carried it. I think that many of those who abstained on the second vote knew in their hearts that the tide had turned, and that logically, from where we were to where we are now, the arguments have changed.

So Cabinet met on Thursday morning. Robin's disappeared and that's that. The tide comes up the beach, the world goes on, and we all should remember that. It is a salutary lesson.

But when I go out and about in my constituency, as I did on the Friday [21 March], to open the £6.5 million Phase 1 of the new Chaucer School and the Meadowhall Training and Resource Centre, and to present the awards to community leaders on Parson Cross, it does bring it home that we are doing good things, that we are changing the world for the better. All those three things were the fruit of work done in the first Parliament.

Then there's asylum. If things go well and we get peace in Iraq, I can really achieve the turn-round. We had the result of the Court of Appeal on Section 55 of the new Immigration, Nationality and Asylum Act on Tuesday morning: what a fiasco. The people we employ manage to give the impression which went out via Press Association that we'd lost when we had changed the idiotic procedure that the IND had engaged in when dealing with applicants. When we first introduced the system, there was one set of people doing interviews, and a different set of people taking the decisions on whether they were entitled to benefits. If you do that you are bound to be challenged, and we had already changed the system. Now the person doing the in-depth interview also makes the decision, and we won on all the key policy points: Article 3 on burden of proof, on timings of judgement, and on whether we had to believe any cock-and-bull story that people came up with. But you wouldn't have thought so. Had the war not been taking place and military action starting, we'd have got a terrible drubbing. As it was, I intervened later in the day and went on Channel 4 news and the BBC ten o'clock news, trying to put the record straight.

We are still having these blasted 8.30 a.m. meetings every day on the conduct of the war (though I managed to miss the one on Saturday because of the Neighbourhood Watch conference). They are a real nuisance, but you need to be in on them otherwise you are out. I have to be there for domestic and internal security, but in truth they are a waste of time. It would make more sense to have them every two or three days.

One of the lighter things of the week, given everything else that was going on and the emotional trauma, was to attend the Privy Council at Buckingham Palace for the clearance of sixty high sheriffs across the country. The Queen was talking to Sadie and asking me about her very strange little turn. I explained to the Queen that Sadie was a half-sister to Lucy, thanks to the wonders of freezing and artificial insemination!

The best part of the week was having two hours out at the cottage late on Friday afternoon and enjoying a walk with Valda and Trevor up on to the edge. I've got to get my case packed for going to the US. I'm in Greece on Thursday and Friday for the Justice and Home Affairs Council and then out to the US on the Sunday.

Just one small footnote on this strange and, in a macabre sort of way, memorable week. On Wednesday morning when we held the first Inner Cabinet, Tony walks in and says, 'Good morning.' I should have cottoned on from his voice that he was tired and not in the mood for a joke, but I said, 'Don't read the morning papers.' He said, 'Why not?' and I said, 'Because it will go to your head.' Not one of my most diplomatic acts, I'm afraid, and it didn't go down well.

Another reflection on that Cabinet: Patricia Hewitt reminded us sardonically, without naming names, of a remark that Robin had made not so long ago in the autumn about Tony having played a blinder. We recalled John Reid saying to Robin that he might regret saying that. But Robin won't. He's now claiming that by the weekend we will all come to regret our diplomatic blunder in supporting the Americans rather than the French, and that we are too close to the Americans and too far away from the Europeans. What on earth he thought we were going to do, God only knows: fall in with the French-German axis as a kind of offshore puppet of Jacques Chirac?

And then on Sunday morning this tragic news:

'BBC Radio 4. It's nine o'clock. This is Broadcasting House. I'm Eddie Mair. Good morning. A Harrier plane returning from a mission over Iraq is missing. It is believed it was shot down by the Americans. Coalition forces have been encountering pockets of resistance as they continue to fan out across Iraq. An American serviceman is being held after a grenade attack in which one soldier died and twelve were wounded. At Broadcasting House, the man who gave up his job over the war, Robin Cook, will be here live. Also, what happens to the Stop the War Coalition, since it failed to stop the war. Three anti-war campaigners will join me. The BBC's Alan Little is keeping a war diary for Broadcasting House. You can hear his first entry just before ten o'clock. You will hear the voice of the major saying, "Are they English or Arabic?" "Arabic." "Then lie flat on the ground, do not move and switch off your mobile phone because if it rings it will give away your position." Plus, away from the war, life tries to go on. We will hear about this year's Oscar ceremony . . .'

So much for BBC non-bias. It's a case of: anyone who is against the war, we will have you on the programme, whoever you are.

But fifteen British servicemen have already died in the helicopter crashes. Oh dear.

This is an absurd situation. Robin Cook wrote an article in the *Sunday Mirror* on the 23rd and the same argument is being peddled very hard now by the anti-war brigade: that the weakness of the Iraqi army proves that Saddam Hussein was not a threat and therefore the war was unnecessary. This ignores the fact that we never argued that the equipment and the traditional military were a threat. Presumably on their argument, we can only be right if Saddam Hussein uses chemical weapons.

Footnote on the week: the Sunday newspapers were making fun of the website advising people what to do to prepare for a domestic attack. They were also poking fun at me, which I find personally irritating even though it's odd to admit it. I had told Huw Evans and officials that I thought the stuff about the storing of bottled water and blankets was really silly and open to ridicule, and it turned out that it was. But the problem is that it is me they ridicule, not officials or special advisers. I was totally against all this silliness but it had already been included before I found out about it. The website went live on 18 March, the day of the Commons vote on Iraq, and I was engaged in anything but trying to second-guess a website. But you just have to live with this sort of situation.

Tom Baldwin recently wrote in *The Times* that I hadn't ruled out standing against Gordon in a future leadership contest, but at the moment there wouldn't be a cat in hell's chance of my standing for the leadership if Tony fell. I could do it, but the honest truth is that I would be only like a slightly more credible Bryan Gould.

I was campaign manager for Bryan Gould – who subsequently returned to his native New Zealand – when, as probably the most intelligent outrider for New Labour in the late 1980s and early 1990s he had stood against John Smith to ensure that there was a contest for the leadership when Neil Kinnock stepped down in 1992. Robin was John's campaign manager and I took up the cudgels for Bryan, having been his No. 2 in the run-up to the 1992 general election when he was Shadow Environment Secretary. We knew it was a hopeless task and I maintained extremely good relations, both with John Smith and with Robin, but Bryan was deeply aggrieved at not winning, as only an individual can be who has given it his best shot and found himself overwhelmed. John was magnanimous to me – but not to Bryan.

Our media are reporting it in a way that was never the case in the First or Second World Wars. If it had been, we would have given up, as there would have been no chance of victory. Just imagine how they would have reported Dunkirk. The reports in the press would have demoralised the whole country rather than mobilising it. It is just remarkable to see it happening and then to realise that we have to fight a war and win through.

We did warn Geoff Hoon in the Cabinet when Geoff was going all gung-ho about smart bombs and the rest of it. John Reid warned caution but someone else said, 'Hear, hear,' and Tony turned to him and said: 'No, no, that's not the way. We need great caution and we don't hype anything.' But I'm afraid Geoff just gets carried away. It just seems to happen to people in the MoD – all this *Boy's Own* stuff again.

Extract from BBC's Tim Franks reporting from British army head-quarters on the Iraqi border: 'The British are having an uncomfortable time in southern Iraq. All units, according to British headquarters, are reporting, in their words, "niggly sniping attacks" . . . As one senior officer put it, "We had the Iraqis at our staff training colleges in the fifties, sixties and seventies, so this is classic counter-insurgency. The biggest problem on the British doorstep may well turn out to be Basra, Iraq's second city. The British insist that they don't want to fight in Basra any more than any other urban area, but military sources clearly believe there are several hundred hard-core well-armed Saddam Hussein loyalists holed up in the city. That is why there were air raids over Basra on Saturday night.'

A very strange meeting of the War Cabinet on Monday morning [24 March]. I arrived about two minutes late and sat at the end of the table. Sir Michael Boyce, Head of the Chiefs of Staff, was waffling on as usual, talking about maps on the table. I had to make the point that I couldn't read the maps but I was as aware as anybody as to exactly what was happening because I had listened to Radio 5 from six a.m. that day! This point was confirmed by Gordon later in the day when I met him to talk about the Budget and he confirmed that we knew more from the media than we were being given at these morning meetings. I said I thought we needed to determine what the strategy was going to be. We were fighting a twenty-first-century technological war but with a medieval strategy – i.e. surrounding the main urban areas and towns, cutting them off but not entering them, and pounding between but over desert. At that point Tony got really angry. I think the tiredness may be getting to him. I said: 'Tony, I am not attacking you. I am trying to work out what we say, what we prepare people for and what they can expect from us, otherwise they only get it from the media – a media that is behind the enemy lines, and is travelling with our troops in a way that would not have been thinkable twenty or even ten years ago.' Thank God, John Prescott and John Reid supported me, saying I was not attacking but asking the questions that are being asked elsewhere. Eventually Tony said that he was sorry, and that he realised that these were perfectly legitimate questions. I pointed out that I'd been canvassing the morning before and that people were supportive. Even the mothers of servicemen in the battle line were supportive, but they wanted answers to questions and they wanted to be sure that the awful images they were seeing on television would in the end transform things. I shall return to it on subsequent mornings because there is no point in getting up early and going to these meetings just to listen to those from the MoD or the Foreign Office mouthing platitudes.

When Gordon and I met later in the day we also spoke about the European Convention on Human Rights. Both of us agreed that it was a fiasco, that nobody had got a grip of it and that things were going drastically wrong. Then later in the day when I was at home doing the box work, I saw the notes. The Foreign Office is upset because I'd attacked the idea of a European Public Prosecutor. Sir John Kerr, who used to be the Foreign Office representative and who is working with the Convention, has said that I'd made life more difficult for him – as though making life easier for him was the objective. It is very worrying that our negotiators are prepared to give away ground on the public prosecutor and justice in order to get agreement on the economic and social security front. As I'd said at Cabinet the previous Thursday, ministers have their eye off the ball, officials have their eye off the ball, and the Convention rolls on. Jack has obviously got more important matters on his mind.

The Americans, as I have discovered, are far more panicky about the war and about casualties than we are. They are not used to what we have been used to, what with Northern Ireland. They panic, they worry, they don't understand that war means that people get killed. It's not clean. It's not a film where people get up afterwards and walk away.

The questions I shall ask at the Tuesday morning meeting will be about who is running the war. Is Colin Powell being overridden by Rumsfeld? Why aren't we taking out the Iraqi television? There is also, of course, the issue of what Turkey is up to in the north, which is really worrying.

Wednesday 26 March: Tony is going to Washington after Prime Minister's Questions, so I shall turn up to the early-morning meeting and see what's what.

The early-morning meeting was quieter and in some ways, more constructive. Sir Michael Boyce started having an argument with John Reid and Clare Short about the issue of whether troops should be switched from Basra to the attack on Baghdad. He didn't seem to understand the politics of Basra at all, that if the people of that city were abandoned when some of them had tried to fight those who were suppressing them, and we just walked away, then we would be held in absolute contempt: the politics, the public relations, the sheer impact of this on support for the military action would be devastating.

Jack is seeing Colin Powell while Tony is at Camp David. Colin Powell needs all the support he can get, because it is clear that Rumsfeld is far too much in charge. He is just overpoweringly confident, and his deputy Paul Wolfowitz is pretty devastating.

It is all very bad at the moment because there are deaths and there are mistakes. Two British soldiers have been killed by our own troops who fired on a tank. These are the terrible casualties of war. There have been mistakes when bombing Baghdad, and because of the intransigence of the

Turks the capitulation and surrender of a whole division in northern Iraq was held up because they would surrender only to regular troops and not to the CIA, and the regular troops couldn't get there because Turkey refused to let them through. So the loyal and political elements from Baghdad managed to get to the brigade in time to stop them capitulating.

I will do my diplomatic bit by going to Greece because I think it will help if we are there and are seen not to have given the cold shoulder to Europe and European meetings.

Thursday, 27 March: there was a panic almost as soon as I had arrived in Greece. There had been a COBR meeting and discussions with Tony in Camp David. Officials and those who are supposed to stay calm are in fact the least calm when these things happen. I had several phone calls from Jonathan Sedgwick, who was just reporting what he was being given and told, and that lasted into Friday, when things started to calm down. It looked at one stage as though I was going to have to come back rather than attend the nine a.m. meeting on Saturday morning, because I am doing *Breakfast with Frost* on Sunday morning as the main government spokesperson. But it calmed down. I was on the *Today* programme about zones and protection for asylum seekers and that went extremely well at the Justice and Home Affairs Council, much better than I could have expected, with Ireland, Holland and even Belgium, Denmark, Austria, Italy, Portugal and Spain all showing real interest. There was opposition from Otto Schily in Germany on the grounds that we could end up with the worst of both worlds – both the zones and the continuing flow, which is a fair point. Opposition also from the Swedish government, but not the Swedish minister, who was wholeheartedly in favour and said that it was time that they all got real. He said he had seen what had happened in Britain with the turning of the tabloids and sensible debate going pear-shaped in January and February, so Jan Karlsson has got the message.

That was a good outcome, and I met Ruud Lubbers from the UNHCR before leaving and had a private chat with him. That was worthwhile, because their convention plus the things the UNHCR is proposing are really incremental steps on the programme that we are trying to lay out. There is going to be a full meeting of all officials involved in Brussels on 7 April, and we are going to see if we can get a number of countries to work together.

I had a very good meal on the waterside across the bay from Thessaloniki on Friday night and then flew back. Unfortunately there was a head wind so it took three and a half hours, and it was midnight before I got home.

But the day in Greece turned out to be a lot better than I thought it would be, ruined by the fact that I got only about four hours' sleep on Thursday night because it was a poor hotel. It was just like being on a building site. There was crashing and banging all night and the sound of running water – in fact everything making a noise. I was woken up at six a.m. their time (four a.m. inside my head) by everybody starting to move about, so that was the end of sleeping.

Saturday morning, 29 March: voice of radio interviewee: 'With any campaign there are periods when you need to redeploy your troops, and you need everything obviously at the peak of fighting ability before you move on to the next objective. There will be periods where things will seem quiet on the fronts, but it is a matter of shaping the battle space, shaping the battlefield, using the air power as and where we can, to get things to our advantage so that when we move on to the next objective, we have the advantage, we call the shots and not the enemy.'

Newsreader: 'A large convoy of American Marines has ground to a halt about 100 miles south of Baghdad. The convoy has become bogged down by pockets of Iraqi resistance and strains on its supply lines. David Willis is with the Marines. Like all our correspondents with coalition forces he is not allowed to say exactly where he is or give details of military plans.'

David Willis: 'Pockets of resistance by Iraqi fighters followed by vicious sandstorms brought this convoy to a halt as hundreds of American Marines are now kicking their heels in the desert and may not be moving for several days. One problem is the supply line. Stretched to the limit on this massive convoy, the infantrymen are now down to one meal a day. Another is the consistent ambush by Iraqi fighters and civilians, some using women and children as human shields. The attacks have prompted commanders to rethink their battle plans. Caution is now the operative word, with the triumphant march on Baghdad currently on hold.'

Newsreader: 'A missile, thought to be Iraqi, has exploded near the shopping centre in Kuwait City during the night. There were no casualties.'

Those reports on the BBC on Saturday morning were all about whether there was going to be a pause of up to a week because of the sandstorm and the difficulties being experienced.

Reuters were with American troops in central Iraq on Saturday morning, and confirmed what had been told to me on Thursday night about how difficult things were. But there was a terrible flap going on. All of these things were highly predictable. If they had put Colin Powell in charge instead of letting Rumsfeld loose with some of the dum-dums who are running the show on the ground, including our Air Marshal, it would have been a lot better. It is self-evident that the massive sandstorms and the over-extension, as well as the failure of Turkey to let troops through in the north, have made a difference.

Above everything – and I am intent on trying to get this across – is the fact that we are fighting a different sort of war.

I did the *Today* programme on the zones, after Bill Morris had attacked me. I then did a Radio 5 Live interview which also touched on Iraq and I managed to get one or two points across, including the fact that older listeners would find what was happening extraordinary: journalists and TV crews behind enemy lines, relaying what the enemy says and reporting on every single incident. How the hell can we fight a war with twenty-four hours a day, seven days a week news-reporting like that, including tactics? Every failure, every mistake is highlighted. I got that message across, and also picked up on the *Daily Telegraph* asking the French Foreign Minister who he hoped would win. I said that that was the question that everybody has to ask themselves and then they know whose side they are really on.

But the question I want to get across on the *Frost show* is: how on earth do you manage to take cities without mass bombardment? It is back to my question to Tony on the previous Monday morning at 8.30: is this a technological war with medieval tactics? It angered him but it is the right question. When was it last possible to take a city without absolute mass bombardment and blitzkrieg? Perhaps that will be something we will discuss before I go to the USA.

The Saturday morning meeting was mainly straightforward. Afterwards I had a chat with Tony about my visit to the USA. He is really jumpy. He is trying to talk to Chirac and Schröder and he sounds so tired. I updated him on the Zones of Protection [for asylum seekers], as well as talking to him about the USA.

The News Quiz on Radio 4 quoted a cutting that I had to laugh at. 'Um Quasa is a city similar to Southampton, the UK Defence Minister said in the Commons yesterday. A British squaddie patrolling the town commented, "Either he has never been to Southampton or he has never been to Um Quasa. There is no beer, no prostitutes and people are shooting at us. It is more like Portsmouth."'

But it wasn't so funny over in America. The trip on Concorde was fantastic – 57,500 feet up, 1,320 miles per hour, three and a half hours across the Atlantic – and yet the plane itself felt as though it was about to fall to pieces. It was like going up in a tin can. It didn't matter that space was fairly restricted. What mattered was that there was really no top-class professional service for the money that would really attract people to it, along with the speed of the flight. They don't even bother giving you any kind of memento any more – though, to be fair, the flight attendants did give me a bottle of champagne. I bought a gift but a little memento would have gone down really well. One of the protection officers managed to persuade the purser to give him a salt and pepper set. When we arrived, we were flying on to Washington rather than staying overnight in New York because it had been decided that the flights between New York and Washington were difficult the next day and that it was better to go that evening. The plane had broken down before we got on it so we sat on the airport bus for ages, waiting while they got another plane. When we got on we had the farce of security, to the point where they wouldn't even let anyone stand up to go to the toilet. Sophie Linden, my assistant, who is six months pregnant, stood up to go, and the guard shouted over the loudspeaker in such a way that everybody jumped out of their seats. He drew his gun and said that if anyone stood up again, they would have to divert the plane away from Reagan airport at Washington. It was curious, because everyone was very quiet. America isn't normally full of quiet people, but people were really subdued on the plane and clearly worried about travelling. There was a very different atmosphere from back home.

Tony Brent, the Chargé d'Affaires, who had taken over from the ambassador because there is an interregnum, was very good. He and his wife looked after us extremely well – a complete contrast to Tom Harris, the Consul-General in New York, who relies entirely on his deputy and others.

We had a quick bite to eat and went to bed, and then on Monday morning [31 March] had a number of meetings, including one with John Ashcroft, the Attorney General, when I signed a new extradition agreement. I also saw the Drugs Tsar, John P. Walters: a very strange man, completely evangelical. I thought we should all get down on our knees and pray to deal with drugs rather than take practical realistic steps. He was totally obsessed with marijuana and how young people should seek treatment for it. What we are struggling to do is to try and treat 250,000 serious drug users. We went on to Capitol Hill and had a look round Congress, sitting in on the Senate. The House of Representatives had gone into partial recess, but in the Senate the Presiding Senator was making a speech – ostensibly about the death of Daniel Patrick Moynihan, the charismatic former Senator for New York, but including material about access to previous records and freedom. I picked up one or two things about Moynihan from the speech that will be useful when I give my lecture on Wednesday night. I saw the British journalistic corps and did some interviews, including one for National Public Radio which, although I was inclined to liken it to getting myself on late-night Radio 3, it did turn out that quite a number of people listened to.

April 2003

In all I did a good number of media interviews around this trip, including both international and domestic CNN and a number of their TV channels, including the *Charlie Rose* show. We then visited Baltimore, and I was surprised to find that there are areas of dereliction on the edge of the city.

In New York I saw Mayor Bloomberg (who didn't impress me) and Commissioner Ray Kelly (who did). I made a little speech at Ground Zero, then saw former Mayor Rudi Giuliani and Kevin Cahill, who turned out to be a man with real expertise, who had diagnosed and treated the people with anthrax and is a world expert in smallpox. He was well worth talking to. I visited a community justice centre at Redhook in Brooklyn, which was so impressive that I will try to get their people across to talk to us about it to see if we can do something similar in the UK.

This is one of the most impressive projects that I ever visited outside our country. I was determined then that we should try to replicate it and, with a visit made by the Lord Chief Justice, Harry Woolf, who was equally impressed, and later by Charlie Falconer, we stood a chance of doing so. Unfortunately the early experiment with the UK's first community justice centre in Liverpool seemed in the early stages to be getting off to a very slow start with regard to changing the whole perspective and way of thinking of those prosecuting, those defending and those responsible for supervising and supporting miscreants.

In simple terms, what we needed was to try to sort out the problem rather than to get either a technical knock-out for the defence, which would get the individual off but not resolve the problem one iota, or get a definable result for the prosecution, which would put a score on the sheet but wouldn't provide a pathway out of criminality. What amazed me then, and still amazes me now, is how little interest the liberal intelligentsia showed in this scheme back in the UK. You would think that with all the spouting on about being 'liberal' and 'helping people out of lifelong criminality' that they would be constantly campaigning – but no such luck. Instead they indulge in hand-wringing at dinner parties on Saturday night and then think they have done their bit.

While we were in New York, I met the *New York Times* editorial board and went out on a police launch to the Statue of Liberty and past Ellis Island. It is amazing what Ellis Island means to so many Americans, particularly those of eastern and central European extraction.

I then delivered my lecture at the John Jay Higher Education College, which deals with crime, terrorism and the like. It was a very good audience, carried live on their C-SPAN television and I think on BBC News 24 as a consequence, but the Press Association (whom Paul Potts had got to come along) were not interested in the philosophy and values, not in the debate about security versus liberty, and balance and proportionality, but only in passing remarks about not treating Saddam Hussein's regime as a moral equivalent in terms of the media and the press, and those who were behind what I called 'enemy lines'. I was roundly abused by those who had neither seen nor heard my words. A man called Benson from the *Mail* appeared on the *Today* programme, attacking me, and they made real mischief with it on Thursday morning. Then there was Roger Mosey in one of the Sunday papers. I have written to him, just to draw attention to the fact that it would have been helpful if he had bothered to read what I had said, especially as he was contrasting it with something he had attended that Jack Straw was doing. This underlines my point that if you are inside, and you see and you know, you can record accurately, but if you are doing it from outside and from a distance and only have partial facts, then you are likely to get it wrong.

The lecture went well, though I felt that I spoke for slightly too long. Then we had all this palaver. I came back on the overnight flight on Thursday night, arriving at 9 a.m. at Heathrow on Friday. A good flight, but if I had managed more than three hours' sleep it would have been better. I felt a bit like the walking wounded. Jet lag is a strange feeling, particularly when you've flown home on what is called the 'Red Eye' (overnight flight across the Atlantic), because you are not entirely knocked out but not entirely with it either. How on earth business people manage when they are supposed to fly in and make important decisions and deal with difficult negotiations, goodness knows.

When I saw Gordon on the Friday morning, we were talking to each other in an easy way so it was not so bad but if we had been knocking seven bells out of each other, I think he would have had the advantage. But we had a good chat about budgetary matters and politics generally, and sorted out where we were on the Budget, including what Sir David Omand had been up to by submitting material about our priorities for internal security while I was away.

I decided to go on the *Today* programme on Saturday morning, when I was interviewed by John Humphrys and dealt with the issue of what I had said and what I hadn't said and all the distortion. I also dealt with the fact that I made the decision on Friday about Abu Hamza and withdrawing his citizenship. Then at Saturday lunchtime on *The World at One* I had to put up with a load of garbage, in which the lawyer for Abu Hamza said he didn't have Egyptian citizenship, and this was believed – then repeated on the Sunday lunchtime programme, which included an interview with Bill Morris: he had written an article for the *Observer* that morning, attacking me and asking when the knock would come on his door, as though we lived under the KGB.

Tony has made John Reid Leader of the House and Ian McCartney Chair of the Party, which should be interesting.

The redistribution of the education budget away from my earmarked Standards Fund spending and key help to inner-city and deprived areas is coming home to roost, with budget cuts in such schools across the country. But Charles Clarke [Secretary of State for Education and Skills] wouldn't listen and officials have got their way, along with the Treasury, as it was at their insistence.

I was really pleased to hear the news this weekend that Sarah and Gordon are expecting a baby in October, and gave Gordon a ring. Sitting in his office dealing with the Budget, he was surprised to hear from me. I said that this was the first time I had ever rung him on a Budget weekend when we hadn't been having words about finance, and that I had just rung to congratulate them both. He said that he was sorry that he hadn't told me the day before, but Sarah had gone off to tell her mother and father and it didn't seem fair to tell people before they knew. I said that I had noticed that he had sounded cheerful the day before.

I found my visit to the USA revealing. They were very anti-French, and very enthusiastic about the British – but from the television coverage you wouldn't even know that the British were participating in the war, let alone that a third of the troops on the ground are ours. They were over the moon about the rescue of Jessica Lynch, the young woman who had been badly shot up and captured and who had then been rescued. Someone will surely be making a film about it soon.

The Americans were friendly towards me and prepared to listen, and I was able to get messages across about how crucial it was to carry the success in Iraq into success in the Middle East – for their security and ours, as well as what needs to be done globally – and to find a settlement for a viable, sustainable secure Palestine as well as for Israel. I kept hammering the point home over and over again, in the lecture and in interviews, just to try to get across how crucial it is that they don't go isolationist. It was absolutely clear though that if Tony had not taken the line he had all the way since Bush's election, then we would have no influence at all in this situation. It would be all waffling in the wind about Palestine and about the rest of the role that the UN could play, as soon as the conflict is over and beyond. If we were in the situation of Chirac or Schröder or Putin we wouldn't have a chance, not a single bit of influence.

As for the BBC, you only have to listen to current-affairs programmes, including things like *Broadcasting House* on Sunday morning, to see that it's overwhelmingly anti-war. Contribution after contribution takes the same line; there's no balance, and it's just awful. We have just got to see it through now and get a conclusion and take it from there. Nobody can say that I have not done my bit. I certainly have.

One lesson from the visit to Washington and New York, apart from the fact that I don't know how Tony Blair does it, and that I am no better at jet lag than I used to be, is that you just end up doing too much. By the time I reached Thursday lunchtime and went to a rather poor project that one of the staff had recommended, I had had enough. I just wanted to go shopping. I had to do some more interviews that afternoon so I missed out a bit, but I did want to get the feel of the place. I would have loved to have just gone to a deli and had lunch. I mustn't get used to flying first class, though. It is going to be a strange life after politics. The seriously rich just take it for granted that the money will be there and they will be carrying on in the same way, but I will have to watch it.

Valda and Julie are keeping things going for me in the constituency office. If it weren't for good friends, if it weren't for those who, while I am whizzing about the world, do the job that matters most of all, then I wouldn't be able to do any of it. And what's more, those are the people who care, really care what happens to me, and care what happens to the job.

My Principal Private Secretary rang me to say that No. 10 were panicking about people being off over Easter and that they were only allowed to be off from Thursday night to Tuesday (and I am off until Wednesday). I wish he had told them that I had spent seven years missing out on Easter holidays and during that time I never expected the Foreign Secretary or the Defence Secretary or anybody else to have to forgo their Easter just because I had to attend teacher conferences.

A footnote on the last few days is just to mention that in my meeting with Gordon we discussed the euro. He made it clear that he was recommending to Tony that we shouldn't go for the euro for the time being, and said that we should make it clear that this was on economic grounds. He asked me not to say anything, but said that he would call me if he needed to ask me to reinforce the position, knowing where I stood. A little bit appeared in the Sunday papers talking about only three out of the five tests being met, but nothing very much. It is quite clear though that Gordon wants to make an announcement this Wednesday to settle the thing once and for all and to discuss it at Cabinet. I don't think Tony will want to do that, so it should be interesting.

Week beginning Monday 7 April: following Bill Morris's article in the *Observer*, criticising me for acting against Abu Hamza, people have come up to me in the street and commended me for it. I'm afraid Bill seems to have lost his marbles. On Tuesday morning John Prescott was chairing the morning breakfast meeting and I deliberately went along to back him up. He did very well. I raised the issue of looting, saying that I was really concerned about it. On Wednesday morning (by which time Tony was back) Clare Short raised the same issue.

At dinner with Alastair Campbell on the following Wednesday evening, he asked me what I thought I was doing backing up Clare Short. I said that in fact she was backing me as I had earlier raised the whole issue of looting and the effect it was having, including the stealing of essential humanitarian aid and medical supplies. By the weekend, this had become a real nightmare of an issue. Our problem at the beginning of the week was with Basra, which we had at least tried to get a grip of. By the end of the week it was Baghdad and the whole thing was unravelling, with people looting hospitals. The military (in our case, Michael Boyce) were insisting that their job was to fight the war, and not to police the area and protect the citizens or vital equipment. They carried on saying this until we told them not to. It is absolutely breathtaking.

On this one I was with Clare. There was a degree of complacency and a feeling along the lines of: why should we be bothered about this when the whole law-and-order situation is falling apart? I immediately went back to the Department and said that I wanted them to look at how we could send people from our police over to help – not to police but to help reorganise their policing so that we could get some civic order back into the place, perhaps using organised volunteers who could be pulled together. The message came back to me via one of the private secretaries that the FCO had said that they had got MoD police so it wasn't necessary. I said that I hadn't asked him to ask what was necessary, I had asked him to organise to offer some help, because it is civilianisation that is needed, not a constant reliance on the military.

This was an important issue because once again it underlined the mistake that was made by the Americans in dismantling the formal mechanisms of local administration and law and order. It was going to take time to rebuild them, and the military police were certainly not the ones to do it.

Those running the show had not quite understood what was about to happen, but they are always about ten leagues behind, even though the military success is overwhelming.

Wednesday was quite a day all round, what with it being Budget Day and the events in Baghdad – the statue of Saddam was toppled – and this wonderful sense that what we wanted was happening in Iraq, and that people were out on the streets rejoicing. The euphoria was spoiled a bit by the US troops deciding to drape the Stars and Stripes over the head of the statue before it was pulled down. How crass can you get? The Americans simply have no feeling at all as to what the attitude to that in the Middle East would be.

It is a great relief to have made such strides in just three weeks. We have not finished, of course, and the fighting is still going on across the country, but what a difference has already been made. Unsurprisingly, there's been no word of apology from those who have been on the other side. Nobody is saying that they were wrong about the outcome, and that there aren't 10 million refugees, as they'd predicted. Nobody is saying that they were wrong about the Iraqi people attacking us with their own hands. Instead of that, they say: where are the chemical weapons, and why haven't they used them?

Budget Day: we had the conventional pre-Budget Cabinet – low key because the Budget was going to be low key, with a hell of a lot of borrowing, although we are still within the cycle of borrowing commitments and the Maastricht Treaty. But there has been something of a row about the euro going on. When I spoke to Gordon the previous Friday I picked this up, and it was running through all the early part of the week. I saw Tony privately for a moment after the Cabinet on Wednesday. He was very nice to me and commended me for what I had done in the USA, then said he wanted to talk to me about the euro (which presumably means that he wants to persuade me that we should go for it!). I have got to decide whether to be all out against or go for suggesting that we should only go for it if we can get the Germans to sign up to unwinding the growth and stability pact (which is nothing to do with growth and nothing to do with stability but all about depression, as they are finding). I am seeing Tony at Monday teatime, privately, and then joining him for dinner with Alan Milburn, John Reid, Hilary Armstrong and Sally Morgan. It is all supposed to be about where we go now on the domestic front, what are we going to do, and what are the next steps in terms of the future – which I am happy to talk about – but in private it is obviously going to be about the euro, and about the upcoming reshuffle, and I want to talk about my idea of where we are going with civil renewal.

Budget Cabinet, and the really good news is that we are going to start the Child Trust Fund, backdated to last September: not enough money and not enough kickstart, but at least it is a start. During Iain Duncan Smith's reply, I made it clear that I thought he was talking rubbish and intervened. He broke off in the middle of his response to attack me and asked if the Home Secretary would stop shouting – and I was shouting because he was talking a load of rubbish. He had attacked the fact that savings had dropped but was then opposing a scheme that encouraged savings.

Dinner with Alastair Campbell and Fiona Millar. Alastair had clearly clocked that Gordon had mentioned the Home Secretary six times in his Budget speech and was very interested, not only in my views on the euro (which I was cautious about) but in my views on other Cabinet ministers in the light of the imminent reshuffle (which I was equally cautious about). He was very positive about Bev Hughes, and euphoric about Margaret Beckett.

Alastair revealed that he had raised £225,000 for his run in the London Marathon [which he undertook to raise funds for leukaemia research], including £50,000 from a neighbour who was an estate agent. Even Michael Heseltine had given him £500. I am afraid I only managed £50 because I was sponsoring several people at the time.

Fiona was very clear that she was out, that she had had enough of Carole Caplin [Cherie Booth's controversial 'lifestyle adviser' in No. 10] and everything else; she was being very positive. Other conversations had led me to believe that she was deeply cynical and negative and was going to pull

Alastair out of the government as well, but I didn't get that impression. I thought that Alastair was very enthusiastic and up for everything. I may be wrong but I got the impression that he had got a new lease of life. On the whole it was an entertaining evening but I felt all the time that I was under scrutiny.

This last week I had meetings about security with Eliza Manningham-Buller [who had succeeded Stephen Lander as Director General of MI5]. A number of us have been wondering what George Galloway [then maverick Labour MP for Glasgow Kelvin] was involved in, and at Prime Minister's Questions when Iain Duncan Smith asked Tony who he thought might accept the surrender in Iraq, David Winnick had shouted 'George Galloway' – which brought the house down.

We had the Anti-Social Behaviour Bill second reading on Tuesday, and the backbenchers were brilliant, offering constant support and generally being very helpful, which made my fifty minutes, with all the interventions, worthwhile – a really good example of how parliamentary colleagues can lift and sustain you. Oliver Letwin was very weak because he wanted to get over to Westminster Hall for a debate on rural post offices at two p.m., and because I had taken so many interventions, not deliberately but just because it seemed right, it just about wiped out his speech. He had got to the point where he was doing a good job illustrating that what we were putting forward was a replica in parts of previous legislation and our lot shouted, 'We'll take your word for it!' rather than allowing him to read it into the record – and he let them get away with it and he didn't read it. I thought: thank goodness for backbenchers, who have turned up in numbers and are willing to do the job.

On Thursday I went to Patricia Hewitt's constituency in Leicester to do a session on faith and cohesion. Patricia couldn't turn up because she had to attend a meeting called by Jack Straw, but had asked me specifically to help with issues around cohesion and growing problems with anti-social behaviour in Leicester. I was glad to do so because the very large Asian community in the area needed to be reassured that we cared. It was rigorous and difficult but worth doing, and it was the top story on the regional news.

On Friday I was in Nottingham doing Home-Start, the gun-crime round table, and the Afro Caribbean Centre.

Home-Start is a really important voluntary sector organisation that I had backed when I was at Education, working in and with families at risk and helping to sustain youngsters when there were real problems with parenting or because of the breakup of families.

I made a terrible *faux pas* by mentioning in the conference that my son Alastair had to use a pseudonym when doing his job because of the difficulties having the name Blunkett created for him. It was stupid of me, because I should have realised that the Press Association locally would pick this up and make his life a misery. I do slip up like this from time to time. I keep secret things that need to be kept secret, but those on the edge I do sometimes let slip, and then kick myself for it.

I had meetings about the constituency and mobile phone masts on Friday afternoon and the surgery on Saturday. Bit of a break at the weekend and then back with a vengeance for the final Budget debate on Monday and then a whole series of meetings before going with my son Alastair on Thursday to see my cousin Pauline in Spain for a day or two.

Just one more reflection this week about the war: on Thursday morning I heard Prince Hassan of Jordan on the radio and I raised at the breakfast War Cabinet meeting the issue of Kirkuk and the fact that there was a real danger of the Kurds taking it. Michael Boyce just dismissed this, saying I didn't know what I was talking about. Later in the day the Kurds invaded Kirkuk. By Saturday they had started to withdraw in favour of the Americans, but it was a very tight moment and provides yet another example of how out of touch many of the military people are. That was reinforced on Saturday morning when I heard Patrick Cordingley, a Major-General in the 1991 Gulf War, waffling on about how unbiased and wonderful the *Today* programme team were and how he had seen them crying over civilian casualties. He then went on to attack the government over the two soldiers who had been reported as assassinated and said that it was just a lie. It was not a lie. But it shows that if the BBC like the message, then it's the truth – and if they don't, it is propaganda.

Week beginning Monday 14 April: Gordon had flown back from the G8 but he was in a really bad way sitting next to me on the bench when Tony made his Statement. It was really a kind of round-up Statement on the end of the main military conflict. Three and a half weeks and very little credit being given to him in the media in Britain – just griping, whining, self-justification. Those who were wrong don't want to be wrong and so resent it, and those who were right still don't seem to want to give Tony any credit for it. But the collapse into anarchy and looting has given them the excuse they wanted. As one professor of physics at Basra University said on Radio

4 (and repeated several times over the following days), 'We want liberty, but there is no liberty without order and security.' That is exactly what I have been trying to say – and what I said in my lecture in New York. And of course it is true.

One of the problems in the Home Office is that even the better people are reactive rather than looking for solutions and getting ahead of the situation as fast as they can. I had this later in the week with organised crime and immigration. Talk about a wet-lettuce approach to a sweep of hundreds of people whom I had authorised to be picked up. 'Prosecution will be the aim and if not we will endeavour to get them out of the country,' said the notice that officials had put up; not 'We will take decisive enforcement action, including removing people from the country as quickly as possible.' We are talking here about massive scams – organised crime, prostitution, and drug- and asylum-running. It is a story that is going to blow up, and I just despair.

I attended the breakfast meetings during the week. Tony wasn't very pleased with me because I asked him whether he was a holiday-phobic. He replied: 'I like holidays but it is inappropriate to take one at the moment.' I don't think it is inappropriate. I think everybody would have told him to get away for a few days. I am always putting my foot in it.

I did have an interesting conversation in private with Tony on Monday evening, followed by dinner. A decent discussion, but still on the lines of 'We need an enemy to attack, we need something big that will allow us to demonstrate our policy and our reform – so who can we take on?' I said that it wasn't difficult to take anybody on, it's what I've been doing for the past six years. Just point me out into the street and I will soon find somebody to take on. But that's not the issue. The issue is that engagement with people is part of the solution, individuals and communities alike, together with civil renewal. I have put a note across to Tony about that and the fact that we are going to produce a pamphlet in June, and I will make a major speech about it so that we can get things moving and see if we can get on to a new trajectory.

But I didn't get the feeling that anybody else was up for it. We had a discussion about foundation hospitals. It was nowhere near as contro-versial or as radical a policy now because they were not going to be allowed to raise substantial additional resources that would fall outside the departmental expenditure limit, but would have to stay within the overall totals. I talked about the reshuffle and he asked me to put in ideas, which is what I have done. I have also put in a paper about ID cards and moving things forward through the Domestic Affairs Cabinet Committee and the Cabinet itself. I am having a hell of a job getting the Department to write the paper. One has been produced that was very similar to the consultation document produced last year.

I gave Tony a note about the reshuffle at the Thursday breakfast meeting. We talked about the euro and I said that I believed Gordon was right about the impact on the economy and having to retrench on public services when there was already a tight situation with the next Spending Review. I said that what I would advocate is that Tony open discussions with Schröder about renegotiating and reshaping the growth and stability pact. Tony said he would when he had dinner with him the following evening, but I haven't yet had a chance to talk to him about whether or not he did. But he has decided that he is not going to go for the euro referendum, thank God, but the door will be kept open so there is still the possibility of a referendum this side of the general election. I think he thinks that we might be able to have a referendum on the day of the European elections, but I think electorally it could be disastrous.

My other reflection on the week: what wonderful weather. Wednesday was the hottest April day ever recorded. Maundy Thursday, when I am flying off to Malaga, is a glorious day, just the sort of day to walk, to talk, to swim – and I am going to an apparently very cloudy, drizzly southern Spain. Past Easters have been foul weather in Britain and Alastair and I go to the south of Spain when the weather is glorious here and poor there. But I will make the best of it. I am taking some books.

Thursday 24 April: back from Pauline's: Alastair put up with me very well, and managed a day skiing. The weather was very poor compared with Britain, so I made a bad choice this time.

Had a terrible dream on Thursday night – a dream that had all the undertones of being on the outside, of being alienated, of being given the cold shoulder, of being friendless and leaning on a stick, having fallen out with Tony Blair and then having challenged him in the middle of a speech in the Commons and humiliating him by raising something that left him floundering. But as with most dreams, I cannot remember what that something was! And we had fallen out about privatising the police service, which is not even something that I would be against, given their performance. Dear, dear.

While I was away, the *Sunday Times* did a front page story on the letter that Derry Irvine had sent to me and that had clearly been leaked. One suggestion was that it was from the Office of the Deputy Prime Minister, but if I tried talking to John Prescott about that he would go ballistic.

So I rang Nick Pearce, who was the only adviser available, and told him to get the press office to quote my Statement to the House on the Second Reading. I also said it in the Statement when I moved the White Paper that was all about anti-social behaviour. That quote was then carried in Monday's papers, but the *Guardian* on Tuesday had to have a go at me. They couldn't resist it. As I found out when I went to Glasgow to campaign for the Scottish elections, people up there are thinking about nothing else but anti-social behaviour – and yet this is the response I get when I lay down what needs to be done. All the things they were talking about in the public meeting we held and all the things that we are doing are as one. We are addressing the issues that matter to them most.

Page five of the *Sunday Times* [20 April] was all about that newspaper having placed somebody as a temp in IND, dealing with the Sangatte intake. This is just indicative of management. It was a story about the total incompetence of the place and people going to sleep on their desks, which is a classic. Then the *Daily Mail* had a real go on the Monday morning [Easter Monday], presumably because Paul Dacre is away.

But the outbreak of this respiratory disease, SARS, will give all the usual suspects on the right the opportunity to have another go about disease coming in with asylum seekers. So I have set in train a defensive reaction, including getting hold of Alan Milburn on Friday while I was in Scotland and saying to him that we really do need to get our act together, not with regard to what his Chief Medical Officer was doing about notifiable diseases, but to how we manage to screen people who have not been through a pre-screening device because they are asylum seekers. Alan seemed to agree and said that we should have a recall meeting of the one with Paul Boateng and Jack Straw and we needed to push on. Then later in the day his office started to back-pedal like mad, and got themselves into a flap about it all. So we take one step forward and several back, I'm afraid.

I am pressing on because we have got to do something to ensure that we have a proper system. I would like all those coming from China, claiming asylum, to be held in secure accommodation while we check them, and they really don't know what to say to me about that!

I spoke to Tony over the weekend while I was away – a very friendly social call. He said he wanted to see me in the week about the reshuffle, but by the time we had made contact with his office they had changed their minds and said that he didn't want to talk to me. I spoke to Sally Morgan and it is absolutely clear that something is going on and things have changed for some reason, and it looks as though the reshuffle has got pushed on from May Bank Holiday way into the future, not even to the Spring Bank Holiday but later, which will cause havoc. Speculation starts, people start backbiting and trying to stitch each other up. We get stupid stories like the one on Saturday morning [26 April]. Two very low-level journalists, Patrick O'Flynn on the *Express* and somebody who I had never heard of on the *Mirror*, had clearly had lunch with somebody and were promoting Mike O'Brien to the Cabinet, even though he is a parliamentary under-secretary, and also floating the idea that I should do a swap with Alan Milburn so that I could sort out foundation hospitals. What a joke – but whoever the joker is, he is going to get his comeuppance if I can find out who it was. I have just about got the management structure at the Home Office sorted and am starting to succeed on immigration and crime, and the suggestion is that I'm demoted to Health. But that's the sort of silliness you get, and it does stir people up.

I chaired a round-table meeting on Thursday night, with Andrew Turnbull, Sir David Omand, John Gieve and other officials, and with Michael Barber and the woman who has been working for him, looking at civil resilience and the structures (the structural and process side of counter-terrorism). Everything they had come up with I know about already and had agreed needed to be done, but it was good to be able to lay it down in terms that everybody could understand, including getting senior officials in each department responsible for doing the job, getting ministerial lines sorted out, getting the other eleven strands of work completed, the twelfth one being CBRN (chemical, biological, radiological and nuclear), which Michael, thank God, found we were now doing well, having put new staff in. But we have really got to pull it together. We have been very fortunate that we haven't been completely done over, so the gods are with us, but I do hope to get this sorted once and for all.

Week beginning Monday 28 April: still massive reverberations from the withdrawal of the substantial part of the Standards Fund and the complete fiasco round it. There was a letter from Andrew Adonis – rather tongue in cheek, seeing that he was partly responsible for not defending the Standards Fund, but acknowledging that I am right and that it is the withdrawal of the Standards Fund that has completely messed up. It has taken David Miliband a very long time to get to grips with this but I think Charles has grasped it.

Estelle told me a lovely story over dinner about the Liberal Democrats in Liverpool. They are inviting her up and making her an honorary member of the Education Committee, showing her round, and treating her decently. When after Cabinet on Thursday I saw Hilary Armstrong to talk to her about the state of play, including the delayed reshuffle, I got the impression that she had had a real mouthful from Estelle, that Estelle had really turned on her. God save me from ever feeling like that – like the terrible dream I had that I was out, with everybody passing me and nobody speaking to me. I have said to Hilary that it is crucial that we give Estelle something in the reshuffle, whenever it eventually happens. If we could just bring her back it would help her.

Busy day, Monday: I went to Dartford in the morning, campaigning. I attended the Press Club lunch and made what I thought was a decent speech, slightly hectoring but amusing. Simon Kelner, editor of the *Independent*, couldn't bring himself to clap. I was quite wound up about that speech, which is curious: all the speeches that I make, and I was so tense about that particular one. Then Home Office Questions; then laying the stone and the buried crystal for the new Home Office building in Marsham Street; and then to Buckingham Palace for the launch, with Sophie, Countess of Wessex, of the Jill Dando Institute of Criminal Science, which is being established at University College, London.

Tuesday, I ended up going to Rhyl to campaign for the Welsh Assembly elections next month: seven and a half hours travelling for an hour and three-quarters' campaigning.

This was a visit to raise the profile of our work with young people, with offenders and with restorative justice – where people who have offended do work that helps either their victim or the community and puts something back in. Ann Treneman, who was then writing profiles for The Times *and has since become a parliamentary sketch-writer for the same paper, accompanied us all day in order to get material for the profile she was doing on me for the following Saturday.*

But what is interesting about my diary is the fact that I make no mention whatsoever, for reasons that will become clear, of a letter I had been passed at dinner the night before going to Rhyl, a letter that revealed that those seeking the renewal of their visa to work legally and legitimately in this country were being told by IND that they would have to wait for up to a year – in most cases, way beyond their right to be in the country – in order to obtain renewal.

In normal circumstances, you may react with 'Incompetent, but so what?', but – and this is really crucial – we had just agreed at my suggestion a programme of charging for the renewal of visas, which would go towards raising the £100 million income that was required to balance the books. A charge of £155 was to be levied from August, and I had given absolute instructions that we were to sort out the administration by then in order to clear much of the backlog and deliver a service worthy of people being charged for it.

I didn't register at the time, but I accept since, that I must have passed that letter in with the response to my usual evening box via my driver, who dropped it off at the office the morning I got the train to Rhyl. The inquiry under Sir Alan Budd into allegations made by the Sunday Telegraph *on 28 November 2004 demonstrated without equivocation that no note accompanying this letter existed. Having examined every piece of evidence, including the hard drive of the computers that would have typed up any note I sent (on cassette tape), it was clear that the letter had simply been passed into the Department for reference and action. I was at meetings and was clearly open about this, raising the whole issue of what on earth was happening with the backlog and explaining that there had been a specific case that had drawn this to my attention, a case that fell within the constituency of a Conservative back-bencher. This made it impossible for me to refer the letter to the MP without bringing down the roof on the Home Office.*

With hindsight, I now accept that I should have dictated a note that indicated that I had, albeit at one remove, a personal connection with the writer of the letter. It would not have changed any of the subsequent events, but it would have protected me from the unjustified allegation that I had sought to help this individual specifically rather than to change the process and the system, which I believed was failing. To this extent I was clearly mistaken, although I make no apology for using individual cases or material drawn to my attention to change the administration and the way that government policy was being carried through by the civil service. I did this (not with any personal connection) over and over again. In many instances, had I not, information would not have been made available to me and changes would not have been made. I believe this is the responsible job of any democratically elected and accountable politician, drawing on day-to-day experience and contact with the public and using individual instances to demonstrate the failure or success of particular policies.

For the record, I did not (and Sir Alan Budd affirms this) request, instigate or demand the fast-tracking of the individual visa renewal, but clearly there was a connection to my office, as demonstrated by Sir Alan, and that connection was the letter that I passed to the office. I deeply regret my own failure to recognise that this might later be used against me in what the public clearly understood, even if others didn't, was a tragic personal and private issue. Together with the breakdown of my health later in the year, it was responsible for my withdrawal from the most senior echelons of government.

Then Wednesday was just another classic busy day. I chaired the gun-crime meeting, and had lunch with the *Sun*. Les Hinton was there, and I made my peace with Rebekah Wade.

May 2003

I saw Prince Charles on Thursday before coming back for the local elections on Thursday [1 May], when we re-took an overall majority in Sheffield after all the years of disaster from the mid-1990s onwards – not as well as we ought to have done, but good enough.

Thursday 6 May was six years to the day since we were elected to government in 1997. Six years as a Cabinet minister: who would have thought it, the lad from Parson Cross? Given that we are in mid term, the atmosphere is better than could have been expected, but we will see what happens.

Bad news of the week locally was the announcement by Corus, the steel company, of massive redundancies in South Yorkshire – over 800 jobs, 370 of them in Stocksbridge, Sheffield – and the sheer gall of the company, who are interested only in treading water, in staying where they are in the world market, rather than looking to expand.

Good news of the week for me was getting an agreement with Tony on ID cards, subject to sorting out the finance and the technology. What a breakthrough. The discussion took place after a very lengthy Cabinet when we discussed the local election results in detail, and in particular the success of the British National Party. Although overall turn-out for the local elections in England was 35.6 per cent, I think Tony is still not of the mind that real disillusionment has set in, and he began to argue with me about whether there would be a less than 50 per cent turnout in the next general election. It is very hard to get across to someone who believes that everything is fine that the electorate are cheesed off with us.

On the turn-out in the next general election, Tony was right and not me. It went up very slightly in 2005 – to 61.2 per cent from 59.4 per cent in 2001 –

but the disillusionment continued. I was guilty of exaggeration, but not of poor perception.

Tony and I had a discussion after the Cabinet meeting, and I persuaded him that we shouldn't introduce another Immigration Bill in June, but should rather introduce a Bill that would fill some gaps and tidy up a lot of things at the beginning of the new session. He wanted me to announce the detail of the Bill on 22 May, when we announce the asylum figures for the first quarter of the year. I persuaded him that we could give an outline and that we were minded to do this in these areas rather than selling the whole lot, and then come back to it and announce it properly at the end of August when we do the second quarter and the first six months. I want at that time to clear the decks on some of this massive backlog of people who have waited for donkey's years.

It is very hard work because asylum is at the top of the agenda again, not just on the back of the BNP and the elections but also because the Home Affairs Select Committee came out with the staggering conclusion that if the intake carried on at the level it had been, then social cohesion would be at risk. I could have told them that on the Sunday after the general election in 2001: indeed, I wrote about it in the *Sunday Times*.

I also had to settle the financing and the future of the Criminal Records Bureau – another wonderful legacy, this time from Jack and Charles. Charles and Alan Milburn were arguing for introducing fees for volunteers. Charles said that the schools could pay. I pointed out that it was hardly an appropriate moment, when the schools are up in arms about what he'd done to them with the withdrawal of the Standards Fund (which is going on and on because they haven't bottomed it). They are starting to blame the local authorities now, and it is not the local authorities' fault.

I batted that off, but we are going to have a massive hike for the professional bodies and try and sort it out. I want to sort out the Criminal Injuries Compensation Scheme once and for all as well. There is so much to do.

The other big news of the week was my announcement on sentencing for murderers – life meaning life, twenty years increased to thirty years, no definable floor up to fifteen years. God! – you'd think I had announced something akin to chopping people's hands off or putting them to death. The libertarians were out in force: the *Guardian* with a leader on the Friday and a piece by Jonathan Freedland on the Saturday. Interesting that it was the leader in the *Guardian* and Routledge in the *Mirror* on the same day. I wonder who is pushing this.

But the world outside agrees with me, because at every meeting, whenever I mention changes in sentencing I get a round of applause. Everybody I've spoken to in the real world is up for it. We have esoteric arguments about the judges' right to decide, as though Parliament and democracy have no jurisdiction over those who put lives at risk, the most heinous murderers who take tiny children apart and rape them and torture them before killing them. They think we should say, 'Oh well, they are open to rehabilitation.' Never. There have to be signals. No more agonising about the Myra Hindleys and Ian Bradys of this world.

Anyway we are going on a charm offensive, if that is the way of describing it, on the back of the *Times* profile by Ann Treneman and an interview with Anne McElvoy in the *Evening Standard* for Monday, mostly about sentencing and the judges.

We had the vote on foundation hospitals on the Wednesday. Clare Short missed the vote and failed to turn up to Cabinet, so that will be that for the reshuffle. It makes it easier for Tony (who incidentally had his fiftieth birthday on Tuesday).

On Wednesday we had the Labour Party gala fundraising dinner at the Hilton, where I sat next to the actor John Mills, who's ninety-five years old: he switched from the Tories in his eighties. What a character.

The tax credit system is a shambles – such a shambles that I've had to help out one of my constituents financially, only the second time that I ever have done this, and the first was for a child. I don't know if I will get the money back. I suppose it is a foolish thing to do, and it has to be on the pain of death that they don't tell people. But what else can you do when the tax credit system is such a total mess?

This was a family that were on the verge of destitution. They had nothing to live on over the May Day Bank Holiday weekend and, with four children to care for, the mother was literally crying and asking me to help. I gave her the money but I said that when she received her tax credit, I would like her to pay me back. I did this because I didn't want to give her charity. I wanted to help her and I believed, and wanted to believe, that she would pay it back – and she did. I should never have done it as it set a terrible precedent, but sometimes it is necessary to put humanity before common sense.

On Sunday [11 May] the *People* had pretty well got the story about what Alan Milburn, Charles Clarke and myself had been discussing on the Criminal Records Bureau last Thursday morning. Amazing.

But probably the silliest thing of the week was all about Tony Martin.

Tony Martin was a Norfolk farmer who in April 2000 was controversially convicted of the murder of a sixteen-year-old boy he had interrupted burgling his remote farmhouse. The case became a cause célèbre, raising issues around the question of a citizen's right to defend his or her own property. Martin was released in July 2003 after serving two-thirds of his five-year sentence.

Two years ago when I came into the Home Office, the Tony Martin case had not been high on the departmental radar. I had therefore put out an instruction in writing that the case would have to be closely monitored, and I expected everybody to be entirely on the ball and to be aware that I wanted regular reports. Then on Bank Holiday Monday, when I was at the G8 Summit and it was difficult to get officials to swing into action, Huw Evans was flipping through the print-out of cuttings, and drew my attention to an article in the *Independent* about Tony Martin – how the Parole Board was being challenged, and inferring that Home Office lawyers were putting forward a case about burglars in general and the rights of the householder. It is worth a study in terms of what then happened. I said to Huw that this was catastrophic and that he should get on the telephone and make sure that those newspapers most likely to get hold of the wrong end of the stick didn't do so. We managed it with the *Daily Mail,* which is remarkable, given that they had been Tony Martin's champion, but they did seem to understand: first, that it wasn't the Home Office, it was Treasury Solicitors; secondly that it was the Parole Board, which is entirely independent of the Home Office; and thirdly that they were speaking for themselves and not for the government.

'Treasury Solicitors' is the term used for the legal advisers to the government as a whole, as opposed to departmental lawyers employed by the major departments to advise them on very specific policy. When the government is going to be represented (other than by the Attorney General himself) it will be Treasury Solicitors who do the work and determine the legal line to be taken.

Huw tried his best with the *Sun* but failed to get anywhere, so that paper got it, then the *Mirror* belatedly got it, and then it sort of rolled forward in a chain reaction throughout the week, so even on Sunday [11 May] articles were still being written about the case. I then get a submission saying would I do the minimum, rather than a broader swathe, with regard to protecting householders from being wrongly accused when defending themselves or their property. This is going back to 27 February, when I indicated publicly on *Any Questions?* that I would back this heavily and that I would amend the Criminal Justice Bill. What made matters worse was that I called a round-table meeting, with the lawyers and everybody there, and what became very clear was the stupidity with which the matter was being handled by the Parole Board barrister. I said that he was being paid out of public funds and if government lawyers, whoever they were, were briefing him, we expected them to adhere to what we were putting forward as policy. It was confirmed that one of our lawyers who had not been consulted had been given what they were going to say, but had not commented on it or passed it on. If he had, we could have intervened – so it was totally mishandled.

It is amazing how this incident echoes the experience of Richard Crossman in his very early period as Housing Minister in 1964–5, when he discovered that a lawyer on behalf of his department was appearing in front of a Public Inquiry with a brief to say exactly the opposite of his view (as Secretary of State) about what should be done – in other words to demonstrate a 'departmental' view as opposed to that of the politicians in charge. Here we were, almost forty years later, having to deal with exactly the same process of reflecting previous policy assumptions rather than current policy direction.

The Tony Martin affair was bizarre in a number of ways, not least because an official in the Home Office had been informed by the Parole Board that they were going to take this line, and he just noted it and took no action one way or the other. He clearly didn't clock that this might be of real concern, as well as having some political significance, nor apparently what had been going on for the previous two years. We also have the head of the probation service flapping about, saying that Tony Martin is dangerous and his release should be accompanied by the highest level of surveillance. I think they have completely lost their marbles.

I have got to announce, before the Tories stand up in the House of Commons for Report and Third Reading, that I am going to do something about civil liability. I've had the Department saying that I should do as little as possible and I've told them not to be ridiculous. It's a major issue and people are beginning to think we're mad.

We've had other similar things that make me livid such as the extraordinary situation of the *Mirror* having been tipped off that during the previous summer Harold Shipman had been allowed to work in the Wakefield Prison hospital unit with elderly and vulnerable prisoners.

We just couldn't believe it. The prison service denied it. I was very angry, because the *Mirror* had a real go at me personally, as though I was in charge of everything that happened in every single prison unit. We were considering taking them to the Press Council, but we then found out that there was some truth in the story: the previous summer some idiot had let Shipman somewhere near other prisoners in a vulnerable situation. I demanded an inquiry, but this is the sort of thing you have to put up with in the Home Office.

My special adviser Huw Evans worked really hard on this story, spending an enormous amount of time rooting out what had gone amiss, why the initial response from the prison had been wrong, and why therefore we had not handled it as well as we should have, then talking to journalists trying to ensure that they understood what had happened, and that they hadn't simply been told lies. The truth is, however, that the briefing I received late in the evening from Huw was a demonstration of how easy it was for me to be run ragged and how often what seemed a major issue disappeared after a day or two into the black hole that constitutes the day-to-day life of a Home Secretary in the twenty-first century!

Week beginning Monday 12 May – and God, what a week that turned out to be: Huw Evans left me a message at 10.21 on Monday morning that it had just flashed up on the news that Clare Short had resigned. He said he was trying to find out more but thought he would let me know. And so mayhem began. They immediately appointed Valerie Amos [who was sitting in the House of Lords as Baroness Amos] to the Cabinet as Secretary of State at the Department for International Development from Parliamentary Under-Secretary at the Foreign Office. Everyone likes Valerie.

That then left mayhem because people rightly said: 'Where do we go from here? We can't have Sally Keeble [junior minister in the Department for International Development] answering in the Commons: the Tories will tear us apart.' In any case, there needs to be a Minister of State.

So then they floundered about. Apparently they wanted to appoint to the Minister-of-State role Chris Mullin who, as Hilary Armstrong rightly pointed out to them, had voted against the government on Iraq, and this would create an enormous problem – not least because the reconstruction of Iraq was a key part of the new job. They then turned to Hilary Benn. I found out as I walked into the office first thing Tuesday morning when they rang me. I pointed out that we had got the Criminal Justice and

Sentencing Bill for a second and third full day's Report and Third Reading coming up very shortly, and that Hilary had taken it all the way through Committee and the first day of Report Stage. Tony said that he would appoint Paul Goggins to replace Hilary, to which I replied: 'I'm very grateful for that. It's exactly what I would want. But this is a real mess. Couldn't we leave the appointment until next week?' Tony said that we couldn't, then said that he'd think about it, and phoned me back twenty minutes later to confirm that he wanted Hilary to move now. To take his call I had to come out of a ministers' meeting that I was chairing, and naturally I couldn't tell them why I had to go out. When I went back in I had to just act professionally, and discuss social cohesion as planned. Then Tony spoke to Hilary, who said that he wouldn't make up his mind until he had spoken to me. I had to persuade him to take this opportunity, as I had had to persuade Jeff Rooker.

I said to Hilary that he was being offered a Minister of State's job and that he would be speaking for the government in the Commons as the lead person. I added that it was a major jumping-off point for him, and that he knew the job because he used to do it as Parliamentary Under-Secretary. Paul Goggins was over the moon, and I'm very pleased for Hilary and for Paul. The decisions, however, did mean that I would have to take on great chunks of the Bill myself, including jury trial and murder sentencing. It is good sometimes to be put on the spot. What is not always understood is what this will mean: not just being in the House of Commons on the day, but taking an enormous amount of time to prepare for it. They don't intend to do the main reshuffle until after the euro announcement.

The major issue of the moment, however, is what to do about the euro and how to involve Cabinet in the decisions. In Cabinet on Thursday morning the solution was presented as being a series of bilateral meetings of Economic Affairs Committees, of a major debate on Thursday 22 May in Cabinet, and either a final debate on 5 June or a special meeting on 6 June, and then the statement to the House on the 9th. We all agreed that this timetable would have to be announced, and No. 10 then managed to do it in a way that looked as though they had asserted themselves. This differed from what Gordon told me on the Wednesday evening – the day before Cabinet – when he had asked me to come across to see him urgently. I'd flown up to the Police Federation conference in Blackpool and back that day (and had got a very good reception, thank goodness). But here we were with Gordon coming out of a meeting to talk to me and telling me that he wanted to have bilaterals.

There had been some pretty rigorous discussions behind the scenes as to whether everything should go through the Economic Affairs Committee of the Cabinet, or whether there should be some mix of bilaterals and what can only be described as 'groups of ministers'. We ended up with a mixture of all three, but not before there had been some real up-and-downers.

So it was decided that they would circulate all eighteen volumes of the Treasury material, that they would later present the assessment and then the announcement in the House on Monday 9 June, although no doubt as soon as we have the Cabinet it will be out all over that weekend, so it's going to be a real dog's dinner.

But we might have the reshuffle, I might get a Minister of State, and we might all be able to get on with the job.

We have an utter fiasco with the tax credits: tens of thousands of people without any money and no sign of their getting it in the near future. But now the media have started to get a bit savvy about what's going on, and I suppose it will be Dawn Primarolo [Paymaster-General] who will take the rap. I imagine she may well lose her job because of it.

The pluses of the week were that the Cabinet Committee on Resilience was the best we've had. We seem to be making real progress at last in getting a grip of internal resilience, which is a good job given the appalling attack in Riyadh (thirty-four is the latest death count, but the Americans think it will be over ninety), and the big scare about Kenya on the back of some arrests in Britain.

I suppose I ought to count the Police Federation as a success. The sentencing in relation to murder convictions has gone down incredibly well with the public. People have really warmed to it – after all the fuss in the Home Office as to what would happen – and to my announcement on presumption of bail for those who do not turn up to court, but the Lord Chief Justice doesn't like it. He has requested to see Tony, but instead of Tony putting him off for a while, he agreed to see him at 9.30 on Monday morning [19 May]. So I've got to talk to Tony over the weekend and get across the message that if he says anything that the Lord Chief Justice can convey as in any sense pulling back from me, even the least hint that he will talk to me, then the whole thing will turn into a fiasco.

I have sent across to Tony a note about what's happened with the judiciary. Woolf had written before I stood up at the Police Federation and attacked Sir Oliver Popplewell [former High Court judge], who had been on the *Today* programme that morning, interviewed by James Naughtie in the most disgraceful fashion I've ever heard: putting words in his mouth, suggesting things about my capturing headlines, and accusing me of being a populist amongst other things. So as part of my speech to the Police Federation, I simply said that he was completely out of touch. I said that I'm not against judges, I'm just in favour of those who are in touch with the real world.

And of course this will now have made matters worse. In fact, Woolf will probably think that this was my riposte, whereas it wasn't. I was simply reacting to Popplewell attacking me and thinking he could get away with it. He has just written a book in which he reveals that even when he was investigating the terrible Bradford football fire [in 1985], he learnt for the first time that people swore at matches and that they could sing well, and that it had put him in touch with the world – hence my references to the real world. But I'm going to press on, whatever the criticisms. It is time to take these people on.

I drove up to Sheffield overnight and then accidentally locked Sadie out. Eventually she woke me up by crashing against the back door the herb pot that she had emptied out. This did terrible damage to the door jamb, but it was entirely my fault. I was able to let her in before it started to pour with rain, which it did for the following sixteen hours. But all this palaver did disrupt my night, and I felt dreadful when I went to address the conference on drugs in Sheffield organised by the Royal College of General Practitioners on Friday morning. Peter Goldsmith was up in Sheffield and we had a really good meeting with the Chief Constable and the Chief Prosecutor.

I then had meetings in the constituency and a visit to the chiropractor. I am trying to catch up on a vast amount of work, including all the tapes. It is not helped by not having a Minister of State. Everybody is having to turn to me, while at the same time, of course, I am understandably having to support and supervise Paul. I've got the summaries of the eighteen Treasury reports on the euro, and I'm going to Spain on Sunday for the meeting of the five interior ministers, flying back Monday morning, then am in the House on Monday afternoon. I really cannot keep this pace up for very much longer.

Recording from the BBC news bulletin: 'The Prime Minister and Chancellor have issued an unprecedented joint statement declaring they are united on the issue of the euro. They have stressed that the Cabinet will have a real say in deciding whether the government should recommend British entry to the single currency.'

We're all over the place on what the Foreign Office are up to and the assessment on terror, and I will take this up urgently. We had the suicide bombers in Morocco on Saturday morning and reports of twenty-four people dead. None of the countries like Uganda and Eritrea that have been put on the Foreign Office risk-to-travel list pose anything like the threat that exists elsewhere. It's just too silly for words.

So we'll have to get a grip of that otherwise we'll be ridiculed but I will deal with it on Monday. I fly back from Spain at lunchtime, then I see Tony and Gordon on the euro, and then I go into the Commons, where it's alleged there will be a revolt of about forty backbenchers in respect of trial without jury for serious fraud.

I had nearly twenty-four hours in Jerez, the sherry-producing area in southern Spain, at the meeting of the interior ministers of Italy, Germany, France, Spain and ourselves. This was extraordinary, because it is absolutely clear that they have no idea what's going on in their countries with regard to counter-terrorism. They didn't appear to know what the security services were doing, and seemed to think that getting them together would be a major move, when of course they meet all the time. I explained to them that there was a Club of Vienna for the security services, and that they had met only a few days before. (The Club of Vienna was set up years ago for the heads of security services in Western Europe to meet and exchange information and ideas and develop better contacts.) The interior ministers hadn't a clue what was going on, and I get blamed for not being on top of this, with the Tories claiming that we need a Tsar to do it all.

I am still getting on well with Nicolas Sarkozy, though I'm afraid that the Home Office officials we are working with are not as good as those I had at the DfEE dealing with European and international affairs. They used to irritate me, but at least they used to punch their weight. When it comes to deciding the agendas, our Home Office lot are ineffective, as I found out with regard to the timing of the meeting in Rome in September under the Justice and Home Affairs banner, when they allowed them to bring the date forward a week. It will mean that I simply cannot go, as I have a crammed diary on Friday and Saturday in the constituency and Sheffield. But they just let it go, then reported back that the date of the meeting had been switched. And they were the same out in Spain: they had no idea how to affect the agenda.

While we were in Jerez, I got the protection officers to fix up that we went to a bodega to see the sherry-making. I had met a man in the street who said that he was from Sheffield, adding that he was there on holiday with his wife but was in fact a beer drinker. I asked him what his wife liked to drink, and he said Bristol Cream. I said she should be all right here, then. He said: 'Aye, *de mek* it here' – classic broad Yorkshire for 'They make it here' – and it took me ten seconds to get the pun, in his reference to Domecq: absolutely classic Sheffield humour.

We'd popped in at the very end of the Jerez Festival and I asked that we stop the cars. The people who were organising the transport were not too pleased but we just sat for quarter of an hour, had a bit of Spanish omelette and a glass of sherry and just enjoyed the music and dancing and people enjoying themselves. Then we had a fascinating trip round the vaults: one is assigned to commemorate Napoleon and another Nelson.

After flying back on Monday morning I went straight to No. 10 to see Gordon and Tony about the euro. It was a very good meeting, and it was clear that they were getting their act together. It was not, as some Cabinet colleagues have been doing both in their meetings and in Cabinet on the Thursday and elsewhere, a case of people parading their knowledge and expertise as world economists to impress everybody. I just thought it was best to talk the politics through and what needed to be done, and it worked very well. Then I had to go into the Chamber for the two days of the Criminal Justice and Sentencing Report and Third Reading. There have been three full days of that but these are the last two. We had bizarre speeches, particularly by the Liberal Democrats and, from our own side, Graham Allen, about how we shouldn't have time limits and how the Bill would have been a lot better if it had had a lot more time, even though it had had thirty-two sessions in Committee. I was saying to colleagues on the front bench that if these ultra-parliamentarians had their way, we'd never manage to pass anything. We would take about three Bills through a year, and they would then grumble that the government weren't doing anything. I repeated on the record that people are not fed up with politicians acting too swiftly and decisively, but they're fed up with politicians who are not acting, who don't respond to what people need and who take years to bring about change – and that is the danger to democracy – but I can't get this through. It was Paul Goggins's first outing and he did very well.

We got the Mode of Trial through, though thirty-three of our back-benchers voted against. A lot of people were away at the farewell do for John Monks [retiring General Secretary of the Trades Union Congress] at Congress House on that night, and I wasn't too pleased with the Whips because they had not got the people in the Chamber to back in. It was easier on the Tuesday with murder and sentencing, but this was completely messed up by Charles Clarke making an announcement about abandoning the primary school targets. I thought the 85 per cent was crazy anyway, but he's gone to the opposite extreme and is now leaving it to schools again. All the pressure on standards and driving forward the literacy and numeracy agenda appears to be reducing, so God knows where we will be in a year or two. The upshot was that the Tories got a Priority Notice Question and Charles had to make a Statement that was self-evident, but because our Bill was timetabled it meant we went until 8 p.m. instead of 7 p.m. before the final vote on third reading.

Iain Duncan Smith came into Third Reading to make sure that Oliver Letwin voted against. You could tell from Oliver's justification for voting against that his heart was not in it, and I think he must have been ordered to vote as he did. What they did miss was the fact that, after the 5.30 p.m. vote, I had nipped off and I made it back too late because a quirk of the timetable meant that, because of the way that Charles's Priority Notice Question had finished, the finish of the Report Stage and the beginning of Third Reading was going to be 6.58 p.m. I arrived back thirty seconds late. (I wouldn't have done if Barry had been driving.) I had expected a vote on the group of amendments and there wasn't one, but thanks to the quick-wittedness of John Heppell, the Whip, and Paul Goggins, they managed to get the backbenchers to call a spurious vote on an amendment on the Criminal Records Bureau, which allowed me to get into the Chamber and sit behind the Dispatch Box. They were able then to call off the vote by not putting tellers on. It avoided what would have been an enormous embarrassment with me not getting back for Third Reading. Some of my opponents would have loved it, and for reasons entirely beyond me neither the Opposition nor the press picked up on what had happened. I thanked Hilary Benn, I thanked the committee members and then I thanked John Heppell. I said in the Third Reading speech: 'Not least, I would like to thank my Honourable Friend for what he's done throughout the Committee Stage, and on the Report and, not least, over the last few minutes' – and they still didn't get it. I thought Alan Beith [Liberal Democrat MP for Berwick-upon-Tweed] may have twigged because I thought I heard him shout out something like, 'The Home Secretary's in his seat!' But the others didn't and nor did the media – a good job too or I would have been up the spout. So I owe John Heppell one in a very big way.

Funny old world. I went home and had half a bottle of red wine and a lasagne that I got from a local restaurant. I needed to sort myself out because I had to go to Southport on the Wednesday. I flew up there and back for the Prison Officers' Association conference which went well: I even managed to get a standing ovation, which is some going.

It was nothing short of a miracle. Until that time, this particular union, representing the middle- and lower-ranking officers, had been about as reactionary as you could get. Things were gradually beginning to change.

I'd had a meeting on the Monday night on counter-terrorism and had to come out of the debate, having done the Single Judge Trials, do that and then go back. I snatched something to eat quickly with Bev before the wind-ups on Monday, but I had a series of meetings when I got back from Southport. I had another counter-terrorism meeting, in which the Met raised the issue of closure of streets and the new bollards but they did not say they were going to rush into doing it – which by Friday they had done. My worry was that people would think we were protecting ourselves in Westminster, rather than them. The Met are a law unto themselves, and SO13 just do what they like. The problem is that I don't have any constitutional hold over them. We have probably got more grip than anyone else before, but it's not enough. We have stopped them doing some really silly things such as the wholesale closure of roads – which they were intending to do over the Bank Holiday weekend, without any thought for the politics of it.

I had a counter-terrorism meeting before the Prime Minister's meeting at three p.m. on the Wednesday afternoon. Tony was obviously not too well. Everybody was saying he looked tired and grey, which was not surprising because Peter Mandelson had gone to a Women's Press Lobby lunch and stupidly opened up all the old wounds again by talking about Gordon stitching up Tony. Firstly I think it's Peter's suicidal tendency, but secondly I think he's trying to push Tony into making a rapid decision about the euro referendum on the grounds that anything but an immediate referendum will be painted as a victory for Gordon. Peter is trying to push Tony into going faster on the referendum than he intends or knows is wise. But by doing so Peter just undoes all Tony's good work in ensuring that when we do make the decision, it is seen to be Tony in charge, not having been pushed into it but determining it all along. It's very hard for Tony when Peter behaves like this.

I nearly had a row with Tony that evening before I went to the Press Gallery Centenary Dinner, where he spoke at the beginning and then understandably departed. I left before the main speeches when it got to 10.30 p.m., as I have been coming down with a cold that I'm fighting. The last thing I want is a cold when I'm going to have a few days' break in the sunshine with Robert Ogden. The upshot is that people in No. 10 had been winding Tony up and trying to get him to say more about the legislation and to push me harder than I'm going. I spoke to him on the telephone and, just before I did, Jonathan Powell said: 'Please don't have a row with him. He's not in a good state, and it won't do you any good. There's a reshuffle coming up and you'll only upset the apple cart.' So I got a grip of myself and we did agree precisely on what should be said, and Tony stuck to it at the press conference after Cabinet on Thursday morning.

Unfortunately, I didn't keep calm. I'm always in a bad temper when I've got a cold coming on, and it was pretty clear that I was getting more and more irritable with everybody, partly because of the pressure – no Minister of State, the switches in the team, taking on all these things that I was having to do on the criminal-justice side, cramming too much in, flying up north, back down and all over the place. The upshot was that I went on the *Today* programme on Thursday morning and just lost my cool at the beginning.

But the statistics on asylum are good. I made it clear we weren't claiming victory and that there was still a mountain to climb, and announced what we were going to look at in legislative terms. The rest of the press was pretty good, and presented this in such a way that I was seen to be doing it rather than Tony forcing me to. So it was good news in that sense, but I know that my performance on the *Today* programme left something to be desired. I just get so irritated when people say that we are fiddling the figures when we have done nothing of the sort. The figures are just the same, the calculations are just the same, the methodologies are what they have always been. They believed them in the past when the figures were going up and when they were very high, but they don't believe them now that they are coming down. They try to mix up clandestine entry and asylum – on which we have got a grip – with work permits and legal migration. As I said on *Today*, even Andrew Green of Migration Watch had written in the *Daily Mail* on the Monday, saying that we had got the wrong countries if we wanted to substitute work permits for asylum. We don't. We just want people to come here legally and openly.

All this was rather overtaken by the idiocy of the fourteen Afghans involved in the hijacked plane at Stansted in 2000 being let off on appeal by a technicality.

It is funny to reflect on exactly the same kind of hoo-hah in May 2006 when
the final nine core hijackers won their legal case to be able to stay, irrespective
of the impact this has on the international efforts to clamp down on hijacking.

So there was another row about that, and the row between me and the
judges has been running on and on. I think people are just getting tired of
the judiciary.

The Queen was in Sheffield on Thursday morning, visiting Fir Vale
School in my constituency and opening the new Winter Garden in the city
centre. I had to forgo being there in order to attend Cabinet.

June 2003

Back from my trip with Robert Ogden to St-Jean-Cap-Ferrat, where there
are the most pretentious restaurants imaginable. I cannot believe that there
are people who spend that sort of money – a bottle of wine that would cost
me £35 from El Vinos costs 1,600 euros. Truly this was a world apart. I
enjoyed Robert's hospitality, which was faultless, but it rained. It rained
virtually all Monday and Tuesday, then improved a bit on Wednesday and
Thursday before deteriorating again in the afternoon and evening with
gale-force winds. It was glorious on the Friday when I flew out from Nice
to Geneva to meet Ruud Lubbers, Nicolas Sarkozy and Otto Schily.

On my return I went to Paul Goggins's little party that his wife had
arranged to celebrate both his becoming a minister and his fiftieth birthday
in two weeks' time. He was just overwhelmed that Bev Hughes and I had
turned up. Then Bev, Tom and I went to the cottage, and the weather was
glorious. We had a most wonderful walk on the Saturday.

I've raised very strongly the whole issue of how domestic policy has been
relegated because of European and international affairs. Tony is in Poland,
then in St Petersburg, then at the G8 Summit in France, and then it's the
euro test, and then the Human Rights Convention, while the row about
Iraq continues. There's no focus on domestic policy at all. We've also got to
sort out the reshuffle and structuring around that.

Derry Irvine has written me a letter saying that he thinks that members
of the House of Lords found guilty of imprisonable offences should not
only be disqualified from voting but should also have their peerages
withdrawn. He went on to say (bearing in mind that he is in charge of
freedom of information and knows that when you mention names, the

person has access to the correspondence): 'and in order not to appear to be persecuting Jeffrey Archer, we should announce this immediately.'

I wrote back: 'Dear Derry, For the very reason you enunciate that we would not wish to be discriminatory against Jeffrey Archer or seen to be vindictive, I do not believe this is the moment to be withdrawing peerages from those who are found guilty or imprisoned. With best wishes . . .'

Big event of the week was the Cabinet discussion on the euro, and a very good discussion it was. When we walked into No. 10, all the journalists in the sunshine were waving and shouting remarks like, 'Are we moving towards consensus?' – and we shouted back, 'We are moving towards convergence.' It was all very good-humoured. There was a picture in one or two of the newspapers, including the *Independent*, taken when I came out, looking cheerful and waving. They asked me what I had got to say and I just lifted my eyebrows, at which they all burst into laughter. But on his way in John Prescott, instead of treating the situation lightly, turned his back on the journalists and gave them a two-fingered sign, about which there was a big fuss for a couple of days. We just have to take the press in good part.

May the Lord forgive me for ever saying that. It is a wonder, when I wrote it, that I wasn't turned into a pillar of salt.

But it was a good Cabinet. Tony started off, followed by Gordon and myself. It had been agreed that Jack and John Prescott should wind up. I set the scene by saying that we had had a good process, that it had been a good learning curve, and that everybody had got something out of it. It had been very helpful and we all now knew a lot more. I said that I was certainly more in favour of the euro and less sceptical than I had been before, and raised the issue as to whether we should be discussing the Convention as well. But Tony didn't want to. I see the two as gelling into each other, especially as the European Council is to be held in a fortnight's time. I said we also had the situation in which people would want to know what will need to have changed and what will have changed in a year's time. I think they have been really struggling on that because everybody joined in and said that that was a key issue. Alistair Darling joined in and backed me when I said that we needed to be clear that the CPI [Consumer Price Index] version of inflation, as opposed to RPI [Retail Price Index], would not be applied to pensions and fixed incomes. Gordon said that it had been made clear all along that the RPI would be used for this but I don't think it had.

Huw rang me Thursday evening to tell me about the stories that had been running. He had had confirmed from inside No. 10 that there is a serious suggestion of a Minister of Justice, and that the position of Lord Chancellor is almost certain to go. Apparently the *Sun* had been briefed very heavily on this and so Huw had briefed the *Sun* back – which was reported on Friday morning [6 June], my birthday, as a flaming row with Tony, complete with my saying that I wasn't going to have it (which is not quite what I had said). I rang Tony and I'm afraid I got him out of the gym – though to do him credit, he was prepared to come out of the gym to speak to me. I said that I just wanted to clear the air because I couldn't carry on like this, finding out from the papers that there is a suggestion of splitting the Department and taking away some of my functions. We had a reasonable conversation, although he gave what some might describe as a lawyer's answer, in that he said that I would be the first to know. First from where though? – that is the question.

I am afraid that by the time I reached my birthday barbecue on Friday night I wasn't in the best of temper, and this was compounded by the fact that my son Andrew, who was supposed to be coming early to help as he was the only one not working or studying, was very late, although he did apologise profusely. A strange birthday, and I fear on this occasion I may have had one or two glasses of very good wine too many. How I felt on Saturday morning put me in mind of Aneurin Bevan, George Brown, Ernest Bevin, Winston Churchill and all those other politicians who took it for granted that pressure would be absorbed in part by the intake of alcohol!

Looking back, I should have had slabs of time out where I arranged for others to take on security warrants and emergencies relating to terrorism and the Home Office. Very often I couldn't relax because I still felt I was on duty, and on the very odd occasion like this when I let myself go, I knew in my heart that I should not – because although it is possible to sober up very quickly, it is not the right thing to do when you are likely to have to deal with potential emergencies.

This week saw a number of very key preparatory meetings and reviews of documents. I spent a good deal of the week preparing for the Edith Kahn Memorial Lecture on 11 June and working with Nick Pearce to get the pamphlet ready.

This was an important statement of policy for me, not just about the reform of the police service but also about the whole relationship between civil society and formal political institutions. I had worked very hard on both the speech and the pamphlet, and intended to ensure that it formed the backcloth for a debate over the summer. In essence it was an attempt by me to get out of the daily grind of immediate issues and try to look forward, and to bring in what Tony and I always called 'the bigger picture'.

Equally, the domestic-violence consultation paper and the preparation of the Statement to the House two weeks later have also taken a hell of a lot of time. I have reflected on this many times in looking at how Green Papers, White Papers and consultations are so time-consuming in simply review-ing and re-reviewing, going through over and over again what needs to be done.

This week I spoke to the Parliamentary Labour Party and separately on the Tuesday to the National Executive Committee of the party. This turned out to be very different from the NEC of old. I thought it would be nostalgic, but it didn't feel like that at all. The NEC has changed beyond all recognition, and I was just very glad that I don't have to sit through it every month.

The PLP meeting went fine. People were very supportive, wanting more action on anti-social behaviour rather than less. It is a very interesting reflection here because, talking to Tony, he was saying to me that we need to be even more radical and bold. I wanted to say – but didn't because it was not an appropriate moment, given everything else that was going on – that the people around him have been trying to stop us from being radical and bold. We have put up things for the Anti-Social Behaviour Bill and the people speaking in his name, euphemistically as ever called 'No. 10', have been the ones saying that they didn't want this in and that they wanted a shorter Bill. They have kept on saying that they wanted a shorter, more focused Bill and that this is what the Prime Minister wanted. Now, of course, he wants anything but a shorter and more focused Bill.

What has struck me, not just from my own experience in government but looking back at previous governments, is the way in which – given time constraints and pressures, perfectly understandably – those around the Prime Minister speak in his name, and therefore 'No. 10' becomes all powerful. There are, however, far too many times when the Prime Minister's thoughts have not been considered in detail and when what is being said to other ministers or departmental civil servants isn't quite what was intended by the Prime Minister in the first place. But of course all of us are heavily reliant on our special advisers and senior civil servants, and they can't get it right all the time.

Mind you, I've got a cheek, because I wanted to distribute all these measures across different pieces of legislation and Tony was certainly right to insist that we focused on an Anti-Social Behaviour Bill that at least everybody could understand and that would put the Opposition on the spot.

And both opposition parties fell for it. The Tories were in a new libertarian mode and didn't like draconian action, dismissing everything as a gimmick, and the Liberal Democrats (whose Home Affairs spokesman, Simon Hughes, was at least consistent – i.e. consistently bad) were against any measure at all that appeared to get tough with anybody. The only amazing thing is how little this permeated the view of the electorate; so Liberal Democrats in by-elections are able to go round saying how tough they are going to be, but when they sit on the benches in Parliament they vote to stop the measures that would ensure that the police, local authorities and local community groups were able to get tough.

I had a meeting on ports and border security during the week, trying to get a grip of what Bob Milton, the man who has taken over looking at co-ordination, has been doing. I also had one of the security DOPIT Cabinet Committees in preparation for that. It is interesting how little Oliver Letwin knows. He keeps on calling for a security Tsar, as though separating the role from departmental responsibilities would help, whereas being involved and knowing what's going on is absolutely crucial.

As ever, many things are in flux all at once. Alison Flashman, who has worked for me many years, has moved with her husband out of London and has stepped down as my parliamentary secretary and Janet Pickering has taken over. Janet had worked with Jeff Rooker when he was an MP. It is always difficult when there are staff changes and it takes time for everyone to get used to each other and new ways of doing things. Sophie Linden is now on maternity leave, which is a great loss to me, although I am glad that she has been able to contribute to the Edith Kahn paper and, of course, to the enormous amount of work that we have done together on the anti-social-behaviour side. On top of this, Hilary Benn has moved out of the Ministerial Team and Paul Goggins has moved in – what a world of change.

But those changes were only the beginning. The real body blow is that Nick Pearce has told me that he has been offered the post of Deputy to Matthew Taylor at the Institute of Public Policy Research. How could I say or do anything other than to congratulate him? This is clearly going to be an opportunity for him to develop his management skills and his independence, and to demonstrate to a wider world the extent of his capabilities. All I can do is wish him well and agonise inside about what on earth I am going to do.

Throughout government I was very fortunate with my special advisers. They made an enormous difference to my ability to do the job and, through good fortune or good choice, I had a group of people around me throughout those near nine years, all of whom made a major contribution to making a difference and to delivering policies despite, as well as on occasions alongside, the bureaucracy.

Both Nick and I were on the verge of tears. He has made such a profound contribution to some of the most difficult issues concerning nationality and citizenship, immigration and asylum, but much more in terms of helping me retain some academic and intellectual input, the ability to involve philosophy and values and not simply be mired in day-to-day administration.

It was a very fortunate move for Nick because, shortly afterwards, Matthew Taylor joined Downing Street and Nick, quite rightly, became Director of the IPPR, in which he was to make a substantial contribution to thinking and policy in the years ahead.

I had a useful meeting with the Speaker before having dinner with Conor Ryan, who is now very distant from me and from what I am doing but seems to be enjoying life. The meeting with the Speaker was about how to clear up Westminster and the Parliament Square area, which is a terrible mess. Michael Martin wants a Bill but I don't think we will quite manage that. We need a bit of action from the Metropolitan Police. I also spoke to the Speaker about office costs.

A bumpy meeting with the Chair of the National Association of Police Authorities, Ruth Henig, who didn't like the idea at all of trying to shake up Police Authorities, nor what I am going to say in the Edith Kahn pamphlet on civil renewal and a new agenda.

On Thursday I was the only Labour MP to turn up to Michael and Carolyn Portillo's fiftieth-birthday celebration – and amazingly it didn't get into the papers.

We were also dealing at this time with a request from the BBC to interview face to face those detained under the Anti-Terrorism, Crime and Security Act (Part 4) in Belmarsh, Woodhill and Broadmoor. With the support of MI5 I have won the struggle to resist this – but it was hard work because the inclination of the lawyers was to give way. I pointed out that if people were certificated and locked up as Category A prisoners, it can be presumed that we did so in order to avoid their passing out messages, sending signals and the like. Nothing could preclude a face-to-face recorded interview from sending out such signals, let alone the propaganda coup that the terrorists would have. It was a bit like thinking that it would have been fine to have put up Lord Haw-Haw on the mainstream BBC in the Second World War – with the Human Rights Act and Freedom of Information Act to ensure full coverage!

Gordon's Statement on the euro was understandably highly technical, but not very educative with regard to wider understanding. Although the Tories did a substantial job on disruption and heckling, in a way that they are unable to do on the Budget Statement, they didn't really get the message across from their point of view – that is, 'And what will have changed in a year's time?' I think the issue is dead, at least for some years to come.

But I suppose that the big event of the week has to be the shock resignation of Alan Milburn in the reshuffle on Thursday [12 June]. I hadn't seen it coming. It is funny how well you think you know someone, but you don't have a clue what they are about to do. When Estelle resigned, at least I knew that she was on the verge of it, even if she didn't want to talk to me during the twenty-four hours leading up to it. But this time I hadn't a clue. Putting family first and trying to lift some of the day-to-day grind and pressure has to be right – but what is the true reason? That is what I am asking myself. Alan is a politician through and through. He loves it. He thrives on it. What enormous traumas have driven him to give it up?

On the Tuesday evening I had chaired a meeting about health screening and immigration, which Alan had put himself out to attend. He was extremely helpful in the face of enormous intransigence, particularly from Paul Boateng. And now he has gone. I am sure if it had simply been pressure, Tony would have offered him the Leader-of-the-House post, where he would have had the whole of the recess free and none of the masses of correspondence and constant Red Boxes. But there we go. Perhaps we will know one day.

I fear that no space was made available for Tony. No events were dropped in order for him to be able to think through the reshuffle, to time it and plan it. All reshuffles appear to be last-minute and under pressure. There is no Anji organising Tony's diary in a way that sorts out the wheat from the chaff. The reshuffle is just shoehorned into everything else that is already there. Does he have to go to see Jacques Chirac and Prime Minister Raffarin? Could it have been postponed? More to the point, does he have to see the German Finance Minister and the Editorial Board of the BBC for lunch? It is courteous and it is commitment – but I think it is crazy.

This is the mid-term, a point of revitalisation and regeneration, and we need a substantial reshuffle to achieve that. But there is no time, space or structure.

The media have presented the reshuffle as a fiasco but how could they not? It was an own goal. It looked like it and it felt like it. And if it feels like it from inside, how must it look from outside? Each bit of the jigsaw on its own had a logic, but when was there time for Tony to put the jigsaw together and to work out the presentation of the whole?

Press speculation is always a killer on the run-up to reshuffles. Jack Straw has copped it with rumour after rumour that there is going to be a Cabinet minister responsible for Europe within the Foreign and Commonwealth Office, while I have had the continuing and repeated speculation about a Ministry of Justice. What a recipe for internal conflict and division. It does make me realise that, other than Gordon himself and in his own way John Prescott, the Foreign Secretary and the Home Secretary are the two bulwarks of balance, power and strength within any government, and particularly in this one.

I am afraid I was very robust when it came to talking to Tony about my team. Everything was running late. Tony was due at the Palace. I was in one of my fed-up, I'm-not-going-to-move moods. Even though I got my way over calling the Lord Chancellor's Department 'Constitutional Affairs' and dropping the term 'Justice', and was happy that Charlie Falconer was taking over, I was still so aggrieved with the process. I even felt sorry for Derry that not a word was said at Cabinet.

This may seem hypocritical, given how angry I was with Derry at that pivotal moment in January when he contributed in such a significant way to derailing what we were doing. But the contribution he has made over the years is substantial. For good or ill, he has been a very big figure. As with Mo Mowlam and Peter Mandelson, so with Derry: you can contribute much but it matters little. I did recognise this at the time, but I didn't fully clock the significance.

If anything I have come out of this reshuffle in a strengthened position – but fancy having to fight such a battle to strengthen my position. To come out of this frustrated and irritated is not good. It is not good for me and it is not good for Tony. And what about those who are not close to Tony and feel frustrated and irritated and left out? Where do they turn? And fancy John Reid being Health Secretary. He's tough, he will stand up to people – but Health Secretary! It's a good job I get on with Charlie and that we have worked together. Let's hope we still can when he's found his feet. There is a lot of nonsense being written and talked. The idea that we could have had a White Paper about what should happen to the Lord Chancellor, that we could have debated it around Derry while he sat there, and that we could have mulled over his future and the future of his office is just ridiculous. It may have been a brutal end and it may have been clumsy, but what else, with regard to the role and position of Lord Chancellor could Tony have done? It is strange, because while all the focus is on the underlying process and that may have been muddled and over-pressurised, it is the substance that we should all be concentrating on. What is it we want to do in the twenty-first century and how best can we do it?

In the end we ended up with the Department of Constitutional Affairs with a wider brief than the Lord Chancellor's Department had had, but we still had the Lord Chancellor and his unique role in Cabinet vis-à-vis the judiciary – albeit with a strengthened hand for the Lord Chief Justice and a muddled and misunderstood comparator with the US Supreme Court who, after all, are scrutinised politically and not just judicially.

Political power was not simply being decentralised and devolved constitutionally – the House of Lords asserting itself with its new legitimacy and economic and social pluralism taking its toll on traditional sources of power – but the judiciary itself was inexorably strengthening its hand within our constitution, and much of it in the area for which I was responsible. No wonder there were constant clashes.

We did our best for the new department. We had a photocall, with Charlie and I slapping each other on the back. I do sometimes think I am in a theatre, except that actors generally appear on stage nightly whereas I seem to be on stage hourly. There is no doubt that we will have problems in terms of demarcation. While I am in charge of criminal justice policy overall, there is no reason to believe that Charlie will be any less ambitious or less subject to fighting his corner than anybody else – in fact probably more so. Both of us have been arguing that the court system should be incorporated into the reform of criminal justice, but it is not going to happen now.

On Friday morning I had half an hour with Tony, still arguing, still discussing. It is a good job we are friends – not for him, but for me. We had been at loggerheads for half an hour, but then got up and gave each other a hug and shook hands. Tony then gave me a bottle of a wonderful 1982 vintage that he had just stored away somewhere, and it completely took the wind out of my sails. It was a good job he gave it to me after we had had the argument and not before, or I would have had to hand it back to him!

At the time of writing, I still haven't opened the bottle. It will have to be for a very special occasion, whatever that might be.

I was just trying to get across to Tony that he should value those who tell him the truth and who are straight and who defend him when no one around is listening. It is good advice for any leader.

People tend to do funny things on these occasions and I'm no different. When things got really tense, I started to hum a tune from *South Pacific* and said, 'Do you know, Tony, when I was very young, I used to think that the words to the song were "There is nothing like a Dane".' Tony said, 'Pardon?', and I said, ' "There is nothing like a Dane", instead of "nothing like a dame".' For a moment I think he thought I had lost my marbles, but then he laughed and the ice was broken.

I have one really big regret about that reshuffle. I had resisted my team being changed wholesale, as we were in the middle of so many critical things that I couldn't face the idea of everyone being shuffled round. But how badly it turned out for my friend Bev Hughes. Had I conceded her move to a much easier Minister of State's job, she would have been spared all the pain and all the difficulty of the following twelve months. There wasn't another Minister of State's job in government anywhere near as difficult as dealing with nationality, immigration and asylum, not to mention supporting me on counter-terrorism, on internal resilience and on the civil-renewal agenda.

Bob Ainsworth became Deputy Chief Whip.

Strange really, because Bob was to reappear once or twice over the next two and a half years, in various ways that I could never have foreseen at the time.

Fiona Mactaggart joined us, backing up Bev on immigration and nationality and dealing with issues around race, at which she is good and which she knows very well from her own experience as MP for Slough. When I rang her, she wasn't just excited, but really surprised that I wanted her in my team. I said: 'The fact that I have robust arguments with people doesn't mean that I don't like them or don't rate them. It just means that I don't soft-soap them.' In fact I do like people with whom I can have a good discussion, who will stand up for themselves, who don't just toady. That is the way to get the best out of people and to blend the team together. At least that is what I try to do. I have always thought that the weakest leaders are those who have to place people around themselves, people who they know will agree with them. Leadership means leadership.

I am pleased that Hazel Blears has joined us as Police Minister, although I had thought before going in to see Tony that Bev might take that job. We have only really done the first stage of reform, and there is such an enormous amount still to do on street crime and on anti-social behaviour. Hazel is really interested and she, Bev and I can do so much on the civil-society and renewal front, on citizenship and on community. It's funny really because I have only just launched Hazel's pamphlet with her at 10 Downing Street, with Tony being away in Paris. Launching my own at the Edith Kahn lecture and hers at the same time was a strange juxtaposition – and here she is now in the team. It looked joined up but it wasn't planned like that. My own pamphlet, *Renewing Civil Society: A New Agenda,* got really good coverage in the *Guardian* on Wednesday morning. I was pleased about that, and that Hazel and I were complementing each other rather than conflicting.

The most surprising part of the reshuffle for my team was Patricia Scotland [Baroness Scotland], who had always fallen out with me when she was in Derry's team. She didn't want to join me and I didn't want her to join, but Tony persuaded both of us. And what an interesting decision it seems to have been. We shall have to see.

It turned out to be a very good decision, as Patricia and I got on extraordinarily well. I turned out not to be the anti-human rights authoritarian bear that she thought I was, and she turned out not to be the non-political rights lawyer that I thought she was. And because we respected each other, we began to find that we could work together very constructively. It just shows how wrong we can be sometimes.

So for the second time in government I have more women members of my team than any other Cabinet minister, with Caroline Flint joining us to deal with organised crime and drugs – that is going to be a hell of a challenge. Paul Goggins is a bit outnumbered now!

The weekend press was dreadful. The briefings that had led to it looking as though there were going to be radical changes to Jack's department and mine managed the extraordinary feat of making Tony look as if he had backed off, when so far as Jack and I were concerned, he had not supported any such changes in the first place. It is funny how in the media it is always about whether someone is strong or weak, often based on the flimsiest of evidence or even on speculation or innuendo – or even on deliberate briefings that should never take place. For once the *Mail on Sunday* has it right, suggesting [on 15 June] that Tony needs the strength around him to be able to sort out the jigsaw. I think we must be the only country in the democratic world to have reshuffles and knock-on consequences on which the Prime Minister is expected to take decisions so rapidly and in such a confined way.

Estelle has bounced back as Minister for Arts, and I hope she will really enjoy it. My old friend Michael Meacher has claimed that he resigned and is in a real grump. He has had six years in government, not as a Cabinet minister but able to make such a difference on the environment, about which he cares so passionately.

Thank goodness that I haven't come out of this weakened. The old adage is still true: the moment you start to slip and someone sees you stumble, the hands come out to give you a push.

This is, of course, not universally true and shows that I was indulging in a moment of cynicism. I was to be very lucky when many hands came out to hold me up and support me, but it was the other hands I was thinking about back in June 2003.

That would be true of the media, not just of those in politics. It is a kind of pack mentality. People get caught up and sometimes they get dragged along. And now all the people I have upset – in the legal profession, the judiciary, and on the liberal Left – are out bad-mouthing me. I should expect nothing else.

And so to Home Office Questions on Monday [16 June]. It is Sod's Law again that we are the first new team in. If I were the Tories I would go on the *News of the World* story about one of their journalists getting a job at Woodhill Prison. You couldn't make it up – he had got dodgy references and his passport said that he was a journalist – but what do you do? You stand there at the Dispatch Box, that's what you do!

The unauthorised briefings are really causing damage – what I described to Tony as *Independent* readers and *Daily Express* briefers, because someone inside Downing Street is briefing the *Express*, of all newspapers. What on earth do they think the mileage is in doing that?

Let me move on. After an intense week or two we were settling in, not to boredom but to the busy pressurised routine that has filled so much of my diary. Perhaps therefore I should include some highlights from the summer of 2003.

Wednesday 18 June saw a really good performance by Tony at Prime Minister's Questions. It cheered up our troops enormously in knocking down Iain Duncan Smith. On the same day I published the consultation on domestic violence: I am pleased with this as I have worked very hard to get the issue on the agenda and, to be fair, many people have put in an enormous effort behind the scenes over the last couple of years, including Harriet Harman and one of our new members, Vera Baird [MP for Redcar]. There has been a small group of women members working on this in the party for some time, and it is really good to be able to see some progress at last. I would like to get the legislation through in this parliament.

I had one of those days when I started at an unearthly hour – in this case 4.10 a.m. because of a security issue – but that is the job. Appearing on the *Today* programme and Radio 5 Live a little later and concentrating on something entirely different is just par for the course. The interviews were as much about the reshuffle and the Head of MI5's speech the day before as they were about domestic violence. It is quite hard to get the broadcasters to concentrate on what it is that you are trying to put across if it is not a row or some form of conflict or has nothing to do with Iraq.

You never know what's round the corner, though. I had thought that I was going to have a quiet weekend on 21 and 22 June, but Prince William's birthday party at Windsor Castle turned out to be something more than expected. A man wearing a dress and a wig managed to get through the whole of the security system and give Prince William a smacker. What on earth SO14 (the royal protection team) was up to, God only knows. I expect I will end up defending them in the House and through the media.

The 7th Earl who was in charge of the Unit (though it has to be said that his appointment was nothing to do with the Royal Family) ended up being promoted rather than sacked, and remained in charge of Royal Protection long after Sir John Stevens and myself had vacated our posts as Commissioner and Home Secretary respectively.

Twenty-one years ago Willie Whitelaw had threatened to resign over such issues, but he was at that time in charge of the Metropolitan Police Authority and I am not. The question for me is: 'Have we done our bit when investing in electronic surveillance and the right resources to do the job?' The answer, from the preliminary information I have, is that we have – in spades. And here we have Oliver Letwin calling for a 'Tsar', as though a Cabinet minister would be wandering around the perimeter of Windsor Park checking that chief superintendents and above are bothering to do their job. Perhaps the Tories think that such an appointment would have ended up with an invitation to Windsor Castle for the evening.

Just another week, with President Putin's visit (which I am involved in), the Report Stage and Third Reading of the Anti-Social Behaviour Bill, the Italian Interior Minister coming across, and now a Statement to the House about Prince William's uninvited guest.

The Statement went fine, but I did make the terrible error of spelling out in graphic detail what had happened at Windsor on the Saturday evening. Of course, the detail was hilarious and I could have kicked myself. A phrase such as 'I think that everyone is aware of the graphic detail' would have been a lot better than the description of a man in a dress! It just shows how important it is to judge the atmosphere in the House of Commons and what is likely to go down well. I should have known better, but I fear that I had spent the hours running up to the Statement on trying to get the facts out of the police – no mean task.

The longer the internal inquiry into what happened at Prince William's party went on, the clearer it became that the three layers of electronic security (the triggers at the boundary and inside) had worked but those who were supposed to be on the job had obviously thought that there was no risk whatsoever. The device at the boundary was so sensitive that it was triggered by rabbits, so they had stopped taking any notice of it. The second trigger did work, but when they swung the cameras across, the contract caterers' vehicle was in the way so they couldn't see anything, and the electronic beam itself on the third trigger was blocked by the contractor's equipment. Then a helpful policeman kindly redirected the man in fancy dress to where the actual events were taking place! That door wasn't manned as it was presumed that all the guests were already there. We must just thank the Lord that it wasn't a dangerous incident. As Prince Andrew said to me at Conrad Black's annual party: 'The man's timing was impeccable!'

During President Putin's visit, the welcoming party were on the dais waiting for his cavalcade to reach us from the airport, and the Queen and Duke of Edinburgh were chatting away to Tony, Jack and myself. In fact the Queen was chatting mostly to Sadie, who seemed to enjoy the occasion until the presentation of arms at the end. She had been grumbling away at the bearskins and I had been feeding her dog chews to quieten her, but when the presentation of arms took place she gave the most enormous bark, which echoed around the Mall, a sound captured for ever by Sky television. It was a surreal occasion, as these always are: a kind of mixture of Ruritania on the one hand and Britain at its ceremonial best on the other. Those in ceremonial dress must have been on the edge of fainting as it was one of those incredibly hot summer days when the last thing you need is to be dressed up.

Peter Hain has had a rough time. Now that he has the dual job of Wales and Northern Ireland, he decided to have a pop about tax policy. Goodness me, the big guns certainly came to bear on him. It is a lonely road when that happens – all the way through to the following Cabinet, where I now sit next to Gordon and can take the temperature through body language and scribbling. I don't need to be able to see to feel it.

It was interesting on the Tuesday evening to sit next to President Musharraf of Pakistan, a very intelligent and thoughtful man, with one hell of a job on his hands in dealing with the very serious threat to the security of his own country, never mind the rest of the world, and at the same time the sheer hatred of the USA within Pakistan itself. Paradoxically, the Deputy Prime Minister of India was over here and I hosted a lunch for him. (As indicated previously, he was also the Interior Minister.) He is very keen that I should go to India, and although I have resisted it so far, I think I will – but I will have to go to Pakistan as well.

During the last week in June I had a meeting with Gordon about civil renewal and the potential for developing a Youth Corps. I am very enthusiastic about this if we can build on the experience of the Millennium Volunteers and not just replicate the AmeriCorps programme in the USA. There is a lot that I can do with Gordon on civil renewal and identity and particularly his interest in engaging young people.

We also came back to the thorny issue of charges for various immigration activities. I just wish I was certain that the efforts I have made on sorting out the charges and the service for visas and renewal would come to fruition. There seems to be no commitment or understanding of how important it is to get this right by August, when the charges come in.

At the end of the month I gave Tony a long note about my feelings about where we are now and where we might be in a year's time. I hope it was helpful. I have given him a number of what I continue to call billets-doux over the years. Perhaps he has them filed away somewhere.

July 2003

Tuesday 15 July was definitely one of those days. The crime stats were out and there was the Second Reading of the Sex Offences/Sex Offenders Bill. (I worked really hard to turn the original proposals into something that could be universally supported.) And here we have the Tories taking out Part 7 of the Criminal Justice and Sentencing Bill in the House of Lords.

They were never taken to task by the right-wing press for a blatant attempt to water down the measures I was putting in place, restoring complete freedom to judges on sentencing, and for doing everything they could to undermine the removal of the double-jeopardy laws that were being used so effectively to stop forensic science being able to catch dangerous criminals and killers.

The last week or two have been amusing when dealing with Oliver Letwin, because having on a number of occasions chided me for having too much to do and having himself not turned up for the Domestic Violence Statement and the Report and Third Reading of the Anti-Social Behaviour Bill, he is beginning to get a reputation, as he did in the 1997 general election, for being 'the missing man'. It was some comfort to see his discomfort.

Went to a John Adams concert at the Barbican. I had never experienced his music and presentation before. I haven't done enough of going to concerts and theatre, but there just isn't enough time. All these years down in London, and hardly ever have I taken advantage of the culture around me. It's my own fault.

The street-crime initiative really has worked over the last year. What has helped enormously is the detailed approach with regular meetings chaired either by Tony or myself, and getting people to report back and to examine where the bottlenecks are and what is happening. We have had people reporting back from the different localities, including ministers, which has made a difference, but above all we have concentrated on getting every-body involved round the table and keeping up the momentum. Every time we think we have resolved one set of issues, something else comes up, whether it is the inability to serve warrants or the failure of the probation service to be able to deal with persistent offenders. It is just one struggle after another, but it is working. And so is the ring-fenced funding.

It is funny how insistent I had been on retaining the ring-fenced funding, and how three years later the statistics were to take a dip in the wrong direction after the ring-fencing had been taken away.

Also during the week starting Monday 14 July we had a postponed meeting on ID cards. I am plugging away but it is hard work. Bev Hughes is helping me enormously with ID cards, and we had a private meeting with Tony, followed by a round-table meeting, in which he was extremely helpful from the chair. He said: 'I know that round the table there are disagreements. There are disagreements by those close to me, but has anyone anything at this stage to say about the proposition that we should go forward with the consultation as agreed?' There was silence. It was a really helpful way of giving me the go-ahead, in providing the Department with the political backing needed, and above all strengthening the hand of our ministerial team and therefore our clout with the civil service in getting the job done.

It was optimistic, as I realised later, but Tony's saying 'Well, if there are no objections, we will go forward together' warmed my heart at the time.

I have just got to win over sufficient Cabinet colleagues to keep up the momentum and carry the day. There are some I will never be able to win over and I will just have to recognise that. I think I am going to have to do the scheme on the back of updating passports. That way the whole thing stays within my hands as Home Secretary, and we can use the existing technology and the developments that are going to be necessary anyway, and we can massively reduce the costs. I would like to incorporate driving licences, but it looks as though the political struggle to get agreement and to ensure that European-wide requirements can be taken into account is going to be too big an obstacle to overcome.

The annual intelligence-and-security debate in the House of Commons was somewhat disrupted. Jack, whose turn it was to lead off, had come back from a trip to Iraq and Iran, stopping off in Afghanistan. He had the most terrible stomach problems, so Denis MacShane did the debate with me. Once again, despite the enormity of the issues and the maturity of the debate, the debate got damn-all coverage. The only downside was Michael Ancram, Shadow Foreign Secretary, who made a very nasty attack on Tony that appeared to me to be a way of the Tory Party, who after all had supported our going into Iraq, having their cake and eating it. It was all about the statement on 3 February and the so-called 'dodgy dossier'.

On these occasions we have civil servants on hand in the Commons – 'in the box', as it is called. I never found their presence to be a great deal of use, but on this occasion it was utterly useless. None of the Foreign Office or Home Office civil servants could come up with anything, and when I was winding up I had to rely on my own memory as Denis MacShane had gone off to Gibraltar and Jack was still ill. Jonathan Sedgwick had come up with extracts from *Hansard* from 3 February, which was the only help I was able to get from anywhere. To be fair, I don't suppose that anyone had anticipated that Jack would be out of action and that Denis MacShane would leave the debate halfway through.

July also saw the beginning of what was to be a devastating series of leaks on ID cards. The Sunday Times, *then and for the following two years, was to print private correspondence and reports for the Domestic Affairs Committee of the Cabinet.*

Apart from the fact that, without agreement having been reached with anyone, private information and material appearing in the newspapers creates controversy, the real worry is the simple fact that those who obviously wish to damage you go round claiming that you have leaked it yourself. I even took the trouble to record the Sunday Times *political editor leaving me an answer-phone message acknowledging that it had nothing to do with me or my ministers and asking that I get back to him to give him a quote on the 'leak'. Of course, I couldn't then or later use such evidence to Cabinet colleagues without reinforcing the view that I was worried about having to defend my integrity on the issue. Ironically, the figure that we were using for stand-alone ID cards (not including the cost of updated passports) was higher than the figure that was used when the Bill became an Act in 2006.*

My diary at the time includes: 'I am sick of this now . . . Someone has really got it in for me, and has my worst interests at heart . . . I've really had it up to here . . . I've already written to John Prescott months ago asking for a new system that has much stronger security in relation to the circulation of sensitive papers.'

But it was only much later, when the leaks were affecting other people, that tougher action was eventually taken.

The other major issue of July was the criminal-justice conference, in which wc had speakers from the USA. The concept of community justice centres is really interesting and I just hope that we can get colleagues on board – Harry Woolf is interested and it is good to have positive agreement with him as Lord Chief Justice and to know that there is an alternative to the 'winner takes all' technical-knock-out system that we call our justice system at the moment.

Huw Evans has told me off for using the conference to have a go at the *Daily Telegraph* for their constant attacks on me. As he quite rightly says, 'The world isn't really interested in your private wars with particular journalists.'

The tragedy of July was the suicide of David Kelly.

On 29 May 2003 BBC reporter Andrew Gilligan had claimed – initially at 6.07 a.m. on the Today *programme – that the dossier about Iraq published the previous autumn had been enhanced shortly before its publication with material that the government knew to be of questionable merit. He repeated the charge in an article in the* Mail on Sunday, *and when giving evidence to the Foreign Affairs Committee on 19 June asserted that his source had been 'one of the senior officials in charge of drawing up the dossier', which triggered even more intense speculation about the identity of his source.*

David Kelly, a biological-weapons expert at the Ministry of Defence, was found dead in woods near his home on 18 July 2003.

We had had speculation all month about who Andrew Gilligan's source was and whether, as the Head of BBC Radio News had claimed on *The*

World at One on 7 July, the source was 'at the very heart of the drafting' in relation to the material drawn up in respect of the debate on Iraq. This was patently wrong. I knew it was wrong because I had been briefed by the Head of MI5, the Terrorism Unit and the Head of the Joint Intelligence Committee on the Monday, indicating that it was someone who had undertaken work for the MoD (in the Defence Intelligence Service, about which so few people knew anything). Andrew Gilligan's description and what was to emerge were quite different, although it was necessary to take a great deal of notice about what was being said, broadcast and written to understand this.

Twenty-four hours later and the BBC had the story. *The World Tonight* on Radio 4 on Tuesday 8 July made it clear that 'the BBC understands' that the description that the BBC has and that given by Andrew Gilligan differ in important respects: 'The description of the person concerned in the MoD statement does not match Mr Gilligan's source in some important ways.

'The MoD say that the person they have talked to gives a different account of his conversation with Andrew Gilligan from the one broadcast on the *Today* programme here on Radio 4 in late May.' That was the report in which it was said that those engaged in drafting the dossier had been 'told at the behest of Downing Street to make it sexier. Tonight's latest twists in this saga come just a day after a committee of MPs decided that allegations of politically inspired meddling could not be credibly established. The Chairman of that committee, the senior Labour MP Donald Anderson, is bemused. He says, "It completely appears to contradict what Mr Gilligan wrote in the *Mail on Sunday* and what he told the committee during the course of our inquiry." We asked our political editor Andrew Marr why the Ministry of Defence published its statement tonight. "It was pretty strange timing. They had just had the lowest majority that Labour have had since coming to power in 1997 on foundation hospitals, a core flagship policy, a big political story, and then this letter drops and knocks that embarrassment off the top of the headlines. Well, it may simply be a coincidence but many people are scratching their heads a bit." '

I talked to Tony about this at dinner the following evening (Tony, Sally Morgan and myself), and about the fact that it was necessary for the MoD to be undertaking an investigation as to who was the leaker, particularly given the spin that had been put on it by Andrew Gilligan. If this person was as close to events as Gilligan had claimed, then we were in obvious serious difficulty over security. If he wasn't, we needed to know what information he did have and what he had said to Andrew Gilligan or any other journalist.

Pam Teare, Head of News for the MoD, had worked for me when I first came into the Home Office, and was a decent, reliable and entirely traditional civil servant. I do not believe for a moment that she would have done anything improper or been bullied into doing so.

Unsurprisingly Tony was the most tired I had ever seen him, and he said quite openly that he is desperate to get a break in Barbados in August. How he is coping is beyond me. He said on a number of occasions during the evening how fit I looked, to which I responded that I didn't feel fit, and in fact I felt as if I had got a dose of whatever it was that Jack Straw had picked up in Kandahar, but without ever having been there.

We also talked about the Special Cabinet that was taking place the following day, and how best to structure it so that it wasn't completely dominated by current events. Sally Morgan floated the idea of Matthew Taylor taking over from Andrew Adonis and thereby letting Nick Pearce move up to Director of the IPPR, which would be extraordinarily good news for all of us.

My diary then records the following words, referring to Tony: 'I like him, I respect him and I despair for him.' My feeling at the time was that he was wearing himself out, that he had taken too much on and that he had not put in place sufficiently robust structures and support systems.

In the throes of so much activity, including the Special Cabinet on Thursday 10 July (whence I think everyone came out a great deal more grumpy than when they went in), I went to see Nelson Mandela, who was visiting London. I was the senior Cabinet minister at the event and had about twenty-five minutes with him before he spoke. I have now met him three times and have found him just as impressive on each occasion, although he is now very frail and very small – that is, small physically but great of status and presence.

I then did the press reception that the Department had set up.

We did a press reception in the summer and also in the run-up to Christmas, and this particular one could not have fallen at a worse moment, given so much activity, so much flurry and so much appearance of government under siege.

My mid-July surgery was 80 per cent nationality and asylum cases. What worries me is not just the stress and strain that this brings for me but also for the staff in my office, as there is not a single case that is easy to handle, otherwise they wouldn't have come to me in the first place. I am deeply concerned that constituents who are long-term residents and voters become disillusioned and, seeing the long queue, walk away. I am going to have to do something to streamline my surgery if I am not to be there hour after hour picking up cases that are not traditional constituency work. But it certainly does bring home the size of the task we have. No one has to tell me any more about the impact of large-scale asylum and the incompetence of the administration of the Immigration and Nationality Directorate. I can feel it for myself.

The day was leavened considerably by three community events. There were over 5,000 people at the Parson Cross Festival, when five years ago there wasn't even a festival and not a cat in hell's chance of getting more than fifty or sixty people at any such event. It is a real turnaround in terms of regeneration, renewal and involvement. I then went to a little fundraising event for a residential complex for older people, and then to the Pilsley festival on the Chatsworth estate in Derbyshire, where I had been asked to do the official opening. There could not have been a bigger contrast than the festival on the big council estate and the archetypal English village summer fête – but both illustrated the importance of community, and both warmed my heart. What was particularly endearing was to get such a warm reception at both the constituency and the Pilsley fête. At the latter it was usually the Duke of Devonshire who carried out the opening so having a Labour Cabinet minister was a very novel experience for them! It just does me so much good when people are so nice. I also enjoyed going on to the Chatsworth farm shop afterwards to stock up for Hugh's birthday barbecue the following day.

I took Tessa Jowell's advice and dropped the idea of making a Parliamentary Statement on ID cards, which would have been when Tony was away in the USA, speaking at Congress. It was better to leave things a little. Sometimes I just push things too much, too fast.

I ended up having to do press on the back of Clare Short's vicious attack on Tony, when she called for his resignation. It is so deeply personal that it can only be presumed that she has a terrible guilt complex from knowing that she agreed with and went along with what we were doing.

One lighter note in an otherwise extremely difficult and deeply unamusing July was at Home Office Questions. The new team had all gathered and went in for Prayers. At the beginning of each day on the floor of the House the Speaker parades and comes in through the door opposite the Speaker's Chair. He has with him his Chaplain who, among other things, has in his prayer that we should not seek popularity (which has always tickled me). However, on this particular afternoon prayers were somewhat disrupted by the fact that as the Speaker came through the doors to make his way through the Chamber, Sadie decided to bark – a great resonant, deep-throated, deep-chested bark. The place was stunned. I quickly gave her a dog chew and all seemed to be well until the Chaplain started his prayers and was obviously so thrown at being barked at by a dog that when it came to 'Have mercy on us' he inadvertently said 'Have mercy on me' – and despite the fact that it was a solemn occasion, everybody laughed.

Even when questions started, Sadie continued to make little woofs in her throat, to the point where I decided that it would be best to get her out of the Chamber and into my room. Room 6 is the first one on the corridor behind the Speaker's Chair, so it was very easy to get one of the team to take her out and settle her. I presume that something had scared her, as she only ever barks when she has been frightened.

Tony's visit to the US, China, Japan and Korea was underpinned by the continuing row about British citizens held at Guantanamo Bay [the detainment camp situated at the US naval base on the south-eastern coast of Cuba].

Being seen as the 'hard man' doesn't worry me, but I am much more sympathetic to the families than people realise. We have a common line although it keeps taking a knock when people feel under pressure from the media. We are all agreed – that is Tony, Jack, Peter Goldsmith, Charlie Falconer and myself – that the fairest way to treat British citizens held there would be a properly conducted trial in the USA, but Peter is quite right in saying that a tribunal in which one of Donald Rumsfeld's neighbours (and all of them government appointees) formulates the legal process is clearly not fair. Tony has accepted my suggestion that we get five of the nine back immediately because the risk assessment on them is so much less than on the others. But local cohesion is a real challenge. It is true in some cases that as time passes (and this is the case with those I have certified under the Anti-Terrorism, Crime and Security Act) the networks erode, links deteriorate, and their will and determination diminish. But it is always a fine judgement, and not one that can be made without the facts – unlike the *Today* programme on Thursday 17 July. The father of one of those not immediately coming back from Guantanamo was being interviewed, and it was presumed by the interviewer that what was being said was simply the truth, that the man's son was simply a charity worker. What a way to start a day. No wonder my blood pressure is up.

This was followed by an early Cabinet at nine a.m. in order to allow Tony to fly to the States to make his speech to the two Houses of Congress. Once again I am just amazed at how he takes the enormous pressure, including the sustained press abuse. Gordon did a presentation on future financing, following up a desultory discussion we had had the week before. The education budget is in a fix and money is being found from underspends on Sure Start, on switching from the social-services element of Health and from John Prescott's Budget to help them out, given that the new strictures are that the final year of the present Spending Review will not effectively be the first year of the new three years because the budget will be frozen, other than for Health at the previously agreed level. I wasn't the only one to point out at Cabinet that we have an election coming up and that while we could lay this down as a general rule, it certainly wasn't going to apply to key pressurised services running up to a projected general election some time in 2005.

At Cabinet I welcomed Gordon's openness about what his thinking was and where we were on budgets and funding for the future. I tried to be helpful by pointing out that we were raising well over £100 million by charging for previously free services in Immigration and Nationality, looking at how to raise money on fixed-penalty notices (which would go back into the criminal-justice budget) and motoring fines arising out of ANPR [Automatic Number Plate Recognition], which allowed easy clocking of unlicensed vehicles or breaches of traffic or other regulations picked up by CCTV. (We haven't reached agreement with the Treasury about the way in which all new fundraising programmes put together by departments are clawed back into the Treasury coffers, which, as I said at the meeting, is a disincentive for people to start raising money rather than just spending it.)

Whenever we discussed finance and public services at Cabinet, I recognise now that I had a bit of a propensity to pomposity and to 'knowing it all'. It must have proved aggravating for my colleagues, but my excuse is that the years I spent in a leading role in local government did at least equip me to know a little of what I was talking about. It was so evident that most of the time departments briefed their own ministers very badly. This is not surprising when, in my experience, it was clear that even those who were in charge of the budgets within departments seemed often to be struggling to hold the detail in their head or to cope with the kind of enormous figures they were dealing with.

For reasons that are very clear, Gordon is reluctant to get into detail, privately or in Cabinet. My reading of history is that every Chancellor in every government has reacted in a very similar fashion. But that said, he doesn't have a very high opinion of other people's grasp of finance. At the end of this Cabinet meeting John Reid and Gordon commenced the most enormous public row (public in the sense of other people being around) that I have seen since 1997. They are going to have to settle how much money will buy what treatment and what targets are attainable.

And so from Cabinet to chairing the Counter-Terrorism Committee. There was a good attendance but the atmosphere was not good. Thank God I hadn't pressed ahead with a Statement to the Commons on ID cards. We have hit – as we seem to every summer but this time with knobs on – that febrile tired state in which everyone is irritable with everyone else and the sooner Parliament goes into recess, the better. How on earth we managed to combine so many different, difficult things, all at the same point in the calendar, is a mystery. I think the crime stats scheduled automatically for this point form just another example of how the business of government is so badly configured. If there had been a Spending Review this July, I think the world would have imploded around us.

By 2006–2007 many departments had been taken out of the Spending Review process altogether, thereby reducing the focused pressure on a few weeks at the end of the internal review of existing and future spending. But in 2002, and to a substantial extent in 2004, the pressure across and within departments was such that friction was bound to arise, and the workload (because there were numerous internal meetings as well as those with the Treasury) would have been one step too far in a summer where tensions were running high, and in danger of breaking out publicly.

In fact the suggestion of the virtual freeze on spending made in July 2003 was only partly implemented because of pressure on services and delivery, and also the approach of the general election. The objective, having been partly met by the separating-out of some departments and a very different treatment for those substantially in the public eye from those that were not, was effectively completed in the Budget announcement of March 2006, although the salience of this seems to have been missed by commentators.

While Tony was receiving seventeen standing ovations at the joint meeting of Congress in Washington, I was chairing a departmental Awayday (or more strictly speaking an Away-afternoon and -evening) following the busy morning of Cabinet and the Terrorism Committee – and yes, several television interviews on the crime stats in between. I found a remarkably positive spirit among senior officials and the ministerial team. Despite tiredness and fractiousness in the light of what was going on around us, it did seem at last as though we were all pulling together and there was a new spirit of reform and modernisation from officials, and a real coming together of the new ministerial team. I think this is remarkable, given the timescale.

I received the news of David Kelly's death on the train as I was returning from London to Sheffield. As is my habit, I was taking the fast route from King's Cross to Doncaster and then across from Doncaster to Sheffield by road. It is hard to describe how I felt when I was phoned and given news that wouldn't be public for just over another twenty-four hours. Although it wasn't confirmed that he had committed suicide, it appeared very clear that he had. I felt sick. It had an impact on me way beyond what I could have expected. After all, in my job I am used to talking to the bereaved parents of murdered children, dealing with counter-terrorism, and the abuse when trying to deal with immigration and asylum issues. (The following day Hugo Young in the *Guardian* wrote that I was the most dangerous Home Secretary in history.) And yet this event hit me as though I had been kicked in the stomach. Sadness and regret, of course, but if I am honest also a feeling that this was a terrible political event, a blow, a failure on everyone's part. Yes, David Kelly was experienced in briefing journalists, but did he really know what Andrew Gilligan was going to do and what the impact would be, and did those around him in those latter days see the state he was in and what he might do?

I didn't know the answers then, and I don't now. I think that even my most vociferous opponent and most cynical critic would agree that I have taken a fair amount of pressure upon myself since the summer of 2004, but even with that experience it is difficult for me to appreciate the despair of someone willing to take their own life – although I have to say it is now a little easier to understand than it was then. How crucial it is that people around you

understand what you are going through, and that there are those who are
alongside you at moments when even they have doubts.

There have been some terrible things written during the days following the
announcement of David Kelly's death. There have been presumptions
made about him and presumptions made posthumously on his behalf. I
have not made a note of all of them here. Suffice it to say that in these few
weeks of July 2003, no one seems to me to have emerged with credit.

Shortly afterwards John Prescott (standing in for Tony during his absence in
the USA) was to slap down quite correctly the so-called 'Downing Street
spokesman' undertaking the lobby briefing in which he used language about
David Kelly that in any circumstances would have been unacceptable. The
reason I note this is that it was the same individual who was responsible for
the lobby on 31 October 2005. This time a life was not being denigrated, nor
was inappropriate language being used about an individual. However, the
inaccuracy, the misinterpretation and the blatant out-of-order assumptions
made took their own toll on my future. I reflect that at least in our democracy,
accountability for politicians is in the end absolute.

When I spoke to Geoff Hoon on Wednesday 23 July he told me that he had
been to see David Kelly's family, who have behaved throughout with great
fortitude and dignity. I think that Geoff too has behaved extremely well in
the circumstances, as it must have been awful for him, expected as he is to
shoulder responsibility. I have written an article in the left-wing weekly
Tribune and undertaken an interview on Channel 4, just trying to get
across that at a time like this it is necessary to see 'the politics behind the
politics'. Let us hope that the report into the affair by Lord Hutton (former
Chief Justice of Northern Ireland) and the Intelligence and Security
Committee report will help clear the air.

Goodness me, how naïve these thoughts appear now, so much later.

For me the adrenalin has gone, and I feel deflated. All the energy has gone
out of me – and this August, for the first time since 1989, I will not be in
Majorca. I am having five days in France and will then spend time at the
cottage. So many hopes dwindling into reality.

I thought that David Aaronovitch, two weeks running in the *Observer*
and in a *Guardian* article on Monday [21 July], was one of those very few

people who genuinely showed some sense of rationality and reason. And on Thursday [24 July] I had a really decent lunch with Robert Thomson, editor of *The Times*. I hope that all the lunches and dinners I have with editors might make some difference in the long run.

I am afraid that was wishful thinking. The very personal relations (often good relations) that I had with all those editors with whom I had regular contact – and that was all except the Express group of newspapers – bore no fruit at all when the chips were down. In one sense, this ought to be the case. Issues and personalities should be judged on their merit. But I can't help feeling that, given the way that journalists support journalists and cover up for journalists' failures, there is a slightly different rule for the relationship of journalists with politicians than there is for journalists with each other. I must have been very naïve not to have realised that it was ever thus.

I have hundreds of cuttings on file relating to the death of David Kelly and the recriminations, and I don't think anyone comes out of this with great credit. The BBC are refusing to release material which they will have to let Lord Hutton have. For very understandable reasons, Alastair Campbell has gone over the top. The political fall-out is awful. I have done an interview with Andrew Rawnsley for the Sunday evening *Westminster Hour* programme on Radio 4, a pre-record for the programme in the run-up to 2 August, when we become the longest-ever continuously serving Labour government. Quite a landmark, though most of my colleagues have gone away on holiday, and to be honest I can't blame them. Everyone needs a break and I shall make the best of being at home and enjoying the cottage.

August 2003

The first week in August saw a very strange snub from Harry Woolf, Lord Chief Justice. I received a message that the judges did not wish to go ahead with a dinner in the autumn, arranged to try and run through issues informally and quietly. They didn't think it was appropriate to meet in an informal setting.

They did meet eventually with Charlie Falconer and myself, with Tony present for part of the time, at 10 Downing Street. On that occasion, it was to ensure that they could put their view about the maintenance of their pension entitlements, so it was more of a shop stewards' meeting than about what is happening to the criminal-justice system.

And in this early recess we had another two letters leaked to David Cracknell on the *Sunday Times* – one from Paul Boateng and one from Patricia Hewitt – on the Criminal Injuries Compensation Scheme. There is clearly someone really out to cause maximum mischief and with access at the highest level to the most sensitive material. Not surprisingly these were the two letters that were least positive about moving forward. I don't believe for a moment that Paul Boateng and Patricia Hewitt connived with the *Sunday Times*, so it has to be someone either working very close to the domestic affairs process or deep in the Downing Street end of the Cabinet Office.

This was all about radical improvements to make sense of the Criminal Injuries Compensation Scheme, where very large sums of money went towards compensating people while I was struggling to get an insurance-based scheme (which I failed to achieve) for low-level injuries, in which treatment and a speedy process within the criminal-justice system was a lot more use to people than low-level compensation. In any case we desperately needed resources to build up victim-support and witness-support systems, and we made some progress, which was built on by Charles Clarke in early 2006.

In the current circumstances and with the pressures of the moment, there is a real danger of becoming paranoid. I am not prepared to put up with this domestic-affairs process any further. The circulation of letters is just like putting material on to the Internet. It is impossible to make policy sensibly and sort out genuine disagreements if every time a radical or controversial policy is put forward, it is leaked. I just despair.

Also in what is supposed to be a slack period, the news is leaked that Alastair Campbell has told Tony that he is going – but only at a time of Tony's agreement. It may be a scalp for those who don't like Tony, and particularly for those who don't like Alastair, but I think it is bad news for Tony, and Lord knows what Alastair will do with himself afterwards. It suggested that Alastair would 'want to clear his name' with regard to what the Hutton Report will say. I gave him a ring and, in Alastair's usual way, he did a bit of f-ing and blinding and then confirmed. But he said he wasn't going to go under pressure from the BBC, and I can't blame him for that.

Alastair eventually stood down on Friday 29 August. He did me the courtesy of giving me a ring before the news broke and I was grateful for that.

Week two of the recess saw arrangements put in place for Tony Martin to be moved out of prison to a safe place before returning home. There will no doubt be another storm around this. It is just another thing to media-manage and explain and make sure that it goes smoothly. The governor of the prison housing Brendon Fearon, one of those who attempted to burgle Tony Martin and was subsequently imprisoned for a range of other activities, has let him out on home domestic curfew. How stupid can you get? It feels to me as though it is a challenge to us for having said that we would back governors in taking difficult decisions over home domestic curfew in order to ease the prison population.

Some people do behave so strangely, so cack-handedly, and it is not always clear what on earth they think they are gaining from it.

We had a farewell reception for the former Head of Immigration and Nationality that was like the end of an era. He is the archetypal civil servant's civil servant, even to the point at the reception of making jokes about past junior ministers. He obviously held in total contempt the junior politicians he had supposedly worked for: a gentle man but with a sting, quiet, unassuming and contemptuous of those attempting to bring about change. He recalled an alleged incident where a Secretary of State had asked the Permanent Secretary how one of his own junior ministers (Parliamentary Under-Secretary) was faring. What a giveaway for the knowledge and competence of the particular Secretary of State – but the reply was even more interesting: 'He won't make a bad executive-officer grade eventually.' Everyone there thought it was hilarious. I didn't.

Peter Goldsmith is flying out to the US for further meetings on Guantanamo Bay. All we can do is to give him whatever backing we can to find a way forward.

As I was coming out from seeing Tony on Wednesday morning, John Prescott tapped on the car window. I wound it down and he made a jocular remark about whether I had got any more leaks coming out. He then told me about what was to appear in the *News of the World* about Pauline and the fact that when she was sixteen she had a baby which she had then had adopted. I sympathised with him and he said everything was fine, but it struck me that the press have no right to do that. They have no right to interfere in someone's life in that way, dragging up something from so long ago. It can turn somebody's existence completely upside down – John and Pauline's, and especially the lad's: it could have destroyed his peace of mind and his relationship with his adoptive parents. It is just an absolute outrage when the press do things like that, and they blithely think they have the right to do it. It certainly isn't in the public interest at all.

Little was I to know that a year later I was to be subjected to the same intrusion.

Before leaving for his holiday, Tony did what I thought was a high-risk end-of-term press conference, with Michael Barber doing a session in front of the media on delivery and Tony taking questions for an hour and a quarter. But it seemed to work. Sensible remarks about needing to sort out the technical issues around ID cards and how that would take time were interpreted in some quarters as Tony going cold on the idea. Well, we will see.

Another court case lost – this time on Section 55 of the Nationality, Immigration and Asylum Act. This is all about how long people should be in the country before they claim asylum and become entitled to asylum support. We have tried so hard to stop people who have been in the country for a long time as illegal immigrants, or have found themselves in difficulty, then claiming asylum to avoid having to return home. But all we get from the judges is a complete failure to understand that people play the system. It is such a difficult area, this – the balance between being fair to those who are genuinely at risk and desperately preventing the whole asylum issue from being distorted and used, not just against us but against any kind of rational cohesion and social integration. People still don't seem to understand that unless we get that balance right, the far right are going to flourish. And what's more, people of goodwill are becoming bewildered and upset, and that being the case, they will turn against us as well, because they will think that it is unfair. So it is absolutely crucial that we get this right, that people aren't seen to take us for granted, and that we extend generosity and a warm welcome to those who need it. And, as I have said so often, how the hell are we going to get legal economic migration sorted when people are so up in arms about clandestine entry and unwarranted asylum claims?

We will appeal. Time and time again we are having to appeal on things that are just straightforward, where for the sake of mutuality and the something-for-something agenda people have got to build up some form of entitlement. They can't just expect us to provide them with hand-outs. What was so bizarre about this judgement was the idea that it was our responsibility to make sure that people had seen the posters and that the posters were prominent enough and in enough languages to ensure that people knew that if they wanted to claim asylum, they had to claim it immediately they arrived at ports or airports. Well, if you want to claim asylum, you claim asylum. You don't need massive posters telling you, 'Here is the point to claim asylum.' It is a kind of *Alice in Wonderland* madhouse – and here I am, as Home Secretary, trying to sort it out.

When I had lunch with Peter Mandelson on 30 July, he asked me what it was that Tony should do to reach out to those who were most antagonistic, particularly the trade unions. I said that he should recognise the real feeling about pensions.

Goodness me. I had no idea how this was to come home to roost when I took over for six months dealing with the pensions issue.

I told him that there are a number of issues on which people will warm to Tony when he talks about their worries, their insecurities, and their desire for some certainty for the future. He is good at this because he does understand that fear of too rapid change and certainties falling apart means increased antagonism to reform and modernisation. Peter said: 'What else for the party and for the Left?' I suggested anti-poverty, world-wide and domestically, and the promotion of Gordon's agenda. I said that he could do it with Valerie Amos in a way that he could never do it with Clare.

At this moment Valerie Amos was the Overseas Development Secretary, and of course when Tony and Gordon worked closely together on the G8 Africa and anti-world poverty agenda in 2005, it was a superb example of how two leading statesmen can bring about significant change.

No. 10 insisted that we should have a street-crime meeting before Tony went away on holiday. I don't know why Tony should be pressurised in this way, but in the end it turned out to be a helpful round-up. We were now really beginning to get to grips with street robbery, theft and mugging. I think that, along with the Literacy and Numeracy Programme, this is one of the best examples of how joined-up thinking and real focus can have results. Of course, the more successful it is, the more people will just take it for granted, but that doesn't matter. It is just so crucial that we are getting a grip of it.

The problem is that when Tony is put under too much pressure, he doesn't have time to prepare. He came into the meeting and, although in his usual way he handled it with great professionalism and expertise, it was absolutely clear that nobody had worked through the agenda with him. Just before the end, he handed over as he had a couple of international calls coming in. Lord knows how he manages to keep his mind on one thing when another is just about to come up.

Like *The Westminster Hour*, I did the *Today* programme on the anniversary of the six years and three months of a continuous Labour government. I am proud to have been able to do this. It is a tremendous moment. I am also proud to have been a member of the Cabinet for this length of time.

I am going out to Beeley to begin having a proper holiday. I will pop in to the Home Office on Thursday [7 August] to do renewal of warrants and one or two other things, and again a week later when I am back from France. But other than that, I am going to take some time out. I am going to read novels and have a break and try and switch off the news, because if I don't it will merely confirm that it is not possible to have a holiday in Britain.

I did in fact have an excellent break in the hottest summer since goodness knows when.

On personal matters: I attended hospital on 31 July for tests and it looks as if the operation on my oesophagus has been successful. I still need to sort out a further problem with my bowel that has been troubling me and then things might pick up.

So just before spending a day or two with Bev Hughes and her husband Tom in the Lake District, I was back at the hospital for further tests. As they were very unpleasant, I had to have a general anaesthetic and the whole experience put me out of action for two or three days. I think I was still suffering from the aftermath of it all while I was with Bev and Tom, but I still very much enjoyed the break. I will have to pull myself round though by the time we are back into it with a vengeance in September.

Ulcerative colitis was eventually identified as the cause of my problem and has responded well to medication.

The whole of August has been dominated by the Hutton Inquiry and the attack on the UN Headquarters in Baghdad: Iraq domestically, Iraq internationally, Iraq everywhere.

Wednesday 27 August: Tony, back from holiday, went with me to the Immigration and Nationality Directorate in Croydon – it is amazing how quickly the holiday disappears – and I chatted to him about a Tom Baldwin article in *The Times* on 8 August. This was all about how he was going to be stepping down as Prime Minister.

It is strange looking back how, over and over again, material has appeared saying that Tony was about to resign. Apart from being untrue, it was also destabilising and extremely unhelpful.

The following day [Thursday 28 August] we got the quarterly asylum statistics out – always a difficult moment, but these were good statistics. We are getting results, and the numbers are coming down rapidly. But what do we get? 'Yes, asylum is coming down but what about illegal immigration?' Well, quite, and that's why I am banging on and on about ID cards and the need to find out who is in the country and who shouldn't be here. But the priority at the moment has to be to deal with asylum. It is just astonishing how quickly things move on. We get a grip in one area and immediately something else pops up. I do think that illegal immigration and clandestine existence in this country will be the long-term issue that we will need to confront. We have now halved the number of asylum seekers coming in, compared with the last quarter of last year. I wonder just how much that will be remembered in years to come.

Of course, it wasn't. No one remembers when you do something that for them is self-evidently something that should have been done a long time before. But what a difference it made, not just then but in the long term, to how we were able to handle these issues.

I had a meeting with Rod Eddington, Chief Executive of British Airways, and Richard Branson of Virgin about new measures I wanted to bring in that were being treated with real scepticism by the Department of Transport. This was all about preventing people in transit to somewhere else from stopping off at one of our airports and claiming asylum. It had become a real problem and, like all scams, when people cotton on to it they then start doing it in really large numbers. Both Rod and Richard were very helpful. I asked Rod if he would sell Richard the remaining Concorde, and I put a £2 coin on the table. It made for a lighter moment.

On the first weekend after August Bank Holiday I held a special surgery in an area from where it is difficult to get to my regular advice surgery, giving constituents a chance to see me rather than the hordes of regulars and immigration and asylum cases. I then went to a community meeting at lunchtime and on to a residential home to visit the mum of a long-standing party member.

Then I literally went to the dogs, because the local Labour Party had linked up with one of the trade unions for an evening of greyhound racing in Sheffield. I had never been before and it was quite an experience: having a small amount of money each way on dogs that inevitably didn't come in, having something to eat in one of the boxes, going round the bars and shaking hands with people surprised to see me there. There were several thousand people having a really nice night out, and the dogs themselves were almost incidental. Then at the end, I presented the awards, taking Sadie along to sniff a greyhound that was well muzzled!

Inevitably Sadie barked at the first race, when she saw the dogs coming out of the traps. I think she could have given them a fair run for their money, with her long legs and being fit as a fiddle, but I don't know what the Guide Dogs for the Blind Association would have thought of that! But it was wonderful, as ever, to get such a good reception. It is so good to be in the constituency and back in Sheffield.

Geoff Hoon has had a terrible week at the Hutton Inquiry. His evidence came across very badly but there is nothing, as a colleague, that anyone can do to help.

This time I didn't think he would survive. I asked myself how much more pressure he could take. When I found out myself just what the pressure was like, I came to realise that he really had enormous internal confidence and determination. It took a lot to come through that.

My big worry about his evidence was the shifting of blame. It looked from outside as though once again Tony was going to have to carry everything, even though Tony is not responsible for everything in the way that people so often think.

The *Daily Mirror* had a very strange little story about how I had talked to Gordon and agreed to step aside and not get in his way in the future for the leadership. I have never been in the way of his desire for the leadership, but nor have I stepped aside. It is curious where these stories come from.

It is even more curious to look back on them. I hadn't got my eyes on the leadership of the Labour Party for the reasons I have explained earlier, but it was strange to read about myself and what I had agreed and hadn't agreed, and to realise that behind the politics continue the politics.

Early evening Thursday I had a drink with Tony at No. 10 – or, to be exact, in the flat at No. 11 – before returning to Sheffield. We talked about the changes to his own office that he was now implementing, with Matthew Taylor coming in and Sally taking on a much more focused role. We talked about the fact that there were so many people in the Cabinet now who were arguing for retrenchment, not pushing ahead with reform and modernisation but just treading water for a time. We agreed how this would risk the momentum of the government running out two years from a general election.

We also talked about ID cards. I had devised a method of avoiding leaks, at least for the time being, although there were some substantial objections from within the Cabinet Office and the Office of the Deputy Prime Minister about this. The idea was to write to each individual Cabinet colleague separately, dealing with the issues that they have raised. If anything was then leaked, it would be fairly self-evident who its original recipient was and therefore which line to follow to find out who did it.

It also has the advantage of allowing us to engage directly with colleagues, which is something I am not good at and might just help in finding out what their fundamental objections are to what we are doing. I know what Alistair Darling has felt because he has been transparently honest all the way along and has engaged. Jack and Paul Boateng are against. I think that the issue of biometrics on passports has still not really got through, and when people do understand that the main cost will be the biometric and therefore what we need to add is a clean database, we might get somewhere.

Tony has promised to be helpful and I really appreciate that. It is, as I said to him, a really important domestic-agenda item at a time of complete focus by the media on Iraq and international issues.

Tony was also testing out at this time thoughts about who might replace the Secretary to the Cabinet.

On a political note, it was good to notice in *The Times* that there was an acknowledgement that whoever else might be running other people's departments, at least I was the one running mine.

Terrorism gets where terrorism is not. The electrical system failed in quite a substantial part of London, and with it the Underground, so that people immediately thought that there had been an attack. There hadn't, but it was a very interesting test of how services would react, how people would get their act together, and they didn't do very well. In particular it was clear that nobody really wanted to take responsibility and the lead in putting things right. So we will certainly have to learn the lessons and do something about that even though it was coincidence – well, not so much coincidence but perhaps a reflection of a lack of forward thinking at the time of privatisation.

The following week I was launching a citizenship report with Professor Sir Bernard Crick, and we decided to do it from a joint public/private partnership, Working Links, which was all about getting people back to work by providing language tuition as well as training. Bernard and I went to Brent, Bernard having steered the material through his working group and done a lot of hard graft, and when we came out he said to me: 'Did your press office tell you what the building is called? It's called Imperial House' – which we both thought was very amusing, given that we had just done this launch on the integration of overseas citizens. The press didn't pick it up so there was no feedback. We all missed it – except Bernard.

I had done an interview that morning on the *Today* programme with John Humphrys that proved one of those rare occasions when the deeper, long-term issues are explored. He told me afterwards that he had received a phone call from the *Observer* newspaper asking him why he had gone so 'easy' on me and not been more aggressive about government policy on immigration and asylum, and he said to me: 'It was because I was trying to get at the deeper issues of what the thinking was on what the report had to say and what the government was going to do about social cohesion and integration – rather than just attack.' It certainly made a change.

It has to be said that I had quite a hard time myself with Bernard, never mind with John Humphrys, because at the press conference he kept making asides like, 'We are trying to make sure that immigrants understand our political parties – that is, of course, if we can understand what they stand for ourselves any more!' I just smiled and it worked because nobody reported it.

It was good to see Nick Pearce on television that day doing his bit from the IPPR. I hope he gets the job of director. I have appointed Matt

Cavanagh to replace him. Matt has been a philosophy tutor at Oxford and then worked for a private-sector management consultancy dealing with the issues around change. We will certainly need all his expertise when handling the Immigration and Nationality Directorate. Jonathan Powell's brother is the Chairman of the Board overseeing the IPPR, so I had better be nice to Jonathan! Despite his obvious capabilities, neither he nor anyone around Tony has a background that would help with public expenditure, but as they appear to balk at the idea of a public-sector economist, I am afraid we go into the Spending Review with Downing Street – well, let me put it as softly as this – at something of a disadvantage.

On a lighter note, Sadie decided to go after a goose in St James's Park. Although she went into the water, she didn't do what Roy Hattersley's dog Buster did and kill it. We just had to nip back home and dry her. The idea of having a smelly wet dog on the train home was not a happy prospect, for me or for other passengers.

We had a Cabinet Committee dealing with the inter-governmental conference and the run-up to trying to sort out the so-called European Constitution. There is far too much emphasis on giving in in one area in order to gain in another, when giving in in one area creates major problems, but at least the discussion was positive and people were pulling together in trying to find a way forward. There is so much wriggle room and so much plasticine about these European discussions, and lack of clarity as to what in the end we are going to see as the bottom line.

I've a busy week because in an effort to get the team and the Executive Board out of London and around the regions, I have arranged an Awayday in Merseyside for ministers and senior officials, but this means that I have to fly from Liverpool to South Wales to attend the superintendents' conference in Newport. It is the only way I am able to speak in Newport and attend the community meetings, then do the business in Merseyside. I will then get a car late at night back to London. It does make it a hell of a hassle but it has to be done.

And then a two-hour Cabinet on Thursday morning: Tony reported on the Intelligence and Security Committee report, and Geoff on what was happening with Hutton and Iraq. We then had a long discussion on ID cards. Tony was very firm on this issue, because unlike Harold Wilson, who would have just 'taken the voices', or Jim Callaghan, who undoubt-edly would have deferred giving any guidance and left it to the Cabinet Committee, he took the bold decision to indicate that drafting time would be made available for the preparation of a Bill, and that the Domestic

Affairs Committee was to address the technical issues and practical barriers rather than the principle. Given how many people were either sceptical or downright antagonistic, this was a genuinely brave decision. As ever there were disagreements with the Treasury over the actual financial detail. There is nothing unusual about this, given that on every major issue there appears to be a formula where Treasury officials are involved with departmental civil servants on reaching agreement. The department thinks it has reached agreement and the Treasury officials report back. There is then a dispute about what has or has not been agreed and the process begins for a second time, with Treasury officials now questioning what they had previously signed up to. This occasion (and this Cabinet) were no different. You do get used to it in the end. It becomes part of the pattern: the arm-wrestling is part of the process. I just wish that I had always seen this process as Round One in a boxing match, and that we would have to go through the form before we could get to the reality of determining what was and wasn't agreed with regard to practical detail.

To make matters worse on this occasion there are all sorts of ifs and buts to be sorted over the likely commercial competition, the potential for reducing unit costs with the volume that will be available, and the way in which the development of the passport will have a major impact on the final cost of the clean database. The issuing of the card is a minor question compared with getting the technology to be able to operate the database correctly.

That afternoon I had the annual shindig of the Home Affairs Select Committee, which is always more difficult in prospect than it is in reality, though it does involve the most enormous amount of work and commitment as you cannot be seen to make a mess of this, and you have to be on top of the issues. It is one of the better pieces of parliamentary scrutiny – much better than on the floor of the House – simply because you have to do your homework. And even if the MPs don't ask the questions, you have asked them of yourself.

I had a gruelling Friday and Saturday morning, including my usual advice surgery in the constituency. I then whizzed back down to London for the Last Night of the Proms at the Albert Hall. It was a disappointment: first, because I banged my head at home before coming out and had blood running down my face; second, because it had been such a rush in terms of getting down to London, I wasn't exactly in the best frame of mind anyway; and third, because I don't think I was at my best at the concert and made one or two *faux pas* that I regretted: I fear I may not have been sufficiently erudite for my companions.

September 2003

The week beginning 8 September saw the publication of Sir Nigel Wickes's final report [on the relationship between politicians and civil servants]. Not surprisingly it was a eulogy to the civil service and a call to politicians to avoid 'interfering'. The need to 'regulate' what a Labour government does was always going to be the logical outcome of putting someone whose roots were deep in the civil service in charge of such a report. My views on these issues are controversial because I know that I am accountable and that if things go wrong, I will have to answer for them. I also know that in the end I will have to defend my civil servants in Parliament at the Dispatch Box, and against the media.

But I also know that I don't really have control – not control in the way that I did when I was Leader of Sheffield City Council and was able to push through efficiency and improvement. This is not true with other politicians across Europe or in North America, where direction is clear, and even where there isn't the US-type system of a separate executive, there is at least a Cabinet system around each Secretary of State. But here special advisers are denigrated rather than being seen as an alternative to a political civil service, and removing someone because they simply cannot do the job is the exception rather than the rule. In fact they are usually promoted.

I am speaking to Tony more often at the moment than in the whole of the time since May 1997, and must be driving him mad. When I am not meeting him, I am talking to him on the phone virtually every other day. I would like to say for posterity that this is normal, but it isn't. It just reflects the enormity of the issues at the moment and the controversies – and the need for mutual support, on ID cards in particular. I made him laugh on the telephone at the weekend by thanking him for not making me the Barbara Castle to his Harold Wilson, as with 'In Place of Strife'.

This was the big industrial-relations reform agenda in the late 1960s that was effectively scuppered by senior members of the Cabinet. Jim Callaghan, then Home Secretary, declared his opposition publicly and rallied Cabinet colleagues against the reform. Had it gone through, who knows whether Labour might have won the general elections in 1970 and even 1979? Had Harold Wilson backed Barbara rather than simply 'counting the voices', then history may well have developed very differently.

On Monday 15 September I was in Brent East prior to the by-election to be held on the Thursday, and made a mistake that appears to have upset the Party Campaign Unit enormously. I can tell the moment I arrive anywhere what the atmosphere is like: after all these years in politics I can smell it and taste it, and I just have to walk around and talk to people to know whether things are going well or badly. It is difficult to describe where this comes from or how it is developed but you either have it or you don't – and on this occasion I could smell that we were in deep trouble. The party had been presenting the by-election as Labour versus Conservative, but it was patently clear that the Liberal Democrats were going to win.

When challenged by both local and national media on the day, I said it was neck and neck. I was asked whether I meant neck and neck with the Conservatives, and I said: 'No, neck and neck with the Liberal Democrats.' I hadn't realised that this was the first time that it had been acknowledged that we were so close to losing the seat. My own belief was that if Labour voters wanted to avoid a defeat, they would vote Labour, and if they didn't think that a defeat was likely, it was quite obvious that they could abstain with impunity. It was hardly going to make voters turn out and vote Liberal Democrat who hadn't already decided to do so. But in any case I felt in my guts that they had.

This didn't stop a lot of bad-mouthing going on when we did lose the by-election spectacularly to the Liberal Democrats. The fact that there was not a cat in hell's chance of my remarks having influenced anybody within the timescale available for people to make up their minds – and how many people would have heard what I said anyway? – seemed to pass people by. They wanted something to blame, and for those who disliked me already, my openness about what was going on was an embarrassment. After all it contradicted the nature of the campaign. Sadly, the same thing happened all over again in early 2006 in Dunfermline West and Fife, where within twenty-four hours of the poll people were telling me that the battle was with the Scottish Nationalists when it was patently with the Liberals. Whatever other things people can criticise me for, self-delusion on the political front is not one of them.

John Kamfpner [of the *New Statesman*] had a book out, the most controversial part of which was about a memo that Jack Straw had sent to Tony *vis-à-vis* Iraq. There seems to be some confusion about exactly when the memo was written or sent or whether it had rested in 'the safe' at the Foreign Office in case the vote was lost in the House of Commons back in March. Given my experience with 'leaks' I would give anybody the benefit of the doubt in relation to the intention, but it is all very odd.

There is a lot of distancing and manoeuvring going on at the moment, but that's just politics. I suppose it makes me an oddball because all my instincts are the other way – to back in when things are difficult rather than to back off.

John Prescott and I had a terrible row before this week's Cabinet. We are so alike in flaring up and standing our ground – and, I fear, standing on our dignity. This was all about what was in the Cabinet minutes or not in the minutes in relation to ID cards and just what the role of the Domestic Affairs Committee would be. John and I were going hammer and tongs at each other before Cabinet, with John coming in and out twice just as we were sitting down. He said that he was going to challenge the minutes and I asked him on what grounds. He said: 'On the process by which the Domestic Affairs Committee should take this through.' I said: 'I have no argument with you at all about the process. By all means, let's take it through the DA Committee.' He said: 'In that case, I will withdraw what I have said to you,' and I said that I would withdraw the remarks I had been making. And as colleagues had gathered round the table, there was a chuckle as we both said that it looked as if we would wait another day for the showdown at the OK Corral! But the tension was broken, thank goodness. The one thing I can do without is an argument about process, on which I am always falling out with John.

I didn't really fully understand until close to the end of my second term in Cabinet just how important process was to John and other colleagues, and I don't think he fully understood, and may still not, just how important the substance was to me. If we had, then some of the misunderstandings may not have occurred – but it's all water under the bridge now.

Appeared on the David Frost programme on Sunday morning, 21 September. I am always saying what I think and that is not always wise. Everybody says that they want politicians who say what they think, but they don't really. David asked me about the Brent East by-election and the accusation that I had been speaking from my experience of Liberals in Sheffield that was made on the Tuesday and Wednesday in response to my 'revelation' that it was the Lib Dems we were fighting and not the Tories. I said that I had been, which is precisely why it would have been helpful if people had taken notice. Thirty-odd years in front-line politics had taught me at least something.

I then went back to Sheffield on the Sunday as I needed to be back in the city before going off to conference the following weekend. I don't like having more than one weekend out from having touched base and feeling that I have had my roots restored.

That week saw Andrew Gilligan in front of the Hutton Inquiry. I think this would make an absolutely admirable case study for citizenship or politics students, looking at the different ways in which both the Hutton Inquiry itself, and in particular this examination, was reported. Depending entirely on the predilection and therefore on the preconceptions of those reporting, people would get an entirely different viewpoint on what had happened, how it had happened, and the conclusions to be drawn from it. This would be a great boon for democracy if it weren't for the fact that only anoraks read through a whole range of reports from different papers, tune in to different broadcast outlets and are able to make comparisons. Most people either don't take any notice whatsoever and get on with their lives, or read, or view, or listen to one particular report, so their view will be dependent on who is reporting it.

Andrew Gilligan did admit that he had made a mistake – but what a mistake! And what a contrast with how the media treated their own, compared with how they would have treated a politician who admitted to such a 'mistake'.

Once again running up to party conference things were very busy. We had a range of Cabinet Committees: the resilience – civil-contingencies – element of our counter-terrorism work; a Special Cabinet leading up to conference where four of us were doing presentations on the reform agenda; and organised crime.

This was the run-up to getting legislation agreed for the Serious Organised Crime Agency, which I was to introduce to Parliament at the end of 2004.

On Friday I did a phone-in on the Jeremy Vine programme on Radio 2. I think if there ever was an example of my saying it as it is, it was probably on that programme.

I also had to contact the French and Spanish Interior Ministers to see if we could stop a piece of ineptitude going through the Competitiveness Agenda of the European Union, which was all about free movement of labour and the danger that people would be given entitlements that would make it impossible for us to cope with cross-border movements, specifically on benefits and housing.

I am having to do a lot of preparation work because there is so much going on: for example, the National Black Police Association Conference, where I need to be both well prepared and clear about what I am going to say. It takes time that is completely over and above all the usual travelling and speaking, holding and chairing meetings, and sorting out all the activity that carries on regardless of how many speaking engagements or other events there are.

I went back down to London for 'stocktake' meetings with Tony on immigration and on drugs policy. Afterwards I walked back to the Department through St James's Park. This time it was a squirrel, not a goose, that Sadie chased, and this time she got herself well and truly lost. It took us about twenty minutes to find out that she hadn't returned to the Department, nor had she stayed in the park. She had in fact made her way across the road and gone back to Downing Street. She obviously felt safer in the presence of the Prime Minister than she did with me. We got the message from the Special Branch based at Downing Street that 'a black Labrador' had arrived at the front door and was it Sadie? When I saw Tony on Thursday morning I said: 'Well, Tony, whatever else is happening with Iraq, at least someone loves you.'

We had another set of leaks on ID cards, allegedly from No. 10 to the *Daily Express*.

Upon reflection, I came to the conclusion that on this occasion the paper had probably made it up in order to cause dissent.

October 2003

The good news is that Sarah and Gordon Brown have a son, John, born on Friday morning [17 October], which is a real cause for rejoicing.

On Thursday 16 October we'd had a pensions presentation at Cabinet. (Tony was not present because of the European Council.) Andrew Smith did a very interesting update, then Gordon joined in, about the spending implications. This was just before he shot off for the birth of John the following morning. It is interesting because I had a meeting with John Prescott immediately afterwards, trying to smooth things out in relation to

ID cards. This was very helpful, as he was reasonable and talked to me sensibly – although he did accuse me of being the one who was leaking the material into the public arena. I told him he had to be bonkers if he thought it was me. Anyway, we came out of it with an understanding that there will be a presentation to his officials on Monday 27 October and that he and I would meet two days after that. We would hold a Cabinet Domestic Affairs Committee on 5 November and would try to go to Cabinet on 6 November.

I saw Ian McCartney and Andrew Smith, and they were being very reasonable. I then had over an hour with Patricia Hewitt, whose objection just comes down to the fact that she doesn't want ID cards to be compulsory. We have decided that at some point they will have to be, otherwise there is no point in having the scheme. It would not be compulsory to carry the card, but it would be compulsory to have one in order to prove identity. So we are working on that presumption.

There were good presentations at conference about the commercial possibilities and what might be done to reduce the costs still further. We are getting there, bit by bit, but it is such a hard struggle.

Another thing that arose was the ongoing story which we had known about for a long time of the infiltration by the BBC into the Greater Manchester Police. We had been trying to get them to give us the material before the programme went out, but they refused. They then briefed the *Scotsman* on the Saturday [18 October] and the *Mail on Sunday* the following day. I commented robustly and my advisers were deeply upset with me. I felt that given that the BBC had refused to let us have the material and we had had to rely on the briefings – which are always exaggerated – my comments were justified at that point. But it was a mistake and I said so on *The World at One* the following Friday [24 October], because the programme did reveal the most horrendous racism in the Manchester force. As a consequence, I felt it was better to cut my losses on that one, and I did get a bit of a drubbing in the liberal papers and on satirical radio programmes. But we have come to a sorry pass when the BBC won't cooperate with us on such a serious matter but are prepared to let the *Mail on Sunday* have a full briefing.

A very entertaining evening for Richard Caborn's sixtieth birthday, where all the past faces associated with Richard were invited. There were 170 of us, a five-course meal, wine and a live band. Very enjoyable.

The following day we were shaken by the news that Tony had been taken into hospital with a heart murmur.

I had flown to France for the meeting of the five Interior Ministers at La Baule and didn't find out about Tony until we had had the first session. I raised it afterwards with Jeremy Heywood, as if anything happens to Tony it is important that his friends know immediately so that we can give support. In fact the French were very good and had already lined up to get me back if they had to, which was thoughtful of them. But thank goodness, it wasn't necessary. Tony told me when I spoke to him on the telephone on the Tuesday that he had had the heart problem, on and off, for fifteen years, but this time he had had to go into hospital, which is why it became public knowledge. He seems fine now and is back in the thick of things immediately, trying to find a way forward on Ireland, having announced on the Monday the resumption of elections for the end of November. He flew to Belfast and thought they had pulled it off but David Trimble panicked at the last moment and wouldn't accept General de Chastelaine's reassurances. He wanted things to be spelled out, which of course the IRA would never agree to and had not been part of the agreement which he had signed up to.

Coincidentally the previous Friday I had been speaking at the Junior Chamber of Commerce. Chris Kelly, a Catholic member of the Parades Commission, was over as Chairman of the National Junior Chamber and was telling me that everybody presumed that David was going to lose his seat on the Northern Ireland Assembly if he signed up. I think perhaps David himself must have realised that and pulled back. But it is a great tragedy for Ireland and a great tragedy for Tony, who has put in the most enormous effort.

Prime Minister's Questions, and Tony did a phenomenal job. Iain Duncan Smith is in a terrible state. The Tory Party is determined to get rid of him but doesn't know how, and is tearing itself apart. This is very good for us while we try to get our act together and reposition ourselves.

Week beginning Monday 20 October: I had a very good meeting with Geoff Mulgan and Matthew Taylor, who have been given the job of pulling together a paper to be launched on 28 November in South Wales, to coincide with the National Policy Forum. We are working with them on the paper, which will set the framework for developing the manifesto and the vision of a third term. We are all thinking extremely hard. I have got the Board and ministers looking at short- and medium-term policies, at further restructuring of the Department, and at trying to get to grips with the difficult issues. This is why on Friday [24 October] I took a difficult decision and announced the provision of indefinite leave to remain for all the immigration family cases that had been presented before 2 October 2000. That date is significant, because up to that point when they finished their asylum claim they were able to claim under the Human Rights legislation, and it pre-dates the National Asylum Support Service, so most of them (around 12,000) are in local authority accommodation. We had to get this cleared once and for all but it brought us a terrible drubbing in some parts of the media on Saturday morning and on the Sunday. I expected that.

On the health front, my situation got worse with regard to weight loss, so I went back to the hospital on Friday, which unfortunately was the same day as the asylum announcement. This couldn't be helped, but it meant that I had to do *The World at One* on Radio 4 before my appointment, and my blood pressure had shot up by the time I got to the hospital. As well as doing a colonoscopy, this time all the way through to the very top of the small bowel, they took blood samples and booked me in for a scan a week later on Friday 31 October, which is Andrew's twenty-first birthday. Meanwhile I have been given some more tablets which I will try.

On a lighter note I have been swotting up on Harry Potter over the past fortnight, having agreed – it has to be said with mixed feelings – to appear on BBC television for a celebrity *Christmas Mastermind* programme for charity: it's being recorded on Sunday 26 October. I thought it a safer bet to choose Harry Potter, because if I chose politics and made a mess of it, it would finish me off. At least with Harry Potter, people can try and answer the questions with me and have a laugh if I get it wrong. And if I make a fool of myself, what does it matter? The most important thing is that it means a £2,500 donation to the hospice in Sheffield.

Thursday 30 October: at Cabinet I did my presentation on Nationality and Asylum and Cohesion. After going through the material and slides three times to get it right, we managed to get a decent slide presentation. It worked smoothly and people were very pleased with it.

The Heslington Lecture at York University went well. This was on faith and inter-faith co-operation, the role of faith in the twenty-first century and the clash between fundamentalism and modernity. There were over 600 people there and they were responsive and asked good questions. With that sort of turn-out, it gives you hope people are interested in these issues.

But the ID cards are a different matter. We had a meeting with John Prescott on Wednesday night, and on this occasion the brief outline of our revised paper was both inaccurate and extremely unhelpful, but despite that John Prescott listened and agreed that we should press on: he could see where they had completely got it wrong. His office then phoned afterwards and were even more positive.

It has to be said that the ID paper is so much better now than it would have been two months ago. The enforced delay has in fact done me a big favour, because what we have produced is a lot better. It is more coherent and adds up in terms of the chronology and the phasing in (or incremental approach, as we are calling it). Of course we would never have introduced a compulsory card from Day One. How could we possibly impose compulsion before sufficient cards have been issued? So it is beginning to come together and we are beginning to get the strategy right. Above all, we are beginning to get the truth out of the officials who have been working on this. Again and again I had banged on to them about the fact that if we were introducing biometrics in passports and driving licences anyway, the costs you would incur would be pretty much that of ID cards and in the long run, because of economies of scale, would be less. Eventually they twigged this and found that the cost of an ID card will only be about £4 higher over the ten years than introducing biometrics on passports and driving licences. It has taken us months to get to this point.

But we are refining the rest of it this weekend, including the Q&A. I am going to do a slide presentation at the Domestic Affairs Committee on Wednesday 5 November, then I hope to take it to Cabinet on Thursday and make a Statement to the House the week after. I just hope I can get it cleared in time and force it through. It is really important politically now, both for Tony and myself.

For all that, the news of the week was the demise of Iain Duncan Smith. It is just amazing how quickly things happen. The word was that they were not going to get in the 25 letters needed for the vote of confidence. There were people going round as late as the morning of the vote on Wednesday [29 October] saying that there were only seven names in and that it couldn't be done. But by teatime he'd had it. The letters were in, the votes were counted and he had lost 90–75. He was out and within half an hour Michael Howard was virtually being crowned as Leader of the Tory Party. It was just an amazing turnaround. Of course, what it has done is lifted the Tories' heads, and above all given the *Daily Mail* and *Daily Telegraph* somebody to believe in and to campaign for. So we will have to see how we get on. It will certainly be a challenge, but one I am looking forward to.

The sideshow of the week was on prison population – to be able to do something meaningful with those in prison and to make some space for those we need to put in. We have to get to grips with this. We got agreement eventually on ejecting foreign nationals from the prison and out of the country, and on an extension of home domestic curfew which we will do for longer serving prisoners shortly. We couldn't get agreement on an avoidance of executive release, which is the release of all short-term prisoners when the prisons get too full. I wanted instead to move an amendment to the Sex Offenders Bill saying that no sex offender could be released early, which was a preliminary to getting into a position where we could release some of the longer serving prisoners slightly early – not those serving more than six years, not murderers and rapists, but other longer serving prisoners – thereby creating some space.

Charlie Falconer wouldn't agree to this and said that we would have to get the judges to find 1,200 places instead. I asked him how on earth he was going to do that.

Anyway, there we are. That's the state we are in. Of course, Tony has far too much on trying to put the Irish talks back on stream again – although I think that's probably had it now until after the Assembly elections.

My good news of the week was that my CT scan showed no cancer.

We had a very pleasant evening with Nicolas Sarkozy, his wife and her two daughters, at the Old Vicarage in Sheffield. This was followed by Andrew's twenty-first birthday celebrations on Saturday.

November 2003

The week beginning 3 November was in my view a fiasco for the Government, self-inflicted by muddle, dithering and weakness. It was not helped by the medication that I had been given making me feel like death warmed up. I felt so nauseous that I thought I was going to be sick in the plane flying to Manchester on Tuesday morning. I had to sit in the toilet for fifteen minutes before I was able to make the speech to the Association of Police Authorities, which went out live on BBC News 24. I don't know where I pulled the reserves of energy and strength from but I did it.

I then held a meeting with the Chief Constable of Greater Manchester and his colleagues, followed by a meeting with Dame Janet Smith, who is chairing the Shipman inquiry. I flew back to London and went to bed feeling absolutely dreadful.

The following day I decided to cut down the number of tablets I had been prescribed, pulled myself round and got on with the job.

It became clear on Monday that No. 10 were getting very cold feet about ID cards because of the volume of opposition from a handful of colleagues in Cabinet. On Sunday I had phoned a couple of them, who she said that they couldn't discuss it with me any further because they hadn't opened their boxes and weren't going to do so until Monday morning and therefore hadn't read the paper. What became very clear is that they still hadn't read it by Wednesday, and it has to be said that a number of other colleagues hadn't read it either. So we were really up against it in the way in which people perceived the programme and what they thought we were doing. All sorts of extraneous issues were being raised, and as a consequence Jeremy Heywood – who, in the end, was very helpful, as was Sally Morgan – was working on watering down the statement to be put to the Domestic Affairs Committee and to Cabinet in order to get maximum support.

There was some doubt on Wednesday about whether Gordon was going to attend the DA Committee that day, but in the end he did. There was criticism from colleagues that they had not had satisfactory answers to the queries which had been raised and that there wasn't a proper programme laid out. I intervened to ask John [Prescott, chairing the meeting] whether he wanted me at that stage to read out my annotated note giving chapter and verse as to precisely where, in the paper which has been produced, the issues have been dealt with. In the end, while there was considerable support from heavyweights such as Charles Clarke and John Reid, there were sufficient voices raised against to warrant John Prescott indicating that a final decision could not be taken on the matter and that he would have to report back to the Prime Minister and Cabinet that we couldn't make a decision on that basis.

I was supposed to be at a meeting at Downing Street to deal with the Correctional Services Review and the whole revamping of prison and probation. The meeting had had to go ahead without me but I went across afterwards, saw the Prime Minister and told him what had happened. Along with Justin Russell, who had been at the meeting, I gave him a complete rundown of who was for and against. It became clear that it was really two thirds to one third in favour with regard to numbers but not with regard to weight. I agreed that we would put a couple of items in that didn't further water down the statement – about the Office of Government Commerce Gateway process and anything that needed to be put in to reassure business.

I then dropped in on the *Mirror* party, went home and took the phones off. It is a long time since I have felt so depressed as I did that evening –

made worse when I realised what a terrible drubbing we were getting in the media by Thursday evening.

But it has all been a terrible mess and there are enormous lessons to be learnt from it, including coming back hard next week, hopefully on Tuesday [11 November] and really going for it and trying to pull all this back by having a proper media strategy – locally, regionally and nationally – and by being very clear in what we are saying in the statement and the revised paper that is going out alongside it, and by having a handling strategy that works. We have really got to go for it now and pull it all back, not least because so few people understand what we are talking about. Everything else pales into insignificance at the moment.

On Thursday I spoke to the Johnson Press annual dinner in Birmingham and they were entirely up for ID cards. They gave me a massive round of applause when I spoke about it. We are going to have to work on the regional media.

I had a Friday in the constituency which took me back to Education days: the inauguration of the start of the building of the Hillsborough College; the celebration of the opening of the nursery at Longley School; the burying of a capsule for the start of the building work at Hinde House joint school; and an interview with Rebecca Smithers of the *Guardian*. It was like the old days. I also had an event at the Town Hall celebrating the work of the Appeals Panels for Education, and to round off the day dinner with Alex Erwin and friends at the Mediterranean Restaurant in the evening to talk about further education. But it was a day that took me out of myself a bit and gave me a bit more spirit for fighting back, not least because it made me realise that people outside the Westminster bubble are not even aware that there has been a defeat.

I suppose my depression is a combination of so much hard work and wanting to get this through and then seeing it all begin to fizzle out, and knowing that this is now about power politics, about having the clout to do other things, including defending Tony. I will fight on.

I have my surgery on Saturday morning and a weekend counter-terrorism exercise that means I have to go down to London at teatime on Saturday and take over the COBR exercise. I have the Remembrance Service on Sunday and dinner planned with Sir John Stevens, John Gieve and Sir Keith Povey on Sunday evening. It was the only time we could fit it in. It's diplomatic because I have to keep everyone on board. But what a struggle and at what a price.

We got the Sex Offenders, Sex Offences Bill through. I did the Third

Reading. Oliver Letwin didn't even bother turning up. If ever there was an example of Parliament working well, this was it, and I reflected on this in my Third Reading speech. Paul Goggins deserves a medal. We now have legislation that people have been afraid to bring in, particularly on sex offences. We have dithered about for the last fifty years, if not for the last century, but we got it through without a whimper in the end and people needn't have been afraid of it.

Not so the Criminal Justice and Sentencing Bill. When I go to the Old Bailey on Monday it will be very interesting to talk to Harry Woolf, following the remarks that he and Lord Judge have made on the record about Charlie Falconer's proposals on revamping the judiciary, Supreme Court and changing the role of the Lord Chancellor.

Just a couple of footnotes on the week.

First, Gordon and Tony had had a dinner arranged for about three months, which took place on Thursday night. I wish I could have been a fly on the wall.

Second, Michael Portillo has announced that he is standing down at the next general election and is pulling out of formal politics.

The following week I was able to make the Statement on ID cards, publish the paper alongside the Statement, deal with the House of Commons on the Statement, and to be able to make progress, thank the Lord.

The debate went well. Fortunately Matthew Seward had come up trumps with quotes from Michael Howard and the quirks of the Liberal Democrats. I managed to save the Michael Howard attack until I got to the end of my response to David Davis, who had just taken over from Oliver Letwin as Shadow Home Secretary, and in the 'inner shadow cabinet' held responsibility for Constitutional Affairs and for Culture, Media and Sport. Julie Kirkbride, who is dealing with Culture, Media and Sport for the Tories at a more junior level, had at the last Home Office Questions declared herself in favour of ID cards. So what with this plus the quote from Michael Howard, I was well armed and able to bring the house down when I said that on 23 September 2001 Michael Howard had nailed his colours to the mast when he said that ID cards were the only solution to clandestine entry and working. Our side were cock-a-hoop, and then when the Liberal Democrat spokesman Mark Oaten said that they had a fundamental objection on principle to ID cards, I was able to ask when the fundamental principle arose, because earlier this year the Honourable

Gentleman voted for a Ten-Minute Rule Bill in favour of ID cards. That again brought the house down, with Dennis Skinner shouting, 'He's knocking 'em round the court!' It really lifted me. Our side were very good and backed in very well.

The atmosphere was so different from a year last July, when I had had such a terrible struggle when I made the initial Statement on the consultation. This time there was such a different atmosphere: it makes what you are doing so much easier and gives you masses of confidence in dealing with the media. Following an interview for Channel 4, I also did a round table with a group of people they had pulled together to cross-question me. The *Today* programme interview also went very well. I was able to use the Barbara Castle 'In Place of Strife' analogy with Jim Naughtie, so that was a good opportunity to get across not just the similarity of Harold Wilson having been engaged with very senior members of the Cabinet split all over the place and, on that occasion, having let Barbara Castle down – but of Tony on this occasion not letting me down.

I also spoke about forward thinking and looking at issues that we don't have to deal with now, issues that are not immediately imperative but will come to bite us in the future. I said that if we don't deal with them now, we will regret it at great length. I made the point that if 'In Place of Strife' had been in place, we might not have won the 1970 election but we would almost certainly have won the 1979 election, because there wouldn't have been a Winter of Discontent.

I believe that what we are doing is setting the scene for the future thinking, of modernising Britain and preparing the country for the challenges of the future, of seeing what's around the corner and doing something before it hits you.

So from my political fortunes on 5 and 6 November taking a massive nosedive, up we come again on the following Tuesday and Wednesday.

There were some amusing sketches, and there was a wonderful cartoon in the *Daily Telegraph*, with two dogs showing each other their ID cards and saying, 'Thank goodness we won't have to sniff bottoms any more,' which I thought was very funny.

There was a slight hiccup, it has to be said, over a speech I made at Chatham House at the Royal Institute of International Affairs on the whole issue of managed migration and getting the balance right. We had worked on the speech over the previous forty-eight hours and made it much better than it would otherwise have been. So many ministerial speeches are tedious repetition of what the Department has already done or recycling what has already been put out in previous speeches or press releases, which is why speeches are so boring. However, what caused some bother in this particular case were two things. Firstly, *Newsnight* wanted an in-depth interview, and allegedly told the press office that they wanted to cover broadbrush immigration and my speech and ID cards. We therefore did a set-piece interview prior to the speech, and basically they stitched me up. It's not that I didn't deal adequately with Jeremy Paxman – I certainly did – but the whole emphasis of the interview was on how many people we could take in this country and whether the balance of inward and outward net migration was out of control.

The officials had not made me aware that statistics on net migration were coming out the following day from the Office of National Statistics. The figures had in fact been put into my overnight box, so when I came out of the interview and was in the car going to supper with Alastair and Fiona, I looked through the papers and there it was: a little note on the statistics coming out. It was quite clear that although they didn't have the actual statistics, *Newsnight* were aware that they were coming out the following day and homed in on this over and over again. Not that it would have made much difference had I had them. Of course, I can't fix an upper limit on our population or on inward migration. As I said, all I can do is to ensure that we have a sensible balance so that people who can contribute, who pay their way, and who pay taxes and National Insurance as opposed to drawing down on benefits can come into the country and fill identified needs.

This was to be an ongoing debate. There is no country which has fixed an upper limit on its population, and the main problem for the older developed nations remains an imbalance between the working age population and those in education or retirement. The Conservatives floated the idea of inventing a figure, but dropped it when the contradictions became apparent. Knowing who is in the country, legally or illegally, is of course a prerequisite to using the levers available to government to influence flows into the country or policy for population expansion.

This was then compounded because of what the press made of it, with headlines such as 'Blunkett says there is no upper limit on migration'. The *Daily Express* ran three whole days of utter and complete nonsense. They cover asylum and immigration virtually every day now, and in a racist fashion, just as they did with the commentary on my speech.

Fortunately for me, Edward Heathcoat-Amory and the *Daily Mail*'s new home affairs editor were at the lecture at Chatham House and understood what I was saying, which modified what the *Daily Mail* did the following day. The *Guardian* wrote it up reasonably responsibly but others didn't. You win some and you lose some. I called for a sensible debate but I didn't get a sensible debate in the days afterwards. Instead I got a load of nonsense.

The last three weeks have been quite stressful. What with my being so unwell when I was launching the Police Reform document, and then the ID card fiasco and then pulling it back, and then this managed migration business, it has been a really hairy time.

Having said that, I am not making this an excuse for my performance on *Mastermind*, yet to be screened!

We are still getting leaks all over the place. David Cracknell had another one in the *Sunday Times* on 9 November, this time about the Child Trust Fund. It was a letter I had sent when Gordon was on paternity leave, prior to the ID card stuff blowing up, saying that I thought the amounts we were putting into the Child Trust Fund were far too small and wouldn't have the kind of impact we needed with regard to building assets. But of course the *Sunday Times* put an entirely different spin on it, with a leader that said that this was an ineffective policy and that I had attacked it – which I hadn't. In fact the Child Trust Fund was partly my idea: I put the money in to research it and worked with Gordon on refining it. Equally I was entertained on Saturday 15 November to learn that David Miliband [then Minister of State for education] is pushing ahead with a major policy for summer camps for teenagers. 'Just a moment,' I thought: 'Didn't I start this three years ago? Didn't I put some money up for the first-year experiment and then £10 million a year?' And there it was, being presented as if it were from scratch. It's a funny old world, politics.

Just thinking about Wednesday night when I was at Alastair Campbell's for supper, and he had been flipping through his diaries for 1995. He was reflecting on when he and Tony went out to Hayman Island [in the Great Barrier Reef] when we were in opposition way back in 1995. I remembered Tony going because on the morning he came back, he stood on Lucy's ear when he was doing Prime Minister's Questions from the Opposition Dispatch Box. He had to apologise to Lucy at the time, and this is recorded in *Hansard*. I remember wondering how he was still on his feet, having flown back overnight from Australia. Alastair was reflecting on how Tony was going to make a speech and they had to get the speech back to London to get it in the papers before he had made it because of the time change. They were talking to Murdoch about this, and when he asked the editors whether they were covering it properly, they all shot off to have a look. This resulted in Tony getting massive coverage just by being with Murdoch, and Murdoch indicating that Tony was the man. So we mustn't believe all we hear about proprietors not interfering!

This coming week I am having lunch with the new editor of the *Daily Telegraph*, Martin Newlands, so we will see how long he lasts. On Wednesday, I am with the greeting party for George Bush in the morning and then at the banquet in the evening – the first ever banquet I have been to at Buckingham Palace, a white tie and tails job. It will be an interesting experience and I am looking forward to it.

I went to an outfitter in Sloane Square to get fitted out. What a bunch of Sloanes. There were two women, obviously very upper-crust and one of them very young, who hadn't a clue how to deal with customers. I think somebody must have bought the shop just to allow them to pass their time.

I saw Gordon for forty-five minutes on Thursday morning between the breakfast meeting we had on bureaucracy and Cabinet. It gave us the chance to talk, and I think we have just about settled the immigration budget for the next two years. We had a sensible discussion about policies relating to mentoring and volunteering.

As well as everything else we have got on, we are now engaged heavily in trying to shape the framework paper which will be published on 28 November as part of the Big Conversation [Labour's major exercise in consulting the votes] to be launched in Newport, South Wales. I will be joining Tony for the launch, followed by the Policy Forum. I am going to have to do something on ID cards there as well, so that's another Friday knocked out. We are trying to be helpful as Geoff Mulgan and Matthew Taylor are struggling with it. They are writing the questions and then writing the text to fit the questions, trying to highlight the issues which are crucial and which they need to get across to people and get people engaged with. So that's the challenge of the moment, and it is going to be another massive drain on time on top of everything else in the next two weeks.

I have also been dealing with some tricky security issues, involving daily discussions with Eliza Manningham-Buller. Then we are into the week when George Bush comes to London, and meetings with John Stevens and David Veness from the Met to sort out what needs to be done about security during the visit. There was an interesting piece in the *Observer* by Martin Bright about what I had and hadn't done. I had intervened to ensure that the President's own security personnel couldn't shoot to kill, they couldn't have indemnity, that we would run the operation, not them, and that there would be a minimal number of officers allowed to be armed, a number which it has to be said was grossly exaggerated by the British media, including the BBC, throughout the week. We obviously had to check that all was done to make it possible for people to be able to demonstrate peacefully, including agreeing a route for the march on Thursday. I have made it clear that if they are peaceful they will be protected, but if there is a riot and people are drawn into it, then we will come down on them like a ton of bricks.

George Bush's visit is just one more thing to worry about in the week when we have the Bills coming back from the Lords. We have Extradition without having to debate it in the Commons, the Courts Bill from the Department of Constitutional Affairs, the Anti-Social Behaviour Bill that went through on Monday, the Sex Offences/Sex Offenders Bill, and then the long debate on the amendments from the Lords on the Criminal Justice and Sentencing Bill which I am dealing with, or kicking off on. That will be the subject of a real ping-pong between the Commons and the Lords.

I did a less than convincing performance in the Chamber at the beginning of the six-hour debate on the Criminal Justice Bill. I was dealing with the issue of intimidation, serious fraud and the right of the individual to choose a judge only, as well as choosing a jury. All of it has been presented very negatively in the media as reducing the right to jury trial – rather than reducing the opportunity of organised criminals to nobble juries and thereby disrupt the trial in order to avoid conviction.

We got all the votes and the rest of it through fine, but I didn't feel that I had performed at my best and went home feeling a bit depressed.

I picked myself up on Wednesday morning, dusted myself down and got on with the job. We had the ceremony at Buckingham Palace to welcome President Bush and his wife Laura. All the same people who were there for Putin's visit came, and again Sadie barked – twice this time. She was fine with the guns, but it was the marching and the drawing of the swords that unnerved her. Again the bark came across on television. It was a very impressive occasion, even for a hard-bitten Northerner like me, and well worth being there.

The banquet in the evening was interesting, in all sorts of ways like stepping back into the 1950s. We used the gold crockery which, as Prince Andrew (who was sitting next to me) pointed out, holds its heat. It did too. It was too hot to touch – but interestingly it then lost its heat very quickly.

Apparently they only bring out the gold crockery for State Banquets. We were treated to all the pomp with the guards playing and the Argyle and Sutherland Highlanders coming in with the pipes. I had to calm Sadie again as she became quite restless when they went round the back of my chair.

It was a very interesting guest list. There were all sorts of people who you would never have expected to be there, including Richard Branson, and the head of Solomon Brothers in the UK. Religious leaders obviously get invited all the time: people like Jonathan Sacks and the Archbishop of Canterbury, who was sitting with Condoleezza Rice and Prince Charles (which must have been an interesting experience).

December 2003

Week beginning Monday 1 December: I am recovering from the stitches that were put in on Friday night after hitting my face on the loft ladder – someone working in my loft had left it down – and the car crash on Monday morning in Leeds where we were very, very lucky indeed to be alive. There was a car coming down a hill at 40 m.p.h. and the police blocked one junction for us to go through but not the other. Nobody was hurt, but it was only by a miracle. I went straight on to the venue with the Prime Minister, on anti-social behaviour as part of the Big Conversation, and then I flew down to London. While we were travelling and Tony was signing Christmas cards, I had a long talk with him about a whole range of things: higher education fees, how in the New Year to highlight anti-social behaviour so that we could get it back up in lights, a few words about Hutton and about broader politics, and where we are going. I joked with him as he was signing cards that I hadn't had a personally signed card from him last year and said that I hoped I would this year!

On *Any Questions?* when I was back in Leeds again on Friday night we had what for me were extremely challenging questions about top-up fees, and about asylum and the distortion that had been made of the issue of what to do with asylum-seeker children when their parents have their subsistence and benefits withdrawn and they refuse to go back home. We also dealt with abortion, which had raised its head again, and asylum seekers being returned to Zimbabwe. The final and only light question of the whole evening allowed me to use the quip about the Christmas card when John Sentamu [Bishop of Birmingham] was chiding me gently for not having sent him a Christmas card.

We have had vigorous debates in Cabinet again about top-up fees.

They never were actual top-up fees, but that's what they were called in debating them.

The *Daily Mail* reported on the Friday morning that I had 'led the assault'. I hadn't. I had contributed and tried to be helpful in putting forward how we might package the proposals differently to achieve the same result. I should have known better than to believe that people wouldn't distort what was said. What I was trying to get across was that we must not end up with a situation where we helped most those who needed help least – namely assisting better-off parents by withdrawing the need to pay up-front contributions to fees, thereby allowing them to be able to pay directly to reduce the debt of those who, given the income of their parents, were most likely to gain from alleviating families from having to find the money there and then. Less well-off families weren't paying the fee, so they weren't going to be alleviated from having to find it. I wasn't sure either that anyone other than myself in the room had heard of Opportunity Bursaries, where grants were paid to the less well-off families targeted on the most deprived parts of the country. But there we go.

This week saw the publication of the Domestic Violence, Crime and Victims Bill, which is about exactly what it says – strengthening the law and powers in relation to domestic violence and giving victims new rights and influence over what goes on. It is not one of those pieces of legislation I will be remembered for, but I would like to think that those who benefited most will sometimes reflect on how important it was. I had given a push to this when speaking on the penultimate day of the Queen's Speech Debate on Tuesday. Unfortunately Patricia Scotland and Harriet Harman were having a bit of a fall-out over which of them was going to go up front on the domestic-violence issues. The truth is that a lot of people have done a lot of work over the past few years to get this issue on to the agenda, and I owe parliamentary colleagues and campaigners outside a great deal.

It makes me think about how real change is brought about. There usually has to be a tide of opinion, with people who have worked tirelessly year after year to keep it on the agenda when other things push it out. They don't get a lot of thanks, so I tried to say thank you to them.

The *Observer* on Sunday 7 December had a thoughtful piece by Andrew

Rawnsley about the to-ing and fro-ing and the nuances of who gains and who loses in government over the issue of higher education funding and the like.

There were more Cabinet Committees, the Resilience and the Counter-Terrorism, and the Drugs Committee. Some are more useful than others. Where something has to be collectively agreed, then they are worthwhile, but where it is just a rubber stamp or where people just read out their departmental brief, then they are a complete waste of space. They just take up time, both in preparation and in being there. Matters could be so much more easily resolved by using the business methodology of decision-taking and getting on with things.

It has started to emerge that there is someone being paid in the Cabinet Office for passing over to the *Sunday Times* at least some of the leaks that have been occurring. I wouldn't be at all surprised. It doesn't, of course, resolve who is briefing the *Daily Express* and the *Independent*, but it certainly helps with regard to things that are passed directly to at least this Sunday newspaper.

The individual was Claire Newell, who went on to work for the Sunday Times, *the very newspaper to which she was leaking.*

Jack Straw and I had a conversation on the secure phone, which I have only used three times since I became Home Secretary. We talked about issues in relation to Europe, but more importantly concerns relating to Iran.

These issues were to gain in salience over subsequent years. Suffice it to say that it looked at the time as though the Iranians might consider coming to an agreement with the International Atomic Energy Agency.

I decided to forgo the pleasure of the reception for the Rugby World Cup champions in order to attend the Archbishop of Canterbury's Advent Carol Service, which I had been to for a number of years and found very comforting. We just avoided a complete mess-up this week over how to handle ID cards. The suggestion from the Secretary to the Cabinet was that we had a separate Cabinet Committee on ID cards (separate, that is, from the Domestic Affairs Committee), to be chaired by Charlie Falconer.

John Prescott was deeply aggrieved because this took away the process and power of the Domestic Affairs Committee, and I was aggrieved as I was the one who was piloting all this through and had just spent two years ensuring that it didn't bite the dust. The trouble with party battles like this is the amount of energy and time it takes and the diversion from getting on with the job.

I attended the Privy Council meeting where, for once, I was the senior government member. After we had done the business I spent twenty minutes talking to the Queen, and Sadie was provided with a bowl of water – the first time that she had been accorded this honour. We talked about the Queen and Prince Philip's visit to Chatsworth a month earlier, and the dreadful rain they had had throughout their visit to Derbyshire. It was good to be able to exchange pleasantries about the wonderful countryside around Chatsworth and the house itself, as well as reflecting on security at Windsor. Even for someone without an ounce of deference in his body, it is endearing to be handed a glass of dry sherry by the Queen and to be able to wish her a Happy Christmas – and also to wish her well as she was to go into hospital the following day for an operation on her knee. She also told me about an incident that hadn't reached the papers, when a drunken intruder had been picked up immediately he came over the wall. His girlfriend was apparently frantic on the outside and had been trying to stop him from carrying out what was obviously an act of bravado and nothing to do with security. I was just relieved that the security system on that occasion had worked.

So Tony and Jack are going off to spend the weekend arguing about the European Constitution, and I go off north to prepare for the end of the trials of Ian Huntley and Maxine Carr [respectively charged with the murder of two girls in Soham and of perverting the course of justice in relation to those murders]. It is highly predictable that Maxine Carr will receive a light sentence because she has put on a bravura performance to save her skin. If, as expected, the judgement is before Thursday 18 December, then the judge will have to take into account both the old rules and the new legislation on life meaning life – but, of course, without the Home Secretary setting the tariff. It appears, however, that prior to the new rules coming in completely on the 18th he would have had to take account of the tariffs that I have recently set, which means that the decisions I have taken in relation to fifty-year sentences will be really important. When taking decisions it is necessary to consider what the implications might be, not just of the individual case (which has to be judged on its own merit) but also with regard to the consequences if you get it wrong. Who would ever have thought that I would come into politics and end up dealing with this?

The big challenge now is to set up the inquiry, make the Statement to

Parliament, and try to get the balance right on where the real blame lies. Of course the blame lies with Ian Huntley, but everyone will be looking for someone else and there is no doubt – although I have to go through the papers for about the third time – that the police in Humberside, and to a lesser extent Cambridgeshire, just didn't do the job. The question for me is: did the Home Office, in overseeing the police and the police technology, also contribute to the tangled web that I hope we can cut through?

A busy weekend preparing for the Asylum Bill Second Reading on Wednesday, on trying to make sense of where we are going on the Criminal Injuries Compensation Scheme, and for Monday's meetings on the proposed National Offender Management Service.

Two years later Charles Clarke as Home Secretary was still having to deal with further consultation on the Criminal Injuries Compensation Scheme, which demonstrates how slowly the wheels of the Home Office and the wider government turn. It is not simply getting sense out of the department you are running, but getting agreement across government when other people are starting from scratch and you provide them with information, and other departments are looking for what implications it might have for them. The advice to Cabinet colleagues comes from their own civil servants who, in part, get it from civil servants in the inter-departmental network but also depend upon their own predilections. You can therefore get the most bizarre objections from other departments, which can take months to sort out when there are misunderstandings.

The National Offender Management Service was also subject to two years of wrangling, explained partly by the intervention of the general election but also by the tremendous resistance of the probation service to radical proposals, arising out of the realisation back in 2002–3 that the service, particularly in London, was massively under-performing, and an enormous increase in staff had done little to turn round the problem. But again, the arguments that we were having in early 2004 were still raging in the spring of 2006.

But the major issue of the moment for me was Tony (Lord) Newton's Privy Council cross-party reform on the Terrorism Act, which had been agreed to as part of the monitoring that was the price of getting the 2001 Act through the House of Lords. Having responded in a very low-key and downbeat fashion, the job now is to study in detail to see if I can come up with ways of meeting the legitimate calls for the use of Control Orders. It makes sense with regard to lower-level activity by those supporting terrorism, but allowing the serious terrorist threat in the community, with people able to walk about and talk to each other, makes no sense whatsoever. It puts the balance firmly on the side of the individual rather than the security of the nation, and it gives enormous ammunition to those who are constantly sniping at us about human rights – as though we don't care about human rights, as though we are not patently aware of the real difficulties involved in the decisions we are taking.

Over the weekend of 14–15 December I talked to Bev about her deep unhappiness with what is happening in the Immigration and Nationality Directorate. I will have to speak to John Gieve about heads rolling, not only if they don't buck up their ideas but if they can't start producing the statistics and information for which we ask them. It is just like a black hole from which nothing ever comes back out. We have got the border controls and security in France working on the things we started to put in train eighteen months ago, but all of that was set up fresh, and even with the complete change in the leadership of IND we are still not seeing anything like the improvements that we expected.

The problem is that everybody out there knows that IND is dysfunctional, so getting people to come and work in the senior management is like asking civil servants to commit hara-kiri. It is true that we have reduced the turn-round time for dealing with asylum cases to two months for at least 80 per cent of cases, but the nitty-gritty of administration, lost papers, failure to answer letters, people's passports missing, the continuing problem with the renewal of visas – all of this is just still mind-blowingly incompetent.

What triggered Bev's deep unhappiness as well was the reaction of colleagues at the parliamentary party last Wednesday. I think we all understood their frustrations, but it really would be helpful if they backed us as ministers, rather than blaming us. I don't think things have been helped either by David Lammy, as the Constitutional Affairs Minister, telling her on Thursday that he wouldn't be able to make next Wednesday's Second-Reading debate so wouldn't be on the bench (because he had got sinusitis). As I said to Bev, I've had sinusitis on and off for the whole of my life – but nothing is a bigger headache than being Home Secretary!

Sunday 14 December: Matthew d'Ancona in the *Sunday Telegraph* has a fairly accurate account of the Cabinet discussion – proof that we have something more akin to a rat than a mole.

The inter-governmental conference has fallen apart over voting arrangements. It reminds me of the more ludicrous times from my days on

Sheffield City Council, when we would have two-hour debates about whether people could keep dogs in flats, when the state of the flats themselves is what we should have been discussing.

But just when you think that you have had a busy enough weekend something else happens, and in this case it wiped out all other news. This was the capture of Saddam Hussein, in a hole in the ground, ignominiously hiding away – no fight, no shoot-out, just a different sort of mole. Downing Street had the courtesy of letting me know on the phone before the news broke but their predicted time of its being released to the news media was slightly, or more than slightly, off beam. We do still have some problems in terms of swift communication.

Down to London on Sunday night. If I thought that Monday and Tuesday were busy, Wednesday was horrendous. There was the planned annual 'interrogation' by the Intelligence and Security Committee in which all senior ministers dealing with terrorism present themselves to answer questions and follow up issues that have been raised in writing. Then the Second Reading of the Asylum and Immigration Bill (I was on my feet for an hour and two minutes, with enormous opposition from our own backbenchers) and the awaited verdict of the Ian Huntley trial for the Soham murders – and therefore the announcement on the setting-up of the Bichard Inquiry. For reasons I do not understand, the Whips have crammed in a Statement on mad-cow disease on the grounds that they thought (or the Department thought) that this was going to be a big issue. All it did was disrupt the day and put off the start of the Second-Reading debate, bringing more pressure to bear on myself and Bev Hughes. Understandably nobody took any notice whatsoever of the Statement on BSE, but my only thought is that if you don't want people to focus on an issue, then don't make a Statement. The whole day was filled with doing radio and television interviews, sorting out precisely where we were going. David Westwood, Chief Constable of Humberside, had walked out on a *Newsnight* interview, but Cambridgeshire got good coverage because they had invited the BBC in and given them footage and background details.

Thursday 18 December: I am getting very tired now and ready for Christmas, but being bad-tempered from the moment I wake up is not good news. I switched on the 7 a.m. news on Radio 4 to find that the Inspectorate of Constabulary had put out their own preliminary look at what had happened in relation to Cambridgeshire and Humberside.

I later found out that no one had bothered to tell my Private Office.

This was the day when the Newton Committee Report was being published. I need to make a full response at the end of February, but I have already decided to try to see if we can pick up the suggestion of incorporating the powers that we gave to the Special Immigration Appeals Commission into the normal court system.

In the end, I wasn't able to persuade people to do this. The lawyers were against doing it on the grounds that it eroded the integrity of the existing procedures on which so much of the defence rests, and the security services were not convinced that there was a reliable system of public interest immunity with regard to being able to provide sufficiently secure private hearings for crucial information, which would put the whole of the surveillance system (and infiltration of organisations) at risk.

Our problem (which eventually Charles Clarke dealt with in the new legislation of 2005) was treating British nationals and non-nationals in the same way, and the objections to dealing with British nationals in this way, without anyone having a solution as to how to deal with those that we had certificated and held in Belmarsh, Broadmoor or Woodhill. Everyone had objections but no one had the answers.

What struck me about the committee was the failure to understand that we are not dealing with a situation after the event – the prosecution and punishment of those who had committed a crime. What we are trying to do is to prevent the crime in the first place.

When I did *The World this Weekend* on Radio 4 that Sunday before Christmas, it really brought home to me that journalists (as well as the world outside) don't know that there is a process, the equivalent of a Superior Court of Record, and therefore that there is proper representation and defence. Human rights lawyers know, but prefer to present it as if they don't. To hear people talk, you'd think that we simply signed a certificate, picked people up and put them in jail, then forgot about them and threw away the key.

I will try to get a rational, balanced debate going again when I respond to the Newton Committee later in the winter.

Sanity returned up north that weekend because I walked into the Christmas lunch for older people on Buchanan Road in my constituency and got the most wonderful round of applause, and going round talking to everyone just lifted my spirits and soul. Being in my constituency in Sheffield is getting plugged into an electric power socket, getting recharged like a renewable battery. It is wonderful. This particular luncheon club was kept going with the assistance of the younger men and women who were on probation and were learning to be social human beings. Two years earlier, when the probation service were going to pull the plug, it had been saved after a bit of robust repartee between the older people (who can often be quite grumpy) and the youngsters, some of whom were rough diamonds.

So the run-up to Christmas – with a document on prostitution and organised crime, the whole issue of setting up a Serious Organised Crime Agency, the alcohol strategy (that the health service had not dealt with and that we were now picking up) and how to relate all three to each other. Oh yes – and the Five-Year Strategic Plan, which sounds a good idea, but I'm worried as to whether it will end up propping a door open.

One of the things worth mentioning over the Christmas period was *Mastermind* on television on Boxing Day. Recording the programme had taken place in the thick of everything, and the last thing on earth I wanted to do was display how little time I had had to prepare. So getting through Boxing Day evening was a trial. I thought I had better watch it, difficult as it was. People were very kind. The fact that I knew anything at all about Harry Potter seemed to go down very well, as it meant that I wasn't too much like a standard politician, and the £2,500 that went to the local children's hospice will have made a difference and made it worthwhile. But I wouldn't appear on such a programme again. That will teach me for not checking out more thoroughly that it wasn't going to be just an entertaining Christmas knockabout but a deadly serious battle to the end. At least the man who won was both extremely capable and very pleasant.

I took a little girl, Alice Clarke, and her mother to the children's Christmas party at Chatsworth House. They loved it – although the conjuror was a bit lost on me – and the Duke and Duchess [of Devonshire] were lovely. They had agreed to Alice coming as her identical twin sister had died in August of a brain tumour, and as so often the family had found some solace in being able to share the experience of losing a child with others, setting up a small charity.

It was only later that I heard that Gordon Brown had written to them and sent them money to help them with, as they put it, 'our little project'. Sarah and Gordon had established a charity – to which Sarah was devoting an enormous amount of time – in memory of Jennifer, which tried to provide some help for

people looking for cash to be able to publish or promote a project or set up a
charity.

Tony rang me on Christmas Eve morning, and it was good to be able to wish him Happy Christmas. He was exercised by the lack of communication over the tremendous news the previous Friday about Libya's willingness to co-operate internationally and cease development of nuclear weapons. He explained that the news wasn't supposed to be coming out, and I said I'd realised that by the fact that he had to do it up in Durham. But it was a bit odd, given that I'd been involved in changing the visa regime a fortnight before, not to have been kept in touch with the final details of what was going on.

The whole of Christmas and New Year was, of course, as in the previous year, disrupted by phone calls and clearance of warrants to do with terrorism. On Boxing Day I had a call from the Permanent Secretary who was at an Arsenal football match and was ringing me at half-time! We were all trying to have a bit of a break for Christmas and do the job effectively at the same time, but I think clearing a series of telephone taps via a mobile phone in the middle of a Premier League match is about as incongruous as it can get.

Shortly after the game had finished I dealt with two calls relating to flights from the east coast of the United States to London, and a threat to these flights that had already been indicated to me earlier in the week. Officials had called a COBR meeting on Boxing Day, and they were about to announce the cancellation of flights and the introduction of sky marshals. Fortunately, with the help of one of my really bright private secretaries, who was later herself to go on placement to Washington, we managed to get the message across, together with Alistair Darling, that anything that looked like panic would finish the airline good and proper. We had real to-ing and fro-ing about whether they could fly out full and fly back empty. I simply said, with Alistair's agreement, that they could fly wherever they liked so long as we didn't ground everybody. This is all about taking a deep breath and working through the consequences of actions to be taken. It reminded me of the 'Sugar Boat' the previous Christmas.

Jack then rang me that evening to say that there had been a hijacking of a Monarch plane out of Bahrain. We have this strange arrangement where the Foreign Secretary is in charge of the arrangements and decision-making when the plane is out of our jurisdiction, but I am in charge when it comes into our air space and when it is landing. Earlier in the year we'd had a mock exercise in how to deal with a hijack, and this wasn't entirely the way we'd planned to deal with things. Without going into too much detail, it turned out that the pilot had turned off his instruments by mistake so it wasn't a hijack after all – but it made for a very disrupted holiday, when I spent as much time on the telephone as I did eating and drinking. It is strange really because all my instincts told me, as they had with the Sugar Boat, that there was something amiss. It just didn't feel right. But of course you can't work from instinct and you have to get to the detail – but it is useful to have the instinct in order to be able to feel when things may not be as they seem. Taking anything to do with terrorism at face value is a big mistake.

Tragically we started 2003 with the death of DC Stephen Oake and we end the year with PC Ian Broadhurst being killed in West Yorkshire. I've been keeping a very low profile and keeping in touch behind the scenes rather than issuing statements and going on the radio.

The saga of sky marshals continued all weekend. We had already had a whole range of phone calls on the Friday about the so-called hijacking, and I then end up with a great palaver on Saturday [27 December] with several more calls – and in the event they didn't issue the statement until Sunday.

I said to my Principal Private Secretary on Monday morning that we cannot have a situation where the officials meet and make such a recommendation over the holiday, with ridiculous deadlines, that I have no choice but to agree it, because if I disagreed and it came out that I had been given that recommendation positively to put sky marshals on – not a range of options but positive recommendations – and had turned it down, I would be in real trouble if anything had then happened. It is simply unacceptable to do it over the holiday, to do it under pressure, to do it without being able to expose to us properly the detail of what new evidence there was of flights at risk. Having agreed to the training of the sky marshals months before and having talked about their use or otherwise, it was very odd to find both Alistair Darling and myself being jumped on this issue.

Looking back, this episode takes on a bizarre hue, for – as many of us had suspected at the time – sky marshals were not appropriate in any but a few circumstances, and although they have been used in the USA, they just don't fit in with our own domestic (or for that matter international) flights. It is just not part of how we like to do things, and in any case monitoring and screening are much more effective than trying to take people out once they are active on the plane.

We now end up with criticism from Gwyneth Dunwoody [Labour MP for Crewe and Nantwich], who is Chair of the Transport Select Committee, the airline pilots' association BALPA, and the pundits on the radio at Monday lunchtime saying: 'Do you think it might be a cynical act by the government?' How can it be a cynical act? A cynical act to do what? And they counterpose it as though sky marshals are an alternative to screening people properly before they go on planes, which clearly they aren't. Screening the baggage is the main issue. No sky marshal would be of any use if there is a terrorist on the plane and the luggage in the hold goes up.

But I think I've done my bit over this so-called holiday. Who else, apart from the Prime Minister, has to deal with all this? Not just one thing, as Alistair Darling is having to deal with, with the sky marshals, but a whole range of things that nobody knows anything about, including authorising two more warrants, one in respect of the man suspected of Ian Broadhurst's murder and the other relating to a threatened New Year gang murder in Sheffield. And all of this is my winter break. This is my holiday!

January/February 2004

Over New Year the job was as extraordinary as ever, with a number of phone calls and warrants during the day on New Year's Eve but none during the evening itself or the early morning of New Year's Day. I had a very nice stay over with Paul and Judith Potts, though the electrics went off from about 12.30 a.m. until 11.30 the following morning. But as they have an Aga, we still had water and facilities to cook breakfast. We then had a walk along the coast, on the cliff just north of Bridlington. It was bitterly cold but not too breezy, so the wind chill wasn't too bad.

But during the day I ended up with two phone calls to John Prescott, one to Alistair Darling, another to Sir Nigel Sheinwald, Tony's special foreign-affairs adviser, and endless phone calls with the office, all about aviation security and the bizarre behaviour of the US in fingering particular flights – not just particular airlines but particular flights. The problems with Air France have now moved through Virgin Atlantic to British Airways, and the fuss started about what was to happen, firstly about the cancellation of

Flight 223 at 3 p.m. on New Year's Day and then into what was going to happen to the flight the following day. John Prescott was going on the *Today* programme on Friday morning [2 January] so was interested in the line to be taken. I was more concerned with what the Americans were up to, as well as where this particular holiday had gone, from Christmas Eve through a particularly bizarre Boxing Day all the way to the weekend. I had more than one phone call on just about every day except Christmas Day, and here we were on New Year's Day having to deal with the issue of what to do.

I fixed up a phone call for the following day with Tom Ridge, Secretary for Homeland Security in the USA, which went very well. He took the point when I said that we had a second 223 flight cancelled that Friday afternoon on evidence provided from the States, because all this evidence is only about overseas planes. They are demanding at very short notice the passenger manifests. They have also been demanding that British Airways should carry sky marshals on transatlantic flights – unlike Virgin Atlantic, who have been resisting this.

I said to Tom Ridge that the terrorists now know that we know there is an issue around Flight 223 and we know there is an issue around Flight 233; we know that they know there is an issue around Flight 223 and they know that we know – and he began to laugh and said that he had got the point. He said the problem is that the terrorists will probably know the source of our information, and I agreed that that was the real danger, and that we would have an interim solution that would get flights back on stream, and that if there was a request for passenger manifests it should be made well in advance, and that we would convene the joint contact group that we had agreed to set up when I was in Washington in March. We also agreed that Sir David Omand would lead a small group to the USA on the following Monday to talk through what needed to be done. Again Tom Ridge echoed my words by saying that we clearly cannot have this *ad hoc* situation going on in the long term; we need a proper permanent solution – and we certainly do.

I am now preparing for the announcement on the new National Offender Management Service and going through the detail. It was only on the morning of New Year's Eve that I realised that they hadn't given me any of the Q&A and background material. I rang my Principal Private Secretary, who was about to fly off to South Africa on holiday, and said that I wasn't doing the Statement next week without the back-up. I said that I couldn't possibly stand up in the Commons and not have answers to questions that would undoubtedly be asked by people like Ann Widde-combe, who has a strong interest and expertise in the prison and probation service – and particularly it has to be said, from people who are interested in prisons rather than probation. Anyway, so much for the final bit of my holiday this weekend, because I shall have to do a lot of work on that.

Week beginning Monday 5 January: the launch of the National Offender Management Service went reasonably well despite the troubles and difficulties of getting the preparation sorted, and I got some accolades with the Parliamentary Labour Party for what I had written in relation to higher-education funding. I am just doing my best to bat in and to keep the wheels on the cart.

I had dinner with Michael Barber and Michael Bichard (who was starting the inquiry into the Soham murders on the following Tuesday) and we were talking about the contrast of the aggravation that the current proposals on higher education were causing, compared with the enormous change that we had managed to put through six years earlier.

Tony wanted a meeting at Chequers followed by dinner on the Friday night, which was the day I was due to be in the constituency seeing refugee groups, meeting the District Labour Party and group leadership and attending my constituency meeting, as well as my advice surgery the following morning. I simply said that I couldn't do it. In the end they gave way and moved it to the following Friday, which was helpful, not least because it means that we can prepare properly. Those attending were to be John Reid, Charles Clarke and myself, but they will probably involve Gordon as well, which will make sense.

I went in for Charles Clarke's Statement and sat with him for the Higher Education Bill launch on the Thursday, again really just as a gesture of goodwill, just trying to be helpful.

The vote on higher-education fees clashes directly with the Holocaust Memorial event on 27 January so I will have to see if I can leave the vote, get to Northolt, fly out, do my bit at the end, and then fly back again. It is crazy but I will have to do it. Otherwise offence will be taken.

With regard to the Hutton Report, the debate and presumably the vote could well fall while I am supposed to be in India and Pakistan. That would be the limit.

Harold Shipman has committed suicide, and at a regional lobby lunch I was asked how I felt when I heard the news. 'Well,' I said, 'when you wake up in the morning and receive a phone call saying that Harold Shipman is dead, you feel like opening a bottle but wonder if it is too early.' Then you hear what the families are feeling and you take it very much more cautiously and have an inquiry. There seems to be a presumption, especially from some of the families, that he would have spilled the beans eventually about all those he had killed – a sort of deathbed confession. I don't share that view at all, which is why it took a little time for me to understand what their feelings were, but I should never have spoken in the terms I did to journalists. It was a very silly mistake on my part.

My propensity to honesty sometimes spills over into looking as if I am a bit of a loose cannon. I need to watch myself.

It was one of those very rare occasions when maintaining the gravitas of Home Secretary was more important than simply saying it as it is. There are times in senior office when it is better not to answer a question, and particularly not to answer it in a way that you may do over supper with friends. This was undoubtedly one of those occasions when a touch of gravitas would have been wiser than a simplistic response, and I should always, always have remembered that journalists are journalists.

But the problem with this job is that there is so much coming at you all the time that if you adopted just the gravitas, you would be permanently po-faced.

Cabinet this week was dealing with the forward legislative programme and I was backing in heavily with John Reid on the Mental Health Bill, which they propose to drop. I think this would be a grave mistake and could involve propositions to amalgamate some of my Bills so that I can get more of them through in a tidy fashion. There is still this terrible propensity around the Leader of the House and the Cabinet Office to believe that lots of small Bills are better than medium-sized ones. I don't know why; what with having to do multiple Second Readings, Report Stages, Committees and so on, it is just crackers, but it is a legacy from the past.

I wonder sometimes about colleagues. I wondered at Cabinet, because colleagues there have long wanted to return to the former hours of the House of Commons, and under great pressure Peter Hain, Leader of the House, has agreed to a vote. They are now having a review and they want to go back to late sittings and the sort of wonderful compromise that we have late sittings on Monday and Tuesday, rather than just Monday. Of course, what they forget is that it wasn't a 10 p.m. finish: it was sometimes midnight, and it was sometimes 2 a.m.

They are all arguing it from the point of view of a 'club'. You hear journalists and old-style reporters saying how wonderful it was when Annie's Bar was open all night and how they could gossip and get to know things. They say that now we are not accessible enough. There were those arguing in Cabinet that we would never manage with a small majority on these hours because it was the camaraderie, the mutuality, the club atmosphere that kept people on board, and that the higher-education problems wouldn't have happened in the old days. What a load of garbage.

The hours were changed and it had no impact whatsoever on camaraderie. Thank goodness we didn't quite go back to the dreadful old days when there were more by-elections due to death than is healthy to contemplate, and when alcoholism was rife both within Parliament and the press.

We have had all sorts of hiccups this week. We have had to deal with Maxine Carr and the fact that she was going to be let out on home/domestic curfew. Of course the liberal media commentary was how awful it was that we were going to stop her automatically being let out. I think it was crucial in order to prevent the whole home/domestic curfew arrangement being brought into disrepute. I notice that not one of them, even on *Any Questions?* when Peter Kilfoyle was on, knew that we had just announced a major change in the National Offender Management Service, a change to intensive community sentences and to dealing with the issues of over-crowding. Not a single one of them seemed to know that. Tim Collins, the Tory, said that those on home/domestic curfew were reoffending and there were dangerous and often violent offences committed by those on HDC. This is a complete distortion of the truth, but it is very difficult because if we have people like Peter Kilfoyle on *Any Questions?*, supposedly representing the Labour Party but hating the government, they don't even get briefed on what we are doing, never mind answering for it. It is very sad.

We are all holding our breath now for the Hutton Inquiry Report on 28 January, and the day before that the vote on the Second Reading of the Higher Education Bill. I have to fly out on the evening of the 28th to India and Pakistan. I think I would have taken a couple of days off sick last week if I wasn't in the job I'm in, so I hope I will feel better in the next day or two.

One interesting event was at Westminster Abbey – 2,500 mainly black men and women at a rally against gun crime. I spoke for the first time ever in the Abbey, just two minutes without notes. It was a moving occasion, with lighting of candles and gospel music.

We are in a sort of interregnum before the 27th and 28th. There is a real dilemma for me because if we lose the vote on the Second Reading there will almost certainly be a vote of confidence on the 29th, which will mean goodbye to the India and Pakistan trip. And if the Hutton Inquiry Report is very bad and there has to be a real head-to-head vote, I shall have to come back early because they are doing it on the following Wednesday. So it is all completely up in the air.

I declined to do the *Today* programme on Tuesday [20 January] and Wednesday, but I needed to do it on Thursday to try and round things up a bit. It was a long interview with John Humphrys which covered cannabis and driving, and I managed to point out that people who were in favour of proportionality and cautions and using common sense on driving were the very ones contradicting us on using proportionality and cautions and common sense on cannabis. The whole interview neatly enabled me to demonstrate that. I also managed to get in that the Lord Chief Justice was clarifying the situation on bail, as well as sensible arguments around civil renewal and what I was putting forward that day at the Local Government Network conference.

This was all about spelling out that we needed to engage with restoring civil society, investing in developing social capital – assisting people to take decisions and change things for themselves – and acknowledging the importance of being able to balance the drive from the centre for rapid change with the decentralisation of power and resources to help communities and individuals to do things for themselves.

At the very beginning of the normal Cabinet, without speaking to me first, John Prescott said that he wanted to raise a serious issue about people speaking beyond their brief and on other people's brief – in this case, local government. He gave as an example the Bicester planning consent, where 'David had rung in the morning when I announced it to thank me, and now uses it on the *Today* programme as an example of the clash between central and local government and decentralisation'. I said that I had said nothing of the sort, and told him not to be ridiculous. I said: 'I do some odd things in politics, John, but ringing to thank you for the decision and then criticising you for it is not one of them.' I said that the introduction for the *Today* programme interview had raised the issue and I had dealt with it by saying that there will always be clashes between local interests and the overall needs of the nation, and that of course I supported the decision that John Prescott had taken.

This was in relation to whether there should be an asylum accommodation centre near Bicester in Oxfordshire, and relates to the issue dealt with earlier in this book on the question of avoiding all asylum seekers being placed in the most disadvantaged and deprived urban communities.

John went on to point out that there were a number of issues in my brief with which he didn't agree but that he did not criticise publicly. He said that there were lots of things that he was unhappy with but didn't speak about. He said that I had only dealt with a junior minister in clearing the material, and that when he had raised the issue of the title of my speech and the conference I was at, it had been dealt with official-to-official and not between him and me. He complained that although I had changed the title, I had not changed the speech, and so on. I said: 'This is just too silly for words. It is not a local-government speech I am making. It is about civil renewal, and I am going to carry on making speeches on civil renewal.' There was absolute silence – then Tony swiftly intervened to close the whole thing down, saying that John had made his point and that was that. Charles Clarke afterwards said that he agreed entirely with me and that we had got to be able to speak. Other people were just shell-shocked.

What I clearly hadn't realised was that, once again, the process adopted was really critical for John. Had I been sensitive and picked up the phone and spoken to him personally there wouldn't have been an issue at all, but as I was so busy and didn't consider that the speech I was making and the pamphlet I was publishing were in the least bit controversial or damaging to his departmental interests, I hadn't felt that it was one of those priorities where I needed to be ultra-sensitive to people's feelings.

Looking back I believe I was right, but it did indicate – and still does – that there were times when I should have thought much more about whether people understood what I was trying to do and therefore did not feel that they were being upstaged. So often these things come home to roost later. Had I read Richard Crossman's diary before rather than after my time as a Cabinet minister, I may have understood the importance of paying as much attention to what other Cabinet colleagues knew about what I was doing, thinking and achieving, as I did to policy development and ideas for the future.

Andrew Smith [Secretary of State for Work and Pensions, with the benefits portfolio] came to talk about something serious that we were dealing with on the major issue running on asylum at the moment, related to accession countries and the habitual-residence test which I have been trying to upgrade. Having changed it once eighteen months ago, I have now for several months been in the process of changing it further. We are going to get it changed because we are determined to do so. Officials are being really awkward in the classic civil service sense, taking legal advice and saying that we will have to do it for overseas visitors generally and we will have to do it for people who have lived here but have been out of Britain for a long time, including British citizens. I said that we would have to do nothing of the sort. I said: 'We are government, not an administration as an advisory body to the civil service.'

The habitual-residence test concerns entitlement to housing and benefits, and once again some two years later the judges were to intervene to offer rights to non-British citizens in relation to housing that would cast doubt on the changes we made, putting the human rights of overseas individuals before the mutual concerns and political and democratic rights of the host population. This is dangerous, because it plays and has played into the hands of the British National Party and others.

But on this occasion the battle was to be won by ensuring that there were extremely tight rules to avoid people claiming benefits or access to housing without building up a fundamental entitlement. It is – and always has been, in my mind – the crucial difference between simply being a soft touch and being uncaring, to allow people to build up in all sorts of ways an entitlement to draw down on the benefits contributed to and therefore available at the time of need for the agreed resident population. This therefore was a fundamental argument in favour of allowing people from the central and eastern European accession countries (from 1 May 2004) to work legally and openly in the UK, rather than clandestinely and in the sub-economy.

Earlier in the week we had had an update with Tony on asylum, as we had on drugs and John Birt's little inquiry wanting to criminalise users of heroin, not the dealers or pushers – but that's a separate issue. Tony made it clear that he wanted the change to benefit entitlement and he wanted it quickly, so there was going to be no argument and that's the end of that one. It is just a question of getting it sorted and out into the public arena.

Media-wise it's been a funny week – with the crime stats showing a drop in burglary, vehicle crime and robbery but an increase in recorded violent crime.

We had a good day on the Tuesday [20 January] with the launch of the measures to curb anti-social behaviour. I would have stayed in bed on the Tuesday if I hadn't had to do this. Tony was going to do it but pulled out to do higher education, so we launched the measures. We got some good coverage on television: in fact I think it went quite well on the Tuesday, and even on the Thursday on crime, my speech and other activities. It is just that it didn't go at all well with the newspapers. It is all about preparing well, feeling well and presenting it well, and I think all three were problematic this week, with lots of reasons why, but nevertheless pretty horrible.

Over the weekend of Saturday 24 and Sunday 25 January, the politics behind the politics got even more complex and Byzantine. I just had a feeling in my bones from listening to the news on Sunday morning that there was something very strange going on with regard to Tuesday's Second Reading of the Higher Education Bill. I suppose it is just having a nose for what is happening. So I rang Charles Clarke, and chatting to him, pretending I knew more than I knew, got more out of him. Putting that together with what I felt in my bones, I then rang Sally Morgan, who, thinking that I knew it already, confirmed it – namely that they were lining up to intervene, presumably with Gordon acting as the 'peacemaker', so that the leaders of the organised opposition, namely Nick Brown and George Mudie, would consider pulling their troops off at the very last minute, leaving some people who would march on and vote against, while the organised opposition to the higher-education measures would collapse.

Strange therefore that two years later in May 2006 it was once again in the run-up to the Report and Third Reading of an Education Bill that we dropped behind in the opinion polls, and grave discontent and organised opposition on a grand scale were to display themselves.

This looked like a positive outcome, but there were real dangers because Tony would not have taken on the challenge and defeated it. He would have had against him the organised group, with a very solid base of sixty to seventy people who will vote together on just about everything, including getting rid of him. He would have allowed them to step back without being defeated, and therefore to be able to hold the sword of Damocles over him on other occasions, so that every modernising, reforming agenda will be entirely subject to the organised gang who form a party within a party.

I have left a message saying that I would like to talk to Tony about this. Obviously he is completely ensconced in preparing his strategy and I understand that, but as I said to Sally, I do think that this is the worst of all worlds. It reminded me of what Arthur Scargill [leader of the National Union of Mineworkers] should have done in 1984, which was to have stepped back in August when he had the chance of doing a deal with Ian MacGregor [Chairman of the National Coal Board] in Edinburgh. Had he done so, he would have been able to claim a tremendous victory, and instead of being remembered as a buffoon who devastated mining communities, mining families and the mining industry he would have been remembered as someone who had won a victory and put Margaret Thatcher on notice that any other time she wanted to take them on, they would be ready and they would have solidarity.

In my view, that's precisely what Nick Brown and George Mudie have worked out, so we will see. I may be wrong, but my feeling is that they have worked out that they can get a great deal more in the long term from stepping back and retaining the theoretical and in one sense real power against any other measures that they don't like. But I am just so glad that I got ID cards through, that I stood up that evening at the Domestic Affairs Committee, refused to be bowed, and got Tony to come on board over the following twenty-four hours and then pushed it through.

Tuesday 27 January was the first of two consecutive momentous days: the parliamentary debate on higher education. Charles Clarke handled himself with great skill, managing to take an intervention from Angela Eagle just at a moment when he would have had to have gone into the detail of whether there was going to be primary legislation for any substantive change to the agreed £3,000 flat-rate fee. By then taking a whole series of questions, he was able to handle it on his own terms rather than the agreed script. Those intervening appeared to be unaware that their efforts to clarify had helped to obfuscate. This often happens when people intervene at just the wrong moment without knowing or instinctively feeling that a moment's pause might place them in a better position to get the true answer. This is all about knowing Parliament, about the skill of handling the House of Commons' Chamber and, contrary to what I thought back in 1987, it takes some learning.

Whether I should have or shouldn't, I got irritated when under pressure Charles denigrated what we'd done in the previous parliament. I'd been through the general election defending our achievements, and knew perfectly well what was likely to be popular and unpopular. If they thought that was difficult and that was real unpopularity, they don't know they were born, but they will certainly know more about it at the next general election. The upshot was that a Tory intervened and said, 'In view of that, would you apologise for having introduced the up-front fee?', and Charles said, 'I just have.' John Reid was on one side of me and Gordon on the other, with Patricia Hewitt on the other side of John, and we were chuntering away about it, when inadvertently Charles happened to accuse the Tories of 'blind opportunism'. So we were having a real laugh: it wasn't meant as offence, rather we were just laughing and wondering what else he was going to say that could be taken amiss. Alan Johnson [Minister of State at the DfES], on the other hand, made an absolutely superb speech in the wind-up. In between we had all been asked to get in touch with likely rebels to see if we could get them to abstain or come and vote with us, and we kept getting messages back that either they were going to vote with us or they were going to abstain, or declared: 'Don't bother with me as I have made it absolutely clear that I am not voting with you.'

Alan Johnson's handling of the higher-education debate was his passport to Cabinet. It is strange how the cards fall; how, if you take a difficult issue and do well, you get promoted, but if you have a difficult issue and things don't go too well, you can find yourself sidelined or even out of government altogether. Quite often this is all about perception from within Downing Street rather than the reality of what has happened on the ground, and sometimes it is those immediately above you who ensure that it isn't they who get the blame for decisions that either were or rightly should have been taken by them. (Thankfully I was free of this, having been in Cabinet from 1997.)

And then we had the vote – and hell's bells, it couldn't have been closer. We won by five, which is really too close for comfort. I went into the Members' Dining Room with Andy Burnham for a meal and was glad I did. We sat with Jack Cunningham and Adam Ingram [Minister of State at the MoD] so it was a bit like *déjà vu* – reliving the old days, which is what Jack loves to do. Entertaining but depressing, because the whole atmosphere was not just one of anti-climax but of real depression, a feeling of a terrible split. It wasn't just the people who voted against (over seventy), and it wasn't just the forty abstentions: it was all the people who had voted with us who had really hated voting with us. We are talking here about nearly 40 per cent of the parliamentary party who were completely offside.

If it hadn't been the Hutton Report the following day, I think that it would have taken us months to have got over that Tuesday.

On the Wednesday Lord Hutton delivered his report, and the atmosphere as he did so that lunchtime was electric. I watched the whole of the presentation, then went into the House for Tony's Statement, which he did very well and in a very balanced way. It completely floored Michael Howard, who didn't have a leg to stand on, and immediately rallied our troops. The atmosphere changed, and it became Us versus Them again. The government was feeling confident. The troops had something to shout about. People were pulling together. But as Tessa Jowell rather wryly put it when I moved over to let her sit nearer to Tony – as Culture Secretary she had a special interest in the BBC's position – 'People like a winner.' That Wednesday, Tony was a winner, and it was so good to feel the atmosphere change. It was a good note on which to depart for India.

In the media over the next couple of days, most of the fall-out from Hutton was predictable.

If a journalist is asked to choose between a fellow journalist and the government, who does he choose? If you have nailed your colours to the mast and have said that the government are liars and cheats and were irresponsible, and then you are told they are not, do you immediately do a double somersault? Not likely. The *Sun* newspaper had been against the BBC all the way along so they were in a good position, but very few other journalists and journals were, and they just revealed their colours as being downright Tory. Boris Johnson, editor of the *Spectator*, lost all journalistic balance with a headline reading 'Whitewash'.

And so to India. Having slept a bit on the plane, as soon as we arrived in New Delhi we received a warm welcome from Sir Michael Arthur, the High Commissioner. The residence was extremely comfortable, with very pleasant rooms and a heated outdoor pool. I thought to myself that I was very lucky because if you are going to go to India, this is the way to travel and the place to stay.

On our first day there we went to the local Hindu temple, one that had been opened by Mahatma Gandhi. The temple was fascinating, but I felt so tired that it was difficult to take everything in. It was weird because we were there as honoured guests, so there weren't people praying: I think there must be a happy medium somewhere between the place being deserted and, as we found at the Golden Temple at Amritsar, being completely overwhelmed and unable to take in any of the spirituality. Then we had to shoot off to the big parade, the finale of the trooping of the colour, with bands. We had been invited by the Deputy Prime Minister, L.K. Advani, and the Prime Minister was also there, together with military generals.

Fortunately the sun had come out, and therefore even though it was getting very cold by five p.m., when we got there, it was still warm enough to sit out. This was an annual event in the calendar of New Delhi and the Indian government was very pleased that a member of the British Cabinet had been able to attend. It was also an opportunity to talk to senior politicians and officials from India and to get a feel of the British legacy, because so much of the atmosphere – piped bands, horse dressage, the lot – was reminiscent of a bygone British era.

I was also to find this in the Punjab when I visited the Police Academy a couple of days later.

We then had a meeting with Islamic leaders – there are 150 million Islamic worshippers in India – and they were very dispirited about their position. This was partly on account of a widespread feeling that they are victims. They had a fair point that the law and the constitution had been improved to protect the outcasts and prevent the caste system discriminating against people, but by doing so it didn't help the very poor Islamic or Christian men and women in society. It did, however, help others who had been specifically mentioned in the constitutional changes, such as Sikhs.

The geographic concentration of particular faiths didn't help either the cohesion or what was felt to be fair political representation at national level. The failure, as they saw it, to investigate properly the massacres in Gujarat also weighed very heavily on them. Despite the privilege of being able to travel in comfort, I did find that by the time I reached the evening – five and a half hours adrift of British time and following many hours of travel – I was on the point of collapse. Goodness knows how Tony does what he does.

The thing about New Delhi that I shall always remember is that there are monkeys all over the place. There was a man with a large monkey of one breed who was paid by residents in the area to have his monkey mark the ground to drive away other, smaller monkeys so that they weren't such a nuisance: he was a kind of wandering environmental health officer getting rid of the pests. There are also cows wandering about, which I found very strange: if cows are to be worshipped, then they shouldn't be meandering about in the road, unmilked and desolate, and trying to find food.

At five in the morning we set off by rail for Agra, to visit the Taj Mahal. It was an excellent train, really fast, clean and with decent service, much better than I had expected. The thing that then began to strike us, as it was described to me, was the fact that there were tips of rubbish everywhere, partly presumably because of modern packaging and plastics. Previous materials would have been easily recycled, whereas modern packaging and materials are different and not biodegradable. This was illustrated most graphically by the polystyrene cups we were given for water, tea or coffee. In the past the cups used would have been made of clay, and when people threw them out of the window they would have disintegrated back into the environment.

The trip to Agra was not simply a tourist visit but also a way of getting into the countryside, and we were able to experience the tremendous contrasts: the wonderful five-star hotel surrounded by puddles of stagnant water in which small children were playing, the rats, the filth, the constant noise and contrasting smells, all of it underpinned by the most sophisticated, highly educated, technologically well-versed people I have ever met. During the monsoon season it must be unbearable, with rats running, pigs snuffling and children being exposed to God knows what – but with the most sophisticated society apparently unable to organise structures to alleviate this enormous inequality. It was quite a contrast to China.

I found Agra bursting with life, full of noise and vigour, with lots of activity – activity that didn't seem to be actually achieving anything, but it was constantly there as a backdrop. We had breakfast in a beautiful hotel overlooking the Taj Mahal, and were given the most wonderful tour of the palace. The guide was excellent, and she persuaded the overseer to do the call within the dome: because we weren't surrounded by hundreds of sightseers the sound was just magic as the echo disappeared into the farthest reaches.

Contrary to the general view, there aren't that many perks in being Home Secretary. The visits to football matches and the visit to the Taj Mahal, and the privilege of travelling comfortably, are those that I recall. If the general public are aggravated that we should have taken a couple of hours out at dawn to see this wonder of the world, then I hope they will forgive us. I think that they would do the same.

We then set off through the really poor area, where we were surrounded by staggering poverty. The sheer squalor was shocking, such as the sight described to me of a beautiful teenage girl in a sari, covered in filth and dirt, beating out metal with a hammer on an anvil. When I raised it with the guide, she said, 'Yes, the tribal women are very beautiful but they have to earn their living.'

After three-quarters of an hour back at the residence for a wash and a cup of tea we were off again on the train down to the Punjab, a journey of nearly four and a half hours. I did a lot of work on these journeys, catching up ready for the Serious Organised Crime Agency launch that Downing Street are insisting should be on Monday 9 February. I wanted to do it alongside publication of a White Paper in March, but they absolutely insist that they need a launch pad to get the internal and domestic issues up and running after Hutton and the subsequent debates. And just as they used to turn to me when I headed Education and Employment and wanted a kickstart, they now want to do it with me at the Home Office. I was also dealing with the Newton Committee, the Anti-Terrorism, Crime and Security Act, and the issues around prevention of suicide terrorism. So I was having to deal with that and the papers alongside it, preliminary material for the visit to the USA in a month's time and a whole range of routine things.

When we arrived in the Punjab we found ourselves in a weird hotel – very large, half empty and rather eerie. We were given a military salute when we arrived and there were people with machine guns all over the place, including outside my room, which was a bit disconcerting. As it was by this time 8.45 in the evening, we had a quick wash and something to eat. All the time throughout this visit I was desperately trying to get food that wasn't curried or heavily spiced, and it was very difficult. I managed to get some food and even when I had eaten things I shouldn't at official events, I managed to survive; that is, until the Sunday at the Police Academy.

I was by this time very relieved that we had done all the necessary official business on the Friday – including meetings with the Deputy Prime Minister and a lunch hosted by him that had been attended by the BBC's veteran correspondent Mark Tully. It was fascinating to talk to Mark, not least because when Indira Gandhi was Prime Minister he had found himself in prison, along with leading activists of the BJP (Nationalist Party) – a party to which he was very close. As part of my preparation for going to India I had started to read his book *India in Slow Motion*, but the book was in such slow motion that given the pressure of work I only managed a couple of chapters.

We visited the Visa Section in New Delhi. This was important, because having clamped down so heavily on asylum we were now getting an avalanche of applications for visitor visas and for what are known as 'working-holiday stays', which entitle people in the Commonwealth to come and work.

This was something that I am afraid we had to clamp down on. All the work was done over the subsequent year for further announcements and changes in early 2005.

One of the main events of the visit was my address, organised by the British Council, to leading human-rights lawyers, interest groups and journalists. Because of the nature of the audience and the real interest in human rights in India, I had chosen (as it turned out, probably mistakenly) to talk about the Newton Committee and the challenges we faced in reshaping the Anti-Terrorism, Crime and Security Act.

I wrote 'probably mistakenly' because although what I was going to say had been circulated, and although it fitted in entirely with the publication of a consultation paper on the issues in February, it irritated some Cabinet ministers and in particular it once again fell foul of John Prescott's concern about process. He thought I was making policy, whereas what I was doing was talking about ideas, which I still believe is absolutely essential in revitalising and renewing government. It is frightening but indisputable that the longer a government is in office, the more afraid of ideas it becomes – this is true of governments of all persuasions – and the more the process takes over rather than the politics, the more people are worried about having genuine public debate or even big disagreements, not between themselves but around the issues: in other words, to share with the British people ideas that can be thrashed out. Would that it were possible in our modern democracy to do this without either total misinterpretation or the usual drawing of lines, the troops gathering on each side, presuming that they are either for you or against you whereas what you are trying to do is get them to address the issues.

Reflecting on the change of Home Secretary in May 2006, The Times expressed the hope – as it had hoped before with Charles Clarke – that John Reid would show 'more respect for liberal values' than I had. I smiled at this. I think that those who claim to themselves the espousing of liberal values would be more respected if they were prepared to engage intellectually and practically with the issues that those making decisions have to address, day in, day out. As with politicians, so with those who analyse, criticise and hold to account politicians, it behoves them to earn respect.

The speech itself went very well, both from the point of view of questions and discussion and the way in which it was received by those present. We had Alan Travis from the *Guardian* and Dave Barratt from the Press

Association with us on the trip, which gave us good coverage back in Britain. *The Times* on the Saturday morning had four items from the visit, none of them very long but nevertheless four items which we would never have got without having the PA with us. But reporting back from this distance could be a problem.

Just how much of a problem I hadn't realised until I got back home, although I ought to have learned the lesson from the way that my speech in New York had been misreported or at least misinterpreted by those wishing to comment without bothering to have seen the content.

I felt that the speech had touched on issues that needed airing, and when I sat at dinner next to the former Lord Chief Justice of India, now Chairman of their All-India Human Rights Commission, and discussed the issues with him, I realised that these were the matters that required addressing: the balance and proportionality, the way in which if we could have a sensible dialogue back home we might be able to see our way through rather than this 'You are trying to take away human rights' on the one hand and 'You couldn't give a damn about security' on the other. But there are no forums in which this is easily done in the UK because we have fallen into such adversarial politics – and such adversarial political reporting – that it is difficult to get these issues across. How do you obtain within the normal judicial process the protection of security information and the avoidance of exploitation of technical knockouts, which is inherent within the system we operate and which is impossible when dealing with suicide terrorists?

We also talked at this dinner about the state of human rights in India and all present, including the women, were clear that it was ridiculous not to make India a safe country with regard to asylum. There was no reason why people shouldn't receive protection from the courts and from the Human Rights Commissions, even if they had to move from their immediate area.

At the Police Academy I found a real willingness for the police to do their job better and more thoroughly. I had given Advani a number of cases where we needed help, and even got the Deputy Prime Minister to release a British prisoner who had been picked up some years earlier with Latvians who on Putin's visit had been released early. This particular man had tuberculosis and his mother was dying, and in all fairness it was right that he should be treated in the same way as those accused with him.

What was astonishing was that, having been released, he never even bothered to write to thank me.

My argument in the speech I made and in the subsequent discussion while travelling with Alan Travis was to get across the need for measures that would provide preventive action and would not simply rest on prosecution once an event had taken place. In other words, we need in a free society to restrict the activities and movements of those about whom there is sufficient concern over their terrorist links, but not to set aside for prosecution purposes the principle of 'beyond reasonable doubt' that people understandably want to keep as an absolutely key element of our legal framework and our democracy.

I did not achieve this. The idea of souped-up Anti-Social Behaviour Orders, which under civil law would control the activities of individuals and which was set out in the subsequent consultation paper and legislation brought in by Charles Clarke, was completely misunderstood and interpreted – not least because the Guardian *asked people to comment on it who had not been there and had no access to the material, knowing that it would create controversy without enlightenment. It was simply presented as though I wished to change the whole nature of our legal system to reduce the 'beyond reasonable doubt' to the formulation used by the Special Immigration Appeals Commission (Superior Court of Record) for terrorist cases, only within the normal court system. The civil law would fall within the bounds of Orders, which would preclude particular actions or access to communication. The tweaking of the rules around admissibility and burden of proof (SIAC already had maintained the 'beyond reasonable doubt' test) would allow for a much more sensible approach to a very different challenge from that of dealing with the burglar or common-or-garden thug.*

But Helena Kennedy (the human-rights activist in the House of Lords) was happy to appear on radio to denounce me and all my works. The fact that she hadn't the faintest idea what I'd said was neither here nor there.

The *Guardian* approached these people, got a quote and made that the story. So what people read was not what I had said, but the story bounced back like a media squash ball off the wall.

Then the *Today* programme picked it up and interviewed Helena Kennedy on the basis of the *Guardian* coverage. Then Tuesday's papers picked up the story, without any recourse to the actual speech made. So we go round in circles. We don't have a sensible debate, we don't address the issues, we just do a dance.

Because all this fed into the febrile atmosphere of the Parliamentary Labour Party, following the handling of the foundation hospitals and higher-education issues, there was a real problem and an issue of process. People had forgotten or didn't know that the Newton Committee had published on 18 December; they didn't know that a debate was going to take place on that report; and they had no idea about the renewal of the Anti-Terrorism, Crime and Security Act Part 4 or the sunset clause on that Part 4 that would wipe it out completely. They didn't know that the Newton Committee had raised a whole range of issues about whether we could integrate what we were doing with the detainees under the Special Immigration Appeals Commission with the normal criminal law and the complications of trying to do that while not allowing terrorists a free run.

John Prescott raised the whole issue at the Parliamentary Committee (the executive of the backbenchers) on the Wednesday, again without contacting me.

So just to finish this particular issue I jump to the Cabinet on Thursday [5 February], where I had decided that I would raise this proactively. Hilary Armstrong had reported on the fact that the future parliamentary debates would include the Newton Committee on 25 February, so I took the opportunity to join in. I explained precisely what I had done, what I had said, the audience I had said it to and why I had done it, and the fact that there would be a consultation and the need for a sensible debate. Tony joined in magnificently. He said he supported me entirely and that I was quite right to raise these issues. He said that if there was a problem over process it was his fault, because of the way in which the higher-education issues had been dealt with, not mine, and that he had for months wanted a debate on them. He also said that I was dealing with the most difficult problems, day in, day out, that I was right to have done what I did and that I deserved support. I could have hugged him. John Reid cleverly joined in and said that he knew that John Prescott would agree, as he had, with encouraging people to take up the Big Conversation, that we needed to make this kind of speech in order to push ideas out and to be ahead of the game. John Prescott said that I had written to him, and that he was satisfied and so long as it went through DA Committee, this was the end of the issue. Charlie Falconer tried to join in and say that the process had been wrong because he hadn't been consulted, but Tony just cut him off.

It was one of those occasions, as with ID cards, when Tony Blair demonstrated how he stands out head and shoulders above earlier Labour Prime Ministers such as Harold Wilson, Jim Callaghan and (from my reading of history) Clement Attlee in his ability to be able to see the bigger picture and give backing at crucial moments – when to equivocate or withdraw support would leave an individual completely isolated, and discourage others from being prepared to put their heads above the parapet.

Sticking your neck out is, in politics, a dangerous game, and as those who avoid it like the plague prosper, it is not surprising that fewer and fewer people are prepared to do so.

But let me return for a moment to the visit to South Asia, because having completed the visit to the Punjab we crossed the border into Pakistan – not, you may think, unusual, but at this time extraordinarily rare. We drove up to the Indian side and had the presentation of arms and the ceremony of departure. We then walked across no man's land carrying our possessions and our clothing, only to find that my trousers had fallen off the hanger. We then had to have a discussion on the Pakistan side in order for one of the protection team to go back and fetch them.

Lahore, the former capital of the Punjab before division, is a magnificent city. We then experienced a flight from Lahore to Miapur in Azad Kashmir in an ex-Soviet helicopter where the doors were opened for the photographer, who was desperately sick on the journey, to relieve himself. I simply put on my earphones and went into what can only be described as a semi-coma, but I couldn't get out of my mind the ground-to-air missiles, which could so easily be fired from vantage points, particularly on the major reservoir in the foothills. It was, after all, Eid and there wasn't a single other craft in the air that morning.

Miapur is one of the wealthier parts of Azad Kashmir, thanks to remittances sent back by very large numbers of those who have emigrated to Sheffield, Rotherham and other areas of Britain. A very large number of those from the Miapur area live in Sheffield, and in my own constituency in particular. Lord Ahmed had organised the welcome, with children throwing rose petals and singing beautifully in English, but my job was to get down to the nitty-gritty of working with the judiciary to be able to prevent forced marriages and the kidnap of girls from Britain, and to gain co-operation from the local police and justice system for the magnificent liaison officers working from the British High Commission in Islamabad.

One of the major events in Miapur was a public meeting at which the High Commissioner and I were speaking. The only person to show any real dissent was a 6' 4" muscular and hairy-armed local resident, with a Yorkshire accent broader than I've heard for a long time in my own constituency. With folded arms and a blunt Yorkshire approach he told me in no uncertain terms what he thought about me and my government in relation to Iraq. The advantage, I said, not only of this meeting but of the country in which, from your accent, you have obviously lived for a very long time, is that we can speak like this, that you can talk to me like this, and that I am prepared to listen like this.

I also raised the issue, with the help of Lord Ahmed, of imams coming from the most rural and unsophisticated villages to Britain, and the crucial need for training and for a proper system that would enable them to do their job while bringing benefit to the community back home.

After meetings with the Pakistan Foreign Minister and a vigorous debate with a very high-level group of academics and judges in Lahore, we had to forgo a planned visit to the Khyber Pass and fly back early to London for the crucial debate on Hutton.

And so to Prime Minister's Questions prior to the Hutton debate, in which Tony opened up the issue of accession countries and benefits and the right to work, on the back of questions from Michael Howard. As I have mentioned before, we have been working on this for months and struggling with the Department for Work and Pensions. It was a clever question from Michael Howard, designed to raise all the usual fears about large-scale immigration and whether those coming across would attempt to claim benefits rather than seek jobs. What I hadn't realised to that point is just how far the Foreign Office had backed down from their previous position in respect of wanting 'open borders'. Jack, as Foreign Secretary, had been a great enthusiast for the expansion and openness of Europe, but now, with the political heat turned up by the Conservatives and the hysteria of some right-wing newspapers, he has changed his mind.

For me this was a matter both of common sense and of sheer practicality. I knew instinctively that if we didn't allow people to come and work legally, we would have the most enormous problem with clandestine working and with illegal presence. Given that it was clear that our opponents were perfectly ready to switch from concentrating on asylum, on which we were being significantly successful, to dealing with clandestine working, illegal use of public services and

a sub-culture of criminality, it was a political imperative to ensure that we had
a regulated, transparent system that worked.

One thing was certain. I was not able to draw on the forces of liberal
England to help, because they significantly steered clear of the short but
vigorous battle that ensued.

How on earth the Foreign Office thought that we were going to cope with a
situation where free movement of labour allowed everyone to be here but
restrictions forbade them to work, goodness only knows.

Later on the Wednesday I organised a meeting that Denis MacShane,
Minister of State for Europe, attended. Denis was very positive indeed and
took an entirely different view. He backed in. But the Thursday papers
were dreadful. They had taken the signal from Prime Minister's Questions
and so this set the scene for our trying to pull it all back.

A further big issue on the Wednesday was the debate. Tony did
extremely well, despite disruption from the Strangers Gallery, where
demonstrators had co-ordinated their shouting and screaming to the
point where the gallery had to be emptied. It was sad, because I had
been arguing against the security services and everyone else wanting to put
up screens to separate out the Gallery from the Chamber. Instead I had
advocated better screening of those going in – that's what we will have to
do for sure – but what happened has not helped my cause.

Tony made a brilliant speech, demolishing Andrew Gilligan totally.
Unfortunately there then arose a row about whether Tony knew that the
45-minute claim [the assertion in the February 2003 dossier that some of
Iraq's supposed weapons of mass destruction could be deployed within
forty-five minutes of an order to use them] referred only to 'battlefield'
weapons with a very short range.

Geoff Hoon, in the wind-up, was unable to clarify this, which I thought
was a great shame as he might have been able to clear up the issue very
quickly. Unfortunately this gave the Tories a new lease of life on the issue,
with Michael Howard on the day after the debate demanding Tony's
resignation. Of course, shells containing chemical or biological weapons
don't know any boundaries and are as much international in the countries
around Iraq as those launching on Cyprus, so it's all very silly and is a
complete re-run of the arguments a year ago, with exactly the same people
putting across the same points.

We've come through this, but part of coming through it is that I've spent
the day not only dealing with the anti-terrorism, crime and security

material and making sure that they start preparing the paper on proper lines (which is very hard work) but also the organised crime announcement. This is because No. 10 are determined to do it now on Monday, which means I will have to come down Sunday night.

Nobody can say that politics isn't interesting but if we lose the election, we will have lost it aided and abetted, in fact engineered and choreographed, by our own side.

On Friday morning [6 February] the BBC 'What the Papers Say' first thing in the morning said that there was a letter from a group of barristers who had acted as special advocates attacking my speech in Delhi, and the letter had appeared in *The Times*. I asked the press office where this letter was, as it did not appear in the cuttings, and they said that it wasn't in *The Times*. But it did appear in *The Times* on the Saturday. So we are going to have to investigate how the hell a letter appeared in *The Times* on the 7th but was announced by the BBC as being in *The Times* on the 6th. We need to know how they knew, why they knew, what they thought they were doing reading it out as an attack on me, and what the agenda was? I only heard the programme because I had woken up so early as I was still suffering from jet lag, and just clocked, as I try to do, what was going on.

We never did find out why the BBC were running a letter a day before it appeared in the paper. I've had a long-standing problem with those operating 'What the Papers Say', to the point where, when I edited the Today programme on 31 December 2005, I asked David Aaronovitch to take a look at how it was produced. The truth is that those editing this particular contribution to the morning news agenda have their own agenda, and until the BBC get a grip of this they will be able to present things that are not in the news but that allow items to be put before the public that would otherwise not be available to the properly screened and edited news bulletins.

Overnight on Thursday/Friday [5/6 February] at least nineteen people of Chinese origin were drowned in Morecambe Bay, picking cockles, working basically as slaves. We may never know the true number of those who died, bearing in mind the nature of the quicksands in the bay. Of course, people are now demanding to know why we haven't legislated, why even though a promise had been made five years before that we would act, gangmasters had not been made to register and be properly regulated. The answer is simple. The DTI had been blocking it. We had put it up for the Asylum

Bill, and the legislative committee had rejected it on the grounds that it extended the Bill and made it too wide-ranging.

In any case the Department for the Environment, Food and Rural Affairs had been very jumpy about the matter all along, and were loath to get involved in the detailed inspection. In fact we had to persuade them to do a pilot in south Lincolnshire, and they had dithered all over the place. So we were unable to get it into the Asylum Bill, but Jim Sheridan, a Scottish Member, had put up a Private Member's Bill. Up to the tragedy of the deaths, we hadn't got agreement across government to back the full Bill.

The government hadn't acted because other people wouldn't go along with us, and therefore inertia led to another example of what looks like complete dithering. On each occasion – whether on this issue of the gangmasters, or ID cards, or the accession countries, or Maxine Carr – we have tried to be ahead of the game. We have been so on asylum as a whole, but you wouldn't think that after reading an article in the *Observer* by the editor of *Prospect* magazine David Goodhart, lecturing us on what we should be doing on balanced asylum policy and work permits, when it was all in the White Paper two years ago and we have been legislating and working on it since. But I just cannot believe how, when I try to get ahead of the game, inertia sets in and I am blocked from taking action. I then get blamed for not taking action, and criticised for taking action in the face of pressure rather than having been in the forefront. This is happening all the time now. The Right criticise us for inaction, the liberal Left criticise us for being pushed by the Right when we do act, and we get no credit for having thought about it and trying to be ahead of the game. I shall try to raise this in a slightly less robust fashion at the Special Political Cabinet this coming Thursday.

We are announcing the Serious Organised Crime Agency this Monday; we are doing the accession countries, all being well, and signing everything off on Tuesday; and we are trying to get a grip on the Licensing Act. I have had another conversation with Tessa Jowell, who I think has realised that there is a big issue around how the Licensing Act plays into all these issues of violence and anti-social behaviour, including film categorisation of what appears on television.

And in the meantime the BNP are leafleting my constituency, raising some of the issues that I myself have been raising: the cost of providing support for asylum seekers and dispersal, why they don't recycle the equipment and materials, why they automatically pay out for things that they don't need to – and we just go round in circles. And this is the inertia of government and the indecision and dithering of politicians.

Paul Potts asked me on the telephone whether, given all the hammering I get, it is worth being Home Secretary – and I had indeed been wondering what the hell am I in this for. If it weren't for good friends, for what I can see I am doing in the constituency, and for what I believe on the whole is the support of the public, I'd jack it in. But I want to achieve something. As Tony said at Cabinet when giving me support, people will only appreciate what we have done and are trying to do on counter-terrorism and getting the balance right when, tragically, someone is blown up by a suicide bomber – and then, of course, we won't have done enough.

I was not to know at that point that 7 July 2005 was to prove Tony right. Unfortunately all those who pooh-poohed all that we did, all those who denigrated the work we were putting in train, will never stand up, will never be counted and will never be held to account.

It was just one of those mornings when I woke up and my heart sank as I realised that another Home Office day was starting.

The Cabinet and the Political Cabinet were very good. For some reason, everybody was affable and pleasant with each other, people were laughing, John Prescott was in one of his very rare good moods – apart from taking a dig at Tessa Jowell about testosterone men, because she had had a dig at macho men in an interview the previous Saturday in the *Daily Telegraph*. We were discussing tactics, so I made the point that we needed a definition and a direction for the European and local-government elections. We sometimes talk round in circles and were more positive on this occasion, but it is planning what we are going to do and getting on with it that are important.

We had a good launch of the Anti-Social Behaviour trailblazer in Sheffield on Friday [13 February]. People are really keen, and I have got to make it work. It is no good just talking about it. People have got to feel that things are being turned round.

In the Department we had a half day on the Spending Review between Board and ministers on Thursday, trying to get a direction and trying to anticipate the googlies. I just feel that there is an inertia settling over the Department. After the big push that we made last year, they have just settled back into tranquillity again, and productivity levels are abysmal. Correspondence has improved in the core department but for immigration and nationality it is still appalling, both in turn-round and in content. I went down to Croydon on Tuesday and addressed the ranks of IND representatives from all over. It went very well and they were very responsive, but I do wonder whether the messages really get across about efficiency and competent administration.

It is a good job it wasn't Thursday, when I saw Geraldine Smith's letter about the cockle pickers. The twentieth victim was found on Sunday the 15th. Geraldine Smith is the MP for Morecambe and Lonsdale and has turned out to be a serial attacker of her own government, someone whom I have never heard saying anything positive about the Labour Party and the Labour government, and who seems to take great pleasure not just (as is her right) in representing her constituency, but in attacking Labour ministers.

Maxine Carr: at last Martin Narey got his act together and blocked her home curfew. The liberal press still don't understand it. Talking of the liberal press, Alan Travis had a piece in the *Guardian* that was an interview I had done with him on the train in India. John Toker, the new Head of News in the Home Office, had given him an instant quote about the cockle pickers, which unfortunately made it look as though I had done the interview over the weekend.

These are the sort of quirks that you have to put up with when in government but, of course, people outside only read what they read.

When I did the interview, I spelled out that I was strongly in favour of avoiding clandestine workers. I didn't know that the cockle pickers were going to be killed. I just knew what I knew and I have stuck to it ever since. We managed to get Tony at the following Prime Minister's Questions not to commit us to blocking the idea of legal registered working for those coming from the central and eastern European states, which is what Jack Straw wants. It appeared to me to be something more than the issue itself because at Cabinet on the Thursday, Jack attacked me over higher education, almost suggesting that it was my fault, that because of my commitment in the previous manifesto to blocking top-up fees, I had made it more difficult to make change. I had, but not the kind of change we were now proposing.

I found out on the Monday that Michael Howard is going up to Morecambe Bay on Wednesday, and I am hoping that, because I have been able to give them advance notice of it, we can organise people who are not us, as government, to get involved and to attack him for opportunism. We are really going to have to be on the ball from now on.

Monday morning's *Financial Times* had reams on Peter Gershon's review of potential savings on procurement, on employees and the operation of the civil service. We had agreed in Cabinet – and Tony had backed in, much to Peter Gershon's dismay – on not circulating the report as written, and certainly not circulating the projected savings, all of which appeared in the *FT* on Monday morning. You have to draw your own conclusions.

Another piece of pre-empting going on is about the screen for the visitors' gallery in the House of Commons which again, on Sunday and Monday, has been leaked to the papers, presumably again to ensure that they get their way.

I continued to put my own view that what we needed to do was to screen the individuals going into the gallery, not place a screen in front of the gallery, but once again circumstance (this time in the middle of May) was to make any argument in this direction meaningless – namely the actions of demonstrators in the gallery throwing coloured powder all over the front bench.

To Munich to the so-called Big Five, way up in the mountains in Garmisch-Partenkirchen, where the 1936 Winter Olympics were held. It was very strange because during the Second World War Otto Schily, German Interior Minister, had been saved by the monks at the monastery we visited.

I raised the issue of the accession countries and it was pretty clear that what both Germany and France are saying is that there are lots of people here clandestinely or working as domestic servants and people don't like to rock the boat. Otto Schily said that when they had tried to regulate it, there was an outcry because virtually every middle-class family had someone working for them who was a clandestine, so it was better to pretend that we were stopping people from working while they carried on employing them. So that just about sums it up!

It was a useful discussion between the five of us but more of a nostalgic homecoming for Otto Schily, who insisted that we should take part in the ceremony in the ancient monastery where he and his family had been hidden. The only problem was that it was ten degrees below and there was no heating, except in the abbot's rooms where we were liberally served with Benedictine. What was also interesting was the fact that they felt no qualms about flying us back to Munich by helicopter, the kind of gesture which in Britain would have brought the national press down on the government for extravagance. This is clear from the fuss that is made about Tony, even as Prime Minister, using the clapped-out planes that are laid on by the Air Force.

After the Lufthansa flight had landed at Heathrow, straight to Downing Street: this time we've got agreement on letting accession-country nationals work legitimately, and the only question remained that of when we should make the announcement. I wanted it to coincide with Michael Howard's trip to Morecambe and Burnley, hoping thereby to put him on the spot: if he wanted to take on the BNP in Burnley, why not take them on by welcoming our sensible, organised and transparent way of letting people work here properly and pay their dues? Jack, who was now won over to the scheme, felt that it should be presented to Parliament.

At the time I was irritated by this, because I felt that dealing with the politics publicly was more important than the niceties about whether a Statement should be made to Parliament or not. But I can see now that very often presenting to Parliament was a way of ensuring that colleagues were carried along with you, thereby avoiding the accusation of giving the Chamber the cold shoulder. The problem, as ever, is that parliamentary arrangements and protocol often make it extremely difficult at short notice to do what you want to do when you want to do it, and it was one of those weeks when political astuteness and parliamentary procedure didn't exactly gel.

Our officials hadn't spotted – and therefore hadn't told us – that the Spring Estimates were coming out and that the reconfiguring of our departmental expenditure limit over the three years, on immigration and asylum, was going to be part of that. They had even written a letter to the Home Affairs Select Committee saying that I ought to spend this before the Spring Estimates, without any political context spelling out at all how it was a reconfiguration and presenting it as though it was £227 million more for immigration and asylum – which is exactly how the papers will present it. Treasury officials have had a hard time in front of the Public Accounts Select Committee and were irritated about this, so you would have thought that our officials would have been on the ball.

Charles Clarke clearly had the same problems in April 2006 over the suggestion that the figures on foreign prisoners who had not been deported should be 'got out' before his Permanent Secretary went before the Public Accounts Committee. It is at times like that when you not only need political nous and inner strength to overrule, but also special advisers who can spot these things coming before it's too late.

Despite the fact that the readjustment is to take account of the failure to get proper agreement back in the Spending Review of 2000, no one will understand the complications of all this when it comes out.

We had that on the Tuesday, and we had Wednesday's big counter-terrorism debate on the Newton Committee, on which I had to spend an enormous amount of preparation time, going through the issues over and over again.

Then on Thursday we had the first of the new citizenship ceremonies. This went extremely well, and despite a heavy news day we got very good coverage on the Friday and over the weekend. Prince Charles and I shared the ceremony between us at Brent Town Hall and all those taking part were not only happy at the ceremony itself but really enthusiastic about the idea of proper recognition of a welcome into citizenship and the concept of developing courses, not just for language but for British values and life.

Rare as these occasions may be, I think I can say, hand on heart, that this was one of those policies that certainly would not have happened when it happened if I had not been Home Secretary. I am therefore very proud to have seen the ceremony ingrained as a natural part of our process of naturalisation.

Michael Howard's speech in Burnley was well put together, with a cleverly chosen audience from the region, balancing an attack on the BNP with an attack on us. He pretended that it is possible to deal with asylum seekers offshore – that is, collect them together and not allow them here until they have been cleared as genuine, which of course you can't. We are partly going down that road in a sensible way with the United Nations High Commissioner for Refugees Gateway, and with the efforts with Tanzania to see if we can get an encampment that we pay for that deals with people being returned. These are horrendous issues that Michael Howard simplified for an audience hungry to hear simple answers.

We are just caught like a pig in the middle – well, at least that's how I feel at the moment. I am desperately trying to hold the line of a balanced approach that recognises legal migration and the right to work, cuts off benefits, deals with asylum decisively and cuts through the incompetence of the administration – and what do I get? I get slagged off by the liberals who never read the *Daily Express*, which is daily now representing racism, not only on its front page but on just about every page. They pretend that the Dutch are suddenly throwing out 26,000 people when they haven't thrown out a quarter of the people we have removed. The Dutch are talking about doing it rather than actually doing it – and all the measures they are talking about to achieve it we have already got in place, including removal centres.

It is absolutely farcical, and extremely demoralising. It is demoralising for me personally, but worse than that it is destructive of democracy, because in the end the more you play to the belief that there are simple answers, the more you play into the hands of the BNP. But it is very hard to galvanise the Department as they are just in sleepy-sleepy land. Now that the liberal Left have decided that I am public enemy No. 1, I can expect no support from them either.

This was one of those occasions when I was clearly feeling isolated and under pressure. I wish I had been able to take a month's holiday and refresh myself. Above all I wish I had simply been able to shake off the irritation I felt about what is sometimes called 'the commentariat', who comment on everything but have experience of nothing.

Tony has gone to Berlin with Jack Straw, Patricia Hewitt, Andrew Smith and John Reid. That means there are five of them in Berlin and Michael Howard in Burnley, where he touches the public – and officials bumble on, not realising that the Spring Estimates were going to clash with the asylum quarterly statistics, not recognising the politics of it.

Instead of getting a month's holiday, I had two days down in Somerset, staying in a farmhouse. Thank goodness it had a wood stove, as it was freezing cold.
  On the Friday night I was woken by one of my protection team running up the stairs. He had been phoned by my office to say that there was an extremely urgent warrant and that my mobile was switched off (which it was!). I had thought, given that I was getting only two days' holiday and that most of the Cabinet had gone away for a week or ten days for the February closure of Parliament, that the office might just have arranged for someone to substitute on warrants, but no such luck. So I phoned and found that it was a warrant

that could easily have been cleared the following morning. There was no urgency. There was no time restriction. Nothing was about to happen. But the night had been ruined and another opportunity for a short break had been interfered with.

So when I got back to London on the Monday for one of the busiest weeks I had had, I was less than pleased when at the Domestic Affairs Committee colleagues began to complain that they hadn't really had time to read the counter-terrorism paper that I intended to publish on the Thursday, because they 'had been on holiday'. Perhaps their officials might have ensured that they took it with them.

We didn't settle things at the committee. It rumbled on all day, with Charlie Falconer and I spatting over the telephone or via officials, so by the time we reached 9.30 in the evening he was still trying to argue about the revised paper because I had had to back down on putting up for discussion specific new offences such as knowingly associating with a terrorist, and had to reword the paper to deal with the same issues but by drawing attention to experience overseas, particularly France, and by toning things down and not making very specific propositions but dealing with it in a more general way.

I decided that that was the only way that I was going to get it through, and I couldn't go running to Tony, crying foul. So we rewrote the final part of the paper and got it out to people, and by eleven p.m. I was the nearest that I've come to thinking that I would be better doing something entirely different – with the exception of the ID cards issue, that is.

Final week of February, and no wonder I am tired. On Wednesday the 25th I agreed reluctantly to do GMTV and other early-morning television, as well as radio broadcasts, having done the *Today* programme the day before. I say reluctantly, because getting up before six a.m., and having not only to be articulate but to look fresh and alive, clean, smart and alert, is a hell of a task for me, not least when I had been working late the night before. Anyone can get up occasionally and do a television broadcast if they are practised enough. It is having to do it when there is so much going on that makes it more difficult. It is rather like the proverbial 'If it's Tuesday, this must be Amsterdam' itinerary.

The Home Office was effectively top of the television news Monday, Tuesday and Wednesday, which was pretty hard work, though it does have the advantage of wiping the Opposition off the news. It also has the advantage of being in charge and getting things done, but it is damned hard work. Where is everyone else?

During the Domestic Affairs Committee, I almost had to burst into laughter because I said that Peter Goldsmith had been kept in touch and that even on holiday we had been taking messages from him. Peter said that he hadn't been on holiday, and I said, 'Well, we've been sending messages to you in the Virgin Islands.' His reply was that he had been there on business. I almost doubled up.

So at the moment I am burning my boats with everybody, but I've just got to keep going, to be me, to do what I think is right and to hover above the shambolic administration.

At the end of the week, I found out that when we were tussling over the publication of the response to the Newton Committee and our ideas on a new approach on counter-terrorism, John Prescott had been ringing the members of the Domestic Affairs Committee specifically to ask them whether they had signed off the version that I was now putting forward, even though their officers had been in touch and indicated that they had agreed to it – as though the individuals concerned would have done so without meaning to, or even inferring that somehow I had persuaded them wrongly to believe that they could sign off something that they were against. I am going to have to have a real session with John because our relationship has broken down so badly that it is damaging the process and operation of government.

We didn't manage to sit down and do this until early August when frankly, in so many ways, it was too late.

An indication of what was going on was an answerphone message I received late on the Wednesday night when the first editions of the newspapers were out. It said: 'David, I need to warn you that we have had a bit of a drubbing in the papers. At least one or two people have been out briefing against the terrorism stuff, so it is widely reported that Prescott put the mockers on it and that Charlie was involved as well. There are varying degrees of detail but you need to be aware and on top of it . . .'

A very useful warning. My capacity to rise to the bait had not diminished over the years, so staying calm had to be the order of the day. We were at this time also dealing with what became known as Operation Crevice, which was all about a cache of ammonium nitrate that had been discovered in a garage in London. A person phoning the hotline had first triggered concerns about the use of the garage, which demonstrates that the hotline was worth having, but also how vigilance and sometimes coincidence can aid otherwise highly sophisticated operations.

As we saw eighteen months later on 7 July 2005, it is often the least sophisticated and most crude – and therefore the least trackable – terrorist plans that cause the greatest devastation. Their very simplicity makes them difficult to identify, and their crudeness almost impossible to avoid.

It has to be remembered that when carrying out their atrocities the Provisional IRA, while almost always giving some sort of limited warning, also sought to protect their own lives and well-being. Suicide for those intent on murder is a new phenomenon, and one with which traditional security and criminal justice procedures struggle to cope.

All this is incredibly time-consuming, and skilling the necessary people to do the job and to switch from the former Northern Ireland threat continued to be a problem.

A nice piece by Steve Richards in the *Independent* was spoilt only by a throwaway remark at the end that wondered whether I was doing more as Home Secretary than was necessary. In itself it was a fair question, and one that I have asked myself over and over again, but it led to diary pieces in the *Mail* and *Mirror* that started to have a life of their own. There is some truth in the fact that you can be over-exposed, and that the more you do, the more resentment this builds up, not only in senior colleagues but junior colleagues, who were the ones being quoted by Paul Routledge of the *Mirror* and Peter McKay of the *Mail*.

That resentment is clearly very strong at the moment and needs watching, without in the least allowing it to intimidate me. By including it in my diary, I suppose I illustrate the point that I am sensitive to criticism and attack, and I really do need to learn not to be.

One example of how difficult it is to evade taking responsibility even if I wanted to, and I don't, was the Clare Short incident. She was being interviewed on the *Today* programme and suddenly, out of the blue, decided to say that she had seen transcripts of private conversations of Kofi Annan, the Secretary-General of the UN, and that he had clearly been spied on. She had no evidence for this at all and she obviously didn't say anything about it at the time. It has since emerged that there is a website with just about everything that Kofi Annan has done and said, including transcripts of his phone calls that his own office had made available, so I presume she is referring to this.

Even on the Friday, when I did the international seminar with French and German socialists as well as the event with the Met Commission, launching the Special Constables Weekend, I was doorstepped. Everyone else was saying absolutely nothing, but I had discovered on Thursday that I had responsibility for the Official Secrets Act. While Jack Straw is responsible for GCHQ, here I am, unbeknown to me, responsible not for the operation of the Official Secrets Act but for overseeing any legislative changes. I am going to get a grip of it, but it does demonstrate that I cannot escape these issues. How on earth, with accession on Monday, immigration on Tuesday, terrorism on Wednesday, naturalisation and Clare Short on Thursday and Friday, could I have avoided being involved? I suppose I could if I didn't care about the job and just wanted to keep my head down.

I fear that at the moment it feels like a government firing on two cylinders. Half the Cabinet seem afraid to say anything radical, if anything at all. I suppose this is born of insecurity and the fact that if you say very little, you don't get noticed but you still survive. So we have got every libertarian and human-rights body and anti-government body having a go now, again linking it all to Iraq: you name it, and there will be a lawyer trying to do us down, including, over this weekend, lawyers trying to sue the Army for killing civilians in Iraq.

This week I have had to deal with Ken Livingstone playing his old games, telling John Stevens that he had wanted John's salary to go up to the amount he was after, while I didn't. I had agreed with John Gieve that I was prepared to go up to £210,000, plus of course everything else that goes with it, including the massively enhanced pension when he goes. But it is deeply unfortunate because quite understandably it turns John Stevens against me and makes it look as if I am being awkward, whereas what I am trying to do is to get some comparability in order to avoid a knock-on effect whereby all the assistant commissioners and Uncle Tom Cobley and all want to ensure that their differentials are not affected, never mind the police service across the country.

I had an interesting conversation with Harry Woolf, who came in for his usual meeting. Everything was very amicable, particularly on trying to get consistency and sense into sentencing, but when we got on to the issue of asylum, having dealt sensibly with counter-terrorism and my having invited him to make a positive contribution, he made it clear that what is now Clause 11, about stopping constant judicial review, he would fight to the death. This was apparently his bête noire, this was *the* issue, he said, that was paramount. So we are obviously going to have a right battle in the Lords, and

I am going to make some suggestions. Again what's going to happen is that Bev and I are going to be the villains of the piece. Charlie and others are going to point the finger and say that it is we who are pressing for it.

Judicial review is a modern invention. It has been substantially in being from the early 1980s, and although it was designed to prevent administrative abuse – where there was no parliamentary authority and where bureaucrats were exercising undue power – it had rapidly become an entirely new arm of our constitution, operated by judges, through judges and without any redress or accountability to Parliament. In fact, unlike statute law, there is a presumption that this is both outside the remit of Parliament and a check on Parliament. I accept, as all democrats do, that it is the right of the independent judiciary to question the implementation of laws where those laws are not in line with the policy intent or the legislative measures passed by Parliament, but not that the intent and policy objective of Parliament can be overturned as though we have a written constitution, and a Supreme Court as a separate arm of that Constitution, as in the United States – not least because in the United States the Supreme Court is appointed through the presidency and is scrutinised by the legislature. In Britain judicial review is all about the rights of the individual over the rights of society.

I am going to have to be smart about this and see if there is any small amount of give that we can offer that will make a difference. We have got the Asylum Report and Third Reading this Monday, 1 March. I shall do the Third Reading and Bev is doing the early part. It clashes with an international seminar on race and Islam, though the Department hadn't noticed that it clashed, and they had arranged the seminar and the dinner at which I am speaking out at Greenwich. It is just as though Parliament doesn't exist for them.

A couple of footnotes to the week.

On *The Week in Westminster* on Radio 4 on Saturday morning Jonathan Baum, General Secretary of the First Division Association of senior civil servants, had the absolute audacity to say that so often ministers blame civil servants for decisions that they had taken. Bev Hughes will demonstrate on Thursday 4 March that so often ministers cover for civil servants who are utterly useless, incompetent and ineffective. In Bev's case, this was demonstrated by the gross misinformation she had been given to put in a letter to Geraldine Smith, about the particular actions and interventions in relation to the gangmasters and cockle pickers.

This was information which officials later admitted had been fabricated because they had kept no records at all about their enforcement activities.

It is just breathtaking how the civil service and those mouthing platitudes can have the cheek to do so. They call Sir Nigel Wickes 'an insider's insider', and it is the civil service that he is defending, the civil service that he believes in, the civil service that he is protecting – not ministers, not the government.

A year on from the publication of Sir Nigel's report we were feeling the impact, more in the change in attitude and culture than in anything tangible or concrete that you could point to. I felt very strongly at the time about what was happening because, as will be seen, Bev Hughes was dealing with the most difficult and heart-rending issues, and regrettably was let down very badly indeed by the civil service, who not only deliberately failed to provide her with information as to what issues were being raised on sensitive matters (including from fellow ministers who sent memoranda rather than talking in detail direct to Bev) but also in failing to act upon instructions given by her. It is the job of the civil service to provide the progress-chasing and monitoring operation on behalf of ministers, but it became clear to me then, as it still is now, that ministers require their own quite separate progress-chasing and review mechanism based in their Private Office and directly responsible to them, not to line management. This would undoubtedly change the relationship of principal private secretaries to Cabinet ministers and private secretaries to ministers in their offices, because there would be an entirely new and separate role being undertaken, but in my view it is crucial that this should be a key part of the reform agenda. The normal process for servicing busy ministers in high-profile and difficult areas – it is much easier in low-key, low-volume areas – simply does not work.

Thank goodness we weren't prepared, despite Sir Nigel's criticism, to rush into a new Civil Service Act, which would entrench all the existing processes and mechanisms dating back to the Northcote-Trevelyan reforms of a bygone era.

March 2004

Tuesday 2 March saw me speaking at a conference on reassurance for the public on crime and policing, calling together chief constables, police authorities and local government. I made the usual speech, answered questions at the end and followed up with a small press conference, then suddenly arose the issue that had already been floated three times, by Peter Goldsmith at the beginning of the year, by me in a pamphlet last summer and by the Director of Public Prosecutions in January: the suggestion that we needed to rename the Crown Prosecution Service. All hell let loose. Suddenly it was a big story. The 'Crown' was going to be dropped from the prosecution service. The Queen was going to have her head chopped off. The world was going to fall apart around us.

The Speaker, God bless him, granted a Private Notice Question on Wednesday on the grounds that the Tories (in this case in the person of Alan Duncan, the Shadow Attorney General) felt that the world was about to collapse. The night before Alan Duncan had said that this was the most enormous outrage, that the prosecution service should be neutral, just as the judges and jury were neutral, leaving only the defence lawyers who are not neutral. The newspapers railed at the terrible insult to the Queen, at the idea that Her Majesty's prisons would no longer be HM prisons, even though this story had arisen from a *Daily Express* article, followed up by the *Sunday Telegraph*, followed by all those who couldn't be bothered to follow up the story properly and therefore just repeated it from the cuts – in this case, repeating a story that's just a load of garbage. Private prisons are not HM prisons, they don't have the insignia on the staff, and the new National Offender Management Service is a commissioning service: those who are public employees in publicly owned prisons will still have the insignia and the prisons will still be HM prisons. But of course all of this passed everybody by.

Harriet Harman did the Private Notice Question because it was the Shadow Attorney General who had put it down, so I sat on the front bench with her.

Even though we had launched the idea on 7 July 2003, and even though it had been cleared through policy, it never happened. It didn't happen because everyone was so jumpy about the idea of talking about a community justice system. I thought this was a great shame, because the idea that the Crown Prosecution Service is somehow neutral is a nonsense. If it doesn't represent the public, and isn't speaking out for the public (while the defence lawyers defend the rights of the individual), then who is speaking for the public?

Our system quite rightly builds in a whole battery of rights for the defence in questioning, drawing information and demanding all sorts of material from the police service. The current Crown Prosecution Service must therefore surely represent the interests of the victims, the victim's immediate family and, of course, the wider community. We still have not sorted out in this country precisely how we wish to proceed in an adversarial system quite different from that of Roman law as per the European model, where the investigatory process does at least offer some opportunity to get at the truth, rather than get at the technical detail to provide a swingeing blow for the defence to be able to gain an acquittal – even if everyone knows that the defendant is guilty. How many documentaries do we have to make about the rights of the individual and how awful anti-social-behaviour measures are – and how few examples can anyone ever register of coverage by the media of the beleaguered communities speaking out on television or radio?

Sally Morgan asked me simply to be nice to everybody, as there are so many people feeling aggrieved and prickly. Huw Evans joined in and persuaded me to be as nice as I possibly could be at the *Daily Telegraph* lunch to which we were about to go. When I arrived, they said that they were surprised that I was there, as they had seen me on the front bench and thought that I had cancelled. I said: 'Why should I cancel?' They said: 'Well, aren't you aggravated with our coverage and our leaders?' I said: 'Why should I be aggravated? You had a story, you've distorted it, you've picked up something from the *Daily Express* and *Sunday Telegraph*, and you've not checked it. It's just one of those things, that's how it is!' The rest of the lunch was sweetness and light. Martin Newlands, the new editor, was excellent. I thought he was a really thoughtful man who had clearly shifted some of the former editorial board out – not enough, but at least some change.

One of those present tried to question whether there was any threat at all from Al Qaeda to Britain. There is a real difficulty because I can't say to these people, 'If you knew about Operation Crevice, which we are involved in at the moment, you wouldn't be asking stupid questions.' There has been massive exchange of information with other countries, and the disabling of the very large quantities of ammonium nitrate that had been discovered – all of this on Operation Crevice. MI5 are really good at this.

The week saw me in front of the Joint Home Affairs/Defence Select Committee. There was a real effort by both the Defence Select Committee and by the Science and Technology Committee to get in on the act of investigating terrorism, even though the Intelligence and Security Committee had the job of doing this. I managed to dampen down any publicity from it, but I reflect that those in the Cabinet who think that we are constantly seeking publicity and hyping things up ought to try damping down the flames and getting on with the job rather than having to deal with the constant eruption (which Tony calls incendiary) of the Home Office.

It is funny reflecting on this because, as we saw in 2006 – particularly around the local elections and immediately afterwards – no Home Secretary in the present era has to seek publicity. Other colleagues, who resented the public profile and who obviously sincerely believed that it had been contrived, lived in an entirely different environment from that experienced by Jack Straw, myself, Charles Clarke and now John Reid. There were many occasions when I would have given anything to have been able to close down the barrage of questions and the constant media attention and simply get on with the job of improving the delivery. But communication is the lifeblood of modern politics in a way that even twenty-five years ago it was not, and as a consequence there is no choice if you are to survive but to be on top of the issue of the day, while desperately ensuring that you are preparing for the issue of tomorrow.

So the week went on. Following two hours at the Joint Home Affairs/ Defence Select Committee, there was a Big Conversation event, followed by open house for parliamentary-party members on the Newton Committee and terrorism. (Six turned up.) The fact that the Joint Home Affairs/Defence Select Committee didn't get any publicity, or very little, was a success rather than a failure. If I had wanted publicity from Tuesday into Wednesday, I would certainly have done it from that committee hearing.

Thursday there was a public-service productivity meeting at 8 a.m. Tony was then going off to Italy and then back to Sedgefield. John Prescott chaired Cabinet. Meetings are always longer when he chairs, not because we deal with more business but because John has always felt that the longer the Cabinet goes on, the more the outside world will take it seriously. So on this occasion we had to have a long discussion on school playing fields and the role of the Department for Culture, Media and Sport. We then endearingly had a request for Gordon to explain the difference between the CPI and the RPIX when it came to inflation.

The Consumer Price Index, which had been the measure used across Europe for many years, was the new formula in relation to the Bank of England's inflation target of 2 per cent, whereas RPIX was the Retail Price Index adjusted in relation to housing costs.

This arose because of the mix-up over precisely what was being used for the definition of increase in council tax and its comparator to inflation, given that we had decided that it would be inappropriate to use the CPI definition for uprating benefits and the like.

Then I was up north for a variety of meetings, then back down to London again for an interview with Adam Boulton for Sky television's Sunday-morning political programme, and then out to Washington on what was Flight 223 – renumbered but only shifted by five minutes!

In between I had done an interview with Roy Hattersley for the *Observer*. I have to have been mad to agree to it, and it was weird at the end. Huw Evans understood for the first time what I was talking about with regard to Roy's attitude to me arising out of our mutual affection for his mum, but his mum's insensitivity to Roy's feelings about me. I have always regretted the clash between two sons of Sheffield, and above all two avid Sheffield Wednesday supporters (though he is a more assiduous one than I am).

Footnote on the week: Robin Butler (Lord Butler) came with members of his committee to see me. It was a good discussion – very positive about the reality of Resolution 1441 and what everybody believed to be the case, even if they had a different solution. There were some revealing thoughts about the nature of the intelligence services, the filtering of material and the credibility and assessment of it, and therefore the recommendations from the Joint Intelligence Committee and whether this was an appropriate way of dealing with things. There was commentary on the role of the Defence Intelligence Service and its resources, but also its lack of focus. I thought it was an interesting discussion to have taken part in. In the end, it does make this job fascinating. The Home Secretary is at the very centre of events, post-11 September in particular.

The Butler Report was the investigation into the decisions taken on the run-up to the action in Iraq, particularly on the issue of weapons of mass destruction and the presentation of that part of the justification. Had I been aware of the significance that would be placed on the dossiers, we might have been more robust about them at the time but, as I have explained earlier, I wasn't, and we weren't.

Thinking about the discussion with the inquiry group made me realise not only what a challenge the job entails, but also how sometimes the responsibility I carry can be really frightening, and how much that has to be put out of mind if I am to get on with it and take difficult decisions quickly and decisively.

And so to the United States on Sunday 7 March, for talks on combating terrorism. Little did I know as the plane took off that afternoon that the hysteria about what became known as the 'Romanian one-legged roofer' (who in the tabloid press personified the issue of self-employed Romanians coming to the UK on work visas) would take off in the media, and that my absence in the USA may well have contributed to the damage done to my very good friend, Bev Hughes, the Immigration Minister, who quite wrongly took the rap for the complete failure of the management in Immigration and Nationality to do their job.

What I hadn't realised until the following day, Monday, was that the Sunday Times *story, given to them by a deeply disaffected, politically motivated employee on a short-term contract in the immigration service in Sheffield and about to be sacked for incompetence, would result in a major row about how such visas were handled from Romania and Bulgaria (associate countries awaiting accession to the EU), and would reveal much deeper problems concerning the decisions taken by middle management without reference to ministers and the failure to follow up ministers' enquiries. The Romania/Bulgaria concession had been agreed long before the negotiations on accession, by Michael Howard back in 1994, but of course none of that was relevant. The relevance was that here was a scheme that fast-tracked people, and there was an accusation that this was to reduce the headline number of people coming in after 1 May.*

This was proved, following the inquiry, to be nonsensical allegation, but it formed the main thrust of the Sunday Times *story that kicked off the controversy. Some wag in the statistical division of the Home Office had inadvertently indicated that the figure for the new accession countries (ten countries, including Malta and Cyprus, where open access had already been the practice for many years) would be around 13,000.*

No minister ever used such a figure, or gave any speculative statistic on how many people would come from the accession countries, but as with the famous misquoting of Jim Callaghan back in the winter of 1978–9 – 'Crisis? What crisis?' – once a myth has got its boots on there is no chance that the truth will ever catch it up. So there we were with allegations about trying to fiddle figures, when no one had given figures. Ministers had not been involved at all in the decision-taking but the impact was, of course, on ministers, while the officials involved simply moved on to pastures new.

No minister knew anything about it, nor did the Head of IND, nor did the people immediately managing the people who had made the decision. But this man, Steve Moxon, had emailed Bev's office and Bev's office had done nothing with the emails, had neither drawn them to Bev's attention nor sought advice on them. So it is a terrible mess. As concerns had been raised previously, Bev Hughes had initiated a request for details.

As enquiries later proved, the report from officials was entirely misleading, presenting the issue as a technical matter of legal interpretation only. The further report she requested had never been acted on by the senior civil servant in IND responsible for this area, and without any progress-chasing facility it is not surprising that her own Private Office, overwhelmed as they were with ministerial correspondence and the detailed work plan that Bev Hughes had set out in chairing the new Immigration Board, simply failed to pick up the significance of the emails complaining about what was happening.

This begs the question as to why on earth a minister should have to deal with a complaint of this sort rather than management having simple and easy systems of access to those with a genuine complaint or grievance, or for that matter with a genuine concern. We addressed this immediately by providing people with a hotline, but it was too late by then.

And there was I in the United States, and Bev gets a Private Notice Question. I had phoned her on the way to the airport and said that I thought that she would get a Private Notice Question and she should be prepared for it. But that's what the Tories requested, and the Speaker granted it and all hell broke loose. The Tories have called for her resignation and it is just a terrible mess. This follows on from what happened with the cockle pickers in Morecambe Bay, and Bev had done an adjournment debate last Thursday on that. I had warned the Board that we weren't having any more of this. I suppose I am really very upset because had I not been in America I would have been able to deal with it.

I think now that this was wishful thinking on my part. The state of play with the audit trail as to what had happened, and the lack of focus and grip by very senior management, would have been no better for me than it was for Bev. My only regret is that at least I would have been taking the heat rather than her, which would have certainly helped in the three weeks ahead.

The then Head of the Immigration and Nationality Directorate took no steps at all on the Monday and in fact I had to ring from Washington on Monday afternoon to get the Permanent Secretary out of a meeting and ask that he concentrate all his time and resources on getting the facts and finding out what needed now to be done.

To this day I don't know why my instincts were so strong from 3,000 miles away, although on reflection I do admit to an element of schizophrenia. One moment I was of the opinion that this was not a serious long-term issue and was perfectly manageable, then the next moment I would become uneasy and call senior officials, telling them to pull their finger out because they were not treating the matter seriously enough, and that the laid-back approach that the Department was taking to this story was a grave mistake.

So on Monday evening UK time I was on the phone first to Bev, who told me what the situation was, and then to John Gieve to get decisive steps taken to help her. I was on the telephone to them both between the meeting with the Attorney General's office – John Ashcroft had been taken seriously ill and rushed into Intensive Care with complications to gall-stones – and during the journey to Reagan airport to fly to Boston. I was talking to Bev and talking to John Gieve and was cut off while talking to John as I walked through security because we were late for the plane. I was getting the message across that I thought that immediate action should have been taken, but it was Sod's Law that in the middle of all this the mobile phone should go dead. I was back on the phone as soon as we landed in Boston, where I was giving lectures at Harvard University (in Cambridge, Massachusetts), and although it was too late to do anything decisive, I did indicate that we would have to have an immediate review, and as part of that we needed to know who had done what, and when. While all this was going on, the Special Immigration Appeals Commission were ruling on the thirteen terrorists whom I had certificated and who had appealed. We won twelve out of the thirteen, including Abu Qatada, and had to go to the Appeal Court on the thirteenth case to gain the right to appeal, as Judge Andrew Collins turned down the right to appeal his own judgement.

Having arrived in Boston in a snowstorm, I discovered that the room that had been allocated to me in Cambridge had a lounge and a small bedroom, but the first thing that struck me was how claustrophobic it was. So I asked a simple question: 'Where are the windows in this bedroom?'

The answer: 'There are none.' I was flabbergasted. I said: 'The fact that I cannot see doesn't mean that I don't like the idea of openness, of light and of having a window. I would rather have one decent bedroom – and a window, preferably one that I can open – than two small rooms described as "a suite".' I was moved within the half-hour to a comfortable small bedroom that suited me very well indeed.

The visit to Harvard went well. My lecture on terrorism wasn't one of my best but was received warmly, and my lecture on civil renewal and community went down a storm. I abandoned my notes and just talked, and I am always better when I do this. It is all about confidence: knowing the information, having the structure in your head, and having done the preparation through detailed notes but not really needing them. The interaction with the audience is always better and the resulting improvement in presentation worth its weight in gold. At the supper afterwards, the Dean of the Kennedy School of Government offered me a visiting professorship – spoilt only by the fact that he then told me that he had only three months left in the job.

Perhaps I should have taken up the offer on the spot!

We flew back on Wednesday morning, and as ever I worked the whole of the journey, as I had done on the previous Sunday flying out to Washington. There had been in one Sunday newspaper on 7 March an interesting memorandum from the Private Secretary of one of my Cabinet colleagues about how other people operated when out of the country. We are all different, but if I worked in that way I would get nothing done. I'm afraid it's a sixteen-hour day wherever you are.

Reflecting on the visit to America, I feel that our discussions with John Gordon, President Bush's security adviser, were helpful and successful, not in getting them to change their minds about Guantanamo Bay and a just and proper process, but more on issues relating to the process of handling joint security measures and the joint group of officials that we had agreed to establish so that we avoid the difficulties we have had over the past few months.

I also think we were successful with the issues we raised with John Ashcroft's people, including making contact with the Head of the Narcotics Unit, a very able woman. The trip to Boston was fascinating, particularly the Grove Hall Community and what they were doing between the police, the various services and the community, which we had visited as part of the arranged look at what Harvard University were doing in their outreach. This is something that I think some of our universities could mirror a lot more successfully, not merely researching but getting stuck in and getting their hands soiled.

And then we came back to the bombing in Madrid. On the Thursday morning, I couldn't initially make contact with my cousin Pauline and her husband Minolo, who live in Madrid, but eventually I did manage to reach them and thank God they and their family were safe.

Our spring conference in Manchester was now dominated wholly by what had happened in Spain, and as Home Secretary that atrocity was central to everything that I was trying to do. So I abandoned much of the speech I was going to make, made a few notes instead, and prepared to speak. Every speaker spoke about the tragedy and our regret. I had a television crew doing a BBC2 short documentary about myself, which in the circumstances seemed a complete irrelevance, and I couldn't concentrate on the questions, never mind on how I looked or how it was going to come across. What had happened in Madrid was what I feared most might happen in Britain. This is what I lived with, not only day in, day out, but during the night and at weekends. Would it happen while I was Home Secretary? I hadn't prepared the phrase 'the tentacles of terror across the world', but I just found myself saying it, and it was that that reached the main news bulletins, plus my comment on having tried to reach my cousin and her family in Madrid. There was also the comment of Lib Dem Foreign Affairs Spokesman Menzies Campbell that being tough on human rights didn't mean that you were soft on terror. I said: 'Let's turn it round – being tough on terror doesn't mean that you are soft when it comes to human rights.' The whole issue dominated the conference.

Tony made a very good speech on Saturday morning, perhaps a little too long, with perhaps a bit too much about education (although I wouldn't have thought so when I was Education Secretary). He underlined the issues surrounding terror and immigration and mentioned ID cards, which was pretty crucial given the appalling letters I have received back to my request for Domestic Affairs Cabinet clearance for the draft ID Bill. How long is this going to go on? John Prescott was dispatched to stand in the rain on behalf of Tony for the mass procession in Madrid, the outpouring by the Spanish people – but outpouring for what? Against the terrorists, and the hurt and distress of the bereaved, or for Spain to be spared? But how do I persuade Cabinet colleagues that what we are doing is protecting us from what happened in Spain, and the sooner that Tony decides that he wants people in the Cabinet who will back him, who are tough and who are going to reach out and reflect the interests of the British people, who understand the nature of terrorism, the international movement of people, and the damage to our services, the better.

Unless they get the message on immigration, we've all had it, as I'm seeing from the terrible time that Bev Hughes has had because of the *Sunday Times* story, the total dysfunctionality of the Immigration and Nationality Directorate, the inability of the management not just to have a grip of but even to know what is going on, and not even to have systems and processes that allow senior management to know which middle manager should know what's going on and to be able to contact them. I sent a memo to this effect on Monday 15 March. So the middle managers don't appear to have a clue what's happening under them, the senior management don't know which middle manager to contact to find out, and if they did, the middle managers wouldn't know in any case.

I am afraid this was reflected in May 2006, when John Reid took over as Home Secretary: he had the most enormous difficulty getting the most basic facts out of his officials. My regret is that I didn't do more, that I didn't press harder, that I didn't insist that the rules were changed in relation to the role of the Secretary of State vis-à-vis the management with regard to appointments, and with regard to transfer or promotion. But of course I could only do what was possible at the time, and what was possible was certainly not a mass upheaval in the Home Office by changing civil-service rules, civil-service practice and the way in which the oversight of the Civil Service Commission constrained rather than liberated government to reform the system.

Bev continues to have a terrible time and it is a co-ordinated attack. The Tory Party have a strategy of trying to pull a minister down, and having got rid of Estelle Morris and Steve Byers they are now absolutely determined to get rid of Bev – and I am absolutely determined that they shouldn't.

I believe I did everything I could. I have looked back and wondered if there was anything more that I could have done but I am convinced that there wasn't. I just remember this particular time with great sadness.

One footnote on the spring conference: Gordon's speech was powerful as ever, but it was an echo of Margaret Thatcher's St Francis of Assisi speech on 4 May 1979, and I just wondered whether his advisers, unusually for them, had advised him badly. The St Francis rerun was probably not appropriate for this moment.

On Sunday 14 March I spoke to Michael Barber, now Head of the Delivery Unit at No. 10, but who formerly ran the Standards Unit and was reverting to his former role in respect of standards in education. He was worried that from 2001 onwards the massive improvement that had been achieved over the previous three years had plateaued out. He told me that he had spoken at a conference of 1,000 heads who were each acting as mentors to at least three other heads in lifting the primary literacy and numeracy results. Michael discovered that they were working on this Excellence and Enjoyment Strategy (that was the title of a document that had been published shortly before by the DfES), and said that there was silence at the end of his speech because he told them that the whole strategy was now off beam and that it had lost its way. I told him that I had seen it vividly on Friday morning, before I went to Manchester, when I visited two schools in my constituency, Southey Green and Hartley Brook. We were back to happy clappy, to children singing, to learning mentors doing problem-solving and questions such as, 'What would you do if someone was touching your hair from behind you?' Not once did they mention literacy or numeracy. Nobody offered to show me youngsters reading.

Of course I never objected to education being fun. The whole point of the literacy and numeracy strategy was to allow youngsters who were completely turned off education to open a window on the world, and to access those things that others took for granted.

But it was the 'reversion' to what we had inherited that worried me. In 2006 the government re-emphasised the importance of the literacy programme and in particular what has become known as 'synthetic' phonics – although there were those commenting at the time that this was something new. In fact synthetic phonics had formed part of the phonics programme from the beginning, but because the early experiments had been with such a limited number of pupils this was part of the literacy hour, rather than the main emphasis running throughout it. It does, however, demonstrate once again that if you take your foot off the accelerator, then the car slows to its normal pace.

I have to laugh sometimes. I was supposed to be cutting a ribbon for the Space for Sports and the Arts building at Southey Green School, which cost

£600,000 and is an excellent facility – and they didn't have any scissors for me to cut the ribbon! So somebody had to rush off and find some scissors which were, for obvious reasons in a school environment, blunt and safe for children to use to cut paper into shapes, and I couldn't cut the ribbon. I was absolutely determined to cut through it, as I didn't know that the scissors were from a classroom for infant children. So I made the most supreme effort to cut the ribbon and eventually managed it, but just about dislocated my fingers in doing so. I could hardly move my middle finger, which swelled up at the knuckle. I do sometimes wonder what on earth I am doing.

The main political issue of the moment was the Second Reading and subsequent stages of the latest Immigration and Asylum Bill going through the Lords. One of the key elements was to cut down the multiple-appeals process and constant judicial review of every step taken, which constituted the existing law. This had bedevilled all our efforts to step up removals from the country and to prevent people using the legal system as a barrier to carrying out properly made and fair decisions, including those who had completed the existing appeals process but were using appeals to the courts as a method of prolonging, over and over again, their stay in the country. The Department for Constitutional Affairs had the lead on this as it was dealing with the judiciary, but we were the ones who had to answer publicly, so there was an internal friction with resistance from the judiciary to more radical change, and (it has to be said) a lack of clarity from my own officials about what would work. It was only by engaging directly and privately with the Chief Adjudicator that I was able to work through and then engage with Charlie Falconer on finding a formula that was acceptable to everybody – except the then Head of the Appeal Tribunal!

Then came the shock of the Socialists winning the election in Spain and the Popular Party, which had been odds-on to win, ending up as losers. I have to say that I hadn't seen this coming, and despite my connections with Spain I hadn't got a clue that the people felt not only that they wanted a change but wanted it in a dramatic fashion. The question of what implications this result has for us concerning our drive against the terrorists – and the likelihood of an attack in Britain – can only be answered in the months and years to come.

By Wednesday afternoon I had made contact with the nominated Interior Minister of the new Spanish government. (It was going to take a long time before confirmation.) I fixed to meet both him and, when nominated, the new Justice Minister when I am in Madrid at the beginning of April for a family wedding.

Had a very good meeting with Gordon on the Thursday [11 March]. He told me that Charles had agreed to settle in advance of the Spending Review, through to 2008, for the education budget. In one sense this makes it easier for me, because the Home Office budget becomes the focal point and therefore getting a decent financial agreement becomes more rather than less likely. Health have already got the budget through to 2008 so the two big spending ministries are really not in the debate any more.

At the Special Cabinet on the Wednesday morning prior to the Budget, I raised the issue of letting people spend money that they had been able to save or at least a substantial portion of it. It didn't go down too well but for the Home Office this is really important, because not only have we got the £100 million plus from the introduction of charges for visa renewals, but also the money for the criminal justice system from fixed-penalty notices (on-the-spot fines) and the revenue from the automatic number-plate-recognition scheme – and therefore the enormous improvement in catching those motorists without tax discs, etc.

We would return to this when I was Secretary of State for Work and Pensions, and I was very pleased to see that John Hutton, who took over from me as Secretary of State in November 2005, was able to make real progress in teeming and ladling on both pensions and welfare reform about money saved or generated in one area being applied to another. After over nine years of government this was a real breakthrough, but is another example of how long it takes to put the bricks in the wall and get anywhere near the coping stone!

I then went and did the Parliamentary Labour Party on Home Office affairs. The session was very badly attended, which Jean Corston, chair of the meeting, interpreted as showing that people are quite satisfied with what's going on in our area.

Well, it was an optimistic way of looking at it, but I think people's minds were elsewhere.

I had what I thought were going to be friendly words with John Prescott about the PLP meeting but, as so often these days, they turned out to be anything but. He was aggrieved by the 'summit' of spending ministers that was being held by Tony at Chequers on the Thursday afternoon and evening.

I checked with Downing Street and advised that if John hadn't been invited, it might be prudent to rectify that – which they did. In the event, I didn't get there. After Chequers I had been due to fly from Northolt to Brussels late that night to attend a specially called meeting of the Justice and Home Affairs Council of the European Union in the aftermath of the Madrid attack, before then flying to Newcastle to pick up the remains of the ministerial and Board visit to the north-east of England, which had been arranged for months. However, by Thursday lunchtime I was laid up in bed. I think it is only the second time in a decade when I've had to drop out of something because of illness but I had to make a snap decision as to whether I should try and get myself in a fit state to fly to Brussels and be available at the crack of dawn on Friday morning, or risk being so ill that having gone to the Chequers meeting, I would not make the meeting in Brussels. With all eyes on what was happening with counter-terrorism and what we were going to do, it seemed to me that I had very little choice but to try and pull myself round. With Tony's agreement therefore I abandoned going to Chequers.

I felt like death warmed up by the time I reached the embassy in Brussels to stay overnight. I went straight to my room, whereas my Principal Private Secretary had to sit with the Ambassador John Grant, when he came back from a meeting, through a long four-course supper (with no wine), with our Europe ambassador confessing that he never knew what was going to be on the menu from one day to the next. I don't know what had struck me down, but whatever it was I still had in spades on Friday morning so I wasn't sorry that a planned breakfast meeting with Nicolas Sarkozy was cancelled because he was flying in on the Friday morning rather than coming the night before. To make matters worse, the alarm went off at five a.m. and I couldn't find it to switch it off. I just managed to get through the television and radio interviews as I went into the building, but no one wants to hear that you feel awful and no one wants to see a politician who looks awful. The meeting itself droned on, but we did make some progress in pushing countries to agree to measures they had already agreed to but failed to implement, and some progress on getting across the seriousness of what was now a European issue and not something that other countries could believe would never happen to them. It was particularly strange to have there the outgoing ministers from the previous Spanish government. They didn't really have an answer about why they had so quickly attempted to blame ETA for the Madrid bombings, but we presume that it was to avoid the link with the stance and support given by the Popular Party to the war in Iraq.

The following Monday I had a bit of a spat with John Stevens. I hadn't intended to be robust, but he and Ken Livingstone had held a high-profile press conference about the Madrid bombing that frankly was likely to scare Londoners rather than gain their confidence and provide them with reassurance. I wondered after the meeting with him whether I had gone too far in saying, 'We've got enough problems with franchised terrorism [the Al Qaeda network] without franchised anti-terrorism.' To be fair, John Stevens and David Veness, Head of SO13 in the Met, had been doing a really good job.

I then went off to an evening that, had I not been so busy, would have been really interesting: the Pride of Britain Awards sponsored by the *Mirror.* This gave me a chance to thank a range of individuals, some never heard of, who have done such a good job throughout life or within their own community, or both. One was the developer of modern DNA fingerprinting from Leicester University, who has helped to transform what we can do with forensics, and there were those overcoming the most horrendous disability, who never cease to amaze me. At my table was Greg Rusedski and his wife, both of whom I liked very much, but I am afraid I still didn't get on with Chris Tarrant, with whom I had fallen out all those years ago when I was wrongly quoted on *Who Wants To Be A Millionaire?* It is funny how people don't bury the hatchet. On the whole, though, I fear that I should have used the evening for something more productive.

There were lots of bits and bobs for the rest of the week, such as giving an award to the Chief Rabbi, Jonathan Sacks, and a doctorate for all his work. I enjoy the evenings with the Jewish community. They are always so warm and supportive.

Lib Dem leader Charles Kennedy didn't turn up for the Budget Speech and people drew all sorts of conclusions. I suspect that he had on this occasion whatever it was that I had caught, because the symptoms described sounded exactly the same, but no doubt with the Liberal Democrat Party there will be an inquest.

I've had another major problem with the leaks to the *Sunday Times.*

It was now clear that more than one person inside the system – and with access to the most confidential material, including the exchange of Cabinet members' letters – was selling material to the Sunday Times.

So there was another round of accusation and counter-accusation over who has leaked what, and for what purpose. Not surprisingly, given the sensitivity of the material, the *Sunday Times* chose to use their leaks on ID cards and cleverly – presuming they have had the material for a day or two – have linked it to their own polling evidence. The fact that they had done a survey on ID cards and 86 per cent were with me doesn't help a bit, as the *Sunday Times* made it look as if we had colluded with them – that they had done a survey, I had given them the letters of opposition, and they had presented it as if I was right and the other people were wrong.

Once again it was the same round of Cabinet objections because the newspaper was not going to print those who were in favour or a list of those who had no objections and had not therefore written. But you can't blame anyone who doesn't understand what is going on or is already deeply opposed to me from drawing entirely the wrong conclusions – which, of course, is presumably what is intended. The more dissent, the more division, the more we fall out, the more there is a story.

By the time the truth was revealed about these leaks the incidents were forgotten, but the resentment had become part of the ether. John Prescott in particular never forgot and, so far as I am aware, never fully accepted that this wasn't some great conspiracy.

Home Office Questions went well on the Monday, which was very good for Bev because she was able to rally the troops without the Opposition scoring heavily. I came out quite relieved. But the issue of the Romanian migrants was not going away, and the more we delved into it the more we found out, and the more that was leaked to the press the more the pressure was building.

There was a sense of déjà vu in April and May 2006 when the same failure to be able to ascertain the facts, the same inability to brief ministers accurately and the same drip, drip, drip of sometimes little but sometimes bigger stories kept the wound festering. In 2004 the issue regained its rightful place as an irritant once the press had gained a scalp, but not so in 2006, where the full realisation of just how much can go wrong hit those who had not been taking that much interest in what operating in the Home Office entailed.

The following Wednesday I spent a great deal of the day on Ken Sutton's internal review of what had happened in relation to Romania and Bulgaria. Ken Sutton is a highly respected official who had knowledge of immigration but was working in the Prison Service. His job with the review was to try to ascertain the facts and precisely who had made decisions, where and when. The frustration for me was the fact that while we could bottom the issue of mis-communication, misunderstanding and downright inertia, Ken Sutton was not getting to the nitty-gritty of which officials were prepared to take accountability seriously, and in particular identify those who had failed to carry out Bev Hughes's specific instructions. A statement had been drawn up and a press release from it, but there were different figures in the press release from those in the statement, and different and contradictory facts within the statement in one part compared with another. It was clear that there was going to have to be some considerable work done on this before it was in a fit state to put out. When dealing with the actual numbers who had been granted self-employed visas we were all over the place. So in one place it said 5,000 when previously they had used 7,000, and then it used 7,000 but gave a different figure, 26,000, rather than the 35,000 that they had given earlier as the aggregate total. It wasn't clear therefore whether it was 5,000 or 7,000 out of 35,000 or out of 26,000!

I had a lot of sympathy with John Reid in May 2006 when he was having exactly the same problems.

In the end I just lost my temper. I said to the Permanent Secretary: 'This is a dysfunctional department. It is impossible to operate when I can't get even basic facts and people seem unable to add up.' It is just so frustrating. In any case, we are publishing the report on Thursday of next week, along with the statement and press release. I've said to Bev that I will do whatever she wants me to, and she's said that she wants to go up front so that she can settle it herself rather than being seen to be second-guessed or protected by me. I've told her that the minute she wants me to get up and do something, she should let me know. I also made it clear to Rebekah Wade on Wednesday night at dinner that Bev Hughes is an excellent minister and is doing a really professional job.

And so to Chepstow for a Labour Party fundraising dinner and then back to the constituency for Big Conversation events, canvassing and a moment out for a celebratory dinner for Alastair's birthday – and also a quick visit to the hospital to see my surgeon and an update (more tablets to take, I'm afraid).

The week beginning Monday 29 March – and what a week: to draw on Tolkien's *Lord of the Rings*, I just felt as though the orcs were gathering, that the press pack were running like hounds, and that they had decided that, whatever happened, a scalp was going to be theirs. As events unfolded, I could feel in the atmosphere the pending crisis. Something was going to have to give.

On Monday I got down to London extremely early for the launch of the Inter-Faith Group Working Party Report, which got virtually no publicity apart from a couple of the papers mentioning it in passing. It is tragic, given that faith activity, particularly drawing in the Muslim community, is so important. The Statement on Serious and Organised Crime went well, and there was a general welcome even from those backbenchers who normally attack me – and I certainly read it better than I have some others recently.

We had known that Shadow Home Secretary David Davis had had an email from a diplomat in Bucharest, but nobody had followed it through, and I am kicking myself now because the minute I heard about it I should have cottoned on. But God help me, nobody else did either. They could have fed the diplomat's name into the system and found out whether he had been in correspondence, with whom, and what sort of things he had been griping about, and it would have turned up material sent over two years to Sheffield (the Home Office facility dealing with Romania). It would have also helped if the ambassador in Bucharest had indicated what sort of gripes the individual had been involved in. If this paper trail, or email trail, had even been touched on, we would have been prepared, and instead this low-level diplomatic individual, under investigation for other matters, caused havoc.

So it was that we were ill prepared when David Davis stood up at the end of the Statement on Serious and Organised Crime and announced that he had received a series of complaints from what he described as a senior diplomat in Bucharest. Initially David Davis raised with the Speaker the fact that he believed that this particular diplomat – James Cameron – was being wrongly persecuted, the individual having been suspended following the emails that he had been sending all over the place.

In fact Bev and I had had a note from officials on 8 March, informing us that this entry clearance officer, James Cameron, had been suspended after having admitted sending an email to David Davis, the contents of which were unknown. As we were later to learn, Home Office officials in Sheffield knew all about James Cameron and his allegations, but no one took the opportunity to tell us what they knew. Had they done so then – on 8 March – we would have discovered the entire history of this issue and would have been in a position to give an accurate and full reply to David Davis's charges.

David Davis then went up to the press gallery and released full details of the email and the material that had been passed to him, with the accusations of forged documents, and of people ignoring indications from Bucharest that people were being fraudulently fast-tracked.

All hell broke loose, and what happened afterwards was the result of another mistake, when Huw Evans and I agreed that Bev should do some interviews because David Davis was out across the whole broadcast media. It was a logical thing to do and No. 10 was pressing Bev to rebut the charges, but in the circumstances devastating, because on the back of the failure to be able to give Bev proper chapter and verse, doing interviews at all was dangerous, especially so after the four weeks that she had had with this issue and the pressure from the media.

Before she did the interviews, the briefing given to Bev was that the Home Office was unaware of James Cameron's allegations, and this was the information she repeated to the media. As with the previous advice about the cockle pickers, that was later shown to be completely untrue. Indeed, the Home Office officials had been receiving numerous emails from the same James Cameron, with the same allegations, since at least April 2002, before Bev became Immigration Minister. They had not disclosed these allegations to Bev, to her predecessor or to me.

In the Newsnight *interview Bev denied that she had had any knowledge of the problem with fraudulent claims from Romania until David Davis had brought the matter up in the House earlier that evening – which turned out to be mistaken.*

The convention has always been that if you lie to the House of Commons you are in deep trouble. Bev made her statements not to the House but to the media, and repeated in good faith the advice she had been given. Everything these days is on the record and therefore undertaking broadcast interviews late at night and not being in full possession of every fact and nuance is something I certainly would counsel even experienced ministers against undertaking. It is, however, a moot point as to whether taking a massive hit and riding it until you are sure of the detail is the best approach: Charles Clarke tried that in April 2006, but to no avail.

On the Monday morning prior to all this blowing up, I had undertaken an interview on the *Today* programme and given absolute support to Bev. I did again later in the week. Bev wanted to be seen to be tough and to handle this herself, so apart from giving 100 per cent support there was nothing more I could do, and I certainly could not have done any better.

So again on the *Today* programme on Tuesday morning I was doing what I could to handle the plethora of accusations made by James Cameron, about whom much was to emerge later but little was known at the time.

I have wondered since whether the fact that I was so robustly determined that Bev shouldn't resign made matters worse for her rather than better. Did it make some branches of the media even more determined that she was to go?

Following the *Newsnight* interview Bob Ainsworth [a junior minister in the Home Office, dealing with serious and organised crime] approached Bev and told her that he remembered writing to her in March 2003, following a meeting in Bucharest expressing concerns from entry clearance officials about the way the Home Office was handling visa applications. He told her this with the best intent because he thought that the letter might emerge. Bev hadn't remembered it when she was doing the interviews, but she did remember it when Bob reminded her. During Tuesday she and I were both occupied in preparing for the Supply Day debate, as the Tories had used one of their allocated days in order to put us on the rack in relation to a whole range of issues. For most of the morning I was chairing the National Criminal Justice Board, and then preparing my speech in response to David Davis. It became very clear in getting into further detail that Bev had asked for a report following Bob Ainsworth's letter. We retrieved this report, which presented the concerns expressed by entry clearance officials not as the allegations of fraud and trafficking but as a technical issue of different legal interpretations of the Accession Agreement by Home Office and Foreign Office officials. It was a side and a half of A4 paper, and simply advised Bev that a definitive legal opinion would be sought and this would be followed through. At the time this advice was given to Bev, Home Office officials had been receiving graphic, detailed emails from James Cameron with cases of people given visas which Cameron was alleging demonstrated fraud. None of this was revealed to ministers, and the fact that officials did not do so when two specific opportunities arose – in March 2003 when Bob Ainsworth wrote and in March 2004 when Cameron was suspended – can only be extreme incompetence or deliberate failure to reveal the full extent of their knowledge.

I wished then, and I wish now, that I had established a progress-chasing unit, accountable solely to ministers, for items that were raised with ministers or where ministers had asked for specific issues to be pursued. There are no such units in the civil service, although I endeavoured to create one when at the Department for Work and Pensions: I was awaiting the new incoming Permanent Secretary before putting it in place, and the matter was then overtaken by my resignation on 2 November 2005.

Given that Home Office ministers were dealing each year with some 5,000 letters passed on by MPs and were responsible for more correspondence than other full Departments of State, with the sole exception of Health, it is not surprising that having dealt with a letter and given instructions on what to do with the issues raised, the minister would then presume that the matter was being handled by management. It is also true that ministers of state and parliamentary under-secretaries are probably under-supported with regard to the number, experience and grading of their civil servants, which have certainly dropped over the last few decades.

Changes to the operation of the Private Office, as well as the potential for creating a non-departmental public body (instead of IND simply being a directorate with everything ending up on ministers' desks), would have been changes that with hindsight would have made a difference. However, there was resistance to any such radical change and, given the enormity of the task at the time, it is not surprising that we did not have the facility or the time and space to take on yet another battle for civil-service reform without support from across government. I was lucky, however, because I built a Private Office team who really did care and supported me.

Bev herself was doing what the civil service should have done. She had started the process of going through the back material and the papers – which, given the total incompetence and failure to have any what I used to call 'collective memory', proper filing and recall systems, was very difficult.

On Tuesday night I abandoned my dinner at the New Zealand embassy for the Foreign and Justice Minister and instead, as it was Bev's birthday, had dinner with her and her husband Tom. By then she had realised that there was a real problem, and said that she was going to go through it all the following day, which she did.

On Wednesday afternoon she met me and told me that she had found the letter from Bob Ainsworth: in response to this she had commissioned a report, which had been produced by an IND official. Three times Bev and I had desperately asked Bill Jeffrey, Head of the Immigration and Nationality

Directorate, to find this official a job more suited to his abilities. Eventually they gave him enhanced early retirement after temporarily moving him into another post, but he was the one who produced what was a misleading response to Bob's letter. Bev had told them to act on the report and they did absolutely nothing. There was no progress-chasing facility at all and all the people who were responsible for this, all those who did absolutely nothing, are all still in their jobs and by Thursday morning Bev Hughes wasn't.

On Wednesday, she told me that she felt she had been placed in an impossible position, but there was no possibility of being able to explain the failure of officials to provide ministers with the truth, and therefore she couldn't continue, as her integrity would not allow her to do so. I tried to dissuade her, against my own integrity in the sense that it was compromising me and my standards, but I knew she had done nothing wrong. Bev decided that all that Home Office officials had known would come out eventually so it was better to present it, and we went to see Tony in his office in the Commons. Bev presented her position and handed over the transcripts of the interviews, indicating to Tony that she thought in order to preserve her own integrity she should step down. She had unwittingly given a false impression, and in doing so she believed that she had damaged the government and that it was therefore better that she should go. Then I said my piece, to the effect that I thought she should stay. Tony looked at the transcripts and said that we should all think about it overnight.

April 2004

Bev then went to see him on the following morning, Thursday [1 April], and told him that she thought she should step down, and Tony agreed. They both felt that it would be better for her and better for the government. I was mortified. The interview was a mistake, but not the way she had handled the actual issue. There was nothing more to be said. We had all done everything we could, firstly to get to the truth, secondly to get management to do something, and thirdly to support and protect a minister who had done a phenomenal job in endeavouring to turn round a directorate that had already pretty well finished the careers of several ministers. I was particularly sad, not just because Bev has been a good friend of mine over many years, but because her work on counter-terrorism, on ID cards, and on citizenship and civil renewal would not be remembered. What would be remembered would be the wretched immigration service, and for my part I had to remember that she would have been in a much easier job with a much more rosy future if I hadn't persuaded Tony that she was the right person to carry on trying to sort out the mess in IND, without the management levers to do so.

So Bev decided to do a Statement to the House that afternoon, and I postponed my flight to Madrid and went into the House to listen. I could have wept. It was all right for me: I was flying off for a weekend in Spain to attend my cousin's wedding, and to meet the incoming ministers of the new Spanish government. Bev was going home with Tom, understandably deeply hurt. Is there anywhere else in the world where a minister would have lost his or her job not because of their own policy decision, not because of incompetence, but because of the failure of others?

I had been up from 5.30 a.m. that Thursday trying to help with what would be said, how it would be said, and what support we could give. I was lucky that I was able to get a seat on a later flight because I would certainly have been in considerable personal difficulties had I not been able to. But it is a period that I shall never forget.

Des Browne entered the Home Office as Immigration Minister that afternoon.

He was later to become Chief Secretary to the Treasury and then Secretary of State for Defence.

We set about immediately planning what he would do while I was away over the weekend. Some of the newspapers that Friday and at the weekend hinted that Bev Hughes had been too 'robust' with the immigration service, and as a consequence the service had felt less loyalty towards her and had been unwilling to take responsibility. Well, she certainly had been robust and had every cause to be, and I had given her every support in being so.

The same thing was pretty much said about me in December of that year: too tough with the civil service, too intolerant of failure. Well, history will be the judge of that. But it is good to reflect that Bev deservedly came back into government as Children's Minister following the 2005 general election. She was one of the most talented ministers I ever worked with.

That weekend there was a bomb on the high-speed line between Madrid and Seville. It was strange to be out there experiencing it – people's real fear, the coverage on Spanish television and radio, and the reaction of my own family out there. It was, in fact, a triumph for the Spanish security services as they genuinely prevented another major catastrophe, but it did bring home very strongly to me that we were dealing with the most dangerous and unscrupulous people, and that the tough stance that we were taking, despite the constant griping and criticism, was entirely right.

Things had been so bad that I couldn't even take pleasure on the Tuesday from winning the argument on going ahead with ID cards – another stage in the almost perennial battle: bit by bit, agreement being reached; bit by bit, taking a step forwards towards legislation in the autumn.

This was a seminal moment. Looking back on it, the agreement to go ahead with preparing for the legislation and my ability to get it into the Queen's Speech in the autumn, and therefore to be able to shape a policy that I had spent years arguing for, has to be a milestone in my political life. Given the continuing and growing media and political interest in clandestine entry, presence and working in this country, the link between the biometric passport, the ID card and the electronic border control and surveillance, all of which I had put in place, may well in years to come be seen as something slightly more than an argument about the effectiveness of government in introducing technology – which at times the debate was reduced to.

John Prescott chaired the meeting extraordinarily well, amazingly so given the battles he and I had had and the personal animosity that had grown up between us, but it is simply a fact. Tony and Tony's staff had done their work, and despite continuing substantial resistance from a handful of colleagues, the heavyweights joined in on the side of ID cards. John Reid said that it was time to stop asking those in favour of something to compromise and for those who were against to either put up or shut up. Charles Clarke joined in positively, as did Tessa Jowell. The battle inside government had been won, but the battle for hearts and minds outside was going to be a continuing war of attrition.

Meanwhile Bev had gone to stay with Hazel Blears and then with her mum, because our media were camped outside her house, phoning incessantly and constantly encroaching on her privacy and her time to get over what she described to me as a sense of total shock.

I was to experience this myself, of course, later in 2004 and in the autumn of 2005, but it is only when you do experience it that you can fully understand just what such a barrage does, not just to the individual but to their family and closest friends. It is what was described to me at the time of Bev's difficulties as a modern form of low-level terrorism, a kind of Stasi treatment experienced by the East Germans for so long, where every movement is tracked, every piece of private life is interfered with, and every right as an individual is completely set aside in what is euphemistically called 'the public interest'. To this day, I wonder how some of those engaging in this activity can live with themselves.

I flew back at the crack of dawn on Monday in order to be in the office early, rather than the later flight that I had originally intended to take in order to give myself a longer weekend – only to discover that the building in which the Home Office was housed in Queen Anne's Gate had transmuted itself in a kind of macabre comment on what was happening politically. It is just impossible to write this without thinking that theatre had taken over reality. I got into the office and went to use the toilet, but was stopped on the way by Denis and Jonathan [Denis O'Reilly and Jonathan Sedgwick, who both worked for me], who told me that there seemed to be something drastically wrong with the bathroom. Sewage was not only coming back up the toilet pan, but also up into the bath and through the washbasin wastepipes. I thought to myself: 'Well, I knew we were in the mire. I knew we were having muck thrown on us from a great height, but to have the damned mire coming up from every orifice in the Department just about sums up the nature of the Home Office.'

Despite some silly briefings to the BBC that because I had emphasised so strongly over the previous two and a half years the issue of nationality and asylum, I had created an environment in which the issue was higher on the agenda than it should have been (an extraordinary twist of anyone's political understanding of what was going on), things were beginning to pull round. On the Tuesday I did both the *Today* programme and a fifty-minute phone-in on Radio 5 Live that went very well. When it is possible to explain to the public what it is that is being done and why, they do get the message and a sensible dialogue becomes possible. The difficulty is getting the opportunity to talk directly to them instead of having everything filtered and interpreted.

But to move on: I had a meeting with Iqbal Sacranie and the Muslim Council of Britain, which was very helpful.

I had a continuing series of meetings relating to cohesion, race and ethnicity, including visits to mosques and temples around the country, and joyous events with the Hindu community, who often feel that they are neglected.

I saw Ian Russell, the Chairman of the new Commission on Volunteering and Young People, who had been appointed by Gordon and myself. Both of us are really enthusiastic to see what can be done to elevate the idea of young people giving time and gaining experience, but it is very difficult to get it on to the political agenda because unless it is a crisis or a 'storm' or something akin to a breakdown in delivery, it is hardly ever possible to get coverage for what is taking place. These meetings can be hard work, and you have to prepare for them in order to be on top of things. At the moment I am crawling towards leaving at Thursday lunchtime and just going home for twenty-four hours, then to stay with Paul and Judith Potts, and then back to the cottage. I'll just rest and collapse. When I get to the cottage, I think I might just go to bed really early and see if I can get some good nights' sleep.

And then, on Thursday morning, Jonathan Sedgwick came to see me and said that he thought that for his own future and career, he should take the opportunity of promotion that was being offered as Director of Criminal Justice Reform, and that we should plan for his departure in the immediate months ahead. This was quite a blow, although I understood perfectly well why he should do this. Doing the job of Principal Private Secretary in my office for two years is as much as can be asked of anyone.

I wonder the same about ministers in this job. I have been thinking lately that ministers are like spark plugs in an engine. When we are worn out, we just get replaced and the engine carries on. We are the firing spark, we are the ones who ignite it and cause forward motion, but we are also expendable and exchangeable.

So after Easter I set about dealing with bogus colleges, and bogus marriages.

My measures here were overturned in early 2006 by a judge who believed that we had been unfair and far too tough in requiring a whole new system that had reduced bogus marriages from over 3,000 annually to less than 300 in eighteen months.

The Duchess of Devonshire has agreed to host the dinner at Chatsworth for the interior ministers in early July, having consulted with her husband Andrew Devonshire, who, from what she said, clearly does not have very long to live. This is very sad. I have got on with the Duke extremely well and his attitude towards opening up the estate and countryside for the enjoyment of the public has been exemplary in helping with 'right to roam' legislation.

It was the weekend after Easter when a very strange event occurred.

It was an event, I am afraid, that proved the precursor to similar ridiculous incursions into my private life by those attempting to make a quick buck.

This was a phone call to my friend Paul Potts, Head of the Press Association, from his editor-in-chief, who knew that Paul was a close friend of mine and as a consequence was checking out a story. The call came while I was with Paul, who answered the editor's query with: 'He's sitting next to me here. I'll ask him.' Then he turned to me and said: 'Jonathan has received a phone call from the *Western Evening Mail*, who have been tipped off that you are dying of throat cancer!' Me: 'Well, perhaps you could tell them that I am sitting next to you and that my throat is fine, but I should be very grateful if the story could be quashed because the last thing I need at the moment is a scurrilous rumour that I am on my way out.' Paul to editor: 'Well, you have it from the horse's mouth' – I don't think a pun was intended – and that was the end of that. But what on earth possesses people to do this?

Thursday 15 April saw me spending several hours at the Thames House headquarters of MI5. It was interesting to see the work that had been going on there over the years in relation to Irish terrorism.

It was one of those very busy days when I had to give lunch to the Belgian Interior Minister and sort out extending controls at Belgian ports and at the Eurostar terminal, matching what we had been doing with France. I also had meetings with the Singapore Prime Minister, with the Head of the National Criminal Intelligence Service, and two meetings on immigration and asylum, to try to look in detail at every single strand of the issues that had been thrown up both by the Moxon/Cameron affair and – because it was uppermost in my mind – the issue of the cockle pickers. Should I have pressed harder on this than I did with Cabinet colleagues the previous summer?

And then up to the constituency for a series of meetings before having dinner with the editor of my local newspaper, only to find that I had to spend most of the evening dealing with information about an alleged threat to the Manchester United v. Liverpool match that was to take place a week the following Saturday [24 April]. Something in my bones told me that we needed to play this down. The Greater Manchester Police were intending to call a press conference, which effectively would have finished the match. The better course is what we did, quietly working it through with the Manchester United management over the following few days. I couldn't explain to my host why it was that I sat in the car for thirty minutes dealing with this on the telephone, rather than coming into the restaurant, but I had to get the Home Office to intervene really strongly to prevent there being an immediate weekend storm.

It turned out in the end that the threat came from low-level miscreants and not high-level terrorists at all. I was so relieved that on this occasion I had followed my instincts.

I am getting really tired now of every part of my life being interrupted, not even being able to enjoy a civilised meal, and beginning to feel so distant from my friends that I worry whether I will ever get them back. It is difficult to describe what I am doing to myself, except that those who are closest to me are saying that I am destroying myself, that I am not behaving the same, that I am not kind and thoughtful any more and that I am so screwed up with personal and political problems that I am just not the same.

And I think they are right. It is a combination of the absurdity of what goes on around me and the fact that I care so much. I know I could just let these things go and pretend I am an amateur, just messing about at the fringe, and go and do something else when it all goes wrong. Does it really matter whether I am there or not? Well, yes, it does. But I know it must be very hard work at the moment for everybody working with me or trying to remain my friend.

Issues like the Manchester United business are really wearing me down, and I had to deal with it again at the beginning of the following week. As soon as I got down to London on Monday we had a round-table meeting with the security services and David Veness from the Counter-Terrorism Branch, to try and pull everything together and decide what to do.

The political world was distracted that weekend by the way in which the decision to announce that there would be a referendum on the proposed European Constitution came out. Suffice it to say that this was not a collective decision but one effectively foisted on the Prime Minister.

In May 2006, Tony was very magnanimous and indicated that he owed those who had been involved a thank you, because the decision to go for a

referendum rather than just parliamentary approval of the proposed European
Constitution had ensured that we had not run into the kind of difficulties that
would certainly have hit us hard politically on the back of discontent and
disaffection over Iraq. Goodness knows what impact it might have had. So it is
amazing how one set of intentions turns out in due course to achieve another.

Tony was clearly tired at the Parliamentary Labour Party meeting on the
Monday evening – and no wonder. It has been a difficult three months.
The opinion polls have been awful and goodness knows the local elections
can hardly be anything but disastrous. What Tony needs around him now
are friends and supporters.

But that week [beginning Monday 19 April] will be remembered by me
for the fact that my friend and long-standing personal assistant (of twenty-
four years' standing) Valda Waterfield has decided, understandably, that
she no longer wants to continue in what is more than a full-time job
running my constituency office. MPs always underestimate the importance
of our constituency offices and the work that is done there. The staff lift an
enormous load from us and make it possible for us to do other things, they
keep us in touch with the electorate, and the electorate themselves believe
that they are cared about. Constituency workers are worth their weight in
gold when working well, and my office was working more than well. So
between now and August comes the daunting task of finding someone to
take on that full-time role, although I hope Valda will continue working for
me at least on a part-time basis in order to keep the ship afloat.

On the political front I've been really worried that in the event of a
referendum, if Tony lost, there would be a massive drive to push him out,
and if he won people would claim that that was his legacy – but not a legacy
that he would want.

Thursday and Friday of that week we had our ministers and Board in the
West Midlands, based in Birmingham. I was distracted on the Friday when
Judge Andrew Collins's verdict came out in relation to a number of
terrorists, including releasing some under 'curfew', which simply means
that MI5 and Special Branch have to devote even more resources to them,
rather than to immediate threats. And then a BBC reporter asked me if I
thought this was bonkers, and I said, 'Your language, not mine' – only to
find that the BBC, and as a consequence a couple of newspapers, were
claiming that I had used the term 'bonkers' about the judgement, when I
had done nothing of the sort. I say things pretty robustly as it is: I don't
have to have things made up or exaggerated.

Anyway, after a busy weekend I came back down to London on Sunday 25 April for the presentation of the Draft Identity Cards Bill (for scrutiny and debate before the final measures were to be put forward). I was really pleased to have got this far.

And here is an example of how misunderstandings occur. Des Browne, as one of his first really high-profile acts, has had his biometric iris scan taken, which the BBC were going to use in their package the following Monday. (Des had had to do it in advance because he simply couldn't get to London to achieve this on the Monday itself.) I had promised John Prescott that I would talk to him over the weekend about precisely what we were doing for the presentation of the Draft Bill and here – Friday – was the BBC breaking the embargo and using as a 'scoop' the issue of the biometric scan and what it would mean for passports and ID cards. I don't think people have the first idea what damage they do when they break their word in this way.

My special advisers are tired out, and everyone is working at the very edge of what is possible. I would have liked to have been able to give the Draft Bill a real push on the David Frost programme on Sunday morning rather than having it dribbled out.

One of the nicest things in the run-up to the start of the local and European elections was a trip to Oldham, where I was joined by Trevor Phillips, the Chairman of the Commission for Racial Equality. We met a group of youngsters who had set up their own programme on a Saturday morning to develop social cohesion and to bring together young people of different ethnicity and background, using art and music and developing citizenship. When I asked them whether they were able to link this to the citizenship curriculum in school (introduced by me when I was Education Secretary) they said: 'Which part of the curriculum is that?' I could only presume that it was either being taught so badly that they hadn't seen any relationship between what they were doing in their own spare time and what we were trying to do, in and out of school, with the support of teachers, or that it wasn't being taught at all. But the young people themselves – and a separate group of really disaffected young white males – were deeply encouraging about work that is taking place on the ground – and that, after all, is where it matters.

At Cabinet on that last Thursday in April [29 April] I was in despair. We didn't seem to have a strategy for the imminent elections, we appeared to be drifting, and we were backbiting each other. In fact I was so fed up that I went back to the Department and Jonathan Sedgwick and I went out to a very good Chinese restaurant for lunch – and just getting a break cheered me up. I was glad that I had abandoned going to the Justice and Home Affairs Council in Luxembourg. Goodness knows how I thought I was going to manage to do that as well as everything else.

On the Friday I did a number of really nice constituency events, including the Child Protection Unit at the specialist Children's Hospital in Sheffield, the launch of the Criminal Justice Interventions Programme (the big investment that we won for putting money into tackling drug abuse, building rapidly the treatment programme that had been desperately needed for so many years, and working with the families who face such heartache). It does make the job feel worthwhile when I see that there is the chance of some progress and that we are helping people on the ground.

And then off to give awards to those in the community who give freely of their time and commitment, sometimes in really difficult circumstances. They are called 'Local Panel Awards', recognising those people who never get accolades nationally, whose only real reward is the satisfaction of helping others. This is what being a constituency MP is all about. This is what being back home is all about. This is what I like best of all.

May 2004

A busy first week in May: sadly the Duke of Devonshire died on the Monday, and regrettably I was unable to attend his funeral a few days later as it clashed with Home Office Questions in the House of Commons. One thing is certain: if you are in the country and there is no overwhelming reason why you shouldn't be present, no Secretary of State ever misses his or her monthly departmental questions. It is just a given convention.

The rest of the week was filled with the usual kind of parliamentary and speaking engagements, a Home Affairs Select Committee hearing, and the absurdity in one or two newspapers (primarily the *Daily Express*) reporting the threat that the whole of Europe opening up its borders to the new accession states would lead to a mass influx of young men threatening the female population here.

This sounds far-fetched but it is what was being said at the time.

Poland was picked on particularly. Of course, none of this happened, but the situation wasn't helped by the fact that we had spent six months trying to get agreement on a tough stance on benefits and housing entitlement and only got that at the very last moment, therefore laying the regulations late. I am afraid this is an example of how when government equivocates and where decisions are not taken quickly and decisively, you end up losing the benefit of the good decisions that you take.

Tony and Gordon launched the European and local election campaign together during the first week of May. We did well in 1999 so we are bound to get a bit of a drubbing in this year's European elections. They have not exactly come at the most auspicious time.

At Cabinet [on 6 May], Charles Clarke did a presentation on the emerging Five-Year Plan for Education and we had a discussion about parental wishes and parental choice. I am afraid I am becoming a bit of a pain in Cabinet, repeating the fact that what people want is a decent school that their children can get to, and that we have no choice but to give them choice because they can buy it themselves. In parts of London, deprived parts like Hackney, over 20 per cent of parents of secondary-school children choose to use their own money to 'go private', very often because they want to avoid thuggery and lack of discipline rather than because of the actual academic results (which are often quite a lot higher than in my constituency, sadly).

But then Cabinet slightly degenerated when Patricia Hewitt understandably raised the issue of the press conference in Leeds on the Tuesday [launching the campaign for the combined local and European elections in early June] and the under-representation of women and the lack of issues that would be appealing to women. John Reid joined in vigorously and said that it was important to see women on the front bench, and that he had been prepared to give up his seat. John Prescott rose to the bait and asked across the table whether he was expected to give up his seat on the front bench. John Reid responded in the way that only John can!

So from a discussion of issues that touched on the electorate, particularly in London and the South, I flew to Scotland and a whole series of meetings, including with the First Minister, Jack McConnell, but what was fascinating was the way in which the Scottish media have a completely different approach on nationality and asylum. Whereas the London-based media think we are not being tough enough, the Scottish media had got the impression that we were authoritarians, uncaring and unkind. It was a really strange juxtaposition and reinforced the cultural and political difference – and why the Scottish National Party play the 'Old Labour' card so hard across Scotland, while playing the Tory card in their rural strongholds – I suppose very much like the Liberal Democrats.

I do wonder whether a left-of-centre government can ever square this circle, because when the Tories are in power we would never attack them for a measured and balanced approach to immigration and asylum, and therefore with the exception of a couple of right-wing newspapers no one would be making it a political issue; whereas when we are in it is open season, with the liberal media thinking we are being awful by tackling these issues in a rational way and allaying people's fears. All we can do is do what is right and get on with it.

Friday [14 May] saw the departure of Piers Morgan as editor of the *Mirror* [following publication of fabricated photographs of British soldiers abusing prisoners in Iraq]. I don't think anyone shed a tear, not least because any kind of journalistic rigour had gone out of the window with his determination to attack the government on Iraq under any circumstances; but abuse of prisoners was an ideal stick with which to beat us, not least because there had been some truth in some of the accusations. I do wonder though whether there has ever been a conflict where so much honest scrutiny has taken place. It is a good thing but it changes the rules under which the public see what we do and how we do it, and we need to adjust to that.

I don't think anyone shed a tear for Piers Morgan because, like so many departing editors, he got an enormous golden handshake, and if rumour is correct he made over £1 million writing what might be described as an 'imaginative diary'. It must indeed be strange to think of what you need to add in, rather than struggle to determine what you take out.

The problem is that the photographs have been shown to be false but have already caused the most enormous damage, and it is never possible to change that. As the old saying has it: 'A lie is halfway round the world before the truth has got its boots on.'

Less tremendous news was the fiasco of Maxine Carr's release. All the arrangements were put in place properly – the original plan overturned, sensible measures, Paul Goggins reporting to me regularly, getting her out of the prison early so that she was in a safe house and couldn't be followed (which was my suggestion), and then the civil servant from the probation service left all the private documents, including the arrangements and procedures for release, in the boot of her car when she went for a drink on her sister's fortieth birthday – and guess what: the car was stolen. There was no problem with her going out to celebrate her sister's birthday, but every problem in believing that she could park her car in London without the risk of it being burgled.

We had focused through the National Criminal Justice Board on what were clearly major problems with the probation service, which is why we were bringing forward the new National Offender Management Service which was causing us so much grief as the probation service resisted reform. But I don't think that any of us was prepared for the difficulties that Charles Clarke had, as Home Secretary, in dealing with the kind of failures that we were concerned about but that had not yet fully revealed themselves. We had in fact asked Harriet Harman to take a lead in London (as the then Solicitor-General) in trying to get a grip of what we had understood to be a fairly dysfunctional operation, but as ever reforms and changes take the most inordinate amount of time.

When they told me what had happened about Maxine Carr, I had one of my calmer moments! When things are very difficult, I stay much calmer, whereas I sometimes hit the roof over more trivial, if irritating, events. They wanted to go for an injunction there and then, to prevent publication, but I overruled that on the grounds that we needed to be clear whether we could find the documents. We didn't know in what circumstances or how they would turn up. It turned out that we had panicked the Met so much that the whole of the area in north London had been flooded with police. Everybody therefore knew that there was something high-profile going on, and obviously the higher echelons had told too many people what it was they were looking for. They had found the car: in fact they made an arrest later in the week of the individual who had done it, a notorious car thief, which means that they can do it when they want to, and when they put their minds to it.

But they leaked it to the press, so there we were on Wednesday night with the whole thing splashed absolutely all over the papers. From Monday to Wednesday night we went from panic (because that's what it was) to calming them down, to having recovered the documents, to believing they were all in order, to the press being given the information about the documents being left in the car and stolen, to controversy about her solicitors then taking out an injunction because of two threats of murder and our backing it, to the press then going to see if they could overturn the injunction, failing to do so – and everybody pouring acrimony on the Home Office. No one could blame my opposite number, David Davis, for having a field day. And all of this at the beginning of an election campaign.

And the same week I was addressing the Annual Conference of Chief Constables and they, not us, raised the issue with the media of the new Licensing Act. This had been a bone of contention for a very long time. In fact when I was Education and Employment Secretary, I had been involved in trying to get major changes to the draft that Jack Straw was dealing with at the time. But it had been a particularly difficult problem for me because Tessa Jowell, as Culture Secretary, had responsibility and as a very close and long-standing friend it was harder to be robust when dealing with the issues with her than it would have been with someone with whom I did not have a close working relationship.

In trying to ensure that I dealt with the issues on their merits rather than letting friendship get in the way I also on some occasions upset Tessa. This was not one of them, except that those around her had clearly given the impression to her that it was the Home Office raising the issue and not the Association of Chief Police Officers. So when on the day of my speech I appeared on the *Today* programme and was challenged about the issues, it appeared as though I had raised the issues, when the seven a.m. news had made it absolutely clear that it was ACPO who had raised it. There was absolutely no way I could refuse to answer questions without either looking a complete prat or making it look as if the government was all over the place. So at 8.10 a.m. I presented what I thought was a decent defence of the government's position, including much broader issues in defence of our position *vis-à-vis* the tortures, and Tony's position *vis-à-vis* the future and the leadership of the party. Having dealt with the licensing issue that they were obsessed with, and having got in some of what I wanted to say about the leadership (the main theme of my speech) and a strenuous clampdown on drugs, with the investment from the Criminal Justice Interventions Programme, I then got a phone call from Tessa when I was on the train to Birmingham. What made it worse from the point of view of trying to calm things was the fact that anyone who has travelled on the line from Euston to New Street will know that mobile phone reception is notoriously bad. I mention it only to show how difficult it is, when you are busy and when technology doesn't always work, to be able to quieten things in a way that would be perfectly reasonable if you could walk round to someone's office, explain what has happened and give them a hug. I think that what we are facing is tiredness and irritation born of the pressure. We are human beings, after all.

So I did my own presentation at Cabinet of the Home Office Strategic Forward Look. I felt a rallying behind the general themes and the direction we were taking, which was very encouraging and uplifting. It is amazing how much better I perform when I am confident, and how much more confident I am when colleagues are backing in. It is a self-evident truth.

But it is a truth that is absolutely vital in sustaining leadership. Whenever the parliamentary party and the Labour Party have fallen in behind the leadership, we have always performed better and have won over the electorate more easily. It is also true at a lower level, when performing within a departmental brief and getting the message across. Confidence and sufficient sleep would be the prescription I would offer for success.

Tony was very kind and said that I had 'characteristically understated' the enormous change that had been brought about, both in the Home Office and in the direction and delivery of services. I was genuinely embarrassed because one of the other problems faced in politics is: the more praise you receive, the more others hate you. I was particularly pleased therefore that Gordon and John Reid joined in and were complimentary – although I have to say that Tony's word 'characteristically' showed him as a friend indeed, because I have never knowingly undersold my achievements! What I was trying to do in truth was to provide a domestic overview of a coherent policy that would match the clear economic strategy of stability and long-termism that Gordon has had from the Treasury, and that Tony and Jack were seeking to achieve with regard to security abroad. I wanted to bring the emphasis within the Cabinet and within politics back on to the domestic agenda. This was something that worried me greatly about the start of the election campaign, which had begun with Tony flying to France to meet Jacques Chirac, followed by all the attention on Iraq.

And I decided that the second half of Ken Sutton's report on what had happened with Bulgaria and Romania and so on should be postponed. The idea of putting this out and fanning the flames all over again in the immediate run-up to the elections struck me as politically inept. I knew that I was bound to get some flak for the delay, but the flak is much less likely to be damaging than throwing the issues on the bonfire and waiting for them to explode once again. The last thing we need is another debate now about immigration.

I had a hell of a battle to get agreement to give all those over the age of seventy-five a free passport. It was only a small amount of money (£3 million) but you would have thought it was billions, with the tussle I had. Agreement was eventually reached, begrudgingly. I just thought that it was a really good thing to do and a valuable announcement to make.

Then came my third visit to the Police Federation conference, which had now become more of a pleasure than a trial. This time I wanted to get across the issue of Respect.

Respect was later to become the title of the wider campaign incorporating issues such as anti-social behaviour as well as parenting.

The issue was covered in only one newspaper (*Daily Mail*) and they did justice to the speech. It is funny how much effort you can put into getting an idea off the ground and then it gets no further than hovering just above your feet. But that particular day [19 May] was dominated by the stunt from the House of Commons Gallery – the throwing of 'the purple powder', as it came to be known. Had it been a real attack with explosive or chemicals, the whole of the front bench for Prime Minister's Questions would have been wiped out. It was a weird feeling to realise that evening that such an event would have left me as the most senior member of the government, and I was just glad that the events in the Commons had turned out to be a protest and nothing more. But it meant that those who wanted a screen across the gallery would now get their way.

The run-up to the elections was full of the usual tours around the country, when maintaining the morale of the troops was as important as trying to win votes. Most votes these days are affected by television and radio and I suppose by immediate perception – for those who bother to vote, that is.

It is worth a mention of the Cabinet that was held on 27 May. It lasted for over two and a quarter hours and was one of the more thoughtful round-table discussions that we had, including the Awaydays at Chequers. It was ostensibly about public-sector reform and a presentation from the Strategy Unit, but it was really about the issue of what can be expected from government, on what timescale and at what price. John Prescott made a powerful contribution on the issue of whether the capacity existed to deliver on the scale that we were envisaging. Bearing in mind that I hadn't prepared in detail, I made one of the most thoughtful contributions that I have made in Cabinet, about how expectation and aspiration had to be managed – and how this related to the way in which we had tried to dampen expectations before the 1997 election, then had seen them take off quite spectacularly in 1999. It was the rolling-up into a three-year announcement of £21 billion and £19 billion for Health and Education respectively, and anticipation of change, of rapid improvement in services, that undermined credibility. I used the example of what we had talked about the previous Thursday on the Early-Years side. What responsibility do we have and what responsibility do the family and the individual have? This was important, because speeches were being made that gave the impression that we, the state, could provide childcare for everyone, whereas while we had a major role in terms of training, quality, building capacity and equality of access, we cannot be responsible for the care of all under-fives and the extension of maternity and paternity leave way beyond what it is either the role or the ability of the state to meet. What we were proposing was radical and imaginative, without its being pushed to the point where we simply wouldn't be able to deliver.

I had to smile at those who advocated 'paying people to stay at home', when on the estates that I represented the real resentment came from those who were working their guts out in order to fund those who were 'staying at home' without ever envisaging being at work.

Gordon warmed to the general point that I was making, that government couldn't be responsible for everything, and I think he and I do see eye to eye on this one. Somewhat robustly – and I think I upset people – I was making the point about the need for radical reform of education and a degree of realism about how long it would take. The point I was making was that it is only because the expectation of people in my constituency with regard to education is so low that the education system works at all, because if they all wanted to get their children into schools in the south-west of the city they couldn't do so, and there would be complete discontent and near revolution. I said that we have done a hell of a lot in the seven years so far, but there is only so much we could do in getting people to cope with change. Therefore the issue of accountability – of mobilising people to make a difference, of having some say, of making a choice, of influencing the service and getting what they want – is very heavily determined by what we can do to change the balance of services.

And then I chaired the Gun Crime round table with representatives of various organisations and agencies, and I promised to go to Brixton and spend time with young black men involved in the effort to reduce gun crime, usually black on black. I then went off for a Big Conversation event in Oxford.

June 2004

I had a few days in Corfu for Spring Bank Holiday and it rained for five consecutive days, including on my birthday.

Gordon invited me to lunch with Nicolas Sarkozy and his wife Cecilia, and Sarah was there too. It was an interesting and pleasant occasion watching the two men who were clearly the outstanding No. 2s in their respective countries – very different but both very able and very driven.

In the run-up to the election itself I had conversations with Charlie Falconer about his wish to change his title to include 'Justice' as well as Constitutional Affairs. I have some sympathy with him in relation to the to-ing and fro-ing about the issue of whether he should remain Lord Chancellor because this was not of his making, but I am afraid that the moment he is known as the Minister for Justice, his department will be the Ministry of Justice, and we will have the most enormous rows about who is responsible for what on reforming the criminal justice system. It is bad enough that nobody has responsibility for reforming the criminal justice system as a key part of their brief, and no senior officials believe that it is their job – because it is seen as the job of the judiciary and the local Criminal Justice Boards to do it. I said slightly mischievously that I would be very happy for Charlie to be called Secretary of State for Judicial Affairs, given that he was responsible for the courts, Peter Goldsmith was responsible for the prosecution service, and I was responsible for trying to get the criminals punished and rehabilitated.

In the end he became known as Lord Chancellor as well as Secretary of State for Constitutional Affairs, so we had really come full circle.

Just before the election Tony was good enough to fulfil a commitment to come to Sheffield to talk with the police and to parents undertaking a parenting course under an imaginative scheme called C'Mon Everybody being run in my own constituency. It gave us all a real boost, particularly given the effort that the BNP were putting in.

For Sheffield it was an 'all out' election because of boundary changes, so all the councillors were up rather than just the one-third at a time that is the usual pattern in the city. Tony was out of the country for the actual election because of the G8 being held off the coast of the USA, and then he had to attend Ronald Reagan's funeral, which, to be honest, seemed to mirror one of his worst B movies, what with kissing the coffins and everything over the top. I was just glad for Tony that he was already out there rather than having to make a separate trip.

The elections: appalling. On the morning after polling day, before the final results were through, I did an interview on the *Today* programme after which there was a tremendous reaction from people at No. 10 to the fact that I said that I was mortified at the losses we were clearly going to sustain, but I was the first one to acknowledge that this was much, much worse than was being portrayed. Cabinet ministers had been out overnight trying to play down the position, but it seemed to me that the best thing was just to tell the truth. What was particularly sad was that one of Tony's staff rang him at six a.m. Washington time to tell him that they thought I had made a *faux pas*. They told him that the media would interpret what I had said as being an attack on Tony, and that it would set up our opposition. It did nothing of the sort. It evoked a reaction of, 'Thank God that people are speaking ordinary language and that David and John [Prescott] are being honest' – and then Gordon joined in and supported the line, and eventually I think the message got through to Tony that he had been sold a pass and that we were doing exactly the opposite of what he had been told.

Coming third in the proportion of votes cast and only getting 26 per cent of the vote – well, what else was there to say? We held on to Sheffield and that cheered me, but it was deeply worrying that the BNP got 3,500 votes in the three wards in my constituency and 8 per cent of the vote in Yorkshire and Humberside. That has got to be a signal.

And then to Lisbon with my sons Alastair and Andrew (at my expense, of course) – as Home Secretary to oversee the policing and as a father to take my boys to see England v. France, England's first game in the European Football Championships. It would have been a really pleasant weekend if we had managed to win. We signed the St George's flag across the square and we joined in with the fans, who were behaving incredibly well, at least in Lisbon: there were just some silly skirmishes in the seaside resorts. It was a moment to be proud of England and the English fans. One amusing aspect of the time out there was when the fans saw me and started to sing, much to my embarrassment: 'One David Blunkett, there's only one David Blunkett'. The *Daily Telegraph* reported it as 'There's only one David Beckham' – which, of course, they did sing in the ground, while the *Daily Mail* reported that they had sung 'There's only one Michael Howard'. I had to pinch myself and ask those I was with whether I had been in a different place, but in any case it was only a bit of fun. The ambassador was very welcoming and laid on a reception for the bigwigs, but also for some of the fans.

There was a brief discussion at Cabinet the following Thursday about the election results, and then the Cabinet Secretary, Andrew Turnbull, revealed that further enquiries were going on into an individual who was being paid to leak material and that he had called in ex-MI5 officers. I upset the applecart once again by suggesting that it was current rather than superannuated security staff we needed to get to the bottom of this, because we couldn't put up with any more of what was causing dissent, friction and downright suspicion. But we will get there eventually. Our problem is that nobody has any idea how much material has been passed across and therefore while they will clearly only use the 'best' in their terms of what they have, and at a time that is most devastating for us, we don't know what, where and when it will be used. It is certainly destabilising. It's like having handed across the whole of your ammunition and then waiting to be shot. I think, however, Andrew Turnbull's report and the discussion have cleared the air a bit: I hope so.

We had a presentation at this Cabinet from John Reid (whose mother had died the day before, so it was strong of him to be there at all) on the forward health strategy. There was a little bit of banter between him and Gordon about how particular programmes were to be achieved, targets met and choice delivered, but I thought that both of them were speaking the same language. It seemed to me that what we were doing was making people an 'offer' in seeking to achieve improvements and the turnaround in waiting times.

No Cabinet minister can get into the detail of someone else's portfolio. For example, it is not possible to start discussing the detail of GP contracts or whether the new tariffs and payment-by-results system will work. All you can do is to get into key questions, seek reassurance and where appropriate give backing to the colleague dealing with such difficult issues.

Then the run-up to 21 June and publication of the Bichard Report on the Soham murders and the role played by the various police forces and agencies. The whole of Tuesday 22 June was spent dealing with Sir Michael's report, which was presented very well, and my Statement to the House. Of course, I knew more than I could put in the Statement or say publicly about the detail and the background to what had happened, particularly to do with the Humberside police. I was very keen indeed not to end up with some silly spat between myself and David Westwood, Chief Constable of Humberside, who had really set himself up by becoming more and more belligerent and failing to accept the responsibility which the Bichard Report was according him in relation to what he did or did not know about the processes and systems being operated in Humberside. What I also knew from Sir Keith Povey, Head of HM Inspectorate of Constabulary, concerned the nature of the force generally and its performance.

It was unfortunate that this began to look like a trial of strength between a Home Secretary and a Chief Constable when it became clear that he was not prepared to offer his resignation or to set a timetable for his departure. At this point I had to act entirely within the law, being so careful in what I said that I wasn't even able to defend properly my own position. This is often the case for the Home Secretary, because the legal advice you are given is that if you are not very careful, what you say will undermine the very case you are putting. Therefore it is better to remain circumspect than to come out with all guns blazing (my usual instinct). In the end David Westwood agreed to go so long as I did not set the date for him and he was allowed to announce it himself. I was happy with this because while I didn't agree with his claim that having been Chief Constable (and Deputy before) for this length of time equipped him to be the best person to put right what he acknowledged was wrong with his force, what really mattered was that the processes and systems were put right and that the people of Humberside received the quality of service they deserved. The Tory Opposition weren't in a strong position, because the previous Shadow Home Secretary, Oliver Letwin, as well as David Davis, had made it clear that they believed that such matters were not the responsibility of national government but of the police forces themselves and of local accountability – although quite clearly the police national computer was the responsibility, in the end, of the Home Office. I certainly accepted that.

Ironically in 2000 it was the Chief Police Officers themselves who put forward the particular model that had been accepted by what is known as the 'tri-partite' grouping of police authorities, police officers and the Home Office. The 'tri-partite' arrangements at all levels kept on being re-sited and recycled – and the opposition parties kept on demanding that this approach should be maintained, whatever the cost.

These things are always forgotten when there is a problem. The tendency to believe that 'it's the government's fault' is understandable, given that it is the government that is accountable, but there are few mechanisms for holding Parliament to account as opposed to the Executive. In simple terms Parliament – Commons and Lords – brings pressure to bear to maintain outdated processes and institutions, and then the government gets the blame when those processes and institutions constrain or pressurise the government away from new directions or putting in place new mechanisms for delivery. Government is held to account as never before because of the rolling news media, but Parliament and the civil service are often protected from this. If they get it wrong, the ministers have to answer for it.

The refusal of the Police Authority to meet until the Friday and to consider seriously the steps I had laid down left me with little choice. No Home Secretary could have a challenge of this sort and simply let it go. Authority, and therefore ability to achieve delivery and improvement across the country, would be undermined, not least in circumstances where there were no direct levers but people had to be persuaded that you meant business and that they couldn't simply duck the responsibility for taking drastic action. So, carefully, and within the procedures laid down in the concordat drawn up with the Police Authorities themselves, Humberside will have to suspend its Chief Constable and undertake the thorough review and analysis of Sir Michael Bichard's report that I required of them. Their refusal to comply, apart from sheer stubbornness, appeared to be based on a number of misunderstandings of what had happened and of what Michael Bichard was saying. For instance, they seemed to presume that this was a purely local matter and appeared not to acknowledge that what had happened and the way in which the force had performed in this area had had a profound and devastating effect on the way in which other forces (in this case Cambridgeshire) could do their job. They seemed to think that they were not overseeing a failing force when they were; that the Chief Constable had been responsible for the improvement over the past six months, when it had been the intervention through the Inspectorate and the Police Standards Unit that had made such a difference; and by refusing to meet immediately and suspend the Chief Constable (not sack him) they had forced me to go down the legal route.

In thinking back on it, my desire to see speedy action and to be decisive probably coloured my judgement. While they were being belligerent, it would have been appropriate if I had asked them to meet me immediately after the Statement. But the actions of the Chairman of the Police Authority had been so bizarre in not signing a confidentiality agreement and therefore not reading the report before it was issued and my Statement was made in the House, that it was difficult to see how such a meeting would have been conducted. Nevertheless I think that the spat between the Home Secretary and David Westwood was not in the interests of either improvement in the service or myself. It simply prolonged the problem, and although in the end what I wanted was achieved, it is always at a political price if there has been a knockabout in the meantime – ammunition for people to make mischief.

I wonder what the *Daily Telegraph* and *The Times* would have said if I had taken no action in the light of the Bichard Report. I suspect that terms like 'ineffective', 'weak' and 'equivocal' would have peppered the headlines. Thank goodness the rest of the press were on board. Certainly anybody who had read the Bichard Report knew that action had to be taken. The only dissenting voice in Parliament was Austin Mitchell, which is astonishing, bearing in mind that he represents Grimsby [in Humberside].

This week I have been preparing again for the Spending Review and trying to finalise the Strategic Plan. I have also had to prepare for numerous speeches, such as the IPPR speech on the issue of identity and belonging, social cohesion and race; the Local Government Association annual conference, where I will try to spell out our new relationship with community and civil society; and a speech to Turning Point [voluntary organisation dealing with drug and alcohol misuse] regarding alcohol, drugs and crime.

Sad news of the week was that while England had a really good victory against Croatia, we lost on penalties after extra time against Portugal on the Thursday night and are out of the European Championships. I missed the match as I was speaking at the Community Security Trust in Manchester, but I caught extra time and the penalty shoot-out on the radio in the car coming back across the Pennines. I was so glad that I had been able to take Alastair and Andrew to the first match, and it was sad now for England to be knocked out.

I've put a cutting on file from the *Independent* that is the first of two quite curious extracts from Simon Walters and Peter Oborne's book on Alastair Campbell. While the context and the reference to Jo Moore are completely wrong – the timing of the discussion in Cabinet and any relevance whatsoever to Jo Moore have simply been made up – the report of my contribution at Cabinet is very accurate indeed. I am absolutely certain that this was a senior civil servant who had spoken to Peter Hennessy, who has long-standing and very close links with the civil service and writes regularly on Whitehall affairs, and who in turn had obviously spoken to Oborne and Walters. As a consequence, it is a very accurate reflection of what I said. However, they conflate two meetings – one where I made the general comments about the civil service and efficiency, and the second, which was much later, in fact earlier this year, in relation to the Civil Service Bill and my comments that the Bill should include protection from the civil service. Nevertheless it is very interesting, particularly that they should have tried to relate it to the Jo Moore affair, which had nothing to do either with the discussion or with the Civil Service Bill.

Sunday 27 June saw the *Sunday Telegraph* doing the most ridiculous front-page story about my past association with the Humane Research Trust. They said that because of this I wasn't an honest broker and wasn't doing my job properly in relation to animal-liberation terrorists and the protection of laboratories. The fact is that the Humane Research Trust is doing exactly what most human beings would want to do: not to attack animal research but to find an alternative for those particular processes where this could be manageable. In any case, I have had no dealings with the HRT for several years, although I am quite proud of my association with them and the work they were doing at the University of Sheffield at the time. So there we are. We even had people calling for my resignation.

Another bit to add to the ongoing saga of David Westwood and the Humberside Police Authority, which has been going on and on – most recently with Richard Brunstrom, the Chief Constable of North Wales, going on the radio and pronouncing that he thought that David Westwood was being made a scapegoat and that he was a good guy. Then it was Kevin Wells – Holly's father – in the *Mail on Sunday*, which we knew was coming in and knew would be supportive of David Westwood. This was just about the last straw. Kevin Wells sent an email to one of the private secretaries in my office, saying that he was deeply sorry, that he hadn't intended to embarrass me and that he understood precisely where I was coming from. So that was decent of him, but it is not something I can put out to the press.

Nor could I put out details that I would want to in relation to Westwood and the police service and police authority. I had to get really tough with our lawyers. We had a very good barrister, and we got sense out of the Head of the Treasury Solicitors who got through to the High Court how important it was that this be dealt with, and the result was that instead of it taking the normal two to three weeks, they agreed to hear it Friday afternoon. The police authority met on Friday morning, and took no notice whatsoever of Ken Williams, the HMIC [Her Majesty's Inspector of Constabulary], who presented facts to them about failings over the years. He said they weren't interested in what they were doing, only interested in fighting for Westwood. We asked for costs and the judge granted them, including Humberside's, which is very unusual: when the government is involved, costs are usually split.

Westwood has his own barrister who turned up in court in support of the Police Authority and I wanted to get across that his very rich friends are going to have to cough up a lot of money if we get into further legal wrangles. So we are through Phase 1 and we now get on with Phase 2. There is a lot of support in the newspapers, including a very sensible article by Steve Richards in the *Independent* on Tuesday, but there was a very silly leader in *The Times* on Saturday which said that I would have to have niftier footwork if I was going to win this one, when I hadn't put a foot wrong and had done it entirely by the book. I have done no interviews, no television or radio, made no extraneous remarks – just statements issued on the Friday and again on the Monday when we announced we were going to the High Court. I spent a massive amount of time dealing with this, getting the statement right, making sure that the lawyers were very clear as to what we wanted and that they were happy with what we were doing. So it's been a bit rum.

I had lunch with the editor of *The Times* earlier in the week and I thought that he might have pulled in the dogs following that, but no such luck.

I called off the dinner with the police authorities that was to be held on Monday night as I thought it would be a farce, with all this going on, and not least because I had had such a dreadful weekend. It reminded me of when I was dealing with Chris Woodhead – firstly when his private affairs were in the papers for eight weeks running and secondly when I was dismissing him.

I had a meeting with Gordon on the Spending Review. We went round the houses, but he seems to have conceded that uniquely there will be some money for the first year of the Spending Review. We are still haggling over how much.

And there was the *New Statesman* interview that Huw Evans had persuaded me to do. I said at the time that these were dangerous interviews – and lo and behold, I repeated what I had said on the Monday at the drugs conference, which was that I intended to remain Home Secretary, I enjoyed the job, it was a tremendous challenge and I wanted to build on the foundations that I had laid. John Kampfner followed that up by trying to probe me about what job I wanted next, and asking me what I thought about Gordon. I simply said that I was talking about myself and I think that we are very privileged to be the cutting edge of politics, at the very centre of the Cabinet, and we should not be seeking to take someone else's job. He immediately made a great song and dance about this, hinting that I was sending a message to Gordon when I was doing nothing of the sort. Huw Evans and Ian Austin, who is Gordon's press adviser, managed to calm most of it down, although the *Daily Telegraph* on the Friday was mischievous.

Not only did I have the Spending Review but I was going up to Scotland to stay with Gordon the following weekend.

I went to the Leicester South by-election on the Friday – not a happy experience [the Liberal Democrats, third in the 2001 general election, took the seat from Labour] – and then flew up from East Midlands airport to Glasgow, went to Dungavel removal centre, across to Kirkcaldy to a volunteer young persons' consultation, then across to Gordon's home in North Queensferry. This visit worked very well, and gave me a chance to make my peace with Gordon, who had been very wound up by a book by former Downing Street insider Derek Scott.

The reception for the Jennifer Brown Research Fund [the charity Gordon and Sarah had set up in memory of Jennifer] was for all those who had helped with the Fund or in the aftermath of Jennifer's death and the birth of John. I said a few words at the reception, which Gordon seemed to appreciate. All the usual Scottish people were there – Michael Martin [Speaker of the House of Commons], Alistair Darling, Nick Brown – plus Tony's pollster Philip Gould, which I found very interesting. There were celebrities such as Joanne Rowling, and Ron Stevenson, the ophthalmologist who had saved Gordon's sight when he was sixteen. I told him the old saying that in the kingdom of the blind, the one-eyed man is king – apparently he hadn't heard it before and thought it was very funny. I stayed overnight, and following a walk with Gordon and Sarah in the morning got the plane back to Birmingham at 10.40 a.m.

It was a very pleasant weekend, enjoyable both for affording the chance to talk and to have in-depth discussions, and on account of the people I met. Those outside the political arena were friendly and open, the kind of acquaintances that any of us would be pleased to have. I felt at the time, and still do, that these are the kind of people who must be very helpful and supportive to Gordon and Sarah, and just the kind of acquaintances that would change the image that Gordon so often has in the Westminster-based media. I wish they could be transported into central London!

I got back to the cottage in time to open the village fête in Beeley, then set about the remaining revisions of the strategic plan: talk about writing and rewriting. I was also preparing for the French, German, Italian and Spanish interior ministers' meeting on Monday and Tuesday and all the diplomacies around that and the dinner at Chatsworth. It is a shame that the summer is nowhere near as good as it was last year, when we got so used to hot summer days and wonderful balmy nights. But no such luck this year.

This year I only put in a twenty-minute appearance at the *Spectator* party, and then went to the American embassy for the Independence Day annual celebration, which I have taken to going to over the past few years, particularly given the build-up of contacts across the Atlantic since September 2001. The ambassador has taken himself off back to America. He has spent the least time in Britain of any US ambassador to our country.

A two-hour Cabinet on the Education Strategic Plan. Tony had asked me to make an early intervention and Gordon had also talked to me about the plan. In fact just about everybody has talked to me about the Strategic Plan – which, of course, is Charles Clarke's baby. The issue in question is ring-fenced funding, which was developed specifically to ensure that the vagaries of what is called the Standard Spending Assessment could be at least offset. The Standard Spending Assessment is a theoretical view of what a particular local authority and school should be spending in relation to the children in their area. But successive governments have failed completely to come up with a solution that is either clearly understandable or fair. The proposition now was pretty well to demolish the ring-fenced funds, including large parts of the Standards Fund, which we had developed specifically to put money into deprived areas and to projects which would otherwise have had no priority and would never have got off the ground. Perversely, the proposition was that all secondary-school funding would be taken out of the allocations for local authorities and provided direct to the schools themselves.

When I was Education Secretary, we had already developed the idea of additional funds being pumped direct to schools rather than simply being distributed by the Local Education Authority at local level, but this proposition was to take all secondary-school funding out of local authorities and deliver it direct. I was against it, not only on the grounds of bureaucracy and under-mining the sensitivities and local knowledge that is crucial to helping schools from one year to another, but also because I feared that government would get the blame for every school that had a deficit and every problem with headteachers who couldn't manage the admittedly increased budgets they were getting.

I spoke at Cabinet about the implications for capping (the proposition of capping the council tax in a locality if authorities went over a particular budgetary increase or council-tax increase) and how if further money was taken out of the distribution of grant, it would inevitably increase what is known as the gearing effect, where the smaller the amount over which the local authority has control, the more they have to increase the local element (council tax) in order to have any impact at all on services. To lose all flexibility in relation to large parts of the education budget when that budget was the largest element of the grant would inevitably distort the system still further. How on earth we were going to deal with funding for what were known as 'extended schools' – namely activity outside and beyond the normal school day – goodness only knows. The specific ring-fenced funding that I had put into the Excellence in Cities programme in the core urban areas, including the Pupil Learning Credits, for out-of-hours activity for the poorer students, was already being withdrawn and put into the general pot, and this would have a major impact anyway on what could be done in the most disadvantaged areas. Anything that further distorted it by treating all secondary schools as though they were the same would make matters grievously worse. Publicly it was thought that we were rowing about whether there were to be 200 city academies, but there were much more fundamental discussions going on about direction.

Of course the 200 city academies and the idea of education trusts were the main bone of contention almost two years later, but it is amazing how time

passes and political focus eventually comes all the way round again, including
those in the political arena refocusing on something that was under discussion
and known about publicly long before it became a substantial political issue.

I had agreement before leaving the Department for Education that city
academies should not be the 'cuckoo in the nest' by knocking out
disadvantaged schools, but by superseding them where they were failing
and where other measures had not achieved substantial change. This
element had to be built back in and Charles Clarke was very amenable to
this, and very much more open to discussion and persuasion than I might
have been in his position.

I remain extremely worried about letting schools do anything they like
without an agreed curriculum or direction. Allowing experimentation is
crucial, but a free-for-all is something that we have managed to set aside in
the last seven years.

I went on a bit about all this in Cabinet – too long – but I did got a lot of
support for what I was saying from around the table. I probably pushed my
luck too far when I said that I thought we were concentrating too much on
the structural matters and teaching methodology, when what was included
in the curriculum and how it was being taught was central to raising
standards. At this point I think Tony was irritated. He certainly said rather
sharply that he thought that sorting out these particular issues of finance
and ring-fencing was critical. I couldn't disagree, but the point I was
making was that if we were not careful we would allow the debate over
funding changes to divert us from our key task. This was entirely in line
with what I had been saying from 1994 onwards.

At the end of the Cabinet meeting I said: 'If you can all take a laugh, after
discussing how badly local authorities are going to react to this and how we
are going to be heavily criticised by councillors, I am the government's
representative in Bournemouth at the annual conference of the LGA on
Friday morning, the day after the publication of the Strategic Plan!'

So it has been a hell of a week, one way or another. It's been quite
stressful and the fact that I had had such a lousy weekend because of
Humberside and not a lot of sleep hasn't helped. I shouldn't be letting
things like Westwood and Humberside get to me, and haven't done so
publicly – nobody would see me blink – but privately it did get to me and
certainly ruined the last weekend of the month [26 and 27 June].

I have decided to appoint Tracey Barker as my personal assistant in the
Sheffield office, so we will see how that works out. The other good news is

that Andrew has got a placement for his sandwich year, and Hugh has got his car back after an accident. Alastair seems to be fine and is considering renting an apartment at 20 Manchester Road in Sheffield, where I went to school and which has now been converted into very nice flats.

It is one of those twists of fate. Alastair didn't even know that it had been my school, and I didn't know that he was looking for an apartment in that area. He did rent the apartment, and I found it very strange when I visited him there and was able to identify where the corridor once ran from the bump in the middle of the lounge floor.

I didn't mention that *Broadcasting House* on Radio 4 on Sunday morning did this twenty-minute programme on me. Everybody who contributed said that the BBC had tried desperately to get them to do a hatchet job, and some people wouldn't take part. Those who did simply wouldn't do the hatchet job, so the programme didn't come out in the way that they intended at all. Radio 5 Live did the same during the week on the Thursday so they are all trying very hard, as with the *New Statesman*.

John Prescott had had a long conversation with me on the Saturday, when he was back from his travels and talked to me about how he had been pulled into No. 10. He had arrived back from India at seven o'clock on Saturday morning and went in and had a conversation with Tony, Charles Clarke and Andrew Adonis (or the Mekon, as he calls him), and was really screwed up about it. This then spilled over, as somebody briefed the Sunday papers about the meeting itself and not just about the issues, and that left John coming to Cabinet in a grumpy mood. There had been further meetings during the week, including mine with Charles and with Tony, so things had calmed down, but it was indicative of the frenzy.

July 2004

Monday and Tuesday went very well. The interior ministers from France, Germany, Italy and Spain seemed both to enjoy and get something out of what was only one day really: Monday lunchtime through to Tuesday lunchtime. We did pack a lot in and it was an incredible strain on me. These international conferences do take it out of you, particularly when you are chairing. I felt exhausted by Tuesday lunchtime, when I went off to the by-election in Birmingham [Birmingham Hodge Hill constituency]. I think it is because you have to concentrate all the time, and when you are dealing with simultaneous translation it is doubly difficult. If you just want waffle that's fine, but if you want to get something out of it and you want to make progress, then it is very much more difficult.

The evening at Chatsworth was a tremendous success. The Duchess hosted it very well indeed and made it a lovely occasion. We saw the paintings and the sculpture gallery. The Orangery is now the shop and it is amazing what they sell in there. We had drinks on the terrace, with a harpist playing, and the sun shone. It was Chatsworth at its best, including a very good dinner.

I had dinner on Tuesday night with Matthew Freud (Clement Freud's son and Sigmund Freud's great-grandson) and his wife Elisabeth, Rupert Murdoch's daughter – another different world.

The whole week was dominated by the Spending Review and trying to get the strategic plan in place. I saw Gordon at 9.30 a.m. on Thursday and Gordon and Tony at 12.30 p.m. This is the day of the launch of the strategic plan for education and my leading off on the intelligence and security debate in the House of Commons, and then the Police Bravery Awards. I was planning to say some nice words about Sir John Stevens, who has formally announced that he is stepping down. (I say 'formally' because we have known about it for some time.) But he did an interview just before 8 a.m. on the *Today* programme, obviously knowing absolutely nothing about what's happened with Westwood and Humberside, and suggested that this should all have been handled quietly behind the scenes rather than through the courts. Well, Ken Williams [from HMIC – Her Majesty's Inspectorate of Constabulary] had been handling it behind the scenes on behalf of the inspectorate. Sir Keith Povey had come back from holiday and gone to Humberside, given David Westwood the report and offered him a way of dealing with it quietly. David Westwood had immediately gone to his lawyers, as he had during the inquiry when he went for an injunction, and sought to scupper the lot. As I had been following the protocol and because he took legal steps and made it clear that he wouldn't step down, we had no choice. We didn't go to the court until we had to.

The speech to the Institute for Public Policy Research on Wednesday went very well – over-spun with regard to incitement to religious hatred, but this was partly because we were appealed to by both the party and by Patricia Hewitt, who as MP for Leicester West got into a terrible state about the fact that we were going to announce the restrictions on imams coming in without English or training in citizenship and life in modern Britain.

They thought it would affect the by-elections, so we had to take that out. That was the story that I would otherwise have placed and instead we got completely hooked on what I had had to deal with in autumn 2001: the incitement issue. But the speech as a whole I think really hung together and read very well.

I had John Humphrys for fifteen minutes on the *Today* programme on Wednesday morning. In the end I just said: 'If there is anybody still listening, this is a game of chess,' and at the end of it I said to John: 'I may not have checkmated you but I put you in check.' It was not an inspiring interview but it was one of my best from the point of view of staying absolutely calm, clear and decisive

At Wednesday lunchtime, after Prime Minister's Questions, I went in to see Tony. A question had been asked about abortion and Tony had answered it in the way he thought was least offensive and least likely to cause problems. Then David Hill [Tony Blair's press spokesman] and co. rushed in while I was there and told him that he had just announced that we were prepared to reconsider the law with regard to the maximum number of weeks during which an abortion could take place. Tony said that he hadn't meant to do that, but they said that that was what he had done. So we are now up for a review and a potential return to the issue, which is not what Tony intended at all. It is amazing how issues like this flare up and then die again, and it is all a question of knowing which ones are going to ignite, which ones are going to keep flaming, and which ones aren't. It is often a fine judgement as to how to play them.

We are now in the final stages of Steve Moxon's sacking. I have told them to concentrate not just on what he did and what he didn't do at the time, but the article that he wrote for the *Daily Telegraph*.

For a civil servant, writing an article attacking the government is itself a sackable offence, and we should have got rid of him just for that.

The intelligence and security debate went OK in the Commons but got no coverage whatsoever. I rewrote my speech about twenty minutes before I went across because the original version – what the civil servants call 'work-through' – was so appalling. We have officials who are supposed to have some knowledge of their own area and it turns out that I know more than they do. I found this in Education, but I never expected to find it with those working in security and intelligence.

We kept going on the Spending Review, not just further meetings with

Gordon and Tony, but letters and papers flying to and fro. In a controlled fashion, I lost my temper at the second of the meetings. I said that I wasn't prepared to sign off or sign up to the kind of budget that Gordon was offering.

Having originally told Tony that he was prepared to fund the correctional-services requirements – we need more prison places but we also need a lot of activity to stop further prison places being needed – Gordon agreed to fund two-thirds of the additional required prison places. We then had real difficulties. I wanted money for preventive work but I also wanted money for the new police community support officers, and Tony wanted money for the CSOs – and as Tony wanted money for the CSOs, there was going to be money for the CSOs. So it is going to take some imagination to restore the balanced package.

Afterwards I tackled my own officials who had previously worked in the Treasury – and we have got some good officials who have come across from there – about how it is that the Treasury officials can adopt the stance they do with the hat that they wear, and then be completely different when taking on the job within the service department. The answer was very simple: 'We were working for a different master then, with a different remit.' I said: 'Well, the impact on all of us is the same, whichever department we are working for, the criminals are the same, the state of the Prison Service is the same, and the consequences and contradictions of getting it wrong are the same.'

So there we are, and the battle will continue while I go to the Local Government Association annual conference in circumstances of a Tory majority, the announcement of capping on Thursday, the ring-fencing of school budgets and everything else in the background that just makes functioning properly extraordinarily difficult – but not impossible because I am still functioning.

I went to the Police Bravery Awards and spoke. I didn't drink a drop of alcohol, as I hadn't on the Wednesday night either as I knew that if I did I wouldn't get to Bournemouth and wouldn't be able to function over another busy weekend – constituency meeting, surgery, Parson Cross Festival, Hillsborough School fundraising and then down again on Sunday night for the Spending Review Cabinet on Monday.

The story about the so-called Islamic scholar runs and runs. It has to be said it has been stirred up by the Jewish community. A letter that was supposed to be from the British Board of Deputies, dated 24 June, never reached me. The Home Office claimed that it had never arrived, it had never been stamped and had never come into the office. When the broadcast and print media said that they had written to me, we eventually got round to asking them for a copy and that is why we know it was dated 24 June – but I hadn't seen it. Originally my office said 'that it had only come in yesterday', which was 7 July, and it was only when I queried what that meant that I found out that it hadn't been sent on 5 or 6 July as implied but on 24 June. One of my private secretaries said that on this occasion she didn't think it was our fault and that it must have been lost by the Post Office. I would love to believe that just for once it wasn't the fault of the Home Office that we didn't receive a letter that would have allowed us to prepare. But that is not the real issue. The real issue is why on earth we have no proper records of controversial figures across the world. I thought such records already existed but apparently not, so I have ordered that wherever anyone is excluded from another country, we register them and have them on the warnings index with a proper system of communication. By Friday [9 June] we were still unable to ascertain from the USA whether this man was excluded from that country in 1999, which is what the papers have reported on the back of briefings from the Jewish community. I don't quite know why the Jewish community have stirred it up in this way, given the massive co-operation we give them.

Just a little anecdote about Thursday night. I got back to get into my dinner suit to go to the Police Bravery Awards and there was a little cat, curled up and obviously hurt, on my doorstep. The protection officers moved her in order to get Sadie in but she was so obviously traumatised that I asked them to take her round to the cattery and said that I would pay for whatever was needed to be done to help her. She was put on a drip and when they called round the following morning, she had started to recover. The owner had responded to a notice that had been put out about a cat being found, and turned up to collect her but paid no money, nor did I receive a note of thanks for taking care of her. It's a strange world. It was like a symbol of life, there on the doorstep. I could easily have just ignored her and left her on the pavement but I was really touched by her plight.

So I went off to the Police Bravery Awards and sat next to Rebekah Wade. The actor David Jason and his wife Jill were there, and I liked them both. Their little girl, who is only three and a half, was diagnosed with diabetes before she was two. Luckily the early diagnosis has meant that they caught it in time before her kidneys and sight were affected. One of the bravery awards had been given to someone who had saved himself from being stabbed by hitting a man over the head several times with a tin of paint. When I was on the platform, I said: 'I liked the story about the tin of paint, it's my sort of justice. It beats fixed-penalty notices any day, doesn't it?' The audience just roared with laughter.

A measure of the growing pressure on me was the fact that, not for the first time, I laid off the wine completely. What is interesting about this period is how, when you have to, you can momentarily lift yourself out of your own concerns to crack a joke and to relate to the audience. I still wonder how on occasions I managed to do it.

Of course, it always helps if the audience has imbibed deeply, as they usually have on occasions like this, because if you hit the right note it really is irrelevant that the joke wouldn't stand up for one minute in the cold light of day. On this occasion, I was fortunate that other branches of the media didn't attempt – as they did on some occasions – to treat a light-hearted remark as a statement of policy.

So I survived that. I also survived the Local Government Association annual conference in Bournemouth by recalling my battles with central government, and how I was involved in trying to find a replacement for the poll tax all those years ago. I said that was all back in the 1980s, and here we were again. I managed to win them over, so instead of getting a rotten reception my speech went down well.

This occasion was in sharp contrast to the Police Bravery Awards evening, not because of the reception but because of what might be described as having to climb a mountain before the audience would warm to the theme. This is something familiar to all those who have ever spoken from the platform of their political party's annual conference. It is interesting now to reflect that after twenty-two consecutive years of speaking from the platform at Labour conferences [a modern record], it never got any easier for me.

From Bournemouth I flew to East Midlands airport and shot up the M1 to get to the Occupational Health Project in Sheffield, arriving only five minutes late. They did a lovely piece about how I had helped get the project off the ground in the 1980s and helped with the black and ethnic minority community, which was the particular focus. I then did constituency business for the rest of the afternoon and evening, and on Saturday morning had the most horrendous advice surgery which lasted two and a half hours. Bill Jeffrey, the Head of IND, was supposed to turn up but never did, even though both Colin and myself had received messages saying that he was coming. Had he done so, he would have seen the fifty or so people queuing down the road for my surgery, the vast majority of them asylum and immigration cases. He would have seen the first person who came into my room and began making funny noises at me. He turned out to be an Afghan asylum seeker who had stitched his lips together with pieces of thread. Fortunately, with a bit of common sense from the protection officers and from Colin, we got him down to the Northern General Hospital. Once there he was seen by a psychiatrist, and was found a place of safety at a unit in Leeds. It appears that he has done this before. This was all pretty traumatic, not only for me but for everybody in the surgery as well. Again I had lots of people coming who had failed their appeals, who can't be removed, who are just dossing out, and others who are halfway through their appeals. It is getting beyond a joke now, having this dispersal facility in the constituency. When they are here at the surgery in such numbers, it disrupts the opportunity of everybody else to see me. I ran out of time as I had to open the Parson Cross Festival and I was already half an hour late.

Rony Robinson and his producer Emma Gilligan from Radio Sheffield were with us all day, and I think Rony got quite a shock. He asked me if I thought he was a member of the liberati, which was a phrase I had used on the *Today* programme. I said: 'Yes, you are a liberal of arty inclinations.' In fact I had been told that Rony had been on the radio, saying that he had never seen an asylum seeker in Sheffield and didn't know what all the fuss was about. Well, he does now!

After the Hillsborough School event, I went back to Beeley and resumed work on the Spending Review. I talked to Tony just after 6 p.m. and from the conversation I had with him it was quite clear that he was now concentrating hard, having had all sorts of other diversions that had obviously taken his attention away from the Review. I mentioned this to my Principal Private Secretary, who spoke to Ivan Rogers, Tony's PPS, who said that Tony was dealing with the Butler Committee and the MoD among other things.

Then on Sunday we had the farce of all farces. I had agreed to speak to Tony and Gordon anytime from 2 p.m., and I went for a decent walk. Firstly Gordon had gone walkabout, then he agreed to speak to me at 3 p.m. When I spoke to him at 3 p.m., he said that he and Tony had reached agreement and that Tony would explain to me what the situation was and run through with me what the compromises were. So I rang Tony. Tony couldn't speak to me because he had gone to bed. Eventually I spoke to him at about 6.30 p.m. and he said: 'I never said that I would speak to you first. Gordon should have briefed you. I haven't got the details.' We spoke briefly about bits of the Spending Review and I then said: 'OK, I'll speak to Gordon.' So I spoke to Gordon: he ran through it and I told him what wasn't acceptable and what needed to be done. Gordon said that he would speak to me again, which he did at about 7.30 p.m. We carried on like this all evening, including during the time I was driving back to London, and at 11.40 p.m. we signed off a compromise.

Huw Evans and officials were up until after 12.30 in the morning trying to deal with it, and Jonathan Sedgwick until after 1 a.m., because during the course of the evening we were writing and rewriting letters in response to their missives, including the settlement letter, so that we could get a reply off. I had to get the compromises and so it was that we got, uniquely in the sense that no other department is having funding in the current financial year, money for CSOs, money for counter-terrorism, and substantial money for correctional services (prison and probation) from April 2005 onwards. Again, apart from the Department of Health, this was a great victory as it was Year 1 of the new Spending Review but the final year of the previous three-year spending cycle and resources at this stage were not being allocated for the coming twelve months – understandably, given that there had to be a Budget before the general election.

In addition there were really important measures within the Office of the Deputy Prime Minister on community-safety funding and on retaining some semblance of the Neighbourhood Renewal Fund, which is really crucial to the most desperate and deprived areas.

We also agreed to return to some of the bigger issues – like prison places – at the end of the year, with a continuing review between the Home Office and the Treasury.

I never saw through the further review because I left government on 15 December 2004.

And so to Special Cabinet, prior to the Spending Review announcement on the Wednesday morning. Gordon was extremely friendly and talked very positively about the Home Office and me. He painted a picture of what would happen from 2008 onwards, of 1.9 per cent average growth, how dreadful things were going to be and how everybody needed to wind down what they wanted to do. I just couldn't resist putting my hand on his shoulder and saying, 'I'm really surprised that you want to continue being Chancellor with such a dreadful scenario.' There was utter silence – I could feel jaws dropping – and then everybody began to laugh. When I saw Tony afterwards for a private meeting, he said, 'Only you could have got away with that.' I thought to myself, 'I wonder if I have!' – but I just couldn't resist it.

Gordon rang me later in the morning to run through what he was putting in his Statement, and was perfectly friendly. As ever, the Statement itself was a triumph, and whatever the struggles of the past few days, I managed a smile.

The weekend [10–11 July] was very bad as the political temperature rose, and an enormous amount of pressure was being exerted on Tony. There have been all sorts of internal rumours about manoeuvres to replace him in the late autumn, and real difficulties dealing with what is always the hothouse of July. We have had the usual fever about reshuffles, and the big five-year strategic plans from Education and Health (with Charles and John appearing on Sunday television to promote them).

Robin Butler presented his report [on intelligence-gathering in the run-up to the Iraq war] on Wednesday 14 July. Given the coverage of this right across the media, it is nothing short of a miracle that we scraped home in the Hodge Hill by-election in Birmingham, and no surprise at all that we lost Leicester South.

The most upsetting thing about the Butler Report was the suggestion that if only we put everything through very formalised Cabinet Committees, then everything would be well, the civil service would be able to give their 'advice' and there would be no danger of wrong decisions – or at least that was the implication.

Of course proper minutes need to be taken, but my own experience is that if we had taken things through formal Cabinet Committees we would have made only a fraction of the progress we have made so far. What we need is more people making firm decisions, not more people talking around issues over and over again until we have talked ourselves into the ground. It is decisive action, with proper accountability, that we need, and if getting ministers together quickly and ensuring that we come out of a meeting with a decision is the way to achieve it, then that's the way it should be done. Whether it is sitting around in the Prime Minister's study or whether it is round the Cabinet table is completely irrelevant. What is important is whether someone, somewhere takes responsibility for deciding something.

Tony is having to lead the debate in Parliament next Tuesday and that probably means that I will have to launch my Home Office strategic plan on the Monday, which is a bind because the moment we have launched it the world will again revolve around Iraq.

Getting the strategic plan right has been quite a task – reading and re-

reading and making lengthy notes, all the while trying to ensure that we don't lose the underlying themes of changing people's lives for the better, giving them the means to take responsibility but also changing the fundamentals.

When I went to the Millan Centre for the Youth Inclusion Programme Awards on Friday, in Firth Park in my constituency, it was absolutely clear that parenting is a crucial issue, and that it is absolutely vital to break generational criminality, engaging the families in being the solution rather than the problem.

We have got a grip of so much. We have transformed the police and reinstated the Beat Teams. We've done as much as we can so far on counter-terrorism and protection, security and stability. We've reversed the upward trend in street robbery and are beginning to get a grip on anti-social behaviour. We have worked nothing short of a minor miracle in reducing asylum by 70 per cent. But there is so much still to be done: to get ID cards in; to implement the Criminal Justice and Sentencing Act and prevent its being overturned on appeal so often; to ensure that the new sex-offenders laws work; and to make the strategic plan not just what we've done but a vision of what we need to do, to draw on the foundations of three years and then to demonstrate that we know what the next steps must be. We also need to counteract the ridiculous view that there is a Year Zero when everything can suddenly be put right, when there is no need for more legislation, no need for more urgent action, when we can just leave everything to itself and it will run like clockwork. Rather, the process is incremental: you lay the bricks and then when they've settled and people have accepted that what you've done makes sense, when originally they perhaps thought you were doing the wrong thing, you can then lay the next bricks on top. Whatever I do now, someone else will be able to build on.

I now have to do interviews with Alan Travis of the *Guardian*, Gaby Hinsliff and Andrew Rawnsley of the *Observer* and Peter Riddell of *The Times*, just to see if we can round up what we've been doing and where we are going. As I also have dinner with Paul Dacre lined up I think I've done my bit for the end of this Session in terms of keeping on top of the messages, as well as delivering them within the system.

It is always a combination of the day-to-day administration and telling the story about the wider picture. Whatever days there were when it was possible to hide your light under a bushel have long gone. What you have to do now is to shine the light to ensure that the message and the delivery go hand in hand, so that if people feel better and feel something is happening – including in the services, like the police – then they'll deliver, they'll do it better, and it will encourage and support them in carrying out what it is you want them to do.

I suppose that's one of my big problems. I don't have the outreach to the judges, and they very often haven't got the first idea what it is that I am trying to do, the balance that I am trying to achieve.

One illustration of the strange political environment we were in was Ed Balls (who had been Gordon's chief economist) appearing on the *Today* programme at 8.10 a.m.. I say strange because as a candidate for the forthcoming general election [he was to win Normanton], but with no formal role, he was being treated as though he was speaking on behalf of government.

Sunday 18 July: had to go down to London for early evening on Sunday for a private meeting. It is critical that I focus on work and concentrate on everything I have got to do and get myself through to the summer break. I am due to go to Italy on Saturday 14 August, which seems a long way away. I think I had only three and a half hours' sleep that night, so I got up at about five a.m. and took some paracetamol, showered and pulled myself round for appearing on the *Today* programme, which I was doing from South Eaton Place. It was a poor interview, not just because I was below par but because Jim Naughtie hadn't done his homework and so we were all over the place with questions. To make things worse, I could hear over my earphones his rapidly turning his papers, which is always a sign that his mind is elsewhere! I was a bit better on Radio 5 Live: they were interested in the strategic plan and where we were going, but of course there always has to be a 'story', whereas what we are doing is setting out a road map of where we are going, which is nowhere near as exciting as an immediate announcement.

Tony's people had briefed that a great many of the troubles we were facing originated back in the 1960s and the 'flower power' era. In the broadcasts, and when we got to the formal launch of the strategic plan in Camden, to get across the message that many of our problems lay in the 1980s, I think between us we managed to square the circle, but only just. I knew precisely what Tony was getting at – a kind of *laissez-faire*, look-after-yourself libertarianism – but mass unemployment, disintegration of the family and downright selfish individualism are just as much to blame as the 'anything goes' attitude of the 1960s and early 1970s. It is perhaps because in the 1960s anything didn't go with me and those immediately around me that colours my view!

So we got back on my more familiar territory of rights and responsibilities, obligations and duties. I just wish we had left it all until September, gone into recess early and got everything to calm down. We usually go up in the opinion polls when we all go away, and certainly this July, as with so many of the previous ones, the fever pitch inside the House of Commons doesn't help.

Tony was good, and between us I think we were getting the message across. It is a solid message that it will take time to bed in, but we have laid the foundation and now we can build on it. We just obviously need the time to be able to do so.

Little did I know that I had only six months left in the job. I had anticipated at least a further year and probably two years, as I thought that all the main players would still be in their jobs a year after the general election.

What we are also doing is building up to the crime stats that come out on Thursday, along with the announcement that police numbers have once again improved. We just have to anticipate what is going to hit us next from around the corner, and try to put in place presentation that effectively gets in first, because we know that whatever the statistics we are bound to be in difficulties on violent crime. The way in which the statistics are now collected makes this inevitable, as we are counting the kind of violent crimes that were never before registered – such as people biffing each other when they turn out of the pub on a Saturday night.

The Statement to the House was as bad as I have ever made, not aided by the restlessness on my own side and the well-organised disruption and destabilisation from Eric Forth [MP for Bromley and Chislehurst, who died in 2006] and a small group of Tory backbenchers on the other side: they did a phenomenal job of shouting, talking, providing verbal interventions at key moments and generally creating as much disruption as possible. I have to say they were very successful at it. Fortunately it doesn't show up on the television, so long as you manage to stay calm and keep going. My problem, as friends keep pointing out, is that I don't watch my body language. I keep my voice calm but I can't always keep my shoulders and my face from displaying the tension or anger. I am going to have to work on this.

As ever, the questions after the Statement were no problem at all. It's just that you do need your own side to back in. Any five-year plan is about reform, and there is enormous suspicion about modernisation, even after seven years in government.

Mind you, when two of my Braille pages stuck together and I turned them over at once, I did think for a second that I had scored the most enormous own goal and that this was going to be the moment when I stood at the Dispatch Box reading out entirely the wrong material – and, unlike past occurrences of this sort, not having had a drop to drink! Fortunately I managed to disentangle the sheets and recognise what the problem was, although there was inevitably an embarrassing pause.

For the second Monday running, David Davis, my opposite number, wasn't in the House – which I thought was pretty crass. He had gone to the USA. There was a great deal of comment about this, given that this was our strategic plan and we were also dealing with the Spending Review. I can only presume that he'd thought we would go into recess earlier.

All the froth that had been going on about the reshuffle came to nothing. Tony had made it clear privately that he wasn't intent on making changes, but nobody took any notice. It would have been far better if there had been a much more robust announcement from No. 10 earlier in the summer to say that there would be no reshuffle: that would have taken some of the heat out of the tea room and the bars inside the Palace of Westminster.

I spoke to Tony on the phone on the Monday evening. There was no point in arguing about the 1960s versus 1980s, and we talked about Peter Mandelson becoming an EU Commissioner. I said that I didn't think it would be a disadvantage in a referendum, if we had to hold one, on the euro. I didn't think that there would be a referendum in any case, because I thought the French would vote No. Tony asked me whether I thought that if he made the announcement, there would be a bad reaction. I said: 'No, I don't think there will. I think the argument about the euro is meaningless because it will be a domestic campaign, not a European one.' I said that there would be kerfuffle for a day or two over the appointment, but it would die away. And, to be frank, Peter having a proper job to do is better than Peter without one!

Tony was helped on the Tuesday in the debate on the Butler Report by what Michael Howard had said to the *Sunday Times*: that he would have voted against the motion because of its wording, but would have voted for the war. Of course that created absolute confusion. Nobody knew what the hell he was talking about so he just made a complete prat of himself. The convoluted presentation of using wording as an excuse for not voting against on one occasion, but voting against on another, was bizarre.

As Alastair Campbell said, another terrible week turned out not to be a terrible week after all. We have had a number of these now.

And then we got out our latest statement on nationality and asylum, including language and citizenship for imams, and on Thursday we got the crime stats out. I wonder sometimes whether Roy Jenkins was right. It doesn't matter how good the overall improvement, it doesn't matter how much crime overall, including street robbery, comes down, there is always something that is going wrong. We are still suffering from the change in the formula for counting the Recorded Crime Statistics – every egg-throwing, every pub brawl, everything is recorded now. It is good for transparency but awful for politics.

The night before, Wednesday [21 July], I had had dinner with Howell James, the new Permanent Secretary for Communications, who used to work with John Major and had now been appointed to do the job of co-ordination across government. I then went on to the fortieth-birthday party for Ross Kemp [*EastEnders* actor]. As I arrived, John Stevens was just saying his farewells to Rebekah Wade [Ross Kemp's wife and editor of the *Sun*]. Gordon had been there earlier, and I think I just arrived at the right time for the cutting of the cake. Everyone was pretty well lubricated, and – lo and behold – Piers Morgan was there as well. Despite their clashes, he and Rebekah have known each other for donkeys' years. God knows how long the party went on but I got home late for me – at 11.45!

The following day my cousin Pauline and her husband Minolo came over from Spain, and we had dinner in the House of Commons, which for me was a moment of tranquillity. I am still not spending enough time with family and friends. People have to be booked in and other diary items shifted around to make it possible.

But I did manage to get to the wedding of John Hutton and his partner Heather on the terrace at the House of Commons on the Saturday – a very enjoyable affair, even though everyone was doing their best to cheer me up because it was pretty obvious that I was down in the dumps.

I was going to go up to the Warwick University Labour Party National Policy Forum, but rather than try to be in three places at once I stayed in London for *Breakfast with Frost* on Sunday morning, which on this particular weekend was being hosted by Andrew Marr.

It proved an important weekend at Warwick – where I relied on junior ministers to ensure that everything was smoothed over in relation to some of our controversial policies – and the 'Warwick Accord' became the foundation for a period of peace within the Labour Party and trade-union movement as agreements were reached on the run-up to the forthcoming election manifesto.

I so often do television programmes 'down the line' rather than in the studio, so appearing 'on the couch' for *Breakfast with Frost* made quite a change. It also made me a little more restrained about how much I drank at the wedding!

And then off up to East Yorkshire to celebrate the tenth wedding anniversary of Paul and Judith Potts, which made this an unusually social weekend for me. Back to Sheffield on Monday morning and down to London for a busy week, clearing up after Parliament has gone into recess. There was a barbecue on Tuesday evening at Jonathan Sedgwick's home, as a farewell from him to everyone he has been working with in our office. We are going to miss him enormously.

Over the previous year and for my remaining time in the Home Office, I had one of the best teams working with me that anyone could wish to have. Despite all my grumbles about incompetence and things going wrong, I can only say that the people who worked with me in my Private Office were committed 100 per cent to me and to what I was trying to do. Hard taskmaster as I always was, I could not have asked for more with regard to their willingness, the enormously long hours they worked, and the care they took in trying to ensure that individuals in the Department and elsewhere understood what was being asked of them, and wherever possible getting them to do it.

I went to GCHQ at Cheltenham and met up with Parmjit Dhanda, MP for Gloucester, then on to community groups, where there has been great upset and bewilderment over the terrorist arrest [the arrest of Saajid Badat, arrested in Gloucester in November 2003 and subsequently convicted].

I had to hold my nerve over this one. In the end the community in Gloucester was very polite and prepared to listen, but it wasn't until the court hearing and the admission of guilt that people realised the enormity of what had been going on under their noses, and that what I had said nationally was in fact true: that we were dealing with a terrorist.

I stayed overnight with Tessa Jowell and David in Warwickshire, then went back up to Sheffield for my gastroscopy test at the Northern General Hospital.

Wednesday 28 July: had dinner with John Prescott in his flat – a very pleasant occasion. In fact it was the most pleasant occasion that John and I have had for a very long time. We talked about all sorts of things, including the dinner he had hosted for Tony and Gordon, acting as a broker and peacemaker, and some of the little quips that had enlivened the evening. We talked about the Warwick Forum and what was happening in the party. There was also a little query about my private life – but my private life is private.

What a strange feeling: to authorise a phone tap warrant in order to protect myself. I am not entirely sure whether or not I should have passed this one to Jack as Foreign Secretary or Geoff Hoon at the MoD, given that it was so personal, but they wanted it urgently and it seemed sensible that if there was a genuine threat – and their evidence was pretty overwhelming – then I should authorise it, whether it was for me or anyone else. Anyway, if there is anything wrong the Commissioner will pick it up.

I never authorised any warrant where I knew the individual myself. There was a clear rule about this, so that any potential conflict of interest would be avoided, but there doesn't appear to be a conflict of interest when your own life is threatened – just a need to stay rational.

On Friday 30 July Valda Waterfield, who had worked with me full-time for twenty-four years, stepped down from running the constituency office, not to stop working for me altogether but to relinquish what by anybody's standards was an extremely stressful job dealing with the day-to-day problems and gripes of people in the constituency. This had become more arduous since I had become Home Secretary, as the constituency office was often the first port of call for asylum and nationality cases from across the country. The job is a combination of psychiatrist and social worker.

Tony Banks was to describe it in much more vivid terms when he stepped down from Parliament and moved into the House of Lords before his tragic death. He said that in his view long-standing constituency personal assistants and secretaries are the unsung heroes of politics. They are virtually never recognised because those doing the recognition have no clue whatsoever as to what they have to do or the conditions under which they do it. But they make a difference to the lives of millions of people in terms of the day-to-day activity and the way in which they use the democratic power of elected parliamentary representatives to change the lives of others, to make representations to departments, to local government and to other agencies.

The fact that so few of them are recognised, including in the Honours List, is a condemnation of those who make the recommendations. The people who do so recommend those whom they know, but they haven't got the first idea of the work that goes on at grass-roots level in the constituency offices of all three main political parties. They can have no such knowledge because none of those who make recommendations on honours, nor those who make final recommendations, have ever touched anything like an advice surgery or a constituency office in the thick of a disadvantaged area.

There isn't an MP worth his or her salt who doesn't think that those who work in their constituency offices, because they are in touch day to day with those we represent, offer the sail and the rudder, to predict the tide and to be able to determine the way in which the current of politics is running. But I have never heard a political broadcast ever mention them.

August 2004

Rejoice, I had a weekend off. I didn't even have a read-out of the papers on Sunday [1 August], and I had Monday off as well. It is impossible to describe how unbelievable it is to have a weekend and a Monday without the papers, and how it can make such a difference to my life – to be free of what appears to be a dark cloud always hanging over me, to walk, to have meals, to drink and to talk to friends, and to do nothing that has anything whatsoever to do with politics and not to have the shadow of condemnation hanging over me for just three days. Bliss.

But back to reality on the Tuesday: thirteen people picked up in a counter-terrorism sweep, one released almost immediately. I am always keen that they don't overdo it. If we get two genuine terrorists, we should concentrate on those, not on a dozen people who may be peripheral to what we are doing.

On Wednesday [4 August] the Joint Committee (of the Lords and

Commons) on Human Rights produced their report on the controversial Part 4 of the Anti-Terrorism, Crime and Security Act, which I had piloted through Parliament three years earlier. It coincided with the anti-terrorism sweep and a great deal of froth from across the Atlantic about new sources of evidence. A great deal of what was now being done was routed back as far as 2001.

The significance of this was that David Davis, Shadow Home Secretary, was going from studio to studio claiming that we should be doing what the Americans were doing. We had chosen to do exactly the opposite, and were wise to do so. Although we had no control whatsoever over the publication of the Joint Committee on Human Rights Report, it did prove to be, by a strange coincidence, appropriate timing.

Once again the balance of reassurance and providing a sense of security while taking care to avoid hiding the truth was uppermost in my mind. Those who think that senior politicians carrying responsibility for such critical issues do not feel and think as they would are gravely mistaken.

I was pressed around a dozen times to do radio and television but chose not to. For someone constantly being accused of using the media to promote government action, it was strange to be refusing to use the media in order to appear to be doing something, and still to be accused of using the press 'to appear to be doing something'.

But I am more resigned to this now. People can only see what they can see.

It is a bit like Donald Rumsfeld's famous convoluted but accurate saying: 'Reports that say that something hasn't happened are always interesting to me, because as we know, there are known knowns; there are things we know we know. We also know there are known unknowns; that is to say, we know there are some things we do not know. But there are also unknown unknowns – the ones we don't know we don't know.'

No one knows when you are not doing something for a reason. They only see what you are doing visibly. I am afraid, particularly as Home Secretary, it was necessary to learn to live with this, although it has to be said that it took me a long time.

In any case, the best way of helping the intelligence and security services to do their job in these circumstances is to keep as quiet as possible. It is unthinkable to reveal to terrorists what we know so that they can then make a judgement on what we don't know.

In Tony's absence on holiday we gave a briefing to John Prescott and to Gordon, who was flying to America. Is this really August?

We spent the whole of Wednesday [4 August] ensconced with our own Terrorism Unit, with Eliza Manningham-Buller's deputy at MI5 (Eliza herself was away) and with David Veness, Head of SO13. COBR meetings of officials had been taking place twice daily for some considerable time, so there was a sense of relief that at least this part of the operation had been successful.

Life was made more difficult by the fact that I had telephone and surveillance warrants to renew from the previous three months, so the changed nature of the job becomes very evident.

I spent the next eight days preparing for events in September, including the Superintendents' Annual Conference, and trying to complete all the outstanding work that needed to be cleared before I went on holiday. Odd things had to be dealt with, like the three Congressmen who were over from the US, and given that there were no other Cabinet ministers around except John Prescott and myself, I agreed to meet them – not an auspicious time for them to be coming when we were so busy, but it had to be done.

I had also had to deal with the Commons Home Affairs Select Committee report on ID cards. I said to the press office that it was really important that we had something ready rather than waiting until the embargo was over.

The report itself was very supportive. The task was to highlight those parts that backed in heavily behind us and to be able to deal with those parts that were critical. Predicting and having something ready in advance of the embargo was, in my view, vital, but it was hard to get across to officials that it was quite likely that the embargo would be broken – and it was. Had we not been ready, a good story could have turned into a very bad one by not spotting the googlies well in advance and having an instant response. Everything now has to be as speedy as possible if we are not to lose the initiative and the momentum.

I was very fortunate that not only did I have high-quality special advisers but that they always got on extremely well with the career civil service. Each knew what their role was and didn't overstep the mark, and in this way we were able to avoid the politicisation of the civil service while ensuring that government policy was understood, and that at least we had some idea what the messages were going to be, in what was always a completely frenetic environment, with a story sometimes almost every hour.

My advisers had been able to take a last-minute look at what the report said and to advise press officers on what were likely to be the headlines coming out of it. There is no reason why career civil servants should always know what the key political messages or controversy will be, and that is why it is crucial to have the advisers assisting them if they are to have any chance of being able to deal with an ever more sophisticated media.

On Thursday [5 August] I talked to Tom Ridge in the USA twice. The main task is to stop the authorities there naming the main suspects we have picked up and blowing the judicial process.

I half succeeded. The unofficial briefings continued, but at least the US administration didn't interfere in a way that would have made it difficult for us.

And I have managed to wrap up the David Westwood affair: he has changed his mind and will take early retirement. I am relieved because a continuing battle would have been a diversion, and Humberside Police can now get back to some sort of long-term reform and improvement programme.

We had a very enjoyable party for Valda on Friday. Dozens of people came, all of them just to say thank you for what she has done over the years in the office – and keeping me afloat. We are all having dinner in Derbyshire with my friends who have come across from Canada, David and Kate Boyce. It is also a special birthday celebration for Kate so it will be a happy joint occasion.

I opened the new sensory garden at Chatsworth House on Saturday afternoon [7 August]. I had worked with the Dowager Duchess on this for a year – well, she had worked on it with her nephew, and I had given encouragement! The police had warned us that there was likely to be a major demonstration by the Anti-Deportation Group, who have indicated that they want to break up the event, which is bringing together a whole range of blind and partially sighted people from across Derbyshire. The group had decided to 'adopt' the asylum seeker who sewed his lips together, and despite the fact that we found him a place of safety he had discharged himself and they now saw him as a suitable cause to adopt. All the security measures automatically went into place but Chatsworth understandably wanted to play it down. They didn't want people being physically evicted, so we were trying to stop the demonstrators getting in in the first place. It was no big deal – in fact it's par for the course. I have got so used to things like this that I rarely mention them in my diary any more.

In fact it was a lovely afternoon. The temperature was about 100 degrees Fahrenheit and we had to shorten the ceremony as both people and guide dogs were beginning to suffer in the heat. In the event the demonstrators didn't come and there was no disruption, so it was all a fuss about nothing. As Home Secretary, I had become used to being public enemy No. 1, but it did become wearing on everybody around me.

What really gets me about these people who are supposedly so 'supportive' of failed asylum seekers is not that many of them don't care, nor even the demonstrations and the *Angst*; it is that some of them are prepared to see someone starve themselves to death (which is what was being encouraged in this case). The only person being damaged is the asylum seeker. It is what we used to call 'coat-holding' of the worst order. I was appalled that Yorkshire Television (in the magazine programme *Calendar*) were giving this so much publicity – just entirely what the Anti-Deportation Group wanted. It only encourages other people to do exactly the same.

All of this made a row about a prisoner who had won £7 million on the National Lottery seem completely trivial, although the papers went to town about it, I suppose because it is the silly season. It has to be said that I was aggravated myself, so we are going to have to do something to stop people from being able to cause this kind of ridiculous publicity (given that it is impossible to stop relatives and friends of prisoners putting on anything they like for the Lottery).

I only gave a very brief mention in the diary at this moment to the fact that the government had won the appeal-court hearing – chaired by the Lord Chief Justice and with some of the more substantial appeal-court judges sitting – in relation to the detainees under the Anti-Terrorism, Crime and Security Act Part 4. What I wasn't to realise at the time was that the fact that they were unanimous lulled me into a false sense of security about what the Law Lords would do on exactly the same issue.

The Attorney General, Lord Peter Goldsmith, had asked me not to press the alternative provisions that we had laid out in our consultation paper, or produce a detailed White Paper, because this would undermine the House of Lords' hearings. I understood this entirely, but it put me in a very awkward situation, as I was unable to pick up and work with those outside the Home Office on the two main alternative options. These were Control Orders – which I had wanted for low-level activity – with low-level restrictions, or getting agreement (which at the time seemed impossible) to taking through the normal court system provisions relating to the rules of evidence, admissibility and crucially an extension of the Public Interest Immunity, to protect the Security and Intelligence Services. Clearly nothing I could have done then could have dealt with the extraordinary judgement of Justice Sullivan at the end of June 2006 in overturning Charles Clarke's legislation. There remained a third option, which was to take the appeal-court ruling of early August 2004 as a benchmark and challenge Parliament to reassert its original position in relation to detention. I wasn't to know that this might have been the most difficult option at the time but the least difficult over the following eighteen months.

I was not to be there to see this through, as that weekend my world – and the world of others – imploded.

On the Saturday I left with my older sons to meet friends at a house we had rented in Italy. The following day – Sunday 15 August – the News of the World *ran a story about my private life, the front-page 'splash' of which is sufficient for here:*

> *Home Secretary David Blunkett is having a secret affair with a married mum, the News of the World can reveal.*
>
> *They have been meeting up for three years but she has so far refused to leave her husband.*
>
> *A source told the News of the World: 'They are torn. There's a deep love but neither of them knows what the future will hold.'*

They did not name the lady in question, and in this book neither will I. My refusal to name names might seem odd to some readers. But throughout these pages I have expressed my conviction that it is proper for my private life to be kept private, and while the events which followed the 'revelations' that weekend were – and continue to be – tempestuous for all involved, they are relevant to the outside world only in so far as they have affected the course of my political life. In subsequent days tabloid newspapers intruded into an aspect of this personal relationship which became subject to the Family Court process from the autumn onwards.

Unsurprisingly the whole of the holiday was completely overshadowed by the necessity to see and provide advice to Huw Evans on the most terrible speculation and invective which poured from the pens of journalists back in Britain.

Other journalists searched for me in Italy. People who had no idea about anything whatsoever to do with this matter pretended they were in the know and were being quoted.

Virtually every day for the next fifteen months was either a nightmare or an anticipated nightmare, with the most gross intrusion into the private lives of several people and massive collateral damage to family and friends. The very fact that my private life had always been kept private in every way, screening me from the presumption that as a public figure I was fair game, seemed to exacerbate the hunger for more and more detail. I owe my special adviser Huw Evans, and many others who helped me, the deepest debt of gratitude, and I owe my sons and my closest friends my thanks beyond measure for putting up with what they had to endure, and for sticking with me. Only those who have experienced this will understand, and it is something I would not wish on anyone, anywhere.

Let me make it clear. The previous decisions I had taken had led to the position I was in. The decisions that I then took at that time and in September were to lead inexorably to my resignation on 15 December. Those decisions were mine. I carry responsibility for my actions. In the full knowledge of what was likely to be done and said, I chose to take my own path. I blame no one else for this. Had I taken a different road, then it is likely that I would have remained as Home Secretary until Tony Blair chose to make a change. But I repeat: I would make the same decisions again, and whatever the British media have to account for, they must account to themselves. All of us have to live with ourselves more than we have to live with others. I know I could not have lived with myself had I taken a different decision on the personal front.

One further point at this stage: I did not believe then or in subsequent months that there was any suggestion that, as with the revelations in August 2006 about phone-tapping the Royal Household, my phone had been tapped by national newspapers – not least because of the complete and gross inaccuracies that were printed over a period of almost two years.

However, by the summer of 2006 I was so deeply worried that I raised the issue with Special Branch officers who had been my protection officers in 2004 in the light of extraordinarily strange interventions on my mobile phone, which led me to believe that someone was verifying that this was my phone. It is extraordinary to have to decide that you will make no private phone calls on your own phone because of the danger that someone is listening and distorting what they hear for their own ends.

That Sunday evening Tony – who himself was on holiday in Tuscany – was extremely understanding and helpful. He and Cherie invited me to join them for supper at the villa of their friends the Strozzis, near San Gimignano. We spent only five minutes discussing my problems and had a wonderfully comfortable and supportive evening.

The Italian security people co-operated extraordinarily well and protected me from being found, or being seen going into the Strozzis' villa. But somehow the papers got their own distorted version of what was happening.

The Strozzis showed us the cellars and the tunnels and the paintings of their family, as the main rivals of the Medicis. They were celebrating a thousand years of wine-growing and farming on the land, and in the year 2000 had produced a Millennium Chianti.

I still have a bottle they gave me that evening.

A week later, we were invited back – this time in the company of Andrea Bocelli, the blind Italian opera singer, more famous in the USA and the rest of Europe than in Italy. He couldn't sing because he had a chest infection and Alastair's girlfriend couldn't play her clarinet because we didn't have the right instruments, but we had a glorious evening nevertheless. It was an opportunity to put aside the troubles for just a couple of hours.

So I came back after what was, with few exceptions, a most stressful holiday, not only for me but for my sons and friends who were with me, to try to pick up the pieces.

I know one thing. I am blessed with some unconditional friends – not uncritical but unconditional. I have a constituency party unequalled in understanding and support. They do believe in mutuality and comradeship.

But who are all these people being quoted in the papers who claim to be 'close to' me? Someone, somewhere is lying and frankly it doesn't matter who it is because the result is the same.

So we carry on saying, 'Private is private.' We carry on saying, 'No one is authorised to say a single thing on my behalf except Huw Evans,' but it continues to make not a halfpenny worth of difference. If I had said anything myself it would have breached my own privacy and justified the dam opening – and to breach my own privacy would allow my opponents to combine the public and the private, which now must be their main concern.

The *Guardian* had a leader condemning voyeurism and *The Times* had a leader condemning the *Guardian*. What a bear pit this is.

What price Bob Boothby and Dorothy Macmillan? What price the great editors, the actions of William Rees-Mogg, as outlined in Roy Hattersley's book *Who Goes Home?* on the most trivial matters? What price the consequences?

The reference to Roy's book illustrates how an amusing episode can briefly light up even the darkest times. Roy recounts how during the Heath government he returned to the Commons from a trip to the Middle East to take part in vote after vote on Labour amendments to a Tory Industrial Relations Bill. Jetlagged and frustrated, he eventually gave up and decided to go home to bed.

> *As I walked through Parliament Square, a polite young man asked me why I was not taking part in the Great Protest. I told him, 'Just because the Shadow Cabinet are making bloody fools of themselves, there is no reason why I should do the same.' The polite young man was a recent recruit to* The Times' *parliamentary staff.*
>
> *My comment on the conduct of my elders and betters appeared on the front page of the first edition. I do not know how William Rees-Mogg – editor of the paper in those days – discovered that my opinion had been obtained by a journalist who had not identified himself. But when he found out he was horrified. In that more gentle age, even when the rules were broken by mistake,* The Times *made amends. The story was taken out of the paper's second edition and Rees-Mogg – who then lived round the corner from me – came to my front door with the offending article and his apologies.*
>
> *It was well after midnight when he rang the bell and I came slowly downstairs expecting a message from the whips, demanding my return to Parliament. My father – who was asleep in the basement bedroom – took longer to regain consciousness and the door had slammed shut before he had made his anxious way into the hall. He was, I knew, a worrier. So I said, at once, 'Nothing to worry about, Dad. Just the editor of* The Times. *He's brought me a copy of tomorrow's paper.' My father's expression changed from anxiety to awe. 'Does he do that every night?' he asked.*

Direct and sustained briefings were now being aimed at linking my private and public life. I know that I must hold my nerve and not bite back.

September 2004

Back in harness on Thursday 2 September, in Manchester to launch the 'Prison Without Bars' satellite tracking system. If we can make this work we can stabilise the prison population and track people, hour by hour, metre by metre. But can we get the technology to work? Well, the three pilots we are putting in place will soon tell us. They have made it work in Florida, where there are 25,000 people on satellite tracking – like a GPS system – but I haven't got the time to go out and see it for myself. The media are in Manchester in droves but they have not come to see the satellite tracking.

David Davis phoned my Private Office to say that he was very sorry, and that he wouldn't be using the coverage politically.

All this changed from the end of November, but understandably so.

What disappoints me most is that the press have now used this opportunity to abandon any pretence of adhering to the universal convention of not identifying my homes. They are now pinpointing where I live, even liberal newspapers like the *Observer*. It is almost an open invitation. They may not know that my security-risk rating has gone up, but the very fact that they don't know should surely make them pause with regard to whether they decide to take a risk with my life and be prepared to do what newspapers have always previously done – respect the request not to put someone at risk.

Of course, I shouldn't have been so naïve. Those who were doing the identifying had an agenda of their own, as became clear a year later.

One thing is certain, when you are back in the maelstrom, it concentrates the mind. Andrew Green of Migration Watch has been causing mischief with the statistics that were published while I was away, and the Department does not have what we call a rebuttal strategy. Again this is anticipating what is likely to come and making sure that you have got absolutely clear lines to do something with it. It is rarely the fault of the press office. It is usually that officials don't understand that if the message is distorted, or we take a hammering, then it makes it less likely that they will be able to do their job properly.

One thing that made me very sad was Margaret Cook, Robin's ex-wife, attacking me in an article in the *New Statesman*. She hasn't the first idea about my circumstances or my relationship, and in any case, bearing in mind what she herself has been through, I would have thought she would have had the nous to understand that my situation was in fact very different from the one that she had experienced.

I spent the whole of the first week in September revising the first draft of the new policy paper on police reform – a kind of stage-two reform – because what we did back in 2001 and 2002 was really to finish an outdated agenda that had never been completed. Now we need to look at the next phase.

I want to concentrate everything on making a difference in the community, on getting the Beat Teams out in every neighbourhood and changing people's perception of the police so that they feel that they are 'on their side'. I have taken a decision that big structural change is not appropriate, that we should encourage small police authorities to amalgamate, and that we should do everything we can to ensure that we run regional structures for organised crime and counter-terrorism. Since the big clash with the police service in the early days there has been tremendous co-operation, and even the Police Federation, as with their reception last May, are now prepared to go along with modernisation if they feel it is in their interests.

God – all my worries about asylum statistics and police reform and continuing counter-terrorism pale into insignificance in the face of the little children murdered in their school in Chechnya. What a terrible, terrible thing. It certainly puts my problems into context.

But politics continues. Sometimes an event can catch you by surprise, and often it triggers action by Tony, totally outside the timescale and the planning that he has put in place. We've had Steve Byers's resignation and then Estelle, Peter Mandelson going twice, Alan Milburn deciding to stand down and now [Monday 6 September] Andrew Smith hands in his resignation. I know Andrew well, and like him. I count him as a political friend, but I had no idea he was going to do it – perhaps in anticipation of the reshuffle and what might happen, or perhaps because he has told me already that he thinks his own constituency is at risk from the Liberal Democrats. He is worried that he is vulnerable as a government minister and cannot devote the time to shoring up support in his constituency. What a choice.

On Radio 4's *PM*, Mark Mardell commented that 'the Chancellor has cut him adrift'. I'm not entirely sure that's fair, but he has certainly put up a good fight from Work and Pensions. He has done a good job at getting the Pension Protection Fund into being and the beginnings of the Financial Assistance Scheme.

I was to pick up both of these when I became Work and Pensions Secretary in May 2005. I know how hard Andrew Smith worked to get these embryo programmes off the ground and how much difficulty he must have faced. But he always had a very low profile, and while some people can make that into a virtue, others fall foul of the press because they are 'invisible'.

On Channel 4 news at 7 p.m. Nick Brown was up. I don't know whether he thought it was helpful to Gordon or anyone else, but if I'm honest we all have a propensity to decide to put our two pennyworth in at times like this. I have tried as much as I can always to be supportive and helpful, but sometimes it is damned difficult.

Week beginning Monday 6 September: it is quite clear that the major issue over the reshuffle is whether Alan Milburn should become Chairman of the Labour Party. There is enough speculation to last a lifetime and I fear some of it that appeared in the *Sunday Times* [on 5 September] may well have come from a lunch that someone I know very closely had with David Cracknell of that paper. Wherever it came from, it is taking hold, but you would have to be a political hermit not to be aware of the forces ranged against the idea. This is all about who should run the general-election campaign and who is in charge of what, when and where. It is tedious and it is energy-sapping, and it is all about the power struggle that has been going on for ten years.

In the end Ian McCartney stayed on as Chairman of the Labour Party and Alan Milburn was reinstated to Cabinet in the post of Chancellor of the Duchy of Lancaster, which had remained vacant from the time when Jack Cunningham left the Cabinet. It was an unhappy and uneasy solution, but it gave Tony the right to determine who his person would be in the build-up to the election campaign and in the campaign itself. But it soon became clear that in reality there was absolutely no way in which Gordon, who had been based in Party HQ for the previous two elections, would not play a key role. It was, however, deeply destabilising.

If I had known then what I know now, I would have asked Tony to move me to a less exacting role where I could have sorted out my private life and been under much less pressure and a little less in the public eye. But hindsight is a wonderful thing.

I was getting a great deal of support, not just from family and friends but from my team and the wider political arena. I was a bit disappointed that one person of whom I expected something better talked at the end of August at a dinner party that was reported back to me about 'the jury being out on whether the publicity would be damaging'. This is not the point. Publicity about your private life is always damaging: the question is whether people are prepared to back in and help. It was a bit disconcerting to have a political ally not realise that words said in any arena are likely to be reported back.

The situation with this ally was put right later.

It is clear that Alan would not have come back into government unless he had a proper role to play, and although he has worked very closely with Gordon as Chief Secretary, there can be no one in any doubt whatsoever about his commitment to supporting Tony.

Alan Johnson has taken over from Andrew at Work and Pensions. I gave him a ring on Wednesday evening as I thought it would be helpful just to run through with him what I had been doing at Employment and the kind of issues that I thought would be relevant, and also to wish him well and give support. I was a bit surprised that Ruth Kelly had been made Alan Milburn's No. 2. It didn't strike me as being entirely up her street.

Before Cabinet on Thursday morning we had one of the famous Cabinet photographs. I quipped: 'If you are in the photo, you are still in the Cabinet. Each photograph that goes by and you are still there, is another notch.' It is very strange. You can be airbrushed out or airbrushed in. You don't have to be there physically for the photograph, as long as you appear in the final version. On this occasion Alistair Darling's plane was late so he was duly airbrushed in later.

It's funny that I should have made a note of this in my diary. It was almost prescient that something traumatic was likely to happen – but, of course, there is nothing more ephemeral than being in the Cabinet.

I had an entertaining occurrence – entertaining because it didn't go seriously wrong – when having prepared for an announcement on tackling prolific offenders and trying to build on best practice, I went to Leeds for the launch. At the press presentation I was joined by a former prolific offender who had been on drugs and who was publishing a book, and my briefing said that his name was Jeremy. It turned out that his name was Ian.

It was a bit like the Labour Party briefing for a visit I made to Hartlepool during the campaign for the by-election [on 30 September 2004, following Peter Mandelson's appointment as an EU Commissioner]. I was told that Hilda was eighty-three years old, and I said to her: 'You're doing very well for eighty-three.' She replied: 'I'm not eighty-three, I'm sixty-three.' Fortunately we had a laugh about it. It does show though, whether in the Department or on political duty, you do have to be enormously careful with the facts you are given.

The weekend of 11–12 September was filled with constituency events and putting the final touches to my speech on police reform and ideas around greater accountability, including letting local people trigger outside intervention when they were sick and tired of the failure of the police and other agencies to come to their assistance. Resistance to this within government, particularly from officials in the Office of the Deputy Prime Minister, has been considerable, but we appear to be winning.

Monday 13 September: I had once again to appear before the House of Commons, this time at ten o'clock at night, to answer for the antics of Fathers 4 Justice, who pulled one of their stunts at Buckingham Palace. My innumerable meetings with John Stevens, the Metropolitan Police Commissioner, and his senior staff did not seem to be getting us anywhere, on account of police resistance to appropriate measures and the fact that I had no power as Home Secretary to remove or even move the senior officer who remained in charge of royal protection.

Indeed, he was promoted following my departure as home secretary.

The same attitudes and culture prevailed. But it was the Home Secretary who appeared at the Dispatch Box to explain that there hadn't really been a major risk to Buckingham Palace, although there had been a considerable risk to those trying to gain access as it was touch and go as to whether they were likely to be shot. I am becoming tired now of apologising for the failure of others. I have authorised whatever policy decisions were needed. I have even offered to talk to those at the Palace myself and I've taken the opportunity to do so informally when I have had the chance, as with my discussions with Prince Andrew last November (and very briefly in my private meetings with Prince Charles). But this is the nature of our Constitution and there is no point in whingeing about it: I just have to get on with it. As ever, it gives a feeling that the Home Office don't know what they are doing, and on this occasion, Lord help us, it is not the fault of the Home Office at all.

And so to a very busy Thursday and Friday: we had arranged to make a Team and Executive Board visit to the South West, as it seemed to me that it was important that we visited areas that so often get neglected, not least because we have so few Labour seats down there. So we arranged to go to Plymouth, taking in other visits on the way down. At each place we followed pretty much the same pattern: meetings with community groups; listening to the gripes and grumbles of people facing anti-social behaviour and vandalism; talking to the police about what might be done; having public forums and the usual phone-ins on local radio.

In between I was dealing with other matters on the telephone and feeling quite dreadful. I then flew to Holland to have a meeting with the Dutch Interior and Justice Ministers on key European Union business. We went from the airport, had dinner with the ministers, went back to the airport and flew back to Britain. Once again I wondered just how Tony does it.

Speculation about my private life continued, almost like a running commentary. But all I could do was concentrate on the job and prepare for party conference. It is absolutely crucial not to let people see that what is happening is affecting me. The moment I look as though I am not on top of the job, that I am not performing as I always do, that I am not ebullient and resilient – that is the moment when I shall fall.

I remember when John Moore, Secretary of State for Health and Social Security under Margaret Thatcher, was clearly being groomed to take over from her in the mid-1980s. He then had a serious illness, coupled I think with the understandable pressures that go with such a high-profile job, and as a consequence of his absence his political star simply dropped from the sky. Within a matter of months, he had fallen from the pinnacle of political expectation to the depths of obscurity.

Party conference is party conference. These days, when you've been to one you've been to them all. The speeches from Tony and Gordon are consistently good but not, this year at least, memorable.

The diary entries for this point have disappeared so I can genuinely say that the conference was not memorable for me, other than the fact that I had to exude good spirits, take the behind-the-hand murmuring in good part, and receive with good humour the Institute for Public Policy Research's 'rubber chicken' award for my remarks about Harold Shipman – saying only that I hope I can have real turkey for Christmas, rather than the rubber chicken. They obliged – and duly sent me a fine turkey at Christmas.

But there was of course one very memorable moment at the end of the 2004 party conference. In an interview Tony revealed that he did not plan to go on and on as Prime Minister, were we to win the next election, and intended to step down before the end of the next parliament. This took me by surprise, as it did many others.

If I'd had any inkling that such an announcement was coming, I would have counselled thinking three times. I understood the pressure that he was under from those wishing him to go there and then, and the need to provide a release of the safety valve, but his decision came to have very severe and perverse consequences, increasing demands for an early departure rather than relieving them.

Two years later we were to have our own 'Black Wednesday' on 6 September 2006, when a combination of public vitriol and minor but co-ordinated resignations and calls for Tony's departure ignited an already febrile and highly combustible situation. I did my utmost in television interviews that day to steady the ship and warned against the outbreak of collective madness that had started to engulf the Labour Party. Having overseen the leadership contest in 1994, I was astonished, and remain so, by the sheer venom which overtook colleagues whose underlying values are supposedly those of fraternity and mutuality. But there is no doubt that the strongly held differences of view reflected a longstanding division between those committed to a progressive Labour Party facing the challenges of the twenty-first century and those with a nostalgia for opposition politics.

My detailed diary kicks back in on 9 October.

October 2004

Saturday 9 October saw one of the longest advice surgeries I have ever had. We were taking two streams simultaneously – asylum seekers who had been before, and those constituents and asylum seekers who were attending for the first time. If we had not done it this way, I think we would have been there for five or six hours. Of course, advice surgeries ensure that you learn something about how the system is failing, about whether changes made are working, about the administrative chaos and delay, and about the silly little things that are nothing to do with ministers or policy but simply to do with a basic grasp of competence. But you also learn about those who are playing the system. You learn about how, even with the rigorous changes we have brought in, we are still not closing the loopholes.

I fear though that a surgery like this distorts my own overview. I see so much of the difficulties, I see so much of those who clearly were not threatened back home and who we have to remove, and I see the problem of those that we can't remove who are sleeping on other people's floors. It is important though that I continue to do my surgeries because it makes a difference to how I approach the job, but it is so wearing and so unbalanced in terms of the constituency workload that I am in danger of getting it out of focus.

After the surgery I did a walk with Radio Sheffield in the Peak District, talking about the area around where I live, my love of the countryside and of the Peak District ever since I was a small child, and the history behind its long having provided an escape for people living in Sheffield.

We had one of those bizarre incidents where a hunt came along: not a fox hunt but a drag hunt with bloodhounds, and what a sound they make. As they came alongside me, there were people leaning down and greeting me warmly – which was really encouraging – and Johnny Nelson, one of Sheffield's famous boxers, leant down and with a massive hand shook mine, almost lifting me off the ground. The twist to this was that it was only a few days earlier that Trevor Phillips had said, as Chairman of the Commission for Racial Equality, that too frequently black people were not welcome in the countryside and there weren't many of them about. Well, at least there was Johnny Nelson.

Back down to London. Meeting with John Prescott cancelled. I have a feeling this is part of the bad temper he is in with all of us at the moment, but it may just be because he is exhausted, having come back this weekend from Vietnam.

The whole week seemed to be taken up with meetings with Tony – on counter-terrorism, on drugs, on organised crime. Tony wants a Drugs Bill. I said to him that he could have a Drugs Bill if he likes, it just means that we pull it out of the serious organised-crime legislation, and as ID cards and the serious organised-crime legislation are the only things that are likely to get through because of the time between now and Parliament being prorogued before Easter, he wouldn't get it until after. So you pays your money and you takes your choice. So we are going to end up with a Serious Organised Crime and Police Bill, an ID Bill, a Corrections Bill (setting up the National Offender Management Scheme to combine prison and probation) and God knows what else.

As became clear, I ended up with about half the Queen's Speech at the end of November. The preparation for it and the inevitable media presentation of it placed me right in the middle of the political maelstrom. The task was to stay steady, to appear calm and, above all, to keep on top of the enormous brief.

We are going to need at least a Draft Bill on Counter-Terrorism, partly to bring forward the measures we have been consulting on and partly to deal with whatever the aftermath of the House of Lords judgement brings, including thoughts from Peter Goldsmith, Attorney General. But I can't do a lot about that until the judgement is through. I can't afford for any of the proposals we are thinking about to leak.

I felt absolutely lousy during the first part of the week, not just ill but a combination of real depression and physical illness. I think all of this is now getting to me. I am getting on with the job behind the scenes and doing the work and I am staying out of the public limelight in a way that I have never done before. I did some media on Wednesday 13 October for the formalised confirmation of the free passports for the over-75s, which didn't get as much publicity as I had hoped – but it was a nice little event at the Cabinet War Rooms. Other than that I have done the *Today* programme only once since coming back from Italy.

I have to smile because I have had one or two dinners over the past few weeks with people who supposedly never read tabloid newspapers, but it is nevertheless amazing how much they know about my private life and what the tabloids have written; or rather, what they don't know, given the garbage that has been written.

I did a presentation to Cabinet on Thursday [14 October] on the police-reform proposals. People were very supportive, although John Prescott still seems worried that I am interfering with local government when what I am trying to do is to seek to extend some forms of democratic accountability at local level, and offer a real chance for local people to have their say and get action rather than just sympathy. At least local authorities are starting to set up their own Scrutiny Committees, particularly in relation to anti-social behaviour. This is a major break-through, because when I argued this a year ago it was very hard to get anyone to take seriously that local government may well have a major role here. But the world has changed, and the attention now on anti-social behaviour has really motivated people to want to do something about the misery that exists in some of our communities.

We had a brief discussion at Cabinet that morning on the European Union referendum. We had had a meeting at 8.30 a.m. prior to Cabinet to try and thrash out the wording that we would use and whether we go into a referendum, and to allow Jack Straw to announce what that wording would be for the preparatory legislation that we would need in order to carry through the promise to have a referendum, whichever way it went.

I was in one of my awkward moods when I was arguing about the detailed wording. Firstly I argued – and was heavily defeated – that we shouldn't be moving the Bill at this stage at all. But I think my colleagues were probably right in saying that it would look as though we had abandoned the commitment if we didn't even have 'paving' legislation. Secondly I argued about the word 'constitution'. There was a lot of sympathy about this, but the problem is the way in which it has been translated in the Giscard d'Estaing version itself. The suggestion on the table that it should be the 'Constitution for Europe' that we were asking people to vote on was changed to 'Constitution for the European Union', but it all felt to me like a suicide pact. John got annoyed with me and said that I was just being awkward. Tony calmed him by saying: 'Look, it's David. He is always deeply pessimistic about these issues, and better to discuss it here than what some people do outside this room.' Alan Milburn has started to really push people on speed of delivery. I suppose, to be honest, he will have few Red Boxes to deal with and little correspondence, so has plenty of time to be taking a look at whether other people are moving fast enough. At the moment I am prepared to play along, see how things go, and get on with the job. We have plenty of innovation, we have lots of ideas and we just need to get on with it and see what other people are up to.

The Alan Milburn approach to issues is relevant because when we got to the end of the presentation on police reform in Cabinet and we had the questions and answers, Tony was talking about 'Citizen Focus'and how it should be written. I said to him that there weren't many pluses in his job, but one of them is that he doesn't have to write White Papers. Everybody laughed and he took it in very good part and said, 'I think I have got the message, Home Secretary.' I think Alan got the point as well, and he was very good-natured about it.

This was one of the longer Cabinets. Gordon did a short presentation, again just warning us all about the tightness of the Budget from 2008 –

better to be forewarned now when we can make plans and wind down expectations.

John Reid and I had a word afterwards and we both agreed that we needed to try to square the circle – to avoid the trap of 'You haven't got authorisation to develop this policy' on the one hand and 'There will be no money' on the other, and yet at the same time be expected to accelerate delivery and to innovate. It is a genuine dilemma, but it does mean that we are going to have to be more robust about allowing free thinking publicly if we are not to run out of steam in the next two years and allow the Opposition free rein.

And we have said farewell, officially, to Jonathan Sedgwick, who has moved to his new post. But his replacement Emma Churchill seems very good, and the whole office is pulling together extremely well.

There are a couple of drugs conferences that have chimed in together at the end of the week, and then off to Florence to an interior ministers' meeting. It is only for forty-eight hours, but I think it will do me good.

It was the last major overseas visit that I made as Home Secretary and it was a productive one. This was the five big countries meeting to exchange information on counter-terrorism, on cross-border policing and organised crime, and crucially on immigration. It was Italy's turn to host the meeting and it was lovely to go to Florence – the first time I had ever been there. We were treated very well, and I remember thinking to myself at the time, 'Don't get too used to this, David.' But I did slip away to see the Santa Croce church, a Franciscan church that has the tombs of some of the most famous men of the Renaissance, among them Galileo, Michelangelo and Machiavelli. The abbot was a lovely man and was kind enough to show us round. This was one of those small perks of the job that should never be taken for granted.

After the tragic murder of Ken Bigley in Iraq, we then had the capture of Mrs Barbara Hassan, who worked for the CARE organisation in Iraq. This all adds to the sense of foreboding that things are not going at all the way we expected, and it is a further pressure on Tony.

I came back from Florence straight into Home Office Questions in the afternoon. This was followed by a Statement on Iraq and a further Statement on 14–19 Education.

We seemed to be repeating at this point what we had decided eight years earlier in the document 'Aiming Higher', but if I have any blame to carry, it's that I didn't push harder between 1997 and 2001 on the whole issue of vocational education. I had, of course, introduced vocational GCSEs and A levels and tried to rationalise the way in which we dealt with adult vocational courses, and to provide more rigour in the NVQ (vocational qualification based on the job), but if I am honest I hadn't really changed the culture away from vocational education being seen as somehow second-rate. The task of changing a century-old culture is a difficult one.

Mike Tomlinson has been very cautious in his report on which the Statement is based. I understand why. In the run-up to a general election we don't want a row about A levels but the report goes nowhere near meeting the requirements or taking us beyond the existing debate. Let's hope we return to it again once the election is over.

I went down to speak for Jim Knight in South Dorset, our most marginal seat with a majority of 153 back in 2001 – better though than in 1997, when it was 37. Jim is an extremely able constituency MP, and it was good to talk to young people down there and to get a feel not only of people's worries but also of their enthusiasm and commitment. The young people told me, however, that they weren't doing citizenship and democracy in their curriculum. This is the umpteenth time I have heard this recently. What on earth is going on in the schools?

Jim Knight became Schools Minister following the 2006 reshuffle – evidence that my regard for him was not misplaced

My older sons are being very supportive. Andrew has had problems with his health but he came to have supper with me and things seem to be a lot better now. They are being extremely thoughtful but we all know that things are going to get much rockier in the weeks ahead.

And then the crime stats, which are extraordinarily good: 7 per cent down on the British Crime Survey measure and 5 per cent down on the Recorded Crime Statistics (even with the new formula), but inevitably everyone concentrated on violent crime once again. I just wish the chief constables who, with all the best intentions, changed the recording system would come out strongly and start defending the reality rather than leaving it to us. It is the new statistical methodology and it accounts for the fact that on the British Crime Survey (that, until we were elected, everyone said was the most accurate measure) violence has gone down but recorded violence has gone up. I would love to have just one measure but it is not politically possible, so we have just got to do our best to get the message across that there are really big problems and we are dealing with them, but that the improvement we promised has taken place and that the reductions in street robbery are phenomenal.

I had been discussing inside the Department the fact that the police chiefs and police authorities didn't like the special funding for the major urban areas on street crime, and the special arrangements for reporting back and holding the continuing cross-departmental meetings, but we would have to press on.

With the benefit of hindsight, I wish I had been even more rigorous in ensuring that we put in place mechanisms for the years ahead to ring-fence funding and to continue the drive on street crime until it became a natural part of what the police service were doing, just as Jack had achieved in relation to domestic burglary.

It is strange that whenever there are crime stats, there is a crime that highlights the issue. The drive-by shooting of Danielle Beccan in Nottingham simply reinforced in people's minds that things were out of control – and on gun crime in Nottingham, there is a real danger that it is.

And, Lord help us, the terrible burglary and stabbing of the cousin of Rosa Monckton, the wife of Dominic Lawson, editor of the *Sunday Telegraph*.

John Monckton had been murdered, and his wife badly injured, by intruders in their London home, and in December 2005 Damien Hanson and Elliot White were convicted of the murder of Mr Monckton and the attempted murder of his wife. Both had been under the supervision of the probation service at the time of the crimes, so this particular stabbing made a big impression on me, not least because I was genuinely concerned that the probation service had not done all they should, although the facts available at the time were very sketchy and were not to fully emerge until much later.

Nevertheless it was clear that the London probation service was in meltdown, as we had already surmised and to correct which we had put in place substantial measures. The legislation and the establishment of the embryo National Offender Management Service were all intended to try to overcome the kind of problems that had led to the lack of supervision of the individuals concerned – including the measures in the 2003 Act to bring in automatic supervision on release for all moderately serious crime. But I was Home Secretary and I knew that in the end people would expect me to take responsibility.

But the usual grind goes on. Now we are arguing about 'corporate killing'. I have got one set of people who want tough action and another set of people who want it watered down. I have a commitment to it, going back to Jack's time as Home Secretary, and I would really like to try and get it sorted by the end of the year.

The next thing I know is that Patrick Wintour, who is usually a very good journalist, has a story about the letter that Jack Straw had sent round. I am presuming that someone who is strongly in favour of the Bill has leaked this letter from the Domestic Affairs Committee in the belief that it would be helpful. It isn't. The only thing that is likely to happen – and it happens all the time – is that people become more entrenched rather than less. It becomes a win-or-lose situation, and finding a way through is made twice as difficult. Please save us all from the well-intentioned.

Lynda Lee-Potter, long-standing columnist on the *Daily Mail*, has died. I shall miss Lynda and her acerbic pen and the all too perceptive enquiry. She could certainly write well.

I knew Jeremy Lee-Potter, Lynda's husband, from way back when I was Shadow Health Secretary and he was Chairman of the British Medical Association. We got on extremely well: our politics were not the same but our objectives were.

I was very sorry that circumstances meant that I was unable to attend Lynda's private funeral on Wednesday the 27th, as I counted it a very thoughtful gesture that the family had invited me. But that day I had the Domestic Violence, Crime and Victims Bill before Parliament – on which Kath Raymond had worked particularly hard in support of Paul Goggins, the minister responsible – and there was no way that I could not be there to see through the final stages of my own legislation. I did, however, manage to pop in for a few minutes earlier in the day to the first-birthday party of John Brown, Sarah and Gordon's little boy. It is heartwarming to see them so happy with him.

Growth figures are down. Well, the Bank of England probably did overdo it but here I go again. I wouldn't mind but house price inflation is falling back, so it isn't as though we have got the traditional gap between trying to do something to modify housing inflation and trying to avoid damaging the whole of the rest of the economy.

Boris Johnson, Tory MP and editor of the *Spectator*, has been to Liverpool to apologise for an article criticising that city – an article that he didn't write but that appeared in his magazine. I suppose it is a little bit like being a minister, having to account for things that you haven't done.

I've been reading Michael Dobbs's book on Churchill, light-hearted but extremely interesting. I wrote a ditty:

> Horace Wilson and Joseph Ball,
> The greatest spin doctors of them all,
> Pro-appeasement through and through,
> Untroubled by things they had to do.
> Protecting Chamberlain by whatever means,
> Prepared to deal with the worst of fiends,
> Corrupt to their very fingertips,
> Poison pouring from their lips.

(Sir Horace Wilson was adviser to Neville Chamberlain, and Joseph Ball was in Conservative Central Office.)

The book is very much like being in politics. It is based on truth but a lot of it is fiction. The characters aren't fictitious and nor are those details like the massive loan in the winter of 1938–9 to save Winston Churchill from having to sell Chartwell – a loan of £1 million that, of course, never had to be registered and that was never repaid. Even with all our faults, it makes our present-day politics totally transparent, open and accountable. That's as it should be but it would be very nice if someone, sometime would acknowledge it.

One of those issues that always comes round at this time of the year is how to ensure that we hold down the council tax for next April without massive cut-backs in local government services. It is clear that all departments are going to have to make a contribution and I thought there was going to be the most enormous row when Gordon chaired a Cabinet subcommittee to look at it – but it was just a preliminary skirmish. My task now is to ensure that I find enough money from within the Department both to hold down the precept and to continue the expansion of police numbers and community support officers.

I was late for the meeting on the Thursday because we had a real mess the night before on the Domestic Violence, Crime and Victims Bill. The Tories had filibustered and wiped out completely the Third-Reading Debate, but we had put together an announcement for Third Reading that I was due to make and a press release to go with it. Unfortunately the press release was worded in such a way that it presumed that the Third Reading had taken place.

This was all about what is called a 'homicide review'. In essence, it is the pressure that's been on for donkeys' years, and particularly over the last year since I passed the Criminal Justice and Sentencing Act, to have a thoroughgoing review of the sentencing for manslaughter and murder, where the line should be drawn between the two and whether judge and jury should be able to determine that if a murder charge didn't stick, a manslaughter one might. It is very complicated because it is all mixed up with domestic violence and the question of how you deal with crimes of passion, where there has been enormous provocation. Should it be manslaughter or should it be murder, and should there be different degrees of murder, not just the three major categories that we built into the Criminal Justice Act, deliberately to stop the lenient sentences that were being handed out?

It was strange in the summer of 2006 to see all these issues debated without any reference back to the end of October 2004. We were painfully aware that what we put in place was not entirely perfect – not so much a holding operation as a necessary step on the road. We knew that there would have to be an overall review but we didn't want it to be in the context of simply going back to letting judges make their own decision on any of these matters, including the sex-offenders law and the changes we had brought about there that had a cross-over to sentencing. This could be seen in June 2006, when there was the most enormous row about the sentencing of a paedophile by the name of Sweeney. How to give judges some leeway, and how to ensure that the leeway is not downwards, was one of those many circles I was asked to square, and I failed to do so.

The Tories had discovered that the press release was out and the nature of the wording, so they decided to use one of those parliamentary tactics to make me look foolish by preventing me from speaking to the House and therefore putting on the record the words in the press release. Of course, we should have reworded it separately, as a parallel announcement, rather than linking it to the Third Reading of the Bill – but that's a lesson learned.

And so on Thursday morning fourteen individuals tried to put down a Priority Notice Question (to get me to the Dispatch Box) and the Speaker chose the one from Douglas Hogg. For reasons I have never understood, Douglas, who had been Secretary of State for Agriculture, Food and Fisheries at the time of the BSE crisis, always sounds as if he is about to bite you. Fortunately I had learned one lesson from earlier in the week when I had been called to the Dispatch Box on a Priority Notice Question in relation to the Justice and Home Affairs Council's deliberations on asylum, which had taken place in Luxembourg on the Monday. The lesson was quite simple: keep calm, play it down, acknowledge my own mistake and let the issue die. And it has.

So I went into the anti-social behaviour conference on the Thursday afternoon feeling a lot better. It is amazing how it lifts you when you feel you have done something well, and how when you are struggling, the struggle seems to get worse. By the afternoon I was able to laugh and joke, even though I didn't feel like it inside.

I just wish I was sleeping better at night. I just wish I could answer the press – but of course I can't. Private means private.

But one uplifting thing came out of Labour Party conference, where I had done one of those very rare fringe meetings that really cheer you, the best-attended I have been to at this year's conference and really worthwhile with regard to the discussion, debate and questions. It was chaired by David Aaronovitch and it gave me the chance to discuss, not simply with delegates but with people who came in from the Brighton area to see what was going on, my philosophy about what I was doing from the Home Office, about securing people from fear, about building stability and respect, about the way in which if people feel that we are on their side they will listen to the difficulties and the problems of government and of changing things.

The uplifting incident was an article that a student had written in the Sussex University magazine. She wasn't a party member, and had just come in to listen to the debate and the questions and answers at the fringe meeting. She said that she had tried to sample meetings across the week and she had enjoyed this one enormously, because it was refreshing to hear someone speak in normal language and tell the problems as they really are and not duck them. I was deeply touched.

And I appointed Sir Ian Blair as the new Commissioner for the Metropolitan Police, the only candidate in the UK that we can appoint. Ken Livingstone and the Met Police Authority and I are all in agreement.

Ian Blair has been instrumental in working with me and with Ken Livingstone on the Beat Teams – real community policing – and on the development of the Community Support Officers initiative. He is not the 'Hail fellow, well met' type, but he is a good copper.

And we are embarking on another round of discussions on ID cards. We have given clear priority from Cabinet for the Queen's Speech and thank God we have got ID cards in there. It means working the whole of

November on making sure that all these Bills that I am going to have to move after the 23rd (Queen's Speech Day) can get under way before Christmas. It is going to be a hell of a few weeks, because if we don't get the Second Reading in very quickly indeed we will never get the legislation through by April. God knows how we are going to do it anyway. It has been agreed that ID cards and serious and organised crime will be the top two priorities, but that means that I have to move both of them as quickly as possible in December.

At this time I was holding meetings almost daily on ID cards to try to sort out realistic and reliable costings, to ensure that we knew precisely what we were saying with regard to biometrics and the clean database that would allow us to know eventually who was in the country illegally: who should be here and entitled to services, and who shouldn't.

I had a busy Friday at Lindholme Prison and in Grimethorpe (a South Yorkshire former pit village hit very badly by massive unemployment and with high levels of incapacity benefit), where I had promised to go and see what was being done for young people and talk to people in the club. I then went back down to London for Margaret Hodge's sixtieth-birthday party on the Saturday evening, where quite a lot of colleagues had gathered at the Old Brewery.

November 2004

I had to circulate to the Domestic Affairs Committee not only the final policy decisions about ID cards but what is called a Regulatory Impact Assessment, which includes at least a substantial piece of work on future costings, even though with the timescales and with the fact that we hadn't gone to competition for anything yet in the commercial arena, we did need at least a very clear view of what the final package would look like: a mix between the costs that had already been agreed in updating passports with biometric identifiers and the clean database and the issuing of the card.

It was strange to hear opposition parties talk as though the money that we were to raise from the renewal of passports and the small addition for the clean database itself was somehow available for spending in other areas. This level of economic illiteracy seemed to pass very many people by. It was quite hard to get across, even in sensible debate in the House of Commons, that if you cancelled the idea of the database of who was in the country and the mechanisms for verifying this – at least initially using the biometric on the card – the only money that you would save would be the set-up costs, and the set-up costs were substantially those that we, Parliament, had agreed to. The Lib Dems at this stage were the most gung ho, suggesting that we could use the money to increase police numbers instead, which was just straight nonsense.

After the departure as Tory leader of Michael Howard, who was in favour of ID cards, David Cameron started to move in the same direction as the Lib Dems had – but this time the money was to be spent on prisons. I had to smile when I thought later of a Tory–Lib Dem coalition – not a lot to smile about – in which they would obviously have to fight it out as to how they would spend non-existent money on either police or prisons, or both.

Getting material round to the Domestic Affairs Committee and ensuring that the Regulatory Impact Assessment stood up to scrutiny was not easy, and we had to do all this before the Queen's Speech, because it was going to take a week or two afterwards to get the Bill into sufficient shape to publish before Christmas.

In the end I did publish the Bill as Home Secretary, but Charles Clarke had to take it through the Second-Reading Debate because by that time I had stepped down from government.

I am not good at this internal schmoozing business, and never have been. In fact some people would call me a bull in a china shop. But frankly I just think that if people have all the information and are able to cross-question their officials rigorously, just as I can, then why ring round and have to schmooze people?

A pretty silly question really. Perhaps a bit more of the schmoozing would have done a great deal for my own personal relations with colleagues and would have meant a lot less final showdowns. But my experiences when I tried to do it were not good: ringing colleagues on a Sunday evening about a committee to take place on Monday or Tuesday, and finding, Lord help me, that they hadn't read the papers – or perhaps I was being naïve.

On that Monday [1 November] Tony and I had three-quarters of an hour talking about how to handle the likely fall-out with regard to my private life. He is more pessimistic than I am about the likely public turn of events, but nevertheless very supportive. I suppose it is his role to paint the worst possible scenario, and it is mine to do what I believe to be right.

To top it all, this was the week of the Home Affairs Select Committee hearing. You have to be an expert when dealing with a particular subject like ID cards in order to get through these, whereas the Annual Report is easier because you are dealing with the whole field and you are almost bound to know more than any other individual in the room, providing you have done your homework. So it has gone well and I was pleased with it. Again I have had to exude confidence.

This was covering the field, and although we got into ID cards at the end, it was just enough for me to get my point across. I was lucky that John Denham in the Chair gave me the chance to do so. I owe him one.

Tuesday 2 November: polling day in the American presidential election. In the evening I went to the American ambassador's residence for dinner, but I didn't go down to the embassy for the reception and television coverage. The result of the election was a foregone conclusion and I need whatever sleep I can get.

One of those coincidences: I sat at the residence next to a Republican supporter who was appearing with me on Friday [5 November] on Radio 4's *Any Questions?*. I had never met her before so it was quite fortuitous.

Then one of our Team and Executive Awaydays, this time in Nottingham and the East Midlands on Thursday and Friday. This was a chance to talk to everyone about gun crime, to talk to young people, to talk to the father of Danielle Beccan, who was killed in the drive-by shooting, and to try and get a feel from the local community about what they think, and why Nottingham is having such enormous problems. We spent quite a time on Friday morning in the St Ann's district, talking both to young people and to those who were working positively with them. One young man had had a friend killed in a shooting incident; his brother had been killed; and now Danielle, whom he knew, had been killed. It shook me to the very core.

I don't think I could have lived with myself if we hadn't already taken action to help, not just with the police and the gun-crime round table and the work we were doing with the families of gun victims, but also the grants that we had allocated earlier in the year to St Ann's. But all of it just seems so inadequate, so meagre compared with the challenge of the problem.

The young man in question did me a great honour when he went on regional television that evening, when he said that he had found me to be a very different person from the one he had expected, and the one he had expected was the image of the Home Secretary. He said: 'He wasn't like a politician.'

I spent the rest of the morning with the police and probation service, talking to people about the projects they were running and about how they might link to the experiences with Operation Trident in London, which has already started to bring success in reducing deaths by guns, and gun- and drug-related crime in general.

I spent a lot of time working on what we might do in relation to gun crime and more serious violence. It is one reason why I was so keen to set up the Serious Organised Crime Agency and to tackle the combined scourges of Class A (hard) drugs and the use of guns – the real challenge in the globalised modern era.

And so to *Any Questions?* in Derbyshire – not far from my home. I am absolutely shattered. I shouldn't have agreed to do the programme, not at the end of this week, not with everything that has happened. But of course these things are agreed months in advance and then when they come round, you just have to get on with it. You can't let people down.

One question – about the referendum in the North East on a regional assembly – was highly predictable. I have never been against some form of accountability for the vast sums of public money that are allocated via regional government offices, but I think that the idea of yet another elected body in areas much more diverse and lacking homogeneity than the North East is just not on. If the North East don't want it, then let's find another solution. But it was tricky on the programme to say this without appearing to put 'the boot in' to colleagues.

I am afraid Jonathan Dimbleby, with whom I get on very well, overdid it by keeping on pressing me to criticise John Prescott's favourite policy of regional assemblies – and in the end I just said, 'Jonathan, sod off.' I shouldn't have said it, and one or two people on *Any Answers?* the following day took exception to it. But Jonathan knew precisely why I had done it, and he knew what he was doing, and there was no offence meant or taken. It is a sign, however, that my nerves are beginning to fray.

I had been working for twelve hours before I got on *Any Questions?* and I had just had time for a quick shower and to grab something to eat. I once thought I couldn't work any harder, but I am doing so.

My problem is that I am either not sleeping at all, or sleeping and then waking up very early. Then on the occasions when I do get to sleep, I get woken up for emergency business. There was an emergency warrant: it was serious and it was necessary to do the warrant. But I do wonder. There is going to have to be some system where we all take it in turns rather than taking our particular warrants and getting woken up in the middle of the night. It isn't easy to do the job with the pressure I am currently under when I am constantly being woken up at night, or over Christmas and New Year, as I was last Christmas. This year I have said that there needs to be a rota for senior politicians. I cannot take any more of what I had.

Saturday morning and to my advice surgery, which I had had to move to accommodate other commitments, and then to finish off the programme with Radio Sheffield.

Jonathan Sedgwick has persuaded me that we ought to go to see *Round the Horne Revisited* – a play based on the wonderful radio series of the 1960s – and that might just give me a laugh. I certainly need one.

The other event worthy of note over these few days was the Youth Justice Board Annual Congress. The Youth Justice Board oversees a budget of around £370 million and is responsible for Youth Offending Teams and for youth-custody provision, among other things. They had not wanted me to do a round-table panel, which was my idea, but preferred a straight speech. I said that I thought it was time that politicians were seen to be listening and engaging and not just speaking, and insisted that if I were to come at all as Home Secretary then we would have a round-table discussion with youngsters who had been in trouble with the law and had been subject to custody. When I got there, they had put us all in a long line facing the audience, not informally sitting round a coffee table engaging with each other – and it was obviously too late to change the arrangements. I thought that this was the last straw. They didn't want me to do this my way and they had no intention of making it easy and making it work. But we managed to get the young people to contribute, even though they were way down a very high and long table. And they were superb. They were counter-intuitive. They wanted stability and structures. I was pressing them over monitoring and mentoring – someone working with them instead of the custodial sentence they had received – and all they could think about was that at least custody had protected them and given them a form by which to live. We have simply got to be able to replicate that without their having to be in institutions. But it is depressing because if those who are running the show can't manage to work out ways of engaging with young people in this environment, then no wonder they are not engaging with them on the ground. One consolation was that the audience were very good. They liked it and they warmed to it, and after I had chaired the panel with the young people, I opened it up to the audience so that they could ask questions of me, as well as the youngsters. That worked as well. But I came out absolutely drained. It was much harder work than making a speech.

And we are still picking up the political flak from the inevitable assault on Faluja. Iraq does not seem ever to go away.

Week beginning Monday 8 November: the issue of keeping council tax down and combating the idea of universal capping of increases is still going on. Gordon and I are completely in agreement on this one. The notion of universal capping is ridiculous: it would just end up with every single reduction in service being put at the door of the government.

I am going to have to find more money, though. The Department has come up with £25 million and I have said that £50 million is the minimum that we need in order to be able to hold down the police precept – and preferably £100 million – but senior officials are having a fit. This is one of those moments when I have to establish that I am in charge and that we find the resources, rather than their squirrelling it away for their own priorities, so that they can pull it out of the hat at a particular moment when there is a 'pressure' that they know is coming up and they anticipated in the reserve. It certainly helps me to have been so heavily involved in budgetary matters, both in local government and in my previous department. I can't help but think of the Children's Fund and how money was suddenly squeezed out of every corner when it was absolutely imperative – and it is imperative now. I've got to get the police grant up to at least 3.75 per cent if we are going to save cuts in service. What a catastrophe that would be: fewer police officers, controversy about community support officers, an inevitable rise in crime, and all of it blamed on the Home Secretary.

What makes this even more important is that at 3.75 per cent, two-thirds of police authorities will be at the 'floor' (the absolute minimum increase), so if we make it the 3.25 per cent that is being pressed on us by the Office of the Deputy Prime Minister, we are going to be in a real mess, with cuts across the country.

I just wish officials had spotted that while a very small number of authorities would do extremely well under the formula for distributing the grant, the bulk (two-thirds) would do extremely badly. So needs must. The small group who were going to gain massively must gain less, and those who were going to lose out need to be stabilised. It is called political reality, but it is also about service on the ground. Happily the two go hand in hand so I have no qualms about this.

One of the things I have already instructed them to do is to raise charges for migration, visa renewals and accession-country registration, but they haven't yet managed to achieve this. If we can only bring some money in, we will have some money to spend, but I am also very keen to see if Gordon will provide new additional cash for a serious expansion of police community support officers. It would be wonderful in the run-up to the general election if we could say that we were going to accelerate recruitment and really get this off the ground.

I was very pleased that with the substantially improved relationship between Gordon and myself it was possible to reach agreement before I stepped down as Home Secretary. Time will tell whether I was right about the development of community support officers, but I believe very strongly that if they are properly used, as part of the neighbourhood Beat Team providing reassurance and visibility within the neighbourhood, then this will turn out to be one of the better things that I did.

Well, having spent the whole of last week to-ing and fro-ing on the exact wording for the White Paper and trying to resolve the continuing disagreements with John Prescott, here we are on Tuesday [9 November] and the launch at last of the police-reform proposals. We have had to agree that council-tax payers won't have to cough up any more money as a result of the White Paper, but at least I have some agreement that we can look at match-funding from local sources to expand policing.

My idea was that local people could make a decision themselves, that they would vote in a defined neighbourhood to provide an additional levy. This is a little bit like the service charge that so many people pay on flats or enclosed housing schemes – or, as I found when I lived near by, the levy to maintain Wimbledon Common in London. In areas designated as deprived – and there is a proper designated programme – we would have to find ways either from regeneration funding or elsewhere to match-fund this so that there was a proper balance and equity – because otherwise the richer the area, the more easy it would be to raise a levy.

I believe this was right, not simply as a way of getting more resources into security, anti-social behaviour and policing at local level, but also because people would feel that they owned what was going on, that they could hold to account those who were employed with the resources, and that they would feel very much part of the programme of stamping out criminality. In simple terms, what the very rich do for themselves we would enable the vast bulk of the population, where appropriate, also to do for themselves. If a parish council wanted a couple of community support officers, then that would be their business. If they wanted a full-time police officer, they could choose to do so in collaboration with, and with the agreement of, the police force.

Nothing is simple, so there were going to be major difficulties in relation to who pays when people are on benefit. But if it is true for housing and council-tax rebate, then why not for the most important thing of all – security in your own home and on the street, which then creates a living, vibrant community in which what we call 'social capital' can be built on and developed, rather than the complete disintegration and alienation that still blight so many of our disadvantaged and deprived areas.

There has been a struggle to keep the levers for ensuring that local communities can trigger action because people across the spectrum appear to be worried that this will be done mischievously and therefore we will end up with quite unwarranted complaints. Well, there is always a way round these things to ensure that there is a filter, so that there has to be a certain number of people and they have to have gone through their local elected representative (councillor or MP), so I'm sure we can find a way round it.

The task now is to make sure that what is going on around me doesn't interfere with doing the job.

Just a thought on the weekend: on Saturday evening, just before one of Tony's Chequers dinners, he gave me a ring to say that all those he had spoken to who had heard *Any Questions?* thought that I had done a first-class job, particularly in relation to Iraq. I was pleased that he had taken the trouble to ring, but it also demonstrated that everyone around Tony now feels quite beleaguered about Iraq. There aren't enough people standing up and being counted.

The Statement I made on Tuesday afternoon on the White Paper was, as ever, too long. I didn't read it too badly, and again questions were fine, but the lesson has to be 'keep it short' – and, for goodness sake, relax.

Dennis Skinner [maverick Labour MP for Bolsover] and I have always got on in quite a remarkable way, but just for once he and I had words after the Statement. It was not because he'd been barracking the Tories barracking me – he does that all the time – but because of some of the things he was saying. We settled our differences quietly.

We had the Civil Partnership Bill on the Tuesday as well, which I voted on.

The *Independent on Sunday* had maligned me. They had taken one sentence from an article I wrote in *Tribune* magazine in 1987 and completely distorted what was a perfectly reasonable argument.

The article related to whether I would like to touch or be touched by another man. In distorting this, the Independent on Sunday *was mistaking equality for personal preference.*

This is exactly what the *Independent* and *Independent on Sunday* do all the time now. They paint people into a corner, where you are either one thing or the other – completely libertarian or completely reactionary.

Tony and I went to Bexley on the morning of the White Paper launch. We had a really good visit, talking about the promotion of community involvement, about community support officers, about turning round anti-social behaviour. The audience, which was very mixed, warmed to all this and weren't daunted by the fact that we were live on television. Ian Blair came down and was very impressive. It is clear that it is this sort of experiment, with a huge drop in crime and in particular anti-social behaviour, that could work right across London, and for that matter right across the country. The residents' representatives were really positive, which is uplifting when you are so often in places where people are grumbling.

So back to the grind of finance – and a Public Expenditure Cabinet committee on Thursday. We had a robust (some might say 'clearing the air') session, but we couldn't reach agreement so we arranged to meet next Thursday, and we will have to take decisions then. John Reid was very complimentary about the part I was playing – I think I may well have got up other people's noses, though – and he is right in saying that there have been rare occasions over the past seven and a half years where we have ensured a really open debate, and where money has been taken from one area and reallocated to another: a simple matter of being absolutely clear about the consequences.

On the following Monday I had dinner with Richard Wallace, editor of the *Daily Mirror*.

I was sorry that later my relationship with the Mirror *was to break down so badly. Despite one or two of their columnists being deeply 'anti-Blunkett' I had always got on very well with the political correspondents. But falling advertising and falling circulation for all the tabloid newspapers leads to a very different approach than would have been the case in the past.*

On the Wednesday I had dinner with Rebekah Wade, editor of the *Sun*, a paper that has been supportive of my agenda: we seem to have got over the tremendous clash in respect of my taking them to task on immigration and asylum. Coverage of Home Office issues in the next few days was very much better than it had been over the previous fortnight – so both dinners were worth it.

And so to my speech on Saturday 13 November, at a conference in London under the auspices of a left-of-centre organisation known as Progress. I'd spent quite a chunk of the week getting the speech right. On the *Today* programme that morning John Humphrys did not give me the space to address philosophical issues in the way that we have on some occasions on Saturdays. This was the first time I had done an interview with him since the end of July. It was a standard interview, in which he wanted to talk about ID cards and terrorism legislation, rather than the issues of how individual rights and rights we hold in common have to be balanced, and how we need to provide people with security in order to be able to address progressive politics – which is the thrust of the speech. I shall try and get more of that across on *The Politics Show* on BBC1 at Sunday lunchtime, after the Remembrance Service.

The conference went fine, with the audience really interested and attentive. Coverage was fairly sparse on the Sunday, although it carried into the week, and as well as *The Politics Show* which again was fine on the Sunday, *The World at One* on Radio 4 picked it up later in the week, and other bits began to appear. Peter Riddell came in for a chat with me and reflected on it in his column in *The Times*. So we are just beginning to get the message across.

There is still coverage coming through suggesting that we are hyping the issues of terrorism, that we are doing so in the likely run-up to a general election, that we want to make it an election issue, and that we want to worry people. The case is entirely the opposite. We need to stop the general election being underpinned by fear and insecurity, which can only help the Tories, not us.

It is amazing how little people have read of history, how little they have looked at what happened only four years ago, or even three years ago, in some parts of Europe. How quickly memories fade. But if you talk about reducing fear and the people who oppose you believe that by talking about it you increase it, you end up with a complete Catch-22. You are telling people what it is you are doing and why you are doing it, but by telling them why you are doing it you are accused of frightening them. That's a road to nowhere and would mean that we would have to say nothing, do nothing and just wait for the hit – and I am just not prepared to have it.

Good discussion at the following Cabinet with the presentation by Philip Gould, who says that we are exaggerating our 'voter identification' – those who are likely to vote and would vote Labour. I don't believe for a minute that it is as high as 42 per cent, and I said so. There was quite a lot of support from Jack Straw, Patricia Hewitt and others about the real danger of the low turn-out and of complacency – coupled, of course, with the backlash on Iraq.

After Cabinet, Tony said to me: 'What was up with you?' I said: 'I was only trying to get people to be realistic. You know I always do, even if sometimes it's irritating.' I think I might have upset the applecart by referring back to the self-delusion we had when people wouldn't address the truth when Neil was leader. It wasn't intended as a knock at Tony, but I can see how he may have interpreted it that way. I think people have become self-deluded by the ICM *Guardian* poll that showed us eight points ahead. I should cocoa!

In my usual way, I have decided to put the world to rights. I have written to Alan Milburn and Ian McCartney (who is ill) about the nature of campaigning. It strikes me that the way in which the Republicans in the USA did the business is something we could all learn from – not big high-profile noise, but getting through to people by text, by internet, by subliminal means, and by targeting audiences very carefully. I haven't forgotten how, when I was in Boston, the organisers of the Democratic Convention dismissed the idea that they needed to reach out to people on the issues of security and stability. I made the point that the Tories are very happy to paint the Liberals, especially in our seats, as being left-wing, so people think that they can vote for them easily, particularly on Iraq. It is a clever ploy, because there are many seats we can't win if the Liberals split the vote. On the other hand, perversely, we need the Liberals to do well nation-wide in order to take right-wing votes off the Tories in the South and in London. This is all the more reason why campaigns should be heavily targeted and very localised.

Peter Kellner was of this view very strongly when he spoke at a seminar held at the conference organised by Progress the previous Saturday, and as Chairman of YouGov and an expert in both polling and political analysis, he is certainly someone worth listening to.

On Sunday morning, Remembrance Day, I attended the early parade of public-service workers, the police, the ambulance service and the fire brigade, and took the salute on behalf of the government. When we got to the Cenotaph itself, I remembered that the year before Sadie had been very jumpy on her first experience of the firing of the guns at eleven o'clock, so I gave her a biscuit and she was fine. I saw the Queen afterwards – the first time when attending the Remembrance Service in London that I have gone out that way and shaken hands with the Queen and Prince Philip – and she patted Sadie and said: 'I see she only barks at swords and not at guns.' I said: 'Yes, I think that's true, Ma'am.' It was nice that she had remembered Sadie's performance from a year ago when George Bush was here, and before that the Putin visit.

I suppose the big political and historic event running up to the Queen's Speech was the Speaker using the Parliament Act to decree that the Bill banning hunting with dogs becomes law, after all the shenanigans in the Lords and Commons. Let's hope that the doom and gloom turns out to be bunkum – but I fear for those in favour of a complete ban that the euphoria will be bunkum as well.

Breakfast time, Monday morning: flew to Dunkirk, then on to Calais. I had a decent morning with Dominique de Villepin but very little publicity out of it. He must have got quite a lot out of it domestically but I got absolutely nothing. The press office couldn't take the point that I had been explaining to them the previous week, that we didn't have a story and they didn't really have a line to sell, so in that sense it was a waste of time; but in diplomatic terms I got on with him better than I had done previously.

The visit was to highlight security and immigration controls and the clampdown that was continuing now that Nicolas Sarkozy had moved to become the Chairman of the UPN, the coalition backing Chirac.

Home Office Questions in the afternoon, which were fairly rough, as they often are now. The Tories are getting tougher and more like an Opposition – not like a government in waiting but certainly more like an Opposition, and they gave Des Browne in particular a very hard time. I think it's the first time he has been really shaken. Immigration Minister is a rotten job, and you are lucky if you get out of it quickly enough not to have been scarred.

On Wednesday I did the IPPR conference on ID cards, which again gave a thrust to the debate about the Queen's Speech, about security, identity and citizenship. There was a reasonable amount of publicity out of it, some of it picking up a bit of a sideswipe that I made at the need for light-touch regulation of loyalty cards and credit cards and the way in which the very big companies use the information they've got. The companies got very upset about this, but nevertheless the tracking of people's spending and shopping and social habits is much greater than anyone realises, and a great deal more than anything that we have ever envisaged in relation to ID cards. The privatised surveillance of our lives in all sorts of respects is now a much greater threat than the twentieth-century surveillance by the state, even if the consequences for most people are nowhere near as bad.

I have spoken to the press office about what we do about promoting the value to the individual of ID cards and how we get the message across. We have done pretty well so far, with 80 per cent of those polled being broadly in favour, but it could slip away just as easily. It is like the drive for education standards and what I did in primary education. You have to keep your foot on the accelerator all the time. The acceptability, and for that matter the delivery, of ID cards is going to be crucially dependent on the understandability and people feeling that this is something that is good for them individually and critical in terms of knowing who is in the country and rooting out illegal migration and illegal working.

Huw Evans has been off all week moving house and getting his own domestic affairs sorted out before he gets married, but we have missed him. We've not scored the goals that we might have done.

Just as I missed Conor Ryan when he stepped down for four months to help Frank Dobson get the Labour Party nomination for the run-off for Mayor of London and Sophie Ryan when over the years she was on maternity leave, so now I really did miss Huw. He certainly needed the break he got in November, because the three weeks from the end of November were to be nothing short of a nightmare for him, almost if not as bad as the whole of the latter part of August, where he had been dealing with the press on an hourly basis for sixteen hours a day. The pressure on him, as well as on me, was absolutely enormous.

And then we are back to the battle for winning minds on why we, as a party, are talking about security and policing. My old mate Robin Cook wrote a piece in the *Guardian* on Friday [19 November] asking why we on the left are messing about with issues such as crime and terrorism – as if people aren't worried about it – and why worry about things that people are worried about? As though if we tell them to stop worrying, they will stop worrying; and if they stop worrying, the issues will go away.

It's interesting though that Paul Routledge in the *Daily Mirror* was saying very much the same thing. It must be the moment for a counter-move against what we are trying to do in learning the lessons from France and Holland, etc. – from Pim Fortuyn to Le Pen's relegating Jospin to third place. Do people never learn?

And now it is all happening again with the murder of the libertarian film-maker Theo van Gogh in Holland. Twenty mosques attacked in two weeks, Pim Fortuyn voted the most significant Dutchman in history by the Dutch people: ephemeral but terrible movements in a country that has prided itself on total tolerance – as though total tolerance could ever work, which is what I was saying at the Progress conference the previous Saturday.

Back on Monday [15 November] I had supper with Edward Heathcoat-Amory, who is on the *Daily Mail*, and his wife Alice Thomson, who writes for the *Daily Telegraph*. I have known them for a very long time.

So many people are being thoughtful and kind but I am letting down my guard – the nicer people are to me, the more naïve I become.

And then Michael Howard sacks Boris Johnson from his front-bench job as Shadow Arts Spokesman. Goodness knows what's been going on there. All I know is that I have known all the way along that I mustn't lie.

But here we go again.

It was no surprise that on Sunday 21 November the News of the World *returned to my private life. The attention that was focused on Boris Johnson and the* Spectator *had a major spin-off in reopening issues around me, just at the time when once again private was genuinely becoming private. This, as with so much in life, was to have consequences.*

And so to the week of the Queen's Speech: we got agreement at the Cabinet Expenditure Committee that we will reverse what was a real danger – namely officials putting to us exactly what the Tories had been putting forward on local-government expenditure – whereas what we are interested in is getting the precept (for counties and police authorities) and council tax for metropolitan and district councils down to the lowest possible level, in this case 5 per cent or lower. In other words, we had to stop this nonsense that was taking off in its own way of following a deeply monetarist policy, believing that it was the expenditure that we should crunch rather than the excessive taxation. It had taken the most enormous struggle in my case to ensure that the police authority precept could not be held down to 5 per cent because it was such a small percentage of the total, and the gearing (that is the ratio of local taxation to the total expenditure) was so great that it would have been absolutely crucifying for services. But you have to understand all this in order to understand what the impact would be, and I got the impression that it wasn't just politicians who didn't understand it, but officials – not surprisingly because none of them felt the impact. Few of them ever went out of London to experience what was taking place on the ground. In other words, they hadn't really got a clue.

John Reid was understandably livid because he had had to find a substantial tranche of his own budget to hold down the council tax. But this is all about having massively underestimated the need for revenue into the local-government grant the year before. It is no good officials from the Treasury or other departments living in Cloud-cuckoo-land. If you don't provide the money you don't provide the service, and the problem is that most officials don't feel the impact of cuts in services because virtually none of them live in a deprived area where the impact is the greatest. This is what irritates me most about the Treasury, but it is true of most other departments as well.

The problem with the Treasury is that there is virtually nobody in the higher echelons who has ever experienced any kind of deprivation whatsoever. I have to hold back on this because if I blow a gasket, it will do nobody any good – least of all my own constituents.

A couple of colleagues at the Cabinet Expenditure Committee (PSX) hadn't got the message from Downing Street that the battle was over, and were still arguing for universal capping. I think I had better spare their blushes.

But both of them survived me as a Cabinet minister, and I don't think either of them would relish being reminded that they were completely wrong.

So while dealing with the Queen's Speech I had the continuing internal battle over expenditure, and the Asian Trader Awards at a Park Lane hotel. This was a massive event, but one in which I felt as though I was simply going through the motions, as I was giving awards and speaking and all the time I was thinking that there was a sword of Damocles hanging over me.

The farewell dinner for John Stevens, Metropolitan Commissioner, on the same evening was one of those strange events because I meant every word I said in praising him but I could tell that there was still a simmering resentment that I hadn't been 100 per cent supportive and that I had given him a hard time. Very big people are prepared to take on big people.

Tuesday [23 November] was Queen's Speech Day. The early part of the day and lunchtime were taken up with radio and television presentations, including from the lobby of the House of Commons at lunchtime on ID cards; and not only ID cards but the fact that I was taking so much of the Queen's Speech, plus the run-up to the general election.

Then to the Queen's Speech Debate in the Commons – the historic ritual of old and new Members moving and seconding the Queen's Speech and then the two party leaders. My task was to leave when Tony left, and his speech was so blissfully brief that I was able to shoot out of the Chamber with him and get to an appointment I could not miss.

And then on to the *Richard and Judy Show* on television, arranged weeks before. 'Smile', said Huw Evans: 'Drop your shoulders and think of anything that will make you look relaxed.' In the car he rubbed my arm and kept talking to me – like keeping a trapped man from falling asleep. The programme was live: I took calls from viewers and tried hard to be me.

Back in the car to Brighton, to the Police Authorities Annual Conference dinner, again to speak, to crack a couple of jokes, as much to make myself feel better as to entertain the audience, while talking to them seriously about police reform. I did manage, with the help of the chairman of the local police authority (a Conservative), to get a decent bottle of burgundy. You would have thought I had asked for a special vintage, not just an alternative to cheap claret.

And then to the airport hotel at Gatwick and an overnight stay. Thank God the triple glazing works so well. At least I got a few hours' sleep. Then at dawn I was on the plane to Liverpool, to meet Prince Charles, to share in the opening of the new immigration and nationality facilities. He was wonderful – good to the staff, supportive and reassuring, and aware of the enormous difficulties that they face in doing their job. And he was very kind to me and understood what I was going through – and, God bless him, he said so.

Then to meet the men and women setting up the new Community Justice Centre in Liverpool. Since visiting Red Hook in New York, I have wanted us to develop these here in Britain, to get close to the community, to share with the community the challenges, to be in tune and in turn to ask the community to be part of the answer, to be the solution.

My great regret at leaving the Home Office in December was underpinned by not being able to carry through small projects that virtually no one had heard of, such as Community Justice Centres, because in government you need a champion, you need a Secretary of State or at the very least a minister who takes up and sees through a project or an idea that the civil service has not previously been engaged in, that isn't the flavour of the month. Citizenship, ID cards, community and civil renewal and Community Justice Centres are such projects.

Thursday 25 November: a sixteen-minute interview on the *Today* programme. To all appearances, I am fine. I listen again to the recording of the programme and, yes, I sound fine. I am still on form. I am still punching my weight. I am still scoring.

And then, at 8.30 a.m., on to a pre-Cabinet meeting on terrorism and the possibility of a draft for a full Counter-Terrorism Bill, and ten minutes with Tony before start of Cabinet, at his request. Just a private word. Not to deal with politics, except insomuch as private and political conjoin. He simply said that I should reflect that this might be the last moment to change my mind from the path I had chosen, as he felt an attack was imminent. But I knew that that moment was long past.

I do not have in my diary reflections of the Cabinet that day. There was a long meeting afterwards on the Home Office five-year programme, concentrating as ever on trying to sort out the Immigration and Nationality Directorate and electronic border controls, and how to tackle illegal migration before ID cards made it easier to do so.

I had lunch with Tom Bradby, with whom I had been in correspondence about his book *White Russians*. It is an excellent read and very well researched. But my mind was elsewhere.

Tom became political editor of ITN when Nick Robinson moved to the BBC in 2005.

Friday 26 November in Sheffield: switching on the Christmas lights at the Firth Park shopping centre; planting a tree at Beck Primary School, newly refurbished and on the up and up; and opening the new Sure Start facility for Firth Park and Shiregreen – all in my constituency, and what a lovely welcome. What an uplifting, embracing, warm and cherishing reception. This is my constituency and my city.

And then to Sunday 28 November and the *Sunday Telegraph* – or rather to 4 p.m. on Saturday the 27th, when the phone rings. It is Huw Evans, and I know there is something wrong. Huw (and Conor before him) would never ring after lunchtime on Saturday unless there was something amiss or there was a news broadcast that had to be done on Sunday. And I could tell from Huw's voice as he said: 'The political editor of the *Sunday Telegraph* has been on to me . . .'

This was a clear indication that we were not now dealing with pure interference in my private life. We were now dealing with the political.

Six allegations have been made, by far the most serious of which is that I used my powers as Home Secretary to do a favour for a close personal friend by 'fast-tracking' a visa application by her nanny, and that my office had processed and delivered the form.

We had collectively remembered giving advice about this application, and I may have raised it within the Department when seeking general advice over tackling the issue of the backlog. But, as Sir Alan Budd subsequently concluded in his official report on the matter, we had not handled that particular form at all.

Less serious is the charge that I gave this friend one of the travel vouchers allowed to a Member's spouse, even though she is not my spouse.

This was true and I said so, but following an investigation by the Parliamentary Commissioner no further action was taken, not least because no one could find any evidence of the use of the voucher (which had allowed for two journeys, out and back). I repaid the appropriate sum and apologised for my mistake.

The other allegations were just nonsense, without the underpinning of any journalistic research or a scintilla of proof. We chose therefore to rebut them one by one.

The Sunday Telegraph *story claimed that these allegations were based on an email sent from my 'friend' to one of her friends which had come into the hands of the paper, but it subsequently emerged that the article was based on a briefing over lunch on the previous Thursday. That article was accompanied in the* Sunday Telegraph *by a malign 3,700-word piece by Olga Craig which cited unnamed 'friends' of my friend.*

However, my big mistake had been to talk to the man purporting to produce a biography of me, for it was his decision to take advantage of this moment to change the arrangements for his publication, which was to be the critical factor in undermining political support, not just in the fateful weeks leading up to Christmas but also a year later when I stepped down for a second time from Cabinet.

Remarks that in one form or another I had undoubtedly made about my colleagues over a two-year period in this man's presence (and I never denied making them) were to be put together in a collage, without context or explanation, in an article in the Daily Mail. *For the rest of my life, I will regret speaking to Stephen Pollard. It was the biggest single mistake of my years in front-line politics, and while I could argue about the circumstances, the nature of the remarks, how they were meant and how they might have been received in entirely different circumstances, in the end there is only one person responsible – and that is me.*

Huw and I agreed that there was only one serious allegation being made, and that was that I had ordered or sought to achieve the fast-tracking of the renewal of a work visa. I was certain that the visa had not been fast-tracked. I said to Huw: 'Eighteen months ago, I set in train a whole range of measures to speed up the renewal of work visas before the charging policy came into operation. In August 2003, the visa would have gone through on that basis.' So we decided – my responsibility – to make it clear that no visa had been 'fast tracked'.

This was a major error. Had I stuck to what I could say with certainty – that I had never instigated or asked others to instigate the speeding-up of an individual visa – then the outcome of Sir Alan Budd's inquiry may have been very different. But I didn't.

Another sleepless night. On Sunday morning Huw calls early: 'It's bad. They have what they have sought for months, a conjoining of the public and private.' We agreed that at some point I should talk to Tony, but I have said to Huw that I have nothing to fear from an inquiry. I am prepared to take the initiative and set one up. Huw is not against this, but cautions regarding what sort of inquiry, and into what.

Very wise, because we should have been much clearer about what the terms of reference were. Having asserted something that I could never have been certain of because I had had nothing to do with the application as it went through the process – only with the letter drawing attention to the catastrophic delays in handling visas back in April 2003 – I was now to determine a set of criteria on the broad assertion that no speeding-up had occurred for this individual visa. It was therefore to become almost irrelevant that no evidence could be found of my requesting or encouraging any individual to pick out or speed up the visa.

But underpinning the reaction that Sunday (and carried forward in the weeks ahead) were entirely false reports about what I was doing, what I was demanding and what I was seeking in my personal life.

That is why Justice Ryder was so angry that he took the unprecedented step of putting on the public record in the High Court Family Division on Friday 3 December 2004 his caustic comments about what was being reported. 'In considering the competing rights, I have come to the clear conclusion that having regard to the quantity of material that is in the public domain, some of it, even in the most responsible commentaries, wholly inaccurate, it is right to give this judgement in public. The ability to correct false impressions and misconceived facts will go further to help secure the Article 6 and 8 rights of all involved, than would the Court's silence which in this case will only promote further speculation and adverse comment that will damage both the interests of those involved and the family justice system itself.'

Unfortunately it made absolutely no difference. In subsequent months the same old garbage was written, on the premise that no one should let the facts get in the way of a good story.

Even now on the public, never mind the private front, I have to be so careful what I say because I could blow everything. So much is *sub judice* – but does anybody seem to clock that? I took over fifty phone calls that Sunday, many from friends and family but also from special advisers, Downing Street and from the Department. I have been inundated with advice, much of it against having an inquiry, but I am committed to it. I am committed to trying to clear the air. I have nothing to hide so let there be an inquiry and let it be open and thorough.

It is worth noting here, given that my whole political future was at stake, that the allegations made on 28 November in the Sunday Telegraph *relating to the renewal of the visa were shown to be entirely wrong. They related to what I had or had not allegedly done with regard to handling the visa application personally, and even its delivery to the Immigration and Nationality Directorate headquarters in Croydon. Over the subsequent three weeks the allegations being made were to change, although remarkably I don't recall commentary on this at all at the time. So here I was, responding to a story that bore no resemblance to my recollections at all, while missing the key question: what had happened to the letter I had been handed on 28 April 2003, which had gone into my office without annotation or commentary but which related to the issue of policy and delivery that I had already raised?*

I was addressing the inquiry on the original allegations made, while the inquiry was delving into the actual facts, which I don't dispute. It was my decision to set up the inquiry – no one else's – and it falls to me to carry the responsibility for not connecting what I considered at the time to be a completely inconsequential act (putting the letter into the office) with subsequent events. Whether, given my emotional and physical situation, I could have seen through the subsequent six months to the general election is debatable. All I know is that I carry responsibility and I blame no one else.

My phone call with Tony was supportive and reassuring. He is good enough to say that I was right all along in my predictions of what might happen, and that he would stand by me – and reluctantly would agree to the inquiry, which he thought would be a rod for my own back. The question now is who should chair the inquiry.

On Monday [29 November] John Gieve and I talked about this. The inquiry must be set up by him, at my request, but he must handle it independently, as Permanent Secretary. He will pick who should chair the inquiry.

Sir Alistair Graham, who chairs the Committee on Standards in Public Life and with whom I had crossed swords when he was Chairman of the Police Complaints Authority before it became independent and his term of office ended, subsequently suggested that there should be a panel of such individuals. This would certainly have helped me at that time, and a year later would have been very helpful. But it would also have opened up a real can of worms, because the question is not who should chair the inquiry into any allegations but whether 'any' allegations of impropriety or breach of the Ministerial Code should be investigated. In simple terms, what constitutes sufficient prima-facie evidence to warrant the inquiry?

There is no doubt whatsoever that given the prurience of the moment and the determination to paint politics and politicians as somehow flawed, allegations would be made on a weekly basis. There would be almost a permanent sitting of inquiry, while the reputation of the individual was destroyed and their ability to do the job completely undermined.

On this occasion, John Gieve put forward the name of Sir Philip Mawer, the Parliamentary Commissioner. This was vetoed by the Speaker of the House, who thought that it would conflict and confuse Sir Philip's role with regard to dealing with parliamentary as opposed to ministerial breaches. Ironically, as could be seen from events around allegations against John Prescott in early July 2006, had Sir Philip chaired the inquiry, I would have been spared the attacks in the House of Commons, not least by Michael Howard and his colleagues at Prime Minister's Questions – something that, combined with the general hysteria, was deeply damaging to my situation, and deeply destabilising for both the Prime Minister and the government, and something that weighed very heavily with me then, as it did later.

I was very happy with the suggestion of Sir Alan Budd, former Chief Economic Adviser to the Tory government, put forward by John Gieve. Sir Alan is someone who knows civil-service procedures, who was a respected academic and had no connection whatsoever with me, the Department or the Labour Party. No one could smear him, so he was ideal. We offered him every possible facility to look at and go into anything he liked.

In his report, published on 21 December 2004, Sir Alan acknowledges that he took full advantage of our openness, including going into the archives, as well as interviewing twenty-two different civil servants, starting in my office and going all the way through the procedure to the hands-on, administrative officers and their supervisors dealing with the handling of the visa renewal.

The trouble is that those who don't know, don't know, so people reading all this material, including about my intimate private life, could believe it. I am standing up for my responsibility and for what I believe to be right – but what are people reading and thinking?

I have had one very nice phone call from a journalist who reminded me of a request that Dominic Lawson and his wife, Rosa Monckton, had made for help when she had left her passport at home. I had set up the immediate emergency turn-round (maximum twenty-four hours) system, but it wasn't yet fully operational. We helped her but I had not only forgotten the incident, but had also forgotten that a strange little story had appeared in the *Sunday Telegraph*, telling the story in a slightly different way, and presumably clearing the decks.

But back to my immediate problems.

Monday 29 November: I have spent all morning dealing with the issue of the inquiry. Sarah Brown suggested that we should continue to have the lunch that we had planned, and I was grateful for this. Now I have to speak on the floor of the House of Commons on the penultimate day of the Queen's Speech Debate. God, the timing is impeccable.

And in the middle of all this, my diary has a fascinating little entry:

I've just discovered that the Department (to be specific, the finance section) had not realised that as we were benefiting on the police grant from the efforts of all departments to put more money into local government generally, we would get more of that local-government grant as part of the police funding so long as we were matching it – which we are – and therefore the average increase for Police Authorities would rise from 4.4 per cent to 4.7 per cent. As a consequence we can do what I've wanted to do all along and lift the amount that constitutes the minimum that any Police Authority will get (the floor). Lord knows why we employ officials at this level if they are unable to spot these things.

The speech in the House went well. I just had to concentrate so hard. It is difficult to describe how you do it. I suppose you go into 'professional mode'. I used to see Jack Cunningham do it when I was working in his team in opposition, but I never thought I would have to do it myself.

From Tony's press conference on Monday morning, no one could ask for more support than he is giving. My job is not to let him down, to get on with the job and to be seen to be doing so, and to hide the hurt, the emotion, the churning that is tearing my guts out.

I went to see Charlie Falconer at his home in Nottinghamshire on the Saturday night. It was good to see the family, but the boyfriend of one of his daughters had the most dreadful cold. Pray God I don't get it.

Cherie Blair rang me at eleven p.m. when I got home to the cottage, which was lovely of her. That is the second time this week she has phoned me.

Every night it has been top of the news, every night when switching on the television or the radio and every morning in every newspaper, so opening up the whole shemozzle to an inquiry has not closed it down. This time the Conservatives smell blood.

December 2004

One story feeds on another, one red herring is followed by another. We've even got newspapers ringing up with the most extraordinary allegations that have been phoned in to the newsdesk. One broadsheet newspaper has set someone on full-time investigating a claim that I had used MI5 or Special Branch (they didn't appear to know the difference) to authorise taps on people's private phones, relating to my personal life.

While it was absurd to think that I would have authorised or even counte-nanced such a thing, it did subsequently turn out (in August 2006) to be a fear that was grounded in reality, with revelations regarding surveillance not by the security services or Special Branch but by private enterprise. This went some way towards explaining the revelations about my private life that had come out on 15 August 2004.

But that was only one of a whole range of the most stupid allegations that some journalists took seriously, and I was to experience this throughout December 2004, and the Sunday newspapers were as ever more imaginative than the daily papers. I bear no grudge, but I would have liked some of the newspaper editors to have gone back over what they wrote and at some point apologised. Alan Budd, in his final report, laid to rest a number of the more ridiculous stories, including those described as being from 'insiders' or 'sources close to' either me or the Department or both. One Sunday newspaper managed to lead the Sunday ITN news with a story that was just completely made up. Alan Budd's report shows that it was fabricated, but the story was all about how the visa had been handled in the Department and how I had 'demanded' in a meeting that action be taken on that individual visa and banged the table. None of it was true, but the fever had gripped everyone and so they were prepared to print, report or broadcast just about anything. Of course, apart from the fact that the story had been running since 15 August (I think this must be a record), I can only put the behaviour down to the fact that they simply thought it was too good a story to drop.

Some of the reports on Sunday 5 and Sunday 12 December 2004 should really have been put in for the Man Booker Prize for fiction. They would certainly have won.

Prime Minister's Questions on 1 December was deeply unpleasant. Michael Howard had picked up from Sir Alastair Graham, who was on the *Newsnight* broadcast the night before, that his Committee had recommended a Standing Panel – a kind of open invitation to anyone to allege anything against any minister. Michael Howard returned to this with a vengeance.

Alastair Graham's suggestion was that 'this sort of thing affects confidence in politics and public life.' Talk about having condemned somebody before they have been found guilty: a presumption of guilt from a man who is supposed to be neutral.

I didn't see it but I have been told that Mary Ann Sieghart did a really good job versus Melanie Phillips on that *Newsnight*. The things that people are having to do. Thank God the *Sun* is totally with me. At least one newspaper is trying to tell the truth.

To top it all I had to be part of the receiving party on 1 December for the President of South Korea. So there we were, with me in the middle of the most enormous controversy, and pictures of myself with Tony and the Queen. I was sorry that Her Majesty had been inadvertently drawn into this.

The same afternoon I kept to my commitment to meet Frances Lawrence, the widow of Philip Lawrence, the head-teacher who had been murdered outside his school when trying to break up a gang fight. The probation service are supervising the killer coming out, as part of the long-term rehabilitation and release, and they have handled it so badly that I am having to intervene. Frances Lawrence was understandably deeply upset, and I simply had to spend time with her. I still wanted to feel I was a human being, even in the middle of the adversity.

Just bizarrely it is worth noting that Thursday 2 December was Pre-Budget Day and that evening I gave dinner to Andrea Bocelli and his party in the House of Commons. He sang a note or two in Westminster Hall. How I managed to get through that evening, I will never know.

Now the press and television cameras are everywhere – every moment of every day and everywhere I go, I am now under 24-hour surveillance.

This was to last not only for the whole of December 2004 but on and off for virtually the whole of 2005.

One most lovely and thoughtful thing: Kevin Wells, father of Holly Wells, the little girl who was killed with Jessica Chapman at Soham, phoned to wish me well. I was touched beyond belief.

All sorts of people who have never known me personally, as well as the great and the good – and the very great – got in touch with me: handwritten notes, emails, phone calls to the office. I had no idea that people cared so much and that they were batting for me. I had no idea there was such goodwill, kindnesses too numerous to mention.

I am a very lucky man. Over 2,500 people – from what my mother would have called the highest to the lowest in the land – wrote to me when I eventually did step down. It has been this, and the love and friendship of family and those closest to me, that have sustained me over a prolonged period that otherwise would have been intolerable.

Hundreds of letters have come into the Department – a complete contrast between the public reaction, from the people I meet and talk to, and what people are writing in the papers. It is just as though there are two nations: those writing and those living; those hating and those caring.

The political editor of the BBC, Andrew Marr, was asked on the six o'clock news, in one of those two-way exchanges with the presenter, 'And will he go?' and replied: 'There are three reasons why I don't think David Blunkett will resign. One is that he has the total support of the Prime Minister. Two, he believes that he's innocent. Three, to call David Blunkett stubborn would be like describing Elton John as a tad flamboyant.'

In a separate two-way, again on the six o'clock news, Andrew Marr was asked: 'If it is a matter of family or political career, which will David Blunkett choose?' His reply was: 'No question, he will choose family.' He was right. In the first interview, unfortunately, he was wrong: not in his three points, which were entirely accurate, but simply because my health started to fail me and my mistaken confidence in my own recollection when responding to the Sunday Telegraph *was to overtake me.*

With the exception of Peter Mandelson on the second occasion (over the Hinduja brothers affair), the resignations we have seen have been when people have simply had enough, simply couldn't take the pressure any longer. I wonder if I can last until Christmas. If I can, then I can rest and recover and carry on. But can I? I am determined to survive, absolutely determined not to be pushed out. I will use every ounce of my reserves to stop them, to stop them doing what they have done to others before me.

Yes, that's what I wrote and that's what I was determined to do, but over the subsequent two weeks my health deteriorated. I wonder now, even if my unequivocal conviction about the visa had been justified, with the enormity of the agenda that I was facing on the political front and the terrible trauma on the private front, whether seriously I could have picked up the pieces again in January. Of course, I will never know. All I know is that I took more in the following year than any human being could be expected to put up with – and I survived it – and as I will show, had circumstances been different, I would not have resigned in November 2005.

It would appear from some of the polling (the *Telegraph* did a YouGov poll and the *Sunday Express* had a poll), that people are still, on the whole, holding firm with me. I have just got to hope that that remains the case. I don't know why, though, because the information they are being fed is awful. If they are still with me after the lies that are being told, then it is nothing short of a miracle. On the other hand, I have to remember the Radio 5 Live phone-in that I caught on Monday morning as I went into the office, where a couple of callers were suggesting that this had happened to me because I was blind and couldn't do the job. God help me.

But I think what really took the biscuit was to read people like Carol Long in the *Daily Mirror* on 1 December, who suggested that if I couldn't sort out my private life, then I couldn't run the Department and be a senior minister. What sort of people are these? But what I had to put up with from Gordon Raynor in the *Mail* and Andrew Neil in his BBC 2 programme was just unforgivable.

Wednesday [1 December] was also the day when we got as near the truth as we could, but in a way that made the waters even murkier. This was all about the letter that I had sent in to the Department on 28 April 2003, which was sold to the *Daily Mail* for a very large sum of money by a nanny who had been seeking to renew her visa to be allowed to work in this country.

Although the individual concerned was not known to me personally, the mother of the child she cared for was central to my personal life.

I immediately said that the letter was perfectly authentic and it was *the* letter. There was no reason why I shouldn't. It was the letter. There was no secret about it. It revealed what I had told the Department back in March 2003: that the system had broken down. Had we had the letter on file, I feel sure that my Private Office would have drawn my attention to it the moment that the *Sunday Telegraph* allegations started. But no one could remember it and there was no reason why they should, because it was completely unexceptional.

The recollections of myself and others on this issue have been made more difficult by the fact that the accusations against us continue to change.

The irony is that the letter was the only explanation that anyone could find as to what had happened, and without it there would have had to have been a presumption that I had given some form of verbal instruction which, although no one could have proved it one way or the other, would for me, at least morally, have been extremely damaging. But – and I blame no one for this – it was presented as being some great piece of revelation. Given the amount of money that had been paid for the letter, this is not surprising as it had to be a real story, and in one sense it was. But as I made my way to the Passport Office to have my biometric identifier taken as part of the ID-card information campaign, I had to stand in front of cameras and simply say it as it was: 'Yes, this is the letter, it is perfectly authentic, I dispute none of it, but I don't remember putting it into the office' – and I didn't.

Paradoxically, Alan Budd told me that it was a perfectly standard letter, but on this occasion sent out in error. It should never have been sent to her because it wasn't a letter designed for her particular type of visa renewal. Why it didn't come across more clearly at the time that the letter itself was inappropriate and therefore whether officials recognised this when the letter reached them (on the back of the policy issue having already been raised weeks earlier when the delay was mentioned to me), I do not know. It would, of course, have explained why, in receiving a copy of the letter down the line, they had examined the fact that the application should have been dealt with and handled in a different way – as it subsequently was. However, this is all water under the bridge and there is absolutely no point in agonising over it now. The only thing that matters to me is to know that what I did was right on every front.

Facts, or someone's version of them, were being presented all over the place. This woman was supposed to have applied for a visa on 19 April and it was actually dated 15 March, which is why I knew that there was a problem by the end of March, because she had been told that there was a massive delay when she applied. The allegation is that I had filled in and delivered the application form.

I hadn't, and Sir Alan Budd found that this was utter nonsense. Conclusion 2 in his offical report reads: 'Neither Mr Blunkett nor anyone in his Private Office was involved in providing the application form, checking it or delivering it to the Immigration and Nationality Directorate (IND) in Croydon.' Not only had it been sent but it had been properly stamped on arrival through the post in the normal way.

God knows who is going to believe what by the time the report comes out. Even I am beginning to doubt myself. I think I am going mad. I know the facts – but these are then widely presented as being completely untrue. I am in the middle of a sustained campaign and because of *sub judice* I can't talk about private matters, and publicly I can't speak about the detail because it would interfere with Sir Alan's investigation and the neutrality of the report. In any case, I can't get stuck in as Home Secretary, even if the inquiry gave me permission to speak – which it won't.

My Private Office, the press office and my special advisers are being run ragged. How the hell we are managing to get any work done I do not know. Our opponents say that I cannot possibly do the job because of the distraction, and then throw everything possible into distracting me and those around me. But we are holding on. We are holding meetings. We are keeping going. We are making decisions. I don't know how, but we are.

And that carried through until Wednesday 15 December. We kept going. Friends and family said, 'God knows how you are keeping going', and I didn't know either.

The broadcast media can do most damage, so being on the news every single night is becoming deeply distressing. (*Newsnight* was particularly unpleasant on Tuesday 30 November: ill informed and venomous.)

This was to become a pattern for Newsnight *over the coming year, leading to a lengthy inquiry into the three broadcasts that systematically attacked me personally in the autumn of 2005. Television is a powerful medium, and when misused can be highly dangerous.*

And aren't there turn-ups for the book? My ex-wife Ruth has turned down £50,000 from a Sunday newspaper to dish the dirt on our marriage. That is the other side of the coin of human nature, and what a contrast.

My sons and their friends are being followed, investigated and harangued by Sunday papers. It is not sufficient to have a go at me, hour by hour.

I have to say that at this time, December 2004, and from May 2005 onwards to my resignation in November 2005 and regrettably beyond, my family and friends were subjected to what can only be described as the equivalent of the Stasi secret service in East Germany. However, with the advent of new technology, of surveillance devices, long-distance microphones and cameras, this sort of harassment has taken on an entirely new dimension compared with the vile but old-fashioned spying techniques of totalitarian regimes of the past. It is, in the words of one fellow minister who has experienced it, 'like a form of privatised non-violent terrorism'. If you are in public life in the twenty-first century you can now expect it personally – but your family and friends should surely be beyond the pale.

Sadly, on the day that the partner of one of my sons was menaced by a journalist, her father was taken seriously ill. They weren't to know this, but even if they had, would it have made any difference? Human tragedies happen all around us: I was rung on the evening of Saturday 27 November, when I was dealing with the *Sunday Telegraph* allegations, to be told that my cousin had died in an accident at home. You have to cope with these things yourself, but how can you help others to cope when they have nothing whatsoever to do with the matter in hand? Where I found the strength on Sunday morning, amongst everything else I was doing that day, to ring his wife to try to comfort her, God knows. But you do find strength from somewhere, and at times like this I just try and think of other people. It's strange but I always think of the troops in the trenches in the First World War and what they endured, and the fact that I am warm, I am strong, and I have family and friends around me.

The second week of December, and there is no doubt that these are the lowest times I have ever had in all my years in politics. Let me lay aside the Sunday papers on the 5th: they speak entirely for themselves and will carry on doing so when the truth is known. Monday [6 December] brought the *Daily Mail*'s carefully choreographed and cleverly put-together extracts from Stephen Pollard's so-called biography of me, and I felt the world opening up beneath me. I recognised that this was a rapier, not a pinprick. You know when something is serious and lasting, and when something is manageable and ephemeral. I spent the early part of Monday morning ringing round and simply saying 'Sorry' to colleagues. Many of them had not seen the extracts, so it was only going to be later that the way in which it was presented would impact on them. I didn't excuse myself. I didn't say, as I so easily could have, that the whole thing had been taken out of context, or that I hadn't really said it at all. I simply told them the truth – that over a two-year period, it was quite likely that the words used could have been used, but in no way in the form presented in the *Daily Mail*, where these words were presented as a whole tirade of commentary on colleagues. But the damage is clearly done.

Without in any way excusing my political ineptitude and, it has to be said, lapse in 'comradeship', I think anyone who has read the context in which these comments arose would realise that in the greater scheme of things they were irritants but nothing more. I regret them most in respect of extremely good friends who have always been, as far as I am aware, loyal and supportive to me. I have a debt to repay to them, and to Jack Straw, my predecessor as Home Secretary, to whom I have apologised. Each of us inherits what our predecessor in government has managed to achieve – the building blocks that I now recognise take us so far, but only so far. It would seem, uniquely in terms of portfolios, that each successive Home Secretary, even of the same party, has tended to see his predecessor as having failed to shift the world – and they would be partly right.

I know this is going to be a humdinger at Prime Minister's Questions on Wednesday. I know that the parliamentary party will be livid with me – and rightly so. But this isn't about here and now. This is a mistake made some time ago, and there is absolutely nothing I can do about it.

To cap it all, I have now gone down with the cold that I have dreaded. I have felt it coming for days. This isn't my usual mardiness about getting a cold. This is something else. I can feel my body and my mind fighting too many battles at once – and I have to present the Second Reading of the Serious Organised Crime and Police Bill, tomorrow [7 December].

At this time I was making my diary almost nightly. I knew that by the time I reached each weekend, it would be impossible to remember what had happened. Even so, I didn't capture all that was going on. I couldn't, because I was trying to do the job. I was still taking home the tapes at night to turn round the work and present the following morning. I was still receiving the 'box' at the weekend. I was still trying to deliver the government's agenda.

Why was I persuaded, or why did I persuade myself, that Pollard's book was going to be a heavyweight biography – that background was needed to get a picture of how government worked, what the pressures were, what the attitudes were, what sort of interaction took place with colleagues and friends? What possessed me to let down my guard on my own political instincts that had stood me in good stead for so long? I don't know the answer.

It is no excuse to say that I couldn't see when the tape recorder was on or off. I had given Stephen Pollard consent to tape the general background conversations we were having. If I stoop to that as an excuse, I am lost. He has made money on the back of my naïvety and I thought he was going to make his name on a serious biography.

What I do resent is that he has used the term 'adviser' when he means the people who generally had dealings of some sort or another with me – but it looks in the article as though he is talking about my special advisers. That is deeply offensive to them, and untrue.

I would have gone by Wednesday 8 December if it hadn't been for the absolute support of Tony Blair, and the love and friendship of my sons and closest friends. I believe I owe them a debt of gratitude that I can never repay. And also for the support of colleagues, even those who had cause to be aggrieved with me – to meet and hug, to have lunch with Charles Clarke, to meet Margaret Beckett in the Members' Dining Room, who said: 'We've all done it, but not in the presence of someone writing it all down. You should hear what I have said about you on occasions!' I just got to my feet and gave her a hug. I was able to make my peace with my long-standing friend, Tessa Jowell, but not, as we will see, with John Prescott.

And so as we approach Friday [10 December], the thirteenth day of unprecedented and sustained pressure, can I get through the barrier that Alastair Campbell describes as the critical test? He says that no one is able to sustain this sort of pressure, or ever has, beyond thirteen days. I want to – but can I?

On Thursday 9 December, Tony joined me in Sheffield. He knew that the pressure on me was relentless, that my physical and emotional health was deteriorating, and that despite all the courage and determination and what Andrew Marr had described as stubbornness, I may well be unable to keep going much longer. We had flown north to present part of our campaign against anti-social behaviour and the promotion of community support officers, a campaign against under-age drinking that we had begun, and fixed-penalty notices, and then to open the new sixth form college, £15 million of investment in giving youngsters in my constituency a chance to stay on beyond the age of sixteen, where staying-on rates were the lowest in the north of England.

We stood on the platform together – before the television cameras which had turned up for entirely different reasons than to cover the event – and he gave me his unequivocal support once again. It was an act of both friendship and defiance on his part, and I am so deeply sorry that a week later I let him down by stepping down.

I am getting support from other colleagues. Gordon has kept in touch and has been supportive. Friends such as Hilary Benn and David Miliband have been really kind, as are my wonderful ministerial team and advisers. How very lucky I am to have them, a Private Office staffed by people who care and a press office that, although run ragged, are giving 100 per cent.

I now know that if I do survive, I have destroyed my chance of promotion. All I can save is my good name. But if only I didn't feel so ill.

During the week before going to Sheffield, I had had dinner on Tuesday night with my old friend and former PPS Jean Corston, now Chair of the Parliamentary Labour Party. On Wednesday my son Alastair came down to London to give me support, which was very thoughtful of him, and joined Louise and Michael Gray, my friends from the village in Derbyshire, for Louise's birthday. Everybody made as good a fist as they could of trying to cheer me.

I needed some cheering because the Cabinet on Thursday morning before flying to Sheffield with Tony hadn't been a freezer or a refrigerator, but what I would call 'a chill cabinet, preserved for a future roasting'. But I can expect no less, and deserve no less.

I had to come back to London on Friday, which must have thrown the media because it meant that I gave them the slip – the last time for some while – and was able to get in and out of my house at South Eaton Place in London without being filmed or photographed. It felt like liberation, but it isn't!

All I can think about is how I can get through the next two weeks: the House of Lords judgement on Part 4 of the Anti-Terrorism, Crime and Security Act on Thursday 16 December, and the Second Reading of the Identity Cards Bill the following Monday.

I wasn't in fact to deal with either.

Back up to Sheffield for my advice surgery and a visit to Firth Park School, to talk with young people who have an arts project going.

And then once again, the Sunday papers.

Down to London and concentrate, just concentrate. Gun-crime round-table meeting for Wednesday: this time we are widening it to consider the issue of knives. I know that this is going to be the next big issue for us to address.

And shall I go to the 'Old Lags' Christmas dinner for MPs? I think I must before I go and eat with the ministerial team and advisers for our Christmas party. Oh dear, they deserve better.

It was a mistake to go to the Christmas dinner. It is called the 'Old Lags' in a friendly way, and has been taking place in a pub near Westminster for years – traditional Christmas fare, a sing-song and a few performances. I think my judgement was beginning to go astray, because I thought it would be a good idea not just to go but to show that I was still bouncing back, still prepared to keep going. By this time I could hardly speak because of the dreadful cold I had, my eyes were running and frankly I was just about dead on my feet. I must have been as near pneumonia as I was in 1988 when my marriage broke up and I moved house. But there I was, with my good colleague Kevin Brennan playing the guitar, attempting to sing 'Pick yourself up, dust yourself off, start all over again'. People joined in and everyone who cared for me said that they had never seen John Prescott look at me with such hatred and bitterness. Little did I know then that he had reason to be slightly more circumspect.

And then to what would have been my father's birthday, Wednesday 15 December 2004: the seminal day in my political life. The day I had not believed would ever come.

The bombshell had been dropped the day before, Tuesday. Sir Alan Budd came in to see me, quietly and unassumingly, and simply said: 'We have gone through everything. We have had full co-operation. We have looked in every corner and on every hard drive. We have interviewed twenty-two men and women in the Immigration Department, all the way down the line. None of them can remember anything. All of them are clear that they did not receive an instruction or a request from you or from the office. But none of them can explain an email.' I asked: 'What email was that?' He replied: 'The one that was sent from IND to your Private Office that said: "The case was in ICU [Initial Consideration Unit] so they pulled it out of the queue and made a decision – no special favours, only what they would normally do – but a bit quicker."'

In his book about me, Stephen Pollard states that this email was 'from a Home Office official to the Immigration Department.' No wonder the press and public got the wrong end of the stick when my so-called biographer managed to get it the wrong way round.

Sir Alan went on to say that it would appear that either as a consequence of my raising the wider issue, or of the letter I passed into the office at the end of April 2003 being then passed down the line, they re-examined the case and switched it from the slow track to the fast track. I asked whether it could have simply been that my directive to try and clear the decks in weeks and months rather than in a year prior to charging coming in, in August of that year, might have made the difference? He said: 'No. It is clear that while there is no evidence and no timeline that links this to you, your office undoubtedly chased the letter that had gone through at the end of April.' I said that if they had made a note, that's exactly what they would do: they would progress-chase. Sir Alan said: 'Yes, but unfortunately we cannot find a note of the exact sequence, nor can we find exactly what was requested.' So I said: 'But it is clear that, in the jargon, this visa renewal was fast-tracked?' Sir Alan replied: 'Yes.' I said, 'Well, in which case, perhaps you would give me twenty-four hours for the things that I need to do and to think about. I am very grateful for the fact that you brought this to my attention as soon as you found it, and for the thoroughness and care with which you have done the job.' I asked how long it would be before he would be able to publish the report, and his reply was: 'Six or seven days, I think, in terms of just clarifying, verifying and writing it up.'

I thanked him. I rang my sons and my very closest friends, but I couldn't tell any of my political friends or acquaintances. I had to think. I had to talk to the special advisers who would lose their jobs, whose livelihood and well-being would go down with me. I had dinner that Tuesday night with Tessa Jowell – a thank-you for restoring our friendship. Tessa may not know this but I think I bought the most expensive bottle of wine I have ever bought in a restaurant. I'd like to say that it was purchased as an act of generosity, but it was because I was no longer taking notice of anything. I had made up my mind by then.

On the day of my resignation came yet another utterly false and scurrilous allegation, this time that I had intervened with the Austrian embassy to get a European transit visa for those outside the European Union wishing to travel direct between London and Vienna. The BBC ran it at the top of the news. The fact that the Daily Mail *had got what they thought was a good story from someone who was absolutely determined to put in the last nail, seemed to be enough for the other news journalists. They were hungry now for anything. The fact that the Austrian ambassador unequivocally knocked the story down*

and said that it was nonsense from beginning to end, didn't make any
difference whatsoever. The pack were now in full flight.

I said to Huw Evans: 'There is no choice, is there, Huw?' He replied: 'I'm
sorry but no there isn't. You and we said that this visa had not been fast-
tracked and it has been, and even if Pollard's book hadn't come out your
integrity would be in doubt if you didn't step down.' So I said: 'Let's fix to
see Tony, and cancel everything. I will go to Prime Minister's Questions
because I want to hold my head high. Despite what is going to happen, I
want to sit there with Tony on the front bench. I want to be strong enough
and brave enough to sit through it with him.' This was because there wasn't
time to see him and to resign before PMQ, and I knew that it was going to
be hell.

I can't even remember now why Tony was so tied up on the Wednesday
morning. Understandably Michael Howard threw everything at Tony, in-
cluding the Pollard book. God knows, it is amazing that any member of the
parliamentary party was speaking to me after it.

We met in Tony's office in Downing Street – David Hill, Jonathan Powell,
Sally Morgan, Huw Evans and myself. I simply spelled out to Tony – who
clearly already knew – the situation. He asked what my decision was. I said
that I believed I had no choice. I said that I was so very sorry that I had let
him down, but that from the very beginning of this last episode I believed
that there was nothing amiss. I said that I wouldn't have asked for the
inquiry and I wouldn't have asked for his support if I had not believed that
to be the case. But it was absolutely clear that the visa was fast-tracked, and
for me to hold my head up high I needed to step down. I needed to also for
my own health, because frankly I wasn't sure I could take any more.

Tony asked Huw Evans what he thought and Huw said that he didn't
think there was any choice whatsoever, and that I wouldn't last five
minutes in the present climate if I tried to face it out. And then we talked
for a minute or two, quietly about what might be done, about the big issues
coming up and the Law Lords' judgement tomorrow, and then everyone
left and Tony and I just hugged each other. I again said that I was sorry and
Tony said: 'Not as sorry as I am. I was relying on you in the build-up to the
general election, and in holding firm.' He also said that the reason I had
received such support from the public, despite everything that has been
said and thrown at me, is because they believe that I am on their side.

I then went into an ante-room and phoned Alastair, Hugh and Andrew and my very closest friends. Tessa Jowell dropped what she was doing and came straight round. And then Huw, and Sophie Linden, who had come across, got me a cup of tea and we began to work out what my letter to Tony would say and what his letter in reply would say, and what Downing Street's press release would say. And it all took for ever. I had already told them that I wouldn't do a parliamentary statement. This wasn't the day for parliamentary statements. I would do no press conference. I would just speak to people in their own homes on the evening news on each main channel. I would just tell them why I was stepping down and give them some idea of the context so that they could make their own judgement. But we got nearer and nearer to six o'clock, and still they hadn't signed off with Tony what needed to be said. So I returned to the Department and told them to get all the crews lined up, to let them know what was happening. The news was already out. Downing Street, on these occasions, is like the Internet, and it can't help itself. But there were other clues by which the outside world could deduce what had happened: I had pulled out of chairing a public meeting about drugs at the Home Office, and Huw had stopped returning calls from journalists.

I phoned my friend Paul Potts, head of the Press Association, so that he knew and so that the PA could carry what I said from the television interviews. I then asked Huw if they could just speed it up because, as I said, 'I don't think I can last much longer. If we don't do it now, I will never be able to do it. I am on the edge of collapse.' And so it was, that one after the other, I did the broadcasts, and then we all gathered ministers, advisers, Private Office – and went downstairs to the press office. I thanked each of them and they clapped and cried. Then we went upstairs and hugged each other and cried some more. Gareth Redmond, one of my private secretaries, produced a mock press release – a Harry Potter press release stating that I was to be moved to the Ministry of Magic – and just for a moment we laughed before crying again.

I went in to see my Permanent Secretary, John Gieve. I thanked him for putting up with me over the very hard time that I had given him, for expecting more of him than probably anyone could have expected. I thanked him for what he had done over the past three weeks, for standing by me, for having to take some of the flak himself, and I wished him well with Charles Clarke, as Tony had told me that Charles would take my place.

I then went and collected my papers – which I had already stacked as I had had twenty-four hours to be able to prepare – and left for South Eaton Place.

3

OUT OF OFFICE

2004–2005

I don't intend to go into detail but Tony agreed that I could keep the house for the time being, on security grounds. I was so sorry that month after month the press raised the issue of my eviction, which would have been inevitable were I not to have returned to government. We all knew there was an election coming.

In retrospect, however, I should have found a way of leaving the house, and I wish I had. It would have been one less pressure point, one less area of criticism, one less accusation of arrogance. Tony's gesture was simple humanity. I no longer had the money. I was in the middle of a private crisis. My health was virtually destroyed. And those newspapers, including those on the liberal Left, who felt it was appropriate to hound me over this should in my view practise what they preach.

I am still being pursued. I've been to Tessa and David's and they gave me a bite of supper. We watched the first twenty-one minutes of the ten o'clock news on BBC television: all of it about me, my time in government and my resignation. And then I went home and tried to sleep. The next phase of my life is about to begin.

Let me spare the reader the blow-by-blow account of the next ten days through to Christmas. Suffice it to say that the media stuck with me, day by day, and the following Tuesday when Sir Alan published his report I dealt with it in my newly allocated office in Portcullis House, next to the Palace of Westminster, as best I could.

I am not proud of those ten days. I wasn't thinking straight and I wasn't behaving sensibly. No excuses. I had simply had enough. I said things to journalists and to other colleagues that should not have been said. I attacked the key person in my personal life, and implied that she was a hedonist and not a good mother. I regret this, and believe it to be untrue. All this was of course at the time of the most unbelievable personal and political pressure, hard even to conceive of without experiencing it.

The political world around me went its own way and the waters started to close behind me. But the letters and messages began to flow, many from people I could never have expected, many from my political opponents who, because they wrote privately, I will not name. I valued that support, and I clung on to the belief that people out there understood. They had seen what had happened *and they reached out to me. The disconnection between the inner world which determined my future and the world outside could not have been greater.*

Just to recall one or two of the sillier things: the newspapers and the broadcast media were still there, day after day, wanting a comment, wanting a photo, wanting to know if I was a broken man. As soon as the Budd Report had been published I went to King's Cross and got the train, avoiding the massed ranks of the media, who were still tied up with the announcement of the report. When I returned to my home in Sheffield (from where I was going out that evening with close friends, and then out to my cottage in Derbyshire) I was met by a posse of television crews and press photographers.

I got into the house as quickly as I could, and then there was a knock on the door. I wasn't prepared to open it, but I asked who was there. A woman's voice replied: 'I'm terribly sorry. I am a producer from BBC television news. We missed the shots of you coming in and we wondered if you would come back out again and do it for us all over again.' I gave one of those ironic laughs and said, 'You really have to be joking, don't you?' She went away and came back a few minutes later and knocked on the door again and said: 'The editors back in London say would you let us film you at the kitchen table using your Braille machine, or just talking to someone?' I said: 'Please, act like a human being and just go away and leave me alone.' There was still a crew outside when I left for the restaurant that evening, but fortunately the cameraman had fallen asleep. God bless him.

One of the twists in this saga is that the fact that I was not personally guilty created bigger problems for me than if I had simply been directly responsible. This becomes clear in paragraph 3.36 of Sir Alan Budd's report, where he states: 'I do not believe that the handling of the case by IND was particularly unusual. Inquiries from the general public or from MPs could trigger the retrieval of a case and the changing of an initial decision. At a time when strenuous efforts were being made to reduce the backlog, it would have been quite normal for a supervisor or senior caseworker to have reviewed the case and to have changed the decision or to have advised or instructed the original caseworker to do so.' Had I been directly responsible, I believe it would have earned me only a reprimand for not having distanced myself from it – and not the destruction of my career.

Wednesday 22 December: the *Today* programme. I cannot believe this. I am listening to John Humphrys interviewing John Prescott. They are talking about me and my demise, and it is absolutely clear that John Prescott hasn't got the first idea what is in the Budd Report or what it is that I am supposed to have done. He said: 'Well, he's been found guilty of the offence, basically, not so much an open verdict. He found that he had intervened and David's argument was that he was not fully aware of that, and I think you have to take that's what he said, but at the end of the day, he has faced up to his full responsibility and resigned. That's the most a minister can do, John.'

No, I wasn't guilty, and I hadn't admitted I was guilty. I had staff in my office and in the Immigration and Nationality Directorate who owed me no favours, given the hard time I had given them throughout the three and a half years I had been there, who had done their job as they had seen it.

So when I heard John Humphrys' Today programme interview with John Prescott on 6 July 2006 I was flabbergasted. The interview was in the wake of allegations that John Prescott had stayed on the Colorado ranch of American billionaire Philip Anschutz, which might have invited accusations of preferential treatment with regard to Anschutz's successful bid to purchase the Millennium Dome. John Prescott said: 'I will say again on your programme, I was never involved in any such action. People had better bring the evidence. But if you say to me, were there some civil servants down the line exercising some judgement about this in view of the circumstances, I wasn't involved in it, didn't even know about it until I read it in the press, and totally reject any idea that I exerted any pressure whatsoever. I know there is a media storm against me. They don't like me and to be quite honest I don't like them, but in reality you have to deal with the facts, not that the papers are doing that too much, but here and what you are saying to me, officials might have been involved, I don't know for sure. I was not involved because the suggestion at the end of day was that my meeting with Mr Anschutz was somehow giving him preference for a bid. It was not. I did not get involved and there is no evidence to that effect at all.' Quite.

Christmas Eve: my invitation to the Nine Lessons and Carols service at King's College, Cambridge, still stood, and with my former Principal Private Secretary and his partner I went to this famous service for the first time in my life. Every Christmas for as long as I can remember, I have listened to it on Radio 4 and now I was there, receiving solace and therapy, an outletting, a great comfort. I was grateful to all those who held out that invitation and allowed me to get close to the spiritual, allowed me the chance to put something inside back together again.

But early on Christmas Day morning, I walked out from the cottage on my own, with Sadie. (I was later due to join my family for lunch at a nearby restaurant.) As I made my way past the church I heard a camera click. Yes: they were still at it on Christmas Day morning.

I grabbed hold of the photographer (just instinctively) and got from him that he was working for the Mail on Sunday, *so I rang the editor, Peter Wright, at home and he agreed to pull it, which he did. But on Boxing Day (Sunday) the* News of the World *ran the photographs instead under the heading 'Lonely Blunkett walks his dog'. And the* Sunday Telegraph *carried three articles on my private life, one of them in the business section, by Robert Peston, now business editor of the BBC. Peston was one of the named journalists on the killer* Sunday Telegraph *article on 28 November, and has also written a biography of Gordon. In addition to the two articles in the main paper, the article in the business section was so ridiculous, so bizarre and so offensive as to be beyond belief. I have not sought to settle scores in this diary. I just draw attention to the facts.*

January 2005

Tony and Gordon had both rung me on the night that I had resigned, and Tony again at the weekend and on the night of 23 December, when he had arrived in Egypt for his Christmas holiday. Gordon and I spoke on 2 January, the day that both of us appeared on *Songs of Praise* with our choice of favourite hymns.

I had recorded the programme way back in November, and had chosen 'Dear Lord and Father of mankind, forgive our foolish ways'.

I was glad they didn't cut me out of the programme, and it was good that people were keeping in touch. Given the clashes that we had had, I was really moved by the fact that Alistair Darling had rung, and had spoken to me separately when I went through the lobbies to vote on the Second Reading of the ID Cards Bill just before Parliament went into recess for Christmas.

I am considering legal action against some of the news media, but honestly all my money is going elsewhere. How many legal actions can I take on? Where will the money come from? And what good would it do?

The Press Complaints Commission is no solution. I've tried using them. They are utterly useless.

I eventually won one of the initial cases, but by summer 2006 I had used my own resources to take legal action in over a dozen cases; in all of these I successfully obtained retractions and apologies. But I was convinced from my experience that the Press Complaints Commission was not worth the paper its name is written on. It has no investigatory power or arm. It simply approaches the newspaper that has perpetrated the untruth or distortion, and they write back saying whether or not they are prepared to do anything – which is usually to say they will print a letter which, by its very nature, will look as though the individual is having to defend themselves against something that they never did in the first place.

Those of us in the very front line of public life can expect no mercy, and perhaps there will never be any redress other than going to court once you are out of office. But for individuals, and particularly for the family and friends of those affected by being in the public eye, it is only right that the system should be changed and protection should be given to them from the gross intrusion into their privacy and lies told about them. No one deserves to be tracked, surveilled, electronically monitored or put under any pressure because they happen to be a family member or a friend of someone on the public platform. In the end, for this reason alone, the nation will get the public representatives that it deserves.

But it's New Year and my life and my woes have been put into some sort of perspective. There has been a tsunami in the Indian Ocean, the most enormous tidal wave, and reports say that 150,000 people are dead. What sort of grumbles have I got? Why should I feel sorry for myself? I am alive. I will be healthy again. I am not poverty-stricken. And I am not without family and friends. Be grateful.

And I don't know why but I put down here in my diary: 'Sir John Gieve, my former Permanent Secretary, has a knighthood. You get a knighthood, if you haven't already got one, the moment you become the Permanent Secretary at the Treasury, so perhaps John Gieve's is four years late.' John was to become the Deputy Governor of the Bank of England when Charles Clarke entered the Home Office and wished to bring with him as Permanent Secretary Sir David Normington, who used to be Director-General of Schools when I was Secretary of State for Education and Employment.

Tony rang me on Thursday 6 January. I thanked him for what he had said the day before on *The Today* programme, when once again he had been supportive and positive about my future. We have agreed to talk in February when I have had a little holiday and time to pull myself round. It compensated for the *Times* leader the same day that urged Tony, before defending me, not only to satisfy himself about the particulars 'but also the question of whether the events were an aberration and not part of a pattern of imperious behaviour and poor judgement': such nasty innuendo and I really don't know why.

I've returned to Westminster before thinking of a holiday. I need to set up a proper diary. I need not to disappear and to give myself something to do. I need to fill the days and make sure that I'm not at a loose end, and if I'm honest, I need to earn some money – and pretty urgently. I could sell everything I've got, but where would that leave my sons, and where would it leave me for the future after all these years? I don't want to go back. I want to be able to go forward. But I cannot give up now on the mission I have set myself.

On two consecutive Sundays there was material in the papers from Robert Peston's biography of Gordon. It is very fortunate indeed that the biography of me didn't come out on the original timetable, as that would have coincided exactly with this biography of Gordon. But the specially picked extracts from mine have clearly diverted attention, which is a good thing for the government, as, while the parliamentary party are seething, the world outside has hardly noticed.

The parliamentary party – all sides, all shades of opinion – really laid down the law at the first parliamentary-party meeting of 2005. Everyone who spoke was simply saying, 'Tony and Gordon – please get your act together. Please stop this conflict and division. Please rein in those around you.' There was more anger than usual at Gordon because of Peston's book, which soon faded into the background.

Politics is like that. Something can have a real salience at a particular moment, and then a few weeks later it has literally disappeared and no one can remember what it was all about. But with an election imminent, every nerve was raw.

Things had come to a head, partly because of continuing friction and partly because of those around Tony and Gordon who had managed to set up a clash of speeches that allowed Sky television to carry pictures of each of them on a split screen, simultaneously talking in different parts of the country. It was a very clever pictorial way of making a point, and the point went home.

Instead of my usual constituency meeting, I have invited all the activists who normally come to have supper at Wortley Hall, an old manor house which has been turned into a trade-union and holiday centre. I just wanted to say thank you – thank you for not equivocating, not flinching, not questioning, for supporting me and being there for me. This is what fraternity and mutuality is all about, but there is so little of it about. Thank God for my constituency and for people who have known me all these years, know who I am and what I am and what I try to do. I have not let them down and they are not letting me down.

In the *Sunday Times* on 16 January, a piece claiming that I had been meeting Tony and was becoming Party Chairman after the election. There has been no such meeting. There has been no such talk or suggestion, and if such an offer was made I would gently decline it. But where on earth do these stories come from?

However, what was fascinating about the *Sunday Times* front page that day was a give-away in relation to the machinery of government, as well as a clear indication that the 'leaked' documents on licensing and on the alcohol strategy could not have come from either the Home Office or DCMS [Department for Culture, Media and Sport] alone, because it carried material relating to officials' advice to both sets of ministers (different advice), and the leaker, whoever that might be in the Cabinet Office or Downing Street, clearly had access to copies of both. This is interesting, not just with regard to the individual concerned having access to both, but also the fact that both sets of preliminary advice, before ministers had made a decision, had been made available outside the departments: in simple terms, preliminary advice before ministers had ruled being circulated not within but between departments and the Cabinet Office. This may be no surprise whatsoever to officials involved, but I think would be a considerable surprise to new ministers and the world outside. This is the world within a world, the civil service, operating entirely outside the ministerial procedures – and the Butler Committee go on about 'formal process'!

I am having to sort out how to continue working at a high level – thinking of speeches and policy documents and, of course, handling the media in the future with so few staff. The contrast is enormous. One day you have the whole of your Private Office, the press office, the Department – and the next day a handful of very dedicated and committed people struggling with the expectation from me that I can carry on as though I still have a department. I am going to have to draw in my horns. I am going to have to remember that I don't have people to direct, or to order about, and I don't have the capacity to draw down on research, to call for immediate information or to have a range of people able to read the papers for me, day in, day out.

Worthy of note are my meetings with Alan Milburn about campaigning and what part I could play, including in the general election, and with David Miliband about the manifesto and what I could do to help. Both of them, interestingly, raised the issue as to whether I thought it would be too soon for me to come back in May.

And in my usual bumptious way I said: 'Well, if I'm not going to come back at the next general election, God knows when the next reshuffle will be – so it's the general election or never.' In retrospect, it would have been a lot better if I had been able to settle my personal and financial affairs and then see how the land lay. It would certainly have avoided the gross irritation of my opponents from all quarters (and a comparison with Peter Mandelson) which my early return evoked.

I am still not sleeping. I am getting up around 6 a.m. and doing what work I can. If I am going to pull round, then I am going to have to sleep. I am going to have to be more relaxed and let things go a bit. I am still seething, but I am desperately trying not to show bitterness or resentment publicly.

I had a very useful lunch with Veronica Wadley, editor of the London *Evening Standard*, on Tuesday 18 January. It was useful to hear her view on why so much that was untrue had been printed and on what basis – basically, because on all fronts, we could say so little.

But what was really amusing was that the *Daily Telegraph* picked up our lunch but the person spying in the restaurant obviously did not recognise Veronica – so the piece appeared in the form of suggesting that I was obviously recovering because I was eating with a very handsome woman and we were clearly getting on extremely well together in one of the booths. They can't even leave me alone when I am eating with journalists!

The last week in January has been dreadful. I am back in the black hole again. Stories have begun to appear about some smart Alec who thinks that it would be funny to put the tragedy of my private life into a play in the West End of London, and they intend to experiment with it somewhere in Yorkshire. There is undoubtedly something extremely sick about them, but the problem is that those they associate with and who are likely to back them are just as sick. You can't even have a rational conversation with such people, but it is not surprising that what I once described as the 'liberati' – a combination of libertarian liberals and the world of the arts – are getting their own back on me. For some of them, I was public enemy No. 1, for speaking out for the people whom I represent and whom they hold in contempt.

But the private pain just wells up, and I still don't appear to be able to shake off, physically or emotionally, the ill health that had worn me down so greatly before Christmas.

I shot up in the late afternoon to speak at Warwick University, and I was hopeless. I am just not functioning properly. I am bumping into things. I've hit my forehead and banged my eye. I am clumsy. I am clearly not thinking straight. But I am not going to take medication. I can see that I am depressed. I can feel that I am and I know it rationally, but I am not going to take some artificial medication. I have seen friends do that and while it does stop you from becoming completely low, it stops you being high as well. So I am just going to plough on.

I am trying to keep in touch. After Prime Minister's Questions, I sat in on the Statement that Charles made on how to deal with the Lords' judgement of 16 December [regarding terrorist suspects held in Belmarsh, Broadmoor and Woodhill]. I can see entirely why Charles is taking the line that he is, but I just feel in my bones that it would have been better to have faced down the Lords' judgement and asked the Commons to reaffirm what we had done, while massively increasing the effort to get countries to take their nationals back so that those held in Belmarsh and Broadmoor can be returned to their country of origin, with guarantees of safety. I still believe in what we floated over a year ago, including seeing how we could have a special tier of the normal court system to deal with issues of prevention and not just prosecution. How can you prosecute a suicide bomber? In order for home detention to work, it has to be detention, and the judgement showed a complete lack of understanding of that simple fact. Indeed, Lord Hoffman suggested that it was Part 4 of the Anti-Terrorism, Crime and Security Act that was a bigger threat to our freedom and our way of life than the terrorists. But when was the last time he travelled by public transport or went into a crowded disco?

Charles took some very difficult decisions, ones which would have fallen to me to take. I wish we had been able to have the discussions leading up to 16 December but quite rightly the Attorney General did not want us to discuss them publicly, and given the complete and utter lack of security across government it wasn't possible in this modern era to discuss them privately without material leaking – which would have been disastrous in fighting the case.

It has to be said that some of the reasoning that was spelled out in the Law Lords' judgement was so totally unrealistic as to be bizarre, in the world we live in. They clearly believed, as so many on the liberal Left did, that we were exaggerating the threat, that we were making all this up, and that it was all part of seeking to scare people. Tragically it was not until 7 July 2005 that some sort of sense of reason returned. People got the message that there is an ongoing, long-term threat. The planning, even of very simple and crude attacks, takes place years in advance and people are schooled, encouraged and indoctrinated in what they need to do, including killing themselves.

I didn't believe then, and I don't believe now, that holding people in perpetuity without any definable way of engineering their release is acceptable. I do believe, however, that what we had put in place with the three-monthly reviews, the right to access to a designated lawyer, and the opportunity to leave the country, was the best we could manage. The later efforts in 2006 of the lower tier of the judiciary to undo even the Control Orders demonstrates that persuading people that reality is reality is a continuous and difficult task. Abuse thrown at those of us who have seen the evidence, who have lived through the threat, who had to countenance it for ourselves, day in, day out, is in part understandable because those who feel so strongly that somehow we are eroding ancient rights personalise this rather than arguing it logically. I have encountered the difficulty of persuading people that those of us who had to take the most difficult decisions of peacetime democracy are as committed to the process of justice, to the upholding of law and to the rights of the individual as anyone else. We just happen to believe that it is not possible to have these unless you protect life itself and the very essence of our democracy.

I can't help myself. The Tories have launched their immigration assault, as I knew they would: I've been waiting for it. The paper we were going to publish in early January has obviously had to be held off while Charles and his ministers consider it, but the policy is there and it's in place.

I am so frustrated that I have written to the *Daily Telegraph* to try to see if we can put the record straight. The legacy, everything we have done so painfully amid so much opposition, is just now being set aside and forgotten. It is as though it never happened.

February 2005

And so to February. I am talking to a consultancy doing work with quite a lot of the former public utilities, advising them on public policy, on government, on how the system works. It is not just the money, welcome as that is, and the ability to pay the bills but also something to focus on, something to be able to feel useful and needed. I have to build confidence in myself again.

And from ORT [Organisation for Research and Technology], a generous offer to give me the opportunity to contribute to this little-known but extremely powerful and highly successful education charity across the world. It was set up by the Jewish community in the Ukraine 100 years ago and now, in countries right across the world, is doing a good job in education and training in the some of the most deprived areas – for all faiths and all creeds. People are being very good to me.

It was at this stage that I failed to write to the Advisory Committee on Ministerial Appointments, a committee set up in the 1990s after controversy about ministers leaving office and taking up highly lucrative appointments as directors or consultants in large companies over which they had recently had ministerial oversight. (The defence industry was a classic example.) It was described as voluntary, although as I was later to realise it was voluntary to take their advice, but mandatory under 5.29 of the Ministerial Code to write to them. They would then publish in their Annual Report what advice they had given.

It was incompetence on my part. I had not read the detail properly, and had I done so I would have consulted at that stage, and would also automatically have done so later when, for two weeks at the end of April, I became a director of DNA Bioscience, in which I also invested £15,000. But more of this later.

I went to see the doctor – not my normal doctor as I wasn't able to get back to Sheffield, but the House of Commons doctor. I have had this bronchitis and chest infection for seven weeks now and I don't seem to be able to shake it off. He offered me therapy, and I turned it down.

What transpired shortly afterwards is breathtaking. Five national newspapers were contacted by one or more individuals claiming that I was in the Priory, a well-known national private clinic working with and supporting people who have had various forms of breakdown and emotional trauma. If I had been an NHS patient and I had wished to take up such a facility, then I would have done so. As one editor said to me, 'There is no shame in accepting help of this sort' – and there isn't. My reply was: 'None at all, but what I'm dealing with are facts. I am not in the Priory Clinic. I am talking to you from my home. I don't want anyone printing that I am in any clinic when I'm not. If ever I am, that's a different matter.' None of them printed the completely false story, for which I am grateful.

However, there was more to come.

On 11 February a serious and well-organised attempt was made to access my records from the medical centre with which I am registered in Sheffield. Efforts were made to con the receptionist into believing that I was in the Priory Clinic, saying that my medical details were required urgently and asking for them to be emailed. The receptionist had the presence of mind to contact one of the senior partners, having requested the caller's contact details and promised to ring back later in the afternoon. The number given to her was in fact that of the Priory Clinic, who had made no such request – but it was a damned near thing. The police were brought in and asked to investigate but we could not conclusively prove who it was, although we could make fair assumptions.

This was one of the many intrusions into my privacy, into my life and into those things that are closest to all of us. I realised then just how low people were prepared to stoop in the early twenty-first century in a way that would never have been considered even twenty years ago.

Just one small note which I forgot from the end of January to put in my diary: for several years I had worked alongside and helped support the Holocaust Memorial Day that had been established by Jack Straw. I had worked throughout the autumn for the 2005 Holocaust Memorial Day, but when it arrived no one bothered sending me an invitation. It has hurt more than so many of the other things thrown at me. It has hurt because it really mattered to me.

But I was invited to the Make a Difference voluntary-sector awards – and people are keeping me in touch from the Active Communities Unit with regard to what's going on and the Respect agenda, and ensuring that I can keep in touch with the Russell Commission that Gordon and I set up on youth volunteering, so that I can at least continue playing a part. I am grateful for this.

I have got to stop feeling sorry for myself and start being realistic. The chances of coming back at the general election are 50–50, and I have got to earn it. I've got to show people that I am strong and confident, back on form and punching my weight. There are lots of colleagues who would like to be in Cabinet and I have no God-given right to be there.

Helen Jackson, my neighbouring MP in Sheffield, has told me that she intends to step down at the general election. I thought she would stay for another parliament and I am going to miss her greatly. We had supper at her son David's flat, which was excellent, but I couldn't persuade her. She said that it was the vote on the reversal of the modernisation programme and the switch of the hours back to ten p.m. on Monday and Tuesday that had done it – because it was never ten p.m., it was often later by the time all the votes were over.

One of the excellent pieces of news as January turned into February was the Iraqi election and the turn-out, despite the bombings and killings and intimidation. Thank goodness for that. There was not a word of apology from those who pooh-poohed the idea and said that it would never happen and that people wouldn't vote. Not a word.

Two interesting points from the second week in February: firstly a good conversation with Gordon, relaxed and easy. It is nice to talk to him in these circumstances; of course, I'm no threat and I don't want anything from him! It was good though to be able to talk about the future, although he is clearly extremely cheesed off about Alan Milburn's role [co-ordinating the general election campaign]. But that's no surprise.

Secondly, a very interesting conversation with Anji Hunter when she came to my office for coffee. She talked about needing to bring the next generation of the party forward and I agree with that. The real question is how to do it while retaining real experience and solidity, a foundation on which younger people can build. It takes a long time to know how government works and how it doesn't and to be able to handle crises. Most parts of the world build on experience in one form or another, rather than throwing it away.

In addition, I had a meeting with someone I used to know from his political days on the *Sunday Times* – Michael Prescott, who now works for Weber Shandwick. I am hoping they will be able to put a little bit of work my way.

My cousins Dorothy and Derek have asked me if I would like to join them for one of their two weeks' holiday in Lanzarote, and I will. I need to in order to get away, to breathe fresh air, to be in a different environment, and to be able to forget about things. It means turning down a major speaking engagement – on the after-dinner circuit – but I know it will be worth it.

People are still being extraordinarily nice. When I'm out and about, the public are just wonderful. The only person (of any consequence) who has not spoken to me since 15 December, and who I know is bad-mouthing me behind the scenes, is John Prescott. I wish I knew what was motivating him.

At the time I thought this very uncomradely, but given later revelations I now find it breathtaking.

On 10 February, Andrea Bocelli came to the Arena in Sheffield to perform before an audience of 8,000 people. I went with Alastair and Hugh and their girlfriends, together with a group of my friends. Andrea Bocelli's manager asked me if I would like to introduce him at the beginning of the evening and invited my sons' girlfriends to present the flowers. Alastair agreed to walk on to the stage with me; and Hugh, to appear at the end of the evening.

This was a big test. How would people from my own city and the region receive me, 8,000 people who hadn't come to see me but to hear Andrea Bocelli? Alastair – in the way that only Alastair can – said to me: 'Dad, no politics, not a whisper, nothing about Bocelli and his campaigning in Italy, nothing about politics – just introduce him.' So we walked to the centre of the platform and when I said, 'Good evening, I'm David Blunkett,' the audience burst into applause – and I could have cried. I said: 'Worry not: Andrea Bocelli is here, and I've no intention of singing' – and they laughed. I then introduced him and left the platform feeling ten feet tall. What a wonderful place Sheffield is. How warm are the people who live in South Yorkshire and North Derbyshire. What a contrast with anything I experience in London.

But back to reality – the reality of a very different life, a backbencher after seventeen years in opposition and government on the front bench, always busy, always having something to contribute, always engaged with policy and, over the past seven and a half years, with delivery.

It is very strange being on the back benches. I am still very busy, but I am busy doing things that other people would have done for me – phone calls that I wouldn't have had to have made, checks on diaries that I didn't have to check, dealing with pieces of information or making contact and organising things that others would have done. And there is a little bit of lethargy. There is no doubt whatsoever that sometimes I just don't feel like being busy because I am not busy. The adrenalin is not running, there is no sense of urgency, there is not the imperative to keep a grip of things, to be on top of everything, to avoid anything slipping, in order not to allow an attack on the government or the policy or myself. It is a very strange feeling of being outside, but still interested as though I was on the inside – but, of course, I'm not.

Saturday 12 February: Matthew Doyle has taken over the difficult task from Huw Evans of dealing with press queries for me, not only on the political front but the private. (It was extremely good of Labour Party Headquarters – and in particular Matthew, who was Chief Press Officer for the Labour Party outside Downing Street – to be prepared to deal with what, by anyone's standards, was a difficult and often embarrassing and sometimes deeply offensive set of queries.)

I have appointed Anna Turley, who used to work with the special advisers in the Home Office, as my researcher. If I get back into government, I will make her a special adviser because she is giving up a very secure job in the civil service to come and work for me, and it is a hell of a risk. God knows how I am going to fund her wages but I will find some resources – if nothing else, from some of the speaking engagements I am doing.

Anna did become a special adviser and stayed with me for six months after I stepped down in November 2005, before becoming a special adviser to Hilary Armstrong at the Cabinet Office. She did a first-rate job.

I had dinner with Alastair Campbell and Fiona Millar on Tuesday 15 February. I travelled down to London from Sheffield, where I had been working in my constituency – it was the half-term recess – and was planning to see Tony on the Wednesday. This would be the first time that we had sat down for a private chat since 15 December 2004, although we had talked many times on the telephone and spoken to each other in the lobbies and corridors of Westminster. The proposed meeting on Wednesday didn't take place after all, but we spoke at length on the phone.

One lighter touch was a programme introduced by William Hague at 10.30 on Saturday morning [26 February] on Radio 4. I had participated in this programme, under the illusion that it was a serious look at reforming the civil service. But it turned out to be a rather entertaining look at *Yes, Minister* and how people saw it. Those taking part included Ken Clarke, Norman Tebbit, Robin Butler, Lord Armstrong (who had been Secretary to the Cabinet and Head of the Civil Service), Michael Bichard, William Hague, Roy Hattersley and myself, and it was reassuring to have our prejudices reinforced.

In the event, I was unable to meet Tony until 28 February.

We had a very interesting discussion. To paraphrase, he told me that if I got my head sorted out there would be no obstacle to my coming back. The people are with me, the party is with me, the parliamentary party wouldn't object. But he said that I would need to be at peace with myself and ready to get embroiled again. He then said that being embroiled would help to get me focused and get my head straightened out. It was clear that he really understood.

Of course, it was right to believe that getting stuck in and being back in government would get my head sorted out. The trouble was that my problems were not going to arise from decisions I took in the political arena or my competence or my ability, and in so far as any decision I took can rationally be seen as the cause of my difficulties in the autumn, it was the period up to election day on 6 May and the ripples thereafter that were to cause me difficulty.

We only won the vote in the House on the Terrorism Bill by fourteen, and had some of the Liberal Democrats, including Charles Kennedy, turned up, it would have been even more embarrassing. God knows what it will be like with a smaller majority after May. We are bound to have a smaller majority, on the back of Iraq, and our own dissidents will be given enormous power.

The Commons sat until midnight but I went home after the key vote around ten p.m. I took a sleeping tablet and got six hours' sleep. This is progress.

When I met Tony on Monday, he had said that it was really important that party HQ organise to get me on television and radio and out on phone-ins, talking to the wider audience. He said that at least I was known by young people, even if all of them didn't agree with me, and that we should therefore try and reach out to the younger generation. Sally Morgan was a bit sceptical about this but Tony was clear.

What has been amazing ever since the first time I stepped down from government is just how many young people do seem to know me. They approach me in the street or they comment as I am passing – mostly in pleasant terms, thankfully – but I fear that recognition is probably to do with the kind of high-profile press coverage that I could have done without.

I'd said that I would do some Big Conversation events as well and told Tony that I would start making some high-profile speeches and that I had events coming up at Balsall Heath in Birmingham and with the IPPR on Englishness, citizenship and identity.

It was time to begin emerging after almost three months of silence, and I had already arranged that I would do Radio 4's Any Questions? *from Sheffield on 18 March and an interview with David Frost (pre-recorded) for the following Sunday morning.*

March 2005

The Joseph Chamberlain Lecture in Birmingham [9 March] went very well. I am pleased that people are so welcoming and enthusiastic: it feels as though I am still in the front line. But of course I am not: on Thursday afternoon I spent four hours in the office and at the end of it, having faffed about, made some phone calls, and made some notes, said to myself: 'And what have I achieved this afternoon?' The answer was: 'Sod all.' But the activity is uplifting, and giving me confidence.

I am very pleased with the paper that we have got together for the IPPR speech. It really does say something about identity and sense of belonging, and how it is possible to be English or Pakistani or Indian – and British. It is just the sort of launch pad I need: not interfering in anyone's department-mental business, not getting up some colleague's nose, but having something to say that touches the public and is newsworthy. It is damned hard to get anything that is newsworthy when I have no government announcement or policy to make something of.

In the end, I did the David Frost interview on the Friday morning after we had had two all-night sittings – ping-pong between Commons and Lords, with Lords as well as MPs sleeping on temporary beds. You would think by the way in which the Lords are behaving that they were fighting on the beaches or against Al Qaeda, not against the government trying to take Al Qaeda on.

The Whips were very helpful. I had chronic colitis late on Thursday night, so we agreed that if I could get in for the votes at breakfast time, that's what I should do. Having voted three times, I then went off to do the Frost interview.

I rang Tony at breakfast time, just to be helpful and to try to suggest a way of getting through the dilemmas – to use the reviewer's powers to give people greater reassurance, and to indicate that we would come back to legislation later in the year. It all seemed to be in tune with the general noises that Charles had been making so it wouldn't look like a climbdown. It was good of Tony to talk to me, given how pressurised he was, and to listen and to respond. I feel as though I am still in there, playing a part.

He invited me to come to his office in the Commons, where Charles and Hilary Armstrong, Chief Whip, were seated. I don't think he had told Charles and Hilary that I was coming as they seemed a bit surprised, and I didn't want to be the spectre at the feast.

There was also Charlie Falconer, who is giving a lot of advice to Tony on this, and David Hill, and of course Justin Russell, Tony's policy adviser. It was afternoon by this time and all virtually over bar the shouting. My contribution was at breakfast time, not in this meeting, but it was good to see that my thoughts had at least been incorporated.

Of course, they may well have already thought of the routes to take so I may have made no contribution at all, but it certainly cheered me up to think that I had.

Tony thanked me as I went out. I thought: 'Thank you.'

Tony had said in the meeting, and I was reflecting on it on my way back up to Sheffield: 'What would all those who are criticising, those who are trying to stop us, say if something happened and we hadn't tried?'

My interview with Jackie Ashley in the *Guardian* on the 12th; the pre-recorded Frost interview shown on the 13th; and then the *Today* programme on Monday the 14th: it feels as if I am coming out of a dark tunnel, that I am breathing again, that there is light and sunshine and there are possibilities, and I am beginning to feel well. I haven't felt well for so long that it is a strange feeling.

The Weber Shandwick dinner on Wednesday night [16 March] went very well. There were two people there whom I would like to follow up because they were really interested in the kind of things that I am interested in, and also what I might do with them – one from Sir Ronald Cohen's finance company Apax and another whose wife is the director of a small company trying to break into a near-monopoly market and whose brother appears to have put up the money for it.

I didn't in the end do any work for Sir Ronald Cohen, although I did liaise with him on corporate social responsibility in the voluntary sector. I did liaise, however, with DNA Bioscience during the course of April, by which time the general-election campaign was well under way. Given that I made more visits round the country than any other senior colleague – with the exceptions of Tony, Gordon and John Prescott – I felt that a few hours out of the campaign when I was already down in London were perfectly justified in trying to hedge my bets in case it was not possible for Tony to bring me back.

If I had my time again, I would do two things. Firstly I would consult more widely about the appropriateness of risking my money, given that I had never been a shareholder before; and secondly, with the considerable benefit of hindsight, I would write to the Advisory Committee on Ministerial Appointments, indicating that I was thinking of involvement with the company. Had I done so there would have been no later problem whatsoever because, as will be seen, there was no conflict of interest. The suggestion that there was constituted a scurrilous piece of muddying the waters into which a motley range of made-up stories would be tossed. So for the sake of clarity, let me at this point explain what was going on in relation to the Advisory Committee.

Private Eye magazine had been in touch with the Secretariat of the Advisory Committee, chaired by Patrick (Lord) Mayhew, a Conservative peer and in my view a man of integrity. The Committee in turn had been in touch with my office in relation to my links with business. (This is entirely separate from the Parliamentary Register of Members' Interests, which had been set up on a mandatory basis – not voluntary – in the late 1990s.) Private Eye, having picked up that I had registered my speeches, seminars, etc., was questioning whether I had sought the advice of the Advisory Committee. I wrote back to Lord Mayhew personally and apologised for not having been in touch.

He replied courteously: 'I think it right, therefore, to point out that the voluntary character of the scheme for former ministers is exactly that: it is voluntary. Accordingly, it is not necessary for you to apologise for having taken up your appointment without referring to my Committee.'

His thoughtfulness in the way he phrased this led me to believe, foolishly as it now turns out, that if I believed that there was clearly no conflict of interest – and I wasn't dealing with Home Office or Home Office-related business – then it was in my hands as to whether or not I wrote to them.

I don't think there is a person alive who hasn't read into something what they wanted to read into it. In the case of someone wanting to return to government (and the rules were, of course, set up for people leaving government and not returning to it) it was foolish in the extreme of me not to have erred on the side of caution and to have perceived ambiguity in returning to the rules at the end of April as justification for not having written. A simple letter would have done, and although it would have been perfectly feasible to have argued in the autumn that at the time in question (towards the end of the general-election campaign) all my normal facilities were barred to me as part of election rules, it would not have been beyond the wit of man to have sent off a letter that would have sufficed. That is why, when this arose in late October 2005, I immediately acknowledged that I had made a mistake and did not attempt to use access to the relevant guidance notes or facilities in the House of Commons as an excuse.

I took a conscious decision not to go into the House of Commons Chamber for the Budget Statement, but instead to watch it on the television. I am glad I didn't go in, as I would have undoubtedly been riddled with nostalgia. Having sat next to Gordon for Budget after Budget and Pre-Budget Statement after Pre-Budget Statement, better not to put myself through torment.

A year later, I was to accept an invitation to commentate on the Budget for Sky television for the same reason.

The follow-through to the Budget didn't go well. The poster campaign was not a roaring success, to say the least, and there were all sorts of messy things in relation to the Internet. This doesn't feel good, given the imminence of the general election. It certainly is possible to see things differently when you are outside than when you are in Cabinet. You perceive them as others do.

I think it is helpful that Huw Evans, my former media adviser, is going to be working at least part of the week with Alastair Campbell on gearing up for the general election. Huw will be excellent at this.

We have a real mess going on in relation to traveller encampments. God knows why the Office of the Deputy Prime Minister has put out a consultation paper, full of ambiguities, in the run-up to the general election. If ever there was an issue (other than immigration) that you don't highlight as you get towards the election, it has got to be travellers' rights. The irony is that they are trying to strengthen the planning guidance, but nobody would believe it.

The Budget as a whole has gone down very well, and I found it easy to defend it when I was on Radio 4's *Any Questions?* on Friday evening [18 March] from Sheffield Hallam University.

I am continuing to have an input into the manifesto, although I don't seem to be having any influence on the campaign and how it is going to be run. I am very worried about wording in relation to education: it's the use of the term 'independent' when describing schools when we mean 'self-governing' – which would be a much better term and less open to misinterpretation.

I wish I had been more vigorous, but I wasn't in a position to be. I didn't have the authority that I had had as Home Secretary, or for that matter as a member of the Cabinet in whatever role, but I did express my concerns. Of course, a word is simply a word, but it didn't help when, six months later, the White Paper came out.

I have tried delivering a speech about quality of life and how work and travel patterns will have to change in future, with regard to the sheer volume of travel, energy and the environment, but also social life and people keeping their families together – but it has got no coverage whatsoever. The audience (at a session arranged by the think tank Progress) were very good and sparky so in terms of discussion it was valuable, but in making a difference to policy and changing anyone's mind it was a failure.

Conor Ryan, my former special adviser, who is going to be working closely with me during the general election, told me that it wouldn't get publicity – and as ever he was right!

I had three good days in Spain, visiting my friends Rob and Judy Glendenning, who have been renovating a derelict farmhouse about twenty-five miles from Malaga. It was very nice to see them and it did me good.

And then back on Sunday the 27th for Alastair's birthday and a big family lunch, which we all enjoyed.

I am so apprehensive at the moment about what's going to happen. As I dictate this there are five and a half weeks to go to general-election day and I am beginning to get really jumpy about what will happen to me. Should I start looking for a rented flat now or prepare to buy? What possibilities exist if I do come back? It's all very difficult. I am undoubtedly stronger. I still have downs, but not as many of them, and I bounce back faster. I've had some nights where I have slept. On the night of Alastair's birthday I slept well – I think mainly because I had eaten in the afternoon and didn't eat in the evening.

The main international news over the weekend was the big earthquake around the Sumatra area. There was no tsunami but very many people were killed.

This week I am campaigning in Oxford, doing a dinner for Andrew Smith; campaigning in Enfield; meetings in the Commons; a fundraising speech on Thursday evening; and a possible interview with Adam Boulton for the Sunday programme on Sky television. Then I need to get stuck in to sorting out my own campaign in Brightside, and awaiting the formal announcement of the election next week.

In the end, the Adam Boulton interview that I undertook as a pre-record on the Friday didn't get used because of the imminent death of the Pope which, at the beginning of the election campaign, dominated so much of the news: he died on 2 April. It must be the first time in history that such an event has put off the visit of the Prime Minister to Buckingham Palace to trigger formally the proroguing of Parliament and a general election – in this case delayed from Monday to Tuesday. And by a twist of fate, it also put off the wedding of Prince Charles and Camilla Parker Bowles. The wedding had been scheduled for 8 April, the day of the Pope's funeral, so it had to be postponed until the Saturday.

It was clear that the Tory Party's decision to drop Howard Flight MP as candidate for Arundel for speaking out of turn about spending cuts and refusing his candidature anywhere else, as well as the death of the Pope, affected the early period of the general-election campaign, when the Conservative Party had chosen, with the advice of their Australian adviser Lynton Crosby to concentrate on core right-wing issues such as immigration and asylum.

It is worth noting that I went to a birthday reception at Lancaster House and George (Lord) Robertson, former Defence Secretary and NATO General Secretary, said to me very quietly: 'Good to see you feeling better, but don't overdo the publicity.' I think it is wise counsel, but I have to be visible and I have to earn my spurs and put in the graft. I know it is dangerous to be too high-profile in case it gets up the noses of members of the Cabinet.

And then one of those pieces of mischief that makes me wonder what goes through people's heads. I am invited to present the awards at the annual Press Club lunch on 13 April. (I have spoken there before, an occasion I remember very well because Simon Kelner, editor of the *Independent*, refused to clap.) This time there's the potential for something a little more serious. I discover that they intend to give an award to the

Sunday Telegraph journalists who 'broke' the attack on me on 28 November, and they want me to give it! I think my presence is required elsewhere. But I ask myself: why would they do that? Why an award for anything? There was no investigative journalism.

April 2005

My launch of the election campaign on 5 April began with a charity breakfast at the Tower of London. It seemed strange to be doing something worthwhile from outside the immediate political arena. The starting gun had fired in 2001 with Tony and myself at that school in south London.

Later that day I had a meeting with John Birt, who has been working in Downing Street on the potential reconfiguration of departments in Whitehall. It was an interesting discussion, but I get the feeling that there is not the stomach for radical change.

And, of course, there was not.

And then into the election proper – to Shropshire and my old stomping ground of Shrewsbury, where Paul Marsden had just announced that he was now back supporting Labour. (Paul was the Labour MP who had moved over to the Liberal Democrats.) But it all felt too late.

In fact, the Conservatives won the seat.

And then, because the Cabinet were all involved in the constitutional meeting with the National Executive Committee of the party to ratify the manifesto, I was asked to do the BBC1 *Question Time* from Stirling University. This involved a mad dash to Birmingham airport, where we just managed to get the scheduled flight to Edinburgh, and then quickly to grab something to eat before going on to record the programme. It was a strange programme, where we were talking mostly about English issues to a Scottish audience – at least in the hall.

I am now writing a twice-weekly column for the *Daily Mirror*, enjoyable but very strange because they didn't use the piece I had written on the contrast of leadership and views about leadership in relation to the death of the Pope. I thought it was probably one of the best articles I have ever written, but maybe they thought it was a bit too deep.

And so the election campaign went on: meeting after meeting, visit after visit – including a visit to Hornchurch in Essex for a return to old-fashioned eyeball-to-eyeball politics, thrashing out crime, nationality and asylum. I thought to myself at the time that we would lose that one by an avalanche but, in the end, it was by less than 500.

I was followed round by camera crews, notably by Michael Crick and *Newsnight* in Redditch and Bromsgrove – with me being too light-hearted and trying to liven up the election campaign, forgetting that Michael Crick is Michael Crick! While travelling I was finishing reading the Alan Clark diaries and it struck me very forcibly how the moment he was out, he wanted to be back – in his case, out of Parliament and then back, in my case in the thick of it and then back.

In retrospect, I wanted it too much – of course to make a difference, to be there affecting policy, campaigning to get the message across and having the platform to do so, but if I'm honest, also for myself, for my self-esteem and to prove something to myself as well as the world. Although that was undoubtedly a subsidiary thought at the back of my mind, I think it is fair to reflect it.

On my way down to the West Country I met Peter Skellern at a motorway service station. You either love or hate Peter Skellern's singing, and I love it, and have several of his LPs. It was nice of him to talk to me, and I really appreciated it. He has done quite a lot with Richard Stilgoe but I have never managed to get to a concert with both of them. It's funny how you bump into people when electioneering, as I did with my cousin Emma Blunkett in the 2001 election.

It is worth recording that on the formal launch of the manifesto I did a couple of media events, both quite low-key: Alastair Stewart on ITV and an interview for Channel 4, but it felt very strange being on the outside. The actual presentation of the launch seemed much more professional than four years earlier in Birmingham and went very well – not least in contrast to the Liberal Democrat launch, where Charles Kennedy got into a terrible tangle at a breakfast session.

His wife Sarah had given birth to their first child a couple of days earlier.

I can't understand why he did a breakfast launch rather than later in the day. Everyone is very pleased for him and Sarah with the new baby, but honestly, who is advising him?

I popped in to DNA Bioscience and they have asked me to become a non-executive director. To do so I have to be a shareholder, and that means buying preference shares so that, if the company ever goes public, the initial shareholding of 3 per cent being offered to me would then be worth that proportion of whatever the company was worth when it floated. They are very optimistic. They think that it will be a tenfold increase, but it is clear that they are going to need all the skills of the recently appointed chairman, John Rowley, who seems a really decent man. He has clearly warned them that the money is needed urgently to set up a laboratory. I said I would come back to them in a day or two, but made it clear that if I decided to invest a little money and then got back into government (and I warned them it was 50–50) I would have to resign my non-executive directorship immediately, and that if I kept the shares, I would put them in trust for my sons.

I was wrong about this. I went to a great deal of trouble to set up a trust, but it transpired that I needn't have done so. The rules in relation to shareholding are that you declare them – which I did – and only if you have multiple sources of shareholding do you need to set up what is then called a 'blind trust'. As I consulted immediately, I was aware that a blind trust would not be appropriate, but what I hadn't realised was that I need not have gone to all this trouble. As will be seen later, the confusion that arose so muddied the water that in the end nobody – including Downing Street – was clear about what the hell was going on I should have taken the advice of David Yelland, the former editor of the Sun *who works for Weber Shandwick and had been at the original dinner in the middle of March. His advice was that I would be wise to steer clear.*

It is hard now, thinking back, to know why I should have made such a misjudgement. It all seemed quite innocent, and the checks we made on the Internet did not lead us to believe, as a family, that there would be a problem. It was my money and a perfectly legitimate operation trying to break into a market in which one major laboratory had a stranglehold. In simple terms, DNA Bioscience appeared to be run by enterprising people, with an important niche market to go at. Of course, with the benefit of hindsight, I should have steered clear of anything that would allow anybody to make even the slightest inference against me.

Given the closeness to the general election, it was frankly a misjudgement to hedge my bets rather than simply to await Tony's final decision about my future (which I really got to know on Sunday 1 May, and had confirmed two days later, at the two rallies where I acted as the warm-up in the final phase of the campaign).

So there was nothing illegal, nothing untoward, nothing surreptitious – but nothing gained. An unnecessary punt which, for other reasons, led to the opportunity for me to be exploited and which I was to regret deeply.

I have learned a lot just talking to the scientist at DNA Bioscience. The changes in biomedical technology that have taken place over the past five years are amazing. I thought I knew something about all this from my visit to the forensic-science laboratories at Solihull.

Anyway I am back in London next week for campaigning so I will see them again and make the decision.

On Wednesday morning [13 April] I appeared on the *Today* programme talking about poetry and the general election, when I read a poem by John Greenleaf Whittier from 1848, and my own little poem 'Echo'. The following day Michael Horowitz was on the programme: he clearly had not understood what my poem was about and criticised me. All very silly.

And surprise, surprise – a number of those accused in the ricin plot have managed to get off. There was so much evidence that couldn't be presented in court – but we will see what happens. Of course, Kamel Bourgass, the man who murdered Detective Constable Stephen Oake, was a failed asylum seeker who couldn't be sent back to Algeria because of the human rights issues. Of course, he would have been tracked had we had ID cards, and had we had the ID card for asylum seekers (which I introduced in 2002 after great effort and expense) up and running properly and linked to a sensible database. I just despair at what happens with the administration. If all of this had been in place, it would have ensured that when he was picked up for shoplifting they would have found out that he was an illegal immigrant and failed asylum seeker, and he could have been held in a secure removal place while we negotiated what to do with him. But it raises the whole issue of those whose asylum applications have failed but who can't immediately be removed, and what we do with them when their presence is undesirable and not conducive to the public good – which incidentally, it has to be said, Michael Howard's policies don't deal with at all.

I spent some time in the constituency and did an interview for the local paper, then went off to campaign in the marginal seats in West Yorkshire. It was freezing cold. I was on a housing estate in Calder Valley, Rastrick, and then going to Garforth and then on to Colne Valley. I did shopping centres on Saturday morning and canvassing on Sunday.

But it was the collapse of Rover on Friday that was the real story of the week. It had been clear for a very long time that they weren't going to survive and that the deal [for the car manufacturer to be sold to the Shanghai Automotive Industry Corporation] wouldn't go through. Tony, Gordon and Patricia Hewitt flew up to Birmingham and I think they handled it very well, but it was impossible to promise the earth. What we have promised is a total of £190 million to try to help with retraining and with relocation. And that's all we can do. It is bound to have an impact on the election and sour things in the West Midlands – what I describe as Sod's Law.

It had been decided that the manifesto would be put on disc for me by the RNIB, but unfortunately it was undertaken in a digital format with a synthetic voice, which made it virtually impossible to listen to. I have been assured that this will not happen again.

The introduction to the manifesto by Tony is almost word for word what I had discussed with him and with Andrew Adonis at the beginning of April, and with David Miliband back in February. Rights and responsibilities, 'on your side', opportunity and security: all the themes I have done my utmost to plug over the last eight years, though no one seems to have been arguing them.

I have started to do a blog. When I say 'I', I mean I give the words to Anna Turley and she puts them on. I am going to have to learn to use the computer! I do wonder how many people read these blogs, but everybody tells me that there's a large number of hits so it has to be worth it. After all, if I attended a public meeting, how many people would I be speaking to?

And so the election runs its inexorable course – for me from Rochdale to Rossendale, pouring down with rain. There was not a good feeling in Rochdale although Lorna Fitzsimons, the MP, is working her guts out. It is a nasty campaign and the Lib Dems are playing all sorts of race cards. In Rossendale I suggested that the babies were probably born with wellies on and nobody demurred. I then went on to Ribble Valley and another classic Blunkettism, when I said to a very senior *Guardian* journalist who was with me: 'I think people in this part of Lancashire must have webbed feet' – and much to my astonishment and chagrin he replied, ' I do have webbed feet.' Oh Lord!

Mary Riddell from the *Observer* had come up as well to write a piece for the following Sunday [24 April], and it was good to talk with her. We don't always see eye to eye, but there is no doubt she is a very nice person.

I had a phone call from Tony on Friday evening, just as I was about to head off to the airport after a visit to Edinburgh and Glasgow.

When I was campaigning in Glasgow in the shopping centre with Jim Murphy, the candidate for Eastwood, a woman stopped and said: 'Mr Blunkett, I have wanted to speak to you for some time. I just want you to know that I detest you.' I replied: 'Well, that's democracy, it's your prerogative – but will you just answer one question for me? Will you be voting for Jim Murphy?' and she said, 'Of course.' I said: 'Well in the end, that's all that matters. Thank you very much.'

I had stayed overnight with Gordon and Sarah on the Thursday and campaigned alongside Alistair Darling in Edinburgh on Friday morning, before driving west to Glasgow.

It was thoughtful of him. I had been into party HQ on the Wednesday [20 April] and things had been very down, but it had given me a chance to talk to Sally: we had arranged that I would do a rally in Sheffield on the Saturday and help with Tony's rallies in the final days of the campaign.

My local evening paper on Friday 22nd was excellent: the interviews I had done for them came out really well. But *Newsnight* that evening was dreadful – filmed earlier in the week when they had trailed round with me in the West Midlands. They simply lied about the reason for my resignation.

I am afraid this was a sign of things to come the following autumn that would become the subject of a detailed inquiry which was still continuing a year after the offending programmes had been broadcast.

But there was a very good piece by Martin Kettle in the *Guardian* on Saturday [23 April], which cheered me up enormously.

I received a warm reception at the South Yorkshire Police Federation dinner in Barnsley on the Saturday night, and then on Sunday morning drove down to appear on BBC1's *The Politics Show* at lunchtime. My interview was preceded by a *One Foot in the Grave*-type film of people grumbling – that 'What have the Romans ever done for us?' attitude.

Jeremy Vine read out an email, supposedly sent to them, querying whether I should come back into government. This email was identical, word for word, with the one read out on Radio 5 earlier in the week – and I gave exactly the same answer. It reminded me of the 'cod' email that supposedly justified the *Sunday Telegraph* writing their attack on me on 28 November last year.

My blog on Yahoo, about which I was so dismissive, has had 160,000 hits so far, so perhaps it is worth doing after all!

Iraq has been the underlying theme throughout this election, and now things are getting worse. Bit by bit, specially chosen extracts of Peter Goldsmith's position note of 7 March 2003 have been leaked: clever, systematic and very damaging. No wonder Tony feels down. No wonder Alan Milburn tells me that it is really hard to lift spirits. But I have not found it unfriendly out there on the ground – just that people are slightly bewildered and a bit fed up with us. The trouble is that expectations are so high. Anything less than a fifty-seat majority will be seen as a disaster, and yet if we get more than seventy it will be a miracle.

Wednesday – off to Blaenau Gwent in South Wales. Gosh, it feels bad; it really feels bad.

In this constituency – which boasts Aneurin Bevan and Michael Foot among its previous Labour MPs – there had been an unholy row over the imposition of an all-woman shortlist for Labour candidate, resulting in the former MP Peter Law standing as an Independent against the official Labour candidate, Maggie Jones. I had known Maggie for many years as a senior official in UNISON, of which I am a member. I was very pleased to go and help, but the atmosphere on the ground was extraordinarily difficult, and it was clear that the aggravation over the all-woman shortlist had gone much deeper. The problem is that the Old Labour solutions to modern challenges would have made matters worse for the people of the constituency, not better – as can be seen in the difference between the approach on health in England as opposed to Wales.

Peter Law took the seat at the 2005 election, but sadly died in 2006, following which his former campaign manager Dai Davies stood as an Independent and won.

Here we are in a greasy café, talking to young people who are nice and sparky, but what an environment. It feels like my constituency ten years ago. John Prescott has been here shortly before me and told a reporter, in no uncertain terms, where to get off. The reporter turned up in the café and it was clear that they thought I would give him the cold shoulder, so I decided to do a bit of theatricals and kissed him on both cheeks. The media were so astonished that they asked me to do it again, and I said, 'Once in a lifetime's enough, thanks very much' – but I don't suppose it won a single vote. It's the travelling that wears me down. I spend so much time on trains and in cars and sometimes on planes, and have to tune in very quickly to where I am. But once I am there I do enjoy it: meeting people, talking to people, trying to win people over. In fact I find it easier to try to win people over to the party across the country than asking people to vote for me personally back home. I feel embarrassed by that: I don't want to have to ask people to vote for me as a person, and it depresses me when people say that we haven't done anything for them. I know I shouldn't but I feel personally hurt. I do wonder sometimes, even though politics is in my blood and I love what I do, whether I am really cut out for it.

I am not missing taking part in the national press conferences. I thought I would but I never liked them and I wasn't all that good at them. I much prefer being on television or radio, and the cut and thrust of a meeting. I am not entirely sure what we are doing with electioneering these days. How are we winning votes? Who are we touching? Whose minds are we changing? I don't know. Perhaps the blog is the answer!

Friday 29 April: I talked to Gordon on the phone in the evening. He confirmed what I had picked up from Sally, that he and Tony were going to talk over the weekend in order to try to keep the wheels on the cart for the reshuffle, but I suspect a great deal will depend on what size majority we get and how strong Tony feels.

May 2005

And so back home, then down to Hastings on Sunday [1 May], by tiny plane to Shoreham. There is massive disruption on the rail service. There would be, given that it is Bank Holiday tomorrow. The roads sound as if they are absolutely gridlocked down towards the south coast, so it is a good job that the party (with the help of UNISON) can afford to fly me down – with Sadie comfortably ensconced in one of the back seats of this four-seater plane.

Tony was there and I had a quick word with him. I tried my best to give him a bit of a boost and the meeting seemed to lift him. It was a very good meeting, with a lot of young people.

And then back to Sheffield, where we arrived just in time for one of my protection team to be able to get to the hospital to see the birth of his baby boy.

The *Sunday Times* ran a piece by me reflecting on an article that I had published on the first Sunday after the 2001 general election, setting out the general direction in which I intended to go. This gave me a chance to consider just how far we had managed to make progress over the three and three-quarter years that I had had, and on the challenges that still remained.

On Tuesday [3 May] I was due to go to Birmingham, but just as we set off the visit was switched and we were asked to go to West Yorkshire and join in the rally taking place in Huddersfield. So I made my way there via my second visit to Phil Woolas's constituency, Oldham East and Saddleworth, where it was neck and neck with the Liberal Democrats. Of all the things I had done during the election campaign, I enjoyed the rally most of all: a final rally with all the British media present, speaking as I love to speak without notes, and just saying it as it is, and Tony telling me that he would like me to come down to London on Friday.

Michael White in the *Guardian* has done an interview with John Prescott in which John made it absolutely clear that there was no way he was going to relinquish his department. So if I hadn't already spoken to Gordon I would have been in no doubt what the position was. I think it narrows Tony's options more broadly – if that is not a contradiction in terms.

I had a late supper in Manchester and an even later drive down to London.

And then to election day in my constituency, to home, to people welcoming me, and to preparing for whatever it is that Tony wishes me to do this time – more modest dreams than I would have had a year ago. It is not possible to go back. In any case, I have given all I can so far as that's concerned – but how can I make a difference? I know I couldn't have done more over the past few weeks. I have given it my best shot and I hope it has been enough for Tony to be able to give me a decent job.

To be on the safe side, I have been trying to place on the House of Commons Register of Members' Interests my association with DNA Bioscience.

Thursday night, polling day: exit polls very bad, everybody down, feeling completely fed up. I expected a majority of sixty-seven realistically, and eighty optimistically, so it looks as if the bottom line is to be a majority in the high sixties.

And so it was: a Commons majority of 67. We would have given our right arm for this in the 1980s and early 1990s, and I suspect that we would have been very happy with it in 1997, but now it felt as though somehow we had lost, when of course we had won a historic third parliament.

Tony Blair had managed the impossible, and yet everyone that weekend was at him. No wonder he felt that his strength had waned and that what he did in the reshuffle had to be the minimum to ensure that we kept the show on the road.

And so on Friday it was down to London, and the strange experience of waiting in the house that without a return to government would no longer be my home.

But before going down, I went to the University of Sheffield for their centenary celebrations and the launch of their Centenary Book, a gesture of goodwill on my part to my old university and to my friend Helen Mathers, who had edited the book. By not pulling out of the launch, there was a recognition on my part that I couldn't in advance presume what Tony was going to do.

In the event, I arrived in London in the afternoon and waited for the phone call from Downing Street. When it came, Tony told me that he intended to give me the job of Work and Pensions Secretary, which covers not only employment – which I had already overseen during the first four years of government – but the whole of the pension and social-security system, disability rights, and health and safety, and carries wider responsibility for policies relating to an ageing population.

I saw this as an opportunity to take initiatives relating to welfare reform as well as influencing Adair Turner's Pensions Commission, but I also had ideas for financial inclusion (as part of the anti-poverty drive) and the development of an occupational-health policy for Britain that would help with productivity and prosperity.

Tony and I agreed that I would come over to Downing Street to talk about this, and I think one of my errors at the time was that when I came out of Downing Street I simply could not help smiling. I was so very pleased to be back in government, to feel that I had a purpose, to have my self-confidence and self-esteem restored. In truth I was too confident, too unaware of the antagonism towards my early return.

Tony and I talked briefly about the challenge ahead. I don't think I have ever known him so tired and deflated. There I was, trying to buoy him up, indicating that we had won a phenomenal third victory, that we were not out for the count, that we had a majority with which we could easily govern – but I think that all he really needed was his family round him, and some sleep.

One of the crucial questions that I asked him at that time was whether I could have an assurance that nothing was going to be ruled in or out and that anything that was said, other than by himself, Gordon or Alan Johnson as the former Secretary of State for Work and Pensions, could therefore be taken as general observation and not as government policy. I received such an assurance, which is crucial to being able to work with Adair Turner and Gordon Brown on getting a sensible package that Tony could back. I therefore left feeling that I had a proper job of work to do.

4

SECRETARY OF STATE

FOR WORK AND PENSIONS

2005

*O*n the evening of Friday 6 May 2005 I went straight from Downing Street across Whitehall to the Department for Work and Pensions in Richmond House.

It was a strange evening, going into the Department for discussions with the Permanent Secretary, Sir Richard Mottram. We talked through the immediate challenges and, of course, the practical side of operating the Braille equipment and getting tapes made. We arranged for Georgina Banton, my PA from the Home Office days, to come across to work with me, as well as getting temporary support from former private secretaries who had volunteered to give a helping hand to the staff of the Work and Pensions department to get used to their new boss. So ex-members of my Private Office from the Home Office, such as Anna Dorricott, came across to give advice.

As ever in these situations I could feel a degree of resistance from existing staff. The idea that I should bring anyone or call on the help of anyone seemed to be viewed with alarm in case this was some sort of 'take-over'. I had experienced exactly the same reaction when I moved from Education to the Home Office, but it does indicate a degree of insularity and defensiveness that is not good.

There is no question that I was much less bumptious, much less directive, than I had been in my previous two posts. I felt that I had to earn my authority rather than to assume it, and in any case I had learned some lessons, both about myself and about the role of Secretary of State. I planned to make much more effort to win people over rather than just presume that they would do as they were told, and to be much more cautious about those who clearly were deeply disaffected with my arrival. A handful of people had had quite an easy time of it and were (and remained) resistant to the complete change of gear. This change of gear involved having to expand not only my own Private Office but those dealing with policy development.

There is no doubt whatsoever that, as ever with me, my arrival created shock waves. I discovered that the workload was something in the region of three-fifths to two-thirds what it had been in the Home Office, and the Secretary of State working through lunch was going to be a shock.

Nevertheless the Private Office knuckled down. There was a real commit-

ment to doing the job and the middle and lower echelons of the Commu-
nication Directorate were enthusiastic and committed to having clear direc-
tion, to knowing what it was that we were saying to the public, and in
particular to the broader agenda that I was intent on inculcating: the
development of a government-wide social policy rather than simply a set of
agencies carrying out disparate and often unrelated policies.

The task now was to get in touch with those to whom I wished to offer
special-adviser posts. Anna Turley would automatically come across as my
researcher, and after spending the best part of the evening in the Department she, Anna Dorricott and myself went for supper at Mimo's on
Elizabeth Street.

Surprise, surprise: Lynton Crosby and members of staff from Conservative Central Office were on the next table. I couldn't resist it. I invited
Lynton Crosby to come across and have a glass of wine, and I found him a
quiet, unassuming man, not the bumptious Australian that I had imagined.
I said that I was pleased that he was returning to Australia on Sunday –
which he took as a compliment – but he said he had just done the job he
had been asked to do. He had come across with a particular perspective
and at least in the early part of the general-election campaign he thought he
had fulfilled his part of the bargain. He was in fact very complimentary
about Tony Blair and New Labour – a very different opponent, he said,
from the Australian Labour Party.

It was strange to sit there, just round the corner from my home, with
Brad Pitt's estranged wife Jennifer Aniston at one table and Lynton Crosby
at another – and me, half celebrating, half still astonished that I was back in
government.

Saturday 7 May: a day devoted to meeting staff, to sorting out a diary, to
pulling in the leaders of a trade-union march on pensions that was
gathering in Whitehall (much to their surprise) in order to indicate that
I wanted to work with the trade-union movement on sorting out some of
the major challenges on the Financial Assistance Scheme, the Pension
Protection Fund, and the big demands of a return to the earnings link for
pensions and compulsory contributions by employers. It was a gesture of
old-fashioned solidarity, and an indication to the Department of the style
to be adopted. But I can see now that it was also a little of the theatre, the
old Blunkett theatre.

And then, because my visit to Buckingham Palace to receive the Seals of
Office could be postponed until the beginning of the following week

(because I was already a Privy Counsellor, and was only receiving the Seals of Office), I made a mad dash back to Derbyshire.

My neighbours Tracy and Gary Wilson had made the highest bid in an auction on Radio 2 to benefit Children in Need, the lot being Katie Melua coming to sing at their home. Instead of simply having a private event, they had asked all of us who could afford it to meet at a local restaurant – the Prospect in Bakewell – in order to raise money for a local children's charity that was set up after the tragic accidental death of a youngster in a swimming pool. So we all gathered for an early supper followed by the Katie Melua concert, with a preview of her forthcoming album, and it felt just for a minute like a private celebration.

A joyful evening and twenty-four hours to remember – and a dangerous piece of self-delusion as well. I was on a high and my guard was down. As journalists were to say to me time and time again over subsequent months, 'You are a celebrity now, so you are fair game.' Had I realised that more clearly, I would have watched my back more carefully.

I was up early on Sunday morning to do *Breakfast with Frost* from Derbyshire, and tried to put into some sort of perspective that we had won, given the vicious attacks that were now being launched against Tony. Following that programme I went on to do my bit on the radio.

So in telling the story of the six months I spent as Secretary of State for Work and Pensions, let me make it clear that I carry my share of responsibility for not spotting the dangers and for not disappearing from the limelight in a manner that would have protected me from attack.

I asked Matthew Doyle, who had worked so well with me as Chief Press Officer of the Party, to come and join me as a special adviser. I also brought in Sue Regan, who was working at Shelter, had been at the IPPR and was extremely well versed and respected in relation to welfare reform and pensions, and Kath Raymond, who had been working for me at the Home Office and now came across part-time.

And then to the ministerial team: Stephen Timms, who had worked with Gordon at the Treasury, to take on pensions; Margaret Hodge to take on welfare reform and disability issues; and Anne McGuire as Parliamentary Under-Secretary. (I had worked with Anne before, both when she was a Whip and long ago when she and I shared a platform at party conference,

778 WORK AND PENSIONS

hammering Militant Tendency, and having the difficult task of persuading people to pay their poll tax.) Tony asked me if I would take James Plaskitt. I don't know James at all so it is a bit of a shot in the dark, but Tony seems very enthusiastic so it's fine with me. And in the House of Lords, Philip Hunt. I like Philip: he resigned over Iraq and he is a really decent man, whom I have known for a long time. I'm sure he will do a really good job in the Lords – and he cares. But I am going to have to give him the Child Support Agency to oversee, and that is a hell of a brief. It feels almost as bad as taking on Immigration and Nationality!

I made a lot of progress in six months in the Department of Work and Pensions on all the fronts I had laid out as critical, but I am afraid the Child Support Agency was merely a holding operation until my successor set up the inquiry under Sir David Henshaw and was to make some progress with getting money to fund the attempt to improve the administration and productivity. The agency and its staff were doing their best in what can only be described as horrendous circumstances, but the best I could do was to sort out the worst of the administration and to give a sense of purpose.

John Heppell is our Whip. He has been very thoughtful to me and I am glad that he is still working with me. Back in January, he was the first MP to invite me to his constituency [Nottingham East], and although I was almost out for the count I received the most warm reception, which really lifted me on a day when I needed it.

I had wanted John Denham to come back into government and did everything I could to bring him into my team, but despite persuading him to talk to Tony there wasn't a job that John considered appropriate, and therefore he chose to continue chairing the Home Affairs Select Committee, where he felt he could have an impact. I was fortunate to have a really good set of ministers, each of them with their own strengths and, like us all – me included – occasional weaknesses, but it didn't take long to build that sense of common purpose and team spirit that, whatever else I have been able to do, I have achieved in the ministerial posts between 1997 and 2006. The old lesson that I learned from Bryan Gould way back in the early 1990s stood me, and I believe the government, in good stead: if the team performs well, then we all perform well.

I am familiar now with coming into office, going through all the briefings, getting people round the table and hearing what they have to say, making a judgement on who seems up for change and reform, who is competent and who is just treading water. I can spot it almost instantly, but I have to hold my judgement just in case I am doing someone a disservice.

And on this Monday, 9 May, The Times *had a leader that I should have read more carefully. It was effectively a warning, saying that I should keep a low profile for a couple of years. I don't quite know how the brains behind this thought that dealing with pensions and welfare reform could be commensurate with a low profile, but perhaps they meant that I should be more cognisant and careful in avoiding thinking that public support and my own competence would protect me from those who thought that I shouldn't be in the job in the first place.*

Back into the thick of things.

Thursday 12 May, and my first Cabinet since December: here I am back in my old seat, next to Gordon, but with John Reid on my left now – and a warm welcome from everyone, except John Prescott. I didn't intend to say anything but I did, because housing benefit was raised as part of the discussion on what should go into the Queen's Speech. There has been a dispute about how much it will cost to bring in the new housing allowance, designed to encourage people to move to more suitable property and to try to cut back on the £12.3 billion we are spending on subsidising rents. The problem is that the original idea was going to cost £500–600 million for about ten years, and I have already made it clear that this is ridiculous. Gordon and I agree that with Des Browne as Chief Secretary now, we will try to find a compromise that involves much less money up front and a much faster break-even time.

I managed to crack a bit of a joke by saying that my intention not to speak had been completely overturned by Des having slipped into his new job so comfortably and made such a good case that there was no way that I couldn't respond. But I do know I have to watch it. If I am too bumptious, I am going to get a rough ride.

I have already rewritten the element of the Queen's Speech from my department. It was unbelievably pedestrian and had no feel of the coherence of what we are trying to put together, how welfare reform and improvement to job opportunities go together, how rights and responsibilities need to be reflected, and how getting more people into work and working longer might have something to do with a decent income in retirement.

I think staff in the Department have found it a terrific shock to get a Secretary of State who rewrites what they have written rather than simply signing it off.

One of the twists of the new job is that I have inherited Jobcentre Plus – the combining of the employment and benefits agencies that I was battling over at the end of my time at the Department for Education and Employment (as it was then). I have also inherited some problems, not least the new computerised management system. I have already heard about this from my own constituency who, as ever, are the eyes and ears on which I rely. Quite a number of staff at middle and lower level work in the constituency and they are pretty quick at getting in touch, so at least I am alerted to what is likely to be a major problem over the summer.

I'm afraid I've had to have words with the Director of Communications. I simply asked him where he was on Friday night when I came into the Department. He said that he was in the South West of England. I said that I didn't mean where was he geographically, I meant why wasn't he here on Friday night or on Saturday, given that he knew that the election was taking place, that he knew there was likely to be a reshuffle, and he knew when the Secretary of State was likely to come into the Department? He said sorry, but the reception I received from the Head of News left me in no doubt as to the view she held, going back to a clash that had taken place some time before in relation to the Home Office and the prison service. So we were facing internal difficulties in a rather crucial area. Thank the Lord that so far as I can see, the rest of the news and communications outfit – and it is very small compared with either Education or the Home Office – are 100 per cent committed to being helpful.

There was a strange end to the week, with Clare Short viciously attacking the government and suggesting that she wasn't elected on the manifesto. Clare got the biggest anti-Labour swing in Britain, of over 20 per cent, so God knows what manifesto she thought she was being elected on!

Then the weekend papers – and here we go all over again.

In the *Mail on Sunday* there was a photograph of me on the pavement outside the building in which an acquaintance of mine had an apartment. I had had supper there and left at around 9.50 p.m. the previous Tuesday. Before the election I had received an invitation to celebrate if we won, and I had indicated that I would come if indeed we were successful and if I got back into Cabinet. Given that my diary was empty for the immediate post-election period – if I hadn't come back into the Cabinet, I would have been up north until the Queen's Speech – I thought nothing of it.

I had written to the lady in question earlier in the year seeking her help on a private matter, following an article she had written in the Mail on Sunday. *We had met a couple of times, as outlined in another article in the* Mail on Sunday *in November 2005. As she spells out in that article, there was no sexual relationship between us – and after May 2005 we had never met again – but a large photograph and a great spread, justifying a follow-up the following week, was enough for the media to reopen their intrusion into my private affairs.*

We had been tipped off about this by Gordon Raynor of the *Daily Mail* on the Friday, so clearly it was widely known in Fleet Street that there was a photograph circulating.

Well, I am really back with a vengeance. I can tell because I am already getting stressed about the way in which the Cabinet reshuffle, or lack of it, is being reported. I have never read such garbage in all my life.

Tony was extremely good at the Parliamentary Labour Party meeting. He had obviously got his strength and vigour back and he really laid into the Liberal Democrats, which has gone down really well with the parliamentary party. There is a lot of dissatisfaction though about junior ministerial posts, including those who expected to move to something better and instead got something that they weren't easy with. It is blindingly obvious that reshuffles are not Tony's forte.

Laura Moffatt has agreed to be my Parliamentary Private Secretary. She now has the smallest Labour majority in Britain – thirty-seven votes – in her Crawley constituency, but is an extremely nice person and will be able to smooth the way a bit within the PLP.

On a lighter note, I ought to confess that I made a terrible mess of taking the oath. I had been promised a Braille version to read out when formally taking my seat – following a general election Cabinet ministers are sworn in first – and was taken aback when it turned out that there wasn't one. It is easy enough to take the oath, but as we now speak through the loudspeaker system it was a trifle embarrassing when instead of committing loyalty to Her Majesty and her 'heirs and successors', I heard myself say 'heirs and graces'! 'Whoops,' I said, 'heirs and successors.' That will teach me not to do my homework. Aficionados of the Parliamentary Channel noticed but nobody else did – except the *Times* diary.

Wednesday 18 May: I did the normal declaration of my interests with Sir

Richard Mottram. I have already made the basic declaration on the evening of 6 May, including the trust for the shareholding in DNA Bioscience, and put the content on the website that evening so that no one can be in any doubt.

I have to laugh out loud. I had declared the shareholding and declared that I had been a director of DNA Bioscience for two weeks, and checked that there was no conflict whatsoever (including with the Child Support Agency, which had already put out a contract for all its appropriate DNA work up until 2008). But I subsequently learned that I could have held on to the shares in any case, given that there was no conflict, and that I had wasted money and time in setting up the trust. Nevertheless it seemed to me to be an additional security. What I didn't know at the time was the terrible trial it was going to be for those whom I had asked to be trustees, who found themselves inadvertently and unjustifiably the centre of attention.

However, the real twist is that, unbeknown to me, a few weeks later the Guardian *newspaper issued a Freedom of Information request for disclosure across government of declarations of interest. I was not made aware of that disclosure request until early 2006. Had it been notified to me and had action been taken to comply at the time, then all of this would have been on the record at the time. It was just one more bizarre twist in an extraordinary story.*

I did the *Today* programme on the 18th on the back of the Queen's Speech the day before, having done a couple of television interviews for BBC and ITV on Monday, all about welfare reform and where we were going. There was a little bit of criticism of my being too conciliatory, although what I was trying to do was achieve the opposite of what politicians are normally accused of. I was trying to talk gently and act decisively. This is too important to simply be bellicose. We have to get it right this time – seven years on.

Anyway I am feeling quite cheerful because on Monday night I went with Valda and Trevor to see Sheffield Wednesday beat Brentford and reach the First Division play-offs final. Thank the Lord for that. We might just make it back into the Championship.

Tony was very good on the Queen's Speech. I said to Cherie that I had no idea he had such a terribly bad back or that he would feel a pain in the back so soon after the general election. We both laughed, but he had clearly been suffering very greatly during the general election, so no wonder he felt stressed.

And then to my second Cabinet – another lesson in diplomacy but also in why it is worth being there. I sat quietly. John Reid [Secretary of State for Defence] gave a long presentation on his visit to Iraq. I had sent a letter the day before to Charlie Falconer in response to a round robin on Lords reform and the setting up of a Joint Committee, which opened up a whole range of issues and a can of worms. What is the Lords for? What is it we intend to do with it and how do we expect it to approach modernisation?

I had expected Charlie to speak to it. I thought it was on the agenda but it wasn't, and therefore I hadn't spoken to him before Cabinet. At the end of the meeting, when Tony said, 'Well, that appears to be that,' I said: 'Just a moment, Tony, I am out of the rhythm of what has been discussed at Cabinet, but I wonder if Charlie can say a word or two about the Lords reform proposals which have been circulated.' There was a stunned silence. Charlie said a few words and I said that that was precisely why I had raised the issue. Because we hadn't had a discussion, we are not clear what we want out of these reforms, or what we want to do with the Lords and how its procedures will be changed.

Then Gordon joined in about how the criteria would open up the possibility of undoing the 1911 Settlement with regard to Finance Bills. In fact he went further and said that he wanted the National Insurance system to be treated the same as tax. I smiled and mumbled to him that the Tories had designated it a tax. Charlie said that the Tories would resist that very strongly, which sounds a bit odd really, given that they had been dubbing it a 'tax' and would want to hang on to the power to argue about National Insurance.

Charlie also said that the Joint Committee and what he was proposing was in the manifesto, and Gordon said, 'Well, it may have been in the manifesto but that's no rationale for doing it,' and everybody just doubled up. It was very funny and Gordon said: 'Clearly we have to go through with the principle.' He obviously didn't mean that we shouldn't fulfil the manifesto commitment, merely that we shouldn't pretend that a couple of lines in the manifesto gave carte blanche for whatever procedure a department came up with – and he is right. In the end, Tony said: 'Charlie, I think you've got the message. We need to have this back and have a proper discussion when your Constitutional Committee has taken a look at this.'

I learned afterwards that Charlie was absolutely livid with me. Had I known that it wasn't going to be raised, I would have raised it with him prior to going into Cabinet – which is a courtesy that is always worth remembering. That was a mistake on my part.

Charles Clarke raised with me that in a short interview in the *Observer* the previous Sunday I had mentioned conditionality in relation to those receiving additional benefits who were drug users. He was right, of course. I should have rung him, but it indicates what I felt at the time when I was Home Secretary. You don't half get defensive when you are under stress, and it is worth my remembering this now that I am in a job with big policy decisions but without the hour-by-hour pressure that I had to put up with as Home Secretary. Charles's words were: 'I can't put up with several home secretaries as well as Shadow home secretaries.' Hell's bells.

Of course it doesn't help with colleagues when Tony was seen to come round the table and thank me for having raised what was a critical issue. I have to remember that I am back in the Cabinet, not that I have been there all this time. I am sorry that I have irritated people, but it was necessary. Reform of the House of Lords is a very important issue and we could easily have got this very badly wrong. What was interesting was the detail that Gordon had in his folder. I suspect that he thought it was on the agenda as well.

It was good to get home on Friday, but I got a real dose on pensions from Rodney Bickerstaffe as he and his wife Pat had joined us for supper at Helen Jackson's home. A very pleasant evening, but Helen has already done some work on women and pensions and I have decided that I am going to make this a really critical centrepiece in trying to get the pension policy right.

I was quite surprised to find that, in discussions, the issue of the unfairness inherent in a system designed for a bygone era when women were dependent on men (and on the male National Insurance contribution) was not up in lights. I was pleased, along with my contribution to making employer contributions mandatory, to be able to change the atmosphere and culture, but it was down to those who campaigned so hard for so long to create an atmosphere and culture in which an incoming Secretary of State could make a difference.

The political agenda of the week has been pretty well dominated by hooded youths, yobbos and lack of respect. It reminded me that it is exactly a year ago at the Police Fed that I talked about the need to reintroduce respect. The only newspaper that covered it in depth was the *Daily Mail* the following day.

Just over a year later David Cameron, the new Conservative Party leader, was talking about hoodies in an entirely different way: 'hug a hoody'!

What I find odd is why the Pupil Referral Units are not fully up and running and being used properly. We spent a fortune developing them, both as learning centres in schools and the independent units to give a full day's education to the youngsters who were excluded. But it raises the issue again as to who is accountable – those at local level who haven't done it or those at national level who put the money and the policy in place?

And all the Tories and Liberals say is, leave it to headteachers – as though an individual school, beleaguered with literally dozens of kids that other schools won't take, can cope with it. That has always been the fallacy of just letting schools float independently. The more deprived, the more disadvantaged and the less popular they are, the more likely they are to have to take the most disruptive pupils simply because they have got spare places. It is a downward spiral.

The problem is – and this is true of hospitals as well – that it was left to those mismanaging the service, it was left to those least able to manage, to struggle with the problem. It is a real paradox about criticism of top-down government and too many 'targets'.

Week beginning Monday 23 May: I'm beginning to think about the European Presidency [the UK was due to assume Presidency of the EU for a six-month period from 1 July] and chairing the Social Affairs and Employment Council. God, this is going to be an incredible waste of time: preparatory meetings, smoothing everyone's ego, being nice but at the same time trying to achieve something meaningful.

And then the wind-up on the final day of the Queen's Speech. It is an important moment because this is the big vote on any Queen's Speech, but it is also awful winding up. It is a long time since I have done it. You have to speak in the House – and we are back to ten p.m. – when everybody has had a good dinner and the last thing they are interested in is what you have to say. But somehow you have to command the House. You have to reply to the day's debate and you have to say something a little broader about the Queen's Speech as a whole. I find I am fighting to get the attention of the House. I don't quite have the authority I had as Home Secretary, and I am going to have to earn it. I get through it, it's fine and nobody notices that I do not feel as in control as I was – but I notice. I am going to have to up everything a notch or two.

I've asked the Department for radical new ideas in updating the previous work on the Welfare to Work Green Paper, as we need something a great deal more imaginative than what we have so far. And what do I get? A shortlist of things that had been excluded from discussion before the general election, about the legislation. Changing bereavement benefit is just not on and I am not prepared to do it, and the rest doesn't add up to a bag of beans. It's clear that, when I talk about 'radical', people are slightly at a loss yet to see what I mean. But I have managed to reverse a decision taken, because of the squeeze on the budget, to cut the Access to Work programme for investment for equipment and support for disabled people going into work. It is crucial that employers feel they are going to get some help with adaptations, equipment or whatever. I can't believe that officials should have expected me, of all people, to ratify a cut in Access to Work. Anyway, we've reversed it. In fact it is one of those programmes we ought to be expanding rather than cutting, speeding up rather than slowing down. God knows how we expect to implement the Welfare to Work programme if we can't help people get the wherewithal to do the job when they get one.

I recall the meeting chaired by Patricia Hewitt (upstairs in the Department of Health, as we share Richmond House). I felt immediately that there was a testing-out here of who is in charge of what. Patricia was chairing because the Working Time Directive had a massive impact on the Department of Health's work because of the hours that junior doctors work, and what is counted as stand-by or cover-time when people are not working but are on call. I am afraid I was deeply sceptical about the ideas being thrown up by the Foreign Office and the DTI that somehow we could challenge this in the European Court. It has absolutely nothing to do with the European Court other than a challenge relating to an amendment. But in any case, governments can't use that route: only individuals, employers or organisations can. Here I am again, upsetting everyone.

I can understand Patricia asserting herself, but given the problems she has in the Department of Health it is best that she leave this issue to the rest of us.

Third Cabinet on the Thursday [26 May], and I still felt odd. Gordon had been good enough to let me have in advance the detail of what he was going to present on the economy, which at least gave me a chance to think about it and to back in very hard in supporting him. I thought he made an excellent presentation.

The thrust was about economic reform in Europe and our taking a lead on bringing about radical economic change, and their view of how the world economy and globalisation was working. It fitted exactly with my own view about trying to reform what they call the 'social model' and getting people to address the real issues involved in what was going on around them, rather than some mythical world that they would like to live in.

But I was clearly once again pushing the boundaries on my return to Cabinet. I think I particularly upset people by saying that the Common Agricultural Policy wasn't simply to do with agriculture or even the distortion of the European budget, but was a clear indication of a concept of welfare and the social model over which, until the French accept that they are going to have to come into the world as it really is, we are always going to have a struggle. They are not really arguing about agriculture. They are arguing about retaining a particular culture. It is very attractive and some of it we would like for ourselves, but unfortunately we don't have the luxury of the rest of Europe subsidising it. It's not about giving up or capitulating; it's about helping people through change and learning the lessons of the 1980s in Britain.

On Thursday afternoon I had a meeting with Tony in the garden at Downing Street. It is always good to be able to sit outside. It feels more natural and less formal. He had just had a session with Gordon and I thought his mind was elsewhere. He had to take two international calls while I was there, and in the end I said that I would leave him to it and that we would talk after the Spring Bank Holiday.

I have had to have a quiet word with Margaret Hodge about a contribution she made to a Progress round-table discussion. (It is not difficult dealing with a friend in your team if you detach yourself temporarily from that and be the team leader.) It is fine for people like Steve Byers, not now in government, to say whatever they think, but for Margaret to start challenging government policy in relation to race and how we were handling the BNP publicly is just not on. I had to point out to her that some of us had been talking about these issues and dealing with them for a very long time.

We've had two or three meetings on pensions and one very interesting one with the Health and Safety Commission, spelling out what I wanted to do on occupational health and upping the ante. I am determined that we should get involved in a really important area that has changed dramatically since the domination of heavy industry.

After three weeks we have partly resolved the problem of an answer-phone in my office that works. They have now installed it and I tried it –

and it lasted ten seconds. This is not rocket science. This is so basic that it is just breathtaking. It is not the fault of my Private Office. It's simply that the Department appears to have no technical expertise whatsoever. Of course, we only oversee a budget of £110 billion.

We are at least getting teas and coffees for meetings, although we are having to rely on the restaurant downstairs that services both ourselves and the Department of Health. I am going to have a bit of a drive to see if we can get healthy eating down there.

We have also had meetings on the Child Support Agency. My instincts are to abolish it, but if you do, how on earth do you deal with the ongoing cases, never mind the poor devils who are in the pipeline? What will happen is that the staff will give up. Ten thousand people dealing with 250,000 new cases a year and something like 1.4 million already in the system, a great chunk of them probably not active cases at all. It is an administrative nightmare.

And so to Spring Bank Holiday weekend, and the play-offs final. Win or lose, we will have a glorious day out in Cardiff on Sunday 29th, and then out to France for three days' holiday. My sons and various friends are coming: 40,000 Sheffield Wednesday supporters in all, the largest ever contingent at the Millennium Stadium outside the Premier League.

Little did I know what the Sunday 29 May was going to hold.

I had to laugh, however, before I went off for Spring Bank Holiday. I had explained that Monday 6 June was my birthday and I thought I would come down on Monday morning rather than Sunday evening. Then I looked at the Braille diary they had produced and my first meeting was 9.30 a.m. in London. I said to the diary secretary, as gently as I could (which is not like me): 'Is the Department laying on a helicopter for me?' 'Pardon?' she said. I knew, of course, that the Department didn't ever do anything that was outside the most basic travel arrangements. They had not been used to flying at all, never mind by helicopter. But I was just having a bit of fun.

The play-off final was a triumph. Wednesday won and we are back in the Championship. It was a lovely, lovely day. The sun shone, we had an excellent lunch before the game – so excellent that when Brian Mawhinney, Chairman of the Football League, inadvertently called us Sheffield United rather than Wednesday, he was forgiven.

In the Millennium Stadium the atmosphere was just magic, and extra time was electric. But we won, and after the match we all had a meal together before we went our separate ways.

And so to a few days in France, blissfully unaware of what was going to hit us: that the knock on the door at three a.m. on the day of the match had been the prelude to something else – a knock on the door because the car that was used for my official northern visits had been found abandoned, with blood in it, and with some of my tapes and papers. Understandably the police were in a panic as to whether something was amiss. Had I been in it? Where was I? In fact I was asleep in bed at the cottage, and when my Protection Officer knocked on the door, there I was in my dressing gown, asking who the hell it was.

When I let him in, I realised what a disrupted night it must have been for all of them. Ensuring that I wasn't hurt was only the beginning. No one could understand quite what my car was doing abandoned, but it soon became clear because the police, finding details of my northern driver's address in the car, broke into her house – to find that her son, who was in his early forties, had guns in his room. What a tragedy for my driver Barbara Smith, and in the end what a blow for me. In 1997 she had inherited me, having already spent twenty-odd years driving ministers of all political persuasions and senior officials, and receiving the MBE. A lovely lady, just doing her job and caring too much, being too soft with her own family. So it was that it became clear that, if not her family, then someone who had leant on the family, had got hold of the car. Her keys had been taken and the car had been used for goodness knows what.

Given the security implications, that was the end of her driving for me, after eight years of loyal service. There was terrible confusion when she was questioned, not just by the police but by the media, firstly in the form of the *Mail on Sunday,* who sent no end of reporters to report on what had happened, and then it was followed up by others. What a personal tragedy and a very sad end to a distinguished driving career. It didn't take a genius to see who must have tipped the papers off.

June 2005

For me the business with Barbara's car was the trigger for yet another set of stories, another opportunity for prying and for gross misreporting, including in *Broadcasting House* on Radio 4 on the Sunday morning [5 June], when during the programme's discussion of the Sunday papers they managed to suggest that I had had guns found in my house.

The BBC tried telling me that it was really only light-hearted, but my special advisers and I had to work very hard to stop others carrying the story in its distorted form. To spare the gory detail, the Mail on Sunday *managed to keep the story going week after week by implying that the speed with which the court hearing and conviction were secured was somehow engineered by me. For four years I had been trying to engineer a speeding-up of the criminal justice system, with only limited success, so the idea that I could intervene in the case of the son of my northern driver in order to get him convicted quickly and kill a story that had nothing to do with me, other than tangentially, was ludicrous. But it linked the private and the public once again.*

At this stage I really should have recognised what was going on. Co-operating with Stephen Pollard had been a misjudgement on my part but, as with other biographers earning themselves a crust, was not exactly a knockout blow. The tragedy of my private life had been private – and yet the world outside Westminster regrettably knew all about it. Photographs of me standing outside someone's apartment or my driver having a family tragedy were irrelevant other than to those involved – but the danger of what might now be forming, irrespective of whether it was fair or true, should have been obvious to me.

This lack of perception of what was happening and might happen in the future, together with my failure to write to the Advisory Committee at the end of April, I believe to have been my fundamental errors.

The main political news of this period has been the defeat of the European Constitution in France and even more heavily in the Netherlands. What a sigh of relief I breathed – and I think everyone around me did the same. If the French were not prepared to vote for it – and it was after all Giscard d'Estaing's drafting we were dealing with – there wasn't a cat in hell's chance of the United Kingdom voting yes, and any campaign would be a political catastrophe. So, like so-called Black Wednesday in September 1992, we have a seminal moment, but this time one that saves our bacon.

Of course, if you send a massive document to every household and your opponents send a slim and easy-to-read analysis of the sillier wording and the aspects that can be most misinterpreted, it is not surprising that you get a bloody nose. But this is all part of the 'out of touch' nature of those embroiled in the European Union and the Euro-enthusiasts. They don't seem to get how people feel; they don't understand the instinct, the almost automatic suspicion of bureaucracy, of the dead hand and, above all, of things that are so far distant that they can't be influenced.

Monday 6 June: my birthday, but not a happy day. In fact the opposite. Early morning and my friend Trevor Waterfield has a heart attack.

It was months before we could breathe easily again and Trevor could resume something like a normal life.

What a strange week, a lot of it spent on non-political matters, and on Friday morning a dash up to Manchester to open the new extension to Manchester City College, which I had promised Willie Knowles, the principal, and Alex Erwin and George Sweeney, my dining companions, that I would undertake, whether in or out of government. It gave me a chance to talk to young people about pensions, of all things. It was all worthwhile because they were so glad that I had gone.

Thursday night I had been to the birthday party of the man I had met at dinner back in March, and who a month later had introduced me to DNA Bioscience.

This was the first of only two occasions when I visited Annabel's, a trendy night-spot which had been the favourite haunt of John Selwyn Gummer, Virginia Bottomley and many other Cabinet ministers years before. While this was not exactly my stamping ground, with hindsight, or perhaps a little more foresight, going there was not a wise move in the light of the attention being paid to me. But I had no intention of gallivanting all night, and it seemed a pretty harmless thing to do. Wrong!

I left early, as I always do, having enjoyed good food, extremely good but expensive wine, and having been introduced to a woman named Sally Anderson, who was charming and talked to me about poetry and Yorkshire. Before I departed, something instinctively told me to ensure that I paid my share (and more) of the bill.

And so back to the constituency for my regular monthly meeting and my advice surgery.

I have written a note for Tony, just reflecting on my first few weeks back and a feeling of treading water, a feeling that colleagues don't want anything too radical or too much rocking the boat, and prefer a kind of comfort zone – but perhaps I'm being unfair.

Jack had done well in a Statement to the House on Monday [6 June]. I had gone in for it to show solidarity. I think Jack has come out of the past six months very well. I think, not least because the presidency is coming up, that he would have remained Foreign Secretary whatever had happened to me and Alan Milburn over the past nine months. But as Margaret Thatcher famously said, 'It's a funny old world.'

President Chirac has reinvented the old issue of the 'British rebate' in a new form.

It has to be said that we didn't do too well in explaining all this over the weeks ahead. The issue was not losing our rebate on the European budget as it had been with just the fifteen members (although that's what Jacques Chirac wanted) but the issue of rebate on the expanded European Union and therefore the expanded budget – in simple terms, whether we got a bigger rebate on a bigger budget. We were run ragged in the papers over this, all the way through to the end of the year, and I did wonder, when I was out of office in November and December, what on earth our communication machine was doing.

As we paid two and a half times more into the European Union than France, *pro rata* to our population, they really do have a cheek. But it's all diversionary tactics, and from France's point of view it's smart.

Tony is in the air again, off to the USA, then on to Russia and Germany. It really is Sod's Law that we have ended up with the presidency in the very early part of the third term. We could have done with Tony being at home, grounding things and accelerating the reform agenda, but on this occasion there is no choice.

And God help us – Channel 4 are going to launch their new digital More4 service with some satirical film purporting to be about my private life. This really is the liberati getting their own back. Those putting this together know perfectly well that I have fought like a tiger to try to keep my private life private, and now they intend to make up what they don't know and present it as entertainment. They know and I know how damaging politically that can be.

It is important to make the point that at no time did I attempt to take legal action to stop this programme going out. Contrary to the briefings put out by senior executives of Channel 4, in referring to private correspondence I merely sought to protect others. I knew perfectly well that I could not protect myself. What I hadn't realised was that, in addition to settling old scores, there was an underlying broader political intent to damage Tony Blair, to take a form of revenge on him in relation to the Iraq conflict. This was made clear by the writer of the script when he appeared on the Today *programme on 16 August as part of the promotion of the digital channel at the Edinburgh Television Festival. Given the assault launched on me in September, this was not insignificant.*

It is a wicked world that we live in. We have newspaper reporters crawling all over Sheffield, trying to dig the dirt on my past and my time when I was Leader of the Council. I understand that one newspaper has five reporters solely devoted to me. My goodness, they must really have some resources and obviously not a lot to do with them. It is beginning to feel just like the end of last year. I am under siege.

Looking back, this was all the more reason that I should have been a great deal more savvy about where I went, who I went with and what they were up to. I can't plead that I was 'an innocent abroad' at my age, because being innocent wasn't the point. Being 'fair game' clearly was.

And the saga of the guns continues. Now I am being accused of not answering questions. Well, of course I am not. The case is *sub judice* and it is absolutely nothing to do with me personally. But not answering daft questions from journalists who simply want a story – presumably along the lines that I have interfered with the legal process – is obviously an irritation, and seems to make them even more determined to dig the dirt.

Now I read in the Sundays that I am 'accident prone'. The fact that it's not my accident but a family tragedy seems to escape them.

Just a note about Cabinet on 9 June: we had an excellent discussion – or rather the Cabinet did because for once in my life I kept quiet – about Europe. Jack wasn't there, but there were some excellent contributions from Charles Clarke and Alistair Darling. People were saying the very things that I believed, so on this occasion I thought it opportune and prudent to let the discussion go with the flow.

Alistair had one of those Cabinet meetings when you realise why he has quietly and unobtrusively been there all the time. He was incisive, he was amusing and he was understated.

Margaret Hodge has raised with me the fact that she has been told by the senior officials in the Department that they intend only to put one name forward for the Head of Jobcentre Plus, the government's biggest agency, where there has been a vacancy for some considerable time. I am going to intervene on this, not with regard to the specific candidate, who seems extremely popular with the managers and certainly knows the ropes, but the principle. We are not having a situation where the head of an agency of this size is decided by the civil service alone. Strictly speaking, under the way in which the Civil Service Commission operates (God knows in whose interests), they could put up a technical case, but I am not having it. We need to know who has applied, what head-hunting has been done, what specification was put forward, and why they think that I, as Secretary of State, and ministers dealing with the agency shouldn't see the final candidate or candidates.

In the end, after examining the short list and seeing the preferred candidate, I made the decision on pragmatic grounds to go along with it, but I wanted to establish that we weren't allowing the Department to see ministers as mere ratifiers of decisions already taken, or arm's-length advisers to which civil servants could refer things if they thought fit and take direction when it suited them. We were either in this together or we were going to be at loggerheads, and bonhomie and 'Hail fellow, well met' was not going to wash with me.

When I saw Brian Mawhinney at the Sheffield Wednesday play-off on 29 May he had reminded me of the tactic adopted by Michael Heseltine, who was extraordinarily astute in dealing with the civil service and very hands-on as a minister – namely to say that if something was claimed to be out of the remit of the ministers, he would find something – like freezing all senior posts – that was within the remit of the minister with regard to financial savings and efficiency. I decided that if push came to shove, that's exactly what I would do.

The workload is picking up. I made twenty-five calls on Sunday [12 June], and it was a bit like the old days. Two of the calls were private – one to Cherie Blair and the other to my former driver Barbara, just to try and cheer her up. Cherie said to me that she was grateful for the call, because nobody knew what it was like to be hounded by the press until they had been through it, while Barbara said that she had never fully understood what I was going through until she experienced it herself. Frankly, no one can.

And so into Work and Pensions Questions on Monday 13 June, and a major departmental seminar on pensions on the Tuesday.

I was very glad that I had stayed for the whole day on the Tuesday. It was certainly appreciated by all those who had taken the trouble to be there, and I was a bit surprised to find that the two opposition spokesmen chose just to pop in and out to make their contributions, given the time that they must have on their hands. I feel as if I have taken a doctorate in pension policy already, and it is certainly complicated. No wonder people get confused.

I had rushed down early on Monday morning for the meeting that re-formed the Terms of Reference for the Joint Committee between the Lords and Commons on the future of the House of Lords, not least to say that one central feature must be the primacy of the Commons. If I have done one thing for this Committee, it is to ensure that we don't drift into ending up with a House of Lords that simply trumps the House of Commons in a kind of gridlock. It is difficult enough to make a difference and to get things moving without snarling up the system even further.

On Wednesday 15 June a meeting with Tony and Gordon about pensions. I am beginning to see where Gordon is coming from, but I don't want some sort of apolitical Beveridge any more than he does. I know, just having worked with Adair Turner, John Hills and Jeannie Drake of the Pensions Commission for five weeks, that it is perfectly possible for us to end up with a package of measures that won't be all that different from what we can agree, even if the timescales are adjusted. But we can't leave it. This is not an issue we have invented. It is one that is at the top of the news.

It is an interesting observation of politics, of timing and of how the tide comes in and goes out, that a year later in the summer of 2006 the programme of measures, as tweaked in the way that we were envisaging back in June 2005, was pretty much accepted as a consensus. The enormous debate in which I was engaged for six months had ebbed, not because the issues had gone away but because there was at least some political direction and sense of purpose. I like to believe that I made a worthwhile contribution in those months to getting this right.

Dominic Lawson, editor of the *Sunday Telegraph*, has gone – and there is nothing more to be said.

My eldest son Alastair and I had a day out on Saturday the 18th, a real break. At the invitation of Sir Robert Ogden we went to Royal Ascot – held at York this year as Ascot racecourse itself is being rebuilt – in top hat and tails on the hottest day I can remember. It was one of those memorable occasions: the lift doors open and who should step out but Her Majesty the Queen? It is amazing how many people I have come across from the North of England who made it to York at one point or other during Royal Ascot week. People from down south may be snooty about going up all that way but it was a damned good week and we had a smashing day – including my winning £146, which is the first time I have ever won anything so far as I can remember. It helped to pay for the top hat and tails, and at the moment every little helps.

Two excellent speeches in the week beginning Monday 20 June: Gordon's at the Mansion House on Wednesday night, and Tony's at the European Parliament the day after. Tony seems to have regained all his strength and confidence. It was a superb speech and even the right-wing papers have had to acknowledge it.

This carried through for some considerable time and was a great uplift. It was something that in my own way I was going to be able to build on in producing in the autumn, as part of our presidency, an alternative to the traditional European social model and the free-market 'anything goes' approach of the United States. It is my regret that we weren't able to carry that forward for all sorts of reasons, so that the informal summit at Hampton Court, while important, didn't provide a jumping-off point for a debate right across Europe about how we configure economic enterprise and deregulation on the one hand; and on the other: protection of employee rights, the acquisition of skills and enabling government to help people through change.

Here we go again, courtesy of the *Daily Mail* on Friday 24th and *Mail on Sunday* on the 26th. They really can't leave me alone. Of course, Norman Baker [Liberal Democrat MP for Lewes] and Christopher Grayling [Conservative MP for Epsom and Ewell] can't resist it either. I think Christopher Grayling has to be one of the most ruthless politicians I have ever come across – and that's saying something.

I had no idea in June just what was in store for me in the autumn, with the oldest trick in the book: come up with a completely fabricated story and get a member of the opposition front bench to comment on it and say that they 'will be taking this up'. The fact that they never do never gets reported, and the fact that they haven't got a clue never precludes them from making exactly the same statement the week after, and the week after that.

But let me not simply discriminate against the Associated Newspaper Group. On Friday 24 June the *Independent* raised the issue of why I was entitled to a severance payment. What a cheek, given the severance pay that editors get when they depart! But of course they had started something running into the weekend.

This was only the beginning of a combination of Associated Newspapers (the Mail group) and the Independent *– a pincer movement between a so-called liberal newspaper and a declared, open and at least transparent right-wing media empire. I have always preferred knowing where my enemies lie to being ambushed by those who pretend to be open-minded and liberal and are in fact anything but.*

Fortunately I was staying with friends in Italy for a long weekend so just for a change my Sunday wasn't ruined, as I didn't pick up the weekend coverage until Monday.

Then to Tuesday 28 June, and ID cards: Simon Davies, who appears to be a part-timer at the London School of Economics, describes himself as 'Privacy International' and undoubtedly represents those who, courtesy of the Internet, are deeply against anything that involves the government in knowing even the most minimal details of who is in the country, who is entitled to services, and who is breaking the law. It reminds me of Migration Watch and the way in which both the *Mail* and the *Telegraph* and the BBC are prepared to present a very small organisation as representative of a large-scale opinion. There's nothing we can do about this, of course, but on this occasion Simon Davies was presenting costings in relation to ID cards that, in my humble opinion, are so completely off the wall that I am really sorry that the London School of Economics have allowed him even to hint that he has any connection with them. I am amazed that Professor Patrick Dunleavy is prepared to risk his academic standing on this particular report.

At Cabinet on Thursday 30 June we had quite a laugh. Tessa Jowell had been held up in traffic and Tony turned to ask her to introduce her paper on the Olympics, only to find that she wasn't there – but almost immediately she appeared through the door. Tony said, 'I thought you were going to miss your big moment,' and quick as a flash she replied: 'Like all big moments, I hope they recur.' Everyone laughed and people started to crack jokes. John Prescott said that he didn't want to have to pronounce 'Milosevic' for goodness knows how many times at Prime Minister's Questions the following Wednesday (when Tony would be in Singapore). While people were laughing, Jack Straw pronounced somebody's unpronounceable name – I can't remember whose – which had obviously taken his fancy, a name that he thought might come up at Prime Minister's Questions!

July 2005

On 1 July we had the launch of our European Presidency at Lancaster House. There weren't all that many of us from the Cabinet there but it was interesting going round the table, and slightly more constructive than I had expected. It was the first time I can remember in the last eight months that John Prescott has been civil to me, so that's a breakthrough.

I rushed back to Sheffield on Friday night to do a fundraising event for children with cancer. This is one of the most wonderful things that you can do when you are in the public eye. You can do some good in a quiet and unassuming way. No one sees it – and nor should they – but it is heartwarming, and although I was pretty stressed because of the day, it was so good to be in Derbyshire and the Dowager Duchess turned up, which was really lovely of her. My task was to talk about Parliament over the years. I had done a bit of research on this so I had got some funny Churchill stories, as well as some of my own. It was good to make people laugh and, if I'm honest, good to make myself laugh as well.

Of course the politics of the time were dominated by the build-up to the G8 Summit at Gleneagles. The pop concert in Hyde Park was the main focus, but the demonstration in Edinburgh was by far the most impressive outpouring of genuine feeling and belief. The Hyde Park concert put me in mind of the phrase 'ageing juveniles' from *Round the Horne*, but if it got the message out across the world, then it's got to be a good thing.

I think that Tony and Gordon between them have worked a miracle here. A small-population country off the edge of Europe, and we have really driven the agenda on both world development (trade, aid and the write-off of debt) and on climate change. There are times – and I've had them – when you think to yourself, 'If I've done nothing else in my life, this was worthwhile,' and for Tony and Gordon, this surely must be worthwhile.

Police estimated that 225,000 people turned out in Edinburgh, and I wish I had been there. I gather from what I can pick up that Gleneagles itself is like a fortress, with police and Special Branch being drawn in from right across the country. It reminds me of the Democratic and Republican Conventions in the USA, but surely no one is going to launch a frontal attack on Gleneagles with all this security going on.

Well, my Department have really dropped one. Fancy managing to have the meeting in Belfast of the twenty-five European countries (and the two pending accession countries) clash with the G8 summit. That's what we are preparing for, and if they think there is going to be any publicity out of it at all, then they must be out of their minds. Talk about awareness of the wider world and what is going on around them.

This gripe faded into insignificance on 7 July with the suicide-bomber attacks on the Underground and on the bus in Tavistock Square. It just shows how petty irritation pales into oblivion with the intrusion of the reality of life. How trivial to have been annoyed because the Department hadn't taken account of what the government as a whole were doing, long before I came back into office. Reality certainly brought home that there were much greater things to concern us.

At last, after six months with the Press Complaints Commission, I've got the *Sunday Telegraph* to retract their Boxing Day story. One small victory, but I am still having to put up with the most appalling vitriol – such as Brian Reade and Paul Routledge in the *Mirror*. Brian Reade compared me to a stalker – referring back to the previous year – and to Freddie Starr. If I weren't in the Cabinet I would take the *Mirror* for all they were worth, but it is just not possible to sue newspapers while a government minister and naturally the journalists know it.

Nor am I the only one. Tessa Jowell and David Mills are having their families pursued. Every other colleague who has hit the headlines has had their family pursued. Those writing don't give a damn what the impact will be or who they are destroying. I wouldn't mind if any single one of them had ever done anything to make a difference to the lives of those around them, achieved something and really changed the world. At least then they would be in a position to throw stones at others.

On Tuesday 28 June I had accepted another invitation to supper at Annabel's. My diary merely records that I had to leave in the middle of the meal to vote on the ID Cards Bill and returned in time to eat the main course before leaving at midnight – before I turned into a pumpkin – and crucially that somehow a Daily Mail photographer had appeared outside the club before I left. After something akin to a farce I left via the kitchens, while shaking off a determined effort by one of the other guests to be seen leaving with me. That guest was Sally Anderson. Nothing appeared in the papers.

This was not my last meeting with Sally Anderson, who that evening had told me all about how she needed to have tests for skin cancer and how much this was worrying her, and of her desperate need to get support for voice training so that she could become an opera singer. And, like a mug, I was deeply sympathetic.

I contacted the club the following day to demand to know what the hell was going on. Obviously no one would accept that anyone inside the club had anything to do with photographers – although clearly I should have expected it – but they did say that a photograph of a woman was being shown round to see if anyone could identify her. It was in fact a photograph of the wife of one of the guests, not Sally Anderson.

I then say in my diary that I need to be a darned sight more careful, and to get to the summer without any further incidents. Goodness me. I couldn't have been less careful when receiving a phone call after the bombing on 7 July from Sally Anderson to see if I was 'all right', and to arrange for me to come down to Berkshire and go out to dinner. I spell this out only to indicate that some of us are sometimes the architect of our own downfall, even though this episode had absolutely nothing to do with my role as a Cabinet minister, my actions regarding policy or delivery, or my skill in campaigning and communicating. In any other way of life it would be completely irrelevant, but not in the life I was leading.

The leaks from the Cabinet Office/Downing Street are still there – this time that there is not enough being done against anti-social behaviour. So Charles is now having to put up with what I had month after month, and the action taken against the 'leaker' has clearly not been enough.

It cannot be rocket science to find out who is doing it. The minutes were those of an update 'stocktake' meeting in relation to the Home Office, about which none of the rest of us had a clue, and the minutes of which had not been circulated. But it does seem as though, with the combined forces of MI5, Special Branch and the Cabinet Office Resilience (anti-terrorism) Operation, we cannot identify who it is.

And ID cards: there seems to be no communications and press operation. The 80 per cent plus rating we were getting in the autumn of last year is disintegrating by the hour. Is anyone explaining what is going on or fighting for it? We have the columnist Simon Jenkins writing that billions could be spent on combating world poverty – a bit like the Lib Dems pretending we could spend it on policing. It is not just economic illiteracy. It is deliberate. I can't believe for a moment that someone like Simon Jenkins doesn't know that the money would not be available if we weren't raising it through the increase in passport fees.

I went along to the 150th anniversary of the Civil Service Commission, marked by the publication of a book. Sir Gus O'Donnell, the new Secretary to the Cabinet, was speaking, and I stood at the back. I think the best thing I can say is that I managed to walk away without commenting. He is a great performer, is Gus, but honestly he can't possibly believe that 150 years on they are really modernising and reforming the civil service.

In June 2006 I was to give evidence alongside Michael Howard to the Public Administration Select Committee and to provide them with a memorandum. A year on from the celebration of the Commission, there appeared to be no sign of radical reform or change, but it is extraordinarily difficult to advocate modernisation without appearing to attack individuals – which I am not doing. I believe there are some excellent people in the civil service, not just nice people but really competent and committed – but that isn't the point. I am trying to get across, and always will, that it is about reforming leadership and management skills, and about the process and the systems, not individuals. Everyone always goes defensive. Everyone always believes you are attacking someone or some individual failure. By doing so, they miss the point.

I will never forget Gus's phrase that 'We seek to influence those with power'. Full of irony, I mused that that's what I thought *we* did.

I had a really good cup of tea with Peter Riddell from *The Times* during the first week in July, and he produced an excellent piece on the back of it. Peter and I reminisced about the time he had come up to Sheffield. He is a good man, but even for those who are interested and well informed it is difficult for them to know what is happening outside London because journalists writing for national newspapers, or for that matter the broadcast media, hardly ever get out of London at all.

Peter said how well I looked. I've put half a stone on since I've been back in government, and shall have to watch it. I have been so much healthier since I had my operation, lost weight and started doing my exercises. Government must be good for me – at least this department.

Talking of weight, I had lunch at Café du Marché with the Royal National Institute for the Blind: Chairman Colin Lowe and Chief Executive Lesley-Anne Alexander and her colleagues. It was really important to learn how they saw what was happening on disability, non-access to work and other issues. There is so much to learn about how people perceive what we are doing on Welfare to Work and how we can work with them. What I gathered was that it was very difficult to get the civil service to talk to big organisations like the RNIB separately, as though there was some fear in seeing people on a one-to-one basis rather than in a big forum. I have always found that listening to people is not a threat. It lets you know what's going on in the real world. You pick up what is happening and that is one of the biggest problems the civil service face – they don't tune in to what's happening on the ground; there are no antennae and they are so frightened of being 'influenced'. So who is influencing?

I have deliberately been doing very few broadcasts but have been getting enormous mentions – it can't be helped, I suppose, what with welfare reform, pensions, Child Support Agency, etc. People are bound to comment because they are top of the news. I have done one pre-interview for the night of 15 July on the launch of J.K. Rowling's latest Harry Potter book. It sounds as if Gordon and I are doing one of those dual acts again, because Joanne Rowling is a personal friend of Sarah and Gordon. Anyway, it is worth doing. Youngsters don't vote but it does get across that politicians are human and they do read the books.

I am noticing one thing: that the almost euphoric public support that I was getting before I was back in government has now eased a bit. I think the drip, drip approach over the past two months is damaging because, after all, people don't know the truth, and if you are not the victim you are not quite so vulnerable, and therefore people don't relate to you quite so well. It was clear, I think, publicly where things stood in the run-up to Christmas, but I am back in government now so I'm part of the establishment.

I've speeches to prepare – one for a work and pensions summer school at King's College, Cambridge, another to the Fabian Society and their review of pensions policy – and articles to write. And a speech to the charity Jewish Care – a way of saying thank you to the Jewish community in London who have been so supportive and kind to me.

I had no idea that private remarks at that forum would be picked up and used against me by the Daily Telegraph. *It would be very unfair to describe them as anti-semitic comments. It was just that my commitment to those who had been so committed to me was interpreted in a quite distorted way, getting into my private life and sneering. I thought that this was way below the ethics and standing of the* Daily Telegraph, *but it was also a lesson that I can't speak anywhere or say anything that can be misinterpreted and used as 'revealing' my private life. In simple terms, as a politician, I am now 'back in my box', speaking always with the voice of someone who expects what's said to be*

misinterpreted, fulfilling the worst expectations of the public, that we talk in
platitudes and never reveal ourselves. And this is a self-fulfilling prophecy for
those who always write about exactly that – that we are stereotyped,
unforthcoming and generally alien to the way that everyone else behaves.
I'm afraid this means we get the politicians we deserve.

It is worth noting that I am again rewriting the letters that go out as part of
ministerial correspondence, just as I did in the last two departments. I am
trying to ensure that the letters that are sent relate to this government, not
the last; to our present policy, not the past. I shouldn't be doing this but I
can't help myself. I just have to redraft the standard letters as well as the
ones that are put to me to send.

I have had three meetings now with those doing the correspondence:
they are very good and they are very amenable but it is quite an effort.
Understandably they are not political, but that's not the issue. The issue
is what the letters say, whether they are sympathetic, and whether
sometimes they indicate that we are prepared to take another look at
policy, rather than reiterating the policy as it is. And crucially, we must
learn from the letters that are coming in. I've said to them that it's a bit
like my advice surgery. If we take note of what's coming in, we can not
only see which issues are really touching people most profoundly, the
questions that are irritating or worrying people most, but we may also
find out where things are going wrong. So let's have a monitoring system
to see precisely where the biggest postbag exists, and whether what they
are saying stands up – and then let's get ministers to do something about
it.

On the private front, I am continuing to adapt the barn that I rent in
Derbyshire to make space so that the family can stay, given that the cottage
has only two small bedrooms and shower room. God knows why I entered
into this financial commitment: it seemed right at the time, even though I
will not be the one to benefit from the investment, as I am tenant rather
than owner. But I am very, very fortunate: what would my mother and
father say if they could see me sitting outside the cottage?

Monday 4 July: lunch with Nick Robinson, who is taking over from
Andrew Marr as political editor of the BBC. I had a good meeting also on
childcare and Sure Start. I have joint responsibility with the Department
for Education and Skills on this, and it is like coming home. I am worried,
however, that Sure Start is not what we started out with, and I am going to
have to do something to try to redeem this.

On Tuesday [5 July] I made my speech at the IPPR on assets and the big challenge we face in overcoming inter-generational poverty. The then Head of News had questioned me in a ministerial team meeting as to whether I thought that anyone would give a damn and whether there would be any publicity at all. I indicated that that was my business. Her business was to ensure that I did get coverage, not whether she thought it was a good idea to be making such a speech.

The Department are so focused on the agencies that they operate and the historic role they have been given that no one can think that maybe we will be firing on entirely new cylinders, across government input and social policy in its broadest sense. In other words, what we used to call 'the big picture'.

As it happened we got good publicity on the Wednesday in the papers and it was well worth doing – and it would have been worth doing even if there had been no publicity at all, because getting the debate back on track is really important.

But all eyes were on two major events this week and I think to write very much about anything else during the week would be to completely miss the point.

Firstly the Olympics, and the presentation in Singapore. Tony had flown out and had spent two days out there. The presentation itself was designed to show London as the epitome of a metropolitan centre – every religion, every nationality and culture.

The bid team was really fantastic. It was strange to think that Seb Coe from Sheffield was there, along with my former researcher Mike Lee, with Jude Kelly, whom I know very well, leading the cultural bid and who I think choreographed large chunks of the final presentation, and of course Richard Caborn from Sheffield, the Sports Minister, and my friend, Tessa Jowell, as Secretary of State for Culture, Media and Sport. It was just one of those coincidences where people you know and people you have known are all deeply involved.

I thought that Paris would win, not London. When the result came through at 12.46, they opened the envelope and announced that it was London. People came out on to the streets, Trafalgar Square was full, people were enjoying themselves. There was an atmosphere of real celebration – and optimism about the G8, as Tony had had to fly straight to Gleneagles for meetings on Wednesday, Thursday and Friday.

On Thursday morning I went to Cabinet. John Prescott was in the chair, and about half an hour in, at about 9.30 a.m., a note was passed in and

Alistair Darling announced that he thought there had been an explosion in an Underground station, but we were not sure about it. Just before we broke up at ten o'clock it became clear that there had been several explosions, and possibly one on a bus, but still no one was entirely sure. The broadcast media, particularly the BBC, had been reporting that there had been a power surge on the Underground. What transpired was that there had been three explosions on the Underground within a minute of each other at approximately 8.50 a.m., and a further explosion on a bus at Tavistock Square.

I was due to leave Cabinet and fly straight to Belfast to start the pre-meetings of trade unions, businesses and non-governmental organisations, prior to the more formal sessions that I was chairing of the European Social Affairs and Employment Council. I immediately indicated that I would not be going until the evening at the earliest. James Plaskitt who, thank goodness, had had the foresight to have left early, managed to get to Belfast to do the diplomacies – although for reasons entirely beyond me, the press office did not.

What astonishes me about that Thursday morning is how long it took before we, as Cabinet members, were fully aware of what had happened, given that the explosions took place ten minutes before Cabinet began. The measures that Alistair Darling and I had put in place, including the exercise on the Underground the previous September, came into play. The emergency services were outstanding, as were acts of individual bravery and commitment, including from passengers. And the calmness of London was frankly stunning. I walked through the streets and into Green Park and found literally thousands of people just walking quietly, hardly speaking – but calm and understanding and brave.

But it was clear that communications were a problem – with the mobile networks jamming up and then being switched off, including those around me. A member of my protection team was desperately trying to contact his daughter, who may well have been on the Underground. Stories like this abound – and mercifully his daughter was safe and sound.

I wasn't sure whether to go to the COBR meeting, and the Department was not geared up to this, as it had never had a minister involved at this level. I thought of going only because given my experience over nearly four years, I thought I might be able to contribute – but when I did go, I felt I wasn't welcome. Tony was not there and Charles chaired the meeting. Gordon was calm and thoughtful – as he had been on 11 September – and asked all the right questions, including the ones that no one wanted asking. But we were in fact merely being updated and much of it was already on Sky television and BBC News 24. A heartbreaking picture was emerging of dozens of people killed or badly injured. It became clear throughout the day – and was particularly apparent when a second COBR meeting was called, which I attended briefly – that in fact the news media were ahead of the material being presented to us. They had had eyewitnesses sending through video footage, photographs and on-the-spot accounts. It was, in essence, the first time I think that reporting was as much about the men and women on the ground as it was about professional reporters them-selves. This posed a difficulty with sorting out the validity and credibility of what was being said and by whom. We were entering a new era.

But there is nothing I can do. I have contributed to putting in place all the necessary work from my Department on bereavement and on benefits for those who have lost loved ones, and I have already said to them that we are not having any deductions from benefits to reflect funds raised for the families – but from the officials' reaction, there is going to be a battle about this. They've started mentioning the benefits regulations already.

Tony had left Gleneagles immediately and was back in London, so there seemed to be nothing more that I could do, other than asking questions that no one wished to answer – such as why had we lowered the threat level? So I went to Northolt and flew to Belfast to pick up the pieces of the European Council.

It was one of those moving moments in life, when at the City Hall in Belfast, a city that had seen so many deaths and tragedies from terrorism, I signed the Book of Condolence and, as events unfolded, realised just how many people had lost their lives.

The final figure was fifty-two innocent deaths, with very many others injured and bereaved.

When we set up the Joint Terrorism Analysis Centre in the aftermath of the attack on 11 September 2001 (reporting in to the Joint Intelligence Commit-tee), we had expected that the domestic as well as the international would be part of the assessment. It was something of a surprise, therefore, to find that while we were extremely well prepared for a more sophisticated chemical or biological attack, the simple expedient of suicide explosives appeared to be something that had been given a lower priority and, for that matter, so had the obvious soft targets at the time of the Gleneagles meeting.

I had not been involved in Intelligence and Security at more than a cursory level since December 2004, and since that date many of the personnel have changed. So has the organisation, effectively breaking up the united Special Branch operation, which may have had some influence over the abortive raid in Forest Gate in the early summer of 2006.

I spoke again to Tony on the telephone on Sunday morning [10 July], and it was a good, honest appraisal. Tony is on top of the situation and has a very clear idea about the importance of getting the signals right. For three and a half years we had driven forward the agenda together, so often facing unpopularity for stating clearly that there was a threat and taking steps to match it. Now all I can do is help from what feels like the sidelines.

When I was at the Home Office I often fell out with David Veness, Head of SO13, but he was thorough, he was committed and he was never, ever, complacent. David moved on to work with the United Nations in the early part of 2005. I think we are missing him.

I am just reflecting on Gleneagles. Despite the tragedy of 7 July and despite not going as far as any of us would have wished on climate change, what we have managed on world development and anti-poverty is really good. It is astonishing when you hear the criticism from Oxfam and from Action Aid. You wonder why they say these things. Why do they snatch defeat from the jaws of victory? Why do they have to pooh-pooh and be so negative? They can still campaign, they can still demand more, they can still pressurise to ensure that what's been agreed is carried out, but they don't always have to be griping and churlish – or do they?

Brussels on Monday 11 July, firstly for a seminar on ageing – I've done a lot of work on this – and then to address the Employment and Social Affairs Committee of the European Parliament.

All of the senior ministers who were chairing European councils had to appear before the appropriate section of the European Parliament to report on the programme for the six-month presidency and to answer questions. My appearance went extremely well, as did the seminar on ageing, which I was very sceptical about when I originally agreed to do it. It turned out to be very worthwhile, not least in understanding the approach that was being taken across Europe in respect of pensions, the demographic changes and their impact on the affordability of the welfare state, and measures in countries like France to stimulate the birth-rate.

What was astonishing was that the Communications Directorate of my

Department clearly felt that anything to do with the European Union, even something as high-profile as the social affairs and employment issues – never mind the major challenges of ageing and demographic change – were so outside the normal remit that they didn't even bother to send a press officer.

I have just read that I've sent my lawyers along to the opening night of this wretched musical about my private life. What a joke. I'm spending so much money on lawyers already that there's not a cat in hell's chance of doing that, even it were likely to do any good. What's even more astonishing is that editors of newspapers are going along to see it. It's a kind of weird voyeurism. I don't know whether people think it is amusing or entertaining, or whether they think it is so vile that they ought to experience it. I just hope that those who wrote and produced it, and for that matter those taking part in it, might one day look back on what they did and regret it.

Anyway it's the Channel 4 film that will be the real killer. I shouldn't get worked up about a tinpot musical that a handful of weirdos go to see.

I've discovered that the press office is keeping a diary of all the requests that I make for press activity. I'd like to believe that this is so they could match the resources to the demands being made. But with one press officer allocated to the Belfast European meeting and none to the two meetings in Brussels, I fear there may be another agenda at play.

The Permanent Secretary, Sir Richard Mottram, has been caught up in the Railtrack court hearing. He was Permanent Secretary when Steve Byers was there and therefore he is inevitably having to give evidence. There is nothing that any of us can do about this, but it is clearly going to be a distraction.

I gave dinner to Melanie Ward on the evening of 10 July, and Hazel Blears joined us in the Churchill Room at the House of Commons. I had met Melanie's father years before on a flight back from Vancouver and he talked to me about her commitment to the Labour Party and the major challenges that her brother faced on account of his special needs. She is a real fighter for the Labour cause amongst students and on the Executive of the National Union of Students – God, what a job.

In the summer of 2006, Melanie came to work for me when Anna Turley moved to be a special adviser to Hilary Armstrong at the Cabinet Office. I had undertaken events that she had organised periodically and it was good to be able to offer her the opportunity of using some of her contacts and experience not only for her benefit, but also for mine.

We have just passed without any upheaval at all the vote on the Immigration Act – but here's a twist. As John Prescott is away, and Jack is away, I've been clearing correspondence as temporary Chair of the Domestic Affairs Committee, and one of the major policy items coming round is the next batch of changes on immigration. I had hoped that we might bottom all of it within this particular Bill but it is like painting the Forth Railway Bridge. Even temporarily it is nice to be back into wider policy issues and feel that I have a part to play.

I went to the First Night of the Proms on Friday night [15 July] before attending the Policy Forum on the Saturday morning. It was about 120 degrees Fahrenheit in the box at the Royal Albert Hall to which I had been invited by Radio 3 and we were all dehydrating – but the music was lovely and there was a great feeling of the courage of London, along with celebration of having won the Olympic bid for 2012.

Afterwards there was a buffet dinner, which gave me a chance to say hello to Robert Thomson of *The Times*. Andrew Marr and Jackie Ashley were also there and one or two other people to whom it was possible to speak, but I escaped as soon as I could. I had to smile because one of those I spoke to had obviously decided that he was in danger of being captured for the evening and said that he would 'find you someone to talk to'. I said, 'That's very kind of you, thank you very much' – and I knew it was time to go home.

I've had a very nice note back from Dominique de Villepin, to whom I'd written when he moved to the Prime Minister's job. I must be the only person who gets on well with both Nicolas Sarkozy and Dominique de Villepin.

I went across to see Charles Clarke. It was the first time I have been in the new Home Office building, even though I was Home Secretary when it was all planned. Charles was telling me that he had had a big fall-out with Nicolas Sarkozy. I think the French had tried to pull a fast one on him. People seem to test each other with regard to the limits of how far they are prepared to go. It is a strange world.

Charles described how helicopters had been laid on to take them from the venue where they had been discussing business to the restaurant on the lakeside. No one blinks an eyelid in France about welcoming visiting politicians and using flights to move people around. I think a happy medium between the way we view things and their profligacy is probably the way forward.

Charles and I also discussed the 7 July bombings and the fact that we had home-grown terror here. We had people who had been brought up in normal communities, with decent people around them who didn't see what was happening. The police seem to be doing a good job at follow-up with regard to identification and being able to track the four terrorists.

Edward Heath has died [on 17 July]. He has been very ill for a long time. I will try to get to his memorial service; the funeral itself will be for family.

I did manage to get to his memorial service but it was after stepping down from Cabinet in November.

I remember the fact that when we were in opposition he had once invited me to come to supper on Christmas Eve. I couldn't go down to Salisbury because I was with my sons, but it was a kind gesture and an indication, I think, of his loneliness.

Monday 18 July: I went down to the Cotswolds to speak at a seminar for senior staff of News International. It was all about leadership and management and they were a very sparky group of people. It was enjoyable even though it was a hell of a drive.

Cabinet on 21 July saw Gordon reporting on his technical change in backdating the 'economic cycle', giving him an extra £12 billion – not to spend but to ensure that the 'golden rule' was met and that by doing so there was no need to increase borrowing. I thought this was very smart and should have been done some time before, because 1997 was the logical starting time for our economic cycle, given that that's when we started in office.

The arrest on this day of those attempting to repeat the attacks of a fortnight earlier made only a marginal impression on me, as at the time I assumed that they were either incompetent or lacking in intent.

Friday 22 July: God, I think the police have shot an innocent man. It sounds as though he was running away from something, but not, from all the descriptions of him flinging himself on to the Underground train, as though he was a terrorist. It is all about split-second decisions and I have always backed the police in these circumstances but in my gut I feel there is something amiss.

It was a year later when the Independent Police Complaints Commission report on the death of Jean Charles de Menezes emerged, in what can only be described as one of the most confused situations I've seen in my time in senior politics.

It is not just a tragedy for the individual, whatever his background, whatever the final truth. It is a tragedy from the point of view of perception of the police. It has given those who are apologists for the terrorists, not just in this country but across the world, something to latch on to – and the papers, particularly on Monday 25 July, were going that way.

One bright spot was the *Today* programme on Tuesday 26 July and their compilation of the 'Citizens' Jury' that I did in Sheffield on the previous Friday, with a range of people who had spent a couple of days examining issues around pensions, and then put me on the spot. I really enjoyed it. I could be myself and speak like a normal human being and not like a politician – and it came across like that on the programme. I just wish I could do more of this, speaking to people and talking with them, not just addressing them. Not only did it work but I think it made sense to the audience as well, since they could relate to the kind of things being raised – and, God willing, to the answers.

I have just been told that Channel 4 are starting to make the film about me, with a caricature of a blind man and a makeshift guide dog. They had the cheek to approach the Guide Dogs for the Blind Association to ask if they could borrow a harness to put on the dog. Fortunately the association had the sense to ring me to find out what was going on, and whether this project was 'friendly'.

I found out much later that one of the Disability Rights Commissioners who also has a guide dog was approached and asked if they could borrow his dog. There seemed no lengths to which they would not go – but, as I was to discover, the ringing of cash registers was to form an orchestra by the time we reached the autumn.

We are in the dog days of July. A meeting on welfare reform was desultory in the extreme: I got agreement to the welfare-reform principles to be published in the autumn and to changes to previous welfare policy, but no one seemed to be interested. We had an aborted meeting between Tony, Gordon and myself on pensions. I can only presume that Gordon wants to buy some time to see how the land lies before the autumn.

Then off to Bristol for a series of meetings and a public round table on pensions.

The moment I got to the DWP I had set in train a whole series of consultations where all or at least part of the ministerial team would visit different regions of the country. They were already going down extremely well, not simply with regard to discussing pensions but showing that ministers were out and about; also, because as it wasn't just one minister making a visit, it was possible to get really decent regional coverage, both on television and in the press. These visits had the great advantage of engaging the public, even if it was only with information, and at the same time demonstrating that government was getting closer to the people and genuinely trying to reach out. It was, in essence, what we had done as a political party with the 'Big Conversation', which I regretted very much that we hadn't pulled together before the general election into a demonstrable set of themes arising out of the consultation with the public. It had been an excellent exercise, but one that really tailed off at the end. There was a desultory effort to reinvent it with 'Let's Talk' in 2006, but there was no real stomach at that moment for widespread political dialogue – and for reasons that are perfectly well understood, the British media had other foxes to chase.

And then we had George Osborne, Shadow Chancellor, spouting nonsense about ministerial pensions.

There is a mind-blowing ignorance about precisely what happens with ministerial pensions. The MPs' pension scheme is a very good one, although unlike the civil-service one it is contributory. But ministers don't see very much at all for the time they spend in government, given how ephemeral and short-lived many ministerial careers are. You don't get your pension on the final salary that you received as a minister, with or without adding it to the MP's salary. It is a contributory scheme so you get out what you've put in.

    But George was not alone in not having done his homework. When I raised the matter with one or two colleagues it was pretty clear that the Cabinet hadn't got the first idea how the ministerial pension scheme worked or didn't work. This is not surprising, given that it was invented by civil servants for ministers on the basis that ministers are, as I have observed before, well-meaning amateurs whose time in government is likely to be limited and whose spell in office is likely to be seen, unlike executives in business, as a mere passing phase before they return to whatever it was they were doing before.

Tuesday 26 July: I must be becoming obsessive. I have been irritated by the fact that *The Times,* having done a preview of this ridiculous musical about me, has now done a review of it. With all that's going on in London in the aftermath of 7 July, and all the things that they might report or even review, they manage to cover it twice. But goodness me, I do have to stop reacting because it is exactly what they want.

And the *Evening Standard* had done a big page-3 review for a second time – which is not surprising, bearing in mind that senior staff have been to see it. But what's the agenda?

And then on the 28th a meeting with Gordon, Jim Callaghan's memorial service, and lunch with Tessa Jowell. Although I am not going away until the middle of August, most people are off at the end of July so everyone is trying to wrap up meetings and events. Unusually for me I will have the early part of August to catch up on what needs to be done inside the Department and in the constituency.

I have had a meeting with Gus O'Donnell about the fact that there are vacancies coming up for permanent secretaries and a potential reshuffle. The Treasury Permanent Secretary comes up on Wednesday the 27th, and I don't know what will happen if John Gieve doesn't get the post, having been pipped for the post of Permanent Secretary to the Cabinet Office. Rumour has it that Charles wants David Normington to come across from Education and Skills, but the atmosphere all round isn't helped by snippets in the *Telegraph* and *Mail* on Tuesday and Wednesday about the Home Office. I am desperately keen to stop people either making comparisons or suggesting that I might want to come back. There is nothing worse in politics than an incumbent thinking their predecessor is having a go.

Thursday [28 July] brought really good news of progress in Ireland. The Provisional IRA decided that they would formally and openly announce the complete cessation of their military action permanently and order a decommissioning of their weaponry. Of course, they won't go as far as the DUP want, with photographs, but they will have verification. Tony has worked really hard on this since the Good Friday Agreement five and a half years ago and if, with what he has managed to do over the past few weeks – the Olympic bid, the G8, handling the terrorist attack – he can manage to pull this off as well, it will be a phenomenal achievement.

Friday 29 July: thank goodness, the last of the bombers from the abortive attack on 21 July has been picked up. I am presuming that their makeshift equipment simply eroded and failed to go off, but this will be a terrific breakthrough.

I am trying to sort out how to update and modernise what we did with the New Deal for the Unemployed, particularly for the young unemployed. I have had meetings with Des Browne and my meeting on the 28th with Gordon touched on this. But there is a game being played that has been going on for the whole of the time I have been in government – namely, when Treasury ministers don't want to make a decision, they indicate that officials in the Treasury have been kept in the dark or don't know exactly what it is that the department is proposing, or that the department has withheld evidence. It happens all the time. It is a clever tactic – simply putting things off – given that Treasury officials are always brought in by the spending departments.

We have a major problem with the budget that I have inherited. It wasn't part of a formal Spending Review. It was signed off on the back of a cigarette packet between Gordon and Andrew Smith. The big problem is with a programme called Work Based Learning for Adults that is not work-based at all: it is work-focused. God knows how we ended up with a title that is a complete misnomer. The difficulty is that it is all over the place. It's bits of programmes here, there and everywhere, and in any case much of it should be funded by the Learning and Skills Council.

I am slipping into the mistake again of trying to fight on too many fronts. I still haven't got out of the habit of having to win every battle.

Then off for a long weekend in Toulouse with my old friend Pat Seyd (Professor of Politics at the University of Sheffield) and his wife Ros. They have bought and renovated a place near Toulouse, and it will be very good to see them.

They had had a heatwave for three months, complete with locusts, but as my plane dipped to land at the airport in Toulouse a tremendous thunderstorm with torrential rain began, and with the exception of a couple of hours, the sun disappeared for the whole of the weekend. Nevertheless it was a really enjoyable break. And I learned something about the social make-up of France and the reality of just how much individuals know about what's going on. An extremely nice former Algerian local resident who grew the most tremendous tomatoes came round, and apart from the fact that he didn't really believe that I was a government minister (because I couldn't see) it soon transpired that he had never even heard of my friend Nicolas Sarkozy. And there was I thinking that everybody in France would have heard of Nicolas Sarkozy.

Nick McPherson has been made Permanent Secretary at the Treasury: he was No. 2 there. Nick and I have had some enormous clashes when dealing with Spending Reviews over the years. I am sure he will be excellent but it does mean that both the Permanent Secretary of the Cabinet and to the Treasury have no experience of spending departments and therefore of hands-on delivery – other than the Revenue and Customs, and of course the in-work tax credits.

While I am on duty through to my holiday, I have agreed to do the security warrants. Charles had already had to postpone his holiday for meetings with Tony so he will be very glad to get away, and as Jack is also away it has fallen to me to do them. John Prescott doesn't seem very pleased. It is almost as if I am taking something off him, but as he doesn't want to do them I am trying to be helpful – and at the same time appear to be getting up his nose. It is a very odd state of affairs. I think it is the fact that the *Sunday Times* spelled out that I was doing the warrants that has really annoyed John. But he's in charge while Tony is away and I'm no threat to him, so I don't really know what this is all about.

When I came back from Toulouse and tapped into my home answerphone from London, I heard a message from a Sunday journalist saying that he had been told that while Tony was away, I was going to be handling Home Office matters, and would I comment? I wouldn't have commented – but I wasn't there to comment so I clearly hadn't been asked any such thing.

However, Matthew Doyle, my special adviser dealing with the media, had also left me a message saying that he was disturbed by a story that had appeared in the Sunday Times, *and that although it was supposedly a 'Downing Street source' that had talked about what part I was playing in relation to security issues while Tony was away, in Matthew's words 'I am slightly concerned about how this has appeared, bluntly because even if all the quotes in the story are from a Downing Street source, it's not very helpful for you. I just wanted to let you know. I am going to make a couple of calls now and try and find out what the actual origin of it is and if I have any more information I will leave you another message.'*

Matthew then agreed a line with Downing Street that John was deputising for the Prime Minister, Hazel Blears for the Home Secretary (which is the obvious answer) and that as a senior minister who is not yet on holiday, I would be available to give support.

Matthew tells me that Mo Mowlam is very close to the end now. We have all known that she has been very ill for some time, but I hadn't realised it was as close as this. ITV had asked him if I would go on and talk about her, but I said that no one can do an obituary for someone who is still alive.

Sadly Mo passed away while I was on holiday in Italy.

In the meantime a little bad news following my gastroscopy and annual check-up. The damage to the oesophagus has continued to extend despite the excellent surgery, and they have advised me that I should take tablets in addition to watching my diet. I don't really want to, but if it's a choice between tablets or the danger of cancer then it will have to be tablets. This has rather thrown me, because I thought that things would have improved – although after the past twelve months it is not really surprising. Apart from the obvious one, all my ailments have something to do with stress, one way or another.

August 2005

On Saturday 6 August at about 4 p.m. I was sitting outside the cottage working when I received a phone call to say that Robin Cook was dead. I was so shocked that I had to hold on to the bench as otherwise I felt I would have fallen to the floor. He had apparently been walking with his wife Gaynor in the far north of Scotland and had collapsed. Then the news began to break publicly that he was ill in hospital, I suppose holding the full news off until those close to him had been informed, as happened when John Smith died.

But Robin is indeed dead. By 6.30 p.m. the news was out. The shock was not only because an able, articulate and in many ways outstanding parliamentarian was dead, but that he was only fifty-nine and we all believed that he had kept himself pretty fit. It just shows that you never know.

On Sunday morning, with Peter Sissons, I was able to say a few words about Robin on BBC television, as I did on Radio 4's *Westminster Hour* later that day with Andrew Rawnsley. I particularly chose to mention Sierra Leone because I think that Robin as Foreign Secretary should be remembered for his part in the prevention of genocide, which is so often forgotten. But there were questions in the interview about what part I was playing while Tony was away, and this upset the applecart. I hadn't meant to suggest that I was 'supporting' John Prescott in the sense of somehow giving him a helping hand. I knew, but others didn't know, that I was doing the warrants – and so did John. But Lord help me, I should have watched every single word. Instead I just chatted, saying it as it is and believing that 'support' was something that you gave to people in a comradely fashion rather than it being interpreted as 'having to give support', which was the way that John had perceived it.

It was the silly season and I know I should have counted to ten and watched everything I said. I think I was speaking as though my five months' absence from Cabinet had not happened. I was forgetting the perception of people who had been glad to see the back of me – and perhaps felt threatened by my return. Whatever the cause, it certainly caused a rumpus, with John having to pronounce that I wasn't a member of his team and that he wouldn't be calling on me. So I rang and left a message asking if they would like to take over the warrants and the day-to-day being on call in order to do the authorisations for tapping and the like in the aftermath of the 7 July attacks and the abortive attacks on 21 July. They declined.

I will go to Robin's funeral. I knew him most closely when we were members of the National Executive Committee of the party and used to sit together month after month, sometimes agreeing, moving and seconding amendments, and sometimes disagreeing, when I was arguing vehemently against spending billions of pounds on an independent nuclear deterrent. Despite our having fallen out over Iraq, I shall miss Robin, and I know the party will. I had hoped that we might have been able to offer him something outside Parliament when he decided to step down from the Cabinet, even with all the acrimony, but it wasn't to be. I am thinking of Gaynor as well, and the loneliness.

All that had taken place the week before paled into insignificance in the face of Robin's death, including my row with Tony McNulty, Immigration Minister, on Thursday [4 August], when after a Fabian speech he had gone off to the South of France and his alleged attack on his predecessors and their handling of ID cards emerged. He claimed that we have exaggerated the effectiveness of ID cards in fighting terrorism and organised crime. Of course we haven't, and we wouldn't: we played down the counter-terrorism issue and played up the way in which we could verify illegal immigration and illegal working. As Charles was away on holiday, I rang one of his special advisers, and indicated that if Tony McNulty didn't get himself on the radio and television and put the record straight then I would do it for him. Tony rang me from the South of France and we had what I think might be called 'words'. But he duly appeared on the Radio 4 *PM* programme – by which time, of course, the damage was done.

But the spat with John Prescott ran on, fuelled it has to be said by a press officer in Downing Street who, having been part of the decision to engage me to back up Hazel Blears, who is pretty much batting on her own, now decided, allegedly under orders from John, to go into complete reverse by indicating that I wouldn't have a role at all while Tony was away.

Matthew tells me that I have got the backwash from John being really aggrieved because he wasn't properly informed and involved prior to Tony's press conference in the run-up to his going on holiday. He is apparently still seething and feels that he has been left out. What a way to carry on!

It is funny what catches your attention. The BBC have been running a series each morning to coincide with the sixtieth anniversary of the dropping of the atomic bomb. One of the things they revealed was that when the bomb was dropped on Nagasaki it didn't even make top of the news: that was the Russians joining in the war against Japan. It makes me realise that people at the time, when there wasn't 24-hour, seven-day week, satellite news, only caught up on the enormity of what was going on across the world way after the impact had been felt.

Closer to home, on 10 and 11 August significant arrests were made. Bakri Mohammed [radical Muslim cleric] has left the country and I have ordered that his benefits be stopped.

It was a strange indication of how my new department considered itself almost isolated from government as a whole, when a press officer asked one of my special advisers whether she should bother ringing back when there was a query from the media about what we were doing about his benefits, because, as she said, 'we don't answer questions on benefits'. I immediately ordered that those who had been arrested and were being deported as non-conducive to the public good, or returned to Belmarsh, should have their benefits stopped. But there was a degree of surprise in the Department that I expected them to be proactive in telling people that we were on the ball and understood the politics of a situation when there was story after story about the massive hand-outs that went to individuals who were abusing the hospitality of this country. But it was damned hard work.

Before Matthew Doyle went to Ireland, we had a very pleasant lunch with Mary Ann Sieghart of *The Times*, unfortunately at the Ivy, where I feel very conspicuous but where journalists do like to go.

I made a visit to the Health and Safety Executive laboratories at Buxton in Derbyshire, a really sophisticated operation. They showed me a piece of the track from the Hatfield rail disaster, which they said had been in that condition for a year before the catastrophe. I have never felt anything so distorted, so obviously and clearly dangerous. They are doing a really good job with limited resources and drawing in new forms of expertise, like industrial psychology, to help with new forms of risk to health and well-being.

It made me acutely aware that I never did get the corporate-manslaughter legislation agreed last December.

Before going on holiday I had a really good visit – on welfare reform – to Derbyshire and Nottinghamshire, and to East Midlands airport, just outside Nottingham, where I met a young woman named Kelly Hill, who got up at 5.30 a.m. in order to get to work because of the difficulty she had in washing and dressing and the challenges she faces. Kelly has no arms and severely damaged legs and operates in a wheelchair. Her mother got up with her to ensure that she got to work. Kelly was so proud to have a job, to be on equal terms, to be working after quite a period of unemployment – and I was proud that we were doing something to make it possible, and that the experimental Pathways to Work programme based in the area was doing its bit.

This is what I want to spell out in the Welfare Green Paper that I am working on at the moment with Margaret Hodge, but the benefits system is so horrendously complex and the additions for disability so disparate that it is no wonder people can't understand what's going on. The important thing is to ensure that we don't get mixed up between disability living allowance (which is not about income but about support) and the benefits system, with all its add-ons and sticking plaster and bits here and there.

Before my holiday I flew up from Manchester to Edinburgh for Robin's funeral service, where I sat behind Pauline and John Prescott. Pauline acknowledged me and then got John to acknowledge me, and we shook hands. He said to me, under his breath: 'You bloody old warrior.' I hope that it will be the beginning of a *rapprochement.*

The service was excellent – well put together and extremely well conducted – and Gordon's oration was powerful and strong. I don't know what Robin would have made of all the tributes to him, not least from those he had fallen out with, but I like to think that his sons and family and Gaynor were lifted a little by the genuine respect and admiration for his political skills, his political contribution and the difference he has made.

Gordon rang me while I was travelling back on the East Coast line to ask if I would like to go round for an informal meal at his house. It was nice of him, but by then I was well on my way back to Sheffield – and to prepare for my holiday.

When the barn conversion is finished and I have cracked the back of the Welfare Green Paper and found an agreement over pensions and been restored by having a break, I'm sure I will smile again. But all the time I feel under surveillance – bit by bit, picking me to pieces, people looking for ways of dragging me down.

While the old adage that 'Just because I'm paranoid doesn't mean that I'm not being followed' stands very firmly, it is absolutely true that feeling sorry for myself is not a pretty picture and, looking back on it, what I needed to be was as smart as those who had it in for me.

While on holiday I have been stupid enough to keep in touch with the papers, so instead of escaping from it all I've finished myself off by reading garbage from the Edinburgh Television Festival about this wretched film. It is just as though, because I had to keep in touch when I was Home Secretary, I now can't leave it alone. I can't avoid it when at home because it doesn't matter how hard I try, I eventually hear the news. But it was very silly of me not to avoid it while I was away.

Now I am back and all hell's let loose. My advisers tell me that Charles is really upset about articles in the *Daily Express* and *Daily Star* about my wanting to come back as Home Secretary.

It would have been funny had it not been so serious, because the Daily Express *and the* Daily Star *were the two newspapers with which, over many years, I have had absolutely no dealings. Their proprietors and editors are the only ones I have never met. Therefore if I or those around me were going to talk to any newspaper – and we had really drawn in the horns as a matter of necessity and survival – it certainly would not have been to the political correspondent of the* Daily Express. *But nevertheless, whatever intent they had, on the back of what had happened at the beginning of August to do with John Prescott and my role as part of the team on duty, it played into the impression Charles had gained.*

September 2005

Sunday 4 September: Sir John Stevens, former Commissioner of the Metropolitan Police and now a columnist for the *News of the World*, has had a book published – an autobiography, in the writing of which he has been 'assisted' by a reporter from the *News of the World*, which paper, together with *The Times*, is carrying extracts. There are five pages in the book relating to his working time with me and these are the five that are highlighted as the only story from the book in the serialisation on 4 September. I have no idea why, but not only does 'What the Papers Say' cover it extensively, so does the news.

My comment, for me, was very low key: 'I wish him luck in selling the book.' I went on to indicate that I had had a very positive working relationship with him, if stormy at times. The newsreader on Radio 4 clearly got the message that this was all about selling the book and making money because I could hear it in her voice, but I had underestimated the way in which this would open a Pandora's Box. It was almost like a starting gun – except of course the pursuit had begun a long time before – so perhaps a better analogy is that the flag came down for the last lap.

It would appear that John Stevens thinks that I bullied him and resents deeply the interview I gave to the crime correspondent of the *Evening Standard* (wrongly referred to in his book as Trevor Kavanagh of the *Sun*) all those years ago. It was an interview about escalating street crime and the action that needed to be taken, and was on the back of Mayor Giuliani's visit to London. Oh dear, how people can harbour resentment for so long.

But what next? My biographer, ever vigilant for an opportunity, appears in *The Times* just days later saying that I am a 'liar' because, according to the *Times* article on which commentators then based their comments, I had made comments to Stephen Pollard about my fall-out with John Stevens and had denied this by writing to John Stevens immediately the biography was published (or at least that was his interpretation of the circumstances). There were only two things wrong with this 'good story'. Firstly, that I never denied what I said to Stephen Pollard, and secondly that I did write to John Stevens, explaining precisely the context of the comments to which Pollard had referred. So Pollard was right, and John Stevens was right. I had made the comments, and I had written the letter. In order to clarify the situation, I decided I would write to both John Stevens and Stephen Pollard.

The significance of this may have paled with the passage of time, but it is impossible to underestimate the impact that the publicity had on the climate of opinion and the way that others then joined in.

As the material being printed did not accord with my recollection of what I had written, I wrote to Sir John Stevens, requesting a copy of the letter I sent him at the time of publication of the Stephen Pollard biography. And as he had asserted that I was a liar, I also wrote to Stephen Pollard, requesting a copy of the same letter on which he based his subsequent articles in The Times. I received no acknowledgement or reply from either of them.

And now it is open season. For anyone with a grudge, anyone seeing an opportunity to make a bob or two, now is the time.

But I am off to the USA and Canada on official business so perhaps the world will calm down while I am away.

This was a piece of optimism on my part that was totally misjudged. The visit had been arranged a long time before and was to allow me to look at welfare-reform programmes in Washington, Chicago and Vancouver, as well as talking with my opposite numbers in the US – and with the Labour Minister from Iraq, who happened to be visiting the US Labour Secretary at the time.

It was an excellent visit: several useful meetings, including one with Congressmen from Louisiana (on the back of Hurricane Katrina), and the chance to meet leading Democrats as well as members of the entourage around George Bush. I had an excellent lunch with John Edwards, former candidate for the Democratic nomination for President, whom I had met previously in Britain.

I had a sixteen-hour visit to downtown Chicago with Mayor Daly – a really interesting character – then flew on to Vancouver to see self-help and ethnic inclusion programmes, followed by an overnight flight home to land on Monday afternoon, 19 September – the day of the first of the Newsnight *attacks.*

Back to the Sally Anderson saga: I had spoken to Sally Anderson a number of times on the telephone since July, when she had told me about the break-up of her relationship with a long-standing boyfriend some months before. She also told me again of her worries about skin cancer and the scan she was having. I explained in early September that I was going to the US and Canada but would be happy to talk to her when I got back. What a mistake.

On the afternoon of the 19th – the day of my return – she rang to suggest that she bring over some fish and chips and have an hour with me. Well, there's a sucker born every day and I was certainly one! I didn't particularly want to cook and had made no arrangement to go out, so I agreed. This was the first and only time that she had been to my home, and in fact the first and only time we had ever been alone together. She told me she was about to have a scan and was booked in for it the following week.

If I am to continue offering help, support and kindness wherever I think it is needed, then I obviously have to put behind me the deception in which Sally Anderson was engaged, as well as the devastating assault on my integrity and credibility. That is why, once I was no longer a Cabinet minister, I sought to clear my name once and for all, though given the amount of publicity that a retraction brings compared with the unrelenting nature of the original coverage absolutely nothing can compensate.

As I have discovered from another bout of intrusion from the News of the World *and* Daily Mail *in the summer of 2006 when I made the mistake of having supper on my own with an attractive woman (with whom I was discussing a potential television programme), my making any friendship and having even the most innocent meeting with any eligible woman was going to be misinterpreted. It is bad enough for me, but it is devastating for anyone who would simply like to meet me and be a friend. When in London I would have to eat in the House of Commons with friends, and always have a third party present if eating with a woman in a restaurant.*

Evening of Monday 19 September: fish and chips arrive from a local take-away restaurant, and I pay for them. Sally Anderson arrives, apologising for being late and not being there in time for the fish and chips, which I have popped into the oven. We talk and she tells me of the difficulty she is having and the terrible hassle to find somewhere decent to live. I sympathise. She talks to me about her desire to become a jazz singer. I sympathise. She leaves at 9.45 p.m., and almost immediately rings me to say that she has been photographed coming out of my house. So I go to the door and ask who is there. A photographer and reporter are outside my house. I ask what they are doing there. The reporter asks if Sally Anderson is my girlfriend. I tell him not to be ridiculous. He says: 'Nothing wrong with that, Mr Blunkett. How long have you known her? What's her name?' – and all the time the camera is clicking. So I ascertain which newspaper they're from – the *Daily Mail* – and ask them why on earth they're pursuing me in this way. I get the reply that must always stay with me if I am going to avoid making a fool of myself in the future: 'Well, you're a celebrity, aren't you?'

I immediately rang Matthew Doyle, who jumped in a taxi and came round. He was with me by ten o'clock. There was not a lot we could do, but I wanted him to be aware of what had happened and above all to see if there were still people hanging about outside. There weren't.

But it wasn't until Saturday the 24th that the *Daily Mail* did the big splash – just before Labour Party conference started on the Sunday. The story took off immediately, followed up by the *Mail on Sunday* and by the *Daily Mirror* on Monday, who managed to cobble together a political story from a detailed political interview (with no private material in it whatsoever) which I had agreed, at late notice, to do with them on a train travelling into London on the Friday. So the two stories were spatchcocked together on the Monday morning, with the addition of aspects from my ITV interview with Jonathan Dimbleby on the Sunday lunchtime. Just right for my appearance on the *Today* programme to be interviewed by John Humphrys.

Full of cold and feeling wretched, I had gone into the studio to do the broadcast in order to talk about the importance of pensions and welfare reform, and while we did do that, John Humphrys couldn't help getting into the *Daily Mirror* front-page story and what purported to be my private life. He asked me whether, given the fact that my private life was being splashed all over the media, I was still able to do my job. I said: 'Well, I could ask you the same thing, John. Given the controversy you've had with the media attention to your own statements, how are you managing to do your job?' The only comfort I got from that was that the people in the control room next door – the technicians and back-up staff – just burst into laughter. But it doesn't help.

I also said that I would seek a retraction from the *Daily Mirror* – which I did, getting a retraction in a limited form on Thursday 29 September – but the damage was done.

For me the party conference was just a matter of survival. People not saying too much, except behind their hands: 'Just what the hell has he been up to this time? Wasn't it enough last time?' If it had been true, then of course they would have been right. But they didn't know – only I did – that it wasn't.

And so the *Daily Mail* continue investigating and discover that they have been traduced as well. There has been no 'close friend' spilling the beans after all: it is Sally Anderson herself. It was her telephone that has been used. But it hasn't stopped the papers.

The News of the World *discovered that there was a new boyfriend called Andy King, whom Sally Anderson married in December 2005. But the papers continue to describe her as my 'lover'.*

I continue to do my job, though if I'm honest with myself it is getting very difficult. I am still concentrating, I am still putting in the hours, but the special advisers are being run ragged. There are all sorts of weird things being thrown at us, including accusations that I didn't pay for my holiday villa in Italy – reported as being a seven-bedroomed affair, which it certainly isn't, and which I rent from complete strangers. They had me down as offering Sally Anderson some enormous sum to buy a place of her own. I should cocoa: I've enough problems paying off the debts I have. But day after day, special advisers have been diverted into having to answer the most ridiculous enquiries from journalists, who had clearly been given a complete free hand and had all the time in the world. We are now getting quotes – the *Daily Mirror* was a classic on 26 September – that are exactly the same as the *Mail on Sunday* printed in relation to an earlier story. In other words, they are just pulling down from the computer quotes purporting to be from 'friends', 'insiders' or 'sources close to' me, and the quotes they are quoting are the same. It is some sort of computer-operated word game: 'Pick a Quote'.

I am determined to keep going but it is very wearing and there is only so much I can take.

I don't know how I got through party conference. The fringe meetings were fine, and I was still getting a really good response. But a combination of feeling ill and, if I'm honest, being so down that I couldn't raise myself, let alone the audience, resulted in my conference speech being probably my least uplifting since 1991. But perhaps oratory is no longer relevant in the politics of the twenty-first century.

I am still being phoned by Sally Anderson and, yes, I am still ringing her back. I want to know where the story has come from and what her game is.

I still had not cottoned on that it was a scam. It wasn't until I rang to ask her what had happened with the skin-cancer scan and she didn't know immediately what I was talking about, that I began to catch on. I suppose, if I'm honest, I was enamoured with a very attractive young woman who told a very good story, and although there was no suggestion of a relationship of the kind being hinted at and later stated openly, I was flattered that she was seeking my advice and help. When she told me she was taking the advice of someone with 'great knowledge' of these issues who had 'told her to go up front and tell her story', then at last the penny dropped for me. I had no experience whatsoever of anyone I'd ever known or ever would want to know going to Max Clifford.

So as she departed to the United States, presumably with her boyfriend, the one who had superseded the long-standing partner – contrary to the allegations being made in the papers that somehow I had broken up that relationship – I breathed a sigh of relief. What I didn't know was what Sally Anderson and Max Clifford had cooked up between them and was likely to be printed. Let it just be said that she was a wonderful actress. She told stories about her grandmother, about her brother, and about her childhood that would make you weep.

And there's me, hard-bitten from years of advice surgeries, contemptuous of those who believe any old sob story, allowing myself to fall for all the old lines.

Tony's advice when I met him on Wednesday [28 September] at conference was very sound. He told me to avoid avoidable publicity and to concentrate on Welfare to Work and pensions. In other words, just do the job well and try to keep out of the public eye – and that is unanswerable. And then he said that it wasn't just pulling me down, it was pulling him down and that getting Peter Mandelson out for a second time, damaging Alan Milburn, and attacking others to attack him was all part of the strategy, not necessarily co-ordinated but because the media acted as a pack. There was nothing I could say because it is true.

He said that everyone is under scrutiny, everyone is under attack, so that what he does and what they do is linked together. I said: 'Well, I'm afraid I do drop myself in it as well.' I told him that I was very sorry and wouldn't have damaged him for the world, because without him I wouldn't have been back in government.

I said to John Reid when I sat next to him at conference for Tony's speech that it was well thought through and well presented, but above all it was well crafted, an elegant speech that said something: it sent a message and told a story.

But Tony is right. If I bite the dust, his decision to support me would then appear very questionable.

All this fuss probably means I have to pull out of doing the Cancer Relief question-and-answer session with Piers Morgan, where I was going to cross-question him. It's far too dangerous and I must not do any of it.

In the end, it was impossible to pull out, as I couldn't find a fellow Cabinet minister willing to do it. This was a major charity lunch where I was to cross-question Piers Morgan – a sort of turning the tables – and Malcolm Rifkind had agreed to do this with Jon Snow. We were to share it. I managed to get

through this – not a great knock-about, but sufficiently insightful to make the
vast sums of money that people had paid for the lunch worthwhile, without
damaging my credibility or integrity.

My advisers breathed a sigh of relief and I asked myself how on earth I had
got myself into it in the first place. But it was for charity, to raise money for
a very good cause, and to try to be something more than just a stereotype
politician.

I made a better speech at the end of Wednesday afternoon, an informal
one replying to the pensions debate, than I had in my set speech on
Monday. I felt the mood of conference, ditched my notes and just spoke.
And even though I was telling the trade unions that they couldn't take,
take, take all the time, and that they couldn't have an agreement at
Warwick University and then expect to unravel it – even that got a round
of applause. There was a warmth that I hadn't felt on the Monday. I just
wish that I had spoken later in the week.

During the week of conference I was attempting to rewrite the Welfare
Green Paper, the first draft of which was completely unacceptable. I was
holding meetings with the TUC and the Equal Opportunities Commission
on the issue of women's pensions, seeing colleagues from Scotland and
Wales, and trying to be full of bonhomie but feeling anything but.

I am looking back now on what I did in America and I am proud of it –
the Centre for American Progress, the Brookings Institution, talking about
welfare reform and pensions to audiences that people would give their
right arms for, and in Victoria on Vancouver Island talking about disability
rights. It is so difficult to get these messages across. We had had the BBC
Politics Show following us round America and I had hoped that they would
do something very serious about what was happening and the lessons we
could learn. In the end, the ten-minute film was a knock-about – trying to
juxtapose radical Democrats from the US against George Bush, when I was
looking at projects that had nothing whatsoever to do with the presidency
or with the American government in general. It was very sad that the BBC
had paid so much, for so many to spend so long doing so little.

My sons are being very supportive. Understandably my closest friends
wonder what on earth is going on, what is true and what isn't. But if
Alastair, Hugh and Andrew didn't believe in me, then I wouldn't be able to
carry on.

Tony was very clear with me on Wednesday afternoon. There would be
no reshuffle for me, and I will stay and do my job for the foreseeable future.

I have to deliver and I have to deliver well. I have to be focused. I have to stop any stories in relation to my private life. I have to question everything I do, every place I go to, every restaurant I go to, as to whether this may be a story and what that would mean. And that has reinforced just about everything that my closest friends and Alastair, Hugh and Andrew have said to me.

The tragedy of what continues to unfold is that for the bulk of the population there is mystification, bewilderment and possibly contempt, along with indifference – but for my very closest friends, there is heartache.

October 2005

Another batch of Sunday papers on 2 October: the *Sunday Times* has an enormous interview with Sally Anderson: unquestioning, unthinking and untrue.

Those who don't read the tabloids or even the so-called broadsheets on a Sunday – tabloids in essence if not in shape – can read a round-up in the *Guardian* on Monday. The *Guardian* and *Independent* don't cover the original story: they just do a kind of photofit of everything that the tabloids have written. I suppose it's quite smart.

Tony repeated to me on the phone on Friday evening that the only way to get on is to get up and get on. The trouble is that once something goes wrong, other things seem to hit you at the same time.

So here I am in the week beginning Monday 3 October, and my old dog Lucy has to be put to sleep. After Val Woolrich, who had fostered her, rang me to say that after several recoveries from what appeared to be the end, this really was the end, I walked up the lane and I am not ashamed to say that I had a little cry. I had seen Lucy in the spring just before the election campaign started, when I had gone over to turn the first sod for the new Guide Dogs for the Blind Association facility in Leigh, near Wigan. She had remembered me and wagged her tail, and she and Sadie had had a little sniff together. Now another part of my life was gone – and at what a time.

And so to the North East on Thursday and Friday for one of our regional team visits. We are doing them so regularly now that it is becoming almost like a pattern – visits around the region, dinner with those representing business, trade unions, communities, the universities and government offices – and then on the Friday concentrated visits to departmental offices, to jobcentres, to programmes to get people off incapacity benefit, to an interesting scheme run by the Salvation Army, to talk to those who found jobs after years of languishing at home, to appear live on an hour-long phone-in on local radio and to have not a single question about my private life or my capacity to do the job. Everyone was interested in what we are doing on pensions, welfare reform and the Child Support Agency.

I spoke to Tony in the afternoon and reported back. He laughed and said: 'I told you so. People out there are interested in what's happening to their lives and to their services, in what you are doing, in the policies and whether we are delivering.' It was such a relief to me that the welcome was so obvious, that people are so kind, and above all, that people are not sneering.

I flew easyJet to Bristol to stay overnight in the West Country, and then to Cardiff on Saturday for the wedding of Huw Evans, who is now working in Downing Street as a key member of the press and communications operation. It was a really relaxed wedding for Huw and Katharine, who used to work in the press office at the Home Office, which is where she and Huw met. They make a wonderful couple and it is joyous to see two people so obviously in love.

And then, just before the dinner, I received a phone call from Matthew Doyle to say that the *Mail on Sunday* had been in touch. He read me out some of what it is that Sally Anderson has been saying. I sat in the car park of the hotel and spent the next three-quarters of an hour on the telephone, as people had drinks and prepared to eat.

I put my neck on the block. I assured Paul Dacre, editor-in-chief of the *Daily Mail* and the *Mail on Sunday* that what I am telling him is the truth. I said that what is intended to be printed is a scurrilous and defamatory lie. He said that he would talk to Peter Wright, the editor, who must make the decision. But for me the only thought now was how on earth could I get through the dinner without Huw and Katharine knowing that there was something terrible going on.

Huw has lived with this kind of nonsense for so long and has seen me through for so long. I couldn't now let his wedding be ruined by it and so, somehow, I sat at the table and managed to eat something. When I left to stay overnight with Tessa Jowell in the Cotswolds, I felt sick to my stomach.

Sunday 9 October: the story does not appear. Little comfort though: the More4 film is on tomorrow.

I didn't view the film, although there were plenty of people to tell me about it: about how the lead actor resembles me visually; how slowly I am supposed to speak; how completely false the fictitious content, and my relationships with constituents, never mind other politicians. But what is astonishing is to hear people I know believing that it is a genuine portrayal and not a piece of fiction made up by someone I have never met who, to the best of my knowledge, has never talked to a single person who could describe themselves as an acquaintance, never mind a friend, and who didn't even bother to come to my constituency to find out precisely how I work, what I do and how people respond. But why bother? It would only spoil a 'good story'.

The objective has been achieved. I am deeply hurt. This is not satire; it is deliberate sabotage – sabotage of my career, and of my standing.

The film was to be transferred from the new channel launched that day to the main Channel 4. In retrospect, I should have just been relieved that it wasn't sufficiently well produced and of sufficient quality to have any standing, but it didn't feel like that to me at the time.

On the Monday evening I had dinner with the Football Association, together with Michael Howard, and with some difficulty managed to take my mind off things. I don't think anyone could have described me as a sparkling guest that evening.

Since 4 September there hasn't been a single day when one news outlet or another wasn't covering some aspect of my life, and on the past three Sundays, virtually every newspaper in the country has been at it – each bit building on the other, each reinforcing an image, each allowing another person, or programme, or journal to piggyback and build on, emphasise or magnify, each bit playing into the other like some play that had already been choreographed. And I had allowed it to happen.

But the significant thing that week was that the *Sunday Times* started another hare running – namely that I had been working for DNA Bioscience for three months, and not just for the two weeks prior to the general election. Had I not been a Cabinet minister I would have sued them. But I had so much on my plate that all we, including my beleaguered special advisers, could do was to deny what was a grossly untrue story. As at the end of November 2004, so now the effort was to try to combine the personal and the private, Sally Anderson and DNA Bioscience, DNA Bioscience and my job at the Department for Work and Pensions (responsible for the Child Support Agency).

The fact that the story was false and that it was calculated to destroy my career and my ability to do my job was obviously of no significance whatsoever to those writing the story. We had been so busy dealing with the main allegation on the Saturday that we hadn't spotted what the *Sunday Times* were up to. And so now we have Christopher Grayling once again, and this time he has got something to get his teeth into. The Conservatives now feel free to make this open season. They have spotted a hare and they are chasing it. Can they bring me down for a second time? What a prize. Another Peter Mandelson. Another blow at Tony Blair.

If I could turn the clock back, if I could make decisions again, I would make the same ones as I made this time last year, but by God, from the middle of April I would run a mile from DNA Bioscience and suppers with Sally Anderson. How can so small a mistake have led to so much? I believe I have managed to hold my head up high since I came into Parliament in 1987 – respected, trusted, held sometimes in fear by my opponents but at least with credit and respect. And look at me now.

I have thought quite a lot about the way in which I was responding at the time – attending public events, getting on with meetings and seminars and with preparation for the publication of the Welfare Green Paper and Adair Turner's Commission on Pensions. Even now I don't know how I managed to continue, and there were another three weeks of this to come. I can only imagine how my sons and my closest family and friends were feeling, as they read what was being written, as they saw the adverts for the Channel 4 film with a dog with its paws over its eyes – and the contradiction, day after day in the papers, that what I was telling them was the truth. My biggest regret of all is to have put them through all this.

One piece of light relief was an excellent lunch with the former Tory Foreign Secretary Geoffrey Howe and his wife Elspeth on Sunday 9 October. It was a really good interlude, talking about the past and Geoffrey's reflections on the world situation. I can see why Margaret Thatcher valued him for so long, even though their views were so very different. Geoffrey and Elspeth live a very short distance from Tessa and David and they gave us a very warm welcome. This is a very different sort of politics. It is sad that it feels as though it is a bygone era.

Meanwhile I had another conversation with Paul Dacre. I think he was genuinely sorry that they had run the original story, certainly in the form they had, and the devastation it had caused, not least because on Saturday 8 October they unravelled their own story by showing what a set of lies Sally

Anderson had already started to engage in, including the fact that she was the one who was pretending to be 'a friend' and setting the whole thing up.

Perhaps more serious for me was the partial leak (including to Channel 4) of a very private memo which my Principal Private Secretary had read over to me on the Saturday evening. This was all to do with welfare reform and the fact that Downing Street knew that I was working hard on a further draft. It wouldn't have mattered if everything else hadn't been going on at the same time.

I didn't know then just how important this would be, because apart from the effort to link quite spuriously my job as Secretary of State with my brief encounter with DNA Bioscience, the other ploy that was to be attempted was to try to present to the public that Tony and I were at loggerheads over welfare reform. This was particularly to emerge in the Sunday papers on 30 October, but it began three weeks earlier. In this instance, very few people indeed had any knowledge of the memorandum, and while substantial leaks were to continue emerging from Downing Street and the Cabinet Office, I couldn't help thinking that someone very senior within my own Department was up to no good. In more stable times I would have been able to take a much more benevolent view, but we were not in stable times.

On Monday 10 October I launched the welfare-reform principles on which the whole of the Green Paper and legislation would be based. We made it a lunch event and it was extremely well covered by television, radio and the press – in fact a great deal more coverage in the broadcast media than would normally have been expected. I think there must be a testing-out of how strong I seem to be – a bit like the early part of December last year.

David Hill and Downing Street were very pleased with the launch, the Parliamentary Labour Party seemed to be rallying round, and many people were being personally supportive, which is nothing short of a miracle, given what they are reading and seeing.

I'm having meetings twice a week now with Adair Turner and John and Jeannie to try to get the final report into a shape where Adair can feel comfortable and remain independent, but knowing that the report is not simply going to be ditched by us all – and at least that it will get a fair wind. The officials working on pensions are beginning to get a feel of what we want now, and Stephen Timms has been working extremely assiduously on it. The fact that he has been a Treasury Minister helps. Philip Hunt and James Plaskitt are working on the Child Support Agency, but the meetings we are having are not yielding fruit. The timescales for action are too long and the amount of money required to put things right is way beyond what even I can think of getting out of the Treasury.

But at least there is a feeling now that we are punching our weight. Officials genuinely seem to feel that they have a set of ministers really fighting for radical change. Margaret and I are going to have to get our act together. I can't have a situation where I write something, Margaret rewrites it and I have to write it again.

We are in a little bit of a cleft stick because without agreement that we can recycle the money we save from the pilot programmes on Welfare to Work, we can't afford to expand the pilots across the country, and of course that means changing Treasury rules regarding ongoing revenue from reductions in benefits and increases in taxes from people being in work and switched into our departmental budget. It is not beyond the wit of man but it isn't in line with usual accountancy practice and therefore everyone gets their knickers in a twist.

A hell of a week from Monday 17th onwards.

I am speaking in Glasgow on Tuesday morning which means flying up from London first thing – a European Union seminar as part of our presidency and coinciding with a speech that Tony is making. I am trying to get my contribution and what we are publishing alongside it coterminous with his.

Then I have ID cards in the House in the afternoon so I will have to get back on the plane immediately. This is one policy and one set of votes that I am determined not to miss.

Regrettably before all this positive activity and getting stuck into the job, we had to put up with the weekend of 15/16 October. We had the usual blanket coverage in all the Sunday newspapers, in one form or another. But the People *newspaper (part of Trinity Mirror Group) printed word for word the material that had been given to the* Mail on Sunday *the week before and that they had declined to use. I don't know to this day why the editor did it or what they thought they were playing at, but this was the last straw.*

One of the twists of my departure from government on 2 November was that it released me to take legal action, although it has to be said that family and friends continued to warn me that I was on very dangerous ground and could lose a very large sum of money (that I didn't have) if I failed in my action against them. But in my view there was no choice: this time I had to act and I had to clear my name. I had made my position clear all along and the accusations against me – that I don't intend to repeat in detail here – called into question not whether I had had a sexual relationship with Sally Anderson but my integrity, approach and care for women, and crucially my personal responsibility.

This is the subsequent retraction by Sally Anderson –

10 March 2006
To whom it may concern
Retraction and apology by Sally King (née Anderson)
I would like to apologise to David Blunkett for the article in the People *on 16 October 2005 headed 'Blunkett's lover loses baby'. Contrary to what I said to the newspaper, Mr Blunkett was not my lover and could not have made me pregnant. He did not callously use me for sex and then abandon me as I claimed in the article. He did not then lie about it.*

I am very sorry for what I said and apologise unreservedly to Mr Blunkett for the hurt and distress I caused him.

Yours faithfully,
Sally King (née Anderson)

And from the People *newspaper –*

12th March 2006
Rt. Hon. David Blunkett MP – an apology
On 16th October 2005 we published an interview with Sally Anderson headed 'Blunkett's lover loses baby'.

Ms Anderson claimed that she had had sex with Mr Blunkett and that when she told him she might be pregnant he abandoned her. Ms Anderson also claimed that Mr Blunkett had used her for sex and had offered valuable gifts as an inducement.

We now accept that these allegations are untrue and that Mr Blunkett did not lie about them. We apologise unreservedly to Mr Blunkett for any hurt and distress caused by the publication. We have agreed to pay him damages and his legal costs.

These – and the similar retraction by Sky Television which was aired nightly for a whole week – require only two comments. Firstly, if I had not been prepared to risk once again large sums of money to take legal action, there is no doubt in my mind that I would not have gained redress and the clearing of my name. Secondly, our legal system is so perverse that had the material printed not been so blatantly untrue and therefore contestable all the way through the courts, I would on winning have received exemplary damages but because, even after months of wrangling and all the stress that goes with it, a complete acceptance was achieved that the story was simply untrue – and all the allegations around it, as can be seen from Sally Anderson's letter – reparation was limited. However, nothing could ever restore the damage that had been done and how it fed into the final assault of the following two and a half weeks.

On 16 October Mary Riddell wrote in the Observer: *'But there is a line between disclosure and savagery. In David Blunkett's case, it has been breached . . . At his best, he is a clever, thoughtful man who has survived more than most people could endure . . . No one, even those guilty of heinous crimes, deserves such cruel treatment. Nor could anyone hold out for ever against what is happening now. David Blunkett, mocked by those without a fraction of his talent, is being systematically ruined.'*

This was picked up on BBC1's Andrew Marr programme that morning and mentioned to me by others, not least because of Alastair Campbell's famous stricture that if under constant pressure you can last more than thirteen consecutive days, there is a chance of survival. The thirteen days had at that point turned into six weeks – and since 15 May almost five months – and there were still sixteen days to go.

Meanwhile I am coping with the aftermath of another set of allegations. The *Evening Standard* on 12 October carried on from the *Mail* and *Daily Telegraph* – this is unbelievable. I am now accused of having used House of Commons letterhead from my constituency office to write about a planning application outside my constituency.

The Daily Telegraph *made it a front-page story!*

Two things strike me. Firstly I had no idea my headed paper was being used: I had simply dictated the letter. And secondly, the Tory councillors who passed it over to the press seem to have missed the point. I wasn't asking for the planning application to be rejected but for environmental protection to be included as part of the approval. I was doing so not at my own behest but at the direct request of my former neighbours at South-fields, near Wimbledon Common. And here's the rub – I am now accused of having bought a former council house.

Another lie that the Evening Standard *retracted but those repeating the story didn't.*

As always when I have made a mistake, I was quick to say so. I indicated that it was not my intention to use headed paper (one sheet) in relation to activity outside my own constituency, and that I would be very happy to pay the 10p or so that it was worth. However, what really got my goat was the sanctimonious nonsense from Tory MPs who saw an opportunity to put the boot in on a piece of complete and utter trivia – and respected newspapers who had so lost any sense of balance that they were prepared to run it as a serious story. The new MP for Monmouth, David Davies, referred the matter to the House of Commons authorities. The reference was dismissed.

But I could feel by this time that every action I took, every part of my life was now under surveillance, and to be honest I began to wonder just how much more of this I could take. Phone calls to family and friends from the House of Commons (free) or the use of the House of Commons free post for something that was marginal in terms of parliamentary activity: which MP could honestly put up his/her hand and plead not guilty?

Well, there are no privacy laws, there is no real redress, and I wonder in ten years' time how many young men, how many young women will feel that front-line politics is a life they would want to lead.

So I met Tony, and Sue Regan, my special adviser, who was with me, said that his face was a picture when I said that in order to make the pensions policy work, we would definitely have to have a mandatory system for employer contributions and an opt-out system for employees. I just know that we have to bite the bullet on this, otherwise not only pensions but savings as a whole will in twenty years' time be a fiasco. This is something that we can secure for the future. If people want a legacy, then Tony and Gordon, never mind me, have got one if we can get all this right.

On 12 October, I managed to find time to go and speak at the farewell do for Joan O'Pray.

Joan and Anne Reyersbach were headteachers in Wandsworth and members of the Labour Party, and from time to time had invited me round to supper. Over a number of years I had found them very cheery companions when I had a spare evening in London.

Joan was retiring and it was nice to be able to go and say farewell to her. It was also nice to feel a welcoming atmosphere from people of all political persuasions and those with none, and to rejoice in the transformation that was taking place in primary education.

Politically there is a strange atmosphere with the Tory leadership campaign and the sudden emergence of David Cameron as the front runner. I think there is a bit of positioning going on, with people like Christopher Grayling trying to ensure that they are prominent enough to get into the Shadow Cabinet as there is bound to be a reshuffle once the leadership contest is over. But it is very unfortunate that Grayling is Shadow Leader of the House because it is just the sort of post that allows him to mouth off to the press on every possible occasion, to be 'Rent-a-Quote', even if (and this has certainly been true) he never follows through.

It is just worth reflecting on the Cabinet on 13 October, when we had a discussion on public pensions. Given everything else that I have got on, I am very glad that I am not leading on this, although we do seem to be getting ourselves in a twist. It was a good discussion but I wasn't entirely clear at the end whether everyone had agreed that the system for public-sector pensions – other than for local government, which John Prescott is having to deal with – should be changed by 2020, when the full changes in relation to the women's retirement age come into effect. That would at least give fifteen years before lifting the retirement age and entitlement to full pension for existing employees.

I am afraid this confusion appeared to lead to a misunderstanding in relation to what Cabinet had or had not agreed, but by the time this became patently obvious I no longer had access to Cabinet minutes.

Once again, just as I'm feeling beleaguered and badly done by, something happens that brings home to you the reality of what other people are facing. Last time it was the tsunami. This time it's the earthquake in Kashmir. The Miapur area that I visited and from where I have so many Islamic constituents seems to have been spared: it is much further across but it sounds absolutely devastating. We will all have to join in locally to see what we can do to raise money to help.

But here we go. The Education White Paper: an extremely good debate at Cabinet, with virtually everyone warning that the issue was the quality of education in the school to which it was most likely that a child in a particular geographical area was going to go. From Geoff Hoon to John Prescott, it was pointed out that the really high-flying and popular schools were full, and they were full of pupils whose homes adjoined and whose primary schools fed directly in. I pointed out that there were many pupils who might historically have travelled from my north-east Sheffield constituency to the affluent south-west where almost all the previous grammar schools had been based, but there was no one clamouring to travel the other way! I said that busing pupils across cities or counties was not an option and that anything other than the local school was not an option either for a very large number of parents. Therefore the issue should remain standards – a point reiterated very heavily by John Prescott who, I think, is more lucid on this than he has been for a very long time. We need to get the wording right if there is not to be an enormous storm and misunderstanding.

In discussions like this at Cabinet a wide range of views are put, normally in a way that doesn't confront or in any way denigrate the Secretary of State, whatever the issue. It is expected that views – particularly the weight of views – will be taken into account in redrafting. My experience was that spending time in redrafting yourself and being very hands-on was worth it with regard to the time you otherwise would have to spend down the line trying to put things right.

Sometimes there are very fundamental differences. When I spoke on the Second-Reading Debate of the Education and Inspections Bill in 2006 (with an eight-minute restriction on backbenchers that came as something of a shock, given that I hadn't spoken as a backbencher since 1988) I tried to distinguish between the fundamentals that we had had to deal with in the 1998 Act and the party conferences in the two years running up to the general election in 1997, and the practical, the nuances and the reality on the ground.

Constituency work carries on – my advice surgery, the annual meeting of relatives of drug abusers, and supper with my old friends John and Grace Vincent. The Revd John Vincent had worked in the inner city in Sheffield for many years, and although now retired still seemed to be as busy as ever. John had been President of the Methodist Conference when, in his waggish way, he had declared himself to be Maoist.

And now we come to the crunch: Friday 21 and Saturday 22 October.

The Mail on Sunday *put to Matthew Doyle, who then put to me, a whole series of bizarre allegations. We knocked down at least a dozen on the Friday, but they returned on Saturday afternoon with a new set, only one of which troubled me. The rest was the kind of fabricated material we'd had week after week – although it has to be said that by this time I virtually did not sleep on a Saturday night, and had not had a Saturday evening when I felt relaxed since the beginning of September.*

If I have a slightly jaundiced view of the liberal press in this country, I might be forgiven, given not only the behaviour of the Independent *over a very lengthy period of time but also the astonishing decision of the* Guardian *newspaper to run a whole week of Steve Bell cartoons, presumably based on their belief that Sally Anderson was telling the truth, painting a graphic picture of me as a Don Juan – including one bizarre cartoon of myself and the Queen in bed. In a different era I might have found the depictions amusing, but at this point they were anything but. How I managed not to become a figure of complete ridicule I will never know, but wherever I went I continued to receive a warm and respected welcome, even if many people were somewhat bemused as to exactly what was going on.*

The *Mail on Sunday* have been told that I didn't write to the Advisory Committee on Ministerial Appointments at the end of April about my directorship of DNA Bioscience. All I could say to Matthew was that we needed a breathing space to check out precisely what it was they were alleging, and for me to check just what I have done. I know we had correspondence with Patrick Mayhew and I know that I apologised for not having contacted him back in February. I know that we are in the middle of that strange time when Parliament is prorogued and therefore I am neither an MP nor a minister, but I am going to have to check the rules.

I rang my friend Estelle Morris, who had been through stepping down from office and taking up appointments as a consequence. She dug out the written material and notes and rang me back to say that my interpretation of what needed to be done was, in her view, mistaken. She said that I should check it out within the Department and the Cabinet Office, and she gave me the name of the person she had been dealing with in the Secretariat of the Advisory Committee.

The Mail on Sunday *did not run the story – presumably they couldn't stand it up – but on Monday we did inform the Department that we thought there was a problem, having tried to contact the Secretariat of the Advisory Committee on Sunday.*

The final ten days of my time as Secretary of State for Work and Pensions was about to start counting down – but day after day I continued with full meetings: on pensions and on welfare reform, and on Child Support. I even managed to have a meeting on financial inclusion and ideas that I was putting together on a complete reform of the Social Fund Budgetary Loan Scheme, and authorisations to the extension of disregards of income from the following April

so that we could bring up to date the social-security system, pending more
radical welfare reform.

Afterwards officials, advisers and ministers were to say that they were
astonished that I managed to keep the focus, to keep the momentum, to keep
on the agenda, when on every day that week I was also holding meetings to try
to work out just how bad the situation had become and how severe my breach
of the Ministerial Code really was.

Everything else is froth but this, I feel, is dangerous. It is not something that
I have done wrong, but a mistake. I have clearly not followed the rules to
the letter, and given what's going on at the moment, the press will have a
field day.

My cousin Pauline, whom I love dearly, phoned me from Spain. She has
been watching on Sky television via satellite what has been going on, and
she cares deeply for me. When I explained to her what had happened, she
said: 'Oh dear, that won't have done your career any good.' I said, 'Pauline,
I had already realised that, I had understood what it meant, thank you very
much.'

I also had dinner with Dorothy and Derek, my cousins, Dorothy being
Pauline's sister, and they too were horrified by what was going on.

So I suppose there are a lot of people thinking that there's no smoke
without fire, that it must be true, and it is getting to me now, this war of
attrition. Who's going to blink first? Can I take it? Can I keep going? The
answer is that I don't know, I honestly don't know.

On the work front, we've been doing a lot of work on pensions. I've
revised the women-and-pensions paper in detail. I've had two meetings,
one very long one on the Child Support Agency, completely revamping
what they were putting forward and trying to get across that we need an
overview that sets the establishment of the Child Support Agency in the
context of where responsibility and consequences should lie, what went
wrong and why, what new steps we intend to take that will affect people on
the ground, what new measures, what enforcement. And then the technical
stuff: it is detailed but the timescales are far too long. They are talking
about not getting this totally right for another three years. I am trying to go
through all this detail and make sure that not just the technical rearrange-
ment and complete revamp of the Child Support Agency but also all the
messages are right.

I am spending a lot of time on welfare reform. I had a separate meeting
with Tony, then a meeting with Tony and Gordon, and we have had the to-

ing and fro-ing within the Department. I am concentrating as hard as I can on getting this right because it will make a difference and it does matter. Nothing going on outside is as important as getting this right.

On the Friday we put together a detailed response to Downing Street, keeping the essence of what we have put forward: the new arrangements with GPs, including sensible pro formas that make information immediately available and insist that a particular pattern is followed by GPs and that they can't just sign a note and send it in.

And we have been ploughing on with all these massive reform changes and preparing for the forum on Monday 24 October with the European Union on the revised social-dimension Social Model for Europe prior to the informal European Council of presidents and prime ministers at the end of that week – including revising the paper, getting the press release sorted out, trying to explain to people how I need to handle the meetings on the Monday when Tony hands over to me to chair. All this is having to be dealt with in detail, as we have in the past, not just signing something off but rewriting it, getting people to see exactly what needs to be done and how it can be sophisticated.

On the political front and the Tory leadership contest: Ken Clarke has been knocked out in the first round and Liam Fox in the second, and it is now between David (or Dave as he prefers to be called) Cameron and David Davis, with David Cameron having got 90 votes and David Davis 57 votes in the final round, with Liam Fox coming a close third on 51. So we will see what comes up. David Cameron has only spoken at the Dispatch Box three times so it will be interesting to see how he performs as he will undoubtedly win – and it will liven politics up, there's no question about it. It is amazing though how quickly he got sympathy for the press when they were unearthing his past and digging into issues around whether he had ever taken drugs. Immediately people began to call it a witch hunt and unfair. Well, they ought to have to endure a witch hunt and being unfairly treated, that's all I can say.

I wrote to Christopher Grayling, who continues every week in the *Mail on Sunday* or *Sunday Times* to say that he is going to take something up, giving him forty-eight hours in which to respond – but he doesn't. Yet he's popped up again in the *Mail on Sunday* [23 October] saying exactly the same, that he is going to take up the latest set of non-allegations – so I shall write to him again, saying that he knows perfectly well that fulfilling the Ministerial Code means that I don't hold shares, and asking him to put in writing just what he is alleging and I will then deal with it. At some point we are going to have to put out the fact that this man appears every Sunday, piggybacking on the *Mail on Sunday* and the *Sunday Times*, saying that he is going to take things up and never doing so. But he has got the publicity, and he has made the smear. So we will see whether he does it this week.

The *Mail on Sunday* carried a nasty piece, again full of innuendo but no facts or actual detail of anything that I'm supposed to have done wrong. I don't hold shares in DNA Bioscience, I haven't interfered on their behalf in any way and I haven't misused my position. The paper didn't use the issue of going to the Advisory Committee and I will deal with that during the week in order to cover the issues there. But no doubt we will be back on another round of it next Sunday, on the back of their determination to go through material at Companies House under the 1985 Companies Act to see precisely who the shareholders are. Anyway, thanks to the efforts of the *Mail on Sunday* and *Sunday Times*, the shares are not worth a bean.

Monday 24 October: the *Today* programme. This is all about the meeting that Tony is partly chairing and that I will take over when he leaves, to discuss the 'social dimension' as it is now being called in relation to the European Union. It is going to be a long day. The Department has worked well on producing the document that will be the backcloth to the discussion at the end of the week at Hampton Court. It will be published today in the name of Alan Johnson, as Secretary of State at the DTI, and myself. After a bit of a dicky start, I think the document now has something to say.

But there I was on the *Today* programme and Carolyn Quinn has been fed, presumably by a researcher, the notion that I am against the banning of smoking. It's a funny old world where people get their ideas from. Here I am, one of only three Cabinet ministers batting away to bring the government into line with the people, and someone is briefing that I am on the other side.

I have just been notified that the fundraising lunch – my clash with Piers Morgan and Malcolm Rifkind's with Jon Snow – raised £76,000 for Cancer Research. I think Malcolm deserves the greater praise because he was genuinely very funny. But, like my *Mastermind* appearance, it does make it feel worthwhile. If you are prepared not to be a stuffed shirt, you can do some real good.

I've had a letter (and I've had to keep his name private) from someone famous in the past for his relationship with someone even more famous. Apparently some blithering idiot intends to make a film and get into his private life all those years ago. It is a cry from the heart. He is asking if there is anything I can do to help him or advise him to do, given my experience. Dear Lord, what can I say? I'm afraid if there's money to be made, they'll make it. If there's privacy to be intruded on, they'll intrude on it. If there's someone, no matter how distant in the past, to make fun of, they'll make fun of it. All I can say to him is that there are no scruples any longer, there are no boundaries, there is no self-restraint – and that I'm sorry.

We have a date now for Leigh Lewis to take over from Richard Mottram as Permanent Secretary. As part of the reshuffle of heads of departments, I have agreed with Gus O'Donnell that Richard Mottram will move to take over from Bill Jeffery at the Cabinet Office end of the counter-terrorism/resilience programme, with Bill Jeffery going to the Ministry of Defence. I am having supper with Leigh so that we can talk through the priorities of what we will do in sorting out Jobcentre Plus, in getting the Department geared up to wider social policy, to financial inclusion and anti-poverty, and to the challenge of ageing.

It had been agreed that Leigh Lewis would take over on 14 November, and although I was able to have the supper with him I left government two weeks before his arrival. It is a regret to me that he and I were not to work together again (for the third time), as I am confident that we could have built an extremely effective partnership.

Tuesday morning, 25 October: meeting with Charles Clarke. It was one of those bizarre moments when I am given an annotated agenda that includes an item explaining that 'departmental policy' is that we are against failed asylum seekers being put to voluntary and community activity in return for bed and board. (This is when they can't be removed immediately from the country.) Of course, this is entirely a government policy and one I insisted on before leaving the Home Office, as an alternative to simply giving people money. So when we reached the item, I said: 'The departmental policy is that I resist co-operating with you, Charles, on implementing the policy that I started before you took over – but I've decided that my policy is that I will implement what the government has agreed.' Lord help us all.

Best to stay calm. I am going to need all the backing I can get from senior officials and Private Office.

And speaking of that, I'm afraid it is clear that I should have written to the Advisory Committee at the end of April. The Secretariat is very clear and so is the section of the Cabinet Office dealing with ethics, although they are being extremely helpful in indicating that it is down to the Prime Minister to make a judgement about by how much the Code has been breached. They think this is a minor technical breach of the Code, particularly with the ambiguity of the correspondence. But it is a breach nevertheless.

All the advice that I was receiving was that the most I should do was to write again to Christopher Grayling, Shadow Leader of the House, and challenge him to put up or shut up on the ridiculous things that he was now saying and the way he was acting simply as a mouthpiece for a couple of national newspapers. But all my instincts were to call a press conference to explain once and for all – even if it breached my privacy by going over my financial arrangements in detail – the truth about each aspect of the lies that were being told. I wanted to lay on the table the fact that there had undoubtedly been a breach by me of the Ministerial Code, to apologise for it and to appeal to public opinion.

I did not do so, which I now regret, for it allowed not only the Independent on Sunday *a free run, but a considerable muddying of the waters to such an extent that, by the time we reached Wednesday 2 November, it is not surprising that even those who did know the truth were, to say the least, confused.*

My Principal Private Secretary is being extraordinarily thoughtful and helpful. In fact the whole office is rallying round. They are keeping me going – keeping the meetings in the diary, making sure that things are focused and that I am clear on agenda items and proper briefings. I have just got to keep going as though nothing is happening.

I don't know how I did it but I was able to keep going – making decisions, clearing papers, signing off the near-final version of the welfare-reform paper.

I want to seek an official ruling from Gus O'Donnell, the Cabinet Secretary, not just on the Ministerial Code but on all the actions I have taken to declare my interests properly and on this ridiculous idea that somehow there is about to be a contract from the Child Support Agency when there clearly isn't. There are some extraordinarily thoughtful people in the Cabinet Office but it is pretty clear that there is a divided view as to whether Gus O'Donnell should be brought into this at all at the moment. Opinion is also divided on just how serious this is. From where I sit, it's not the individual issue, it's the whole froth, it's everything that's going on that's the problem.

It is what I call Sod's Law. At this stage, I should have had a sit-down with Tony and discussed things, but he was phenomenally busy and, as he said to me the following Sunday when we spoke on the telephone in the evening, 'What I want you to do is to get on with the big issues – welfare reform and pensions.' So did I. The problem was that I was not going to be able to do so without sorting out the sustained attack.

I can see why Gus O'Donnell would not wish to be embroiled, because, given the delicacy of my position at the time, he probably felt – though I haven't had a detailed conversation with him about this – that his duty lay both in advising the Prime Minister and being seen to be independent of any internal political pressure. As a new Head of the Civil Service and Secretary of the Cabinet, that is a perfectly understandable and respectable point of view – but for me it was disastrous.

So it was that by Friday evening, when we thought that we might have an exchange of correspondence that would stand me in good stead, we had nothing in writing.

I already knew from the approach of the *Mail on Sunday* that journalists had been alerted to a potential story, but it wasn't until Saturday 29 October that Francis Elliott of the *Independent on Sunday* approached Matthew Doyle (who was in the USA, preparing a best man's speech) with a set of queries, which were answered openly and candidly. Francis Elliott had been given information by the Secretary of the Advisory Committee, and when the Cabinet Office learned of this they alerted my Private Office.

I authorised Matthew to say to Elliott that we accepted that I had made a mistake and that I had breached the Ministerial Code. Surprisingly, two hours later the *News of the World* made contact with Matthew, asking exactly the same questions that the *Independent on Sunday* had raised with us. They too printed the story.

It was my son Andrew's birthday on Monday so we had a dinner on Saturday evening. I desperately tried not to make it a sombre affair – though I decided a few days ago that I am best to have an absolutely clear head, and so until all this is cleared up I will stay clear of my treasured burgundy. We had as pleasant an evening as we could, in the company of Louise and Michael Gray, who live in the village. Everyone locally is being very kind, though they are under siege again from the media – camera crews, people knocking on doors, intrusion into everyone else's lives. It's a wonder anybody is still speaking to me. Gloria and Roger Sherwood, who live next door to me, have been very kind and supportive. Roger's mum,

Hilda, ran the hairdressing salon at Southey Green when I was a boy and Roger jokes that he spent fifty years trying to get away from me, only to find me ending up as his next-door neighbour! Like so many neighbours here and those who have supported me in Sheffield, they don't agree with my politics but it doesn't make any difference. They are decent human beings and I owe them a great debt of gratitude.

But the worst thing is what the press are doing to the trustees of my small shareholding, which is now worth absolutely nothing: they are being harassed with phone calls, knocking on doors and windows, people sitting outside their homes at 7.30 a.m. – all in the misguided belief that there is something amiss.

And my misguided belief that it was necessary to put the now-defunct shareholding into a trust in the first place, when I could have saved enormous pain to those I care about by just holding on to the shares myself – or by selling them back, an option I considered in the week before my resignation when what was tantamount to hysteria reached a point where there was no rational discussion, no ability to put across facts any more. What the world outside did not appreciate – and the public couldn't – was that because of the publicity (which some associated with the company astonishingly contributed to) the company was going bust. For the fifteen people employed it was a personal tragedy, and I regret that their good idea and hard work came to nothing. For me it was a harsh lesson learned.

On the Thursday, the day after the *Independent on Sunday* had approached the Advisory Committee Secretariat, the *Daily Telegraph* produced a lengthy compilation piece under the byline of George Jones that I never, ever expected to see. This is a once-respected, reliable, heavyweight newspaper, a broadsheet in every way. People have a go at the tabloids but everyone understands and expects what they get from them: they are, in the old saying when I was a child, no better than they ought to be. But the *Daily Telegraph*, *The Times* and even the *Sunday Times* can be more hypocritical because they purport to work to much higher standards.

And to cap it all, Tom Utley, the son of the highly respected Tom Utley senior, writing the day after, describes me as 'mad'. Well, I'm mad all right but not in the way he thinks.

The weekend of 29–30 October: another sleepless night. Another waking up to the Sunday papers and the speculation. This is now the eighth weekend on the trot. Saturday inquisition – Sunday accusation. But I feel it slipping away. I need to talk to Tony but he has overseas visitors and he is up to his neck in it. And now there is a new strand. Someone is briefing that Tony and I are at loggerheads over policy. Not just the *Observer*. Not just one newspaper. But someone who has been out and about.

Sometimes Sunday newspapers simply insert stories that they pick up from the early editions of their rivals. (In fact they keep space specifically for these.) But it struck me on this particular Sunday that someone had deliberately and systematically sought to create a divide.

When I spoke to Tony on Sunday evening, by which time I felt so screwed up that I had to concentrate like mad in order to sound rational, I explained to him that although the feedback from Gus O'Donnell and the Cabinet Office was that the mistake I had made could be explained by the ambiguity of the correspondence and the wording of the Ministerial Code, I felt that this was going to be an incredibly difficult week. Tony was very bullish – not complacent, but deeply concerned about the briefing in relation to policy. He reiterated yet again that the critical thing was that I was able to get on with my job, and all I could say was that, for the past eleven years, he and I had worked on reform and modernisation, on rights and responsibilities, on everything that I believe in and he believes in. And we left it at that.

Monday 31 October: Andrew's birthday. The papers are dreadful. The Tories have decided to up the ante over the shareholding. But they clearly don't believe that my mistake in not writing to the Advisory Committee is anywhere bad enough to warrant my resignation.

In fact Sir Malcolm Rifkind, who deserves a great deal of credit for the dignified, statesmanlike and honest way he dealt with the situation, refused four times to call for my resignation when interviewed by John Humphrys on the Today *programme, even though John did everything he possibly could to get him to say the words. And at Work and Pensions Questions in the House of Commons that Monday afternoon neither he nor any other opposition MP attempted to use the press campaign against me. I am proud that despite the enormity of the difficulty I was facing, there was no time during the run-up to my stepping down when I felt any ridicule or undermining of my authority in the House of Commons. In fact it is worth putting on record the amusing exchange with Denis MacShane, MP for Rotherham and former European minister:*

Question – Denis MacShane:
My Right Hon. Friend is a very youthful, energetic, virile kind of chap with many years of service on the Front Bench.

Will he welcome the German government's decision to move the retirement age in Germany from sixty-five to sixty-seven? Bismarck chose a retirement age of sixty-five at a time when the average life expectancy of a German worker was forty-nine, which resulted in a wonderful pension scheme – everybody paid in, and if they lived, they waited until they were sixty-five to draw out. We live in a different world, and I urge my Right Hon. Friend to get away from sixty, sixty-five and any other arbitrary age limit and to bury the idea that there is a time when people must retire or when he must leave the Front Bench.

Answer – Mr Blunkett:
I plead guilty to being energetic – my virility has been over-exaggerated! [Laughter] . . .

But I wasn't counting on an own goal.

As I drove down to London on Monday morning Tom Kelly, the official spokesman of the day doing the first of the twice-daily lobby briefings for journalists, was changing the terms of the debate by another crucial notch. I heard about this in three phone calls prior to David Hill, Director of Communications at 10 Downing Street, ringing me. In briefing the lobby Kelly, who knew absolutely nothing about my shareholding, indicated that the Prime Minister would be investigating the matter.

When David came on the phone, he said, 'There's a firestorm.' I replied: 'I'm not surprised: it's been lit by the remarks of the government official spokesman.' Understandably David defended him and indicated that that was not what he had meant, but I'm afraid the firestorm had indeed started.

My advice for the future for Downing Street would be to stop having twice-daily lobby briefings because this system cannot be good for anyone. Once every other day, or when there is something sensible to say, would be more appropriate. It simply sets them up as Aunt Sally – and on this occasion, I was the Aunt Sally.

'Can't you get rid of the shares?' is the cry from all around me. Well, to begin with, they are not mine. Secondly, they are worthless. Thirdly, if I do ask my sons to ask the trustees to sell them, it will take ages. But I will ask them.

And I did. They told me to do whatever I had to, to save the day.

And so top of the news on Monday night, once again. How many times is this now that I have been top of the news for all the wrong reasons? And we stagger through Tuesday. I am still holding meetings. I am still pulling everyone together. I am still ensuring that we write and rewrite, that we get things right. But it is going like sand between my fingers.

November 2005

Wednesday 2 November: I wake up at six a.m. I must have slept, which is remarkable. I listen to the early-morning news and the paper review at 6.45. It feels very bad. God knows – colleagues in Parliament can't be blamed if they're listening to this and they think enough is enough.

I ring Downing Street. I need to see Tony. I leave a message as he is ensconced with Jonathan Powell, David Hill and co. I have the Select Committee annual hearing at 9.30 a.m.

I had been preparing through the weekend, goodness knows how, for this Select Committee hearing, the annual review of the Department's work and finances and a very major challenge. You have to be totally on top of the job and all aspects of the departmental work and, despite what was happening to me, I felt I was. However, this time it was more than just a Select Committee hearing: this was a public spectacle. This was either an opportunity to demonstrate that I was strong and on top of the job, that I could see this through, that policy mattered and nothing else – or that I was on the slide, that I had lost the plot and that I had been distracted from being able to command the detail. I have always prepared thoroughly for Select Committee hearings. I have always been on top of the detail and I always took it for granted that I had to know more than the people questioning me.

I waited and I waited, and then Jonathan Powell came on the line and said, 'Can you get over here?' I said that I had been trying to for the past hour and a half. I told him that I had a Select Committee hearing at 9.30 a.m. and that I had to be there. 'Cancel it,' he said. I said: 'Well, if I cancel it, I might as well put it out on the internet that I have resigned. I can postpone it for half an hour and perhaps get away with it, but that's all.' 'Well, do what you have to,' he said. So I spoke for the fourth time that morning to my long-suffering and deeply caring Principal Private Secretary. I was seeing a side of her that I don't think anyone, other than her partner, has seen. We agreed that one of the junior private secretaries must go across and ask the chairman to hold for half an hour, on the grounds that I am temporarily delayed. It didn't feel good, but it was the best I could do. I then got in the car and made for Downing Street.

In the office, besides Tony, are Jonathan Powell, David Hill, Ruth Turner (Tony's Director of Government Relations), a junior briefing official, my special adviser Matthew Doyle and myself. The conversation was robust. It had been clear to me from the moment I entered the room that Tony was already vigorously embroiled in defending my corner. The conversation continued in this vein for a minute or two before I joined in, trying to put straight some of the misconceptions that clearly existed around Tony and had been reinforced forty-eight hours earlier in the ill-fated lobby briefing.

It was clear that some present were totally unfamiliar with the detail. I do not, for understandable reasons, have a detailed record here of the conversation, but at one stage I had to ask Tony to request the young briefing official to leave the room. Those remaining were doing their best to ensure that the Prime Minister was protected. That is their job. Matthew was doing his best to ensure that the truth I have been telling them is reinforced by evidence. But it was also clear – and this must be a mistake by me – that Gus O'Donnell had not spoken to Tony in detail about the exchanges.

Gus O'Donnell had on Monday answered a direct query from Christopher Grayling. It is not for me to make a judgement on the construction of the letter itself. Suffice it to say that it confirmed the blindingly obvious that I had already confirmed on Sunday – that I had made a mistake and that by not writing to the Advisory Committee I had technically breached the Ministerial Code.

I indicated as calmly as I could that the issue of the Code was not in dispute but only the severity of the mistake and the judgement to be made by the

Prime Minister as to whether it warranted resignation. I indicated that everything else was lies – but I have to say that I do not believe that, with the exception of Tony, and of course Matthew who knew the detail, anyone else believed me.

And if they didn't, it's not surprising that others didn't either. So I bear no resentment.

I asked that if everyone would leave, Tony and I could have a conversation, one to one. They did and we did – and without giving away confidence, it was clear that there were two choices. Either we could see it through – and I indicated that unlike the previous December I was strong physically and, although deeply bruised, I was angry and determined inside and felt I could see it through; or I went now, given the damage that was being done to Tony and to the government at a very difficult time.

And one of the those twists of fate was that the government itself was under enormous pressure. There was turmoil in the Parliamentary Labour Party. We were on a knife edge with regard to further votes on the Terrorism Bill, and therefore the credibility of the government itself was at stake. My problems were clearly deeply unhelpful to Tony at this moment. I regretted it but I still wanted a decision made, and I wanted to avoid a second close confidant, a second friend, a second senior minister biting the dust for a second time.

Tony stood silent for a very long time and then we hugged and he said, 'Go and do the Select Committee.' I took his hand and then I left. I said nothing to anyone as I walked to the car. When we arrived some 200 metres away at Portcullis House, which adjoins the House of Commons and houses the major committee rooms, it was clear that there was something wrong. As we mounted the escalator and came on to the main open floor, journalists were milling about. I could feel the atmosphere and one of my private secretaries came to me to say that, just before I had arrived, the select committee had disbanded. The chairman, Terry Rooney, Labour MP for Bradford West, had received an indication that I had resigned.

I think that, in entire good faith, Terry believed this to be the case.

I will never know whether assumptions had been made. The Deputy Chief Whip, Bob Ainsworth, was over in Portcullis House, presumably because of the enormity of the Select Committee hearing and the fact that the nation's press were gathered. But it is clearly all up. Whatever agreement the Prime Minister and I had reached, it is time to go back to Downing Street and face the truth. I have lost sufficient support to be able to carry on and do the job properly.

So I returned to Downing Street to see Tony alone. I indicated to him what had happened and that I would call a press conference. I asked him whether he would like to do Prime Minister's Questions before that and he said he would. This was helpful to me, both in pulling myself together and calming everyone, and ensuring that we at least could go out with dignity. I needed to talk to my special advisers – another set of advisers who had lost their jobs – and to my Private Office, who had been so supportive, to the middle and junior ranks of the press office, who had been so thoughtful and kind (and remained so throughout the day). And I needed to prepare what I was going to say.

I addressed the press at the Foreign Press Association in Carlton House Terrace, hurriedly called together but a packed room, and I believe that it was one of my more dignified occasions – no bitterness, no anger, no turning on those who had turned on me, but an enunciation of the truth that I had been telling, week after week, day after day.

Now I can start taking legal action to clear my name. As a Cabinet minister I could not. Now I can – and I will.

And I did, not just against the People *newspaper and Sky television, but a whole range of untruths then and since on which I have taken successful legal action for retraction.*

Shortly after my press conference I receive a phone call asking if I will come down to meet Rupert Murdoch at six p.m. at Wapping. I agree to do so.

I feel a strange calm in the afternoon – as though a terrible time is over, although I know it's not. There is still the grieving to come.

On the way down to Wapping, I am reflecting on a question put to me by Michael White, the long-standing and highly respected political editor of the *Guardian*. I have known Michael for many years and, as with all politicians and journalists, we have had our ups and downs; but he is thorough, does his homework and is very perceptive. So what did he mean when he asked me in the press conference if I thought that I had been bugged over the past few months? I could have said, 'Well, if I had, a great deal more truth might have been told than what's been made up,' but instead I just looked at the ceiling and said, 'Well, when I walk in the countryside, and I hear the birds, I do sometimes wonder whether they are wired for sound.'

I am afraid the surveillance of me by the press didn't cease. Even in the summer of 2006, my Protection Officer discovered a man ensconced in the undergrowth opposite my driveway at the cottage. It was clear from the indentations in the ground that he must have been there for some considerable time. Unfortunately by the time he was spotted he had run away, but given the continuing interest in my whereabouts and my comings and goings, it was soon to become clear that the nightmare of almost continuous surveillance may have eased but certainly hadn't gone away. With attempts around the same time to verify surreptitiously whether my mobile phone was in fact correctly identified – two people ringing within the space of ten minutes and pretending to be someone else – I think I can be forgiven for being what might be described as a tad suspicious.

But before going to Wapping I went back into the Commons to vote – much to the surprise of the Whips. It seemed fairly fruitless to have found myself out of government in the morning and then to fail to support the government in the afternoon, because the only value of my departure in my own eyes must be to help Tony and the government at this critical moment. So I went back into the Commons and voted, and we won – by one!

We were to lose by thirty-one votes on the issue of extending from fourteen to ninety days the length of time (with review by a judge) that suspected terrorists could be held under investigation before charge.

It is a strange world. The atmosphere has changed in the parliamentary party in a matter of hours. Many people are friendly. Many, I think, are sorry. But if I don't delude myself, there must be some who are really pleased.

And so to Wapping – with Rupert Murdoch, Les Hinton, Rebekah Wade and others. After three-quarters of an hour, having a pleasant drink and a talk, Rupert Murdoch offers me a column in the *Sun*. I accept. What immediately goes through my head is firstly, you don't refuse Rupert twice, and secondly, I am going to have to move pretty smartish out of my house, and if I'm going to live anywhere within spitting distance of Westminster, it is going to cost me an arm and a leg.

I left in time for a predicted vote at 7 p.m. that never occurred, then went on to a dinner that had been arranged weeks before with trusted and good friends from Home Office days – and at their suggestion, as an act of friendship, one of my protection team who is a Coldplay fanatic, insisted on cheering me up by playing one of their CDs over the restaurant hi-fi. There wasn't a lot to cheer about and it was nice to be with people who had supported and cared about me over quite a long period of time.

And then home to bed.

Thursday 3 November, and another extraordinary set of occurrences. It appeared that Rebekah Wade had been to a party and there was a fracas with Ross Kemp, her husband, that hit the headlines. It isn't that that I'm concerned with. It's the reaction of the media. The rumour-mongers began putting it about that I had been drinking with Rebekah Wade, some of them insisting that I had had bottles of champagne, which for medical reasons I can no longer drink. And then the *coup de grâce*: the BBC Radio 4 news reported that I had been out drinking with Rebekah Wade before the 'incident' that they were reporting on. Lord help me, what has happened to basic standards of checking factual accuracy and of some sense of proportion? No wonder they are running a two-part series on television on the decline of Rome. It feels like it here to me.

Sunday 6 November: articles all over the *Mail on Sunday* and the *Independent on Sunday*. Here goes this combination all over again. The *Sunday Times* carries a bizarre story about 'tabloids' – goodness me, what is this paper if not a tabloid? – tapping into the answerphones of people I know. Surprise, surprise. It is a bit like living in *Alice in Wonderland* now.

I listened to *The World Tonight* on Radio 4 this last week – it all fades into one – who did a vox pop asking people why I had resigned. Some thought it had something to do with shares, some thought it had to do with 'some affair that he has had', but most hadn't got the first idea. And in truth, that was true of most of those who had been reporting.

My constituency has been extremely supportive once again. We had a little gathering of very close party friends and colleagues for supper at my old friend Helen Jackson's home, on Sunday night, and then a constituency meeting the following Friday. I am not sure I deserve the unswerving – though not unquestioning – support, the friendship, the belief. This is the kind of thing we used to talk about when I was young – about comradeship and fraternity, about people who help each other. These are my roots. 'A tree that is detached from its roots forms merely the logs from which the fire can be fuelled.' No, it's not a Chinese proverb: I've just made it up!

One shining light in the very dark days of this period was that on Sunday [13 November] my son Hugh walked with me on the ridge above my home in Derbyshire and told me that he and his girlfriend Alyson were to be married next year. In the old-fashioned way, he asked for my blessing, and I was glad to give it. I wish them both all the happiness in the world.

It is time now to get on with life, to take action to try to clear my name, bit by bit, to take the legal cases I could never have taken before (and the risk that my friends and family are telling me I can't afford to take and shouldn't take, but over which I have no control). I have to clear my name and restore my integrity, to set aside the lies about Sally Anderson, about DNA Bioscience and conflict of interest, about shareholdings and declarations – and about how when I challenge the BBC over their reports of my alleged partying on the evening of 2 November, their response is, 'Well, it must be an urban myth.' I have to challenge the surveillance and the monitoring of every aspect of my life and that of my family and friends, the photographs snatched outside people's apartments or restaurants, the assumption that private lives are no longer private, and above all I have to put straight the truth about my alleged impropriety.

So I write to Sir Gus O'Donnell, Head of the Civil Service and Secretary to the Cabinet. I ask him to clarify, as I had sought to clarify the week before my departure from Cabinet, what was the truth about the often-repeated allegations against me. I can do no better than to print the relevant paragraphs of his reply of 25 November 2005 – just over three weeks too late to save my job but not too late to save my reputation:

In my letter to you of 31 October, I said I was taking steps to ensure that the status of the business appointments system is clear. I have now reviewed the standard letters that are issued to former Ministers by the Cabinet Office and have made amendments to ensure that there is no doubt that former Ministers are required to seek the advice of the Advisory Committee on Business Appointments for any appointments that they wish to take up within two years of leaving office. The letters now make clear that this is a mandatory process. I understand that the Advisory Committee has made similar amendments . . .

The issue of shareholdings and trusts and the handling of private interests more generally is of course covered quite extensively in Section 5 of the Ministerial Code. There is no ban on a Minister, or his or her immediate family members, holding such interests but where they do the Minister must ensure that no conflict arises, or appears to arise, between his or her public duties and such private interests.

In terms of the handling of your interests, and those of your family, you followed correct procedure in notifying your Permanent Secretary of your interests. Neither the DWP nor the CSA were in any contractual relationship with DNA Bioscience, and the CSA's contract for biometric testing was not due to be renewed for some years. The fact that the department's officials were aware of your history with DNA Bioscience would have enabled appropriate safeguards to have been put in place should contractual issues have arisen, including consideration as to whether your sons could have continued to have held onto such a shareholding.

So there was no conflict of interest, and there was no failure to declare either my shareholding or my brief business connection with the company. In short, there was no impropriety. I had failed to write to the Advisory Committee, but had this letter from the Head of the Civil Service been received before 2 November, it would have been clear that there was no requirement for me to step down.

However, as Tony Blair and I agreed later, the pressure that had existed upon me for the whole of my time back in government, and the understandable if sad fact that the lies told had eroded support, made it very difficult to do the job with the focus and full commitment which I had always endeavoured to give.

The reader will make his or her own judgement regarding the part I played in my own downfall – and also, I trust, regarding my contribution to making a difference to the lives of the people from whom I sprang and whom I have sought to serve.

INDEX